# Tolley's Con

# Handbook 2016

Whilst care has been taken to ensure the accuracy of the contents of this book, no responsibility for loss occasioned to any person acting or refraining from action as a result of any statement in it can be accepted by the author or the publisher. Readers should take specialist professional advice before entering into any specific transaction.

# Tolley's Company Law Handbook 2018

by

Emma Manuel Szelepet

LexisNexis® | 2⃝⃝

**Members of the LexisNexis Group worldwide**

| | |
|---|---|
| United Kingdom | RELX (UK) Limited trading as LexisNexis, 1-3 Strand, London WC2N 5JR and 9-10 St Andrew Square, Edinburgh EH2 2AF |
| Australia | Reed International Books Australia Pty Ltd trading as LexisNexis, Chatswood, New South Wales |
| Austria | LexisNexis Verlag ARD Orac GmbH & Co KG, Vienna |
| Benelux | LexisNexis Benelux, Amsterdam |
| Canada | LexisNexis Canada, Markham, Ontario |
| China | LexisNexis China, Beijing and Shanghai |
| France | LexisNexis SA, Paris |
| Germany | LexisNexis GmbH, Dusseldorf |
| Hong Kong | LexisNexis Hong Kong, Hong Kong |
| India | LexisNexis India, New Delhi |
| Italy | Giuffrè Editore, Milan |
| Japan | LexisNexis Japan, Tokyo |
| Malaysia | Malayan Law Journal Sdn Bhd, Kuala Lumpur |
| New Zealand | LexisNexis New Zealand Ltd, Wellington |
| Singapore | LexisNexis Singapore, Singapore |
| South Africa | LexisNexis, Durban |
| USA | LexisNexis, Dayton, Ohio |

© RELX (UK) Ltd 2018

Published by LexisNexis
This is a Tolley title

ISBN for this volume: 9781474307826

**Visit LexisNexis at www.lexisnexis.co.uk**

# About This Book

Tolley's Company Law Handbook is intended to be a first book of reference for accountants, solicitors, company secretaries and all those involved in company law.

The twenty sixth edition includes full coverage of the Companies Act 2006 (CA 2006). The Act extends to the whole of the UK, so that there is no separate regime for Northern Ireland.

This edition covers, in alphabetical order, the relevant topics of CA 2006.

Among tax law development and other changes, this edition includes:

- an update of the regime governing the need for companies to keep a register of 'people with significant control' over the company;

- the further refinement of the scope of directors' duties, particularly with regard to the impact of s 172 in insolvency;

- the ongoing developments of the duty of disclosure in respect of directors' and secretaries' address;

- the introduction of the Insolvency and Companies Court Judges;

- recent case law reflecting the court's response to an application to restrain the presentation of a winding-up petition;

- MiFID II, which came into force on 3 January 2018;

- the continuing roll-out of the new Prospectus Regulation;

- consideration of the GDPR, which took effect in May, with the UK's data protection laws changing accordingly (almost every business in the UK collects, keeps and accesses personal information about existing and potential customers, and so potentially faces stiff penalties for non-compliance); and

- consideration of gender pay gap reporting, as, since April 2018, UK companies with at least 250 employees have been required to reveal data about the differences in pay between men and women, with roughly half of the UK workforce affected by the new reporting rules.

Chapters are in alphabetical order for ease of reference to a particular subject, and cross-references, an index and a table of statutes provide further ways of quickly finding the matter required.

Comments on the publication and suggestions for improvement of future editions are always welcome.

I am indebted to a number of people for the very kind assistance they have given to me in the production of this latest edition. Firstly, I must continue to pay tribute to my predecessor, the author of the Handbook's 24th edition, Janet Rosser, for her excellent and meticulously accurate rendition of the law in this area. Hers were very challenging shoes to fill. I am also enormously grateful to my former colleague and fellow Senior Lecturer at the University of Law Angela Delbourgo for her invaluable input on the public companies aspects. Angela Delbourgo is a practising barrister at 12 Old Square Chambers, Lincoln's Inn who has nearly twenty years' experience teaching Corporate Finance (debt and equity) at the University of Law and almost 18 years' experience working as an in-house lawyer for various banks mostly in the City of London; she has also spent some time working in Brussels and New York. My grateful thanks must go to Glynis D Morris, Chartered Accountant, for her authorship of the accounts chapters, and the audit and strategic reports and directors' reports chapters, along with her invaluable support in reviewing the accountancy aspects of further chapters, such as that on public listed companies. I am also grateful to Richard A Dollimore, Special Counsel, K&L Gates, for his update to the reconstruction and mergers chapter.

# About This Book

I would dedicate this edition to my parents, the late Mr Jan Szelepet and Dr Diana Manuel, (respectively, architectural engineer and academic); they have been a huge source of inspiration and support to me, past and present.

# Contents

# Contents

# Abbreviations and References

## Abbreviations

| | | |
|---|---|---|
| **AGM** | = | Annual General Meeting |
| **AIM** | = | Alternative Investment Market |
| **Art** | = | Article |
| **BNA 1985** | = | Business Names Act 1985 |
| **CA 1948** | = | Companies Act 1948 |
| **CA 1985** | = | Companies Act 1985 |
| **CA 1989** | = | Companies Act 1989 |
| **CA 2006** | = | Companies Act 2006 |
| **C(AICE)A 2004** | = | Companies (Audit, Investigations and Community Enterprise) Act 2004 |
| **CC(CP)A 1985** | = | Companies Consolidation (Consequential Provisions) Act 1985 |
| **CDDA 1986** | = | Company Directors Disqualification Act 1986 |
| **Ch** | = | Chapter |
| **CS(ID)A 1985** | = | Company Securities (Insider Dealing) Act 1985 |
| **EA 2002** | = | Enterprise Act 2002 |
| **EC** | = | European community |
| **ECUs** | = | European Currency Units |
| **EEA** | = | European Economic Area |
| **EEC** | = | European Economic Community |
| **EGM** | = | Extraordinary General Meeting |
| **EmA 2002** | = | Employment Act 2002 |
| **FRS** | = | Financial Reporting Standard |
| **FSA** | = | Financial Services Authority |
| **FSA 1986** | = | Financial Services Act 1986 |
| **FSMA 2000** | = | Financial Services and Markets Act 2000 |
| **FTA 1973** | = | Fair Trading Act 1973 |
| **IA 1985** | = | Insolvency Act 1985 |
| **IA 1986** | = | Insolvency Act 1986 |
| **IA 2000** | = | Insolvency Act 2000 |
| **IAS** | = | International Accounting Standards |
| **ICTA 1988** | = | Income and Corporation Taxes Act 1988 |
| **LLP** | = | Limited Liability Partnership |
| **LLPA 2000** | = | Limited Liability Partnership Act 2000 |
| **LLPR 2001** | = | Limited Liability Partnership Regulations 2001 |
| **NI** | = | Northern Ireland |
| **No** | = | Number |
| **Para** | = | Paragraph |
| **POS Regulations** | = | Public Offers of Securities Regulations 1995 |
| **PPERA 2000** | = | Political Parties, Elections and Referendum Act 2000 |
| **Pt** | = | Part |
| **Reg** | = | Regulation |
| **RIE** | = | Recognised Investment Exchange |
| **RIS** | = | Regulatory Information Service |
| **s(s)** | = | Section(s) |
| **Sec** | = | Section |
| **Sch** | = | Schedule [*4 Sch 10* = 4th Schedule, paragraph 10] |
| **SFS** | = | Summary Financial Statement |
| **SI** | = | Statutory Instrument |
| **SSAP** | = | Standard Statement of Accounting Practice |
| **STA 1963** | = | Stock Transfer Act 1963 |

# Abbreviations and References

| | | |
|---|---|---|
| STA 1982 | = | Stock Transfer Act 1982 |
| VAT | = | Value Added Tax |

# References

| | | |
|---|---|---|
| AC | = | Law Reports, Appeal Cases |
| All ER | = | All England Law Reports (1936 onwards) |
| App Cas | = | Law Reports Appeal Cases (1875–90) |
| BCC | = | British Company Law Cases (CCH Editions Ltd) |
| BCLC | = | Butterworths Company Law Cases |
| [1891] Ch | = | Law Reports, Chancery (1891 onwards) |
| ChD | = | Law Reports, Chancery Division (1876–90) |
| CLR | = | Commonwealth Law Reports (1903 onwards) |
| CPD | = | Common Pleas Division (1875–80) |
| E & B | = | Ellis and Blackburn's Queen's Bench Reports (1852–58) |
| Ex D | = | Exchequer Division (1875–80) |
| Hare | = | Hare's Vice-Chancellor's Reports (1841–53) |
| HL Cas | = | House of Lords Cases (Clark) (1847–66) |
| [1901] KB | = | Law Reports, King's Bench (1901 onwards) |
| Lloyd's Rep | = | Lloyd's List Law Reports |
| LR CP | = | Law Reports, Common Pleas (1865–75) |
| LR Eq | = | Law Reports, Equity (1865–75) |
| LR Ex | = | Law Reports, Exchequer (1865–75) |
| LR HL | = | Law Reports, English and Irish Appeal Cases (1865–75) |
| LR QB | = | Law Reports, Queen's Bench (1865–75) |
| LT | = | Law Times (1843 onwards) |
| Macq | = | Macqueen's Scotch Appeal Cases (1851–65) |
| [1891] QB | = | Law Reports, Queen's Bench (1891 onwards) |
| QBD | = | Law Reports, Queen's Bench Division (1876–90) |
| [1907] SC | = | Court of Session Cases (1907 onwards) |
| TLR | = | Times Law Reports (1885 onwards) |
| WLR | = | Weekly Law Reports |
| WN | = | Weekly Notes (1886 onwards) |

# 1  Introduction

1.1    Territorial extent
1.2    Meaning of 'company' and 'Companies Acts'

## 1.1   TERRITORIAL EXTENT

The *Companies Act 2006* (*CA 2006*) creates a single company law regime which applies to the whole of the UK and unless the context otherwise requires, the provisions of the *'Companies Acts'* (see **1.2**) as described in this book apply to the whole of the UK.

[*CA 2006, s 1299*].

**Northern Ireland.** Before *CA 2006*, the provisions of GB company law were generally replicated in separate Northern Ireland legislation. However, as the provisions of *CA 2006* were commenced, they were extended to Northern Ireland and the separate Northern Ireland legislation was repealed.

[*CA 2006, s 1284*].

See **28** Northern Ireland.

## 1.2   MEANING OF 'COMPANY' AND 'COMPANIES ACTS'

Unless the context requires otherwise, *'company'* means a company formed and registered under *CA 2006*, ie

- a company so formed and registered after 1 October 2009; or
- a company that immediately before that date

  (i)    was formed and registered under *CA 1985* or the *Companies (Northern Ireland) Order 1986* (*SI 1986 No 1032*); or

  (ii)   was an existing company for the purposes of that *Act* or that *Order*,

  (which is to be treated on commencement as if formed and registered under *CA 2006*).

Certain provisions of the 'Companies Acts' apply to

- companies registered, but not formed, under *CA 2006* (see **11** Companies Not Formed Under the Companies Acts); and
- bodies incorporated in the UK but not registered under *CA 2006*.

[*CA 2006, s 1*].

See **12** Company Formations and Types of Companies for types of companies which can be formed and registered under *CA 2006* and **30** Overseas Companies for the provisions applying to companies incorporated outside the UK.

## 1.2 Introduction

Any reference to the *'Companies Acts'* is a reference to

(a)     the company law provisions of *CA 2006*, ie *CA 2006, Pts 1–39* together with *CA 2006, Pts 45–47* in so far as they apply for the purposes of those *Parts*;

(b)     *C(AICE)A 2004, Pt 2* (community interest companies); and

(c)     the provisions of *CA 1985* and *CC(CP)A 1985* that remain in force.

The provisions under (*b*) and (*c*) above are extended to Northern Ireland by *CA 2006, s 1284*.

[*CA 2006, s 2*].

# 2  Accounts General and Accounting Reference Dates and Periods

**Cross-references.** See 3 ACCOUNTS: LARGE COMPANIES; 4 ACCOUNTS: MEDIUM-SIZED COMPANIES; 5 ACCOUNTS: SMALL COMPANIES AND MICRO-ENTITIES; 6 ACCOUNTS: STAND-ALONE STRATEGIC REPORTS; 8 AUDIT; 20 STRATEGIC REPORTS AND DIRECTORS' REPORTS; 36.5–36.8 RECORDS.

**Background.** The provisions in this chapter apply, unless otherwise stated, to accounts and reports for financial years beginning on or after 6 April 2008. [*SI 2007 No 3495, Sch 4 para 6*]. The corresponding provisions of *CA 1985* continue to apply to accounts and reports for financial years beginning before 6 April 2008. There is no historical information for pre 6 April 2008 in the text of this chapter. The *Companies Act 2006 (Strategic Report and Directors' Report) Regulations 2013* ("the *2013 Regulations*") which are referred to in various parts of this chapter, brought into force the requirement for a company to produce a strategic report for financial years ending on or after 30 September 2013. [*SI 2013 No 1970*].

## 2.1  INTRODUCTION TO ACCOUNTS

The provisions described in this chapter cover the requirements which relate to accounts generally, whether individual or group including accounting reference dates and periods.

## 2.2  PREPARATION, APPROVAL AND SIGNING OF ACCOUNTS

The directors of every company must prepare accounts for the company for each of its financial years unless the company is exempt from that requirement under *Companies Act 2006 (CA 2006), s 394A* (certain dormant subsidiaries). The accounts must be approved by the board of directors and signed on behalf of the board by a director of the company. The signature must be on the balance sheet. If the accounts are prepared in accordance with the small companies regime (see 5 ACCOUNTS: SMALL COMPANIES AND MICRO-ENTITIES), the balance sheet must contain in a prominent position above the signature

- in the case of individual accounts prepared in accordance with the micro-entity provisions, a statement to that effect or

- in the case of accounts not prepared in accordance with those provisions, a statement to the effect that the accounts have been prepared in accordance with the provisions applicable to companies subject to the small companies' regime.

If annual accounts are approved that do not comply with the requirements of *CA 2006* (or, where applicable, the requirements of adopted International Accounting Standards), every director of the company who

- knew that they did not comply, or was reckless as to whether they complied, and
- failed to take reasonable steps to secure compliance with those requirements or, as the case may be, to prevent the accounts from being approved,

commits an offence. A person guilty of such an offence is liable (i) on conviction on indictment, to a fine; and (ii) on summary conviction, to a fine not exceeding the statutory maximum. See **29.1** OFFENCES AND LEGAL PROCEEDINGS for the statutory maximum.

[*CA 2006, ss 394, 414; SI 2013 No 3008, Reg 5(4); SI 2012 No 2301, Reg 8*].

**Corporate governance statements**. In relation to financial years beginning on or after 29 June 2008 and which did not end before 27 June 2009, any separate corporate governance statement must be approved by the board of directors and signed on behalf of the board by a director or the secretary of the company. [*CA 2006, s 419A; SI 2009 No 1581, Reg 2*].

### 2.3   PUBLICATION OF ACCOUNTS AND REPORTS

There are a number of provisions which must be complied with in *CA 2006* in connection with the publication of accounts and reports. These are considered in **2.4–2.8**. Note also that, in certain circumstances, a company can send out a copy of the strategic report with supplementary material in place of the full accounts and reports. See **6** ACCOUNTS: STAND-ALONE STRATEGIC REPORTS.

### 2.4   Name of signatory to be stated in published copies of accounts and reports

Every copy of the following document that is 'published' by or on behalf of a company must state the name of the person who signed it on behalf of the board under **2.2**.

- In the case of an unquoted company,
  - (i)    the company's balance sheet;
  - (ii)   the strategic report; and
  - (iii)  the directors' report.
- In the case of a quoted company,
  - (i)    the company's balance sheet;
  - (ii)   the directors' remuneration report;
  - (iii)  the strategic report; and
  - (iv)   the directors' report.

A quoted company is defined in *CA 2006, s 385* as a company whose equity share capital is either included in the UK official list or is officially listed in an EEA state or is admitted to trading on Nasdaq or New York Stock Exchange. A company is regarded as '*publishing*' a document if it publishes, issues or circulates it or otherwise makes it available for public inspection in a manner calculated to invite members of the public generally, or any class of members of the public, to read it.

If a copy is published without the required statement of the signatory's name, an offence is committed by the company and every officer of the company who is in default. A person guilty of such an offence is liable, on summary conviction, to a fine not exceeding level 3 on the standard scale. See **29.1** OFFENCES AND LEGAL PROCEEDINGS for the standard scale.

[*CA 2006, s 433; SI 2013 No 1970, Schedule, para 6*].

**2.5      Requirements in connection with publication of accounts**

(1) *Statutory accounts*

If a company publishes any of its 'statutory accounts', they must be accompanied by the auditor's report on those accounts (unless the company is exempt from audit and the directors have taken advantage of that exemption).

A company that prepares statutory group accounts for a financial year must not publish its statutory individual accounts for that year without also publishing with them its statutory group accounts.

'*Statutory accounts*' are a company's accounts for a financial year as required to be delivered to the Registrar of Companies (see **2.11**). They include

(i)      abridged accounts delivered to the Registrar of Companies under the special provisions for micro-entities and small companies (see **5.6** and **5.40** ACCOUNTS: SMALL COMPANIES AND MICRO-ENTITIES) and accounts with slightly reduced disclosures that can be filed by medium-sized companies (see **4.5** ACCOUNTS: MEDIUM-SIZED COMPANIES); and

(ii)     any additional copy of the annual accounts delivered in euros (see **2.11**).

In the case of an unlimited company, the statutory accounts are the accounts as prepared in accordance with *CA 2006* and approved by the board of directors.

If a company contravenes any of the above provisions, an offence is committed by the company and by every officer of the company who is in default. A person guilty of such an offence is liable on summary conviction to a fine not exceeding level 3 on the standard scale. See **29.1** OFFENCES AND LEGAL PROCEEDINGS for the standard scale.

[*CA 2006, ss 434, 448(4)(a), 449(5), 469(4)*].

(2) *Non-statutory accounts*

A company must not publish with 'non-statutory accounts' the auditor's report on the company's statutory accounts. But it must publish with non-statutory accounts a statement indicating

•        that they are not the company's statutory accounts;

•        whether statutory accounts dealing with any financial year with which the non-statutory accounts purport to deal have been delivered to the Registrar of Companies (or in the case of an unlimited company, that the company is exempt from the requirement to deliver statutory accounts); and

•        whether an auditor's report has been made on the company's statutory accounts for any such financial year, and if so whether the report

        (i)      was qualified or unqualified, or included a reference to any matters to which the auditor drew attention by way of emphasis without qualifying the report; or

(ii)     contained a statement under *CA 2006, s 498(2)* (accounting records or returns inadequate or accounts or directors' remuneration report not agreeing with records and returns), or *CA 2006, s 498(3)* (failure to obtain necessary information and explanations).

See (1) above for '*statutory accounts*'.

'*Non-statutory accounts*' means either of the following which is published otherwise than as part of the company's statutory accounts.

(i)      Any balance sheet or profit and loss account relating to, or purporting to deal with, a financial year of the company.

(ii)     An account in any form purporting to be a balance sheet or profit and loss account for 'a group headed by the company' relating to, or purporting to deal with, a financial year of the company.

A '*group headed by the company*' means a group consisting of the company and any other undertaking (regardless of whether it is a subsidiary undertaking of the company) other than a parent undertaking of the company.

If a company contravenes any of the above provisions, an offence is committed by the company, and by every officer of the company who is in default. A person guilty of such an offence is liable on summary conviction to a fine not exceeding level 3 on the standard scale. See **29.1 OFFENCES AND LEGAL PROCEEDINGS** for the standard scale.

[*[CA 2006, ss 435, 448(4)(b), 469(4)].*].

For the purposes of both (1) and (2) above, a company is regarded as publishing a document if it publishes, issues or circulates it or otherwise makes it available for public inspection in a manner calculated to invite members of the public generally, or any class of members of the public, to read it. [*CA 2006, s 436*].

**2.6   Circulation to members, debenture holders and other entitled persons**

Subject to the provisions on issuing a stand-alone strategic report with supplementary material in place of the full accounts and reports (see **6 ACCOUNTS: STAND-ALONE STRATEGIC REPORTS**) a company must send a copy of its 'annual accounts and reports' for each financial year to

•     every member of the company;

•     every holder of the company's debentures; and

•     every person who is entitled to receive notice of general meetings.

See **APPENDIX 1 DEFINITIONS** for the meaning of '*annual accounts and reports*'.

**Exceptions.** Copies need not be sent to the following persons.

(a)     A person for whom the company does not have a 'current address'. It has a current address for a person if

(i)      an address has been notified to the company by the person as one at which documents may be sent to him; and

(ii)     the company has no reason to believe that documents sent to him at that address will not reach him.

As a result of (ii) above, a company does not have a current address if previous correspondence has been returned marked not known at this address (or its electronic equivalent).

(b)     In the case of a company not having a share capital, copies need not be sent to anyone who is not entitled to receive notices of general meetings of the company.

See **16.33** DEALINGS WITH THIRD PARTIES for general provisions about supplying documents to joint holders.

[*CA 2006, s 423(1)–(4), (6)*].

Where copies are sent out over a period of days, references in the *Companies Acts* to the day on which copies are sent out are to be read as references to the last day of that period. [*CA 2006, s 423(5)*].

**Time allowed for sending out copies of accounts and reports.**

•       *A public company* must comply with the above provisions at least 21 days before the date of the general meeting of the company at which the accounts and reports in question are to be laid in accordance with **2.10**. If copies are sent out later than this, they will still be deemed to have been duly sent if all the members entitled to attend and vote at that meeting so agree.

•       *A private company* must comply with the above provisions not later than

        (i)      the end of the period for filing accounts and report (see **2.12**), or

        (ii)     if earlier, the date on which it actually delivers its accounts and reports to the Registrar of Companies.

Whether the time allowed is that for a private company or a public company is determined by reference to the company's status immediately before the end of the accounting reference period by reference to which the financial year for the accounts in question was determined.

[*CA 2006, s 424*].

**Offences.** In default in complying with any of the above provisions, an offence is committed by the company and every officer of the company who is in default. A person guilty of such an offence is liable (i) on conviction on indictment, to a fine; and (ii) on summary conviction, to a fine not exceeding the statutory maximum. See **29.1** OFFENCES AND LEGAL PROCEEDINGS for the statutory maximum. [*CA 2006, s 425*].

**Method of sending accounts.** For the provisions explaining how a company can communicate with members, etc (including in electronic form and by means of a website) see **16.29–16.33** DEALINGS WITH THIRD PARTIES.

**2.7     Right to demand copies**

In addition to any copy to which a person is entitled under **2.6**, a member or debenture holder of a company is entitled to be provided, on demand and without charge, with a single copy of

•       the company's last annual accounts;

•       the strategic report (if any) for the last financial year;

•       the last directors' report;

•       in the case of a quoted company, the last directors' remuneration report; and

•       the auditor's report on those accounts (including the report on the directors' report and, where applicable, the directors' remuneration report *and* (where applicable) on the strategic report).

If a demand made under these provisions is not complied with within seven days of receipt by the company, an offence is committed by the company and by every officer of the company who is in default. A person guilty of such an offence is liable (i) on summary conviction, to a fine not exceeding level 3 on the standard scale, and (ii) for continued contravention, a daily default fine not exceeding one-tenth of level 3 on the standard scale. See **29.1** OFFENCES AND LEGAL PROCEEDINGS for the standard scale.

[*CA 2006, ss 431, 432; SI 2013 No 1970, Schedule, para 4*]

**2.8    Quoted companies: availability of accounts and reports on website**

A quoted company (see **2.4** for a definition) must ensure that its annual accounts and reports are made available on a website and remain so available until the annual accounts and reports for the company's next financial year are made available on the website.

If the directors' remuneration policy is revised in accordance with *CA 2006, s 422A* (see **19.19**) the company must ensure that the revised policy is made available on the website on which its annual accounts and reports are made available.

**Website availability.** The accounts and reports must be made available on a website that is maintained by, or on behalf of, the company and identifies the company in question. They must be made available as soon as reasonably practicable, must be kept available until the report and accounts for the company's next financial year are made available and, where *CA 2006, s 430(2A)* applies (quoted company's revised remuneration policy), the material in question must also be made available as soon as reasonably practicable and must be kept available until the next directors' remuneration report is made available on the website. Access to the materials made available under *CA 2006, s 230*, and the ability to obtain a hard copy of such material from the website, must not be conditional on the payment of a fee or otherwise restricted (except so far as necessary to comply with any enactment or regulatory requirement in the UK or elsewhere).

A failure to make the material available on a website throughout the period mentioned in *CA 2006, s 420(4) or (4A)* as the case may be, is disregarded if

*   it is made available on the website for part of that period; and

*   the failure is wholly attributable to circumstances that it would not be reasonable to have expected the company to prevent or avoid.

**Offences.** In default in complying with the above provisions, an offence is committed by every officer of the company who is in default. A person guilty of such an offence is liable, on summary conviction, to a fine not exceeding level 3 on the standard scale. See **29.1** OFFENCES AND LEGAL PROCEEDINGS for the standard scale.

[*CA 2006, s 430; ERRA, ss 81(6), (7), (8), (9)*].

**2.9    Website publication of information by other companies**

All companies with shares traded on the Alternative Investment Market (AIM) are required by the AIM Rules to make both annual and interim accounts and reports available on a company website, and with effect from 28 September 2018, this is extended to cover details of a recognised corporate governance code that the board of directors has decided to apply, how the company complies with that code, and an explanation of the reasons for any departures. The Quoted Companies Alliance publishes a corporate governance code designed specifically for smaller quoted and AIM companies and this was updated in April 2018 in conjunction with these changes.

For periods beginning on or after 1 January 2019, the *Companies (Miscellaneous Reporting) Regulations 2018, SI 2018 No 860*, amend *CA 2006* to require the following details to be published on a website maintained by or on behalf of the company:

- for all companies other than those that qualify as small or medium-sized, the directors' statement within the strategic report explaining how they have had regard to the matters specified in *CA 2006, s 172* (see **20.5** for further details); and

- in the case of larger unlisted companies (both public and private), the directors' statement on the company's corporate governance arrangements (see **20.8** for further details).

## 2.10   LAYING OF ACCOUNTS AND REPORTS BEFORE GENERAL MEETING

### (1) Public companies

The directors of a public company must lay before the company in general meeting copies of its annual accounts and reports. They must do so not later than the end of the period for filing the accounts and reports in question (see **2.12**).

If these requirements are not complied with before the end of the period allowed, every person who immediately before the end of that period was a director of the company commits an offence. A person guilty of such an offence is liable (i) on summary conviction, to a fine not exceeding level 5 on the standard scale, and (ii) for continued contravention, a daily default fine not exceeding one-tenth of the greater of £5,000 or level 4 on the standard scale. See **29.1** Offences and Legal Proceedings for the standard scale. It is a defence for a person charged with such an offence to prove that he took all reasonable steps for securing that those requirements would be complied with before the end of that period. It is not a defence to prove that the documents in question were not in fact prepared as required.

[*CA 2006, ss 437, 438; SI 2015 No 664, Sch 3*].

### (2) Private companies

Private companies are no longer under a statutory obligation to hold an AGM or to lay accounts and reports in general meeting (although they may be required to do so under the articles). This applies to financial years ending on or after 1 October 2007 [*SI 2007 No 2194 Sch 3 Para 49*]. If a private company's articles require it to lay accounts and reports in general meeting, a special resolution can be passed to amend the articles and remove the requirement.

## 2.11   FILING ACCOUNTS AND REPORTS WITH THE REGISTRAR OF COMPANIES

The directors of a company must deliver to the Registrar of Companies for each financial year a copy of its accounts and reports unless it is exempt from filing because it is an unlimited company or a qualifying dormant subsidiary. See **12** Company Formation and Types of Companies for details of these exemptions.

[*CA 2006, s 441; SI 2008 No 393, Reg 6(6); SI 2012 No 2301, Reg 10*].

(1)   **Companies subject to the small companies regime**

The directors of a company subject to the small companies' regime (see **5.7–5.8** Accounts: Small Companies and Micro-entities)

(a)   must deliver to the Registrar of Companies for each financial year a copy of the balance sheet drawn up as at the last day of that year (and this must include a prominent statement on adoption of the small companies regime – see **5.10** Accounts: Small Companies and Micro-entities);

(b)    may also deliver to the Registrar of Companies

    (i)    a copy of the company's profit and loss account for that year; and

    (ii)    a copy of the directors' report for that year; and

(c)    where the directors deliver a copy of the company's profit and loss account ((b)(i) above) they must also deliver to the Registrar of Companies a copy of the auditor's report on the accounts (and any directors' report) that it delivers unless the company is exempt from audit and the directors have taken advantage of that exemption.

Where the balance sheet or profit and loss account is abridged pursuant to *SI 2008 No 409* (see **5.11**) the directors must also deliver to the Registrar a statement by the company that all the members of the company have consented to the abridgement.

Where the directors of a company subject to the small companies regime do not deliver to the Registrar a copy of the company's profit and loss account or directors' report, the copy of the balance sheet delivered to the Registrar of Companies must contain, in a prominent position, a statement that the company's annual accounts and reports have been delivered in accordance with the provisions applicable to companies subject to the small companies regime.

Subject to the exception below, where the directors of a company subject to the small companies regime do not deliver a copy of the company's profit and loss account to the Registrar

- the copy of the balance sheet delivered to the Registrar must disclose that fact; and

- unless the company is exempt from audit and the directors have taken advantage of that exemption, the notes to the balance sheet must satisfy the following requirements

    (i)    the notes must state whether the auditor's report was qualified or unqualified;

    (ii)    where the report was qualified, disclose the basis of the qualification (reproducing any statement under *CA 2006, s 498(2)(a)* or *(b)* or *s 498(3)* if applicable);

    (iii)    where the report was unqualified include a reference to any matters to which the auditor drew attention by way of emphasis; and

    (iv)    state the name of the auditor and (where the auditor is a firm) the name of the person who signed the auditor's report as senior statutory auditor or if the conditions in *CA 2006, s 506* (circumstances in which names may be omitted) are met, that a resolution has been passed and notified to the Secretary of State in accordance with that section.

Exception. The above does not apply if the company qualifies as a micro-entity in relation to a financial year and the company's accounts are prepared for that year in accordance with any of the micro-entity provisions (see **5.2–5.6** ACCOUNTS: SMALL COMPANIES AND MICRO-ENTITIES).

The copies of the balance sheet and any directors' report delivered to the Registrar of Companies under these provisions must state the name of the person who signed it on behalf of the board.

The copy of the auditor's report delivered to the Registrar of Companies under these provisions must

- state the name of the auditor and (where the auditor is a firm) the name of the person who signed it as senior statutory auditor; or

- if the conditions in *CA 2006, s 506* are met (circumstances in which names may be omitted, see **8.42 Audit**), state that a resolution has been passed and notified to the Secretary of State in accordance with those provisions.

[*CA 2006, s 444; SI 2008 No 393, Reg 12; SI 2013 No 3008, Reg 6; SI 2015 No 980, Reg 8(g)*].

(2) **Companies entitled to the small companies' exemption in relation to the directors' report**

Where a company is entitled to the small companies exemption in relation to its directors' report for a financial year but does not fall within (1) above only because it is a member of an ineligible group, (see **5.8 Accounts: Small Companies and Micro-entities**), the report must include the statement referred to at **20.22 Strategic Reports and Directors' Reports** and the directors of the company

- must deliver to the Registrar of Companies a copy of the company's annual accounts for that year;

- may also deliver to the Registrar of Companies a copy of the directors' report; and

- must also deliver to the Registrar of Companies a copy of the auditor's report on the accounts (and any directors' report) that it delivers unless the company is exempt from audit and the directors have taken advantage of that exemption.

The copies of the balance sheet and any directors' report delivered to the Registrar of Companies under these provisions must state the name of the person who signed it on behalf of the board.

The copy of the auditor's report delivered to the Registrar of Companies under these provisions must

- state the name of the auditor and (where the auditor is a firm) the name of the person who signed it as senior statutory auditor; and

- if the conditions in *CA 2006, s 506* (circumstances in which names may be omitted, see **8.42 Audit**) are met, state that a resolution has been passed and notified to the Secretary of State in accordance with that section.

[*CA 2006, s 444A; SI 2008 No 393, Reg 6(7); SI 2009 No 1581, Reg 10*].

(3) **Medium-sized companies**

The directors of a company that qualifies as a medium-sized company (other than a company within (1) above) in relation to a financial year (see **4.2 Accounts: Medium-Sized Companies**) must deliver to the Registrar of Companies a copy of

- the company's annual accounts;

- the strategic report;

- the directors' report;

- the auditor's report on those accounts (and on the strategic report and directors' report) unless the company is exempt from audit and the directors have taken advantage of that exemption.

# 2.11 Accounts (General): Accounting Reference (Dates/Periods)

The copies of the balance sheet and strategic report and directors' report delivered to the Registrar of Companies under these provisions must state the name of the person who signed it on behalf of the board.

The copy of the auditor's report delivered to the Registrar of Companies under these provisions must

- state the name of the auditor and (where the auditor is a firm) the name of the person who signed it as senior statutory auditor; or

- if the conditions is *CA 2006, s 506* are met (circumstances in which names may be omitted, see **8.42 AUDIT**), state that a resolution has been passed and notified to the Secretary of State in accordance with those provisions.

[*CA 2006, s 445, SI 2008 No 393, Reg 6(8); SI 2013 No 1970, Schedule, para 9; SI 2015 No 980, Reg 8*].

(4)    **Unquoted companies**

The directors of an unquoted company (which does not fall within (1)–(3) above) must deliver to the Registrar of Companies for each financial year of the company a copy of

- the company's annual accounts;

- the strategic report;

- the directors' report;

- any separate corporate governance statement; and

- the auditor's report on those accounts, the strategic report (where this is covered by the auditor's report), the directors' report and any separate corporate governance statement unless the company is exempt from audit and the directors have taken advantage of that exemption.

The copies of the balance sheet, and strategic report and directors' report and any separate corporate governance statement delivered to the Registrar of Companies under these provisions must state the name of the person who signed it on behalf of the board.

The copy of the auditor's report delivered to the Registrar of Companies under these provisions must

- state the name of the auditor and (where the auditor is a firm) the name of the person who signed it as senior statutory auditor; or

- if the conditions is *CA 2006, s 506* are met (circumstances in which names may be omitted, see **8.42 AUDIT**), state that a resolution has been passed and notified to the Secretary of State in accordance with that section.

[*CA 2006, s 446; SI 2008 No 393, Reg 6(9) and 6(9)(a); SI 2009 No 1581, Reg 3(2), 3(3) and 3(6); SI 2013 No 1970, Schedule, para 10*].

(5)    **Quoted companies**

The directors of a quoted company must deliver to the Registrar of Companies for each financial year of the company a copy of

- the company's annual accounts;

- the strategic report;

- the directors' remuneration report;

- the directors' report;

- any separate corporate governance statement; and

- the auditor's report on those accounts and on the directors' remuneration report, the strategic report (where this is covered by the auditor's report), the directors' report and any separate corporate governance statement.

The copies of the balance sheet, directors' remuneration report, the strategic report and directors' report and any separate corporate governance statement delivered to the Registrar of Companies under these provisions must state the name of the person who signed it on behalf of the board.

The copy of the auditor's report delivered to the Registrar of Companies under these provisions must

- state the name of the auditor and (where the auditor is a firm) the name of the person who signed it as senior statutory auditor; or

- if the conditions is *CA 2006, s 506* are met (circumstances in which names may be omitted, see **8.42** AUDIT), state that a resolution has been passed and notified to the Secretary of State in accordance with that section.

[*CA 2006, s 447; SI 2009 No 1581, Reg 4(2), 4(3) and 4(6); SI 2013 No 1970, Schedule, para 11*].

**Failure to file accounts and reports.** There are three possible consequences of failing to comply with the requirements under (1) to (5) above (as the case may be) before the end of the period for filing those accounts and reports (see **2.12**).

(a)   *Offences.* Every person who immediately before the end of that period was a director of the company commits an offence. A person guilty of such an offence is liable (i) on summary conviction, to a fine not exceeding level 5 on the standard scale; and (ii) for continued contravention, to a daily default fine not exceeding one-tenth of the greater of £5,000 or level 4 on the standard scale. See **29.1** OFFENCES AND PENALTIES for the standard scale. It is a defence for a person charged with such an offence to prove that he took all reasonable steps for securing that those requirements would be complied with before the end of that period. It is not a defence to prove that the documents in question were not in fact prepared as required. [*CA 2006, s 451; SI 2015 No 664, Sch 3*].

(b)   *Court orders.* If the directors of the company fail to make good the default within 14 days after the service of a notice on them requiring compliance, the court may, on the application of any member or creditor of the company or of the Registrar of Companies, make an order directing the directors (or any of them) to make good the default within such time as may be specified in the order. The court's order may provide that all costs (in Scotland, expenses) of, and incidental to, the application are to be borne by the directors. [*CA 2006, s 452*].

(c)   *Civil penalty (the late filing penalty).* In addition to any liability of the directors under (*a*) above, the company is liable to a civil penalty. The amount of the penalty depends upon the length of the period between the end of the period for filing the accounts and reports in question and the date of eventual compliance and on whether the company is a private or public company, as follows.

## 2.11 Accounts (General): Accounting Reference (Dates/Periods)

*Accounts filed on or after 1 February 2009*

*Note.* If there was a failure to comply with the filing requirements in relation to the previous financial year of the company, and that previous financial year began on or after 6 April 2008, the penalties in the table below are doubled.

| Length of period | Public company | Private company |
|---|---|---|
| Not more than 1 month | £750 | £150 |
| More than 1 month but not more than 3 months | £1,500 | £375 |
| More than 3 months but not more than 6 months | £3,000 | £750 |
| More than 6 months | £7,500 | £1,500 |

Whether a company is a public company or a private company depends upon its status at the end of the financial year in question.

It is not a defence in proceedings under these provisions to prove that the documents in question were not in fact prepared.

[*CA 2006, s 453; SI 2008 No 497*].

**Filing of accounts in euros.** The amounts set out in the annual accounts of a company may also be shown in the same accounts translated into euros. When complying with (1) to (4) above, the directors may deliver to the Registrar of Companies an additional copy of the company's annual accounts in which the amounts have been translated into euros. In both cases, the amounts must have been translated at the exchange rate prevailing on the date to which the balance sheet is made up and the rate must be disclosed in the notes to the accounts. The requirement to disclose the rate in the notes to the accounts does not apply to the individual accounts of a company for a financial year in which the company qualifies as a micro-entity. For the meaning of 'micro-entity' see **5.3 ACCOUNTS: SMALL COMPANIES AND MICRO-ENTITIES**,

[*CA 2006, ss 469(1)–(3), (3A); SI 2013 No 3008, Reg 7(2)*].

**For the form, authentication and manner of delivery of accounts sent to the Registrar of Companies.** See **39.6 REGISTRAR OF COMPANIES**.

## 2.12 Period allowed for filing accounts

Subject to below, the period allowed for the directors of a company to deliver accounts and reports for a financial year to the Registrar of Companies under **2.11** is

- *for a private company*, nine months after the end of the relevant accounting reference period; and

- *for a public company*, six months after the end of the relevant accounting reference period.

The '*relevant accounting reference period*' is the accounting reference period by reference to which the financial year for the accounts in question was determined (see **2.17**).

Whether the period allowed is that for a private company or a public company is determined by reference to the company's status immediately before the end of the relevant accounting reference period.

**Exceptions.**

(1)    If the relevant accounting reference period is the company's first and is a period of more than twelve months, the period is

- nine months or six months, as the case may be, from the first anniversary of the incorporation of the company; or

- three months after the end of the accounting reference period;

whichever expires last.

(2)    If the relevant accounting reference period is treated as shortened by virtue of a notice given by the company under **2.19**, the period is

- that applicable in accordance with the above provisions; or

- three months from the date of the notice;

whichever expires last.

(3)    Applying for extra time to file. If for any special reason the Secretary of State thinks fit, he may, on an application made before the expiry of the period otherwise allowed, give notice in writing to a company extending that period by such further period as may be specified in the notice but any such extension must not have the effect of extending the filing period to more than 12 months after the end of the relevant accounting reference period.

An application for such an extension, giving reasons why the extension should be granted, should be sent before the normal filing deadlines. The application must be in writing (by e-mailing the enquiries section at Companies House) or in hard copy (for companies incorporated in England and Wales) to Companies House, Crown Way, Cardiff, CF14 3UZ or (for companies incorporated in Scotland) to Companies House, 4th Floor, Edinburgh Quay 2, 139 Fountainbridge, Edinburgh, EH1 9FF. ('Companies House Guidance' (July 2018), section 7 – available at www.gov.uk.)

**Calculation of the period allowed.** For the purposes of calculating the period for filing a company's accounts and reports which is expressed as a specified number of months from a specified date (or after the end of a specified previous period), the period ends with the date in the appropriate month corresponding to the specified date or the last day of the specified previous period. For example, if the end of the accounting reference period is 5 June, six months from then is 5 December. But this is overridden in two circumstances.

(a)    If the specified date (or the last day of the specified previous period) is the last day of a month, the period ends with the last day of the appropriate month (whether or not that is the corresponding date). For example, if the end of the accounting reference period is 30 June, six months from then is 31 December (not 30 December).

(b)    If the specified date (or the last day of the specified previous period) is not the last day of a month but is the 29th or 30th, and the appropriate month is February, the period ends with the last day of February. For example, if the end of the accounting reference period is 29 or 30 August, six months from then is the last day of the following February.

[*CA 2006, ss 442, 443; SI 2015 No 980, Reg 8(3)(b)*].

**Companies House policy.** Companies House rigidly applies the deadline. If a filing deadline expires on a Sunday or Bank Holiday, the accounts must still be filed by that date and therefore should be posted in time to arrive before such a deadline.

## 2.12 Accounts (General): Accounting Reference (Dates/Periods)

Companies House cannot accept accounts until they meet the requirements of *CA 2006*. If, for example, a signature is missing, the accounts will be returned for amendment. This might result in a penalty if the corrected accounts are delivered late and it is therefore recommended that accounts are delivered as soon as they are completed and as far in advance as possible of the last date for delivery.

(Companies House Guidance 'Life of a company: annual requirements – Filing accounts', sections 6 and 8 – available at www.gov.uk).

### 2.13 REVISION OF DEFECTIVE ACCOUNTS AND REPORTS

If it appears to the directors of a company that

- the annual accounts or

- strategic report or

- directors' report, or

- directors' remuneration report

did not comply with the requirements of *CA 2006* (or, where applicable, adopted international accounting standards), they may prepare revised accounts or a revised report. Where copies of the previous accounts or report have been sent out to members, delivered to the Registrar of Companies or (in the case of a public company) laid before the company in general meeting, the revisions must do no more than correct those respects in which the previous accounts, etc did not comply with the said requirements and make any necessary consequential alterations.

[*CA 2006, s 454(1) (2); SI 2013 No 1970, Reg 1(3), Schedule, paras 12(b), 12(c)*].

For provisions relating to defective reports, see **19.20–19.25** DIRECTORS' REMUNERATION REPORTS and **20.23–20.29** STRATEGIC REPORTS AND DIRECTORS' REPORTS.

(1)     **Contents of revised accounts**

The provisions of *CA 2006* (and, where applicable, *IAS Regulations*) as to the matters to be included in a company's annual accounts apply to revised accounts as if they had been prepared and approved by the directors as at the date of approval of the original accounts. In particular,

- the revised accounts must show a true and fair view as at the date of the original accounts; and

- the requirement to deal in the accounts with liabilities arising between the balance sheet date and the date the accounts are signed is to be treated as a reference to the date of the original accounts.

Where the accounts provisions in *CA 2006* are amended after the date of approval of the original accounts but before the date of revision, it is the provisions before amendment that apply. [*SI 2008 No 373, Regs 2, 3(1)–(3), 19(1)*]. See **2.16** for '*true and fair view*'.

(2)     **Approval and signature**

The provisions under **2.2** as regards the approval and signing of accounts apply equally to revised accounts, but if the revision is by way of '*supplementary note*' (ie a note indicating corrections to be made to the original accounts or reports), it is that note rather than the balance sheet which must be signed. The approved revised accounts (or supplementary note) must state the date of approval. Where copies of the original accounts have been sent out to members, etc under **2.6**, laid before the company in general meeting under **2.10** or delivered to the Registrar of Companies under **2.11**, the directors must, before approving the revised accounts, cause the following matters to be made in a prominent position in the revised accounts (or the supplementary note).

- In the case of revisions by replacement (ie where revision is by way of a replacement set of accounts in substitution for the originals):

  (i) that the revised accounts replace the original annual accounts for the specified financial year;

  (ii) that they are now the company's statutory accounts for that financial year;

  (iii) that they have been prepared as at the date the original accounts were approved and not as at the date the revised accounts were approved and so do not deal with events between those dates;

  (iv) the respects in which the original accounts did not comply with the requirements of *CA 2006*; and

  (v) any significant amendments made as a consequence of remedying those defects.

- In the case of revision by supplementary note:

  (i) that the note revises in certain respects the original annual accounts and is to be treated as forming part of those accounts; and

  (ii) that the annual accounts have been revised as at the date the original accounts were approved and not as at the date of the revised accounts were approved and so do not deal with events between those dates.

The penalty provisions in **2.2** apply in the case of non-compliance.

[*SI 2008 No 373, Regs 2, 4*].

(3)    **Effect of revision and publication of accounts**

Upon the directors approving revised accounts, the provisions of *CA 2006* have effect as if the revised accounts were, as from the date of their approval, the annual accounts of the company in place of the original annual accounts. This applies in particular for the purposes of

- *CA 2006, ss 431, 432* (the right to demand copies of accounts, see **2.7**);

- *CA 2006, s 434(3)* (meaning of 'statutory accounts', see **2.5**); and

- *CA 2006, s 423* (persons entitled to receive copies, see **2.6**), *CA 2006, s 437* (accounts, etc of public company to be laid before company in general meeting, see **2.10**) and *CA 2006, s 441* (accounts, etc to be delivered to Registrar of Companies, see **2.11**) if the requirements of those provisions have not been complied with prior to the date of revision.

Where the directors have prepared a revised report and copies of the original report have been sent to any person under *CA 2006, s 423* (persons entitled to receive copies, see **2.6**) or *CA 2006, s 146* (traded companies: nomination of persons to enjoy information rights, see **26.4** Members), the directors must send to any such person

- in the case of a revision by replacement, a copy of the revised accounts, together with a copy of the auditor's report on those accounts; or

- in the case of revision by supplementary note, a copy of that note together with a copy of the auditor's report on the revised accounts.

This must be done not more than 28 days after the date of the revision (ie the date on which the revised report is approved by the directors).

The directors must also, not more than 28 days after the revision, send a copy of the revised accounts and auditor's report on those accounts to any person who is not entitled to receive a copy under the above provisions but who is, as at the date of revision,

(a)   a member of the company,

(b)   a holder of the company's debentures, or

(c)   a person who is entitled to receive notice of general meetings

unless the company would be entitled at that date to send to that person a strategic report and supplementary material.

The exceptions from the requirement to send copies of the annual accounts and reports in **2.6** equally apply to sending out copies of the revised directors' report.

References in *CA 2006* to the day on which the accounts are sent out refer to the original accounts (with *CA 2006, s 423(5)* – see **2.6** – applying where necessary) in cases where the sending out of the original accounts has been completed prior to the date of the directors' approval of the revised accounts. In other cases, such references are to the day, or the last day, on which the revised accounts are sent out.

In default in complying with the above provisions, an offence is committed by each of the directors who approved the revised accounts. A person guilty of such an offence is liable (i) on conviction on indictment, to a fine; and (ii) on summary conviction, to a fine not exceeding the statutory maximum. See **29.1** OFFENCES AND LEGAL PROCEEDINGS for the statutory maximum.

[*SI 2008 No 373, Regs 10, 12; SI 2013 No 2224, Reg 11*].

(4)   **Laying of revised accounts**

Where the directors of a public company have prepared revised accounts and copies of the original annual accounts have been laid before a general meeting under **2.10**, a copy of the revised accounts (together with the auditor's report thereon) must be laid at the next general meeting held (after the date of the directors' approval to the revised accounts) at which the annual accounts for a financial year are laid (unless the revised accounts have already been laid before an earlier general meeting). The same penalty provisions as in **2.10** apply, except that the reference to 'the period allowed' was a reference to the period between the date of approval of the revised accounts and the date of the, next general meeting, referred to above. [*SI 2008 No 373, Reg 13*].

(5)   **Delivery to Registrar of Companies**

Where the directors have prepared revised accounts and a copy of the original accounts has been delivered to the Registrar of Companies, the directors must deliver, within 28 days of their approval of the revised accounts, a copy of the revised accounts (or supplementary note) together with the auditor's report on the revised accounts.

The same offences apply as in **2.11**(*a*) (Failure to file accounts and reports) for failure to deliver the replacement accounts in the period of 28 days referred to above. [*SI 2008 No 373, Reg 14*].

## 2.14   Powers of the Secretary of State and authorised persons

Where

- copies of a company's annual accounts strategic report or directors' report have been sent out in accordance with **2.6**, or

- a copy of a company's annual accounts strategic report or directors' report has been laid before the company in general meeting under **2.10** or delivered to the Registrar of Companies under **2.11**

the Secretary of State (or a person authorised by him for these purposes, see below) may apply to the court for a declaration (or, in Scotland, a declarator) that the annual accounts of the company do not comply (or a strategic report or directors' report do not comply) with the requirements of *CA 2006*.

If at the end of the period specified in the notice (which must be at least one month), it appears to the Secretary of State that the directors have not

- given a satisfactory explanation of the accounts or report, or

- revised the accounts or report so as to comply with the requirements of *CA 2006*,

the Secretary of State (or a person authorised by him for these purposes, see below) may apply to the court for a declaration (or, in Scotland, a declarator) that the annual accounts of the company do not comply (or a directors' report does not comply) with the requirements of *CA 2006* and for an order requiring the directors to prepare revised accounts (or a revised report).

The applicant must give notice of the application, together with a general statement of the matters at issue, to the Registrar of Companies for registration. At the end of the proceedings, he must similarly give the Registrar of Companies a copy of the court order for registration or, where applicable, notice that the application has either failed or been withdrawn.

If the court orders revised accounts to be prepared, it may give directions with respect to

- auditing of the accounts;

- the revision of any directors' report, strategic report (or strategic report and supplementary material) or directors' remuneration report;

- the taking of steps by the directors to bring the order to the notice of those person likely to rely on the previous accounts; and

- any other matters which it thinks fit.

If the court orders a revised strategic report or directors' report to be prepared, it may give directions with respect to

- the review of the directors' report by the auditor;

- the taking of steps by the directors to bring the order to the notice of persons likely to rely on the previous report; and

- any other matters which it thinks fit.

If the court finds that the accounts or report did not comply with the requirements of *CA 2006* (or, where applicable, adopted international accounting standards), it may order that those directors who were party to the approval of the defective accounts, etc should bear all or part of both the costs (in Scotland, expenses) of the application (including incidental costs) and any reasonable expenses incurred by the company in connection with, or in consequence of, the preparing of the revised accounts, etc.

Every director of the company at the time of the approval of the annual reports and accounts is deemed to have been party to the approval unless he shows that he took all reasonable steps to prevent that approval. The court may, however, take account of whether the directors party to the approval knew, or ought to have known, that the accounts, etc did not comply with the requirements of *CA 2006* (or, where applicable, adopted international accounting standards) and may exclude one or more directors from the order or order the payment of different amounts by different directors.

**Revised accounts.** The above provisions apply equally to revised annual accounts revised strategic reports and revised directors' reports, in which case they have effect as if the references to revised accounts or reports were references to further revised accounts or reports.

**Authorised person.** The Secretary of State can authorise persons to act on his behalf for the purposes of the above provisions. The Conduct Committee of the Financial Reporting Council (established under the articles of the Financial Reporting Council Ltd) has been the authorised body since 2 July 2012.

[*CA 2006, ss 455–457; SI 2012 No 1439; SI 2013 No 1970, Schedule, para 14*].

**Disclosure of tax information by HM Revenue and Customs (HMRC).** HMRC can disclose information to a person authorised under the above provisions to facilitate his application to the court for a declaration that a company's accounts do not comply with the legislation. Any personal data cannot be disclosed in contravention of the *Data Protection Act 1998*. The authorised person can only use the information to determine whether there are grounds for an application, to determine whether or not to make an application, and in any court proceedings. The authorised person cannot further disclose the information except to the person to whom it relates or in connection with court proceedings.

In contravention of use or disclosure, a person is guilty of an offence and liable (i) on conviction on indictment, to imprisonment for a term not exceeding two years or a fine (or both); and (ii) on summary conviction, to imprisonment for a term not exceeding 12 months (in Scotland and Northern Ireland, six months) or a fine up to the statutory maximum (or both). See **29.1** OFFENCES AND LEGAL PROCEEDINGS for the statutory maximum. It is a defence for a person charged with such an offence to prove he did not know, and had no reason to suspect, that the information has been disclosed under these provisions or that he took all reasonable steps and exercised all due diligence to avoid the commission of the offence. Where such an offence is committed by a body corporate, every officer of the body who is in default also commits the offence. For this purpose, any person who purports to act as a director, manager or secretary of the body is treated as an officer of the company and is, if the body is a company, any shadow director (see **18.1(2)** DIRECTORS). [*CA 2006, s 458*]. Proceedings for such an offence can only be brought with the consent of the Secretary of State or the Director of Public Prosecutions (in Northern Ireland the Director of Public Prosecutions for Northern Ireland). [*CA 2006, s 1126*].

**Powers of an authorised person to require documents, information and explanations.** Where it appears to an authorised person that a company's annual accounts, strategic report or directors' report may not comply with the requirements of *CA 2006* (or, where applicable, *IAS Regulation, Art 4*) he may require

(a)     the company,

(b)     any officer, employee or auditor of the company, and

(c)     any person who fell within (*b*) above at the time to which the document or information relates

to produce any document (which includes information recorded in any form, eg on computer) or provide him with any information or explanations that he may reasonably require for the purposes of discovering whether there are grounds for an application to the court or determining whether or not to make such an application. A statement made by any person under these provisions cannot be used in evidence against him in any criminal proceedings. Nothing in the above provisions compels any person to disclose documents or information in respect of which a claim to legal professional privilege (in Scotland, a claim to confidentiality of communications) could be maintained. Subject to this, on failure to comply, a court can grant an order directing that the information or explanations are provided.

Information relating to the private affairs of an individual can only be disclosed, during the lifetime of that individual, with his consent. Similarly, any information which relates to any particular business can only be disclosed, so long as that business continues to be carried on, with the consent of the person for the time being carrying on the business. These restrictions do not apply to the disclosure of information

•       that is or has been available to the public from another source;

•       for the purposes of facilitating the carrying out by the authorised person of his functions under *CA 2006, s 456*;

•       to the Secretary of State, the Department of Enterprise, Trade and Investment for Northern Ireland, the Treasury, the Bank of England, the Financial Services Authority, or the Commissioners of Revenue and Customs;

•       for certain specified circumstances including

   (i)     assisting the Financial Reporting Council to exercise its functions under *CA 2006, Pt 42* (statutory auditors);

   (ii)    facilitating the carrying out of inspections under *CA 2006, Sch 10, para 23* (arrangements for independent monitoring of auditors of listed companies and other major bodies);

   (iii)   disciplinary proceedings relating to the performance of his professional duties by an accountant or auditor;

   (iv)    enabling the Secretary of State or Treasury to exercise any of their functions under the *Companies Acts, CJA 1993, Pt 5* (insider dealing), *IA 1986* (or the *Insolvency (Northern Ireland) Order 1989*), *CDDA 1986* (or the *Company Directors Disqualification (Northern Ireland) Order 2002*), and *FSMA 2000*;

   (v)     enabling the Department of Enterprise, Trade and Investment for Northern Ireland to exercise any powers conferred on it relating to companies, directors' disqualification or insolvency;

   (vi)    enabling the Bank of England or the Commissioners of Revenue and Customs to exercise their functions;

   (vii)   enabling the FCA to exercise its functions under the *Building Societies Act 1986, CA 1989, Part 7, FSMA 2000*, or the legislation relating to friendly societies or to industrial and provident societies; or

(viii)   in pursuance of any EU obligation.

•   to a body that exercises functions of a public nature under legislation in any country or territory outside the UK similar in function to those of the authorised person and which is made for the purpose of enabling or assisting that body to exercise those functions.

But this does not authorise the making of a disclosure in contravention of data protection legislation.

A person who discloses information in contravention of the above provisions commits an offence and is liable (i) on conviction on indictment, to imprisonment for two years or a fine (or both); and (ii) on summary conviction, to imprisonment for a term not exceeding 12 months (in Scotland and Northern Ireland, six months) or a fine up to the statutory maximum (or both). See **29.1** OFFENCES AND LEGAL PROCEEDINGS for the statutory maximum. It is a defence for a person charged with such an offence to show that he did not know, and had no reason to suspect, that the information has been disclosed under these powers or that he took all reasonable steps and exercised all due diligence to avoid the commission of the offence. Where such an offence is committed by a body corporate, every officer of the body who is in default also commits the offence. For this purpose, any person who purports to act as a director, manager or secretary of the body is treated as an officer of the company and is, if the body is a company, any shadow director (see **18.1**(2) DIRECTORS).

[*CA 2006 ss 459–461; SI 2008 No 948, Sch 1, paras 245, 246; SI 2013 No 1970, Schedule, para 16*].

Proceedings for such an offence can only be brought with the consent of the Secretary of State or the Director of Public Prosecutions (in Northern Ireland the Director of Public Prosecutions for Northern Ireland). [*CA 2006, s 1126*].

## 2.15   ACCOUNTING STANDARDS

**Companies Act accounts**. Accounts of large companies must disclose by way of note that they have been prepared in accordance with applicable accounting standards. This requirement does not apply to small and medium-sized companies.

A new framework for UK accounting was introduced for financial reporting periods beginning on or after 1 January 2015 and all previous UK accounting standards and related pronouncements were withdrawn from this date. UK accounting standards take the form of Financial Reporting Standards (FRS), with the following standards currently in issue (and most of these have been updated since they were first issued, some on a number of occasions).

| | |
|---|---|
| FRS 100 | Application of Financial Reporting Requirements |
| FRS 101 | Reduced Disclosure Framework |
| FRS 102 | The Financial Reporting Standard applicable in the UK and Republic of Ireland |
| FRS 103 | Insurance Contracts |
| FRS 104 | Interim Financial Reporting |
| FRS 105 | The Financial Reporting Standard applicable to the Micro-entities Regime |

The FRC carried out the first triennial review of the new framework in 2016–17 and new editions of all six UK accounting standards were issued in March 2018 incorporating all amendments made to date, including those that resulted from the triennial review.

**IAS accounts.** Where a company must, or (as the case may be) opts to, prepare IAS accounts rather than Companies Act accounts, its accounts must be prepared on the basis of the accounting standards issued by the International Accounting Standard Board (IASB) which is the standard setting body of the IFRS. The international accounting standards currently in issue are as follows.

| | |
|---|---|
| IFRS 1 | First-time adoption of international financial reporting standards |
| IFRS 2 | Share-based payment |
| IFRS 3 | Business combinations |
| IFRS 4 | Insurance contracts (superseded by IFRS 17 for periods beginning on or after 1 January 2021) |
| IFRS 5 | Non-current assets held for sale and discontinued operations |
| IFRS 6 | Exploration for and evaluation of mineral resources |
| IFRS 7 | Financial Instruments: disclosures |
| IRFS 8 | Operating segments |
| IRFS 9 | Financial Instruments |
| IRFS 10 | Consolidated financial statements |
| IRFS 11 | Joint arrangements |
| IRFS 12 | Disclosure of interests in other entities |
| IRFS 13 | Fair value measurement |
| IFRS 14 | Regulatory deferral accounts |
| IFRS 15 | Revenue from contracts with customers |
| IFRS 16 | Leases |
| IFRS 17 | Insurance contracts |
| IAS 1 | Presentation of financial statements |
| IAS 2 | Inventories |
| IAS 7 | Statements of cash flow |
| IAS 8 | Accounting policies, changes in accounting estimates and errors |
| IAS 10 | Events after the reporting period |
| IAS 11 | Construction contracts (superseded by IFRS 15 for periods beginning on or after 1 January 2018) |
| IAS 12 | Income taxes |
| IAS 16 | Property, plant and equipment |
| IAS 17 | Leases (superseded by IFRS 16 for periods beginning on or after 1 January 2019) |
| IAS 18 | Revenue (superseded by IFRS 15 for periods beginning on or after 1 January 2018) |
| IAS 19 | Employee benefits |
| IAS 20 | Accounting for government grants and disclosure of government assistance |
| IAS 21 | The effects of changes in foreign exchange rates |
| IAS 23 | Borrowing costs |
| IAS 24 | Related party disclosures |
| IAS 26 | Accounting and reporting by retirement benefit plans |
| IAS 27 | Separate financial statements |
| IAS 28 | Investments in associates and joint ventures |
| IAS 29 | Financial reporting in hyperinflationary economies |

# 2.15 Accounts (General): Accounting Reference (Dates/Periods)

| IAS 32 | Financial instruments: presentation |
| IAS 33 | Earnings per share |
| IAS 34 | Interim financial reporting |
| IAS 36 | Impairment of assets |
| IAS 37 | Provisions, contingent liabilities and contingent assets |
| IAS 38 | Intangible assets |
| IAS 39 | Financial instruments: recognition and measurement (largely superseded by IFRS 9 for periods beginning on or after 1 January 2018) |
| IAS 40 | Investment property |
| IAS 41 | Agriculture |

## 2.16 TRUE AND FAIR VIEW

The directors of a company must not approve annual accounts unless they are satisfied that they give a true and fair view of the assets, liabilities, financial position and profit or loss

• in the case of the company's individual accounts, of the company; and

• in the case of the company's group accounts, of the undertakings included in the consolidation as a whole so far as concerns the members of the company.

The auditor of a company, in carrying out his functions in relations to the company's annual accounts must have regard to the directors' duty under the above provisions.

Where a company qualifies as a micro-entity in relation to a financial year and prepares accounts under the micro-entity financial reporting regime (see 5 ACCOUNTS: SMALL COMPANIES AND MICRO-ENTITIES) the following applies to the directors in their consideration of whether the individual accounts of the company for that year give a true and fair view

• where the accounts comprise only micro-entity minimum accounting items (as defined in CA 2006, s 474(1)), the directors must disregard any provision of an accounting standard which would require the accounts to contain information additional to those items

• in relation to a micro-entity minimum accounting item contained in the accounts, the directors must disregard any provision of an accounting standard which would require the accounts to contain further information in relation to that item and

• where the accounts contain an item of information additional to the micro-entity minimum accounting items, the directors must have regard to any provision of an accounting standard which relates to that item.

[CA 2006, ss 393, 474(1); SI 2013 No 3008, Reg 5].

**Counsels' opinions on the meaning of 'true and fair view'.** There is no definition of 'true and fair view' in CA 2006 (or earlier legislation) and the courts have never attempted to define it although there has been some commentary in case law. In 2008 the FRC took counsel's opinion. A copy of the 2008 opinion given by Martin Moore QC is available on the FRC website together with his 2013 commentary on an opinion given by George Bompas QC. Martin Moore's 2008 Opinion confirms that the introduction of IFRS did not change the fundamental requirement for accounts to give a true and fair view. The FRC believe that this 2008 Opinion is an important confirmation of a key contributor to the integrity of financial reporting in the UK. In 2014 the FRC published a paper 'True and Fair' which confirms that the concept of true and fair remains of fundamental importance in both UK GAAP and IFRS.

## 2.17 ACCOUNTING REFERENCE DATES AND PERIODS

A company must prepare accounts for each financial year. The financial year is determined by the company's 'accounting reference period' which, in turn, is determined according to its 'accounting reference date' in each calendar year (see **2.18**). [*CA 2006, s 391(1)*]. This date can only be altered in certain defined circumstances (see **2.19**).

A company's first accounting reference period is the period of more than six months, but not more than 18 months, beginning with its date of incorporation and ending with its accounting reference date. Its subsequent accounting reference periods are successive periods of 12 months beginning immediately after the end of the previous accounting reference period and ending with its accounting reference date. [*CA 2006, s 391(5), (6)*].

## 2.18 ACCOUNTING REFERENCE DATE

The '*accounting reference date*' is the date on which a company's accounting reference period ends in each calendar year. Subject to **2.19**, the accounting reference date of a company is determined as follows.

**For companies incorporated in Great Britain before 1 April 1996**, the accounting reference date is

- the date specified by notice to the Registrar of Companies in accordance with *CA 1985, s 224(2)* (notice specifying accounting reference date given within nine months of incorporation); or

- failing such notice

    (i)   in the case of a company incorporated before 1 April 1990, 31 March; and

    (ii)  in the case of a company incorporated on or after 1 April 1990, the last day of the month in which the anniversary of its incorporation falls.

**For companies incorporated in Northern Ireland before 22 August 1997**, the accounting reference date is

- the date specified by notice to the Registrar of Companies in accordance with *Companies (Northern Ireland) Order 1986, Art 232(2)* (notice specifying accounting reference date given within nine months of incorporation); or

- failing such notice

    (i)   in the case of a company incorporated before the coming into operation of *Companies (Northern Ireland) Order 1990, Art 5*, 31 March; and

    (ii)  in the case of a company incorporated after the coming into operation of that *Article*, the last day of the month in which the anniversary of its incorporation falls.

**For companies incorporated in Great Britain after 31 March 1996 or Northern Ireland after 21 August 1997**, the accounting reference date is the last day of the month in which the anniversary of its incorporation falls.

[*CA 2006, s 391(2)–(4), (7)*].

## 2.19 Alteration of an accounting reference date

A company may, by notice to the Registrar of Companies, specify a new accounting reference date having effect in relation to either

- its current and subsequent accounting reference periods; or

- its immediately preceding and subsequent accounting reference periods. This option is not available if the period for filing accounts and reports for the financial year determined by reference to the immediately preceding accounting reference period has already expired (normally six months after the end of the relevant accounting reference period for public companies and nine months for private companies).

The notice must state whether the current or immediately preceding accounting reference period is to be shortened or extended (ie whether it is to end on the first or second occasion on which the new accounting reference date falls).

**Notice to shorten.** A company may give notice to shorten the current or immediately preceding accounting reference period as often as it likes.

**Notice to extend.** A notice to extend a company's current or immediately preceding accounting reference period is not effective if given less than five years after the end of an earlier accounting reference period of the company which was extended under these provisions unless

(a)   it is given by a company that is a 'subsidiary undertaking' or 'parent undertaking' (see APPENDIX 1 DEFINITIONS ) of another 'EEA undertaking' and the new accounting reference date coincides with that of the other EEA undertaking (or, where that undertaking is not a company, the last day of its financial year);

(b)   the company is in administration under *IA 1986, Pt II* or *Insolvency (Northern Ireland) Order 1989, Pt III*; or

(c)   the Secretary of State directs otherwise.

But in any case, unless (*b*) above applies, an accounting reference period may not be extended so as to exceed 18 months and any notice attempting to do this is ineffective.

'*EEA undertaking*' means an undertaking established under the law of any part of the UK or any other EEA State.

[*CA 2006, s 392*].

**EEA States.** See Appendix 1 Definitions for the current EEA States.

**Listed companies.** See 33 PUBLIC AND LISTED COMPANIES for additional requirements for listed companies.


**2.20   OVERSEAS COMPANIES**

**With effect from 1 October 2009, see 30 OVERSEAS COMPANIES.**

# 3 Accounts: Large Companies

**Cross-references.** See 2 ACCOUNTS GENERAL AND ACCOUNTING REFERENCE DATES AND PERIODS; 4 ACCOUNTS; MEDIUM-SIZED COMPANIES; 5 ACCOUNTS: SMALL COMPANIES AND MICRO-ENTITIES; 6 ACCOUNTS: STAND-ALONE STRATEGIC REPORTS; 19 DIRECTORS' REMUNERATION REPORTS AND POLICIES—QUOTED COMPANIES; APPENDIX 1 DEFINITIONS.

**Background.** The provisions as described in this chapter are, unless otherwise stated, taken from *CA 2006* and supporting Regulations which apply to accounts for financial years beginning on or after 6 April 2008. The requirements of the *Companies, Partnerships and Groups (Accounts and Reports) Regulations 2015 (SI 2015 No 980)* are referred throughout this chapter where they amend either CA 2006 or the 2008 Regulations. The 2015 Regulations apply in respect of financial years beginning on or after 1 January 2016.

# 3.1  Accounts: Large Companies

## 3.1  INTRODUCTION TO ACCOUNTS REQUIREMENTS

The provisions described in this chapter relate to the requirements for accounts of all companies other than those that are subject to the small companies regime, which have the option of preparing abridged accounts, and those that qualify as micro-entities and have the option of preparing accounts under the micro-entity regime (see 5 ACCOUNTS: SMALL COMPANIES AND MICRO-ENTITIES). Where a company qualifies as 'medium-sized' in relation to a financial year, it is not entitled to prepare individual accounts in abridged form in the same way as a company subject to the small companies regime, but it is entitled to certain exemptions with respect to its accounts. See 4 ACCOUNTS: MEDIUM-SIZED COMPANIES for the definition of 'medium-sized' and the provisions relating to accounts of medium-sized companies generally.

## 3.2  INDIVIDUAL ACCOUNTS: DUTY TO PREPARE

The directors of every company must prepare accounts for the company for each of its financial years unless the company is exempt under *CA 2006, s 394A* (certain dormant subsidiaries – see 5.9). Those accounts are referred to in the legislation and in this chapter as the company's 'individual accounts'. [*CA 2006, s 394; SI 2012 No 2301, Reg 8*].

Subject to below, these accounts may be prepared in accordance with

- *CA 2006, s 396* ('*Companies Act individual accounts*'); or

- international accounting standards ('*IAS individual accounts*').

But

- the individual accounts of a company that is a charity *must* be Companies Act individual accounts; and

- after the first financial year in which the directors of a company prepare IAS individual accounts ('*the first IAS year*'), all subsequent individual accounts of the company must be prepared in accordance with international accounting standards unless there is a '*relevant change of circumstance*'. This is subject to the right to change to Companies Act accounts set out in *CA 2006, s 395(4A)* (see below) A relevant change of circumstance occurs if, at any time during or after the first IAS year

  (i)   the company becomes a subsidiary undertaking of another undertaking that does not prepare IAS individual accounts;

  (ii)  the company ceases to be a subsidiary undertaking;

  (iii) the company ceases to be a company with securities admitted to trading on a regulated market in an EEA State; or

  (iv)  a parent undertaking of the company ceases to be an undertaking with securities admitted to trading on a regulated market in an EEA State.

After a financial year in which IAS individual accounts are prepared, the directors may change to preparing Companies Act individual accounts for a reason other than a relevant change of circumstance, provided they have not changed to Companies Act accounts in the five years preceding the first day of that financial year.

If, having changed to preparing Companies Act individual accounts, the directors again prepare IAS individual accounts for the company, the above provisions apply again as if the first financial year for which such accounts are again prepared were the first IAS year.

[*CA 2006, s 395; SI 2008 No 393, Reg 9; SI 2012 No 2301, Reg 12*].

See Appendix 1 Definitions for the current EEA States.

**Companies Act individual accounts.** Companies Act individual accounts must state

(a)     the part of the UK in which the company is registered;

(b)     the company's registered number;

(c)     whether the company is a public or private company and whether it is limited by shares or by guarantee;

(d)     the address of the company's registered office; and

(e)     where appropriate, the fact that the company is being wound up

and must comprise

•     a balance sheet as at the last day of the financial year; and

•     a profit and loss account.

The balance sheet must give a true and fair view of the state of affairs of the company as at the end of the financial year and the profit and loss account must give a true and fair view of the profit or loss of the company for the financial year. See **2.16** Accounts: General for the interpretation of '*true and fair view*'.

Companies Act individual accounts must comply with the *Large and Medium Sized Companies and Groups (Accounts and Reports) Regulations 2008 (SI 2008 No 410)* as amended by subsequent regulations as described in **3.3** to **3.35**. The regulations prescribe the form and content of the balance sheet and profit and loss account and additional information to be provided by way of notes to the accounts. If compliance with those provisions, and other provisions made by or under *CA 2006* (see **3.36** to **3.54**) as to the matters to be included in a company's individual accounts or in notes to those accounts, would not be sufficient to give a true and fair view, the necessary additional information must be given in the accounts or notes. If, in special circumstances, compliance with any of those provisions is inconsistent with the requirement to give a true and fair view, the directors must depart from that provision to the extent necessary to give a true and fair view. Particulars of any such departure, the reasons for it and its effect must be given in a note to the accounts.

[*CA 2006, s 396; SI 2015 No 980, Reg 5(4)*].

**IAS individual accounts.** The provisions as described in **3.3** to **3.35** do not apply to IAS individual accounts. Instead, individual accounts must be prepared on the basis of the accounting standards issued by the International Accounting Standard Board (IASB). [*EC Council Regulation 1606/2002, Art 4*]. In place of the profit and loss account and balance sheet, companies must prepare primary financial statements and supporting notes as required under international accounting standards. See **2.15** Accounts: General for a list of standards.

However, the provisions relating to

•     information about related undertakings (see **3.36** to **3.44**),

•     directors' remuneration and benefits (see **3.45** to **3.52**),

•     auditor's remuneration and liability limitation agreements (see **3.53**), and

•     off balance sheet arrangements (see **3.54**)

continue to apply where IAS individual accounts are prepared, as do aspects of *CA 2006* that deal with matters outside the scope of international accounting standards (eg the requirements relating to directors' reports, publication (as opposed to preparation) of accounts, and audit).

## 3.2 Accounts: Large Companies

Where the directors of a company prepare IAS individual accounts, they must state in the notes to the accounts that the accounts have been prepared in accordance with international accounting standards. They must also state

- the part of the UK in which the company is registered;

- the company's registered number;

- whether the company is a public or private company and whether it is limited by shares or by guarantee;

- the address of the company's registered office; and

- where appropriate, the fact that the company is being wound up.

[*CA 2006, s 397; SI 2015 No 980, Reg 5(5)*].

**Consistency of accounts within a group.** Subject to the exceptions below, the directors of a parent company must secure that the individual accounts of

(a)    the parent company, and

(b)    each of its subsidiary undertakings

are all prepared using the same financial reporting framework (ie Companies Act or IAS), except to the extent that in their opinion there are good reasons for not doing so. BIS indicated, in their 2008 guidance to companies on the introduction of IAS accounts, that 'good reasons' could include the following.

- Where a group using IAS acquires a subsidiary undertaking that had not been using IAS, in the first year of acquisition it might not be practical for the newly acquired company to switch to IAS straight away.

- Where a group contains subsidiary undertakings that are themselves publicly traded, market pressures or regulatory requirements to use IAS might come into play, without necessarily justifying a switch to IAS by the non-publicly traded subsidiaries.

- Where a subsidiary undertaking or the parent is planning to list and so might wish to convert to IAS in advance, but the rest of the group is not listed.

- Where the group contains minor or dormant subsidiaries and the costs of switching accounting framework would outweigh the benefits.

*Exceptions.* The general requirement to prepare individual accounts using the same financial framework is subject to the following specific exceptions, It:

- does not apply if the directors do not prepare group accounts for the parent company;

- only applies to the accounts of subsidiary undertakings that are required to be prepared under *CA 2006*;

- does not require accounts of undertakings that are charities to be prepared using the same financial reporting framework as accounts of undertakings which are not charities; and

- does not apply where the directors of a parent company prepare both group accounts and individual accounts under IAS. In this case the parent company is not required to ensure that all its subsidiary undertakings also use IAS. However it must ensure that all its subsidiary undertakings use the same accounting framework, unless there are good reasons for not doing so.

[*CA 2006, s 407(2)–(4) and (5)*].

## 3.3 INDIVIDUAL ACCOUNTS: FORM AND CONTENT OF COMPANIES ACT ACCOUNTS

The directors of a company

- for which they are preparing Companies Act individual accounts, and

- which is not a banking company or an insurance company,

must comply with the provisions in this paragraph and in **3.4** to **3.35** as to the form and content of the balance sheet and profit and loss account, and additional information to be provided by way of notes to the accounts. The only exceptions are that medium-sized companies need not comply with the disclosure requirements relating to compliance with accounting standards (see **3.18**) and the requirements on the disclosure of related party transactions (see **3.19**) apply with modifications as explained at **4.4** ACCOUNTS: MEDIUM-SIZED COMPANIES.

[*SI 2008 No 410, Regs 3(1), 4(2A), (2B); SI 2015 No 980, Reg 26*].

Every balance sheet of a company must show the items listed in either of the balance sheet formats in **3.4** and every profit and loss account must show the items listed in either of the profit and loss account formats in **3.5**, in both cases in the order and under the headings and sub-headings given in the format used, but subject to the following.

(1)     The notes to the formats may permit alternative positions for any particular items.

(2)     The heading or sub-heading for any item does not have to be distinguished by any letter or number assigned to that item in the format used.

(3)     Any item required to be shown in a company's balance sheet or profit and loss account may be shown in greater detail than required by the particular format used.

(4)     A heading or sub-heading corresponding to an item in the balance sheet or profit and loss account format used must not be included if there is no amount to be shown for that item for the financial year in question unless an amount must be disclosed for the immediately preceding financial year (see below).

(5)     The balance sheet or profit and loss account may include an item representing or covering the amount of any asset or liability, income or expenditure not otherwise covered by any of the items listed in the format used, except that none of the following may be treated as assets in any balance sheet.

- Preliminary expenses.

- Expenses of, and commission on, any issue of shares or debentures.

- Costs of research.

(6)     Where the special nature of the company's business requires it, the company's directors

(a)     *must* adapt the arrangement, headings and sub-headings otherwise required in respect of items given an Arabic number in the balance sheet or profit and loss account format used; and

(b)     *may* combine items to which Arabic numbers are given in any of the formats if

(i)    their individual amounts are not material to assessing the state of affairs or profit or loss of the company for the financial year in question; or

(ii)    the combination facilitates that assessment (but in this case the individual amounts of any items which have been combined must be disclosed in a note to the accounts).

(7)    The company's directors may adapt one of the balance sheet formats so to distinguish between current and non-current items in a different way, provided that—

(a)    the information given is at least equivalent to that which would have been required by the use of such format had it not been thus adapted; and

(b)    the presentation of those items is in accordance with generally accepted accounting principles or practice.

The company's directors may adapt one of the profit and loss account formats provided that—

(a)    the information given is at least equivalent to that which would have been required by the use of such format had it not been thus adapted; and

(b)    the presentation is in accordance with generally accepted accounting principles or practice.

*[SI 2008 No 410, Sch 1 paras 1, 3–5; SI 2015 No 980, Reg 27(2)(c)].*

The flexibility provided by (7) above is intended to allow companies to adopt a presentation closer to that used in IAS accounts, but note that FRS 102 specifies the minimum line items that must be presented in the balance sheet and profit and loss account in this situation and sets out certain additional requirements.

**Consistency in use of formats.** Where a company's balance sheet or profit and loss account for any financial year has been prepared by reference to one of the said formats, the company's directors must use the same format in preparing Companies Act individual accounts for subsequent financial years, unless in their opinion there are special reasons for a change. Particulars of any such change must be given in a note to the accounts in which the new format is first used, and the reasons for the change must be explained. *[SI 2008 No 410, Sch 1 para 2].*

**Profit before taxation.** Every profit and loss account must show the amount of a company's profit or loss before taxation.

*[SI 2008 No 410, Sch 1 para 6; SI 2015 No 980, Reg 27(2)(d)].*

**Preceding financial year.** For every item shown in the balance sheet or profit and loss account the corresponding amount for the immediately preceding financial year must also be shown. Where that corresponding amount is not comparable with the figure for the current year, the former amount may be adjusted, in which case particulars of the non-comparability and of any adjustment must be disclosed in a note to the accounts. Note that FRS 102 generally requires corresponding amounts to be restated where necessary but may specify a different approach in certain circumstances (for instance, as a transitional measure on the implementation of new requirements where restatement would be onerous and this would outweigh the related benefits).

*[SI 2008 No 410, Sch 1 para 7].*

**Set-offs.** Amounts in respect of items representing assets or income may not be set off against amounts in respect of items representing liabilities or expenditure, or vice versa.

[*SI 2008 No 410, Sch 1 para 8*].

**Presentation in accordance with accounting principles.** The company's directors must, in determining how amounts are presented within items in the profit and loss account and balance sheet, have regard to the substance of the reported transaction or arrangement, in accordance with generally accepted accounting principles or practice. Where an asset or liability relates to more than one item in the balance sheet, the relationship of such asset or liability to the relevant items must be disclosed either under those items or in the notes to the accounts.

[*SI 2008 No 410, Sch 1 paras 9, 9A; SI 2015 No 980, Reg 27(2)(e)*].

**Materiality.** Amounts which in the particular context are not material may be disregarded for the purposes of that provision.

[*SI 2008 No 410, Sch 10 para 10*].

**Accounts in euros.** The amounts set out in the annual accounts of a company may also be shown in the same accounts translated into euros. If so, the amounts must have been translated at the exchange rate prevailing at the balance sheet date and that rate must be disclosed in the notes to the accounts.

[*CA 2006, s 469(1)(3)*].

**Listed companies.** In addition to the requirements of *CA 2006* and supporting Regulations, listed companies must also comply with the requirements of the FCA Listing Rules as to the content of annual accounts (annual financial report). See **33.32** PUBLIC AND LISTED COMPANIES.

## 3.4    Balance sheet formats

The two balance sheet formats set out in *SI 2008 No 410, Sch 1 as amended by SI 2015 No 980* and referred to in **3.3** are reproduced below, and are followed by the notes also set out in the *Regulations*.

### Format 1

A.    Called up share capital not paid (see note (1))

B.    Fixed assets (see below)

    I    Intangible assets

        1.    Development costs

        2.    Concessions, patents, licences, trademarks and similar rights and assets (see note (2))

        3.    Goodwill (see note (3))

        4.    Payments on account

    II    Tangible assets

        1.    Land and buildings

        2.    Plant and machinery

        3.    Fixtures, fittings, tools and equipment

        4.    Payments on account and assets in course of construction

    III    Investments

        1.    Shares in group undertakings

        2.    Loans to group undertakings

        3.    Participating interests

# 3.4  Accounts: Large Companies

        4.   Loans to undertakings in which the company has a participating interest

        5.   Other investments other than loans

        6.   Other loans

        7.   Own shares (see note (4))

C.   Current assets (see below)

   I    Stocks

        1.   Raw materials and consumables

        2.   Work in progress

        3.   Finished goods and goods for resale

        4.   Payments on account

   II   Debtors (see note (5))

        1.   Trade debtors

        2.   Amounts owed by group undertakings

        3.   Amounts owed by undertakings in which the company has a participating interest

        4.   Other debtors

        5.   Called up share capital not paid (see note (1))

        6.   Prepayments and accrued income (see note (6))

   III  Investments

        1.   Shares in group undertakings

        2.   Own shares (see note (4))

        3.   Other investments

   IV  Cash at bank and in hand

D.   Prepayments and accrued income (see note (6))

E.   Creditors: amounts falling due within one year

   1.   Debenture loans (see note (7))

   2.   Bank loans and overdrafts

   3.   Payments received on account (see note (8))

   4.   Trade creditors

   5.   Bills of exchange payable

   6.   Amounts owed to group undertakings

   7.   Amounts owed to undertakings in which the company has a participating interest

   8.   Other creditors including taxation and social security (see note (9))

   9.   Accruals and deferred income (see note (10))

F.   Net current assets (liabilities) (see note (11))

G.   Total assets less current liabilities

H.   Creditors: amounts falling due after more than one year

   1.   Debenture loans (see note (7))

   2.   Bank loans and overdrafts

   3.   Payments received on account (see note (8))

   4.   Trade creditors

   5.   Bills of exchange payable

6.   Amounts owed to group undertakings

7.   Amounts owed to undertakings in which the company has a participating interest

8.   Other creditors including taxation and social security (see note (9))

9.   Accruals and deferred income (see note (10))

I.   Provisions for liabilities (see below)

    1.   Pensions and similar obligations

    2.   Taxation, including deferred taxation

    3.   Other provisions

J.   Accruals and deferred income (see note (10))

K.   Capital and reserves

    I    Called up share capital (see note (12))

    II   Share premium account

    III  Revaluation reserve

    IV  Other reserves

        1.   Capital redemption reserve

        2.   Reserve for own shares

        3.   Reserves provided for by the articles of association

        4.   Other reserves including the fair value reserve

    V   Profit and loss account

**Format 2**

ASSETS

A.   Called up share capital not paid (see note (1))

B.   Fixed assets (see below)

    I    Intangible assets

        1.   Development costs

        2.   Concessions, patents, licences, trademarks and similar rights and assets (see note (2))

        3.   Goodwill (see note (3))

        4.   Payments on account

    II   Tangible assets

        1.   Land and buildings

        2.   Plant and machinery

        3.   Fixtures, fittings, tools and equipment

        4.   Payments on account and assets in course of construction

    III  Investments

        1.   Shares in group undertakings

        2.   Loans to group undertakings

        3.   Participating interests

        4.   Loans to undertakings in which the company has a participating interest

        5.   Other investments other than loans

        6.   Other loans

7.   Own shares (see note (4))

C.   Current assets (see below)

    I    Stocks

        1.   Raw materials and consumables

        2.   Work in progress

        3.   Finished goods and goods for resale

        4.   Payments on account

    II   Debtors (see note (5))

        1.   Trade debtors

        2.   Amounts owed by group undertakings

        3.   Amounts owed by undertakings in which the company has a participating interest

        4.   Other debtors

        5.   Called up share capital not paid (see note (1))

        6.   Prepayments and accrued income (see note (6))

   III  Investments

        1.   Shares in group undertakings

        2.   Own shares (see note (4))

        3.   Other investments

    IV  Cash at bank and in hand

D.   Prepayments and accrued income (see note (6))

## CAPITAL, RESERVES AND LIABILITIES

A.   Capital and reserves

    I    Called up share capital (see note (12))

    II   Share premium account

   III  Revaluation reserve

   IV  Other reserves

        1.   Capital redemption reserve

        2.   Reserve for own shares

        3.   Reserves provided for by the articles of association

        4.   Other reserves including the fair value reserve

    V   Profit and loss account

B.   Provisions for liabilities (see below)

    1.   Pensions and similar obligations

    2.   Taxation, including deferred taxation

    3.   Other provisions

C.   Creditors (see note (13))

    1.   Debenture loans (see note (7))

    2.   Bank loans and overdrafts

    3.   Payments received on account (see note (8))

    4.   Trade creditors

    5.   Bills of exchange payable

    6.   Amounts owed to group undertakings

7.   Amounts owed to undertakings in which the company has a participating interest

8.   Other creditors including taxation and social security (see note (9))

9.   Accruals and deferred income (see note (10))

D.   Accruals and deferred income (see note (10))

**Notes**

(1)   *Called up share capital not paid.* This item may be shown in either of the two positions given in each format.

(2)   *Concessions etc.* Amounts in respect of assets are to be included under this item only if the assets in question either were acquired for valuable consideration (and are not required to be shown under 'goodwill') or were created by the company itself.

(3)   *Goodwill.* Amounts representing goodwill are to be included only to the extent that the goodwill was acquired for valuable consideration.

(4)   *Own shares.* Where own shares are included under investments, the nominal value of the shares held must be shown separately (but note that this accounting treatment for own shares held is precluded by accounting standards).

(5)   *Debtors.* The amount falling due after more than one year must be shown separately for each item included under debtors.

(6)   *Prepayments and accrued income.* This item may be shown in either of the two positions given in each format.

(7)   *Debenture loans.* The amount of any convertible loans must be shown separately.

(8)   *Payments received on account.* Payments received on account of orders must be shown in so far as they are not shown as deductions from stocks.

(9)   *Other creditors including taxation and social security.* The amount for creditors in respect of taxation and social security must be shown separately from the amount for other creditors.

(10)   *Accruals and deferred income.* The two positions given for this item in Format 1 at E.9 and H.9 are an alternative to the position at J, but if the item is not shown in a position corresponding to that at J it may be shown in either or both of the other two positions (as the case may require). The two positions given for this item in Format 2 are alternatives.

(11)   *Net current assets (liabilities).* In determining the amount to be shown for this item, any amounts shown under 'prepayments and accrued income' must be taken into account wherever shown.

(12)   *Called up share capital.* The amount of allotted share capital and the amount of called up share capital which has been paid up must be shown separately.

(13)   *Creditors.* Amounts falling due within one year and after one year must be shown separately for each of these items and for the aggregate of all of these items.

[*SI 2008 No 410, Sch 1 Part 1 Section B; SI 2015 No 980, Reg 27(3)*].

'*Fixed assets*' means assets of a company which are intended for use on a continuing basis in the company's activities. [*SI 2008 No 410, Sch 10 para 4*].

*'Current assets'* means assets not intended for use as fixed assets. [*SI 2008 No 410, Sch 10 para 4*].

*Provision for liabilities.* A provision for liabilities means any amount retained as reasonably necessary for the purpose of providing for any liability the nature of which is clearly defined and which is either likely to be incurred, or certain to be incurred but uncertain as to amount or as to the date on which it will arise. [*SI 2008 No 410, Sch 9 para 2*].

**3.5 Profit and loss account formats**

The two profit and loss account formats set out in *SI 2008 No 410, Sch 1 as amended by SI 2015 No 980* and referred to in **3.3** are reproduced below, and are followed by the notes also set out in the *Regulations*. Reference should also be made to the detailed requirements of FRS 102 on the presentation of the profit and loss account and related disclosures in the notes.

**Format 1 (see note (4))**
1. Turnover
2. Cost of sales (see note (1))
3. Gross profit or loss
4. Distribution costs (see note (1))
5. Administrative expenses (see note (1))
6. Other operating income
7. Income from shares in group undertakings
8. Income from participating interests
9. Income from other fixed asset investments (see note (2))
10. Other interest receivable and similar income (see note (2))
11. Amounts written off investments
12. Interest payable and similar expenses (see note (3))
13. Tax on profit or loss
14. Profit or loss after taxation
15. Other taxes not shown under the above items
16. Profit or loss for the financial year

**Format 2**
1. Turnover
2. Change in stocks of finished goods and in work in progress
3. Own work capitalised
4. Other operating income
5. (a) Raw materials and consumables
   (b) Other external expenses
6. Staff costs:
   (a) wages and salaries (see below)
   (b) social security costs (see below)
   (c) other pension costs (see below)
7. (a) Depreciation and other amounts written off tangible and intangible fixed assets (see below)
   (b) Amounts written off current assets to the extent that they exceed write-offs which are normal in the undertaking concerned

8.   Other operating expenses
9.   Income from shares in group undertakings
10.  Income from participating interests
11.  Income from other fixed asset investments (see note (2))
12.  Other interest receivable and similar income (see note (2))
13.  Amounts written off investments
14.  Interest payable and similar expenses (see note (3))
15.  Tax on profit or loss
16.  Profit or loss after taxation
17.  Other taxes not shown under the above items
18.  Profit or loss for the financial year.

**Notes**

(1)   *Cost of sales: distribution costs: administrative expenses.* These items must be stated after taking into account any necessary provisions for depreciation or diminution in value of assets.

(2)   *Income from other fixed asset investments: other interest receivable and similar income.* Income and interest derived from group undertakings must be shown separately from income and interest derived from other sources.

(3)   *Interest payable and similar expenses.* The amount payable to group undertakings must be shown separately.

(4)   *Format 1.* Where this format is used, the amount of any provisions for depreciation and diminution in value of tangible and intangible fixed assets falling to be shown under item 7(*a*) in Format 2 must be disclosed in a note to the accounts.

[*SI 2008 No 410, Sch 1 Part 1, Section B; SI 2015 No 980, Reg 27(3)*].

*Staff costs.*

•   '*Social security costs*' means any contributions by the company to any state social security or pension scheme, fund or arrangement.

•   '*Pension costs*' includes

(i)    any costs incurred by the company in respect of any pension scheme established for the purpose of providing pensions for persons currently or formerly employed by the company;

(ii)   any sums set aside for the future payment of pensions directly by the company to current or former employees; and

(iii)  any pensions paid directly to such persons without having first been set aside.

Any amount stated in respect of the item 'social security costs' or in respect of the item 'wages and salaries' in the company's profit and loss account must be determined by reference to payments made or costs incurred in respect of all persons employed by the company during the financial year under contracts of service.

[*SI 2008 No 410, Sch 10 para 14*].

## 3.5 Accounts: Large Companies

*Depreciation, etc.* Any reference in the profit and loss account formats (or the notes to them) to the depreciation of, or amounts written off, assets of any description is to any provision for depreciation or diminution in value of assets of that description. [*SI 2008 No 410, Sch 9 para 1(2)*].

'*Fixed assets*' means assets of a company which are intended for use on a continuing basis in the company's activities. [*SI 2008 No 410, Sch 10 para 4*].

### 3.6 Accounting principles

The amounts to be included in respect of all items shown in a company's accounts must be determined in accordance with the principles set out in (*a*)–(*e*) below. But if it appears to the directors that there are special reasons for departing from any of those principles in preparing the company's accounts for any financial year, they may do so, in which case particulars of the departure, the reasons for it and its effect must be given in a note to the accounts.

(a)    The company is presumed to be carrying on business as a going concern.

(b)    Accounting policies and measurement bases must be applied consistently within the same accounts and from one financial year to the next.

(c)    The amount of any item must be determined on a prudent basis, and in particular

    (i)    only profits realised at the balance sheet date are to be included in the profit and loss account;

    (ii)   all liabilities which have arisen in respect of the financial year to which the accounts relate or a previous financial year must be taken into account. This includes those which only become apparent between the balance sheet date and the date on which it is signed on behalf of the board of directors (see **2.2** ACCOUNTS: GENERAL). Where revised accounts are prepared (see **2.13** ACCOUNTS: GENERAL) it is the date on which the original accounts were signed that is taken into account for this purposes; and

    (iii)  all provisions for diminution in value must be recognised whether the result of the financial year is a profit or a loss.

(d)    All income and charges relating to the financial year to which the accounts relate must be taken into account, without regard to the date of receipt or payment.

(e)    In determining the aggregate amount of any item, the amount of each individual asset or liability that falls to be taken into account must be determined separately and the opening balance sheet for each financial year shall correspond to the closing balance sheet for the preceding financial year.

[*SI 2008 No 410, Sch 1 paras 10–15A; SI 2015 No 980, Reg 28(2)*].

FRS 102 sets out further detailed guidance on these issues, including practical interpretation of the legislative requirements. Additional guidance on going concern can be found in the Financial Reporting Council document 'Guidance on the Going Concern Basis of Accounting and Reporting on Solvency and Liquidity Risk' (available at www.frc.org.uk).

### 3.7 Historical cost accounting rules

Subject to

*    the alternative accounting rules in **3.14** to **3.16**, and

*    the fair value accounting provisions in **3.17**

40

the amounts to be included in respect of all items shown in a company's accounts must be determined in accordance with the rules set out in 3.8 to 3.12. [*SI 2008 No 410, Sch 1 para 16*].

**3.8** *Fixed assets*

*General rules.* Fixed asset (ie assets of a company which are intended for use on a continuing basis in the company's activities) must be included at their 'purchase price' or 'production cost' (see **3.12**). [*SI 2008 No 410, Sch 1 para 17, Sch 10 para 4*].

*Rules for depreciation and diminution in value.*

(a) In the case of any fixed asset which has a limited useful economic life, its purchase price or production cost, less the amount of any estimated residual value at the end of the asset's useful economic life, must be reduced by provisions for depreciation calculated to write off that amount systematically over the asset's useful economic life. [*SI 2008 No 410, Sch 1 para 18*].

(b) Where a fixed asset investment falling to be included under item B.III of either of the balance sheet formats set out in **3.4** has diminished in value, provisions for diminution in value may be made in respect of it and the amount to be included in respect of it may be reduced accordingly. Such provisions must be made in respect of *any* fixed asset which has diminished in value if the reduction in its value is expected to be permanent (whether it's useful economic life is limited or not), and the amount to be included in respect of it must be reduced accordingly. Provisions made must be charged to the profit and loss account and disclosed separately in a note to the accounts if not shown separately in the profit and loss account. [*SI 2008 No 410, Sch 1 para 19; SI 2015 No 980, Reg 28(3)*].

(c) Where the reasons for which any provision was made have ceased to apply to any extent, that provision must be written back to the extent that it is no longer necessary but provisions made in accordance with Sch 1, para 19(2) in respect of goodwill must not be written back to any extent. [*SI 2008 No 410, Sch 1 para 20(1); SI 2015 No 1672, Reg 4*].

Any amounts written back under (c) must be recognised in the profit and loss account and disclosed separately in a note to the accounts if not shown separately in the profit and loss account. [*SI 2008 No 410, Sch 1 para 20(2); SI 2015 No 980, Reg 28(3)(b)*].

Reference should also be made to the detailed requirements of FRS 102 on measuring the cost of property, plant and equipment, useful economic lives, residual values and depreciation. The standard also includes specific requirements on accounting for investment property and heritage assets.

**3.9** *Intangible assets*

Where this is in accordance with generally accepted accounting principles or practice, development costs may be included in 'other intangible assets' under 'fixed assets' in the balance sheet formats set out in Section B of Part 1 of the Schedule to the 2008 Regulations. If any amount is included in a company's balance sheet in respect of development costs, the note on accounting policies must include the following information—

(a) the period over which the amount of those costs originally capitalised is being or is to be written off; and

(b) the reasons for capitalising the development costs in question.

Intangible assets must be written off over the useful economic life of the intangible asset. Where in exceptional cases the useful life of intangible assets cannot be reliably estimated, such assets must be written off over a period chosen by the directors of the company but this period must not exceed ten years and both the period and the reasons for choosing it must be disclosed in the notes to the accounts.

## 3.9 Accounts: Large Companies

[*SI 2008 No 410, Sch 1 paras 21 and 22; SI 2015 No 980, Reg 28(3)(c)*].

Reference should also be made to the requirements of FRS 102 on the recognition, measurement and amortisation of intangible assets and goodwill, and the need for impairment reviews to be carried out in certain circumstances.

**3.10** *Current assets*

The amount to be included in respect of any current asset must be its 'purchase price' or 'production cost' (see **3.12**) or, if lower, its net realisable value. Where the reasons for which any provision for diminution in value has been made (ie to reduce the assets to its net realisable value) have ceased to apply to any extent, that provision must be written back to the extent that it is no longer necessary. [*SI 2008 No 410, Sch 1 paras 23, 24*].

**3.11** *Miscellaneous provisions*

(1) *Excess of money owed over value received*

Where the amount repayable on any debt owed by a company is greater than the value of the consideration received in the transaction giving rise to the debt, the amount of the difference may be treated as an asset. But in the case of such treatment, the amount of the difference must be written off by reasonable amounts each year and must be completely written off before repayment of the debt. If the current amount is not shown as a separate item in the company's balance sheet, it must be disclosed in a note to the accounts. [*SI 2008 No 410, Sch 1 para 25*]. However, note that the requirements of FRS 102 will usually preclude adoption of this accounting treatment.

(2) *Assets included at a fixed amount*

Assets which fall to be included either amongst the

- fixed assets of a company under the item 'tangible assets', or

- current assets of a company under the item 'raw materials and consumables',

may be included at a fixed quantity and value where the assets are of a kind which are constantly being replaced and where their

- overall value is not material to assessing the company's state of affairs; and

- quantity, value and composition are not subject to material variation.

[*SI 2008 No 410, Sch 1 para 26*].

**3.12** *Determination of purchase price or production cost*

The '*purchase price*' of an asset is the actual price paid plus any expenses incidental to its acquisition and then subtracting any incidental reductions in the cost of the acquisition.

'*Purchase price*', in relation to an asset of a company or any raw materials or consumables used in the production of such an asset, includes any consideration (whether in cash or otherwise) given by the company in respect of that asset or those materials or consumables, as the case may be.

The '*production cost*' of an asset is the purchase price of the raw materials and consumables used plus the costs incurred by the company which are directly attributable to the production of that asset. In addition, there may be included

- a reasonable proportion of the costs so incurred by the company which are only indirectly attributable to the production of that asset, but only to the extent that they relate to the period of production; and

- interest on capital borrowed to finance the production of that asset, to the extent that it accrues in respect of the period of production. The inclusion of interest in determining the cost and the amount of the interest so included must be disclosed in a note to the accounts. Note that FRS 102 also sets out detailed requirements on the capitalisation of finance costs.

In the case of current assets, production costs must not include distribution costs.

[*SI 2008 No 410, Sch 1 para 27, Sch 10 para 12; SI 2015 No 980, Reg 28(3)(d)*].

Where

- there is no record of the purchase price or production cost of any asset (of any price, expenses or costs relevant to its determination), or

- any such record cannot be obtained without unreasonable expense or delay,

the purchase price or production cost of the asset must be taken to be the value ascribed to it in the earliest available record of its value made on or after its acquisition or production by the company. [*SI 2008 No 410, Sch 1 para 29*].

*Equity method in respect of participating interests.* Participating interests may be accounted for using the equity method but if they are accounted for in such a way—

- the proportion of profit or loss attributable to a participating interest and recognised in the profit and loss account may be that proportion which corresponds to the amount of any dividends; and

- where the profit attributable to a participating interest and recognised in the profit and loss account exceeds the amount of any dividends, the difference must be placed in a reserve which cannot be distributed to shareholders. The reference to 'dividends' includes dividends already paid and those whose payment can be claimed.

[*SI 2008 No 410, Sch 1, para 29A; SI 2015 No 980, Reg 28(f)*].

*Stocks and fungible assets.* The purchase price or production cost of

- any assets which fall to be included under any item shown in a company's balance sheet under the general item 'stocks', and

- any assets which are 'fungible assets' (including investments),

may be determined by applying any of the following methods in relation to any such assets of the same class, provided that the method chosen is one which appears to the directors to be appropriate in the circumstances of the company.

(1)   'First in, first out' (FIFO).

(2)   'Last in, first out' (LIFO) – but see below.

(3)   A weighted average price.

(4)   Any other method reflecting generally accepted best practice.

However, the detailed requirements of FRS 102 must also be taken into account, and these specifically prohibit the use of LIFO to measure the cost of stocks.

'*Fungible assets*' means assets of any description which are substantially indistinguishable one from another.

But where the result of such determination differs materially from the 'relevant alternative amount', the difference must be disclosed in a note to the accounts.

The *'relevant alternative amount'* is the amount which would have been shown in respect of the item in question if assets of any class included under that item had instead been included at their replacement cost as at the balance sheet date. If, however, the directors consider it a more appropriate standard of comparison in the case of assets of a particular class, the relevant alternative amount may instead be determined by reference to the most recent actual purchase price or production cost before the balance sheet date of assets of that class.

[*SI 2008 No 410, Sch 1 para 28, Sch 10 para 5; SI 2015 No 980, Reg 28(e)*].

**3.13**  *Equity method in respect of participating interests*

Participating interests may be accounted for using the equity method.

If participating interests are accounted for using the equity method:

- the proportion of profit or loss attributable to a participating interest and recognised in the profit and loss account may be that proportion which corresponds to the amount of any dividends; and

- where the profit attributable to a participating interest and recognised in the profit and loss account exceeds the amount of any dividends, the difference must be placed in a reserve which cannot be distributed to shareholders.

The reference to 'dividends' includes dividends already paid and those whose payment can be claimed.

[*SI 2008 No 410, Sch 1 para 29A; SI 2015 No 980, Reg 28(3)(f)*].

Note that this treatment is not currently permitted under accounting standards and the FRC has indicated that it does not intend to incorporate it into UK accounting practice at present.

**3.14  Alternative accounting rules**

Any of the accounting rules set out below may be used (as alternatives to the historical cost accounting rules in **3.7** to **3.12**) to determine the amounts to be included in respect of the assets in question (but note that not all of these options are acceptable under current accounting standards).

(a)  *Intangible fixed assets*, other than goodwill, may be included at their current cost.

(b)  *Tangible fixed assets* may be included at a market value (determined as at the date of their last valuation) or at their current cost.

(c)  *Investments of any description falling to be included under item B III* of either of the balance sheet formats in **3.4** may be included either at

 (i)  market value determined as at the date of their last valuation; or

 (ii)  a value determined on any basis which appears to the directors to be appropriate in the circumstances of the company (but in this case particulars of the method of valuation adopted and of the reasons for adopting it must be disclosed in a note to the accounts).

**Application of the depreciation rules.** Where the value of any asset is determined on any basis within (*a*)–(*c*) above, that value (instead of the purchase price, production cost or any value previously so determined for that asset) must be (or, as the case may require, must be the starting point for determining) the amount to be included in respect of that asset in the accounts. The historical cost depreciation rules in **3.8** to **3.11** above (other than those in *SI 2008 No 410, Sch 1, paras 22* and *26–29*) apply accordingly in relation to any such asset with the substitution for any reference to its purchase price or production cost of a reference to the value most recently determined for that asset under (*a*)–(*c*) above (the '*adjusted depreciation rules*').

In the case of a fixed asset, any provision for depreciation in respect of that asset which is

- included in any item shown in the profit and loss account in respect of amounts written off assets of the description in question, or

- taken into account as required by note (1) to the profit and loss account formats in **3.5**

will normally be included or taken into account at the amount calculated under the adjusted depreciation rules above. It may, however, be included or taken in account under the historic cost depreciation rules instead of the adjusted depreciation rules, provided that the amount of any difference between the two is shown separately in the profit and loss account or in a note to the accounts.

[*SI 2008 No 410, Sch 1 paras 30–33*].

Reference should also be made to the detailed requirements of FRS 102 on accounting for revalued assets.

**3.15**   *Additional information to be provided in case of departure from historical cost accounting rules*

Where the amounts to be included in respect of assets covered by any items shown in the accounts have been determined on any basis in **3.14**(*a*)–(*c*), the following additional information must be disclosed in a note to the accounts or alternatively, in the case of (*b*) below, shown separately in the balance sheet.

(a)   The items affected and the basis of valuation adopted in determining the amounts of the assets in question in the case of each such item must be disclosed in the note on accounting policies (see *SI 2008 No 410, Sch 1, para 44* and **3.18** below).

(b)   In the case of each balance sheet item affected the 'comparable amounts determined according to the historical cost accounting rules' must be shown in a note to the accounts. The '*comparable amounts determined according to the historical cost accounting rules*' are—

- the aggregate amount which would be required to be shown in respect of that item if the amounts to be included in respect of all the assets covered by that item were determined according to the historical cost accounting rules; and

- the aggregate amount of the cumulative provisions for depreciation or diminution in value which would be permitted or required in determining those amounts according to those rules.

[*SI 2008 No 410, Sch 1 para 34; SI 2015 No 980, Reg 28(4)*].

**3.16**   *Revaluation reserve*

The amount of any profit or loss arising from the determination of the value of an asset on any basis mentioned in **3.14**(*a*)–(*c*) (after allowing, where appropriate, for any provisions for depreciation or diminution in value) must be credited or, as the case may be, debited to a separate reserve, the 'revaluation reserve'.

The amount of the revaluation reserve must be shown in the balance sheet under a separate sub-heading in the position given for the item 'revaluation reserve' under 'Capital and Reserves' in either of the balance sheet formats in **3.4**.

# 3.16   Accounts: Large Companies

The revaluation reserve must be reduced to the extent that the amounts transferred to it are no longer necessary for the purposes of the valuation method used. In addition, an amount may be transferred

- from the revaluation reserve to the profit and loss account, if the amount was previously charged to that account or represents realised profit;

- from the revaluation reserve on capitalisation (ie by applying the amount in wholly or partly paying up unissued shares in the company to be allotted to members as fully or partly paid shares); and

- to or from the revaluation reserve in respect of the taxation relating to any profit or loss credited or debited to the reserve.

The revaluation reserve must not be reduced except as mentioned above.

The treatment for taxation purposes of amounts credited or debited to the revaluation reserve must be disclosed in a note to the accounts.

[*SI 2008 No 410, Sch 1 para 35; SI 2015 No 980, Reg 28(4)*].

## 3.17   Fair value accounting

(1) *Financial instruments*

Financial instruments (including 'derivatives') may be included at fair value with the following exceptions.

- Financial instruments which constitute liabilities unless

  (i)    they are held as part of a 'trading portfolio';

  (ii)   they are derivatives; or

  (iii)  they are financial instruments which under international accounting standards may be included in accounts at fair value, provided that the disclosures required by such accounting standards are made.

- Any of the following, namely

  (i)    financial instruments (other than derivatives) 'held to maturity',

  (ii)   loans and 'receivables' originated by the company and not 'held for trading purposes',

  (iii)  interests in subsidiary undertakings, associated undertaking (see **3.65**) and joint ventures (see **3.64**),

  (iv)   'equity instruments' issued by the company,

  (v)    contracts for contingent consideration in a 'business combination',

  (vi)   other financial instruments with such special characteristics that the instruments, according to generally accepted accounting principles or practice, should be accounted for differently from other financial instruments,

  unless they are financial instruments that, under international accounting standards adopted by the European Commission before 6 September 2006 in accordance with the IAS Regulation, may be included in accounts at fair value, provided that the disclosures required by such accounting standards are made.

- If the fair value of a financial instrument cannot be determined reliably under the rules set out below.

'*Derivatives*' include 'commodity-based contracts' that give either contracting party the right to settle in cash or in some other financial instrument, except when such contracts

- were entered into for the purpose of, and continue to meet, the company's expected purchase, sale or usage requirements;

- were designated for such purpose at their inception; and

- are expected to be settled by delivery of the commodity.

*Determination of fair value.* The fair value of a financial instrument is determined as follows.

(a)   If a 'reliable market' can readily be identified for the financial instrument, its fair value is determined by reference to its market value.

(b)   If a reliable market cannot readily be identified for the financial instrument but can be identified for its components or for a similar instrument, its fair value is determined by reference to the market value of its components or of the similar instrument.

(c)   If neither (*a*) or (*b*) above applies, the fair value of the financial instrument is a value resulting from generally accepted valuation models and techniques which ensure a reasonable approximation of the market value.

*Hedged items.* A company may include any assets and liabilities, or identified portions of such assets or liabilities, that qualify as hedged items under a 'fair value hedge accounting system' at the amount required under that system.

The expressions '*business combination*', '*commodity-based contracts*', '*derivative*', '*equity instrument*', '*fair value hedge accounting system*', '*financial instrument*', '*hedge accounting*', '*hedge accounting system*', '*hedged items*', '*held for trading purposes*', '*held to maturity*', '*receivables*', '*reliable market*' and '*trading portfolio*' have the same meaning as they have in Directive 2013/34/EU on the annual accounts of certain types of undertakings.

(2) *Stocks, investment property, and living plants and animals*

Stocks, investment property and living plants and animals may be included at fair value, provided that, as the case may be, all such stocks, investment property and living plants and animals are so included where its fair value can reliably be determined. For these purposes, 'fair value' means fair value determined in accordance with generally accepted accounting principles or practice.

**Accounting for changes in value.** Where a financial instrument or asset is valued in accordance with (1) to (2) above, a change in the value of the financial instrument or asset must be included in the profit and loss account. But

(A)   where

(i)   the financial instrument accounted for is a 'hedging instrument' under a hedge accounting system that allows some or all of the change in value not to be shown in the profit and loss account, or

(ii)   the change in value relates to an 'exchange difference' arising on a 'monetary item' that forms part of a company's net investment in a 'foreign entity',

the amount of the change in value *must* be credited to or (as the case may be) debited from a separate reserve ('*the fair value reserve*'); and

(B)   where the instrument accounted for

(i)   is an 'available for sale financial asset', and

(ii)      is not a derivative,

the change in value *may* be credited to or (as the case may be) debited from the fair value reserve.

The expressions '*available for sale financial asset*', '*exchange difference*', '*financial instrument*', '*foreign entity*', '*hedge accounting*', '*hedge accounting system*', '*hedging instrument*', and '*monetary item*' have the same meaning as they have in Directive 2013/34/EU on the annual accounts of certain types of undertakings.

**The fair value reserve.** The fair value reserve must be adjusted to the extent that the amounts shown in it are no longer necessary for the purposes of (A) or (B) above.

The treatment for taxation purposes of amounts credited or debited to the fair value reserve must be disclosed in a note to the accounts.

[*SI 2008 No 410, Sch 1 paras 36–41, Sch 10 paras 2, 3; SI 2015 No 980, Reg 28(5)*].

Reference should also be made to the detailed requirements of FRS 102 in respect of items included at fair value, and those in respect of financial instruments in particular.

### 3.18   Notes to the accounts: general

Any information required in the case of a company by the provisions of SI 2008 No 409, Part 3, Sch 1 must be given by way of a note to the accounts. The notes must be presented in the order in which, where relevant, the items to which they relate are presented in the balance sheet and in the profit and loss account.

**Information about employee numbers and costs.** The notes to a company's annual accounts must disclose:

(a)      the average number of persons employed by the company in the financial year; and

(b)      in the case of a company not subject to the small companies regime they must also disclose the average number of persons within each category of persons so employed.

The categories by reference to which the number required to be disclosed by (b) is to be determined must be such as the directors may select having regard to the manner in which the company's activities are organised.

The average number required by (a) or (b) is determined by dividing the relevant annual number by the number of months in the financial year.

The relevant annual number is determined by ascertaining for each month in the financial year—

(i)      the number of persons employed under contracts of service by the company in that month (whether throughout the month or not);

(ii)     for the purposes of (b), the number of persons in the category in question of persons so employed.

Except in the case of a company subject to the small companies regime, the notes to the accounts or the profit and loss account must disclose, with reference to all persons employed by the company during the financial year, the total staff costs of the company relating to the financial year broken down between—

•      wages and salaries paid or payable in respect of that year to those persons;

- social security costs incurred by the company on their behalf; and

- other pension costs so incurred.

**Information about directors' benefits: advances, credit and guarantees**. In the case of a company that does not prepare group accounts, details of advances and credits granted by the company to its directors, and guarantees of any kind entered into by the company on behalf of its directors, must be shown in the notes to its individual accounts.

In the case of a parent company that prepares group accounts, details of advances and credits granted to the directors of the parent company, by that company or by any of its subsidiary undertakings, and guarantees of any kind entered into on behalf of the directors of the parent company, by that company or by any of its subsidiary undertakings must be shown in the notes to the group accounts.

See 3.52 for the detailed disclosure requirements.

**Reserves and dividends**. There must be stated

(a)  any amount set aside or proposed to be set aside to, or withdrawn or proposed to be withdrawn from, reserves;

(b)  the aggregate amount of dividends paid in the financial year (other than those for which a liability existed at the immediately preceding balance sheet date);

(c)  the aggregate amount of dividends that the company is liable to pay at the balance sheet date; and

(d)  the aggregate amount of dividends that are proposed before the date of approval of the accounts, and not otherwise disclosed under (*b*) or (*c*) above.

**Disclosure of accounting policies**. The accounting policies adopted in determining the profit or loss and the amounts of balance sheet items (including policies with respect to the depreciation and diminution in value of assets) must be stated.

**Accounting standards**. It must be stated whether the accounts have been prepared in accordance with applicable accounting standards. Particulars of any material departure from those standards, and the reasons for it, must also be given.

**Foreign currency translation**. Where any sums originally denominated in foreign currencies have been brought into account under any items shown in the balance sheet or profit and loss account, the basis on which those sums have been translated into sterling (or the currency in which the accounts are drawn up) must be stated.

**Dormant companies acting as agents**. Where the directors of a company take advantage of the exemption from audit conferred on dormant companies by *CA 2006, s 480* (see **8.34** Audit) and the company has during the financial year in question acted as an agent for any person, the fact that it has so acted must be stated.

[*CA 2006, s 411; SI 2008 No 410, Sch 1 paras 42-45, 70, 71; SI 2015 No 980, Reg 5*].

**Listed companies**. In addition to the requirements of *CA 2006* and supporting Regulations, listed companies must also comply with the requirements of the FCA Listing Rules as to content of annual accounts. See **33.32** Public and Listed Companies.

## 3.19    Related party transactions

Particulars *may* be given of transactions that the company has entered into with 'related parties' and *must* be given if such transactions are material and have not been concluded under normal market conditions.

## 3.19   Accounts: Large Companies

Where disclosure is required, the details disclosed must include

- the amount of such transactions;

- the nature of the related party relationship; and

- other information about the transactions necessary for an understanding of the financial position of the company.

Information about individual transactions may be aggregated according to their nature, except where separate information is necessary for an understanding of the effects of related party transactions on the financial position of the company.

Particulars need not be given of transactions entered into between two or more members of a group, provided that any subsidiary undertaking that is a party to the transaction is wholly-owned by such a member.

'*Related party*' has the same meaning as in international accounting standards.

[*SI 2008 No 410, Sch 1 para 72*].

Reference should also be made to the detailed requirements of FRS 102 on the disclosure of related party transactions.

## 3.20   Post-balance sheet events

The nature and financial effect of material events arising after the balance sheet date which are not reflected in the profit and loss account or balance sheet must be stated.

[*SI 2008 No 410, Sch 1, para 72A; SI 2015 No 980, Reg 29(11)*].

## 3.21   Appropriations

Particulars must be given of the proposed appropriation of profit or treatment of loss or, where applicable, particulars of the actual appropriation of the profits or treatment of the losses.

[*SI 2008 No 410, Sch 1, para 72B; SI 2015 No 980, Reg 29(11)*].

## 3.22   Notes to the accounts: information supplementing the balance sheet

The information required, as set out in **3.23** to **3.30**, being information which either supplements that given with respect to particular items in the balance sheet or is otherwise relevant to assessing the company's state of affairs, must be given by way of notes to the accounts (if not given in the accounts themselves). [*SI 2008 No 410, para 46*].

### 3.23   *Share capital and debentures*

(1) *Share capital*

The following information must be given with respect to the company's share capital.

- Where shares of more than one class have been allotted, the number and aggregate nominal value of shares of each class allotted.

- Where shares are held as treasury shares, the number and aggregate nominal value of the treasury shares and, where shares of more than one class have been allotted, the number and aggregate nominal value of the shares of each class held as treasury shares.

If any part of the allotted share capital consists of redeemable shares, the following information must be given.

- The earliest and latest dates on which the company has power to redeem those shares.

- Whether those shares must be redeemed in any event or are liable to be redeemed at the option of the company or of the shareholder.

- Whether any (and, if so, what) premium is payable on redemption.

If the company has allotted any shares during the financial year, the following information must be given.

- The classes of shares allotted.

- As respects each class of shares, the number allotted, their aggregate nominal value, and the consideration received by the company for the allotment.

[*SI 2008 No 410, Sch 1 paras 47, 48*].

With respect to any contingent right to the allotment of shares in the company (meaning any option to subscribe for shares and any other right to require the allotment of shares to any person whether arising on the conversion into shares of securities of any other description or otherwise), the following particulars must be given.

- The number, description and amount of the shares in relation to which the right is exercisable.

- The period during which it is exercisable.

- The price to be paid for the shares allotted.

[*SI 2008 No 410, Sch 1 para 49*].

(2) *Debentures*

If the company has issued any debentures during the financial year, the following information must be given.

- The classes of debentures issued.

- As respects each class of debentures, the amount issued and the consideration received by the company for the issue.

Where any of the company's debentures are held by a nominee of, or trustee for, the company, the nominal amount of the debentures and the amount at which they are stated in the company's accounting records must be stated.

[*SI 2008 No 410, Sch 1 para 50*].

FRS 102 includes detailed requirements on the classification of financial instruments as either liabilities or equity based on the substance of the contractual arrangements and the definitions in the standard. For accounts purposes, this can result in certain preference shares being classified as liabilities rather than as share capital and dividends on those shares being treated as an interest expense in the profit and loss account. Particular care is required over disclosure in these circumstances.

**3.24**   *Fixed assets*

The information set out below must be given for each item which is shown under the general item 'fixed assets' in the balance sheet (or which would be shown there were it not for 3.3(6)(*b*)(ii)).

## 3.24   Accounts: Large Companies

(a)     The 'appropriate amounts' in respect of that item as at both the beginning of the financial year and at the balance sheet date.

(b)     The effect on any amount shown in the balance sheet in respect of that item of

   (i)     any revision of the amount in respect of any assets included under that item made during that year on any basis in **3.14**(*a*)–(*c*);

   (ii)     acquisitions and disposals during that year of any assets; and

   (iii)     any transfers of assets of the company to and from that item during that year.

(c)     In respect of each item

   •     the cumulative amount of provisions for depreciation or diminution in value of assets included under that item both as at the beginning of the financial year and at the balance sheet date;

   •     the amount of any such provisions made in respect of the financial year; and

   •     the amount of any adjustments made in respect of any such provisions during that year, distinguishing between adjustments made in consequence of disposals and other adjustments.

For the purposes of (*a*) above, the '*appropriate amounts*' in respect of any item as at either of the dates there mentioned are the aggregate amounts determined, as at that date, in respect of assets falling to be included under that item, either on the basis of purchase price or production cost (see **3.12**) or on any basis in **3.14**(*a*)–(*c*) but in either case leaving out of account in either case any provisions for depreciation or diminution in value.

[*SI 2008 No 410, Sch 1 para 51*].

*Assets included at valuation.* The following additional information must be given where any fixed assets (other than listed investments, see **3.25**) are included under any balance sheet item at an amount determined on any basis in **3.14**(*a*)–(*c*).

(i)     The years (so far as they are known to the directors) in which the assets were severally valued, and the several values.

(ii)     In the case of assets valued during the financial year, the bases of valuation used and either the names or qualifications of the valuers.

[*SI 2008 No 410, Sch 1 para 52*].

*Land and buildings.* In relation to any amount shown in the balance sheet in respect of the item 'land and buildings' (or which would be shown there but for **3.3**(6)(*b*)(ii)), the following must be stated.

•     How much of that amount is ascribable to land of freehold tenure and how much to land of leasehold tenure (in Scotland, land in respect of which the company is the owner and land of which the company is the tenant under a lease).

•     How much of the amount ascribable to land of leasehold tenure (in Scotland, land of which the company is the tenant under a lease) is ascribable to land held on 'long lease' and how much to land held on 'short lease'. '*Long lease*' means a lease with an unexpired term at the end of the financial year of not less than 50 years and '*short lease*' means a lease which is not a long lease. '*Lease*' includes an agreement for a lease.

[*SI 2008 No 410, Sch 1 para 53, Sch 10 paras 7, 15*].

Additional disclosure requirements may also apply under FRS 102.

**3.25** *Investments*

In respect of the amount of each item shown in the balance sheet under the general item 'investments' (whether as fixed or current assets) (or which would be shown there were it not for **3.3**(6)(*b*)(ii)) there must be stated how much is ascribable to 'listed investments'.

Where the amount of any listed investments is stated (as required above), there must also be stated

- their aggregate market value where this differs from the amount so stated; and

- both the market value and the stock exchange value of any investments of which the former value is, for the purposes of the accounts, taken as being higher than the latter.

A *'listed investment'* is an investment which has been granted a listing either on a recognised investment exchange other than an overseas investment exchange (which terms have the same meaning as in *FSMA 2000, Pt 18*) or on any stock exchange of repute outside the UK.

[*SI 2008 No 410, Sch 1 para 54, Sch 10 para 8*].

See also **3.36** to **3.44** for disclosure of shares in related undertakings.

**3.26** *Fair value of assets and liabilities*

(1) *Financial instruments*

*Financial instruments or other assets.* Where financial instruments or other assets have been valued in accordance with **3.17** the following must be stated.

(a)     Where the fair value of the instruments has been determined in accordance with **3.15**(1)(*c*)—

- the significant assumptions underlying the valuation models and techniques used.

- for each category of financial instrument or other asset, the fair value of the assets in that category and the changes in value—

    (i)      included directly in the profit and loss account, or

    (ii)     credited to or (as the case may be) debited from the fair value reserve, in respect of those assets.

(b)     For each class of 'derivatives', the extent and nature of the instruments, including significant terms and conditions that may affect the amount, timing and certainty of future cash flows.

(c)     Where any amount is transferred to or from the fair value reserve during the financial year, there must be stated in tabular form

    (i)      the amount of the reserve as at the date of the beginning of the financial year and as at the balance sheet date respectively;

    (ii)     the amount transferred to or from the reserve during the year; and

    (iii)    the source and application respectively of the amounts so transferred.

*Derivatives not included at fair value.* Where the company has derivatives that it has not included at fair value, there must be stated for each class of such derivatives

- the fair value of the derivatives in that class, if such a value can be determined in accordance with **3.17**(1), and

- the extent and nature of the derivatives.

*Financial fixed assets.* If

- the company has 'financial fixed assets' that could be included at fair value by virtue of **3.17(1)**,

- the amount at which those items are included under any item in the company's accounts is in excess of their fair value, and

- the company has not made provision for diminution in value of those assets in accordance with **3.8**,

there must be stated

- the amount at which either the individual assets or appropriate groupings of those individual assets are included in the company's accounts;

- the fair value of those assets or groupings; and

- the reasons for not making a provision for diminution in value of those assets, including the nature of the evidence that provides the basis for the belief that the amount at which they are stated in the accounts will be recovered.

[*SI 2008 No 410, Sch 1 paras 55–57; SI 2015 No 980, Reg 29(3)*].

See **3.17** for the meaning of '*derivatives*'.

(2) *Stocks, investment property, and living animals and plants*

Where the amounts to be included in the accounts in respect of stocks, investment property or living animals and plants have been determined in accordance with **3.17(2)**, the balance sheet items affected and the basis of valuation adopted in determining the amounts of the assets in question in the case of each such item must be disclosed in a note to the accounts.

In the case of investment property, for each balance sheet item affected there must be shown, either separately in the balance sheet or in a note to the accounts

- the 'comparable amounts' determined according to the historical cost accounting rules; or

- the differences between those amounts and the corresponding amounts actually shown in the balance sheet in respect of that item.

'*Comparable amounts*' mean

- the aggregate amount which would be required to be shown in respect of that item if the amounts to be included in respect of all the assets covered by that item were determined according to the historical cost accounting rules; and

- the aggregate amount of the cumulative provisions for depreciation or diminution in value which would be permitted or required in determining those amounts according to those rules.

[*SI 2008 No 410, Sch 1 para 58; SI 2015 No 980, Reg 29(4)*].

Reference should also be made to the detailed disclosure requirements of FRS 102, and those in respect of financial instruments and investment property in particular.

**3.27**  *Reserves and provisions*

Where any amount is transferred

- to or from any reserves,

- to any 'provisions for liabilities', or

- from any such provision for liabilities, otherwise than for the purpose for which the provision was established,

and the reserves or provisions are shown as separate items in the balance sheet (or would be so shown were it not for 3.3(6)(*b*)(ii)), the following information must be given in respect of the aggregate of reserves or provisions included in the same item.

- The amount of the reserves or provisions at the beginning of the financial year and at the balance sheet date.

- Any amounts transferred to or from the reserves or provisions during the year.

- The source and application of the amounts so transferred.

Where the amount of the provision is material, particulars must be given of each provision included in the item 'other provisions' in the balance sheet.

References to *provisions for liabilities* are to any amount retained as reasonably necessary for the purpose of providing for any liability the nature of which is clearly defined and which is either likely to be incurred, or certain to be incurred but uncertain as to amount or as to the date on which it will arise.

[*SI 2008 No 410, Sch 1 para 59, Sch 9 para 2*].

*Provision for deferred taxation.* The amount of any provision for deferred taxation must be stated separately from the amount of any provision for other taxation. [*SI 2008 No 410, Sch 1 para 60*].

**3.28** *Details of indebtedness*

In respect of each item shown in the balance sheet under 'creditors' (or which would be shown there were it not for 3.3(6)(*b*)(ii)), the following information is required.

(a) The aggregate amount of any debts included under that item which are payable or repayable otherwise than by instalments and which fall due for payment or repayment after the end of a five-year period beginning with the day after the end of the financial year.

(b) In the case of any debts so included which are payable or repayable by instalments, the aggregate amount of any instalments which fall due for payment after the end of the period specified in (*a*) above.

(c) The aggregate amount of any debts included under that item in respect of which any security has been given by the company.

(d) An indication of the nature and form of the securities so given.

In relation to each debt falling to be taken into account under (*a*) and (*b*) above, the terms of payment or repayment and the rate of any interest payable on the debt must be stated. But if the number of debts is such that, in the opinion of the directors, compliance with this requirement would result in a statement of excessive length, it is sufficient to give a general indication of the terms of payment or repayment and the rates of any interest payable on the debts.

Where a distinction is made in the balance sheet between amounts falling due to creditors within one year and those falling due after more than one year, (*a*) and (*b*) above apply only to items shown under the latter of those categories and (*c*) and (*d*) above apply to items shown under either category.

# 3.28 Accounts: Large Companies

[*SI 2008 No 410, Sch 1 para 61; SI 2015 No 980, Reg 29(6)*].

*Fixed cumulative dividends.* If any fixed cumulative dividends on the company's shares are in arrear, there must be stated the amount of the arrears and the period for which the dividends (or, if there is more than one class, each class of them) are in arrear. [*SI 2008 No 410, Sch 1 para 62*].

**3.29** *Guarantees and other financial commitments*

The following information must be given.

(a) Particulars of any charge on the assets of the company to secure the liabilities of any other person, including the amount secured.

(b) Particulars and the total amount of any financial commitments, guarantees and contingencies that are not included in the balance sheet must be disclosed. The total amount of any commitments concerning pensions must be separately disclosed and where any commitment relates wholly or partly to pensions payable to past directors of the company separate particulars must be given of that commitment.

The total amount of any commitments etc in this provision which are undertaken on behalf of or for the benefit of—

- any parent undertaking or fellow subsidiary undertaking if the company;

- any subsidiary undertaking of the company; or

- any undertaking in which the company has a participating interest must be separately stated and those must all also be stated separately from each other.

(c) An indication of the nature and form of any valuable security given by the company in respect of commitments, guarantees and contingencies within (b) must be given.

(d) Particulars of any pension commitments which are included in the balance sheet and where any commitment relates wholly or partly to pensions payable to past directors of the company separate particulars must be given of that commitment.

[*SI 2008 No 410, Sch 1 para 63; SI 2015 No 980, Reg 29(7)*].

*Guarantees and other financial commitments in favour of group undertakings.* Commitments within any of (a)–(e) above which are undertaken on behalf of or for the benefit of

(i) any parent undertaking or fellow subsidiary undertaking, or

(ii) any subsidiary undertaking of the company,

must be stated separately from the other commitments within each of (a)–(e) above, distinguishing commitments within (i) from those within (ii) above.

[*SI 2008 No 410, Sch 1 para 73*].

Reference should also be made to the requirements of FRS 102 on the disclosure of contingent liabilities and contingent assets.

**3.30** *Miscellaneous matters*

The following information must be given.

(a) Particulars of any case where the purchase price or production cost of any asset is for the first time determined *SI 2008 No 410, Sch 1 para 29* (see **3.12**).

(b) The aggregate amount, for each item in question, of any outstanding loans made under the authority of *CA 2006, s 682(2)(b), (c)* or *(d)* (various cases of financial assistance by a company for purchase of its own shares, see **34.26(***i***)(***j***)(***k***)** PURCHASE OF OWN SHARES) included under any item shown in the company's balance sheet.

[*SI 2008 No 410, Sch 1 para 64*].

**3.31**   **Notes to the accounts: information supplementing the profit and loss account**

The information required, as set out in **3.32** to **3.35**, being information which either supplements that given with respect to particular items in the profit and loss account or otherwise provides particulars of income or expenditure or of circumstances affecting items shown in the profit and loss account, must be given by way of notes to the accounts (if not given in the accounts themselves).

[*SI 2008 No 410, Sch 1 para 65*].

**3.32**   *Separate statement of loan interest*

The amount of the interest on (or any similar charges in respect of)

- bank loans and overdrafts, and

- loans of any other kind made to the company

   must be stated.

This does not apply to interest or charges on loans to the company from group undertakings, but, with that exception, it applies to interest or charges on all loans, whether made on the security of debentures or not.

[*SI 2008 No 410, Sch 1 para 66*].

**3.33**   *Particulars of tax*

Particulars must be given of any special circumstances which affect liability in respect of taxation of profits, income or capital gains for the financial year in question and/or succeeding financial years.

In respect of each of the amounts shown under the items 'tax on profit or loss on ordinary activities' and 'tax on extraordinary profit or loss' in the profit and loss account (or which would be shown were it not for 3.3(6)(*b*)(ii)), the following must be stated.

- The amount of the charge for UK corporation tax.

- If that amount would have been greater but for double taxation relief, the amount which it would have been but for such relief.

- The amount of the charge for UK income tax.

- The amount of the charge for taxation imposed outside the UK of profits, income and (so far as charged to revenue) capital gains.

These amounts must be stated separately in respect of each of the amounts which is or would but for para 4(2)(b), Sch 1 be shown under the item 'tax on profit or loss' in the profit and loss account.

[*SI 2008 No 410, Sch 1 para 67*].

Reference should also be made to the tax accounting and disclosure requirements of FRS 102. In particular, the standard requires the notes to the accounts to include a reconciliation of the tax charge shown in the profit and loss account to the amount that would result from applying a relevant standard rate of tax to the profit before tax.

**3.34**   *Particulars of turnover*

If, in the course of the financial year, the company has

- carried on business of two or more classes that, in the directors' opinion, differ substantially from each other, there must be stated in respect of each class

    (i)      a description of the class concerned; and

    (ii)     the amount of the turnover attributable to it; and

- supplied different markets ('market' meaning a market delimited by geographical bounds) that, in the directors' opinion, differ substantially from each other, there must be stated the amount of the turnover attributable to each such market.

Where, in the directors' opinion, the disclosure of any information required above would be seriously prejudicial to the interests of the company, that information need not be disclosed, but the fact that any such information has not been disclosed must be stated.

In analysing for the above purposes the source (in terms of either business or market) of turnover, the directors must have regard to the manner in which the company's activities are organised. Classes of business and markets which, in the opinion of the directors, do not differ substantially from each other must be treated as one class or one market respectively. Any amounts properly attributable to one class of business or (as the case may be) to one market which are not material may be included in the amount stated in respect of another.

[*SI 2008 No 410, Sch 1 para 68*].

**3.35**  *Miscellaneous matters*

*Prior year adjustments*. Where any amount relating to any preceding financial year is included in any profit and loss account item, the effect must be stated.

*Exceptional items*. The amount, nature and effect of any individual items of income or expenditure which are of exceptional size or incidence must be stated.

[*SI 2008 No 410, Sch 1, para 69; SI 2015 No 980, Reg 29(9)*].

**3.36**    **INDIVIDUAL ACCOUNTS: INFORMATION ABOUT RELATED UNDERTAKINGS**

Where a company is not preparing group accounts, its Companies Act or IAS individual accounts must comply with the provisions in **3.37** to **3.44** as to the information about related undertakings to be given in notes to the company's accounts. The only exception is that the information (other than that in **3.41** and **3.43**) need not be disclosed with respect to an undertaking that

- is established under the law of a country outside the UK, or

- carries on business outside the UK,

but only if

- in the opinion of the directors of the company, the disclosure would be seriously prejudicial to the business of

    (i)      that undertaking;

    (ii)     the company;

    (iii)    any of the company's subsidiary undertakings; or

    (iv)    any other undertaking which is included in the consolidation; and

- the Secretary of State agrees that the information need not be disclosed.

Where advantage is taken of this exemption, a note to that effect must be included in the company's accounts.

[*CA 2006, s 409(4), (5); SI 2008 No 410, Reg 7*].

The provision in *CA 2006, s 410* that permitted an alternative approach in order to avoid disclosure of excessive length was repealed by *SI 2015 No 980* in respect of accounts approved on or after 1 July 2015.

## 3.37    Subsidiary undertakings

Subject to **3.36**, where, at the end of the financial year, the company has subsidiary undertakings, there must be stated in respect of each one of them

•     its name;

•     the address of its registered office (whether inside or outside the UK);

•     if it is unincorporated, the address of its principal place of business.

[*SI 2008 No 410, Sch 4 para 1; SI 2015 No 980, Reg 37(2)*].

**Reason for not preparing group accounts.** There must also be stated the reason why the company is not required to prepare group accounts. If the reason is that all the company's subsidiary undertakings fall within the exclusions in *CA 2006, s 405* (see **3.58**), there must be stated, for each subsidiary undertaking, which of those exclusions applies.

[*SI 2008 No 410, Sch 4 para 10*].

## 3.38    *Holdings in subsidiary undertakings*

Subject to **3.36**, in relation to shares of each class 'held by the company' in a subsidiary undertaking, there must be stated

•     the identity of the class; and

•     the proportion of the nominal value of the shares of that class represented by those shares.

The shares held by or on behalf of the company itself must be distinguished from those attributed to the company which are held by or on behalf of a subsidiary undertaking.

[*SI 2008 No 410, Sch 4 para 11*].

In ascertaining the shares '*held by the company*',

•     there must be attributed to the company any shares held by a subsidiary undertaking, or by a person acting on behalf of the company or a subsidiary undertaking. Any shares held on behalf of a person other than the company or a subsidiary undertaking must be treated as not held by the company; and

•     shares held by way of security must be treated as held by the person providing the security where

    (i)     the rights attached to the shares are exercisable only in accordance with his instructions; and

    (ii)     the shares are held in connection with the granting of loans as part of normal business activities and the rights attached to the shares are exercisable only in his interests

disregarding, in each case, any right to exercise the rights for the purpose of preserving the value of the security, or of realising it.

## 3.38 Accounts: Large Companies

[*SI 2008 No 410, Sch 4 para 14*].

**3.39** *Financial information about subsidiary undertakings*

Subject to **3.36** and the exceptions below, there must be disclosed with respect to each subsidiary undertaking not included in consolidated accounts by the company

- the aggregate amount of its capital and reserves as at the end of its 'relevant financial year'; and

- its profit or loss for that year.

For this purposes, the '*relevant financial year*' of a subsidiary undertaking is, if its financial year ends with that of the company, that year and, if it does not, its financial year ending last before the end of the company's financial year.

*Exceptions.* The above information need not be given if

- the company is exempt under **3.57** from the requirement to prepare group accounts (parent company included in accounts of larger group);

- the company's investment in the subsidiary undertaking is included in the company's accounts by way of the equity method of valuation;

- the subsidiary undertaking is not required by any provision of the *CA 2006* to deliver a copy of its balance sheet for its relevant financial year and does not otherwise publish that balance sheet in the UK or elsewhere *and* the shares '*held by the company*' (see **3.38**) are less than 50% of the nominal value of the shares in the undertaking; or

- it is not material.

[*SI 2008 No 410, Sch 4 para 2*].

**3.40** *Financial years of subsidiary undertakings*

Where disclosure is made under **3.39** with respect to a subsidiary undertaking and that undertaking's financial year does not end with that of the company, there must be stated in relation to that undertaking the date on which its last financial year ended (ie last before the end of the company's financial year).

[*SI 2008 No 410, Sch 4 para 12*].

**3.41** *Shares and debentures of company held by subsidiary undertakings*

The number, description and amount of shares in the company held by, or on behalf of, its subsidiary undertakings must be disclosed. This does not apply in relation to shares in the case of which the subsidiary undertaking is concerned as

- personal representative; or

- trustee unless the company, or any subsidiary undertaking of the company, is 'beneficially interested under the trust', otherwise than by way of security only for the purposes of a transaction entered into by it in the ordinary course of a business which includes the lending of money.

[*SI 2008 No 410, Sch 4 para 3*].

In determining whether the company is '*beneficially interested under the trust*', certain residual interests under pension and employees' share schemes, employer's charges and other rights of recovery under such schemes, and a trustee's right to expenses, remuneration, indemnity, etc are disregarded. See *SI 2008 No 410, Sch 4 paras 24–27* for full details.

**3.42   Significant holdings in undertakings other than subsidiary undertakings**

Subject to **3.36**, where at the end of the financial year the company has a 'significant holding' in an undertaking which is not a subsidiary undertaking, the following must be stated.

(a)   The name of the undertaking.

(b)   The address of its registered office (whether inside or outside the UK).

(c)   If it is unincorporated, the address of its principal place of business.

(d)   The identity of each class of shares in the undertaking held by the company.

(e)   The proportion of the nominal value of the shares of that class represented by those shares.

(f)   Subject to the exemption below, the aggregate amount of the capital and reserves of the undertaking as at the end of its 'relevant financial year'.

(g)   Subject to the exemption below, its profit or loss for that year.

A '*significant holding*' is a holding which amounts to 20% or more of the nominal value of any class of shares in the undertaking *or* the amount of which (as stated or included in the company's individual accounts) exceeds one-fifth of the amount (as so stated) of the company's assets.

The '*relevant financial year*' of an undertaking for these purposes is, if its financial year ends with that of the company, that year, and if it does not, its financial year ending last before the end of the company's financial year.

**Exemption.** The information in (*f*) and (*g*) above need not be given in respect of an undertaking if

•   the undertaking is exempt under **3.57** from the requirement to prepare group accounts (parent company included in accounts of larger group) *and* the investment of the company in all undertakings in which it has a significant holding is shown, in aggregate, in the notes to the accounts by way of the equity method of valuation;

•   the undertaking in question is not required by any provision of *CA 2006* to deliver a copy of its balance sheet for its relevant financial year and does not otherwise publish that balance sheet in the UK or elsewhere *and* the company's holding is less than 50% of the nominal value of the shares in the undertaking; or

•   it is not material.

[*SI 2008 No 410, Sch 4 paras 4–6, 13; SI 2015 No 980, Reg 37(3)*].

In ascertaining, for any of the above purposes, the company's holding,

•   there must be attributed to the company shares held on its behalf by any person but any shares held on behalf of a person other than the company must be treated as not held by the company; and

•   shares held by way of security must be treated as held by the person providing the security where

(i)   the rights attached to the shares are exercisable only in accordance with his instructions; and

(ii)   the shares are held in connection with the granting of loans as part of normal business activities and the rights attached to the shares are exercisable only in his interests

## 3.42   Accounts: Large Companies

disregarding, in each case, any right to exercise the rights for the purpose of preserving the value of the security, or of realising it.

[*SI 2008 No 410, Sch 4 para 14*].

### 3.43   Membership of certain undertakings

Where at the end of the financial year a company is a member of an undertaking with unlimited liability the following must be stated.

- The name and legal form of the undertaking (unless it is not material).

- The address (whether in or outside the UK) of its registered office or, if it does not have such an office, its head office (unless it is not material).

- Where the undertaking is a qualifying partnership, either

    (i)    a statement that a copy of the latest accounts of the undertaking has been or is to be appended to the copy of the company's accounts sent to the Registrar of Companies; or

    (ii)   the name of at least one body corporate (which may be the company) in whose group accounts the undertaking has been or is to be dealt with on a consolidated basis. This information need not be given if the notes to the company's accounts disclose that advantage has been taken of the exemption in *regulation 7* of the *Partnerships (Accounts) Regulations 2008*.

A '*qualifying partnership*' is a partnership formed under the law of any part of the UK, each of whose members or, in the case of a limited partnership, each of whose general partners is:

(a)    a limited company;

(b)    an unlimited company each of whose members is a limited company;

(c)    a Scottish partnership which is not a limited partnership, each of whose members is a limited company; or

(d)    a Scottish partnership which is a limited partnership, each of whose general partners is a limited company,

and, for these purposes, references to a limited company, an unlimited company and a Scottish partnership include a comparable undertaking incorporated in, or formed under, the law of a country or territory outside the UK.

[*SI 2008 No 410, Sch 4 para 7; SI 2008 No 569, Reg 3; SI 2015 No 980, Reg 37(1), (4)*].

### 3.44   Parent undertaking drawing up accounts for larger group

Subject to **3.36**, where the company is a subsidiary undertaking, the following information must be given.

(a)    Particulars as follows with respect to the parent undertaking of the largest and smallest group of undertakings for which group accounts are drawn up and of which the company is a member.

    (i)    The name of the parent undertaking.

    (ii)   The address of its registered office (whether inside or outside the UK).

(iii)   If it is unincorporated, the address of its principal place of business.

(iv)   If copies of the group accounts referred to above are available to the public, the addresses from which copies of the accounts can be obtained.

(b)   Particulars as follows with respect to the company (which includes any body corporate) regarded by the directors as being the company's ultimate parent company.

(i)   Its name.

(ii)   If that company is incorporated outside the UK, the country in which it is incorporated (if known to the directors).

[*SI 2008 No 410, Sch 4 paras 8, 9; SI 2015 No 980, Reg 37(5)*].

### 3.45   INDIVIDUAL ACCOUNTS: DIRECTORS' REMUNERATION AND BENEFITS, UNQUOTED COMPANIES

The information as described in **3.46** to **3.52** must be given in the notes to a company's individual accounts, except that the information in **3.48** to **3.51** only applies to unquoted companies. The provisions in **3.46** apply equally to quoted companies and they must continue to give the disclosures in **3.47** in the notes to the accounts. In addition to this, they are required to prepare a separate directors' remuneration report (see **19** Directors' Remuneration Reports). The detailed legislative requirements may result in a difference between the total remuneration disclosures given in the directors' remuneration report and the aggregate remuneration disclosures given in the notes to the accounts, and the FRC has encouraged directors to include an explanation of any difference that arises.

The provisions apply whether the company is preparing Companies Act or IAS accounts.

[*SI 2008 No 410, Reg 8*].

In addition, the AIM Rules require an AIM company to provide in the notes to the accounts separate disclosure of the remuneration earned in respect of that financial year by each person who acted as director during the year. Some AIM companies voluntarily prepare a directors' remuneration report similar to that required from quoted companies, and in this case the notes to the accounts should include a cross-reference to where the relevant disclosures can be found.

FRS 102 also requires the total compensation of key management personnel to be disclosed. The term 'key management personnel' is defined in the glossary to FRS 102 and includes, but is not necessarily restricted to, directors.

**Listed companies.** In addition to the requirements of *CA 2006* and supporting Regulations, listed companies must also comply with the requirements of the FCA Listing Rules. See **33.32**(*q*) Public and Listed Companies.

### 3.46   Directors' remuneration

The information on directors' remuneration as described in **3.47** to **3.51** must be given in the notes to a company's annual accounts. [*CA 2006, s 412(1)*]. It is the duty of

•   any director of a company, and

•   any person who is or has at any time in the preceding five years been a director of the company

to give notice to the company of such matters relating to himself as may be necessary for these purposes. A person in default commits an offence and is liable, on summary conviction to a fine not exceeding level 3 on the standard scale. See **29.1** Offences and Legal Proceedings for the standard scale.

[*CA 2006, s 412(5)(6)*].

Information is to be given only so far as it is contained in the company's books and papers or the company has the right to obtain it from the persons concerned. [*SI 2008 No 410, Sch 5 para 6(1)*].

Where it is necessary for the purpose of making any distinction required in **3.47** to **3.51**, the directors may apportion payments between the matters in respect of which they have been paid or are receivable in such manner as they think appropriate. [*SI 2008 No 410, Sch 5 para 7(6)*].

**Meaning of 'subsidiary undertakings'.** Any reference in these provisions to a subsidiary undertaking of the company, in relation to a person who is or was, while a director of the company, a director also, by virtue of the company's nomination (direct or indirect) of any other undertaking, includes that undertaking (whether or not it is or was in fact a subsidiary undertaking of the company). [*SI 2008 No 410, Sch 5 para 14(1)*].

**3.47** *Total amount of directors' remuneration*

The following must be shown. Any information is treated as being shown if it is capable of being readily ascertained from other information which is shown.

(a)    The aggregate amount of 'remuneration' paid to or receivable by directors in respect of 'qualifying services'.

'*Remuneration*' of a director includes

- salary, fees and bonuses;

- sums paid by way of expenses allowance (so far as they are chargeable to UK income tax); and

- the estimated money value of any other benefits received by the director otherwise than in cash

but does not include

- the value of any share options granted to the director or the amount of any gains made on the exercise of any such options;

- any company contributions paid, or treated as paid, under any pension scheme or any benefits to which the director is entitled under any such scheme; or

- any money or other assets paid to or received or receivable by the director under any 'long term incentive scheme'.

(b)    For quoted companies and companies whose equity share capital is listed on the AIM only, the aggregate of the amount of gains made by directors on the exercise of share options in shares of the company or a group undertaking.

(c)    The aggregate of

(i)    the amount of money paid to or receivable by directors under 'long-term incentive schemes' in respect of 'qualifying services'; and

(ii)   the 'net value' of assets (other than money and share options and, in the case of a company which is not a quoted company and whose equity share capital is not listed on the market known as AIM, shares in the company or any group undertaking) received or receivable by directors under long-term incentive schemes in respect of qualifying services. '*Net value*' means the value after deducting any money paid or other value given by the director in respect of those assets.

(d)    The aggregate value of any 'company contributions' paid, or treated as paid, to a pension scheme in respect of directors' 'qualifying services', being contributions by reference to which the rate or amount of any 'money purchase benefits' that may become payable will be calculated.

'*Company contributions*' mean any payments (including insurance premiums) made, or treated as made, to the scheme in respect of the director by any person other than the director.

'*Money purchase benefits*' are retirement benefits payable under a pension scheme, the rate or amount of which is calculated by reference to payments made, or treated as made, by the director or by any other person in respect of the director and which are not average salary benefits.

(e)    The number of directors (if any) to whom retirement benefits are accruing in respect of 'qualifying services' under each of

    (i)    '*money purchase schemes*' (ie, pension schemes under which all of the benefits that may become payable to, or in respect of, the director are 'money purchase benefits', see (*d*) above); and

    (ii)    '*defined benefit schemes*' (ie any pension scheme which is not a money purchase scheme).

(f)    In the case of a company which is not a quoted company and whose equity share capital is not listed on the market known as AIM, both the number of directors

    (i)    who exercised share options in shares in the company or a group undertaking; and

    (ii)    in respect of whose 'qualifying services' shares in the company or a group undertaking were received or receivable under 'long-term incentive schemes'.

'*Qualifying services*' in respect of any person means

•    his services as director of the company; and

•    his services while director of the company

    (i)    as director of any of its subsidiary undertakings; or

    (ii)    otherwise in connection with the management of the company's affairs or those of any of its subsidiary undertakings.

Reference to a subsidiary undertaking of the company is to an undertaking which is a subsidiary undertaking at the time the services were rendered.

A '*long term incentive scheme*' means any agreement or arrangement under which money or other assets may become receivable by a director and which includes one or more qualifying conditions with respect to service or performance which cannot be fulfilled in a single financial year, but disregarding

•    bonuses determined by reference to service or performance in a single financial year;

•    compensation for loss of office, payments for breach of contract and other termination payments; and

•    retirement benefits.

*Notes*

(1)     Remuneration paid or receivable or share options granted in respect of a person's accepting office as director are treated as remuneration paid or receivable or share options granted in respect of his services as director.

(2)     For the purpose of determining whether a pension scheme is a money purchase scheme or defined benefit scheme, any death in service benefits provided are to be disregarded.

(3)     Where a pension scheme provides for any benefits that may become payable to or in respect of any director to be whichever are the greater of money purchase benefits and defined benefits (in each case as determined under the scheme), the company may assume that those benefits will be whichever appears more likely at the end of the financial year.

(4)     Amounts paid to or receivable by a person include amounts paid to or receivable by a connected person or a body corporate controlled by him (both to be construed in accordance with *CA 2006, ss 252–255*, see **18 DIRECTORS**), but not so as to require an amount to be counted twice.

(5)     The amounts to be shown include all relevant sums paid by or receivable from the company, its subsidiary undertakings and any other person. They do not, however, include sums to be accounted for

•         to the company or any of its subsidiary undertakings; or

•         under **18 DIRECTORS** (payments in connection with shares transfers, duty to account) to persons who sold their shares as a result of the offer made.

(6)     The amounts to be shown for any financial year are the sums receivable in respect of that financial year (whenever paid) or, in the case of sums not payable in respect of a period, the sums paid during the year. However, in either of the two circumstances set out below, the sums in question must be shown (and distinguished as such), to the extent appropriate, in a note to the first accounts in which it is practicable to show them. The said circumstances are where

(i)     any sums are not shown for the relevant financial year on the grounds that the person receiving them is liable to account for them as mentioned above, but the liability is later released (wholly or partly) or is not enforced within a period of two years; or

(ii)    sums paid by way of expenses allowances are charged to UK income tax after the end of the relevant financial year.

[*SI 2008 No 410, Sch 5 paras 1, 6(2), 7(2)–(5), 8, 9, 11, 12, 13(3) (4) (6) (7), 14(2), 15*].

**3.48**    *Details of highest paid director's remuneration*

*Note.* The provisions in this paragraph only apply to unquoted companies.

Where the aggregate shown under **3.47**(*a*)–(*c*) is £200,000 or more, the following information must be shown. Any information is treated as being shown if it is capable of being readily ascertained from other information which is shown.

(a)     So much of the total of the aggregate of **3.47**(*a*)–(*c*) which is attributable to the '*highest paid director*' (ie the director to whom is attributable the greatest part of that aggregate).

(b)     So much of the aggregate in **3.47**(*d*) as is attributable to the 'highest paid director'.

(c)    If the highest paid director has performed 'qualifying services' during the financial year by reference to which the rate or amount of any 'defined benefits' that may become payable will be calculated,

(i)    the amount at the end of the year of his 'accrued pension'; and

(ii)    where applicable, the amount at the end of the year of his 'accrued lump sum'.

'*Accrued pension*' and '*accrued lump sum*' mean respectively the amount of the annual pension and the amount of the lump sum which would be payable under the pension scheme on his attaining normal pension age under the scheme if

•    he had left the company's service at the end of the financial year;

•    there were no increases in the general level of prices in the UK from the end of the financial year until his attaining that age;

•    no question arose of any commutation of the pension or inverse commutation of the lump sum; and

•    any amounts attributable to voluntary contributions paid by the director to the scheme, and any 'money purchase benefits' which would be payable under the scheme, were disregarded.

(d)    In the case of a company which is not a listed company, whether

(i)    the highest paid director exercised any share options in the shares of the company or any group undertaking; and

(ii)    any shares were received or receivable by that director in respect of qualifying services under a long term incentive scheme.

If the highest paid director has not been involved in any of the transactions specified in (i) or (ii) above, that fact need not be stated.

See **3.47** for the definitions of '*qualifying services*', '*defined benefits*', '*money purchase benefits*' and '*long-term incentive scheme*'.

Notes (1)–(6) in **3.47** equally apply for the above purposes.

[*SI 2008 No 410, Sch 5 paras 2, 6(2), 7(2)–(5), 8, 10, 11, 12, 13(2), (4), (6), (7), (15)*].

**3.49**    *Excess retirement benefits of directors and past directors*

*Note.* The provisions in this paragraph only apply to unquoted companies.

Subject to below, there must be shown the aggregate amount of

(a)    so much of 'retirement benefits' paid to or receivable by directors under 'pension schemes', and

(b)    so much of retirement benefits paid to or receivable by past directors under such schemes,

as (in each case) is in excess of the retirement benefits to which they were respectively entitled on the date on which the benefits first became payable (or 31 March 1997, if later). The amounts shown must include the estimated money value of any benefits paid otherwise than in cash, and the nature of any such benefit must also be disclosed.

Amounts paid or receivable under a pension scheme need not be included in the aggregate amount if

(i)    the funding of the scheme was such that the amounts were or, as the case may be, could have been paid without recourse to additional contributions; and

(ii)   amounts were paid to or receivable by all pensioner entitled to the present payment of retirement benefits under the scheme on the same basis.

Notes (4)–(6) in **3.47** equally apply for the above purposes.

[*SI 2008 No 410, Sch 5 paras 3, 7(2)-(5), 8, 13(1), 15(2)*].

**3.50**   *Compensation to directors for loss of office*

*Note.* The provisions in this paragraph only apply to unquoted companies.

There must be shown the aggregate amount of any compensation to directors or past directors in respect of loss of office. The amount shown must include the estimated money value of any benefits paid otherwise than in cash, and the nature of any such compensation must be disclosed. The necessary information is treated as shown if it can be readily ascertained from other information which is shown.

There must be included compensation received or receivable for

(a)     loss of office as director of the company; or

(b)     loss, while director of the company or on (or in connection with) his ceasing to be a director of it, of

(i)     any other office in connection with the management of the company's affairs; or

(ii)     any office (as director or otherwise) in connection with the management of the affairs of any subsidiary undertaking of the company.

References above to compensation for loss of office include

•     compensation in consideration for (or in connection with) a person's retirement from office; and

•     where such a retirement is occasioned by a breach of the person's contract with the company or with a subsidiary undertaking of the company

(i)     payments made by way of damages for the breach; or

(ii)     payments made by way of settlement or compromise of any claim in respect of the breach.

Reference to a subsidiary undertaking of the company is to a subsidiary undertaking immediately before the loss of office as director.

Notes (4)–(6) in **3.47** equally apply for the above purposes.

[*SI 2008 No 410, Sch 5 paras 4, 6(2), 7(2)–(5), 8, 14(2), 15(2)*].

**3.51**   *Sums paid to third parties in respect of directors' services*

*Note.* The provisions in this paragraph only apply to unquoted companies.

There must be shown the aggregate amount of any consideration paid to or receivable by 'third parties' for making available the services of any person

•     as a director of the company; or

•     while director of the company

(i)     as director of any of its subsidiary undertakings; or

(ii)   otherwise in connection with the management of the affairs of the company or any of its subsidiary undertakings.

The amount shown must include the estimated money value of benefits paid otherwise than in cash, and the nature of any such consideration must be disclosed.

A '*third party*' means a person other than

- the director himself or a person connected with him or a body corporate controlled by him; or

- the company or any of its subsidiary undertakings.

Notes (4)–(6) in **3.47** equally apply for the above purposes.

[*SI 2008 No 410, Sch 5 paras 5, 7(2)–(5), 8, 15(2)*].

## 3.52   Directors' benefits: advances, credit and guarantees

In the case of a company that does not prepare group accounts, the notes to its individual accounts must show the following.

(a)   In respect of any advance or credit granted by the company to a director, details of

(i)    its amount;

(ii)   an indication of the interest rate;

(iii)  its main conditions;

(iv)  any amounts repaid;

(v)   any amounts written off; and

(vi)  any amounts waived.

(b)   In respect of any guarantee of any kind entered into by the company on behalf of a director, details of

(i)    its main terms;

(ii)   the amount of the maximum liability that may be incurred by the company; and

(iii)  any amount paid and any liability incurred by the company for the purpose of fulfilling the guarantee (including any loss incurred by reason of enforcement of the guarantee).

The totals of amounts stated under (*a*)(i), (*a*)(iv), (*a*)(v), (*a*)(vi), (*b*)(ii) and (*b*)(iii) must also be given.

The provisions apply to

- persons who were directors of the company at any time in the financial year to which the accounts relate; and

- every advance, credit or guarantee subsisting at any time in the financial year to which the accounts relate

(i)    whenever it was entered into; and

(ii)   whether or not the person concerned was a director of the company in question at the time it was entered into.

## 3.52 Accounts: Large Companies

[*CA 2006, s 413(1), (3)–(7); SI 2015 No 980, Reg 5*].

### 3.53 INDIVIDUAL ACCOUNTS: AUDITOR'S REMUNERATION AND LIABILITY LIMITATION AGREEMENTS

**Remuneration.** The following must be disclosed in the notes to the annual accounts.

(a)  The amount of any 'remuneration' receivable by the company's auditor or any associate of the company's auditors for the auditing of the accounts.

(b)  The amount of any remuneration receivable in respect of the period to which the accounts relate by

- the company's auditor, or

- any person who was, at any time during the period to which the accounts relate, an 'associate of the company's auditor'

for the supply of other services to the company or any 'associates of the company'.

This requirement is subject to two exceptions.

(i)  Disclosure is not required of remuneration receivable for the supply of services falling within *SI 2008 No 489, Sch 2A, para 8* (ie all other non-audit services) supplied by a 'distant associate' of a company's auditor where the total remuneration receivable for all those services supplied by that associate does not exceed either

- £10,000; or

- 1% of the 'total audit remuneration received' by the company's auditor in the most recent 'financial year of the auditor' which ended no later than the end of the financial year of the company to which the accounts relate.

'*Total audit remuneration received*' means the total remuneration received for auditing pursuant to legislation (including that of countries and territories outside the UK) of any accounts of any person.

'*Financial year of the auditor*' means the period of not more than 18 months in respect of which the auditor's profit and loss account is required to be made up *or*, failing any such requirement, the period of 12 months beginning with 1 April.

(ii)  The notes to the individual accounts of

- a 'parent company' which is required to prepare (and does prepare) group accounts in accordance with *CA 2006*, and

- a 'subsidiary company' where its parent is required to prepare (and does prepare) group accounts in accordance with *CA 2006*, the subsidiary company is included in the consolidation, and (for periods beginning on or after 17 June 2016) the statutory auditor is the same for both the subsidiary and its parent

need not disclose this information if the group accounts are required to disclose it and the individual accounts state that the group accounts are so required.

Where more than one person has been appointed as the company's auditor during the period to which the accounts relate, separate disclosure must be given in respect of each such person and his associates.

Where the remuneration includes benefits in kind, the nature and estimated money-value of those benefits must also be disclosed.

*Types of other services in respect of which separate disclosure is required.* In the case of (b) above, separate disclosure is required in respect of each of the following types of service.

(1)    The auditing of accounts of any associate of the company.

(2)    Audit-related assurance services.

(3)    Taxation compliance services.

(4)    All taxation advisory services not falling with (3) above.

(5)    Internal audit services.

(6)    All assurance services not falling within (1)–(5) above.

(7)    All services relating to corporate finance transactions entered into or proposed to be entered into by or on behalf of the company or any of its associates not falling within paras (1)–(6) above.

(8)    All non-audit services not falling within (2)–(7) above.

It is not necessary to disclose separately each service falling within a type of service listed above.

Separate disclosure is required in respect of services supplied to the company and its subsidiaries on the one hand and to 'associated pension schemes' on the other.

Detailed guidance on these disclosure requirements can be found in TECH 14/13 'Disclosure of auditor remuneration' issued by the Institute of Chartered Accountants in England and Wales (ICAEW) and available at www.icaew.com/en/technical/technical -releases/financial-reporting. Audit-related services are defined in *para* **5.42** of the Ethical Standard issued by the Financial Reporting Council in June 2016 (available at www.frc.org.uk).

*Duty of auditor to supply information.* The auditor must supply the directors of the company with such information as is necessary to enable the disclosure required by (*b*) above.

*Definitions.*

(1)    *Remuneration*

Remuneration includes payments in respect of expenses and benefits in kind. Where it includes benefits in kind, the nature and estimated money value must also be disclosed in the notes.

(2)    *Associate of a company's auditor*

(a)    Each of the following is regarded as an associate of a company's auditor.

(i)    Any person controlled by the company's auditor or by any associate of the company's auditor (whether alone or through two or more persons acting together to secure or exercise control). This only applies if that control does *not* arise solely by virtue of the company's auditor or any associate of the company's auditor acting as an insolvency practitioner in relation to any person *or* acting in the capacity of a receiver, or a receiver or manager, of the property of a company or other body corporate (including a receiver or, as the case may be, a receiver or manager, of part only of that property) *or* acting as a judicial factor on the estate of any person.

(ii) Any person who, or group of persons acting together which, has control of the company's auditor.

(iii) Any person using a trading name which is the same as or similar to a trading name used by the company's auditor, but only if the company's auditor uses that trading name with the intention of creating the impression of a connection between him and that other person.

(iv) Any person who is party to an arrangement with the company's auditor, with or without any other person, under which costs, profits, quality control, business strategy or significant professional resources are shared.

(b) Where a company's auditor is a partnership, each of the following is also regarded as an associate of the auditor.

(i) Any other partnership which has a partner in common with the company's auditor.

(ii) Any partner in the company's auditor.

(iii) Any body corporate which is in the same group as a body corporate which is a partner in the company's auditor.

(iv) Any body corporate which is in the same group as a body corporate which is a partner in a partnership which has a partner in common with the company's auditor.

(v) Any body corporate of which a partner in the company's auditor is a director.

(c) Where a company's auditor is a body corporate (other than one which is also a partnership as defined for these purposes below), each of the following is also regarded as an associate of the auditor.

(i) Any other body corporate which has a director in common with the company's auditor.

(ii) Any director of the company's auditor.

(iii) Any body corporate which is in the same group as a body corporate which is a director of the company's auditor.

(iv) Any body corporate which is in the same group as a body corporate which has a director in common with the company's auditor.

(v) Any partnership in which a director of the company's auditor is a partner.

(vi) Any body corporate which is in the same group as the company's auditor.

(vii) Any partnership in which any body corporate which is in the same group as the company's auditor is a partner.

A '*distant associate*' of the company's auditor is a person who is an associate of that auditor by reason only that that person is an associate within one or more of

• (a)(i) above where the person in question is controlled by a distant associate of the company's auditor but not by the auditor or by an associate who is not a distant associate;

- (*b*)(i)(iv) or (v); or

- (*c*)(i)(iv) or (v).

For these purposes, '*partner*' includes a member of an LLP and '*partnership*' includes an LLP and a partnership constituted under the law of a country or a territory outside the UK.

A person able, directly or indirectly, to control or materially to influence the operating and financial policy of another person is to be treated as having control of that other person.

A body corporate is in the same group as another body corporate if it is a parent or subsidiary of that body corporate, or a subsidiary of a parent of that body corporate.

(3) *Associate of a company*

References to an associate of a company are references to

- any subsidiary of that company, other than a subsidiary in respect of which severe long-term restrictions substantially hinder the exercise of the rights of the company over the assets or management of the subsidiary; and

- any scheme which is an 'associated pension scheme' in relation to that company.

(4) *Parent/subsidiary*

See Appendix 1 Definitions.

(5) *Associated pension scheme*

Associated pension scheme means, in relation to a company, a scheme for the provision of benefits for or in respect of directors or employees (or former directors or employees) of the company or any subsidiary of the company where

- the benefits consist of or include any pension, lump sum, gratuity or other like benefit given or to be given on retirement or on death or in anticipation of retirement or, in connection with past service, after retirement or death; and

- either

  (i) a majority of the trustees are appointed by (or by a person acting on behalf of) the company or a subsidiary of the company; or

  (ii) the company, or a subsidiary of the company, exercises a dominant influence over the appointment of the auditor (if any) of the scheme.

[*SI 2008 No 489, Regs 3, 5, 6(2), (3), 7, Sch 1, Sch 2A; SI 2011 No 2198, Regs 2–5; SI 2016 No 649, Reg 18(1)(3)*].

**Liability limitation agreements.** A company is able to enter into a liability limitation agreement with its auditors, the effect of which is to limit the auditor's liability to not less than such amount as it is fair and reasonable in all the circumstances of the case having regard in particular to

- the auditor's responsibilities under *CA 2006*

- the nature and purpose of the auditor's contractual obligations to the company; and

- the professional standards expected of an auditor.

## 3.53   Accounts: Large Companies

A company which has entered into a liability limitation agreement must have it approved by its shareholders (unless it is a private company whose shareholders have waived the need for approval) and must disclose the following in a note to its annual accounts for the financial year to which the agreement relates.

•   Its principal terms.

•   The date of the resolution approving the agreement or the agreement's principal terms or, in the case of a private company, the date of the resolution waiving the need for such approval.

The annual accounts in which the required disclosure must be made are those for the financial year to which the agreement relates unless the agreement was entered into too late for it to be reasonably practicable for the disclosure to be made in those accounts. In such a case, the disclosure must be made in a note to the company's next following annual accounts.

[*CA 2006, ss 534–538; SI 2008 No 489, Reg 8*].

Practical guidance on using auditor liability limitation agreements can be found in 'Guidance on Auditor Liability Limitation Agreements' available at www.frc.org.uk.

## 3.54   INDIVIDUAL ACCOUNTS: OFF-BALANCE SHEET ARRANGEMENTS

If in any financial year

•   the company is, or has been, party to arrangements that are not reflected in its balance sheet, and

•   at the balance sheet date the risks or benefits arising from those arrangements are material,

the following information must be given in notes to the company's annual accounts.

(a)   The nature and business purpose of the arrangements.

(b)   The financial impact of the arrangements on the company.

The information need only be given to the extent necessary for enabling the financial position of the company to be assessed.

[*CA 2006, s 410A(1)–(3); SI 2008 No 393, Reg 8; SI 2015 No 980, Reg 5*].

## 3.55   INTRODUCTION TO GROUP ACCOUNTS REQUIREMENTS

The provisions in **3.56** to **3.78** cover the general requirements on the preparation of accounts for groups of companies. Unless otherwise stated, the provisions apply irrespective of whether the accounts are Companies Act group accounts or IAS group accounts (see **3.56**).

## 3.56   GROUP ACCOUNTS: DUTY TO PREPARE

If, at the end of a financial year, a company is a parent company (see APPENDIX 1 DEFINITIONS) the directors, as well as preparing individual accounts for the year *must* prepare group accounts for the year. This does not apply where—

•   for periods beginning before 1 January 2017, the company is subject to the small companies regime under **5.7–5.8** ACCOUNTS: SMALL COMPANIES AND MICRO-ENTITIES, or would be subject to that regime but for being a public company, and it is not a traded company;

- for periods beginning on or after 1 January 2017, the company is subject to the small companies regime under **5.7–5.8** ACCOUNTS: SMALL COMPANIES AND MICRO-ENTITIES, or would be subject to that regime but for being a public company, and it is not a member of a group which, at any time in the financial year, has as a member an undertaking falling within *CA 2006, s 399(2B)* – this section encompasses an EEA undertaking that is required to prepare accounts and reports under the EU Accounting Directive and that has been designated as a public interest entity (PIE) under that Directive, has transferable securities admitted to trading on a regulated market in an EEA State, is a credit institution or is an insurance undertaking: or

- exemption applies under **3.57** (company included in EEA or non-EEA group accounts of a larger group) or **3.58** (all subsidiary undertakings from consolidation).

However a company to which these provisions apply and which is exempt from the requirement to prepare group accounts, *may* nevertheless do so. Any group accounts prepared on a voluntary basis form part of the company's annual accounts for all legislative purposes.

[*CA 2006, ss 399, 471(1); SI 2015 No 980, Reg 5; SI 2016 No 1245, Reg 3(4)*].

**Applicable accounting framework.** Subject to below

(a) companies, governed by the law of a Member State (ie incorporated in a Member State), whose securities (including debt securities) are admitted to trading on a regulated market in any EEA State *must* prepare their group accounts in accordance with international accounting standards ('*IAS group accounts*', see below); and

(b) companies not falling within (*a*) above may

    (i) prepare their group accounts in accordance with *CA 2006, s 404* ('*Companies Act group accounts*', see below); or

    (ii) prepare IAS group accounts.

But

- the group accounts of a parent company that is a charity must be Companies Act group accounts; and

- after the first financial year in which the directors of a parent company prepare IAS group accounts ('*the first IAS year*'), all subsequent group accounts of the company must be prepared in accordance with international accounting standards unless there is a '*relevant change of circumstance*'. This is subject to the right to change to Companies Act accounts set out in *CA 2006, s 403(5A)* (see below) A relevant change of circumstance occurs if, at any time during or after the first IAS year

    (i) the company becomes a subsidiary undertaking of another undertaking that does not prepare IAS group accounts;

    (ii) the company ceases to be a company with securities admitted to trading on a regulated market in an EEA State; or

    (iii) a parent undertaking of the company ceases to be an undertaking with securities admitted to trading on a regulated market in an EEA State.

After a financial year in which IAS group accounts are prepared, the directors may change to preparing Companies Act individual accounts for a reason other than a relevant change of circumstance, provided they have not changed to Companies Act accounts in the five years preceding the first day of that financial year

If, having changed to preparing Companies Act group accounts, the directors again prepare IAS group accounts for the company, the above provisions again apply as if the first financial year for which such accounts are again prepared were the first IAS year.

[*CA 2006, s 403; SI 2012 No 2301, Reg 15, 16, 17*].

See APPENDIX 1 DEFINITIONS for the current EEA States.

**Companies Act group accounts**. Companies Act group accounts must state in respect of the parent company—

- the part of the UK in which the company is registered;

- the company's registered number;

- whether the company is a public or private company and whether it is limited by shares or by guarantee;

- the address of the company's registered office;

- where appropriate, the fact that the company is being wound up

and must comprise;

- a consolidated balance sheet dealing with the state of affairs of the parent company and its 'subsidiary undertakings' (see APPENDIX 1 DEFINITIONS); and

- a consolidated profit and loss account dealing with the profit or loss of the parent company and its subsidiary undertakings.

The accounts must give a true and fair view of the state of affairs as at the end of the financial year, and the profit or loss for the financial year, of the undertakings included in the consolidation as a whole, so far as concerns members of the company.

Companies Act group accounts must comply with the provisions made by Regulations as described in **3.60–3.67** as to the form and content of the consolidated balance sheet and consolidated profit and loss account and additional information to be provided by way of notes to the accounts. If compliance with those provisions, and any other provisions made by or under *CA 2006*, as to the matters to be included in a company's group accounts or in notes to those accounts would not be sufficient to give a true and fair view, the necessary additional information must be given in the accounts or notes. If, in special circumstances, compliance with any of those provisions is inconsistent with the requirement to give a true and fair view, the directors must depart from that provision to the extent necessary to give a true and fair view. Particulars of any such departure, the reasons for it and its effect must be given in a note to the accounts.

[*CA 2006, s 404; SI 2015 No 980, Reg 5*].

See **2.16** ACCOUNTS: GENERAL for 'true and fair view'. Companies Act group accounts must also comply with all relevant requirements of FRS 102.

**IAS group accounts**. The provisions described in **3.60–3.67** do not apply to IAS group accounts. Instead, consolidated accounts must be prepared on the basis of the accounting standards issued by the International Accounting Standard Board (IASB) that are adopted by the European Commission. [*EC Council Regulation 1606/2002, Art 4*]. Instead of the profit and loss account and balance sheet required under *CA 2006*, a company must prepare primary financial statements and supporting notes as required under international accounting standards. See **2.15** ACCOUNTS: GENERAL for a list of accounting standards.

Where the directors of a company prepare IAS group accounts, the accounts must state in the notes to those accounts that the accounts have been prepared in accordance with international accounting standards. The accounts must also state—

- the part of the UK in which the company is registered;

- the company's registered number;

- whether the company is a public or private company and whether it is limited by shares or by guarantee;

- the address of the company's registered office; and

- where appropriate, the fact that the company is being wound up.

[*CA 2006, s 406; SI 2015 No 980, Reg 5*].

### 3.57   Exemption for parent companies included in accounts of larger groups

(1) *Where a company's immediate parent undertaking is established under the law of an EEA State*

Subject to *all* the conditions below being fulfilled, a company is exempt from the requirement to prepare group accounts if

- it is itself a subsidiary undertaking; and

- its immediate parent undertaking is established under the law of an EEA State; in the following cases—

    (i)    where the company is a wholly-owned subsidiary of that parent undertaking;

    (ii)   where that parent undertaking holds 90% or more of the allotted shares in the company and the remaining shareholders have approved the exemption; or

    (iii)  where that parent undertaking holds more than 50% (but less than 90%) of the company's allotted shares and no notice requesting the preparation of group accounts has been served on the company by shareholders holding in aggregate at least 5% of the allotted shares in the company. Such notice must be served not later than six months after the end of the financial year before that to which it relates.

For the purposes of (ii) above, shares held by a wholly-owned subsidiary of the parent undertaking are attributed to the parent undertaking, as are shares held on behalf of the parent undertaking or a wholly-owned subsidiary of it.

The conditions are as follows.

(i)    The company must be included in consolidated accounts for a larger group drawn up to the same date, or to an earlier date in the same financial year, by a parent undertaking established under the law of an EEA State.

(ii)   Those accounts must be drawn up and audited, and the parent undertaking's annual report must be drawn up, according to that law, in accordance with the EC Directive 2013/34/EU of the European Parliament and Council on the annual financial statements, consolidated financial statements and related reports of certain types of undertakings or in accordance with international accounting standards.

(iii)  The company must disclose in the notes to its individual accounts that it is exempt from the obligation to prepare and deliver group accounts.

(iv)    The company must state in its individual accounts the name of the parent undertaking that draws up the group accounts referred to above and

   •        the address of the undertaking's registered office (whether in or outside the UK); or

   •        if it is unincorporated, the address of its principal place of business.

(v)     The company must deliver to the Registrar of Companies under **2.11** ACCOUNTS: GENERAL, and within the period allowed for delivering its individual accounts under **2.12** ACCOUNTS: GENERAL, copies of the group accounts and the parent undertaking's annual report, together with the auditor's report on them.

(vi)    If any document comprised in accounts and reports delivered under (v) above is in a language other than English, there must be annexed thereto a certified translation of it into English.

(vii)   The exemption does not apply to a company which is a traded company.

Shares held by directors of a company for the purpose of complying with any share qualification requirement are disregarded for the above purposes in determining whether the company is a wholly-owned subsidiary.

[*CA 2006, s 400(1)–(5); SI 2015 No 980, Reg 5(7)*].

*(2) Where a company's parent undertaking is not established under the law of an EEA State*

Subject to *all* the conditions below being fulfilled, a company is exempt from the requirement to prepare group accounts if

•        it is itself a subsidiary undertaking;

•        its parent undertaking is not established under the law of an EEA State; and

•        either

   (i)     where the company is a wholly-owned subsidiary of that parent undertaking;

   (ii)    where that parent undertaking holds 90% or more of the allotted shares in the company and the remaining shareholders have approved the exemption; or

   (iii)   where parent undertaking holds more than 50% (but less that 90%) of the company's allotted shares and notice requesting the preparation of group accounts has not been served on the company by shareholders holding in aggregate at least 5% of the allotted shares in the company. Such notice must be served at least six months before the end of the financial year to which it relates.

   For the purposes of (ii) above, shares held by a wholly-owned subsidiary of the parent undertaking are attributed to the parent undertaking, as are shares held on behalf of the parent undertaking or a wholly-owned subsidiary of it.

The conditions are as follows.

(i)     The company and all of its subsidiary undertakings must be included in consolidated accounts for a larger group drawn up to the same date, or to an earlier date in the same financial year, by a parent undertaking.

(ii)    Those accounts and, where appropriate, the group's annual report, must be drawn up—

- in accordance with the provisions of Directive 2013/34/EU of the European Parliament and of the Council of 26 June 2013 on the annual financial statements, consolidated financial statements and related reports of certain types of undertakings;

- in a manner equivalent to consolidated accounts and consolidated reports so drawn up;

- in accordance with international accounting standards adopted pursuant to the IAS Regulation; or

- in accordance with accounting standards which are equivalent to such international accounting standards, as determined pursuant to Commission Regulation (EC) No 1569/2007.

Guidance on the interpretation of equivalence for these purposes is set out in FRS 100.

(iii)    The consolidated accounts must be audited by one or more persons authorised to audit accounts under the law under which the parent undertaking which draws them up is established.

(iv)    The company must disclose in its individual accounts that it is exempt from the obligation to prepare and deliver group accounts.

(v)    The company must state in its individual accounts the name of the parent undertaking which draws up the group accounts referred to above and

- the address of the undertaking's registered office (whether in or outside the UK); or

- if it is unincorporated, the address of its principal place of business.

(vi)    The company must deliver to the Registrar of Companies under **2.11** Accounts: General, and within the period allowed for delivering its individual accounts under **2.12** Accounts: General, copies of the group accounts and, where appropriate, the consolidated annual report, together with the auditor's report on them.

(vii)    If any document comprised in accounts and reports delivered under (vi) above is in a language other than English, there must be annexed thereto a translation of it into English.

(viii)    The exemption does not apply if the company is a traded company.

Shares held by directors of a company for the purpose of complying with any share qualification requirement are disregarded for the above purposes in determining whether the company is a wholly-owned subsidiary.

[*CA 2006, s 401(1)–(5); SI 2015 No 980, Reg 5(8)*].

### 3.58    Exclusion of subsidiary undertakings from consolidation

Where a parent company prepares Companies Act group accounts (see **3.56**) all subsidiary undertakings of the company must normally be included in the consolidation. There are, however, exclusions, as listed below. If *all* of a parent company's subsidiary undertakings could be excluded from consolidation in Companies Act group accounts, the parent company need not prepare group accounts.

(a)    A subsidiary undertaking may be excluded from consolidation if its inclusion is not material for the purpose of giving a true and fair view (see **2.16** Accounts: General). Two or more undertakings can be excluded only if they are not material taken together.

## 3.58    Accounts: Large Companies

(b)    A subsidiary undertaking may be excluded from consolidation where

   (i)    severe long-term restrictions substantially hinder the exercise of the parent company's rights over the assets or management of the undertaking; or

   (ii)    extremely rare circumstances mean that the information necessary to prepare group accounts cannot be obtained without disproportionate expense or undue delay; or

   (iii)    the interest of the parent company is held exclusively with a view to subsequent resale.

The references in (i) and (iii) above to, respectively, the rights and the interest of the parent company are references to rights and interests held by or attributed to it for the purposes of the definition of 'parent undertaking' (see APPENDIX 1 DEFINITIONS) in the absence of which it would not be the parent company.

[*CA 2006, ss 402, 405; SI 2015 No 980, Reg 5(10)*].

Note also that, although the legislation permits exclusion in these situations, FRS 102 requires exclusion in the case of (b)(i) above, does not allow exclusion under (b)(ii) for undertakings that are individually or collectively material in the context of the group, and imposes more stringent requirements in the case of (b)(iii) in that it only allows exclusion if the subsidiary undertaking has not previously been included in consolidated group accounts prepared by the parent. Where a subsidiary undertaking is excluded from consolidation under (b)(i) or (b)(iii), FRS 102 specifies the accounting treatment to be adopted.

### 3.59    GROUP ACCOUNTS: PARENT COMPANY PROFIT AND LOSS ACCOUNT

Where a company prepares group accounts in accordance with *CA 2006* and the company's individual balance sheet shows the company's profit or loss for the financial year (determined in accordance with *CA 2006*), its individual profit and loss account may be omitted from the company's annual accounts, although it must still be approved in accordance with *CA 2006, s 414(1)* (see **2.2** ACCOUNTS: GENERAL).

The above exemption is conditional upon the company's annual accounts disclosing the fact that the exemption applies.

[*CA 2006, s 408; SI 2008 No 393, Reg 10; SI 2008 No 410, Reg 3(2); SI 2015 No 980, Reg 5*].

### 3.60    GROUP ACCOUNTS: FORM AND CONTENT OF COMPANIES ACT GROUP ACCOUNTS

Where the directors of a parent company

•    prepare Companies Act group accounts, and

•    the company is not a banking company or an insurance company,

the accounts must comply with the provisions in this paragraph and in **3.61–3.67** as to the form and content of the consolidated balance sheet and consolidated profit and loss account, and additional information to be provided by way of notes to the accounts. [*SI 2008 No 410, Reg 9(1)*].

The group accounts must comply, so far as practicable, with the provisions of

- *SI 2008 No 410, Sch 1* (see **3.3** to **3.35**),

- *CA 2006, s 411* (employee numbers and cost, see **3.18**),

- *SI 2008 No 489, Reg 5(1)(b)* (disclosure of auditor's remuneration, see **3.53**), and

- *CA 2006 s 410A* (off-balance sheet arrangements, see **3.54**)

as if the '*group*' (meaning, for these purposes, all the undertakings included in the consolidation) were a single company.

[*CA 2006, ss 410A(5), 411(7); SI 2008 No 393, Reg 11; SI 2008 No 410, Sch 6 para 1; SI 2008 No 489, Reg 6(1)*].

The consolidated balance sheet and profit and loss account must incorporate in full the information contained in the individual accounts of the undertakings included in the consolidation, subject to the adjustments authorised or required under this paragraph and **3.61** to **3.66** and to such other adjustments (if any) that are appropriate in accordance with generally accepted accounting principles or practice, and the group accounts must be drawn up as at the same date as the accounts of the parent company.

**Subsidiaries with different financial years.** If the financial year of a subsidiary undertaking included in the consolidation does not end with that of the parent company, the group accounts must be made up

- from the accounts of the subsidiary undertaking for its financial year last ending before the end of the parent company's financial year (provided that year ended no more than three months before that of the parent company) – and in this situation FRS 102 requires the accounts to be adjusted for the effects of any significant transactions or events that occur between the year ends of the subsidiary undertaking and the parent; or

- from interim accounts prepared by the subsidiary undertaking as at the end of the parent company's financial year.

[*SI 2008 No 410, Sch 6 para 2; SI 2015 No 980, Reg 39(2)*].

But note that the directors of a parent company must secure that, except where in their opinion there are good reasons against it, the financial year of each of its subsidiary undertakings coincides with the company's own financial year. [*CA 2006, s 390(5)*].

**Assets and liabilities.** Where assets and liabilities to be included in the group accounts have been valued or otherwise determined by undertakings according to accounting rules differing from those used for the group accounts, the values or amounts must be adjusted so as to accord with the rules used for the group accounts (unless such adjustments are not material for the purpose of giving a true and fair view). If it appears to the parent company's directors that there are special reasons for doing so, they may depart from this requirement, but particulars of the departure, the reasons for it and its effect must be given in a note to the accounts. [*SI 2008 No 410, Sch 6 para 3*].

**Accounting rules.** Any differences between the accounting rules used for a parent company's individual accounts for a financial year and those used for its group accounts must be disclosed in a note to the group accounts. The reasons for the difference must be given. [*SI 2008 No 410, Sch 6 para 4*].

**Materiality.** Amounts that in the particular context of any provision in this paragraph and **3.61–3.67** are not material may be disregarded for the purposes of that provision. [*SI 2008 No 410, Sch 6 para 5*].

## 3.60    Accounts: Large Companies

**Accounts in euros.** The amounts set out in the annual accounts of a company may also be shown in the same accounts translated into euros. If so, the amounts must have been translated at the exchange rate prevailing at the balance sheet date and that rate must be disclosed in the notes to the accounts. [*CA 2006, s 469(1), (3)*].

### 3.61    Elimination of group transactions

In preparing group accounts, the following must be eliminated (unless the amounts concerned are not material for the purpose of giving a true and fair view, see **2.16 ACCOUNTS: GENERAL**).

•       Debts and claims between undertakings included in the consolidation.

•       Income and expenditure relating to transactions between such undertakings.

•       Profits and losses resulting from transactions between such undertakings and included in the book value of assets. (Note also that the legislation allows this elimination to be effected in proportion to the group's interest in the shares of the undertakings concerned but FRS 102 requires full elimination).

[*SI 2008 No 410, Sch 6 para 6*].

### 3.62    Acquisition and merger accounting

The following provisions apply where an undertaking becomes a subsidiary undertaking of the parent company, such an event being referred to as an '*acquisition*'. An acquisition must be accounted for by the 'acquisition method of accounting' unless the conditions for accounting for it as a merger are met and the 'merger method of accounting' is adopted. [*SI 2008 No 410, Sch 6 paras 7, 8*]. Note, however, that FRS 102 only allows merger accounting to be used for group reconstructions (as defined in the standard) and certain public benefit entity combinations, in each case subject to strict conditions.

(1)    **Acquisition method of accounting**

Under the '*acquisition method of accounting*'

•       the identifiable assets and liabilities of the undertaking acquired must be included in the consolidated balance sheet at their fair values as at the date of acquisition;

•       the income and expenditure of the undertaking acquired must be brought into the group accounts only as from the date of the acquisition; and

•       the interest of the parent company and its subsidiary undertakings in the adjusted capital and reserves of the undertaking acquired must be set off against the acquisition cost of the interest in the shares of the undertaking held by the parent company and its subsidiary undertakings. The resulting amount, if positive, must be treated as goodwill and, if negative, as a negative consolidation difference. Negative goodwill may be transferred to the consolidated profit and loss account where such a treatment is in accordance with the principles and rules of *SI 2008 No 409, Sch 1, Part 2*.

[*SI 2008 No 410, Sch 6 para 9; SI 2015 No 980, Reg 39(3)*].

Where a group is acquired, references above to shares of the undertaking acquired should be read as references to shares of the parent undertaking of the group acquired. Other references to the undertaking acquired should be read as references to the group acquired. References to the assets and liabilities, income and

82

expenditure and capital and reserves of the undertaking acquired should be read as references to those of the group acquired, after making the set-offs and other adjustments required by **3.60–3.67** in the case of group accounts. [*SI 2008 No 410, Sch 6 para 12*].

(2)    **Merger method of accounting**

The '*merger method of accounting*' can only be used if the following conditions are satisfied (and in the limited situations where FRS 102 allows its use – see above).

- The undertaking whose shares are acquired is ultimately controlled by the same party both before and after the acquisition.

- The control referred to above is not transitory.

- Adoption of the merger method accords with generally accepted accounting principles or practice.

[*SI 2008 No 410, Sch 6 para 10; SI 2015 No 980, Reg 39(4)*].

Where the above conditions are satisfied

- the assets and liabilities of the undertaking acquired must be brought into the group accounts at the figures at which they stand in the undertaking's accounts, subject to any adjustment authorised or required by the provisions in **3.60–3.67**;

- the income and expenditure of the undertaking acquired must be included in the group accounts for the entire financial year, including the period before the acquisition;

- the group accounts must show comparative figures for the previous financial year as if the undertaking acquired had been included in the consolidation throughout that year; and

- the nominal value of the issued share capital of the undertaking acquired held by the parent company and its subsidiary undertakings must be set off against the aggregate of

    (i)    the appropriate amount in respect of 'qualifying shares' issued by the parent company or its subsidiary undertakings in consideration for the acquisition of shares in the undertaking acquired; and

    (ii)    the fair value of any other consideration for the acquisition of shares in the undertaking acquired, determined as at the date when those shares were acquired.

The resulting amount must be shown as an adjustment to the consolidated reserves.

'*Qualifying shares*' means

- shares to which *CA 1985, s 131* or *CA 2006, s 612* applies (merger relief, see **46.2** SHARE PREMIUM), in respect of which the appropriate amount is the nominal value; or

- shares to which *CA 1985, s 132* or *CA 2006, s 611* applies (relief in respect of group reconstructions, see **46.3** SHARE PREMIUM), in respect of which the appropriate amount is the nominal value together with any 'minimum premium value' as there defined.

[*SI 2008 No 410, Sch 6 para 11*].

Where a group is acquired, references above to shares of the undertaking acquired should be read as references to shares of the parent undertaking of the group acquired. Other references to the undertaking acquired should be read as references to the group acquired. References to the assets and liabilities and to income and expenditure of the undertaking acquired should be read as references to those of the group acquired, after making the set-offs and other adjustments required by **3.60–3.67** in the case of group accounts. [*SI 2008 No 410, Sch 6 para 12*].

(3)    **Information to be given in the notes to the accounts**

Subject to below, the following information with respect to acquisitions taking place in the financial year must be given in a note to the accounts (although the information in (*c*) and (*d*) below need only be given in relation to an acquisition which significantly affects the figures shown in the group accounts).

(a)    The name of the undertaking acquired or, where a group was acquired, the name of the parent undertaking of that group.

(b)    Whether the acquisition has been accounted for by the acquisition or the merger method of accounting.

(c)    The composition and fair value of the consideration for the acquisition given by the parent company and its subsidiary undertakings.

(d)    Where the acquisition method of accounting has been adopted, the book values immediately prior to the acquisition, and the fair values at the date of acquisition, of each class of assets and liabilities of the undertaking (or group) acquired in tabular form. This must include a statement of the amount of any goodwill or negative consolidation difference arising on the acquisition, together with an explanation of any significant adjustments made.

In ascertaining for these purposes the profit or loss of a group, the book values and fair values of assets and liabilities of a group or the amount of the assets and liabilities of a group, the set-offs and other adjustments required by **3.60–3.67** in the case of group accounts must be made.

[*SI 2008 No 410, Sch 6 para 13*].

Subject to below, the following information must also be stated in a note to the accounts.

(i)    The cumulative amount of goodwill resulting from acquisitions in that and earlier financial years which has been written off otherwise than in the consolidated profit and loss account for that or any earlier financial year. That figure must be shown net of any goodwill attributable to subsidiary undertakings or businesses disposed of prior to the balance sheet date.

(ii)    Where, during the financial year, there has been a disposal of an undertaking or group which significantly affects the figure shown in the group accounts, the name of that undertaking (or parent undertaking of that group) and the extent to which the profit or loss shown in the group accounts is attributable to profit or loss of that undertaking or group.

[*SI 2008 No 410, Sch 6 paras 14, 15*].

The information required by (*a*) to (*d*) and (i) and (ii) above need not be disclosed with respect to an undertaking which is either

•    established under the law of a country outside the UK, or

•    carries on business outside the UK

if, in the opinion of the directors of the parent company, the disclosure would be seriously prejudicial to the business of that undertaking or to the business of the parent company or any of its subsidiary undertakings *and* the Secretary of State agrees that the information should not be disclosed.

Where an acquisition has taken place in the financial year and the merger method of accounting has been adopted, the notes to the accounts must also disclose—

- the address of the registered office of the undertaking acquired (whether in or outside the UK);

- the name of the party who controls the acquired undertaking both before and after the acquisition;

- the address of the registered office of that party (whether in or outside the UK); and

- the amount of the adjustment to the consolidated reserves required by *SI 2008 No 410, Sch 6, para 11(6)*.

[*SI 2008 No 410, Sch 6 para 16; SI 2015 No 980, Reg 39(5)*].

Reference should also be made to the detailed disclosure requirements of FRS 102 in respect of business combinations and goodwill.

### 3.63    Non-controlling interests

The formats for the balance sheet (see **3.4**) and profit and loss account (see **3.5**) have effect in relation to group accounts with the following additions.

(1)    *Balance sheet formats*

There must be shown, as a separate item and under the heading 'non-controlling interests', the amount of capital and reserves attributable to shares in subsidiary undertakings included in the consolidation held by or, on behalf of, persons other than the parent company and its subsidiary undertakings.

For the purposes of *SI 2008 No 410, Sch 1 para 4(1)(2)* (power of directors to adapt or combine items, see **3.3(6)**), this additional item is treated as one to which a letter is assigned (and not an Arabic number).

(2)    *Profit and loss account formats*

There must be shown, as a separate item and under the 'non-controlling interests' heading,

- the amount of any profit or loss attributable to shares in subsidiary undertakings included in the consolidation held by, or on behalf of, persons other than the parent company and its subsidiary undertakings.

For the purposes of *SI 2008 No 410, Sch 1 para 4(1)(2)* (power of directors to adapt or combine items, see **3.3(6)**), these additional items are treated as ones to which an Arabic number is assigned.

[*SI 2008 No 410, Sch 6 para 17; SI 2015 No 980, Reg 39(6)*].

### 3.64    Joint ventures

Where an undertaking included in the consolidation manages another undertaking (the 'joint venture') jointly with one or more undertakings not included in the consolidation, the joint venture may, if it is not

- a body corporate, or

- a subsidiary undertaking of the parent company,

be dealt with in the group accounts by the method of proportional consolidation (but note that FRS 102 does not allow this treatment).

The provisions in **3.60** to **3.67** relating to the preparation of consolidated accounts and *CA 2006, ss 402* and *405* apply, with any necessary modifications, to proportional consolidation under this provision.

In addition to the average number of employees employed during the financial year (see **3.18**) there must be a separate disclosure in the notes to the accounts of the average number of employees employed by undertakings that are proportionately consolidated.

[*SI 2008 No 410, Sch 6 para 18; SI 2015 No 980, Reg 39(7), (8)*].

### 3.65 Associated undertakings

**Definition.** An '*associated undertaking*' means an undertaking in which an undertaking included in the consolidation has a 'participating interest' (see APPENDIX 1 DEFINITIONS) and over whose operating and financial policy it exercises a significant influence, and which is not

- a subsidiary undertaking of the parent company; or

- a joint venture dealt with in **3.64**.

Where an undertaking holds 20% or more of the voting rights in another undertaking, it is presumed to exercise such an influence over it unless the contrary is shown. The voting rights in an undertaking means the rights conferred on shareholders in respect of their shares (or, if the undertaking does not have a share capital, on members) to vote at general meetings of the undertaking on all (or substantially all) matters.

In determining whether 20% or more of the voting rights are held, the provisions in APPENDIX 1 DEFINITIONS apply.

FRS 102 includes detailed guidance on what constitutes significant influence in this context.

**Disclosure requirements.** The balance sheet and profit and loss account formats in **3.4** and **3.5** respectively are modified as below in relation to group accounts to give information in respect of associated undertakings.

(1) *Balance sheet formats*

The item 'Participating interests' in each of the two formats (item B.III.3 in Format 1 and item B.III.3 under 'ASSETS' in Format 2) is replaced by two items, 'Interests in associated undertakings' and 'Other participating interests'.

(2) *Profit and loss account formats*

The item 'Income from participating interests' in each of the formats (item 8 in Format 1, and item 10 in Format 2) is replaced by two items, 'Income from interests in associated undertakings' and 'Income from other participating interests'.

The interest of an undertaking in an associated undertaking, and the amount of profit or loss attributable to such an interest, must be shown by the equity method of accounting (including dealing with any goodwill arising in accordance with **3.8**). But the equity method of accounting need not be applied if the amounts in question are not material for the purpose of giving a true and fair view. FRS 102 also includes specific requirements on accounting for associates, with detailed guidance on the practicalities of the equity method of accounting.

Where the associated undertaking is itself a parent undertaking, the net assets and profits or losses to be taken into account are those of the parent and its subsidiary undertakings (after making any consolidation adjustments).

[*SI 2008 No 410, Sch 6 paras 19–21; SI 2015 No 980, Reg 39(9)*].

### 3.66   Related party transactions

Particulars must be given of transactions (other than intra-group transactions) which the parent company, or other undertakings included in the consolidation, have entered into with 'related parties' if these transactions are material and have not been concluded under normal market conditions.

The particulars must include

•      the amounts of such transactions;

•      the nature of the related party relationship; and

•      other information about the transactions necessary for an understanding of the financial position of the undertakings included in the consolidation taken as a whole.

Information about individual transactions may be aggregated according to their nature, except where separate information is necessary for an understanding of the effects of related party transaction on the financial position of the undertakings included in the consolidation taken as a whole.

'*Related party*' has the same meaning as in international accounting standards.

[*SI 2008 No 410, Sch 6 para 22*].

Reference should also be made to the requirements of FRS 102 on the disclosure of related party transactions.

### 3.67   Deferred tax balances

Deferred tax balances must be recognised on consolidation where it is probable that a charge to tax will arise within the foreseeable future for one of the undertakings included in the consolidation.

[*SI 2008 No 410, Sch 6 para 22B; SI 2015 No 980, Reg 39(10)*].

### 3.68   GROUP ACCOUNTS: INFORMATION ABOUT RELATED UNDERTAKINGS

Where a company is preparing group accounts, its Companies Act or IAS accounts must comply with the provisions in **3.69** to **3.77** as to the information about related undertakings to be given in the notes to the company's accounts. The only exception is that the information (other than that in **3.72** and **3.76**) need not be disclosed with respect to an undertaking that

•      is established under the law of a country outside the UK, or

•      carries on business outside the UK,

but only if

•      in the opinion of the directors of the company, the disclosure would be seriously prejudicial to the business of

       (i)      that undertaking;

    (ii)    the company;

    (iii)    any of the company's subsidiary undertakings; or

    (iv)    any other undertaking which is included in the consolidation; and

- the Secretary of State agrees that the information need not be disclosed.

Where advantage is taken of this exemption, a note to that effect must be included in the company's accounts.

*[CA 2006, s 409(4), (5); SI 2008 No 410, Reg 7].*

The provision in *CA 2006, s 410* that permitted an alternative approach in order to avoid disclosure of excessive length was repealed by *SI 2015 No 980* in respect of accounts approved on or after 1 July 2015.

For the purposes of these disclosure requirements:

- *'The group'* means the group consisting of the parent company and its subsidiary undertakings. *[SI 2008 No 410, Sch 4 para 15].*

- References to shares held by the group are to any shares held by or on behalf of the parent company or any of its subsidiary undertakings. But any shares held on behalf of a person other than the parent company or any of its subsidiary undertakings are not to be treated as held by the group. *[SI 2008 No 410, Sch 4 para 22(3)].*

- Shares held by way of security must be treated as held by the person providing the security

    (i)    where the rights attached to the shares are exercisable only in accordance with that person's instructions (disregarding any right to exercise them in order to preserve the value of, or realise, the security); and

    (ii)    as regards shares held in connection with the granting of loans as part of normal business activities, where the rights attached to the shares are exercisable only in that person's interests (disregarding any right to exercise them in order to preserve the value of, or realise, the security).

*[SI 2008 No 410, Sch 4 para 22(4)].*

### 3.69 Subsidiary undertakings

Subject to **3.68**, where, at the end of the financial year, the company has subsidiary undertakings the following must be stated in respect of each of them.

(a)    Its name.

(b)    The address of the undertaking's registered office (whether in or outside the UK).

(c)    If it is unincorporated, the address of its principal place of business.

(d)    Whether the subsidiary undertaking is included in the consolidation and, if it is not, the reasons for excluding it.

(e)    Which of the conditions in APPENDIX 1(*a*)–(*f*) DEFINITIONS applies to make it a subsidiary undertaking of its immediate parent undertaking. But that information need not be given if the relevant condition is that specified in APPENDIX 1(*a*) DEFINITIONS (holding of a majority of the voting rights) and the immediate parent undertaking holds the same proportion of the shares in the undertaking as it holds voting rights.

*[SI 2008 No 410, Sch 4 paras 1, 16; SI 2015 No 980, Reg 37(2)].*

**3.70**  *Holdings in subsidiary undertakings*

Subject to **3.68**, with respect to the shares of a subsidiary undertaking held by

- the parent company, and

- the group,

there must be stated

- the identity of each class of shares held, and

- the proportion of the nominal value of the shares of that class represented by those shares.

This information must (if different) be shown separately as regards the parent company and group.

*[SI 2008 No 410, Sch 4 para 17].*

For the above purposes, there must be attributed to the parent company shares held on its behalf by any person. But shares held on behalf of a person other than the parent company must be treated as not held by that company. *[SI 2008 No 410, Sch 4 para 22(2)].*

**3.71**  *Financial information about subsidiary undertakings not included in the consolidated accounts*

Subject to **3.68**, with respect to each subsidiary undertaking not included in the consolidated accounts, there must be shown

- the aggregate amount of its capital and reserves as at the end of its relevant financial year; and

- its profit or loss for that year.

This information need not be given if

- the company is exempt under **3.57** from the requirement to prepare group accounts (parent company included in the accounts of a larger group);

- the company's investment in the subsidiary undertaking is included in the company's accounts by way of the equity method of valuation;

- the company's holding is less than 50% of the nominal value of the shares in the undertaking *and* the subsidiary undertaking is not required by any provision of *CA 2006* to deliver to the Registrar of Companies a copy of its balance sheet for its 'relevant financial year' and does not otherwise publish that balance sheet in the UK or elsewhere; or

- it is not material.

The *'relevant financial year'* of a subsidiary undertaking is

- if its financial year ends with that of the company, that year; and

- if not, its financial year ending last before the end of the company's financial year.

*[SI 2008 No 410, Sch 4 para 2].*

**3.72**  *Shares and debentures of company held by subsidiary undertakings*

The number, description and amount of the shares in the company held by, or on behalf of, its subsidiary undertakings must be disclosed. This does not apply in relation to shares in the case of which the subsidiary undertaking is concerned as

- personal representative; or

- trustee, unless the company, or any of its subsidiary undertakings is 'beneficially interested under the trust', otherwise than by way of security only for the purposes of a transaction entered into by it in the ordinary course of a business which includes the lending of money.

[*SI 2008 No 410, Sch 4 para 3*].

In determining whether the company is '*beneficially interested under the trust*', certain residual interests under pension and employees' share schemes, employer's charges and other rights of recovery under such schemes, and a trustee's right to expenses, remuneration, indemnity, etc are disregarded. See *SI 2008 No 410, Sch 4 paras 24–27* for full details.

### 3.73 Joint ventures

Subject to **3.68**, where an undertaking is dealt with in the consolidated accounts by the method of proportional consolidation in accordance with **3.64** (but note that accounting standards do not currently permit this treatment), the following information must be given in respect of the undertaking.

- Its name.

- The address of the undertaking's registered office (whether in or outside the UK).

- The factors on which joint management of the undertaking is based.

- The proportion of its capital held by undertakings included in the consolidation.

- Where its financial year did not end with that of the company, the date on which a financial year of the undertaking last ended before that date.

[*SI 2008 No 410, Sch 4 para 18; SI 2015 No 980, Reg 38(2); SI 2016 No 575, Reg 66*].

### 3.74 Associated undertakings

Subject to **3.68**, the following information must be given where an undertaking included in the consolidation has an interest in an associated undertaking.

(a) The name of the associated undertaking.

(b) If the undertaking is incorporated outside the UK, the country in which it is incorporated.

(c) The address of the undertaking's registered office (whether in or outside the UK).

(d) With respect to the shares of the undertaking held by the parent company and by the group,

- the identity of each class of shares held, and

- the proportion of the nominal value of the shares of that class represented by those shares,

giving details for the parent company and group separately.

'*Associated undertaking*' has the same meaning as in **3.65**.

[*SI 2008 No 410, Sch 4 para 19; SI 2015 No 980, Reg 38(3)*].

For the above purposes, there must be attributed to the parent company shares held on its behalf by any person. But shares held on behalf of a person other than the parent company must be treated as not held by that company. [*SI 2008 No 410, Sch 4 para 22(2)*].

**3.75   Other significant holdings of parent company or group**

**Parent company holdings.** Subject to **3.68**, where at the end of the financial year the parent company has a 'significant holding' in an undertaking which is not one of its subsidiary undertakings and does not fall within **3.73** or **3.74**, the following must be stated.

(a)   The name of the undertaking.

(b)   The address of the undertaking's registered office (whether in or outside the UK).

(c)   If it is unincorporated, the address of its principal place of business.

(d)   The identity of each class of shares of the undertaking held by the parent company.

(e)   The proportion of the nominal value of the shares of that class represented by those shares.

(f)   The aggregate amount of the capital and reserves of the undertaking as at the end of its 'relevant financial year'.

(g)   Its profit or loss for that year.

A *'significant holding'* is a holding which amounts to 20% or more of the nominal value of any class of shares in the undertaking *or* the amount of which (as stated or included in the parent company's individual accounts) exceeds one-fifth of the amount (as so stated) of the parent company's assets.

The *'relevant financial year'* of an undertaking for these purposes is, if its financial year ends with that of the company, that year, and if it does not, its financial year ending last before the end of the company's financial year.

*Exemption.* The information in (*f*) and (*g*) above need not be given if

•   the undertaking in question is not required by any provision of *CA 2006* to deliver a copy of its balance sheet for its relevant financial year and does not otherwise publish that balance sheet in the UK or elsewhere *and* the company's holding is less than 50% of the nominal value of the shares in the undertaking; or

•   it is not material.

*[SI 2008 No 410, Sch 4 paras 4–6; SI 2015 No 980, Reg 37(3)].*

For the above purposes, there must be attributed to the parent company shares held on its behalf by any person. But shares held on behalf of a person other than the parent company must be treated as not held by that company. *[SI 2008 No 410, Sch 4 para 22(2)].*

**Group holdings.** Subject to **3.68**, where at the end of the financial year the group has a 'significant holding' in an undertaking which is not a subsidiary undertaking of the parent company and does not fall within **3.73** or **3.74**, the same information must be given as under (*a*) to (*g*) above (and with the same exemption as above), substituting 'group' for 'parent company' in (*d*) and in the definition of 'significant holding'. *[SI 2008 No 410, Sch 4 para 20].*

**3.76   Parent company's or group's membership of certain undertakings**

Where, at the end of the financial year, the company or group is a member of an undertaking having unlimited liability the following must be stated.

(a)   The name and legal form of the undertaking.

(b)   The address of its registered office (whether in or outside the UK) or, if it does not have such an office, its head office (whether in or outside the UK).

(c)  Where the undertaking is a qualifying partnership (see **3.43**), either

   (i)   a statement that a copy of the latest accounts of the partnership has been or is to be appended to the copy of the company's accounts sent to the Registrar of Companies; or

   (ii)  the name of at least one body corporate (which may be the company itself) in whose group accounts the undertaking has been, or is to be, dealt with on a consolidated basis.

The information required by (*a*) and (*b*) above need not be given if not material and the information required by (*c*)(ii) above need not be given if the notes to the company's accounts disclose that advantage has been taken of the exemption in *regulation 7* of the *Partnerships (Accounts) Regulations 2008 (SI 2008 No 569)*.

[*SI 2008 No 410, Sch 4 paras 7, 21; SI 2015 No 980, Reg 38(4)*].

### 3.77  Information where parent company is a subsidiary undertaking

Subject to **3.68**, where the parent company is itself a subsidiary undertaking, the following information must be given.

(a)  Particulars, as follows, with respect to the parent undertaking of the largest and smallest group of undertakings for which group accounts are drawn up and of which that company is a member.

   (i)    The name of the parent undertaking.

   (ii)   The address of the undertaking's registered office (whether in or outside the UK).

   (iii)  If it is unincorporated, the address of its principal place of business.

   (iv)   If copies of the above-mentioned group accounts are available to the public, the addresses from which copies of the accounts can be obtained.

(b)  Particulars, as follows, with respect to the company (which includes any body corporate) regarded by the directors as being that company's ultimate parent company.

   (i)    Its name.

   (ii)   If that company is incorporated outside the UK, the country in which it is incorporated (if known to the directors).

[*SI 2008 No 410, Sch 4 paras 8, 9; SI 2015 No 980, Reg 37(5)*].

### 3.78  GROUP ACCOUNTS: DIRECTORS' REMUNERATION AND BENEFITS

**Directors' remuneration.** Companies Act and IAS group accounts must comply with all relevant provisions of *SI 2008 No 409, Sch 5* on the disclosure of directors' remuneration in the notes to the accounts (see **3.45–3.51**). However, in the case of group accounts, the requirements of *SI 2008 No 409, Sch 1, para 1* on disclosure of the total amount of directors' remuneration apply with the modification that only the amounts and values referred to in that paragraph received or receivable by the directors of the parent company from the parent company and any of its subsidiary undertakings must be disclosed in the notes to the accounts.

[*SI 2008 No 410, Reg 8, Sch 6 para 22A; SI 2015 No 980, Reg 39(10)*].

For the additional reporting requirements in respect of directors' remuneration in quoted companies, see **19 DIRECTORS' REMUNERATION REPORTS AND POLICIES—QUOTED COMPANIES**.

**Directors' benefits: advances, credits and guarantees.** In the case of a parent company that prepares group accounts, the notes to the group accounts must show the following.

(a)   In respect of any advance or credit granted to the directors of the parent company, by that company or by any of its subsidiary undertakings, details of

    (i)   its amount;

    (ii)   an indication of the interest rate;

    (iii)   its main conditions;

    (iv)   any amounts repaid;

    (v)   any amounts written off; and

    (vi)   any amounts waived.

(b)   In respect of any guarantee of any kind entered into on behalf of the directors of the parent company, by that company or by any of its subsidiary undertakings, details of

    (i)   its main terms;

    (ii)   the amount of the maximum liability that may be incurred by the company (or its subsidiary); and

    (iii)   any amount paid and any liability incurred by the company (or its subsidiary) for the purpose of fulfilling the guarantee (including any loss incurred by reason of enforcement of the guarantee).

The totals of amounts stated under (a)(i), (a)(iv), (a)(v), (a)(vi), (b)(ii) and (b)(iii) must also be given.

The provisions apply to

•   persons who were directors of the company at any time in the financial year to which the accounts relate; and

•   every advance, credit or guarantee subsisting at any time in the financial year to which the accounts relate

    (i)   whenever it was entered into; and

    (ii)   whether or not the person concerned was a director of the company in question at the time it was entered into; and

    (iii)   in the case of an advance, credit or guarantee involving a subsidiary undertaking of that company, whether or not that undertaking was such a subsidiary undertaking at the time it was entered into.

[*CA 2006, s 413(2)–(7); SI 2015 No 980, Reg 5(16)*].

# 4 Accounts: Medium-sized Companies

**Background.** The provisions in this chapter apply, unless otherwise stated, to accounts for financial years beginning on or after 6 April 2008. The *Companies Act 2006 (Strategic Report and Directors' Report) Regulations 2013* ('the *2013 Regulations*') which are referred to in various parts of this chapter brought into force the requirement for a company to produce a strategic report for financial years ending on or after 30 September 2013. The requirements of the *Companies, Partnerships and Groups (Accounts and Reports) Regulations 2015 (SI 2015 No 980)* are referred to throughout this chapter where they amend either *CA 2006* or the 2008 Regulations. The 2015 Regulations apply in respect of financial years beginning on or after 1 January 2016.

## 4.1 INTRODUCTION TO MEDIUM-SIZED COMPANY ACCOUNTS

A company which qualifies as 'medium-sized' (see **4.2**) is, for most purposes, treated the same as a large company so that the provisions in 3 ACCOUNTS: LARGE COMPANIES and 2 ACCOUNTS: GENERAL apply to it as for a large company. However, when preparing Companies Act accounts, the company

(i)     need not comply with the provisions on disclosure of compliance with accounting standards;

(ii)    need not comply with the full requirements relating to the disclosure of related party transactions; and

(iii)   need not disclose the more detailed information on auditor's remuneration that must be given in the accounts of larger companies.

See **4.4**.

## 4.2 MEANING OF 'MEDIUM-SIZED'

(1) *Companies qualifying as medium-sized: general*

Subject to (2) below, a company qualifies as medium-sized

(a)     in relation to its first financial year if the qualifying conditions below are met in that year; and

(b)     in relation to a subsequent financial year if

    (i)     the qualifying conditions are met in that year and the preceding financial year;

    (ii)    the qualifying conditions are met in that year and the company qualified as medium-sized in relation to the preceding financial year; or

    (iii)   the qualifying conditions were met in the preceding financial year and the company qualified as medium-sized in relation to that year.

## 4.2 Accounts: Medium-sized Companies

The qualifying conditions are met by a company in a year in which it satisfies two or more of the following requirements.

| | |
|---|---|
| Turnover | Not more than £36m |
| 'Balance sheet total' | Not more than £18m |
| 'Number of employees' | Not more than 250 |

*Notes.*

- For a period that is a company's financial year but not in fact a year, the maximum figures for turnover must be proportionately adjusted.

- The '*balance sheet total*' means the aggregate of the amounts shown as assets in the company's balance sheet.

- The '*number of employees*' means the average number of persons employed by the company in the year, calculated as

$$A \div B$$

where

A = the sum of the number of persons employed under contracts of service by the company for each month in the financial year (whether throughout the month or not)

B = the number of months in the financial year

[*CA 2006, s 465; SI 2008 No 393, Regs 2, 4; SI 2015 No 980, Reg 9*].

(2) *Companies qualifying as medium-sized: parent companies*

A parent company qualifies as a medium-sized company in relation to a financial year only if the group headed by it qualifies as a medium-sized group. A group qualifies as medium-sized

(a) in relation to the parent company's first financial year if the qualifying conditions below are met in that year; and

(b) in relation to a subsequent financial year of the parent company if

    (i) the qualifying conditions are met in that year and the preceding financial year;

    (ii) the qualifying conditions are met in that year and the group qualified as medium-sized in relation to the preceding financial year; or

    (iii) the qualifying conditions were met in the preceding financial year and the group qualified as medium-sized in relation to that year.

The qualifying conditions are met by a group in a year in which it satisfies two or more of the following requirements.

| | |
|---|---|
| Aggregate turnover | Not more than £36m net (or £43.2m gross) |
| Aggregate balance sheet total | Not more than £18m net (or £21.6m gross) |
| Aggregate number of employees | Not more than 250 |

*Notes.*

- The aggregate figures are ascertained by aggregating the relevant figures determined as under (1) above for each member of the group.

- In relation to the aggregate figures for turnover and balance sheet total, 'net' means after any set-offs and other adjustments made to eliminate group transactions and 'gross' means without those set-offs and other adjustments.

  A company may satisfy any relevant requirement on the basis of either the net or the gross figure.

- The figures for each subsidiary undertaking are those included in its individual accounts for the relevant financial year, ie

  (i)     if its financial year ends with that of the parent company, that financial year; and

  (ii)    if not, its financial year ending last before the end of the financial year of the parent company.

  If those figures cannot be obtained without disproportionate expense or undue delay, the latest available figures can be taken.

[*CA 2006, s 466, SI 2008 No 393, Regs 2, 4; SI 2015 No 980, Reg 9*].

All of the financial thresholds given above are those that apply for periods beginning on or after 1 January 2016 (and may be applied for periods beginning on or after 1 January 2015 where the directors so decide). The monetary amounts are increased from time to time and the regulations implementing such increases usually provide that, in determining whether a company qualifies as medium-sized in relation to a financial year for which the amendments have effect, it is treated as having qualified as medium-sized in any previous year in which it would have so qualified if the increased thresholds had applied in that year.

### 4.3    Companies excluded from being treated as medium-sized

A company is not entitled to take advantage of any of the provisions relating to medium-sized companies if it was at any time within the financial year in question

(a)     a public company;

(b)     a company that has permission under *FSMA 2000, Pt 4A* to carry on a regulated activity, carries on insurance market activity or is an e-money issuer; or

(c)     a member of an 'ineligible group'.

A group is an '*ineligible group*' if any of its members is

(i)     a traded company;

(ii)    a body corporate (other than a company) whose shares are admitted to trading on a regulated market;

# 4.3 Accounts: Medium-sized Companies

    (iii)    a person (other than a small company) who has permission under *FSMA 2000, Pt 4A* to carry on a regulated activity;

    (iv)    an e-money issuer;

    (v)    a small company that is an authorised insurance company, a banking company, a 'MiFID investment firm' or a UCITS management company; or

    (vi)    a person who carries on insurance market activity;

and a company is a small company for these purposes if it qualified as small in relation to its last financial year ending on or before the end of the financial year in question.

The legislation provides that the above provisions do not prevent a company from taking advantage of *CA 2006, s 417(7)* (business review: non-financial information) by reason only of its having been a member of an ineligible group at any time within the financial year in question. However, note that *CA 2007, s 417* was repealed by *SI 2013 No 1970* and replaced with new requirements in *CA 2006, ss 414A–414D* on the preparation of a strategic report (see **20 STRATEGIC REPORTS AND DIRECTORS' REPORTS**).

See **APPENDIX 1 DEFINITIONS** for the meaning of 'MiFID investment firm'.

[*CA 2006, s 467; SI 2008 No 393, Reg 7; SI 2015 No 980, Reg 9*].

## 4.4    FORM AND CONTENT OF INDIVIDUAL ACCOUNTS

Apart from the exceptions below, there are no special provisions for the form and content of the individual accounts of 'medium-sized' companies. Such companies must therefore prepare individual accounts complying with the full requirements in **3 ACCOUNTS: LARGE COMPANIES**.

The exceptions to this general are as follows.

    (1)    Where the directors of the company are preparing Companies Act individual accounts, those individual accounts *need not* comply with the requirements of *SI 2008 No 410, Sch 1 para 45* (disclosure with respect to compliance with accounting standards, see **3.18 ACCOUNTS: LARGE COMPANIES**) – but this does not affect its obligation to comply with all relevant standards.

    (2)    Where the directors of the company are preparing Companies Act individual accounts, those individual accounts *need not* comply with the full requirements of *SI 2008 No 410, Sch 1 para 72* (disclosure of related party transactions – see **3.19 ACCOUNTS: LARGE COMPANIES**) in that a medium-sized company is only required to give details of transactions that have not been concluded under normal market conditions with the following:

        (i)    owners of a participating interest in the company;

        (ii)    companies in which the company has a participating interest; and

        (iii)    the company's directors.

        However, note that all of the related party disclosure requirements of FRS 102 continue to apply.

    (3)    The accounts do not have to comply with the more detailed requirements on disclosure of auditor's remuneration required by larger companies (see **3.53 ACCOUNTS: LARGE COMPANIES**).

        Instead, a note to the annual accounts of a medium-sized company must disclose

- the amount of any remuneration receivable by the company's auditor for the auditing of those accounts (note that, in this case, the disclosure requirement does not encompass any remuneration receivable by an associate of the auditor for auditing the company's accounts); and

- where the remuneration includes benefits in kind, the nature and estimated money-value of those benefits.

Where more than one person has been appointed as a company's auditor in respect of the period to which the accounts relate, separate disclosure is required in respect of the remuneration of each such person.

Note, however, that a medium-sized company must still comply with the requirements on disclosure of liability limitation agreements. See **3.53** ACCOUNTS: LARGE COMPANIES.

[*CA 2006, s 410A(4); SI 2008 No 393, Reg 8; SI 2008 No 410, Reg 4(1), (2A), (2B); SI 2008 No 489, Reg 4; SI 2015 No 980, Reg 26*].


**4.5    ACCOUNTS DELIVERED TO THE REGISTRAR OF COMPANIES**

**Accounts generally**. The directors of a company that qualifies as a medium-sized company in relation to a financial year must deliver to the Registrar of Companies

- the company's annual accounts,

- the strategic report;

- the directors' report, and

- unless the company is exempt from audit and the directors have taken advantage of that exemption, the auditor's report on those accounts (and on the strategic report and directors' report).

But the above provisions do not apply to companies within

- *CA 2006, s 444* (filing obligations of companies subject to the small companies regime, see **2.11**(1) ACCOUNTS: GENERAL), or

- *CA 2006, s 444A* (filing obligations of companies entitled to small companies exemption in relation to the directors' report, see **2.11**(2) ACCOUNTS: GENERAL

[*CA 2006, s 445(1)–(2), (7); SI 2008 No 393, Reg 6(8); SI 2013 No 1970, Schedule, para 9*].

**Names appearing on accounts**. The copies of the balance sheet and strategic report and directors' report delivered to the Registrar of Companies under these provisions must state the name of the person who signed it on behalf of the board.

The copy of the auditor's report delivered to the Registrar of Companies under these provisions must either

- state the name of the auditor and (where the auditor is a firm) the name of the person who signed it as senior statutory auditor; or

- if the conditions is *CA 2006, s 506* are met (circumstances in which names may be omitted, see **8.42** AUDIT), state that a resolution has been passed and notified to the Secretary of State in accordance with those provisions.

## 4.5  Accounts: Medium-sized Companies

[*CA 2006, s 445(5), (6); SI 2013 No 1970, Schedule, para 9*].

# 5 Accounts: Small Companies and Micro-entities

*Cross-references.* See 2 ACCOUNTS: GENERAL; 3 ACCOUNTS: LARGE COMPANIES; 4 ACCOUNTS: MEDIUM-SIZED COMPANIES; APPENDIX 1 DEFINITIONS.

**Background.** The provisions as described in this chapter are, unless otherwise stated, taken from *CA 2006* and the *Small Companies and Groups (Accounts and Directors' Report) Regulations 2008 (SI 2008 No 409)*. The requirements of the *Companies, Partnerships and Groups (Accounts and Reports) Regulations 2015 (SI 2015 No 980)* are referred where they amend either *CA 2006* or the *2008 Regulations*. The *2015 Regulations* apply in respect of financial years beginning on or after 1 January 2016 (with adoption for periods beginning on or after 1 January 2015 also generally permitted) and they significantly reduce the amount of detail that needs to be given in accounts prepared under the small companies regime. A separate financial reporting regime, with even more limited disclosure, is available to a company that qualifies as a micro-entity and is eligible for the exemptions.

### 5.1 INTRODUCTION TO SMALL COMPANY ACCOUNTS

A company which qualifies as 'small' (see **5.7**) in relation to a financial year and is eligible for the small companies regime is entitled to various exemptions with respect to

(a)    the preparation of individual accounts (see **5.9** to **5.39**);

(b)    the requirement to prepare group accounts (see **5.41**);

(c)    the form and content of group accounts where these are prepared (see **5.43–5.62**).

Such a company is also exempt from the preparation of a strategic report and from certain of the requirements on the contents of the directors' report. See **20 STRATEGIC REPORTS AND DIRECTORS' REPORTS**.

Certain very small companies (micro-entities) can choose to prepare their annual accounts under the micro-entities financial reporting regime provided that they meet the qualification and eligibility requirements (see **5.2–5.6**).

See also **8.29–8.31** Audit for the audit exemptions available to small companies that satisfy certain conditions.

### 5.2 THE MICRO-ENTITY REGIME

Micro-entities are often owner-managed and funded mainly from owner resources, so the full legislative financial reporting regime may be unnecessarily burdensome for them. It was therefore considered appropriate that the smallest companies should be given the opportunity to prepare simplified accounts if these meet their business and shareholder needs. However, not all of the available options available under the relevant EU Directive have been taken up in the UK.

### 5.3 Companies qualifying as micro-entities

A company qualifies as a micro-entity

(a)    in relation to its first financial year if the qualifying conditions below are met in that year;

(b)    subject to the provision set out in (c), in relation to a subsequent financial year if the qualifying conditions are met in that year; and

(c)    in relation to a subsequent financial year, where on its balance sheet date a company meets or ceases to meet the qualifying conditions, that affects its qualification as a micro-entity only if it occurs in two consecutive financial years.

The qualifying conditions are met by a company in a year in which it satisfies two or more of the following requirements.

| | |
|---|---|
| Turnover | Not more than £632,000 |
| 'Balance sheet total' | Not more than £316,000 |
| 'Number of employees' | Not more than 10 |

**Notes**

- For a period that is a company's financial year but not in fact a year the maximum figures for turnover must be proportionately adjusted.

- The balance sheet total means the aggregate of the amounts shown as assets in the company's balance sheet.

- The number of employees means the average number of persons employed by the company in the year determined as follows

  (i) find for each month in the financial year the number of persons employed under contracts of service by the company in that month (whether throughout the month or not);

  (ii) add together the monthly totals; and

  (iii) divide by the number of months in the financial year.

- In the case of a company which is a parent company, the company qualifies as a micro-entity in relation to a financial year only if the company qualifies as a micro-entity in relation to that year as determined by the provisions in this section and the group headed by the company qualifies as a small group as determined by the provisions set out in **5.7**.

[*CA 2006, s 384A; SI 2013 No 3008, Reg 4(4)*].

**5.4 Companies excluded from being treated as micro-entities**

The micro-entity provisions do not apply in relation to a company's accounts for a particular financial year if the company was at any time within that year

(a) a company excluded from the small companies regime by virtue of *CA 2006, s 384* (see **5.8**);

(b) an investment undertaking as defined in *Article 2(14)* of *Directive 2013/34/EU* on the annual financial statements etc of certain types of undertakings;

(c) a financial holding undertaking as defined in *Article 2(15)* of the above *Directive*;

(d) a credit institution as defined in *Article 4 of Directive 2006/48/EC* relating to the taking up and pursuit of the business of credit institutions, other than one referred to in *Article 2* of that *Directive*;

(e) an insurance undertaking as defined in *Article 2(1)* of *Council Directive 91/674/EEC* on the annual accounts of insurance undertakings; or

(f) a charity.

The micro-entity provisions also do not apply in relation to a company's accounts for a financial year if

(a) the company is a parent company which prepares group accounts for that year as permitted by *CA 2006, s 399(4)* (see **5.41**); or

(b) the company is not a parent company but its accounts are included in consolidated group accounts for that year.

## 5.4　Accounts: Small Companies and Micro-entities

[*CA 2006, ss 384A, 384B; SI 2013 No 3008, Reg 4*].

Overseas companies, unregistered companies and companies registered pursuant to *CA 2006, s 1040* and *Regulation 18* of the *Companies (Companies Authorised to Register) Regulations 2009 (SI 2009 No 2437)* are also specifically excluded from the micro-entities regime. The original regulations also excluded qualifying partnerships and limited liability partnerships (LLPs), but for financial years beginning on or after 1 January 2016 the *Limited Liability Partnerships, Partnerships and Groups (Accounts and Audit) Regulations 2016 (SI 2016 No 575)* amend

(i)　　*SI 2013 No 3008* so that qualifying partnerships are no longer excluded from the regime; and

(ii)　　the LLP accounts regulations so that they provide for a micro-entity regime.

[*SI 2013 No 3008, Reg 3; SI 2016 No 575, Parts 2, 3 and 5*].

### 5.5　Preparing accounts under the micro-entity regime

The micro-entity financial reporting regime is incorporated into the small company accounts regulations and applies only where the company prepares *Companies Act* accounts. Under the regime, a micro-entity has the option of preparing an abridged balance sheet and profit and loss account (see **5.14**). There is a choice of two formats for the abridged balance sheet but only one format for the abridged profit and loss account. Once chosen, the same format must be used in future years unless there are special reasons for a change. A company preparing accounts under the micro-entity regime is specifically prohibited from adopting either the alternative accounting rules or fair value accounting.

No detailed notes to the accounts are required, but the following details must be given at the foot of the abridged balance sheet

(a)　　the details of guarantees and other financial commitments required by *paragraph 57* of *Schedule 1* to *SI 2008 No 409* (see **5.34**); and

(b)　　the information on directors' advances, credits and guarantees that must be given in the accounts under *CA 2006, s 413* (see **5.28**).

The accounts must also continue to give the basic information about the company required by *CA 2006, s 396(A1)* (see **5.9** below).

Accounts prepared in accordance with the micro-entity provisions must include a prominent statement to that effect on the balance sheet, immediately above the director's signature.

[*CA 2006, ss 413, 472(1A); SI 2008 No 409, Regs 3(1A), 5A, Sch 1, paras 1(1A), 2A; SI 2013 No 3008, Regs 7, 9*].

In the case of accounts prepared under the micro-entity regime, inclusion of the minimum accounting items in the company's accounts for the year is presumed to give the true and fair view required by *CA 2006, s 396(2)* (see also **2.16** TRUE AND FAIR VIEW). A 'micro-entity minimum accounting item' means an item of information required by *CA 2006, Part 15* or by regulations made under those provisions to be contained in the individual accounts of a company for a financial year in relation to which it qualifies as a micro-entity.

[*CA 2006, ss 396(2A), 474(1)*].

A company that chooses to adopt the micro-entity financial reporting regime must also apply the detailed requirements of FRS 105 'The Financial Reporting Standard applicable to the Micro-entities Regime'.

**5.6    Delivering micro-entity accounts to the Registrar of Companies**

A micro-entity that prepares abridged accounts under the micro-entity regime must deliver a copy of those accounts to the registrar. However, the small company filing exemption in respect of the profit and loss account continues to apply (see **5.40**).

[*CA 2006, s 444 (1), (3A) and (3B); SI 2013 No 3008, Reg 6*].


**5.7    MEANING OF 'SMALL COMPANY'**

The small companies regime applies to a company for a financial year in relation to which the company

*   qualifies as small (see (1) and (2) below); and

*   is not excluded from the regime (see **5.8**).

[*CA 2006, s 381; SI 2008 No 393, Reg 6(1)*].

(1)    **Companies qualifying as small: general**

Subject to (2) below, a company qualifies as small

(a)    in relation to its first financial year if the qualifying conditions below are met in that year;

(b)    subject to the provision set out in (c) in relation to a subsequent financial year if the qualifying conditions are met in that year and the preceding financial year; and

(c)    in relation a subsequent financial year where on its balance sheet date a company meets or ceases to meet the qualifying conditions, that affects its qualification as a small company only if it occurs in two consecutive financial years.

The qualifying conditions are met by a company in a year in which it satisfies two or more of the following requirements.

| | |
|---|---|
| Turnover | Not more than £10.2m |
| 'Balance sheet total' | Not more than £5.1m |
| 'Number of employees' | Not more than 50 |

*Notes.*

*   For a period that is a company's financial year but not in fact a year, the maximum figures for turnover must be proportionately adjusted.

*   The '*balance sheet total*' means the aggregate of the amounts shown as assets in the company's balance sheet.

*   The '*number of employees*' means the average number of persons employed by the company in the year, calculated as

$$A \div B$$

where

A = the sum of the number of persons employed under contracts of service by the company for each month in the financial year (whether throughout the month or not)

B = the number of months in the financial year

[*CA 2006, s 382; SI 2008 No 393, Regs 2, 3; SI 2013 No 3008, Reg 4(2); SI 2015 No 980, Reg 4*].

(2) **Companies qualifying as small: parent companies**

A parent company qualifies as a small company in relation to a financial year only if the group headed by it qualifies as a small group. A group qualifies as small

(a) in relation to the parent company's first financial year if the qualifying conditions below are met in that year;

(b) subject to the provision in (c) in relation to a subsequent financial year of the parent company if the qualifying conditions are met in that year; and

(c) in relation to a subsequent financial year of the parent company, where on the parent company's balance sheet date the group meets or ceases to meet the qualifying conditions, that affects the group's qualification as a small group only if it occurs in two consecutive financial years.

The qualifying conditions are met by a group in a year in which it satisfies two or more of the following requirements.

| | |
|---|---|
| Aggregate turnover | Not more than £10.2m net (or £12.2m gross) |
| Aggregate balance sheet total | Not more than £5.1m net (or £6.1m gross) |
| Aggregate number of employees | Not more than 50 |

*Notes.*

- The aggregate figures are ascertained by aggregating the relevant figures determined as under (1) above for each member of the group.

- In relation to the aggregate figures for turnover and balance sheet total, 'net' means after any set-offs and other adjustments made to eliminate group transactions and 'gross' means without those set-offs and other adjustments.

  A company may satisfy any relevant requirement on the basis of either the net or the gross figure.

- The figures for each subsidiary undertaking are those included in its individual accounts for the relevant financial year, ie

  (i) if its financial year ends with that of the parent company, that financial year; and

  (ii) if not, its financial year ending last before the end of the financial year of the parent company.

If those figures cannot be obtained without disproportionate expense or undue delay, the latest available figures can be taken.

[*CA 2006, s 383; SI 2008 No 393, Regs 2, 3; SI 2013 No 3008, Reg 4(3); SI 2015 No 980, Reg 4*].

All of the financial thresholds given above are those that apply for periods beginning on or after 1 January 2016 (and may be applied for periods beginning on or after 1 January 2015 where the directors so decide). The monetary amounts are increased from time to time and the regulations implementing such increases usually provide that, in determining whether a company qualifies as small in relation to a financial year for which the amendments have effect, it is treated as having qualified as small in any previous year in which it would have so qualified if the increased thresholds had applied in that year.

**5.8    Companies excluded from the small companies regime**

The small companies regime does not apply to a company that is, or was at any time within the financial year to which the accounts relate,

(a)    a public company;

(b)    a company that

    (i)    is an authorised insurance company, a banking company, an e-money issuer, a 'MiFID investment firm' or a UCITS management company; or

    (ii)    carries on insurance market activity; or

(c)    a member of an 'ineligible group'.

A group is an *'ineligible group'* if any of its members is

(i)    a traded company;

(ii)    a body corporate (other than a company) whose shares are admitted to trading on a regulated market in an EEA State;

(iii)    a person (other than a small company) who has permission under *FSMA 2000, Pt 4A* to carry on a regulated activity;

(iv)    an e-money issuer;

(v)    a small company that is an authorised insurance company, a banking company, a 'MiFID investment firm' or a UCITS management company; or

(vi)    a person who carries on insurance market activity;

and a company is a small company for these purposes if it qualified as small in relation to its last financial year ending on or before the end of the financial year to which the accounts relate.

[*CA 2006, s 384; SI 2007 No 2932, Reg 3; SI 2015 No 980, Reg 4*].

See Appendix 1 Definitions for the meaning of *'MiFID investment firm'*.

**5.9    SMALL COMPANY INDIVIDUAL ACCOUNTS: DUTY TO PREPARE**

The directors of every company, including a small company, must prepare accounts for the company for each of its financial years (the only exception to this is for certain dormant subsidiaries as explained below). [*CA 2006, ss 394, 394A*]. Those accounts are referred to in the legislation and in this chapter as the company's *'individual accounts'*. Subject to below, these accounts may be prepared in accordance with

## 5.9  Accounts: Small Companies and Micro-entities

- *CA 2006, s 396* ('*Companies Act individual accounts*'); or

- international accounting standards ('*IAS individual accounts*').

But

- the individual accounts of a company that is a charity *must* be Companies Act individual accounts; and

- after the first financial year in which the directors of a company prepare IAS individual accounts ('*the first IAS year*'), all subsequent individual accounts of the company must be prepared in accordance with international accounting standards unless there is a '*relevant change of circumstance*'. This is subject to the right to change to Companies Act accounts set out in *CA 2006, s 395(4A)* (see below) A relevant change of circumstance occurs if, at any time during or after the first IAS year,

  (i)   the company becomes a subsidiary undertaking of another undertaking that does not prepare IAS individual accounts;

  (ii)  the company has ceased to be a subsidiary undertaking;

  (iii) the company ceases to be a company with securities admitted to trading on a regulated market in an EEA State; or

  (iv)  a parent undertaking of the company ceases to be an undertaking with securities admitted to trading on a regulated market in an EEA State.

After a financial year in which IAS individual accounts are prepared, the directors may change to preparing Companies Act individual accounts for a reason other than a relevant change of circumstance, provided they have not changed to Companies Act accounts in the five years preceding the first day of that financial year.

If, having changed to preparing Companies Act individual accounts, the directors again prepare IAS individual accounts for the company, the above provisions apply again as if the first financial year for which such accounts are again prepared were the first IAS year.

[*CA 2006, s 395; SI 2008 No 393, Reg 9; SI 2012 No 2301, Reg 13*].

See APPENDIX 1 DEFINITIONS for the current EEA States.

**Companies Act individual accounts.** Companies Act individual accounts must state—

(a)   the part of the UK in which the company is registered;

(b)   the company's registered number;

(c)   whether the company is a public or private company and whether it is limited by shares or by guarantee;

(d)   the address of the company's registered office; and

(e)   where appropriate, the fact that the company is being wound up

and must comprise—

(a)   a balance sheet as at the last day of the financial year; and

(b)   a profit and loss account.

The balance sheet must give a true and fair view of the state of affairs of the company as at the end of the financial year and the profit and loss account must give a true and fair view of the profit or loss of the company for the financial year. See **2.16** Accounts: General for the interpretation of '*true and fair view*'.

Where a company qualifies as 'small' in relation to the financial year (see **5.7–5.8**) and its individual accounts for the year are Companies Act individual accounts, those accounts may either

•    be prepared in compliance with the provisions explained in **5.10** to **5.39** as to form and content of the balance sheet and profit and loss account and additional information to be provided by way of notes to the accounts; or

•    comply with the fuller provisions as described in **3.3** to **3.35** Accounts: Large Companies.

If compliance with the chosen method would not be sufficient to give a true and fair view, the necessary additional information must be given in the accounts or notes. If, in special circumstances, compliance with any of those provisions is inconsistent with the requirement to give a true and fair view, the directors must depart from that provision to the extent necessary to give a true and fair view. Particulars of any such departure, the reasons for it and its effect must be given in a note to the accounts. (See **5.5** above and **2.5** Accounts: General for the different requirements that apply under the micro-entity financial reporting regime.)

[*CA 2006, s 396; SI 2008 No 409, Sch 1, para 10(2); SI 2013 No 3008, Reg 5; SI 2015 No 980, Reg 5(4)*].

**IAS individual accounts.** The provisions relating to the individual accounts of small companies as described in **5.10** to **5.39** do not apply to IAS individual accounts. Instead IAS individual accounts must state in the notes to the accounts that they have been prepared in accordance with international accounting standards. They must also state

•    the part of the UK in which the company is registered;

•    the company's registered number;

•    whether the company is a public or private company and whether it is limited by shares or by guarantee;

•    the address of the company's registered office; and

•    where appropriate, the fact that the company is being wound up.

[*CA 2006, s 397; SI 2015 No 980, Reg 5(5)*].

**Consistency of accounts within a group.** Subject to the exceptions below, the directors of a parent company must secure that the individual accounts of

(a)    the parent company, and

(b)    each of its subsidiary undertakings

are all prepared using the same financial reporting framework (ie Companies Act or IAS), except to the extent that in their opinion there are good reasons for not doing so. BIS indicated, in their 2008 guidance to companies on the introduction of IAS accounts, that 'good reasons' could include the following.

•    Where a group using IAS acquires a subsidiary undertaking that had not been using IAS, in the first year of acquisition it might not be practical for the newly acquired company to switch to IAS straight away.

- Where a group contains subsidiary undertakings that are themselves publicly traded, market pressures or regulatory requirements to use IAS might come into play, without necessarily justifying a switch to IAS by the non-publicly traded subsidiaries.

- Where a subsidiary undertaking or the parent is planning to list and so might wish to convert to IAS in advance, but the rest of the group is not listed.

- Where the group contains minor or dormant subsidiaries and the costs of switching accounting framework would outweigh the benefits.

*Exceptions.* The general requirement to prepare individual accounts using the same financial framework is subject to the following specific exceptions. It

- does not apply if the directors do not prepare group accounts for the parent company;

- only applies to the accounts of subsidiary undertakings that are required to be prepared under *CA 2006*;

- does not require accounts of undertakings that are charities to be prepared using the same financial reporting framework as accounts of undertakings which are not charities; and

- does not apply where the directors of a parent company prepare both group accounts and individual accounts under IAS. In this case the parent company is not required to ensure that all its subsidiary undertakings also use IAS. However it must ensure that all its subsidiary undertakings use the same accounting framework, unless there are good reasons for not doing so.

[*CA 2006, s 407(2)–(4) and (5)*].

**Exemption for dormant subsidiaries.** A company is exempt from the requirement to prepare individual accounts if

- it is itself a subsidiary undertaking;

- it has been dormant throughout the whole of that year;

- its parent undertaking is established under the law of an EEA state; and

- all of the conditions set out in *CA 2006, s 394A(2)* are met.

The detailed conditions include a requirement that the subsidiary is included in audited consolidated accounts prepared by the parent, and detailed requirements on a guarantee to be given by the parent in respect of the subsidiary's liabilities. The subsidiary company's shareholders must also declare their unanimous agreement to use of the exemption for the relevant financial year. Reference should be made to *CA 2006, s 394A(2)* for full details of the conditions that must be met.

[*CA 2006, s 394A; SI 2012 No 2301, Regs 1, 9; SI 2015 No 980, Reg 5*].

A company is not entitled to the dormant subsidiary exemption if it was at any time within the financial year in question—

- a traded company;

- a company that is an authorised insurance company, a banking company, an e-money issuer, a MIFID investment firm or a UCITS management company or carries on insurance market activity; or

- a special register body as defined in *TULR(C)A 1992, s 117(1)* or an employees' association as defined in *s 122* of that Act or *Article 4 of SI 1992 No 807*.

[*CA 2006, s 394B; SI 2015 No 980, Reg 5*].

## 5.10    SMALL COMPANY INDIVIDUAL ACCOUNTS: FORM AND CONTENT

Subject to *regulations 3* and *5A* of *SI 2008 No 409* (the *Small Companies and Groups (Accounts and Directors' Reports) Regulations 2008*), Companies Act individual accounts for small companies must comply with the provisions of that SI described in this paragraph and in **5.12** to **5.39** as to the form and content of the balance sheet and profit and loss account, and additional information to be provided by way of notes to the accounts. However, accounts are treated as having complied with those provisions if they comply instead with the corresponding provision of *SI 2008 No 410, Sch 1* (see **3.3** to **3.35** Accounts: Large Companies). *Sections C* (alternative accounting rules) and *D* (fair value accounting) in *SI 2008 No 409, Schedule 1, Part 2* do not apply to a company which qualifies as a micro-entity in relation to a financial year and whose accounts for that year are prepared in accordance with the exemption permitted by *SI 2008 No 409, Reg 5A* or *section A, Part 1, Schedule 1, para 1(1A)* (see **5.2–5.6**).

Accounts prepared under the small companies regime must include a statement in a prominent position on the balance sheet, above the signature of the director(s), that they are prepared in accordance with the provisions applicable to companies subject to the small companies regime. [*CA 2006, s 414(3)*].

Every balance sheet of a small company must show the items listed in either of the balance sheet formats in **5.12** and every profit and loss account must show the items listed in either of the profit and loss account formats in **5.13**. Subject to the provisions for abridged balance sheets (see **5.11**), the items must be shown in the order and under the headings and sub-headings given in the particular format used, but subject to the following.

(1)    The notes to the formats may permit alternative positions for any particular items.

(2)    The heading or sub-heading for any item does not have to be distinguished by any letter or number assigned to that item in the format used.

(3)    Any item required to be shown in a company's balance sheet or profit and loss account may be shown in greater detail than required by the particular format used.

(4)    A heading or sub-heading corresponding to an item in the balance sheet or profit and loss account format used must not be included if there is no amount to be shown for that item for the financial year in question unless an amount must be disclosed for the immediately preceding financial year (see below).

(5)    The balance sheet or profit and loss account may include an item representing or covering the amount of any asset or liability, income or expenditure not otherwise covered by any of the items listed in the format used, except that none of the following may be treated as assets in any balance sheet.

- Preliminary expenses.

- Expenses of, and commission on, any issue of shares or debentures.

- Costs of research.

(6)    Where the special nature of the company's business requires it, the company's directors

(a)    *must* adapt the arrangement, headings and sub-headings otherwise required in respect of items given an Arabic number in the balance sheet or profit and loss account format used; and

(b)    *may* combine items to which Arabic numbers are given in any of the formats if

(i)    their individual amounts are not material to assessing the state of affairs or profit or loss of the company for the financial year in question; or

(ii)   the combination facilitates that assessment (but in this case the individual amounts of any items which have been combined must be disclosed in a note to the accounts).

(7)    The company's directors may adapt one of the balance sheet formats so to distinguish between current and non-current items in a different way, provided that

(a)    the information given is at least equivalent to that which would have been required by the use of such format had it not been thus adapted; and

(b)    the presentation of those items is in accordance with generally accepted accounting principles or practice.

The company's directors may adapt one of the profit and loss account formats provided that

(a)    the information given is at least equivalent to that which would have been required by the use of such format had it not been thus adapted; and

(b)    the presentation is in accordance with generally accepted accounting principles or practice.

(8)    In relation to a company which qualifies as a micro-entity in relation to a financial year (see **5.2–5.6**), the only items which must be shown in the company's balance sheet for that year are those listed in either of the balance sheet formats in **5.14** and the only items which must be shown in the company's profit and loss account for that year are those listed in the profit and loss format in **5.14**.

[*SI 2008 No 409, Reg 3, 5, Sch 1, paras 1, 1B, 3–5; SI 2013 No 3008, Reg 9, 10; SI 2015 No 980, Reg 16(2)(c)*].

The flexibility provided by (7) above is intended to allow companies to adopt a presentation closer to that used in IAS accounts, but note that FRS 102 specifies the minimum line items that must be presented in the balance sheet and profit and loss account in this situation and sets out certain additional requirements.

**Consistency in use of formats.** Where a company's balance sheet or profit and loss account for any financial year has been prepared by reference to one of the said formats, the company's directors must use the same format in preparing Companies Act individual accounts for subsequent financial years, unless in their opinion there are special reasons for a change. Particulars of any such change must be given in a note to the accounts in which the new format is first used, and the reasons for the change must be explained. [*SI 2008 No 409, Sch 1, para 2; SI 2013 No 3008, Reg 10*].

**Profit before taxation.** Every profit and loss account, other than one prepared by reference to the format in 5.7A, must show the amount of a company's profit or loss before taxation. [*SI 2008 No 409, Sch 1, para 6; SI 2013 No 3008, Reg 10; SI 2015 No 980, Reg 16*].

**Preceding financial year.** For every item shown in the balance sheet or profit and loss account the corresponding amount for the immediately preceding financial year must also be shown. Where that corresponding amount is not comparable with the figure for the current year, the former amount may be adjusted, in which case particulars of the non-comparability and of any adjustment must be disclosed in a note to the accounts. [*SI 2008 No 409, Sch 1 para 7*]. Note that FRS 102 generally requires corresponding amounts to be restated where necessary but may specify a different approach in certain circumstances (for instance, as a transitional measure on the implementation of new requirements where restatement would be onerous and this would outweigh the related benefits).

**Set-offs.** Amounts in respect of items representing assets or income may not be set off against amounts in respect of items representing liabilities or expenditure, or vice versa. [*SI 2008 No 409, Sch 1 para 8*].

**Presentation in accordance with accounting principles.** The company's directors must, in determining how amounts are presented within items in the profit and loss account and balance sheet, have regard to the substance of the reported transaction or arrangement, in accordance with generally accepted accounting principles or practice. Where an asset or liability relates to more than one item in the balance sheet, the relationship of such asset or liability to the relevant items must be disclosed either under those items or in the notes to the accounts [*SI 2008 No 409, Sch 1 para 9; SI 2015 No 980, Reg 16*].

**Materiality.** Amounts which in the particular context of any provision of *SI 2008 No 409, Sch 1* (see above and **5.12** to **5.39**) are not material may be disregarded for the purposes of that provision. [*SI 2008 No 409, Sch 8 para 7*].

**Accounts in euros.** The amounts set out in the annual accounts of a small company may also be shown in the same accounts translated into euros. If so, the amounts must have been translated at the exchange rate prevailing at the balance sheet date and that rate must be disclosed in the notes to the accounts. The requirement to disclose the rate in the notes to the accounts does not apply to accounts prepared under the micro-entity regime (see **5.2–5.6**).

[*CA 2006, s 469(1) (3) (3A); SI 2013 No 3008, Reg 7 (2)*].

### 5.11   Abridged balance sheets

(a) Where appropriate to the circumstances of a company's business, the company's directors may, with reference to one of the formats in **5.12** below draw up an abridged balance sheet showing only those items in that format preceded by letters and roman numerals, provided that—

• in the case of Format 1, note (5) of the notes to the formats is complied with;

• in the case of Format 2, notes (5) and (10) of those notes are complied with; and

• all of the members of the company have consented to the drawing up of the abridged balance sheet.

(b) Where appropriate to the circumstances of a company's business, the company's directors may, with reference to one of the formats in **5.13** below draw up an abridged profit and loss account, combining under one item called 'Gross profit or loss'—

(i)     items 1, 2, 3 and 6 in the case of Format 1;

(ii)    items 1 to 5 in the case of Format 2; and

(iii)   provided that, in either case, all of the members of the company have consented to the drawing up of the abridged profit and loss account.

Such shareholder consent as is referred to above may only be given as regards the preparation of, as appropriate, the balance sheet or profit and loss account in respect of the preceding financial year.

# 5.11    Accounts: Small Companies and Micro-entities

Neither of the above apply in relation to the preparation of, as appropriate, a company's balance sheet or profit and loss account for a particular financial year if the company was a charity at any time within that year.

The company's directors may also adapt one of the balance sheet formats in 5.12 below so to distinguish between current and non-current items in a different way, provided that—

• the information given is at least equivalent to that which would have been required by the use of such format had it not been thus adapted; and

• the presentation of those items is in accordance with generally accepted accounting principles or practice.

The company's directors may, otherwise than pursuant to (b) above, adapt one of the profit and loss account formats in 5.13 below provided that—

• the information given is at least equivalent to that which would have been required by the use of such format had it not been thus adapted; and

• the presentation is in accordance with generally accepted accounting principles or practice.

So far as is practicable, the provisions of *SI 2008 No 409, Sch 1*, Section A, Part 1 apply to the balance sheet or profit or loss account of a company notwithstanding any such abridgment or adaptation pursuant to the above.

[*SI 2008 No 409, Sch 1, para 1A; SI 2015 No 980, Reg 16*].

FRS 102 specifies the minimum line items that must be presented in a balance sheet and profit and loss account where the format is adapted under these provisions.

## 5.12    Balance sheet formats for companies other than micro-entities

The two balance sheet formats set out in *SI 2008 No 409, Sch 1* and referred to in 5.10 are reproduced below and in 5.14, and are followed by the notes also set out in the SI. The balance sheet format for micro-entities is reproduced in 5.14.

### Format 1 – the required format for companies other than micro-entities

A.    Called up share capital not paid (see note (1))

B.    Fixed assets

    I    Intangible assets

        1.    Goodwill (see note (2))

        2.    Other intangible assets (see note (3))

    II    Tangible assets

        1.    Land and buildings

        2.    Plant and machinery etc

    III    Investments

        1.    Shares in group undertakings and participating interests

        2.    Loans to group undertakings and undertakings in which the company has a participating interest

        3.    Other investments other than loans

        4.    Other investments (see note (4))

C.    Current assets

I    Stocks

    1.    Stocks

    2.    Payments on account

II   Debtors (see note (5))

    1.    Trade debtors

    2.    Amounts owed by group undertakings and undertakings in which the company has a participating interest

    3.    Other debtors (see notes (1) and (6))

III  Investments

    1.    Shares in group undertakings

    2.    Other investments

IV   Cash at bank and in hand

D.    Prepayments and accrued income (see note (6))

E.    Creditors: amounts falling due within one year

    1.    Bank loans and overdrafts

    2.    Trade creditors

    3.    Amounts owed to group undertakings and undertakings in which the company has a participating interest

    4.    Other creditors (see note (7))

F.    Net current assets (liabilities) (see note (8))

G.    Total assets less current liabilities

H.    Creditors: amounts falling due after more than one year

    1.    Bank loans and overdrafts

    2.    Trade creditors

    3.    Amounts owed to group undertakings and undertakings in which the company has a participating interest

    4.    Other creditors (see note (7))

I.    Provisions for liabilities

J.    Accruals and deferred income (see note (7))

K.    Capital and reserves

    I    Called up share capital (see note (9))

    II   Share premium account

    III  Revaluation reserve

    IV   Other reserves

    V    Profit and loss account

**Format 2**

A.    Called up share capital not paid (see note (1))

B.    Fixed assets

    I    Intangible assets

        1.    Goodwill (see note (2))

        2.    Other intangible assets (see note (3))

    II   Tangible assets

        1.    Land and buildings

        2.    Plant and machinery etc

      III   Investments
1. Shares in group undertakings and participating interests
2. Loans to group undertakings and undertakings in which the company has a participating interest
3. Other investments other than loans
4. Other investments (see note (4))

  C.   Current assets

      I   Stocks
1. Stocks
2. Payments on account

      II   Debtors (see note (5))
1. Trade debtors
2. Amounts owed by group undertakings and undertakings in which the company has a participating interest
3. Other debtors (see notes (1) and (6))

      III   Investments
1. Shares in group undertakings
2. Other investments

      IV   Cash at bank and in hand

  D.   Prepayments and accrued income (see note (6))

CAPITAL, RESERVES AND LIABILITIES

  A.   Capital and reserves

      I   Called up share capital (see note (9))

      II   Share premium account

      III   Revaluation reserve

      IV   Other reserves

      V   Profit and loss account

  B.   Provisions for liabilities

  C.   Creditors (see note (10))
1. Bank loans and overdrafts
2. Trade creditors
3. Amounts owed to group undertakings and undertakings in which the company has a participating interest
4. Other creditors (see note (7))

  D.   Accruals and deferred income (see note (7))

**Notes**

(1)   *Called up share capital not paid.* This item may be shown at item A or included under item C.II.3 in format 1 or 2.

(2)   *Goodwill.* Amounts representing goodwill must be included only to the extent that the goodwill was acquired for valuable consideration.

(3)    *Other intangible assets.* Amounts in respect of concessions, patents, licences, trademarks and similar rights and assets must only be included under this item if the assets in question were either acquired for valuable consideration (and are not required to be shown under 'goodwill') or created by the company itself.

(4)    *Own shares.* Where own shares are included under investments, the nominal value of the shares held must be shown separately (but note that this accounting treatment for own shares held is precluded by accounting standards).

(5)    *Debtors.* The amount falling due after more than one year must be shown separately for each item included under debtors and in the case of Format 2 the aggregate amount falling due after more than one year must also be shown.

(6)    *Prepayments and accrued income.* This may be shown at item D or included under item C.II.3 in format 1 or 2.

(7)    *Other creditors.*

   (a)    The amount of any convertible loans must be shown separately.

   (b)    The amount for creditors in respect of taxation and social security must be shown separately.

   (c)    Payments received on account of orders must be included in so far as they are not shown as deductions from stocks.

   (d)    In format 1, accruals and deferred income may be shown under item J or included under item E.4 or H.4, or both (as the case may require). In format 2, accruals and deferred income may be shown under item D or within item C.4 under Liabilities.

(8)    *Net current assets (liabilities).* In determining the amount to be shown under this item, any 'prepayments and accrued income' (see note (6) above) are to be taken into account wherever shown.

(9)    *Called up share capital.* The amount of allotted share capital and the amount of called up share capital which has been paid up must be shown separately.

(10)   *Creditors.* In format 2, amounts falling due within one year and after one year must be shown separately for each item under this heading and for the aggregate of all these items. [*SI 2008 No 409, Sch 1 Section B*].

**5.13   Profit and loss account formats for companies other than micro-entities**

The two small company profit and loss account formats set out in *SI 2008 No 409, Sch 1, Section B* and referred to in **5.10** are reproduced below, followed by the notes also set out in the regulations. The profit and loss account format for micro-entities is reproduced in **5.14**.

**Format 1** (see note (4)) – formats for companies other than micro-entities
   1.    Turnover
   2.    Cost of sales (see note (1))
   3.    Gross profit or loss
   4.    Distribution costs (see note (1))
   5.    Administrative expenses (see note (1))
   6.    Other operating income
   7.    Income from shares in group undertakings
   8.    Income from participating interests

9.   Income from other fixed asset investments (see note (2))
10.  Other interest receivable and similar income (see note (2))
11.  Amounts written off investments
12.  Interest payable and similar expenses (see note (3))
13.  Tax on profit or loss
14.  Profit or loss after taxation
15.  Other taxes not shown under the above items
16.  Profit or loss for the financial year

**Format 2**
1.   Turnover
2.   Change in stocks of finished goods and in work in progress
3.   Own work capitalised
4.   Other operating income
5.   (a)   Raw materials and consumables
     (b)   Other external charges
6.   Staff costs:
     (a)   wages and salaries (see below)
     (b)   social security costs (see below)
     (c)   other pension costs (see below)
7.   (a)   Depreciation and other amounts written off tangible and intangible fixed assets
     (b)   Amounts written off current assets to the extent that they exceed write-offs which are normal in the undertaking concerned
8.   Other operating expenses
9.   Income from shares in group undertakings
10.  Income from participating interests
11.  Income from other fixed asset investments (see note (2))
12.  Other interest receivable and similar income (see note (2))
13.  Amounts written off investments
14.  Interest payable and similar expenses (see note (3))
15.  Tax on profit or loss
16.  Profit or loss after taxation
17.  Other taxes not shown under the above items
18.  Profit or loss for the financial year

**Notes**

(1)   *Cost of sales: distribution costs: administrative expenses.* These items must be stated after taking into account any necessary provisions for depreciation or diminution in value of assets.

(2)   *Income from other fixed asset investments: other interest receivable and similar income.* Income and interest derived from group undertakings must be shown separately from income and interest derived from other sources.

(3)   *Interest payable and similar expenses.* The amount payable to group undertakings must be shown separately.

[*SI 2008 No 409, Sch 1 Section B; SI 2015 No 980, Reg 16*].

*Staff costs.*

• '*Social security costs*' means any contributions by the company to any state social security or pension scheme, fund or arrangement.

• '*Pension costs*' includes

(i)    any costs incurred by the company in respect of any pension scheme established for the purpose of providing pensions for persons currently or formerly employed by the company;

(ii)    any sums set aside for the future payment of pensions directly by the company to current or former employees; and

(iii)    any pensions paid directly to such persons without having first been set aside.

Any amount stated in respect of the item 'social security costs' or in respect of the item 'wages and salaries' in the company's profit and loss account must be determined by reference to payments made or costs incurred in respect of all persons employed by the company during the financial year under contracts of service.

[*SI 2008 No 409, Sch 8 para 14*].

*Depreciation, etc* Any reference in the profit and loss account formats (or the notes to them) to the depreciation of, or amounts written off, assets of any description is to any provision for depreciation or diminution in value of assets of that description. [*SI 2008 No 409, Sch 7 para 1(2)*].

'*Fixed assets*' means assets of a company which are intended for use on a continuing basis in the company's activities. [*SI 2008 No 409, Sch 8 para 3*].

### 5.14    Balance sheet and profit and loss formats for micro-entities

**Format 1 –Balance sheet**
A.    Called up share capital not paid
B.    Fixed assets
C.    Current assets
D.    Prepayments and accrued income
E.    Creditors: amounts falling due within one year
F.    Net current assets (liabilities)
G.    Total assets less current liabilities
H.    Creditors: amounts falling due after more than one year
I.    Provisions for liabilities
J.    Accruals and deferred income (see note (7))
K.    Capital and reserves

**Format 2 –Balance sheet**
A.    Called up share capital not paid
B.    Fixed assets

C.    Current assets

D.    Prepayments and accrued income

CAPITAL, RESERVES AND LIABILITIES

A.    Capital and reserves

B.    Fixed assets

C.    Creditors[1]

D.    Accruals and deferred income

[1] Creditors. In format 2, amounts falling due within one year and after one year must be shown separately.

Format 1 –profit and loss account format

A.    Turnover

B.    Other income

C.    Cost of raw materials and consumables

D.    Staff costs

E.    Depreciation and other amounts written off assets

F.    Other charges

G.    Tax

H.    Profit or loss

[*SI 2008 No 409, Sch 1, Section C; SI 2013 No 3008, Reg 10(4)*].

## 5.15    Accounting principles

The amounts to be included in respect of all items shown in a company's accounts must be determined in accordance with the principles set out in (*a*)–(*e*) below. But if it appears to the directors that there are special reasons for departing from any of those principles in preparing the company's accounts for any financial year, they may do so, in which case particulars of the departure, the reasons for it and its effect must be given in a note to the accounts.

(a)    The company is presumed to be carrying on business as a going concern.

(b)    Accounting policies and measurement bases must be applied consistently within the same accounts and from one financial year to the next.

(c)    The amount of any item must be determined on a prudent basis, and in particular

    (i)    only profits realised at the balance sheet date are to be included in the profit and loss account;

    (ii)    all liabilities which have arisen in respect of the financial year to which the accounts relate or a previous financial year must be taken into account. This includes those which only become apparent between the balance sheet date and the date on which it is signed on behalf of the board of directors (see **2.2** Accounts: General). Where revised accounts are prepared (see **2.13** Accounts: General) it is the date on which the original accounts were signed that is taken into account for this purposes; and

    (iii)    all provisions for diminution in value must be recognised whether the result of the financial year is a profit or a loss.

(d)    All income and charges relating to the financial year to which the accounts relate must be taken into account, without regard to the date of receipt or payment.

(e)    In determining the aggregate amount of any item, the amount of each individual asset or liability that falls to be taken into account must be determined separately.

(f)    The opening balance sheet for each financial year shall correspond to the closing balance sheet for the preceding financial year.

[*SI 2008 No 409, Sch 1 paras 10–15; SI 2015 No 980, Reg 17*].

FRS 102 sets out further detailed guidance on these issues, including practical interpretation of the legislative requirements. Additional guidance on going concern can be found in the Financial Reporting Council document 'Guidance on the Going Concern Basis of Accounting and Reporting on Solvency and Liquidity Risk' (available at www.frc.org.uk).

## 5.16    Historical cost accounting rules

Subject to

•    the alternative accounting rules in **5.23** to **5.25**, and

•    the fair value accounting provisions in **5.26**

the amounts to be included in respect of all items shown in a company's accounts must be determined in accordance with the rules set out in **5.17** to **5.21**. [*SI 2008 No 409, Sch 1 para 16*].

## 5.17    *Fixed assets*

*General rules.* Fixed asset (ie assets of a company which are intended for use on a continuing basis in the company's activities) must be included at their 'purchase price' or 'production cost' (see **5.21**). [*SI 2008 No 409, Sch 1 para 17, Sch 8 para 3*].

*Rules for depreciation and diminution in value.*

(a)    In the case of any fixed asset which has a limited useful economic life, its purchase price or production cost, less the amount of any estimated residual value at the end of the asset's useful economic life, must be reduced by provisions for depreciation calculated to write off that amount systematically over the asset's useful economic life. [*SI 2008 No 409, Sch 1 para 18*].

(b)    Where a fixed asset investment falling to be included under item B.III of either of the balance sheet formats set out in **5.12** has diminished in value, provisions for diminution in value may be made in respect of it and the amount to be included in respect of it may be reduced accordingly. Such provisions must be made in respect of *any* fixed asset which has diminished in value if the reduction in its value is expected to be permanent (whether it's useful economic life is limited or not), and the amount to be included in respect of it must be reduced accordingly. Provisions so made must be charged to the profit and loss account and disclosed separately in a note to the accounts if not shown separately in the profit and loss account. [*SI 2008 No 409, Sch 1 para 19*].

(c)    Where the reasons for which any provision was made have ceased to apply to any extent, that provision must be written back to the extent that it is no longer necessary. Any amounts so written back must be recognised in the profit and loss account and disclosed separately in a note to the accounts if not shown separately in the profit and loss account but provisions made in respect of goodwill under *Sch 1, para 19(2)* (above) must not be written back to any extent. [*SI 2008 No 409, Sch 1, para 20(1), (2); SI 2015 No 1672, Reg 3*].

Reference should also be made to the detailed requirements of FRS 102 on measuring the cost of property, plant and equipment, useful economic lives, residual values and depreciation. The standard also includes specific requirements on accounting for investment property and heritage assets.

**5.18**    *Intangible assets*

Where this is in accordance with generally accepted accounting principles or practice, development costs may be included in 'other intangible assets' under 'fixed assets' in the balance sheet formats set out in **5.12** above. If any amount is included in a company's balance sheet in respect of development costs, the note on accounting policies must include the following information—

*    the period over which the amount of those costs originally capitalised is being or is to be written off; and

*    the reasons for capitalising the development costs in question.

Intangible assets must be written off over the useful economic life of the intangible asset. Where in exceptional cases the useful life of intangible assets cannot be reliably estimated, such assets must be written off over a period chosen by the directors of the company. This period must not exceed ten years and both the period and the reasons for choosing it must be disclosed in the notes to the accounts.

[*SI 2008 No 409, Sch 1, paras 21, 22; SI 2015 No 980, Reg 17(3)(c)*].

Reference should also be made to the requirements of FRS 102 on the recognition, measurement and amortisation of intangible assets and goodwill, and the need for impairment reviews to be carried out in certain circumstances.

**5.19**    *Current assets*

The amount to be included in respect of any current asset must be its 'purchase price' or 'production cost' (see **5.21**) or, if lower, its net realisable value. Where the reasons for which any provision for diminution in value has been made (ie to reduce the assets to its net realisable value) have ceased to apply to any extent, that provision must be written back to the extent that it is no longer necessary. [*SI 2008 No 409, Sch 1 paras 23, 24*].

**5.20**    *Miscellaneous provisions*

(1) *Excess of money owed over value received*

Where the amount repayable on any debt owed by a company is greater than the value of the consideration received in the transaction giving rise to the debt, the amount of the difference may be treated as an asset. But in the case of such treatment, the amount of the difference must be written off by reasonable amounts each year and must be completely written off before repayment of the debt. If the current amount is not shown as a separate item in the company's balance sheet, it must be disclosed in a note to the accounts. However, note that the requirements of FRS 102 will usually preclude adoption of this accounting treatment.

[*SI 2008 No 409, Sch 1 para 25*].

(2) *Assets included at a fixed amount*

Assets which fall to be included either amongst the

*    fixed assets of a company under the item 'tangible assets', or

*    current assets of a company under the item 'raw materials and consumables',

may be included at a fixed quantity and value in the balance sheet formats set out in **5.12** where the assets are of a kind which are constantly being replaced and where their

- overall value is not material to assessing the company's state of affairs; and

- quantity, value and composition are not subject to material variation.

[*SI 2008 No 409, Sch 1 para 26; SI 2013 No 3008, Reg 11*].

**5.21**   *Determination of purchase price or production cost*

The '*purchase price*' of an asset is the actual price paid plus any expenses incidental to its acquisition and then subtracting any incidental reductions in the cost of acquisition.

'*Purchase price*', in relation to an asset of a company or any raw materials or consumables used in the production of such an asset, includes any consideration (whether in cash or otherwise) given by the company in respect of that asset or those materials or consumables, as the case may be.

The '*production cost*' of an asset is the purchase price of the raw materials and consumables used plus the costs incurred by the company which are directly attributable to the production of that asset. In addition, there may be included

- a reasonable proportion of the costs so incurred by the company which are only indirectly attributable to the production of that asset, but only to the extent that they relate to the period of production; and

- interest on capital borrowed to finance the production of that asset, to the extent that it accrues in respect of the period of production. The inclusion of interest in determining the cost and the amount of the interest so included must be disclosed in a note to the accounts. Note that FRS 102 also sets out detailed requirements on the capitalisation of finance costs.

In the case of current assets, production costs must not include distribution costs.

[*SI 2008 No 409, Sch 1 para 27; Sch 8 para 9; SI 2015 No 980, Reg 17*].

Where

- there is no record of the purchase price or production cost of any asset (of any price, expenses or costs relevant to its determination), or

- any such record cannot be obtained without unreasonable expense or delay,

the purchase price or production cost of the asset must be taken to be the value ascribed to it in the earliest available record of its value made on or after its acquisition or production by the company. [*SI 2008 No 409, Sch 1 para 29*].

*Stocks and fungible assets.* The purchase price or production cost of

- any assets which by virtue of *SI 2008 No 409, reg 3* (see **5.10**) and the balance sheet formats set out in **5.12** fall to be included under any item shown in a company's balance sheet under the general item 'stocks', and

- any assets which are 'fungible assets' (including investments),

may be determined by applying any of the following methods in relation to any such assets of the same class, provided that the method chosen is one which appears to the directors to be appropriate in the circumstances of the company.

(1)   'First in, first out' (FIFO).

(2)   'Last in, first out' (LIFO) – but see below.

(3)     A weighted average price.

(4)     Any other method reflecting generally accepted best practice.

However, the detailed requirements of FRS 102 must also be taken into account, and these specifically prohibit the use of LIFO to measure the cost of stocks.

'*Fungible assets*' means assets of any description which are substantially indistinguishable one from another.

[*SI 2008 No 409, Sch 1 para 28; SI 2015 No 980, Reg 17(e)*].

**5.22**   *Equity method in respect of participating interests*

Participating interests may be accounted for using the equity method.

If participating interests are accounted for using the equity method—

•       the proportion of profit or loss attributable to a participating interest and recognised in the profit and loss account may be that proportion which corresponds to the amount of any dividends; and

•       where the profit attributable to a participating interest and recognised in the profit and loss account exceeds the amount of any dividends, the difference must be placed in a reserve which cannot be distributed to shareholders.

The reference to 'dividends' includes dividends already paid and those whose payment can be claimed.

[*SI 2008 No 409, Sch 1, para 29A; SI 2015 No 980, Reg 17(f)*].

Note that this treatment is not currently permitted under accounting standards and the FRC has indicated that it does not intend to incorporate it into UK accounting practice at present.

**5.23**   **Alternative accounting rules**

Any of the accounting rules set out below may be used (as alternatives to the historical cost accounting rules in **5.16** to **5.21**) to determine the amounts to be included in respect of the assets in question (but note that not all of these options are acceptable under current accounting standards).

(a)     *Intangible fixed assets*, other than goodwill, may be included at their current cost.

(b)     *Tangible fixed assets* may be included at a market value (determined as at the date of their last valuation) or at their current cost.

(c)     *Investments of any description falling to be included under item B III* of either of the balance sheet formats in **5.12** may be included either at

(i)      market value determined as at the date of their last valuation; or

(ii)     a value determined on any basis which appears to the directors to be appropriate in the circumstances of the company (but in this case particulars of the method of valuation adopted and of the reasons for adopting it must be disclosed in a note to the accounts).

(d)     *Investments of any description falling to be included under item C III* of either of the balance sheet formats in **5.12** may be included at their current cost.

(e)     *Stocks* may be included at their current cost.

**Application of the depreciation rules.** Where the value of any asset is determined on any basis within (a)–(e) above, that value (instead of the purchase price, production cost or any value previously so determined for that asset) must be (or, as the case may require, must be the starting point for determining) the amount to be included in respect of that asset in the accounts. The historical cost depreciation rules in 5.17 to 5.20 (other than those in *SI 2008 No 409, Sch 1, paras 22 and 26–29*) apply accordingly in relation to any such asset with the substitution for any reference to its purchase price or production cost of a reference to the value most recently determined for that asset under (a)–(e) above (the '*adjusted depreciation rules*').

In the case of a fixed asset, any provision for depreciation in respect of that asset which is

• included in any item shown in the profit and loss account in respect of amounts written off assets of the description in question, or

• taken into account as required by note (1) to the profit and loss account formats in 5.13

will normally be included or taken into account at the amount calculated under the adjusted depreciation rules above. It may, however, be included or taken in account under the historic cost depreciation rules instead of the adjusted depreciation rules, provided that the amount of any difference between the two is shown separately in the profit and loss account or in a note to the accounts.

[*SI 2008 No 409, Sch 1, paras 30–33*].

Reference should also be made to the detailed requirements of FRS 102 on accounting for revalued assets.

**5.24** *Additional information to be provided in case of departure from historical cost accounting rules*

Where the amounts to be included in respect of assets covered by any items shown in the accounts have been determined on any basis in 5.23(a)–(e), the following additional information must be disclosed in a note to the accounts or alternatively, in the case of (b) below, shown separately in the balance sheet.

(a)    The items affected and the basis of valuation adopted in determining the amounts of the assets in question in the case of each such item.

(b)    In the case of each balance sheet item affected (except stocks), either

•    the 'comparable amounts determined according to the historical cost accounting rules'; or

•    the differences between those amounts and the corresponding amounts actually shown in the balance sheet in respect of that item.

The '*comparable amounts determined according to the historical cost accounting rules*' are

•    the aggregate amount which would be required to be shown in respect of that item if the amounts to be included in respect of all the assets covered by that item were determined according to the historical cost accounting rules; and

•    the aggregate amount of the cumulative provisions for depreciation or diminution in value which would be permitted or required in determining those amounts according to those rules.

[*SI 2008 No 409, Sch 1 para 34*].

**5.25**   *Revaluation reserve*

The amount of any profit or loss arising from the determination of the value of an asset on any basis mentioned in **5.23**(*a*)–(*e*) (after allowing, where appropriate, for any provisions for depreciation or diminution in value) must be credited or, as the case may be, debited to a separate reserve, the 'revaluation reserve'.

The amount of the revaluation reserve must be shown in the balance sheet under a separate sub-heading in the position given for the item 'revaluation reserve' in either of the balance sheet formats in **5.12**, although it need not be shown under that name.

The revaluation reserve must be reduced to the extent that the amounts transferred to it are no longer necessary for the purposes of the valuation method used. In addition, an amount may be transferred

- from the revaluation reserve to the profit and loss account, if the amount was previously charged to that account or represents realised profit;

- from the revaluation reserve on capitalisation (ie by applying the amount in wholly or partly paying up unissued shares in the company to be allotted to members as fully or partly paid shares); and

- to or from the revaluation reserve in respect of the taxation relating to any profit or loss credited or debited to the reserve.

The revaluation reserve must not be reduced except as mentioned above.

The treatment for taxation purposes of amounts credited or debited to the revaluation reserve must be disclosed in a note to the accounts.

[*SI 2008 No 409, Sch 1 para 35*].

**5.26   Fair value accounting**

(1) *Financial instruments*

Financial instruments (including 'derivatives') may be included at fair value with the following exceptions.

- Financial instruments which constitute liabilities unless

  (i)    they are held as part of a 'trading portfolio';

  (ii)   they are derivative; or

  (iii)  they are financial instruments which under international accounting standards may be included in accounts at fair value, provided that the disclosures required by such accounting standards are made.

- Any of the following, namely

  (i)    financial instruments (other than derivatives) 'held to maturity',

  (ii)   loans and 'receivables' originated by the company and not 'held for trading purposes',

  (iii)  interests in subsidiary undertakings, associated undertaking (see **5.49**) and joint ventures (see **5.48**),

  (iv)   'equity instruments' issued by the company,

  (v)    contracts for contingent consideration in a 'business combination',

(vi)      other financial instruments with such special characteristics that the instruments, according to generally accepted accounting principles or practice, should be accounted for differently from other financial instruments,

unless they are financial instruments which may be included in accounts at fair value, provided that the disclosures required by such accounting standards are made.

- If the fair value of a financial instrument cannot be determined reliably under the rules set out below.

*'Derivatives'* include 'commodity-based contracts' that give either contracting party the right to settle in cash or in some other financial instrument, except when such contracts

- were entered into for the purpose of, and continue to meet, the company's expected purchase, sale or usage requirements;
- were designated for such purpose at their inception; and
- are expected to be settled by delivery of the commodity.

*Determination of fair value.* The fair value of a financial instrument is determined as follows.

(a)      If a 'reliable market' can readily be identified for the financial instrument, its fair value is determined by reference to its market value.

(b)      If a reliable market cannot readily be identified for the financial instrument but can be identified for its components or for a similar instrument, its fair value is determined by reference to the market value of its components or of the similar instrument.

(c)      If neither (*a*) or (*b*) above applies, the fair value of the financial instrument is a value resulting from generally accepted valuation models and techniques which ensure a reasonable approximation of the market value.

*Hedged items.* A company may include any assets and liabilities that qualify as hedged items under a 'fair value hedge accounting system', or identified portions of such assets or liabilities, at the amount required under that system.

The expressions 'business combination', 'commodity-based contracts', 'derivative', 'equity instrument', 'fair value hedge accounting system', 'financial instrument', 'hedge accounting', 'hedge accounting system', 'hedged items', 'held for trading purposes', 'held to maturity', 'receivables', 'reliable market' and 'trading portfolio' have the same meaning as they have in *Directive 2013/34/EU* on the annual accounts of certain types of undertakings.

*(2) Stocks, investment property, and living animals and plants*

Stocks, investment property and living animals and plants may be included at fair value provided that, as the case may be, all such stocks, investment property and living animals and plants are so included where their fair value can reliably be determined. For these purposes, 'fair value' means fair value determined in accordance with generally accepted accounting principles or practice.

**Accounting for changes in value.** Where a financial instrument or asset is valued in accordance with (1) to (2) above, a change in the value of the financial instrument or asset must be included in the profit and loss account. But

(A)      where

(i)      the financial instrument accounted for is a 'hedging instrument' under a hedge accounting system that allows some or all of the change in value not to be shown in the profit and loss account, or

(ii)    the change in value relates to an 'exchange difference' arising on a 'monetary item' that forms part of a company's net investment in a 'foreign entity',

the amount of the change in value *must* be credited to or (as the case may be) debited from a separate reserve (*'the fair value reserve'*); and

(B)    where the instrument accounted for

(i)     is an 'available for sale financial asset', and

(ii)    is not a derivative,

the change in value *may* be credited to or (as the case may be) debited from the fair value reserve.

The expressions *'available for sale financial asset'*, *'exchange difference'*, *'financial instrument'*, *'foreign entity'*, *'hedge accounting'*, *'hedge accounting system'*, *'hedging instrument'*, and *'monetary item'* have the same meaning as they have in *Directive 2013/34/EU* on the annual accounts of certain types of undertaking.

**The fair value reserve.** The fair value reserve must be adjusted to the extent that the amounts shown in it are no longer necessary for the purposes of (A) or (B) above.

[*SI 2008 No 409, Sch 1, paras 36–41, Sch 8, paras 1, 2; SI 2015 No 980, Reg 17*].

Reference should also be made to the detailed requirements of FRS 102 in respect of items included at fair value, and those in respect of financial instruments in particular.

**5.27    Notes to the accounts: general**

Any information required by the following provisions must be given by way of a note to the accounts and the notes must be presented in the order in which, where relevant, the items to which they relate are presented in the balance sheet and in the profit and loss account.

**Off-balance sheet arrangements.** If in any financial year

•    the company is, or has been, party to arrangements that are not reflected in its balance sheet; and

•    at the balance sheet date the risks or benefits arising from those arrangements are material,

the nature and business purpose of the arrangements must be disclosed in the notes to the accounts, to extent necessary for enabling the financial position of the company to be assessed.

**Average number of employees.** For periods beginning on or after 1 January 2016, the notes to the accounts of a small company must disclose the average number of employees during the reporting period, calculated as specified in the legislation. Further details of the calculation requirements are given at **3.18**. A small company continues to be exempt from the related disclosures in respect of staff costs.

**Relationship between assets and liabilities.** Where an asset or liability relates to more than one item in the balance sheet, the relationship of this asset or liability to the relevant items must be disclosed either under those items or in the notes to the accounts.

**Disclosure of accounting policies.** The accounting policies adopted in determining the profit or loss and the amounts of balance sheet items (including policies with respect to the depreciation and diminution in value of assets) must be stated.

[*CA 2006, ss 410A(1)–(4), 411(1); SI 2008 No 409, Sch 1, paras 9A, 42, 44; SI 2015 No 980, Regs 5(14), 5(15)(a), 16(2)(e), 18*].

The amount of information that needs to be disclosed in small company accounts has been considerably reduced for periods beginning on or after 1 January 2016. However, the accounts are still required to give a true and fair view and additional details over and above those required by the legislation may need to be given to achieve this. FRS 102 encourages additional disclosure where relevant and paragraph 1A.17 and Appendix D to Section 1A of the standard include guidance for directors on additional disclosures that may need to be given.

**5.28**  *Directors' benefits: advances, credits and guarantees*

A small company that does not prepare group accounts must disclose the following details of advances and credits granted by the company to its directors, and guarantees of any kind entered into by the company on behalf of its directors, in the notes to its individual accounts.

(a)  In respect of any advance or credit granted by the company to a director, details of

(i)   its amount;

(ii)  an indication of the interest rate;

(iii) its main conditions;

(iv)  any amounts repaid;

(v)   any amounts written off; and

(vi)  any amounts waived.

(b)  In respect of any guarantee of any kind entered into by the company on behalf of a director, details of

(i)   its main terms;

(ii)  the amount of the maximum liability that may be incurred by the company; and

(iii) any amount paid and any liability incurred by the company for the purpose of fulfilling the guarantee (including any loss incurred by reason of enforcement of the guarantee).

The totals of amounts stated under (*a*)(i), (*a*)(iv), (*a*)(v), (*a*)(vi), (*b*)(ii) and (*b*)(iii) must also be given.

The provisions apply to

•   persons who were directors of the company at any time in the financial year to which the accounts relate; and

•   every advance, credit or guarantee subsisting at any time in the financial year to which the accounts relate

(i)   whenever it was entered into; and

(ii)  whether or not the person concerned was a director of the company in question at the time it was entered into.

[*CA 2006, s 413(1), (3)–(7); SI 2015 No 980, Reg 5*].

**5.29**  Notes to the accounts: information supplementing the balance sheet

Paragraphs **5.30** to **5.34**, require information which either supplements the information given with respect to particular items in the balance sheet or is otherwise relevant to assessing the company's state of affairs. [*SI 2008 No 409, Sch 1 paras 42, 45*].

**5.30**  *Fixed assets*

The information set out below must be given for each item which is shown under the general item 'fixed assets' in the balance sheet (or which would be shown there were it not for **5.10**(6) (*b*) (ii)).

(a)  The 'appropriate amounts' in respect of that item as at both the beginning of the financial year and at the balance sheet date.

(b)  The effect on any amount shown in the balance sheet in respect of that item of

(i)  any revision of the amount in respect of any assets included under that item made during that year on any basis in **5.23**(*a*)–(*e*);

(ii)  acquisitions and disposals during that year of any assets; and

(iii)  any transfers of assets of the company to and from that item during that year.

(c)  In respect of each item

•  the cumulative amount of provisions for depreciation or diminution in value of assets included under that item both as at the beginning of the financial year and at the balance sheet date;

•  the amount of any such provisions made in respect of the financial year; and

•  the amount of any adjustments made in respect of any such provisions during that year, distinguishing between adjustments made in consequence of disposals and other adjustments.

For the purposes of (*a*) above, the '*appropriate amounts*' in respect of any item as at either of the dates there mentioned are the aggregate amounts determined, as at that date, in respect of assets falling to be included under that item, either on the basis of purchase price or production cost (see **5.21**) or on any basis in **5.23**(*a*)–(*e*) but in either case leaving out of account in either case any provisions for depreciation or diminution in value.

[*SI 2008 No 409, Sch 1 para 48*].

*Assets included at valuation.* The following additional information must be given where any fixed assets are included under any balance sheet item at an amount determined on any basis in **5.23**(a)–(e).

(i)  The years (as far as they are known to the directors) in which the assets were severally valued, and the several values.

(ii)  In the case of assets valued during the financial year, the bases of valuation used and either the names or qualifications of the valuers.

[*SI 2008 No 409, Sch 1 para 49*].

**5.31**  *Information about fair value of assets and liabilities*

Where financial instruments or other assets have been included at fair value in accordance with **5.26**(1), the following must be stated.

(a)  The significant assumptions underlying the valuation models and techniques used.

(b)   For each category of financial instrument or other asset, the fair value of the assets in that category and the changes in value

   (i)   included directly in the profit and loss account, or

   (ii)   credited to or (as the case may be) debited from the fair value reserve,

in respect of those assets.

(c)   For each class of 'derivatives', the extent and nature of the instruments, including significant terms and conditions that may affect the amount, timing and certainty of future cash flows.

(d)   Where any amount is transferred to or from the fair value reserve during the financial year, there must be stated in tabular form

•   the amount of the reserve as at the beginning of the financial year and as at the balance sheet date; and

•   the amount transferred to or from the reserve during that year.

[*SI 2008 No 409, Sch 1, para 51*].

See **5.26** for the meaning of '*derivatives*'.

**5.32**   *Information about revalued fixed assets*

Where fixed assets are measured at revalued amounts, the following information must be given in tabular form—

•   movements in the revaluation reserve in the financial year, with an explanation of the tax treatment of items therein; and

•   the carrying amount in the balance sheet that would have been recognised had the fixed assets not been revalued.

[*SI 2008 No 409, Sch 1, para 54; SI 2015 No 980, Reg 18(11)*].

**5.33**   *Details of indebtedness*

For the aggregate of all items shown in the balance sheet under 'creditors' the following information is required.

(a)   The aggregate amount of any debts included under that item which are payable or repayable otherwise than by instalments and which fall due for payment or repayment after the end of a five-year period beginning with the day after the end of the financial year.

(b)   In the case of any debts so included which are payable or repayable by instalments, the aggregate amount of any instalments which fall due for payment after the end of the period specified in (*a*) above.

In respect of each item shown under 'creditors' in the balance sheet there must be stated the aggregate amount of any debts included under that item in respect of which any security has been given by the company with the indication of the nature and form of any such security.

Where a distinction is made in the balance sheet between amounts falling due to creditors within one year and those falling due after more than one year, (*a*) and (*b*) above apply only to items shown under the latter of those categories. The disclosure requirements in respect of security apply to items shown under either category.

[*SI 2008 No 409, Sch 1, para 55; SI 2015 No 980, Reg 18(12)*].

## 5.34 Accounts: Small Companies and Micro-entities

**5.34** *Guarantees and other financial commitments*

The following information must be given.

(a) The total amount of any financial commitments, guarantees and contingencies that are not included in the balance sheet together with an indication of the nature and form of any valuable security given by the company in respect of such commitments, guarantees and contingencies.

(b) The total amount of any of the above commitments concerning pensions must be stated separately.

(c) The total amount of any commitments under (a) which are undertaken on behalf of or for the benefit of—

    (i) any parent undertaking, fellow subsidiary undertaking or any subsidiary undertaking of the company; or

    (ii) any undertaking in which the company has a participating interest

must be stated separately and those within (i) must be stated separately from those within (ii).

[*SI 2008 No 409, Sch 1 para 57; SI 2015 No 980, Reg 18(14)*].

### 5.35 Notes to the accounts: information supplementing the profit and loss account

*Prior year adjustments.* Where any amount relating to any preceding financial year is included in any profit and loss account item, the effect must be stated.

*Exceptional items.* The amount and nature of any individual items of income and expenditure of exceptional size or incidence must be stated.

[*SI 2008 No 409, Sch 1, para 61; SI 2015 No 980, Reg 18(18)*].

### 5.36 Post-balance sheet events

The nature and financial effect of material events arising after the balance sheet date which are not reflected in the profit and loss account or balance sheet must be stated.

[*SI 2008 No 409, Sch 1, para 64; SI 2015 No 980, Reg 18(21)*].

### 5.37 Parent undertaking information

Where the company is a subsidiary undertaking, the following information must be given in respect of the parent undertaking of the smallest group of undertakings for which group accounts are drawn up of which the company is a member—

(a) the name of the parent undertaking which draws up the group accounts;

(b) the address of the undertaking's registered office (whether in or outside the United Kingdom); or

(c) if it is unincorporated, the address of its principal place of business.

[*SI 2008 No 409, Sch 1, para 65; SI 2015 No 980, Reg 18(21)*].

### 5.38 Related party transactions

Particulars *may* be given of transactions which the company has entered into with related parties, and *must* be given if such transactions are material and have not been concluded under normal market conditions with—

- owners holding a participating interest in the company;

- companies in which the company itself has a participating interest; and

- the company's directors.

Where disclosure is required, the details disclosed must include—

- the amount of such transactions;

- the nature of the related party relationship; and

- other information about the transactions necessary for an understanding of the financial position of the company.

Information about individual transactions may be aggregated according to their nature, except where separate information is necessary of an understanding of the effects of the related party transactions on the financial position of the company.

Particulars need not be given of transactions entered into between two or more members of a group, provided that any subsidiary undertaking which is a party to the transaction is wholly-owned by such a member.

In this paragraph, 'related party' has the same meaning as in international accounting standards.

[*SI 2008 No 409, Sch 1, para 66; SI 2015 No 980, Reg 18(21)*].

## 5.39 SMALL COMPANY INDIVIDUAL ACCOUNTS: AUDITOR'S REMUNERATION AND LIABILITY LIMITATION AGREEMENTS

For financial years beginning on or after 1 January 2016, there is no longer any requirement for a small company to disclose details of auditor remuneration in the notes to the accounts.

[*SI 2016 No 649, Reg 18(2)*].

The disclosure requirements in respect of liability limitation agreements continue to apply in the case of a small company although use of these agreements is relatively rare in practice, particularly in the case of small companies. Further details about such agreements and the related disclosure requirements can be found at 3.53 ACCOUNTS: LARGE COMPANIES.

## 5.40 SMALL COMPANY INDIVIDUAL ACCOUNTS: DELIVERY TO THE REGISTRAR OF COMPANIES

**Small company accounts generally**. For each financial year, the directors of a company subject to the small companies regime

(a)     *must* deliver to the Registrar of Companies a copy of the balance sheet drawn up as at the last day of that year;

(b)     *may* also deliver to the Registrar of Companies

 (i)     a copy of the company's profit and loss account for that year; and

 (ii)     a copy of the directors' report for that year.

In addition

- where the directors deliver a copy of the company's profit and loss account under (b)(i) they *must* also deliver to the Registrar of Companies a copy of the auditor's report on the accounts (and on any directors' report) unless the company is exempt from audit and the directors have taken advantage of that exemption;

- where the directors take advantage of the option not to deliver a copy of the profit and loss account, the balance sheet must disclose that fact and, unless the company is exempt from audit and the directors have taken advantage of this, the notes to the balance sheet must

  (i)    state whether the auditor's report was qualified or unqualified;

  (ii)   if the report was qualified, disclose the basis of any qualification and, if applicable, reproduce any statement under *CA 2006, s 498(2)(a)* or *(b)* or *CA 2006, s 498(3);*

  (iii)  if the report was unqualified, include a reference to any matters to which the auditor drew attention by way of emphasis; and

  (iv)   state the name of the auditor and, in the case of a firm, the name of the person who signed as senior statutory auditor (unless these details are omitted in accordance with *CA 2006, s 506*, in which case the usual disclosures required by that section must be given).

These disclosures do not have to be given in accounts prepared under the micro-entity financial reporting regime.

Where the balance sheet or profit and loss account is abridged pursuant to *SI 2008 No 409* (see **5.11**) the directors must also deliver to the Registrar a statement by the company that all the members have consented to the abridgement.

Where the accounts delivered to the Registrar of Companies are either

- IAS accounts, or

- Companies Act accounts that are not abridged accounts

and the directors take the option under (*b*) above of not delivering a copy of the company's profit and loss account or directors' report, the copy of the balance sheet delivered to the Registrar of Companies must contain, in a prominent position, a statement that the company's annual accounts and reports have been delivered in accordance with the provisions applicable to companies subject to the small companies regime.

[*CA 2006, s 444(1)–(3), (5)–(5C); SI 2008 No 393, Reg 12; SI 2015 No 980, Reg 8(3)*].

**Small companies' exemption in relation to directors' report**. A company is entitled to small companies exemption in relation to the directors' report for a financial year if

- it is entitled to prepare accounts for the year in accordance with the small companies regime; or

- it would be so entitled but for being or having been a member of an ineligible group.

This grants exemption from the disclosure of dividend details in the report (see **20.10**). A company falling within the first category will be subject to the filing requirements in *CA 2006, s 444* described above. A company falling within the second category above *must* deliver a copy of its annual accounts and *may* deliver a copy of its directors' report. It must also deliver a copy of the auditor's report on the accounts and directors' report, unless it is exempt from audit and the directors have taken advantage of this.

[*CA 2006, ss 415A, 444A; SI 2008 No 393, Reg 6*].

**Names appearing on accounts**. The copies of the balance sheet and any directors' report delivered to the Registrar of Companies under these provisions must state the name of the person who signed it on behalf of the board.

The copy of the auditor's report delivered to the Registrar of Companies under these provisions must either

- state the name of the auditor and (where the auditor is a firm) the name of the person who signed it as senior statutory auditor; or

- if the conditions in *CA 2006, s 506* are met (circumstances in which names may be omitted, see **8.42 AUDIT**), state that a resolution has been passed and notified to the Secretary of State in accordance with those provisions.

[*CA 2006, ss 444(6) (7), 444A(3) (4); SI 2007 No 3495, Sch 1, para 6; SI 2008 No 2860, Art 6*].

## 5.41   SMALL COMPANY GROUP ACCOUNTS

For periods beginning before 1 January 2017, a company is exempt from the requirement to prepare group accounts if, at the end of the financial year, it is subject to the small companies regime or would be subject to that regime but for the fact that it is a public company and provided that it is not a traded company (as defined in *CA 2006, s 474(1)*).

For periods beginning on or after 1 January 2017, a company is exempt from the requirement to prepare group accounts if, at the end of the financial year, it is

(a)   subject to the small companies regime, or would be subject to that regime but for the fact that it is a public company; and

(b)   it is not a member of a group which, at any time during the year, has an undertaking falling with *CA 2006, s 399(2B)* (see **3.56** for further details of this condition).

However, any company that is exempt from the requirement to prepare group accounts may prepare them on a voluntary basis. Any group accounts prepared on a voluntary basis form part of the company's annual accounts for all legislative purposes.

[*CA 2006, ss 399(2A), (2B), (4), 471(1); SI 2015 No 980, Reg 5(6); SI 2016 No 1245, Reg 3(4)(c)*].

Where group accounts are prepared, the provisions below and in **5.42** to **5.62** apply to the accounts.

**Applicable accounting framework**. Subject to below, the group accounts may be prepared in accordance with

- *CA 2006, s 404* ('*Companies Act individual accounts*'); or

- international accounting standards ('*IAS individual accounts*').

But

- the group accounts of a parent company that is a charity must be Companies Act group accounts; and

- after the first financial year in which the directors of a parent company prepare IAS group accounts ('*the first IAS year*'), all subsequent group accounts of the company must be prepared in accordance with international accounting standards unless there is a '*relevant change of circumstance*'. This is subject to the right to change to Companies Act accounts in *CA 2006, s 403(5A)* (see below). A relevant change of circumstance occurs if, at any time during or after the first IAS year

(i)     the company becomes a subsidiary undertaking of another undertaking that does not prepare IAS group accounts;

(ii)    the company ceases to be a company with securities admitted to trading on a regulated market in an EEA State; or

(iii)   a parent undertaking of the company ceases to be an undertaking with securities admitted to trading on a regulated market in an EEA State.

After a financial year in which IAS group accounts are prepared, the directors may change to preparing Companies Act group accounts for a reason other than a relevant change of circumstance, provided they have not changed to Companies Act group accounts in the five years preceding the first day of that financial year.

If, having changed to preparing Companies Act group accounts the directors again prepare IAS group accounts for the company, the above provisions again apply as if the first financial year for which such accounts are again prepared were the first IAS year.

[*CA 2006, s 403; SI 2012 No 2301, Reg 15, 16, 17*].

See Appendix 1 Definitions for the current EEA States.

**Companies Act group accounts**. Companies Act group accounts must comprise

•       a consolidated balance sheet dealing with the state of affairs of the parent company and its 'subsidiary undertakings' (see Appendix 1 Definitions); and

•       a consolidated profit and loss account dealing with the profit or loss of the parent company and its subsidiary undertakings,

and must state the following in respect of the parent company—

(a)     the part of the UK in which the company is registered;

(b)     the company's registered number;

(c)     whether the company is a public or private company and whether it is limited by shares or by guarantee;

(d)     the address of the company's registered office; and

(e)     where appropriate, the fact that the company is being wound up.

The accounts must give a true and fair view of the state of affairs as at the end of the financial year, and the profit or loss for the financial year, of the undertakings included in the consolidation as a whole, so far as concerns members of the company.

Companies Act group accounts must comply with the provisions in **5.44–5.51** as to the form and content of the consolidated balance sheet and consolidated profit and loss account and additional information to be provided by way of notes to the accounts. If compliance with those provisions, and any other provisions made by or under *CA 2006*, as to the matters to be included in a company's group accounts or in notes to those accounts would not be sufficient to give a true and fair view, the necessary additional information must be given in the accounts or notes. If, in special circumstances, compliance with any of those provisions is inconsistent with the requirement to give a true and fair view, the directors must depart from that provision to the extent necessary to give a true and fair view. Particulars of any such departure, the reasons for it and its effect must be given in a note to the accounts.

[*CA 2006, s 404*].

See **2.16 Accounts: General** for 'true and fair view'. Companies Act group accounts must also comply with all relevant requirements of FRS 102.

**IAS group accounts**. The provisions described in **5.44–5.51** do not apply to IAS group accounts. Instead, consolidated accounts must be prepared on the basis of the accounting standards issued by the International Accounting Standard Board (IASB) that are adopted by the European Commission. [*EC Council Regulation 1606/2002, Art 4*]. Instead of the profit and loss account and balance sheet required under *CA 2006*, a company must prepare primary financial statements and supporting notes as required under international accounting standards. See **2.15 Accounts: General** for a list of standards.

Where the directors of a company prepare IAS group accounts, they must state in the notes to those accounts that the accounts have been prepared in accordance with international accounting standards.

They must also state

- the part of the UK in which the company is registered;

- the company's registered number;

- whether the company is a public or private company and whether it is limited by shares or by guarantee;

- the address of the company's registered office; and

- where appropriate, the fact that the company is being wound up.

[*CA 2006, s 406; SI 2015 No 980, Reg 5*].

### 5.42   Exclusion of subsidiary undertakings from consolidation

Where a parent company prepares Companies Act group accounts (see **5.41**) all subsidiary undertakings of the company must normally be included in the consolidation. There are, however, exclusions, as listed below. If *all* of a parent company's subsidiary undertakings could be excluded from consolidation in Companies Act group accounts, the parent company need not prepare group accounts.

(a)   A subsidiary undertaking may be excluded from consolidation if its inclusion is not material for the purpose of giving a true and fair view (see **2.16 Accounts: General**). Two or more undertakings can be excluded only if they are not material taken together.

(b)   A subsidiary undertaking may be excluded from consolidation where

(i)   severe long-term restrictions substantially hinder the exercise of the parent company's rights over the assets or management of the undertaking; or

(ii)   extremely rare circumstances mean that the information necessary to prepare group accounts cannot be obtained without disproportionate expense or undue delay; or

(iii)   the interest of the parent company is held exclusively with a view to subsequent resale.

The references in (i) and (iii) above to, respectively, the rights and the interest of the parent company are references to rights and interests held by or attributed to it for the purposes of the definition of 'parent undertaking' (see **Appendix 1 Definitions**) in the absence of which it would not be the parent company.

[*CA 2006, ss 402, 405; SI 2015 No 980, Reg 5(10)*].

Note also that, although the legislation permits exclusion in these situations, FRS 102 requires exclusion in the case of (b)(i) above, does not allow exclusion under (b)(ii) for undertakings that are individually or collectively material in the context of the group, and imposes more stringent requirements in the case of (b)(iii) in that it only allows exclusion if the subsidiary undertaking has not previously been included in consolidated group accounts prepared by the parent. Where a subsidiary undertaking is excluded from consolidation under (b)(i) or (b)(iii), FRS 102 specifies the accounting treatment to be adopted.

### 5.43   SMALL COMPANY GROUP ACCOUNTS: PARENT COMPANY PROFIT AND LOSS ACCOUNT

Where a small company prepares group accounts in accordance with *CA 2006* and the notes to its individual balance sheet show the parent company's profit or loss for the financial year (determined in accordance with *CA 2006*), the parent company's individual profit and loss account may be omitted from the company's annual accounts, although it must still be approved in accordance with *CA 2006, s 414(1)* (see **2.2** ACCOUNTS: GENERAL).

The above exemption is conditional upon the company's annual accounts disclosing the fact that the exemption applies.

[*CA 2006, s 408; SI 2008 No 393, Reg 10; SI 2008 No 409, Reg 3(2); SI 2015 No 980, Reg 5*].

### 5.44   SMALL COMPANY GROUP ACCOUNTS: FORM AND CONTENT

Where the directors of a parent company which

- is subject to the small companies regime, and
- has prepared Companies Act individual accounts

prepare Companies Act group accounts, those accounts must comply with the provisions in this paragraph and in **5.45–5.51** as to the form and content of the consolidated balance sheet and consolidated profit and loss account, and additional information to be provided by way of notes to the accounts. Accounts are treated as having complied with any of those provisions if they comply instead with the corresponding provision in **3.61** to **3.66** ACCOUNTS: LARGE COMPANIES. [*SI 2008 No 409, Reg 8*].

The group accounts must comply, so far as practicable, with the provisions of *SI 2008 No 409, Sch 1* (see **5.10** to **5.38**) as if the '*group*' (meaning, for these purposes, all the undertakings included in the consolidation) were a single company, except that

(a)     for item B.III in each balance sheet format in **5.12** substitute:

   B.III. Investments

     (1)     Shares in group undertakings

     (2)     Interests in associated undertakings

     (3)     Other participating interests

     (4)     Loans to group undertakings and undertakings in which a participating interest is held

     (5)     Other investments other than loans

     (6)     Others

(b)     In the profit and loss account formats in **5.13**, replace the items headed 'income from participating interests' in—

- format 1, item 8, and

- format 2, item 10,

by two items: 'Income from interests in associated undertakings' and 'Income from other participating interests'.

*SI 2008 No 409, Sch 1, para 4A* (rules relating to micro-entities) does not apply to group accounts.

[*SI 2008 No 409, Sch 6, paras 1; SI 2015 No 980, Reg 22*].

Note, however, that there is no option for a small company to prepare an abridged group balance sheet or an abridged group profit and loss account.

[*SI 2008 No 409, Sch 6, para 1 (1A); SI 2015, Reg 22(3)*].

The consolidated balance sheet and profit and loss account must incorporate in full the information contained in the individual accounts of the undertakings included in the consolidation, subject to the adjustments authorised or required under this paragraph and **5.45–5.51** and to such other adjustments (if any) that are appropriate in accordance with generally accepted accounting principles or practice, and the group accounts must be drawn up as at the same date as the accounts of the parent company.

**Subsidiaries with different financial years.** If the financial year of a subsidiary undertaking included in the consolidation does not end with that of the parent company, the group accounts must be made up

- from the accounts of the subsidiary undertaking for its financial year last ending before the end of the parent company's financial year (provided that year ended no more than three months before that of the parent company) – and in this situation FRS 102 requires the accounts to be adjusted for the effects of any significant transactions or events that occur between the year ends of the subsidiary undertaking and the parent; or

- from interim accounts prepared by the subsidiary undertaking as at the end of the parent company's financial year.

[*SI 2008 No 409, Sch 6, para 2; SI 2015 No 980, Reg 22*].

But note that the directors of a parent company must secure that, except where in their opinion there are good reasons against it, the financial year of each of its subsidiary undertakings coincides with the company's own financial year. [*CA 2006, s 390(5)*].

**Assets and liabilities.** Where assets and liabilities to be included in the group accounts have been valued or otherwise determined by undertakings according to accounting rules differing from those used for the group accounts, the values or amounts must be adjusted so as to accord with the rules used for the group accounts (unless such adjustments are not material for the purpose of giving a true and fair view). If it appears to the parent company's directors that there are special reasons for doing so, they may depart from this requirement, but particulars of the departure, the reasons for it and its effect must be given in a note to the accounts. [*SI 2008 No 409, Sch 6, para 3*].

**Accounting rules.** Any differences between the accounting rules used for a parent company's individual accounts for a financial year and those used for its group accounts must be disclosed in a note to the group accounts. The reasons for the difference must be given. [*SI 2008 No 409, Sch 6, para 4*].

**Materiality.** Amounts that in the particular context of any provision in this paragraph and 5.45–5.51 are not material may be disregarded for the purposes of that provision. [*SI 2008 No 409, Sch 6, para 5*].

**Accounts in euros.** The amounts set out in the annual accounts of a company may also be shown in the same accounts translated into euros. If so, the amounts must have been translated at the exchange rate prevailing at the balance sheet date and that rate must be disclosed in the notes to the accounts.

[*CA 2006, s 469(1)–(3)*].

## 5.45    Elimination of group transactions

In preparing group accounts, the following must be eliminated (unless the amounts concerned are not material for the purpose of giving a true and fair view, see **2.16 ACCOUNTS: GENERAL**).

•    Debts and claims between undertakings included in the consolidation.

•    Income and expenditure relating to transactions between such undertakings.

•    Profits and losses resulting from transactions between such undertakings and included in the book value of assets. (Note also that the legislation allows this elimination to be effected in proportion to the group's interest in the shares of the undertakings concerned but FRS 102 requires full elimination.)

[*SI 2008 No 409, Sch 6, para 6*].

## 5.46    Acquisition and merger accounting

The following provisions apply where an undertaking becomes a subsidiary undertaking of the parent company, such an event being referred to as an '*acquisition*'. An acquisition must be accounted for by the 'acquisition method of accounting' unless the conditions for accounting for it as a merger are met and the 'merger method of accounting' is adopted. [*SI 2008 No 409, Sch 6, paras 7, 8*]. Note, however, that FRS 102 only allows merger accounting to be used for group reconstructions (as defined in the standard) and certain public benefit entity combinations, in each case subject to strict conditions.

(1)    **Acquisition method of accounting**

Under the '*acquisition method of accounting*'

•    the identifiable assets and liabilities of the undertaking acquired must be included in the consolidated balance sheet at their fair values as at the date of acquisition;

•    the income and expenditure of the undertaking acquired must be brought into the group accounts only as from the date of the acquisition;

•    the interest of the parent company and its subsidiary undertakings in the adjusted capital and reserves of the undertaking acquired must be set off against the acquisition cost of the interest in the shares of the undertaking held by the parent company and its subsidiary undertakings. The resulting amount, if positive, must be treated as goodwill and, if negative, as a negative consolidation difference; and

•    negative good will may be transferred to the consolidated profit and loss account where such a treatment is in accordance with the principles and rules of *SI 2015 No 980, Sch 1, part 2*.

[*SI 2008 No 409, Sch 6, para 9; SI 2015 No 980, Reg 22(6)*].

Where a group is acquired, references in (1) above to shares of the undertaking acquired should be read as references to shares of the parent undertaking of the group acquired. Other references to the undertaking acquired should be read as references to the group acquired. References to the assets and liabilities, income and expenditure and capital and reserves of the undertaking acquired should be read as references to those of the group acquired, after making the set-offs and other adjustments required by **5.44–5.51** in the case of group accounts. [*SI 2008 No 409, Sch 6, para 12*].

(2)   **Merger method of accounting**

The 'merger method of accounting' can only be used if the following conditions are satisfied (and in the limited situations where FRS 102 allows its use – see above).

- The undertaking whose shares are acquired is ultimately controlled by the same party both before and after the acquisition.

- The control referred to above is not transitory.

- Adoption of the merger method of accounting accords with generally accepted accounting principles or practice.

[*SI 2008 No 409, Sch 6, para 10; SI 2015 No 980, Reg 22(7)*].

Where the above conditions are satisfied

- the assets and liabilities of the undertaking acquired must be brought into the group accounts at the figures at which they stand in the undertaking's accounts, subject to any adjustment authorised or required by the provisions in **5.44–5.51**;

- the income and expenditure of the undertaking acquired must be included in the group accounts for the entire financial year, including the period before the acquisition;

- the group accounts must show comparative figures for the previous financial year as if the undertaking acquired had been included in the consolidation throughout that year; and

- the nominal value of the issued share capital of the undertaking acquired held by the parent company and its subsidiary undertakings must be set off against the aggregate of

  (i)   the appropriate amount in respect of 'qualifying shares' issued by the parent company or its subsidiary undertakings in consideration for the acquisition of shares in the undertaking acquired; and

  (ii)   the fair value of any other consideration for the acquisition of shares in the undertaking acquired, determined as at the date when those shares were acquired.

The resulting amount must be shown as an adjustment to the consolidated reserves.

'*Qualifying shares*' means

- shares to which *CA 2006, s 612* applies (merger relief, see **46.2 Share Premium**), in respect of which the appropriate amount is the nominal value; or

- shares to which *CA 2006, s 611* applies (relief in respect of group reconstructions, see **46.3** S<small>HARE</small> P<small>REMIUM</small>), in respect of which the appropriate amount is the nominal value together with any 'minimum premium value' as there defined.

[*SI 2008 No 409, Sch 6, para 11*].

Where a group is acquired, references above to shares of the undertaking acquired should be read as references to shares of the parent undertaking of the group acquired. Other references to the undertaking acquired should be read as references to the group acquired. References to the assets and liabilities and to income and expenditure of the undertaking acquired should be read as references to those of the group acquired, after making the set-offs and other adjustments required by **5.44–5.51** in the case of group accounts. [*SI 2008 No 410, Sch 6, para 12*].

(3)   **Information to be given in the notes to the accounts**

Subject to below, the following information with respect to acquisitions taking place in the financial year must be given in a note to the accounts (although the information in (*c*) and (*d*) below need only be given in relation to an acquisition which significantly affects the figures shown in the group accounts).

(a)   The name of the undertaking acquired or, where a group was acquired, the name of the parent undertaking of that group.

(b)   Whether the acquisition has been accounted for by the acquisition or the merger method of accounting.

(c)   The composition and fair value of the consideration for the acquisition given by the parent company and its subsidiary undertakings.

(d)   Where the acquisition method of accounting has been adopted, the book values immediately prior to the acquisition, and the fair values at the date of acquisition, of each class of assets and liabilities of the undertaking (or group) acquired in tabular form. This must include a statement of the amount of any goodwill or negative consolidation difference arising on the acquisition, together with an explanation of any significant adjustments made.

In ascertaining for these purposes the profit or loss of a group, the book values and fair values of assets and liabilities of a group or the amount of the assets and liabilities of a group, the set-offs and other adjustments required by **5.44–5.51** in the case of group accounts must be made.

[*SI 2008 No 409, Sch 6, para 13*].

Subject to below, the following information must also be stated in a note to the accounts.

(i)   The cumulative amount of goodwill resulting from acquisitions in that and earlier financial years which has been written off otherwise than in the consolidated profit and loss account for that or any earlier financial year. That figure must be shown net of any goodwill attributable to subsidiary undertakings or businesses disposed of prior to the balance sheet date.

(ii)   Where, during the financial year, there has been a disposal of an undertaking or group which significantly affects the figure shown in the group accounts, the name of that undertaking (or parent undertaking of that group) and the extent to which the profit or loss shown in the group accounts is attributable to profit or loss of that undertaking or group.

*[SI 2008 No 409, Sch 6, paras 14, 15]*.

The information required by (*a*) to (*d*) and (i) and (ii) above need not be disclosed with respect to an undertaking which is either

- established under the law of a country outside the UK, or

- carries on business outside the UK

if, in the opinion of the directors of the parent company, the disclosure would be seriously prejudicial to the business of that undertaking or to the business of the parent company or any of its subsidiary undertakings *and* the Secretary of State agrees that the information should not be disclosed.

Where an acquisition has taken place in the financial year and the merger method of accounting has been adopted, the notes to the accounts must also disclose—

- the address of the registered undertaking of the acquired (whether in or outside the UK);

- the name of the party referred to in **5.46(2)**;

- the address of the registered office of that party (whether in or outside the UK); and

- the information referred to in *Sch 1, para 11(6)* (the resulting amount to be shown as an adjustment to the consolidated account).

*[SI 2008 No 409, Sch 6, para 16; SI 2015 No 980, Reg 22(8)]*.

### 5.47    Non-controlling interests

The formats for the balance sheet (see **5.12**) and profit and loss account (see **5.13**) have effect in relation to group accounts with the following additions.

(1)    *Balance sheet formats*

There must be shown, as a separate item and under the heading 'non-controlling interests', the amount of any profit or loss on ordinary activities, attributable to shares in subsidiary undertakings included in the consolidation held by, or on behalf of, persons other than the parent company and its subsidiary undertakings.

(2)    *Profit and loss account formats*

There must be shown, as a separate item and under the heading 'non-controlling interests', the amount of any profit or loss on ordinary activities, attributable to shares in subsidiary undertakings included in the consolidation held by, or on behalf of, persons other than the parent company and its subsidiary undertakings.

For the purposes of *SI 2008 No 409, Sch 1 para 4* (power of directors to adapt or combine items, see **5.5(6)**) the additional item required by (1) (above) is treated as one to which a letter is assigned and, the additional item required by (2) (above) is treated as one to which an Arabic number is assigned.

*[SI 2008 No 409, Sch 6, para 17; SI 2015 No 980, Reg 22(9)]*.

### 5.48    Joint ventures

Where an undertaking included in the consolidation manages another undertaking (the 'joint venture') jointly with one or more undertakings not included in the consolidation, the joint venture may, if it is not

- a body corporate, or

- a subsidiary undertaking of the parent company,

be dealt with in the group accounts by the method of proportional consolidation (but note that FRS 102 does not allow this treatment).

The provisions in **5.44–5.51** relating to the preparation of consolidated accounts and *CA 2006, ss 402* and *405* apply, with any necessary modifications, to proportional consolidation under this provision.

In addition to the disclosure of the average number of employees employed during the financial year (see *CA 2006, s 411(7)*), there must be a separate disclosure in the notes to the accounts of the average number of employees employed by undertakings that are proportionately consolidated.

[*SI 2008 No 409, Sch 6, para 18; SI 2015 No 980, Reg 22(10), (11)*].

### 5.49 Associated undertakings

**Definition.** An '*associated undertaking*' means an undertaking in which an undertaking included in the consolidation has a 'participating interest' (see APPENDIX 1 DEFINITIONS) and over whose operating and financial policy it exercises a significant influence, and which is not

- a subsidiary undertaking of the parent company; or

- a joint venture dealt with in **5.48**.

Where an undertaking holds 20% or more of the voting rights in another undertaking, it is presumed to exercise such an influence over it unless the contrary is shown. The voting rights in an undertaking means the rights conferred on shareholders in respect of their shares (or, if the undertaking does not have a share capital, on members) to vote at general meetings of the undertaking on all (or substantially all) matters.

In determining whether 20% or more of the voting rights are held, the provisions in APPENDIX 1 DEFINITIONS apply.

FRS 102 includes detailed guidance on what constitutes significant influence in this context.

**Disclosure requirements.** The interest of an undertaking in an associated undertaking, and the amount of profit or loss attributable to such an interest, must be shown by the equity method of accounting (including dealing with any goodwill arising in accordance with **5.17–5.18**. But the equity method of accounting need not be applied if the amounts in question are not material for the purpose of giving a true and fair view.

Where the associated undertaking is itself a parent undertaking, the net assets and profits or losses to be taken into account are those of the parent and its subsidiary undertakings (after making any consolidation adjustments).

[*SI 2008 No 409, Sch 6, paras 19, 20*].

### 5.50 Deferred tax

Deferred tax balances must be recognised on consolidation where it is probable that a charge to tax will arise within the foreseeable future for one of the undertakings included in the consolidation.

[*SI 2008 No 409, Sch 6, para 20A; SI 2015 No 980, Reg 22(12)*].

**5.51   Related party transactions**

The disclosure requirements in respect of related party transactions (*SI 2008 No 409, Sch 1, para 66*) apply to transactions which the parent company or other undertakings included in the consolidation have entered into with related parties, unless they are intra-group transactions.

[*SI 2008 No 409, Sch 6, para 20B; SI 2015 No 980, Reg 22(12)*].

**5.52   SMALL COMPANY GROUP ACCOUNTS: INFORMATION ABOUT RELATED UNDERTAKINGS**

Where a small company prepares group accounts, the notes to those accounts must include the information about related undertakings set out in **5.53–5.61**. In this case, the same requirements apply to both *Companies Act* and IAS group accounts. The only exception is that the information (other than that in **5.56** and **5.60**) need not be disclosed with respect to an undertaking that

- is established under the law of a country outside the UK, or

- carries on business outside the UK,

but only if

- in the opinion of the directors of the company, the disclosure would be seriously prejudicial to the business of

    (i)     that undertaking;

    (ii)    the company;

    (iii)   any of the company's subsidiary undertakings; or

    (iv)   any other undertaking which is included in the consolidation; and

- the Secretary of State agrees that the information need not be disclosed.

Where advantage is taken of this exemption, a note to that effect must be included in the company's accounts.

[*CA 2006, s 409(4), (5); SI 2008 No 409, Reg 10*].

The provision in *CA 2006, s 410* that permitted an alternative approach in order to avoid disclosure of excessive length was repealed by *SI 2015 No 980* in respect of accounts approved on or after 1 July 2015.

For the purposes of these disclosure requirements

- 'The group' means the group consisting of the parent company and its subsidiary undertakings.

- References to shares held by the group are to any shares held by or on behalf of the parent company or any of its subsidiary undertakings. But any shares held on behalf of a person other than the parent company or any of its subsidiary undertakings are not to be treated as held by the group.

- Shares held by way of security must be treated as held by the person providing the security

    (i)     where the rights attached to the shares are exercisable only in accordance with that person's instructions (disregarding any right to exercise them in order to preserve the value of, or realise, the security); and

145

(ii)   as regards shares held in connection with the granting of loans as part of normal business activities, where the rights attached to the shares are exercisable only in that person's interests (disregarding any right to exercise them in order to preserve the value of, or realise, the security).

[*SI 2008 No 409, Sch 6, paras 21, 37(3), (4)*].

## 5.53   Subsidiary undertakings

Subject to **5.52**, the following information must be given with respect to each of the subsidiary undertakings of the parent company at the end of the financial year.

(a)   Its name.

(b)   If the undertaking is incorporated outside the UK, the country in which it is incorporated.

(c)   If it is unincorporated, the address the undertaking's registered office (whether in or outside the UK).

(d)   Whether the subsidiary undertaking is included in the consolidation and, if it is not, the reasons for excluding it.

(e)   Which of the conditions in APPENDIX 1 DEFINITIONS applies to make it a subsidiary undertaking of its immediate parent undertaking. But that information need not be given if the relevant condition is that specified in APPENDIX 1 DEFINITIONS (holding of a majority of the voting rights) and the immediate parent undertaking holds the same proportion of the shares in the undertaking as it holds voting rights.

[*SI 2008 No 409, Sch 6, para 22; SI 2015 No 980, Reg 23(2)*].

## 5.54   *Holdings in subsidiary undertakings*

Subject to **5.52**, with respect to the shares of a subsidiary undertaking held by

•   the parent company, and

•   the group,

there must be stated

•   the identity of each class of shares held, and

•   the proportion of the nominal value of the shares of that class represented by those shares.

This information must (if different) be shown separately as regards the parent company and group.

[*SI 2008 No 409, Sch 6, para 23*].

For the above purposes, there must be attributed to the parent company shares held on its behalf by any person. But shares held on behalf of a person other than the parent company must be treated as not held by that company. [*SI 2008 No 409, Sch 6, para 37(2)*].

## 5.55   *Financial information about subsidiary undertakings not included in the consolidated accounts*

Subject to **5.52**, with respect to each subsidiary undertaking not included in the consolidated accounts, there must be shown

•   the aggregate amount of its capital and reserves as at the end of its relevant financial year; and

- its profit or loss for that year.

This information need not be given if

- the company's investment in the subsidiary undertaking is included in the company's accounts by way of the equity method of valuation;

- the company's holding is less than 50% of the nominal value of the shares in the undertaking *and* the subsidiary undertaking is not required to deliver to the Registrar of Companies a copy of its balance sheet for its 'relevant financial year' and does not otherwise publish that balance sheet in the UK or elsewhere; or

- it is not material.

The '*relevant financial year*' of a subsidiary undertaking is

- if its financial year ends with that of the company, that year; and

- if not, its financial year ending last before the end of the company's financial year.

[*SI 2008 No 409, Sch 6, para 24*].

**5.56** *Shares of company held by subsidiary undertakings*

The number, description and amount of the shares in the company held by, or on behalf of, its subsidiary undertakings must be disclosed. This does not apply in relation to shares in the case of which the subsidiary undertaking is concerned as

- personal representative; or

- trustee, unless the company, or any of its subsidiary undertakings is 'beneficially interested under the trust', otherwise than by way of security only for the purposes of a transaction entered into by it in the ordinary course of a business which includes the lending of money.

[*SI 2008 No 409, Sch 6, para 25*].

In determining whether the company is '*beneficially interested under the trust*', certain residual interests under pension and employees' share schemes, employer's charges and other rights of recovery under such schemes, and a trustee's right to expenses, remuneration, indemnity, etc are disregarded. See *SI 2008 No 409, Sch 2, paras 12–17* for full details.

**5.57   Joint ventures**

Subject to **5.52**, where an undertaking is dealt with in the consolidated accounts by the method of proportional consolidation in accordance with **5.48** (but note accounting standards do not allow this treatment), the following information must be given in respect of the undertaking.

- Its name.

- The address of the undertaking's registered office (whether in or outside the UK).

- The factors on which joint management of the undertaking is based.

- The proportion of its capital held by or on behalf of undertakings included in the consolidation.

- Where its financial year did not end with that of the company, the date on which a financial year of the undertaking last ended before that date.

## 5.57 Accounts: Small Companies and Micro-entities

[*SI 2008 No 409, Sch 6, para 26; SI 2015 No 980, Reg 23(3), (4)*].

### 5.58 Associated undertakings

Subject to **5.52**, the following information must be given where an undertaking included in the consolidation has an interest in an associated undertaking.

(a)     The name of the associated undertaking.

(b)     The address of the undertaking's registered office (whether in or outside the UK).

(c)     If it is unincorporated, the address of its principal place of business.

(d)     With respect to the shares of the undertaking held by the parent company and by the group,

- the identity of each class of shares held, and

- the proportion of the nominal value of the shares of that class represented by those shares,

giving details for the parent company and group separately.

'Associated undertaking' has the same meaning as in **5.49** and the information specified above must be given notwithstanding that the provision on materiality in that paragraph applies in relation to the accounts themselves.

[*SI 2008 No 409, Sch 6, para 27; SI 2015 No 980, Reg 23(5)*].

For the above purposes, there must be attributed to the parent company shares held on its behalf by any person. But shares held on behalf of a person other than the parent company must be treated as not held by that company. [*SI 2008 No 409, Sch 6, para 37(2)*].

### 5.59 Other significant holdings of parent company or group

**Parent company holdings.** Subject to **5.52**, where at the end of the financial year the parent company has a 'significant holding' in an undertaking which is not one of its subsidiary undertakings and does not fall within **5.57** or **5.58**, the following must be stated.

(a)     The name of the undertaking.

(b)     The address of the undertaking's registered office (whether in or outside the UK).

(c)     If it is unincorporated, the address of its principal place of business.

(d)     The identity of each class of shares of the undertaking held by the parent company.

(e)     The proportion of the nominal value of the shares of that class represented by those shares.

(f)     The aggregate amount of the capital and reserves of the undertaking as at the end of its 'relevant financial year'.

(g)     Its profit or loss for that year.

A '*significant holding*' is a holding which amounts to 20% or more of the nominal value of any class of shares in the undertaking *or* the amount of which (as stated or included in the parent company's individual accounts) exceeds 20% of the amount (as so stated) of the parent company's assets.

The '*relevant financial year*' of an undertaking for these purposes is, if its financial year ends with that of the parent company, that year, and if it does not, its financial year ending last before the end of the parent company's financial year.

148

*Exemption.* The information in (*f*) and (*g*) above need not be given if

- the undertaking in question is not required to deliver a copy of its balance sheet for its relevant financial year and does not otherwise publish that balance sheet in the UK or elsewhere *and* the company's holding is less than 50% of the nominal value of the shares in the undertaking; or

- it is not material.

[*SI 2008 No 409, Sch 6, paras 28–30; SI 2015 No 980, Reg 23(6)*].

For the above purposes, there must be attributed to the parent company shares held on its behalf by any person. But shares held on behalf of a person other than the parent company must be treated as not held by that company. [*SI 2008 No 409, Sch 6, para 37(2)*].

**Group holdings.** Subject to **5.52**, where at the end of the financial year the group has a 'significant holding' in an undertaking which is not a subsidiary undertaking of the parent company and does not fall within **5.57** or **5.58**, the same information must be given as under (*a*) to (*g*) above (and with the same exemption as above), substituting 'group' for 'parent company' in (*d*) and in the definition of '*significant holding*'. [*SI 2008 No 409, Sch 6, paras 31–33*].

**5.60   Parent company's or group's membership of certain undertakings**

Where, at the end of the financial year, the company or group is a member of a 'qualifying undertaking' the following must be stated.

(a)   The name and legal form of the undertaking.

(b)   The address of its registered office (whether in or outside the UK) or, if it does not have such an office, its head office (whether in or outside the UK).

(c)   Where the undertaking is a qualifying partnership (see **3.43**), either

(i)   a statement that a copy of the latest accounts of the partnership has been or is to be appended to the copy of the company's accounts sent to the Registrar of Companies; or

(ii)   the name of at least one body corporate (which may be the company itself) in whose group accounts the undertaking has been, or is to be, dealt with on a consolidated basis.

The information required by (*a*) and (*b*) above need not be given if not material and the information required by (*c*) (ii) above need not be given if the notes to the company's accounts disclose that advantage has been taken of the exemption in *Regulation 7* of the *Partnerships (Accounts) Regulations 2008 (SI 2008 No 569)*.

A 'qualifying undertaking' means

(a)   a qualifying partnership (see **3.43**); or

(b)   an unlimited company each of whose members is

(i)   a limited company;

(ii)   another unlimited company each of whose members is a limited company;

(iii)   a Scottish partnership which is not a limited partnership, each of whose members is a limited company; or

(iv)   a Scottish partnership which is a limited partnership, each of whose general partners is a limited company, and, for these purposes, references to a limited company, another unlimited company and a Scottish partnership (either limited or not) include a comparable undertaking incorporated in, or formed under, the law of a country or territory outside the UK.

[*SI 2008 No 409, Sch 6, para 34; SI 2008 No 569, Reg 17; SI 2013 No 2005, Reg 5*].

### 5.61   Information where parent company is a subsidiary undertaking

Subject to **5.52**, where the parent company is itself a subsidiary undertaking, the following information must be given.

(a)    Particulars, as follows, with respect to the parent undertaking of the largest and smallest group of undertakings for which group accounts are drawn up and of which that company is a member.

    (i)    The name of the parent undertaking.

    (ii)    If the undertaking is incorporated outside the UK, the country in which it is incorporated.

    (iii)    If it is unincorporated, the address of its principal place of business.

    (iv)    If copies of the above-mentioned group accounts are available to the public, the addresses from which copies of the accounts can be obtained.

(b)    Particulars, as follows, with respect to the company (which includes any body corporate) regarded by the directors as being that company's ultimate parent company.

    (i)    Its name.

    (ii)    If that company is incorporated outside the UK, the country in which it is incorporated (if known to the directors).

[*SI 2008 No 409, Sch 6, paras 35, 36*].

### 5.62   SMALL COMPANY GROUP ACCOUNTS: DIRECTORS' BENEFITS

In the case of a parent company that prepares group accounts, the notes to the group accounts must also show the following.

(a)    In respect of any advance or credit granted to the directors of the parent company, by that company or by any of its subsidiary undertakings, details of

    (i)    its amount;

    (ii)    an indication of the interest rate;

    (iii)    its main conditions;

    (iv)    any amounts repaid;

    (v)    any amounts written off; and

    (vi)    any amounts waived.

(b)    In respect of any guarantee of any kind entered into on behalf of the directors of the parent company, by that company or by any of its subsidiary undertakings, details of

    (i)    its main terms;

    (ii)    the amount of the maximum liability that may be incurred by the company (or its subsidiary); and

(iii)    any amount paid and any liability incurred by the company (or its subsidiary) for the purpose of fulfilling the guarantee (including any loss incurred by reason of enforcement of the guarantee).

The totals of amounts stated under (*a*)(i), (*a*)(iv), (*a*)(v), (*a*)(vi), (*b*)(ii) and (*b*)(iii) must also be given.

The provisions apply to

•    persons who were directors of the company at any time in the financial year to which the accounts relate; and

•    every advance, credit or guarantee subsisting at any time in the financial year to which the accounts relate

     (i)    whenever it was entered into; and

     (ii)    whether or not the person concerned was a director of the company in question at the time it was entered into; and

     (iii)    in the case of an advance, credit or guarantee involving a subsidiary undertaking of that company, whether or not that undertaking was such a subsidiary undertaking at the time it was entered into.

[*CA 2006, s 413(2)–(7); SI 2015 No 980, Reg 5(16)*].

## 5.63   SMALL COMPANY GROUP ACCOUNTS: DELIVERY TO THE REGISTRAR OF COMPANIES

Companies Act group accounts delivered to the Registrar of Companies need not give the information required by *SI 2009 No 409, Sch 6, para 25* (shares of company held by subsidiary, see **5.56**).

[*SI 2009 No 409, Reg 11*].

# 6   Accounts: Stand-alone Strategic Reports

**Background.** The *Companies Act 2006 (Strategic Report and Directors' Report) Regulations 2013* ("the *2013 Regulations*") which are referred to in various parts of this chapter, bring into force the requirement for a company to produce a strategic report for financial years ending on or after 30 September 2013. Subject to certain conditions, the changes made by these regulations also enable a company to issue a stand-alone strategic report with supplementary material to certain entitled persons in place of the full annual report and accounts.

## 6.1   INTRODUCTION TO STAND-ALONE STRATEGIC REPORTS

CHAPTER 20 STRATEGIC REPORTS AND DIRECTORS' REPORTS explains the requirement for each company (other than certain small companies) to prepare a strategic report for each financial year. A company may also send just a copy of the strategic report with supplementary material instead of copies of the full accounts and reports to

(a)   a person specified as entitled to receive those accounts in *CA 2006, s 423*, ie

- every member of the company;

- every holder of the company's debentures; and

- every person who is entitled to receive notice of general meetings; and

(b)   a person nominated by a member to enjoy information rights under *CA 2006, s 146* (see **26.4** MEMBERS).

But copies of the full reports and accounts must be sent to any person entitled to be sent them under those provisions and who wishes to receive them. See **6.3** for the manner in which this is determined.

A strategic report and supplementary material must comply with the minimum require-ments as to form and content in **6.6** but this does not prevent a company from including additional information derived from its annual accounts and reports.

[*CA 2006, ss 426(1) (2) (4), 427(3), 428(3); SI 2013 No 1970, Regs 9, 10, 11; SI 2013 No 1973, Reg 4*].

**Offences.** In case of a failure to comply with the requirements to prepare a strategic report, an offence is committed by every person who was a director of the company immediately before the end of the period for filing accounts and reports for the financial year in question and failed to take all reasonable steps for securing compliance with that requirement. A person guilty of such an offence is liable, on summary conviction, to a fine not exceeding the statutory maximum and on conviction on indictment to a fine. See **29.1** OFFENCES AND LEGAL PROCEEDINGS.

## 6.1 Accounts: Stand-alone Strategic Reports

*[CA 2006, s 414A(5) (6); SI 2013 No 1970, Reg 3]*

**Defective strategic reports.** See **20.23–20.28** for details of the provisions on the revision of defective strategic reports.


## 6.2 CONDITIONS FOR SENDING OUT A STAND-ALONE STRATEGIC REPORT

A company may not send a copy of its strategic report and supplementary material to any person within **6.1** in the following circumstances.

- It is prohibited from doing because

    (i)    of any relevant provision of its constitution, or

    (ii)   in the case of a debenture-holder, a relevant provision in any instrument constituting or otherwise governing any of the company's debentures of which that person is a holder or

    (iii)  in the case of any such person (whether or not a debenture holder ) where it is prohibited from sending a summary financial statement to any such person by any relevant provision of its constitution.

- Where, in relation to the financial year in question, no auditor's report has been made in respect of

    (i)    the annual accounts of the company under *CA 2006, s 495*;

    (ii)   the strategic report (if any) and the directors' report under *CA 2006, s 496*; or

    (iii)  the auditable part of the directors' remuneration report (where relevant) under *CA 2006, 497*.

- Where, in relation to the financial year, the period for filing accounts and reports for that year under *CA 2006, s 442* (see **2.12** ACCOUNTS: GENERAL) has expired.

- Where the strategic report in respect of that financial year has not been approved by the board of directors and the original statement has not been signed on behalf of the board by a director of the company.

- Where it has not ascertained the wishes of that person under **6.3**.

    *[SI 2013 No 1973, Reg 5; SI 2013 No 1970, Schedule, para 21]*.


## 6.3 Ascertainment of wishes

A company may not send a copy of the strategic report with supplementary material to any person within **6.1** unless it has ascertained that the person does not wish to receive copies of its full accounts and reports. In ascertaining this:

- Where such a person has expressly notified the company either

    (i)    that he wishes to receive copies of the full accounts and reports, or

    (ii)   that he wishes, instead of copies of those documents, to receive a copy of the strategic report with supplementary information

    the company must send copies of the full accounts and reports or copies of the strategic report with supplementary material, as appropriate, to that person in respect of the financial years to which the notification applies.

For these purposes, a notification has effect in relation to a financial year if it relates to that year (whether or not it has been given at the invitation of the company) and if it has been received by the company not later than 28 days before the first date on which copies of the full accounts and reports for that year are sent out to the person specified in **6.1**.

• Where there has been no such express notification to the company by such a person, that person may be taken to have elected to receive a strategic report with supplementary information if he fails to respond to an opportunity to elect to receive copies of the full accounts and reports given to him either

(i)    by a consultation notice under **6.4**, or

(ii)   as part of a relevant consultation of his wishes by the company under **6.5**.

The company communications provisions (see **16.23** DEALINGS WITH THIRD PARTIES) apply to any notice or other communication required or authorised to be sent to or by the company under the above provisions.

[*SI 2013 No 1973, Reg 6*].

## 6.4   Consultation by notice

A consultation notice is notice given by a company to a person within **6.1** (or a person who is entitled to become such a person but who has not yet become one) which complies with the following requirements.

• It must state that for the future, so long as he is such a person he will be sent a copy of the strategic report with supplementary material for each financial year instead of a copy of the company's full accounts and reports, unless he notifies the company that he wishes to receive full accounts and reports.

• It must be accompanied by a card or form so worded as to enable the person to notify the company (by marking a box and returning the card or form) that he wishes to receive full accounts and reports for the next financial year for which he is entitled to receive them and for all future financial years thereafter.

If sent by post, any postage for the return of the card or form has been or will be paid by the company unless the address of a person concerned is not within an EEA State (see APPENDIX 1 DEFINITIONS).

• It must state that the card or form accompanying the notice must be returned by a date set out in the notice, being a date at least 21 days after service of the notice and not less than 28 days before the first date on which copies of the full accounts and reports for the next financial year for which that person is entitled to receive them are sent out.

• It must include a statement in a prominent position to the effect that a copy of the strategic report with supplementary material will not contain sufficient information to allow as full an understanding of the results and state of affairs of the company or group as would be provided by the full annual accounts and reports and that persons requiring more detailed information have the right to obtain, free of charge, a copy of the company's last full accounts and reports.

The company communications provisions (see **16.23** DEALINGS WITH THIRD PARTIES) apply to any notice or other communication required or authorised to be sent to or by the company under the above provisions.

[*SI 2013 No 1973, Regs 7, 9*].

## 6.5 Accounts: Stand-alone Strategic Reports

### 6.5 Relevant consultation

A company may conduct a 'relevant consultation' to ascertain the wishes of a person within 6.1 or a person who is entitled to become such a person but who has not yet become one.

For these purposes, a *'relevant consultation'* of the wishes of such a person is a notice given to that person which complies with the following requirements.

- It states that for the future, so long as he is a such a person, he will be sent a copy of the strategic report with supplementary material instead of the full accounts and reports of the company, unless he notifies the company that he wishes to continue to receive full accounts and reports.

- It accompanies a copy of the full accounts and reports.

- It accompanies a copy of the strategic report with supplementary material for the same financial year covered by those full accounts and reports and which is identified in the notice as an example of the document which that person will receive for the future, so long as he is a such a person, unless he notifies the company to the contrary.

- It is accompanied by a card or form so worded as to enable the person to notify the company (by marking a box and returning the card or form) that he wishes to receive full accounts and reports for the next financial year for which he is entitled to receive them and for all future financial years after that.

   If sent by post, any postage for the return of the card or form must be paid by the company unless the address of a person concerned is not within an EEA State (see APPENDIX 1 DEFINITIONS).

The company communications provisions (see **16.23** DEALINGS WITH THIRD PARTIES) apply to any notice or other communication required or authorised to be sent to or by the company under the above provisions.

[*SI 2013 No 1973, Regs 8, 9*].

### 6.6 FORM AND CONTENT OF A STAND-ALONE STRATEGIC REPORT WITH SUPPLEMENTARY MATERIAL

The purpose of the strategic report is to inform members of the company and help them assess how the directors have performed their duty under *CA 2006, s 172* (Duty to promote the success of the company) (see **18.24**). The strategic report must:

- contain a fair review of the company's business ie a balanced and comprehensive analysis of the development and performance of the company's business during the financial year and the position of the business at the end of that year

- contain a description of the principal risks and uncertainties facing the company

- to the extent necessary for an understanding of the development, performance or position of the company's business include analysis using key performance indicators and where appropriate analysis using other key performance indicators including information relating to environmental and employee matters. For these purposes 'key performance indicators' means factors by reference to which the development, performance or position of the company's business can be measured effectively. If a company qualifies as a medium-sized company in relation to a financial year (see **4** ACCOUNTS: MEDIUM-SIZED COMPANIES), the strategic report for that year does not need to comply with this requirement so far as it relates to non-financial information.

- where appropriate include references to, and additional explanations of, amounts included in the company's annual accounts

- contain such of the matters otherwise required by regulations made under CA 2006 s 416(4) to be disclosed in the directors' report as the directors consider are of strategic importance to the company

The company is not required to disclose information in the strategic report about impending developments or matters in the course of negotiation if the disclosure would, in the opinion of the directors, be seriously prejudicial to the interests of the company.

For further information on the contents and signing of strategic reports, and on the relationship between the strategic and directors' report, see **20 STRATEGIC REPORTS AND DIRECTORS' REPORTS.**

For periods beginning on or after 1 January 2019, the *Companies (Miscellaneous Reporting) Regulations 2018, SI 2018 No 860*, amend *CA 2006* to require directors to include in the strategic report a clearly identifiable statement explaining how they have had regard to the matters specified in *CA 2006, s 172* (see **20.8** for further details).

The FCA Listing Rules require any strategic report with supplementary information issued by a listed company to disclose earnings per share in addition to the contents specified in the legislation.

**Supplementary material.** The supplementary material referred to in *CA 2006, s 426A* must:

- Contain a statement that the strategic report is only a part of the company's annual accounts and reports

- State how a person entitled to them can obtain a full copy of the company's annual report and accounts

- State whether the auditor's report on the annual accounts was unqualified or qualified and, if the latter, set out the report in full together with any further material needed to understand the qualification.

- State whether, in that auditor's report, the auditor's statements under *CA 2006, s 496* (whether strategic report and the directors' report consistent with the accounts see **8.36 AUDIT**) was qualified or unqualified and, if qualified, set out the qualified statement in full together with any further material needed to understand the qualification.

- In the case of a quoted company contain a copy of that part of the directors' remuneration report which sets out the single total figure table in respect of the company's directors' remuneration in accordance with the requirements of SI 2008 No 410 Schedule 8 (as amended)

[*CA 2006, s 426A; SI 2013 No 1970, Reg 12*].

## 6.7    Additional issues to consider

Section 9 of the July 2018 version of the Financial Reporting Council document 'Guidance on the Strategic Report' (available from www.frc.org.uk) highlights a number of issues that companies may need to consider when taking advantage of the option to issue just a strategic report with supplementary material. These include:

(a)    the legislation requires the complete strategic report, as it appears in the annual report , to be sent out – sending out a summarised version or extracts from the report will not be sufficient to comply with the legislative requirements;

(b)   any required disclosures that are included in the strategic report by cross-reference to another part of the annual report must also be sent out with the stand-alone strategic report;

(c)   if the strategic report signposts or otherwise refers to complementary information provided elsewhere in the annual report, it may be appropriate for the directors to clarify that this is not included as part of the document that has been sent out.

# 7   Annual Returns/Confirmation Statements

**Background.** As from 30 June 2016 the duty to deliver an annual return has been replaced by the duty to deliver a "confirmation statement". The provisions which applied before that date, set out in paras **7.1–7.4** continue to apply to annual returns to be made up to a return date before 30 June 2016.

## 7.1   DUTY TO DELIVER

An annual return (or, now, a confirmation statement) is a snapshot of general information about such matters as a company's directors, registered office address, shareholders and share capital. There are different requirements for shareholder details and the company's principal business activities (SIC codes) depending on whether the annual return is made up to 30 September 2011 or 1 October 2011 or later. Companies House sends a letter to the company's registered office reminding the company when it's annual return is due and advising how to file the return. See **7.3**.

Every company must deliver successive annual returns to the Registrar of Companies. Each such return must contain all the required information in **7.2** and be submitted to the Registrar of Companies within 28 days of the date to which it is made up. A filing fee is payable. See APPENDIX 3 COMPANIES HOUSE FEES.

The return must be made up to a date not later than:

•   in the case of a new company, the anniversary of incorporation; or

•   in any other case, the anniversary of the previous return.

[*CA 2006, s 854*].

## 7.2   CONTENTS OF ANNUAL RETURNS

Every annual return must state the date to which it is made up and contain the following information.

(a)   Name, registered number and address of the company's registered office and the address (single alternate inspection location (SAIL)) where the company keeps certain records if they are not kept at the registered office. See **36.2**.

(b)   Business. Its principal business activities as described by SIC 2007 which is the UK Standard Industrial Classification of Economic Activities. This is available from the gov.uk website.

## 7.2 Annual Returns/Confirmation Statements

(c)    The type of company it is according to the following classifications.

        T1    Public limited company

        T2    Private company limited by shares

        T3    Private company limited by guarantee

        T4    Private company limited by shares exempt from the requirement to use 'limited' as part of its name

        T5    Private company limited by guarantee exempt from the requirement to use 'limited' as part of its name

        T6    Private unlimited company with share capital

        T7    Private unlimited company without share capital

(d)    Directors.

    (i)    where the director is an individual, the particulars required by *CA 2006, s 163* to be entered in the register of directors (except that the former name of a director is required in relation to an annual return only if the director was known by the name for business purposes during the period covered by the return); and

    (ii)    where the director is a body corporate or a firm that is a legal person under the law by which it is governed, the particulars required by *CA 2006, s 164* to be entered in the register of directors.

See **38.3 R**EGISTERS for *CA 2006, ss 163, 164.*

(e)    Company Secretary. In the case of a private company with a secretary or a public company,

    (i)    where the secretary is an individual, the particulars required by *CA 2006, s 277* to be entered in the register of secretaries (except that the former name of a secretary is required in relation to an annual return only if the secretary was known by the name for business purposes during the period covered by the return); and

    (ii)    where the secretary is a body corporate or a firm that is a legal person under the law by which it is governed, the particulars required by *CA 2006, s 278(1)* to be entered in the register of directors.

See **38.6 R**EGISTERS for *CA 2006, ss 277, 278(1).*

Where all the partners in a firm are joint secretaries, the required particulars are those that would be required to be entered in the register of secretaries if the firm were a legal person and the firm had been appointed secretary.

(f)    Company Records. If any company records are kept at a place other than the company's registered office, the address of that place (the single alternative inspection location (SAIL) and the records that are kept there.

(g)    Traded Company. If the return is made up to 30 September 2011 whether the company was a 'traded company' at any time during the period covered by the return. If the return is made up to 1 October 2011 or later, whether the company's shares have been admitted to trading on a "relevant market" at any time during the return period.

A '*traded company*' is a company any of whose shares are shares admitted to trading on a regulated market (so that a '*non-traded company*' means a company none of whose shares are admitted to trading on a regulated market). For these purposes an AIM company is not a 'traded company'. '*Relevant market*' is one of the current UK recognised investment exchanges and regulated markets found on the FCA Financial Services register.

(h)     Details of share capital. In the case of a company having a share capital, a statement of capital stating with respect to the company's share capital at the date to which the return is made up:

(i)     The total number of shares of the company.

(ii)    The aggregate nominal value of those shares.

(iii)   For each class of shares

- the voting rights attached to the shares;

- the total number of shares of that class; and

- the aggregate nominal value of shares of that class; and

(iv)    The amount paid up and the amount (if any) unpaid on each share (whether on account of the nominal value of the share or by way of premium). If a company has converted shares into stock, it must give the corresponding information in relation to that stock, stating the amount of stock instead of the number and nominal value of the shares.

Where a return to be made up to a return date before 30 June 2016 is delivered to the Registrar of Companies on or after that date, the statement of capital must state with respect to the company's share capital at the return date

(i)     The total number of shares of the company.

(ii)    The aggregate nominal value of those shares.

(iii)   The aggregate amount (if any) unpaid on those shares (whether on account of their nominal value or by way of premium).

(iv)    For each class of shares

- prescribed particulars of the rights attached to the shares;

- the total number of shares of that class; and

- the aggregate nominal value of shares of that class.

(i)     *Shares and shareholdings Private and Non-traded public companies (or for returns made up to 1 October 2011 or later a company whose shares have not been admitted to trading on a "relevant market" (see above for the meaning)).* If the company was a private or a non-traded public company throughout the period covered by the return, the company has to provide a "full list" of shareholders ie the information in (i)–(iv) in the first annual return following incorporation and in every third annual return after the company has provided a full list. The intervening two annual returns only need to report any changes during that year ie shares transferred and details of people who have become or ceased to be shareholders.

(i)     The name (as it appears in the company's register of members) of every person who was a member or joint member of the company at the made-up date.

To enable the entries relating to any given person to be easily found, either the entries must be listed in alphabetical order by name or the return must have annexed to it an index that is sufficient to enable the name of the person in question to be easily found. Joint shareholders should be listed consecutively. Companies House recommends that private and non-traded public companies with a large number of shareholders may find it more convenient to provide a full list of shareholders with each annual return but in that case the list must not include the shareholders' addresses. Companies that file paper returns may provide this information on a CD Rom if the list is 50 pages or more.

(ii) The name of every person who became or ceased to be a shareholder or joint shareholder during the period covered by the return (or in the case of a first return since the incorporation of the company).

(iii) The number of shares of each class held by each shareholder at the made up date.

(iv) The date of registration and the number of shares of each class transferred by each shareholder or past shareholder during the period covered by the return (or in the case of the first return since the date of incorporation of the company).

Shareholder addresses must not be included on paper returns or the form will be returned to the company.

(j) *Shares and Shareholdings—Traded companies/shares traded on a "relevant market".* If the company was a traded public company at any time during the period covered by the return, the following information must be given for returns made up to 30 September 2011 or earlier.

(i) The name and address (as they appear on the company's register of members) of every shareholder or joint holder who held at least 5% of the issued shares of any class of the company at any time during the period covered by the return.

To enable the entries relating to any given person to be easily found, *either* the entries must be listed alphabetical order by name *or* the return must have annexed to it an index that is sufficient to enable the name of the person in question to be easily found. Joint shareholders should be listed consecutively.

(ii) The number of shares of each class held at the end of the date to which the return is made up.

(iii) The number of shares of each class transferred during the period coved by the return by or to each person who held at least 5% of the issued shares of any class of the company at any time during the period covered by the return.

(iv) The dates of registration of those transfers.

If either of the two immediately preceding annual returns has given the full particulars required by (i)–(iv) above, the return need only give such particulars as relate to

• persons who came to hold, or ceased to hold, at least 5% of the issued shares of any class of the company during the period covered by the return; and

• shares transferred during that period.

If the company's shares were admitted to trading on a relevant market (see above) at any time during the period covered by the return, the following information must be given for returns made up to 1 October 2011 or later.

The names and addresses (as they appear on the company's register of members) of every person or joint holder who hold 5% or more of the company's issued share capital of any class of the company as at the made-up date of the return. There is an exception for a company whose shares were admitted to trading on a relevant market throughout the period covered by the return and which were subject to the Vote Holder and Issuer Notification Rules in Chapter 5 of the FCA Disclosure and Transparency Rules. See 33 PUBLIC AND LISTED COMPANIES for references to those Rules. In this case shareholder details (ie other than their names and addresses) do not have to be provided.

For shareholders who hold less than 5% of the company's issued share capital of any class,

(i)     Returns made up to 30 September 2011 or earlier- no details must be given of members who hold or continue to hold less than 5% of shares of any class during the return period.

(ii)    Returns made up to 1 October 2011 or later – the names and addresses of members who held less than 5% of the company's issued share capital at the made up date of the return must not be given. If a company shares were subject to the FCA Disclosure and Transparency Rules no shareholder details are required.

Companies with a class of shares that are traded and a class of shares that are not traded.

(i)     Returns made up to 30 September 2011 or earlier – if shares are traded on a regulated market during the period of the annual return, the box marked "traded" on the annual return must be ticked and on paper annual returns Schedule B must be completed for all classes of shares whether or not that class of shares is traded.

(ii)    Returns made up to 1 October 2011 or later – if shares have been traded on a relevant market at any time during the period covered by the return, for each person who held at least 5% of the issued shares of any class of the company at the made-up date of the return, the annual return must show the person's name and address (as they appear in the company's register of members) and the number of shares of each class held by the person at that time. The entries must be listed in alphabetical order by name or an index must be annexed to the return that is sufficient to enable the name of the person to be easily found.

[*CA 2006, ss 855, 855A, 856, 856A, 856B; SI 2008 No 3000, Regs 2–7, Schs 1, 2; SI 2011 No 1487*].

Companies House will reject the annual return if it does not include all the above required information. If the information is completed but does not match their records Companies House may accept the annual return but mark it 'inconsistent with the public register'. If you need any further help see Companies House guide GP6 Registrar's Rules and Powers.

**Non-disclosure of subsidiaries in the accounts.** In relation to financial years beginning on or after 6 April 2008, a company need not disclose full particulars of all its subsidiaries in its annual accounts if it would result in a statement of excessive length. In such a case, it must annex the full information required (ie both that which has been disclosed in the notes to the accounts and that which has not) in the next annual return following the approval of the accounts in question. See **3.36 ACCOUNTS: LARGE COMPANIES** for full details.

[*CA 2006, ss 410(3)*].

## 7.3 METHOD OF FILING

Annual returns may be delivered electronically using Companies House Software Filing or Webfiling services. For more information, see the Companies House website at:

www.companieshouse.gov.uk

If the company does not have the facility to file online, it can download a hard copy form AR01 which can be completed and delivered by hand (personally or by courier), including outside office hours, bank holidays and weekends to the Registrar at Cardiff or Edinburgh (see below) or London. Companies which file paper returns may provide shareholder information on a CD-ROM if the list is 50 pages or more.

Alternatively, the completed hard copy annual return can also be sent by post, by DX or (in Scotland) by LP to

*For companies incorporated in England and Wales*

Companies House
Crown Way
Cardiff CF14 3UZ

DX33050 Cardiff 1 (Documents Exchange Service)

*For companies incorporated in Scotland:*

Companies House
4th Floor
Edinburgh Quay 2
139 Fountainbridge
Edinburgh EH1 9FF

DX ED235 Edinburgh 1 (Documents Exchange Service)

LP–4 Edinburgh 2 (Legal Post)

Companies House
4 Abbey Orchard Street
Westminster
London SW1P 2HT

Documents are only acknowledged if a copy of the covering letter and a prepaid addressed return envelope are provided.

**Additional security for directors' and registered office addresses and shareholder details (Companies House PROOF system). Electronic delivery of directors' details and registered office address.** Companies House offers companies a free, fully electronic and secure system for notifying changes of directors, changes to the registered office address and annual returns. If a company opts to notify these electronically, it (or its authorised agents) will need a company authentication code and Companies House will not accept notices from the company delivered in any other format. The service is voluntary and the company may opt-out at any time. Companies House will then revert to accepting notices from the company delivered electronically or on paper returns.

**Change of information**: The annual return should confirm the information already held by Companies House but if any of the following specific information needs to be changed the relevant forms must also be sent (either electronically as above or in hard copy). The following changes have to be notified separately:

- change of registered office (Form AD01);

- appointment of company director or secretary (Forms AP01, AP02, AP03 or AP04);

- change of details of director or secretary (Form CH01. CH02, CH03 or CH04);

- termination of appointment of director or secretary (Form TM01 or TM02);

- notification of address or change of address where company records are available for inspection (SAIL) (Form AD02). If a SAIL notification has been given, the annual return will need to show the SAIL address;

- notification of company records held at an alternate address or if they are being returned to the registered office (Form AD0301 or AD04);

- allotment of new shares (Form SH01);

- change to the company's total share capital.

(Companies House Guidance GP2 Life of a Company – Part 1 Annual Requirements Annual Return, Chapter 1, para 5).

## 7.4    FAILURE TO DELIVER ANNUAL RETURN

If a company fails to deliver a fully completed annual return within the 28 days allowed, an offence is committed by

- the company,

- subject to below, every director (including shadow director, see **18.1** DIRECTORS) of the company and, in the case of a private company with a secretary or a public company, every secretary of the company; and

- every other officer of the company who is in default.

A person guilty of such an offence is liable, on summary conviction, to a fine not exceeding level 5 on the standard scale and, for continued contravention, a daily default fine not exceeding one-tenth of level 5 on the standard scale until such time as the return is delivered. See **29.1** OFFENCES AND LEGAL PROCEEDINGS for the standard scale. It is a defence for a director or secretary to show that he took all reasonable steps to avoid the commission or continuation of the offence. It is not a defence that another person was required to make the return (*Gibson v Barton* (1875) LR 10 QB 329).

In the case of continued contravention, an offence is also committed by every officer of the company who did not commit an offence in relation to the initial contravention but is in default in relation to the continued contravention. A person guilty of such an offence is liable, on summary conviction, to a fine not exceeding one-tenth of the greater of £5,000 or level 4 on the standard scale for each day on which the contravention continues and he is in default.

[*CA 2006, s 858; SI 2008 No 3000, Reg 8; SI 2015 No 664, Sch 3*].

See also **39.16** REGISTRAR OF COMPANIES for the Registrar's powers of enforcement.

## 7.5 Annual Returns/Confirmation Statements

### 7.5 ANNUAL CONFIRMATION STATEMENTS

As from 30 June 2016 the requirement to deliver an annual return has been replaced by the duty to deliver a confirmation statement. Every company must, before the end of the period of 14 days after the end of each "review period", deliver to the Registrar of Companies such information as is necessary to ensure that the company is able to make a "confirmation statement".

For the purpose of making a confirmation statement, a company is entitled to assume that any information has been properly delivered to the Registrar if it has been delivered within the period of five days ending with the date on which the statement is delivered. This does not apply where the company has received notice from the Registrar that such information has not been properly delivered.

The confirmation statement confirms that all information required to be delivered by the company to the Registrar in relation to the "confirmation period" concerned under any of the duties set out below either

(i)      has been delivered; or

(ii)     is being delivered at the same time as the confirmation statement.

The duties are

•        any duty to notify a relevant event (see **7.7** below); or

•        any duty under *CA 2006, ss 853C–853I* (see **7.8–7.14**).

**Transitional provision.** Any reference in *CA 2006, 853A* to a "review period" is to be read as including the period of 12 months beginning with the day after the company's last return date.

[*SBEE 2015, s 92; CA 2006, s 853A; SI 2016 No 321, Reg 6, Schedule, para 8*].

### 7.6   Definitions

"Confirmation period"

(a)      in relation to a company's first confirmation statement, means the period beginning with the day of the company's incorporation and ending with the date specified in the statement (the "confirmation date"); and

(b)      in relation to any other confirmation statement of a company, means the period beginning with the day after the confirmation date of the last such statement and ending with the confirmation date of the confirmation statement concerned.

The confirmation date of a confirmation statement must be no later than the last day of the review period concerned.

"Review period" means

(a)      the period of 12 months beginning with the day of the company's incorporation; and

(b)      each period of 12 months beginning with the day after the end of the previous review period.

Any reference to a review period includes the period of 12 months beginning with the day after the company's last return date.

Where a company delivers a confirmation statement with a confirmation date which is earlier than the last day of the review period concerned, the next review period is the period of 12 months beginning with the day after the confirmation date.

[*SBEE 2015, s 92; CA 2006, s 853A; SI 2016 No 321, Reg 6*].

## 7.7    Duties to notify a relevant event

The following duties are duties to notify a relevant event

- the duty to give notice of a change in the address of the company's registered office;

- in the case of a company in respect of which an election is in force under *CA 2006, s 128B* (election to keep membership information on central register), the duty to deliver anything as mentioned in *CA 2006, s 128E*;

- the duty to give notice of a change as mentioned in *CA 2006, s 167* (change in directors or in particulars required to be included in register of directors or register of directors' residential addresses);

- in the case of a company in respect of which an election is in force under CA 2006, s 167A (election to keep information in register of directors or register of directors' residential addresses on central register), the duty to deliver anything as mentioned in *CA 2006, s 167D*;

- in the case of a private company with a secretary or a public company, the duty to give notice of a change as mentioned in *CA 2006, s 276* (change in secretary or joint secretaries or in particulars required to be included in register of secretaries);

- in the case of a private company with a secretary in respect of which an election is in force under *CA 2006, s 279A* (election to keep information in register of secretaries on central register), the duty to deliver anything as mentioned in *CA 2006, s 279D*;

- in the case of a company in respect of which an election is in force under *CA 2006, s 790X* (election to keep information in PSC register on central register), the duty to deliver anything as mentioned in *CA 2006, s 790ZA*; and

- in the case of a company which, in accordance with regulations under *CA 2006, s 1136*, keeps any company records at a place other than its registered office, any duty under the regulations to give notice of a change in the address of that place.

[*SBEE 2015, s 92; CA 2006, s 853B; SI 2016 No 321, Reg 6*].

## 7.8    Duty to notify a change in company's principal business activities

Where a company makes a confirmation statement, and there has been a change in the company's principal business activities during the confirmation period concerned, the company must give notice to the Registrar of the change at the same time as it delivers the confirmation statement.

The information as to the company's new principal business activities may be given by reference to one or more categories of any prescribed system of classifying business activities (see **7.2**).

[*SBEE 2015, s 92; CA 2006, s 853C; SI 2016 No 321, Reg 6*].

## 7.9 Annual Returns/Confirmation Statements

### 7.9 Duty to deliver statement of capital

Where a company having a share capital makes a confirmation statement, the company must deliver a statement of capital to the Registrar at the same time as it delivers the confirmation statement. This requirement does not apply if there has been no change in any of the matters required to be dealt with by the statement of capital since the last such statement was delivered to the Registrar.

The statement of capital must state with respect to the company's share capital at the confirmation date

(i)     the total number of shares of the company;

(ii)    the aggregate nominal value of those shares; and

(iii)   the aggregate amount (if any) unpaid on those shares (whether on account of their nominal value or by way of premium).

For each class of shares

(i)     prescribed particulars of the rights attached to the shares;

(ii)    the total number of shares of that class; and

(iii)   the aggregate nominal value of shares of that class.

[*SBEE 2015, s 92; CA 2006, s 853D; SI 2016 No 321, Reg 6*].

### 7.10 Duty to notify trading status of shares

Where a company having a share capital makes a confirmation statement, the company must deliver a statement to the Registrar dealing with the following matters at the same time as it delivers the confirmation statement

- whether any of the company's shares were, at any time during the confirmation period concerned, shares admitted to trading on a relevant market or on any other market which is outside the United Kingdom; and

- if so, whether both of the conditions below were satisfied throughout the confirmation period concerned.

The conditions are that

- there were shares of the company which were shares admitted to trading on a relevant market; and

- the company was a DTR5 issuer.

In this part

- "DTR5 issuer" means an issuer to which Chapter 5 of the Disclosure Rules and Transparency Rules sourcebook made by the Financial Conduct Authority (as amended or replaced from time to time) applies; and

- "relevant market" means any of the markets mentioned in Article 4(1) of the Financial Services and Markets Act 2000 (Prescribed Markets and Qualifying Investments) Order 2001.

  The company is not required to deliver the above statement if and to the extent that the last statement delivered to the Registrar under this section applies equally to the confirmation period concerned.

**Transitional provision.** The reference in the above to the "last confirmation statement" is to be read as including the last annual return delivered in accordance with CA 2006.

[*SBEE 2015, s 92; CA 2006, s 853E; SI 2016 No 321, Reg 6, Schedule, para 9*].

### 7.11    Duty to deliver shareholder information: non-traded companies

Where

(a)    a non-traded company makes a confirmation statement; and

(b)    there is no election in force under *CA 2006, s 128B* (election to keep certain information on the central register – (see **38.2**)) in respect of the company, the company must deliver the following information to the Registrar at the same time as it delivers the confirmation statement. The information is

- the name (as it appears in the company's register of members) of every person who was at any time during the confirmation period a member of the company;

- the number of shares of each class held at the end of the confirmation date concerned by each person who was a member of the company at that time;

- the number of shares of each class transferred during the confirmation period concerned by or to each person who was a member of the company at any time during that period; and

- the dates of registration of those transfers.

The duty to deliver the information does not apply if and to the extent that the information most recently delivered to the Registrar under this section applies equally to the confirmation period concerned.

A "non-traded company" is a company none of whose shares were, at any time during the confirmation period concerned, shares admitted to trading on a relevant market or on any other market which is outside the United Kingdom.

**Transitional provision.** The reference in the above to the "information most recently delivered" is to be read as including information in the last annual return delivered in accordance with CA 2006.

[*SBEE 2015, s 92; CA 2006, s 853F; SI 2016 No 321, Reg 6, Schedule, para 10*].

### 7.12    Duty to deliver shareholder information: certain traded companies

Where a traded company makes a confirmation statement, the company must deliver the following information to the Registrar at the same time as it delivers the confirmation statement. The information is

- the name and address (as they appear in the company's register of members) of each person who, at the end of the confirmation date concerned, held at least 5% of the issued shares of any class of the company; and

- the number of shares of each class held by each such person at that time.

This does not apply if and to the extent the information most recently delivered to the Registrar under this section applies equally to the confirmation period concerned.

A "traded company" is a company any of whose shares were, at any time during the confirmation period concerned, shares admitted to trading on a relevant market or on any other market which is outside the United Kingdom.

But a company is not a traded company if throughout the confirmation period concerned

- there were shares of the company which were shares admitted to trading on a relevant market; and

- the company was a DTR5 issuer.

**Transitional provision.** The reference in the above to the "information most recently delivered" is to be read as including information in the last annual return delivered in accordance with CA 2006.

[*SBEE 2015, s 92; CA 2006, s 853G; SI 2016 No 321, Reg 6, Schedule, para 10*].

## 7.13 Duty to deliver information about exemption from CA 2006, Part 21A

Where a company which is not a DTR5 issuer, and to which *CA 2006, Part 21A* does not apply (information about people with significant control (see s **38.18**)), makes a confirmation statement, the company must deliver to the Registrar a statement of the fact that it is a company to which *CA 2006, Part 21A* does not apply at the same time as it delivers the confirmation statement.

This does not apply if the last statement delivered to the registrar under this section applies equally to the confirmation period concerned.

[*SBEE 2015, s 92; CA 2006, s 853H; SI 2016 No 321, Reg 6*].

## 7.14 Duty to deliver information about people with significant control

Where a company to which *CA 2006, Part 21A* (information about people with significant control) applies makes a confirmation statement, and there is no election in force under *CA 2006, s 790X* (right to elect to keep information on the central register) in respect of the company, the company must deliver the information stated in its PSC register to the Registrar at the same time as it delivers the confirmation statement.

This does not apply if and to the extent that the information most recently delivered to the registrar under this section applies equally to the confirmation period concerned.

"PSC register" has the same meaning as in *CA 2006, Part 21A* (see **38.18**). See **38** REGISTERS for more details on the PSC regime.

[*SBEE 2015, s 92; CA 2006, s 853I; SI 2016 No 321, Reg 6*].

## 7.15 *Failure to deliver confirmation statement*

If a company fails to deliver a confirmation statement before the end of the period of 14 days after the end of a review period an offence is committed by

- the company;

- subject to below, every director (including shadow director, see **18.1** Directors) of the company and in the case of a private company with a secretary or a public company, every secretary of the company; and

- every other officer of the company who is in default.

A person guilty of such an offence is liable, on summary conviction, in England and Wales to a fine, and, for continued contravention, a daily default fine not exceeding the greater of £500 and one-tenth of level 4 on the standard scale and in Scotland or Northern Ireland, to a fine not exceeding level 5 on the standard scale and, for continued contravention, a daily default fine not exceeding one-tenth of level 5 on the standard scale. See 29.1 Offences and Legal Proceedings for the standard scale. It is a defence for a director or secretary to prove that he took all reasonable steps to avoid the commission or continuation of the offence.

The contravention continues until such time as a confirmation statement specifying a confirmation date no later than the last day of the review period concerned is delivered by the company to the registrar.

In the case of continued contravention, an offence is also committed by every officer of the company who did not commit an offence in relation to the initial contravention but who is in default in relation to the continued contravention. A person guilty of such an offence is liable on summary conviction in England and Wales, to a fine not exceeding the greater of £500 and one-tenth of level 4 on the standard scale for each day on which the contravention continues and the person is in default and in Scotland or Northern Ireland, to a fine not exceeding one-tenth of level 5 on the standard scale for each day on which the contravention continues and the person is in default.

*[CA 2006, s 853A–853L; SBEE 2015, s 92; SI 2016 No 321, Reg 6].*

# 8 Audit

**Cross-references.** See **6.6** ACCOUNTS: STAND-ALONE STRATEGIC REPORTS for disclosures in respect of the auditor's report in a strategic report with supplementary information; **22.4** DISTRIBUTIONS for report when qualified accounts are relevant for the purposes of a proposed distribution; **34.13** PURCHASE OF OWN SHARES for report when a private company wishes to redeem or purchase its own shares out of capital; **41.4** RE-REGISTRATION for report when a private company wishes to re-register as a public company.

The *Companies Act 2006 (Strategic Report and Directors' Report) Regulations 2013* ("the *2013 Regulations*") which are referred to in this chapter, brought into force the requirement for a company to produce a strategic report for financial years ending on or after 30 September 2013.

## 8.1 Audit

Significant changes are made to audit requirements for periods beginning on or after 17 June 2016 by the *Statutory Auditors and Third Country Auditors Regulations 2016 (SI 2016 No 649)*, which introduce into UK legislation new obligations under Directive 2014/56/EU. The key points are summarised at 8.1 and the details are incorporated into the relevant section of this chapter.

### 8.1 IMPACT OF RECENT EU AUDIT CHANGES

Following a lengthy period of consultation and debate, significant amendments to the EU Statutory Audit Directive, together with a new Regulation (*Regulation EU 537/2014*), were approved in 2014. Member States were required to transpose the amending Directive (*Directive 2014/56/EU*) into their national law by 17 June 2016 and the requirements of the Regulation generally apply from the same date. Key changes to the Directive include

(a)  considerable expansion of the detailed requirements on independence;

(b)  expansion of the detailed requirements in respect of group audits, with more emphasis on the group auditor bearing full responsibility for the audit report and, where applicable, the additional report to the audit committee (see below);

(c)  the addition of detailed requirements on the form and content of the auditor's report;

(d)  a prohibition on contractual clauses that restrict the choice of auditor, with any existing clauses becoming null and void;

(e)  a new requirement that, in the case of a public-interest entity, shareholders representing 5% or more of the voting rights or of the share capital, and certain other bodies, including the competent authorities, must be able to bring a claim before the national court for dismissal of the auditor where there are proper grounds for this; and

(f)  expanded requirements on the constitution and role of the audit committee of a public-interest entity.

The new Regulation applies only to the statutory audit of public interest entities but key changes include the following

(a)  the auditor is prohibited from providing a wide range of non-audit services to an audited entity;

(b)  the audit committee can assess whether other non-audit services should be provided by the auditor but if they are provided for three or more consecutive years, the total fees for those services must be limited to no more than 70% of the average of the fees paid for the statutory audit of the company (or, where relevant, the group) over the last three consecutive years;

(c)  more detailed requirements on the content of the auditor's report;

(d)  the auditor must submit an additional report to the audit committee explaining the results of the audit and including as a minimum the content specified in the Regulation:

(e)  a specific process must be followed where a new auditor is to be appointed;

(f)  an auditor cannot continue in office for more than ten years in total, and cannot be reappointed until a further period of four years has elapsed – however, Member States have the option to extend the maximum period to 20 years where a public tendering is conducted and to 24 years where joint auditors are appointed (the competent authority may also grant an extension of up to two years in exceptional circumstances); and

(g)     key audit partners must not serve for more than seven years, and cannot participate in the audit again until a further three years have elapsed.

The *Statutory Auditors and Third Country Auditors Regulations 2016 (SI 2016 No 649)* generally come into force on 17 June 2016 and establish the Financial Reporting Council (FRC) as the competent authority for the purposes of the Directive. They also amend *CA 2006* and other relevant legislation to implement the new requirements for periods beginning on or after 17 June 2016. The changes are explained in more detail in the relevant paragraphs below.

In conjunction with the changes, the FRC revised the UK Corporate Governance Code (see **15 CORPORATE GOVERNANCE**) and its related 'Guidance on Audit Committees', issued a new Ethical Standard and revised UK auditing standards. All of these changes apply for periods beginning on or after 17 June 2016. The Code was revised again in July 2018, with this version applying for periods beginning on or after 1 January 2019.

## 8.2    APPOINTMENT OF AUDITOR

Every company must appoint an auditor or auditors except where exemption from audit applies (see **8.29** to **8.35**). Different requirements apply, depending on whether the company is a private company or a public company, and on whether or not it is a public interest entity (PIE). For these purposes, a PIE is

- a company that is an issuer with transferable securities admitted to trading on a regulated market;

- a credit institution (defined as including a bank or building society, but not a credit union); or

- an insurance undertaking.

[*CA 2006, s 519A(1); SI 2016 No 649, Reg 15, Sch 3, Part 3, para 26(1), (2)*].

## 8.3    Appointment by private companies

A private company must appoint an auditor or auditors for each financial year of the company, unless the directors reasonably resolve otherwise on the grounds that audited accounts are unlikely to be required.

For each financial year for which an appointment is made (other than the company's first financial year), the appointment must be made before the end of the period of 28 days beginning with

- the end of the time allowed for sending out copies of the company's annual accounts and reports for the previous financial year under *CA 2006, s 424* (see **2.6 ACCOUNTS: GENERAL**); or

- if earlier, the day on which copies of the company's annual accounts and reports for the previous financial year are sent out under *CA 2006, s 423* (see **2.6 ACCOUNTS: GENERAL**).

This is the 'period for appointing auditors'.

Without prejudice to any deemed re-appointment under **8.4**, an auditor or auditors of a private company may only be appointed by the directors or members as below or, in default, by the Secretary of State under **8.7**.

## 8.3 Audit

(a) *Appointment by directors.* The directors may appoint an auditor or auditors of the company

 •  at any time before the company's first period for appointing auditors;

 •  following a period during which the company did not have any auditor (because it was exempt from audit) at any time before the company's next period for appointing auditors; or

 •  to fill a casual vacancy in the office of auditor.

(b) *Appointment by members.* The members may appoint an auditor or auditors by ordinary resolution (see **42.2 RESOLUTIONS AND MEETINGS**)

 •  during a period for appointing auditors;

 •  if the company should have appointed an auditor or auditors during a period for appointing auditors but failed to do so; or

 •  where the directors could have appointed as above but have failed to do so.

[*CA 2006, s 485*].

For periods beginning on or after 17 June 2016, where the company is a PIE (see **8.2**) and an auditor is appointed by the members by ordinary resolution under *CA 2006, s 485(4)*, additional provisions apply under *CA 2006, s 485A* if the company has an audit committee or under *CA 2006, s 485B* if it does not (although neither section applies to the appointment of an Auditor General as auditor, or one of the auditors, of the company). The effect is that all appointments of a new auditor to a PIE must now be based on an audit tender, although there are certain exceptions for companies that qualify as small or medium-sized enterprises and companies with reduced market capitalisation.

If the company has an audit committee

(a) the audit committee or the directors must carry out a selection procedure (ie a formal audit tender) in accordance with *Article 16(3)* of the Audit Regulation (*Regulation EU 537/2014*) unless the company is a small or medium-sized enterprise within *Article 2(1)(f)* of *Directive 2003/71/EC*;

(b) following this selection procedure, the audit committee must make a recommendation to the directors, identifying its first and second choice candidates for appointment, give reasons for these choices, and state that the recommendation is free from any third party influence and that no contractual clause has been imposed on the company to restrict its choice of auditor; and

(c) the directors must propose an auditor for appointment with details of the recommendation made by the audit committee and, if the directors' proposal does not accord with that recommendation, the reasons for not following it.

However, there is no requirement for the audit committee to carry out the specified selection procedure when recommending or proposing the reappointment of an incumbent auditor who was appointed as a result of such a procedure within the last ten years, although the audit committee must still make a recommendation to the directors in respect of the appointment.

[*CA 2006, s 485A; SI 2016 No 649, Reg 15, Sch 3, Part 3, para 4*].

If the company does not have an audit committee, the directors must carry out the specified selection procedure (unless the company is a small or medium-sized enterprise within *Article 2(1)(f)* of *Directive 2003/71/EC*) and propose an auditor for appointment. However, there is no requirement for the directors to carry out the required selection procedure when recommending or proposing the reappointment of an incumbent auditor who was appointed as a result of such a procedure within the last ten years.

[*CA 2006, s 485B; SI 2016 No 649, Reg 15, Sch 3, Part 3, para 4*].

Various transitional provisions are included in *CA 2006, ss 485A* and *485B* depending on when the current auditor was first appointed and on whether that appointment was made following an audit tender.

**8.4**   *Term of office of auditors of private company*

An auditor or auditors of a private company hold office in accordance with the terms of their appointment, subject to the requirements that

- he does not take office until any previous auditor or auditors cease to hold office; and

- he ceases to hold office at the end of the next period for appointing auditors unless re-appointed.

This is without prejudice to the provisions as to removal and resignation of auditors.

An auditor's term of office will therefore typically run from the end of the 28-day period following the circulation of the accounts until the end of the corresponding period in the following year.

In addition, for periods beginning on or after 17 June 2016, if the company is a PIE (see **8.2**) the auditor ceases to hold office on the expiry of the period for appointing auditors in respect of the first complete financial year following the expiry of the maximum engagement period. This provision is introduced to comply with the requirement under the EU Audit Directive that a PIE audit must be put out to tender at least every ten years and that there must be a change of auditor at least every 20 years. *CA 2006, s 487 (1C)–(1E)* sets out additional requirements on the operation of this restriction and also enables the competent authority (ie the FRC) to approve an extension of the maximum engagement period by up to two years in exceptional circumstances. Once the overall maximum period of 20 years has been reached the auditor, and any member of the auditor's network, is prohibited from undertaking the statutory audit of the PIE (either individually or as joint auditor) within the following four years. *CA 2006, s 487A* sets out various transitional provisions, depending on when the current auditor was last appointed and on whether that appointment was made following an audit tender.

*Deemed re-appointment.* Where no auditor has been appointed by the end of the next 'period for appointing auditors' (see **8.3**), any auditor in office immediately before that time is deemed to be re-appointed at that time unless

(a)   he was appointed by the directors;

(b)   the company's articles require actual re-appointment;

(c)   the deemed re-appointment is prevented by the members (see below);

(d)   the members have resolved that he should not be re-appointed;

(e)   the directors have resolved that no auditor or auditors should be appointed for the financial year in question; or

(f)   for periods beginning on or after 17 June 2016, the auditor has ceased to hold office by virtue of *CA 2006, s 487(1A)* (ie on expiry of the maximum engagement period – see above).

No account is to be taken of any loss of the opportunity of deemed re-appointment under the above provisions in determining the amount of any compensation or damages payable to an auditor on his ceasing to hold office for any reason.

**8.4  Audit**

*Prevention by members of deemed re-appointment.* An auditor of a private company is not deemed to be re-appointed if the company has received notices from members representing at least 5% (or such lower percentage as is specified in the company's articles) of the total voting rights of all members who would be entitled to vote on a resolution that the auditor should not be re-appointed.

Such a notice may be in hard copy or electronic form. It must be authenticated by the person or persons giving it and must be received by the company before the end of the accounting reference period immediately preceding the time when the deemed re-appointment would have effect (ie before the end of the financial year the accounts for which he is auditing).

[*CA 2006, ss 487, 487A, 488; SI 2007 No 2194, Sch 1 para 18, Sch 3 para 44: SI 2016 No 649, Reg 15, Sch 3, Part 3, para 6, 7*].

*Transitional provisions*–the effect of resolutions in force before 1 October 2007.

(1)  Where a private company elected under *CA 1985, s 386* to dispense with the annual appointment of auditors and that election was in force immediately before 1 October 2007, (*a*) above does not prevent the deemed re-appointment of auditors first appointed before 1 October 2007.

(2)  Where, immediately before 1 October 2007, a resolution of a private company under *CA 1985, s 390A* (auditors' remuneration) was in force and was expressed to continue to have effect so long as a resolution under *CA 1985, s 386* continued in force, the repeal of *CA 1985, s 386* does not affect the continued operation of the resolution which continues to have effect until

- it is revoked or superseded by a further resolution;

- the auditors to which it applied cease to hold office; or

- it otherwise ceases to have effect in accordance with its terms.

[*SI 2007 No 2194, Sch 3 paras 44, 45*].

**8.5  Appointment by public companies**

A public company must appoint an auditor or auditors for each financial year of the company, unless the directors reasonably resolve otherwise on the ground that audited accounts are unlikely to be required.

For each financial year for which an appointment is made (other than the company's first financial year), the appointment must be made before the end of the accounts meeting of the company at which the company's annual accounts and reports for the previous financial year are laid.

An auditor or auditors of a public company may only be appointed by the directors or members as below or, in default, by the Secretary of State under **8.7**.

(a)  *Appointment by directors.* The directors may appoint an auditor or auditors of the company

- at any time before the company's first accounts meeting;

- following a period during which the company did not have any auditor (because it was exempt from audit), at any time before the company's next accounts meeting; or

- to fill a casual vacancy in the office of auditor.

(b)    *Appointment by members.* The members may appoint an auditor or auditors by ordinary resolution

- at an accounts meeting;

- if the company should have appointed an auditor or auditors at an accounts meeting but failed to do so; or

- where the directors could have appointed as above but failed to do so.

[*CA 2006, s 489*].

See APPENDIX 1 – DEFINITIONS for the meaning of "accounts meeting".

For periods beginning on or after 17 June 2016, where the company is a PIE (see **8.2**) and an auditor is appointed by the members by ordinary resolution under *CA 2006, s 489(4)*, additional provisions apply under *CA 2006, s 489A* if the company has an audit committee or under or *CA 2006, s 489B* if it does not (although neither section applies to the appointment of an Auditor General as auditor, or one of the auditors, of the company). The effect that all appointments of a new auditor to a PIE must now be based on an audit tender, although there are certain exceptions for companies that qualify as small or medium-sized enterprises and companies with reduced market capitalisation.

[*CA 2006, s 519A(1); SI 2016 No 649, Reg 15, Sch 3, Part 3, para 26(1), (2)*].

If the company has an audit committee

(a)    the audit committee or the directors must carry out a selection procedure (ie a formal audit tender) in accordance with *Article 16(3)* of the Audit Regulation (*Regulation EU 537/2014*) unless the company is a small or medium-sized enterprise within *Article 2(1)(f)* of *Directive 2003/71/EC*;

(b)    following the selection procedure, the audit committee must make a recommendation to the directors, identifying its first and second choice candidates for appointment, give reasons for these choices, and state that the recommendation is free from any third party influence and that no contractual clause has been imposed on the company to restrict its choice of auditor; and

(c)    the directors must propose an auditor for appointment with details of the recommendation made by the audit committee and, if the directors' proposal does not accord with that recommendation, the reasons for not following it.

However, there is no requirement for the audit committee to carry out the specified selection procedure when recommending or proposing the reappointment of an incumbent auditor who was appointed as a result of such a procedure within the last ten years, although the audit committee must still make a recommendation to the directors in respect of the appointment.

[*CA 2006, s 489A; SI 2016 No 649, Reg 15, Sch 3, Part 3, para 8*].

If the company does not have an audit committee, the directors must carry out the specified selection procedure (unless the company is a small or medium-sized enterprise within *Article 2(1)(f)* of *Directive 2003/71/EC*) and propose an auditor for appointment. However, there is no requirement for the directors to carry out the required selection procedure when recommending or proposing the reappointment of an incumbent auditor who was appointed as a result of such a procedure within the last ten years.

[*CA 2006, s 489B; SI 2016 No 649, Reg 15, Sch 3, Part 3, para 8*].

Various transitional provisions are included in *CA 2006, ss 489A* and *489B* depending on when the current auditor was first appointed and on whether that appointment was made following an audit tender.

## 8.6 Audit

*Term of office of auditors of public company*

The auditor or auditors of a public company hold office in accordance with the terms of their appointment, subject to the requirements that

- they do not take office until the previous auditor or auditors have ceased to hold office; and

- they cease to hold office at the conclusion of the accounts meeting next following their appointment, unless re-appointed.

This is without prejudice to the provisions as to removal and resignation of auditors.

In addition, for periods beginning on or after 17 June 2016, if the company is a PIE (see **8.2**), the auditor ceases to hold office on the expiry of the period for appointing auditors in respect of the first complete financial year following the expiry of the maximum engagement period. This provision is introduced to comply with the requirement under the EU Audit Directive that a PIE audit must be put out to tender at least every ten years and that there must be a change of auditor at least every 20 years. *CA 2006, s 491 (1C)–(1E)* sets out additional requirements on the operation of this restriction and also enables the competent authority (ie the FRC) to approve an extension of the maximum engagement period by up to two years in exceptional circumstances. Once the overall maximum period of 20 years has been reached the auditor, and any member of the auditor's network, is prohibited from undertaking the statutory audit of the PIE (either individually or as joint auditor) within the following four years. Various transitional provisions apply under *CA 2006, s 491A*, depending on when the current auditor was last appointed and on whether that appointment was made following an audit tender.

[*CA 2006, ss 491, 491A; SI 2016 No 649, Reg 15, Sch 3, Part 3, paras 10, 11*].

## 8.7 Default appointment by the Secretary of State

Where

- a private company fails to appoint an auditor or auditors before the end of the 'period for appointing auditors' in accordance with **8.3**, or

- a public company fails to appoint an auditor or auditors before the end of the accounts meeting in accordance with **8.5**

the company must, within one week of the end of that period/meeting, give notice to the Secretary of State of his power having become exercisable to appoint one or more persons to fill the vacancy.

If a company fails to give the required notice, an offence is committed by the company and every officer of the company who is in default. A person guilty of such an offence is liable, on summary conviction, to a fine not exceeding level 3 on the standard scale and, for continued contravention, to a daily default fine not exceeding one-tenth of level 3 on the standard scale. See **29.1** OFFENCES AND LEGAL PROCEEDINGS for the standard scale.

[*CA 2006, ss 486, 490; SI 2016 No 649, Reg 15, Sch 3, paras 5, 9*].

## 8.8 Disclosure of terms of auditor's appointment and auditor's remuneration

*CA 2006, s 493* provides that the Secretary of State may make regulations for the disclosure of the terms on which a company's auditor is appointed, remunerated or performs his duties. [*CA 2006, s 493*]. No regulations have been made under this section.

*CA 2006, s 494* provides that the Secretary of State may make regulations on the disclosure of the nature of services provided by a company's auditor and that auditor's associates, and the amount of remuneration received or receivable in respect of those services. The *Companies (Disclosure of Auditor Remuneration and Liability Limitation Agreements) Regulations 2008 (SI 2008 No 489)* provide that

- for small companies, there is no longer any requirement to disclose any details of auditor remuneration;

- for medium-sized companies, the amount of any remuneration receivable by the auditor for auditing the accounts must be disclosed in a note to the annual accounts (and where the remuneration includes benefits in kind, the nature and estimated money-value of those benefits must also be disclosed); and

- for all other companies, the notes to the accounts must disclose:

    (i)   the amount of any remuneration receivable by the auditor and any associate of the auditor for auditing the accounts (and where the remuneration includes benefits in kind, the nature and estimated money-value of those benefits must also be disclosed); and

    (ii)  any remuneration receivable by the auditor or any associate of that auditor for the supply of any other services to both the company and any associate of the company.

The types of services for which disclosure must be made under (ii) are set out in *SI 2008 No 489, Sch 2A*.

Separate disclosure is required in respect of

- the auditing of the accounts in question and of each type of service specified in *Schedule 2A* but not in respect of each type of service falling within a type of service;

- services supplied to the company and its subsidiaries on the one hand and to associated pension schemes on the other; and

- each person and his associates where more than one person has been appointed as a company's auditor in respect of the period to which the accounts relate.

Disclosure is not required for the supply of services falling within *SI 2008 No 489, Sch 2A, para 8* (see **3.53** Accounts: Large Companies) that are supplied by a distant associate of the auditor where the total remuneration receivable for all the services supplied by that associate does not exceed £10,000 or 1% of the total auditor remuneration received by the company's auditor in the most recent financial year of the auditor which ended no later than the end of the financial year of the company to which the accounts relate.

See **3.53** Accounts: Large Companies for additional detail on these disclosure requirements.

[*SI 2008 No 489 as amended by SI 2011 No 2198 and SI 2016 No 649*].

In the UK there have been stringent professional requirements for some time on the circumstances in which an audit firm can provide non-audit services to an audit client and these have been enhanced for periods beginning on or after 17 June 2016 in line with new EU requirements (see **8.1**). Full details can be found in the FRC Ethical Standard.

**8.9   Cap on remuneration for non-audit services provided to a PIE**

As explained at **8.1**, under the EU Audit Regulation (*Regulation EU 537/2014*), where the auditor of a PIE (see **8.2**) provides permitted non-audit services to the audited entity for three or more consecutive years, the total fees for those services must be limited to no more than

**8.9 Audit**

70% of the average of the fees paid for the statutory audit of the company (or, where relevant, the group) over the last three consecutive years. This is incorporated into section 4 of Part B of the FRC Ethical Standard, which is effective for periods beginning on or after 17 June 2016. Particular issues to note include:

(a) certain differences in approach between the prohibition on the provision of specified non-audit services and the cap in respect of permitted non-audit services – for instance, the cap applies only to non-audit services provided by the audit firm itself (and so excludes any provided by associates of the auditor) but it covers fees for services provided by the audit firm to any other member of the PIE group (not just to group members based in the EU);

(b) the cap only applies once the auditor has provided services for three or more consecutive years, so for practical purposes it will not apply until periods beginning on or after 17 June 2019; and

(c) any non-audit services that are required under EU or national law are excluded, and this applies even if the law does not specifically require the auditor to provide those services.

In exceptional circumstances, *Regulation 13* of *SI 2016 No 649* enables the FRC (as UK competent authority) to grant an exemption from these requirements for no more than two consecutive years.

**8.10 ELIGIBILITY FOR APPOINTMENT AS AUDITOR**

The main purposes of *CA 2006, Pt 42* (statutory auditors) are to secure that

• only persons who are properly supervised and appropriately qualified are appointed as statutory auditors; and

• audits by persons so appointed are carried out properly, with integrity and with a proper degree of independence.

[*CA 2006, s 1209*].

Many of the functions of the Secretary of State under *CA 2006, Pt 42* are transferred to the FRC as the designated body under the *Statutory Auditors (Amendment of Companies Act 2006 and Delegation of Functions etc) Order 2012 (SI 2012 No 1741)*.

The *Statutory Auditors and Third Country Auditors Regulations 2016 (SI 2016 No 649)* make a number of changes to *CA 2006, Pt 42* (and to *SI 2012 No 1741*) to reflect the requirements of the amended EU Audit Directive and related Regulation (see 8.1). These are reflected in the sections below and apply with effect from 17 June 2016.

**(1) Eligibility for appointment**

An individual or 'firm' is eligible for appointment as a statutory auditor if the individual or firm is

(a) a member of a recognised 'supervisory body' (see (2) below), *and*

(b) eligible for appointment under the rules of that body. A person cannot be eligible for appointment unless

(i) in the case of an individual who is not an EEA auditor (ie an individual approved by an EEA competent authority to carry out audits), he holds an 'appropriate qualification';

(ii)   in the case of a firm which is not an EEA auditor, each individual responsible for statutory audit work on behalf of the firm is eligible for appointment as a statutory auditor *and* the firm is controlled by qualified persons (see below);

(iii)  in the case of an individual who is an EEA auditor, he

- holds an appropriate qualification;

- has been authorised on or before 5 April 2008 to practise the profession of company auditor under *EC (Recognition of Professional Qualifications) Regs 2005 (SI 2005 No 18)* and has fulfilled any requirement imposed pursuant to *Regulation 6* of those Regulations;

- already holds a professional qualification which covers all subjects covered by a recognised professional qualification and which are subjects the knowledge of which is essential for the pursuit of the profession of statutory auditing; or

- holds a professional qualification that does not cover all those subjects and (as specified in the rules of the relevant body) has passed an appropriate aptitude test or completed an adaptation period (in both cases as specified in the legislation);

(iv)   in the case of a firm which is an 'EEA auditor'

- each individual responsible for statutory audit work on behalf of the firm is eligible for appointment as a statutory auditor;

- the firm would be eligible for appointment as a statutory auditor if it were not an EEA auditor or is eligible for a corresponding appointment as an auditor under the law of an EEA State or part of an EEA State, other than the UK; and

- if the firm is eligible for a corresponding appointment as an auditor under the law of an EEA State or part of an EEA State, other than the UK, the firm provides proof of its eligibility in the form of a certificate dated not more than three months before it is provided by the firm, from the competent authority of the EEA State concerned.

In the case of *(b)*(ii) above, a firm is to be treated as controlled by qualified persons if, and only if, both a majority of the members of the firm are qualified persons and (where the firm's affairs are managed by a board of directors, committee or other management body) a majority of that body are qualified persons. If the body consists of two persons only, at least one of them must be a qualified person.

A firm which has ceased to comply with the conditions in *(b)*(ii) above may be permitted to remain eligible for appointment as a statutory auditor for a period of not more than three months.

'*Firm*' means any entity, whether or not a legal person, which is not an individual and includes a body corporate, a corporation sole and a partnership or other unincorporated association.

[*CA 2006, ss 1212(1), 1261, Sch 10 paras 6, 7; SI 2007 No 3494, Reg 17, 18; SI 2016 No 649, Reg 15, Sch 3 Part 5, paras 53, 57*].

(2)    **Supervisory body**

A *'supervisory body'* means a body 'established in the UK' which maintains and enforces binding rules as to eligibility of persons for appointment as a statutory auditor, the conduct of statutory audit work and specified requirements in respect of professional integrity, independence and confidentiality. [*CA 2006, s 1217; SI 2007 No 3494, Reg 4; SI 2016 No 649, Reg 15, Sch 3 Part 5, para 29(1) (3)*].

See *CA 2006, Sch 10* for provisions on the recognition of supervisory bodies.

*Part 1* covers the grant and revocation of recognition.

*Part 2* deals with the requirements for recognition including rules for

- holding of appropriate qualifications by auditors;
- the necessity for auditors to be fit and proper persons;
- professional integrity and independence;
- technical standards;
- technical standards for group audits;
- public interest entity reporting requirements;
- public interest entity independence requirements;
- procedures for maintaining competence;
- monitoring and enforcement of compliance;
- monitoring of audits;
- membership, eligibility and discipline;
- investigation of complaints;
- independent investigation for enforcement purposes;
- transfer of papers to third countries;
- meeting of claims arising out of audit work;
- maintenance of a register of auditors;
- taking account of costs of compliance; and
- the promotion and maintenance of standards.

*Part 3* previously covered arrangements in which recognised supervisory bodies were required to participate, including those for

- setting standards in relation to professional integrity and independence;
- setting technical standards;
- setting standards relating to public interest entity reporting requirements;
- setting standards relating to public interest entity independence requirements;
- independent monitoring of audits of listed and other major bodies; and
- independent investigation for disciplinary purposes of public interest cases.

*Part 3* is repealed by *SI 2016 No 649* with effect from 17 June 2016.

For these purposes, a body is to be regarded as '*established in the UK*' if and only if it is incorporated or formed under the law of the UK (or a part of the UK) or its central management and control are exercised in the UK. [*CA 2006, s 1261(2)*].

(3)    **Appropriate qualification**

A person holds an '*appropriate qualification*' in the following circumstances.

(a)    He holds a 'recognised professional qualification' obtained in the UK.

See *CA 2006, Sch 11* for provisions relating to 'recognised professional qualifications'.

*Part 1* covers the grant and revocation of recognition of a professional qualification.

*Part 2* deals with the requirements for recognition. The qualification must only be open to persons who have attained university entrance level or have a sufficient period of professional expertise. It must be restricted to persons who have completed a course of theoretical instruction and passed an examination (at least part of which is in writing) testing theoretical knowledge and the ability to put that knowledge into practice and requiring a standard of attainment at least equivalent to that required to obtain a degree in the UK.

The subjects for theoretical instruction are prescribed by Regulations made by the Professional Oversight Board.

The qualification may be awarded to a person without his theoretical knowledge of a subject being tested by examination if he has passed a university or other examination of equivalent standard in that subject or holds a university degree or equivalent qualification in it. The qualification may also be awarded to a person without his ability to apply his theoretical knowledge of a subject in practice being tested by examination if he has received practical training in that subject which is attested by an examination or diploma recognised by the Professional Oversight Board for these purposes.

The qualification must also be restricted to persons who have completed at least three years' practical training, part of which must be spent being trained in statutory audit work by a person qualified for appointment as a statutory auditor.

(b)    Immediately before 6 April 2008, he held (or was treated as holding) an appropriate qualification for the purposes of *CA 1989, Part 2* (eligibility for appointment as company auditor) by virtue of *CA 1989, s 31*.

(c)    Immediately before 6 April 2008, he held (or was treated as holding) an appropriate qualification for the purposes of *Companies (Northern Ireland) Order 1990 (SI 1990 No 593) Pt 3* by virtue of *Article 34* of that *Order*.

(d)    Before 1 January 1990, he began a course of study or practical training leading to a professional qualification in accountancy offered by a body 'established in the UK' (see above); he obtained that qualification on or after that date and before 1 January 1996; and the Secretary of State approves his qualification as an appropriate qualification for these purposes.

(e)    He is regarded as holding an approved third country qualification as a result of a declaration by the Secretary of State under *CA 2006, s 1221*.

[*CA 2006, ss 1219, 1220; SI 2007 No 3494, Reg 5*].

## 8.10 Audit

A person whose only appropriate qualification is based upon his retention of an authorisation granted by the Board of Trade or the Secretary of State under the CA 1967, s 13(1) is eligible only for appointment as auditor of an unquoted company. For these purposes, a company is unquoted if, at the time of the person's appointment, neither the company, nor any parent undertaking of which it is a subsidiary undertaking, is a quoted company (see APPENDIX 1 – DEFINITIONS). [*CA 2006, ss 1212(2), 1222; SI 2005 No 2337*].

The following are currently recognised by the FRC as a Recognised Supervisory Body (RSB) for the purposes of statutory audit

- the Institute of Chartered Accountants in England and Wales;

- the Institute of Chartered Accountants of Scotland;

- Chartered Accountants Ireland; and

- the Association of Chartered Certified Accountants.

Previously, the Association of Authorised Public Accountants (AAPA) was also a recognised supervisory body but the FRC revoked this recognition with effect from 31 December 2016. Consequently, AAPA members with an appropriate audit qualification can now only act as a statutory auditor if they are registered with an RSB listed above.

### 8.11 Independence requirement

A person may not act as statutory auditor of an audited person if

(a)     he is an 'officer' or employee of the audited person;

(b)     he is a partner or employee of a person within (*a*) above or a partnership of which such a person is a partner;

(c)     he is an officer or employee of an 'associated undertaking' of the audited person;

(d)     he is a partner or employee of a person within (*c*) above or a partnership of which such a person is a partner; or

(e)     there exists between

    (i)     the person or an 'associate' of his, and

    (ii)     the audited person or an associated undertaking of the audited person,

a connection of any such description as may be specified by Regulations made by the Secretary of State.

An auditor of an audited person is not to be regarded as an officer or employee of that person for the purposes of (*a*)–(*d*) above.

'*Officer*', in relation to a body corporate, includes a director, a manager, a secretary or, where the affairs of the body are managed by its members, a member.

'*Associated undertaking*' for these purposes, in relation to an audited person, means

- a parent undertaking or subsidiary undertaking of the audited person; or

- a subsidiary undertaking of a parent undertaking of the audited person.

'*Associate*', in relation to a person, for these purposes means

- in relation to an individual,

  (i)   that individual's spouse, civil partner or minor child or step-child;

  (ii)  any body corporate of which that individual is a director; and

  (iii) any employee or partner of that individual;

- in relation to a body corporate,

  (i)   any body corporate of which that body is a director;

  (ii)  any body corporate in the same group as that body; and

  (iii) any employee or partner of that body or of any body corporate in the same group;

- in relation to a partnership constituted under the law of Scotland, or any other country or territory in which a partnership is a legal person,

  (i)   any body corporate of which that partnership is a director;

  (ii)  any employee of or partner in that partnership; and

  (iii) any person who is an associate of a partner in that partnership; and

- in relation to a partnership constituted under the law of England and Wales or Northern Ireland, or the law of any other country or territory in which a partnership is not a legal person, any person who is an associate of any of the partners. [*CA 2006, ss 1214, 1260*].

## 8.12   Effect of ineligibility or lack of independence

If at any time during his term of office a statutory auditor becomes

- ineligible for appointment as a statutory auditor under **8.10**, or

- prohibited from acting through lack of independence under **8.11**

he must immediately resign his office (with immediate effect) and give notice in writing to the audited person that he has resigned by reason of becoming ineligible for appointment or, as the case may be, lack of independence.

A person is guilty of an offence if he

(a)   acts as a statutory auditor in contravention of the above; or

(b)   fails to give the required notice.

A person guilty of such an offence is liable (i) on conviction on indictment, to a fine; and (ii) on summary conviction, to a fine not exceeding the statutory maximum. See **29.1** Offences and Legal Proceedings for the statutory maximum.

A person is also guilty of an offence if, having been convicted of an offence under (*a*) or (*b*) above, he continues to act as a statutory auditor (when still ineligible or prohibited through lack of independence) or continues to fail to give the required notice. A person guilty of such an offence is liable (i) on conviction on indictment, to a fine; and (ii) on summary conviction, to a fine not exceeding one-tenth of the greater of £5,000 or level 4 on the standard scale for each day on which the act or the failure continues.

In proceedings against a person for an offence under these provisions it is a defence for him to show that he did not know and had no reason to believe that he was, or had become, ineligible for appointment as a statutory auditor or, as the case may be, prohibited from acting through lack of independence.

## 8.12   Audit

[*CA 2006, ss 1213, 1215; SI 2015 No 664, Regs 3, 5, Sch 3 Part 1, para 9(24)*].

### 8.13   Power to require second audit

Where a person appointed as statutory auditor of a company was not an 'appropriate' person for any part of the period during which the audit was conducted, the Secretary of State may direct the company concerned to retain an appropriate person to

- conduct a second audit of the relevant accounts; or

- review the first audit and to report (giving his reasons) whether a second audit is needed.

For the above purposes, a person is *'appropriate'* if he is eligible for appointment as a statutory auditor under **8.10** and is not ineligible under **8.11** through lack of independence.

The Secretary of State must send a copy of any direction made to the Registrar of Companies. The company must

(i)     comply with the direction within 21 days of it being given;

(ii)    send a copy of any report from the second auditor to the Registrar of Companies within 21 days of receipt; and

(iii)   if that report states that a second audit is needed, take such steps as are necessary for the carrying out of that audit.

The company is guilty of an offence if it

(a)     fails to comply with the direction within the 21-day period;

(b)     fails to send a copy of a report from the second auditor to the Registrar of Companies within the 21-day period;

(c)     where (iii) above applies, fails to take the necessary steps to carry out the audit immediately it receives the report; and

(d)     has been convicted of a previous offence under (*a*)–(*c*) above and the failure which led to the conviction continues after the conviction.

A company guilty of such an offence is liable, on summary conviction, in a case within (*a*)–(*c*) above to a fine not exceeding level 5 on the standard scale and in a case within (*d*) above to a fine not exceeding one-tenth of the greater of £5,000 or level 4 on the standard scale for each day on which the failure continues. See **29.1** Offences and Legal Proceedings for the standard scale.

If a person accepts an appointment, or continues to act, as statutory auditor of a company when he knows he is not an appropriate person, the company may recover from him any costs incurred by it in complying with the above requirements.

Where a second audit is carried out, any statutory or other provision applying in relation to the first audit applies also, in so far as practicable, in relation to the second audit.

A direction under these provisions is, on the application of the Secretary of State, enforceable by injunction or, in Scotland, by an order under *Court of Session Act 1988, s 45*.

[*CA 2006, ss 1248, 1249; SI 2015 No 664, Regs 3, 5, Sch 3, para 9(26)*].

### 8.14   Effect of appointment of partnership

The appointment of a partnership constituted under the law of

- England and Wales,

- Northern Ireland, or

- any other country or territory in which a partnership is not a legal person

as statutory auditor is, unless a contrary intention appears, the appointment of the partnership as such and not of the partners.

Where the partnership ceases, the appointment is treated as extending to

- any partnership which succeeds to the practice of that partnership provided the membership of the successor partnership is substantially the same as that of the former partnership; or

- any other person who succeeds to that practice having previously carried it on in partnership.

In each case, the succeeding partnership or other person must

(a)    be eligible for the appointment as a statutory auditor;

(b)    not be prohibited from acting as the statutory auditor because of lack of independence (see **8.11–8.12**); and

(c)    succeed to the whole, or substantially the whole, of the business of the former partnership.

Where a partnership ceases and no person succeeds under the above rules, the appointment may, with the consent of the audited company, be treated as extending to a partnership or person satisfying the conditions in (*a*) and (*b*) above who succeeds to the business of the former partnership or such part of it as is agreed by the audited person as comprising the appointment.

[*CA 2006, s 1216*].

## 8.15    Register of auditors

The Secretary of State must make regulations requiring the keeping of a register of

- persons eligible for appointment as a statutory auditor (see **8.10**); and

- third country auditors who apply to be registered in the specified manner and in relation to whom specified requirements are met.

As the UK competent authority responsible for the public oversight of auditors, the FRC is responsible for the registration of persons eligible for appointment as statutory auditor, keeping the register and making it available for inspection. The FRC is also responsible for maintaining the separate register of third country auditors (see **8.16**).

[*CA 2006, s 1239; SI 2007 No 3494, Reg 30; SI 2016 No 649, Regs 3, 15, Sch 3 Part 5, para 37*].

The FRC issued the *Statutory Auditors (Registration) Instrument 2016* in June 2016 (available at www.frc.org.uk/Our-Work/Audit-and-Actuarial-Regulation/ Professional -oversight/Oversight-of-Audit/Statutory-Instruments.aspx).

*Contents of the register.* The register must contain the following information.

(a)    In relation to an individual eligible for appointment as a statutory auditor

(i)    the individual's name and address;

(ii)     the individual's registered number;

(iii)    the name and address of the registration body under whose rules the individual is eligible for appointment as a statutory auditor;

(iv)     if the individual is responsible for statutory audit work on behalf of any firm, the firm's name, address, registered number, and if it has a website, its address; a

(v)      the name of any EEA competent authority with whom the individual is registered for audit purposes and any registration number which such an authority has allocated to the individual; and

(vi)     the name and address of any body which has authorised the individual to conduct audits in accordance with the law of a third country.

(b)     In relation to a person eligible for appointment as a statutory auditor which is a firm,

(i)      its name and address;

(ii)     its registered number;

(iii)    the address of each of its offices in which it carries out statutory audit work;

(iv)     information as to how the firm is to be contacted, the primary contact person and, if it has a website, its address;

(v)      the name, business address and registration number of each individual responsible for statutory audit work on behalf of the firm;

(vi)     its legal form and

•        in the case of a limited liability partnership, the name and business address of each member of the partnership;

•        in the case of a body corporate, other than a limited liability partnership, the name and business address of each person who is a director of the body or holds any shares in it;

•        in the case of a corporation sole, the name and address of the individual for the time being holding the office by the name of which he is the corporation sole;

•        in the case of a partnership, the name and business address of each partner

(vii)    the name and address of the registration body under whose rules it is eligible for appointment as a statutory auditor;

(viii)   in the case of a firm which is a member of a 'network', the name of the network and either

•        a list of the names and addresses of the other members of that network and of the affiliates of all the members of that network; or

•        a reference to the address of a website or any other place where that information is available to the public;

(ix)     the name of any EEA competent authority or third country authority with whom it is registered for audit purposes and any registration number which such an authority has allocated to it;

(x)     the name and address of any body which has authorised the firm to conduct audits in accordance with the law of a third country; and

(xi)    whether the firm is eligible for appointment as a statutory auditor by virtue of being an EEA auditor which meets the requirements in *CA 2006, Sch 10, para 6(1)(c)*.

References under (vi) above to a limited liability partnership, a body corporate, a corporation sole or a partnership include references to any comparable undertaking incorporated in or formed under the law of any country or territory outside the UK.

'*Network*' means an association of persons other than a firm co-operating in audit work by way of

- profit-sharing;
- cost-sharing;
- common ownership, control or management;
- common quality control policies and procedures;
- common business strategy; or
- use of a common name.

*Maintenance and inspection.* The FRC (as competent authority) is the '*maintaining body*' responsible for keeping an up-to-date register in electronic form and making it available for inspection on a website accessible to the public or by other electronic means. It must ensure that the information contained in the register may be inspected

- alphabetically by name of person;
- by reference to registered individuals or registered firms;
- by reference to the registration number of the registered person;
- by reference to registration body of the registered person; and
- by address of the registered person.

Information on the register relating to a person may be excluded from being made available for inspection to the extent that making such information available would create, or be likely to create, a serious risk that any individual would be subject to violence or intimidation as a result.

A registration body that is not the maintaining body must co-operate with the maintaining body for the purpose of enabling the maintaining body to keep the register up to date and must send to the maintaining body for entry on the register, in electronic form

(i)     the information specified in (a) and (b) above in relation to each person that the registration body has determined to be eligible for appointment as a statutory auditor; and

(ii)    any changes in that information of which it becomes aware.

Each registration body must take reasonable care to ensure that the information is accurate at the time of sending and is sent to the maintaining body within ten working days beginning with the day on which the registration body makes the determination in the case of (i) above or becomes aware of the change in (ii) above.

## 8.15 Audit

The register is available at www.auditregister.org.uk.

*Duty to provide updated information.* Any person eligible for appointment as a statutory auditor must take all reasonable steps to notify the relevant registration body, without undue delay, of any information necessary to ensure that the information in the register relating to that person is correct.

[*CA 2006, s 1239; SI 2007 No 3494, Reg 30; SI 2016 No 649, Regs 2, 15, Sch 3 Part 5, para 37; Statutory Auditors (Registration) Instrument 2016*].

### 8.16 Registered third country auditors

A *'registered third country auditor'* means a third country auditor who is entered in the register to be kept in accordance with regulations under *CA 2006, s 1239(1)*. [*CA 2006, s 1241; SI 2007 No 3494, Reg 31*].

A registered third country auditor who audits the accounts of a 'UK-traded non-EEA company' is subject to arrangements for independent monitoring of audits and independent investigations for disciplinary purposes in the UK in accordance with *CA 2006, Sch 12*. These provisions are similar to supervision arrangements for statutory auditors under **8.10**. The Secretary of State may direct in writing that these provisions are not to apply, in whole or in part, in relation to a particular registered third country auditor or class of registered third country auditors. [*CA 2006, s 1242; SI 2007 No 3494, Reg 32*]. He may do this, for example, if satisfied that the third company auditor is already subject to equivalent supervision in his home country.

A *'UK-traded non-EEA company'* means a body corporate

- which is incorporated or formed under the law of a third country;

- whose transferable securities are admitted to trading on a regulated market situated or operating in the UK; and

- which has not been excluded from the definition by the Secretary of State. A large debt securities issuer (ie a body corporate whose only issued transferable securities admitted to trading are debt securities with a denomination of not less than 50,000 euros or its equivalent in the case of securities admitted before 31 December 2010 or 100,000 euros or an equivalent amount in the case of securities admitted after 31 December 2010) has been excluded.

[*CA 2006, s 1241(2); SI 2007 No 3494, Regs 31; SI 2016 No 649, Reg 21(1)–(3)*].

**Register of third country auditors.** The Secretary of State must make regulations requiring the keeping of a register of third country auditors (see **8.15**). The FRC, as the designated body, must keep a register of third country auditors containing specified information detailed in the *Statutory Auditors and Third Country Auditors Regulations 2013 (SI 2013 No 1672)*. The register must be kept in electronic form and the information on it must be available for inspection by any person by electronic means (unless making the information so available would create a serious risk that the individual, or any other person, would be subject to violence or intimidation). [*SI 2013 No 1672, Reg 6*]. The register is available at www.frc.org.uk.

**Application for registration.** A third country auditor may apply to the FRC in writing for registration. The application must comply with the requirements in *SI 2013 No 1675, Regs 7 and 8* which include an application statement that he holds the necessary qualifications, is a fit and proper person to conduct audits and conducts audits under the necessary standards. If satisfied with the application, the FRC will duly register him and allocate him a registered number. If it refuses registration, the FRC must give him written notice to that effect stating the reason for the refusal. [*SI 2013 No 1672, Regs 7, 8, 9; SI 2016 No 649, Reg 20(2)*].

**Duty to provide updated information.** Once registered a third country auditor must take all reasonable steps to notify the FRC without undue delay of any change or addition to the information specified in *Reg 11* (the name, registered number, third country or territory in which it is incorporated or under the law of which it is formed and the accounting period to which the audit relates in respect of each UK traded non EEA company for which the third country auditor provides a service), any information or event which may lead the FRC to consider that the application statement required by *Reg 8* made by the third country auditor is not correct, and any information necessary to ensure that the information in the register relating to the third country auditor is correct. [*SI 2013 No 1672, Reg 11*].

## 8.17   FIXING OF AUDITOR'S REMUNERATION

The 'remuneration' of an auditor appointed by the members of a company must be fixed by the members by ordinary resolution (or in such manner as the members may by ordinary resolution determine). The remuneration of an auditor appointed by the directors or the Secretary of State must be fixed by the directors or Secretary of State (as the case may be).

*'Remuneration'* includes sums paid in respect of expenses and the provisions apply to benefits in kind as to payments of money.

[*CA 2006, s 492*].

## 8.18   REMOVAL OF AUDITOR FROM OFFICE

The members of a company can remove an auditor from office at any time. This power is exercisable only by ordinary resolution at a meeting and in accordance with the procedure set out below. Nothing in these provisions is to be taken as depriving the person removed of compensation or damages payable to him in respect of the termination

- of his appointment as auditor; or

- of any appointment terminating with that as auditor.

However, an auditor cannot be removed from office before the expiration of his term of office other than

(a)    by resolution under *CA 2006, s 510* in accordance with the procedure below; or

(b)    in accordance with *CA 2006, s 511A* (public interest entities: application to court to remove an auditor from office).

*Procedure for removal by ordinary resolution.* Special notice (see **42.19** Resolutions and Meetings) is required for a resolution at a general meeting of a company removing an auditor from office. On receipt of notice of such an intended resolution, the company must immediately send a copy of it to the person proposed to be removed. That person may then make written representations to the company, not exceeding a reasonable length, and request their notification to the members. The company must then, unless the representations are received too late to do so, state the fact that representations have been made in the notice of any resolution to the members and send a copy of the representations to every member to whom notice of the meeting is or has been sent.

If a copy of the representations is not sent because it is received too late or because of the company's default, the auditor can, without prejudice to his right to be heard orally, require that the representations be read out at the meeting.

Copies of the representations need not be sent out, and the representations need not be read at the meeting if, on the application either of the company or of any other person claiming to be aggrieved, the court is satisfied that the auditor is using these provisions to secure needless publicity for defamatory matter. The court may order the company's costs (in Scotland, expenses) on the application to be paid in whole or in part by the auditor, notwithstanding that he is not a party to the application.

*Application to the court under CA 2006, s 511A.* The competent authority (which in the UK is the FRC) or members holding at least 5% of the voting rights, or at least 5% of the nominal value of the share capital, may apply to the court for the removal from office of the auditor of a public interest entity where there are proper grounds for this. This applies for financial years beginning on or after 17 June 2016. *CA 2006, s 511A(6)* states categorically that, for the purposes of this section, divergence of opinions on accounting treatments or audit procedures are not to be taken as proper grounds for removing an auditor from office.

*Rights of auditor who has been removed from office.* An auditor who has been removed by ordinary resolution under *CA 2006, s 510* or as a result of an application to the court under *CA 2006, s 511A* still has the right under **8.44** to attend the general meeting of the company at which

•        his term of office would otherwise have expired; or

•        it is proposed to fill the vacancy caused by his removal.

[*CA 2006, ss 510–513; SI 2007 No 3495, Sch 4 para 13; SI 2016 No 649, Reg 15, Sch 3, paras 22, 23*].

**8.19    Failure to re-appoint auditor: special procedure required for written resolution**

Where:

(a)      a resolution is proposed as a written resolution of a private company, the effect of which would be to appoint a person as auditor in place of a person (the '*outgoing auditor*') who, at the time that the resolution is proposed, is an auditor of the company and who is to cease to hold office at the end of a period for appointing auditors; or

(b)      a resolution is proposed as a written resolution of a private company, the effect of which would be to appoint a person as auditor where, at the time that the resolution is proposed, the company does not have an auditor and the person proposed to be appointed is not a person (the '*outgoing auditor*') who was an auditor of the company when it last had an auditor

the company must send a copy of the proposed resolution to the person proposed to be appointed and to the outgoing auditor. However, this does not apply if

•        in the case of (a) above, the auditor is to cease to hold office by virtue of *CA 2006, ss 510, 511A or 516* (see **8.18**); or

•        in the case of (b) above

         (i)       a period for appointing auditors has ended since the outgoing auditor ceased to hold office;

         (ii)      the outgoing auditor ceased to hold office by virtue of *CA 2006, ss 510, 511A or 516* (see **8.18**); or

         (iii)     the outgoing auditor has previously had the opportunity to make representations with respect to a proposed resolution under *CA 2006, s 514(4)* or an intended resolution under *CA 2006, s 515(5)* (see **8.20**).

Where the company is required to send a copy of the proposed resolution, the outgoing auditor may, within 14 days of receiving the notice, make representations in writing to the company (not exceeding a reasonable length) about the proposed resolution and request their circulation to members of the company.

The company must circulate the representations together with the copy or copies of the written resolution circulated in accordance with *CA 2006, s 291* (resolution proposed by directors, see **42.7** RESOLUTIONS AND MEETINGS) or, as the case may be, *CA 2006, s 293* (resolution proposed by members, see **42.8** RESOLUTIONS AND MEETINGS). Where the latter applies, the period allowed for service of copies of the proposed resolution is 28 days (instead of 21 days).

**Application to the court.** Copies of the representations need not be circulated if, on the application either of the company or of any other person claiming to be aggrieved, the court is satisfied that the auditor is using these provisions to secure needless publicity for defamatory matter. The court may order the company's costs (in Scotland, expenses) on the application to be paid in whole or in part by the auditor, notwithstanding that he is not a party to the application.

If any of the requirements above are not complied with, the resolution is ineffective.

[*CA 2006, s 514; Deregulation Act 2015, s 18(5), Sch 5 Part 2, paras 13, 14(1)–(3); SI 2016 No 649, Reg 15, Sch 3 Part 3, para 24*].

8.20 **Failure to re-appoint auditor: special notice required for resolution at general meeting**

Special notice (see **42.19** Resolutions and Meetings) is required for a resolution at a general meeting of a company the effect of which would be

(a)     to appoint a person as auditor in place of a person (the '*outgoing auditor*') who, at the time that the notice is given

•     in the case of a private company, is an auditor of the company and is to cease to hold office at the end of the 'period for appointing auditors' (see **8.3**), unless he is to cease to hold office by virtue of *CA 2006, ss 510, 511A or 516* (see **8.18**); or

•     in the case of a public company, is an auditor of the company and is to cease to hold office at the end of the next accounts meeting, unless he is to cease to hold office by virtue of *CA 2006, ss 510, 511A or 516* (see **8.18**); or

(b)     to appoint a person as auditor where, at the time that the notice is given, the company does not have an auditor and the person proposed to be appointed is not a person (the '*outgoing auditor*') who was an auditor of the company when it last had an auditor – however, special notice is not required if:

(i)     in the case of a private company, a period for appointing auditors has ended since the outgoing auditor ceased to hold office; or

(ii)     in the case of a public company, an accounts meeting has been held since the auditor ceased to hold office; or

(iii)     the outgoing auditor ceased to hold office by virtue of *CA 2006, ss 510, 511A or 516* (see **8.18**); or

(iv)     the outgoing auditor has previously had the opportunity to make representations with respect to a proposed resolution under *CA 2006, s 515(4)* (see **8.19**) or an intended resolution under *CA 2006, s 515(5)*.

On receipt of notice of such an intended resolution, the company must immediately send a copy of it to the person proposed to be appointed and to the outgoing auditor. The outgoing auditor may then make written representations to the company, not exceeding a reasonable length, and request their notification to the members. The company must then, unless the representations are received too late to do so, state the fact that representations have been made in the notice of any resolution to the members and send a copy of the representations to every member to whom notice of the meeting is or has been sent.

If a copy of the representations is not sent because it is received too late or because of the company's default, the auditor can, without prejudice to his right to be heard orally, require that the representations be read out at the meeting.

*Application to the court.* Copies of the representations need not be sent out, and the representations need not be read at the meeting if, on the application either of the company or of any other person claiming to be aggrieved, the court is satisfied that the auditor is using these provisions to secure needless publicity for defamatory matter. The court may order the company's costs (in Scotland, expenses) on the application to be paid in whole or in part by the auditor, notwithstanding that he is not a party to the application.

[*CA 2006, s 515; Deregulation Act 2015, s 18(5), Sch 5 Part 2, paras 13, 15(1)–(3); SI 2016 No 649, Reg 15, Sch 3 Part 3, para 25*].

## 8.21    RESIGNATION OF AUDITOR

An auditor may resign his office by sending a notice to that effect at the company's registered office. Where the company is a public interest company, the notice is only effective if it is accompanied by a statement required under **8.23**. The auditor's term of office then ends on the date on which the notice is received or on such later date as may be specified in the notice.

There is no longer any requirement for the company to send a copy of the resignation notice to the Registrar of Companies.

[*CA 2006, s 516; Deregulation Act 2015, s 18(5), Sch 5, Part 1, paras 1, 3, 4 and Part 2, paras 13, 16(1)–(3)*].

## 8.22    Rights of resigning auditor

Where an auditor's notice of resignation is accompanied by a statement of the circumstances connected with his resignation (see **8.23**), he may send with the notice a signed requisition calling on the directors to convene a general meeting of the company for the purpose of receiving and considering such explanation of the reasons for, and matters connected with, his resignation as he may wish to place before the meeting. However, this does not apply if the company is a non-public interest company and the auditor's statement of circumstances includes a statement to the effect that none of the reasons for his ceasing to hold office, and no matters (if any) connected with his ceasing to hold office, need to be brought to the attention of the members or creditors of the company.

Where the auditor sends a notice under these provisions, he may also request the company to circulate to members

(a)    before the meeting convened on his requisition, or

(b)    before any general meeting at which his term of office would otherwise have expired or at which it is proposed to fill the vacancy caused by his resignation

a written statement of reasonable length of the reasons for, and matters connected with, his resignation.

The company must then, unless the statement is received too late for it to comply, state the fact of the statement having been made in any notice of the meeting to the members and send a copy of the statement to every member to whom notice of the meeting is or has been sent.

The directors must then, within 21 days from the date on which the company receives the requisition, proceed to convene a meeting for a day not more than 28 days after the date on which the notice convening the meeting is given. In default, every director who failed to take all reasonable steps to secure that a meeting was convened commits an offence. A person guilty of such an offence is liable (i) on conviction on indictment, to a fine; and (ii) on summary conviction, to a fine not exceeding the statutory maximum. See **29.1** OFFENCES AND LEGAL PROCEEDINGS for the statutory maximum.

Where a copy of the statement is not sent out because it was received too late or because of the company's default, the auditor can, without prejudice to his right to be heard orally, require that the statement be read out at the meeting.

*Application to the court.* Copies of a statement need not be sent out and the statement need not be read out at the meeting if, on the application either of the company or of any other person who claims to be aggrieved, the court is satisfied that the auditor is using these provisions to secure needless publicity for defamatory matter. The court may order the company's costs (in Scotland, expenses) on such an application to be paid in whole or in part by the auditor, notwithstanding that he is not a party to the application.

An auditor who has resigned still has the right to receive notices of, attend and be heard at, any general meeting mentioned in (*a*) or (*b*) above.

[*CA 2006, s 518; Deregulation Act 2015, s 18(5), Sch 5, Part 1, paras 5(1)–(4) and Part 2, paras 13, 17(1)–(3)*].


## 8.23    STATEMENT BY AUDITOR CEASING TO HOLD OFFICE

An auditor of a public interest company (see **8.2**) who ceases to hold office at any time and for any reason (ie whether removed or by resignation) *must* send to the company a statement of his reasons for doing so.

An auditor of a non-public interest company who is ceasing to hold office *must* send to the company a statement of his reasons for doing so unless he satisfies either of the following conditions:

(a)    he is ceasing to hold office at the end of a period for appointing auditors (in the case of a private company) or at the end of an accounts meeting (in the case of a public company); or

(b)    his reasons for ceasing to hold office are all exempt reason and there are no matters connected with his ceasing to hold office that he considers need to be brought to the attention of the members or creditors of the company – exempt reasons are defined in *CA 2006, s 591A(3)* and cover the following:

    (i)    the auditor is no longer carrying out statutory audit work within the meaning of *Part 42* of *CA 2006*;

    (ii)   the company is, or is to become, exempt from audit under *CA 2006, ss 477, 479A or 480*, or from the audit requirements of *CA 2006* as a result of *s 482* (non-profit-making companies subject to public sector audit – see **8.35**);

(iii)   the company is a subsidiary undertaking of a parent undertaking incorporated in the UK that prepares group accounts and the auditor is being replaced by the auditor who conducts, or is to conduct, the audit of the group accounts (but only if the group auditor conducts or will conduct the audit of every UK incorporated subsidiary undertaking that is included in the consolidated accounts);

(iv)   the company is being wound up.

A statement required under these provisions must include

(1)   the auditor's name, address and registered number;

(2)   the company's name and registered number;

(3)   details of any matters connected with the auditor's ceasing to hold office that the auditor considers should be brought to the attention of the members or creditors; and

(4)   in the case of a non-public interest company, if the auditor considers that none of the reasons for, and no matters (if any) connected with, his ceasing to hold office need to be brought to the attention of the company's members or creditors, a statement to that effect.

The statement must be sent

• in the case of resignation, along with the notice of resignation;

• in the case of failure to seek re-appointment, not less than 14 days before the end of the time allowed for appointing the next auditor; and

• in any other case, not later than 14 days after he ceases to hold office.

If a person ceasing to hold office as auditor fails to comply with these provisions, he commits an offence. A person guilty of such an offence is liable (i) on conviction on indictment, to a fine; and (ii) on summary conviction, to a fine not exceeding the statutory maximum. See **29.1 OFFENCES AND LEGAL PROCEEDINGS** for the statutory maximum. However, it is a defence for the person charged to show that he took all reasonable steps and exercised all due diligence to avoid the commission of the offence. Where such an offence is committed by a body corporate, every officer of the body (which includes any person who purports to act as a director, manager or secretary of the body and, if the body is a company, any shadow director) who is in default also commits an offence.

[*CA 2006, s 519; Deregulation Act 2015, s 18(1), (2), (5), Sch 5, Part 1, paras 1, 6 and Part 2, paras 13, 18(1)–(3)*].

## 8.24   Company's duties in relation to the auditor's statement

Where a non-public interest company receives a statement from the auditor under *CA 2006, s 519* and the auditor states that he does not consider that any of the reasons for, or matters connected with, his ceasing to hold office need to be brought to the attention of the members or creditors of the company, no further action is required.

In all other cases where an auditor sends a statement under *CA 2006, s 519* the company must, within 14 days of receipt, either

(a)   send a copy of the statement to every person who is entitled to be sent copies of the accounts under *CA 2006, s 423*; or

(b)    apply to the court, in which case the company must notify the auditor of this application.

If the court is satisfied that the auditor is using the statement to secure needless publicity for defamatory matter, it must direct that the statement need not be sent out and may order the auditor to meet all or part of the company's costs in making the application. In this case, the company has 14 days in which to send a statement of the effect of the court order to every person entitled to receive a copy of the company's accounts.

If no such direction is made, the company must, within 14 days of the date of the court's decision (or of the discontinuance of the proceedings), notify the auditor of that decision and send a copy of the auditor's statement to every person entitled to receive copies of the accounts.

In the event of default in complying with these provisions, an offence is committed by every officer of the company who is in default. A person guilty of such an offence is liable (i) on conviction on indictment, to a fine; and (ii) on summary conviction, to a fine not exceeding the statutory maximum. See **29.1** OFFENCES AND LEGAL PROCEEDINGS for the statutory maximum. However, it is a defence for the person charged to show that he took all reasonable steps and exercised all due diligence to avoid the commission of the offence.

[*CA 2006, s 520; Deregulation Act 2015, s 18(5), Sch 5 Part 1, paras 1, 7(1)–(3) and Part 2, paras 13, 19*].

**8.25    Copy of statement to be sent to the Registrar of Companies**

Where the company is a non-public interest company and the auditor's statement under *CA 2006, s 519* states that he does not consider that any of the reasons for, or matters connected with, his ceasing to hold office need to be brought to the attention of the members or creditors of the company, no further action is required.

In all other cases where an auditor sends a statement under *CA 2006, s 519*

(a)    if the auditor has not received notice of an application to the court 21 days after the day that his statement was sent to the company, he must send a copy of his statement to the Registrar of Companies within a further seven days (ie within 28 days of the date on which the statement was originally sent to the company);

(b)    if the company applies to the court and the auditor subsequently receives notice that no direction has been made under *CA 2006, s 520(4)*, the auditor must send a copy of his statement to the Registrar of Companies within seven days of receiving that notice.

An auditor who fails to comply with these provisions commits an offence. A person guilty of such an offence is liable (i) on conviction on indictment, to a fine; and (ii) on summary conviction, to a fine not exceeding the statutory maximum. See **29.1** OFFENCES AND LEGAL PROCEEDINGS for the statutory maximum. However, it is a defence for the person charged to show that he took all reasonable steps and exercised all due diligence to avoid the commission of the offence. Where such an offence is committed by a body corporate, every officer of the body (which includes any person who purports to act as a director, manager or secretary of the body and, if the body is a company, any shadow director) who is in default also commits an offence.

[*CA 2006, s 521; Deregulation Act 2015, s 18(5), Sch 5 Part 1, paras 1, 8(1)–(3) and Part 2, paras 13, 20*].

**8.26    Duty to send statement to the appropriate audit authority**

Where an auditor sends a statement to a company under *CA 2006, s 519*, he must at the same time send a copy to the appropriate audit authority.

Also, in any case where an auditor is ceasing to hold office at any time other than at the end of a period for appointing auditors (in the case of a private company) or at the end of an accounts meeting (in the case of a public company, the company must give notice to the appropriate audit authority within 28 days of the auditor ceasing to hold office. However, this does not apply where the company reasonably believes that the only reasons for the auditor ceasing to hold office are exempt reasons (see **8.23**).

Where the company is required to give such notice it must be either

(a)     in the form of a statement by the company of what it believes to be the reasons for the auditor ceasing to hold office, including the information required by *CA 2006, s 519(3)* (see **8.23** items (1) and (2)); or

(b)     where the auditor sends a statement to the company under *CA 2006, s 519* within the timescale required by that section and the company agrees with the contents, in the form of a copy of the auditor's statement endorsed to show the company's agreement with it.

The appropriate audit authority may forward a copy of any statement or notice to the accounting authorities (ie the Secretary of State or the FRC) together with any other relevant information.

'*Appropriate audit authority*' means (i) in relation to an auditor of a public interest company (other than an Auditor General), the Secretary of State or, if the Secretary of State has delegated functions under *CA 2006, s 1252* to a body whose functions include receiving the notice in question, that body (the FRC has delegated functions given by *SI 2012 No 1741*); (ii) in relation to an auditor of a non-public interest company (other than an Auditor General), the relevant supervisory body (see **8.10**); and (iii) in relation to an Auditor General, the Independent Supervisor.

A person ceasing to hold office as auditor who fails to comply with these provisions commits an offence. If that person is a firm an offence is committed by the firm and every officer of the firm who is in default. Similarly, if a company fails to comply with these provisions, an offence is committed by the company and every officer of the company who is in default. A person guilty of such an offence is liable (i) on conviction on indictment, to a fine; and (ii) on summary conviction, to a fine not exceeding the statutory maximum. See **29.1** OFFENCES AND LEGAL PROCEEDINGS for the statutory maximum. However, it is a defence for the person charged to show that he took all reasonable steps and exercised all due diligence to avoid the commission of the offence.

[*CA 2006, ss 522–525; SI 2007 No 3494, Reg 41; 2012 No 1741, Reg 8; Deregulation Act 2015, s 18(1), (4), (5), Sch 5 Part 1, paras 1, 9(1)–(3), 10(1)–(4), 11(1)–(4)*].

## 8.27   EFFECT OF CASUAL VACANCIES WHERE JOINT AUDITORS

If an auditor ceases to hold office for any reason, any surviving or continuing auditor or auditors may continue to act. [*CA 2006, s 526*]. The effect of this is that when one out of two or more joint auditors cease to be an auditor of the company, the remaining auditors can continue in office.

## 8.28   REQUIREMENT FOR AUDITED ACCOUNTS

A company's annual accounts must be audited in accordance with *CA 2006, Pt 16* unless the company is

(a)     exempt from audit under the provisions relating to

- small companies (see **8.29** to **8.31**) or subsidiary companies (see **8.32**);

- dormant companies (see **8.34**); or

- charitable companies (see **8.35**); or

(b)    exempt from the requirements under the provisions relating to non-profit-making companies subject to public sector audit (see **8.35**).

*Statement on the balance sheet confirming exemption.* A company is not entitled to any exemption

- under (*a*) or (*b*) above unless its balance sheet contains a statement by the directors to that effect; or

- under (a) above unless its balance sheet also contains a statement by the directors to the effect that

    (i)    the members have not required the company to obtain an audit of its accounts for the year in question under the provisions below; and

    (ii)   the directors acknowledge their responsibilities for complying with the requirements of *CA 2006* with respect to accounting records and the preparation of accounts.

The statement required must appear on the balance sheet above the signature of the director of the company who signs the company's accounts on behalf of the board.

[*CA 2006, s 475; SI 2012 No 2301, Reg 6*].

*Right of members to require audit.* The members of a company that would otherwise be entitled to exemption from audit under any of the provisions in (*a*) above may by notice require it to obtain an audit of its accounts for a financial year. The notice must be given by

- members representing not less in total than 10% in nominal value of the company's issued share capital, or any class of it; or

- if the company does not have a share capital, not less than 10% in number of the members of the company.

The notice may not be given before the financial year to which it relates and must be given not later than one month before the end of that year. [*CA 2006, s 476*].

## 8.29    Exemption from audit: small companies

Subject to the

- requirement for a statement on the balance sheet (see **8.28**),

- right of members to require an audit (see **8.28**),

- companies excluded from small companies exemption (see **8.30**), and

- availability of small companies exemption in case of a group company (see **8.31**)

a company that qualifies as a small company in relation to a financial year is exempt from the requirements of *CA 2006* relating to the audit of accounts for that year.

[*CA 2006, s 477; SI 2012 No 2301, Reg 4*].

## 8.30    *Companies excluded from small companies exemption*

A company is not entitled to the exemption under **8.29** if it was at any time in the financial year in question

## 8.30  Audit

(a)   a public company (see 33.1 PUBLIC AND LISTED COMPANIES);

(b)   a company that

(i)   is an authorised insurance company, a banking company, an e-money issuer, a 'MiFID investment firm' or a UCITS management company; or

(ii)  carries on an insurance market activity; or

(c)   a special register body or an employers' association as defined by, respectively, the *Trade Union and Labour Relations (Consolidation) Act 1992, s 117(1) and s 122.*

See APPENDIX 1 – DEFINITIONS for the meaning of '*MiFID investment firm*'

[*CA 2006, s 478*].

**8.31**  *Small companies exemption in case of a group company*

A company that is a group company for any part of a financial year is not entitled to the exemption under **8.29** for that year unless the group qualifies as a small group in relation to that financial year and was not at any time in that year an ineligible group (see **5.7** and **5.8** ACCOUNTS: SMALL COMPANIES) or throughout the whole of the period or periods during the financial year when it was a group company, it was both a subsidiary undertaking and dormant.

'*Group company*' means a company that is a parent company or a subsidiary undertaking.

'*The group*', in relation to a group company, means that company together with all its associated undertakings. For this purpose undertakings are associated if one is a subsidiary undertaking of the other or both are subsidiary undertakings of a third undertaking.

[*CA 2006, s 479; SI 2012 No 2301, Reg 5*].

**8.32**  **Subsidiary companies: conditions for exemption from audit**

A company is exempt from the requirements of CA 2006 relating to the audit of individual accounts for a financial year if

(a)   it is a subsidiary undertaking, and

(b)   its parent undertaking is established under the law of an EEA State.

Exemption is however conditional upon compliance with all the following conditions

(a)   all members of the company must agree to the exemption in respect of the financial year in question;

(b)   the parent undertaking must give a guarantee in respect of that year (see **8.33**):

(c)   the company must be included in the consolidated accounts drawn up for that year or to an earlier date in that year by the parent undertaking in accordance with the provisions of the 2013/34/EU of the European Parliament and of the Council on the annual financial statements, consolidated statements and related reports of certain types of undertakings or international accounting standards;

(d)   the parent undertaking must disclose in the notes to the consolidated accounts that the company is exempt from the requirements of CA 2006 relating to the audit of individual accounts by virtue of *CA 2006, s 479A*: and

(e)   the directors of the company must deliver to the Registrar of Companies on or before the date that they file the accounts for that year

(i)     a written notice of the agreement referred to in (a) (above)

(ii)    a statement of guarantee (see **8.33** below)

(iii)   a copy of the consolidated accounts referred to in (c) (above) and a copy of the auditor's report on those accounts

(iv)    a copy of the consolidated account drawn up by the parent undertaking.

A company is not entitled to the subsidiary company exemption above if it was at any time within the financial year in question a traded company (as defined in *CA 2006, s 474(1)*), an authorised insurance company, a banking company, an e-money issuer, a MiFID investment firm, a UCITS management company, or if it carries on insurance market activity or is a special register body as defined in *s 117(1)* of the *Trade Union and Labour Relations (Consolidation) Act 1992* or an employers' association as defined in *s 122* of that *Act* or *Article 4* of the *Industrial Relations (Northern Ireland) Order 1992*.

[*CA 2006 s 479A, 479B; SI 2012 No 2301, Reg 7; SI 2015 No 980, Reg 16*].

**8.33    Parent undertaking guarantee**

A guarantee is only given by a parent undertaking when the subsidiary company delivers to the Registrar of Companies a statement by the parent undertaking that it guarantees the subsidiary company under CA 2006 s 479C. The statement must be authenticated by the parent and must specify

(a)     the name of the parent undertaking

(b)     if the parent is incorporated in the United Kingdom, its registered number (if any)

(c)     if the parent is incorporated outside the United Kingdom and registered in the country in which it is incorporated, the identity of the register on which it is registered and the number with which it is registered

(d)     the name and registered number of the subsidiary company in respect of which the guarantee is being given

(e)     the date of the statement and

(f)     the financial year to which the guarantee relates.

The guarantee given under *CA 2006, s 479C* has the effect that the parent guarantees all outstanding liabilities to which the subsidiary company is subject at the end of the financial year to which the guarantee relates until they are satisfied in full and the guarantee is enforceable against the parent by any person to whom the subsidiary is liable in respect of those liabilities.

[*CA 2006, s 479C; SI 2012 No 2301, Reg 7*]

**8.34    Exemption from audit: dormant companies**

Subject to the

•     requirement for a statement on the balance sheet (see **8.28**),

•     right of members to require an audit (see **8.28**), and

•     companies excluded from dormant companies exemption (see below)

a company is exempt from the requirements relating to the audit of accounts in respect of a financial year if

(a)      it has been 'dormant' since its formation, or

(b)      it has been dormant since the end of the previous financial year and

        (i)      as regards its individual accounts for the financial year in question, it is entitled to prepare accounts in accordance with the small companies regime or would be so entitled but for having been a public company or a member of an ineligible group (see **5.7** and **5.8** Accounts: Small Companies); and

        (ii)      is not required to prepare group accounts for that year.

[*CA 2006, s 480*].

See Appendix 1 Definitions for the meaning of 'dormant company'.

*Excluded companies.* A company is not entitled to the above exemption if it was at any time within the financial year in question a company that

- is a traded company as defined in *CA 2006, s 474(1)*;

- is an authorised insurance company, a banking company, an e-money issuer, a 'MiFID investment firm' or a UCITS management company; or

- carries on insurance market activity.

[*CA 2006, s 481; SI 2015 No 980, Reg 10*].

See Appendix 1 – Definitions for the meaning of 'MiFID investment firm'.

## 8.35    Exemption from audit: other circumstances

(1) *Public sector audits*

Subject to the requirement for a statement on the balance sheet (see **8.28**), the requirements of *CA 2006, Pt 16* as to audit of accounts do not apply to a company for a financial year if it is non-profit-making and its accounts

- are subject to audit by

        (i)      the Comptroller and Auditor General by virtue of an order under *Government Resources and Accounts Act 2000, s 25(6)*; or

        (ii)      the Auditor General for Wales by virtue of *Government of Wales Act 1998, s 96* or an order under *Government of Wales Act 1998, s 144*;

- are accounts

        (i)      in relation to which *Public Finance and Accountability (Scotland) Act 2000, s 21* applies; or

        (ii)      that are subject to audit by the Auditor General for Scotland by virtue of an order under *CA 2006, s 483* (see below); or

- are subject to audit by the Comptroller and Auditor General for Northern Ireland by virtue of an order under *Audit and Accountability (Northern Ireland) Order 2003 (SI 2003 No 418), Art 5(3)*.

In the case of a company that is a parent company or a subsidiary undertaking, the above provisions apply only if every group undertaking is non-profit-making. [*CA 2006, s 482*].

(2) *Scottish public sector companies: audit by Auditor General for Scotland*

The Scottish Ministers may, by *Order*, provide for the accounts of a company having its registered office in Scotland to be audited by the Auditor General for Scotland. Such an *Order* may be made in relation to a company only if it appears to the Scottish Ministers that the company

•      exercises in or as regards Scotland functions of a public nature none of which relate to reserved matters (within the meaning of the *Scotland Act 1998*); or

•      is entirely or substantially funded from a body having accounts

     (i)      in relation to which $S$ applies; or

     (ii)      which are subject to audit by the Auditor General for Scotland by virtue of an order under these provisions. [*CA 2006, s 483*].

(3) *Charitable companies*

A charitable company is one which is formed and registered under *CA 2006* and is established for exclusively charitable purposes.

*England and Wales.* Small charitable companies are now subject to the same audit and independent examination requirements as unincorporated charities. However, if the directors of a small charitable company do not elect to take advantage of any audit exemption available under company law, the accounts will need to be audited under company law, and the charity law requirements do not apply.

Under charity law, the accounts of a charitable company must be subject to full audit where

(a)      gross income is more than £1 million; or

(b)      gross income is more than £250,000 and the aggregate value of the charity's assets is more than £3.26 million.

Also, a parent charity is required to prepare group accounts where the gross income of the group is more than £1 million (after eliminating all group transactions from income for the year) and to have those accounts audited.

[*Charities Act 2011, ss 138, 139, 144; SI 2015 No 321, Art 3; SI 2015 No 322, Reg 2*].

For other charitable companies, the following scrutiny requirements apply:

(i)      the accounts of charitable companies with gross income of less than £25,000 do not require any independent scrutiny; and

(ii)      the trustees of a charitable company with gross income of more than £25,000 but not more than £500,000 may elect for an independent examination in place of a full audit – where gross income is more than £250,000, the independent examiner must be from one of the recognised professional bodies specified in the legislation (and the examiner's report must state the qualification held).

[*Charities Act 2011, s 145*].

## 8.36   AUDITOR'S REPORT

A company's auditor must make a report to the company's members on all annual accounts of the company of which copies are, during his tenure of office

- in the case of a private company, to be sent out to members under *CA 2006, s 423*, see **2.6 ACCOUNTS: GENERAL**; or

- in the case of a public company, to be laid before the company in general meeting under *CA 2006, s 437*, see **2.10 ACCOUNTS: GENERAL**.

Despite this obligation to report to the *members*, the auditor's obligation is satisfied by forwarding the signed report to the company secretary, leaving him or the directors to convene the meeting and send copies of the account and report to the members (*Re Allen, Craig & Co (London) Ltd* [1934] Ch 483, 103 LJ Ch 193).

The *Statutory Auditors and Third Country Auditors Regulations 2016 (SI 2016 No 649)* make a number of changes to the detailed requirements on the form and content of auditor reports. These are reflected in the sections below and apply to audits for financial periods beginning on or after 17 June 2016.

The report must specifically deal with the following matters.

*Annual accounts.* The report must

(a) include the identity of the company whose accounts are the subject of the audit;

(b) include a description of the annual accounts that are the subject of the audit and the period covered;

(c) include a description of the financial reporting framework applied in preparing the accounts;

(d) include a description of the scope of the audit, identifying the auditing standards in accordance with which the audit was conducted;

(e) state clearly whether, in the auditor's opinion, the annual accounts

    (i) give a 'true and fair view (see **2.16 ACCOUNTS GENERAL**)'

- in the case of an individual balance sheet, of the state of affairs of the company as at the end of the financial year;

- in the case of an individual profit and loss account, of the profit or loss of the company for the financial year;

- in the case of group accounts, of the state of affairs as at the end of the financial year and of the profit or loss for the financial year of the undertakings included in the consolidation as a whole, so far as concerns the company;

    (ii) have been properly prepared in accordance with the relevant financial reporting framework; and

    (iii) have been prepared in accordance with the requirements of *CA 2006* (and, where applicable, *IAS Regulation, Art 4*).

(f) be either unqualified or 'qualified' (and 'qualified' means that the report does not state the auditor's unqualified opinion that the accounts have been properly prepared in accordance with *CA 2006* or, in the case of an undertaking not required to prepare accounts in accordance with *CA 2006*, under any corresponding legislation under which it is required to prepare accounts);

(g) include a reference to any matters to which the auditor wishes to draw attention by way of emphasis without qualifying the report;

# Audit   8.36

(h)     include a statement on any material uncertainty relating to events that may cast significant doubt about the company's ability to continue to adopt the going concern basis of accounting; and

(i)     identify the auditor's place of establishment.

*Micro-entity accounts.* The following additional requirements apply in the case of a company that qualifies as a micro-entity and prepares its accounts under the micro-entity financial reporting regime (see **5.2–5.6 SMALL COMPANIES AND MICRO-ENTITIES**)

–       where the accounts comprise only micro-entity minimum accounting items, the auditor must disregard any provision of an accounting standard which would require the accounts to contain information additional to those items;

–       in relation to a micro-entity minimum accounting item contained in the accounts the auditor must disregard any provision of an accounting standard which would require the accounts to contain further information in relation to those items; and

–       where the accounts contain an item of information additional to the micro-entity minimum accounting items, the auditor must have regard to any provision of an accounting standard which relates to that item.

For the meaning of 'micro-entity minimum accounting item' and 'micro-entity provisions' see **APPENDIX 1 – DEFINITIONS**.

*Additional requirements in the case of joint auditors.* Where more than one person is appointed as auditor, all the persons appointed must jointly make a report under *CA 2006, s 495* and the report must include a statement as to whether all those appointed agree on the matters contained in the report. If all the persons appointed cannot agree on the matters contained in the report, the report must include the opinions of each person appointed and give reasons for the disagreement.

[*CA 2006, ss 495, 539; SI 2013 No 3008, Reg 8; SI 2016 No 649, Reg 15, Sch 3 Part 3, para 13(1)–(4)*].

*Strategic report and Directors' report.* In his report on the company's annual accounts, the auditor must also

•       state whether, in his opinion, based on the work undertaken in the course of the audit

        (i)     the information given in the strategic report (if any) or the directors' report for the financial year for which the accounts are prepared is consistent with those accounts; and

        (ii)    any such strategic report and the directors' report have been prepared in accordance with applicable legal requirements;

•       state whether, in the light of the knowledge and understanding of the company and its environment obtained in the course of the audit he has identified material misstatements in the strategic report (if any) and the directors' report; and

•       if applicable give an indication of the nature of each of the misstatements referred to above.

*Additional requirements in the case of joint auditors.* Where more than one person is appointed as auditor, the report must include a statement as to whether all those appointed agree on the statements and indications set out above. If they cannot agree on those statements and indications, the report must include the opinions of each person appointed and give reasons for the disagreement.

## 8.36  Audit

[*CA 2006, s 496; SI 2015 No 980, Reg 11; SI 2016 No 649, Reg 15, Sch 3 Part 3, para 14*].

*Directors' remuneration report.* In the case of a quoted company, the auditor, in his report on the company's annual accounts for the financial year, must also

- report to the company's members on the '*auditable part*' of the directors' remuneration report (see **19.9** to **19.15** DIRECTORS' REMUNERATION REPORTS); and

- state whether in his opinion that part of the directors' remuneration report has been properly prepared in accordance with *CA 2006*.

[*CA 2006, s 497*].

*Corporate governance statement.* Where a company prepares a separate corporate governance statement (see **15.5(2)** CORPORATE GOVERNANCE and **20.21** STRATEGIC REPORTS AND DIRECTORS' REPORTS) in respect of a financial year, the auditor must in his report on the company's annual accounts for that year

(i)   state whether, in his opinion, based on the work undertaken in the course of the audit, the information given in the statement is in accordance with Disclosure and Transparency

- rule 7.2.5 (a description of the main features of the issuer's internal control and risk management systems in relation to the financial reporting process); and

- rule 7.2.6 (information about share capital where the issuer is subject to those requirements)

is consistent with those accounts and has been prepared in accordance with applicable legal requirements;

(ii)  state whether, in the light of the knowledge and understanding of the company and its environment obtained in the course of the audit he has identified material misstatements in the information in the statement referred to above;

(iii) if applicable give an indication of the nature of each of the misstatements referred to above; and

(iv)  state whether in his opinion, based on the work undertaken in the course of the audit, rules 7.2.2, 7.2.3 and 7.2.7 in the Disclosure Rules and Transparency Rules made by the FCA have been complied with if applicable (these rules cover information about the company's corporate governance code and practices, and its administrative, management and supervisory bodies and their committees).

*Additional requirements in the case of joint auditors.* Where more than one person is appointed as auditor, the report must include a statement as to whether all those appointed agree on the statements and indications set out above. If they cannot agree on those statements and indications, the report must include the opinions of each person appointed and give reasons for the disagreement.

Where a company is required to prepare a corporate governance statement and no such statement is included in the directors' report, the auditor, in preparing his report on the company's accounts

- must ascertain whether a corporate governance statement has been prepared and

- if it appears to the auditor that no such statement has been prepared he must state that fact in his report.

[*CA 2006, ss 497A, 498A; SI 2015 No 980, Reg 11; SI 2016 No 649, Reg 15, Sch 3 Part 3, para 15*].

**8.37   Related requirements of UK auditing standards**

All statutory audits must be carried out in accordance with UK auditing standards (International Standards on Auditing (UK) – ISAs (UK) issued by the FRC) and in compliance with the FRC Ethical Standard. [*SI 2016 No 649, Reg 4*]. In particular, the requirements of ISA (UK) 700 'Forming an Opinion and Reporting on Financial Statements' apply whenever an opinion is expressed in terms of whether the financial statements give a true and fair view. The standard sets out detailed requirements on the structure and content of the auditor's report and additional requirements that apply to PIE audits (for instance, the report must state by whom the auditor was appointed, state the date of appointment and the period of total uninterrupted engagement, confirm that the audit opinion is consistent with the additional report provided to the audit committee, and declare that no non-audit services prohibited under the FRC Ethical Standard were provided to the entity). In addition, the requirements of ISA (UK) 701 'Communicating Key Audit Matters in the Independent Auditor's Report' apply to audits of PIEs and of any other entities that report on compliance with the UK Corporate Governance Code, irrespective of whether this is under regulatory requirements or on a voluntary basis.

An auditor must also comply with ISA (UK) 705 'Modifications to opinions in the independent auditor's report' when issuing a qualified report, and with ISA (UK) 706 'Emphasis of matter paragraphs and other matter paragraphs in the independent auditor's report' where relevant.

Example auditor reports and additional guidance on auditor reporting can be found in the FRC Bulletin 'Compendium of illustrative auditor's reports on United Kingdom private sector financial statements for periods commencing on or after 17 June 2016' (available at www.frc.org.uk).

**8.38   Auditor's report following defective accounts or report**

The annual accounts, directors' report or directors' remuneration report of a company may, in certain circumstances, be replaced or partially revised because the original was defective. See 2.13 ACCOUNTS: GENERAL. A special auditor's report is then required (unless the company is exempt from audit). [*SI 2008 No 373, Reg 18*] and in those circumstances the following provisions apply.

(1)   *Auditor's Report on either revised accounts or revised strategic report or directors' report or* revised remuneration report

Who can prepare the auditor's report – a company's current auditor must make a report or (as the case may be) further report to the company's members on any revised accounts prepared. But if the auditor's report on the original annual accounts was not made by the company's current auditor, the directors of the company may resolve that the report is to be made by the person or persons who made that report, provided that that person or those persons agree to do so and would be qualified for appointment as auditor of the company.

What must be included in the report – the provisions in **8.39** also apply to this report and the report must state whether in the auditor's opinion:

• The revised accounts have been properly prepared in accordance with *CA 2006* (and, where applicable, *IAS Regulations, Art 4*) and in particular whether a true and fair view, seen as at the date the original annual accounts were approved, is given by the revised accounts with respect to the matters set out in **8.36(e)(i)**. For this purpose, where any provision of *CA 2006* as to matters to be included in the annual accounts or report have been amended after the date of the original annual accounts or report but before the date of revision, the relevant provisions are those in force at the date of the original accounts or report.

•   The original annual accounts failed to comply with the requirements of *CA 2006* (and, where applicable, *IAS Regulations, Art 4*) in the respects identified by the directors

(i)   in the case of a revision by replacement, in the statement the directors are required to make in the revised accounts as to how the original accounts failed to comply; or

(ii)   in the case of a revision by supplementary note, in the supplementary note.

The auditor must also state whether the information contained in the strategic report or directors' report for the financial year for which the annual accounts are prepared (which is, if the report has been revised under these provisions, that revised report) is consistent with those accounts.

Signature – The provisions in **8.41** relating to signature of the auditor's report also apply to the auditor's report under these provisions (with any necessary modifications) which, as from the date that report is signed, becomes the auditor's report on the annual accounts of the company in place of the report on the original annual accounts.

[*SI 2008 No 373, Regs 7, 19(1); SI 2013 No 2224, Regs 8, 9; SI 2015 No 980, Reg 43(1)–(3)*].

(2)   *Report where company ceases to be exempt from audit*

Where, as a result of the revisions to its accounts, a company is no longer entitled to exemption from audit, the company must cause an auditor's report on the revised accounts to be prepared. The auditor's report must be delivered to the Registrar of Companies within 28 days after the date of revision of the accounts. If the report is not delivered within the 28 day period then every person who immediately before the end of that period was a director of the company commits an offence. A person guilty of such an offence is liable (i) on summary conviction, to a fine not exceeding level 5 on the standard scale; and (ii) for continued contravention, to a daily default fine not exceeding one-tenth of the greater of £5,000 or level 4 on the standard scale. See **29.1** OFFENCES AND PENALTIES for the standard scale. It is a defence for a person charged with such an offence to prove that he took all reasonable steps for securing that those requirements would be complied with before the end of that period. It is not a defence to prove that the documents in question were not in fact prepared as required. [*CA 2006, s 451; SI 2015 No 664, Regs 3, 5, Sch 3 Part 1, para 9(1) (13)*].

If the directors of the company fail to make good the default within 14 days after the service of a notice on them requiring compliance, the court may, on the application of any member or creditor of the company or of the Registrar of Companies, make an order directing the directors (or any of them) to make good the default within such time as may be specified in the order. The court's order may provide that all costs (in Scotland, expenses) of, and incidental to, the application are to be borne by the directors. [*CA 2006, s 452*].

[*SI 2008 No 373, Reg 8*].

(3)   *Auditor's report on revised directors' report alone*

A company's current auditor must make a report or (as the case may be) further report to the company's members on any revised report prepared if the relevant annual accounts have not been revised at the same time. But where the auditor's report on the annual accounts for the financial year covered by the revised report was not made by the company's current auditor, the directors of the company may resolve that the required report should be made by the person or persons who made that report, provided that that person or those persons agree to do so and would be qualified for appointment as auditor of the company.

Where a revised strategic report or directors' report is prepared, the auditor's report must state whether in his opinion the information given in that revised report is consistent with the annual accounts for the relevant year and must specify the relevant year.

Where a revised directors' remuneration report is prepared, the auditor's report must state whether in his opinion any 'auditable part' (see **19.2** DIRECTORS' REMUNERATION REPORTS) of that revised report has been properly prepared.

The provisions in **8.41** relating to signature of the auditor's report also apply to the auditor's report under these provisions (with any necessary modifications).

[*SI 2008 No 373, Reg 9; SI 2013 No 2224, Reg 9; SI 2015 No 980, Reg 43(1)–(3)*].

## 8.39   Duties of auditor in connection with report

A company auditor must have regard to the directors' duty under *CA 2006, s 393(1)* (ie that the directors must not approve annual accounts unless they are satisfied that they give a true and fair view).

An auditor of a company, in addition to the matters which he must deal with in his report under **8.36**, also has a duty to consider and include the following in his report where relevant.

(a)     The auditor must carry out such investigations as will enable him to form an opinion as to

    (i)     whether adequate accounting records have been kept by the company and returns adequate for their audit have been received from branches not visited by him;

    (ii)     whether the company's individual accounts are in agreement with the accounting records and returns; and

    (iii)     in the case of a quoted company, whether the auditable part of the company's directors' remuneration report (see **19.9** to **19.15** DIRECTORS' REMUNERATION REPORTS) is in agreement with the accounting records and returns.

If the auditor is of the opinion that (i), (ii) or (iii) above has not been complied with he must state that fact in his report.

(b)     If the auditor fails to obtain all the information and explanations which, to the best of his knowledge and belief, are necessary for the purposes of his audit, he must state that fact in his report.

(c)     If

    (i)     the requirements of regulations under *CA 2006, s 412* (disclosure of directors' benefits: remuneration, pensions and compensation for loss of office, see **3.46** ACCOUNTS: LARGE COMPANIES are not complied with in the annual accounts, or

    (ii)     in the case of a quoted company, the requirements of regulations under *CA 2006, s 421* as to information forming the auditable part of the directors' remuneration report are not complied with in that report (see **19.9** to **19.15** DIRECTORS' REMUNERATION REPORT) the auditor must include in his report, so far as he is reasonably able to do so, a statement giving the required particulars.

(d)     If the directors of the company have

(i)      prepared accounts in accordance with the small companies regime, or

(ii)     have taken advantage of small companies exemption from the requirement to prepare a *strategic report* or in preparing the directors' report

and in the auditor's opinion they were not entitled so to do, the auditor must state that fact in his report.

Where more than one person is appointed as auditor, the report must include a statement as to whether all those appointed agree on the statements given under (a)–(d) above. If they cannot agree on those statements, the report must include the opinions of each person appointed and give reasons for the disagreement.

[*CA 2006, s 498; SI 2008 No 393, Reg 6; SI 2013 No 1970, Reg 14, Sch para 22; SI 2016 No 649, Reg 15, Sch 3 Part 3, para 16*].

**8.40**   *Case law explaining auditor's standard of care*

In *Re London and General Bank (No 2)* [1895] 2 Ch 673, CA, the court held that an auditor is not bound to do more than exercise reasonable care and skill in making enquiries and investigations. What is reasonable care in any particular case must depend upon the circumstances of that case. Where suspicion is aroused more care is necessary. An auditor is a watch-dog not a bloodhound (*Re Kingston Cotton Mill Co (No 2)* [1896] 2 Ch 279, CA).

However, the standard of skill and care may be more exacting since these earlier cases were decided and, where suspicion ought emphatically to be aroused, the auditor should take steps to investigate in depth and cannot make such excuses as shortage of time (*Re Thomas Gerrard & Son Ltd* [1968] Ch 455, [1967] 2 All ER 525). In *Lloyd Cheyham & Co Ltd v Littlejohn & Co* [1987] BCLC 303, [1986] PCC 389 the court adopted the test of whether the defendant had acted in accordance with a practice accepted as proper by a body of responsible and skilled opinion. Current accounting standards (see **2.15**) and auditing standards (see below) were relied upon by the court as setting the appropriate standards and must now be considered of paramount importance.

In applying the necessary standard of care, the auditor should be aware of the content of the company's articles. See *Leeds Estate, Building and Investment Co v Shepherd* (1887) 36 Ch D 787 where dividends were paid out of capital. As to whether auditor should rely on a bank certificate, etc for verification of ownership of securities, see *Re City Equitable Fire Insurance Co Ltd* [1925] Ch 407, 94 LJ Ch 445, CA.

**Auditing standards.** International standards on auditing are set by the International Auditing and Assurance Standards Board. In the UK, these are adopted by the Financial Reporting Council (FRC), often with certain amendments specific to the UK, and known as International Standards of Auditing (UK) (see also **8.37**). The amended EU Audit Directive (see **8.1**) places increased emphasis on compliance with international auditing standards as adopted by the European Commission (EC), with Member States allowed to impose additional procedures only if these are necessary to meet national legal requirements on the scope of a statutory audit or to add to the credibility and quality of financial statements. However, no auditing standards have yet been adopted by the EC and so the FRC's own auditing standards continue to apply at present. All UK statutory audits must be carried out in accordance with ISAs (UK) and auditors must also comply with the requirements of the FRC Ethical Standard. [*SI 2016 No 649, Reg 4*].

The FRC also issues Practice Notes, Bulletins and other explanatory material for auditors. These documents give guidance on the procedures by which ISAs (UK) may be applied and deal with current auditing techniques and particular auditing problems.

## 8.41   Signature of auditor's report

The auditor's report must state the name of the auditor and be signed and dated. Where the auditor is an individual, the report must be signed by him. Where the auditor is a firm, the report must be signed by the 'senior statutory auditor' in his own name, for and on behalf of the auditor.

'*Senior statutory auditor*' means the individual identified by the firm as senior statutory auditor in relation to the audit in accordance with standards issued by the EC (or, if there is no applicable standard so issued, any relevant guidance issued by the Secretary of State or a body appointed by order of the Secretary of State). The FRC is the body appointed for this purpose. The person identified as senior statutory auditor must be eligible for appointment as auditor of the company in question (see **8.10** and **8.11**).

The senior statutory auditor is not, by reason of being named or identified as senior statutory auditor or by reason of his having signed the auditor's report, subject to any civil liability to which he would not otherwise be subject.

Where more than one person is appointed as auditor, the report must be signed by all those appointed.

[*CA 2006, ss 503, 504; SI 2012 No 1741, Art 15; SI 2016 No 649, Reg 15, Sch 3 Part 3, para 17*].

*Statement of names in published copies of auditor's report.* Every copy of the auditor's report that is published by or on behalf of the company must

- state the name of the auditor and (where the auditor is a firm) the name of the person who signed it as senior statutory auditor; or

- if that information may be omitted (see below), state that a resolution has been passed and notified to the Secretary of State in accordance with those provisions.

If more than one person is appointed as auditor, the reference to the name of the auditor is to be read as a reference to the names of all the auditors.

For these purposes, a company is regarded as publishing the report if it publishes, issues or circulates it or otherwise makes it available for public inspection in a manner calculated to invite members of the public generally, or any class of members of the public, to read it.

If a copy of the auditor's report is published without the required statement, an offence is committed by the company and every officer of the company who is in default. A person guilty of such an offence is liable on summary conviction to a fine not exceeding level 3 on the standard scale. See **29.1** OFFENCES AND LEGAL PROCEEDINGS for the standard scale.

*Circumstances in which names may be omitted.* The auditor's name and, where the auditor is a firm, the name of the person who signed the report as senior statutory auditor, may be omitted from published copies of the report and the copy of the report delivered to the Registrar of Companies for filing if the following conditions are met.

- The company, considering on reasonable grounds that statement of the name would create or be likely to create a serious risk that the auditor or senior statutory auditor (or any other person) would be subject to violence or intimidation, has resolved that the name should not be stated.

- The company has given notice of the resolution to the Secretary of State, stating

    (i)   the name and registered number of the company;

    (ii)  the financial year of the company to which the report relates; and

(iii) the name of the auditor and (where the auditor is a firm) the name of the person who signed the report as senior statutory auditor.

[*CA 2006, ss 505, 506; SI 2016 No 649, Reg 15, Sch 3 Part 3, para 18*].

**8.42 Offences in connection with auditors' reports**

The following offences apply in relation to auditors' reports on accounts:

(a) where the auditor is an individual, to that individual and any employee or agent of his who is eligible for appointment as auditor of the company; and

(b) where the auditor is a firm, to any director, member, employee or agent of the firm who is eligible for appointment as auditor of the company.

A person within (*a*) or (*b*) above commits an offence if he knowingly or recklessly causes an auditor's report on a company's annual accounts to

- include any matter that is misleading, false or deceptive in a material particular; or

- omit a statement required by **8.39**(*a*)(ii), (*b*) or (*d*).

A person guilty of such an offence is liable (i) on conviction on indictment, to a fine; and (ii) on summary conviction, to a fine not exceeding the statutory maximum. See **29.1** Offences and Legal Proceedings for the statutory maximum.

[*CA 2006, s 507*].

*Guidance for regulatory and prosecuting authorities.* The Secretary of State (in Scotland, the Lord Advocate) may issue guidance about handling matters where the same behaviour by an auditor could give rise to prosecution under the above provisions and disciplinary proceedings by a certain regulatory body. [*CA 2006, ss 508, 509; SI 2016 No 649, Reg 15, Sch 3 Part 3, paras 19, 20*]. General guidance for regulatory and prosecuting authorities in England, Wales and Northern Ireland on the principles to be applied when making decisions about prosecution under *CA 2006, s 507* was issued in 2010 (available at www.gov.uk/government/publications/companies-act-2006-offences-in-connection-with -auditors-reports).

**8.43 AUDITOR'S RIGHT TO INFORMATION**

(1) *General right to information*

An auditor of a company

- has a right of access at all times to the company's books, accounts and vouchers (in whatever form they are held); and

- can require such information or explanations as he thinks necessary for the performance of his duties as auditor from

(i) any officer or employee of the company;

(ii) any person holding or accountable for any of the company's books, accounts or vouchers;

(iii) any subsidiary undertaking of the company which is a body corporate incorporated in the UK;

(iv)    any officer, employee or auditor of any such subsidiary undertaking or any person holding or accountable for any books, accounts or vouchers of any such subsidiary undertaking; and

(v)     any person who fell within any of (i)–(iv) above at a time to which the information or explanations required by the auditor relates.

A company cannot rely on any of its regulations which restricts the rights of auditors to information to which they are entitled under these provisions (*Newton v Birmingham Small Arms Co Ltd* [1906] 2 Ch 378, 75 LJ Ch 627).

A statement made by a person in response to a requirement under the above provisions may not be used in evidence against him in any criminal proceedings except proceedings for an offence as below.

*Offences.* A person commits an offence who knowingly or recklessly makes a statement (oral or written) to an auditor of a company that

•       conveys or purports to convey any information or explanations which the auditor requires, or is entitled to require; under the above provisions; and

•       is misleading, false or deceptive in a material particular.

A person guilty of such an offence is liable (i) on conviction on indictment, to imprisonment for a term not exceeding two years or a fine (or both); and (ii) on summary conviction, to imprisonment for a term not exceeding 12 months (in Scotland or Northern Ireland, 6 months) or a fine up to the statutory maximum (or both). See **29.1** OFFENCES AND LEGAL PROCEEDINGS for the statutory maximum.

A person who fails to comply with a requirement under the above provisions without delay commits an offence unless it was not reasonably practicable for him to provide the required information or explanations. A person guilty of such an offence is liable, on summary conviction, to a fine not exceeding level 3 on the standard scale. See **29.1** OFFENCES AND LEGAL PROCEEDINGS for the standard scale.

[*CA 2006, ss 499(1)–(3), 501(1)–(3)(5)*].

(2) *Overseas subsidiaries*

Where a parent company has a subsidiary undertaking that is not a body corporate incorporated in the UK, the auditor of the parent company may require it to obtain such information or explanations as he may reasonably require for the purposes of his duties as auditor from

(a)     the undertaking;

(b)     any officer, employee or auditor of the undertaking;

(c)     any person holding or accountable for any of the undertaking's books, accounts or vouchers; and

(d)     any person who fell within (*b*) or (*c*) above at a time to which the information or explanations relates.

If so required, the parent company must take all such steps as are reasonably open to it to obtain the information or explanations from the person concerned.

A statement made by a person in response to a requirement under the above provisions may not be used in evidence against him in any criminal proceedings except proceedings for an offence as below.

*Offences.* If a parent company fails to comply with the above provisions, an offence is committed by the company and every officer of it who is in default. A person guilty of such an offence is liable, on summary conviction, to a fine not exceeding level 3 on the standard scale. See **29.1 Offences and Legal Proceedings** for the standard scale.

[*CA 2006, ss 500(1)–(4), 501(4)(5)*].

(3) *Professional privilege*

Nothing in the above provisions compels any person to disclose information in respect of which a claim to legal professional privilege (in Scotland, to confidentiality of communications) could be maintained in legal proceedings. [*CA 2006, ss 499(4), 500(5), 501(6)*].


**8.44  AUDITOR'S RIGHTS IN RELATION TO RESOLUTIONS AND MEETINGS**

A company's auditor is entitled to

- receive all notices of, and other communications relating to, any general meeting of the company which a member is entitled to receive;

- attend any general meeting of the company; and

- be heard at any general meeting which he attends on any part of the business which concerns him as auditor.

Where a written resolution has been proposed by a private company (see **42.5 Resolutions and Meetings**) the company's auditor is entitled to receive all such communications relating to the resolution which must be supplied to members.

Where the auditor is a firm, the right to attend or be heard at a meeting is exercisable by an individual authorised by the firm in writing to act as its representative at the meeting.

[*CA 2006, s 502*].


**8.45  AUDITOR'S LIABILITY**

In addition to the cases listed in **8.39**, liability of the auditors to the members has been considered in *London Oil Storage Co Ltd v Seear Hasluck & Co* (1904) 30 Acct LR 93 (verification of assets); *AE Green & Co v Central Advance and Discount Corpn Ltd* (1920) 63 Acct LR 1 (bad debts provision); and *Pendleburys Ltd v Ellis Green & Co* (1936) 80 Acct LR 39 (insufficient internal control in a private company where the directors were the sole shareholders).

In *Hedley Byrne & Co Ltd v Heller & Partners Ltd* [1964] AC 465, [1963] 2 All ER 575, HL, the House of Lords approved of the dissenting judgment of Denning LJ in *Candler v Crane, Christmas and Co* [1951] 2 KB 164, [1951] 1 All ER 426, CA, which included the comment that ' . . . accountants owe a duty of care not only to their own clients, but also to those whom they know will rely on their accounts in the transactions for which the accounts are prepared'. On this basis, an auditor could be held liable for negligence to third parties (eg investors) where he knows, or ought to know, that his work is liable to be relied upon by such a person and that person suffers a financial loss as a result. Subsequent cases have, however, tended to restrict this liability. In *Caparo Industries plc v Dickman* [1990] 2 AC 605, [1990] BCLC 273, HL, the House of Lords considered the auditor's duty of care to shareholders and potential shareholders. It held that the purpose of the audit report was to enable shareholders to exercise their proprietary powers as shareholders by giving them reliable intelligence on the company's affairs, sufficient to allow them to scrutinise the management's conduct and to exercise their collective powers to control the management through general meetings. To meet the requirements for a duty of care to exist, the report must be used for the purpose for which it was intended and the precise purpose for which the accounts are required must be known to the wrongdoer. In the circumstances of a shareholder (or potential shareholder) simply dealing in the company's shares on the basis of the report, these requirements were not met.

**Liability for false or misleading statements in directors' reports, etc.** No person (including therefore an auditor) can be subject to any liability to a person other than the company resulting from reliance, by that person or another, on information in the strategic report, the directors' report or the directors' remuneration report. This does not affect liability for a civil penalty or a criminal offence. [*CA 2006, s 463(1), (4), (6); SI 2013 No 1970, Reg 14, Sch, para 16*].

### 8.46   Provisions protecting auditor from liability

Except as permitted under **8.47** and **8.48** below, any provision (whether contained in the company's articles or in any contract with the company or otherwise)

* exempting an auditor of a company (to any extent) from any liability that would otherwise attach to him, or

* by which a company (directly or indirectly) provides an indemnity (to any extent) for an auditor of the company, or of an associated company, against any liability attaching to him

in connection with any negligence, default, breach of duty or breach of trust in relation to the company occurring in the course of the audit of accounts is void.

For these purposes, companies are associated if one is a subsidiary of the other or both are subsidiaries of the same body corporate.

[*CA 2006, s 532*].

**Before 6 April 2008**, any provision (whether contained in the company's articles or in any contract with the company or otherwise) exempting any person employed by a company as auditor from, or indemnifying him against, any liability was, subject to **8.47**, void. This applied to any liability which by virtue of any rule of law would otherwise attach to that person in respect of any negligence, default, breach of duty or breach of trust of which he might be guilty in relation to the company. [*CA 1985, s 310(1)(2)*].

### 8.47   Indemnity for costs of defending proceedings

The provisions in **8.46** do not prevent a company from indemnifying an auditor against any liability incurred by him

* in defending proceedings (whether civil or criminal) in which judgment is given in his favour or he is acquitted; or

* in connection with an application under *CA 2006, s 1157* or, before 1 October 2008, *CA 1985, s 727* (power of court to grant relief in case of honest and reasonable conduct, see **29.10** OFFENCES AND LEGAL PROCEEDINGS) in which relief is granted to him by the court.

[*CA 2006, s 533*].

**Before 6 April 2008**, the provisions in **8.46** did not prevent a company from

* purchasing and maintaining for any such auditor insurance against any such liability; or

- from indemnifying any such auditor against any liability incurred by him

  (i) in defending any proceedings (whether civil or criminal) in which judgment was given in his favour or he was acquitted; or

  (ii) in connection with any application under *CA 1985, s 727* (general power to grant relief in case of honest and reasonable conduct) in which relief was granted to him by the court.

[*CA 1985, s 310; CA 1989, s 137; C(AICE)A 2004, s 19*].

**8.48 Liability limitation agreements**

The provisions in **8.46** do not affect the validity of a liability limitation agreement that

- complies with the terms in **8.49**; and
- is authorised by the members of the company as in **8.50**.

Such an agreement is not subject

- in England and Wales or Northern Ireland, to *Unfair Contract Terms Act 1977, s 2(2)* or *3(2)(a)*; or
- in Scotland, to *Unfair Contract Terms Act 1977, s 16(1)(b)* or *17(1)(a)*.

A '*liability limitation agreement*' is an agreement that purports to limit the amount of a liability owed to a company by its auditor in respect of any negligence, default, breach of duty or breach of trust, occurring in the course of the audit of accounts, of which the auditor may be guilty in relation to the company.

[*CA 2006, s 534*].

*Disclosure of agreement by company.* A company which has entered into a liability limitation agreement must make such disclosure in connection with the agreement as the Secretary of State may require by Regulations. [*CA 2006, s 538*]. Disclosure requirements are currently set out in the *Companies (Disclosure of Auditor Remuneration and Liability Limitation Agreements) Regulations 2008 (SI 2008 No 489)* – see **3.53** ACCOUNTS: LARGE COMPANIES.

**8.49** *Terms of liability limitation agreement*

A liability limitation agreement must

- not apply in respect of acts or omissions occurring in the course of the audit of accounts for more than one financial year; and
- specify the financial year in relation to which it applies.

Subject to the above, it is immaterial how a liability limitation agreement is framed. In particular, the limit on the amount of the auditor's liability need not be a sum of money, or a formula, specified in the agreement.

[*CA 2006, s 535*].

No regulations have been made under this section.

**8.50** *Authorisation of agreement by members of the company*

A liability limitation agreement must be authorised by the members of the company in one of the following ways for each financial year of the company.

Private companies. A liability limitation agreement auditor may be authorised—

(i)     by the company passing an ordinary resolution, before it enters into the agreement, waiving the need for approval;

(ii)    by the company passing an ordinary resolution, before it enters into the agreement, approving the agreement's 'principal terms'; or

(iii)   by the company passing an ordinary resolution, after it enters into the agreement, approving the agreement;

Public companies. A liability limitation agreement may be authorised—

(i)     by the company passing an ordinary resolution in general meeting, before it enters into the agreement, approving the agreement's principal terms; or

(ii)    by the company passing an ordinary resolution in general meeting, after it enters into the agreement, approving the agreement.

The '*principal terms*' of an agreement are terms specifying, or relevant to the determination of

•       the kind (or kinds) of acts or omissions covered;

•       the financial year to which the agreement relates; or

•       the limit to which the auditor's liability is subject.

*Withdrawal of authorisation.* Authorisation may be withdrawn by the company passing an ordinary resolution to that effect

(a)     at any time before the company enters into the agreement; or

(b)     if the company has already entered into the agreement, before the beginning of the financial year to which the agreement relates. This applies notwithstanding anything in the agreement.

[*CA 2006, s 536*].

**8.51**   *Effect of liability limitation agreement*

A liability limitation agreement is not effective to limit the auditor's liability to less than such amount as is fair and reasonable in all the circumstances of the case having regard (in particular) to

•       the auditor's responsibilities under *CA 2006, Pt 16*;

•       the nature and purpose of the auditor's contractual obligations to the company; and

•       the professional standards expected of him.

A liability limitation agreement that purports to limit the auditor's liability to less than such an amount has effect as if it limited his liability to that amount.

In determining what is fair and reasonable in all the circumstances of the case, no account is to be taken of

•       matters arising after the loss or damage in question has been incurred; or

•       matters (whenever arising) affecting the possibility of recovering compensation from other persons liable in respect of the same loss or damage.

## 8.51    Audit

[*CA 2006, s 537*].

## 8.52   QUOTED COMPANIES: MEMBERS' POWER TO REQUIRE WEBSITE PUBLICATION OF AUDIT CONCERNS

**Requests from members**. The members of a 'quoted company' may require the company to publish on a website a statement setting out any matter relating to

- the audit of the company's accounts (including the auditor's report and the conduct of the audit) that are to be laid before the next accounts meeting, or

- any circumstances connected with an auditor of the company appointed for such a year ceasing to hold office since the previous accounts meeting,

that the members propose to raise at the next accounts meeting of the company. A request from a member may be sent to the company in hard copy or electronic form and must identify the statement to which it relates. It must be authenticated by the person or persons making it and must be received by the company at least one week before the meeting to which it relates.

See APPENDIX 1 – DEFINITIONS for the meaning of '*quoted company*' which applies for these purposes and definition of '*accounts meeting*'.

[*CA 2006, ss 527(1)(4), 531*].

**Duties of company**. Unless the court directs otherwise (see below), the company must publish the statement, on a website that is maintained by or on behalf of the company and which identifies the company in question, once it has received requests to that effect from

- members representing at least 5% of the total voting rights of all the members who have a 'relevant right to vote' (excluding any voting rights attached to any shares in the company held as treasury shares); or

- at least 100 members who have a relevant right to vote and hold shares in the company on which there has been paid up an average sum, per member, of at least £100.

See 26 MEMBERS for different criteria where members have exercised their rights in relation to shares held on behalf of others.

A '*relevant right to vote*' means a right to vote at the accounts meeting.

Access to the information on the website, and the ability to obtain a hard copy of the information from the website, must not be conditional on the payment of a fee or otherwise restricted.

The statement must be made available within three working days of the company being required to publish it on a website and must be kept available until after the meeting to which it relates. A failure to make the information available on a website throughout this period is disregarded if

- the information is made available on the website for part of that period; and

- the failure is wholly attributable to circumstances that it would not be reasonable to have expected the company to prevent or avoid.

*Application to court*. A quoted company is not required to place a statement on a website if, on an application by the company or another person who claims to be aggrieved, the court is satisfied that the rights conferred by these provisions are being abused. The court may order the members requesting website publication to pay the whole or part of the company's costs (in Scotland, expenses) on such an application, even if they are not parties to the application.

*[CA 2006, ss 527(2), (3), (5), (6), 528]*.

*Supplementary duties of company.* The quoted company must in the notice it gives of the accounts meeting draw attention to

•     the possibility of a statement being placed on a website in pursuance of members' requests;

•     the fact that the company must pay its expenses in complying with these requirements;

•     the fact that it must (and has) forwarded the statement to the company's auditor not later than the time when it makes the statement available on the website; and

•     the fact that the business which may be dealt with at the accounts meeting includes any statement that the company has been required to publish on a website.

*[CA 2006, s 529]*.

**Offences.** In the event of the company defaulting in complying with its above duties, an offence is committed by every officer of the company who is in default. A person guilty of such an offence is liable (i) on conviction on indictment, to a fine; and (ii) on summary conviction, to a fine not exceeding the statutory maximum. See **29.1** OFFENCES AND LEGAL PROCEEDINGS for the statutory maximum.

*[CA 2006, s 530]*.

# 9 Class Rights

**Background.** The provisions in this chapter apply, unless otherwise stated, with effect from 1 October 2009. They retain the earlier provisions in *CA 1985* (with some simplification) but notably extend them to cover companies without a share capital.

## 9.1 VARIATION OF CLASS RIGHTS: COMPANIES WITH A SHARE CAPITAL

Where a company's share capital is divided into different classes (eg ordinary shares and preference shares), there are special provisions concerned with the 'variation' of the rights attached to any class of shares in a company. Class rights might cover such matters as voting rights, rights to dividends and right to a return of capital on a winding up. Where all the shares in a company fall within one class, there are no class rights, only shareholder rights.

**Classes of shares.** For the purposes of the *Companies Acts*, shares are of one class if the rights attached to them are in all respects uniform. The rights attached to shares are not regarded as different from those attached to other shares by reason only that they do not carry the same rights to dividends in the twelve months immediately following their allotment. [*CA 2006, s 629*]. Apart from this, what amounts to a 'class' is not defined in the legislation.

**Meaning of variation.** For these purposes, and (except where the context requires otherwise) in any provision in a company's articles for the variation of rights attached to a class of shares, references to the '*variation*' of those rights includes references to their abrogation. [*CA 2006, s 630(6)*]. Otherwise, the meaning of 'variation' has been strictly construed by the courts, so that where the value of the rights of a class of shareholders has effectively been reduced, but those rights themselves have not been affected as such, this has been held not to be a variation (see *Greenhalgh v Arderne Cinemas Ltd* [1946] 1 All ER 512, 90 Sol Jo 248, CA). See also *White v Bristol Aeroplane Co Ltd* [1953] Ch 65, [1953] 1 All ER 40, CA; *Re John Smith's Tadcaster Brewery Co Ltd, John Smith's Tadcaster Brewery Co Ltd v Gresham Life Assurance Society Ltd* [1953] Ch 308, [1953] 1 All ER 518, CA; *Re Saltdean Estate Co Ltd* [1968] 3 All ER 829, [1968] 1 WLR 1844; and *House of Fraser plc v ACGE Investments Ltd* [1987] AC 387, [1987] BCLC 478, HL.

For a right to be a class right, it must be given to members of a class in their capacity as members, although such a right need not be attached to particular shares. See *Cumbrian Newspapers Group Ltd v Cumberland and Westmorland Herald Newspaper and Printing Co Ltd* [1987] Ch 1, [1986] BCLC 286.

Any amendment of a provision contained in a company's articles for the variation of the rights attached to a class of shares, or the insertion of any such provision into the articles, is itself to be treated as a variation of those rights. [*CA 2006, s 630(5)*].

**Conditions for variation.** Subject to **9.7**, the rights attached to a class of a company's shares may only be varied

## 9.1 Class Rights

- in accordance with provisions in the company's articles for variation of the rights; or

- where the company's articles contain no such provision, if the holders of shares of that class consent to the variation.

The consent must take the form of either

- consent in writing from the holders of at least three-quarters in nominal value of the issued shares of that class (excluding any shares held as treasury shares); or

- a special resolution passed at a separate general meeting of the holders of that class sanctioning the variation.

This is without prejudice to any other restrictions on the variation of the rights. Thus, if the company has adopted a more onerous regime in its articles for the variation of class rights (eg a higher percentage) it must comply with the more onerous regime. Also, if and to the extent that the company has protected class rights by making provisions for entrenchment of those rights under *CA 2006, s 22* (see **14.7** CONSTITUTION – MEMORANDUM AND ARTICLES) that protection cannot be circumvented by changing the class rights under these provisions.

[*CA 2006, s 630(2)–(4)*].

### 9.2 Right to object to variation

Where the rights attached to any class of shares in a company are varied under **9.1**, the holders of not less than 15% of the issued shares of the class in question (being persons who did not consent to, or vote in favour of, the resolution for variation) may apply to the court to have the variation cancelled. The application must be made within 21 days after the date on which the consent to the variation was given or the resolution for the variation was passed (as the case may be). Such application may be made, on behalf of the shareholders entitled to make it, by such one or more of their number as they may appoint in writing for the purpose.

If such an application is made, the variation has no effect unless and until it is confirmed by the court.

In determining whether any application is made by the holders of 15% of the issued shares of the class in question, any of the company's share capital held as treasury shares is disregarded.

[*CA 2006, s 633(1)–(4)*].

The court may disallow the variation if satisfied that, having regard to all the circumstances of the case, the variation would unfairly prejudice the shareholders of the class represented by the applicant. If the court is not so satisfied, it must confirm the variation. The decision of the court is final. [*CA 2006, s 633(5)*].

For an example of what could constitute unfair prejudice in this context, see *Re Holders Investment Trust Ltd* [1971] 2 All ER 289, [1971] 1 WLR 583, a case on reduction of capital.

The company must, within 15 days after the court makes an order by the court, forward a copy of the order to the Registrar of Companies. In default, an offence is committed by the company and every officer of the company who is in default. A person guilty of such an offence is liable, on summary conviction, to a fine not exceeding level 3 on the standard scale and, for continued contravention, a daily default fine not exceeding one-tenth of level 3 on the standard scale. [*CA 2006, s 635*]. See **29.1** OFFENCES AND LEGAL PROCEEDINGS for the standard scale.

**9.3    Registration of particulars**

Under certain circumstances, a company is required to provide the Registrar of Companies with particulars of the rights attaching to its shares.

(a)    **Variation of rights.** Where the rights attached to any shares of a company are varied, the company must, within one month from the date on which the variation is made, deliver to the Registrar of Companies a notice giving particulars of the variation. [*CA 2006, s 637(1)*].

(b)    **Name or other designation of class of shares.** Where a company assigns a name or other designation, or a new name or other designation, to any class or description of its shares, it must, within one month from doing so deliver to the Registrar of Companies a notice giving particulars of the name or designation so assigned. [*CA 2006, s 636(1)*].

If default is made in complying with either (*a*) or (*b*) above, an offence is committed by the company and every officer of the company who is in default. A person guilty of such an offence is liable, on summary conviction, to a fine not exceeding level 3 on the standard scale and, for continued contravention, a daily default fine not exceeding one-tenth of level 3 on the standard scale. [*CA 2006, ss 636(2)(3), 637(2)(3)*]. See **29.1** OFFENCES AND LEGAL PROCEEDINGS for the standard scale.

**Allotment of shares.** Under *CA 2006, s 555*,

• a company limited by shares, or

• a company limited by guarantee and having a share capital

must, within one month of allotting shares, deliver to the Registrar of Companies a statement of capital which, amongst other things, gives details, for each class of shares, of prescribed particulars of the rights attached to the share. See **47.12** SHARES.

Similarly, under *CA 2006, s 556*, if an unlimited company allots shares with rights which are not in all respects uniform with shares previously allotted, it must, within one month of the allotting the shares, deliver to the Registrar of Companies a return of allotments containing prescribed particulars of those rights. See **47.12** SHARES.

**9.4    VARIATION OF CLASS RIGHTS: COMPANIES WITHOUT SHARES**

Where a company does not have a share capital but has different classes of members, there are special provisions concerned with the variation of the rights attached to any class of members in the company. These might apply, for example, where a company limited by guarantee has different classes of members with different voting rights. Where all the members in a company fall within one class, there are no class rights, only members' rights.

**Meaning of variation.** For these purposes, and (except where the context requires otherwise) in any provision in a company's articles for the variation of the rights of a class of members, references to the variation of those rights includes reference to their abrogation.

Any alteration of a provision contained in a company's articles for the variation of the rights of a class of members, or the insertion of any such provision into the articles, is itself to be treated as a variation of those rights.

[*CA 2006, s 631(5)(6)*].

## 9.4 Class Rights

**Conditions for variation.** Subject to **9.7**, rights of a class of members may only be varied

- in accordance with provisions in the company's articles for variation of the rights; or

- where the company's articles contain no such provision, if the members of that class consent to the variation.

The consent must take the form of either

- consent in writing from at least three-quarters of the members of the class; or

- a special resolution passed at a separate general meeting of the members of that class sanctioning the variation.

This is without prejudice to any other restrictions on the variation of the rights. Thus, if the company has adopted a more onerous regime in its articles for the variation of class rights (eg a higher percentage) it must comply with the more onerous regime. Also, if and to the extent that the company has protected class rights by making provisions for entrenchment of those rights under *CA 2006, s 22* (see **14.5** CONSTITUTION – MEMORANDUM AND ARTICLES) that protection cannot be circumvented by changing the class rights under these provisions.

[*CA 2006, s 631(2)–(4)*].

## 9.5 Right to object to variation

Where the rights attaching to any class of members of a company are varied under **9.4**, members amounting to not less than 15% of the members of the class in question (being persons who did not consent to, or vote in favour of, the resolution for variation) may apply to the court to have the variation cancelled. The application must be made within 21 days after the date on which the consent to the variation was given or the resolution for the variation was passed (as the case may be). The application may be made, on behalf of the members entitled to make it, by such one or more of their number as they may appoint in writing for the purpose.

If an application is made, the variation has no effect unless and until it is confirmed by the court.

[*CA 2006, s 634(1)–(4)*].

The court may disallow the variation if satisfied that, having regard to all the circumstances of the case, the variation would unfairly prejudice the members of the class represented by the applicant. If the court is not so satisfied, it must confirm the variation. The decision of the court is final. [*CA 2006, s 634(5)*].

The company must, within 15 days after the court makes an order, forward a copy of the order to the Registrar of Companies. In default, an offence is committed by the company and every officer of the company who is in default. A person guilty of an offence under these provisions is liable, on summary conviction, to a fine not exceeding level 3 on the standard scale and, for continued contravention, a daily default fine not exceeding one-tenth of level 3 on the standard scale. [*CA 2006, s 635*]. See **29.1** OFFENCES AND LEGAL PROCEEDINGS for the standard scale.

## 9.6 Registration of particulars

Under certain circumstances, a company is required to provide the Registrar of Companies with particulars of the rights attaching to any class of members.

The following apply after 1 October 2009.

(a)    **Creation of a new class of members.** If, a company creates a new class of members, the company must, within one month from the date on which the new class is created, deliver to the Registrar of Companies a notice containing particulars of the rights attached to that class. [*CA 2006, s 638(1)*].

(b)    **Variation of class rights.** If the rights of any class of members are varied, the company must, within one month from the date on which the variation is made, deliver to the Registrar of Companies a notice (Form SH 10) containing particulars of the variation. [*CA 2006, s 640(1)*].

(c)    **Name or other designation of class of members.** Where a company assigns a name or other designation, or a new name or other designation, to any class of its members, it must, within one month of doing so, deliver to the Registrar of Companies a notice (Form SH08) giving particulars of the name or designation so assigned. [*CA 2006, s 639(1)*].

If default is made in complying with (a)–(c) above, an offence is committed by the company and every officer of the company who is in default. A person guilty of such an offence is liable, on summary conviction, to a fine not exceeding level 3 on the standard scale and, for continued contravention, a daily default fine not exceeding one-tenth of level 3 on the standard scale. [*CA 2006, ss 638(2)(3), 639(2)(3), 640(2)(3)(6)*]. See **29.1** OFFENCES AND LEGAL PROCEEDINGS for the standard scale.

## 9.7    POWERS OF THE COURT

Nothing in **9.1** or **9.4** (variation of class rights) affects the power of the court under the following provisions.

•    *CA 2006, s 98* (application to cancel resolution for public company to be re-registered as private). See **41.9** RE-REGISTRATION.

•    *CA 2006, Pt 26* (arrangements and reconstructions). See **35** RECONSTRUCTIONS AND MERGERS.

•    *CA 2006, Pt 30* (protection of members against unfair prejudice). See **26.5** MEMBERS.

[*CA 2006, s 632*].

# 10   Community Interest Companies

## 10.1   INTRODUCTION TO COMMUNITY INTEREST COMPANIES

With effect from 1 July 2005 (6 April 2007 for Northern Ireland), a community interest company ('CIC') was created by *Companies (Audit, Investigations and Community Enterprise) Act 2004.* [*C(AICE)A 2004, s 26(1)*]. CICs can be used by non-profit-distributing enterprises providing benefit to a community in areas such as childcare, social housing, leisure and community transport. The special characteristics of the CIC make it a particularly suitable vehicle for social enterprises that wish to work for community benefit within the relative freedom of the non-charitable company form, but with a clear assurance of non-profit-distribution status.

Companies that are formed as, or become, CICs are formed under *CA 2006* and continue to be subject to the general framework of company law. In particular, CICs and directors of CICs have to comply with their obligations and duties under the *CA 2006* and the common law. CICs must register as companies with the Registrar of Companies in the usual way, and are subject to the usual regulatory constraints and powers associated with company status (including the oversight of the BIS Companies Investigation Branch).

The distinguishing features of a CIC are as follows.

- In order to become a CIC, a company must satisfy a community interest test, confirming that it will pursue purposes beneficial to the community and will not serve an unduly restricted group of beneficiaries. Certain companies may be excluded from CIC status. See **10.2**.

- Even if a CIC is established for charitable purposes, it is not treated as being established for such purposes, and therefore is not a charity. [*C(AICE)A 2004, s 26(3); SI 2006 No 242*]. This means that CICs are not subject to the benefits or obligations of charitable status; nor are they subject to regulation by the

Charity Commission or the charitable jurisdiction of the High Court. CICs, and outright bequests to them, are not eligible for any tax reliefs or exemptions which are only available to charities or for charitable giving. However, a donation to a charitable trust of which a CIC is trustee will be eligible for relief. The charitable status of the trust is unaffected by the status of the trustee.

Charities (and all other organisations except political parties) are able to establish CICs as subsidiaries.

- Every CIC is required to produce an annual community interest company report containing key information relevant to CIC status. The report must be placed on the public register of companies. See **10.16**.

- CICs have an asset lock, ie they are ordinarily prohibited from distributing any profits they make to their members. See **10.7**. However, CICs limited by shares can issue dividend-paying 'investor shares' although the dividend payable on such shares is subject to a maximum aggregate cap. See **10.9**.

- When a CIC is wound up, its surplus residual assets are not distributed to its members but pass to another suitable organisation that has restrictions on the distribution of its profits (eg another CIC or a charity). See **10.30**.

- A Regulator (see **10.17**) must approve applications for CIC status, receive copies of the community interest company reports and police the requirements of CIC status, including compliance with the asset lock. He has powers to investigate abuses of CIC status and to take action where necessary (eg to remove directors, freeze assets or apply to the courts for a CIC to be wound up). He also sets the cap on CIC dividends.

## 10.2 ELIGIBLE COMPANIES

**Community interest test.** A '*community interest test*' is used to determine the eligibility of a company to be formed as a CIC (see **10.4**) or to become a CIC if already incorporated (see **10.5**). The Regulator can also exercise certain supervisory powers if a CIC ceases to satisfy the community interest test (see **10.18**).

A company satisfies the community interest test if

- it is not an excluded company; and

- a reasonable person might consider that its activities are being carried on for the benefit of the 'community'.

    '*Community*' includes a 'section of the community' (whether in the UK or anywhere else). For the purposes of the CIC test, any group of individuals may constitute a '*section of the community*' if

    (i)   they share a common characteristic which distinguishes them from other members of the community; and

    (ii)  a reasonable person might consider that they constitute a section of the community.

[*C(AICE)A 2004, s 35; SI 2005 No 1788, Reg 5*].

**Excluded companies.** The following are excluded companies.

- A company which is (or when formed would be) a 'political party' or a 'political campaigning organisation'.

- A company which is (or when formed would be) a subsidiary of a political party or of a political campaigning organisation.

A *'political party'* includes any person standing, or proposing to stand, as a candidate at any 'election', and any person holding public office following his election to that office. *'Election'* means any election to public office held in the UK or elsewhere.

A *'political campaigning organisation'* means any person carrying on, or proposing to carry on, activities

- to promote or oppose

    (i)     changes in any law applicable in the UK or elsewhere, or

    (ii)    any policy of a 'governmental authority' or 'public authority', or

- which could reasonably be regarded as intended

    (i)     to affect public support for a political party, or

    (ii)    to influence voters in relation to any election or 'referendum'

unless, in either case, such activities are incidental to other activities carried on by that person.

*'Governmental authority'* includes

- any national, regional or local government in the UK or elsewhere,

- the European Community,

- any inter-governmental organisation, and

- any organisation which is able to make rules or adopt decisions which are legally binding on any governmental authority falling within either of the above three categories

or any of their organs, institutions or agencies.

*'Public authority'* includes a court or tribunal and any person certain of whose functions are functions of a public nature whether in the UK or elsewhere.

*'Referendum'* includes any national or regional referendum or other poll held in pursuance of any provision made by or under the law of any state on one or more questions or propositions specified in or in accordance with any such provision.

[*SI 2005 No 1788, Regs 2, 6*].

**Activities not treated as for the benefit of the community.** For the purposes of the community interest test, subject to below, the following activities are to be treated as *not* being activities which a reasonable person might consider are activities carried on for the benefit of the community.

(a)    The promotion of, or the opposition to, changes in

    (i)     any law applicable in the UK or elsewhere; or

    (ii)    the policy adopted by any 'governmental authority' or 'public authority' (see above) in relation to any matter.

(b)    The promotion of, or the opposition (including the promotion of changes) to, the policy which any governmental authority or public authority proposes to adopt in relation to any matter.

(c)   Activities which can reasonably be regarded as intended or likely to

   (i)   provide or affect support (whether financial or otherwise) for a 'political party' or 'political campaigning organisation' (see above); or

   (ii)   influence voters in relation to any 'election' or 'referendum' (see above).

(d)   Activities to the extent that a reasonable person might consider that they benefit only the members of a particular body or the 'employees' of a particular 'employer'.

But activities within (*a*) to (*c*) above *are* to be treated as being activities which a reasonable person might consider are activities carried on for the benefit of the community if

- they can reasonably be regarded as incidental to other activities, which a reasonable person might consider are being carried on for the benefit the community; and

- those other activities cannot reasonably be regarded as incidental to activities within (*a*) to (*c*) above.

'*Employee*' means a person who has entered into or works under (or, where the employment has ceased, worked under)

- a contract of service or apprenticeship; or

- a contract for services under which it is agreed that a specified individual is to perform services

whether express or implied, and (if it is express) whether oral or in writing.

'*Employer*' means the person by whom an employee is (or, where the employment has ceased, was) employed.

[*SI 2005 No 1788, Regs 1, 3, 4*].

## 10.3   BECOMING A COMMUNITY INTEREST COMPANY

A new organisation applying to be incorporated as a CIC can be incorporated as a public or private company and either

- a company limited by shares; or

- a company limited by guarantee and not having a share capital.

An existing registered company can also apply to be converted into a CIC if it is currently

- limited by shares;

- limited by guarantee and not having a share capital; or

- limited by guarantee having a share capital.

[*C(AICE)A 2004, s 26(2); CA 2006, s 6*].

## 10.4   Requirements for new companies

Since CICs are companies under the *Companies Acts*, the normal company formation provisions apply, together with additional provisions specific to CICs.

If a company is to be formed as a CIC, the documents delivered to the Registrar of Companies under *CA 2006, s 9* (see 12 COMPANY FORMATION AND TYPES OF COMPANY) must be accompanied by the 'prescribed formation documents'. [*C(AICE)A 2004, s 36(1), (2)*].).

Note that the articles of a CIC must comply with the requirements of *CA 2006, s 18* and *C(AICE)A 2004* and the regulations made under that *Act* (See **10.13**). A CIC cannot rely on the default articles under *CA 2006, s 20*. Model constitutional documents are available on the Regulator's website at www.cicregulator.gov.uk on the guidance page. A filing fee of £35 is payable. See Appendix 3 Fees.

The *'prescribed formation documents'* are

(a)    a community interest statement (Form CIC36) (signed by each person who is to be a first director of the company) in a form approved by the Regulator and which

   (i)    contains a declaration that the company will carry on its activities for the benefit of the community or a section of the community; and

   (ii)   indicates how it is proposed that the company's activities will benefit the community (or a section of the community); and

(b)    a declaration made by each person who is to be a first director of the company that the company, when formed, will not be an excluded company (see **10.2**).

On receiving the documents, the Registrar of Companies must (instead of registering them) forward a copy of each of the documents to the Regulator (see **10.17**) and retain the documents pending the Regulator's decision. Same day registration service is not available for a CIC.

The Regulator must decide whether the company is eligible to be formed as a CIC, ie whether

•    the articles comply with the requirements under **10.13**;

•    the company's name complies with the provisions in **10.15**; and

•    having regard to the documents delivered and any other relevant considerations, the company will satisfy the community interest test and is not an excluded company (see **10.2**).

The Regulator must give notice of the decision to the Registrar of Companies (but the Registrar is not required to record it).

If the Regulator decides that the company is eligible to be formed as a CIC, the Registrar of Companies must proceed with the registration of the company and issue a certificate of incorporation. If the company is entered on the register, the Registrar must retain and record the prescribed formation documents. The certificate of incorporation must state that the company is a CIC and is conclusive evidence that the company is a CIC.

If the Regulator decides that the company is not eligible to be formed as a CIC, any subscriber to the memorandum may appeal against the decision (see **10.27**).

[*C(AICE)A 2004, ss 36, 36A, 36B; SI 2005 No 1788, Regs 2, 11*].

**10.5    Requirements for existing companies to become CICs**

If an existing private company is to become a CIC, the following conditions must be satisfied.

•    The company must by special resolution

   (i)    alter its articles to state that it is to be a CIC;

   (ii)   make such alterations of its articles by special resolution as it considers necessary to comply with requirements imposed under **10.13** or otherwise appropriate in connection with becoming a CIC; and

(iii)    change its name by special resolution to comply with **10.15**.

A model special resolution to comply with the above is available in a guidance booklet "CIC business activities: forms and step by step guide" from the website of the Office of the Regulator of CICs.

• An application to become a CIC must be delivered to the Registrar of Companies, together with certain other documents (see below).

*[C(AICE)A 2004, s 37(1)(2)].*

*Application to court to cancel special resolutions.* Where special resolutions have been passed with a view to the company becoming a CIC, an application to the court for the cancellation of the resolutions may be made

• by the holders of not less in the aggregate than 15% in nominal value of the company's issued share capital or any class of the company's issued share capital (disregarding any shares held by the company as treasury shares),

• if the company is not limited by shares, by not less than 15% of its members, or

• by the holders of not less than 15% of the company's debentures entitling the holders to object to an alteration of its objects

but not by a person who has consented to or voted in favour of the resolutions.

The application must be made within 28 days after the date on which the resolutions are passed or made (or, if the resolutions are passed or made on different days, the date on which the last of them is passed or made). It may be made on behalf of the persons entitled to make it by such one or more of their number as they may appoint for the purpose.

On making such an application, the applicants (or the person making the application on their behalf) must immediately give notice to the Registrar of Companies. The company must also immediately give notice to the Registrar of Companies on being served with notice of such an application.

The court must make an order (on such terms as it thinks fit) either cancelling or confirming the resolutions. The order may provide (where relevant) for the purchase by the company of the shares of any of its members and for the reduction accordingly of the company's capital (making such alteration in the company's articles as may be required in consequence).

Within 15 days of the making of the court's order on the application, or such longer period as the court may at any time direct, the company must deliver to the Registrar of Companies a copy of the order.

If a company fails to comply with the above requirement to notify the Registrar of Companies of service of an application or to deliver to him a copy of the court order, an offence is committed by the company and every officer of the company who is in default. A person guilty of such an offence is liable on summary conviction to a fine not exceeding level 3 on the standard scale and, for continued contravention, a daily default fine not exceeding one-tenth of level 3 on the standard scale. See **29.1** OFFENCES AND LEGAL PROCEEDINGS for the standard scale.

*[C(AICE)A 2004, ss 37A, 37B].*

*Application and accompanying documents.* An application to the Registrar of Companies to become a CIC must be accompanied by

• a copy of the special resolution;

- Form NMO1-notice of change of name by CIC

- resolution fee of £25

- a printed copy of the company's articles as altered by the special resolutions; and

- Form CIC37, the community interest statement. The form contains declarations that the company will provide benefit to the community by describing its activities, who they will help and how. Form CIC 37 also contains the following

  (a)  a declaration that the company is not an excluded company (see **10.2**); and

  (b)  either

    (i)   a declaration that the company is not a charity or

    (ii)  in the case of a company that is an English charity, a declaration that the Charity Commission has consented to the change of name of the company. The company will cease to be a charity on becoming a CIC; or

    (iii) in the case of a company that is a Scottish charity, a declaration that the Scottish Charity Regulator and, where applicable, the Charity Commission, has given the company the written consent required by *C(AICE)A 2004, s 40* (see **10.6**).

The statement under (*a*) above must be signed, and the declarations under (*b*) and (*c*) above must be made, by each person who is a director of the company and each must be in a form approved by the Regulator.

On receiving an application to become a CIC together with the other documents required to accompany it, the Registrar of Companies must (instead of recording the documents and entering a new name on the register) forward a copy of each of the documents to the Regulator and retain the documents pending the Regulator's decision whether the company is eligible to form a CIC.

A company is treated as complying with the requirements of *CA 2006, s 30* (copies of resolutions to be forwarded to the Registrar of Companies, see **14.8** Constitution – Memorandum and Articles) by forwarding copies of the resolutions together with the application in accordance with the above provisions. Copies of the resolutions must not be so forwarded before the 'relevant date' and *CA 2006, s 30(1)* has effect in relation to the resolutions as if it referred to 15 days after the relevant date. The '*relevant date*' is

- if an application is made for cancellation of the special resolutions (see above)

    (i)   the date on which the court determines the application (or if there is more than one application, the date on which the last to be determined by the court is determined); or

    (ii)  such later date as the court may order; or

- if there is no such application

    (i)   if having regard to the number of members who consented to or voted in favour of the resolutions, no such application may be made, the date on which the resolutions were passed or made (or, if the resolutions were passed or made on different days, the date on which the last of them was passed or made);

    (ii)  in any other case, the end of the period for making such an application.

[*C(AICE)A 2004, ss 37(3)(4), 37C; SI 2005 No 1788, Regs 2, 12*].

## 10.5 Community Interest Companies

*Decision by the Regulator.* The Regulator must decide whether the company is eligible to become a CIC, ie whether

- its articles as proposed to be amended comply with the requirements imposed under **10.13**;

- its proposed name complies with the provisions in **10.15**; and

- having regard to the application and accompanying documents and any other relevant considerations, the Regulator considers that the company will satisfy the community interest test and is not an excluded company (see **10.2**).

The Regulator must give notice of the decision to the Registrar of Companies (but the Registrar is not required to record it).

If the Regulator gives notice of a decision that the company is eligible to become a CIC, the Registrar of Companies must proceed in accordance with *CA 2006, s 80* (registration and issue of new certificate of incorporation on change of name, see **27.17** NAMES AND BUSINESS NAMES). If the Registrar of Companies enters the new name of the company on the register, he must retain and record the application to become a CIC together with the other documents required to accompany it. The new certificate of incorporation must state that it is issued on the company's conversion to a CIC, the date on which it is issued, and that the company is a CIC. On the issue of the certificate, the company by virtue of the issue of the certificate becomes a CIC and the changes in the company's name and articles take effect. The certificate is conclusive evidence that the company is a CIC.

If the Regulator decides that the company is not eligible to become a CIC, the company may appeal to the Appeal Officer against the decision.

The above provisions refer to an existing private limited company becoming a CIC. The guidance booklet referred to also contains details of how to convert

- a charitable company to a CIC;

- a registered society to a CIC;

- a private company to a CIC PLC; and

- a PLC to a CIC.

[*C(AICE)A 2004, ss 38, 38A*].

## 10.6 Charities

**English charities.** A CIC must be a limited company. Therefore an unincorporated charity cannot convert to a CIC. Similar provisions apply as in **10.5** where a company which is a charity wishes to become a CIC except that the company cannot become a CIC without the prior written consent of the Charity Commission. In contravention of this requirement, the Charity Commission may apply to the High Court for an order quashing any altered certificate of incorporation issued.

If a company that is an English charity becomes a CIC, that does not affect the application of

- any property acquired under any disposition or agreement previously made otherwise than for full consideration in money or money's worth, or any property representing property so acquired,

- any property representing income which has previously accrued, or

236

- the income from any such property

which remains applicable to the company's original charitable purposes.

[*C(AICE)A 2004, s 39*].

**Scottish charities**. A company that is a Scottish charity cannot become a CIC without the prior written consent

(a)     if the company's registered office is situated in Scotland, of the Scottish Charity Regulator; or

(b)     if the company's registered office is situated in England and Wales (or Wales), of both the Scottish Charity Regulator and the Charity Commission.

In contravention of (*a*) above, the Scottish Charity Regulator may apply to the Court of Session for an order quashing any altered certificate of incorporation issued. In contravention of (*b*) above, the Scottish Charity Regulator or the Charity Commission may apply to the High Court for such an order.

If a company that is a Scottish charity becomes a CIC, it continues to be under a duty to apply

- any property previously acquired or any property representing property previously acquired,

- any property representing income which has previously accrued, or

- the income from any such property

in accordance with its purposes as set out in its entry in the Scottish Charity Register immediately before it become a CIC.

[*C(AICE)A 2004, s 40(3)–(9); SI 2006 No 242*].

**Northern Ireland**. A company that is a NI charity may not become a CIC. If such a company purports to become a CIC, HMRC may apply to the High Court for an order quashing any altered certificate of incorporation. [*C(AICE)A 2004, s 40A*].

**10.7   RESTRICTIONS ON THE TRANSFER OF ASSETS (DISTRIBUTIONS AND INTEREST)**

*Asset lock*

*Section 30* of *C(AICE)A 2004* and Regulations made under the *Act* provide for asset locking by:

- a ban on distribution of assets to members. Assets must either be retained within the CIC to be used for the community purposes for which the CIC was formed or, if they are transferred out of the CIC the transfer must either be made for full consideration (ie at market value) or be transferred to another asset locked body specified in the CIC's Articles of Association or transferred to another asset locked body with the consent of the CIC Regulator or be made for the benefit of the community. Asset locked bodies specified in the Articles of Association can be changed by special resolution (see a model special resolution in the Guidance referred to in 10.5).

- limits on the extent to which distributions may be made

## 10.7 Community Interest Companies

- limits on the payment of interest on debentures
- provisions for caps on dividends
- regulation on the return of capital to members and
- restriction on the transfer of assets.

See **10.8** to **10.12** and, for distributions of assets on a winding up, **10.29**.

### 10.8 Declaration of dividends

A CIC which is either a company limited by shares or a company limited by guarantee with a share capital may only pay dividends out of distributable profits and may declare a dividend to its members only

(a)   to the extent that its articles permit it to do so;

(b)   if an ordinary or special resolution of the company's members has approved the declaration of the dividend; and

(c)   (subject to below) if the declaration of the dividend does not cause

the total amount of all the dividends declared on shares in the relevant company for the financial year for which it is declared to exceed the maximum aggregate dividend for that financial year (see **10.9**).

*Exempt dividends*

To qualify as an exempt dividend, the conditions in each of the following (with alternatives) must be satisfied.

- the dividend is declared on a share which is held by an 'asset-locked body' (but this condition is not satisfied in respect of a share which the directors recommending the dividend are aware is being held on trust for a person who is not an asset-locked body); or

- The dividend is declared on a share which is held on behalf of an asset-locked body (or is believed by the directors recommending the dividend to be so held).

- The Regulator has consented to the declaration of the dividend; or

- The asset-locked body by or on behalf of which the share on which the dividend is declared is held (or on behalf of which the directors declaring the dividend believe that it is held) is named in the memorandum or articles of the company as a possible recipient of the assets of the company.

*'Asset-locked body'* (See APPENDIX 1 DEFINITIONS)

The benefits of an exempt dividend are:

- the dividend only needs to be authorised by the articles and approved by an ordinary or special resolution; and

- conditions (c)(i) and (ii) above do not apply to exempt dividends so that there is no limit on the sum that can be paid by way of an exempt dividend (other than the general rules on distributions).

*[SI 2005 No 1788, Regs 2, 17; SI 2014 No 2483, Reg 4].*

**10.9    Dividend cap**

**Maximum aggregate dividend**. The maximum aggregate dividend for a financial year of a relevant company is declared when the total amount of all dividends declared on its shares for that year, less the amount of any exempt dividends (see **10.8**), equals (when expressed as a percentage of the relevant company's 'distributable profits') the aggregate dividend cap which had effect in relation to that company on the first day of the financial year in respect of which the dividends are declared. Examples of how to work out dividend calculations can be found on the Community Interest Companies pages on the BIS website – www.gov.uk.

'*Distributable profits*' means, in relation to a company, its accumulated realised profits (so far as not previously utilised by distribution or capitalisation) less its accumulated realised losses (so far as not previously written off in a reduction or reorganisation of capital duly made).

[*SI 2005 No 1788, Regs 2, 19*].

**Rates of caps**.

For shares in issue between 1 July 2005 and 5 April 2010 the share dividend cap is that percentage of the paid-up value of a share in a relevant company which is 5% higher than the Bank of England's base lending rate. For shares in issue between 6 April 2010 and 30 September 2014, the dividend cap is 20% of the paid-up value of a share in a relevant company. From 1 October 2014 the dividend per share cap has been removed.

The maximum aggregate dividend cap is 35% of a relevant company's distributable profits. This *aggregate* cap continues to apply from 1 October 2014, even after the removal of the *per share* cap by the *Community Interest Company (Amendment) Regulations 2014*. The rationale is to preserve the notion that the CIC's assets benefit the community, insofar as dividends are not disproportionate to the sum invested by the investor, nor to the profit generated by the CIC.

The Regulator may from time to time, with the approval of the Secretary of State, set an aggregate dividend cap. Any such new cap, cannot take effect from a date less than three months after it is published.

[*SI 2005 No 1788, Reg 22; SI 2014 No 2483, Reg 1*].

**10.10    The interest cap**

In relation to debentures issued by, and debts of, a CIC

- on which a '*performance-related rate*' (ie any rate which is linked to the company's profits or turnover or to any item in the balance sheet of the company) of interest is payable, and

- where the agreement to pay interest at a performance-related rate was entered into by the company on or after the date on which it became a CIC,

a CIC must not be liable to pay, and must not pay, interest at a higher rate than the 'applicable interest cap'.

The '*applicable interest cap*' is the interest cap which had effect at the time that the agreement to pay interest at a performance-related rate was made.

Where the expression of the interest cap includes reference to a rate or figure determined by any person other than the company, the Regulator or the Secretary of State (in NI, the Department of Enterprise, Trade and Investment for NI) (eg by reference to the Bank of England base rate), the interest payable on any debt or debenture to which the interest cap applies must be calculated by reference to that rate or figure as it had effect at the beginning of the first day of the financial year in which the interest became due.

## 10.10 Community Interest Companies

Nothing in the above provisions is to be taken as releasing a CIC from liability to pay, or as preventing a CIC from paying

- interest which accrued before the company became a CIC; or

- arrears of interest which, if it had been paid at the time it became due, would not have breached those provisions.

[*SI 2005 No 1788, Reg 21*].

**Rate of interest cap**. The CIC Regulations set the first interest cap as that percentage of the average amount of a CIC's debt, or the sum outstanding under a debenture issued by it, during the 12-month period immediately preceding the date on which the interest on that debt or debenture becomes due which is 4% higher than the Bank of England's base lending rate. This applies to agreements made between 1 July 2005 and 5 April 2010. Further changes were made in 2010 and 2014.

For agreements made between 6 April 2010 and 30 September 2014 the interest cap is 10% of the average amount of a CIC's debt, or sum outstanding under a debenture issued by it, during the 12-month period immediately preceding the date on which the interest on that debt or debenture becomes due.

For agreements made on or after 1 October 2014, the interest cap is 20% of the average amount of a CIC's debt, or sum outstanding under a debenture issued by it, during the 12-month period immediately preceding the date on which the interest on that debt or debenture becomes due.

[*SI 2005 No 1788, Reg 22, Sch 4*].

## 10.11 Redemption and purchase of shares

A CIC may not distribute assets to its members by way of the redemption or purchase of the company's own shares unless the amount to be paid by the company in respect of any such share does not exceed the paid-up value of the share (see **10.9**). [*SI 2005 No 1788, Reg 24*].

## 10.12 Reduction of share capital

A CIC may not distribute assets to its members by way of a reduction of the company's share capital unless

- the reduction is made by extinguishing or reducing the liability of any of the members on any of the company's shares in respect of share capital not paid up; or

- the amount to be paid by the company to members in paying off paid-up share capital does not exceed the paid-up value (see **10.9**) of their respective shares.

[*SI 2005 No 1788, Reg 25*].

## 10.13 ARTICLES OF ASSOCIATION

Every CIC must have articles of association. A CIC cannot be registered without supplying articles. The articles of a CIC must state that the company is to be a CIC and must at all times include the provisions (and must also not include certain other provisions) set out in *Regulations* (see below). Subject to this and the requirements of company law, a CIC can include any other provisions in its articles it wishes.

If a CIC's constitution contains any provision which is inconsistent with the *C(AICE) Act 2004* and such Regulations, that provision will have no effect.

[*C(AICE)A 2004, s 32*].

The following Regulations set out what a CIC must include in its articles:

For companies without share capital – *SI 2005 No 1788, Regs 2, 7, 9, 10, Sch 1; SI 2006 No 242; SI 2007 No 1093, Sch 4 paras 27, 29, 42; SI 2008 No 948, Sch 1 para 242; SI 2009 No 1942, Regs 3, 6, 7, 19–22;*

For companies with share capital – *SI 2005 No 1788, Regs 2, 8–10, Schs 2, 3; SI 2006 No 242; SI 2007 No 1093, Sch 4, paras 27, 43, 44; SI 2008 No 948, Sch 1 para 242; SI 2009 No 1942, Regs 3, 6, 8, 19–22.*

## 10.14  Alteration of objects

As from 1 October 2009 the constitution of any company (including a CIC) is set out in its articles by virtue of *section 8* of the *CA 2006*. This includes the company's objects. So if a company wants to alter its objects unless

- a CIC ceases being a CIC by becoming a charity; and

- a special resolution to alter the articles of the company with respect to the statement of its objects is forwarded to the Registrar of Companies as required by *C(AICE)A 2004, s 54* (see **10.30**).

then any alteration of the articles of a CIC with respect to the statement of the company's objects does not have effect unless it is approved by the Regulator.

If notice under *CA 2006, s 31(2)(a)* (see **14.10** CONSTITUTION – MEMORANDUM AND ARTICLES) is given to the Registrar of Companies on form CC04 of an amendment of the articles so as to add, remove or alter a statement of the company's objects the company must also deliver an application form CIC 14 (application to alter the objects of a CIC) which includes

- a statement of the steps that have been taken to bring the proposed alteration to the notice of persons affected by the company's activities; and

- a special resolution changing the object statement. A model resolution is available in the Guidance referred to in **10.5**.

The forms must be signed by each person who is a director of the company.

On receiving these documents, the Registrar of Companies must forward a copy of each to the Regulator and retain the documents pending the Regulator's decision (but take no further action at that time).

The Regulator must decide whether to approve the proposed alteration of the articles of the CIC with respect to the statement of the company's objects. He may do so if he considers that

- the altered objects will comply with the requirements imposed on CICs under the provisions in **10.13**;

- the company will continue to satisfy the community interest test; and

- the company has taken reasonable steps to bring the proposed alteration to the notice of persons affected by its activities.

The Regulator must give notice of the decision to the Registrar of Companies (but the Registrar is not required to record it). The Registrar of Companies must not

- register the notice under *CA 2006, s 31(2)(a)*,

- register any copy of the amended articles as delivered to him, or

- cause notice of that alteration to be published in the Gazette

unless and until the Regulator has given notice of his decision to approve the proposed alteration.

If the Regulator gives such notice, the Registrar of Companies must also record the community interest statement and the statement of the steps that have been taken to bring the proposed alteration to the notice of persons affected by the company's activities.

If the Regulator does not to approve the proposed alteration, the company may appeal (see **10.26**).

[*C(AICE)A 2004, s 32(6); SI 2005 No 1788, Regs 13–16*].

## 10.15   NAMES OF COMMUNITY INTEREST COMPANIES

*The name of a CIC which is not a public company* must end with 'community interest company' or 'cic'. In the case of a Welsh company, its name may instead end with 'cwmni buddiant cymunedol' or 'cbc'.

*The name of a CIC which is a public company* must end with 'community interest public limited company' or 'community interest plc'. In the case of a Welsh company, its name may instead end with 'cwmni buddiant cymunedol cyhoeddus cyfyngedig' or 'cwmni buddiant cymunedol ccc'.

[*C(AICE)A 2004, s 33*].

## 10.16   REPORT ON ACTIVITIES

The directors of a CIC must prepare in respect of each financial year a report about the company's activities during the financial year (a 'CIC report'). A copy of the report must be delivered to the Registrar of Companies and the Registrar must forward a copy to the Regulator. [*C(AICE)A 2004, s 34(1)(2)(4)*]. A filing fee is payable. See APPENDIX 3 FEES.

**Contents of report.**

(1)   *General.*

   (a)   Every CIC report must contain

      (i)   a fair and accurate description of the manner in which the company's activities during the financial year have benefited the community;

      (ii)   a description of the steps, if any, which the company has taken during the financial year to consult persons affected by the company's activities, and the outcome of any such consultation

   (b)   If, during a financial year, a CIC has transferred any of its assets other than for full consideration

- to any 'asset-locked body' (other than by way of an 'exempt dividend'); or

- for the benefit of the community other than by way of transfer to an asset-locked body, its community interest report for that financial year must specify the amount, or contain a fair estimate of the value, of such transfer.

See **10.8** for '*asset-locked body*' and '*exempt dividend*'.

(2) *Dividends*.

Where a CIC has declared (or its directors propose to declare) a dividend for the financial year to which a report relates, its report must state the amount of any dividend declared, or proposed to be declared, by the company on each of its shares *for the financial year to which the report relates*. There is no longer a requirement to set out details of dividends paid in the four years preceding the year to which the report relates. The report must also explain how the declaration or proposed declaration of any dividend declared, or proposed to be declared, by the company in respect of the financial year to which the report relates complies, or will comply, with the provisions in **10.8** and **10.9**. This explanation must include details of

• in the case of an exempt dividend (see **10.8**), why it is an exempt dividend;

• in the case of any other dividend

the maximum aggregate dividend (see **10.8**),

and how each of these has been determined.

(3) *Debts or debentures on which a performance-related rate is payable*.

Where a CIC has at any time during the financial year a debt outstanding, or a debenture in issue, to which the interest cap provisions in **10.10** apply, its CIC report must state

• the rate of interest payable on that debt or debenture as calculated over a 12-month period ending with the most recent date on which interest became payable in respect of that debt or debenture during the financial year; and

• the applicable interest cap (see **10.10**) applying to that debt or debenture,

and how each of these has been determined.

Where the company has at any time during the financial year a debt outstanding, or a debenture in issue, to which the interest cap provisions in **10.10** do not apply, but on which a performance-related rate (ie any rate which is linked to the company's profits or turnover or to any item in the balance sheet of the company) is payable, its CIC report must state

• the rate of interest payable on that debt or debenture as calculated over a 12-month period ending with the most recent date on which interest became payable in respect of that debt or debenture during the financial year; and

• why the interest cap provisions do not apply to that debt or debenture.

**Application of provisions relating to directors' reports (and from 1 October 2013 strategic reports).** The following provisions of *CA 2006* apply to the CIC report as they apply to the directors' and strategic report.

• *CA 2006, s 419* (approval and signing, see **20.20** Directors' Reports);

• *CA 2006, ss 423–425* (circulation, see **2.6** Accounts: General);

• *CA 2006, s 430* (quoted companies; website availability, see **2.8** Accounts: General);

• *CA 2006, ss 431–432* (right to demand copies, see **2.7** Accounts: General);

## 10.16  Community Interest Companies

- *CA 2006, s 433, 436* (name of signatory to be stated in published copies, see **2.4** ACCOUNTS: GENERAL);

- *CA 2006, ss 437, 438* (public companies: laying of accounts and reports before general meeting, see **2.10** ACCOUNTS: GENERAL);

- *CA 2006, ss 441–443, 445(1)* and *445(5), 446(1)* and *446(3), 447(1)* and *447(3), 451–453. Sections 444(1)* and *444(6)* have effect as if the directors of a CIC subject to the small companies regime must deliver a copy of the CIC report for each financial year to the Registrar of Companies and s 444A(1) has effect as if the directors of a CIC subject to the small companies exemption in relation to the directors' report for a financial year must deliver a copy of the CIC report for that year to the Registrar of Companies (filing obligations, see **2.11, 2.12** ACCOUNTS: GENERAL); and

- *CA 2006, s 454* (revision of defective accounts, see **2.13** ACCOUNTS: GENERAL).

[*SI 2005 No 1788, Regs 26–29; SI 2012 No 2335 Reg 2; SI 2014 No 2483, Reg 8*].

## 10.17  THE REGULATOR AND HIS POWERS

The role of Regulator of CICs came into force at the same time as the *C(AICE) Act*. The Regulator is appointed by the Secretary of State for Business, Innovation and Skills and is an independent public office holder. Full details can be found on the CIC website at www.bis.gov.uk/cicregulator. He has such functions relating to CICs as are conferred or imposed on him by virtue of *C(AICE)A 2004* or any other enactment.

The Regulator must adopt an approach to the discharge of those functions which is based on good regulatory practice, that is an approach adopted having regard to

- the likely impact on those who may be affected by the discharge of those functions,

- the outcome of consultations with, and with organisations representing, CICs and others with relevant experience, and

- the desirability of using the Regulator's resources in the most efficient and economic way.

The Regulator may issue (or the Secretary of State may require him to issue) guidance, or otherwise provide assistance, about any matter relating to CICs.

[*C(AICE)A 2004, s 27*].

*C(AICE)A 2004, Sch 3* sets out the Regulator's terms of appointment and makes provisions about his remuneration, staffing, and financial and reporting framework. The Regulator is subject to investigation by the Parliamentary Commissioner and is disqualified from membership of the House of Commons.

The Office of the Regulator of Community Interest Companies is a partner of the Department for Business, Innovation and Skills (BIS).

## 10.18  Conditions for exercising powers

In deciding whether and how to exercise the powers conferred on him by **10.19** to **10.25**, the Regulator must adopt an approach which is based on the principle that those powers should be exercised only to the extent necessary to maintain confidence in CICs. In particular:

- No power conferred under **10.23, 10.24** or **10.5** is exercisable in relation to a CIC unless the 'company default condition' is satisfied in relation to the power and the company.

The '*company default condition*' is satisfied if it appears to the Regulator necessary to exercise the power in relation to the company because

(a)    there has been misconduct or mismanagement in the administration of the company,

(b)    there is a need to protect the company's property or to secure the proper application of that property,

(c)    the company is not satisfying the community interest test, or

(d)    if the company has community interest objects, the company is not carrying on any activities in pursuit of those objects.

- The power conferred to transfer shares (see **10.24**) is not exercisable unless it appears to the Regulator that the company is an excluded company (see **10.2**).

[*C(AICE)A 2004, s 41*].

## 10.19 Investigation of the affairs of a CIC

The Regulator may

- investigate the affairs of a CIC; or

- appoint any person (other than a member of his staff) to investigate the affairs of a CIC on his behalf.

[*C(AICE)A 2004, s 42*].

The Regulator may also authorise members of his own staff to carry out investigations under *C(AICE)A 2004, Sch 3 para 5*.

**Power to require documents and information.** The investigator of a CIC may require the company or any other person to produce such documents or provide such information as the investigator may specify. Such a requirement must be complied with at such time and place as may be specified by the investigator. The production of a document does not affect any lien which a person has on the document.

The investigator may take copies of or extracts from a document produced. In relation to information recorded otherwise than in legible form, the power to require production of it includes power to require the production of a copy of it in legible form or in a form from which it can readily be produced in visible and legible form.

**Privileged information.** Nothing in the above requires a person to produce a document or provide information in respect of which a claim could be maintained

- in an action in the High Court, to legal professional privilege, or

- in an action in the Court of Session, to confidentiality of communications,

but a person who is a lawyer may be required to provide the name and address of his client.

A person carrying on the business of banking cannot be required to produce a document, or provide information, relating to the affairs of a customer unless a requirement to produce the document, or provide the information, has been imposed on the customer.

**Use of information as evidence.** A statement made by a person in compliance with a requirement imposed under the above provisions may be used in evidence against the person. But in criminal proceedings

- no evidence relating to the statement may be adduced by or on behalf of the prosecution, and

- no question relating to it may be asked by or on behalf of the prosecution,

unless evidence relating to it is adduced or a question relating to it is asked in the proceedings by or on behalf of that person.

However, this does not apply to proceedings in which a person is charged with an offence under *Perjury Act 1911, s 5, Criminal Law (Consolidation) (Scotland) Act 1995, s 44(2)* or *Perjury (NI) Order 1979, Art 10* (false statement made otherwise than on oath) or the provisions below relating to false information.

**Failure to comply with requirement.** If a person fails to comply with a requirement relating to the production of documents or information, the investigator may certify that fact in writing to the court. Where, after hearing any witnesses who may be produced against or on behalf of the alleged offender and any statement which may be offered in defence, the court is satisfied that the offender failed, without reasonable excuse, to comply with the requirement, it may deal with him as if he had been guilty of contempt of the court.

**False information.** A person commits an offence if in purported compliance with a requirement to provide information as above, the person

- provides information which he knows to be false in a material particular, or

- recklessly provides information which is false in a material particular.

A prosecution may be instituted in England and Wales only with the consent of the Director of Public Prosecutions (in NI only with the consent of the Director of Public Prosecutions for NI).

A person guilty of such an offence is liable,

- on conviction on indictment, to imprisonment for a term not exceeding two years or a fine or to both;

- on summary conviction in England and Wales, to imprisonment for a term not exceeding twelve months (six months before the commencement of *Criminal Justice Act 2003, s 154(1)*) or a fine of an amount not exceeding the statutory maximum or to both, and

- on summary conviction in Scotland, to imprisonment for a term not exceeding six months or a fine of an amount not exceeding the statutory maximum or to both.

See **29.1 OFFENCES AND LEGAL PROCEEDINGS** for the statutory maximum.

[*C(AICE)A 2004, Sch 7*].

## 10.20   Audit of annual accounts

The Regulator may, by order, require a CIC to allow its annual accounts to be audited by a qualified auditor appointed by him. *CA 2006, ss 499–501* (auditor's rights to information, see **8.44 AUDIT**) apply in relation to such an auditor.

On completion of the audit, the auditor must make a report to the Regulator on such matters and in such form as the Regulator specifies. The expenses of the audit, including the remuneration of the auditor, are to be paid by the Regulator.

An audit under these provisions is in addition to, and does not affect, any audit required by or by virtue of any other enactment.

[*C(AICE)A 2004, s 43*].

### 10.21  Appointment and removal of directors

**Note.** The powers conferred by this paragraph can only be exercised if the 'company default condition' in **10.18** is satisfied.

**Appointment of director.** The Regulator may, by order, appoint anyone he thinks fit (other than a member of his staff) to be a director of a CIC although the company may appeal against the order (see **10.26**).

A person may be appointed as a director of a company under this provision

* whether or not the person is a member of the company, and

* irrespective of any provision made by the articles of the company or a resolution of the company.

Any such order must specify the terms on which the director is to hold office; and those terms have effect as if contained in a contract between the director and the company. The terms specified must include the period for which the director is to hold office, and may include terms as to the remuneration of the director by the company.

A director appointed under this provision has all the powers of the directors appointed by the company (including powers exercisable only by a particular director or class of directors). He may not be removed by the company but may be removed by the Regulator at any time (see below).

Where a person is appointed to be a director of the company under this provision (or a person so appointed ceases to be a director), the obligation which would otherwise be imposed on the company to notify the Registrar of Companies of the change within 14 days is instead an obligation of the Regulator. But if a person so appointed ceases to be a director otherwise than by removal by the Regulator, the company must give notification of that fact to the Regulator within 14 days and the Regulator must then send a notification to the Registrar of Companies within 14 days from the date on which he receives notification from the company. If a company fails to give notice to the Regulator as required, an offence is committed by the company and every officer of the company who is in default. A person guilty of such an offence is liable, on summary conviction, to a fine not exceeding level 5 on the standard scale and, for continued contravention, a daily default fine not exceeding one-tenth of level 5 on the standard scale. See **29.1** OFFENCES AND LEGAL PROCEEDINGS for the standard scale. For the purposes of this offence a shadow director (see **18.1** DIRECTORS) is treated as an officer of the company.

[*C(AICE)A 2004, s 45*].

**Removal of director.** The Regulator may, by order:

(a)    Remove a director of a CIC, in which case

    (i)    the company may not subsequently appoint that person a director of the company, and

    (ii)    any assignment to the person of the office of director of the company is of no effect (even if approved by special resolution of the company).

The Regulator may discharge any such order. The discharge does not reinstate the person removed as a director of the company, but (i) and (ii) above then cease to apply to the person.

(b)    Suspend a director of the company, for a maximum period of one year, pending a decision whether to remove him. The Regulator may then give directions in relation to the performance of the director's functions.

The Regulator must, from time to time, review any such order and, if appropriate, discharge the order.

Before making an order under (*a*) or (*b*) above, the Regulator must give at least 14 days' notice to the director and the company. The director may appeal against the order (in England and Wales and Northern Ireland to the High Court and in Scotland to the Court of Session).

The Regulator must, before the end of the period of 14 days beginning with the date on which an order under (*a*) or (*b*) above is made, discharged or quashed on appeal (or an order under (*b*) above expires) give notification of that event to the Registrar of Companies. Where the event involves a change in the company's directors, the company is not also obliged to notify the Registrar under *CA 2006, s 167(1)(a)*.

[*C(AICE)A 2004, s 46*].

## 10.22 Appointment of a manager

**Note**. The powers conferred by this paragraph can only be exercised if the 'company default condition' in **10.18** is satisfied.

The Regulator may, by order, appoint a manager in respect of the property and affairs of a CIC although the company may appeal against any such order. The person appointed may be anyone whom the Regulator thinks appropriate, other than a member of his staff.

The Regulator must give notice of the appointment of the manager to the Registrar of Companies, specifying an address at which service of documents (including legal process) can be effected on the person appointed. The Regulator must also give notice of any subsequent change in this address.

In carrying out his functions, the manager acts as the company's agent; and a person dealing with the manager in good faith and for value need not inquire whether the manager is acting within his powers.

The appointment of the manager does not affect

- any right of any person to appoint an interim manager of the company's property (including any right under *IA 1986, s 51* – power to appoint receiver under laws of Scotland); or

- the rights of an interim manager appointed by a person other than the Regulator.

The manager's functions are to be discharged by him under the supervision of the Regulator; and the Regulator must, from time to time, review the order by which the manager is appointed and, if it is appropriate to do so, discharge it in whole or in part. In particular, the Regulator must discharge the order on the appointment of a person to act as administrative receiver, administrator, provisional liquidator or liquidator of the company.

[*C(AICE)A 2004, s 47; CA 2006, s 1154(1)–(3)*].

**Remuneration**. The Regulator is authorised to determine the amount of a manager's remuneration. Any remuneration is payable out of the income of the CIC in respect of which the manager was appointed.

The Regulator may disallow any amount of a manager's remuneration if, having served a notice on him for failure to give security or discharge any of his functions (see below), the time specified in the notice for replying has expired and the Regulator, having considered such representations (if any) as are duly made, is satisfied that the manager has failed in his obligations.

**Security.** The Regulator may require the manager to give security to him for the due discharge of the manager's functions within such time and in such form as the Regulator may specify.

**Failure and removal.** Where

(a)     it appears to the Regulator that a manager has failed

    (i)     to give security within such time or in such form as the Regulator has specified; or

    (ii)    satisfactorily to discharge any function imposed on him; and

(b)     the Regulator wishes to consider exercising his powers to disallow any amount of remuneration (see above) or remove the manager (see below), the Regulator must give the manager, in person or by post, a written notice informing him of

- any failure under (*a*) above in respect of which the notice is issued;

- the Regulator's power to authorise the disallowance of any amount of remuneration if satisfied as to any such failure;

- the Regulator's power to remove the manager if satisfied as to any such failure; and

- the manager's right to make representations to the Regulator in respect of any such alleged failure within such reasonable time as is specified in the notice.

The Regulator may remove a manager (whether or not he also exercises the power to disallow any remuneration) if, having served a notice on him for failure to give security or discharge any of his functions (see above), the time specified in the notice for replying has expired and the Regulator, having considered such representations (if any) as are duly made, is satisfied that the manager has failed in his obligations.

The Regulator must give notice of the termination of the appointment of a manager to the Registrar of Companies.

**Reports.** The manager must make such reports to the Regulator as the Regulator may from time to time require on such matters and in such form as the Regulator specifies.

[*CA 2006, s 1154(4); SI 2005 No 1788, Regs 30–33*].

### 10.23   Powers in relation to property

**Note.** The powers conferred by this paragraph can only be exercised if the 'company default condition' in **10.18** is satisfied.

The Regulator may

(a)     by order, vest in the Official Property Holder, (who is an officer appointed by the Regulator from his own staff) any property held by or in trust for a CIC;

(b)     by order, require persons in whom such property is vested to transfer it to the Official Property Holder;

(c)     order a person who holds property on behalf of a CIC, or on behalf of a trustee of a CIC, not to part with the property without the Regulator's consent;

(d)     order any debtor of a CIC not to make any payment in respect of the debtor's liability to the company without the Regulator's consent; and

(e)      by order, restrict the transactions which may be entered into by a CIC or the nature or amount of the payments that a CIC may make.

The Regulator must, from time to time, review any order made and, if appropriate, discharge the order in whole or in part. On discharging an order made under (*a*) or (*b*) above, the Regulator may make any order as to the vesting or transfer of the property, and give any directions which he considers appropriate.

**Penalties, etc.** If a person fails to comply with an order under (*b*) above, the Regulator may certify that fact in writing to the court. If the court is satisfied that the offender failed without reasonable excuse to comply with the order, it may deal with him as if he had been guilty of contempt of the court.

A person who contravenes an order under (*c*) to (*e*) above commits an offence although a prosecution may be instituted in England and Wales only with the consent of the Regulator or the Director of Public Prosecutions (in NI only with the consent of the Regulator or the Director of Public Prosecutions for NI). A person found guilty of such an offence is liable on summary conviction to a fine not exceeding level 5 on the standard scale. See **29.1** OFFENCES AND LEGAL PROCEEDINGS for the standard scale.

Any criminal proceedings as above do not prevent the bringing of civil proceedings in respect of a contravention of an order under (*b*) to (*e*) above.

**Appeals.** The company may appeal against an order under (*a*) to (*e*) above and any person to whom it is directed may appeal against an order under (*a*) to (*d*) above.

[*C(AICE)A 2004, s 48*].

## 10.24 Transfers of shares

**Note.** The power conferred under this paragraph is not exercisable unless it appears to the Regulator that the company is an excluded company (see **10.2**). [*C(AICE)A 2004, s 41(4)*].

Subject to below,

(a)      if a CIC has a share capital, the Regulator may, by order, transfer specified shares in the company to specified persons; and

(b)      if a CIC is a company limited by guarantee, the Regulator may by order

      (i)      extinguish the interests in the company of specified members of the company (otherwise than as shareholders), and

      (ii)     appoint a new member in place of each member whose interest has been extinguished.

However

(1)      he may not transfer any shares under (*a*) above in respect of which

      (i)      a dividend may be paid, or

      (ii)     a distribution of the company's assets may be made if the company is wound up; and

(2)      an order in relation to a company may only transfer shares to, and appoint as new members, persons who have consented to the transfer or appointment.

The Regulator may make an order irrespective of any provision made by the articles of the company or a resolution of the company in general meeting.

**Appeals**. The company, and any person from whom shares are transferred by the order, may appeal against an order under (*a*) above. The company, and any person whose interest is extinguished by the order, may appeal against an order under (*b*) above.

[*C(AICE)A 2004, s 49*].

## 10.25  Dissolution and striking off

If a CIC has been dissolved or struck off the register, the Regulator may apply to the court for an order restoring the company's name to the register. These powers will enable the Regulator to safeguard the assets of a CIC for the community interest where the CIC has been struck off the register without having been wound up, or where an asset has been overlooked in a winding up.

If an application is made under *CA 2006, s 1003* by the director's of a CIC which is a private company to have the company struck off the register, the directors must send a copy of the application to the Regulator.

[*C(AICE)A 2004, s 51*].

## 10.26  APPEALS AND COMMUNITY INTEREST COMPANIES

The Secretary of State must appoint a person to be known as the Appeal Officer for CICs ('the Appeal Officer'). He has the function of determining appeals against decisions and orders of the Regulator which under or by virtue of *C(AICE)A 2004* or any other enactment lie with him.

An appeal to the Appeal Officer against a decision or order of the Regulator may be brought on the ground that the Regulator made a material error of law or fact. On such an appeal, the Appeal Officer must dismiss the appeal, allow the appeal, or remit the case to the Regulator. In the latter case, the Regulator must reconsider it in accordance with any rulings of law and findings of fact made by the Appeal Officer.

[*C(AICE)A 2004, s 28*].

*C(AICE)A 2004, Sch 4* sets out the Appeal Officer's terms of appointment, remuneration and financing and provides for the Secretary of State to make regulations about the procedures to be followed by the Appeal Officer. The Appeal Officer is subject to investigation by the Parliamentary Commissioner and is disqualified from membership of the House of Commons.

## 10.27  CHANGE OF STATUS – RE-REGISTRATION

A CIC is excluded from re-registering under *CA 2006, s 102* ie as an unlimited company.

If a CIC re-registers as a public company under *CA 2006, s 90* or re-registers as a private company under *CA 2006, s 97* the new certificate of incorporation must contain a statement that the company is a CIC and the fact that is does so is conclusive evidence that the company is a CIC.

[*C(AICE)A 2004, s 52(2)*].

## 10.28  CEASING TO BE A COMMUNITY INTEREST COMPANY

A CIC can only cease to be a CIC

- by dissolution (see **10.25** for the powers of the Regulator following a dissolution and **10.29** for distribution of assets on a winding up);

- by becoming a charity (see **10.30**); or

- by becoming an industrial and provident society (see **10.31**).

[*C(AICE)A 2004, s 53*].

## 10.29 Distribution of assets on a winding up

Where a CIC is wound up under *IA 1986* and some property of the company (the '*residual assets*') remains after satisfaction of the company's liabilities, the residual assets must be distributed to those members of the CIC (if any) who are entitled to share in any distribution of assets on the winding up of the company according to their rights and interests in the company. But no member must receive an amount which exceeds the 'paid-up value' of the shares which he holds in the company.

'*Paid-up value*' means, in respect of any share in a company, the sum of

- so much of the share's nominal value as has been paid up; and

- any premium on that share paid to the company.

If any residual assets remain after any such distribution to members, they must be distributed as follows.

(a)   If the articles of the company specify an 'asset-locked body' to which any remaining residual assets of the company should be distributed, then, unless either of the conditions in (*b*) (ii) or (iii) below is satisfied, the remaining residual assets must be distributed to that asset-locked body in such proportions or amounts as the Regulator directs.

(b)   If

    (i)   the articles of the company do not specify an asset-locked body to which any remaining residual assets of the company should be distributed,

    (ii)   the Regulator is aware that the asset-locked body to which the articles of the company specify that the remaining residual assets of the company should be distributed is itself in the process of being wound up, or

    (iii)   the Regulator

- has received representations from a member or director of the company stating, with reasons, that the asset-locked body to which the articles of the company specify that the remaining residual assets of the company should be distributed is not an appropriate recipient of the company's remaining residual assets; and

- has agreed with those representations,

then the remaining residual assets must be distributed to such asset-locked bodies, and in such proportions or amounts, as the Regulator directs.

'*Asset-locked body*' means

- a CIC, a charity or a permitted industrial and provident society; or

- a body established outside the UK that is equivalent to either of those.

In considering any direction to be made under these provisions, the Regulator must consult the directors and members of the company to the extent that he considers it practicable and appropriate to do so. He must also have regard to the desirability of distributing assets in accordance with any relevant provisions of the company's articles.

The Regulator must give notice of any direction under these provisions to the company and the liquidator. Any member or director of the company can appeal to the Appeal Officer against such a direction. See **10.26** APPEALS.

[*SI 2005 No 1788, Reg 23*].

## 10.30 Becoming a charity

If a company is to cease to be a CIC and become a charity, the following conditions must be satisfied.

*   The company must by special resolution

    (i)     state that it is to cease to be a CIC;

    (ii)    make such alterations of its articles as it considers appropriate; and

    (iii)   change its name so that it no longer complies with **10.15**.

A model special resolution to convert from a CIC to a charity is available in the Guidance referred to in **10.5**.

The following must be sent to the Registrar of Companies

*   a copy of the special resolution;

*   amended Articles of Association (see the Charity Commission website for model Articles);

*   form NM01 ( notice of change of name);

*   a £10 fee; and

*   either a statement from the Charity Commissioners that in its opinion if the proposed changes take effect the company will be an English charity and will not be an exempt charity or a statement from the Scottish Charity Regulator that if the proposed changes take effect the company will be entered into the Scottish Charity Register or a statement from HMRC that the company has claimed exemption under *ICTA 1988, s 505(1)* (for Northern Ireland).

[*C(AICE)A 2004, s 54(1)(2)*].

*Application to court to cancel special resolutions.* Where special resolutions have been passed with a view to the company ceasing to be a CIC and becoming a charity, an application to the court for the cancellation of the resolutions may be made

*   by the holders of not less in the aggregate than 15% in nominal value of the company's issued share capital or any class of the company's issued share capital (disregarding any shares held by the company as treasury shares),

*   if the company is not limited by shares, by not less than 15% of its members, or

*   by the holders of not less than 15% of the company's debentures entitling the holders to object to an alteration of its objects

but not by a person who has consented to or voted in favour of the resolutions.

The application must be made within 28 days after the date on which the resolutions are passed or made (or, if the resolutions are passed or made on different days, the date on which the last of them is passed or made). It may be made on behalf of the persons entitled to make it by such one or more of their number as they may appoint for the purpose.

On making such an application, the applicants (or the person making the application on their behalf) must immediately give notice to the Registrar of Companies. The company must also immediately give notice to the Registrar of Companies on being served with notice of such an application.

The court must make an order (on such terms as it thinks fit) either cancelling or confirming the resolutions. The order may provide for the purchase by the company of the shares of any of its members and for the reduction accordingly of the company's capital (making such alteration in the company's articles as may be required in consequence).

Within 15 days of the making of the court's order on the application, or such longer period as the court may at any time direct, the company must deliver to the Registrar of Companies a copy of the order.

If a company fails to comply with the above requirement to notify the Registrar of Companies of service of an application or to deliver to him a copy of the court order, an offence is committed by the company and every officer of the company who is in default. A person guilty of such an offence is liable on summary conviction to a fine not exceeding level 3 on the standard scale and, for continued contravention, a daily default fine not exceeding one-tenth of level 3 on the standard scale. See **29.1** Offences and Legal Proceedings for the standard scale.

[*C(AICE)A 2004, ss 54A, 54B*].

*Application and accompanying documents.* An application to the Registrar of Companies to cease to be a CIC and become a charity must be accompanied by

•     a copy of the special resolutions;

•     a copy of the company's articles as proposed to be amended; and

•     a statement

   (i)     where the company is to become an English charity, by the Charity Commission that, in its opinion, if the proposed changes take effect the company will be an English charity and will not be an exempt charity;

   (ii)    where the company is to become a Scottish charity, by the Scottish Charity Regulator that if the proposed changes take effect the company will be entered in the Scottish Charity Register; or

   (iii)   where the company is to become a Northern Ireland charity, by the Commissioners of Her Majesty's Revenue and Customs that the company has claimed exemption under *ICTA 1988, s 505(1)*.

On receiving an application to cease to be a CIC and become a charity, together with the other documents required to accompany it, the Registrar of Companies must (instead of recording the documents and entering a new name on the register) forward a copy of each of the documents to the Regulator and retain the documents pending the Regulator's decision.

[*C(AICE)A 2004, ss 54(3)(4), 54C*].

*Decision by the Regulator.* The Regulator must decide whether the company is eligible to cease being a CIC, ie whether it has complied with *C(AICE)A 2004, ss 54 and 54C* above and that *none* of the following apply.

- The Regulator has appointed an auditor to audit the company's annual accounts and the audit has not been completed.

- Civil proceedings instituted by the Regulator in the name of the company under *C(AICE)A 2004, s 44* have not been determined or discontinued.

- A director of the company holds office by virtue of an order under *C(AICE)A 2004, s 45* (see **10.21**).

- A director of the company is suspended under *C(AICE)A 2004, s 46(3)* (see **10.21**).

- There is a manager in respect of the property and affairs of the company appointed under *C(AICE)A 2004, s 47* (see **10.22**).

- The Official Property Holder holds property as trustee for the company.

- An order under *C(AICE)A 2004, s 48(2)*, re the company's property, debtors or transactions (see **10.23**).

- A petition has been presented for the company to be wound up.

The Regulator must give notice of the decision to the Registrar of Companies (but the Registrar is not required to record it).

If the Regulator gives notice of a decision that the company is eligible to cease being a CIC and become a charity, the Registrar of Companies must proceed in accordance with *CA 2006, s 80* (registration and issue of new certificate of incorporation on change of name, see **27.17 NAMES AND BUSINESS NAMES**). If the Registrar of Companies enters the new name of the company on the register, he must retain and record the application to cease to become a CIC together with the other documents required to accompany it. The new certificate of incorporation must state that it is issued on the company's ceasing to be a CIC and the date on which it is issued. On the issue of the certificate, the changes in the company's name and articles take effect and the company ceases to be a CIC.

If the Regulator decides that the company is not eligible to cease being a CIC, the company may appeal to the Appeal Officer against the decision.

[*C(AICE)A 2004, ss 55, 55A*].

## 10.31  Becoming an industrial and provident society

*Section 56* of the *C(AICE)A 2004* provides that 'unless Regulations make provision to the contrary' a CIC may not convert itself into an industrial or provident society. However *regulation 5* of the *Community Interest Companies (Amendment) Regulations 2009 (SI 2009/1942)* allows a CIC to convert itself to a permitted industrial and provident society by special resolution of its members and provided it complies with *section 53* of the *Industrial and Provident Societies Act 1965* (as modified by the *2009 Regulations*).

## 10.32  Becoming a charitable incorporated organisation ('CIO')

Currently, no conversion process exists by which a CIC may convert itself into a CIO. Such a process would potentially allow a CIC to enjoy the benefit of having a corporate structure while retaining its existing identity and reducing the administration and costs which conversion entails.

The Government initiated a consultation in April 2016 inviting views as to whether regulations should be introduced under the *Charities Act 2011* providing for such a conversion process. Legislation was drafted in the shape of three draft regulations: The *Charitable Incorporated Organisations (Conversion) Regulations 2016*, the *Charitable Incor-*

*porated Organisations (Consequential Amendments) Order 2016*, and the *Index of Company Names (Listed Bodies) (England and Wales) Order 2016*. The consultation, initiated by the Cabinet Office and the Charity Commission, ran from 1 April to 10 June 2016. However, at the date of finalising this edition, no legislation to this effect has been enacted.

## 10.33 DISCLOSURE OF INFORMATION

A public authority may disclose to the Regulator, for any purpose connected with the exercise of the Regulator's functions, information received by it in connection with its functions.

The Regulator may disclose to a public authority any information received by him in connection with his functions

- for a purpose connected with the exercise of those functions, or

- for a purpose connected with the exercise by the authority of its functions.

The powers to disclose information are subject to

- any restriction on disclosure imposed by, or by virtue of, an enactment, and

- any express restriction on disclosure subject to which information was supplied.

A person who discloses information in contravention of a restriction imposed is guilty of an offence, but a prosecution may be instituted in England or Wales only with the consent of the Regulator or the Director of Public Prosecutions (in NI only with the consent of the Regulator or the Director of Public Prosecutions for NI). A person guilty of such an offence is liable on summary conviction to a fine not exceeding level 3 on the standard scale. See **29.1 OFFENCES AND LEGAL PROCEEDINGS** for the standard scale.

[*C(AICE)A 2004, s 59*].

## 10.34 DUTIES

The Court of Appeal has recently published a key decision which should help to clarify the scope of the duties owed in the case of a charitable company limited by guarantee (*Lehtimaki v Children's Investment Fund Foundation (UK)* [2018] EWCA Civ 1605 (6 July 2018)).

In essence, the Court of Appeal upheld the High Court's finding that a member of the Children's Investment Fund Foundation (UK) ('CIFF'), a charitable company limited by guarantee, owed fiduciary duties to act in the best interests of the company.

The Court of Appeal did not rule on the precise extent or scope of the fiduciary duties. However, it did express the view that the duties arising here corresponded to those imposed on members of a CIO by the *Charities Act 2011, s 220* (which only came into force on 2 January 2013, so is not yet the subject of its own case law). Hence, a member of CIFF had to exercise the power he or she had in that capacity in the way that he or she decided, in good faith, would be most likely to further the purposes of the company. The duty was subjective. The key issue was the member's state of mind. However, the court had no power to direct a fiduciary how to exercise their powers unless he or she was acting in breach of duty. In other words, the judgment reaffirms the principle that, provided a fiduciary in respect of a charity acts in good faith, reasonably and responsibly, and informs himself or herself of relevant matters before making a decision, it is not for the court or the Commission to interfere with his or her decisions.

On the present facts, the court had found no significant evidence that the member had been acting (or proposing to act) in breach of duty. The Court of Appeal therefore allowed the appeal.

The issue of whether members of charitable companies owe fiduciary duties has long been debated by charity lawyers, so the outcome of this appeal will be of great interest to charity practitioners in particular. The decision does not apply to *all* charitable companies or structures. Further clarification will be welcomed in the future as to the exact nature and extent of the duties owed in the charitable sphere. The decision may in any event be subject to a further appeal to the Supreme Court.

## 10.35 OFFENCES AND COMMUNITY INTEREST COMPANIES

If an offence committed by a body corporate is proved

- to have been committed with the consent or connivance of an 'officer', or

- to be attributable to any neglect on the part of an officer,

the officer, as well as the body corporate, is guilty of the offence and liable to be proceeded against and punished accordingly.

'*Officer*' means a 'director', manager, secretary or other similar officer of the body corporate, or a person purporting to act in any such capacity. '*Director*' includes a shadow director and, if the affairs of a body corporate are managed by its members, means a member of the body. [*C(AICE)A 2004, s 60*].

# 11   Companies not Formed under the Companies Acts

This chapter relates to companies which were not incorporated under the companies' legislation, but which are permitted to register under it. Effectively, this means that the Companies Act is applied more widely to unregistered companies. In short, a non-Companies Act corporation may still enjoy the benefit of separate legal personality and the limited liability of its members, save where statutory provisions preclude this.

**Background.** The *CA 2006* provisions of this chapter apply, under otherwise stated, to applications for registration received by the Registrar of Companies on or after 1 October 2009. If a resolution was agreed to, or other thing done, before 1 October 2009 it may be relied upon for the purposes of meeting the requirements of these provisions.

[*SI 2008 No 2860, Sch 2 para 93*].

## 11.1   COMPANIES NOT FORMED UNDER THE COMPANIES ACTS BUT AUTHORISED TO REGISTER

Subject to the exceptions below, any company

- in existence on November 1862 (including any company registered under the *Joint Stock Companies Acts*), or

- formed after that date (whether before or after the commencement of *CA 2006*)

  (i)   in pursuance of any Act of Parliament other than *CA 2006* or any of the 'former Companies Acts' (such as, for example, trustees of the British Museum, incorporated as a body corporate under the *British Museum Act 1963*),

  (ii)   in pursuance of letters patent, or

  (iii)   that is otherwise duly constituted according to law

may, on making application, register under *CA 2006*. It may register as an unlimited company, as a company limited by shares or as a company limited by guarantee. Registration is not invalid because it has taken place with a view to the company's being wound up (in fact registration is often sought for this very purpose).

Letters patent are documents recording an exercise of the sovereign's authority (whether prerogative or statutory); they are written by or in the name of the monarch pursuant to the *Great Seal Act 1884* and the *Letters Patent Act 1571*. Letters patent can be used to create corporations or government offices, and to grant city status or coats of arms.

## 11.1  Companies not Formed under the Companies Acts

**Exceptions**. This procedure cannot be used

- by a company having the liability of its members limited by Act of Parliament or letters patent which is either

    (i)     not a 'joint stock company'; or

    (ii)    seeking to register as an unlimited company or a company limited by guarantee; or

- by a company that is not a joint stock company seeking to register as a company limited by shares.

[*CA 2006, s 1040*].

See Appendix 1 Definitions for the meaning of the '*Companies Acts*' and '*Former Companies Acts*'.

'*Joint stock company*' for these purposes means a company having a permanent paid-up or nominal share capital of fixed amount *either* divided into shares of fixed amount *or* held and transferable as stock *or* divided and held partly in one way and partly in the other. It must be formed on the principle of having for its members the holders of those shares or that stock and no other persons. Such a company when registered with limited liability under the *CA 2006* is deemed to be a company limited by shares. [*CA 2006, s 1041*]. The joint stock company legislation provided a simple administrative mechanism whereby any group of seven people could register a limited liability company – with separate corporate identity – for themselves. The joint stock company legislation is thus essentially the predecessor of the modern Companies Act.

## 11.2  REGISTRATION REQUIREMENTS

Regulations made under *CA 2006* (the *Companies (Companies Authorised to Register) Regulations 2009*) provide the registration requirements for non Companies Act companies [*CA 2006, s 1042*; *SI 2009 No 2437*].

On compliance with the registration requirements, the Registrar of Companies must register the documents delivered to him.

The following is a summary of the registration requirements.

## 11.3  Consent of members

A company must have the consent of a majority of members present in person or by proxy (in cases where proxies are allowed) at a general meeting summoned for the purpose of registration.

If the company wants to register as a limited company and the liability of the company's members is not limited by an enactment or letters patent, the majority required must be not less than 75% of the members present in person or by proxy at the meeting.

In computing any majority when a poll is demanded, regard is to be had to the number of votes to which each member is entitled according to the company's regulations.

**Guarantee companies**. Where a company wishes to register as a company limited by guarantee, the consent to its being so registered must be accompanied by a resolution by each member undertaking to contribute to the company's assets, in the event of its being wound up while he is a member or within one year after he ceases to be a member, such amount as may be required for

- payment of the company's debts and liabilities contracted before he ceases to be a member,

- payment of the costs, charges and expenses of winding up, and

- the adjustment of the rights of the contributories among themselves,

such amount as may be required, not exceeding a specified amount "(a statement of guarantee)".

[*SI 2009 No 2437 Regs 3 and 6*].

## 11.4   Companies other than joint stock companies

Before the registration of a company other than a 'joint stock company' (see **11.1**) an application for registration 'the application for registration' must be delivered to the Registrar of Companies together with the documents required by *regulation 4* of *SI 2009 No 2437* and a statement of compliance.

The application for registration must state.

(a)    The name with which the company is proposed to be registered. See **11.7**.

(b)    Whether the company's registered office is to be situated in England and Wales (or in Wales), in Scotland or in Northern Ireland.

(c)    Whether the liability of the members is to be limited, and if so whether it is to be limited by shares or by guarantee and whether the company is to be a private or public company and must contain

    (i)    (for guarantee companies) a statement of guarantee (see above)

    (ii)   a statement of the company's proposed officers (directors, and, where relevant, secretary (see *Regulation 7* of *SI 2009 No 2437* for the required details)

    (iii)  a statement of the intended address of the company's registered office

(d)    A copy of any enactment, royal charter, letters patent, deed of settlement, contract of partnership or other instrument constituting or regulating the company and must be accompanied by a statement of compliance ie a statement that the requirements of registration have been complied with. The Registrar may accept the statement of compliance as evidence of that compliance.

[*SI 2009 No 2437 Regs 4, 5, 6, 7 and 8*].

## 11.5   Joint stock company

Before the registration of a joint stock company, the following must be delivered to the Registrar of Companies.

(a)    The application for registration and documents as for other companies and the statement of compliance (see **11.4**);

(b)    A statement of capital and initial shareholdings complying with *Reg 5* of *SI 2009 No 2437*.

[*SI 2009 No 2437 Regs 4, 5, 6, 7 and 8*].

## 11.6   *Registration of a joint stock company as a public company*

A joint stock company may apply to be registered as a public company subject to meeting the following conditions.

## 11.6 Companies not Formed under the Companies Acts

(a) It must satisfy the requirements set out in

    (i) *CA 2006, s 91(1)* (requirements as to share capital, see **41.3**(*a*)–(*d*) RE-REGISTRATION));

    (ii) *CA 2006, s 92* (requirements re net assets); and

    (iii) (where applicable) *CA 2006, s 93(2)(a)*, namely it must not allot shares as fully or partly paid up (as to their nominal value and any premium on them) otherwise than in cash unless the consideration for the allotment has been independently valued and the valuer's report has been made to the company in the six months immediately preceding the allotment of the shares.

(b) Before the registration, the following must be delivered to the Registrar of Companies.

    (i) All the documents required under **11.5**.

    (ii) A copy of the resolution that the company be a public company.

    (iii) A copy of the balance sheet, and other documents referred to *CA 2006, s 92(3)*.

    (iv) A copy of any valuation report prepared under (*a*)(iii) above.

[*SI 2009 No 2437 Regs 4 and 9*].

## 11.7 Company name

The following provisions apply with respect to the name of the company registering (whether or not it is a joint stock company).

(a) If the company is to be registered as a public company, its name must end with the words

    (i) 'public limited company', or,

    (ii) where it is stated that the company's registered office is to be situated in Wales, with those words or their equivalent in Welsh ('cwmni cyfyngedig chyoeddus')

and those words (or that equivalent) may not be preceded by the word 'limited' or its equivalent in Welsh ('cyfyngedig').

(b) In the case of a company limited by shares or by guarantee (not being a public company), the name must have as its last word

    (i) 'limited", or

    (ii) where the company's registered office is to be situated in Wales, 'cyfyngedig'

but this is subject to *CA 2006, s 60* which exempts a company, in certain circumstances, from having 'limited' as part of the name. See **27.5** NAMES AND BUSINESS NAMES.

(c) If the company is registered with limited liability, then any additions to the company's name set out in the statement specifying the name with which the company is proposed to be registered must form and be registered as the last part of the company's name.

(d) Where the name of a company seeking registration is a name by which it is precluded from registration by

    • *CA 2006, s 53* (prohibited names), see **27.4** NAMES AND BUSINESS NAMES,

- *CA 2006, s 54* (name suggesting connection with government or public authority) or *CA 2006, s 55* (other sensitive words or expressions), see **27.7** NAMES AND BUSINESS NAMES,

- *CA 2006, s 57* (permitted characters), see **27.8** NAMES AND BUSINESS NAMES,

- *CA 2006, s 65* (inappropriate use of indications of company type or legal form), see **27.5** NAMES AND BUSINESS NAMES, or

- *CA 2006, s 66* (name not to be the same as another in the index), see **27.6** NAMES AND BUSINESS NAMES

the company may change its name with effect from the date on which it is registered. Such a change of name requires the like consent of the company's members as is required by **11.3** for registration.

[*SI 2009 No 2437, Reg 10*].

## 11.8   Issue of certificate of incorporation

On the registration of a company, the Registrar of Companies must give a certificate that the company is incorporated. The certificate must state

- the name and registered number of the company;

- the date of its incorporation;

- whether it is a limited or unlimited company, and if it is limited whether it is limited by shares or limited by guarantee;

- whether it is a private or a public company; and

- whether the company's registered office is situated in England and Wales (or in Wales), in Scotland or in Northern Ireland.

The certificate must be signed by the Registrar of Companies or authenticated by his official seal and is conclusive evidence that the requirements relating to registration have been complied with.

[*SI 2009 No 2437, Reg 12*].

## CONSEQUENCES OF REGISTRATION

## 11.9   Transfer of property, rights and liabilities

All property belonging to or vested in the company at the date of its registration passes to and vests in the company on registration but registration does not affect the company's rights or liabilities in respect of any debt or obligation incurred, or contract entered into, by, to, with or on behalf of the company before registration.

[*SI 2009 No 2437, Reg 14*].

## 11.10   Pending legal proceedings

Subject to below, all actions and other legal proceedings which, at the time of the company's registration, are pending by or against the company, or the public officer or any member of it, may be continued in the same manner as if the registration had not taken place.

But execution cannot be issued against the effects of any individual member of the company on any judgment, decree or order obtained in such an action or proceeding. In the event of the company's property and effects being insufficient to satisfy the judgment, decree or order, an order may be obtained for winding up the company.

[*SI 2009 No 2437, Reg 15*].

## 11.11 The company's constitution

Although the *2009 Regulations* provide that all provisions contained in any enactment or other instrument constituting or regulating the company are deemed to be conditions and regulations of the company, as if, had the company been formed under *CA 2006*, they had been contained in registered articles of association, there are limits to the changes the company can make to its constitution.

[*SI 2009 No 2437, Regs 16 and 20*].

## 11.12 Power to substitute articles of association for deed of settlement

A company authorised to register may, by special resolution, alter the form of its constitution by substituting articles of association for any instrument constituting or regulating the company, other than an enactment, a royal charter or letters patent.

[*SI 2009 No 2437, Reg 17*].

## 11.13 Application of the Companies Act

The provisions of the *Companies Acts* apply to a registered company and to its members, contributories and creditors, in the same manner as if the company had been formed under *CA 2006*, except that

(a)     the model articles of association prescribed by the Secretary of State do not apply unless adopted by special resolution; (see APPENDIX 4 MODEL ARTICLES OF ASSOCIATION) and

(b)     provisions relating to the numbering of shares do not apply to any joint stock company whose shares are not numbered;

The company does not have the power

•       to alter any provision contained in an enactment relating to the company

•       (without the consent of the Secretary of State) to alter any provision in letters patent relating to the company; or

•       to alter any provision in a royal charter or letters patent with respect to the company's objects

•       and in each case does not have the power to ratify the acts of the directors which contravene such provisions.

For these purposes the *Companies Acts'* include the *Companies (Cross-Border Mergers) Regulations 2007* and do not include *Part 2 of the C(AICE) A 2004*.

[*SI 2009 No 2437, Reg 18, 19, 20*].

## 11.14 Capital structure

Provisions in *CA 2006* with respect to

•       the re-registration of an unlimited company as limited,

- the powers of an unlimited company on re-registration as a limited company and to provide that a portion of its share capital is not capable of being called up except in the event of winding up, and

- the power of a limited company to determine that a portion of its share capital is not capable of being called up except in that event,

of an unlimited company on re-registration as a limited company and to provide that a portion of its share capital is not capable of being called up except in the event of winding up, and

[*SI 2009 No 2437, Reg 21*].

# 12   Company Formation and Types of Companies

Cross-references. See 14 CONSTITUTION – MEMORANDUM AND ARTICLES.

## 12.1   PRE-INCORPORATION

### Promoters

A *'promoter'* is a person who undertakes to form a company with reference to a given project and to set it going, and who takes the necessary steps to accomplish that purpose (*Twycross v Grant* (1877) 2 CPD 469, CA).

A promoter has duties towards the company before it comes into existence and may continue to be in a fiduciary relation to it after incorporation (*Emma Silver Mining Co v Lewis & Son* (1879) 4 CPD 396). If he sells property to the company he is bound to take care that he sells it through the medium of the board of directors who can and do exercise an independent judgement on the transaction (*Erlanger (Emile) v New Sombrero Phosphate Co* (1878) 3 App Cas 1218, HL). Where a promoter makes any undisclosed profit, this should be handed over to the company (*Whaley Bridge Calico Printing Co v Green and Smith* (1879) 5 QBD 109). See also *Gluckstein v Barnes* [1900] AC 240, HL.

### Pre-incorporation contracts

A contract that purports to be made by or on behalf of a company at a time when the company has not been formed has effect, subject to any agreement to the contrary, as one made with the person purporting to act for the company or as agent for it, and that person or agent is personally liable on the contract.

This also applies to

- the making of a deed under the law of England and Wales or Northern Ireland, and

- the undertaking of an obligation under the law of Scotland

as it applies to the making of a contract.

[*CA 2006, s 51*].

For cases involving the enforceability of pre-incorporation contracts by and against the agent or promoter, see *Kelner v Baxter* (1866) LR 2 CP 174; *Newborne v Sensolid (Great Britain) Ltd* [1954] 1 QB 45, [1953] 1 All ER 708, CA; *Black v Smallwood* (1965) 117 CLR 52, [1966] ALR 744, Aust HC; and *Phonogram Ltd v Lane* [1982] QB 938, [1981] 3 All ER 182, CA. As the company has not yet been formed, it cannot be bound by the contract (*Re English and Colonial Produce Co Ltd* [1906] 2 Ch 435, 75 LJ Ch 831, CA) and cannot sue on it (*Natal Land and Colonization Co Ltd v Pauline Colliery and Development Syndicate* [1904] AC 120, 73 LJPC 22, PC).

## 12.2 Company Formation and Types of Companies

### 12.2 METHOD OF FORMING A COMPANY

**For companies incorporated on or after 1 October 2009** a company is formed by one or more persons

- subscribing their names to a memorandum of association; and

- complying with the requirements as to registration.

A company may not be so formed for an unlawful purpose.

[*CA 2006, s 7*].

Any type of company can be formed by a single subscriber and can continue as a single member company. If that is the case *CA 2006, s 38* provides that any enactment or rule of law applicable to companies formed by two or more persons or having two or more members applies with any necessary modification in relation to a company formed by one person or having only one person as a member. [*CA 2006, s 38*].

### 12.3 REGISTRATION OF A COMPANY

A company seeking registration must deliver to the Registrar of Companies

- the memorandum of association. The memorandum of a company incorporated on or after 1 October 2009 is in a short form only and states only that the subscribers wish to form a company under *CA 2006* and agree to become members of the company and in the case of a company that is to have a share capital, to take at least one share each (see **14 CONSTITUTION – MEMORANDUM AND ARTICLES**);

- an application for registration of the company (form INO1) including a statement of compliance and the fee (see **APPENDIX 3**); and

- a copy of the company's articles (unless the company decides that the relevant model articles should apply in their entirety - see **14 CONSTITUTION – MEMORANDUM AND ARTICLES** and **APPENDIX 4 STANDARD ARTICLES OF ASSOCIATION**).

- additional information if the application includes a prescribed or sensitive word or expression in its name – see **27 NAMES AND BUSINESS NAMES**.

**Application for registration.** Companies Form IN01 (Application to register a company) requires the following information.

(a)   The company's proposed name and, if the proposed name contains a sensitive or restricted word or expression, confirmation that the company has requested the views of a government department or other body (see **27 NAMES AND BUSINESS names**).

(b)   Whether the company's registered office is to be situated in England and Wales, Wales, Scotland or Northern Ireland and the address of the registered office, which must be the same as the situation of the registered office.

(c)   Whether the liability of the members of the company is to be limited, and if so whether it is to be limited by shares or by guarantee.

(d)   Whether the company is to be private, public or unlimited company (see **TYPES OF COMPANY 12.7**).

(e)   If the application is delivered by a person as agent for the subscribers to the memorandum of association, it must state his name and address.

(f)   In the case of a company that is to have a share capital, a statement of capital and a statement of initial shareholdings. The statement of capital must

- state the total number of shares to be taken on formation by the subscribers to the memorandum the total aggregate nominal value of issued share capital and the aggregate amount (if any) to be unpaid on those shares (whether on account of their nominal value or by way of premium) and must set out the number of shares held in sterling and any shares held in other currencies;

- state for each class of shares

  (i)    particulars of any voting rights attached to the shares, including rights that arise only in certain circumstances;

  (ii)   particulars of any rights attached to the shares, as respects dividends, to participate in a distribution;

  (iii)  particulars of any rights attached to the shares, as respects capital, to participate in a distribution (including on a winding up);

  (iv)   whether the shares are to be redeemed or are liable to be redeemed at the option of the company or the shareholder and any terms or conditions relating to redemption of those shares;

  (v)    the total number of shares of that class; and

  (vi)   the aggregate nominal value of shares of that class;

- state the amount to be paid up and the amount (if any) unpaid on each share (whether on account of the nominal value of the share or by way of premium).

  The statement of initial shareholdings must

- state the name(s) (in alphabetical order) and address of each subscriber to the memorandum of association;

- state, with respect to each subscriber to the memorandum,

  (i)    the number, nominal value (of each share), currency and class of shares to be taken by him on formation, and

  (ii)   the amount to be paid up and the amount (if any) unpaid on each share (whether on account of the nominal value of the share or by way of premium).

  Where a subscriber to the memorandum is to take shares of more than one class, the information required under (i) above is required for each class.

(g)    In the case of a company that is to be limited by guarantee, a statement of guarantee. This must

- contain the name and address of each subscribers to the memorandum of association. The address does not have to be the subscriber's usual residential address;

- state that each member undertakes that, if the company is wound up while he is a member, or within one year after he ceases to be a member, he will contribute to the assets of the company such amount as may be required for

  (i)    payment of the debts and liabilities of the company contracted before he ceases to be a member;

  (ii)   payment of the costs, charges and expenses of winding up; and

  (iii)  adjustment of the rights of the contributories among themselves, not exceeding a specified amount.

(h)     A statement of the company's proposed officers containing the particulars of

- the person who is, or the persons who are, to be the first director or directors of the company as will be required or, in the absence of an election under *CA 2006, s 167A or 279A* (option to keep details on the central register) (see **38.4**) to be stated in the company's register of directors and register of directors' residential addresses (see **38.3** and **38.5 Registers**). Private companies must appoint at least one director and public companies must appoint at least two directors. In either case one director of a company must be an individual (but see **18.2** for the effect of changes to be brought about by the *SBEE 2015* in relation to corporate directors); or

- the person who is (or the persons who are) to be the first secretary (or joint secretaries) of the company as will be required to be stated in the company's register of secretaries (see **38.6 Registers**). Additional information is required if the secretary or director is a corporate secretary or director and is registered within the EEA (Companies House guidance provides full details of EEA countries). The secretary must supply a service address.

The statement must also contain

- a statement by the subscribers to the memorandum that each of the persons named as a director, as secretary or as one of the joint secretaries has consented to act in the relevant capacity; and

- a statement by the company that the person named as secretary or each of the persons named as joint secretaries has consented to act in the relevant capacity.

(i)     A statement of initial significant control (*SBEE 2015, Sch 3, paras 4 and 5*).

(j)     Each director must supply a service address and a usual residential address. The service address is the address which will appear on the public record. When supplying the usual residential address, the director must also complete details of any *CA 2006, s 243* exemption which has been applied for or already granted (see **18 Directors**).

(k)     A copy of any proposed articles of association (to the extent that these are not supplied by the default application of model articles under *CA 2006, s 20*, see **14.3 Constitution – Memorandum and Articles**).

(l)     A statement of the type of company it is to be and its intended principal business activities. The information as to the company's type must be given by reference to the classification scheme prescribed for the purposes of *CA 2006, s 9* and the information as to the company's principal business activities may be given by reference to one or more of the categories of any prescribed system of classifying business activities.

(m)    Whether a private company limited by guarantee wishes to apply to be exempt from the requirement to use 'limited' or 'cyfyngedig' in its name.

(n)     A statement of compliance. The statement of compliance required to be delivered to the Registrar of Companies is a statement that the requirements of *CA 2006* as to registration have been complied with. The statement must be signed by all the subscribers or by an agent acting on behalf of all the subscribers. The Registrar of Companies may accept the statement of compliance as sufficient evidence of compliance.

The application must be delivered to the Registrar of Companies for England and Wales (if the registered office of the company is to be situated in England and Wales or in Wales), to the Registrar of Companies for Scotland (if the registered office of the company is to be situated in Scotland) or to the Registrar of Companies for Northern Ireland (if the registered office of the company is to be situated in Northern Ireland) together with the memorandum and articles (if relevant). If the company does not send a copy of its articles then by default the relevant model articles will apply (see *CA 2006, s 20* and **14 Constitution – Memorandum and Articles**). The application can be filed either electronically or by paper application. From 6 April 2011 an application for web incorporation can also be made via Companies House Businesslink service. See **Appendix 3** for fees payable.

[*CA 2006, ss 9–13; SBEE 2015, ss 93, 100–101, Sch 6, para 2; SI 2015 No 1689, Reg 4; SI 2016 No 321, Reg 6*].

There is also a useful checklist on Form IN01.

**Registration.** If the Registrar of Companies is satisfied that the above requirements have been complied with, he must register the documents delivered to him. [*CA 2006, s 14*].

## 12.4   Certificate of incorporation

On the registration of a company, the Registrar of Companies must give a certificate that the company is incorporated. The certificate must state

* the name and registered number of the company;

* the date of its incorporation;

* whether it is a limited or unlimited company, and if it is limited whether it is limited by shares or limited by guarantee;

* whether it is a private or a public company; and

* whether the company's registered office is situated in England and Wales, Wales) Scotland or Northern Ireland.

The certificate must be signed by the Registrar of Companies or authenticated by the Registrar's official seal.

The certificate is conclusive evidence that the requirements of *CA 2006* as to registration have been complied with and that the company is duly registered under that *Act*. [*CA 2006, s 15*].

## 12.5   Effect of registration

The registration of a company has the following effects as from the date of incorporation.

* The subscribers to the memorandum, together with such other persons as may from time to time become members of the company, are a body corporate by the name stated in the certificate of incorporation.

* That body corporate is capable of exercising all the functions of an incorporated company.

* The status and registered office of the company are as stated in the application for registration.

* In the case of a company having a share capital, the subscribers to the memorandum become holders of the shares specified in the statement of capital and initial shareholdings.

* A person named in the statement of proposed officers (see **12.3**(*h*)) as a director or secretary is deemed to have been appointed to that office.

[*CA 2006, s 16*].

A public company, however, cannot do business or borrow money until it receives a trading certificate from the Registrar of Companies under *CA 2006, s 761*. A trading certificate will not be issued unless the Registrar is satisfied that the company's allotted share capital is not less the authorised minimum (currently £50,000 or the prescribed equivalent). For the purposes of calculating the amount allotted, any shares allotted pursuant to an employees' share scheme must not be taken into account unless they are paid up to at least one quarter of their nominal value plus the whole of any premium. (see **33.3** PUBLIC AND LISTED COMPANIES).

## 12.6   COMPANY AS A SEPARATE LEGAL PERSON

Once a company has been validly formed and incorporated, it is a legal person distinct from its members. This applies even where a controlling shareholder effectively owns all the shares in the company (*Salomon v A Salomon & Co Ltd* [1897] AC 22, HL). See also *Lee v Lee's Air Farming Ltd* [1961] AC 12, [1960] 3 All ER 420, PC, where such a person may function in a dual capacity and a contractual relationship may be established between the shareholder and the company.

Once incorporated, the company is bound by the decision of a majority of its members in general meeting and the courts will not normally interfere in the internal management of a company acting within its powers (*Foss v Harbottle* (1843) 2 Hare 461).

*Foss v Harbottle* also established the fundamental rule that to redress a wrong done to a company or to recover moneys or damages due to it, action must *prima facie* be brought by the company itself. Subsequent case law, however, established exceptions to the rule in *Foss v Harbottle* for the protection of minority interests and *CA 2006* provides a statutory remedy for the protection of members who may take action against the directors. See **26.6** MEMBERS.

**Lifting the veil.** In certain circumstances, the court may pull aside the corporate veil and look through the transactions of the company to see what really lies behind them. See *Wallersteiner v Moir* [1974] 3 All ER 217, [1974] 1 WLR 991, CA, and *Littlewoods Mail Order Stores Ltd v IRC* [1969] 3 All ER 855, [1969] 1 WLR 1241, CA. The courts have frequently done this and looked at the personal relationships of the shareholders when deciding if a family company should be wound up (see, for example, *Ebrahimi v Westbourne Galleries Ltd* [1973] AC 360, [1972] 2 All ER 492, HL); to determine whether a company is an 'enemy' at time of war (*Daimler Co Ltd v Continental Tyre and Rubber Co (Great Britain) Ltd* [1916] 2 AC 307, 85 LJKB 1333, HL); where a company is used to carry out a fraud (*Re Darby, ex p Brougham* [1911] 1 KB 95, 80 LJKB 180); and to treat a group of companies as one company (*DHN Food Distributors Ltd v Tower Hamlets London Borough Council* [1976] 1 WLR 852, [1976] 1 WLR 852, CA).

In *Prest v Petrodel Resources Ltd* [2013] UKSC 34, [2013] 2 AC 415, [2013] 4 All ER 673, the facts of which arose out of litigation following divorce proceedings, the Supreme Court fundamentally changed the guidelines which determine the circumstances in which the Court may depart from the *Salomon* rule. The Supreme Court held that there was a principle of English law which enabled a court in very limited circumstances to pierce the corporate veil. It applied when a person was under an existing legal obligation or liability, or subject to an existing legal restriction, which he or she deliberately evaded or whose enforcement he or she deliberately frustrated by interposing a company under his or her control. The Court may then pierce the corporate veil solely for the purpose of depriving the company or its controller of the advantage which they would otherwise have obtained by the company's separate legal personality. If there is another legal remedy, piercing the corporate veil will not be necessary and will not be available.

A further interesting development in this area arises in the case of *AAA v Unilever plc* [2018] EWCA Civ 1532. Here, the Court of Appeal dismissed an appeal against a decision that the English court did not have jurisdiction to hear a tort claim against an English company

(Unilever) and its Kenyan subsidiary (UTKL). It held that, in relation to the claim against Unilever, the second limb of the test in *Caparo Industries plc v Dickman* [1990] 2 AC 605 (proximity) had not been satisfied. Hence, the claim against Unilever, as 'anchor defendant', could not succeed. It followed that the claimants could not establish that the English court had jurisdiction to hear the claim against UTKL on the 'necessary or proper party' jurisdictional test (*PD 6B.3.1(3) and (4)*).

This decision is a further example of a claimant looking to an English company for compensation in respect of alleged torts of that English company's *overseas* subsidiaries. The claimants had relied on *Chandler v Cape plc* [2012] EWCA Civ 525. The judge at first instance had found that the claimants had no arguable claim against either Unilever or UTKL, as neither company owed the claimants a duty of care in tort to take effective steps to protect them from post-election violence in Kenya, which had spilled from the surrounding area to the relevant tea plantation. However, the judge also considered that the claimants had an arguable case that the proximity requirement had been satisfied, on the basis that there was a sufficient degree of connection between the activities of Unilever, as the holding company of UTKL, and the damage suffered by the claimants.

The Court of Appeal gave significant attention to the proximity issue in its decision. It held that a *parent* company will only be found to be subject to a duty of care owed to claimant in relation to an activity of its (the parent's) *subsidiary* if ordinary, general principles of the law of tort on duty of care were satisfied. *Chandler v Cape* provided helpful guidance, but did not lay down a separate test, distinct from general principle (namely the *Caparo* test). However, although the same broad legal principles applied here, there were some cases in which a parent company, having greater scope to intervene in the affairs of its subsidiary than another third party may have, might have taken action which would merit the imposition of a duty of care (that is, upon the parent in respect of its subsidiary's acts). There were two basic types of case where this might be the position:

- where the parent had in effect taken over the management of the relevant activity of the subsidiary in place of the subsidiary's own management (*Lungowe v Vedanta Resources plc* [2017] EWCA Civ 1528 and *Okpabi v Royal Dutch Shell plc* [2018] EWCA Civ 191); and

- where the parent had given relevant advice to the subsidiary about how it should manage a particular risk.

The claimants in *AAA v Unilever* had relied on the second case above in seeking to establish proximity and hence in arguing that a duty of care existed. But the Court of Appeal was not persuaded that this scenario had not arisen on the evidence. On the contrary, said the Court, the facts showed that UTKL carried out its own crisis management training programme. UTKL had sole responsibility for devising its own relevant policies and for deciding what to do when the crisis arose.

Admittedly, the decision seems to turn significantly on its facts. Nonetheless, it provides useful guidance on the application of the proximity requirement to 'lifting the veil' disputes. It also demonstrates that, when assessing whether a duty of care should be imposed on a parent company, the court will apply the three-limb test established in *Caparo*.

Further guidance in relation to tort claims against English multi-nationals is anticipated when the Supreme Court hands down its eagerly awaited decision in *Lungowe v Vedanta Resources plc* [2017] EWCA Civ 1528.

## 12.7 Company Formation and Types of Companies

### 12.7 TYPES OF COMPANIES FORMED UNDER THE COMPANIES ACT

#### Limited and unlimited companies

A company is a '*limited company*' if the liability of its members is limited by its constitution. Liability may be limited in two ways.

- The company is '*limited by shares*' if the liability of members is limited to the amount, if any, unpaid on the shares held by them.

- The company is '*limited by guarantee*' if the liability of members is limited to such amount as the members undertake to contribute to the assets of the company in the event of its being wound up.

If there is no limit on the liability of its members, the company is an '*unlimited company*'. [*CA 2006, s 3*].

#### Private and public companies

A '*private company*' is any company that is not a public company.

A '*public company*' is a company limited by shares or limited by guarantee and having a share capital

- whose certificate of incorporation states that it is a public company; and

- in relation to which the requirements of the *CA 2006* or the '*former Companies Acts*' (see APPENDIX 1 DEFINITIONS) as to registration or re-registration as a public company have been complied with on or after

  (i) in relation to registration or re-registration in Great Britain, 22 December 1980; and

  (ii) in relation to registration or re-registration in Northern Ireland, 1 July 1983.

[*CA 2006, s 4*].

For some of the major differences between private and public companies, see 33 PUBLIC AND LISTED COMPANIES.

#### Companies limited by guarantee

A company limited by guarantee is a company having the liability of its members limited to such amount as the members undertake to contribute to the assets of the company in the event of its being wound up. Such companies are widely used by schools, professional and trade associations, clubs and for management companies of blocks of flats in which all the tenants are members.

A company cannot be formed as, or become, a company limited by guarantee with a share capital. Provision to this effect has been in force in Great Britain since 22 December 1980 and in Northern Ireland since 1 July 1983. Any provision in the constitution of a company limited by guarantee that purports to divide the company's undertaking into shares or interests is a provision for a share capital (whether or not the nominal value or number of the shares or interests is specified by the provision). [*CA 2006, s 5*].

As the definition of a public company only includes companies limited by guarantee which have a share capital, it follows that a guarantee company can only be formed as a private company.

See **14.3 Constitution – Memorandum and Articles** for requirements of the articles of association; formation for requirements of the memorandum of association and registration; **27.2 Names and Business Names** for exemption from requirement as to the use of 'limited'.

*Right to participate in profits otherwise than as member void*

In order to prevent members of a company limited by guarantee and not having a share capital being given rights equivalent to those of shareholders, any provision in the company's articles, or in any resolution of the company, purporting to give a person a right to participate in the divisible profits of the company otherwise than as a member is void. [*CA 2006, s 37*]. In the case of a company formed before 1 October 2009, this also applies to any provision of its memorandum (which, from that date, is deemed to be part of its articles under *CA 2006, s 28*, see **14 Constitution – Memorandum and Articles**).

There is no statutory restriction on the members of such a company participating in their profits except where it has sought exemption from the use of the word 'limited' in its name (see **27 Names and Business Names**).

## Unlimited companies

An unlimited company is a company having no limit on the liability of its members. Such a company can only be a private company and cannot be a public one. [*CA 2006, s 4(2)*]. This liability arises only on the company being insolvent on winding up. Whilst the company is a going concern, liability is limited to the amount unpaid on shares.

See **14 Constitution** for requirements of the articles of association; and **41 Re-Registration** for private limited company becoming unlimited, an unlimited private company becoming limited, and a public company becoming private and unlimited.

*Exemption for unlimited companies from obligation to file accounts*

Subject to below, the directors of an unlimited company are not required to deliver accounts and reports to the Registrar of Companies in respect of a financial year unless at any time during the 'relevant accounting reference period'

- the company was a subsidiary undertaking or a parent of an undertaking which was then limited

   Relevant accounting reference period' in relation to a financial year means the accounting reference period by reference to which the financial year was determined.

   [*CA 2006, s 448(1)–(3)(5); SI 2008 No 393, Reg 13*].

   References to an undertaking being limited at a particular time are to an undertaking (under whatever law established) the liability of whose members is at that time limited.

- the company was a banking or insurance company or the parent company of a banking or insurance group or each of the company's members was

   (i)     a limited company; or

   (ii)    another unlimited company or Scottish partnership, each of whose members is a limited company.

   References in (i) or (ii) above to a limited company, another unlimited company or Scottish partnership include references to any comparable undertaking incorporated in, or formed under, the law of a country or territory outside the UK.

## 12.7 Company Formation and Types of Companies

### Unregistered companies

Only specific provisions of the *Companies Act* apply to '*unregistered companies*'. See *Schedule 1* to the *Companies (Unregistered Companies) Regulations 2009 (SI 2009 No 2436)* which apply provisions of *CA 1985* and *CA 2006* with modifications to unregistered companies and *Schedule 2* to that *Order* which contains transitional provisions applying to companies incorporated before 1 October 2009. The *2009 Regulations* also revoked the *Companies (Unregistered Companies) Regulations 2007*. So, for example, the same naming requirements do not apply to unregistered companies; hence, an unregistered 'Bridge Society' would be permissible without the Secretary of State's approval, and this would not violate the *Company, Limited Liability Partnership and Business Names (Sensitive Words and Expressions) Regulations 2014*. See **27.7** SENSITIVE WORDS AND EXPRESSION.

'*Unregistered companies*' means any body corporate, incorporated in and having a principal place of business in the UK, other than

(a)     any body incorporated by or registered under, a public general Act of Parliament;

(b)     any body not formed for the purpose of carrying on a business which has for its object the acquisition of gain by the body or its individual members;

(c)     any body exempted by statutory instrument; and

(d)     any open-ended investment company.

*Section 1043* of the *CA 2006* does not repeal or revoke any enactment, Royal Charter or other instrument constituting or regulating any unregistered company or restrict the power to grant a charter in lieu of, or supplementary to, any such charter. However, the operation of any such enactment, etc which is inconsistent with any of those provisions is suspended to the extent of that inconsistency.

[*CA 2006, s 1043*].

The majority of unregistered companies have been formed by royal charter. Over 900 such companies have been formed since the 13th century although only around 400 are now still actively within the remit of the Privy Council. Today, charters are now chiefly granted to non-trading corporations acting for the public good, such as professional institutions and charities, which display permanence in their own sphere – such as the Institute of Chartered Accountants. Hence, most current charter companies fall *outside* the scope of unregistered companies, since they do not satisfy the element of the definition set out at (b) above. As at the date on which the *Companies (Unregistered Companies) Regulations 2009* came into force (1 October 2009), fewer than 50 unregistered companies had filed documents at Companies House. By contrast, there were 2.5 million active companies formed under the *Companies Acts*.

### Community interest companies

With effect from 1 October 2009, a company

•     limited by shares or a company limited by guarantee and not having a share capital may be formed as or become a community interest company; and

•     limited by guarantee and having a share capital may become a community interest company.

[*CA 2006, s 6*]

Such companies are intended for use by non-profit-distributing enterprises providing benefit to a community in areas such as childcare, social housing, leisure and community transport. They are subject to the general framework of company law. See **10** COMMUNITY INTEREST COMPANIES.

### Open-ended investment companies

A company can be incorporated as an open-ended investment company (OEIC). The regulations making provision for OEICs are the *Open-Ended Investment Companies Regulations 2001 (SI 2001 No 1228)*. These regulations are concerned with

- the formation and subsequent control and supervision of OEICs; and

- the corporate framework within which an OEIC operates.

Under *SI 2001 No 1228, Reg 6*, the FCA are given powers to make additional rules on both the constitution and management of OEICs and the publication of scheme particulars.

Detailed coverage of the provisions of these rules and regulations is beyond the scope of this book.


## 12.8   OTHER REGISTRABLE CORPORATE VEHICLES

### Private fund limited partnerships

As from 6 April 2017, it has been possible to register a new form of entity; namely, the private fund limited partnership (PFLP), in accordance with the *Limited Partnerships Act 1907* as amended by the *Legislative Reform (Private Fund Limited Partnerships) Order 2017 (SI 2017 No 514)*.

Private fund limited partnerships are a new sub-category of Limited Partnerships (LPs), the latter being formed under the *Limited Partnerships Act 1907* (as amended). In short, an LP (under the *Limited Partnerships Act 1907*) needed to have at least one 'general partner' who took on unlimited liability for partnership debts, whilst the other partners – classed as 'limited partners' – could enjoy limited liability. These limited partners were however not allowed to take part in the active management of the business.

For present purposes, the PFLP is effectively a modern 'evolution' of the old LP structure.

The PFLP structure was introduced primarily for use by private investment funds (that is, funds that are not authorised to be promoted to retail consumers) – for example, private equity and venture capital funds.

The key advantages of using the PFLP rather than the existing English LP structure are:

- A PFLP benefits from a 'white list' of permitted actions which 'limited partners' in the PFLP can take without being regarded as participating in the management of the limited partnership and hence losing their limited liability. This includes, for example, voting on amendments to the limited partnership agreement. The white list is not intended to destroy the general principle that limited partners cannot actively participate in the management of the limited partnership. However, it should extend the scope of what limited partners in private funds can safely do without jeopardising their limited liability.

- Limited partners in a PFLP are not required to contribute any capital to the partnership.

- A PFLP is exempt from the administratively onerous requirement imposed on the limited partnership that any assignment of a limited partnership interest be advertised in the London Gazette.

- A PFLP benefits from a right given to limited partners to appoint a person to wind up the partnership if the 'general partner' is unable to do so.

- A PFLP is also exempt from certain statutory duties imposed on limited partners not to compete with the limited partnership and to render accounts and information on matters affecting the partnership to any limited partner.

Given that other jurisdictions (such as Luxembourg and the Channel Islands) have laws which offer flexible structures for private fund sponsors, the rationale behind the PFLP structure was to make the UK an attractive domicile for such funds.

It is widely anticipated that the PFLP will become established as the default choice for private fund managers that use an English limited partnership structure.

Further detail about the PFLP is beyond the scope of this Handbook. It will be interesting to observe in what contexts this new form of business medium is applied in years to come, particularly in light of the current Government's stated aims of enforcing the UK tax obligations of foreign businesses, and given the uncertain climate in light of Brexit.

# 13   Company Secretaries

## 13.1   PRIVATE COMPANIES AND COMPANY SECRETARIES

As from 6 April 2008 a private company is not required to have a company secretary unless its articles expressly require it (although it may choose to do so). In the case of a private company 'without a secretary',

*   anything authorised or required to be given or sent to, or served on, the company by being sent to its secretary

    (i)   may be given or sent to, or served on, the company itself; and

    (ii)   if addressed to the secretary is treated as addressed to the company; and

*   anything else required or authorised to be done by or to the secretary of the company may be done by or to

    (i)   a director; or

    (ii)   a person authorised generally or specifically in that behalf by the directors.

Any reference in the *Companies Acts* to a company *'without a secretary'* is to a private company which has taken advantage of the exemption (as opposed to one which normally has a company secretary but which for some reason, such as death of the office holder, is without a secretary at a given time). References to a private company 'with a secretary' are construed accordingly.

[*CA 2006, ss 270, 271*].

If the articles of a private company immediately before 6 April 2008 expressly required it to have a secretary it is a company 'with a secretary' for the above purposes until its articles are amended to remove the requirement. For this purpose a provision

*   requiring or authorising things to be done by or in relation to a secretary, or

*   as to the manner in which, or terms on which, a secretary is to be appointed or removed,

is not a provision expressly requiring the company to have a secretary.

[*SI 2007 No 3495, Sch 4 para 4*].

### Provisions applying to all secretaries

**Acts done by person in a dual capacity.** Although a director can act as secretary note that a provision requiring or authorising a thing to be done by or to a director *and* the secretary of a company is not satisfied by its being done by or to the same person acting both as director and as, or in place of, the secretary. So for example if the articles required countersignature of company documents by both a director and the secretary, the same person could not countersign in each capacity. [*CA 2006, s 280*].

## 13.1 Company Secretaries

**Secretary not also to be auditor.** It should be noted that an officer of the company (which includes the company secretary) cannot act as the statutory auditor of the company. [*CA 2006, s 1214*]. It follows from this that an existing auditor cannot be appointed company secretary.

## 13.2 PUBLIC COMPANIES AND COMPANY SECRETARIES

A public company, unlike a private one, must have a secretary. [*CA 2006, s 271*].

### Qualifications of a public company secretary

The directors of a public company must take all reasonable steps to secure that the secretary (or each joint secretary) is a person who appears to them to have the requisite knowledge and experience to discharge the functions of secretary of the company and who has one or more of the following qualifications.

- He has held the office of secretary of a public company for at least three of the five years immediately preceding his appointment as secretary.

- He is a member of

    (i)     the Institute of Chartered Accountants in England and Wales;

    (ii)    the Institute of Chartered Accountants of Scotland;

    (iii)   the Chartered Association of Certified Accountants;

    (iv)    the Institute of Chartered Accountants in Ireland;

    (v)     the Institute of Chartered Secretaries and Administrators;

    (vi)    the Chartered Institute of Management Accountants; or

    (vii)   the Chartered Institute of Public Finance and Accountancy.

- He is a barrister, advocate or solicitor called or admitted in any part of the UK.

- He is a person who, by virtue of his holding or having held any other position or his being a member of any other body, appears to the directors to be capable of discharging the functions of secretary of the company.

[*CA 2006, s 273*].

### Direction requiring public company to appoint secretary

If it appears to the Secretary of State that a public company is in breach of the requirement to have a company secretary, he may give the company a direction to that effect, specifying

- what it must do to comply with the direction;

- the period, which must be not less than one month or more than three months after the date on which the direction is given, in which the company must comply with the direction; and

- the consequences failing to comply.

Where the company does not have a secretary, it must make the necessary appointment and notify the Registrar of Companies of the appointment before the end of the period specified in the direction. If the company has already made the necessary appointment, it must still ensure that it notifies the Registrar of Companies before the end of the period specified.

If a company fails to comply with a direction under these provisions, an offence is committed by the company and every officer of the company who is in default. For this purpose a shadow director (see directors) is treated as an officer of the company. A person guilty of such an offence is liable on summary conviction to a fine not exceeding level 5 on the standard scale and, for continued contravention, a daily default fine not exceeding one-tenth of the greater of £5,000 or level 4 on the standard scale. See **29** OFFENCES AND LEGAL PROCEEDINGS for the standard scale.

[*CA 2006, s 272; SI 2015 No 664, Sch 3*].

### 13.3   APPOINTMENT AND REMOVAL

Particulars of the first secretary (or joint secretaries) of a company must be given in the statement of the company's proposed officers required to be delivered to the Registrar of Companies at the time of application for formation under *CA 2006, s 12* (see **12.3(h)** COMPANY FORMATION). On registration, the person or persons so named are deemed to be appointed. [*CA 2006, s 16(6)*].

Appointment of subsequent secretaries is regulated by the articles. Where the company has adopted standard Table A articles, see *Table A 1985 Reg 99.*

The model articles for both private and public companies made under *CA 2006* are silent on the subject of re-appointment or appointment of subsequent secretaries and so companies incorporated on after 1 October 2009 will if necessary either have to modify the model articles (if adopted) or draft bespoke articles to include such provision. Table A and the Model Articles are set out in APPENDIX **4** STANDARD ARTICLES OF ASSOCIATION.

Where the articles are silent, it is likely that analogous powers are within the board's scope of authority. In relation to listed companies, the the UK Corporate Governance Code states that any question of the removal of the secretary should be a matter for the board of directors as a whole (Code provision B.5.2).

Details of the first secretary and all subsequent changes must be recorded in the company's register of secretaries. See **38.6** REGISTERS.

### 13.4   Notification of changes to Companies House

A company must, within 14 days of

- a person becoming or ceasing to become its secretary, or

- any change in the particulars contained in its register of secretaries (see **38.6** REGISTERS),

give notice to the Registrar of Companies of the change and of the date on which it occurred. Notification is given on Form TM02 (Termination of appointment of secretary) or CH03 (Change of secretary's details).

Any notice of a person having become secretary (or one of joint secretaries) of the company must be accompanied by a consent by that person to act in the relevant capacity.

In default in complying with the above provisions, an offence is committed by every officer of the company who is in default. For this purpose a shadow director (see **18.1** DIRECTORS) is treated as an officer of the company. A person guilty of such an offence is liable on summary conviction to a fine not exceeding level 5 on the standard scale and, for continued contravention, a daily default fine not exceeding one-tenth of level 5 on the standard scale. See **29.1** OFFENCES AND LEGAL PROCEEDINGS for the standard scale.

## 13.4    Company Secretaries

[*CA 2006, s 276*].

## 13.5    VACANCY IN OFFICE OR SECRETARY UNABLE TO ACT

If the office of secretary is vacant, or there is for any other reason no secretary capable of acting, anything required or authorised to be done by or to the secretary may be done

* by or to an assistant or deputy secretary (if any); or

* if there is no assistant or deputy secretary or none capable of acting, by or to any person (before 1 October 2009, an officer of the company) authorised generally or specially in that behalf by the directors.

[*CA 2006, s 274*].

See also **13.2** for the power of the Secretary of State to direct a public company to appoint a secretary.

## 13.6    LIABILITY OF A COMPANY SECRETARY

An '*officer*' in relation to a company includes a secretary. [*CA 2006, s 1173*].

A secretary is, therefore, potentially liable for any of the penalties and fines imposed under the *Companies Acts* for default by officers. Penalties are dealt with in the appropriate part of the text but see also

* **29.3** OFFENCES AND LEGAL PROCEEDINGS for the liability of the company secretary where an offence is committed by the company;

* **18.33–18.38** and **18.41** DIRECTORS for liabilities under the *Insolvency Act 1986* and the *Theft Act 1968* which also apply to the company secretary; and

* **29.10** OFFENCES AND LEGAL PROCEEDINGS for the power of the court to grant relief.

Note that the general prohibition on indemnifying directors against liabilities in *CA 2006, s 232* does not expressly include other officers (including the company secretary) so companies may provide (and often do provide in their articles) indemnities for the secretary. The company can also take out personal legal liability insurance for the benefit of the secretary.

## 13.7    POWERS OF A COMPANY SECRETARY

A company secretary has been held to be a mere servant whose position is to do what he is told so that he has no authority to represent anything at all (*Barnett, Hoares & Co v South London Tramways Co* (1887) 18 QBD 815, CA). But a modern company secretary is a much more important person. He is an officer of the company normally with extensive duties and responsibilities. He may regularly make representations on behalf of the board and enter into contracts on its behalf which come within the day-to-day running of the company's business. Signing contracts connected with the administrative side of the company's affairs therefore comes within his ostensible authority (*Panorama Developments (Guildford) Ltd v Fidelis Furnishing Fabrics Ltd* [1971] 2 QB 711, [1971] 3 All ER 16, CA).

The range of responsibilities and duties of a company secretary will depend on the size and nature of the company, on whether the company is listed, and on its particular sphere of business. The duties may encompass the giving of support to the board and to the company generally on a range of commercially sophisticated matters, and to assisting on a range of corporate transactions. The company secretary is likely also to be responsible for maintaining the statutory registers and books of minutes (for both directors and shareholders). See **38.18** Rᴇɢɪsᴛᴇʀ ᴏꜰ ᴘᴇᴏᴘʟᴇ ᴡɪᴛʜ sɪɢɴɪꜰɪᴄᴀɴᴛ ɪɴᴛᴇʀᴇsᴛs for the obligation to maintain the PSC register, and to file certain information in this regard with Companies House. It is likely that responsibility to discharge these obligations will fall primarily on the company secretary. The company secretary could also be personally liable for the specific statutory penalties for default on the various filing obligations.

# 14   Constitution – Memorandum and Articles

**Cross-references.** See 12 COMPANY FORMATION AND TYPES OF COMPANIES and APPENDIX 4 STANDARD ARTICLES OF ASSOCIATION.

**Background.** The provisions in this chapter apply, unless otherwise stated, with effect from 1 October 2009.

## 14.1   A COMPANY'S CONSTITUTION

Before 1 October 2009 the constitution of a company incorporated under the Companies Act was comprised in the memorandum of association and the articles of association. Articles (typically based on *Table A 1985 (SI 1985 No 805)*), were concerned with the company's internal management and as such could be changed by special resolution by the members. The memorandum of association could only be changed in ways specified by *CA 1985* given that it contained the company's objects and the basis on which the company was incorporated (for example the authorised share capital of the company).

From 1 October 2009 the constitution of a company has been defined [*CA 2006, s 17*] as;

•      the company's articles; and

•      any resolutions and agreements to which *CA 2006, Chapter 3* applies (see *section 29*). *Section 29* then sets out which resolutions and agreements affect a company's constitution.

Other parts of *CA 2006* give a wider meaning to "constitution"– see *CA 2006, s 257* where references to a company's constitution include resolutions and decisions made by members of the company.

**Before 1 October 2009,** where any provision of *CA 2006* which came into force before that date refers to the company's articles (including above), this is to be taken as including a reference to the company's memorandum. [*SI 2007 No 2194, Sch 1 para 1*].

## 14.2   MEMORANDUM OF ASSOCIATION

The memorandum of a company incorporated on or after 1 October 2009 is markedly different from that of a company registered under *CA 1985*. The 'modern' memorandum is a statement that the subscribers wish to form a company under *CA 2006* and agree to become members of the company and, in the case of a company with share capital, to take at least one share each [*CA 2006, s 8*]. It must be in a prescribed form set out in the *Companies (Registration) Regulations 2008 (SI 2008 No 3014)* in order to comply with the registration requirements of *CA 2006* [*ss 7–12*]. It is in effect a short form, historical document used only on incorporation. It has no real continuing significance and is not thereafter capable of alteration. Matters that were contained in the memorandum of a company incorporated under *CA 1985* (such as the company's name, its objects, the type of company, its liability status and its registered office address) are no longer part of the memorandum but are either addressed in the articles or, in the case of the name, simply recorded on the certificate of incorporation.

**Effect on the memorandum of companies incorporated before 1 October 2009.** Provisions that immediately before 1 October 2009 were contained in a company's memorandum but are not provisions of the kind to be included in the new-style memorandum under *CA 2006, s 8* (see **12 COMPANY FORMATION AND TYPES OF COMPANIES**) are treated, with effect from 1 October 2009, as provisions of the company's articles. This applies not only to substantive provisions but also to provisions for entrenchment. Where the memorandum of a company incorporated before that date contained entrenching provisions, those provisions are deemed with effect from that date, to be entrenching provisions of the company's articles .[*CA 2006, s 28*].

**Objects.** As from 1 October 2009 a company's objects are unrestricted unless the company's articles provide otherwise [*CA 2006, s 31(1)*]. A company incorporated on or after 1 October 2009 may adopt restricted objects which would have to be set out in the articles of association. A company incorporated before that date whose objects are restricted but which wants to have unrestricted objects will need to amend its articles.

**Share capital.** From 1 October 2009 companies have not been required to have an upper limit on share capital (authorised share capital). Effectively, *CA 2006* has abolished the concept of authorised share capital which previously all companies were required to state in their memorandum. If the memorandum of a company incorporated before 1 October 2009 provides for an authorised share capital this is deemed to form a provision of its articles (see above) and can be removed by ordinary resolution.

**Limitation of liability.** For companies incorporated on or after 1 October 2009, the prescribed form memorandum (see above and *CA 2006, s 8*) does not include a limitation of liability statement. The statement has instead in the case of a company limited by shares or by guarantee, to be included in the articles. The Model Articles for both private and public companies (see **APPENDIX 4 STANDARD ARTICLES OF ASSOCIATION**) provide for limitation of members liability. If a company's articles exclude the Model Articles it should ensure that a limited liability statement is included in its articles.

## 14.3    ARTICLES OF ASSOCIATION

Historically companies' articles of association adopted *Table A 1985* (or *Table A 1948* for companies incorporated before *Table A 1985* came into force) in whole or in part. *Table A 1985* was replaced on 1 October 2009 by the Model Articles for private and public companies (see *Schedules 1* and *3* to the *Companies (Model Articles) Regulations 2008 (SI 2008 No 3229)* set out in **APPENDIX 4**).

The Model Articles were amended with effect from 28 April 2013 to remove the provision which allowed companies to terminate a director's appointment on the grounds of mental health. See further at **14.6 REMOVAL OF DIRECTORS**.

The Model Articles do not duplicate provisions in *CA 2006* (for example the provisions for resolutions and meetings). It is therefore important to bear this in mind if a company incorporated on or after 1 October 2009 is either adopting the Model Articles (unamended) on incorporation or, after incorporation if it is adopting new articles based on the Model Articles. In most cases thought needs to be given whether amendments or additions need to be made to the articles whether or not a company was incorporated before 1 October 2009 and still has *Table A* or is adopting the Model Articles. (See **14.6** ALTERATION OF ARTICLES – THE PRACTICAL ISSUES).

The starting point in law is that every company must have articles of association on incorporation. It must register the articles with the Registrar of Companies at the same time as it registers the memorandum of association. See **12.3** COMPANY FORMATION AND TYPES OF COMPANIES.

Articles of association registered by a company must

- be contained in a single document; and

- be divided into paragraphs numbered consecutively

[*CA 2006, s 218*].

A company's articles are rules, chosen by the members, governing the company's internal affairs and form an integral and, after 1 October 2009, the main part of the company's constitution. All the company's key internal rules on matters such as the allocation of powers between members and its directors are set out in the articles.

### 14.4   Form and content of articles

The form of a company's articles depends on the date of incorporation (see **14.1** and **14.3**). The important thing to note is that the articles adopted by a company (or as subsequently altered) will continue to apply to that company unless and until they are changed.

A company incorporated on after 1 October 2009 may adopt all or any of the provisions of the Model Articles which can be made by reference. This is common where a company wishes to incorporate specific provisions of the model articles. For example, a company's registered articles may read 'The Model Articles apply except for articles X, Y and Z' or 'Model Article A applies but is amended as follows'.

**Default application of Model Articles.** On the formation of a limited company

- if articles are not registered, or

- if articles are registered, in so far as they do not exclude or modify the relevant Model Articles,

the relevant Model Articles prescribed for a company of that description (so far as applicable) form part of the company's articles in the same manner and to the same extent as if articles in the form of those articles had been duly registered.

[*CA 2006, s 20*].

**Companies not limited by shares.** In the case of company incorporated between 1 July 1985 and 30 September 2009 which is

- a company limited by guarantee and not having a share capital,

- a company limited by guarantee and having a share capital, or

- an unlimited company having a share capital,

the form of the articles must be respectively in accordance with *Table C, D,* or *E* set out in *SI 1985 No 805* or as near as circumstances permit. [*CA 1985, s 8(4)* before repeal by *CA 2006*]. In the case of a company incorporated on or after 1 October 2009 as a private company limited by guarantee, the form of the model articles is in *SI 2008 No 3229, Sch 2*. None of these model articles are reproduced in this book.

## 14.4 Constitution – Memorandum and Articles

**Charitable companies.** A model memorandum and articles of association for use by charitable companies can be downloaded from the Law Commission website at www.charity -commission.gov.uk.

## 14.5 Alteration of articles – the law

**Alteration by special resolution of members.** Subject to the rules on entrenchment in **14.7**, a company may amend its articles by special resolution (see **42.3** RESOLUTIONS AND MEETINGS). But this does not apply to the provisions of the articles (including provisions of the company's memorandum that are treated as provisions of the articles) of a company incorporated before 1 October 2009 where the articles were not capable of being so amended immediately before 1 October 2009.

The *Small Business, Enterprise and Employment Act 2015 (SBEE 2015)*, ss 84 and 85 provide (in summary) that a company may not (after May 2015) issue share warrants to bearer. If the company's articles authorise the company to issue share warrants, the articles can be amended to remove that provision without the need for a special resolution and without complying with any provision for entrenchment which is relevant to the provision for share warrants. A copy of the articles when amended must be sent to the Registrar of Companies (see **14.8**).

[*SBEE 2015, ss 84, 85, 164*].

**Charities.** Note also that the amendment of articles by special resolution is, in the case of a company that is

- a charity, subject to *Charities Act 2011, ss 197* and *198* (in Northern Ireland *Charities (Northern Ireland) Order 1987 (SI 1987 No 2048), Art 9*); and

- registered in the Scottish Charity Register, subject to *CA 1989, s 162* and *Charities and Trustee Investment (Scotland) Act 2005, s 16*.

[*CA 2006, s 21; SI 2008 No 2860, Sch 2 para 4*].

*Private companies* may also alter their articles without a special resolution in meeting by means of a written resolution. See **42.5** RESOLUTIONS AND MEETINGS.

**Restrictions on alteration.** Apart from the above restrictions and specific statutory restrictions, any requirements of the Listing Rules and the rules on entrenchment in **14.7**, a company is free to alter its articles as it wishes, and it must not nullify or restrict its ability to alter them. See *Allen v Gold Reefs of West Africa Ltd* [1900] 1 Ch 656, CA, and *Russell v Northern Bank Development Corpn Ltd* [1992] 3 All ER 161, [1992] BCLC 1016, HL. This applies even if to do so would involve a breach of contract with a third party. Such a third party would, however, be entitled to damages for the breach (*Southern Foundries (1926) Ltd v Shirlaw* [1940] AC 701, [1940] 2 All ER 445, HL).

Any alteration must be made *bona fide* for the benefit of the company as a whole. See *Allen v Gold Reefs of West Africa Ltd* above (creation of a lien on fully paid shares); *Brown v British Abrasive Wheel Co* [1919] 1 Ch 290, 88 LJ Ch 143 (compulsory purchase of minority shares); and *Sidebottom v Kershaw, Leese & Co Ltd* [1920] 1 Ch 154, 89 LJ Ch 113, CA (forced sale of shares by shareholders carrying on business in direct competition). Whether such an alteration is for the company's benefit is for the shareholders to decide, and the court will intervene only if it considers the alteration to be such that no reasonable person would consider it to be in the interests of the company (*Shuttleworth v Cox Bros & Co (Maidenhead) Ltd* [1927] 2 KB 9, 96 LJKB 104, CA). As to the meaning of 'bona fide for the benefit of the company as a whole', see *Greenhalgh v Arderne Cinemas Ltd* [1951] Ch 286, [1950] 2 All ER 1120, CA.

See also generally *Peter's American Delicacy Co Ltd v Heath* (1939) 61 CLR 457, Aust HC.

**14.6    Alteration of articles – the practical issues**

The following practical issues are based on:

- the fact that pre 1 October 2009 articles based on *Table A* may not reflect changes made by *CA 2006* or any subsequent legislation; and

- the *Model Articles* are in minimal form and do not repeat or amend any provisions of *CA 2006* (for example provisions for proxies).

The practical issues are categorised for the purposes of this chapter as: 1) general issues with, where relevant, references to *Table A 1985* and/or the *Model Articles* 2) issues specific to *Table A 1985*, where relevant referring to numbered regulations in *Table A* and 3) issues specific to the *Model Articles* (again where relevant) referring to numbered articles and also whether the issue affects only the *Model Articles* for private companies or the *Model Articles* for public companies (or both).

*Table A 1985* and the *Model Articles* are set out in Appendix 4 standard articles of association.

**1. General issues**

**Electronic communication.** Do the articles contain provision for electronic communication to and from members? Under *CA 2006* companies are able to send a wide range of documents both electronically and by posting them on a website provided that the requirements of *CA 2006 ss 308, 309, 333, 1143–1148* and *Schedules 4* and *5* are complied with and in the case of fully listed companies they comply with the electronic communication provisions in the FCA's Disclosure and Transparency Rules.

There is no statutory requirement to amend the articles to permit electronic communication but:

- a company can assume that a member has agreed to accept communications posted on a website (the so called 'deemed' agreement in *CA 2006*) if either the member has agreed to receive documents by means of a website or an ordinary resolution has been passed resolving that the company can send documents to members by means of a website or there is a provision in the articles to that effect

- there is some debate whether *CA 2006, s 1134* which sets out what can be sent to and from a company includes for example online voting as it refers only to 'documents or information'. It is preferable therefore to make this clear in the articles

- if members send documents to the company there are two relevant provisions. The first is that if the company includes an electronic address in either a notice of meeting or proxy, it is deemed to have agreed to receive documents relating to that meeting or proxy by electronic means and at the address set out. Secondly for all other documents *CA 2006, Sch 4, Part 3, para 6* provides that documents can only be sent electronically to the company if the company expressly agrees. The articles therefore could be amended to provide that only specific types of documents can be sent electronically and to set out how the company wants the sender's identity to be confirmed. If the articles do not expressly set this out then the default position is that a document is 'authenticated' if it contains or is accompanied by a statement of identity of the sender and the company has no reason to doubt the truth of the statement [*CA 2006, s 1146*].

- it is better practice to ensure the articles are consistent with *CA 2006* provisions to avoid confusion and make it clear what can or cannot be sent electronically.

**2. Company objects**

See **14.2** above that as from 1 October 2009 a company has unrestricted objects unless its articles provided otherwise. The *Model Articles* therefore do not include an objects clause. If a company is incorporated after 1 October 2009 and adopts the model articles but wants to have restricted objects it will have to amend its articles.

The objects of a company incorporated before 1 October 2009 and which are contained in its memorandum are deemed to form part of its articles [*CA 2006, s 28*]. If such a company whose objects are restricted wants to have unrestricted objects, the articles will need to be amended either to remove the objects altogether or to amend them.

Charitable companies. Any amendment of the articles of a charitable company to add, remove or alter the company's objects is a "regulated" alteration which requires the prior written consent of the Charity Commission and is ineffective if such consent has not been obtained. Any such regulated alteration is governed by *CA 2006, ss 26, 30* and *31* as to the requirements to notify the Registrar of Companies (see **14.8, 14.10**)

[*Charities Act 2011, s 198*]

**3. Consolidation/sub-division of share capital/purchase of own shares**

*CA 2006* does not require a company to have shareholder approval to consolidate or sub-divide capital or purchase its own shares. If there are such restrictions in pre 1 October 2009 articles (see *Table A 1985, regulations 32* and *34*) removing them means that the articles will not need to be amended (and filed) on each change of capital. Alternatively a pre 1 October 2009 company could retain such restrictions and a post 1 October 2009 could include them as *CA 2006, s 618(5)* provides that a company's articles can exclude or restrict the power to change capital without authority and *s 690(1)* provides that a company can purchase its own shares subject to any prohibition or restriction in the company's articles.

**4. Share capital reduction (private companies only)**

See **47.51** SHARES that as from 1 October 2008 a private company has been able to reduce share capital without the need for a court application provided it complies with *CA 2006, ss 641–644.*

This is subject to any provision of the company's articles which restricts or prohibits a reduction of capital. Any such restrictions or prohibitions would need to be removed. *Table A, regulation 32* only requires an ordinary resolution to cancel shares and diminish share capital, The Model Articles for private companies contain no restrictions or prohibitions.

**5. Directors' age restrictions**

Provisions which prevent a director remaining in office or being re-elected to office after a specific age are potentially discriminatory and should be removed. Neither *Table A* or the *Model Articles* contain such provisions.

**6. Authorised share capital**

(Formerly found in the memorandum of association but sometimes provision was, pre 1 October 2009, also included in the articles). See **47.6** SHARES, that as from 1 October 2009 there is no requirement to have an upper limit on authorised share capital. Companies incorporated before that date with an upper limit in the memorandum, which is deemed as from that date to form provisions of the articles by virtue of *CA 2006, s 28* continue to be subject to that limit unless and until the articles are amended. The *Model Articles* contain no provision for authorised share capital.

**7. Proxies**

On a vote on a show of hands if a proxy has been appointed by more than one member the proxy has one vote 'for' and one vote 'against' the resolution provided that the proxy has been instructed by one or more of those members to vote for the resolution and by one or more of those members to vote against it [*CA 2006, s 285(2)*]. This is subject to anything in the company's articles. See *Table A, regulation 54* which only provides for single voting and note that if a company was incorporated before 1 October 2007, *regulation 54* (if not later amended) did not refer to a right for a proxy to vote on a show of hands. The *Model Articles* make no provision for how proxies should vote.

## 8. AGMs (private companies only)

As from 1 October 2007 *CA 2006* removed the requirement for private companies to hold an AGM. There is however nothing in *CA 2006* which prevents a private company holding an AGM. Consider whether the company needs to hold an AGM and, if not, check the articles for any provision which requires the holding of an AGM (see for example *Table A 1985* which does not require the holding of an AGM but does, pre 1 October 2007, at *regulations 36* and *38* refer to notice of AGM). If the company does not intend to hold AGMs other changes to the articles may also be needed (see for the example the need for directors to retire by rotation in pre 1 October 2007 *Table A 1985* at *regulations 73–76*).

If a company was incorporated after 1 October 2007 and adopted *Table A 1985* unamended or after 1 October 2009 and adopted the *Model Articles* unamended and wants to hold AGMs, it may need to add provisions back in to the articles to regulate both notice of AGM and the holding of an AGM. The Model Articles for public companies contain provisions which could be included in the articles of a private company where necessary.

## 9. Notice of general meetings

The Model Articles for private companies are silent on the issue of calling and providing notice of general meetings.

*CA 2006* provides that only 14 days notice of general meetings (ie not AGMs or meetings requiring special notice to remove directors or auditors) needs to be given. Check the articles to see whether longer notice (eg 21 days) needs to be given and amend if necessary.

**Traded companies**. If the company is 'traded' (see APPENDIX 1 DEFINITIONS for the meaning of traded) the following conditions must be met to take advantage of the 14 day notice period

• the general meeting must not be an AGM

• the company must offer the facility for members to vote by electronic means. This condition is met if there is a facility to appoint a proxy by means of a website. ICSA guidance (ICSA Guidance on the Implementation of the Shareholder Rights Directive July 2009) suggests that offering electronic voting through CREST does not meet the 'electronic means' requirement. To comply a company would need to offer electronic proxy appointment to all their shareholders by means of a website. The facility does not necessarily have to be on the company's own website – it could be hosted for example on a registrar's website.

• a special resolution reducing the notice period to not less than 14 days has been passed either at the preceding AGM or at a general meeting held since the AGM. If the company has not held an AGM the resolution has to be passed at a general meeting (see *CA 2006, ss 307* and *307A*).

All companies: the company's articles may require a longer period of notice (see *CA 2006, s 307(3)* and *307A(6)* and *Table A 1985, regulation 85*). See **42.15 RESOLUTIONS AND MEETINGS**.

## 10. Share capital redenomination

## 14.6    Constitution – Memorandum and Articles

*Section 622* of *CA 2006* allows a company to redenominate the whole, or any class of, share capital, into other currencies but provides that the company's articles may prohibit or restrict the power to do this.

### 11. Directors' conflicts of interest

The directors of a private company can authorise other directors' conflicts of interests [*CA 2006, s 175(5)(a)*] provided that

- there is nothing in the company's constitution that invalidates that authorisation (*s 175(5)(a)*)

- the quorum for the meeting is met without counting the conflicted director and any other interested director (*s 175(6)(a)*)

- the matter is agreed without the conflicted director or any other interested director voting (or would have been agreed if their votes had not been counted) (*s 175(6)(b)*).

Consider whether any limits should be imposed in the articles either on the types of conflicts which can be authorised and/or any procedures to be followed or restrictions to be imposed.

**Public companies**. Similar provisions (as above) apply as for private companies except that the company's constitution must positively provide for directors' authorisation of conflicts ie provision must be made in the company's articles. *Table A 1985, regulations 84* and *85* provide for limited situations in which a director may be a party to or interested in transactions or arrangements with the company but do not expressly provide for other conflicts of interest. *Regulation 94* limited the situations in which a director can vote and be counted in the quorum where he has a conflict of interest. The *Model Articles* (at *article 14* for private companies and *article 16* for public companies) provide for participation in the quorum and voting where conflicts arise.

### 12. Company name

*CA 2006, s 77(1)(b)* allows a company to change its name by any means provided for in the articles, for example by allowing the directors to change the name. This is in addition to the usual means of changing a name by special resolution of the shareholders. Neither *Table A 1985* nor the *Model Articles* contain alternate means of changing the company name.

### 13. Employees

*CA 2006, s 247* enables the directors to make provision for employees/former employees employed either by the company or any of its subsidiaries on cessation or transfer of the company's business provided that any board resolution is authorised by the articles. *Section 247* largely reproduces *CA 1985, s 719. Table A 1985* made no such provision (although *regulation 87* enables the directors to provide for directors' gratuities and pensions). The *Model Articles* at *article 51* for private companies and *84* for public companies enable the directors to make such provision for employees.

### 14. Nomination and information rights

The articles can enable a shareholder to nominate a third party to 'enjoy or exercise all or any of the specified rights of the member' (see *CA 2006, s 145*). If a company is traded company (see APPENDIX 1 DEFINITIONS) members can nominate third parties to enjoy information rights ie the right to receive copies of communications that the company sends to its members and the right to require copies of accounts and reports and to require hard copies of documents provided 'in other forms' (see *CA 2006, s 146*). These statutory information rights do not depend on anything in the company's articles.

Neither *Table A 1985* or the *Model Articles* contain such provisions.

## 15. Conflicting provisions of *CA 2006*

Certain provisions of *CA 2006* may conflict with or override the company's articles. Check the following to determine whether the articles need amending

- appointment of proxies (see *CA 2006, s 324, 327(2)* and *330(6)*)

- time for delivery of proxies (see *CA 2006, s 327(3)*)

- voting on a poll (see *CA 2006, s 285A*)

- appointment of multiple corporate representatives (see *CA 2006, s 323*)

- refusal of transfer of shares (see *CA 2006, s 771*)

- percentage of members who can requisition a general meeting of a private or non traded public company (see *CA 2006, s 303*)

## 16. Attendance and speaking at general meetings

The Model Articles do not, in the way that Table A attempted to, set out provisions for attending and speaking at general meetings. Instead they are permissive and allow the directors to make any arrangements appropriate to enable those attending a general meeting to exercise their rights to speak or vote at it. The Model Articles do not set out what those arrangements should be.

**Issues specific to Table A 1985 (or articles based on Table A 1985)**

**EGMs and extraordinary resolutions.** *CA 2006* refers only to AGMs and general meetings and special and ordinary resolutions (see *CA 2006, ss 281, 282* and *283*) and not to EGMs and extraordinary resolutions. *Table A 1985* refers to extraordinary resolutions (see for example *regulation 117* 'winding up') and that all general meetings other than AGMs are called EGMs (see *regulation 36*).

Although it is not strictly incorrect to continue to refer to EGMs and extraordinary resolutions, for consistency with *CA 2006* the terms should be changed. If not transitional provisions in *paragraph 23* of *Sch 3* to the *CA 2006 Third Commencement Order 2007 (SI 2007 No 2194)* expressly say that any reference to an extraordinary resolution in a company's articles continues to have effect and shall continue to be construed in accordance with *CA 1985, s 378* "as if that section had not been repealed".

**Old statutory references.** Old statutory references to provisions which have either been repealed or replaced by provisions of *CA 2006* need to be checked for any inconsistency/change in meaning.

**Share capital (private companies only).** Private companies no longer need shareholder approval to allot redeemable shares or to redeem or purchase shares out of capital. Consider removing any restrictions in the articles (see for example *regulation 3* of *Table A* which says that redeemable shares may only be issued subject to 'the Act' ie *CA 1985*).

**Company secretary (private companies only).** As from 6 April 2008 private companies have not been required to have a company secretary but if, at that time, the articles expressly required the company to have a secretary it must have one. *Table A 1985* does not specifically require companies to appoint a secretary.

**Notice of members' meetings (private companies only).** *CA 2006, s 307(6)* reduced the percentage required to consent to short notice from 95% to 90%. If the articles require 95% consent, consider reducing it to the statutory limit although this is not obligatory as *s 307(6)(a)* does say "90% or such higher percentage (not exceeding 95%) as may be specified in the company's articles".

**Written resolutions (private companies only).** Under *CA 2006, s 296(4)* written resolutions do not need unanimous consent to be passed but only the required majority. Consider removing the need for unanimous consent if it is included in the articles. *Table A 1985* does not refer to the majority required for written resolutions.

**2007 changes.** SIs *2007 No 2541* and *2007 No 2826* made substantial changes to *Table A 1985* as a consequence of which companies incorporated on or after 1 October 2007 adopted an amended *Table A*.

### Issues specific to the Model Articles

**Share capital (private companies only).** The *Model Articles (Article 21.8)* for private companies assume that all shares are issued fully paid and so make no provisions for liens, calls on shares or forfeiture of shares.

**Directors' meetings.** The following amendments need to be considered for the *Model Articles* for both private and public companies:

- Calling the meeting. The *Model Articles* do not provide a period of notice for calling a directors meeting but do provide that the notice of meeting does not need to be in writing.

- Unanimous decisions. It is not clear whether the *Model Articles* anticipate that if directors sign multiple copies of written resolutions each copy has to be signed by each director.

- Participating in meetings. The *Model Articles* enable directors to participate in meetings wherever the directors are and however they communicate with each other.

**Alternate directors (private companies only).** The *Model Articles* for private companies do not provide for the appointment of alternates.

**Authority to allot shares.** Private companies with one class of shares incorporated after 1 October 2009 do not need authority in the articles to allot shares. The company can however choose to include in its articles an express prohibition on allotment without authority [*CA 2006, s 550*]. This type of private company incorporated before 1 October 2009 needs to 'opt in' to the new *CA 2006* regime by passing an ordinary resolution (which may also have the effect of altering the articles).

Private companies with more than one class of shares/public companies incorporated after 1 October 2009 still need to give directors authority in the articles (or by ordinary resolution) to allot shares [*CA 2006, s 551*].

*Article 43* of the *Model Articles* for public companies provides that the company may issues shares with such rights or restrictions as the company may by ordinary resolution determine.

**Removal of directors.** An important amendment was made to the Model Articles in 2013 on the issue of mental health. *Section 3(1)* of the *Mental Health (Discrimination) Act 2013* amended the Model Articles to remove the provisions requiring the automatic termination of a director's appointment if that director's rights or powers are restricted by a court order made on mental health grounds. The Act therefore revoked *Article 18(e)* of both the *Model Articles* for private companies limited by shares and of private companies limited by guarantee, and *Article 22(e)* of the *Model Articles* for public companies.

It is not a statutory requirement for a company to remove this provision from its articles. However, reliance on such a provision could be seen as potentially discriminatory. Discrimination on the grounds of disability relating to mental health is caught in English law by the *Equality Act 2010*.

**14.7    Entrenched provisions of the articles**

A company's articles may contain *provisions for entrenchment* to the effect that specified provisions of the articles may be amended or repealed only if conditions are met, or procedures are complied with, that are more restrictive than those applicable in the case of a special resolution. [*CA 2006, s 22(1)*]. In other words, the articles of association may contain some provisions which themselves may only be amended or repealed if certain restrictive conditions or procedures are met that are *more* demanding than those applicable in the case of a special resolution.

Such provision for entrenchment may only be adopted either

- in the company's articles on formation; or

- by an amendment of the company's articles agreed to by *all* the members of the company. (*CA 2006, s 22(2)*).

There can no longer be absolute entrenchment since, unlike under *CA 1985*, provisions cannot be included in the *memorandum* which were incapable of amendment.

However, following concerns that *CA 2006, s 22* will catch variation of class rights provisions and thus impede the amendment of articles to include such provisions, *s 22(2)* has not yet been brought into force, and the Government is understood to be considering the issue further (see the *Companies Act 2006 and LLPs (Transitional Provisions and Savings) (Amendment) Regulations 2009 (SI 2009 No 2476)*.

Provision for entrenchment does not prevent amendment of the company's articles

(a)    by agreement of all the members of the company; or

(b)    by order of a court or other authority having power to alter the company's articles.

The members cannot (as in (a) above) agree to amend provisions of the articles (including provisions of the company's memorandum that are treated as provisions of the articles of a company incorporated before 1 October 2009) which were not capable of being so amended immediately before that date.

**Notice to Registrar of Companies**. Where a company's articles

(a)    on formation contain provision for entrenchment (but see above for the non-commencement of *s 22(2)*)

(b)    are amended so as to include such provision,

(c)    are altered by order of a court or other authority so as to restrict or exclude the power of the company to amend its articles under (*b*),

(d)    are amended so as to remove provision for entrenchment, or

(e)    are altered by order of a court or other authority so as to remove

    (i)    such provision under (*d*), or

    (ii)    any other restriction on, or any exclusion of, the power of the company to amend its articles,

the company must give notice of that fact to the Registrar of Companies.

[*CA 2006, s 23*].

**Statement of compliance where amendment of articles restricted**. Where a company's articles are subject to

- provision for entrenchment, or

- an order of a court or other authority restricting or excluding the company's power to amend the articles

if the company amends its articles and is required to send to the Registrar of Companies a document making or evidencing the amendment, the company must deliver with that document a statement of compliance. This is a statement certifying that the amendment has been made in accordance with the company's articles and, where relevant, any applicable order of a court or other authority. The Registrar of Companies may rely on the statement of compliance as sufficient evidence of the matters stated in it.

[*CA 2006, s 24*].

## 14.8 Filing requirements, etc

**Copies of amended articles to Registrar of Companies.** If a company amends its articles, it must send a copy of the articles as amended to the Registrar of Companies, not later than 15 days after the amendment takes effect. If the company's articles are amended on or after 1 October 2009 (or pre 1 October 2009 amendments take effect after that date) the company can either append a copy of the old style memorandum to its articles or send a copy of the old style memorandum indicating which provisions are deemed to be part of the articles. If a company fails to comply with these provisions, an offence is committed by the company and every officer of the company who is in default. A person guilty of such an offence is liable, on summary conviction, to a fine not exceeding level 3 on the standard scale and, for continued contravention, a daily default fine not exceeding one-tenth of level 3 on the standard scale. See **29.1** Offences and Legal Proceedings for the standard scale.

[*CA 2006, s 26; SI 2008 No 2860, Sch 2 para 6*].

The Registrar of Companies must ensure that notice of receipt of the amended articles is published (see **39.8** Registrar of Companies). A company cannot rely on any amendment of its articles unless, at the material time, the amendment has been published or the company shows that the person concerned knew of the amendment. But if the material time falls within 15 days of publication and the person concerned can show that he was unavoidably prevented from knowing of the event at that time, the company still cannot rely on the amendment as against that person. [*CA 2006, s 1079*]. See **16.19** Dealings with Third Parties.

**Notice to comply by Registrar of Companies.** If it appears to the Registrar of Companies that a company has failed to comply with the above provisions (or a similar requirement in earlier legislation) requiring it to send to him

- a document making or evidencing an alteration in the company's articles, or

- a copy of the company's articles as amended,

the Registrar of Companies may give notice to the company requiring it to comply. The notice must state the date on which it is issued and require the company to comply within 28 days from that date.

If the company complies with the notice within the specified time, no criminal proceedings may be brought in respect of the failure to comply. But if the company does not comply with the notice within the specified time, it is liable to a civil penalty of £200. This is in addition to any liability to criminal proceedings in respect of the failure.

[*CA 2006, s 27*].

### 14.9   Effect of alteration of articles on company's members

Unless a member agrees to the alteration in writing (before or after the alteration is made), he is not bound by an alteration to the articles if and so far as the alteration

- requires him to take or subscribe for more shares than the number held by him at the date on which the alteration is made; or

- in any way increases his liability as at that date to contribute to the company's share capital or otherwise to pay money to the company.

[*CA 2006, s 25*].

### 14.10   RESOLUTIONS AND AGREEMENTS AFFECTING A COMPANY'S CONSTITUTION

A copy of each of the following resolutions or agreements (or, in the case of a resolution or agreement that is not in writing, a written memorandum setting out its terms) must be forwarded to the Registrar of Companies within 15 days after it is passed or made.

- Any special resolution. (see **42.3** RESOLUTIONS AND MEETINGS).

- Any resolution or agreement agreed to by all the members of a company that, if not so agreed to, would not have been effective for its purpose unless passed as a special resolution.

- Any resolution or agreement agreed to by all the members of a class of shareholders that, if not so agreed to, would not have been effective for its purpose unless passed by some particular majority or otherwise in some particular manner.

- Any resolution or agreement that effectively binds all members of a class of shareholders though not agreed to by all those members.

- Any other resolution or agreement to which this paragraph applies by virtue of any enactment.

References above to a member of a company, or of a class of members of a company, do not include the company itself where it is such a member by virtue only of its holding shares as treasury shares.

If a company fails to comply with the above provisions, an offence is committed by the company and every officer of it (which for these purposes includes a liquidator) who is in default. A person guilty of such an offence is liable, on summary conviction, to a fine not exceeding level 3 on the standard scale and, for continued contravention, a daily default fine not exceeding one-tenth of level 3 on the standard scale. See **29.1** OFFENCES AND LEGAL PROCEEDINGS for the standard scale.

[*CA 2006, ss 29, 30*].

### 14.11   CONSTITUTIONAL DOCUMENTS TO BE PROVIDED TO MEMBERS

A company must on request send a member the following documents.

- An up-to-date copy of the company's articles.

  When complying with the obligation to send the articles, if the articles are deemed to incorporate provisions of the memorandum a company can either append a copy of the provisions of the old style memorandum which are deemed to be provisions of the articles or can send a copy of the old-style memorandum indicating which provisions are deemed to be provisions of the articles (*SI 2008 No 2860, art 5, Sch 2, para 9*).

## 14.11 Constitution – Memorandum and Articles

- A copy of any resolution or agreement relating to the company to which *CA 2006, ss 29, 30* apply (see **14.10**).

- A copy of any document required to be sent to the Registrar of Companies under *CA 2006, s 34(2)* (notice where company's constitution altered by special enactment) or *CA 2006, s 35(2)(a)* (notice where order of court or other authority alters company's constitution).

- A copy of any court order under *CA 2006, s 899* (order sanctioning compromise or arrangement) or *CA 2006, s 900* (order facilitating reconstruction or amalgamation). See 35.3 and 35.4 RECONSTRUCTIONS AND MERGERS.

- A copy of any court order under *CA 2006, s 996* (protection of members against unfair prejudice: powers of the court) that alters the company's constitution. See **26.5**, MEMBERS.

- A copy of the company's current certificate of incorporation, and of any past certificates of incorporation.

- In the case of a company with a share capital, a current statement of capital, ie

  (a) the total number of shares of the company;

  (b) the aggregate nominal value of those shares and the aggregate amount (if any) unpaid on those shares (whether on account of their nominal value or by way of premium).

  (c) for each class of shares

   (i) particulars of any voting rights attached to the shares, including rights that arise only in certain circumstances;

   (ii) particulars of any rights attached to the shares, as respects dividends, to participate in a distribution;

   (iii) particulars of any rights attached to the shares, as respects capital, to participate in a distribution (including on a winding up);

   (iv) whether the shares are to be redeemed or are liable to be redeemed at the option of the company or the shareholder;

   (v) the total number of shares of that class; and

   (vi) the aggregate nominal value of shares of that class; and

  (d) the amount paid up and the amount (if any) unpaid on each share (whether on account of the nominal value of the share or by way of premium).

- In the case of a company limited by guarantee, a copy of the statement of guarantee.

If a company defaults in complying with the above provisions, an offence is committed by every officer of the company who is in default. A person guilty of such an offence is liable, on summary conviction, to a fine not exceeding level 3 on the standard scale. See **29.1** OFFENCES AND LEGAL PROCEEDINGS for the standard scale.

[*CA 2006, s 32; SI 2009 No 388, Art 2; SBEE 2015, Sch 6, para 3; SI 2016 No 321, Reg 6*].

**Inspection of the articles.** Any person may inspect a copy of the articles at Companies House and may obtain a certified copy of the articles on payment of the prescribed fee. See APPENDIX 3 FEES.

## 14.12 EFFECT OF COMPANY'S CONSTITUTION

The provisions of a company's constitution bind the company and its members to the same extent as if there were covenants on the part of the company and of each member, to observe those provisions.

In relation to liabilities arising on or after 1 October 2009, money payable by a member to the company under its constitution is a debt due from him to the company. In England and Wales and Northern Ireland it is of the nature of an ordinary contract debt. (The provisions in *CA 1985, s 14(2)* continue to apply to liabilities arising before 1 October 2009 and for this purpose, a liability is treated as arising when the limitation period starts to run for the purposes of the *Limitation Act 1980*.)

[*CA 2006, s 33; SI 2009 No 1941, Art 11*].

The above wording (which broadly follows the earlier wording in *CA 1985, s 14(1)* except that it refers to 'a company's constitution' rather than its 'memorandum and articles') does not make very clear the nature of the relationship which it creates between one member and another and between a member and the company. As a result, there have been numerous court cases on the relationships.

**Between members**. The cases seem to indicate that, even if the articles do constitute a contract between the members of a company, generally the rights bestowed by the articles can only be enforced through the company or, where the company is being wound up, through the liquidator (*Welton v Saffery* [1897] AC 299, HL).

However, in some cases, the court has adopted a different approach, most notably in *Rayfield v Hands* [1960] Ch 1, [1958] 2 All ER 194 where the company's articles required the directors to be members of the company, and also required any member proposing to transfer shares in the company to inform the directors 'who will take the shares equally between them at a fair value'. It was held that a member could compel the directors to purchase his shares in accordance with this provision as the relationship was between the plaintiff as a member and the defendants not as directors but as members.

Nevertheless, the general view appears to be that *Welton v Saffery* still represents the principle which will normally be applied and the reasoning in *Rayfield v Hands* is probably only applicable where the articles give one member a personal right as against another member.

**Between the company and its members**. The general principle is that the articles constitute a contract between the company and its members in relation to their rights and obligations as members. In *Hickman v Kent or Romney Marsh Sheep-Breeders' Association* [1915] 1 Ch 881, 84 LJ Ch 688 the court granted the company a stay of proceedings brought against it by a member who was disputing his expulsion from the company. The articles provided that disputes between the company and its members were to go to arbitration, and by bringing the action, the member was acting contrary to the articles. Similarly, in *Wood v Odessa Waterworks Co* (1889) 42 Ch D 636, a member was granted an injunction restraining the company from acting on a resolution which was contrary to the articles.

However, the general principle applies only where the articles confer a right on a member in his capacity as a member. Thus, in *Eley v Positive Government Security Life Assurance Co Ltd* (1876) 1 Ex D 88, CA, the articles stated that the plaintiff was to be employed for life as the company's solicitor. When the company ceased to employ him, the plaintiff was held not to be entitled to damages for breach of contract, because the articles did not constitute a contract between the company and the plaintiff in a capacity other than as a member. (See also *Beattie v E & F Beattie Ltd* [1938] Ch 708, [1938] 3 All ER 214, CA.)

**14.13    ALTERATION OF COMPANY'S CONSTITUTION BY ENACTMENT OR ORDER**

**Alteration by enactment.** *In relation to any enactment coming into force on or after 1 October 2009*, where a company's constitution is altered by an enactment (other than an enactment amending the general law), the company must give notice of the alteration to the Registrar of Companies, specifying the enactment, not later than 15 days after the enactment comes into force. In the case of a 'special enactment' the notice must be accompanied by a copy of the enactment. [*CA 2006, s 34(1)(2); SI 2008 No 2860, Sch 2 para 12*].

If the enactment amends

- the company's articles, or

- a resolution or agreement under **14.10**,

the notice must be accompanied by a copy of the company's articles, or the resolution or agreement in question, as amended.

A '*special enactment*' means an enactment that is not a public general enactment, and includes

- an Act for confirming a provisional order;

- any provision of a public general Act in relation to the passing of which any of the standing orders of the House of Lords or the House of Commons relating to Private Business applied; or

- any enactment to the extent that it is incorporated or applied for the purposes of a special enactment.

[*CA 2006, s 34(3)(4)*].

*In relation to any enactment coming into force before 1 October 2009, CA 1985, s 18* continues to apply.

**Alteration by order.** *In relation to orders made on or after 1 October 2009*, where a company's constitution is altered by an order of a court or other authority, the company must give notice to the Registrar of Companies of the alteration not later than 15 days after the alteration takes effect. The notice must be accompanied by

(a)    a copy of the order; and

(b)    if the order amends

　　(i)    the company's articles, or

　　(ii)   a resolution or agreement under **14.10**

a copy of the company's articles, or the resolution or agreement in question, as amended.

These provisions do not apply where another enactment provides for the delivery of a copy of the order in question to the Registrar of Companies.

[*CA 2006, s 35(1)(2)(5)*].

**Penalties.** If a company fails to comply with either of the above provisions, an offence is committed by the company and every officer of the company who is in default. A person guilty of such an offence is liable, on summary conviction, to a fine not exceeding level 3 on the standard scale and, for continued contravention, a daily default fine not exceeding one-tenth of level 3 on the standard scale. See **29.1** OFFENCES AND LEGAL PROCEEDINGS for the standard scale.

*[CA 2006, ss 34(5)(6), 35(3)(4)]*.

## 14.14 SHAREHOLDERS' AGREEMENTS

The arrangements reflected in the letter of a company's Memorandum and Articles of Association may, in practice, be overshadowed by 'free-standing' agreements reached between shareholders. Courts will potentially be required to construe such agreements using normal contractual principles. In the absence of ambiguity, courts will give effect to the ordinary and literal meaning of the words in the agreement. Courts will not consider the commercial context save where this is necessary to interpret the language used (*Alberta Ltd v EML Relocation Services* [2007] ABQB 742 at [6] (CANLII) (Alta QB)).

Even if a shareholders' agreement is not expressly designed to alter the constitution, but is merely a private agreement (for example, on how members shall use their votes), it can in practice alter how the company's constitution works. In practice, however, courts have sometimes been slow to enforce such agreements unless they are very clearly drawn up (*Halton International Inc (Holding) SARL v Guernroy Ltd* [2005] EWHC 1968 (Ch), [2006] 1 BCLC 78, [2005] All ER (D) 44 (Sep)).

# 15   Corporate Governance

**Cross-references.** See **19** Directors' Remuneration Reports—Quoted Companies; **33** Public Companies; **42** Resolutions and Meetings.

## 15.1   INTRODUCTION TO CORPORATE GOVERNANCE

Corporate Governance is not a term which is defined in *CA 2006*. but is generally accepted as meaning the system by which companies are managed and controlled. The general framework for corporate governance is:

•   *CA 2006* (see **15.6** below)

•   the Listing Rules (see **15.4** below) and the Disclosure Guidance and Transparency Rules (see **15.5** below) and

•   the UK Corporate Governance Code (see **15.2** below) and the UK Stewardship Code for institutional shareholders ("the Stewardship Code" see **15.3** below)

The Financial Reporting Council (FRC) is responsible for corporate governance in the United Kingdom and as such also has responsibility to publish and maintain a single code of good corporate governance practice. This is now known as the UK Corporate Governance Code ("The Code") (formerly known as the Combined Code). Adherence to the Code is expected by institutional shareholders and committees of those shareholders (in particular NAPF and PIRC) publish their own best practice guidelines.

In general the system of corporate governance set out in the Code applies to larger listed companies ie companies with securities admitted to trading on the London Stock Exchange main market. Some of its provisions apply to companies in the FTSE 350 and are not obligatory for smaller listed companies. Smaller listed companies and unlisted companies (for example those companies with securities traded on the Alternative Investment Market) may choose to comply with the Code or comply with the QCA (Quoted Companies Alliance) corporate governance guidelines. Additionally the London Stock Exchange publishes a corporate governance guide 'Corporate Governance for main market and AIM companies'. The FRC in its publication 'The UK approach to corporate governance' (available from the FRC website) says that the key aspects of corporate governance in the UK are:

•   a single board collectively responsible for the sustainable success of the company;

## 15.1   Corporate Governance

- checks and balances including a separate chairman and chief executive, a balance of executive and independent non-executives, strong, independent audit and remuneration committees (see **15.8** and **15.10**) and annual evaluation by the board of its performance;

- transparency on appointments and remuneration; and

- effective rights for shareholders who are encouraged to engage with the companies in which they invest.

In July 2018, the FRC published a new version of the UK Corporate Governance Code which will apply to accounting periods starting on or after 1 January 2019. The 2018 Code broadens the definition of governance and emphasises the importance of positive relationships between companies, shareholders and other stakeholders (including engaging with the workforce), providing a clear purpose and strategy aligned with a healthy corporate culture, high quality board composition (including strengthening consideration of 'over-boarding') and a focus on diversity and remuneration which is proportionate (including reporting on alignment of executive pay with workforce remuneration) and supports long-term success. The 2018 Code is shorter and sharper than the previous version, with fewer provisions, as the 'Supporting Principles' have been removed and largely relegated to the 2018 Guidance on Board Effectiveness, also published by the FRC.

### THE UK REGULATORY FRAMEWORK

### 15.2   The UK Corporate Governance Code

The Code sets out standards of good practice re board leadership and effectiveness, remuneration, accountability and relations with a company's shareholders. The Listing Rules require all companies with a premium listing of equity shares in the United Kingdom to report on how they have applied the main principles of the Code in their annual report and accounts and either to confirm that they have complied with the Code's provisions or, where they have not complied, explain why they have not (the so called 'comply or explain' principle). To help companies with the comply or explain principle, in 2012 the FRC published a paper 'What constitutes an explanation under "comply or explain"' which sets out a number of features of a meaningful explanation. The paper can be found on the FRC website. For corporate governance systems to work effectively shareholders need rights to enable them to influence board behaviour when they are not happy with the approach the board has taken. Comply or explain therefore needs to be underpinned by a regulatory framework. This is achieved by provisions of *CA 2006* relating to voting and disclosure rights (see **42.41** RESOLUTIONS AND MEETINGS and **19** DIRECTORS' REMUNERATION REPORTS-QUOTED COMPANIES) and provisions of the Listing Rules (see **15.4** below). The comply or explain principle has also been reinforced by the UK Stewardship Code (see **15.3** below) under which institutional investors report on their policies for monitoring and engaging with companies in which they invest.

The Code comprises main principles, supporting principles and framework provisions. It includes best practice in relation to:

- the role of non-executive directors ('NEDS') (see **15.13** below);

- remuneration of directors and the role of the remuneration committee (see **15.10** below);

- appointment of directors and the role of the nomination committee (see **15.9** below).

The FRC publishes guidance notes to assist companies in applying the principles of the Code. The Guidance on Board Effectiveness is an example of this. See the FRC website at www.frc.org.uk for details.

The present Code is set out in full in the Appendix to this chapter. The Code is reviewed every two years and was amended in July 2018 (with changes taking effect for reporting periods beginning on or after 1 January 2019). This chapter will flag key differences between the present Code and the 2018 Code by reference to the Revised UK Corporate Governance Code 2018 highlights published by the FRC.

## 15.3    The UK Stewardship Code

The Stewardship Code, published by the FRC, aims to:

- enhance the quality of engagement between institutional investors and companies;

- help improve the long term returns for investors; and

- help to promote the efficient exercise of governance responsibilities by setting out good practice on engagement with companies in which shareholders invest.

The FRC sees the Stewardship Code as complementary to the Code and that like the Code it should be applied on a comply or explain basis (see **15.2**). In the case of the Stewardship Code, the FRC expects signatories of the Code to publish on their website, or if they do not have a website, in another accessible form a statement that describes how the signatory has applied each of the seven principles of the Code and discloses the specific information requested in the guidance to the principles or if more than one of the principles have not been applied or the specific information requested in the guidance has not been disclosed, explains why the signatory has not complied with those elements of the Code. From October 2010 the FRC have been listing on its website all investors that have published reporting statements and encourages all institutional investors to publish on their websites a statement of the extent to which they have complied with the Stewardship Code and to notify the FRC when they have done so.

The Stewardship Code is aimed principally at those firms who manage assets on behalf of institutional investors and the Financial Conduct Authority (FCA) amended its Conduct of Business sourcebook to require a UK authorised firm managing investments to disclose:

- the nature of its commitment to the Stewardship Code; or

- if it does not commit to the Stewardship Code, its alternative Business Strategy (COBS 2.2.3).

The Stewardship Code comprises seven principles, each with related guidance. The principles require institutional investors to:

- publicly disclose their policy on how they will discharge their stewardship responsibilities (Principle 1);

- have a robust policy on managing conflicts of interest in relation to stewardship and publicly disclose this policy (Principle 2);

- monitor their investee companies (Principle 3);

- establish clear guidelines on when and how they will escalate their stewardship activities (Principle 4);

- be willing to act collectively with other investors where appropriate (Principle 5);

- have a clear policy on voting and disclosure of voting activity (Principle 6); and

- report periodically on their stewardship and voting activities (Principle 7).

The Stewardship Code is, like the Corporate Governance Code, reviewed regularly and was last updated in September 2012. The FRC is presently consulting on amendments to the Stewardship Code.

## 15.4 Corporate Governance

### 15.4 The Listing Rules

The Listing Rules require a UK company with a premium listing of equity shares in the UK and an overseas company with a premium listing in the UK of equity shares to include in its annual report:

- a statement of how the listed company has applied the main principles set out in the Code, in a manner that would enable shareholders to evaluate how the principles have been applied; and

- a statement as to whether the listed company has complied throughout the accounting period with all relevant provisions of the Code or has not complied throughout the accounting period with all relevant provisions of the Code and, if so, setting out those provisions, if any, it has not complied with and, in the case of provisions of a continuing nature, the period within which, if any, it did not comply and the company's reasons for non-compliance.

(FCA Listing Rules 9.8.6(5), 9.8.6(6) and 9.8.7.)

For the meaning of 'premium listing' and 'equity shares' see the Glossary to the FCA handbook.

### 15.5 The Disclosure Guidance and Transparency Rules

The provisions of the Disclosure Guidance and Transparency Rules ('DTR') set out below apply to financial years of a company beginning on or after 29 June 2008.

(1)     *Application*

The provisions in (2) below apply to an issuer:

- whose transferable securities are admitted to trading; and

- which is a company within the meaning of *CA 2006, s 1(1)*,

but subject to the provisions in DTR 1B.1.6 for issued shares traded on an MTF (defined in the FCA Glossary as a 'multilateral trading facility') as opposed to a regulated market.

(DTR 1B.1.5, 1B.1.6).

(2)     *Statements*

An issuer to which these provisions apply must:

- include a corporate governance statement as a specific section of its directors' report; or

- elect to set out the required information in a separate report published together with, and in the same manner as, its annual report or set out the required information in a document publicly available on the issuer's website to which reference is made in the directors' report.

In either case the corporate governance statement must contain the information required by DTR 7.2.6 (information about accounts) or a reference to the directors' report where that information is made available.

The corporate governance statement must contain a reference to the following where applicable:

(a)     Subject to the exemption below:

(i)      the corporate governance code to which the issuer is subject;

(ii)     the corporate governance code which the issuer may have voluntarily decided to apply; and

(iii)    all relevant information about the corporate governance practices applied over and above the requirements of national law.

An issuer which is complying with (i) or (ii) above must:

- state in its directors' report where the relevant corporate governance code is publicly available; and

- where it departs from that corporate governance code, explain which parts of the corporate governance code it departs from and the reasons for doing so.

Where (iii) above applies, the issuer must make details of its corporate governance practices publicly available and state in its directors' report where they can be found.

If an issuer has decided not to refer to any provisions of a corporate governance code referred to under (i) and (ii) above, it must explain its reasons for that decision.

A listed company which complies with the comply or explain rule in relation to the Code will satisfy the above requirements.

(b)   A description of the main features of the issuer's internal control and risk management systems in relation to the financial reporting process.

(c)   The information about share capital required by Art 20(1)(*d*) of the Accounting Directive where the issuer is subject to those requirements.

(d)   A description of the composition and operation of the issuer's administrative, management and supervisory bodies and their committees.

In the FCA's view, the information specified in provisions A.1.1, A.1.2, B.2.4, C.3.3, C.3.8 and D.2.1 of the Code will satisfy the requirements of (*d*). This provision will need to be amended when the 2018 Rules become effective because provisions A.1.1 and C.3.3 of the present Code will be relegated to guidance, A.1.2 will be incorporated into provision 14 of the 2018 Code, B2.4 will be incorporated into provisions 23 and 24, C.3.8 incorporated into provision 26 and D.2.1 into provisions 32 and 35.

(e)

(1)   A description of:

(i)      the diversity policy which applies to the issuers administrative, management and supervisory bodies with regard to aspects such as, for instance, age, gender, or educational and professional backgrounds;

(ii)     the objectives of the diversity policy; and

(iii)    how the diversity policy has been implemented and the results in the reporting period.

(2)   If no diversity policy is applied by the issuer the corporate governance statement must contain an explanation as to why this is the case.

## 15.5 Corporate Governance

The above provision does not apply to an issuer which is a small or medium company.

*Group directors' reports.* An issuer which is required to prepare a group directors' report must include in that report a description of the main features of the group's internal control and risk management systems in relation to the financial reporting process for the undertakings included in the consolidation taken as a whole. In the event that the issuer presents its own annual report and its consolidated annual report as a single report, this information must be included in the corporate governance statement in its directors' report. If the issuer elects to include its corporate governance statement in a separate report, it must provide the information in that report. If the issuer elects to include its corporate governance statement in a document publicly available on its website to which reference is made in the directors' report, it must provide the information in that document.

(DTR 1B.1.6, 7.2.1–7.2.11).

### Approval and signing of separate corporate governance statement

**15.6** *CA 2006 Requirements*

In relation to financial years beginning on or after 29 June 2008 any separate corporate governance statement must be approved by the board of directors and signed on behalf of the board by a director or the secretary of the company. [*CA 2006, s 419A; SI 2009 No 1581, Reg 2*].

See also **8.36** DUTIES OF AUDITORS in connection with the corporate governance report (*CA 2006, s 498A*).

## COMPANY COMMITTEE STRUCTURE

### 15.7 The Structure

There are various provisions which regulate the setting up of committees which are responsible for regulating and monitoring corporate governance in a company. The Code (see **15.2**) in particular says that the company should establish formal and transparent arrangements for considering how they should apply the corporate reporting and risk management and internal control principles and for maintaining an appropriate relationship with the company's auditors through an audit committee (Code principle C3). The Code also regulates the setting up of a remuneration committee (see **15.10** below) and a nomination committee (see **15.9** below) the role generally of NEDS (see **15.13**) and those matters which are reserved wholly to the board (see **15.12**).

### 15.8 The Audit Committee

See **15.7** above for provisions of the Code regulating the establishment of an audit committee. Additionally the FRC has published guidance ('Guidance on Audit committees') to help companies when implementing the Code provisions on audit committees. Boards are not required to follow the Guidance, it is designed to assist them. The Guidance also assists directors serving on audit committees in carrying out their role. The 2016 edition of the Guidance is available to download from the FRC website at www.frc.org.uk or printed copies can be obtained free of charge from FRC publications.

The Code says in particular that:

- a company to which the Code applies should establish an audit committee (Code provision C.3.1);

- the committee should comprise at least three or, in the case of smaller companies outside the FTSE 350 throughout the year immediately prior to the reporting period, two independent NEDS (Code provision C.3.1). The board is required to identify in its annual report which of its NEDS are considered to be 'independent' (Code provision B.1.1). In smaller companies the company chairman may be a member of, but not chair, the audit committee in addition to the independent NEDs provided the chair was considered independent on appointment as chairman. The board should satisfy itself that at least one member of the audit committee has recent and relevant financial experience;

- the main roles and responsibilities of the audit committee should be set out in written terms of reference (Code provision C.3.2) and the terms of reference should be 'made available' (Code provision C.3.3). The requirement to be 'made available' would be met by including the information on a website maintained by or on behalf of the company. Model terms of reference are published by the Institute of Chartered Secretaries and Administrators (ICSA) and further details of what the terms of reference should include are found in Code provision C.3.2;

- where requested by the board the audit committee should provide advice on whether the annual report and accounts, taken as a whole, is fair, balanced and understandable and provides the information necessary for shareholders to assess the company's performance, business model and strategy (Code provision C. 3.4)

- the audit committee must review arrangements for staff "whistleblowing" (Code provision C.3.5 and also see the FRC Guidance above at paras 4.9–4.16)

- the audit committee should monitor and review the effectiveness of the internal audit activities (Code provision C.3.6) and should have primary responsibility for making recommendations on the appointment, re-appointment and removal of the company's external auditors. FTSE companies should put the external audit contract out to tender at least every ten years. If the board does not accept the audit committee's recommendation, it should include in the annual report and in any papers recommending appointment or reappointment a statement from the audit committee explaining the recommendation and should set out reasons why the board has taken a different position.(Code provision C.3.7); and

- a separate section of the company's annual report should describe the work of the audit committee in discharging its responsibilities and the annual report should include the significant issues that the audit committee considered in relation to the financial statements and how these issues were addressed, an explanation of how it has assessed the effectiveness of the external audit process and the approach taken to the appointment or reappointment of the external auditor, and information on the length of tenure of the current audit firm and when a tender was last conducted and how, if the auditor provides non-audit services to the company, auditor independence and objectivity is safeguarded (Code provision C.3.8).

The Disclosure Guidance and Transparency Rules also apply to audit committees in a company

- whose transferable securities are admitted to trading; and

- which is required to appoint a statutory auditor;

except for

- any issuer which is a subsidiary undertaking of a parent undertaking where the parent undertaking is required to appoint a statutory auditor;

- any issuer, the sole business of which is to act as the issuer of asset-backed securities, provided the entity makes a statement available to the public setting out the reasons why it considers it is not appropriate to have either an audit committee or an administrative or supervisory body entrusted to carry out the functions of an audit committee; or

- a credit institution whose shares are not admitted to trading and which has, in a continuous or repeated manner, issued only debt securities provided that

  (i)   the total nominal amount of all such debt securities remains below €100 million; and

  (ii)  the credit institution has not been subject to a requirement to publish a prospectus in accordance with *FSMA 2000, s 85.*

(DTR 1B.1.2, 1B.1.3).

An issuer must have a body which is responsible for performing the functions set out below. At least one member of that body must be independent and at least one member must have competence in accounting and/or auditing. The requirements for independence and competence may be satisfied by the same member or by different members of the relevant body.

An issuer must:

(a)   ensure that, as a *minimum*, the relevant body must:

   (i)    monitor the financial reporting process;

   (ii)   monitor the effectiveness of the issuer's internal control, internal audit where applicable, and risk management systems;

   (iii)  monitor the statutory audit of the annual and consolidated accounts; and

   (iv)   review and monitor the independence of the statutory auditor, and in particular the provision of additional services to the issuer.

(b)   base any proposal to appoint a statutory auditor on a recommendation made by the relevant body; and

(c)   make a statement available to the public disclosing which body carries out the functions required by (a) above and how it is composed. This statement may be included in any corporate governance statement required under **15.5**.

In the FCA's view, compliance with the requirements of A.1.2, C.3.1, C.3.2, C.3.3 and C.3.8 of the Code will result in compliance with the above.

(DTR 7.1.1–7.1.7).

## 15.9   The Nomination Committee

In addition to the setting up of an audit committee, the Code says that there should be a formal, rigorous and transparent procedure for the appointment of new directors to the board (Code Principle B.2) and companies to which the Code applies (see above) should establish a nomination committee to lead the process for board appointments and make recommendations to the board (Code provision B.2.1). The following supporting principles to main principle B.2 should also be adhered to:

- the search for board candidates should be conducted, and appointments made, on merit, against objective criteria and with due regard for the benefits of diversity on the board including gender. Note here the Lord Davies independent review into Women on Boards published on 24 February 2011. The main recommendations were that FTSE 100 companies should be aiming for a minimum of 25% female board representation by the year 2015 and FTSE 350 companies should be setting their own challenging targets for appointing women to the board. The Code provides that a separate section of the annual report should describe the work of the nomination committee (and) should include a description of the board's policy on diversity, including gender, any measurable objectives that it has set for implementing the policy, and progress on achieving objectives (Code provision B.2.4). Annual progress reports are published; and

- the board should satisfy itself that plans are in place for orderly succession for appointments to the board and to senior management, so as to maintain an appropriate balance of skills and experience within the company and on the board and to ensure progressive refreshing of the board.

The nomination committee should:

- in the majority comprise independent NEDS (Code provision B.2.1);

- be chaired by the chairman of the company or an independent NED but the chairman should not chair the committee when it is dealing with the appointment of (his) successor. (Code provision B.2.1);

- lead the process for board appointments and make recommendations to the board (Code provision B.2.1);

- before making an appointment evaluate the balance of skills, experience, independence and knowledge of the board and, in light of this evaluation, prepare a description of the role and capabilities required for a particular appointment ( Code provision B.2.2);

- have terms of reference which are made "available" for example by publication on the company's website (Code provision B.2.1). For what should be included in the terms of reference see the ICSA Model terms of reference for a nomination committee available from the ICSA website;

- in relation to all appointments be mindful of the Code main principle that all directors should be able to allocate sufficient time to the company to discharge their responsibilities effectively (Code provision B.3);

- appoint NEDS for specified terms subject to re-election and to statutory provisions relating to the removal of a director. Any term of office beyond six years should be subject to particularly rigorous review and should take into account the need for progressive refreshing of the board (Code provision B.2.3);

- for the appointment of a new chairman, prepare a job specification which includes an assessment of the time commitment expected, recognising the need for availability in times of crises. (Code provision B.3.1); and

- have sufficient resources to undertake its duties (Code provision B.5.1).

The 2018 Code gives the Nomination Committee responsibility for more effective succession planning that develops a more diverse pipeline and requires reporting on the gender balance of senior managers and their direct reports. This is part of the emphasis the 2018 Code places on the importance of independence and constructive challenge of the board room and strengthening consideration of 'overboarding'. The focus is to be on diversity, the length of service of the board as a whole and effective board refreshment. A 'comply or explain' provision will be introduced for a maximum nine-year length of service, allowing flexibility to extend 'to facilitate effective succession planning and the development of a diverse board . . . particularly in those cases where the chair was an existing non-executive director on appointment'. The 2018 Code will prescribe higher quality external board evaluations emphasising the importance of the evaluator's direct contact with the board and individual directors.

*Shareholder and board access to information*

The ICSA guidance referred to above provides that the chairman of the nomination committee should attend the company's annual general meeting each year to answer any questions which may be raised by shareholders on matters within the committee's area of responsibility. Additionally the Code provides that:

- a separate section of the annual report should describe the work of the committee including the process it has used in relation to board appointments. The section of the annual report should include a description of the board's policy on diversity, including gender, any measurable objectives that it has set for implementing the policy, and progress on achieving the objectives. An explanation should be given if neither an external search consultancy nor open advertising has been used in the appointment of a chairman or non executive director. Where an external search consultancy has been used, it should be identified in the report and a statement should be made as to whether it has any other connection with the company (Code provision B.2.4).

- the chairman and members of the committee should be identified in the annual report (Code provision A.1.2)

- other significant commitments of the chairman and any NEDS should be disclosed to the board before appointment and, for the chairman only, should be included in the annual report. Changes to any such commitments should be reported to the board as they arise, and, in the case of the chairman, included in the next annual report (Code provision B.3.1 and B.3.2)

- the terms of appointment of NEDS should be made available for inspection by any person at the company's registered office during normal business hours and at the annual general meeting both for fifteen minutes before the meeting and during that meeting (Code provision B.3.2).

The 2018 Code regards the role of investors and their advisers as very important. Investors should engage constructively and discuss with the company any departures from recommended practice. When considering explanations, investors and proxy advisers should pay due regard to a company's individual circumstances. Proxy advisers have every right to challenge explanations if they are unconvincing, but explanations must not be evaluated in a mechanistic way. Investors and proxy advisers should also give companies sufficient time to respond to enquiries about corporate governance reporting.

Moreover, the 2018 Code places an emphasis on improving the quality of the board and company's relationships with a wider range of stakeholders. Not only does it require effective action to be taken when receiving significant shareholder votes against resolutions and reporting back more promptly, but also it requires the board to take responsibility for workforce policies and practices which reinforce a healthy culture – including by engaging with the workforce through one or a combination of a director appointed from the workforce, a formal workforce advisory panel and a designated non-executive director or other arrangements which meet the circumstances of the company and the workforce. There should be an ability for directors and the workforce to be able to raise concerns and for effective enquiry about those concerns.

## 15.10  The Remuneration Committee

The Code also requires listed companies to establish a remuneration committee to ensure the company complies with the Code principle that there should be a formal and transparent procedure for developing policy on executive remuneration and for fixing the remuneration packages of individual directors, and that no director should be involved in deciding (his) own remuneration (Code principle D.2 and Code provision D.2.1). Additionally *CA 2006* requires quoted companies to prepare a directors' remuneration report for each financial year (see **19 DIRECTORS' REMUNERATION REPORTS—QUOTED COMPANIES**).

The remuneration committee should:

- consist of three, or in the case of smaller companies outside the FTSE 350, two independent NEDS (Code provision D.2.1);

- not be chaired by the chairman of the company although (he) may serve on the committee (Code provision D.2.1);

- be given delegated responsibility for setting the remuneration of all executive directors and the chairman including pension rights and any compensation payments and be expected to recommend and monitor the level and structure of remuneration for senior management. The definition of "senior management" should be determined by the board but should normally include the first level of management below board level. (Code provision D.2.2);

- take care to recognise and manage conflicts of interest when receiving views from executive directors or senior managers or consulting the chief executive officer about their proposals relating to the remuneration of other executive directors (Supporting principles to Code main principle D.2);

- be responsible for appointing any consultants in respect of executive directors' remuneration (supporting principle to Code main principle D.2); and

- have terms of reference which are made "available" for example by publication on the company's website. Its terms of reference should explain the committee's role and the authority delegated to it by the board (Code provision D.2.1). For what should be included in the terms of reference see the ICSA Model terms of reference for a remuneration committee available from the ICSA website(these are only available to members of ICSA).

### *Setting levels of remuneration including performance related*

The Code provides that executive directors' remuneration should be designed to promote the long-term success of the company and that performance-related elements should be transparent, stretching and rigorously applied (Code main principle D.1).

Specifically the Code says:

- remuneration committees should judge where to position their company relative to others but should use such comparisons with caution in view of the risk of an upward ratchet of remuneration levels with no corresponding increase in corporate and individual performance and should avoid paying more than is necessary and should also be sensitive to pay and employment conditions elsewhere in the group, especially when determining annual salary increases (Supporting principle to main Code principle D.1);

- levels of remuneration for NEDS should reflect the time commitment and responsibilities of the role (Code provision D.1.3);

- the board itself or, where required by the company's articles of association, the shareholders should determine the remuneration of the NEDS within the limits set out in the articles. However, where permitted by the articles, the board may delegate this responsibility to a committee, which may include the chief executive (Code provision D.2.3);

- remuneration for NEDS should not include share options or other performance related elements (although if exceptionally options are granted, shareholder approval should be sought in advance and any shares acquired by the exercise of options should be held until at least one year after the NED leaves the company) (Code provision D.1.3);

- notice or contract periods should be set at one year or less and if it is necessary to offer longer notice or contract periods to new directors recruited from outside the company, such periods should reduce to one year or less after the initial period (Code provision D.1.5). See also the *CA 2006, s 188* requirement that directors' service agreements must not exceed two years duration without shareholder approval;

- the remuneration committee should carefully consider what compensation commitments (including pension contributions and other entitlements) their directors' terms of appointment would entail in the event of early termination. The aim should be to avoid rewarding poor performance and the committee should take a robust line on reducing compensation to reflect departing directors' obligations to mitigate loss (Code provision D.1.4); and

- shareholders should be invited specifically to approve all new long–term incentive schemes and significant changes to existing schemes, save in the circumstances permitted by the Listing Rules (Code provision D.2.4). The Listing Rules require all share option and long-term incentive schemes to be approved by the shareholders (by ordinary resolution) unless participation in the scheme is offered to all or substantially all employees of the group or the scheme is established specifically to facilitate, in unusual circumstances, the recruitment or retention of a director (in which case detailed information of the special scheme must be given in the company's next annual report). (LR 9.4.1. and 9.4.2).

*Shareholder and board access to information*

The Code provides that:

- the annual report should identify members of the remuneration committee and set out the number of meetings held by the committee with details of each director's attendance (Code provision A.1.2) and should include a statement of how the board operates, including a high level statement of which types of decisions are to be taken by the board and which are delegated (Code provision A.1.1); and

- where remuneration consultants are appointed a statement should be made available as to whether they have any other connection with the company (Code provision D.2.1).

The 2018 Code sets more demanding criteria for remuneration policies and practices. It requires clearer reporting on remuneration, how it delivers company strategy, long-term success and its alignment with workforce remuneration. Directors should exercise independent judgement and discretion on remuneration outcomes, taking account of wider circumstances. The remuneration committee chair should have served on a remuneration committee for at least 12 months.

## 15.11  The Risk Committee

The Code does not expressly require a company to set up a risk committee It says in the first instance that the board is responsible for determining the nature and extent of the significant risks it is willing to take in achieving its strategic objectives and for maintaining sound risk management and internal control systems (Code Main Principle C.2). Further guidance can be found in the Walker Review ('A review of corporate governance in UK banks and other financial industry entities 2009') and in ICSA Model terms of reference--Risk Committee (as above that these are only available to ICSA members).

Guidance suggests that:

- the board of a bank or other financial institution should establish a board risk committee separate from the audit committee (Walker recommendations 23–27). The role of the risk committee in such institutions is set out in detail in the Walker recommendations referred to;

- the chairman of the risk committee should attend the company's annual general meeting to answer any questions on the risk committee's activities (ICSA Model terms of reference);

- the committee should have access to sufficient resources to carry out its duties including access to the services of the company secretary; and

- the frequency of committee meetings will vary from company to company and may change from time to time but the ICSA Model terms of reference say that the committee should meet at least three times a year at appropriate times and otherwise as required.

## 15.12  Matters reserved to the board

The Code requires the board to establish a formal schedule of matters specifically reserved for their decision and to include in the annual report a statement of how the board operates which should include a high-level statement of which types of decisions are to be taken by the board and which are delegated to management (Code provision A.1.1). Apart from those general provisions the Code does not specify what should be included in the matters reserved for the board. Instead guidance can be found in the original 1992 Cadbury Report (the Cadbury Code on the financial aspects of corporate governance) and in ICSA Guidance: Matters reserved for the board (available only to ICSA members). Generally it is suggested that matters to be reserved should include:

- the acquisition and disposal of material assets of the company or its subsidiaries (Cadbury report para 4.24);

- investments, capital projects, authority levels, treasury policies and risk management policies (Cadbury report para 4.24); and

- responsibility for the overall management of the group.

As indicated in **15.9**, the 2018 Code will require the board to take responsibility for workforce policies and practices which reinforce a healthy culture.

## 15.13  Non-Executive Directors (NEDS)

The starting point for any consideration of the role of NEDS in corporate governance is the Higgs review (Review of the role and effectiveness of non-executive directors 2003). The Higgs guidance was itself reviewed in 2009 by ICSA and a Guidance on Board Effectiveness was published by the FRC in March 2011 (as indicated in **15.1**, in conjunction with the 2018 Code, the FRC has published 2018 Guidance on Board Effectiveness to which the Supporting Principles contained in the present Code have largely been relegated). The 2011 Guidance:

•      replaces "Good practice suggestions from the Higgs Report"; and

•      is intended to help companies apply the provisions of the Code.

In January 2013 ICSA published guidance on the liability of non –executive directors. Entitled "ICSA guidance on liability of non-executive directors: care, skill and diligence" the guidance suggests ways in which non-executive directors can approach their work in a way which would allow them to demonstrate to a regulator (eg the FCA) or in a court of law that they had taken appropriate steps to exercise care, skill and diligence in the execution of their roles and responsibilities. The guidance expressly refers to provisions of the Code which are likely to be relevant in a court's assessment. These are mainly Code provisions A.4 and B3, B4, and B5.

The Code requires that:

•      a board should include an appropriate combination of executive directors and NEDS (and in particular independent NEDS) such that no individual or small group of individuals can dominate the board's decision making (Code Main principle B.1);

•      at least half the board of FTSE 350 companies, excluding the chairman, should be independent. Companies outside the FTSE 350 should have at least two independent NEDS. (Code provision B.1.2);

•      the board identifies in the annual report each NED they consider is independent for the purposes of the Code (Code provision B.1.1). Code provision B.1.1 contains a non-exhaustive list of circumstances which would indicate that a director is not independent and if the board determines that a NED is independent despite one of the list of circumstances applying, it should state its reasons for finding that the NED is independent in the annual report (Code provision B.1.1);

•      NEDS should constructively challenge and help develop proposals on strategy (Code main principle A.4). They are responsible for scrutinising the performance of management in meeting agreed goals and objectives, monitoring the reporting of performance, satisfying themselves on the integrity of financial information and that financial controls and systems of risk management are robust and defensible, for determining appropriate levels of remuneration of executive directors and have a prime role in appointing and where necessary removing executive directors and in succession planning. (Code supporting principles to main principle A.4);

•      the board should appoint one of the independent NEDS as the senior independent director and identify that person in the company's annual report (Code provision A.4.1 and A.1.2). Provisions A.4.1, A.4.2 and E.1.1 contain details of the role of the senior independent director; and

•      NEDS fees should be decided either by the board or a committee of the board if the company's articles permit such delegation or, where required by the company's articles, the shareholders (Code provision D.2.3).

For the appointment and remuneration of NEDS see **15.10** (above).

*Election and re-election*

All directors should be submitted for re-election at regular intervals subject to satisfactory performance and directors of FTSE 350 companies should be subject to annual election by shareholders. All other directors should be subject to election at the first annual general meeting after their appointment and then to re-election at intervals of no more than three years. (Code main principle B.7 and provision B.7.1). There are no specific provisions for the development and training of NEDS, instead there are general provisions relating to all directors (Code main principle B.4 and provisions B.4.1 and supporting principles B.4 and B.5).

*FRC Guidance*

The FRC Guidance on Board Effectiveness is not intended to be prescriptive. Instead it says in the Preface that it is intended to stimulate boards' thinking on how they can carry out their role most effectively. The Guidance also does not contain all the information (for example board terms of reference) which was in the Higgs guidance. Rather the FRC Guidance provides links to information available from other organisations. In relation to NEDS (and the senior independent director) the FRC Guidance provides as follows:

### Senior independent directors

- In normal times the senior independent director should act as a sounding board for the chairman, providing support for the chairman in the delivery of his or her objectives, and leading the evaluation of the chairman on behalf of the other directors, as set out in the Code. The senior independent director might also take responsibility for an orderly succession process for the chairman.

- When the board is undergoing a period of stress, however, the senior independent director's role becomes critically important. He or she is expected to work with the chairman and other directors, and/or shareholders, to resolve significant issues. Boards should ensure they have a clear understanding of when the senior independent director might intervene in order to maintain board and company stability. Examples might include where:

  - there is a dispute between the chairman and CEO;

  - shareholders or non-executive directors have expressed concerns that are not being addressed by the chairman or CEO;

  - the strategy being followed by the chairman and CEO is not supported by the entire board;

  - the relationship between the chairman and CEO is particularly close, and decisions are being made without the approval of the full board; or

  - succession planning is being ignored.

These issues should be considered when defining the role of the senior independent director, which should be set out in writing. (FRC Guidance paras 1.9-1.11)

**NEDS**

- A non-executive director should, on appointment, devote time to a comprehensive, formal and tailored induction which should extend beyond the boardroom. Initiatives such as partnering a non-executive director with an executive board member may speed up the process of him or her acquiring an understanding of the main areas of business activity, especially areas involving significant risk. The director should expect to visit, and talk with, senior and middle managers in these areas.

- Non-executive directors should devote time to developing and refreshing their knowledge and skills, including those of communication, to ensure that they continue to make a positive contribution to the board. Being well-informed about the company, and having a strong command of the issues relevant to the business, will generate the respect of the other directors.

- Non-executive directors need to make sufficient time available to discharge their responsibilities effectively. The letter of appointment should state the minimum time that the non-executive director will be required to spend on the company's business, and seek the individual's confirmation that he or she can devote that amount of time to the role, consistent with other commitments. The letter should also indicate the possibility of additional time commitment when the company is undergoing a period of particularly increased activity, such as an acquisition or takeover, or as a result of some major difficulty with one or more of its operations.

- Non-executive directors have a responsibility to uphold high standards of integrity and probity. They should support the chairman and executive directors in instilling the appropriate culture, values and behaviours in the boardroom and beyond.

- Non-executive directors should insist on receiving high-quality information sufficiently in advance so that there can be thorough consideration of the issues prior to, and informed debate and challenge at, board meetings. High-quality information is that which is appropriate for making decisions on the issue at hand – it should be accurate, clear, comprehensive, up-to-date and timely; contain a summary of the contents of any paper; and inform the director of what is expected of him or her on that issue.

- Non-executive directors should take into account the views of shareholders and other stakeholders, because these views may provide different perspectives on the company and its performance. (FRC Guidance paras 1.18-1.23)

## 15.14   The 2018 Code

The FRC says that the 2018 Code is designed to set high standards of corporate governance to promote transparency and integrity in business and thereby attract investment in the UK for the long-term benefit of the economy and wider society.

The 2018 Code does not set out a rigid set of rules; instead it is designed to offer flexibility through the application of principles and through 'comply or explain' provisions and supporting guidance.

The FRC says that it is the responsibility of Boards to use this flexibility wisely and of investors and their advisers to assess differing company approaches thoughtfully.

By placing renewed focus on the principles and requiring reporting on their application in a manner that can be evaluated, companies are required to demonstrate how the governance of the company contributes to its long-term sustainable success and the achievement of wider objectives.

The corporate governance statement should cover the application of the principles in the context of the particular circumstances of the company, saying how the board has set the company's purpose and strategy, met objectives and achieved outcomes through its decisions.

The 2018 Code will require the effective application of the principles to be supported by high-quality reporting on the provisions, including signposting and cross-referencing to other relevant parts of the annual report.

The provisions establish good practice on a 'comply or explain' basis. Companies should avoid a 'tick box approach'. An alternative to complying with a provision may be justified in particular circumstances based on a range of factors, including the size, complexity, history and ownership structure of a company. Explanations should set out the background, provide a clear rationale for the action the company is taking and explain the impact that the action has had. When a departure from a provision is intended to be limited in time, the explanation should indicate when the company expects to conform to the provisions.

Explanations are intended to be a positive opportunity to communicate, not an onerous obligation.

As indicated in **15.9**, the role of investors and their advisers is very important.

See **19** Directors' Remuneration reports-Quoted Companies for details of provisions which came into effect in October 2013.

# APPENDIX: THE UK CORPORATE GOVERNANCE CODE (JULY 2018)

The UK Corporate Governance Code is available on the Financial Reporting Council's website.

## THE UK CORPORATE GOVERNANCE CODE (JULY 2018)

### INTRODUCTION

The first version of the UK Corporate Governance Code (the Code) was published in 1992 by the Cadbury Committee. It defined corporate governance as 'the system by which companies are directed and controlled. Boards of directors are responsible for the governance of their companies. The shareholders' role in governance is to appoint the directors and the auditors and to satisfy themselves that an appropriate governance structure is in place.' This remains true today, but the environment in which companies, their shareholders and wider stakeholders operate continues to develop rapidly.

Companies do not exist in isolation. Successful and sustainable businesses underpin our economy and society by providing employment and creating prosperity. To succeed in the long-term, directors and the companies they lead need to build and maintain successful relationships with a wide range of stakeholders. These relationships will be successful and enduring if they are based on respect, trust and mutual benefit. Accordingly, a company's culture should promote integrity and openness, value diversity and be responsive to the views of shareholders and wider stakeholders.

Over the years the Code has been revised and expanded to take account of the increasing demands on the UK's corporate governance framework. The principle of collective responsibility within a unitary board has been a success and – alongside the stewardship activities of investors – played a vital role in delivering high standards of governance and encouraging long-term investment. Nevertheless, the debate about the nature and extent of the framework has intensified as a result of financial crises and high-profile examples of inadequate governance and misconduct, which have led to poor outcomes for a wide range of stakeholders.

At the heart of this Code is an updated set of Principles that emphasise the value of good corporate governance to long-term sustainable success. By applying the Principles, following the more detailed Provisions and using the associated guidance, companies can demonstrate throughout their reporting how the governance of the company contributes to its long term sustainable success and achieves wider objectives.

Achieving this depends crucially on the way boards and companies apply the spirit of the Principles. The Code does not set out a rigid set of rules; instead it offers flexibility through the application of Principles and through 'comply or explain' Provisions and supporting guidance. It is the responsibility of boards to use this flexibility wisely and of investors and their advisors to assess differing company approaches thoughtfully

### *Reporting on the Code*

The 2018 Code focuses on the application of the Principles. The Listing Rules require companies to make a statement of how they have applied the Principles, in a manner that would enable shareholders to evaluate how the Principles have been applied. The ability of investors to evaluate the approach to governance is important. Reporting should cover the application of the Principles in the context of the particular circumstances of the company and how the board has set the company's purpose and strategy, met objectives and achieved outcomes through the decisions it has taken.

It is important to report meaningfully when discussing the application of the Principles and to avoid boilerplate reporting. The focus should be on how these have been applied, articulating what action has been taken and the resulting outcomes. High-quality reporting will include signposting and cross-referencing to those parts of the annual report that describe how the Principles have been applied. This will help investors with their evaluation of company practices.

The effective application of the Principles should be supported by high-quality reporting on the Provisions. These operate on a 'comply or explain' basis and companies should avoid a 'tick-box approach'. An alternative to complying with a Provision may be justified in particular circumstances based on a range of factors, including the size, complexity, history and ownership structure of a company. Explanations should set out the background, provide a clear rationale for the action the company is taking, and explain the impact that the action has had. Where a departure from a Provision is intended to be limited in time, the explanation should indicate when the company expects to conform to the Provision. Explanations are a positive opportunity to communicate, not an onerous obligation.

In line with their responsibilities under the UK Stewardship Code, investors should engage constructively and discuss with the company any departures from recommended practice. In their consideration of explanations, investors and their advisors should pay due regard to a company's individual circumstances. While they have every right to challenge explanations if they are unconvincing, these must not be evaluated in a mechanistic way. Investors and their advisors should also give companies sufficient time to respond to enquiries about corporate governance.

Corporate governance reporting should also relate coherently to other parts of the annual report – particularly the Strategic Report and other complementary information – so that shareholders can effectively assess the quality of the company's governance arrangements, and the board's activities and contributions. This should include providing information that enables shareholders to assess how the directors have performed their duty under section 172 of the Companies Act 2006 (the Act) to promote the success of the company. Nothing in this Code overrides or is intended as an interpretation of the statutory statement of directors' duties in the Act.

The Code is also supported by the Guidance on Board Effectiveness (the Guidance). We encourage boards and companies to use this to support their activities. The Guidance does not set out the 'right way' to apply the Code. It is intended to stimulate thinking on how boards can carry out their role most effectively. The Guidance is designed to help boards with their actions and decisions when reporting on the application of the Code's Principles. The board should also take into account the Financial Reporting Council's Guidance on Audit Committees and Guidance on Risk Management, Internal Control and Related Financial and Business Reporting.

*Application*

The Code is applicable to all companies with a premium listing, whether incorporated in the UK or elsewhere. The new Code applies to accounting periods beginning on or after 1 January 2019. For parent companies with a premium listing, the board should ensure that there is adequate co-operation within the group to enable it to discharge its governance responsibilities under the Code effectively. This includes the communication of the parent company's purpose, values and strategy.

Externally managed investment companies (which typically have a different board and company structure that may affect the relevance of particular Principles) may wish to use the Association of Investment Companies' Corporate Governance Code to meet their obligations under the Code. In addition, the Association of Financial Mutuals produces an annotated version of the Code for mutual insurers to use.

## 1 BOARD LEADERSHIP AND COMPANY PURPOSE

*Principles*

**A.** A successful company is led by an effective and entrepreneurial board, whose role is to promote the long-term sustainable success of the company, generating value for shareholders and contributing to wider society.

**B.** The board should establish the company's purpose, values and strategy, and satisfy itself that these and its culture are aligned. All directors must act with integrity, lead by example and promote the desired culture.

**C.** The board should ensure that the necessary resources are in place for the company to meet its objectives and measure performance against them. The board should also establish a framework of prudent and effective controls, which enable risk to be assessed and managed.

**D.** In order for the company to meet its responsibilities to shareholders and stakeholders, the board should ensure effective engagement with, and encourage participation from, these parties.

**E.** The board should ensure that workforce policies and practices are consistent with the company's values and support its long-term sustainable success. The workforce should be able to raise any matters of concern.

*Provisions*

**1.** The board should assess the basis on which the company generates and preserves value over the long-term. It should describe in the annual report how opportunities and risks to the future success of the business have been considered and addressed, the sustainability of the company's business model and how its governance contributes to the delivery of its strategy.

**2.** The board should assess and monitor culture. Where it is not satisfied that policy, practices or behaviour throughout the business are aligned with the company's purpose, values and strategy, it should seek assurance that management has taken corrective action. The annual report should explain the board's activities and any action taken. In addition, it should include an explanation of the company's approach to investing in and rewarding its workforce.

**3.** In addition to formal general meetings, the chair should seek regular engagement with major shareholders in order to understand their views on governance and performance against the strategy. Committee chairs should seek engagement with shareholders on significant matters related to their areas of responsibility. The chair should ensure that the board as a whole has a clear understanding of the views of shareholders.

**4.** When 20 per cent or more of votes have been cast against the board recommendation for a resolution, the company should explain, when announcing voting results, what actions it intends to take to consult shareholders in order to understand the reasons behind the result. An update on the views received from shareholders and actions taken should be published no later than six months after the shareholder meeting. The board should then provide a final summary in the annual report and, if applicable, in the explanatory notes to resolutions at the next shareholder meeting, on what impact the feedback has had on the decisions the board has taken and any actions or resolutions now proposed.[1]

5. The board should understand the views of the company's other key stakeholders and describe in the annual report how their interests and the matters set out in section 172 of the Companies Act 2006 have been considered in board discussions and decision-making. 2 The board should keep engagement mechanisms under review so that they remain effective. For engagement with the workforce,[3] one or a combination of the following methods should be used:

- a director appointed from the workforce;
- a formal workforce advisory panel;
- a designated non-executive director.

If the board has not chosen one or more of these methods, it should explain what alternative arrangements are in place and why it considers that they are effective.

6. There should be a means for the workforce to raise concerns in confidence and – if they wish – anonymously. The board should routinely review this and the reports arising from its operation. It should ensure that arrangements are in place for the proportionate and independent investigation of such matters and for follow-up action.

7. The board should take action to identify and manage conflicts of interest, including those resulting from significant shareholdings, and ensure that the influence of third parties does not compromise or override independent judgement.

8. Where directors have concerns about the operation of the board or the management of the company that cannot be resolved, their concerns should be recorded in the board minutes. On resignation, a non-executive director should provide a written statement to the chair, for circulation to the board, if they have any such concerns.

## 2 DIVISION OF RESPONSIBILITIES

### Principles

F. The chair leads the board and is responsible for its overall effectiveness in directing the company. They should demonstrate objective judgement throughout their tenure and promote a culture of openness and debate. In addition, the chair facilitates constructive board relations and the effective contribution of all non-executive directors, and ensures that directors receive accurate, timely and clear information.

G. The board should include an appropriate combination of executive and non-executive (and, in particular, independent non-executive) directors, such that no one individual or small group of individuals dominates the board's decision-making. There should be a clear division of responsibilities between the leadership of the board and the executive leadership of the company's business.

H. Non-executive directors should have sufficient time to meet their board responsibilities. They should provide constructive challenge, strategic guidance, offer specialist advice and hold management to account.

I. The board, supported by the company secretary, should ensure that it has the policies, processes, information, time and resources it needs in order to function effectively and efficiently.

### Provisions

9. The chair should be independent on appointment when assessed against the circumstances set out in Provision 10. The roles of chair and chief executive should not be

exercised by the same individual. A chief executive should not become chair of the same company. If, exceptionally, this is proposed by the board, major shareholders should be consulted ahead of appointment. The board should set out its reasons to all shareholders at the time of the appointment and also publish these on the company website.

10. The board should identify in the annual report each non-executive director it considers to be independent. Circumstances which are likely to impair, or could appear to impair, a non-executive director's independence include, but are not limited to, whether a director:

- is or has been an employee of the company or group within the last five years;
- has, or has had within the last three years, a material business relationship with the company, either directly or as a partner, shareholder, director or senior employee of a body that has such a relationship with the company;
- has received or receives additional remuneration from the company apart from a director's fee, participates in the company's share option or a performance-related pay scheme, or is a member of the company's pension scheme;
- has close family ties with any of the company's advisers, directors or senior employees;
- holds cross-directorships or has significant links with other directors through involvement in other companies or bodies; • represents a significant shareholder; or
- has served on the board for more than nine years from the date of their first appointment.

Where any of these or other relevant circumstances apply, and the board nonetheless considers that the non-executive director is independent, a clear explanation should be provided.

11. At least half the board, excluding the chair, should be non-executive directors whom the board considers to be independent.

12. The board should appoint one of the independent non-executive directors to be the senior independent director to provide a sounding board for the chair and serve as an intermediary for the other directors and shareholders. Led by the senior independent director, the non-executive directors should meet without the chair present at least annually to appraise the chair's performance, and on other occasions as necessary.

13. Non-executive directors have a prime role in appointing and removing executive directors. Non-executive directors should scrutinise and hold to account the performance of management and individual executive directors against agreed performance objectives. The chair should hold meetings with the non-executive directors without the executive directors present.

14. The responsibilities of the chair, chief executive, senior independent director, board and committees should be clear, set out in writing, agreed by the board and made publicly available. The annual report should set out the number of meetings of the board and its committees, and the individual attendance by directors.

15. When making new appointments, the board should take into account other demands on directors' time. Prior to appointment, significant commitments should be disclosed with an indication of the time involved. Additional external appointments should not be undertaken without prior approval of the board, with the reasons for permitting significant appointments explained in the annual report. Full-time executive directors should not take on more than one non-executive directorship in a FTSE 100 company or other significant appointment.

16. All directors should have access to the advice of the company secretary, who is responsible for advising the board on all governance matters. Both the appointment and removal of the company secretary should be a matter for the whole board.

# Corporate Governance Appendix

## 3 COMPOSITION, SUCCESSION AND EVALUATION

*Principles*

J. Appointments to the board should be subject to a formal, rigorous and transparent procedure, and an effective succession plan should be maintained for board and senior management. Both appointments and succession plans should be based on merit and objective criteria[5] and, within this context, should promote diversity of gender, social and ethnic backgrounds, cognitive and personal strengths.

K. The board and its committees should have a combination of skills, experience and knowledge. Consideration should be given to the length of service of the board as a whole and membership regularly refreshed.

L. Annual evaluation of the board should consider its composition, diversity and how effectively members work together to achieve objectives. Individual evaluation should demonstrate whether each director continues to contribute effectively.

*Provisions*

17. The board should establish a nomination committee to lead the process for appointments, ensure plans are in place for orderly succession to both the board and senior management positions, and oversee the development of a diverse pipeline for succession. A majority of members of the committee should be independent non-executive directors. The chair of the board should not chair the committee when it is dealing with the appointment of their successor.

18. All directors should be subject to annual re-election. The board should set out in the papers accompanying the resolutions to elect each director the specific reasons why their contribution is, and continues to be, important to the company's long-term sustainable success.

19. The chair should not remain in post beyond nine years from the date of their first appointment to the board. To facilitate effective succession planning and the development of a diverse board, this period can be extended for a limited time, particularly in those cases where the chair was an existing non-executive director on appointment. A clear explanation should be provided.

20. Open advertising and/or an external search consultancy should generally be used for the appointment of the chair and non-executive directors. If an external search consultancy is engaged it should be identified in the annual report alongside a statement about any other connection it has with the company or individual directors.

21. There should be a formal and rigorous annual evaluation of the performance of the board, its committees, the chair and individual directors. The chair should consider having a regular externally facilitated board evaluation. In FTSE 350 companies this should happen at least every three years. The external evaluator should be identified in the annual report and a statement made about any other connection it has with the company or individual directors.

22. The chair should act on the results of the evaluation by recognising the strengths and addressing any weaknesses of the board. Each director should engage with the process and take appropriate action when development needs have been identified.

23. The annual report should describe the work of the nomination committee, including:

- the process used in relation to appointments, its approach to succession planning and how both support developing a diverse pipeline;

- how the board evaluation has been conducted, the nature and extent of an external evaluator's contact with the board and individual directors, the outcomes and actions taken, and how it has or will influence board composition;
- the policy on diversity and inclusion, its objectives and linkage to company strategy, how it has been implemented and progress on achieving the objectives; and
- the gender balance of those in the senior management[6] and their direct reports.

## 4 AUDIT, RISK AND INTERNAL CONTROL

*Principles*

M. The board should establish formal and transparent policies and procedures to ensure the independence and effectiveness of internal and external audit functions and satisfy itself on the integrity of financial and narrative statements.[7]

N. The board should present a fair, balanced and understandable assessment of the company's position and prospects.

O. The board should establish procedures to manage risk, oversee the internal control framework, and determine the nature and extent of the principal risks the company is willing to take in order to achieve its long-term strategic objectives.

*Provisions*

24. The board should establish an audit committee of independent non-executive directors, with a minimum membership of three, or in the case of smaller companies, two.[8] The chair of the board should not be a member. The board should satisfy itself that at least one member has recent and relevant financial experience. The committee as a whole shall have competence relevant to the sector in which the company operates.

25. The main roles and responsibilities of the audit committee should include:

- monitoring the integrity of the financial statements of the company and any formal announcements relating to the company's financial performance, and reviewing significant financial reporting judgements contained in them;
- providing advice (where requested by the board) on whether the annual report and accounts, taken as a whole, is fair, balanced and understandable, and provides the information necessary for shareholders to assess the company's position and performance, business model and strategy;
- reviewing the company's internal financial controls and internal control and risk management systems, unless expressly addressed by a separate board risk committee composed of independent non-executive directors, or by the board itself;
- monitoring and reviewing the effectiveness of the company's internal audit function or, where there is not one, considering annually whether there is a need for one and making a recommendation to the board;
- conducting the tender process and making recommendations to the board, about the appointment, reappointment and removal of the external auditor, and approving the remuneration and terms of engagement of the external auditor;
- reviewing and monitoring the external auditor's independence and objectivity;
- reviewing the effectiveness of the external audit process, taking into consideration relevant UK professional and regulatory requirements;
- developing and implementing policy on the engagement of the external auditor to supply non-audit services, ensuring there is prior approval of

non-audit services, considering the impact this may have on independence, taking into account the relevant regulations and ethical guidance in this regard, and reporting to the board on any improvement or action required; and

- reporting to the board on how it has discharged its responsibilities.

26. The annual report should describe the work of the audit committee, including:

- the significant issues that the audit committee considered relating to the financial statements, and how these issues were addressed;
- an explanation of how it has assessed the independence and effectiveness of the external audit process and the approach taken to the appointment or reappointment of the external auditor, information on the length of tenure of the current audit firm, when a tender was last conducted and advance notice of any retendering plans;
- in the case of a board not accepting the audit committee's recommendation on the external auditor appointment, reappointment or removal, a statement from the audit committee explaining its recommendation and the reasons why the board has taken a different position (this should also be supplied in any papers recommending appointment or reappointment);
- where there is no internal audit function, an explanation for the absence, how internal assurance is achieved, and how this affects the work of external audit; and
- an explanation of how auditor independence and objectivity are safeguarded, if the external auditor provides non-audit services.

27. The directors should explain in the annual report their responsibility for preparing the annual report and accounts, and state that they consider the annual report and accounts, taken as a whole, is fair, balanced and understandable, and provides the information necessary for shareholders to assess the company's position, performance, business model and strategy.

28. The board should carry out a robust assessment of the company's emerging and principal risks.[9] The board should confirm in the annual report that it has completed this assessment, including a description of its principal risks, what procedures are in place to identify emerging risks, and an explanation of how these are being managed or mitigated.

29. The board should monitor the company's risk management and internal control systems and, at least annually, carry out a review of their effectiveness and report on that review in the annual report. The monitoring and review should cover all material controls, including financial, operational and compliance controls.

30. In annual and half-yearly financial statements, the board should state whether it considers it appropriate to adopt the going concern basis of accounting in preparing them, and identify any material uncertainties to the company's ability to continue to do so over a period of at least twelve months from the date of approval of the financial statements.

31. Taking account of the company's current position and principal risks, the board should explain in the annual report how it has assessed the prospects of the company, over what period it has done so and why it considers that period to be appropriate. The board should state whether it has a reasonable expectation that the company will be able to continue in operation and meet its liabilities as they fall due over the period of their assessment, drawing attention to any qualifications or assumptions as necessary.

## 5 REMUNERATION

*Principles*

P. Remuneration policies and practices should be designed to support strategy and promote long-term sustainable success. Executive remuneration should be aligned to company purpose and values, and be clearly linked to the successful delivery of the company's long-term strategy.

Q. A formal and transparent procedure for developing policy on executive remuneration and determining director and senior management[10] remuneration should be established. No director should be involved in deciding their own remuneration outcome.

R. Directors should exercise independent judgement and discretion when authorising remuneration outcomes, taking account of company and individual performance, and wider circumstances.

*Provisions*

32. The board should establish a remuneration committee of independent non-executive directors, with a minimum membership of three, or in the case of smaller companies, two. 11 In addition, the chair of the board can only be a member if they were independent on appointment and cannot chair the committee. Before appointment as chair of the remuneration committee, the appointee should have served on a remuneration committee for at least 12 months.

33. The remuneration committee should have delegated responsibility for determining the policy for executive director remuneration and setting remuneration for the chair, executive directors and senior management.[12] It should review workforce[13] remuneration and related policies and the alignment of incentives and rewards with culture, taking these into account when setting the policy for executive director remuneration.

34. The remuneration of non-executive directors should be determined in accordance with the Articles of Association or, alternatively, by the board. Levels of remuneration for the chair and all non-executive directors should reflect the time commitment and responsibilities of the role. Remuneration for all non-executive directors should not include share options or other performance-related elements.

35. Where a remuneration consultant is appointed, this should be the responsibility of the remuneration committee. The consultant should be identified in the annual report alongside a statement about any other connection it has with the company or individual directors. Independent judgement should be exercised when evaluating the advice of external third parties[14] and when receiving views from executive directors and senior management.

36. Remuneration schemes should promote long-term shareholdings by executive directors that support alignment with long-term shareholder interests. Share awards granted for this purpose should be released for sale on a phased basis and be subject to a total vesting and holding period of five years or more. The remuneration committee should develop a formal policy for post-employment shareholding requirements encompassing both unvested and vested shares.

37. Remuneration schemes and policies should enable the use of discretion to override formulaic outcomes. They should also include provisions that would enable the company to recover and/or withhold sums or share awards and specify the circumstances in which it would be appropriate to do so.

38. Only basic salary should be pensionable. The pension contribution rates for executive directors, or payments in lieu, should be aligned with those available to the workforce. The

# Corporate Governance Appendix

pension consequences and associated costs of basic salary increases and any other changes in pensionable remuneration, or contribution rates, particularly for directors close to retirement, should be carefully considered when compared with workforce arrangements.

39. Notice or contract periods should be one year or less. If it is necessary to offer longer periods to new directors recruited from outside the company, such periods should reduce to one year or less after the initial period. The remuneration committee should ensure compensation commitments in directors' terms of appointment do not reward poor performance. They should be robust in reducing compensation to reflect departing directors' obligations to mitigate loss.

40. When determining executive director remuneration policy and practices, the remuneration committee should address the following:

- clarity – remuneration arrangements should be transparent and promote effective engagement with shareholders and the workforce;
- simplicity – remuneration structures should avoid complexity and their rationale and operation should be easy to understand;
- risk – remuneration arrangements should ensure reputational and other risks from excessive rewards, and behavioural risks that can arise from target-based incentive plans, are identified and mitigated;
- predictability – the range of possible values of rewards to individual directors and any other limits or discretions should be identified and explained at the time of approving the policy;
- proportionality – the link between individual awards, the delivery of strategy and the long-term performance of the company should be clear. Outcomes should not reward poor performance; and
- alignment to culture – incentive schemes should drive behaviours consistent with company purpose, values and strategy.

41. There should be a description of the work of the remuneration committee in the annual report, including:

- an explanation of the strategic rationale for executive directors' remuneration policies, structures and any performance metrics;
- reasons why the remuneration is appropriate using internal and external measures, including pay ratios and pay gaps;
- a description, with examples, of how the remuneration committee has addressed the factors in Provision 40;
- whether the remuneration policy operated as intended in terms of company performance and quantum, and, if not, what changes are necessary;
- what engagement has taken place with shareholders and the impact this has had on remuneration policy and outcomes;
- what engagement with the workforce has taken place to explain how executive remuneration aligns with wider company pay policy; and
- to what extent discretion has been applied to remuneration outcomes and the reasons why.

---

1    Details of significant votes against and related company updates are available on the Public Register maintained by The Investment Association – www.theinvestmentassociation.org/publicregister.html.

2    The Companies (Miscellaneous Reporting) Regulations 2018 require directors to explain how they have had regard to various matters in performing their duty to promote the success of the company in section 172 of the Companies Act 2006. The Financial Reporting Council's Guidance on the Strategic Report supports reporting on the legislative requirement.

3    See the Guidance on Board Effectiveness Section 1 for a description of 'workforce' in this context.

4    The definition of 'senior management' for this purpose should be the executive committee or the first layer of management below board level, including the company secretary.

5    Which protect against discrimination for those with protected characteristics within the meaning of the Equalities Act 2010.

6    See footnote 4.

7   The board's responsibility to present a fair, balanced and understandable assessment extends to interim and other price-sensitive public records and reports to regulators, as well as to information required to be presented by statutory instruments.

8   A smaller company is one that is below the FTSE 350 throughout the year immediately prior to the reporting year

9   Principal risks should include, but are not necessarily limited to, those that could result in events or circumstances that might threaten the company's business model, future performance, solvency or liquidity and reputation. In deciding which risks are principal risks companies should consider the potential impact and probability of the related events or circumstances, and the timescale over which they may occur.

10   See footnote 4.

11   See footnote 8.

12   See footnote 4.

13   See the Guidance on Board Effectiveness Section 5 for a description of 'workforce' in this context.

14   See footnote 4.

# 16   Dealings with Third Parties

Cross references. See **12.1** COMPANY FORMATION AND TYPES OF COMPANY (for pre-incorporation contracts) and **14** CONSTITUTION – MEMORANDUM AND ARTICLES.

## 16.1   A COMPANY'S CAPACITY

The basis for whether a company has capacity to carry out transactions was based historically on the objects as set out in its memorandum of association and the doctrine of ultra vires. If a company exceeded the powers given by the objects its actions were ultra vires, the transaction would be void and the officers in breach responsible for breach of duty (*Ashbury Railway Carriage and Iron Co Ltd v Riche* (1875) LR 7 HL 653, HL). Changes brought about by *CA 1985, s 35* were designed to ensure that the validity of any transactions could not be challenged on the ground of lack of corporate capacity. *CA 2006, s 39* replaced *CA 1985, s 35* as from 1 October 2009 with little change other than substituting "constitution" for "memorandum" given the other constitutional changes brought in on that date (see **14** CONSTITUTION – MEMORANDUM AND ARTICLES). *Section 39* provides that the validity of an act done by a company cannot be called into question on the ground of lack of capacity by reason of anything in the company's constitution. But see **16.3** for certain transactions where a director (or a person connected with him) is a party to the contract and **16.4** for charitable companies.

Additionally the scope of the *ultra vires* doctrine has been further limited by the introduction of *CA 2006, s 31* which provides that a company's objects are unrestricted unless the company's articles restrict them. This means that a company incorporated on or after 1 October 2009 has unlimited capacity (unless it chooses to have some restrictions in

## 16.1 Dealings with Third Parties

its articles) and companies incorporated before that date the provisions of whose memorandum are deemed to form provisions of their articles (see **14 COMPANY CONSTITUTION**) can amend or remove any restrictions by changing their articles.

## 16.2 Power of directors to bind the company

Although for reasons given in **16.1** a company's objects do not limit the company's capacity, they do restrict the directors' authority. If the directors exceed the authority given by the objects, the transaction will not be invalid as a consequence but only voidable and provided that the other party satisfies the 'good faith' requirement they will be protected. See below for the definition of good faith. If the third party cannot show good faith and the transaction is outside the company's objects then it will be void.

Subject to **16.3** and **16.4**, where a person 'deals with' a company in good faith, the power of the directors to bind the company, or authorise others to do so, is deemed to be free of any limitation under the company's constitution. This includes limitations deriving from

- a resolution of the company or of any class of shareholders; or

- any agreement between the members of the company or of any class of shareholders.

[*CA 2006, s 40(1), (3), (6)*].

A person '*deals with*' a company if he is a party to any transaction or other act to which the company is a party. A person dealing with a company is

- not bound to enquire as to any limitation on the powers of the directors to bind the company or authorise others to do so;

- presumed to have acted in good faith unless the contrary is proved; and

- not to be regarded as acting in bad faith by reason only of his knowing that an act is beyond the powers of the directors under the company's constitution.

[*CA 2006, s 40(2)*].

The above provisions do not affect

- any right of a member of the company to bring proceedings to restrain the doing of an action that is beyond the powers of the directors. No such proceedings can be brought if the action is done to fulfil a legal obligation arising from a previous act of the company; or

- any liability incurred by the directors, or any other person, by reason of the directors exceeding their powers.

[*CA 2006, s 40(4), (5)*].

## 16.3 Transactions involving directors or their associates

Where a company enters into a transaction and the validity of that transaction depends on the provisions in *CA 2006, s 40* (ie that the powers of the directors are deemed to be free of any limitations under the company's constitution) if the third party is acting in good faith and the parties to the transaction include

(i)     a director of the company or of its holding company, or

(ii)    a person '*connected with*' any such director,

the transaction is voidable at the instance of the company. 'Connected with' has the same meaning as in *CA 2006, s 252* (see **18.1 DIRECTORS**).

Whether or not the transaction is avoided, any party to the transaction and any director of the company who authorised the transaction, is liable to

- account to the company for any gain he has made directly or indirectly by the transaction, and

- indemnify the company for any loss or damage resulting from the transaction

except that a person other than a director of the company is not liable if he shows that, at the time the transaction was entered into, he did not know that the directors were exceeding their powers.

The transaction ceases to be voidable if

- restitution of any money or other asset which was the subject-matter of the transaction is no longer possible;

- the company is indemnified for any loss or damage resulting from the transaction;

- rights acquired *bona fide* for value and without actual notice of the directors' exceeding their powers by a person who is not party to the transaction would be affected by the avoidance; or

- the transaction is affirmed by the company (but see **16.4** where the company is a charity).

Nothing in the above provisions affects the rights of any party to the transaction not within (i) or (ii) above, but the court may, on the application of the company or any such party, make an order affirming, severing or setting aside the transaction on such terms as appear to the court to be just.

[*CA 2006, s 41*].

## 16.4 Charitable companies

**England and Wales and Northern Ireland.** The provisions in **16.1** and **16.2** do not apply to the acts of a company that is a charity, except in favour of a person who

(a) does not know at the time the act is done that the company is a charity; or

(b) gives full consideration in money or money's worth in relation to the act in question and does not know that the act is not permitted by the company's constitution or, as the case may be, is beyond the powers of the directors.

In any proceedings, the burden of proof that (*a*) or (*b*) above is not satisfied lies with the person asserting that fact.

But where a company that is a charity purports to transfer or grant an interest in property, the title of a person who subsequently acquires the property or an interest in it and who satisfies the conditions in (*b*) above is not affected by the fact that the act was not so permitted or beyond the directors' powers.

[*CA 2006, s 42(1)–(3)*].

In the case of a company that is a charity the affirmation of a transaction to which **16.3** applies is ineffective without the prior written consent of

- in England and Wales, the Charity Commission; or

- in Northern Ireland, the Department for Social Development (the functions of this department have been transferred to the Charities Commission for the purposes of *CA 2006, s 42(4)(b)*)

## 16.4  Dealings with Third Parties

[*CA 2006, s 42(4); Charities Act (Northern Ireland) 2013, s 5*].

**Scotland**. Corresponding provisions apply to charitable companies that are registered in Scotland. [*CA 1989, s 112(3)–(5)*].


## 16.5  CONTRACTS

Under the law of England and Wales or Northern Ireland, a contract may be made

- by a company, by writing under its common seal; or

- on behalf of a company, by a person acting under its authority, express or implied.

Unless a contrary intention appears, any formalities required by law in the case of a contract made by an individual also apply to one made by or on behalf of a company.

[*CA 2006, s 43*].


## 16.6  DEEDS AND DOCUMENTS: PROVISIONS APPLYING IN ENGLAND AND WALES AND NORTHERN IRELAND

(1) *Execution of documents*

A document is executed by a company in either of the following ways.

(a)     By the affixing of its common seal (see **16.8**)

(b)     If it is signed on behalf of the company by

  (i)     two 'authorised signatories'; or

  (ii)    a director of the company in the presence of a witness who attests the signature.

  '*Authorised signatories*' are every director of the company and, in the case of a private company with a secretary or a public company, the secretary (or any joint secretary) of the company.

  A document so signed and expressed, in whatever words, to be executed by the company has the same effect as if executed under the common seal of the company.

In favour of a 'purchaser', a document is deemed to have been duly executed by a company if it purports to be signed in accordance with (*b*) above. A '*purchaser*' means a purchaser in good faith for valuable consideration and includes a lessee, mortgagee or other person who, for valuable consideration, acquires an interest in property.

Where a document is to be signed by a person on behalf of more than one company, it is not duly signed by that person for the purposes of these provisions unless he signs it separately in each capacity.

References above to a document being (or purporting to be) signed by a director or secretary are to be read, in a case where that office is held by a firm, as references to its being (or purporting to be) signed by an individual authorised by the firm to sign on its behalf.

The above provisions apply to a document that is (or purports to be) executed by a company in the name of or on behalf of another person whether or not that person is also a company.

[*CA 2006, s 44*].

(2) *Execution of deeds*

A document is validly executed by a company as a deed for the purposes of *Law of Property (Miscellaneous Provisions) Act 1989, s 1(2)(b)* and the law of Northern Ireland if, and only if, it is

- duly executed by the company; and

- delivered as a deed.

A document is presumed to be delivered for these purposes upon its being executed, unless a contrary intention is proved.

[*CA 2006, s 46*].

(3) *Execution of deeds or other documents by attorney*

A company may, by instrument executed as a deed, empower a person, either generally or in respect of specified matters, as its attorney to execute deeds or other documents on its behalf. A deed or other document so executed, whether in the UK or elsewhere, has effect as if executed by the company. [*CA 2006, s 47*].

*Where the power to act as a company's attorney was conferred before 1 October 2009,* (including in relation to instruments executed by the attorney on behalf of the company on or after that date), *CA 1985, s 38* continues to apply.

Special rules apply to overseas companies (that is, companies incorporated outside the UK) (see **30.59** COMPANY CONTRACTS AND EXECUTION OF DOCUMENTS).

## 16.7   EXECUTION OF DOCUMENTS: PROVISIONS APPLYING IN SCOTLAND

Despite the provisions of any enactment, a company need not have a company seal (see **16.8**). For the purposes of any enactment

- providing for a document to be executed by a company by affixing its common seal, or

- referring (in whatever terms) to a document so executed,

a document signed or subscribed by or on behalf of the company in accordance with the provisions of the *Requirements of Writing (Scotland) Act 1995* has effect as if so executed. [*CA 2006, s 48*].

Except where an enactment provides otherwise, a document is signed by a company if it is signed in its behalf by a director, or by the secretary, or by a person authorised to sign the document on its behalf. [*Requirements of Writing (Scotland) Act 1995, Sch 2 para 3*].

## 16.8   COMMON SEAL

A company may have a common seal, but need not have one. [*CA 2006, ss 45(1), 48(2)*].

**Under the law of England and Wales and Northern Ireland,** a company which has a common seal must have its name engraved on it in legible characters. An offence is committed by

- the company, and every officer of the company who is in default, if the company fails to have the common seal so engraved; and

- by an officer of a company, or a person acting on behalf of a company, if he uses, or authorises the use of, a seal purporting to be a seal of the company on which its name is not engraved.

A person guilty of such an offence is liable, on summary conviction, to a fine not exceeding level 3 on the standard scale. See **29.1** OFFENCES AND LEGAL PROCEEDINGS for the standard scale.

[*CA 2006, s 45*].

**Authority to use seal.** Where a company has adopted standard articles, see

- *Table A, 1985, Reg 101*

- *Model Articles, Art 49* (private companies)

- *Model Articles, Art 81* (public companies)

Set out in APPENDIX 4 standard articles of association.

Table A 1985 provides (in summary) that the seal can only be used if the directors, or a committee of the directors, authorise its use and any instruments to which the seal is affixed shall be signed either by a director and the secretary or by two directors.

The Model Articles provide (in summary) that the seal can only be used if the directors authorise its use and that any document to which the seal is affixed must be signed by either one director or by the company secretary or by any other person authorised by the directors. The Model Articles for public companies additionally provide for the use of the official seal for use abroad (see **16.9** below) and the use of the securities seal (if any) (see **16.10** below).

## 16.9    Official seal for use abroad

A company which has a common seal may have an official seal for use outside the UK. It must be a facsimile of the common seal with the addition on its face of place or places where it is to be used. In England and Wales and Northern Ireland, when duly affixed to a document, the official seal has the same effect as the company's common seal.

A company which has an official seal for use outside the UK may, by writing under its common seal (or, as respects Scotland, by writing subscribed in accordance with the *Requirements of Writing (Scotland) Act 1995*), authorise any person appointed for the purposes to affix the official seal to any deed or other document to which the company is a party. As between the company and a person dealing with such an agent, the agent's authority continues

- during the period mentioned in the instrument conferring the authority; or

- if no period is mentioned, until notice of the revocation or termination of the agent's authority has been given to the person dealing with him.

The person affixing the official seal must certify in writing on the deed or other document to which the seal is affixed the date on which, and place at which, it is affixed.

[*CA 2006, s 49*].

## 16.10   Official seal for share certificates, etc

A company that has a common seal may have an official seal for use for sealing securities issued by the company or for sealing documents creating or evidencing securities so issued. The official seal must be a facsimile of the company's common seal, with the addition on its face of the word 'Securities'. When duly affixed to the document, it has the same effect as the company's common seal. [*CA 2006, s 50*].

The foregoing provisions are without prejudice to the right of a company to subscribe such securities and documents in accordance with the *Requirements of Writing (Scotland) Act 1995*. [*Requirements of Writing (Scotland) Act 1995, Sch 4, paras 55, 57*].

## 16.11 BILLS OF EXCHANGE AND PROMISSORY NOTES

A bill of exchange or promissory note is deemed to have been made, accepted or endorsed on behalf of a company if made, accepted or endorsed in the name of, or by or on behalf or on account of, the company by a person acting under its authority. [*CA 2006, s 52*].

## 16.12 TRADING DISCLOSURES

Regulations made under *CA 2006, s 82* require a company to disclose specified trading information [*CA 2006, s 82*] and make it a criminal offence where the company fails, without reasonable excuse, to comply with the provisions. [*CA 2006, s 84*]. These requirements fall into three categories.

- Displaying a sign with the company name and certain other information at specific locations (see **16.13**).

- Including the company name and specified other information in certain documents and communications (see **16.15**).

- Providing the company name and specified other information to those who request it in the course of business (**16.16**).

### 16.13 Display of registered name at registered office, etc

Every company must display its registered name at

(a)   its registered office;

(b)   any '*inspection place*' ie any location (other than its registered office) at which it keeps available for inspection any 'company record' which it is required under the Companies Acts to keep available for inspection; and

(c)   any other location at which it carries on business unless that location is primarily used for living accommodation.

But

- (*a*) and (*b*) above do not apply to a company which has at all times since its incorporation been dormant; or

- (*a*)–(*c*) above do not apply to a registered office, inspection place or other location where

  (i)    in respect of that company, a liquidator, administrator or administrative receiver has been appointed; and

  (ii)   the registered office inspection, place or location is also a place of business of that liquidator, etc; and

- (*c*) above does not apply to any location at which business is carried on by a company of which every director is an individual in respect of whom the Registrar of Companies is required to refrain from disclosing protected information to a credit reference agency. See **18.70 DIRECTORS**.

## 16.14   Dealings with Third Parties

### 16.14   Manner of display of registered name

Where the office, place or location is shared by no more than five companies, the registered name must be so positioned that it may be easily seen by any visitor to the office, place or location and must be displayed continuously.

Where the office, place or location is shared by six or more companies, each such company must ensure that either its registered name is displayed continuously for at least 15 continuous seconds at least once in every three minutes or its registered name is available for inspection on a register by any visitor to that office, place or location.

Any display or disclosure of the company name must be in characters that can be read with the naked eye.

For permitted minor variations in the displayed name see *CA 2006, s 85.*

Where the name of a charitable company does not include the word 'charity' or 'charitable', the fact that the company is a charity must be stated in legible characters in every location required by the regulations made under *CA 2006*. [*Charities Act 2011, s 194(1)*]

There are civil consequences for failure to make the disclosures required by *Charities Act 2011, s 194*. [*Charities Act 2011. s 195*]

'*Company records*' means

- any register, index, accounting records, agreement, memorandum, minutes or other documents required to be kept by a company under the Companies Acts; and

- any register kept be a company of its debenture holders.

*Penalties.* Where a company fails, without reasonable excuse, to comply with the above requirements, an offence is committed by the company and every officer of the company who is in default. A person guilty of such an offence is liable, on summary conviction, to a fine not exceeding level 3 on the standard scale and, for continued contravention, a daily default fine not exceeding one-tenth of level 3 on the standard scale. See **29.1 OFFENCES AND LEGAL PROCEEDINGS** for the standard scale. For these purposes, a 'shadow director' (see **18.1 DIRECTORS**) is treated as an officer of the company.

[*SI 2015 No 17, Regs 20–23, 28*].

### 16.15   Inclusion of name and other specified information in documents and communications

Every company must:

(a)   Disclose its registered name on

(i)     its business letters, notices and other official publications;

(ii)    its bills of exchange, promissory notes, endorsements, and order forms;

(iii)   cheques purporting to be signed by or on behalf of the company;

(iv)    orders for money, goods or services purporting to be signed by or on behalf of the company;

(v)     its bills of parcels, invoices and other demands for payment, receipts, letters of credit;

(vi)    its applications for licences to carry on a trade or activity;

(vii)    all other forms of its business correspondence and documentation; and

(viii)   its websites.

(b)      Disclose the following particulars on its business letters, order forms, and websites.

   (i)     The part of the UK in which the company is registered.

   (ii)    The company's registered number.

   (iii)   The address of the company's registered office.

   (iv)   In the case of a limited company exempt from the obligation to use the word 'limited' as part of its name under *CA 2006, s 60* (see **27.2** NAMES AND BUSINESS NAMES), the fact that it is a limited company.

   (v)    In the case of a community interest company which is not a public company, the fact that it is a limited company.

   (vi)   In the case of an investment company (see **22.1** DISTRIBUTIONS), the fact that it is such a company.

   If, in the case of a company having a share capital, there is a disclosure as to the amount of share capital, it must be to paid up share capital.

(c)      Where its business letter includes the 'name' of any director of the company (other than in the text or as a signatory), the letter must disclose the name of every director of that company. '*Name*' means

   (i)     in the case of a director who is an individual, Christian name (or other forename) and surname (except that in the case of a peer or individual usually known by a title, the title may be stated instead of the Christian name (or other forename) and surname or in addition to either or both of them); and

   (ii)    in the case of a director who is a body corporate or a firm that is a legal person under the law by which it is governed, corporate or firm name.

A reference to any type of document is a reference to a document of that type in hard copy, electronic or any other form. The classification of a communication (for example, as a business letter, invoice, or other) will depend not on its format (email, compliments slip or other) but on its content. So, for example, an email or compliments slip could constitute a business letter for the purposes of these rules.

Any disclosure of information required must be in characters that can be read with the naked eye.

A company must disclose its name on its websites. For this purpose, 'websites' includes any part of a website relating to a company which that company has caused or authorised to appear. Whilst it is not necessary to put the registered name on every page of the website, the name should be placed where it can easily be read.

Charitable companies. Where the name of a charitable company does not include the word "charity" or "charitable" the fact that the company is a charity must be stated in English in legible characters in every description of document or communication in which it is required by the regulations made under *CA 2006, s 82* to state its name. This does not apply to any document that is wholly in Welsh and the company's name includes the Welsh equivalent of "charity" or "charitable".

[*Charities Act 2011, ss 194(1) and 194(2)*]

There are civil consequences for failure to make the disclosures required by *Charities Act 2011, s 194.*

## 16.15 Dealings with Third Parties

[*Charities Act 2011, s 195*]

*Penalties.* Similar penalties apply as under **16.13**.

[*SI 2015 No 17, Regs 20, 24, 25, 26, 28*].

### 16.16 Provision of information on request

A company must disclose

- the address of its registered office,

- any inspection place (see **16.13**(*b*)), and

- the type of company records kept at that office or place

to any person it deals with in the course of business who makes a written request to the company for that information. It must do so in writing within five working days of the receipt of that request.

*Penalties.* Similar penalties apply as under **16.13** above.

[*SI 2015 No 17, Regs 27, 28*].

### 16.17 Civil consequences of failure to disclose the information required by CA 2006, s 82

If a company is obliged to make statutory trading disclosures and brings legal proceedings to enforce a contract made in the course of a business and the company was at the time the time the contract was made, in breach of the trading disclosure regulations made under *s 82* (ie the *Company, Limited Liability Partnerships and Business (Names and Trading Disclosures) Regulations 2015 (SI 2015 No 17)* then

- the proceedings must be dismissed if the defendant can show that he has a claim against the company that he has been unable to pursue because of the company's breach of the regulations; and

- the defendant's claim arises from the same contract; and

- the defendant has suffered some financial loss in connection with the contract as a consequence of the company's breach of the regulations.

The proceedings will not be dismissed if the court is satisfied that it is just and equitable to permit the proceedings to continue. For Scottish proceedings read 'defender' for 'defendant' and 'pursuer' for 'claimant'.

[*CA 2006, s 83*]

### 16.18 EFFECT OF FAILURE TO GIVE PUBLIC NOTICE

A company is not entitled to rely against other persons on the happening of any of the following events, namely

(a) an amendment to the company's articles (before 1 October 2009, memorandum and articles),

(b) a change in the directors,

(c) (as regards the service of any document on the company) a change of the company's registered office,

(d)   the making of a winding-up order in respect of the company or the appointment of a liquidator in a voluntary winding up,

unless

- that event has been 'officially notified' at the material time, or

- the company shows that the person concerned knew of the event at the material time.

Where the material time falls on or before the 15th day after the date of official notification (or, where the 15th day was not a working day, on or before the next day that was) the company is not entitled to rely on the happening of the event as against a person who shows that he was unavoidably prevented from knowing of the event at that time.

'*Officially notified*' means notified in accordance with *CA 2006, s 1077* (see **39.8 REGISTRAR OF COMPANIES**) or, in relation to the appointment of a liquidator in a voluntary winding up, notification in accordance with *IA 1986, s 109* or *Insolvency (NI) Order 1989, Art 95*. [*CA 2006, s 1079*].

## 16.19   FRAUDULENT TRADING

If any business of a company is carried on with 'intent to defraud' creditors (of the company or any other person) or for any fraudulent purpose, every person who is knowingly a 'party' to the carrying on of the business in that manner commits an offence. This applies whether or not the company has been, or is in the course of being, wound up. For the meaning of a '*party*' see *Re Maidstone Buildings Provisions Ltd* [1971] 3 All ER 363, [1971] 1 WLR 1085.

A person guilty of such an offence is liable (i) on conviction on indictment, to imprisonment for a term not exceeding 10 years or a fine (or both); and (ii) on summary conviction, to imprisonment for a term not exceeding 12 months (six months in Scotland and Northern Ireland) or to a fine not exceeding the statutory maximum (or both). See **29.1 OFFENCES AND LEGAL PROCEEDINGS** for the statutory maximum.

[*CA 2006, s 993*].

In addition, if the company is in the course of winding up, the court may, on the application of the liquidator, declare that such a person is liable to make such a contribution to the company's assets as it thinks proper [*IA 1986, s 213*]. Technically, the amount of any such contribution cannot include a punitive element (*Morphitis v Bernasconi* [2003] EWCA Civ 289, [2003] Ch 552, [2003] 2 WLR 1521). Where the person concerned is a director, he may also be disqualified from acting as a director (see **18.12(*c*) DIRECTORS**).

There is '*intent to defraud*' where the company continues to carry on business and to incur debts at a time when there is to the knowledge of the directors no reasonable prospect of the creditors ever receiving payment for those debts (*William C Leitch Bros Ltd, Re* [1932] 2 Ch 71, 101 LJ Ch 380). However, it is not enough that the company had incurred debts when the directors knew it was insolvent. There has to be 'actual dishonesty, involving . . . real moral blame' (*Re Patrick & Lyon Ltd* [1933] Ch 786, 102 LJ Ch 300).

Only those who were knowingly party to the fraudulent trading are caught. However, this does not necessarily encompass only the company's directors. Anyone who is knowingly party to carrying on the business with intent to defraud may be found liable for fraudulent trading. Indeed, even a bank could be held liable as a party to fraudulent trading by virtue of its employees' knowledge (*Bank of India v Morris* [2005] EWCA Civ 693, [2005] 2 BCLC 328, (2005) Times, 19 July 16.18).

Actions for fraudulent trading are relatively rare in practice since establishing fraud constitutes a high evidential burden.

## 16.20    Dealings with Third Parties

### 16.20  SERVICE ADDRESSES

A '*service address*' in relation to a person, means an address at which documents may be effectively served on that person.

The address must be a place where

- the service of documents can be effected by physical delivery, and

- the delivery of documents is capable of being recorded by the obtaining of an acknowledgement of delivery

and must not be a post office box number or a document exchange box number.

Any obligation to give a person's address is, unless otherwise expressly provided, to give a service address for that person.

[*CA 2006, ss 1141, 1142; SI 2008 No 3000, Reg 10*].

### 16.21  SERVICE OF DOCUMENTS ON COMPANY

A document may be served on

- a company registered under *CA 2006* by leaving it at, or sending it by post to, the company's registered office; and

- an overseas company whose particulars are registered under *CA 2006, s 1046*

    (i)     by leaving it at, or sending it by post to, the registered address of any person resident in the UK who is authorised to accept service of documents on the company's behalf (registered address meaning any address for the time being shown as the current address on the part of the register available for public inspection); or

    (ii)    if there is no such person, or if any such person refuses service or service cannot for any other reason be effected, by leaving it at, or sending it by post to, any place of business of the company in the UK.

Where a company registered in Scotland or Northern Ireland carries on business in England and Wales, the process of any court in England and Wales may be served on the company by leaving it at, or sending it by post to, the company's principal place of business in England and Wales, addressed to the manager or other head officer in England and Wales of the company.

Where process is served on a company under these provisions, the person issuing out the process must send a copy of it by post to the company's registered office.

[*CA 2006, s 1139*].

See also **16.23** *et seq* below.

### 16.22  SERVICE OF DOCUMENTS ON DIRECTORS, SECRETARIES AND OTHERS

*CA 2006, s 1140* was introduced by *CA 2006* (ie there was no corresponding provision in *CA 1985*). It provides that a document may be served on any of the following persons by leaving it at, or sending it by post to, the person's registered address, ie any address for the time being shown as a current address in relation to that person in the part of the register available for public inspection (see **18.29** provisions for protecting the disclosure of directors' addresses.)

(a)     A director or secretary of a company.

(b)     In the case of an overseas company whose particulars are registered under *CA 2006, s 1046*, a director, secretary or permanent representative.

(c)     A person appointed in relation to a company as a judicial factor (in Scotland), an interim manager appointed under *Charities Act 2011, s 76* or a manager appointed under *Companies (Audit, Investigations and Community Enterprise) Act 2004*, s 47.

This applies whatever the purpose of the document in question and is not restricted to service for purposes arising out of, or in connection with, the appointment or position mentioned or in connection with the company concerned.

**Change of address.** If notice of a change of address (above) is given to the Registrar of Companies, a person may validly serve a document at the address previously registered until the end of the period of 14 days beginning with the date on which notice of the change is registered.

Service cannot be effected under these provisions at an address

•       if notice has been registered of the termination of the appointment in relation to which the address was registered and the address is not a registered address of the person concerned in relation to any other appointment; and

•       where (*b*) above applies, if the overseas company has ceased to have any connection with the UK by virtue of which it is required to register particulars under *CA 2006, s 1046*.

[*CA 2006, s 1140; SI 2009 No 1801, Reg 75*].

See also **16.24** *et seq* below.


## 16.23   SENDING DOCUMENTS AND INFORMATION (THE 'COMPANY COMMUNICATIONS PROVISIONS')

The following provisions and those in **16.24** to **16.35** (the '*company communications provisions*') have effect for the purposes of any provision of the *Companies Acts* that authorises or requires 'documents' or information to be sent or supplied by or to a company (including documents or information sent or supplied by or to the directors of a company acting on behalf of the company). [*CA 2006, ss 1143(1), 1148(3)*].

The provisions have effect subject to any requirement imposed, or contrary provision made, by or under any enactment (but a provision is not to be treated as contrary to the company communications provisions only on the grounds that it expressly authorises a document or information to be sent in hard copy form, in electronic form or by means of a website). In particular, the provisions have effect subject to the provisions in **39 REGISTRAR OF COMPANIES** in relation to documents and information sent or supplied to the Registrar. [*CA 2006, s 1143(2)–(4)*].

'*Document*' includes summons, notice, order or other legal process and registers. [*CA 2006, s 1148(1)*].

Documents or information to be sent or supplied

(a)     *to a company*, must be sent or supplied in accordance with the provisions in **16.24** to **16.27**; and

(b)     *by a company*, must be sent or supplied in accordance with the provisions in **16.28** to **16.33**.

## 16.23    Dealings with Third Parties

In relation to documents or information that are to be sent or supplied by one company to another, the provisions of (*b*) apply and not the provisions in (*a*) above.

[*CA 2006, s 1144*].

Where standard articles have been adopted, see

- *Model Articles, Art 48* (private companies)

- *Model Articles, Arts 79, 80* (public companies)

set out in APPENDIX 4 standard articles of association

These are expressed in very general terms and provide (in summary) that anything which is sent or supplied by or to the company under the articles can be sent or supplied in any way. *CA 2006* provides that any notice or document to be sent or supplied to a director in connection with directors' decision making can be sent by the means that director has asked for documents or notices to be sent or supplied.

### 16.24    Documents and information sent or supplied to a company

The provisions in **16.25** to **16.27** apply to documents and information sent or supplied to a company. They do not apply to documents or information sent or supplied by one company (eg a corporate shareholder) to another. In that case the provisions in **16.29** to **16.34** apply ie communications by a company. [*CA 2006, Sch 4 para 1*].

### 16.25    *Communications in hard copy form*

A document or information is validly sent or supplied to a company in '*hard copy*' form (see APPENDIX 1 DEFINITIONS) if it is sent or supplied

- by hand, or

- by posting a prepaid envelope

to

- an address specified by the company for the purpose;

- the company's registered office; or

- an address to which any provision of the *Companies Acts* authorises the document or information to be sent or supplied.

[*CA 2006, Sch 4 paras 2–4*].

*Authentication.* A document or information sent or supplied in hard copy form is sufficiently authenticated if it is signed by the person sending or supplying it. Despite this, where a document or information is sent or supplied by one person on behalf of another, a company's articles may require reasonable evidence of the authority of the former to act on behalf of the latter. [*CA 2006, s 1146(2)(4)*].

### 16.26    *Communications in electronic form*

A document or information is validly sent or supplied to a company in 'electronic form' (see APPENDIX 1 DEFINITIONS) if

- the company

    (i)    has agreed (generally or specifically) that the document or information may be sent or supplied in that form (and has not revoked that agreement); or

(ii)    is deemed to have so agreed by a provision in the *Companies Acts*;

- where the document or information is sent or supplied by electronic means, it is sent or supplied to an 'address'

(i)    specified for the purpose by the company (generally or specifically); or

(ii)    deemed by a provision in the *Companies Acts* to have been so specified; and

- where the document or information is sent or supplied in electronic form by hand or by post, it is sent or supplied to an address to which it could be validly sent if it were in hard copy form (see **16.25**).

'*Address*' includes a number or address used for the purposes of sending or receiving documents or information by electronic means.

[*CA 2006, s 1148(1), Sch 4 paras 5–7*].

*Authentication.* A document or information sent or supplied in electronic form is sufficiently authenticated

- if the identity of the sender is confirmed in a manner specified by the company; or

- where no such manner has been specified by the company, if the communication contains, or is accompanied by, a statement of the identity of the sender and the company has no reason to doubt the truth of that statement.

Despite this, where a document or information is sent or supplied by one person on behalf of another, a company's articles may require reasonable evidence of the authority of the former to act on behalf of the latter.

[*CA 2006, s 1146(3)(4)*].

**16.27**  *Other agreed forms of communication*

A document or information that is sent or supplied to a company otherwise than in hard copy form (see **16.25**) or electronic form (see **16.26**) is validly sent or supplied if it is sent or supplied in a form or manner that has been agreed by the company.

[*CA 2006, Sch 4 para 8*].

**16.28  Communications by a company**

The provisions in **16.29** to **16.33** below apply to documents or information sent or supplied by a company. [*CA 2006, Sch 5 para 1*].

**16.29**  *Communications in hard copy form*

A document or information is validly sent or supplied by a company in '*hard copy*' form (see APPENDIX 1 DEFINITIONS) if it is

- handed to the intended recipient; or

- sent or supplied by hand or by posting a prepaid envelope to

(i)    an address specified for the purpose by the intended recipient;

(ii)    a company at its registered office;

(iii)    a person in his capacity as a member of the company at his address as shown in the company's register of members;

(iv)    a person in his capacity as a director of the company at his address as shown in the company's register of directors;

(v)     an address to which any provision of the *Companies Acts* authorises the document or information to be sent or supplied; or

(vi)    where the company is unable to obtain an appropriate address falling within (i)–(v) above, the intended recipient's last address known to the company.

The requirement to supply in hard copy has effect, where an election is in force under *CA 2006, s 128B* (option to keep information on the central register) as if the reference in (iii) to the register of members was a reference to the register kept by the Registrar of companies and as if the reference in (iv) to the register of directors was a reference to the register kept by the Registrar of companies.

[*CA 2006, Sch 5, paras 2–4; SBEE 2015, Sch 5, paras 34, 35; SI 2015 No 321, Reg 6*].

See **16.35** below for deemed delivery of documents and information.

**16.30** *Communications in electronic form*

A document or information is validly sent or supplied by a company in electronic form if

(a)    it is sent or supplied to

(i)     a person who has agreed (generally or specifically) that the document or information may be sent or supplied in that form (and has not revoked that agreement); or

(ii)    a company that is deemed to have so agreed by a provision in the *Companies Acts*;

(b)    where the document or information is sent or supplied by electronic means, it is sent or supplied to an 'address'

(i)     specified for the purpose by the intended recipient (generally or specifically); or

(ii)    where the intended recipient is a company, deemed by a provision of the *Companies Acts* to have been so specified; and

(c)    where the document or information is sent or supplied in electronic form by hand or by post, it is

(i)     handed to the intended recipient; or

(ii)    sent or supplied to an address to which it could be validly sent if it were in hard copy form (see **16.29**).

'*Address*' includes a number or address used for the purposes of sending or receiving documents or information by electronic means.

[*CA 2006, s 1148(1), Sch 5 paras 5–7*].

See **16.34** below for the right of a member or debenture holder to require any document or information in hard copy form and **16.35** below for deemed delivery of documents and information.

**16.31** *Communications by means of a website*

A document or information is validly sent or supplied by a company if it is made available on a website and the following conditions are satisfied.

(1)    *Agreement to use of website*. A document or information may only be sent or supplied by the company to a person by being made available on a website if the person

(i)      has agreed (generally or specifically) that the document or information may be sent or supplied to him in that manner; or

(ii)     is taken to have so agreed under the provisions relating to deemed agreement by members or debenture holders (see below)

and has not revoked that agreement.

(2)   *Availability of document or information.* A document or information authorised or required to be sent or supplied by means of a website must be made available in a form, and by a means, that the company reasonably considers will enable the recipient to read it and to retain a copy of it. For this purpose, a document or information can be read only if

(i)      it can be read with the naked eye; or

(ii)     to the extent that it consists of images (eg photographs, pictures, maps, plans or drawings), it can be seen with the naked eye.

(3)   *Notification of availability.* The company must notify the intended recipient of

(i)      the presence of the document or information on the website;

(ii)     the address of the website;

(iii)    the place on the website where it may be accessed; and

(iv)     how to access the document or information.

The document or information is taken to be sent on the date on which that notification is sent (or, if later, the date on which the document or information first appears on the website after that notification is sent).

(4)   *Period of availability on website.* The company must make the document or information available on the website throughout

(i)      the period specified by any applicable provision of the *Companies Acts*;

(ii)     if no such period is specified, the period of 28 days beginning with the date on which the notification required as above is sent to the person in question.

For these purposes, a failure to make a document or information available on a website throughout the period required is disregarded if it is made available on the website for part of that period and the failure to make it available throughout that period is wholly attributable to circumstances that it would not be reasonable to have expected the company to prevent or avoid.

*Deemed agreement of members of company, etc to use of website.* Where a document or information is to be sent or supplied to a person

•      as a member of the company,

•      as a person nominated by a member (in accordance with the company's articles) to enjoy or exercise all or any specified rights of the member in relation to the company, or

•      as a person nominated by the member under *CA 2006, s 146* to enjoy information rights (see **26.11** MEMBERS)

to the extent that

•      the members of the company have resolved that the company may send or supply documents or information to members by making them available on a website, or

349

- the company's articles contain provision to that effect,

a person is taken to have agreed that the company may send or supply documents or information to him in that manner provided the following conditions are met.

(a) The person has been asked individually by the company to agree that the company may send or supply documents or information generally, or the documents or information in question, to him by means of a website.

(b) The company has not received a response within 28 days of the date on which the request was sent.

A person is not taken to have so agreed if the company's request did not state clearly what the effect of a failure to respond would be or if it was sent less than twelve months after a previous such request was made to him in respect of the same or a similar class of documents or information.

*CA 2006, ss 29, 30* (resolutions affecting a company's constitution, see **14.10** CONSTITUTION – MEMORANDUM AND ARTICLES) apply to a resolution under these provisions.

*Deemed agreement of debenture holders to use of website.* Where a document or information is to be sent or supplied to a person as holder of a company's debentures, to the extent that

- the 'relevant debenture holders' have duly resolved that the company may send or supply documents or information to them by making them available on a website, or

- the instrument creating the debentures in question contains provision to that effect,

a debenture holder is taken to have agreed that the company may send or supply documents or information to him in that manner provided the following conditions are met.

(i) The debenture holder has been asked individually by the company to agree that the company may send or supply documents or information generally, or the documents or information in question, to him by means of a website.

(ii) The company has not received a response within 28 days of the date on which the request was sent.

A person is not taken to have so agreed if the company's request did not state clearly what the effect of a failure to respond would be or if it was sent less than twelve months after a previous such request was made to him in respect of the same or a similar class of documents or information.

For these purposes, the '*relevant debenture holders*' are the holders of debentures of the company ranking pari passu for all purposes with the intended recipient and a resolution of the relevant debenture holders is duly passed if they agree in accordance with the provisions of the instruments creating the debentures.

*[CA 2006, Sch 5 paras 8–14].*

See **16.34** below for the right of a member or debenture holder to require any document or information in hard copy form and **16.35** below for deemed delivery of documents and information.

## 16.32 *Other agreed forms of communication*

A document or information that is sent or supplied otherwise than in hard copy (see **16.29**) or electronic form (see **16.30**) or by means of a website (see **16.31**) is validly sent or supplied if it is sent or supplied in a form or manner that has been agreed by the intended recipient.

[*CA 2006, Sch 5 para 15*].

16.33 *Supplementary provisions*

*Joint holders of shares or debentures.* Subject to anything in the company's articles, in relation to documents or information to be sent or supplied to joint holders of shares or debentures of a company

•    anything to be agreed or specified by the holder must be agreed or specified by all the joint holders;

•    anything authorised or required to be sent or supplied to the holder may be sent or supplied either

   (i)    to each of the joint holders; or

   (ii)   to the holder whose name appears first in the register of members or the relevant register of debenture holders.

[*CA 2006, Sch 5 para 16*].

*Death or bankruptcy of holder of shares.* Subject to anything in the company's articles, following the death or bankruptcy of a holder of a company's shares, documents or information required or authorised to be sent or supplied to the member may be sent or supplied to the persons claiming to be entitled to the shares in consequence of the death or bankruptcy

(a)    by name, or

(b)    by the title of representatives of the deceased, or trustee of the bankrupt, or by any like description,

at the 'address' in the UK supplied for the purpose by those so claiming.

Until such an address has been supplied, a document or information may be sent or supplied in any manner in which it might have been sent or supplied if the death or bankruptcy had not occurred.

'*Address*' includes a number or address used for the purposes of sending or receiving documents or information by electronic means.

For these purposes, bankruptcy of a person includes the sequestration of the estate of a person or a person's estate being the subject of a protected trust deed (within the meaning of the *Bankruptcy (Scotland) Act 1985*). In such a case, the reference (*b*) above to the trustee of the bankrupt is to be read as the permanent or interim trustee on the sequestrated estate or, as the case may be, the trustee under the protected deed.

[*CA 2006, s 1148(1), Sch 5 para 15*].

16.34 **Right of members and debenture holders to hard copy version**

Where a member of a company or a holder of a company's debentures has received a document or information from the company otherwise than in hard copy form, he is entitled to require the company to send him a version of the document or information in hard copy form.

The company must send the document or information in hard copy form within 21 days of receipt of the request. It may not make a charge for doing so.

If a company fails to comply with these provisions, an offence is committed by the company and every officer of it who is in default. A person guilty of such an offence is liable, on summary conviction, to a fine not exceeding level 3 on the standard scale and, for continued contravention, a daily default fine not exceeding one-tenth of level 3 on the standard scale. See **29.1** OFFENCES AND LEGAL PROCEEDINGS for the standard scale.

## 16.34    Dealings with Third Parties

[*CA 2006, s 1145*].

### 16.35 Deemed delivery of documents and information

The following provisions apply to determine when documents or information are deemed to have been delivered but subject to

- in their application to documents or information sent or supplied by a company to its members, any contrary provision of the company's articles;

- in their application to documents or information sent or supplied by a company to its debentures holders, any contrary provision in the instrument constituting the debentures; and

- in their application to documents or information sent or supplied by a company to a person otherwise than in his capacity as a member or debenture holder, any contrary provision in an agreement between the company and that person.

**Items sent by post.** Where

- a document or information is sent by post (whether in hard copy or electronic form) to an address in the UK, and

- the company is able to show that it was properly addressed, prepaid and posted,

it is deemed to have been received by the intended recipient 48 hours after it was posted (ignoring any part of a day that is not a working day).

**Items sent by electronic means.** Where

- a document or information is sent or supplied by electronic means, and

- the company is able to show that it was properly addressed,

it is deemed to have been received by the intended recipient 48 hours after it was sent (ignoring any part of a day that is not a working day).

**Items sent by means of a website.** Where a document or information is sent or supplied by means of a website, it is deemed to have been received by the intended recipient

- when the material was first made available on the website; or

- if later, when the recipient received (or is deemed to have received) notice of the fact that the material was available on the website. [*CA 2006, s 1147*].

# 17   Debt Finance – Debentures and Other Forms of Borrowing

**Cross-references.** See 2.6 ACCOUNTS: GENERAL for the right of debenture-holders to receive copies of the accounts; 2.7 ACCOUNTS: GENERAL for the right of debenture holders to demand an additional copy of the accounts; 22.5 DISTRIBUTIONS for restriction on paying up debentures out of unrealised profit; 38.16 REGISTERS for the register of debenture holders; 40 REGISTRATION OF CHARGES; 47.21 SHARES for the prohibition of public offers by private companies which provisions also apply to debentures; 45 SECURITY FOR COMPANY BORROWING.

**Background.** The provisions in this chapter apply, unless otherwise stated, with effect from 6 April 2008. They restate the provisions in *CA 1985* without making any change in the law.

## 17.1   WHAT IS "BORROWING"?

For the purposes of this chapter "borrowing" means debt obligations incurred by a company as a consequence of loans made to the company. The term "borrowing" is not defined in legislation and the interpretation of its meaning derives from common law – see for example *IRC v Port of London Authority* [1923] AC 507, 92 LJKB 655, HL, *Potts' Executors v IRC* [1951] AC 443, [1951] 1 All ER 76, HL (it is the legal nature and form of the transaction which determines whether it is "borrowing") This chapter does not therefore deal with other aspects of company financing such as:

- Share capital
- Factoring/invoice discounting
- Conditional and/or credit sales of goods (including retention of title)
- Lease financing

## 17.2   COMPANY'S POWER TO BORROW GENERALLY

A power to borrow for the purposes of the company's business is implied in the case of a trading or commercial company as long as the power is not expressly prohibited (see, for example, *David Payne & Co Ltd, Re, Young v David Payne & Co Ltd* [1904] 2 Ch 608, 73 LJ Ch 849, CA). A non-trading company will generally include in its articles an express power to borrow for the purposes of the business.

## 17.2    Debt Finance – Debentures and Other Forms of Borrowing

Restrictions on borrowing may be

*        contained in a company's articles;

*        imposed on the company by resolution of the members; or

*        included in the terms of a contract, loan agreement or trust deed.

Even where there are limitations on a company's power to borrow, any further borrowing cannot be called into question on the grounds of lack of capacity by reason of anything in the company's constitution and, in favour of a person dealing with a company in good faith, the power of the directors to bind the company is deemed to be free of any limitation under the company's constitution. [*CA 2006, ss 39, 40*]. See **16.1** and **16.2 DEALINGS WITH THIRD PARTIES**.

### 17.3    Directors' powers to authorise borrowing and charge company property

A company's articles will usually contain a provision allowing the directors to exercise the company's powers to borrow money (but only up to any limit in the articles, see *Irvine v Union Bank of Australia* (1877) 2 App Cas 366, PC). Where a company has adopted standard articles, see

*        *Table A 1985, Art 70*

*        *Model Articles, Arts 3, 4* (private companies

*        *Model Articles, Arts 3, 4* (public companies)

These all provide (in summary) that the business of the company will be managed by the directors who may exercise all the powers of the company including, (although this is not expressly set out in the standard articles) the power to borrow on behalf of the company.

Where a company has the power to borrow, it also has an implied or incidental power to charge all or any part of its property to secure past or future debts (*Patent File Co, Re, ex p Birmingham Banking Co* (1870) 6 Ch App 83) including a charge by way of fixed security or by way of a floating charge (see **17.5**). The directors have authority to grant security and, notwithstanding any limitations in the company's constitution, a third party who deals with the company in good faith (*CA 2006 ss 39, 40* and *41*) is entitled to rely on the power of the directors to bind the company, free of any limit under the company's constitution.

### 17.4    Types of borrowing

Companies are able to borrow from a wide range of sources including banks ,venture capital companies and their own directors and shareholders. Borrowings from directors can be in the form of unsecured directors' loan accounts or more formally by the granting of a debenture. Venture capital funding is usually provided in return for an equity stake in the company.

Loan facilities (secured or unsecured) – A common type of borrowing is a loan facility (typically from a bank) which can either be

*        Committed (eg term/revolving loan) ie the lender makes the funds available subject to certain specified conditions precedent, the right to demand repayment arises only on certain specific acts of default, provisions for repayment and provision is made in the agreement for draw down of the facilities and for lender's returns (for example interest and commissions). The distinction between a term loan and a revolving facility is that a term loan is provided over a specific period of time and is repayable at or by the end of that specified period. A revolving facility by contrast allows the company to draw down and repay funds as required (and as provided for in a facilities agreement); or

- On-demand (eg an overdraft/working capital facility) ie the lender makes funds available and demands repayment at its own discretion.

These types of loans can be syndicated by several lenders. In this case the loan is made by several lenders, each one puts forward a percentage of the principal sum but then one or more of them act as agent and administer the loan on behalf of the syndicate.

Project/property finance. This can used to finance large scale projects such as infrastructure. Project finance involves not only debt borrowings provided by banks but also (and typically) some equity finance and often some government funding.

Debt securities. In this category are debentures, a term which describes both the document itself and the type of transaction and includes debenture stock and bonds – see **17.6**.

Asset based lending. These are loans secured by a variety of the company's assets (liquid or fixed assets).

Loans of any description can be secured or unsecured – see **45** SECURITY FOR COMPANY BORROWING and **17.5** FIXED AND FLOATING CHARGES)

## 17.5  Fixed and Floating charges

As with the term "borrowing" the terms fixed and floating charge are not defined in legislation. A fixed charge is a present charge over present or future property which fastens on the property when the charge is executed (*Illingworth v Houldsworth* [1904] AC 355, 73 LJ Ch 739, HL) or in the case of future property when the property comes into existence as long as it is capable of being ascertained (*Yorkshire Woolcombers Association Ltd, Re, Houldsworth v Yorkshire Woolcombers Association Ltd* [1903] 2 Ch 284, 72 LJ Ch 635, CA). The company cannot deal with or dispose of property subject to a fixed charge without the consent of the chargee.

A 'floating charge' is an immediate and present security which floats over a company's assets so that the company is allowed to carry on its business and is left free to manage the assets which are subject to the charge. Management of the assets continues by the borrower until some event occurs or some act is done which causes the charge to attach to specific assets which are subject to the charge (see *Re Yorkshire Woolcombers* (above) and *Brightlife Ltd, Re* [1987] Ch 200, [1986] BCLC 418). At this point the charge crystallises and:

- the chargee's rights are converted into the individual assets in the fund and any property acquired thereafter which falls within the scope of the charge;

- the company is no longer free to manage the property or deal with the property without the consent of the chargee; and

- no new charge is created and therefore no new registration at Companies House of the security under *CA 2006, s 860* is required – see **40** REGISTRATION.

The essence of a floating charge is that it is a charge, not on any particular asset, but on a fluctuating body of assets which remain under the management and control of the company who can dispose of and deal with the charged asset and, if necessary, remove it from the security without the consent of the chargee.

The instrument creating a charge will say whether it is to take effect as a fixed or floating charge but in deciding whether a charge is fixed or floating: (1) the instrument of charge is construed to establish the intention of the parties with regard to their mutual rights and obligations in respect of the charged assets; and (2) the charge is then characterised as a matter of law (*Agnew v IRC* [2001] UKPC 28, [2001] 2 AC 710, [2001] 2 BCLC 188 followed in *Spectrum Plus Ltd, Re, National Westminster Bank plc v Spectrum Plus Ltd* [2005] UKHL 41, [2005] 2 AC 680, [2005] 2 BCLC 269.)

**17.6    DEBENTURES**

A company may raise capital by means of loans evidenced by 'debentures'. '*Debentures*' include debenture stock, bonds and any 'other securities' of a company, whether or not constituting a charge on the assets of the company. [*CA 2006, s 738*]. The term is thus used to cover a variety of loan transactions depending upon the circumstances and is not confined to a document actually describing itself as a debenture. In *Slavenburg's Bank NV v Intercontinental Natural Resources Ltd* [1980] 1 All ER 955, [1980] 1 WLR 1076 a debenture was held to be a document which creates or acknowledges an indebtedness. A note by which a company undertook to repay a loan but gave no security was held to be a debenture in *British India Steam Navigation Co v IRC* (1881) 7 QBD 165. The document may need to disclose an agreement to repay the advance (*Topham v Greenside Glazed Fire-Brick Co* (1887) 37 Ch D 281 and *R v Findlater* [1939] 1 KB 594, [1939] 1 All ER 82, CA). '*Other securities*' includes a guarantee (*Temperance Loan Fund Ltd v Rose* [1932] 2 KB 522, 101 LJKB 609, CA; *IRC v Henry Ansbacher & Co* [1963] AC 191, [1962] 3 All ER 843, HL).

**17.7    Debenture stock and loan stock**

Where money is to be borrowed from many lenders, it may be more convenient to issue 'debenture stock' or 'loan stock'.

**Debenture stock**. The term 'debenture stock' is normally used for stock which is secured by a mortgage or charge. The lender has a certificate which gives him a right to a certain sum, which is a proportion of a larger sum, and which may be transferred, in whole or in part, subject to the terms of the issue.

The usual charge is a floating charge (ie on unascertained assets and property of the company). For cases of debenture stock accompanied by floating charges see, for example, *Robson v Smith* [1895] 2 Ch 118 and *George Barker (Transport) Ltd v Eynon* [1974] 1 All ER 900, [1974] 1 WLR 462, CA. Where there is a fixed charge on specific assets of the company, once the charge is registered (see **40 REGISTRATION OF CHARGES**) the holder has an immediate security over those assets so that the company may not realise them without his consent.

In the event of default by the company, the holder of secured debenture stock has, in addition to the remedies of an unsecured creditor (see below), the power to appoint a receiver or administrator and the power of sale (although in practice these powers will generally be enforced on his behalf by the trustees where there is a trust deed). See, however, **17.14** for the rights of preferential creditors in the case of a floating charge.

**Loan stock**. If the stock is unsecured, the term 'loan stock' is generally used. It is usual for the loan stock to be constituted by a trust deed which contains a covenant by the company for the payment of capital (either at a fixed date or on the happening of a certain event, eg a winding up) and interest. In the event of default by the company, the holder may sue for his money and present a petition for winding up.

**17.8    Convertible debentures**

A convertible debenture contains an option entitling the holder to convert into ordinary or preference shares of the company at stated times and in stated proportions.

**17.9    Irredeemable and perpetual debentures**

A condition imposed in debentures, or in a deed for securing debentures, is not invalid by reason only that the debentures are made irredeemable or redeemable only on the

•        happening of a contingency (however remote), or

- expiration of a period (however long),

any rule of equity to the contrary notwithstanding.

This applies to debentures whenever issued and to deeds whenever executed.

[*CA 2006, s 739*].

The company must be authorised by its articles to issue irredeemable debentures but where it has issued such stock, the stock is irredeemable only as long as the company is a going concern (*Southern Brazilian Rio Grande do Sul Rly Co Ltd, Re* [1905] 2 Ch 78, 74 LJ Ch 392).

## 17.10 ISSUE OF DEBENTURES

For the duties of a company as to the issue of debentures and certificates of debenture stock, see **44 Securities: Certification and Transfers**.

Debentures, unlike shares, can be issued at a discount. There must, however, be no possibility that *shares* could be issued at a discount as a result, eg because debentures are, or will be, convertible into shares (see *Moseley v Koffyfontein Mines Ltd* [1904] 2 Ch 108, 73 LJ Ch 569, CA).

Debentures may also be issued (or redeemed) at a premium.

A contract with a company to take up and pay for debentures may be enforced by an order for specific performance. [*CA 2006, s 740*]. In *Kuala Pahi Rubber Estates Ltd v Mowbray* (1914) 111 LT 1072, CA it was held that where a company had forfeited debentures it was not in a position to ask for specific performance on calls made to a shareholder and not paid.

## 17.11 Registration of allotments

A company must register an allotment of debentures as soon as practicable and in any event within two months after the date of allotment.

If the company fails to do so, an offence is committed by the company and every officer of the company who is in default. A person guilty of such an offence is liable, on summary conviction, to a fine not exceeding level 3 on the standard scale and, for continued contravention, a daily default fine not exceeding one-tenth of level 3 on the standard scale. See **29.1 Offences and Legal Proceedings** for the standard scale.

[*CA 2006, s 741*].

## 17.12 POWER TO RE-ISSUE REDEEMABLE DEBENTURES

Where a company has redeemed debentures previously issued, it has, and is always deemed to have had, power to re-issue the debentures (either by re-issuing the same debentures or issuing other debentures in their place). This is subject to the conditions that

(a) no expressed or implied provision to the contrary is contained in the company's articles or in any contract made by the company; and

(b) the company has not, by passing a resolution to that effect or by some other act, manifested its intention that the debentures should be cancelled.

On the re-issue, the person entitled to the debentures has (and is deemed always to have had) the same priorities as if the debentures had never been redeemed.

# 17.12   Debt Finance – Debentures and Other Forms of Borrowing

The re-issue of a debenture or the issue of another debenture in its place under these provisions is treated as the issue of a new debenture for stamp duty purposes but it is not so treated for the purposes of any provision limiting the amount or number of debentures to be issued.

A person lending money on the security of a re-issued debenture which appears to be duly stamped may give the debenture in evidence in any proceedings to enforce his security without payment of the stamp duty or any penalty in respect of it unless

(i)     he had notice that the debenture was not duly stamped; or

(ii)    but for his negligence he might have discovered that fact.

In that case the company is liable to pay the proper stamp duty and penalty.

[*CA 2006, s 752*].

## 17.13   DEPOSIT OF DEBENTURES TO SECURE ADVANCES

Where a company has deposited any of its debentures to secure advances from time to time on current account or otherwise, the debentures are not treated as redeemed by reason only of the company's account ceasing to be in debit while the debentures remain so deposited. [*CA 2006, s 753*].

## 17.14   PRIORITIES WHERE DEBENTURES SECURED BY A FLOATING CHARGE

See 17.5 for fixed and floating charges.

Where debentures of a company registered in England and Wales or Northern Ireland are secured by a charge that, as created, was a floating charge, then if

*   possession is taken, by or on behalf of the holders of the debentures, of any property comprised in or subject to the charge, and

*   the company is not at that time in the course of being wound up,

the company's preferential debts must be paid out of assets coming to the hands of the person taking possession in priority to any claims for principal or interest in respect of the debentures. Payments must be recouped, as far as possible, out of the assets of the company available for payment of general creditors.

Preferential creditors are:

*   Contributions to occupational pension schemes and state scheme premiums.

*   Remuneration due to employees in respect of the whole or any part of the period of four months before the 'relevant date' up to a maximum (currently £800)

*   Any amount owed as accrued holiday remuneration in respect of any period of employment before the relevant date to a person whose employment has been terminated, whether before, on or after that date.

*   Any money advanced to the company that has been applied in paying remuneration or accrued holiday pay which would otherwise have been preferential.

The '*relevant date*' is the date of possession being taken.

[*CA 2006, s 754; IA 1986, Sch 6; EmA 2002, Sch 26*].

## 17.15  LIABILITIES OF TRUSTEES OF DEBENTURES

Subject to below, any provision contained in a trust deed for securing an issue of debentures (or any contract with the holders of debentures secured by a trust deed) is void in so far as it would have the effect of exempting a trustee from, or indemnify him against, liability for breach of trust where he fails to show the degree of care and diligence required of him as a trustee, having regard to the provisions of the trust deed conferring on him any powers, authorities or discretions.

The above does not, however,

(a)   invalidate a release otherwise validly given in respect of anything done, or omitted to be done, by a trustee before the release is given;

(b)   invalidate any provision allowing such a release to be given

   (i)   on the agreement of a majority of not less than 75% in value of the debenture-holders present and voting in person or, where proxies are permitted, by proxy at a meeting summoned for the purpose; and

   (ii)   either with respect to specific acts or omissions or on the trustee dying or ceasing to act;

(c)   invalidate any provision in force on

   (i)   1 July 1948 in a case where *CA 1985, s 192* was in force immediately before 6 April 2008, or

   (ii)   1 July 1961 in a case when *Companies (Northern Ireland) Order 1986* then applied

   so long as any person then entitled to the benefit of that provision remains a trustee; or

(d)   deprive any person of any exemption or right to be indemnified in respect of anything done or omitted to be done by him while any provision within (*c*) above was in force.

While *any* trustee remains entitled to the benefit of a provision under (*c*) or (*d*) above, the benefit may also be given to

•   all trustees of the deed (present and future), or

•   any named trustees or proposed trustees of it

by a resolution passed by a majority of not less than 75% in value of the debenture holders present in person or, where proxies are permitted, by proxy at a meeting summoned for the purpose. A meeting for that purpose must be summoned in accordance with the provisions of the deed or, if the deed makes no provision for summoning meetings, in a manner approved by the court.

[*CA 2006, ss 750, 751*].

## 17.16  RIGHT OF DEBENTURE HOLDERS TO A COPY OF THE DEED

A debenture holder is entitled, on request and on payment of a fee (see APPENDIX 3 – COMPANIES HOUSE FEES), to be provided with a copy of any trust deed which secures the debentures.

## 17.16   Debt Finance – Debentures and Other Forms of Borrowing

See **36.2** Records for the provisions relating to providing copies.

In default, of providing a copy, an offence is committed by every officer of the company who is in default. A person guilty of such an offence is liable, on summary conviction, to a fine not exceeding level 3 on the standard scale and, for continues contravention, a daily default fine not exceeding one-tenth of level 3 on the standard scale. See **29.1** Offences and Legal Proceedings for the standard scale.

In the case of such a default, the court may direct that the copy required is sent to the person concerned.

[*CA 2006, s 749*].

### 17.17 DEBENTURES TO BEARER (SCOTLAND)

Debentures to bearer issued in Scotland are valid and binding according to the terms of their issue despite anything in the statute of the Scots Parliament of 1696, chapter 25. [*CA 2006, s 742*].

# 18 Directors

**Cross-references.** See **16.2** DEALINGS WITH THIRD PARTIES for the power of directors to bind a company; **16.3** DEALINGS WITH THIRD PARTIES for transactions involving directors or their associates; **39.1** REGISTRAR OF COMPANIES.

## 18.1 Directors

### 18.1 MEANING OF THE TERM 'DIRECTOR' AND OTHER ASSOCIATED TERMS

(1) The definition of a director in *Companies Act 2006 (CA 2006)* is not exhaustive – *section 250* provides that the term *Director* includes any person occupying the position of director, by whatever name called. [*CA 2006, s 250*].

In *Re Eurostem Maritime Ltd* (1987) PCC 190, Mervyn Davies J thought that the words 'occupying the position of director' (which were also used in *CA 1985*) covered any person who *de facto* acted as a director despite his appointment being invalid or whether the person had in fact been appointed at all.

However in *Lo-Line Electric Motors Ltd, Re* [1988] Ch 477, [1988] BCLC 698 Browne-Wilkinson V-C thought the words "by whatever names called" (in *CA 1985*) were merely a recognition of the use of alternative terms for 'director' in a company's constitution eg governor or manager.

Because the only definition given in *CA 2006* is not exhaustive, in practice, it is necessary to examine the function of the person, the constitution of the company, and the terms of any contract between the company and the person, to decide whether a person is occupying the position of director.

The *chairman* is a member of the board (usually acting in a non-executive capacity) who is usually elected to that position by the board. Strictly, the chairman is chairman of the board and not chairman of the company.

The *managing director/CEO* is an executive director whose duties may be prescribed by the articles and who is presumed to have authority to deal with all areas of the business.

A *de facto director* a person acting as a director whether or not that person has been validly appointed, invalidly appointed or is just assuming to act as a director without any appointment at all – see the *Re Lo-Line Electric Motors* case referred to above and see also the case *Re Paycheck Services 3 Ltd (Holland v Revenue & Customs)* [2010] UKSC 51. This latter case decide that the critical test in deciding whether a person is a de facto director is whether the person has assumed to act as a director, exercising the powers and discharging the functions of a director. See below for the link between a de facto director and a shadow director

An *executive director* is a member of the board authorised to carry out certain day-to-day functions including entering into contracts, managing staff and assets, etc. In many cases executive directors have a full time service contract with the company and can be treated as employees.

A *non-executive director* is a director who sits as part of the decision-making board but without executive authority and who is brought onto the board for other skills. In particular non-executives play an important part in the corporate governance of a company (see **15 Corporate Governance**).

An *alternate director* acts as a proxy for the person who appoints him and has the right to receive all documents etc (eg notices of meeting) sent to the other directors (see **18.10**). The rights of an alternate are usually set out in the company's articles of association. The Model Articles for private companies do not contain such provisions but the Model Articles for public companies do (Articles 25–27) (see **Appendix 4 Standard Articles of Association**)

(2) *Shadow director*

*Companies Act 2006, s 251(1)* defines a '*shadow director*', in relation to a company, as a person in accordance with whose directions or instructions the directors of the company are 'accustomed to act'. But

- so that a person is not to be deemed a shadow director by reason only that the directors act on advice given by him in a professional capacity, in accordance with instructions, a direction, guidance or advice given by that person in the exercise of a function conferred by or under an enactment or in accordance with guidance or advice given by that person in that person's capacity as a Minister of the Crown (within the meaning of the Ministers of the *Crown Act 1975*); and

- a body corporate is not to be regarded as a shadow director of any of its subsidiary companies for the purposes of

  (i) *CA 2006, ss 170–181* (general duties of directors, see **18.23** to **18.26**),

  (ii) *CA 2006, ss 188, 189* (service contracts, see **18.54**),

  (iii) *CA 2006, ss 190–196* (substantial property transactions, see **18.59** and **18.60**),

  (iv) *CA 2006, ss 197–214* (loans, quasi-loans and credit transactions, see **18.61** to **18.67**),

  (v) *CA 2006, ss 215–222* (payment for loss of office, see **18.47** to **18.51**), or

  (vi) *CA 2006, s 231* (contracts with sole member who is also a director, see **18.58**)

only because the directors of the subsidiary are accustomed to act in accordance with its directions or instructions.

[*CA 2006, s 251; SBEE s 89, 90*].

The acts of any one of several directors in complying with the directions of an outsider cannot make that outsider a shadow director of the company. Such an outsider cannot be a shadow director unless the whole of the board, or at very least a governing majority of it, are accustomed to act on that outsider's directions. '*Accustomed to act*' refers to acts on more than one occasion, over a period of time and as a regular course of conduct (*Unisoft Group Ltd (No 3), Re* [1994] 1 BCLC 609, [1994] BCC 766). See also the *Re Paycheck* case (above) which decided that a person can be both a shadow director and a de facto director simultaneously. Before this case was decided it was always thought that the roles were mutually exclusive.

(3) *Persons connected with a director*

The following persons (and only those persons) are connected with a director of a company unless the person is himself a director of the company.

(a) Members of the director's family, ie

  (i) the director's spouse or civil partner;

  (ii) any other person (whether of a different sex or the same sex) with whom the director lives as partner in an enduring family relationship (other than the director's grandparent or grandchild, sister, brother, aunt or uncle, or nephew or niece);

  (iii) the director's children or stepchildren;

  (iv) any children or stepchildren of a person within paragraph (ii) above (and who are not children or step-children of the director) who live with the director and have not attained the age of 18;

  (v) the director's parents.

(b) A body corporate with which the director is connected (see (4) below).

(c) A person acting in his capacity as trustee of a trust,

    (i)    the beneficiaries of which include the director or a person who by virtue of (*a*) or (*b*) is connected with him, or

    (ii)    the terms of which confer a power on the trustees that may be exercised for the benefit of the director or any such person,

other than a trust for the purposes of an employees' share scheme or a pension scheme.

(d)    A person acting in his capacity as partner of

    (i)    the director; or

    (ii)    a person who, by virtue of (*a*), (*b*) or (*c*) above, is connected with that director.

(e)    A firm that is a legal person under the law by which it is governed and in which

    (i)    the director is a partner;

    (ii)    a partner is a person who, by virtue of (*a*), (*b*) or (*c*) above, is connected with the director; or

    (iii)    a partner is a firm in which the director is a partner or in which there is a partner who, by virtue of (*a*), (*b*) or (*c*) above, is connected with the director.

[*CA 2006, ss 252, 253*].

(4) *Director 'connected with' a body corporate*

A director is connected with a body corporate if, but only if, he and the persons connected with him are together

- interested in shares comprised in the equity share capital of that body corporate of a nominal value equal to at least 20% of that share capital; or

- entitled to exercise or control the exercise of more than 20% of the voting power at any general meeting of that body. This includes voting power whose exercise is controlled by a body corporate controlled by the director.

See (6) below for the interpretation of 'an interest in shares'.

Shares in a company held as treasury shares, and any voting rights attached to such shares, are disregarded for these purposes. See **34.19** for the meaning of 'treasury shares'.

For the avoidance of circularity in the application of *s 252* above (the meaning of 'connected person'),

- a body corporate with which a director is connected is not treated for these purposes as connected with him unless it is also connected with him by virtue of (3)(*c*) or (*d*) above (connection as a trustee or partner); and

- a trustee of a trust, the beneficiaries of which include (or may include) a body corporate with which a director is connected is not treated for these purposes as connected with a director by reason only of that fact.

[*CA 2006, s 254*].

(5) *Director 'controlling' a body corporate*

A director of a company is taken to control a body corporate if, but only if

- he or any person connected with him is

    (i)    interested in any part of the equity share capital of that body; or

    (ii)   entitled to exercise or control the exercise of any part of the voting power at any general meeting of that body; and

- he, the persons connected with him and the other directors of that company, together are

    (i)    interested in more than 50% of that share capital; or

    (ii)   entitled to exercise or control the exercise of more than 50% of that voting power.

'*Voting power*' includes voting power whose exercise is controlled by a body corporate controlled by the director.

See (6) below for the interpretation of 'an interest in shares'.

Shares in a company held as treasury shares, and any voting rights attached to such shares, are disregarded for these purposes.

For the avoidance of circularity in the application of *s 252* above (the meaning of connected person),

- a body corporate with which a director is connected is not treated for these purposes as connected with him unless it is also connected with him by virtue of (3)(*c*) or (*d*) above; and

- a trustee of a trust, the beneficiaries of which include (or may include) a body corporate with which a director is connected is not treated for these purposes as connected with a director by reason only of that fact.

[*CA 2006, s 255*].

(6) *Interest in shares*

The following provisions have effect for the interpretation of references to an interest in shares under (4) and (5) above. Note that although the provisions are expressed only in relation to shares they apply also to debentures.

A reference to an interest in shares includes any interest of any kind whatsoever in shares. Any restraints or restrictions to which the exercise of any right attached to the interest is or may be subject are disregarded. It is immaterial that shares in which a person has an interest are unidentifiable.

Persons having a joint interest in shares are each deemed to have that interest.

(a)    *Rights to acquire shares.* A person is taken to have an interest in shares if he

- enters into a contract to acquire them;

- has a right to call for delivery of the shares to himself or to his order (whether the right or obligation is conditional or absolute); or

- has a right to acquire an interest in shares or is under an obligation to take an interest in shares (whether the right or obligation is conditional or absolute).

Rights or obligations to *subscribe* for shares are not to be taken for these purposes to be rights to acquire or obligations to take an interest in shares.

A person ceases to have an interest in shares by virtue of this provision

- on the shares being delivered to another person at his order either in fulfilment of a contract for their acquisition by him or in satisfaction of a right of his to call for their delivery;

- on a failure to deliver the shares in accordance with the terms of such a contract or on which such a right falls to be satisfied; and

- on the lapse of his right to call for the delivery of shares.

(b) *Right to exercise or control exercise of rights.* A person is taken to have an interest in shares if, not being the registered holder, he is entitled to

- exercise any right conferred by the holding of the shares, or

- control the exercise of any such right

and, for this purpose, a person is taken to be entitled to exercise or control the exercise of a right conferred by the holding of shares if he

- has a right (whether subject to conditions or not) the exercise of which would make him so entitled; or

- is under an obligation (whether or not so subject) the fulfilment of which would make him so entitled.

But a person is not taken to be interested in shares by these provisions by reason only that he has been appointed

- a proxy to exercise any of the rights attached to the shares; or

- by a body corporate to act as its representative at any meeting of a company or of any class of its members.

(c) *Bodies corporate.* A person is taken to be interested in shares if a body corporate is interested in them and

(i) the body corporate or its directors are accustomed to act in accordance with his directions or instructions; or

(ii) he is entitled to exercise or control the exercise of more than 50% of the voting power at general meetings of the body corporate.

For the purposes of (ii) above, where

- a person is entitled to exercise or control the exercise of more than 50% of the voting power at general meetings of a body corporate, and

- that body corporate is entitled to exercise or control the exercise of any of the voting power at general meetings of another body corporate,

the voting power mentioned in (ii) above is taken to be exercisable by that person.

(d) *Trusts.* Where an interest in shares is comprised in property held on trust, every beneficiary of the trust is taken to have an interest in shares, subject to the following.

- So long as a person is entitled to receive, during the lifetime of himself or another, income from trust property comprising shares, an interest in the shares in reversion or remainder or (as regards Scotland) in fee is disregarded.

- A person is treated as not interested in shares if and so long as he holds them under the law in force in any part of the UK as a bare trustee or as a custodian trustee or under the law in force in Scotland as a simple trustee.

- Any interest of a person is disregarded if subsisting by virtue of an authorised unit trust scheme (within the meaning of *FSMA 2000, s 237*); a scheme made under *Charities Act 1960, s 22* or *22A, Charities Act (Northern Ireland) 1964, s 25, Charities Act 1993, s 24, Charities Act 2011, s 96* or *100, Trustee Investments Act 1961, s 11* or *Administration of Justice Act 1982, s 42*; or the scheme set out in the *Schedule* to the *Church Funds Investment Measure 1958.*

- There is to be disregarded any interest of the Church of Scotland General Trustees or of the Church of Scotland Trust in shares held by them (and of any other person in shares held by those Trustees or that Trust otherwise than as simple trustees)

[*CA 2006, Sch 1*].

## 18.2 MINIMUM NUMBER OF DIRECTORS

A private company must have at least one director and a public company must have at least two directors. [*CA 2006, s 154*]. There is no longer an exception for public companies registered before 1 November 1929 to have only one director.

The articles of a company may provide for a higher minimum number. Where a company has adopted standard articles, see

- *Table A 1985, Reg 64*

set out in APPENDIX 4 STANDARD ARTICLES OF ASSOCIATION.

Where a public company has adopted standard articles, see

- *Model Articles (public companies), Art 28*

set out in APPENDIX 4 STANDARD ARTICLES OF ASSOCIATION for the power of members to call a meeting if the company has fewer than two directors and the director (if any) is unable or unwilling to appoint sufficient directors to make up the quorum or to call a general meeting to do so.

**One director to be a natural person.** Every company must have at least one director who is a natural person (ie an individual). This requirement is met if the office of director is held by a natural person as a corporation sole (eg the Archbishop of Canterbury) or otherwise by virtue of an office.

This provision will be replaced by provisions contained in *Small Business, Enterprise and Employment Act 2015 (SBEE 2015), ss 87 and 88* which provide (in summary) that a company will not be able to appoint a corporate director once the relevant provisions of *SBEE 2015* are in force. From that date all directors must be a natural person other than ones holding office as a corporation sole or otherwise by virtue of an office. Anyone who is a corporate director ceases to be one 12 months after *CA 2006, s 156A* (as provided for in *SBEE 2015*) comes into force. Regulations may make exceptions to these provisions. As at September 2018 the relevant provisions of *SBEE 2015* are not in force.

[*CA 2006, s 155* and *SI 2007 No 3495, Sch 4, para 46*].

## 18.2 Directors

The transition period for companies with corporate directors is dealt with in *CA 2006, s 156C*. This provides that after one year of *s 156A* coming into force, any remaining corporate directors will automatically cease to be directors (subject to any exceptions set out in regulations made under *s 156B*).

These provisions were originally scheduled to come into force in October 2016. However, BEIS has further delayed implementation of *s 87*. While no implementation date has been set for the time being, BEIS has indicated that it does intend to implement the prohibition, and publish regulations setting out exceptions to the prohibition, in due course.

As explained above, this anticipated ban on corporate directors is to be introduced by the *Small Business, Enterprise and Employment Act 2016* (*SBEEA 2016*), which will amend *CA 2006*. At the time this edition goes to press, there still remains no indication of when the ban is likely to come into force. The date has been pushed back yet again. No official announcement or indication of a new implementation date has been made by the Government, but it is understood that it still intends to implement the prohibition in future. Moreover, on 5 April 2018, Companies House published its 2018 to 2019 business plan, in which it confirms an intention to work in partnership with BEIS to implement the prohibition.

**Direction to make an appointment.** If a company is in breach of either of the above requirements (ie number of directors or requirement to have at least one director who is a natural person), the Secretary of State may direct the company to comply within a period of not less than one month or more than three months after the date of the direction. The company must comply by making the necessary appointment or appointments (if it has not already done so) and giving the required notice of them under *CA 2006, s 167* to the Registrar of Companies (see **18.4**) before the end of the period specified in the direction.

If a company fails to comply with a direction, an offence is committed by the company and every officer of the company who is in default. A person guilty of such an offence is liable, on summary conviction, to a fine not exceeding level 5 on the standard scale and, for continued contravention, a daily default fine not exceeding one-tenth of the greater of £5,000 or level 4 on the standard scale. See **29.1** Offences and Legal Proceedings for the standard scale. For this purpose, a shadow director (see **18.1(2)**) is treated as an officer of the company.

[*CA 2006, s 156; SI 2015 No 664, Sch 3*].

## 18.3 DIRECTOR ALSO ACTING AS SECRETARY

A director may also act as secretary.

**Acts done by person in a dual capacity.** A provision requiring or authorising a thing to be done by or to a director *and* the secretary of a company is not satisfied by its being done by or to the same person acting both as director and as, or in place of, the secretary. [*CA 2006, s 280*]. (See **13.1**.)

## 18.4 CHANGES IN DIRECTORS

Whenever there is a change either of directors (appointment or removal) or a change of directors' details, the company must update its own internal registers and notify Companies House.

**Notifying Companies House.** A company must give notice to the Registrar of Companies of any person becoming or ceasing to become a director on forms APO1 (appointment of director) or TMO1 (termination of appointment of director) or CHO1 (change of director's details) within 14 days of the change. Where a person becomes a director, the notice must contain a statement of the particulars of the new director that are required to be included in the company's register of directors and its register of directors' residential addresses (see **38.3** and **38.5** REGISTERS respectively) and be accompanied by a consent, by that person, to act in that capacity.

If default is made in complying with these provisions, an offence is committed by the company and every officer of the company who is in default. A person guilty of such an offence is liable, on summary conviction, to a fine not exceeding level 5 on the standard scale and, for continued contravention, a daily default fine not exceeding one-tenth of the greater of £5,000 or level 4 on the standard scale. See **29.1** OFFENCES AND LEGAL PROCEEDINGS for the standard scale. For this purpose, a shadow director (see **18.1(2)**) is treated as an officer of the company. [*CA 2006, s 167; SI 2015 No 664, Sch 3*].

**Listed companies.** See **33.30** PUBLIC AND LISTED COMPANIES for requirements to notify change of details of directors to a RIS under the FCA Listing Rules.

**18.5    Appointment and retirement by rotation**

The first directors of a company are appointed at the time of registration of the company (see **12.3** COMPANY FORMATION). Thereafter, the appointment of directors and their retirement by rotation is determined by the company's articles. Where a company has adopted standard articles, see

- *Table A 1985, Regs 73–80, 84*

- *Model Articles, Art 17* (private companies)

- *Model Articles, Arts 20, 21* (public companies)

set out in APPENDIX **4** STANDARD ARTICLES OF ASSOCIATION.

The UK Corporate Governance Code (see **15** CORPORATE GOVERNANCE) requires all directors of FTSE 350 companies to be subject to annual election by shareholders. For all other companies listed on the London Stock Exchange main market, directors should be subject to election by shareholders at the first annual general meeting after their appointment and then to re-election at intervals of no more than three years (Code main principle B.7 and Code provision B.7.1).

Where a company removes a director before the expiry of his term of office under *CA 2006, s 168* (see **18.9**)

- a vacancy created by the removal, if not filled at the meeting at which he is removed, may be filled as a casual vacancy; and

- a person appointed director in place of a person removed is treated, for the purpose of determining the time at which he or any other director is to retire, as if he had become director on the day on which the person in whose place he is appointed was last appointed a director.

[*CA 2006, s 168(3)(4)*].

**Appointment of directors of public company to be voted on individually.** Where it is proposed to appoint two or more persons as directors at a general meeting of a public company, a motion for the appointment must not be made by a single resolution unless a resolution that it should be so made has first been agreed to by the meeting without any vote being given against it. A resolution moved in contravention of this provision is void (whether or not its being so moved was objected to at the time) but where a resolution so moved is passed, no provision for the automatic reappointment of retiring directors in default of another appointment applies.

For these purposes, a motion for approving a person's appointment, or for nominating a person for appointment, is treated as a motion for his appointment.

Nothing in these provisions applies to a resolution amending the company's articles.

[*CA 2006, s 160*].

**18.6**  *Restrictions on appointments*

(1) *Minimum age requirement*

A person may not be appointed a director of a company until he is 16 years old. But the appointment of a director that does not take effect until he is 16 years old is a valid appointment.

Where the office of director of a company is held by a corporation sole, or otherwise by virtue of another office, the appointment to that other office of a person who has not attained the age of 16 years is not effective also to make him a director of the company until he attains the age of 16 years.

An appointment made in contravention of the above provisions is void. But this does not affect any liability of a person under any provision of the *Companies Acts* if he purports to act as director or acts as a shadow director (see **18.1(2)**) although he could not, because of these provisions, be validly appointed as a director.

*Exceptions.* The Secretary of State may provide, by Regulations, for cases in which a person who has not attained the age of 16 years may be appointed a director of a company.

*Transitional provisions.* Where

- a person was appointed a director of a company before 1 October 2008 and was not 16 years old on that date, or

- the office of director of a company was held by a corporation sole, or otherwise by virtue of another office, and the person appointed to that other office was not 16 years old on that date,

and the case is not one excepted by Regulations, that person ceased to be a director on that date.

The company must make the necessary consequential alteration in its register of directors but need not give notice to the Registrar of Companies of the change. If it appears to the Registrar of Companies (from other information) that a person has so ceased to be a director of a company, the Registrar must note that fact on the register.

[*CA 2006, ss 157–159*].

(2) *Upper age limit*

There is no upper age restriction unless the articles provide otherwise. Neither Table A nor the Model Articles contain such restrictions. The repeal of *CA 1985, s 293(3)* (age limit of 70 for a director not affecting the validity of acts done before it is discovered that his appointment has terminated) does not affect the validity of any acts done on or after 6 April 2007 by a person who was appointed and reached the age of 70 before 6 April 2007. [*SI 2006 No 3428, Sch 5 para 7*].

(3) *Other restrictions*

A person cannot be appointed a director of a company if

- he is an undischarged bankrupt (unless the court has given him permission to act for a particular company), or

- he has been disqualified from acting as a company director (unless the court has given him permission to act for a particular company) (see **18.11** et seq), or

- he is under the age of 16

(Companies House Guidance Booklet GP 1 Incorporation and names Chapter 2).

*Certain non-British or EEA nationals* are under restrictions as to what work they can do whilst in the UK. Further information can be obtained from the Home Office (Visas and Immigration). Details are available on the Home Office website at www.homeoffice.gov.uk

**18.7** *Validity of acts of directors*

The acts of a person acting as a director are valid even though that it is afterwards discovered that

- there was a defect in his appointment;

- he was disqualified from holding office;

- he had ceased to hold office; or

- he was not entitled to vote on the matter in question.

This applies even if the resolution for his appointment is void under *CA 2006, s 160* (appointment of directors of public company to be voted on individually, see **18.5**).

*Transitional provisions. CA 2006, s 161* applies to acts done by a director on or after 1 October 2007 but *CA 1985, s 285* continues to apply to acts done by a director before that date.

[*CA 2006, s 161; SI 2007 No 2194, Sch 3 para 4*].

See *Morris v Kanssen* [1946] AC 459, [1946] 1 All ER 586, HL, where a distinction was drawn between a defective appointment and no appointment at all.

**18.8** *Appointment of managing directors/other executive appointments*

Although the power to run a company is vested in the board as a whole, in practice the day to day decision making is delegated to committees of the board and/or the managing director or other executive officers usually under provisions in the company's articles of association- see for example *Table A 1985, reg 84* and *Model Articles, article 5* which provide for such delegation of authority.

**18.9 Removal of directors**

A company may by ordinary resolution remove a director before the expiration of his period of office, despite anything in any agreement between it and the director. Special notice (see **42.19** RESOLUTIONS AND MEETINGS) is required of the resolution (and of any resolution to appoint somebody at the same meeting instead of the director being removed). [*CA 2006, s 168(1)(2)*].

The provisions are not to be taken as

- depriving a person removed under them of compensation or damages payable to him in respect of the termination of his appointment as director or of any appointment terminating with that as director; or

- derogating from any power to remove a director that may exist apart from these provisions.

[*CA 2006, s 168(5)*].

## 18.9 Directors

It should also be noted that, although any provision in the articles requiring a special or extraordinary resolution to remove a director is overridden by *CA 2006, s 168* above, a company is not prevented from 'weighting' votes attached to shares even if the effect is to nullify the effects of *s 168*. See, for example, *Bushell v Faith* [1970] AC 1099, [1970] 1 All ER 53, HL, where the articles stated that, in the event of a resolution to remove a director, any shares held by that director carried three votes per share. This effectively increased each director's share of the votes on such a resolution from one-third to 60% so that a director could not be removed by an ordinary resolution.

**Director's right to protest removal.** On receipt of notice of an intended resolution to remove a director under the above provisions, the company must immediately send a copy of the notice to the director who is entitled to be heard on the resolution at the meeting (whether or not he is a member of the company). He may also make written representations of reasonable length to the company and request their notification to the members of the company. Unless received too late, the company must

- state the fact that representations have been made in any notice of the resolution given to members; and

- send a copy of the representations to every member to whom notice of the meeting is sent (whether before or after receipt of the representations by the company).

Where the representations are received too late or are not sent through the default of the company, the director may require the representations to be read out at the meeting (without affecting his right to be heard orally).

Copies of the representations need not be sent out, and the representation need not be read at the meeting, if, on application by the company or any other person claiming to be aggrieved, the court is satisfied that the rights conferred by these provisions are being abused. The court may order the company's costs (in Scotland, expenses) on the application to be paid, in whole or in part, by the director even if he is not a party to the application.

[*CA 2006, s 169*].

See also **18.21** for the possible removal of a director under the provisions of the company's articles.

## 18.10 ALTERNATE DIRECTORS

A company may make provision under its articles for directors to appoint alternates to act on their behalf. Where the company has adopted standard articles, see

- *Table A 1985, Regs 65–69*

- *Model Articles, Arts 25–27* (public companies)

set out in APPENDIX 4 STANDARD ARTICLES OF ASSOCIATION.

The Model Articles for private companies do not contain provision for the appointment etc of alternate directors. The provisions set out in the Model Articles for public companies can however be adapted as appropriate for private companies.

## 18.11 DISQUALIFICATION OF DIRECTORS

A court may (and in certain cases must) make a disqualification order against a person if one of the grounds in **18.12** to **18.18** is established. The effect of such an order is that, for the period specified in the order, the person must

(a)     not, without the leave of the court,

  (i)     be a director of a company;

  (ii)    act as receiver of a company's property (which includes acting as a manager, or as both receiver and manager but does not include acting as an administrative receiver); or

  (iii)   in any way, directly or indirectly, be concerned or take part in the promotion, formation or management of a company. In *R v Campbell* (1984) 78 Cr App Rep 95, [1984] BCLC 83, CA, the Court of Appeal held that a person subject to a disqualification order who, as a management consultant, advised on the financial management and restructuring of a company, could be (and, on the facts of the case, was) 'concerned . . . in the management' of that company, and thereby in breach of the order; and

(b)     not act as an insolvency practitioner.

Where a disqualification order is made against a person who is already subject to such an order or a disqualification undertaking, the periods specified in the orders (or the order and undertaking) run concurrently.

[*CDDA 1986, ss 1(1)(3), 22(10); IA 2000, s 5, Sch 4 para 2; Employment Act 2002 (EmA 2002), s 204(3)*].

Similar provisions apply in Northern Ireland where a person is subject to a disqualification order or undertaking under *Companies Directors Disqualification (Northern Ireland) Order 2002.* [*CDDA 1986, ss 12A, 12B; IA 2000, s 7(1); SI 2004 No 1941, Art 2; SI 2009 No 1941, Sch 1 para 85*].

Where a court contemplates making a compensation order against a director, it must be careful not to reduce or inhibit his means to pay such an order. See *R v Holmes* [1991] BCC 394 where the Court of Appeal held that a compensation order made against a director in the Crown Court was inconsistent with the disqualification order also made since the latter order would seriously diminish his ability to earn the means with which to pay the compensation.

In addition to the above, a person is automatically disqualified, without the need for a disqualification order, in the circumstances in **18.19** and may be disqualified under the provisions of the company's articles where **18.21** applies.

**Building societies and friendly societies.** The provisions above and in **18.12** to **18.19** apply to a building society or an incorporated friendly society as they apply to a company.

[*CDDA 1986, ss 22A, 22B; CA 1989, s 211; Friendly Societies Act 1992, Sch 21 para 8; SI 2008 No 948, Sch 1 para 106; SI 2009 No 1941, Sch 1 para 85*].

**Open-ended investment companies.** The provisions above and in **18.12** to **18.19** apply to open-ended investment companies with modifications. [*CDDA 1986, s 22E; SI 2009 No 1941, Sch 1 para 85*].

### 18.12 Disqualification for general misconduct

A court may make a disqualification order against a person in the following circumstances.

(a)     *He is convicted of an indictable offence* (whether on indictment or summarily) in connection with

  •     the promotion, formation, management, liquidation or striking off of a company;

- the receivership of a company's property; or

- his being an administrative receiver of a company.

The maximum period of disqualification is five years where the disqualification order is made by a court of summary jurisdiction and 15 years in any other case. For the wide interpretation given to 'in connection with the management of the company' see *R v Goodman* [1993] 2 All ER 789, [1994] 1 BCLC 349, CA.

An order under this provision may be made by

(i)     any court having jurisdiction to wind up the company involved;

(ii)    the court by or before which the person is convicted of the offence; or

(iii)   in the case of a summary conviction in England and Wales, any other magistrates' court acting in the same local justice area.

[*CDDA 1986, s 2; Deregulation and Contracting Out Act 1994, Sch 11 para 6; IA 2000, Sch 4 para 3; Courts Act 2003, Sch 8 para 300*].

(b)     *He has been 'persistently in default' in relation to provisions of the 'companies legislation'* requiring any return, account or other document to be filed with, delivered or sent, or notice of any matter to be given, to the Registrar of Companies.

'*Persistently in default*' may (without prejudice to its proof in any other matter) be conclusively proved by showing that, in the five years ending with the date of the application to the court, he has been 'adjudged guilty' (whether or not on the same occasion) of three or more defaults in relation to such provisions. See also *Arctic Engineering Ltd (No 2), Re* [1986] 2 All ER 346, [1986] BCLC 253.

'*Companies legislation*' means the Companies Acts and *IA 1986, Pts 1–7* (insolvency and winding up).

A person is treated as being '*adjudged guilty*' of a default in relation to any such provision if *either* he is convicted of an offence for contravention or failure to comply with that provision *or* a default order is made against him under

(i)     *CA 2006, s 452* (order requiring delivery of company's accounts, see **2.11** ACCOUNTS: GENERAL under the heading *Failure to file accounts and reports*);

(ii)    *CA 2006, s 456* (order requiring preparation of revised accounts, see **2.15** ACCOUNTS: GENERAL);

(iii)   *CA 2006, s 1113* (enforcement by the Registrar of Companies of company's filing obligations);

(iv)    *IA 1986, s 41* (enforcement of receiver's or manager's duty to make returns); or

(v)     *IA 1986, s 170* (corresponding provision for liquidator in winding up).

The maximum period of disqualification is five years.

An order may be made by any court having jurisdiction to wind up any of the companies involved.

[*CDDA 1986, s 3; CA 1989, Sch 10 para 35; SI 2008 No 948, Sch 1 para 106; SI 2009 No 1941, Sch 1 para 85*].

(c)     *In the course of the winding up of a company* it appears that he has

(i)  been guilty of an offence for which he is liable (whether he has been convicted or not) under *CA 2006, s 993* (fraudulent trading, see **16.19** DEALINGS WITH THIRD PARTIES); or

(ii)  otherwise been guilty, while an officer or liquidator of the company, receiver of the company's property or administrative receiver of the company, of any fraud in relation to the company or any breach of duty as such officer, etc.

The maximum period of disqualification is 15 years.

An order may be made by any court having jurisdiction to wind up any of the companies involved.

[*CDDA 1986, s 4; IA 2000, Sch 4 para 4; SI 2007 No 2194, Sch 4 para 46*].

(d)  *He is convicted of a 'summary offence'* (either on indictment or summarily) in consequence of a contravention of any provision of the 'companies legislation' requiring a return, account or other document to be filed with, delivered or sent, or notice of any matter to be given, to the Registrar of Companies where

(i)  during the five years ending with the date of the conviction, he has been convicted of a similar offence or offences or has had made against him one or more default orders under the provisions listed in (*b*)(i)–(v) above; and

(ii)  the number of convictions and/or default orders made against him (including the current summary conviction) totals three or more.

The maximum period of disqualification is five years.

An order may be made by the court by which he is convicted (or in England and Wales by any other magistrates' court acting in the same local justice area).

'*Companies legislation*' means the Companies Acts and *IA 1986, Pts 1–7* (insolvency and winding up).

[*CDDA 1986, s 5; Courts Act 2003, Sch 8 para 300; SI 2009 No 1941, Sch 1 para 85*].

(e)  *He has been convicted of a 'relevant foreign offence'.*

A relevant foreign offence is an offence committed outside Great Britain in connection with the promotion, formation, management, liquidation or striking off of a company (or any similar procedure) or the receivership of a company's property (or any similar procedure) in each case which corresponds to an indictable offence in Great Britain. If however the person has offered to give a disqualification undertaking, and it appears to the Secretary of State that the person has been convicted of a relevant foreign offence, the Secretary of State may accept the undertaking if it is expedient in the public interest that the Secretary of State should accept the undertaking (instead of applying or proceeding with an application for a disqualification order).

[*CDDA 1986, s 5A; SBEE 2015, s 104; SI 2015 No 1689, Reg 2*].

An application (to a court with jurisdiction to wind up companies) for the making against any person of a disqualification order under (*a*) to (*c*) above may be made by the Secretary of State; the official receiver; the liquidator; or any past or present member or creditor of any company in relation to which that person has committed, or is alleged to have committed, an offence or other default. [*CDDA 1986, s 16(2); IA 2000, Sch 4 para 11*].

In determining whether to make a disqualification order the court must in every case have regard to the matters set out in paras 1–4 (see **18.16**) and in a case where the person concerned is, or has been, a director of a company or overseas company also have regard to the matters set out in paras 5–7 (see **18.16**).

## 18.12 Directors

[*CDDA 1986, s 106; SBEE 2015, s 12C; SI 2015 No 1689, Reg 2*].

### 18.13 Disqualification for unfitness

There are both mandatory grounds (**18.14**) and discretionary grounds (**18.15**) whereby a court can make a disqualification order against a person as being unfit to act as a director. In either case the court must have regard to the provisions of **18.16** in determining his unfitness.

In determining whether to make a disqualification order the court must in every case have regard to the matters set out in paras 1–4 (see **18.16**) and in a case where the person concerned is, or has been, a director of a company or overseas company also have regard to the matters set out in paras 5–7 (see **18.16**).

[*CDDA 1986, s 106; SBEE 2015, s 12C; SI 2015 No 1689, Reg 2*].

### 18.14 *Mandatory grounds*

A court *must* make a disqualification order against a person if it is satisfied that

(a)     he is or has been a director (or shadow director, see **18.1**(2)) of a company which has at any time become insolvent (whether while he was a director or subsequently); and

(b)     his conduct as a director of that company (whether taken alone or taken together with his conduct as a director of one or more other companies or overseas companies) makes him unfit to be concerned in the management of a company. References to a person's conduct as a director of any company or overseas company include, where that company or overseas company has become insolvent, reference to that person's conduct in relation to any matter connected with or arising out of the insolvency.

A person may be included under (*a*) above where he has acted as a director even though not validly appointed or not appointed at all. To be disqualified as a *de facto* director, there must be clear evidence that either he had been the sole person directing the affairs of the company or, if there were others who were true directors, he acted on an equal footing with them in directing the affairs of the company. Where it is unclear whether his actions are referable to an assumed directorship or some other capacity (eg shareholder or consultant) the person must be given the benefit of doubt (*Re Richborough Furniture Ltd* [1996] 1 BCLC 507, [1996] BCC 155).

The minimum period of disqualification is two years and the maximum is 15 years.

A company becomes insolvent for these purposes if

•       it goes into liquidation at a time when its assets are insufficient for the payment of its debts and other liabilities and the expenses of winding up;

•       it enters administration; or

•       an administrative receiver of the company is appointed.

An application for the making of a disqualification order against any person may be made by the Secretary of State or, if he so directs, the official receiver in the case of a director or former director of a company which is being or has been wound up by the court in England and Wales. Except with the leave of the court, such an application cannot be made more than three years from the date on which the company became insolvent. In deciding whether an application can be made out of time, the court will consider the length of, and reasons for, the delay, the strength of the case against the director and the degree of prejudice caused to the director by the delay (*Probe Data Systems Ltd (No 3), Re* [1992] BCLC 405, [1992] BCC 110, CA). See also, *inter alia, Re Lo-Line Electric Motors Ltd* [1988] Ch 477, [1988] BCLC 698, [1988] 2 All ER 692 and *Re Crestjoy Products Ltd* [1990] BCLC 677, [1990] BCC 23.

If it appears, as the case may be, to the official receiver, liquidator, administrator or administrative receiver that the conditions for making an order under these provisions are satisfied, he must report that fact to the Secretary of State. See the *Insolvent Companies (Reports on Conduct of Directors) Rules 1996* (*SI 1996 No 1909*) and the *Insolvent Companies (Reports on Conduct of Directors) (Scotland) Rules 1996* (*SI 1996 No 1910*) for the form and content of such a report.

**Transitional provisions.** The amendments to *CDDA 1986, s 8* in respect of overseas companies apply in respect of the person's conduct as a director of an overseas company where that conduct occurs on or after 1 October 2015.

[*CDDA 1986, ss 6, 7; IA 2000, Sch 4 paras 5, 6; EmA 2002, Sch 17, paras 40–42; SBEE 2015, ss 106,108; SI 2015 No 1689, Reg 2, Sch 1*].

**Report of office holder.** The office-holder in respect of a company which is insolvent must prepare a report (a 'conduct report') about the conduct of each person who was a director (which includes shadow director) of the company

- on the insolvency date; and

- at any time during the period of three years ending with that date.

The 'insolvency date' means

- in the case of a company being wound up by the court, means the date on which the court makes the winding-up order (*see IA 1986, s 125*);

- in the case of a company being wound up by way of a members' voluntary winding up, means the date on which the liquidator forms the opinion that the company will be unable to pay its debts in full (together with interest at the official rate) within the period stated in the directors' declaration of solvency under *IA 1986, s 89*;

- in the case of a company being wound up by way of a creditors' voluntary winding up where no such declaration under *IA 1986, s 89* has been made, means the date of the passing of the resolution for voluntary winding up;

- in the case of a company which has entered administration, means the date the company did so; and

- in the case of a company in respect of which an administrative receiver has been appointed, means the date of that appointment.

For these purposes a company is insolvent if

- the company is in liquidation and at the time it went into liquidation its assets were insufficient for the payment of its debts and other liabilities and the expenses of the winding up;

- the company has entered administration; or

- an administrative receiver of the company has been appointed.

And for these purposes the 'office-holder' in respect of a company which is insolvent is

- in the case of a company being wound up by the court in England and Wales, the official receiver;

- in the case of a company being wound up otherwise, the liquidator;

- in the case of a company in administration, the administrator; and

- in the case of a company of which there is an administrative receiver, the receiver.

A conduct report must, in relation to each person, describe any conduct of the person which may assist the Secretary of State in deciding whether to exercise the power under *CDDA 1986, s 7(1)* (application by the Secretary of State) or *(2A)* (acceptance of a disqualification undertaking) in relation to the person.

The office-holder must send the conduct report to the Secretary of State before the end of

- the period of three months beginning with the insolvency date; or

- such other longer period as the Secretary of State considers appropriate in the particular circumstances.

If new information comes to the attention of an office-holder, the office-holder must send that information to the Secretary of State as soon as reasonably practicable. 'New information' is information which an office-holder considers should have been included in a conduct report prepared in relation to the company, or would have been so included had it been available before the report was sent.

If there is more than one office-holder in respect of a company at any particular time (because the company is insolvent by virtue of falling within more than one of the definitions of insolvency (above) at that time) the requirement to prepare a conduct report applies only to the first of the office-holders to be appointed.

In the case of a company which is at different times insolvent by virtue of falling within one or more different definitions of insolvency (above) references to the insolvency date are to be read as references to the first such date during the period in which the company is insolvent and the requirement to prepare a conduct report does not apply to an office-holder if at any time during the period in which the company is insolvent a conduct report has already been prepared and sent to the Secretary of State.

[*CDDA 1986, s 7A; SBEE 2015, s 107; SI 2016 No 321, Reg 3*].

In *Re Deaduck Ltd (in liq), Baker v Secretary of State for Trade and Industry* [2000] 1 BCLC 148, Neuberger J held that, in considering disqualification applications under *CDDA 1986, s 6* where the director had not been guilty of dishonest or commercially flagrantly culpable behaviour, there were two competing factors to be balanced

- the protection of the public against someone who had been found liable in respect of a charge which constituted conduct as a director which made him unfit to be concerned in the management of a company

as against

- the consideration that it would involve going further than *CDDA 1986* or relevant authorities contemplated, if every time a director was found to have failed in his duty, he was liable to be disqualified.

In *Cathie v Secretary of State for Business, Innovation and Skills* [2012] 2All ER (D) 86 the court at first instance said that once misconduct is found, a finding of unfitness (to be concerned in the management of a company) must necessarily follow unless there are "exceptional circumstances" and the burden is on the director to establish those exceptional circumstances. The Court of Appeal disagreed saying that the phrase "exceptional circumstances" should be avoided. The correct approach is for the court to consider the evidence as a whole including any extenuating circumstances and to decide whether the director has fallen below the standards of probity and competence appropriate for a director of a company.

*Disqualification undertakings.* Instead of applying for a disqualification order, the Secretary of State, if it appears to him to be expedient in the public interest that he should do so, may accept a 'disqualification undertaking' from any person that, for the period specified in the undertaking, he will comply with the conditions in **18.11**(*a*) and (*b*). The maximum period which may be specified in such an undertaking is 15 years and the minimum period is seven years. Where a disqualification undertaking is accepted by a person who is already subject to such an undertaking or to a disqualification order, the periods specified in those undertakings and orders run concurrently. In determining whether to accept a disqualification undertaking by any person, the Secretary of State

- may take account of matters other than criminal convictions; and

- as respects the person's conduct as a director of any company concerned, must have regard to the matters listed in **18.16**.

The court may, on the application of a person who is subject to a disqualification undertaking, reduce the period for which it is to be in force or provide for it to cease altogether.

[*CDDA 1986, ss 1A, 7, 8A (1), 12C; IA 2000, s 6, Sch 4 para 6; EmA 2002, Sch 17 paras 40, 42; SBEE 2015, s 106; SI 2015 No 1689, Reg 2*].

**18.15** *Discretionary grounds*

If it appears to the Secretary of State from investigation material, that is

- a report made by inspectors under *CA 1985, s 437* (see **25.4** INVESTIGATIONS) or *FSMA 2000, ss 167, 168, 169* or *284*, or

- information or documents obtained under *CA 1985, ss 437, 446E, 447, 448, 451A* or *453A* (see **25** INVESTIGATIONS), *Criminal Justice Act 1987, s 2, Criminal Law (Consolidation) (Scotland) Act 1995, s 28, CA 1989, s 83*, or *FSMA 2000, ss 165, 171, 172, 173* or *175*

that it is expedient in the public interest for a disqualification order to be made against any director, former director or shadow director of the company (either taken alone or taken together with his conduct as a director or shadow director of one or more other companies or overseas companies), he may apply to the High Court (in Scotland, the Court of Sessions) for such an order to be made against that person. The court may make a disqualification order where it is satisfied that the person's conduct in relation to the company makes him unfit to be concerned in the management of the company.

The maximum period of disqualification is 15 years.

[*CDDA 1986, s 8(1)(1A)(2); C(AICE)A 2004, Sch 2 para 28; CA 2006, s 1039; SI 2001 No 3649, Art 39; SI 2009 No 1941, Sch 1 para 85*].

*Disqualification undertakings.* Instead of applying for a disqualification order, the Secretary of State, if it appears to him to be expedient in the public interest that he should do so, may accept a 'disqualification undertaking' from any person that his conduct in relation to a company of which he is or has been a director or shadow director (either taken alone or taken together with his conduct as a director or shadow director of one or more other companies or overseas companies) makes him unfit to be concerned in the management of a company and, for the period specified in the undertaking, he will comply with the conditions in **18.11**(*a*) and (b) above. The maximum period which may be specified in such an undertaking is 15 years. Where a disqualification undertaking is accepted by a person who is already subject to such an undertaking or to a disqualification order, the periods specified in those undertakings and orders run concurrently. In determining whether to accept a disqualification undertaking by any person, the Secretary of State

- may take account of matters other than criminal convictions; and

- as respects the person's conduct as a director of any company concerned, must have regard to the matters listed in **18.16**.

The court may, on the application of a person who is subject to a disqualification undertaking, reduce the period for which it is to be in force or provide for it to cease altogether.

[*CDDA 1986, ss 1A, 8(2A), 8A, 9(1A); IA 2000, s 6; EmA 2002, s 204; SBEE 2015, s 106; SI 2015 No 1689, Reg 2*].

### Disqualification of persons who instruct unfit directors

*Section 105* of the *SBEE 2015* inserts new *CDDA, ss 8ZA–E*. They provide (in summary) that a court may make a disqualification order against a person ('P') if it is satisfied that either a disqualification order under *CDDA, s 6* or *s 8* has been made against a person who is, or has been, a director or that the Secretary of State has accepted a disqualification undertaking from such a person, and that P exercised the requisite amount of influence over that person. 'Requisite amount of influence' is defined in *CDDA, s 8ZA (2)–(3)*. Disqualification undertakings may also be accepted in either case.

**Transitional provisions.** These new provisions apply where 'P's' conduct and the exercise by 'P' of the requisite amount of influence occur on or after 1 October 2015.

[*SBEE 2015, s 105; CDDA 1986, ss 8ZA–E; SI 2015 No 1689*].

**18.16**   *Matters for determining unfitness of directors*

In determining whether either a person's conduct as a director of more companies or overseas companies makes him unfit to be concerned in the management of a company or whether the court should exercise any discretion to make a disqualification order under any of *CDDA 1986, ss 2–4, 5A, 8 or 10* or what the period of disqualification should be, the court or the Secretary of State (as the case may be) must have regard in particular to the following matters.

*Matters applicable in all cases*

- The extent to which the person was responsible for the causes of any material contravention by a company or overseas company of any applicable legislative or other requirement.

- Where applicable the extent to which the person was responsible for the causes of a company or overseas company becoming insolvent.

- The frequency of the conduct of the person which falls within either of the above.

- The nature and extent of any loss or harm caused, or any potential loss or harm which could have been caused, by the person's conduct in relation to a company or overseas company.

*Additional matters to be taken into account where person is or has been a director*

- Any misfeasance or breach or any fiduciary duty by the director in relation to a company or overseas company.

- Any material breach of any legislative or other obligation of the director which applies as a result of being a director of a company or overseas company.

- The frequency of the conduct of the director which falls within either of the above.

*[SBEE 2015, s 106; SI 2015 No 1689, Reg 2].*

In considering the question of unfitness, the court is concerned with the director's conduct generally and is not restricted in making a finding of unfitness to cases where the director could be disqualified on some other ground. The words '*in particular*' suggest that the court is not confined to looking at the matters set out in the legislation (*Re Bath Glass Ltd* [1988] BCLC 329, 4 BCC 130).

The court is required to have regard to a person's conduct as a director regardless of whether he has been validly appointed or is merely assuming to act as a director. The conduct relevant to his future suitability to act depends on his past record irrespective of the circumstances in which he came to act as a director (*Re Lo-Line Electric Motors Ltd* [1988] Ch 477, [1988] BCLC 698).

### 18.17 Disqualification for competition infringements

The High Court (in Scotland, the Court of Session) must make a disqualification order against a person if the following two conditions are satisfied in relation to him.

(1)  A company of which he is a director commits a breach of competition law.

A company commits a breach of competition law if it engages in conduct which infringes any of the following:

- The Chapter 1 prohibition (within the meaning of the *Competition Act 1998*) (prohibition on agreements, etc preventing, restricting or distorting competition).

- The Chapter 2 prohibition (within the meaning of that *Act*) (prohibition on abuse of a dominant position).

- *Article 81* of the Treaty establishing the European Community (prohibition on agreements, etc preventing, restricting or distorting competition).

- *Article 82* of that Treaty (prohibition on abuse of a dominant position).

(2)  The court considers that his conduct as a director makes him unfit to be concerned in the management of a company.

For these purpose the court

- *must* have regard to whether, as a director of the company,

  (i)  his conduct contributed to the breach of competition law mentioned in (1) above (and for this purpose it is immaterial whether the person knew that the conduct of the company constituted the breach);

  (ii)  his conduct did not contribute to the breach but he had reasonable grounds to suspect that the conduct of the company constituted the breach and he took no steps to prevent it; or

  (iii)  he did not know, but ought to have known, that the conduct of the company constituted the breach;

- *may* have regard to his conduct as a director of a company in connection with any other breach of competition law; and

- *must not* have regard to the matters mentioned in *CDDA 1986, Sch 1* (see **18.16**).

For the above purposes, 'conduct' includes omission and 'director' includes shadow director (see **18.1(2)**).

The maximum period of disqualification is 15 years.

An application under these provisions for a disqualification order may be made by the OFT or by a *'specified regulator'*, ie each of the following for the purposes of a breach of competition law in relation to a matter in respect of which he or it has a function, namely

- the Office of Communications (Ofcom);

- the Gas and Electricity Markets Authority;

- the Water Services Regulation Authority (Ofwat);

- the Office of Rail and Road (ORR); and

- the Civil Aviation Authority.

*Competition undertakings.* Instead of applying for a disqualification order, the OFT or the specified regulator (as the case may be) may accept a 'disqualification undertaking' from any person that, for the period specified in the undertaking, he will not

(a) be a director of a company,

(b) act as receiver of a company's property,

(c) in any way, whether directly or indirectly, be concerned or take part in the promotion, formation or management of a company, or

(d) act as an insolvency practitioner

but a disqualification undertaking may provide that a prohibition falling within (*a*) to (*c*) above does not apply if the person obtains the leave of the court.

The maximum period which may be specified in a disqualification undertaking is 15 years. Where a disqualification undertaking is accepted from a person who is already subject to such an undertaking or to a disqualification order, the periods specified in those undertakings or the undertaking and the order (as the case may be) run concurrently.

*Competition investigations.* If the OFT or a specified regulator has reasonable grounds for suspecting that a breach of competition law has occurred, it or he (as the case may be) may carry out an investigation for the purpose of deciding whether to make an application for a disqualification order (in which case, for the purposes of such an investigation, *Competition Act 1998, ss 26–30* apply as they apply to the OFT for the purposes of an investigation under *Competition Act 1998, s 25*). Where, as a result of such an investigation, the OFT or a specified regulator proposes to apply for a disqualification order under the above provisions, before making the application the OFT or regulator (as the case may be) must

- give notice to the person likely to be affected by the application; and

- give that person an opportunity to make representations.

[*CDDA 1986, ss 9A–9E; EmA 2002, s 204; Communications Act 2003, Sch 17 para 83; Railway and Transport Safety Act 2003, Sch 2 para 19; Water Act 2003, Sch 7 para 25*].

**18.18  Disqualification for participation in wrongful trading**

Where the court makes a declaration under *IA 1986, ss 213* (fraudulent trading) or *214* (wrongful trading) that a person is liable to contribute to a company's assets, then the court may also make a disqualification order against the person to whom the declaration relates. This applies whether or not an application for such an order is made by any person.

The maximum period of disqualification is 15 years.

[*CDDA 1986, s 10; SI 2009 No 1941, Sch 1 para 85*].

**18.19  Automatic disqualification for bankruptcy etc**

A person may not act as a director of, or directly or indirectly take part in or be concerned in the promotion, formation or management of, a company (including a company incorporated outside Great Britain that has a an established place of business in Great Britain) in the following circumstances.

(a)  Either

- he is an undischarged bankrupt,

- a moratorium period under a debt relief order applies in relation to him, or

- a bankruptcy restriction order or a debt relief restrictions order is in force in respect of him

and the court by which he was adjudged bankrupt (or, in Scotland, by which sequestration of his estates was awarded) has not given leave for him so to act, etc. See *R v Brockley* (1993) 99 Cr App Rep 385, [1994] 1 BCLC 606, CA.

In England and Wales, the court must not give leave unless notice of intention to apply for it has been served on the official receiver, who has a duty to attend the hearing and oppose the application if he considers that it is contrary to the public interest that the application should be granted.

[*CDDA 1986, s 11; EmA 2002, Sch 21 para 5; Tribunals, Courts and Enforcement Act 2007, Sch 20 para 16; SI 2009 No 1941, Sch 1 para 85*].

(b)  A county court revokes an administration order made in respect of that person because either

- he failed to make two payments (whether consecutive or not) required by the order, or

- at the time the order was made, the total amount of his qualifying debts was more than the prescribed maximum for the purposes *IA 1986, Pt 6* but because of information provided, or not provided, by him, that amount was thought to be less than, or the same as, the prescribed maximum,

and the court, at the time it revokes the administration order, makes an order directing that he shall not act, etc for such period (not exceeding one year) as may be specified in the order. [*CDDA 1986, s 12; Tribunals, Courts and Enforcement Act 2007, Sch 16 para 5; SI 2009 No 1941, Sch 1 para 85*].

# 18.20 Directors

## 18.20 Consequences of contravention

*Criminal penalties.* A person who acts in contravention of a disqualification order or disqualification undertaking or in contravention of the provisions of **18.19** is guilty of an offence and liable (i) on conviction on indictment, to imprisonment for not more than two years or a fine (or both); and (ii) on summary conviction, to imprisonment for not more than 6 months or a fine (or both). [*CDDA 1986, s 13; IA 2000 Sch 4 para 8; SI 2004 No 1941, Art 2*].

Where a body corporate is guilty of an offence of acting in contravention of a disqualification order or disqualification undertaking, a director, manager, secretary, or other similar official of the body corporate is also guilty of the offence if it is proved that the offence occurred with the consent or connivance of, or was attributable to any neglect on the part of, that person. [*CDDA 1986, s 14(1); IA 2000, Sch 4 para 9; SI 2004 No 1941, Art 2*]. Similarly, where the affairs of a body corporate are managed by its members, a member will be liable for his acts and defaults in connection with his functions of management as if he were a director of the body corporate. [*CDDA 1986, s 14(2)*].

*Personal liability.* Where a person, in contravention of a disqualification order or disqualification undertaking or of **18.19**(*a*), is a director of, or is concerned or takes part in the management of, a company, he is personally responsible for such debts and other liabilities of the company as are incurred while he is so involved.

In addition, where a person (A) involved in the management of a company acts (or is willing to act) on instructions given, without leave of the court, by another person (B) whom A knows at that time to be the subject of a disqualification order or disqualification undertaking or to be an undischarged bankrupt, then A is personally responsible for such debts and other liabilities of the company as are incurred while he is acting (or willing to act) on such instructions. For these purposes, where A has at any time acted on instructions given, without the leave of the court, by B, and A knew at that time that B was the subject of a disqualification order or disqualification undertaking or to be an undischarged bankrupt, then A is presumed to have been willing to act on B's instructions at any time thereafter, unless the contrary is shown.

Where a person is personally responsible, he is jointly and severally liable for the debts referred to above with

- the company; and

- any other person who is so liable, whether under these provisions or otherwise.

[*CDDA 1986, s 15; IA 2000, Sch 4 para 10; SI 2004 No 1941, Art 2; SI 2009 No 1941, Sch 1 para 85*].

*Compensation orders.* The court may make a compensation order against a person on the application of the Secretary of State if it is satisfied that the following conditions mentioned are met.

The conditions are that—

- the person is subject to a disqualification order or disqualification undertaking under *CDDA 1986*; and

- conduct for which the person is subject to the order or undertaking has caused loss to one or more creditors of an insolvent company of which the person has at any time been a director.

If it appears to the Secretary of State that the above conditions are met in respect of a person who has offered to give the Secretary of State a compensation undertaking, the Secretary of State may accept the undertaking instead of applying, or proceeding with an application, for a compensation order.

An 'insolvent company' is a company that is or has been insolvent and a company becomes insolvent if—

- the company goes into liquidation at a time when its assets are insufficient for the payment of its debts and other liabilities and the expenses of the winding up;

- the company enters administration; or

- an administrative receiver of the company is appointed.

The Secretary of State may apply for a compensation order at any time before the end of the period of two years beginning with the date on which the disqualification order referred to in the first condition (above) was made, or the disqualification undertaking referred to was accepted.

In the case of a person subject to a disqualification order under *CDDA 1986, s 8ZA* or *8ZD*, or a disqualification undertaking under *CDDA 1986, s 8ZC* or *8ZE*, the reference in the second condition to 'conduct' is a reference to the conduct of the main transgressor in relation to which the person has exercised the requisite amount of influence.

For these purposes 'the court' means—

- in a case where a disqualification order has been made, the court that made the order; and

- in any other case, the High Court or, in Scotland, the Court of Session.

Amounts payable under compensation orders and undertakings.

A compensation order is an order requiring the person against whom it is made to pay an amount specified in the order—

(a)    to the Secretary of State for the benefit of—

- a creditor or creditors specified in the order; and

- a class or classes of creditor so specified.

(b)    as a contribution to the assets of a company so specified.

A compensation undertaking is an undertaking to pay an amount specified in the undertaking

(a)    to the Secretary of State for the benefit of—

- a creditor or creditors specified in the undertaking; and

- a class or classes of creditor so specified.

(b)    as a contribution to the assets of a company so specified.

When specifying an amount the court (in the case of an order) and the Secretary of State (in the case of an undertaking) must in particular have regard to—

(a)    the amount of the loss caused;

(b)    the nature of the conduct mentioned in the second condition (above); and

(c)    whether the person has made any other financial contribution in recompense for the conduct (whether under a statutory provision or otherwise).

An amount payable by virtue of the above under a compensation undertaking is recoverable as if payable under a court order.

An amount payable under a compensation order or compensation undertaking is provable as a bankruptcy debt.

Variation and revocation of compensation undertakings

The court may, on the application of a person who is subject to a compensation undertaking—

(a)    reduce the amount payable under the undertaking, or

(b)    provide for the undertaking not to have effect.

On the hearing of such an application the Secretary of State must appear and call the attention of the court to any matters which the Secretary of State considers relevant, and may give evidence or call witnesses.

**Transitional provision.** The above provisions apply in respect of a person's conduct under *CDDA 1986, s 15A(3)(b)* or exercise of the requisite amount of influence under *CDDA 1986, s 15A(6)*.

[*SBEE 2015, s 110; SI 2015 No 1689, Reg 2, Sch 1, para 4*].

*Register of orders.* The Secretary of State is required to keep a register of disqualification orders and undertakings and can require court officers to furnish him with certain particulars. See *CDDA 1986, s 18* and the *Companies (Disqualification Orders) Regulations 2009 (SI 2009 No 2471)*.

### 18.21  Disqualification under the company's articles

Generally, a company's articles will contain provisions either for the removal of a director (see **18.9**) or requiring a director to vacate office on grounds additional to those set out in **18.12** to **18.19**. Where a company has adopted standard articles, see

•      *Table A 1985, Reg 81*

•      *Model Articles, Art 18* (private companies)

•      *Model Articles, Art 22* (public companies)

set out in APPENDIX **4** STANDARD ARTICLES OF ASSOCIATION.

### 18.22  FOREIGN DISQUALIFICATIONS

The Secretary of State may make Regulations disqualifying a person 'subject to foreign restrictions' from

(a)    being a director of a 'UK company';

(b)    acting as receiver of a UK company's property; or

(c)    in any way, whether directly or indirectly, being concerned or taking part in the promotion, formation or management of a UK company.

'*UK company*' means a company registered under *CA 2006*.

[*CA 2006, s 1184*].

A person is '*subject to foreign restrictions*' if under the law of a country or territory outside the UK

- he is, by reason of misconduct or unfitness, disqualified to any extent from acting in connection with the affairs of a company incorporated or formed under the law of that country or territory;

- he is, by reason of misconduct or unfitness, required to

  (i)    obtain permission from a court or other authority, or

  (ii)   meet any other condition,

  before acting in connection with the affairs of a company incorporated or formed under the law of that country or territory; or

- he has, by reason of misconduct or unfitness, given undertakings to a court or other authority of a country or territory outside the UK

  (i)    not to act in connection with the affairs of a company incorporated or formed under the law of that country or territory; or

  (ii)   restricting the extent to which, or the way in which, he may do so.

The references to '*acting in connection with the affairs of a company*' are to doing anything within (*a*)–(*c*) above.

[*CA 2006, s 1182*].

## 18.23  DUTIES OF DIRECTORS

The general duties specified in **18.24** (modified, in the case of charitable companies, as in **18.26**) are owed by a director of a company to the company. Even where a person ceases to be a director, on or after 1 October 2008 he continues to be subject to the duty to

- to avoid conflicts of interest (see **18.24(5)**) as regards the exploitation of any property, information or opportunity of which he became aware at a time when he was a director; and

- not to accept benefits from third parties (see **18.24(6)**) as regards things done or omitted by him before he ceased to be a director.

To that extent those duties apply to a former director as to a director (subject to any necessary adaptations).

These general duties

- are based on certain common law rules and equitable principles as they apply in relation to directors and have effect in place of those rules and principles as regards the duties owed to a company by a director;

- are to be interpreted and applied in the same way as common law rules or equitable principles, so that regard must be had to the corresponding common law rules and equitable principles in interpreting and applying the general duties;

- apply to shadow directors (see **18.1(2)**) where, and to the extent that either, the corresponding common law rules or equitable principles apply or regulations to be made under *SBEE 2015, s 89* provide how the general duties will apply to shadow directors. *Section 89* of the *SBEE 2015* came into force in May 2015 but regulations made under that section have not been made; and

- are owed to the company (*CA 2006, s 170(1)*). Only the company will be able to enforce the duties. Directors do not, in their capacity as directors, owe fiduciary duties to the company's shareholders or creditors. In certain circumstances, however, shareholders may be able to bring a derivative action on the company's behalf (see **26.12 DERIVATIVE CLAIMS IN ENGLAND AND WALES OR NORTHERN IRELAND**).

[*CA 2006, s 170; SBEE 2015, ss 89, 164; SI 2007 No 2194, Sch 1 para 6; SI 2007 No 3495, Art 10*].

Where a particular situation triggers more than one duty, the director must comply with *every* relevant duty (*CA 2006, s 179*). For example, the obligation to promote the success of the company (*s 172*) will not excuse a director from his or her concurrent duty to act within his or her powers (*s 171*), even if he or she believes that action which contravened *s 171* would be most likely to promote the success of the company. Nor do the general duties require or authorise a director to breach any other law.

**Civil consequences of breach of general duties**. The consequences of breach (or threatened breach) of any of the general duties in **18.24** are the same as would apply if the corresponding common law rule or equitable principle applied. The duties (with the exception of **18.24(4)**) are, accordingly, enforceable in the same way as any other fiduciary duty owed to a company by its directors. [*CA 2006, s 178*]. In the case of fiduciary duties, the consequences of breach may include:

- an injunction;

- damages or compensation where the company has suffered loss;

- restoration of the company's property;

- an account of profits made by the director; and

- rescission of a contract where the director fails to disclose an interest.

The typical remedy for a breach of the duty of care, skill and diligence (**18.24(4)**) is damages.

A breach of duty may also create grounds for the termination of an executive director's service contract, or for his or her disqualification as a director under the *Company Directors Disqualification Act 1986*.

## 18.24 General duties

(1) *Duty to act within powers*

A director of a company must act in accordance with the 'company's constitution' and only exercise powers for the purposes for which they are conferred. [*CA 2006, s 171*].

The Supreme Court decision in *Eclairs Group Ltd and Glengary Overseas Ltd v JKX Oil & Gas plc* [2015] UKSC 71, [2016] 3 All ER 641, [2016] 2 All ER (Comm) 413, sheds light on the correct rationale for applying this broad duty. The Supreme Court was scrutinising a decision, made by the board of a public company listed on the London Stock Exchange, to issue 'restriction notices' (the nature of which merit brief explanation below) in reliance on the company's articles.

By *CA 2006, Part 22*, where a *public* company knows or suspects that a person has (or within the past three years has had) an interest in its shares, the company can send to the (potentially) interested party a *s 793* 'disclosure notice', demanding certain information. (So, for example, the company can investigate the beneficial owner of shares held via a nominee.) If the recipient fails to comply, the company may be able, by virtue of its articles, to serve a 'restriction notice' automatically preventing the disobedient recipient from voting on 'their' shares or appointing a proxy.

The directors of J plc perceived that it had become the target of a corporate raid by two minority shareholders (E Ltd and G Ltd), both companies controlled by trusts. E Ltd was pressing for shareholder resolutions removing two J directors and appointing new ones. There were even reports in the media in Ukraine that an individual behind one of the trusts was trying to take control of J's main Ukrainian subsidiary.

J plc issued disclosure notices to E Ltd and G Ltd, and to individuals behind the trusts. Unsatisfied with the responses, and relying on provisions in J's articles (*article 42*), the J board issued restriction notices for the E Ltd and G Ltd shares, suspending (for those shares) the right to vote at general meetings and restricting the right of transfer.

E Ltd and G Ltd applied to court challenging the restriction notices. They argued that the J board had acted for an improper purpose.

The Supreme Court unanimously allowed the appeals by E Ltd and G Ltd, holding that the proper purpose rule applied to the J board's exercise of its power under *article 42*, and that the board had indeed acted for an improper purpose. The Supreme Court explained that the *s 171* duty was not focussed on the question of whether a board had technically *exceeded* its power by going beyond the scope of the relevant provision as a matter of construction or implication. Rather, the duty was designed to catch an *abuse* of power, where a board had committed an act which fell within its scope but was done for an improper reason (here, to influence the outcome of a *shareholders'* general meeting). It followed, said the Court, that the test under *s 171* was necessarily subjective.

This decision would seem potentially to widen the future application of this duty and the scope of the evidence which a court may consider in scrutinising alleged breaches.

Please see also the discussion below, in relation to the *s 172* duty, of the recent case of *Ball (liquidator of PV Solar Solutions Ltd) v Hughes* [2017] EWHC 3228 (Ch), [2018] 1 BCLC 58, [2017] All ER (D) 90 (Dec).

*(2) Duty to promote the success of the company*

A director of a company must act in the way he considers, in good faith, would be most likely to promote the success of the company for the benefit of its members as a whole. In doing so, he must have regard (amongst other matters) to

- the likely consequences of any decision in the long term;

- the interests of the company's employees;

- the need to foster the company's business relationships with suppliers, customers and others;

- the impact of the company's operations on the community and the environment;

- the desirability of the company maintaining a reputation for high standards of business conduct; and

- the need to act fairly as between members of the company.

Where (or to the extent that) the purposes of the company consist of or include purposes other than the benefit of its members (eg charitable companies and community interest companies), the above provisions have effect as if the reference to promoting the success of the company for the benefit of its members were to achieving those purposes.

The duty imposed by these provisions has effect subject to any enactment or rule of law requiring directors, in certain circumstances, to consider or act in the interests of creditors of the company (see, for example, *IA 1986, s 214* at **18.39**).

## 18.24 Directors

[*CA 2006, s 172*].

In having regard to the factors listed, the duty to exercise reasonable care, skill and diligence (see (4) below) will apply.

There remains some ambiguity as to the meaning of the term 'success'. The government has explained that 'success' for this purpose will usually mean 'long-term increase in value' for commercial companies; also, that the issue of what will promote the success of the company, and of what constitutes success for it, in a particular case are issues for the director's good faith judgment. The government's view was that this would keep strategic/tactical business decisions within the purview of the *directors*, and are not of the courts – provided the directors were acting in good faith.

In *Southern Counties Fresh Foods Ltd, Re* [2008] EWHC 2810 (Ch), [2008] All ER (D) 195 (Nov), the court compared the new form of words in *s 172* with the old case law wording (acting 'bona fide in the interests of the company'). It concluded that the two wordings essentially meant the same thing, with the modern formulation giving a clearer definition of the scope of the duty. The court in *Re Southern Counties* also confirmed that the test under (at least the first limb of) *s 172(1)* remains subjective in nature. Hence, the question is whether the director honestly believed that he or she was acting in a way most likely to promote the company's success. This mirrors the pre-*CA 2006* position as established in *Smith & Fawcett Ltd, Re* [1942] Ch 304, [1942] 1 All ER 542.

Nevertheless, a court may be more likely to find that a decision was not taken in good faith where it was not a decision that a reasonable and intelligent director could have concluded would promote the success of the company (*Charterbridge Corpn Ltd v Lloyds Bank Ltd* [1970] Ch 62, [1969] 2 All ER 1185; *Hellard v Carvalho, In the Matter of HLC Environmental Projects Ltd (in liq)* [2013] EWHC 2876 (Ch), [2013] All ER (D) 240 (Sep), CSRC vol 37 iss 16/1 at para 92).

The subjective test will only apply where there is evidence that the director actually considered the best interests of the company. Where there is no such evidence, the proper test is objective. The question then becomes one of whether an intelligent and honest man in the position of a director of the company concerned could, in the circumstances, reasonably have believed that the transaction was for the benefit of the company (*Hellard (Liquidators of HLC Environmental Projects Ltd) v Carvalho*).

The *s 172* duty is displaced when the company is insolvent. It may be transformed into a duty to have regard to the interests of *creditors*, where the company is of doubtful solvency or on the verge of insolvency. Where creditors' interests become influential, the director's duty will be to have regard to the interests of the creditors *as a class* – not to advance the interests of a *particular* creditor (*GHLM Trading Ltd v Maroo* [2012] EWHC 61 (Ch), [2012] 2 BCLC 369, [2012] 07 LS Gaz R 18). The precise point at which the duty to consider creditors' interests arises remains a moot point. Courts have considered various formulations – that the company must be at 'a real (as opposed) to remote risk of insolvency', 'on the verge of insolvency', or of 'doubtful' or '*marginal*' solvency. The position seems to be that these are essentially different ways of phrasing the same test. Ultimately, the key principle is that the directors ought to be anticipating the prospect of the insolvency of the company because, if and when that occurred, the creditors would then have a greater claim to the assets of the company than the shareholders (*BTI 2014 LLC v Sequana SA* [2016] EWHC 1686 (Ch), [2017] Bus LR 82, [2017] 1 BCLC 453).

In order to evidence directors' compliance with *s 172*, the usual practice is for the minutes to state, in relation to a particular decision (where the circumstances made it particularly necessary or relevant), that the directors have taken the statutory *s 172* factors into account in arriving at their decision.

In *Ball (liquidator of PV Solar Solutions Ltd) v Hughes* [2017] EWHC 3228 (Ch), [2018] 1 BCLC 58, [2017] All ER (D) 90 (Dec), the High Court explored the application of the duty imposed on directors to consider the interests of a company's *creditors* under *s 172(3)*. In this recent case, the court scrutinised the position of two directors of a private company, who had caused their company to adopt a modified employer-financed retirement benefit scheme in order to shield their own remuneration from tax, and had then gone on to apply three credit entries against their respective directors' loan accounts. The court considered whether, in applying those credits, the directors had breached their fiduciary duties and been guilty of misfeasance.

The High Court held that the two directors had, in applying those credits, breached their fiduciary duties and had been guilty of misfeasance for the purposes of *IA 1986, s 212* (which is discussed further at **18.33** and **18.37**).

The case did not fundamentally concern whether or not the retirement benefit scheme was itself an effective scheme for the avoidance of tax. The key issue was whether the directors, neither of whom had a contract of employment with the company, were entitled to withdraw remuneration, and to make the credit entries, in the way they did. Registrar Barber in the High Court held that they were not so entitled.

As to whether the directors had breached their duty under *CA 2006, s 172* to promote the success of the company, Registrar Barber found that, at the time of each credit entry, the duty to prioritise *creditors*' interests had arisen such that, in order to discharge the *s 172* duty, the directors were required to have regard to the interests of the company's creditors as a whole. In part because of the directors' failure to do so, an *objective* test, rather than the usual subjective test, was to be applied to *s 172*. The registrar was satisfied on the evidence that an intelligent and honest man in the position of a director of the company could not reasonably have believed that the credits were for the benefit of the company's creditors. On this basis, the directors had breached the *s 172* duty.

The case thus throws valuable light on the application of the *s 172* duty to an insolvency situation. In the Registrar's view, the key point was that directors were not free to take action which put at *real* (as opposed to remote) risk the creditors' chances of being paid, without first having considered their (ie creditors') interests rather than those of the company and its shareholders. The point at which the risk to creditors' interests becomes *real* for these purposes must be determined on a case-by-case basis.

References in certain formulations of the *s 172* test to be applied to a company being of 'dubious' or 'doubtful' solvency had to be viewed in the context of the underlying principle. The 'doubt' in this context is not purely whether, on the figures, the numbers add up on a given day. The test is broader than that. The court must ask itself, in relation to a given company, whether, at the time of (or as a result of) the director's actions, there is a real risk of the company's creditors being left unpaid. In some cases, this may involve considering the wider context in which that company operates; such as, known significant trading events, which it is reasonably foreseeable will impact materially in the near future on the trading viability of the company.

The directors had also failed to exercise their powers for proper purposes as required by *CA 2006, s 171*.

The court found that the directors were not entitled to be remunerated as a *quantum meruit*.

The registrar made an order (under *IA 1986, s 212*) compelling the directors jointly and severally to repay slightly in excess of £750,000 to the company, with interest.

This case also impacts on the *Duomatic* principle, which is discussed below at **42.1**.

(3) *Duty to exercise independent judgment*

A director of a company must exercise independent judgment. This duty is not infringed by his acting

- in accordance with an agreement duly entered into by the company that restricts the future exercise of discretion by its directors; or

- in a way authorised by the 'company's constitution'.

[*CA 2006, s 173*].

(4) *Duty to exercise reasonable care, skill and diligence*

A director of a company must exercise reasonable care, skill and diligence. This means the care, skill and diligence that would be exercised by a reasonably diligent person with the general knowledge, skill and experience:

- that may reasonably be expected of a person carrying out the functions carried out by the director in relation to the company; and

- that this director actually has.

[*CA 2006, s 174*].

This codifies the more recent case law formulations of a director's common law duty of care, skill and diligence; notably, as expressed in *Re D'Jan of London Ltd, Copp v D'Jan* [1994] 1 BCLC 561, [1993] BCC 646.

So, as a minimum, a director must demonstrate the knowledge, skill and experience set out in the objective test (under the first limb above). However, where a director has specialist knowledge, he or she must meet the higher subjective standard (set by the second limb above). In applying the test, one should consider the functions carried out by the particular director, including his or her specific responsibilities, and the circumstances of the particular company.

Accordingly, a person should not take on a directorship unless he or she is sufficiently qualified or experienced to be able to fulfil the functions that he or she might reasonably be expected to carry out. A particularly highly qualified or experienced director will be obliged to exercise a commensurately high level of skill and expertise.

A director will also be required to exercise his or her duties diligently, to keep himself or herself informed about the company's affairs and to join with his or her co-directors in supervising and controlling them. This does not prevent a director from relying on the experience and expertise of their colleagues. Nor does it, in principle, prohibit prudent delegation or distribution of tasks, provided that the director does not seek to divest themselves of all personal responsibility for what is done by the 'subordinates'.

(5) *Duty to avoid conflicts of interest*

A director of a company must avoid a situation in which he has, or can have, a direct or indirect interest that conflicts, or possibly may conflict, with the interests of the company. This applies, in particular, to the exploitation of any property, information or opportunity (and it is immaterial whether the company could take advantage of the property, information or opportunity).

The test of whether there has been a breach of the *s 175* duty is objective. It does not depend on whether the director is aware that what they are doing is a breach of duty (*Richmond Pharmacology Ltd v Chester Overseas Ltd* [2014] EWHC 2692 (Ch), [2014] Bus LR 1110, [2014] All ER (D) 92 (Aug), Stephen Jourdan QC at paras 69–72).

This duty

(a)    does not apply to a conflict of interest arising in relation to a transaction or arrangement with the company; and

(b)       is not infringed if the situation cannot reasonably be regarded as likely to give rise to a conflict of interest or if the matter has been authorised by the directors.

For these purposes, a conflict of interest includes a conflict of interest and duty and a conflict of duties.

Companies can cater in their articles for potential *s 175* dilemmas. For example, the articles may provide that directors are allowed to hold additional directorships (of other companies), and that they need not disclose confidential information which they obtain through such other positions.

*Authorisation by the directors.* Authorisation may be given by the directors

(i)       where the company is a private company and nothing in the company's constitution invalidates such authorisation, by the matter being proposed to and authorised by the directors; and

(ii)      where the company is a public company and its constitution includes provision enabling the directors to authorise the matter, by the matter being proposed to and authorised by them in accordance with the constitution.

For the authorisation to be effective, any requirement as to the quorum at the meeting at which the matter is considered must be met without counting the director in question or any other interested director. The matter must then be agreed to without their voting (or, where they vote, would still have been agreed to if their votes had not been counted).

*Transitional provisions*

1. In relation to conflicts of interest situations which arose before 1 October 2008, the law that applied before that date continues to apply; and

2. In relation to companies incorporated before 1 October 2008, (i) (above) applies where the members of a private company resolved (before, on or after that date) that authorisation could be given in accordance with *CA 2006, s 175.*

[*CA 2006, s 175*].

(6) *Duty not to accept benefits from third parties*

A director of a company must not accept a benefit from a 'third party' conferred by reason of his being a director or his doing (or not doing) anything as director.

'*Third party*' means a person other than the company, an associated body corporate or a person acting on behalf of the company or an associated body corporate. For these purposes, bodies corporate are associated if one is a subsidiary of the other or both are subsidiaries of the same body corporate.

This duty is not infringed if

•         benefits are received by a director from a person by whom his services (as a director or otherwise) are provided to the company; or

•         the acceptance of the benefit cannot reasonably be regarded as likely to give rise to a conflict of interest. For these purposes, a conflict of interest includes a conflict of interest and duty and a conflict of duties. Benefits conferred on the director by the company itself, by its holding company or by its subsidiaries, and benefits received from a person who provides the director's services to the company, are excluded.

[*CA 2006, ss 176, 256*].

'Benefit' is not defined in the statute. The government stated, during the parliamentary debates, that it intended the word to bear its ordinary dictionary meaning, and noted that the Oxford English Dictionary defined 'benefit' as being a favourable or helpful factor, circumstance, advantage or profit (*House of Commons, Company Law Reform Bill [Lords] in Standing Committee D, Solicitor-General, column 622*).

(7) *Duty to declare interest in proposed transaction or arrangement*

If a director of a company is in any way, directly or indirectly, interested in a proposed transaction or arrangement with the company, he must declare the nature and extent of that interest to the other directors. The declaration may (but need not) be made at a meeting of the directors or by notice to the directors in accordance with *CA 2006, s 184* (notice in writing) or *CA 2006, s 185* (general notice). See **18.59**. It must be made before the company enters into the transaction or arrangement in question.

If a declaration of interest as above proves to be, or becomes, inaccurate or incomplete, a further declaration must be made.

These provisions do not require a declaration of an interest

- where the director is not aware of the interest or is not aware of the transaction or arrangement in question (and for this purpose a director is treated as being aware of matters of which he ought reasonably to be aware);

- if it cannot reasonably be regarded as likely to give rise to a conflict of interest;

- if, or to the extent that, the other directors are already aware of it (and for this purpose the other directors are treated as aware of anything of which they ought reasonably to be aware); or

- if, or to the extent that, it concerns terms of his service contract that have been or are to be considered

  (i) by a meeting of the directors; or

  (ii) by a committee of the directors appointed for the purpose under the 'company's constitution'.

[*CA 2006, s 177*].

Transitional provisions

(1) *CA 1985, s 317* continues to apply in relation to a duty arising before 1 October 2008.

(2) A declaration of interest in a proposed transaction or arrangement made before 1 October 2008 which proves to be, or becomes, inaccurate or incomplete on or after 1 October 2008, is treated as made on or after that date for the purposes of any further declaration that must be made.

[*SI 2007 No 3495, Sch 4, para 48*].

**Company's constitution.** For the above purposes, a company's constitution includes

- the company's articles;

- any resolutions and agreements to which *CA 2006, ss 29, 30* apply (see **14.9** CONSTITUTION – MEMORANDUM AND ARTICLES);

- any resolution or other decision come to in accordance with the constitution; and

- any decision by the members of the company, or a class of members, that is treated by virtue of any enactment or rule of law as equivalent to a decision by the company (eg a decision taken by the informal unanimous consent of all the members).

[*CA 2006, s 257*].

**Cases within more than one of the general duties.** Except as otherwise provided, more than one of the general duties may apply in any given case. [*CA 2006, s 179*]. It is therefore necessary to comply with every duty that applies in any given case. For example, the duty to promote the success of the company under (2) above will not authorise a director to breach his duty to act within his powers under (1) above, even if he considers that it would be most likely to promote the success of the company.

The one exception relates to the duty to avoid conflicts of interest under (5) above which does not apply to a conflict of interest arising in relation to a transaction or arrangement with the company. In such cases, the duty to declare interests in proposed transactions or arrangements under (7) above or the requirement to declare interests in existing transactions or arrangements under **18.57** will apply instead.

**18.25** *Consent, approval or authorisation by members*

In a case where a duty to avoid a conflict of interest is authorised by the directors or the director declares an interest in a proposed transaction or arrangement with the company, the transaction or arrangement is not liable to be set aside by virtue of any common law rule or equitable principle requiring the consent or approval of the members of the company. This is without prejudice to any enactment, or provision of the 'company's constitution', requiring such consent or approval.

Where a particular case falls within the transactions with directors requiring approval of members under

- *CA 2006, ss 188, 189* (service contracts, see **18.54**),

- *CA 2006, ss 190–196* (substantial property transactions, see **18.59** and **18.60**),

- *CA 2006, ss 197–214* (loans, quasi-loans and credit transactions, see **18.61** to **18.67**), or

- *CA 2006, ss 215–222* (payment for loss of office, see **18.47** to **18.51**), or

- *CA 2006, ss 226A–226F* (payments for loss of office-quoted companies, see **18.52**)

then

(a)  the application of the general duties is not affected except that it is not necessary also to comply with **18.24**(5) or **18.24**(6)

　(i)  where any of the above provisions apply and the necessary approval is given (including approval given by a resolution passed before 1 October 2007 if it complies with the requirements of those provisions); or

　(ii)  the matter is one for which approval is not needed; and

(b)  compliance with the general duties does not remove the need for approval under the appropriate provision.

The general duties have effect (except as otherwise provided or the context otherwise requires) notwithstanding any enactment or rule of law, except that

- they have effect subject to any rule of law enabling the company to give authority, specifically or generally, for anything to be done (or omitted) by the directors, or any of them, that would otherwise be a breach of duty; and

- where the company's articles contain provisions for dealing with conflicts of interest, the general duties are not infringed by anything done (or omitted) by the directors, or any of them, in accordance with those provisions.

## 18.25 Directors

[*CA 2006, s 180; SI 2007 No 2194, Sch 3 paras 6(2), 7(2), 8(2), 12(2); SI 2007 No 3495, Sch 4 para 49*].

*Company's constitution.* For the purposes of **18.23**(7), **18.25** and **18.26** (below), a company's constitution includes

- the company's articles;

- any resolutions and agreements to which *CA 2006, ss 29, 30* apply (see **14.1** CONSTITUTION – MEMORANDUM AND ARTICLES);

- any resolution or other decision come to in accordance with the constitution; and

- any decision by the members of the company, or a class of members, that is treated by virtue of any enactment or rule of law as equivalent to a decision by the company (eg a decision taken by the informal unanimous consent of all the members).

[*CA 2006, s 257*].

### 18.26 *Charitable companies*

In England and Wales and Northern Ireland, the provisions in **18.23** to **18.25** also apply to a company that is a charity, but with the following modifications.

(a) Conflicts of interest arising in relation to a transaction or arrangement with the company are excluded from the duty only if, or to the extent that, the charitable company's articles so allow. The articles must describe the transactions or arrangements which are excluded from the duty.

(b) Authorisation by the directors may only be given where the 'company's constitution' includes provision enabling the directors to authorise the matter and by the matter being proposed to and authorised by them in accordance with the constitution.

(c) If the matter falls within **18.25** (transactions requiring approval of members) matters not needing approval must be set out it the company's articles and only to the extent that the articles allow those duties to be disapplied.

[*CA 2006, s 181*].

## 18.27 Other statutory duties

In addition to the general duties in **18.24**, other statutory provisions extend and modify the general principles that directors must not abuse their positions and must deal fairly in certain transactions with the company or its shares. In particular, these arise in connection with the following.

- Payments for loss of office (see **18.47** to **18.51**).

- Service contracts (see **18.53**).

- Disclosure of interests in contracts (see **18.56**).

- Substantial property transactions (see **18.59**).

- Loans, quasi-loans and credit transactions (see **18.61**).

- Insider dealing (see **23** INSIDER DEALING AND MARKET ABUSE).

**Duties of internal management under the** *CA 2006.* A director has a considerable number of duties under *CA 2006* which he must perform or ensure are performed. To a large extent they relate to matters of internal management and are dealt with in the appropriate chapters of this book. They include provisions relating to the keeping of accounting records, the preparation of annual accounts, the filing of documents with the Registrar of Companies, and the keeping of the statutory books of the company. The company is punishable for failure by a fine and in some cases a daily default fine; directors can suffer fines, daily default fines, and, in some cases, imprisonment.

## 18.28 Duties to third parties

Although a director in his capacity as such owes his duties to the company, he may in the course of carrying out those duties find that he puts himself in a position where he also owes obligations to other persons. These include:

- Shareholders and employees of the company.

- Subscribers for, and purchasers of, securities. Subscribers for listed securities are protected by *FSMA 2000, s 90*. This provides that the persons responsible for any listing particulars or a prospectus are liable to pay compensation to any person who has acquired any of the securities in question and suffered loss in respect of them as a result of any untrue or misleading statements in them or the omission of any matter required to be included in them.

- Customers, suppliers and other contracting parties.

## 18.29 POWERS OF DIRECTORS

Subject to any provision to the contrary in the *Companies Acts* or the company's articles, the directors are responsible for the management of the company and they may exercise all the powers of the company.

Where a company has adopted standard articles, see

(a)    for general powers of directors,

- *Table A, Regs 70, 71*

- *Model Articles, Art 3* (private companies)

- *Model Articles, Art 3* (public companies);

(b)    for delegation of powers

- *Table A, Reg 72*;

- *Model Articles, Arts 5, 6* (private companies)

- *Model Articles, Arts 5, 6* (public companies);

(c)    for discretion to make further rules

- *Model Articles, Art 16* (private companies)

- *Model Articles, Art 19* (public companies);

set out in APPENDIX 4 STANDARD ARTICLES OF ASSOCIATION.

Where the articles give the directors the authority to manage the business of the company, the shareholders cannot, by ordinary resolution, give directions to the board or overrule a decision without first altering the articles (*Automatic Self-Cleansing Filter Syndicate Co Ltd v Cunninghame* [1906] 2 Ch 34, 75 LJ Ch 437, CA, and *John Shaw & Sons (Salford) Ltd v Shaw* [1935] 2 KB 113, 104 LJKB 549, CA).

## 18.29 Directors

**Assignment of office.** A director of a company may be empowered by the articles to assign his office to another person. *Before 1 October 2009*, an assignment had to be approved by a special resolution of the company; otherwise the assignment had no effect despite anything to the contrary in the provision. [*CA 1985, s 308*]. *Section 308* of *CA 1985* has not been reproduced in *CA 2006*.

### 18.30 Power to make provision for employees on cessation or transfer of business

The powers of the directors of a company include (if they would not otherwise do so) power to make provision for the benefit of persons employed (or formerly employed)

- by the company, or
- any of its subsidiaries

in connection with the cessation or the transfer to any person of the whole or part of the undertaking of the company or that subsidiary. This power is exercisable notwithstanding

- the general duty imposed by *CA 2006, s 173* (duty to promote the success of the company, see **18.24**); and
- in the case of a company that is a charity, any restrictions on the directors' powers (or the company's capacity) flowing from the objects of the company.

The power may be exercised by complying with any requirement of the company's articles and, only then, by being sanctioned by

(a) resolution of the company; or

(b) a resolution of the directors if specifically authorised by the company's articles. But a resolution of the directors is not sufficient sanction for payments to or for the benefit of directors, former directors or shadow directors.

Any payment under these provisions must be made before the commencement of any winding up of the company and out of profits of the company that are available for dividend. [*CA 2006, s 247; SI 2008 No 2860, Sch 2 para 40*].

Where a company has adopted standard articles, see

- *Model Articles, Art 51* (private companies)
- *Model Articles, Art 84* (public companies)

set out in Appendix 4 Standard Articles of Association which authorise the provision for the benefit of employees (and so enable the directors to pass a resolution to sanction the exercise of the power).

### 18.31 DIRECTORS' LIABILITIES

A director is not liable for the acts of co-directors and company officers solely by virtue of his position, although he will be if he participates in the wrong. Merely signing minutes approving a misapplication of property attracts liability (*Re Lands Allotment Co* [1894] 1 Ch 616, CA) as does unquestioningly signing a cheque for an unauthorised payment (*City Equitable Fire Insurance Co Ltd, Re* [1925] Ch 407, 94 LJ Ch 445, CA). A director is liable for, though actually ignorant of, another's wrong where he ought to have supervised the activity or ought to have known that it was wrong (*Selangor United Rubber Estates Ltd v Cradock (a bankrupt) (No 3)* [1968] 2 All ER 1073, [1968] 1 WLR 1555).

## 18.32 Liabilities and offences under Companies Acts provisions

There are a large number of offences for failure to comply with the requirements of the *Companies Acts*. These are dealt with in the appropriate part of the text. See also **29.3** OFFENCES AND LEGAL PROCEEDINGS for directors' liabilities where a body corporate is guilty of certain offences.

## 18.33 Liabilities and offences under IA 1986

In addition to offences under the *Companies Acts*, *IA 1986, ss 206–217* contain a number of other offences for malpractice before and during winding up. These are considered in **18.34** to **18.40**.

### 18.34 *Fraud in anticipation of winding up*

Where company is

- ordered to be wound up by the court, or

- passes a resolution for voluntary winding up,

any past or present officer of a company (including a shadow director, see **18.1(2)**) is deemed to have committed an offence if, within the twelve months immediately preceding the commencement of winding up or any time thereafter, he has

(a)    concealed or fraudulently removed company property valued at £500 or more;

(b)    concealed any debt due to or from the company;

(c)    concealed, destroyed, mutilated, falsified or made any false entry in any books or papers relating to the company;

(d)    fraudulently parted with, altered or made an omission in any document relating to the company;

(e)    pawned, pledged or disposed of property of the company obtained on credit and not paid for (unless done in the normal course of business); or

(f)    been privy to the doing by others of any act within (*c*) or (*d*) above.

Where appropriate, it is a defence to prove there was no intent to defraud or conceal.

A person guilty of an offence under the above provisions is liable (i) on indictment, to imprisonment for a period of up to seven years or a fine (or both); and (ii) on summary conviction, to imprisonment for a period of up to six months or a fine up to the statutory maximum (or both). See **29.1** OFFENCES AND LEGAL PROCEEDINGS for the statutory maximum.

[*IA 1986, s 206, Sch 10; SI 1986 No 1996*].

### 18.35 *Transactions in fraud of creditors*

Where company is

- ordered to be wound up by the court, or

- passes a resolution for voluntary winding up,

an officer of the company is deemed to have committed an offence if he has

- made (or caused to be made) any gift or transfer of, or charge on, or has caused or connived at the levying of any execution against, the company's property in the five years before winding up; or

## 18.35 Directors

- concealed or removed any part of the company's property since, or in the two months before, the date an unsatisfied judgment or order for payment of money has been obtained against the company.

It is a defence to prove that there was no intent to defraud the company's creditors.

A person guilty of an offence under the above provisions is liable (i) on indictment, to imprisonment for a period of up to two years or a fine (or both); and (ii) on summary conviction, to imprisonment for a period of up to six months or a fine up to the statutory maximum (or both). See **29.1** OFFENCES AND LEGAL PROCEEDINGS for the statutory maximum.

[*IA 1986, s 207, Sch 10*].

**18.36** *Misconduct in the course of winding up*

When a company is being wound up, an officer of the company commits an offence if he

- (a) does not to the best of his knowledge give the liquidator details of all the company's property and any disposals of that property not in the ordinary course of business;

- (b) does not deliver up to the liquidator any of the company's property or books in his custody;

- (c) fails to inform the liquidator as soon as practicable if he knows that a false debt has been proved;

- (d) prevents the production of any books or papers relating to the company's property or affairs;

- (e) attempts to account for any of the company's property by fictitious losses or expenses (and he is deemed to have committed that offence if he so attempted at any meeting of the company's creditors within the 12 months immediately preceding the commencement of winding up);

- (f) destroys, mutilates, alters or falsifies any of the company's books or papers or is privy to the making of a false entry therein;

- (g) makes any material omission in any statement relating to the company's affairs (including any such omission in the period from the date the company is ordered to be wound up by the court or has passed a resolution for voluntary winding up until the date of winding up); or

- (h) makes any false representation or commits any other fraud (whether before or after the date of winding up) to obtain the consent of any of the company's creditors to an agreement in connection with the company's affairs or the winding up.

The provisions also apply, except for (*f*), to past officers and shadow directors (see **18.1(2)**).

It is a defence under (*a*), (*b*), (*d*) and (*g*) to prove that there was no intent to defraud or conceal.

A person guilty of an offence under the above provisions is liable (i) on indictment, to imprisonment for a period of up to seven years or a fine (or both); and (ii) on summary conviction, to imprisonment for a period of up to six months or a fine up to the statutory maximum (or both). See **29.1** OFFENCES AND LEGAL PROCEEDINGS for the statutory maximum.

[*IA 1986, ss 208–211, Sch 10*].

**18.37** *Summary remedy against delinquent officers*

If in the course of winding up it appears that a past or present officer of the company has

- misapplied or retained, or become accountable for, any money or other property of the company, or

- been guilty of any misfeasance or breach of fiduciary or other duty in relation to the company,

the court may examine the conduct of the person concerned and compel him to

- repay, restore or account for the money or property with interest; or

- contribute such sum to the company's assets by way of compensation as the court thinks fit.

[*IA 1986, s 212; EmA 2002, Sch 17 para 18*].

The above is a procedural remedy only and does not give any additional right of action so that it cannot be invoked where the director has been negligent only (*Re B Johnson & Co (Builders) Ltd* [1955] Ch 634, [1955] 2 All ER 775, CA). However, 'misfeasance' comprehends any breach of duty involving a misapplication or wrongful retention of the company's assets and does not necessarily involve moral turpitude (see *Selangor United Rubber Estates Ltd v Cradock* [1967] 2 All ER 1255, [1967] 1 WLR 1168).

**18.38** *Fraudulent trading*

If in the course of the winding up of a company it appears that any business has been carried on 'with intent to defraud creditors' (whether of the company or any other person) or for any fraudulent purpose, the court may declare that any persons knowingly involved are liable to make such contributions to the company's assets as the court thinks proper. [*IA 1986, s 213*].

If while a company is in administration it appears that any business of the company has been carried on with intent to defraud creditors of the company or creditors of any other person, or for any fraudulent purpose, the court, on the application of the administrator, may declare that any persons who were knowingly parties to the carrying on of the business in the manner mentioned above are to be liable to make such contributions (if any) to the company's assets as the court thinks proper.

[*IA 1986, s 246ZA; SBEE 2015, s 117; SI 2015 No 1689*].

For a consideration of the phrase '*with intent to defraud creditors*' see *Re William C Leitch Bros Ltd* [1932] 2 Ch 71, 101 LJ Ch 380 and for '*fraudulent purposes*' see *Re Patrick & Lyon Ltd* [1933] Ch 786, 102 LJ Ch 300. It does not matter that only one creditor was defrauded (*Re Gerald Cooper Chemicals Ltd* [1978] Ch 262, [1978] 2 All ER 49).

**18.39** *Wrongful trading*

*Wrongful trading—insolvent liquidation or insolvent administration.* If a company has gone into insolvent liquidation and before that time a director (or shadow director) knew, or ought to have concluded, that there was no reasonable prospect that the company would avoid going into insolvent liquidation or entering into insolvent administration, the court may declare that that person is liable to make such contribution to the company's assets as it thinks proper. The court must not make such a declaration if satisfied that, once the director knew, etc, he took every step which a reasonably diligent person having both

- the general knowledge, skill and experience that may be reasonably expected of a person carrying out his functions, and

- the general knowledge, skill and experience that the director himself has

would have taken to minimise the potential loss to the company's creditors he ought to have taken on the assumption that he had the knowledge referred to above.

For the purposes of *IA 1986, s 214* a company enters insolvent administration if it enters administration at a time when its assets are insufficient for the payment of its debts and other liabilities and the expenses of the administration.

[*IA 1986, s 214*].

Once it has been established that a director knew or ought to have concluded that there was no reasonable prospect that the company would avoid going into insolvent liquidation, the burden of proving that the *s 214(3)* defence applies – namely, that he or she had taken every step to minimise the potential loss to the company's creditors – falls on *the director*. The onus is not on the liquidator to establish that the director had *not* taken the necessary steps (*Brooks v Armstrong* [2015] EWHC 2289 (Ch), [2016] BPIR 272, [2015] All ER (D) 45 (Aug)). This case also provides a useful analysis of the elements of a wrongful trading claim. (The decision in the case was overturned on the facts on appeal, however, in *Philip Anthony Brooks and Julie Elizabeth Willetts (Joint Liquidators of Robin Hood Centre plc in liquidation) v Kieron Armstrong and Ian Walker* [2016] EWHC 2893 (Ch),the court found that the liquidators had not established that the wrongful trading in this case had caused any increase in the company's net deficiency.)

In interpreting *ss 214(2)*, *(3)* and *246ZB(2)*, *(3)*, the facts that a director of a company ought to know or ascertain, the conclusions that he ought to reach and the steps that he ought to take are those that would be known or ascertained, or reached or taken, by a reasonably diligent person having both the general knowledge, skill and experience that may reasonably be expected of a person carrying out the same functions as are carried out by that director in relation to the company, and the general knowledge, skill and experience which that director has (*ss 214(4)* and *246ZB(4)*). The test under *ss 214(4)* and *246ZB(4)* is thus both subjective and objective.

Dishonesty is not required for wrongful trading. Hence, it carries a lower burden of proof than does fraudulent trading under *IA 1986, ss 213* and *246ZA*. In principle, therefore, it should be considerably easier for a liquidator or administrator to obtain an order for wrongful trading than for fraudulent trading against an errant director.

Nonetheless, to succeed in proving wrongful trading, a liquidator or an administrator will still need to obtain a considerable amount of evidence, which may entail significant cost and time.

*Wrongful trading—administration.* If while a company is in administration it appears that the conditions set out below apply in relation to a person who is or has been a director (which includes a shadow director) of the company, the court, on the application of the administrator, may declare that that person is to be liable to make such contribution (if any) to the company's assets as the court thinks proper.

The conditions which apply in relation to a person—

- the company has entered insolvent administration;

- at some time before the company entered administration, that person knew or ought to have concluded that there was no reasonable prospect that the company would avoid entering insolvent administration or going into insolvent liquidation; and

- the person was a director of the company at that time.

The court must not make such a declaration with respect to any person if it is satisfied that, after the second condition specified above was first satisfied in relation to the person, the person took every step with a view to minimising the potential loss to the company's creditors as (on the assumption that the person had knowledge of the matter mentioned in in that condition) the person ought to have taken.

For the purposes of the above, the facts which a director of a company ought to know or ascertain, the conclusions which the director ought to reach and the steps which the director ought to take are those which would be known or ascertained, or reached or taken, by a reasonably diligent person having both—

• the general knowledge, skill and experience that may reasonably be expected of a person carrying out the same functions as are carried out by that director in relation to the company; and

• the general knowledge, skill and experience that that director has.

The reference to the functions carried out in relation to a company by a director of the company includes any functions which the director does not carry out but which have been entrusted to the director.

For the purposes of *IA 1986, s 246ZB* a company enters insolvent administration if it enters administration at a time when its assets are insufficient for the payment of its debts and other liabilities and the expenses of the administration and company goes into insolvent liquidation if it goes into liquidation at a time when its assets are insufficient for the payment of its debts and other liabilities and the expenses of the winding up.

**Transitional provisions.** The above provisions apply in respect of the carrying on of business on or after 1 October 2015.

[*IA 1986, s 246ZB; SBEE 2015, s 117; SI 2015 No 1689, Sch, para 15*].

**18.40** *Re-use of company name*

Where a company goes into insolvent liquidation, a director or shadow director of that company is prohibited from

• being a director of another company,

• in any way being involved in the promotion, formation or management of another company, or

• in any way being concerned in the carrying on of a business

using the same, or a similar, name to that used by the company at any time in the 12 months before it went into liquidation. Except with the leave of the court, the prohibition applies to any person who was a director or shadow director within that twelve-month period and continues to apply to him for the five years beginning with the date that the company went into liquidation.

A person guilty of an offence under the above provisions is liable (i) on indictment, to imprisonment for a period of up to two years or a fine (or both); and (ii) on summary conviction, to imprisonment for a period of up to six months or a fine up to the statutory maximum (or both). See **29.1 OFFENCES AND LEGAL PROCEEDINGS** for the statutory maximum.

[*IA 1986, s 216*].

If, in contravention of the above provisions, a person is involved in the 'management' of a company re-using the name, he is personally responsible for the debts of the company incurred when so involved. Additionally, any other person involved in the management of the company who acts, or is willing to act, on instructions given by a person whom he knows at the time to be in contravention of the provisions, is also personally responsible for debts incurred when so acting.

For these purposes, a person is involved in the '*management*' of a company if he is a director of the company or if he is concerned, whether directly or indirectly, or takes part, in the management of the company.

## 18.40　Directors

[*IA 1986, s 217*].

### 18.41　Criminal liability

Where any officer of a company (or person purporting to act as such) publishes or concurs in publishing a written statement which to his knowledge is or may be misleading, false or deceptive in a material particular, he is liable on conviction on indictment, to imprisonment for up to seven years if he acted with intent to deceive the members or creditors about the company's affairs. [*Theft Act 1968, s 19*].

**Malpractice discovered during winding up**. If it appears in the course of a winding up that any past or present officer of the company has been guilty of an offence in relation to the company for which he is criminally liable, then the liquidator must report the matter to the official receiver in a winding up by the court or the Secretary of State (Lord Advocate in Scotland) in a voluntary liquidation. [*IA 1986, ss 218, 219; IA 2000, s 10*].

### 18.42　Relief from liability by court

If a director is or will be liable for negligence, default, breach of duty or breach of trust, a court may relieve him wholly or partly from liability under *CA 2006, s 1157*. See **29.10** OFFENCES AND LEGAL PROCEEDINGS.

### 18.43　Indemnification and provisions protecting directors from liability

*Sections 232–237* of *CA 2006* allow (to a limited extent) a company to indemnify its directors and to provide insurance against certain liabilities. The general prohibition in *s 232* (provisions for exemption of liability and indemnification are void) is then qualified by *sections 233–237* which allow the company to purchase insurance for directors and for directors to be indemnified against liabilities to a "qualifying third party" and against liabilities incurred in connection with the company's activities as trustee of a "qualifying pension scheme" but not against liabilities to the company itself. There is no specific prohibition against providing indemnities to former directors or other officers of the company.

[*CA 2006, ss 232, 256*].

(1)　**Provision of insurance**

A company is not prevented from purchasing and maintaining for a director of the company, or of an associated company, insurance against liabilities for negligence, default, breach of duty or breach of trust in relation to the company. [*CA 2006, s 233*].

A company is an associated company of another company if one of the companies is a subsidiary of the other or both are subsidiaries of the same body corporate [*CA 2006, s 256*].

(2)　**Qualifying third party indemnity provision**

The provisions against providing an indemnity above do not apply to 'qualifying third party indemnity provision'. 'Third party indemnity provision' means provision for indemnity against liability incurred by the director to a person other than the company or an associated company (see above). Such provision is '*qualifying third party indemnity provision*' if the following requirements are met.

- The provision must not provide any indemnity against any liability of the director to pay

    (i)　a fine imposed in criminal proceedings; or

(ii)    a sum payable to a regulatory authority by way of a penalty in respect of non-compliance with any requirement of a regulatory nature (however arising).

•    The provision must not provide any indemnity against any liability incurred by the director

(i)    in defending any criminal proceedings in which he is convicted;

(ii)    in defending any civil proceedings brought by the company, or an associated company (see above), in which judgment is given against him; or

(iii)    in connection with any application under *CA 2006, s 1157* (general power of court to grant relief in case of honest and reasonable conduct, see **29.10 OFFENCES AND LEGAL PROCEEDINGS**) or *CA 2006, s 661(3)(4)* own in which the court refuses to grant him relief.

References in (i)–(iii) above to a conviction, judgment or refusal of relief are to the final decision in the proceedings. This occurs, if not appealed against, at the end of the period for bringing an appeal or, if appealed against, at the time when the appeal (or any further appeal) is disposed of. An appeal is disposed of if it is determined and the period for bringing any further appeal has ended or if it is abandoned or otherwise ceases to have effect.

[*CA 2006, s 234; SI 2007 No 2194, Sch 1 para 12; SI 2007 No 3495, Art 10; SI 2008 No 674, Sch 3 paras 1, 5; SI 2008 No 2860, Art 6*].

(3)    **Qualifying pension scheme indemnity provision**

The general prohibition referred to above in *CA 2006, s 232* does not apply to 'qualifying pension scheme indemnity provision'. 'Pension scheme indemnity provision' means provision indemnifying a director of a company that is a trustee of an occupational pension scheme (as defined in *FA 2004, s 150(5)*) against liability incurred in connection with the company's activities as trustee of the scheme. Such provision is '*qualifying pension scheme indemnity provision*' if the following requirements are met.

•    The provision must not provide any indemnity against any liability of the director to pay

(i)    a fine imposed in criminal proceedings; or

(ii)    a sum payable to a regulatory authority by way of a penalty in respect of non-compliance with any requirement of a regulatory nature (however arising).

•    The provision must not provide any indemnity against any liability incurred by the director in defending criminal proceedings in which he is convicted.

The reference to a conviction is to the final decision in the proceedings. For this purpose a conviction becomes final, if not appealed against, at the end of the period for bringing an appeal or, if appealed against, at the time when the appeal (or any further appeal) is disposed of. An appeal is disposed of if it is determined and the period for bringing any further appeal has ended or if it is abandoned or otherwise ceases to have effect.

[*CA 2006, s 235*].

**Standard articles.** Where a company has adopted standard articles, see

## 18.43  Directors

- *Table A, Reg 118* (which provides for indemnification only)

- *Model Articles, Arts 52, 53* (private companies) (which provide for both indemnity and insurance)

- *Model Articles, Arts 85, 86* (public companies) (which provide for both indemnity and insurance)

set out in APPENDIX 4 STANDARD ARTICLES OF ASSOCIATION.

**18.44** *Inspection of qualifying indemnity provision*

Where a qualifying indemnity provision (or a variation of the provision) is made for a director of a company the company or (in the case of an associated company), as the case may be, each of them must keep available for inspection a copy of the qualifying indemnity provision. If the provision is not in writing, a written memorandum setting out its terms must be kept.

*Inspection.* The copy (or memorandum) must be kept available for inspection at the company's registered office or a place specified in the regulations made under *CA 2006, s 1136* (see **36.2** RECORDS) for details.

The copy (or memorandum) must be open to inspection by any member of the company without charge. Any member of the company is also entitled, on request and on payment of such fee as may be prescribed, to be provided with a copy of any such copy (or memorandum) within seven days after the request is received by the company.

*Availability for inspection and copying.* See **36.2** RECORDS.

*Retention.* The copy (or memorandum) must be retained by the company for at least one year from the date of termination or expiry of the provision and must be kept available for inspection during that time.

*Notice to Registrar of Companies.* The company must, within 14 days, give notice to the Registrar of Companies of the place at which the copy or memorandum is kept available for inspection and any change in that place (unless it has at all times been kept at the company's registered office).

*Offences.* If inspection is refused or default is made in complying with the above provisions, an offence is committed by every officer of the company who is in default. A person guilty of such an offence is liable, on summary conviction, to a fine not exceeding level 3 on the standard scale and, for continued contravention, a daily default fine not exceeding one-tenth of level 3 on the standard scale. See **29.1** OFFENCES AND LEGAL PROCEEDINGS for the standard scale.

In the case of any such refusal or default, the court may by order compel an immediate inspection or, as the case may be, direct that the copy required be sent to the person requiring it.

[*CA 2006, ss 237, 238, 256*].

## 18.45  Ratification of acts of directors

In addition to any indemnity or insurance which the company may provide, or any statutory authorisation by the directors of conflicts of interest (see **18.24**(5)) or any common law approval by members of such conflicts of interest (whether by provision in the company's articles or in shareholder meeting), *s 239* of *CA 2006* also preserves the common law rule that breaches of directors' duties can be ratified by the company's members. Neither the director in breach nor any person connected with him (and for the extended definition of "connected" see **18.1(3)**) can, as a member, vote on the ratification. "Ratification" in this context means a release of a claim for breach of duty against a director. *CA 2006, s 239* provides that any decision of a company to ratify any acts or omissions by a director (including a former director or a shadow director) amounting to negligence, default, breach of duty or breach of trust in relation to the company must be made by resolution of the members of the company. Where the resolution is

- proposed as a written resolution, neither the director (if a member of the company) nor any member 'connected' with him is an eligible member; and

- proposed at a meeting, it is passed only if the necessary majority is obtained disregarding votes in favour of the resolution by the director (if a member of the company) and any member connected with him. But this does not prevent the director or any such member from attending, being counted towards the quorum and taking part in the proceedings at any meeting at which the decision is considered.

The above provisions do not affect

- the validity of a decision taken by unanimous consent of the members of the company;

- any power of the directors to agree not to sue, or to settle or release a claim made by them on behalf of the company; or

- any other enactment or rule of law imposing additional requirements for valid ratification or any rule of law as to acts that are incapable of being ratified by the company.

[*CA 2006, s 239*].

## 18.46 EMPLOYMENT, REMUNERATION, ETC

The remuneration, etc of directors is determined in accordance with the articles. Where a company has adopted standard articles,

(a)     for remuneration, see

- *Table A, Reg 82*

- *Model Articles, Art 19* (private companies)

- *Model Articles, Art 23* (public companies);

(b)     for pensions and gratuities, see

- *Table A, Reg 87*; and

(c)     for expenses, see

- *Table A, Reg 83*

- *Model Articles, Art 20* (private companies)

- *Model Articles, Art 24* (public companies)

set out in APPENDIX 4 STANDARD ARTICLES OF ASSOCIATION.

## 18.47 Payments for loss of office

Subject to the exceptions in **18.50** below, any 'payment for loss of office'

- by a company to a director of the company or its holding company,

- by any person to a director of a company in connection with the transfer of the undertaking or property of the company or a subsidiary of the company, or

- by any person to a director of a company in connection with the transfer of shares in the company or in a subsidiary company resulting from a takeover bid

requires approval by the appropriate members. See **18.48** to **18.50** for full details.

Where approval by the members is required under more than one set of provisions (see **18.48–18.50**), the requirements of each applicable provision must be met but a separate resolution for each provision is not required. [*CA 2006, s 225*].

**Meaning of payment for loss of office.** *Payment for loss of office'* means a payment made to a director or past director of a company

(a)   by way of compensation for loss of office as director of the company;

(b)   by way of compensation for loss, while director of the company or in connection with his ceasing to be a director of it, of

    (i)   any other office or employment in connection with the management of the affairs of the company; or

    (ii)   any office (as director or otherwise) or employment in connection with the management of the affairs of any subsidiary undertaking of the company;

(c)   as consideration for, or in connection with, his retirement from his office as director of the company; or

(d)   as consideration for, or in connection with, his retirement, while director of the company or in connection with his ceasing to be a director of it, from

    (i)   any other office or employment in connection with the management of the affairs of the company; or

    (ii)   any office (as director or otherwise) or employment in connection with the management of the affairs of any subsidiary undertaking of the company.

The references to 'compensation' and 'consideration' include benefits otherwise than in cash. [*CA 2006, s 215(1)(2)*].

**18.48**   *Approval by members of payment*

Subject to the exceptions in **18.50**, a company cannot make a payment for loss of office or payment for loss of office in connection with the transfer of the whole or part of the undertaking of the company to

(a)   a director of the company unless the payment has been approved by a resolution of the members of the company; or

(b)   a director of its holding company (or in the case of a transfer of undertaking to a director of a subsidiary) unless the payment has been approved by a resolution of the members of each of those companies.

No approval is required on the part of the members of a body corporate that is a wholly-owned subsidiary of another body corporate or is not a UK-registered company.

Director for these purposes includes shadow director but loss of office as a director does not apply in relation to loss of a person's status as a shadow director.

*Memorandum of particulars.* The resolution must not be passed unless a memorandum setting out particulars of the proposed payment (including its amount) is made available to the members of the company.

- Where members' approval is sought by way of a written resolution, the memorandum must be sent or submitted to every eligible member at or before the time at which the proposed resolution is sent or submitted to him. Any accidental failure to send or submit the memorandum to one or more members is disregarded for the purpose of determining whether the requirement has been met (subject to any provision of the company's articles).

- Where members' approval is sought by a resolution at a meeting, the memorandum must be made available for inspection by the members both

  (i)    at the company's registered office for not less than 15 days ending with the date of the meeting; and

  (ii)   at the meeting itself.

*Payment.* For the above purposes,

- payment to a person connected with a director (see **18.1**(3)) is treated as payment to the director;

- payment to any person at the direction of, or for the benefit of, a director or a person connected with him is treated as payment to the director; and

- payment by a person includes payment by another person at the direction of, or on behalf of, the person referred to.

And in relation to a transfer of undertaking "payment" also means

- payment made in pursuance of an arrangement

  (i)    entered into as part of the agreement for the transfer in question, or within one year before or two years after that agreement, and

  (ii)   to which the company whose undertaking or property is transferred, or any person to whom the transfer is made, is privy,

  is presumed, except in so far as the contrary is shown, to be a payment to which these provisions apply; and

- where a director is to cease to hold office or is to cease to be the holder of

  (i)    any other office or employment in connection with the management of the affairs of the company, or

  (ii)   any office (as director or otherwise) or employment in connection with the management of the affairs of any subsidiary undertaking of the company,

  payment for loss of office includes

    (a)    the excess of the price to be paid to the director for any shares in the company held by him over the price which could at the time have been obtained by other holders of like shares; and

    (b)    the money value of any valuable consideration given to the director by a person other than the company.

[*CA 2006, ss 215(3)(4), 216, 217, 218, 223, 224*].

*Charitable companies.* Where a company is a charity in England and Wales, any approval given by the members of the company for the above purposes is ineffective without the prior written permission of the Charity Commission. Such written permission is also required where the payment for loss of office would require approval but for the exemption on the part of the members of a body corporate that is a wholly-owned subsidiary of another body corporate. [*Charities Act 2011, ss 201, 202; CA 2006, s 226*].

**18.49**  *Payment in connection with share transfer resulting from takeover bids*

Subject to the exceptions in **18.50**, no payment for loss of office may be made by any person to a director of a company in connection with a transfer of shares in

- the company, or

- a subsidiary of the company,

resulting from a takeover bid unless the payment has been approved by a resolution of the relevant shareholders. The relevant shareholders are the holders of the shares to which the bid relates and any holders of shares of the same class as any of those shares.

Director for these purposes includes shadow director but loss of office as a director does not apply in relation to loss of a person's status as a shadow director.

No approval is required on the part of the members of a body corporate that is a wholly-owned subsidiary of another body corporate or is not a UK-registered company.

*Memorandum of particulars*. The resolution must not be passed unless a memorandum setting out particulars of the proposed payment (including its amount) is made available to the members of the company.

- Where members' approval is sought by way of a written resolution, the memorandum must be sent or submitted to every eligible member at or before the time at which the proposed resolution is sent or submitted to him. Any accidental failure to send or submit the memorandum to one or more members is disregarded for the purpose of determining whether the requirement has been met (subject to any provision of the company's articles).

- Where members' approval is sought by a resolution at a meeting, the memorandum must be made available for inspection by the members both

  (i)   at the company's registered office for not less than 15 days ending with the date of the meeting; and

  (ii)  at the meeting itself.

*Voting on the resolution*. Neither the person making the offer, nor any associate of his, is entitled to vote on the resolution, but

- where the resolution is proposed as a written resolution, they are entitled (if they would otherwise be so entitled) to be sent a copy of it; and

- at any meeting to consider the resolution they are entitled (if they would otherwise be so entitled) to be given notice of the meeting, to attend and speak and if present (in person or by proxy) to count towards the quorum.

*Deemed approval where no quorum*. If at a meeting to consider the resolution a quorum is not present, and after the meeting has been adjourned to a later date a quorum is again not present, the payment is deemed to have been approved.

*Payment*. For the above purposes,

- payment to a person connected with a director (see **18.1(3)**) is treated as payment to the director;

- payment to any person at the direction of, or for the benefit of, a director or a person connected with him is treated as payment to the director;

- payment by a person includes payment by another person at the direction of, or on behalf of, the person referred to;

- payment made in pursuance of an arrangement

  (i)   entered into as part of the agreement for the transfer in question, or within one year before or two years after that agreement, and

  (ii)   to which the company whose undertaking or property is transferred, or any person to whom the transfer is made, is privy,

  is presumed, except in so far as the contrary is shown, to be a payment to which these provisions apply; and

- where a director is to cease to hold office or is to cease to be the holder of

  (i)   any other office or employment in connection with the management of the affairs of the company, or

  (ii)   any office (as director or otherwise) or employment in connection with the management of the affairs of any subsidiary undertaking of the company,

  payment for loss of office includes

  (a)   the excess of the price to be paid to the director for any shares in the company held by him over the price which could at the time have been obtained by other holders of like shares; and

  (b)   the money value of any valuable consideration given to the director by a person other than the company.

[*CA 2006, ss 215(3), (4), 216, 219, 223, 224*].

**18.50** *Exceptions*

Approval is not required under **18.47** to **18.49** for the following payments.

(1)   *Payments in discharge of legal obligations, etc*

Approval is not required for a payment made in good faith:

(a)   In discharge of an '*existing legal obligation*', ie

  (i)   in relation to a payment within **18.47**, an obligation of the company, or any body corporate associated with it, that was not entered into in connection with, or in consequence of, the event giving rise to the payment for loss of office; or

  (ii)   in relation to a payment within **18.49**, an obligation of the person making the payment that was not entered into for the purposes of, in connection with or in consequence of, the transfer in question.

In the case of a payment within both **18.47** or both **18.47** and **18.49**, then (i) applies and not (ii).

(b)   By way of damages for breach of such an obligation.

(c)   By way of settlement or compromise of any claim arising in connection with the termination of a person's office or employment.

(d)   By way of pension in respect of past services.

A payment part of which falls within (*a*)–(*d*) above and part of which does not is treated as if the parts were separate payments.

For these purposes, bodies corporate are associated if one is a subsidiary of the other or both are subsidiaries of the same body corporate.

[*CA 2006, ss 220, 256*].

(2)   *Small payments*

Approval is not required if

- the payment in question is made by the company or any of its subsidiaries; and

- the amount or value of the payment, together with the amount or value of any 'other relevant payments', does not exceed £200.

'*Other relevant payments*' are payments for loss of office in relation to which the following conditions are met.

- Where the payment in question is one to which **18.47** applies, the other payment was or is paid

  (i)     by the company making the payment in question or any of its subsidiaries;

  (ii)    to the director to whom that payment is made; and

  (iii)   in connection with the same event.

- Where the payment in question is one to which **18.49** applies, the other payment was (or is) paid in connection with the same transfer

  (i)     to the director to whom the payment in question was made; and

  (ii)    by the company making the payment or any of its subsidiaries.

[*CA 2006, s 221*].

*Payment*. For the above purposes,

- payment to a person connected with a director (see **18.1(3)**) is treated as payment to the director;

- payment to any person at the direction of, or for the benefit of, a director or a person connected with him is treated as payment to the director; and

- payment by a person includes payment by another person at the direction of, or on behalf of, the person referred to.

[*CA 2006, s 215(3), (4)*].

**18.51** *Civil consequences of payments made without approval*

The following consequences apply where payments are made in contravention of **18.47** to **18.49** above.

(a)     If a payment is made in contravention of *CA 2006, s 217* (payment by a company to a director)

  (i)     it is held by the recipient on trust for the company making the payment; and

  (ii)    any director who authorised the payment is jointly and severally liable to indemnify the company that made the payment for any loss resulting from it.

(b)    If a payment is made in contravention of *CA 2006, s 218* (payment in connection with the transfer of an undertaking) it is held by the recipient on trust for the company whose undertaking or property is or is proposed to be transferred.

(c)    If a payment is made in contravention of *CA 2006, s 219* (payment in connection with share transfers)

(i)    it is held by the recipient on trust for persons who have sold their shares as a result of the offer made; and

(ii)   the expenses incurred by the recipient in distributing that sum amongst those persons is borne by him and not retained out of that sum.

(d)    If a payment is made in contravention of both *ss 217* and *218*, then (*b*) above applies rather than (*a*) above.

(e)    If a payment is made in contravention of both *ss 217* and *219*, then (*c*) above applies rather than (*a*) above, unless the court directs otherwise.

[*CA 2006, s 222*].

## 18.52 PAYMENTS FOR LOSS OF OFFICE – QUOTED COMPANIES

A quoted company may not make a remuneration payment to a person who is, or is to be or has been, a director of the company unless

(a)    the payment is consistent with the approved directors' remuneration policy, or

(b)    the payment is approved by resolution of the members of the company.

'Remuneration payment' means any form of payment or other benefit made to or otherwise conferred on a person as consideration for the person holding, agreeing to hold or having held, office as director of a company or holding, agreeing to hold or having held during a period when the person is or was such a director any other office or employment in connection with the management of the affairs of the company or any office (as director or otherwise) or employment in connection with the management of the affairs of any subsidiary undertaking of the company, other than a payment for loss of office.

For details of remuneration policy requirements see **19**.

*Payment for loss of office*

No payment for loss of office may be made by any person to a person who is, or has been, a director of a quoted company unless

(a)    the payment is consistent with the 'approved directors' remuneration policy', or

(b)    the payment is approved by resolution of the members of the company.

The approved directors' remuneration policy is the most recent remuneration policy to have been approved by a resolution passed by the members of the company in general meeting.

A resolution approving a payment for loss of office must not be passed unless a memorandum setting out particulars of the proposed payment (including its amount) is made available for inspection by the members of the company

(a)    at the company's registered office for not less than 15 days ending with the date of the meeting at which the resolution is to be considered, and

(b)     at that meeting itself.

The memorandum must explain the ways in which the payment is inconsistent with the approved directors' remuneration policy (see above for its meaning) and .the company must ensure that the memorandum is made available on the company's website from the first day on which the memorandum is made available for inspection until its next accounts meeting. Failure to comply with this requirement does not affect the validity of the meeting at which a resolution is passed approving a payment to which the memorandum relates or the validity of anything done at the meeting .See APPENDIX 1 for the meaning of 'accounts meeting'.

Nothing in the above either

•       authorises a payment for loss of office in contravention of the articles of the company concerned. or

•       applies in relation to a remuneration payment or (as the case may be) a payment for loss of office made to a person who is, or is to be or has been, a director of a quoted company before the earlier of

(a)     the end of the first financial year of the company to begin on or after the day on which it becomes a quoted company, and

(b)     the date from which the company's first directors' remuneration policy to be approved under *CA 2006, s 439A* takes effect.

The "company's website" is the website on which the company makes material available under *CA 2006, s 430*.

*Civil consequences of contravention*

(a)     An obligation (however arising) to make a payment which would be in contravention of the above has no effect.

(b)     If a payment is made in contravention of the above provisions

(i)     it is held by the recipient on trust for the company or other person making the payment, and

(ii)    in the case of a payment by a company, any director who authorised the payment is jointly and severally liable to indemnify the company that made the payment for any loss resulting from it.

(c)     If a payment for loss of office is made in contravention of *CA 2006, s 226C* to a director of a quoted company in connection with the transfer of the whole or any part of the undertaking or property of the company or a subsidiary of the company

(i)     (b) above does not apply, and

(ii)    the payment is held by the recipient on trust for the company whose undertaking or property is or is proposed to be transferred.

(d)     If in proceedings against a director for the enforcement of a liability under (b)(ii)

(i)     the director shows that he or she has acted honestly and reasonably, and

(ii)    the court considers that, having regard to all the circumstances of the case, the director ought to be relieved of liability,

the court may relieve the director, either wholly or in part, from liability on such terms as the court thinks fit.

[*CA 2006, ss 226A–226F; Enterprise and Regulatory Reform Act 2013, s 80*]

**18.53  DIRECTORS' SERVICE CONTRACTS**

**Definition of director's service contract.** A director's *'service contract'*, in relation to a company, means a contract under which

(a)     a director of the company undertakes personally to perform services (as director or otherwise) for the company, or for a subsidiary of the company; or

(b)     services (as director or otherwise) that a director of the company undertakes personally to perform are made available by a third party to the company, or to a subsidiary of the company.

[*CA 2006, s 227(1)*].

Provisions relating to directors' service contracts apply to the terms of a person's appointment as a director of a company. They are not restricted to contracts for the performance of services outside the scope of the ordinary duties of a director. [*CA 2006, s 227(2)*].

**Execution formalities.** It is essential that, prior to the execution of a director's service contract on behalf of the company, the correct formalities are followed. Where a company has adopted standard articles,

(i)      for general powers of directors, see

•        *Table A, Reg 70*

•        *Model Articles, Art 3* (private companies)

•        *Model Articles, Art 3* (public companies); and

(ii)     for directors powers to enter into agreements regarding directors employment, see

•        *Table A, Reg 84*

set out in Appendix 4 Standard Articles of Association.

However, it is not uncommon for companies to have specialised articles which require the consent of members. See also **18.54** below for members' approval of long-term service contracts.

The effect of *CA 2006, s 39*, see **16.1** Dealings With Third Parties, is that there should be no question of entry into the contract being beyond the company's capacity. However, the articles of the company should be checked to ascertain whether or not the matter requires the approval of shareholders.

Where the board of directors does have sufficient authority, any quorum and voting requirements of the articles in respect of directors' meetings should be checked. See **42.42** Resolutions and Meetings.

**Listed companies: periods of notice.** Listed companies must consider the provisions of the Combined Code. Notice or contract periods should be set at one year or less. If it is necessary to offer longer notice or contract periods to new directors recruited from outside, such periods should reduce to one year or less after the initial period. (Combined Code, para B.1.6).

**Compensation, etc for termination.** Where a resolution is passed removing a director from office under *CA 2006, s 168* (see **18.9**), such action is not to be taken as depriving the person removed of compensation or damages in respect of the termination of his appointment as director or of any appointment terminating with that as director. [*CA 2006, s 168(5)*]. Where a company has adopted standard articles, see also

## 18.53 Directors

- *Table A, Reg 84*

set out in APPENDIX 4 STANDARD ARTICLES OF ASSOCIATION.

### 18.54 Members' approval of long-term service contracts

*CA 2006, ss 188* and *189* apply to agreements made on or after 1 October 2007. If however a resolution had been passed before that date approving a long term service agreement, the resolution is effective for the purposes of *sections 188* and *189* if it complies with those sections and *CA 1985, s 319* continues to apply to agreements made before that date. [*SI 2007 No 2194, Sch 3 para 6*].

Where the 'guaranteed term' of a director's employment under a service contract

- with the company of which he is a director, or
- where he is the director of a holding company, within the group consisting of that company and its subsidiaries,

is, or may be, longer than two years, the company cannot agree to such provision unless it has been approved

- by resolution of the members of the company; and
- in the case of a director of a holding company, by resolution of the members of that company.

No approval is required under these provisions on the part of the members of a body corporate that is a wholly-owned subsidiary of another company or is not a UK-registered company.

Director for these purposes includes shadow director (see **18.1(2)**).

*Guaranteed term.* The '*guaranteed term*' of a director's employment is

(a) the period (if any) during which the director's employment

    (i) is to continue, or may be continued otherwise than at the instance of the company (whether under the original agreement or under a new agreement entered into in pursuance of it); and

    (ii) cannot be terminated by the company by notice, or can be so terminated only in specified circumstances; or

(b) in the case of employment terminable by the company by notice, the period of notice required to be given,

or, in the case of employment having a period within (*a*) above and a period within (*b*) above, the aggregate of those periods.

If, more than six months before the end of the guaranteed term of a director's employment, the company enters into a further service contract (otherwise than in pursuance of a right conferred by or under the original contract on the other party to it), these provisions apply as if there were added to the guaranteed term of the new contract the unexpired period of the guaranteed term of the original contract. This applies whether the original contract was entered into before or on or after 1 October 2007. (This is intended to cover the situation where, for example, at the end of the first year of a two-year contract, a director enters into another two-year contract commencing on the expiry of the original two-year contract. In these circumstances the period for which he is to be employed would be three years.)

*Memorandum of proposed contract.* The resolution must not be passed unless a memorandum setting out the proposed contract is made available to the members of the company.

- Where members' approval is sought by way of a written resolution, the memorandum must be sent or submitted to every eligible member at or before the time at which the proposed resolution is sent or submitted to him. Any accidental failure to send or submit the memorandum to one or more members is disregarded for the purpose of determining whether the requirement has been met (subject to any provision of the company's articles).

- Where members' approval is sought by a resolution at a meeting, the memorandum must be made available for inspection by the members both

    (i)   at the company's registered office for not less than 15 days ending with the date of the meeting; and

    (ii)  at the meeting itself.

[*CA 2006, ss 188, 223, 224*].

*Civil consequences of contravention.* If a company agrees to provision of a service contract in contravention of the above provisions, the provision is void to the extent of the contravention. The contract is deemed to contain a term entitling the company to terminate it at any time by the giving of reasonable notice. [*CA 2006, s 189*].

*Charitable companies.* Where a company is a charity in England and Wales, any approval given by the members of the company for the above purposes is ineffective without the prior written permission of the Charity Commission. Such written permission is also required where the payment would require approval but for the exemption on the part of the members of a body corporate that is a wholly-owned subsidiary of another body corporate.

[*Charities Act 2011, ss 201, 202; CA 2006, s 226*].

## 18.55  Inspection of service contracts

A company must keep available for inspection

- a copy of every director's service contract (or a variation of that contract) with the company or with a subsidiary of the company; or

- if the contract is not in writing, a written memorandum setting out the terms of the contract.

All the copies and memoranda must be kept available for inspection at the company's registered office or at one other location. That location must be notified to the Registrar of Companies (see *Companies (Company Records) Regulations 2008 (SI 2008 No 3006)*.

The copy (or memorandum) must be open to inspection by any member of the company without charge. Any member of the company is also entitled, on request and on payment of such fee as may be prescribed, to be provided with a copy of any such copy (or memorandum) within seven days after the request is received by the company.

*Availability for inspection and copying.* See **36.2 Records**.

**Retention.** The copy (or memorandum) must be retained by the company for at least one year from the date of termination or expiry of the contract and must be kept available for inspection during that time.

**Notice to Registrar of Companies.** The company must, within 14 days, give notice to the Registrar of Companies of the place at which the copy or memorandum is kept available for inspection and any change in that place (unless it has at all times been kept at the company's registered office).

**Offences.** If inspection is refused or default is made in complying with the above provisions, an offence is committed by every officer of the company who is in default. A person guilty of such an offence is liable, on summary conviction, to a fine not exceeding level 3 on the standard scale and, for continued contravention, a daily default fine not exceeding one-tenth of level 3 on the standard scale. See **29.1** Offences and Legal Proceedings for the standard scale.

In the case of any such refusal or default, the court may by order compel an immediate inspection or, as the case may be, direct that the copy required be sent to the person requiring it.

**Shadow directors.** A shadow director is treated as a director for the above.

[*CA 2006, ss 228–230*].

**Transitional provisions.** The above provisions apply to

- contracts within *CA 2006, s 227(1)* (see **18.53**) entered into on or after 1 October 2007;

- appointments within *CA 2006, s 227(2)* (see **18.53**) made on or after 1 October 2007; and

- contracts to which the earlier provisions in *CA 1985, s 318(1)* applied immediately before that date.

The provisions of *CA 1985, s 318* continue to apply in relation to

- any default before 1 October 2007 in complying with *CA 1985, s 318(1)* or *(5)*;

- any request for inspection under *CA 1985, s 318(7)* made before that date; and

- any duty to give notice under to the Registrar of Companies under *CA 1985, s 318(4)* arising before that date.

[*SI 2007 No 2194, Sch 3 para 13*].

## 18.56 INTERESTS IN CONTRACTS, TRANSACTIONS, ETC

*Sections 177* and *182* of *CA 2006* provide that if a director is interested in a proposed transaction or arrangement with the company (*s 177*) or an existing transaction or arrangement (*s 182*) he must declare both the nature and extent of that interest to the other directors. Subject to making such a declaration and to anything to the contrary in *CA 2006* or the company's articles, a director may have an interest in such a transaction or arrangement.

The distinctions between *ss 177* and *182* are:

- *section 177* is expressly categorised as a statutory duty whereas *section 182* (which replaced *CA 1985, s 317*) is expressed as an obligation to make a declaration

- breach of *section 182* is a criminal offence

- *section 177* is expressly subject to *section 180* of *CA 2006* which provides that so long as a director has complied with *s 177* the transaction cannot be set aside" by virtue of any common law rule or equitable principle requiring the consent or approval of the members of the company". In other words if the board authorises a transaction it cannot be set aside simply because the members have not given their consent (subject to anything in law or the company's constitution which may otherwise require that consent).

## 18.57   Declaration of interest in existing transactions and arrangements

Subject to the exemptions below, where a director of a company is in any way, directly or indirectly, interested in a transaction or arrangement that has been entered into by the company, he must declare the nature and extent of the interest to the other directors in accordance with the following provisions. The provisions do not apply if, or to the extent that, the interest has been declared under the general duty to declare interest in *a proposed* transaction or arrangement.

The declaration must be made

- at a meeting of the directors, or

- by notice in writing or by general notice (see below)

and if a declaration proves to be, or becomes, inaccurate or incomplete, a further declaration must be made.

Any required declaration must be made as soon as is reasonably practicable, but failure to comply with this requirement does not affect the underlying duty to make the declaration.

*Exemptions.* A declaration is not required

- of an interest of which the director is not aware or where the director is not aware of the transaction or arrangement in question (and, for this purpose, a director is treated as being aware of matters of which he ought reasonably to be aware);

- if it cannot reasonably be regarded as likely to give rise to a conflict of interest;

- if, or to the extent that, the other directors are already aware of it (and for this purpose the other directors are treated as aware of anything of which they ought reasonably to be aware); or

- if, or to the extent that, it concerns terms of his service contract that have been or are to be considered

    (i)    by a meeting of the directors; or

    (ii)   by a committee of the directors appointed for the purpose under the 'company's constitution'.

[*CA 2006, s 182; SI 2007 No 3495, Sch 4 para 50*].

For the above purposes, a '*company's constitution*' includes

- the company's articles;

- any resolutions and agreements to which *CA 2006, ss 29, 30* apply (see **14.1** Constitution – Memorandum and Articles);

- any resolution or other decision come to in accordance with the constitution; and

- any decision by the members of the company, or a class of members, that is treated by virtue of any enactment or rule of law as equivalent to a decision by the company (eg a decision taken by the informal unanimous consent of all the members).

[*CA 2006, s 257*].

*Offence of failure to declare interest.* A director who fails to comply with the above requirements commits an offence. If found guilty, he is liable (i) on conviction on indictment, to a fine; and (ii) on summary conviction, to a fine not exceeding the statutory maximum. See **29.1** OFFENCES AND LEGAL PROCEEDINGS for the statutory maximum.

[*CA 2006, s 183; SI 2007 No 3495, Sch 4 para 50*].

*Declaration made by notice in writing.* A declaration made by notice in writing must be sent to the other directors. It may be sent

- in hard copy form by hand or by post; or

- if the recipient has agreed to receive it in electronic form, in an agreed electronic form by an agreed electronic means.

Where a director declares an interest by notice in writing, the making of the declaration is deemed to form part of the proceedings at the next meeting of the directors after the notice is given. The provisions of *CA 2006, s 248* (minutes of meetings of directors, see **42.43** RESOLUTIONS AND MEETINGS) apply as if the declaration had been made at that meeting.

[*CA 2006, s 184; SI 2007 No 3495, Sch 4 para 50*].

*General notice.* General notice is notice given to the directors of a company to the effect that a director

- has an interest (as member, officer, employee or otherwise) in a specified body corporate or firm and is to be regarded as interested in any transaction or arrangement that may, after the date of the notice, be made with that body corporate or firm; or

- is connected with a specified person (other than a body corporate or firm) and is to be regarded as interested in any transaction or arrangement that may, after the date of the notice, be made with that person. See **18.1**(3) for persons connected with a director.

General notice must state the nature and extent of the director's interest in the body corporate or firm or (as the case may be) the nature of his connection with the person. It is then sufficient declaration of interest in relation to the matters to which it relates provided

- it is given at a meeting of the directors; or

- the director takes reasonable steps to secure that it is brought up and read at the next meeting of the directors after it is given.

[*CA 2006, s 185; SI 2007 No 3495, Sch 4 para 50*].

*Company with sole director.* A sole director need not comply with the above requirements (as there are no other directors to whom he can declare his interests). But where a company is required to have more than one director (eg because it is a public company) and has only a sole director, a declaration is required and

- the declaration must be recorded in writing;

- the making of the declaration is deemed to form part of the proceedings at the next meeting of the directors after the notice is given; and

- the provisions of *CA 2006, s 248* (minutes of meetings of directors, see **42.43** RESOLUTIONS AND MEETINGS) apply as if the declaration had been made at that meeting.

This requirement does not affect the operations of the provisions in **18.58** below.

[*CA 2006, s 186; SI 2007 No 3495, Sch 4 para 50*].

*Shadow directors.* The above provisions apply to a shadow director (see **18.1**(2)) as to a director, but with the following adaptations.

•    The requirement for the declaration to be made at a meeting of directors does not apply.

•    In the requirements for general notice, the requirement for general notice to be given at a meeting of directors or brought up and read at the next meeting of directors does not apply. Instead, general notice by a shadow director is not effective unless given by notice in writing in accordance with the provisions of *CA 2006, s 185* above.

[*CA 2006, s 187; SI 2007 No 3495, Sch 4 para 50*].

*Non-compliance* with the above provisions makes the contract voidable not void (*Hely-Hutchinson v Brayhead Ltd* [1968] 1 QB 549).

*Listed companies.* See **33.32**(*h*) PUBLIC AND LISTED COMPANIES for disclosure of significant contracts in the annual accounts.

**Transitional provisions at 1 October 2008.**

(1)    *CA 1985, s 317* continues to apply in relation to transactions and arrangements entered into before 1 October 2008.

(2)    For the purposes *CA 2006, s 182(1)* above (declaration of interest in existing transaction not previously declared under *CA 2006, s 177*), a declaration of interest made before 1 October 2008 under *CA 1985, s 317* is treated on and after that date as if made under *CA 2006, s 177*.

(3)    For the purposes of *CA 2006, s 182(3)* above (previous declaration under that section proving or becoming inadequate), a declaration of interest made before 1 October 2008 under *CA 1985, s 317* is treated on and after that date as if made under *CA 2006, s 182*.

[*SI 2007 No 3495, Sch 4 para 50*].

## 18.58  Contracts with sole member who is also a director

Where

•    a limited company having only one member enters into a contract with the sole member,

•    the sole member is also a director (or shadow director, see **18.1**(2)) of the company, and

•    the contract is not entered into in the ordinary course of the company's business

the company must, unless the contract is in writing, ensure that the terms of the contract are either set out in a written memorandum or recorded in the minutes of the first meeting of the directors of the company following the making of the contract.

If a company fails to comply with these provisions, an offence is committed by every officer of the company who is in default. A person guilty of such an offence is liable, on summary conviction, to a fine not exceeding level 5 on the standard scale. See **29.1** OFFENCES AND LEGAL PROCEEDINGS for the standard scale. But failure to comply the provisions in relation to a contract does not affect the validity of the contract.

Nothing in these provisions is to be read as excluding the operation of any other enactment or rule of law applying to contracts between a company and a director of the company.

*[CA 2006, s 231; SI 2007 No 2194, Sch 3 para 14]*.

## 18.59 SUBSTANTIAL PROPERTY TRANSACTIONS: MEMBERS' APPROVAL

*Sections 190–196* of *CA 2006* apply to arrangements or substantial property transactions entered into on or after 1 October 2007. A resolution passed before that date approving an arrangement or transaction is effective for the purposes of *CA 2006 ss 190–196* if it complies with the requirements of those provisions. *CA 1985, ss 320–322* continue to apply in relation to substantial property transactions entered into before that date.

*[SI 2007 No 2194, Sch 3 para 7]*.

Subject to the exceptions below, a company must not enter into an arrangement under which

(a)     a director of the company or of its holding company, or a person connected with such a director, acquires (or is to acquire) a 'substantial' non-cash asset from the company (directly or indirectly), or

(b)     the company acquires (or is to acquire) a substantial non-cash asset (directly or indirectly) from such a director or a person so connected,

unless the arrangement has been approved by a resolution of the members of the company or is conditional on such approval being obtained. If the director or connected person is a director of the company's holding company or a person connected with such a director, the arrangement must also have been approved by a resolution of the members of the holding company or be conditional on such approval being obtained.

For these purposes, a shadow director is treated as a director.

*'Substantial'* non-cash asset. An asset is a substantial asset in relation to a company if its value, determined as at the time the arrangement is entered into, exceeds

•     10% of the company's 'asset value' and is more than £5,000; or

•     £100,000.

A company's *'asset value'* at any time is the value of its net assets determined by reference to its most recent annual accounts or, if no annual accounts have been prepared, the amount of the company's called-up share capital. The most recent annual accounts are those in relation to which the time for sending them out to members is most recent.

An arrangement involving more than one non-cash asset or an arrangement that is one of a series involving non-cash assets is treated as if it involved a non-cash asset of a value equal to the aggregate value of all the non-cash assets involved in the arrangement or, as the case may be, the series.

*Exceptions* to the above are as follows.

•     No approval is required on the part of the members of a body corporate that is a wholly-owned subsidiary of another body corporate or is not a UK-registered company.

•     The provisions do not apply to a transaction so far as it relates to

(i)     anything to which a director of a company is entitled under his service contract; or

(ii)     to payment for loss of office as defined in **18.47**.

• No approval is required for a transaction between

(i)      a company and a person in his character as a member of that company; or

(ii)     a holding company and its wholly-owned subsidiary; or

(iii)    two wholly-owned subsidiaries of the same holding company.

• Where a company is being wound up (unless the winding up is a members' voluntary winding up) or is in administration (within the meaning of *IA 1986, Sch B1* or *Insolvency (Northern Ireland) Order 1989 (SI 1989 No 2405)*), no approval is required

(i)      on the part of the members of a company to which these provisions apply; or

(ii)     for an arrangement entered into by a company to which these provisions apply.

• No approval is required for a transaction on a recognised investment exchange effected by a director, or a person connected with him, through the agency of a person who, in relation to the transaction, acts as an independent broker.

[*CA 2006, ss 190–194, 223*].

**Listed companies.** In addition to the requirements of *CA 2006*, listed companies must also comply with the requirements of the Listing Rules on related party transactions. See **33.38** PUBLIC AND LISTED COMPANIES.

**Charitable companies.** Where a company is a charity in England and Wales, any approval given by the members of the company for the above purposes is ineffective without the prior written permission of the Charity Commission. Such written permission is also required where the payment would require approval but for the exemption on the part of the members of a body corporate that is a wholly-owned subsidiary of another body corporate.

[*Charities Act 2011, ss 201, 202; CA 2006, s 226*].

## 18.60   Consequences of contravention

Where a company enters into an arrangement which has not been approved by members or is conditional on such approval, the company is not subject to any liability by reason of a failure to obtain the required approval. [*CA 2006, s 190(3)*]. But the arrangement, and any transaction entered into in pursuance of the arrangement (whether by the company or any other person), is voidable at the instance of the company, unless

• restitution of any money or other asset that was the subject-matter of the arrangement or transaction is no longer possible;

• the company has been indemnified by any other persons for the loss or damage suffered by it; or

• rights acquired in good faith, for value and without actual notice of the contravention by a person who is not a party to the arrangement or transaction would be affected by the avoidance.

Whether or not the arrangement or any such transaction has been avoided, each of the following persons is liable to account to the company for any gain that he has made (directly or indirectly) by the arrangement or transaction, and (jointly and severally with any other person so liable) to indemnify the company for any loss or damage resulting from the arrangement or transaction.

(a)   Any director of the company or of its holding company with whom the company entered into the arrangement in contravention of the provisions in **18.59**.

(b)   Any person with whom the company entered into the arrangement in contravention of those provisions who is connected with a director of the company or of its holding company.

(c)   The director of the company or of its holding company with whom any such person is connected.

(d)   Any other director of the company who authorised the arrangement or any transaction entered into in pursuance of such an arrangement.

For these purposes, director includes shadow director.

This is subject to two exceptions.

(1)   In the case of an arrangement entered into by a company in contravention of *s 190* (which has not been approved by members) with a person connected with a director of the company or of its holding company, that director is not liable if he shows that he took all reasonable steps to secure the company's compliance with *s 190*.

(2)   In any case,

•   a person connected with a director of the company or of its holding company is not liable by virtue of (*b*) above (ie a connected person with whom the company entered into a transaction which was not approved), and

•   a director is not liable by virtue of (*d*) above (ie a director who authorised the arrangement),

if he shows that, at the time the arrangement was entered into, he did not know the relevant circumstances constituting the contravention.

Nothing in the above provisions is to be read as excluding the operation of any other enactment or rule of law by virtue of which the arrangement or transaction may be called in question or any liability to the company may arise.

[*CA 2006, s 195*].

**Effect of subsequent affirmation.** Where a transaction or arrangement is entered into by a company in contravention of the substantial property transactions set out in **18.59** but, within a reasonable period, it is affirmed by resolution of the members of the company (and also, where appropriate, by resolution of the members of the holding company) the transaction or arrangement may no longer be avoided under *CA 2006, s 195* above. [*CA 2006, s 196*].

*Charitable companies.* Where a company is a charity in England and Wales, any affirmation given by the members of the company for the above purposes is ineffective without the prior written permission of the Charity Commission.

[*Charities Act 2011, s 201; CA 2006, s 226*].

## 18.61   LOANS, QUASI LOANS AND CREDIT TRANSACTIONS

The provisions in **18.62** to **18.67** below require, with certain exceptions, members' approval for loans, quasi–loans, credit transactions and related guarantees or security made by a company for directors and connected persons.

## 18.62  Members' approval of loans and quasi-loans

*Loans and quasi-loans to directors and connected persons*

Subject to the exceptions in **18.65**,

(a)    any company may not

    (i)    make a loan to a director of the company or of its holding company, or

    (ii)   give a guarantee or provide security in connection with a loan made by any person to such a director, and

(b)    a public company or a company associated with a public company may not

    (i)    make a 'quasi-loan' to a director or to a person connected with a director of the company or of its holding company, or

    (ii)   give a guarantee or provide security in connection with a quasi-loan made by any person to such a director or to a person connected with such a director,

unless the transaction has been approved by a resolution of the members of the company. If the director is a director of the company's holding company, the transaction must also have been approved by a resolution of the members of the holding company.

No approval is required under these provisions on the part of the members of a body corporate that is a wholly-owned subsidiary of another body corporate or is not a UK-registered company.

For these purposes, a shadow director is treated as a director.

**'Quasi-loan'.** A 'quasi-loan' is a transaction under which one party ('the creditor') agrees to pay, or pays otherwise than in pursuance of an agreement, a sum for another ('the borrower') or agrees to reimburse, or reimburses otherwise than in pursuance of an agreement, expenditure incurred by another party for another ('the borrower')

*   on terms that the borrower (or a person on his behalf) will reimburse the creditor; or

*   in circumstances giving rise to a liability on the borrower to reimburse the creditor.

Any reference to the person to whom a quasi-loan is made is a reference to the borrower. The liabilities of the borrower under a quasi-loan include the liabilities of any person who has agreed to reimburse the creditor on behalf of the borrower.

*Memorandum of loan.* The resolution must not be passed unless a memorandum setting out

*   the nature of the transaction,

*   the amount of the loan/quasi-loan and the purpose for which it is required, and

*   the extent of the company's liability under any transaction connected with the loan/quasi-loan

is made available to members.

Where members' approval is sought by way of a written resolution, the memorandum must be sent or submitted to every eligible member at or before the time at which the proposed resolution is sent or submitted to him. Any accidental failure to send or submit the memorandum to one or more members is disregarded for the purpose of determining whether the requirement has been met (subject to any provisions in the company's articles).

Where members' approval is sought by a resolution at a meeting, the memorandum must be made available for inspection by the members both

(i)     at the company's registered office for not less than 15 days ending with the date of the meeting; and

(ii)    at the meeting itself.

[*CA 2006, ss 197–199, 200, 223, 224*].

Charitable companies. Where a company is a charity in England and Wales, any approval given by the members of the company for the above purposes is ineffective without the prior written permission of the Charity Commission. Such written permission is also required where the loan or guarantee would require approval but for the exemption on the part of the members of a body corporate that is a wholly-owned subsidiary of another body corporate.

[*Charities Act 2011, ss 201, 202; CA 2006, s 226*].

## 18.63   Members' approval of credit transactions

Subject to the exceptions in **18.65**, a public company or a company associated with a public company may not

(a)     enter into a 'credit transaction' as creditor for the benefit of a director of the company or of its holding company, or a person connected with such a director, or

(b)     give a guarantee or provide security in connection with a credit transaction entered into by any person for the benefit of such a director, or a person connected with such a director,

unless the transaction (that is, the credit transaction, the giving of the guarantee or the provision of security, as the case may be) has been approved by a resolution of the members of the company. If the director or connected person is a director of its holding company or a person connected with such a director, the transaction must also have been approved by a resolution of the members of the holding company.

No approval is required under these provisions on the part of the members of a body corporate that is a wholly-owned subsidiary of another body corporate or is not a UK-registered company.

For these purposes, a shadow director is treated as a director.

'**Credit transaction**'. A 'credit transaction' is a transaction under which one party ('the creditor')

•       supplies any goods or sells any land under a hire-purchase agreement or a conditional sale agreement;

•       leases or hires any land or goods in return for periodical payments; or

•       otherwise disposes of land or supplies goods or services on the understanding that payment (whether in a lump sum or instalments or by way of periodical payments or otherwise) is to be deferred.

Any reference to the person for whose benefit a credit transaction is entered into is to the person to whom goods, land or services are supplied, sold, leased, hired or otherwise disposed of under the transaction.

**Memorandum of credit transaction, etc.** The resolution must not be passed unless a memorandum setting out

(1)    the nature of the transaction,

(2)    the value of the credit transaction and the purpose for which the land, goods or services sold or otherwise disposed of, leased, hired or supplied under the credit transaction are required, and

(3)    the extent of the company's liability under any transaction connected with the credit transaction

is made available to the members of the company.

•    Where members' approval is sought by way of a written resolution, the memorandum must be sent or submitted to every eligible member at or before the time at which the proposed resolution is sent or submitted to him. Any accidental failure to send or submit the memorandum to one or more members is disregarded for the purpose of determining whether the requirement has been met (subject to any provision of the company's articles).

•    Where members' approval is sought by a resolution at a meeting, the memorandum must be made available for inspection by the members both

(i)    at the company's registered office for not less than 15 days ending with the date of the meeting; and

(ii)   at the meeting itself.

[*CA 2006, s 201, 202, 223, 224*].

**Charitable companies.** Where a company is a charity in England and Wales, any approval given by the members of the company for the above purposes is ineffective without the prior written permission of the Charity Commission. Such written permission is also required where the transaction would require approval but for the exemption on the part of the members of a body corporate that is a wholly-owned subsidiary of another body corporate.

[*Charities Act 2011, ss 201, 202; CA 2006, s 226*].

## 18.64  Members' approval of related arrangements

A company may not

(a)    take part in an arrangement under which

(i)    another person enters into a transaction that, if it had been entered into by the company, would have required approval under **18.62** or **18.63**, and

(ii)   that person, in pursuance of the arrangement, obtains a benefit from the company or a body corporate associated with it, or

(b)    arrange for the assignment to it, or assumption by it, of any rights, obligations or liabilities under a transaction that, if it had been entered into by the company, would have required such approval,

unless the arrangement in question has been approved by a resolution of the members of the company. If the director or connected person for whom the transaction is entered into is a director of its holding company or a person connected with such a director, the arrangement must also have been approved by a resolution of the members of the holding company.

No approval is required under these provisions on the part of the members of a body corporate that is a wholly-owned subsidiary of another body corporate or is not a UK-registered company.

For these purposes, a shadow director is treated as a director and bodies corporate are associated if one is a subsidiary of the other or both are subsidiaries of the same body corporate.

**Memorandum of arrangement, etc**. The resolution must not be passed unless a memorandum setting out

(1)      the matters that would have to be disclosed if the company were seeking approval of the transaction to which the arrangement relates,

(2)      the nature of the arrangement, and

(3)      the extent of the company's liability under the arrangement or any transaction connected with it

is made available to the members of the company.

•      Where members' approval is sought by way of a written resolution, the memorandum must be sent or submitted to every eligible member at or before the time at which the proposed resolution is sent or submitted to him. Any accidental failure to send or submit the memorandum to one or more members is disregarded for the purpose of determining whether the requirement has been met (subject to any provision of the company's articles).

•      Where members' approval is sought by a resolution at a meeting, the memorandum must be made available for inspection by the members both

(i)      at the company's registered office for not less than 15 days ending with the date of the meeting; and

(ii)      at the meeting itself.

In determining for these purposes whether a transaction is one that would have required approval under **18.62** or **18.63** if it had been entered into by the company, the transaction is to be treated as having been entered into on the date of the arrangement.

[*CA 2006, ss 203, 223, 224, 256*].

**Charitable companies**. Where a company is a charity in England and Wales, any approval given by the members of the company for the above purposes is ineffective without the prior written permission of the Charity Commission. Such written permission is also required where the arrangement would require approval but for the exemption on the part of the members of a body corporate that is a wholly-owned subsidiary of another body corporate.

[*Charities Act 2011, ss 201, 202; CA 2006, s 226*].

## 18.65 Exceptions

Approval is not required for the following payments.

(1)      **Expenditure on company business**

Approval is not required for anything done by a company when making a loan or quasi loan or entering into a credit transaction

•      to provide a director of the company or of its holding company, or a person connected with any such director, with funds to meet expenditure incurred or to be incurred by him for the purposes of

(i)      the company; or

(ii)    enabling him properly to perform his duties as an officer of the company; or

•    to enable any such person to avoid incurring such expenditure.

But this does not authorise a company to enter into a transaction if the aggregate of the value of the transaction in question and the value of any 'other relevant transactions or arrangements' (see below) exceeds £50,000.

[*CA 2006, s 204*].

(2)    **Expenditure on defending proceedings, etc**

Approval is not required for anything done by a company when making a loan or quasi loan or entering into a credit transaction

(a)    to provide a director of the company or of its holding company with funds to meet expenditure incurred or to be incurred by him

(i)    in defending any criminal or civil proceedings in connection with any alleged negligence, default, breach of duty or breach of trust by him in relation to the company or associated company; or

(ii)    in connection with an application for relief under CA 2006, s 1157 (general power of court to grant relief in case of honest and reasonable conduct, see **29.10 OFFENCES AND LEGAL PROCEEDINGS**) or *CA 2006, s 661(3)(4)*; or

(b)    to enable any such director to avoid incurring such expenditure,

if it is done on the following terms.

The terms are

•    that the loan is to be repaid, or (as the case may be) any liability of the company incurred under any transaction connected with the thing done is to be discharged, in the event of

(i)    the director being convicted in the proceedings;

(ii)    judgment being given against him in the proceedings; or

(iii)    the court refusing to grant him relief on the application; and

•    that it is to be so repaid or discharged not later than

(i)    the date when the conviction becomes final;

(ii)    the date when the judgment becomes final; or

(iii)    the date when the refusal of relief becomes final.

For these purposes, a conviction, judgment or refusal of relief becomes final, if not appealed against, at the end of the period for bringing an appeal and, if appealed against, when the appeal (or any further appeal) is disposed of. An appeal is disposed of if it is determined and the period for bringing any further appeal has ended or if it is abandoned or otherwise ceases to have effect.

[*CA 2006, s 205; SI 2007 No 2194, Sch 1 para 11; SI 2007 No 3495, Art 10; SI 2008 No 674, Sch 3 paras 1, 5; SI 2008 No 2860, Art 6*].

(3)    **Expenditure in connection with regulatory action or investigation**

Approval is not required for anything done by a company when making a loan or quasi loan or entering into a credit transaction

(a)    provide a director of the company or of its holding company with funds to meet expenditure incurred or to be incurred by him in defending himself

    (i)    in an investigation by a regulatory authority, or

    (ii)    against action proposed to be taken by a regulatory authority,

in connection with any alleged negligence, default, breach of duty or breach of trust by him in relation to the company or associated company; or

(b)    enable any such director to avoid incurring such expenditure.

[*CA 2006, s 206*].

(4)    **Minor and business transactions**

Approval is not required for a company to make a loan or quasi-loan, or to give a guarantee or provide security in connection with a loan or quasi-loan, if the aggregate of

- the value of the transaction, and

- the value of any 'other relevant transactions or arrangements' (see below),

does not exceed £10,000.

Approval is not required for a company to enter into a credit transaction, or to give a guarantee or provide security in connection with a credit transaction, if the aggregate of

- the value of the transaction (that is, of the credit transaction, guarantee or security), and

- the value of any 'other relevant transactions or arrangements' (see below),

does not exceed £15,000, or if

- the transaction is entered into by the company in the ordinary course of the company's business; and

- the value of the transaction is not greater, and the terms on which it is entered into are not more favourable, than it is reasonable to expect the company would have offered to, or in respect of, a person of the same financial standing but unconnected with the company.

[*CA 2006, s 207*].

(5)    **Intra-group transactions**

Approval is not required for

- the making of a loan or quasi-loan to an associated body corporate; or

- the giving of a guarantee or provision of security in connection with a loan or quasi-loan made to an associated body corporate.

Approval is not required

- to enter into a credit transaction as creditor for the benefit of an associated body corporate; or

- to give a guarantee or provide security in connection with a credit transaction entered into by any person for the benefit of an associated body corporate.

For these purposes, bodies corporate are associated if one is a subsidiary of the other or both are subsidiaries of the same body corporate.

[*CA 2006, ss 208, 256*].

(6)     **Money-lending companies**

Approval is not required for the making of a loan or quasi-loan, or the giving of a guarantee or provision of security in connection with a loan or quasi-loan, by a 'money-lending company' if

(a)     the transaction (that is, the loan, quasi-loan, guarantee or security) is entered into by the company in the ordinary course of its business; and

(b)     (subject to below) the value of the transaction is not greater, and its terms are not more favourable, than it is reasonable to expect the company would have offered to a person of the same financial standing but unconnected with the company.

A '*money-lending company*' means a company whose ordinary business includes the making of loans or quasi-loans, or the giving of guarantees or provision of security in connection with loans or quasi-loans.

The condition specified in (*b*) above does not of itself prevent a company from making a 'home loan' to

- a director of the company or of its holding company, or

- an employee of the company,

if loans of that description are ordinarily made by the company to its employees and the terms of the loan in question are no more favourable than those on which such loans are ordinarily made. A '*home loan*' means a loan

(i)     for the purpose of facilitating the purchase, for use as the only or main residence of the person to whom the loan is made, of the whole or part of any dwelling-house together with any land to be occupied and enjoyed with it;

(ii)    for the purpose of improving a dwelling-house or part of a dwelling-house so used or any land occupied and enjoyed with it; or

(iii)   in substitution for any loan made by any person and falling within (i) or (ii) above.

[*CA 2006, s 209*].

'Other relevant transactions or arrangements'. For the purposes of the above exceptions, '*other relevant transactions or arrangements*' are those previously entered into, or entered into at the same time as the transaction or arrangement in question, in relation to which the following conditions are met.

- Where the transaction or arrangement in question is entered into

(i)     for a director of the company entering into it, or

(ii)    for a person connected with such a director,

the conditions are that the transaction or arrangement was (or is) entered into for that director, or a person connected with him, by virtue of the relevant exception by that company or by any of its subsidiaries.

- Where the transaction or arrangement in question is entered into

  (i)     for a director of the holding company of the company entering into it, or

  (ii)    for a person connected with such a director,

  the conditions are that the transaction or arrangement was (or is) entered into for that director, or a person connected with him, by virtue of the relevant exception by the holding company or by any of its subsidiaries.

A transaction or arrangement entered into by a company that at the time it was entered into

- was a subsidiary of the company entering into the transaction or arrangement in question, or

- was a subsidiary of that company's holding company,

is not a relevant transaction or arrangement if, at the time the question arises whether the transaction or arrangement in question falls within a relevant exception, it is no longer such a subsidiary.

[*CA 2006, s 210*].

## 18.66 Value of transactions and arrangements

For the purposes of loans, quasi loans, credit transactions and related arrangements, the value of a transaction or arrangement is determined as follows. The value of any other relevant transaction or arrangement is taken to be the value so determined reduced by any amount by which the liabilities of the person for whom the transaction or arrangement was made have been reduced.

- The value of a loan is the amount of its principal.

- The value of a quasi-loan is the amount, or maximum amount, that the person to whom the quasi-loan is made is liable to reimburse the creditor.

- The value of a credit transaction is the price that it is reasonable to expect could be obtained for the goods, services or land to which the transaction relates if they had been supplied (at the time the transaction is entered into) in the ordinary course of business and on the same terms (apart from price) as they have been supplied, or are to be supplied, under the transaction in question.

- The value of a guarantee or security is the amount guaranteed or secured.

- The value of an arrangement to which **18.64** applies is the value of the transaction to which the arrangement relates.

- If the value of a transaction or arrangement is not capable of being expressed as a specific sum of money

  (i)     whether because the amount of any liability arising under the transaction or arrangement is unascertainable, or for any other reason; and

  (ii)    whether or not any liability under the transaction or arrangement has been reduced,

  its value is deemed to exceed £50,000.

[*CA 2006, s 211*].

**18.67 Consequences of contravention**

Where a company enters into a transaction or arrangement in contravention of the provisions set out in **18.62** to **18.64**, the transaction or arrangement is voidable at the instance of the company, unless

- restitution of any money or other asset that was the subject-matter of the transaction or arrangement is no longer possible;

- the company has been indemnified for any loss or damage resulting from the transaction or arrangement; or

- rights acquired in good faith, for value and without actual notice of the contravention by a person who is not a party to the transaction or arrangement would be affected by the avoidance.

Whether or not the transaction or arrangement has been avoided, each of the following persons is liable to account to the company for any gain that he has made (directly or indirectly) by the transaction or arrangement and (jointly and severally with any other person so liable) to indemnify the company for any loss or damage resulting from the transaction or arrangement.

(a)     Any director of the company or of its holding company with whom the company entered into the transaction or arrangement in contravention of the provisions in **18.62** to **18.64**.

(b)     Any person with whom the company entered into the transaction or arrangement in contravention of any of those provisions who is connected with a director of the company or of its holding company.

(c)     The director of the company or of its holding company with whom any such person is connected.

(d)     Any other director of the company who authorised the transaction or arrangement.

For these purposes, director includes shadow director.

This is subject to two exceptions.

(1)     In the case of a transaction or arrangement entered into by a company in contravention of the provisions in **18.62** to **18.64** with a person connected with a director of the company or of its holding company, that director is not liable by virtue of (*c*) above if he shows that he took all reasonable steps to secure the company's compliance with the provisions concerned.

(2)     In any case,

- a person connected with a director of the company or of its holding company is not liable by virtue of (*b*) above, and

- a director is not liable by virtue of (d) above,

if he shows that, at the time the transaction or arrangement was entered into, he did not know the relevant circumstances constituting the contravention.

Nothing in the above provisions is to be read as excluding the operation of any other enactment or rule of law by virtue of which the transaction or arrangement may be called in question or any liability to the company may arise.

[*CA 2006, ss 213, 223*].

**Effect of subsequent affirmation**. Where a transaction or arrangement is entered into by a company in contravention of the provisions in **18.62** to **18.64** but, within a reasonable period, it is affirmed by resolution of the members of the company (and also, where appropriate, by resolution of the members of the holding company) the transaction or arrangement may no longer be avoided under *CA 2006, s 213* above.

[*CA 2006, s 214*].

*Charitable companies*. Where a company is a charity in England and Wales, any affirmation given by the members of the company for the above purposes is ineffective without the prior written permission of the Charity Commission.

[*Charities Act 1993, s 66; CA 2006, s 226*].

## 18.68   DIRECTORS' RESIDENTIAL ADDRESSES: PROTECTION FROM DISCLOSURE

Because directors are obliged to give both a service address and a usual residential address to Companies House, details of a director's address is on public record at both the Registrar of Companies and in the register of directors which all companies must keep. Directors have the option of

- providing their residential addresses (as the service address) for the public record (which the vast majority do); or

- providing both a service address and a residential address, with the service address being on the public record and the residential address being on a separate secure register to which access is restricted.

The provisions in **18.69** to **18.73** protect, in the case of a company director who is an individual,

- information as to his usual residential address; and

- the information that his service address is his usual residential address.

From 1 October 2009 that information is referred to as '*protected information*'. Addresses already on the public register at that time continue to be available for public inspection unless the director had applied for a confidentiality order (see below).

Information does not cease to be protected information on the individual ceasing to be a director of the company. To that extent, references to a director include a former director.

[*CA 2006, s 240*].

**Before 1 October 2009**, under *CA 1985, ss 723B–723E* the only effective way that a director at risk of violence or intimidation could protect his address was to apply for a confidentiality order. A director with a confidentiality order provided a single service address in addition to his usual residential address. The service address was entered on the public record. The usual residential address was kept on a secure register to which access was restricted to specified enforcement authorities.

**Companies incorporated before 1 October 2009**. In the case of a company incorporated before 1 October 2009, on or after that date the service address for a director of the company is deemed to be

(a)     the service address for that director that appeared in the company's register of directors and secretaries and in the register of companies as having been notified under a confidentiality order; or

(b)     if no such address appeared, the address that immediately before that date appeared as his usual residential address.

Where (*b*) applies, that address is not protected information for the purposes of the provisions in **18.69** to **18.73**.

[*SI 2008 No 2860, Sch 2 para 33*].

### 18.69   Restriction on use or disclosure of protected information

(1) *By the company*

A company must not use or disclose 'protected information' (see **18.68**) about any of its directors, except

•     for communicating with the director concerned;

•     in order to comply with any requirement of the *Companies Act*s as to particulars to be sent to the Registrar of Companies; or

•     to comply with a court order (see **18.72**).

But this does not prohibit any use or disclosure of protected information with the consent of the director concerned.

[*CA 2006, s 241*].

(2) *By the Registrar of Companies*

(a)     The Registrar of Companies must omit 'protected information' (see **18.68**) from the material on the register that is available for inspection where

   (i)     it is contained in a document delivered to him in which such information is required to be stated, and

   (ii)    in the case of a document having more than one part, it is contained in a part of the document in which such information is required to be stated.

(b)     The Registrar is not obliged

   (i)     to check other documents or (as the case may be) other parts of the document to ensure the absence of protected information; or

   (ii)    to omit from the material that is available for public inspection anything registered before 1 October 2009;

   but otherwise must not use or disclose protected information except as permitted under **18.70** or **18.72**.

[*CA 2006, s 242*].

Transitional provisions.

•     The provisions in (*a*) above do not apply to

   (i)     material delivered to the Registrar of Companies before 1 October 2009; or

   (ii)    material delivered to him on or after that date but which related to notification of changes to directors particulars occurring before that date.

•     In (*b*)(ii) above, the material available for public inspection registered before 1 October 2009 is treated as including changes to directors particulars notified on or after that date in respect of changes occurring before that date.

But these transitional provisions are subject to the continuation of protection afforded by a confidentiality order under *SI 2008 No 2860, Sch 2 para 36.*

[*SI 2008 No 2860, Sch 2 para 34*].

### 18.70   Permitted use or disclosure by the Registrar of Companies

The Registrar of Companies may use 'protected information' (see **18.68**) in the following ways.

(1)   **Directors**

For communicating with the director in question.

[*CA 2006, s 243(1)*].

(2)   **Disclosure to specified public authorities**

To disclose the protected information to the public authorities specified in regulations made under *CA 2006* where the conditions set out in those regulations are satisfied For full details of the specified public authorities and conditions see the *Companies (Disclosure of Address) Regulations 2009 (SI 2009 No 214).*

[*CA 2006, s 243(2); SI 2009 No 214, Reg 2, Sch 1, Sch 2 paras 1–4, 11*].

(3)   **Disclosure to credit agencies**

To disclose the protected information to a '*credit reference agency*' (ie a person carrying on a business comprising the furnishing of information relevant to the financial standing of individuals, being information collected by the agency for that purpose) where the conditions set out in regulations referred to in **18.70(2)** are satisfied. The Registrar must however refrain from disclosing protected information to a credit reference agency if the information relates to a "section 243 beneficiary" or a "section 243 applicant". See **18.71** for the meaning of section 243 beneficiary.

[*CA 2006, s 243(2)(7); SI 2009 No 214, Regs 3, 4, Sch 2 paras 6–10*].

### 18.71   *Application not to disclose protected information to credit reference agencies*

An application can be made to the Registrar of Companies requiring the Registrar to refrain from disclosing protected information relating to a director. The application can be made:

(1)   *By an individual who is, or proposes to become, a director* on the grounds that the individual making the application

(a)   considers that there is a serious risk that he, or a person who lives with him, will be subjected to violence or intimidation as a result of the activities of at least one of

(i)   the companies of which he is, or proposes to become, a director;

(ii)   the companies of which he was a director;

(iii)   the overseas companies of which he is or has been a director, secretary or permanent representative; or

(iv)   the limited liability partnerships of which he is or has been a member; or

(b)   is or has been employed by a 'relevant organisation'.

The application on form SRO4 (together with a fee of £100) must contain

•   a statement of the grounds on which the application is made;

- the name and any former name of the applicant;

- the date of birth of the applicant;

- the usual residential address of the applicant;

- where the Registrar of Companies has allocated a unique identifier to the applicant, that unique identifier;

- the name and registered number of each company of which the applicant is, or proposes to become, a director;

- where the grounds of the application are those described in (a)(ii), (iii) or (iv), the name and registered number of the company, overseas company or limited liability partnership.

Where the grounds of the application are those described in (a) above, the application must be accompanied by evidence which supports the applicant's statement of the grounds of the application. See Companies House Guidance GR7 for examples of evidence which could be supplied. The Registrar of Companies may request additional information or evidence and may also refer to a 'relevant body' any question relating to an assessment of the nature and extent of any risk of violence or intimidation.

Where the grounds of the application are that the applicant is or has been employed by a "relevant organisation", the application must be accompanied by evidence which establishes that the applicant is or has been employed by a relevant organisation. The Registrar of Companies may request additional information or evidence and may also refer to a 'relevant body' any question relating to an assessment of whether the applicant is or has been employed by a relevant organisation.

The Registrar of Companies may accept any answer from a relevant body as sufficient evidence of the matter referred to it.

A 'relevant organisation' means the Government Communications Headquarters, the Secret Intelligence Service, the Security Service or a police force.

A 'relevant body' means any police force and any other person whom the Registrar of Companies considers may be able to assist in answering a question referred to that person by him.

The Registrar of Companies must determine the application and send the applicant notice of the decision to the applicant's usual residential address, as stated in his application, within five working days of the determination being made.

(2)   *By a company on behalf of any of its directors who are individuals* on the grounds that the company making the application considers that there is a serious risk that the director on behalf of whom the application is made, or a person who lives with that director, will be subjected to violence or intimidation as a result of the activities of the company making the application.

The application on form SRO5 (together with a fee of £100) must contain

- a statement of the grounds on which the application is made;

- the name and registered number of the applicant;

- the name and any former name of each director on behalf of whom the application is made;

- the date of birth of each such director;

- the usual residential address of each such director;

- where the Registrar of Companies has allocated a unique identifier to any such director, that unique identifier; and

- the name and registered number of each company of which each such director is a director.

The application must be accompanied by evidence which supports the applicant's statement of the grounds of the application.

The Registrar of Companies may request additional information or evidence. He may also refer to a 'relevant body' (see (1) above) any question relating to an assessment of the nature and extent of any risk of violence or intimidation and may accept any answer as sufficient evidence of that risk.

The Registrar of Companies must then determine the application and send notice of the decision to the company's registered office and to each director concerned (to his usual residential address as stated in the application) within five working days of the determination being made.

(3)    *By a subscriber to a memorandum of association on behalf of any of the proposed directors of a proposed company who are individuals* on the grounds that the subscriber considers that there is a serious risk that those directors on behalf of whom the application is made, or persons who live with them, will be subjected to violence or intimidation as a result of the proposed activities of that proposed company.

The application must contain

- a statement of the grounds on which the application is made;

- the name of the applicant;

- the address of the applicant;

- the name of the proposed company;

- the name and any former name of each of the proposed directors on behalf of whom the application is made;

- the date of birth of each such proposed director;

- the usual residential address of each such proposed director; and

- the name and registered number of each company of which each such proposed director is a director.

The application must be accompanied by evidence which supports the applicant's statement of the grounds of the application.

The Registrar of Companies may request additional information or evidence. He may also refer to a 'relevant body' (see (1) above) any question relating to an assessment of the nature and extent of any risk of violence or intimidation and may accept any answer as sufficient evidence of that risk.

The Registrar of Companies must then determine the application and send the applicant (to the address stated in the application) and each of the proposed directors concerned (to their usual residential address as stated in the application) notice of his determination within five working days of that determination being made.

The Registrar of Companies must not make available for public inspection any application under the above provisions or any documents provided in support of that application.

*Appeals.* Unsuccessful applicants may, with leave of the court, appeal to the High Court (in Scotland, the Court of Session) on the grounds that the decision is unlawful, irrational or unreasonable, or has been made on the basis of a procedural impropriety or otherwise contravenes the rules of natural justice. Any appeal must be brought within 21 days of the date of the Registrar's notice (or later with the court's permission). The court may dismiss the appeal or quash the decision. In the later case, it may refer the matter to the Registrar of Companies with a direction to reconsider it and make a determination in accordance with the findings of the court.

*Duration of decision.* Any decision will continue to have effect until either

•    the beneficiary of the decision or his personal representative has notified the Registrar of Companies in writing that he wishes the decision to cease to apply; or

•    the Registrar of Companies revokes the decision (see below),

whichever happens first.

*Revocation.* The Registrar of Companies may revoke a decision at any time if he is satisfied that the 'beneficiary' of that decision or any other person, in purported compliance with any of the above provisions, is found guilty of an offence under *CA 2006, s 1112* (general false statement offence). A *'beneficiary'* includes an individual in relation to whom confidentiality order was in force immediately before 1 October 2009.

If the Registrar of Companies proposes to make a revocation decision, he must send the beneficiary notice of his intention

•    informing the beneficiary that he may, within 28 days of the notice, deliver representations in writing to the Registrar; and

•    stating that if representations are not received by the Registrar within that period, the revocation decision will be made at the expiry of that period.

If the beneficiary delivers representations in the time allowed, the Registrar of Companies must consider them and, within five working days of making his decision, send notice of it to the beneficiary.

[*CA 2006, s 243(4)–(6); SI 2009 No 214, Regs 5–8, 14–16*].

A person who has had a decision made in their favour is known as a section 243 beneficiary. Any forms delivered to Companies House must indicate this (either paper forms or electronic filing). Failure to do so risks the protected information being disclosed to credit reference agencies.

## 18.72 Disclosure under a court order

The court may make an order for the disclosure of protected information by the company or by the Registrar of Companies if

•    there is evidence that service of documents at a service address other than the director's usual residential address is not effective to bring them to the notice of the director; or

•    it is necessary or expedient for the information to be provided in connection with the enforcement of an order or decree of the court, and the court is otherwise satisfied that it is appropriate to make the order. An order for disclosure by the Registrar of Companies can only be made if the company does not have the director's usual residential address or has been dissolved.

A court order can be made on the application of a liquidator, creditor or member of the company, or any other person appearing to the court to have a sufficient interest.

[*CA 2006, s 244*].

### 18.73  Circumstances in which the Registrar of Companies can put a usual residential address on the public record

The Registrar of Companies can put a director's usual residential address on the public record if

- communications sent by the Registrar to the director and requiring a response within a specified period remain unanswered; or

- evidence comes to the Registrar's attention that service of documents at a service address provided in place of the director's usual residential address is not effective to bring them to the notice of the director.

Before doing so, the Registrar must give notice of the proposed course of action to the director and to every company of which the Registrar has been notified that the individual is a director. The notice must state the grounds for doing so and specify a period within which representations may be made. It must be sent to the director at his usual residential address, unless it appears to the Registrar that service at that address may be ineffective to bring it to the individual's notice, in which case it may be sent to any service address provided in place of that address.

On deciding that a director's usual residential address is to be put on the public record, the Registrar of Companies must proceed as if notice of a change of registered particulars had been given stating

- the usual residential address as the director's service address; and

- that the director's usual residential address is the same as his service address.

The Registrar must give notice of having done so to the director and to the company.

On receipt of the notice the company must

- enter the director's usual residential address in its register of directors as his service address; and

- state in its register of directors' residential addresses that his usual residential address is the same as his service address.

unless it has been notified by the director in question of a more recent address as his usual residential address, in which case the company must enter that address in its register of directors as the director's service address and give notice to the Registrar as on a change of registered particulars.

The requirement to enter the address and state that it is a directors' usual address does not apply if an election under *CA 2006, s 167A* is in force (see **38.4**—Option to keep information on the central register). If such an election is in force and the director has notified a more recent address, the company must deliver the particulars to the Registrar of Companies in place of entering the address in its register.

If a company fails to comply with these requirements, an offence is committed by the company and every officer of the company who is in default. A person guilty of such an offence is liable, on summary conviction, to a fine not exceeding level 5 on the standard scale and, for continued contravention, a daily default fine not exceeding of the greater of £5,000 or level 4 on the standard scale. See **29.1** Offences and Legal Proceedings for the standard scale.

A director whose usual residential address has been put on the public record by the Registrar of Companies under the above provisions cannot register a service address other than his usual residential address for a period of five years from the date of the Registrar's decision.

[*CA 2006, ss 245, 246; SBEE 2015, s 94, Sch 5, para 15; SI 2008 No 2860, Sch 2 para 35; SI 2015 No 664, Sch 3; SI 2016 No 321, Reg 6*].

See generally Companies House Guidance GP7 "Restricting the disclosure of your address".

## 18.74 Application to make an address unavailable for inspection

Where the usual residential address of an individual was placed on the public register on or after 1 January 2003, the individual can, in certain circumstances, make an application to make that address unavailable for public inspection. See **39.19** for full details.

# 19   Directors' Remuneration Reports and Policies – Quoted Companies

**Background.** The provisions in this chapter apply, unless otherwise stated, to financial years beginning on or after 1 October 2013 in respect of the annual remuneration report (prepared that year on directors' remuneration in the preceding year) and the remuneration policy (which contains forward-looking disclosures and will be required to be submitted to shareholders for approval for the first time at a general meeting held during that year).Regulations which came into effect on 1 October 2013 are the *Large and Medium-sized Companies and Groups (Accounts and Reports) Amendment Regulations 2013*. They amend earlier regulations by substituting a new Schedule 8 into the 2008 *Large and Medium-sized Companies and Groups (Accounts and Reports) Regulations*. The amendments made by the 2013 regulations do not apply to a company in respect of a financial year ending before 30th September 2013 and the 2008 Regulations continue to apply in that case. This chapter only sets out the new provisions ie the 2008 Regulations as amended by the *2013 Regulations*.

[*SI 2013 No 1981, Reg 3 and 4*]

## 19.1   DUTY TO PREPARE AND DISCLOSE

The directors of a quoted company must prepare a directors' remuneration report for each financial year of the company. In the case of failure to do so, every person who

- was a director of the company immediately before the end of the period for filing accounts and reports for the financial year in question (see **2.12** ACCOUNTS: GENERAL), and

- failed to take all reasonable steps for securing compliance with that requirement,

commits an offence. A person guilty of such an offence is liable (i) on conviction on indictment, to a fine; and (ii) on summary conviction, to a fine not exceeding the statutory maximum. See **29.1** OFFENCES AND PENALTIES for the statutory maximum.

[*CA 2006, s 420*].

The report must contain:

- a statement by the chair of the company's remuneration committee (see 19.15),

- the company's policy on directors' remuneration (see below), and

- information on how the remuneration policy was implemented in the financial year being reported on.

**Duty to disclose.** It is the duty of any director of a company, and any person who is or has at any time in the preceding five years been a director of the company, to give notice to the company of such matters relating to himself as may be necessary for the purposes of a directors' remuneration report. A person who defaults in complying with this requirement commits an offence and is liable, on summary conviction, to a fine not exceeding level 3 on the standard scale. See **29.1** OFFENCES AND PENALTIES for the standard scale.

[*CA 2006, s 421(3), (4)*].

**Remuneration policy to be set out in a separate part of the report**.

*Section 79* of the *Enterprise and Regulatory Reform Act 2013* (*E and RR Act 2013*) inserted *CA 2006, s 421(2A)*. It provides that any information about company policies with respect to the making of remuneration payments and payments for loss of office have to be set out in a separate part of the remuneration report. Regulations made under that provision are the *Large and Medium-sized Companies and Groups (Accounts and Reports) (Amendment) Regulations 2013*, Part 4 of which sets out the requirements for a directors' remuneration policy. Revisions to that policy must be approved and signed by the board of directors.

[*E and RR Act 2013, s 79(1), 79(2)*]

[*CA 2006, s 421(2A), 422A; E and RR Act 2013, s 79(1), 79(2); SI 2013 No 1981, Schedule, Part 4*]

## 19.2    GENERAL PROVISIONS

The regulations made under *s 421* of *CA 2006* referred to above regulate the contents and presentation of the directors' remuneration report and what is to be subject to audit. [See *CA 2006, s 421(1), (2)* and the *Large and Medium-sized Companies and Groups (Accounts and Reports) Regulations 2008 (SI 2008 No 410)* (the *2008 regulations*) as amended by the *Large and Medium-sized Companies and Groups (Accounts and Reports) (Amendment) Regulations 2013*].

Under *regulation 11* of the *2008 regulations*, the remuneration report which the directors of a quoted company are required to prepare must contain the information in **19.4** to **19.25** and must comply with any requirement in those paragraphs as to how information is to be set out in the report.

- The information in **19.4** relates to information about remuneration committees. The information in **19.5** relates to the remuneration policy

- The information in **19.16** to **19.21** relates to detailed information about directors' remuneration and is required to be reported upon by the auditors. It forms the 'auditable part' of a directors' remuneration report for the purposes of *CA 2006, s 497* (see **8.36** AUDIT).

[*SI 2008 No 410, Reg 11; SI 2013 No 1981, Reg 2*]

Information required to be shown in the report for, or in respect of, a particular person must be shown in a manner that links the information to that person identified by name. Nothing prevents the directors setting out in the report any such additional information as they think fit and any item which may be shown in the report may be shown in greater detail than required by *Schedule 8* to the *2008 Regulations* (as amended).

Where the requirements of *Schedule 8* to the *2008 Regulations* refer to a "director" those requirements may be complied with in such manner as to distinguish between directors who perform executive functions and those who do not (see **18.1** for the meaning of executive director).

Any requirement of that Schedule to provide information in respect of a director may, in respect of those directors who do not perform executive functions be omitted or otherwise modified where that requirement does not apply to such a director. In such a case particulars of, and the reason for, the omission or modification must be given in the report.

Any requirement of that *Schedule* to provide information in respect of performance measures or targets does not require the disclosure of information which, in the opinion of the directors, is commercially sensitive in respect of the company. Where the directors rely on this provision particulars of, and the reason for the omission, must be given in the report and an indication given of when (if at all) the information is to be reported to members of the company.

Where any provision of that *Schedule* requires a sum or figure to be given in respect of any financial year preceding the relevant financial year, in the first remuneration report prepared in accordance with that *Schedule* that sum or figure may, where the sum or figure is not readily available from the reports and accounts of the company prepared for those years, be given as an estimate and a note of explanation provided in the report.

[*SI 2008 No 410, Sch 8, paras 2, 41; SI 2013 No 1981, Reg 2*].

## 19.3  Interpretation

(1) *Amounts to be shown*

(a) With respect to the amounts to be shown the amount in each case includes all relevant sums paid by or receivable from

    (i)   the company,

    (ii)  the company's subsidiary undertakings, and

    (iii) any other person

except sums to be accounted for to the company or any of its subsidiary undertakings or any other undertaking of which any person has been a director while director of the company, by virtue of *CA 2006, s 219* (payment in connection with share transfer resulting from a takeover bid: requirement of members' approval, see **18.51** DIRECTORS), to past or present members of the company or any of its subsidiaries or any class of those members.

Amounts paid to or receivable by a person include amounts paid to or receivable by a person connected with him or a body corporate controlled by him (but not so as to require an amount to be counted twice).

(b)     The amounts to be shown for any financial year under **19.16** to **19.26** are the sums receivable in respect of that year (whenever paid) or, in the case of sums not receivable in respect of a period, the sums paid during that year. But where

      (i)     any sums are not shown in the directors' remuneration report for the relevant financial year on the ground that the person receiving them is liable to account for them as mentioned in (*a*) above, but the liability is thereafter wholly or partly released or is not enforced within a period of two years, or

      (ii)    any sums paid by way of expenses allowance are charged to UK income tax after the end of the relevant financial year (or, in the case of any such sums paid otherwise than to an individual, it does not become clear until the end of the relevant financial year that those sums would be charged to such tax were the person an individual),

those sums must, to the extent to which the liability is released or not enforced or they are charged as mentioned above (as the case may be), be shown in the first directors' remuneration report in which it is practicable to show them and must be distinguished from the amounts to be shown apart from this provision.

Where it is necessary to do so for the purposes of making any distinction required by paragraphs (a) or (b) in any amount to be shown, the directors may apportion any payments between the matters in respect of which these have been or are receivable in such manner as they think appropriate.

[*SI 2008 No 410, Sch 8, paras 46, 47, 48; SI 2013 No 1981, Reg 3*].

(2) *Compensation*

Compensation includes benefits otherwise than in cash; and in relation to such compensation references to its amount are to the estimated money value of the benefit.

[*SI 2008 No 410, Sch 8, para 44(3); SI 2013 No 1981, Reg 3*].

(3) *Compensation in respect of loss of office*

Compensation in respect of loss of office includes compensation received or receivable by a person for

(a)     loss of office as director of the company;

(b)     loss, while director of the company or on or in connection with his ceasing to be a director of it, of

      •      any other office in connection with the management of the company's affairs, or

      •      any office as director or otherwise in connection with the management of the affairs of any undertaking that, immediately before the loss, is a subsidiary undertaking of the company or an undertaking of which he is a director by virtue of the company's nomination (direct or indirect);

(c)     compensation in consideration for, or in connection with, a person's retirement from office; and

(d)     where such a retirement is occasioned by a breach of the person's contract with the company or with an undertaking that, immediately before the breach, is a subsidiary undertaking of the company or an undertaking of which he is a director by virtue of the company's nomination (direct or indirect)

- payments made by way of damages for the breach; or

- payments made by way of settlement or compromise of any claim in respect of the breach.

[*SI 2008 No 410, Sch 8, para 44(2); SI 2013 No 1981, Reg 3*].

(4) *'Pension scheme'*

Pension scheme means a retirement benefits scheme within the meaning given by *section 150(1)* of the *Finance Act 2004* which is one in which the company participates or one to which the company paid a contribution during the financial year

[*SI 2008 No 410, Sch 8, para 44(1)*].

(5) *'Performance measure'*

Performance measure is the measure by which performance is to be assessed but does not include any condition relating to service

[*SI 2008 No 410, Sch 8, para 44(1)*].

(6) 'Performance target'

Performance target is the specific level of performance to be attained in respect of that performance measure

[*SI 2008 No 410, Sch 8, para 44(1)*].

(7) *'Qualifying services'*

Qualifying services, in relation to any person, means his services as a director of the company, and his services at any time while he is a director of the company

- as a director of an undertaking that is a subsidiary undertaking of the company at that time;

- as a director of any other undertaking of which he is a director by virtue of the company's nomination (direct or indirect); or

- otherwise in connection with the management of the affairs of the company or any such subsidiary undertaking or any such other undertaking.

[*SI 2008 No 410, Sch 8, para 44(1)*].

(8) *'Remuneration committee'*

Remuneration committee means a committee of directors of the company having responsibility for considering matters related to the remuneration of directors.

[*SI 2008 No 410, Sch 8, para 44(1)*].

(9) *'Retirement benefits'*

Retirement benefits means relevant benefits within the meaning given by *section 393B* of the *Income Tax (Earnings and Pensions) Act 2003* read as if *section 393B(2)* were omitted.

[*SI 2008 No 410, Sch 8, para 44(1)*].

(10) *'Scheme'*

Scheme (other than a pension scheme) means any agreement or arrangement under which money or other assets may become receivable by a person and which includes one or more qualifying conditions with respect to service or performance that cannot be fulfilled within a single financial year, and for this purpose the following must be disregarded, namely

• any payment the amount of which falls to be determined by reference to service or performance within a single financial year

• compensation in respect of loss of office, payments for breach of contract and other termination payments and

• retirement benefits

and 'scheme interest' means an interest under a scheme.

[*SI 2008 No 410, Sch 8, para 44(1)*].

(11) *Shares*

Shares means shares (whether allotted or not) in the company, or any undertaking which is a group undertaking in relation to the company, and includes a share warrant as defined by *CA 2006, s 779* (see **44.12** SECURITIES: CERTIFICATION AND TRANSFERS). Note the provisions of *SBEE 2015* (see **44.12**) which abolish share warrants to bearer.

[*SI 2008 No 410, Sch 8, para 44(1); SI 2013 No 1981, Reg 3*].

## 19.4    Consideration by the directors of matters relating to directors' remuneration

If a committee of the company's directors has considered matters relating to the directors' remuneration for the relevant financial year, the directors' remuneration report must

(a) name each director who was a member of the committee at any time when the committee was considering any such matter;

(b) state whether any person provided to the committee advice, or services, that materially assisted the committee in their consideration of any such matter and name any person that has done so;

(c) in the case of any person named under (b) above who is not a director of the company (other than a person who provided legal advice on compliance with any relevant legislation), state

  (i) the nature of any other services that that person has provided to the company during the relevant financial year;

  (ii) by whom that person was appointed, whether or not by the committee and how they were selected;

  (iii) whether and how the remuneration committee has satisfied itself that the advice received was objective and independent; and

  (iv) the amount of fee or other charge paid by the company to that person for the provision of advice or services referred to in (b) and the basis on which it was charged.

[*SI 2008 No 410, Sch 8, para 22; SI 2013 No 1981, Reg 3*].

## 19.5    Statement of company's policy on directors' remuneration

For financial years beginning on or after 1 October 2013 the directors' remuneration report must contain a statement of the company's policy on directors' remuneration for the following financial year and which must

- be set out in a separate part of the report

- set out all the matters for which the company needs approval from shareholders under *CA 2006, Part 4A* (see **18.52** for *Part 4A* and **19.26** for shareholder approval)

- where any provision in the policy provides for the exercise by the directors of a discretion on any aspect of the policy, set out clearly the extent of that discretion in respect of any such variation, change or amendment.

The report must also contain a statement

- describing how the company intends to implement the approved policy in the financial year following the relevant financial year

- including, where applicable, the performance measures and relative weightings for each performance measure and performance targets determined for the performance measures and how awards will be calculated

- where this is not the first year of the approved remuneration policy, details of any significant changes in the way the policy will be implemented in the next financial year compared to how it was implemented in the relevant financial year and

- need not include information that is elsewhere in the report including any disclosed in the policy.

The policy may be omitted from the report for a financial year if the company does not intend, at the accounts meeting at which the report is to be laid, to move a resolution to approve the policy in accordance with *CA 2006, s 439A* (see **19.26**).

If the policy is omitted from the report in accordance with the above provision, the following information must be set out in the report

- the date of the last general meeting of the company at which a resolution was moved by the company in respect of that directors' remuneration policy and at which the policy was approved and

- where on the company's website or at some other place a copy of the policy may be inspected by members of the company.

[*SI 2008 No 410, Sch 8, para 1, 21, 24(1), (3), (4); SI 2013 No 1981, Reg 3*]

## 19.6   Contents of company's policy on directors' remuneration

In addition to the matters set out in **19.5** the policy must contain

- a future policy table (see **19.7**)

- the principles for a remuneration package when appointing directors (see **19.8**)

- details of service contracts (see **19.9**)

- illustrations of how the policy will apply (see **19.10**)

- policy on payments for loss of office (see **19.11**)

- statement of consideration of employment conditions elsewhere in the group (see **19.12**) and

- statement of consideration of shareholder views (see **19.13**)

[*SI 2008 No 410, Sch 8, Part 4; SI 2013 No 1981, Reg 3*]

## 19.7   Future policy table

A description of each of the components of the remuneration package for directors, comprised in the remuneration policy, must be set out in tabular form and where provisions apply to all directors generally, the table must also include any particular arrangements which are specific to any individual director. In respect of directors not performing an executive function, the information may be set out in a separate table which must also set out the approach of the company to the determination of the fee payable to such directors, any additional fees payable for any other duties to the company and such other items as are to be considered in the nature of remuneration.

In respect of each of the components in the table, the following information must be set out

(a)     how that component supports the long and short-term strategic objectives of the company (or where the company is a parent company, the group)

(b)     an explanation of how that component of the remuneration package operates

(c)     the maximum that must be paid in respect of that component (which may be expressed in monetary terms or otherwise)

(d)     where applicable a description of the framework used to assess performance including

   •      a description of any performance measures which apply and, where more than one performance measure applies, an indication of the weighting of the performance measures or group of performance measures

   •      details of any performance period and

   •      the amount (which may be expressed in monetary terms or otherwise) that may be paid in respect of the minimum level of performance under the policy and any further levels of performance set in accordance with the policy, and

(e)     an explanation as to whether there are any provisions for the recovery of sums paid or the withholding of the payment of any sum.

Notes must accompany the table which set out in respect of any component

   •      which falls within (d) above, an explanation of why any performance measures were chosen and how any performance targets are set

   •      (other than salary, fees, benefits or pension) which is not subject to performance measures, an explanation of why there are no such measures

   •      if the component did not form part of the remuneration package in the last approved directors' remuneration policy, why that component is now contained in the remuneration package

   •      which did not form part of such a package, what changes have been made to it and why and

   •      an explanation of the difference (if any) in the company's policy on the remuneration of directors from the policy on the remuneration of employees generally (within the company or where the company is a parent company, the group).

References to 'component parts of the remuneration package' include, but are not limited to, all those items which are relevant for the purposes of the single total figure table.

[*SI 2001 No 410, Sch 8, para 25–28; SI No 2013 No 1981, Reg 3*]

**19.8   Principles for remuneration package—appointing directors**

The policy must contain a statement

- of the principles which would be applied by the company when agreeing the components of a remuneration package for the appointment of directors

- which sets out the various components which would be considered for inclusion in that package and the approach to be adopted by the company in respect of each component and

- which sets out the maximum level of variable remuneration which may be granted (which can be expressed in monetary terms or otherwise). This does not apply to compensation for the forfeit of any award under variable remuneration arrangements entered into with a previous employer (this is however subject to the above two requirements).

[*SI 2008 No 410, Sch 8, para 29; SI No 2013 No 1981, Reg 3*]

**19.9   Service contracts**

The directors' remuneration policy must contain a description of any obligation on the company which

- is contained in all directors' service contracts.

- is contained in the service contracts of any one or more existing directors or

- it is proposed would be contained in directors' service contracts to be entered into by the company.

Where the directors' service contracts are not kept available for inspection at the company's registered office, the remuneration report must give details of where the contracts are kept and, if the contracts are available on a website, a link to that website.

All of the above apply in like manner to the terms of letters of appointment of directors.

[*SI 2008 No 410, Sch 8, para 30–32; SI 2013 No 1981, Reg 3*].

**19.10   Illustrations of how the policy will apply**

Other than a director who is not performing an executive function, an indication of the level of remuneration that would be received by each director in accordance with the directors' remuneration policy in the first year to which the policy applies must be set out in the form of a bar chart which must contain

(a)   separate bars representing minimum remuneration receivable ie including, but not limited to, salary, fees, benefits and pension

(b)   separate bars representing the remuneration receivable if the director was, in respect of any performance measures or targets, performing in line with the company's expectations

(c)   separate bars representing maximum remuneration receivable (not allowing for any share price appreciation)

(d)   each bar divided into separate parts representing salary, fees, benefits, pension and any other item falling within (a), remuneration where performance measures or targets relate to one financial year and remuneration where performance measures or targets relate to more than one financial year

(e)      each bar showing the percentage of the total comprised by each of the parts and the total value of remuneration expected for each bar

A narrative description of the basis of calculation and assumptions used to compile the bar chart must be set out to enable an understanding of the charts presented but it is not necessary for any matter to be included in the narrative description which has been set out in the future policy table.

[*SI 2008 No 410, Sch 8, para 33–35; SI 2013 No 1981, Reg 3*].

## 19.11  Policy on payment for loss of office

The directors' remuneration policy must set out

(a)      the company's policy on the setting of notice periods under directors' service contracts

(b)      the principles on which the determination of payments for loss of office will be calculated including

     (i)      an indication of how each component of the payment will be calculated

     (ii)     whether, and if so how, the circumstances of the director's loss of office and performance during the period of qualifying services are relevant to any exercise of discretion and

     (iii)    any contractual provision agreed prior to 27 June 2012 that could impact on the quantum of that payment.

[*SI 2008 No 410, Sch 8, para 36–37; SI 2013 No 1981, Reg 3*].

## 19.12  Statement of consideration of employment conditions elsewhere in the company

The directors' remuneration policy must

(a)      contain a statement of how pay and employment conditions of employees (other than directors) of the company and, where the company is a parent company, of the group or other undertakings within the same group as the company, were taken into account when setting the policy for directors' remuneration

(b)      set out whether, and if so how, the company consulted with employees when drawing up the directors' remuneration policy set out in this part of the report and whether any remuneration comparisons measurements were used and if so, what they were, and how that information was taken into account.

[*SI 2008 No 410, Sch 8, para 38–39; SI 2013 No 1981, Reg 3*].

## 19.13  Statement of consideration of shareholder views

The directors' remuneration policy must contain a statement of whether, and if so how, any views in respect of directors' remuneration expressed to the company by shareholders (whether at a general meeting or otherwise) have been taken into account in the formulation of the directors' remuneration policy.

[*SI 2008 No 410, Sch 8, para 40; SI 2013 No 1981, Reg 3*].

**19.14   Contents of remuneration report**

In addition to the provisions of the remuneration policy (above) which forms a separate part of the remuneration report, the report must also contain

- a statement by the chair of the remuneration committee (**19.15**)

- single total figure of remuneration for each director and some additional information (**19.16** and **19.17**)

- pensions (**19.18**)

- scheme interests (**19.19**)

- payments to past directors (**19.20**)

- payments for loss of office (**19.21**)

- share holdings and share interests (**19.22**)

- performance graph and table (**19.23**)

- percentage change in remuneration of director undertaking the role of CEO (**19.24**)

- relative importance of spend on pay (**19.25**)

- statement of voting at general meeting (**19.26**)

**19.15   Statement by chair of the remuneration committee**

The directors' remuneration report must contain a statement by the chair of the remuneration committee (or where there is no such person by a director nominated by the directors to make the statement) summarising for the relevant financial year the major decisions on directors' remuneration, any substantial changes relating to directors' remuneration made during the year and the context in which those changes occurred and decisions have been taken.

[*SI 2008 No 410, Sch 8, para 3; SI 2013 No 1981, Reg 3*].

**19.16   Single total figure of remuneration for each director**

The directors' remuneration report must for the relevant financial year show the information in respect of each person who has served as a director of the company at any time during that year set out in a table( below) ('the single total figure table'). The directors may choose to display the table using an alternative orientation, in which case references to columns in *Schedule 8* to the *2008 Regulations* are to be read as references to rows and where it is necessary to assist in the understanding of the table by the creation of sub-totals the columns headed 'a'–'e' may be set out in an order other than the one set out below.

| Single figure total table | | a | b | c | d | e | Total |
|---|---|---|---|---|---|---|---|
| Director 1 | | | | | | | |
| Director 2 | | | | | | | |

In the single figure total table the sums required to be set out in the columns are

(a)     In the column headed 'a' the total amount of salary and fees .The method to be used to calculate the sums required in this column is the cash paid to or receivable by the person in respect of the relevant financial year.

(b)   In the column headed 'b' all taxable benefits. The method to be used to calculate the sums required in this column is the gross value before payment of tax. Taxable benefits are defined as including

    (i)   sums paid by way of expenses allowances that are chargeable to United kingdom income tax (or would be if the person were an individual or would be if the person were resident in the United Kingdom for tax purposes) and paid to or receivable by the person in respect of qualifying services and

    (ii)  any benefits received by the person, other than salary, (whether or not in cash) that are emoluments of the person and are received by the person in respect of qualifying services. A payment or other benefit received in advance of a director commencing qualifying services, but in anticipation of performing qualifying services, is to be treated as if received on the first day of performance of the qualifying services.

(c)   In the column headed 'c' money or other assets received or receivable for the relevant financial year as a result of the achievement of performance measures and targets relating to a period ending in that financial year other than

•   those which result from awards made in a previous financial year and where final vesting is determined as a result of the achievement of performance measures or targets relating to a period ending in the relevant financial year or

•   those receivable subject to the achievement of performance measures or targets in a future financial year.

Where the performance measures or targets are substantially (but not fully) completed by the end of the relevant financial year, the sum given in the 'c' column may include sums which relate to the following financial year but where such sums are included, those sums must not be included in the corresponding column of the single total figure table prepared for that following year and a note must explain the basis of the calculation.

The method to be used to calculate the sums required in this column is the total cash equivalent including any amount deferred, other than where the deferral is subject to the achievement of further performance measures or targets in a future financial year.

(d)   In the column headed 'd' money or other assets received or receivable for periods of more than one financial year where final vesting

•   is determined as a result of the achievement of performance measures or targets relating to a period ending in the relevant financial year or

•   is not subject to the achievement of performance measures or targets in a future financial year

The method to be used to calculate the sums required in this column is

•   the cash value of any monetary award

•   the value of any shares or share options awarded, calculated by multiplying the original number of shares granted by the proportion that vest (or an estimate) and multiplying that total arrived at by the market price of shares at the date on which the shares vest. Where the market price of shares at the date on which the shares vest is not ascertainable by the date on which the remuneration report is approved by the directors, an estimate of the market price of the shares shall be calculated on the basis of an average market value over the last quarter of the relevant financial year and where the award was an award of shares or share options, the cash amount the individual was or will be required to pay to acquire the shares must be deducted from the total

- the value of any additional cash or shares receivable in respect of dividends accrued (actually or notionally)

(e)    In the column headed 'e' all pension related benefits including payments (whether in cash or otherwise) in lieu of retirement benefits and all benefits in year from participating in pension schemes. The method to be used to calculate the sums required in this column is, for payments in lieu of retirement benefits, the cash benefit and for all benefits in year from participating in pension schemes, what the aggregate pension input amount would be across all the pension schemes of the company or group in which the director accrues benefit, calculated using the method set out in *Finance Act 2004, s 229*. Where there has not been a company contribution to the pension scheme in respect of the director (but if such a contribution had been made it would have been measured for pension input purposes under *Finance Act 2004, s 223(1)(b)*), when calculating the pension input amount for the purposes of this provision, it should be calculated as follows. As if the cash value of any contribution notionally allocated to the scheme in respect of the person (by or on behalf of the company) including any adjustment made for any notional investment return achieved during the relevant financial year were a contribution paid by the employer in respect of the individual for the purposes of *Finance Act 2004, s 223(1)(b)*.

(f)    In the column headed 'total' the total amount of the sums set out in the previous columns.

In addition columns must be included to set out any other items in the nature of remuneration which are not set out in columns 'a' to 'e' (other than payments to past directors) and columns may be included if there are any sub-totals or other items which the directors consider necessary in order to assist in the understanding of the table.

*'Emoluments'* of a person includes salary, fees and bonuses, sums paid by way of expenses allowance (so far as they are chargeable to UK income tax or would be if the person were an individual) but does not include the following.

- The value of any share options granted to him.

- The amount of any gains made on the exercise of any such options (ie the difference between the market price of the shares on the day on which the option was exercised and the price actually paid for the shares).

- Any 'company contributions' paid, or treated as paid, in respect of him under any pension scheme or any benefits to which he is entitled under any such scheme. 'Company contributions' means any payments (including insurance premiums) made, or treated as made, to the scheme in respect of the person by anyone other than the person.

- Any money or other assets paid to or received or receivable by him under any long-term incentive scheme.

Any emoluments paid or receivable or share options granted in respect of a person's accepting office as a director are treated as emoluments paid or receivable or share options granted in respect of his services as a director.

[*SI 2008 No 410, Sch 8, paras 4, 5, 6, 7, 8(1), 10, 11, 44, 45; SI 2013 No 1981, Reg 3*]

## 19.17 Remuneration Reports/Policies (Quoted Companies)

### 19.17 Additional requirements for single total figure table

**Withholding and recovery.** Where any money or assets are reported in the single figure table prepared in respect of any previous financial year and are the subject of a recovery of sums paid or the withholding of any sum for any reason in the relevant financial year then

- the recovery or withholding so attributable must be shown in a separate column in the table as a negative value and deducted from the column headed 'total' and

- an explanation for the recovery or withholding and the basis of the calculation must be given in a note to the table.

**Negative values.** Where the calculations in the table (other than in respect of a recovery or withholding) result in a negative value, the result must be expressed as zero in the relevant column in the table.

**Comparisons.** In order to permit a comparison, each column in the single figure table must contain two sums as follows

- the sum set out in the corresponding column in the report prepared in respect of the financial year preceding the relevant year and

- the sum for the relevant financial year.

**Estimates.** Where a sum is given in the column which relates to the preceding financial year and, was given as an estimated sum, then in the relevant financial year

- it must be given as an actual sum

- the amount representing the difference between the estimate and the actual must not be included in the column relating to the relevant financial year and

- details of the calculation of the revised sum must be given in a note to the table.

**Value of taxable benefits.** In respect of the taxable benefits sum (see **19.16(b)**) after the table a summary must be set out identifying the types of benefits the value of which is included in the sum set out in column 'b' and the value (where significant)

**Money or other assets for achievement of performance measures (see 19.16(c) and (d)).** For every component, the value of which is included in columns 'c' and 'd' of the table, after the table the following relevant details must be set out

- details of any performance measures and the relative weighting of each

- within each performance measure, the performance targets set out at the beginning of the performance period and the corresponding value of the award achievable

- for each performance measure, details of actual performance relative to the targets set and measured over the relevant reporting period, and the resulting level of award and

- where any discretion has been exercised in respect of the award, particulars must be given of how the discretion was exercised and how the resulting level of award was determined.

For every component, the value of which is included in columns 'c' of the table the remuneration report must state if any amount was deferred, the percentage deferred, whether it was deferred in cash or shares, if relevant, and whether the deferral was subject to any conditions other than performance measures.

**Additional columns.** Where additional columns are included a note to the table must set out the basis on which the sums in the column were calculated and such other details as are necessary for an understanding of the sums set out in the column, including any performance measures relating to that component of remuneration or if there are none, an explanation of why not.

[*SI 2008 No 410, Sch 8, para 8(2), 9, 10; SI 2013 No 1981, Reg 3*]

## 19.18 Pensions

The directors' remuneration report must, for each person who has served as a director of the company at any time during the relevant financial year and who has a prospective entitlement to defined benefits or cash balance benefits (or to benefits under a hybrid arrangement which includes such benefits) in respect of qualifying services, contain the following information in respect of pensions.

(a)    details of those rights as at the end of that year, including the person's normal retirement date

(b)    a description of any additional benefit that will become receivable by a director in the event that that director retires early and

(c)    where a person has rights under more than one type of pension benefit identified in column 'e' of the single total figure table (see **19.16**), separate details relating to each type of pension benefit.

'Defined benefits', 'cash balance benefits' and 'hybrid arrangement' have the same meaning as in *Finance Act 2004, s 152*.

'Normal retirement date' means an age specified in the pension scheme rules (or otherwise determined) as the earliest age at which, while the individual continues to accrue benefits under the pension scheme, entitlement to a benefit arises without consent (whether of an employer, the trustees or managers of the scheme or otherwise) and without any actuarial reduction but disregarding any special provision as to early repayment on grounds of ill health, redundancy or dismissal.

[*SI 2008 No 410, Sch 8, para 13; SI 2013 No 1981, Reg 3*].

## 19.19 Scheme interests including share options

The directors' remuneration report must, subject to below, contain a table setting out the following information in respect of each person who has served as a director of the company at any time during the relevant financial year.

(a)    Details of the 'scheme interests' awarded to the person during the relevant financial year and

(b)    For each scheme interest

(i)    a description of the type of interest awarded

(ii)    a description of the basis on which the award is made

(iii)    the face value of the award

(iv)    the percentage of scheme interests that would be receivable if the minimum performance was achieved

(v)    for a scheme interest that is a share option, an explanation of any difference between the exercise price per share and the price specified below

(vi)     the end of the period over which the performance measures and targets for that interest have to be achieved (or if there are different periods for different measures and targets, the end of whichever of those periods ends last) and

(vii)     a summary of the performance measures and targets if not set out elsewhere in the report.

Where the report sets out the face value of an award in respect of a scheme interest relating to shares or share options, the report must specify

(a)     whether the face value has been calculated using the share price at date of grant or the average share price

(b)     where the share price at date of grant is used, the amount of that share price and the date of grant

(c)     where the average share price is used, what that price was and the period used for calculating the average.

In respect of a scheme interest relating to shares or share options 'face value' means the maximum number of shares that would vest if all performance measures and targets are met multiplied by either the share price at date of grant or the average share price used to determine the number of shares awarded.

Where the report sets out the face value of an award in respect of a scheme interest relating to shares or share options, the report must specify

(a)     whether the face value has been calculated using the share price at date of grant or the average share price

(b)     where the share price at date of grant is used, the amount of that share price and the date of grant and

(c)     where the average share price is used, what that price was and the period used for calculating the average.

[*SI 2008 No 410, Sch 8, para 14; SI 2013 No 1981, Reg 3*].

## 19.20 Payments to past directors

The directors' remuneration report must for the relevant financial year contain details of any payments of money or other assets to any person who was not a director of the company at the time the payment was made but had been a director of the company before that time, excluding,

(a)     any payments falling within **19.21** 'payments for loss of office'

(b)     any payments shown in the single total figure table (see **19.16**)

(c)     any payments which have been disclosed in a previous directors' remuneration report of the company

(d)     any payments which are below a de minimis threshold set by the company and stated in the report

(e)     payments by way of regular pension benefits commenced in a previous year or dividend payments in respect of scheme interests retained after leaving office and

(f)     payments in respect of employment with or any other contractual service performed for the company other than as a director.

*[SI 2008 No 410, Sch 8, para 15; SI 2013 No 1981, Reg 3].*

### 19.21  Payments for loss of office

The directors' remuneration report must, for the relevant financial year set out, for each person who has served as a director of the company at any time during that year, or any previous year, excluding payments which are below a de minimis threshold set by the company and stated in the report

(a)    the total amount of any payment for loss of office paid to or receivable by the person in respect of that financial year, broken down into each component comprised in that payment and the value of each component

(b)    an explanation of how each component was calculated

(c)    any other payments paid to or receivable by the person in connection with the termination of qualifying services, whether by way of compensation for loss of office or otherwise, including the treatment of outstanding incentive awards that vest on or following termination and

(d)    where any discretion was exercised in respect of the payment, an explanation of how it was exercised.

*[SI 2008 No 410, Sch 8, para 16; SI 2013 No 1981, Reg 3].*

### 19.22  Statement of directors' shareholdings and share interests

The directors' remuneration report for the relevant financial year must contain for each person who has served as a director of the company at any time during that year

(a)    a statement of any requirements or guidelines for the director to own shares in the company and state whether or not those requirements or guidelines have been met

(b)    in tabular form or forms

    (i)    the total number of interests in shares in the company of the director including interests of connected persons (as defined for the purposes of *FSMA 2000*)

    (ii)    the total number of scheme interests differentiating between shares and share options and those with or without performance measures

    (iii)    details of those scheme interests (which may exclude any details included elsewhere in the report) and

    (iv)    details of share options which are vested but unexercised and exercised in the relevant financial year.

*[SI 2008 No 410, Sch 8, para 17; SI 2013 No 1981, Reg 3].*

### 19.23  Performance graph and table

(1) The directors' remuneration report must

(a)    contain a line graph that shows for each of

    (i)    a holding of shares of that class of the company's equity share capital whose listing, or admission to dealing, has resulted in the company falling within the definition of quoted company, and

(ii)    a hypothetical holding of shares made up of shares of the same kinds and number as those by reference to which a broad equity market index is calculated,

a line drawn by joining up points plotted to represent, for each of the financial years in the relevant period, the total shareholder return on that holding; and

(b)    state the name of the index selected for the purposes of the graph and set out the reasons for selecting that index.

The '*total shareholder return*' for a relevant period on a holding of shares must be calculated using a fair method that

- takes as its starting point the percentage change over the period in the market price of the holding;

- involves making the 'assumptions as to reinvestment of income' and 'assumptions as to the funding of liabilities' specified below, and

- makes provision for any replacement of shares in the holding by shares of a different description;

and the same method must be used for each of the holdings mentioned above.

The '*assumptions as to reinvestment of income*' are

(i)    that any benefit in the form of shares of the same kind as those in the holding is added to the holding at the time the benefit becomes receivable; and

(ii)    that any '*benefit*' in cash, and an amount equal to the value of any benefit not in cash and not falling within (i) above, is applied at the time the benefit becomes receivable in the purchase at their market price of shares of the same kind as those in the holding and that the shares purchased are added to the holding at that time;

and for this purpose 'benefit' means any benefit (including, in particular, any dividend) receivable in respect of any shares in the holding by the holder from the company of whose share capital the shares form part.

The '*assumption as to the funding of liabilities*' is that, where the holder has a 'liability' to the company of whose capital the shares in the holding form part, shares are sold from the holding

- immediately before the time by which the liability is due to be satisfied, and

- in such numbers that, at the time of the sale, the market price of the shares sold equals the amount of the liability in respect of the shares in the holding that are not being sold;

and for this purpose '*liability*' means a liability arising in respect of any shares in the holding or from the exercise of a right attached to any of those shares.

(2) The report must also set out in tabular form the following information for each of the financial years in the relevant period in respect of the director undertaking the role of chief executive officer

(a)    total remuneration as set out in the single total figure table (see **19.16**)

(b)    the sum set out in the table in column headed 'c' in the single total figure table expressed as a percentage of the maximum that could have been paid in respect of that component in the financial year and

(c)     the sum set out in the table in column headed 'd' in the single total figure table restated as a percentage of the number of shares vesting against the maximum number of shares that could have been received, or, where paid in money and other assets, as a percentage of the maximum that could have been paid in respect of that component in the financial year.

This provision may be complied with by use of either

(a)     a sum based on the information supplied in the directors' remuneration reports for those previous years or

(b)     where no such report has been compiled, a suitable corresponding sum.

In each of the above '*relevant period*' means the 'specified' period of financial years of which the last is the relevant financial year. Where the relevant financial year

*       is the company's first financial year for which the performance graph is prepared in accordance with these provisions, 'specified' means five

*       is the company's second, third, fourth, fifth financial year in which the report is prepared in accordance with *Schedule 8* to *SI 2008 No 418* (as amended), 'specified' means six, seven, eight, nine as the case may be and

*       is any financial year after the fifth financial year in which the report is prepared in accordance with *Schedule 8* to *SI 2008 No 418* (as amended), 'specified' means ten.

[*SI 2008 No 410, Sch 8, para 18; SI 2013 No 1981, Reg 3*].

**19.24  Percentage change in remuneration of director undertaking the role of chief executive officer**

The directors' remuneration report must set out (in a manner which permits comparison) in relation to each of the kinds of remuneration required to be set out in each of the columns headed 'a', 'b', and 'c' of the single total figure table (see **19.16**) the following information

(a)     the percentage change from the financial year preceding the relevant financial year in respect of the director undertaking the role of chief executive officer and

(b)     the average percentage change from the financial year preceding the relevant financial year in respect of the employees of the company taken as a whole.

Where for the purposes of (b) a comparator group comprising the employees taken as a whole is considered by the company as an inappropriate comparator group of employees, the company may use such other comparator group of employees as the company identifies, provided the report contains a statement setting out why that group was chosen.

Where the company is a parent company, the statement must relate to the group and not the company and the director reported on is the director undertaking the role of chief executive officer of the parent company, and the employees are the employees of the group.

[*SI 2008 No 410, Sch 8, para 19; SI 2013 No 1981, Reg 3*].

**19.25  Relative importance of spend on pay**

The directors' remuneration report must set out in a graphical or tabular form that shows in respect of the relevant financial year and the immediately preceding financial year the actual expenditure of the company, and the difference in spend between those years, on

(a)     remuneration paid to or receivable by all employees of the group

# 19.25  Remuneration Reports/Policies (Quoted Companies)

(b)    distributions to shareholders by way of dividend and share buyback and

(c)    any other significant distributions and payments or other uses of profit or cash-flow deemed by the directors to assist in understanding the relative importance of spend on pay.

There must be set out in a note to the report an explanation in respect of (c) why the particular matters were chosen by the directors and how the amounts were calculated.

Where the matters chosen for the report in (c) in the relevant financial year are not the same as the other items set out in the report for previous years, an explanation for that change must be given.

[*SI 2008 No 410, Sch 8, para 20; SI 2013 No 1981, Reg 3*].

## 19.26  Statement of voting at general meeting

The directors' remuneration report must contain a statement setting out in respect of the last general meeting at which a resolution of the following kind was moved by the company

(a)    in respect of a resolution to approve the directors' remuneration report, the percentage of votes cast for and against and the number of votes withheld

(b)    in respect of a resolution to approve the directors' remuneration policy, the percentage of votes cast for and against and the number of votes withheld and

(c)    where there was a significant percentage of votes against either such resolution, a summary of the reasons for those votes, as far as known to the directors, and any actions taken by the directors in response to those concerns.

[*SI 2008 No 410, Sch 8, para 23; SI 2013 No 1981, Reg 3*].

## 19.27  APPROVAL AND SIGNING OF THE REMUNERATION REPORT AND POLICY

**Board approval.** The directors' remuneration report must be approved by the board of directors and signed on its behalf by a director or the secretary of the company. If such a report is approved that does not comply with the requirements of *CA 2006*, every director of the company who

•    knew that it did not comply, or was reckless as to whether it complied, and

•    failed to take reasonable steps to secure compliance with those requirements or, as the case may be, to prevent the report from being approved,

commits an offence. A person guilty of such an offence is liable (i) on conviction on indictment, to a fine; and (ii) on summary conviction, to a fine not exceeding the statutory maximum. See **29.1** OFFENCES AND LEGAL PROCEEDINGS for the statutory maximum.

[*CA 2006, s 422*].

*Revisions to directors' remuneration policy*

*Section 79(2)* of the E and RR Act 2013 inserted a new *CA 2006, s 422A* as from 1 October 2013. It provides that the remuneration policy may be revised but that such revision must be approved by the board of directors and the policy as so revised must be set out in a document signed on behalf of the board by a director or the Company Secretary. The document setting out a revised directors' remuneration policy must contain the information specified in *SI 2008 No 410, Schedule 8, para 42* (as amended) and must be set out in the same manner as required by *part 4* of that *Schedule.*

**Quoted companies: members' approval of the report.** Before each "accounts meeting" (see APPENDIX 1 DEFINITIONS for the meaning) a quoted company must give to the members entitled to be sent notice of the meeting notice of the intention to move at the meeting, as an ordinary resolution, a resolution approving the directors' remuneration report for the financial year other than the part containing the directors' remuneration policy The notice may be given in any manner permitted for the service on the member of notice of the meeting (see **42.16** RESOLUTIONS AND MEETINGS).

The business that may be dealt with at the accounts meeting includes the resolution to approve the report despite any default in complying with the above provisions.

The existing directors (ie persons who are directors of the company immediately before the meeting) must ensure that the resolution is put to the vote of the meeting. But no entitlement of a person to remuneration is made conditional on the resolution being passed by reason only of the provisions made above.

*Penalties.* An offence is committed

(a)     in the event of failure to give members notice of the resolution for approval of directors' remuneration report or remuneration policy (see below), by every officer of the company who is in default; and

(b)     if the resolution is not put to the vote of the meeting to which it relates, by each existing director.

A person guilty of such an offence is liable, on summary conviction, to a fine not exceeding level 3 on the standard scale. See **29.1** OFFENCES AND LEGAL PROCEEDINGS for the standard scale.

It is a defence for a person charged with an offence under (*b*) above to prove that he took all reasonable steps for securing that the resolution was put to the vote of the meeting.

[*CA 2006, ss 422A, 439, 440; ERRA 2013, s 81 (10); SI 2013 No 1981, Regs 2, 42, 43*].

*Quoted companies: members' approval of the remuneration policy*

Prior to the "accounts meeting" (see APPENDIX 1 DEFINITIONS) held in the first financial year which begins on or after the day on which the company becomes a quoted company and at an accounts or other general meeting held no later than the end of the period of three financial years beginning with the first financial year after the last accounts or other general meeting in relation to which notice is given under CA 2006, s 439A (see APPENDIX 1 DEFINITIONS for the meaning of "accounts meeting" ) a quoted company must give to the members entitled to be sent notice of the meeting notice of the intention to move at the meeting, as an ordinary resolution, a resolution approving the relevant directors' remuneration policy .The notice may be given in any manner permitted for the service on the member of notice of the meeting (see **42.16** RESOLUTIONS AND MEETINGS).

*A quoted company must also give to the members entitled to be sent notice of the meeting notice of the intention to move at the meeting, as an ordinary resolution, a resolution approving the relevant directors' remuneration policy if:*

(a)     *a resolution required to be put to the vote under CA 2006, s 439 was not passed at the last accounts meeting of the company and*

(b)     *no notice under CA 2006, s 439A was given in relation to that meeting or any other general meeting held before the next accounts meeting.*

## 19.27    Remuneration Reports/Policies (Quoted Companies)

This provision does not apply before the first meeting in relation to which a quoted company gives notice as above in relation to approval.

For the purposes of these provisions 'relevant directors' remuneration policy' is

(a)    in a case where notice is given in relation to an accounts meeting, the remuneration policy contained in the directors' remuneration report in respect of which a resolution (as above) is required to be put to the vote at that accounts meeting

(b)    in a case where notice is given in relation to a general meeting other than an accounts meeting

    (i)    the remuneration policy contained in the directors' remuneration report in respect of which such a resolution was required to be put to the vote at the last accounts meeting to be held before that other general meeting or

    (ii)    where that policy has been revised in accordance with CA 2006, s 422A, the policy as so revised.

Where a company intends to move a resolution to approve a directors' remuneration policy and it is intended that some or all of the provisions of the last approved policy are to continue to apply after the resolution is approved, that fact must be stated in the policy which is the subject of the resolution and it must be made clear which provisions of the last approved policy are to continue to apply and for what period of time it is intended that they shall apply.

On the first occasion that a resolution to approve a directors' remuneration policy (or revised policy) is moved after 1 October 2013, the policy must set out a date from which it is intended by the company that the policy is to take effect.

[CA 2006, s 439A; SI 2008 No 410, Sch 8, para 24(2), 24(4)]

## 19.28  DEFECTIVE REMUNERATION REPORT AND POLICY

A directors' remuneration report or policy may be replaced or partially revised because it was originally defective. See 2.13 ACCOUNTS: GENERAL. The provisions of CA 2006 as to the matters to be included in a directors' remuneration report or policy apply to a revised report or policy as if the revised report or policy were prepared and approved by the directors of the company as at the date of the original report or policy.

[SI 2013 No 2224, Reg 5].

## 19.29  Approval and signing of revised remuneration report and policy

The requirement that a directors' remuneration report must be approved by the board of directors and signed on its behalf by a director or the secretary of the company (see 19.27) also applies to a revised directors' remuneration report or revised remuneration policy (see 19.27), except that (in either case) in the case of revision by supplementary note, the provisions apply as if they required the signature to be on the supplementary note.

Where copies of the original directors' remuneration report have already been sent out to members, laid before the company in general meeting in the case of a public company, or delivered to the Registrar of Companies, the directors must, before approving the revised report, cause statements as to the following matters to be made in a prominent position in the revised report (or, in the case of revision by supplementary note, in that note).

(a)    In the case of revision by replacement

- that the revised report replaces the original report for the financial year (specifying it);

- that it has been prepared as at the date of the original directors' remuneration report and not at the date of revision and accordingly does not deal with any events between those dates;

- the respects in which the original directors' remuneration report did not comply with the requirements of *CA 2006*; and

- any significant amendments made consequential upon the remedying of those defects.

(b)    In the case of a revision by supplementary note

- that the note revises in certain respects the original directors' remuneration report of the company and is to be treated as forming part of that report; and

- that the directors' remuneration report has been revised as at the date of the original directors' remuneration report and not as at the date of revision and accordingly does not deal with any events between those dates.

The date of approval of the revised report must be stated on the face of the report (or, in the case of revision by supplementary note, in that note).

The penalty for failure to comply with these provisions is as in **19.27**.

[*SI 2008 No 373, Regs 6, 6A; SI 2013 No 2224, Reg 7*].

## 19.30  Effect of revision of report or policy

On approval of a revised report or policy by the directors, the provisions of *CA 2006* have effect as if the revised report or policy was, as from the date of its approval, the directors' remuneration report or revised remuneration policy (as the case may be) in place of the original report or policy (as the case may be). This applies in particular for the purposes of

- *CA 2006, ss 431, 432* (right to demand copies of accounts, etc, see **2.7** ACCOUNTS: GENERAL); and

- *CA 2006, s 423* (persons entitled to receive copies, see **2.6** ACCOUNTS: GENERAL), *CA 2006, s 437* (accounts, etc of public companies to be laid before company in general meeting, see **2.10** ACCOUNTS: GENERAL) and *CA 2006, s 441* (accounts, etc to be delivered to Registrar of Companies, see **2.11** ACCOUNTS: GENERAL) if the requirements of those provisions have not been complied with prior to the date of revision.

[*SI 2008 No 373, Reg 11; SI 2013 No 2224, Reg 10]*].

## 19.31  Publication of revised report

Where the directors have prepared a revised directors' remuneration report and copies of the original report have been sent to any person under *CA 2006, s 423* (persons entitled to receive copies, see **2.6** ACCOUNTS: GENERAL) or *CA 2006, s 146* (traded companies: nomination of persons to enjoy information rights, see **26.4** MEMBERS), the directors must send to any such person

- in the case of a revision by replacement, a copy of the revised report, together with a copy of the auditor's report on that report; or

- in the case of revision by supplementary note, a copy of that note, together with a copy of the auditor's report on the revised report.

## 19.31 Remuneration Reports/Policies (Quoted Companies)

This must be done not more than 28 days after the date of the revision (ie the date on which the revised report is approved by the directors).

The directors must also, not more than 28 days after the revision, send a copy of the revised report and auditor's report thereon to any person who is not entitled to receive a copy under the above provisions but who is, at the date of the revision,

(a)    a member of the company,

(b)    a holder of the company's debentures, or

(c)    a person who is entitled to receive notice of general meetings

unless the company would be entitled at that date to send to that person a strategic report and supplementary material.

The exceptions from the requirement to send copies of the annual accounts and reports in **2.6 ACCOUNTS: GENERAL** equally apply to sending out copies of the revised directors' remuneration report.

In default in complying with the above provisions, an offence is committed by each of the directors who approved the revised report. A person guilty of such an offence is liable (i) on conviction on indictment, to a fine; and (ii) on summary conviction, to a fine not exceeding the statutory maximum. See **29.1 OFFENCES AND LEGAL PROCEEDINGS** for the statutory maximum.

[*SI 2008 No 373, Reg 12; SI 2013 No 2224, Reg 11*].

### 19.32 Laying of revised report

Where the directors of a public company have prepared a revised directors' remuneration report and the original report has already been laid before the company in general meeting, a copy of the revised report, together with a copy of the auditor's report on that report, must be laid before the next annual general meeting of the company held after the date of revision at which any annual accounts for a financial year are laid (unless they have already been laid before an earlier general meeting).

In default, every person who is a director of the company immediately before that annual general meeting commits an offence. A person guilty of such an offence is liable, on summary conviction, to a fine not exceeding level 5 on the standard scale and, for continued contravention, a daily default fine not exceeding one-tenth of level 5 on the standard scale. See **29.1 OFFENCES AND LEGAL PROCEEDINGS** for the standard scale. It is a defence for a person charged with such an offence to prove that he took all reasonable steps for securing that the requirements would be complied with before that annual general meeting; it is not a defence to prove that the revised report was not in fact prepared.

[*SI 2008 No 373, Reg 13*].

### 19.33 Delivery of revised report to the Registrar of Companies

Where the directors have prepared a revised directors' remuneration report and a copy of the original report has been delivered to the Registrar of Companies, the directors must, within 28 days of the revision, deliver to the Registrar

•    in the case of a revision by replacement, a copy of the revised report, together with a copy of the auditor's report on that report; or

•    in the case of a revision by supplementary note, a copy of that note, together with a copy of the auditor's report on the revised report.

*CA 2006, ss 451* and *452* (offences and court order for default in filing accounts and reports, see **2.11** Accounts: General) also apply to a failure to comply with the above requirements but as if the reference to 'the period for filing those accounts and reports' was a reference to the 28 day period above.

*[SI 2008 No 373, Reg 14].*

## 19.34 LIABILITY FOR FALSE OR MISLEADING STATEMENTS IN REPORT

A director of a company is liable to compensate the company for any loss suffered by it as a result of

* any untrue or misleading statement, or

* the omission of anything required to be included

in a directors' report or a directors' remuneration report or a strategic report so far as it is derived from that report. No liability arises in respect of a report or summary financial statement first sent out before 20 January 2007.

A director is so liable only if

* he knew the statement to be untrue or misleading or was reckless as to whether it was untrue or misleading; or

* he knew the omission to be dishonest concealment of a material fact.

No person can be subject to any liability to a person other than the company resulting from reliance, by that person or another, on information in a report to which CA 2006, s 463 applies. The reference to a person being 'subject to a liability' includes a reference to another person being entitled as against him to be granted any civil remedy or to rescind or repudiate an agreement.

The effect of this is that no persons (including directors) are liable to individual investors or third parties but auditors remain liable to the company for negligence in preparing their own report.

The above provisions do not affect liability for a civil penalty or liability for a criminal offence.

*[CA 2006, s 463; SI 2006 No 3428, Sch 5 para 3; SI 2013 No 1970, Schedule, para 17].].*

# 20   Strategic Reports and Directors' Reports

**Cross-references.** See **2 ACCOUNTS: GENERAL** for publication of directors' report, laying it before members and delivery to Registrar of Companies; **8.36 AUDIT** for the auditor's duty concerning the directors' report.

The *Companies Act 2006 (Strategic Report and Directors' Report) Regulations 2013* ("the *2013 Regulations*") which are referred to in various parts of this chapter, require a company to produce a strategic report for financial years ending on or after 30 September 2013. For periods beginning on or after 1 January 2017, the *Companies, Partnerships and Groups (Accounting and Non-Financial Reporting) Regulations 2016 (SI 2016 No 1245)* introduce new requirements on the disclosure of non-financial information within the strategic report by certain larger companies.

## 20.1   REQUIREMENT TO PREPARE A STRATEGIC REPORT

The directors of a company must prepare a strategic report for each financial year of the company unless the company qualifies for the small companies exemption (this exemption is available to a company that is entitled to prepare accounts under the small companies regime or would be entitled to do so but for the fact that it is a member of an ineligible group – see **5 ACCOUNTS: SMALL COMPANIES**).

**Parent companies preparing group accounts.** The directors of a parent company that prepares group accounts must prepare a consolidated strategic report, although where appropriate this may give greater emphasis to matters significant to the consolidated undertakings taken as a whole.

**Penalties.** In the case of failure to comply with the requirement to prepare a strategic report, an offence is committed by every person who

- was a director of the company immediately before the end of the period for filing accounts and reports for the financial year in question; and

- failed to take all reasonable steps for securing compliance with that requirement.

A person guilty of such an offence is liable (i) on conviction on indictment, to a fine; and (ii) on summary conviction, to a fine not exceeding the statutory maximum. See **29.1 OFFENCES AND LEGAL PROCEEDINGS** for the statutory maximum.

[*CA 2006, ss 414A, 414B; SI 2013 No 1970, Reg 2, 3*].

**Audit requirements.** The auditor must state in his report

(a) whether, in his opinion, based on the work undertaken in the course of the audit

    (i) the information given in the strategic report is consistent with the accounts; and

    (ii) the strategic report has been prepared in accordance with applicable legal requirements; and

(b) whether, in the light of his knowledge and understanding of the company and its environment gained during the course of the audit, he has identified any material misstatement in the strategic report – and the nature of any such misstatements must also be disclosed.

[*CA 2006, s 496(1); SI 2015 No 980, Reg 11*].

## 20.2 CONTENTS OF THE STRATEGIC REPORT

The purpose of the strategic report is to inform members of the company and help them assess how the directors have performed their duty under *CA 2006, s 172* (Duty to promote the success of the company) (see **18.24**). The strategic report must:

- Contain a fair review of the company's business (ie a balanced and comprehensive analysis of the development and performance of the company's business during the financial year and the position of the business at the end of that year).

- Describe the principal risks and uncertainties facing the company.

- To the extent necessary for an understanding of the development, performance or position of the company's business, include analysis using financial key performance indicators (KPIs) and where appropriate analysis using other KPIs including information relating to environmental and employee matters. For these purposes, KPIs are the factors by reference to which the development, performance or position of the company's business can be measured effectively. A company that qualifies as a medium-sized company in relation to a financial year (see **4 ACCOUNTS: MEDIUM-SIZED COMPANIES**), need not comply with this requirement so far as it relates to non-financial information but must still provide financial KPIs.

- Where appropriate, include references to, and additional explanations of, amounts included in the company's annual accounts.

In the case of a group report, references to the company are to be taken as references to the undertakings included in the consolidation.

If information that would otherwise need to be disclosed in the directors' report (see **20.9–20.21**) is considered by the directors to be of strategic importance to the company, it can be given instead in the strategic report.

There is no requirement to disclose information about impending developments or matters in the course of negotiation if disclosure would be seriously prejudicial the company's commercial interests, provided that non-disclosure does not prevent a fair and balanced understanding of the company's development, performance and position or the impact of its activity.

[*CA 2006, s 414C (1)–(6), (11)–(14)*].

Detailed guidance on the form and content of a strategic report can be found in the Financial Reporting Council (FRC) document 'Guidance on the Strategic Report' (available at www.frc.org.uk/Narrative-Reporting). This was first issued in 2014 and was revised and updated in July 2018 to take account of developments in the intervening period, including the introduction of the non-financial reporting statement and the statement on compliance with CA 2006, s 172 (see **20.4** and **20.5** below). The FRC's Financial Reporting Lab has also undertaken a project on risk and viability reporting, and the report issued in November 2017 includes a number of practical examples to illustrate the disclosures that investors find particularly helpful.

**20.3   Additional requirements for quoted companies**

In addition to the matters set out above, the following requirements apply to the strategic report of a quoted company.

- To the extent necessary for an understanding of the development, performance or position of the company's business, the report must include

  (i)   the main trends and factors likely to affect the future development, performance and position of the company's business; and

  (ii)   information about environmental matters (including the impact of the company's business on the environment), the company's employees, social, community and human rights issues – the disclosures should include information about any policies of the company in relation to these matters and the effectiveness of those policies.

  If the report does not contain the information on environmental matters, employees and social, community and human rights issues, it must state which of those kinds of information it does not contain.

- Include a description of the company's strategy and a description of the company's business model (the FRC Financial Reporting Lab has undertaken a project on business model reporting and the related report includes examples of good practice).

- Contain a breakdown showing at the end of the financial year the number of persons of each sex who were directors of the company, the number of persons of each sex who were senior managers of the company (other than persons who are directors) and the number of each person of each sex who were employees of the company. For these purposes 'senior manager' means a person who has responsibility for planning, directing or controlling the activities of the company or a strategically significant part of the company and is an employee of the company. In the case of a group strategic report:

  (i)   the breakdown in respect of directors should be given for directors of the parent company only; and

  (ii)   the breakdown in respect of senior managers should include the directors of other undertakings included in the consolidation.

[*CA 2006, s 414C (7)–(10); SI 2013 No 1970, Reg 3*].

For periods beginning on or after 1 January 2017, a quoted company may also need to comply with the requirements on the inclusion of a non-financial information statement within the strategic report (see **20.4**). A non-financial information statement that complies with *CA 2006, s 414CB(1)–(6)* is treated as complying with the requirements of *CA 2006*,

## 20.3 Strategic Reports and Directors' Reports

*s 414C* in respect of the additional information required by *CA 2006, s 414C(7)* (other than community issues), the company's business model and additional information on items included in the financial statements in respect of these matters, as well as the requirements on the disclosure of non-financial KPIs.

[*CA 2006, s 414CB (7); SI 2016 No 1245, Reg 4*].

### 20.4 Non-financial information statement

For periods beginning on or after 1 January 2017, unless it qualifies for one of the exemptions set out below, a company that is a traded company, a banking company, an authorised insurance company or a company carrying on insurance market activity must include a non-financial information statement in its strategic report, and if the strategic report is a group report, the non-financial information statement must cover all undertakings included in the consolidation.

Exemption from this disclosure requirement is granted to

- a company that is subject to the small companies regime for the relevant financial year;

- a company that qualifies as medium-sized for the relevant financial year;

- a company that is not a parent company and that has no more than 500 employees in the financial year (calculated as specified in the legislation);

- a company that is a parent company but heads a group in which the aggregate number of employees in the financial year was no more than 500 (calculated as specified in the legislation);

- a company that is a subsidiary undertaking and is included in the group strategic report of a parent undertaking that

    (i)    relates to undertakings that include the company and its subsidiary undertakings (if any);

    (ii)   is prepared for a financial year of the parent that ends at the same time as, or before, the end of company's financial year; and

    (iii)  includes a group non-financial information statement in respect of all the undertakings included in the consolidation; or

- the company is a subsidiary undertaking that is included in a consolidated management report of a parent undertaking established under the law of an EEA State (or in a separate report under Article 19a(3) or 29a(3) of Directive 2013/34/EU) and that report

    (i)    relates to undertakings that include the company and its subsidiary undertakings (if any); and

    (ii)   includes the non-financial information required under Article 19a (non-financial statement) or Article 29a (consolidated non-financial statement), as appropriate, of Directive 2013/34/EU.

However, any company may include a non-financial information statement in its strategic report on a voluntary basis. This gives quoted companies close to the size threshold the flexibility to adopt a consistent reporting approach each year, even if they are not technically required to prepare a non-financial information statement in some years.

[*CA 2006, s 414CA; SI 2016 No 1245, Reg 4*].

As a minimum, and to the extent necessary for an understanding of the company's development, performance and position and the impact of its activity, a non-financial statement must include information on

(a)    environmental matters, including the impact of the company's business on the environment;

(b)    the company's employees;

(c)    social matters;

(d)    respect for human rights; and

(e)    anti-corruption and anti-bribery matters.

The information must include:

•    a description of the company's business model;

•    a description of its policies in respect of (a)–(e) above, together with their outcome, and details of any due diligence processes adopted in pursuance of those policies;

•    a description of the principal risks relating to (a)–(e) above in connection with the company's operations and, where relevant and proportionate, a description of the business relationships, products and services that are likely to cause adverse impacts in those risk areas and a description of how the company manages the principal risks;

•    a description of the non-financial KPIs relevant to its business.

A clear and reasoned explanation must be provided if the company does not pursue policies in respect of any of the matters in (a)–(e) above.

Where relevant, the non-financial information statement should include references to, and additional explanations of, amounts shown in the financial statements.

If any of the required details are published by means of a national, EU or international reporting framework, the statement should specify the framework used instead of giving the required information.

In the case of a group report, references to the company are to be taken as references to the undertakings included in the consolidation.

There is no requirement to disclose information about impending developments or matters in the course of negotiation if disclosure would be seriously prejudicial the company's commercial interests, provided that non-disclosure does not prevent a fair and balanced understanding of the company's development, performance and position or the impact of its activity.

[*CA 2006, s 414CB; SI 2016 No 1245, Reg 4*].

The FRC has issued a short Factsheet to help companies who come within the scope of these reporting requirements (available at www.frc.org.uk) and more detailed guidance can be found in the July 2018 version of the FRC's 'Guidance on the Strategic Report'.

## 20.5    Statement on compliance with CA 2006, s 172

The *Companies (Miscellaneous Reporting) Regulations 2018, SI 2018 No 860*, inserts a new *CA 2006, s 414CZA* to require directors of all companies other than those that qualify as medium-sized to include in the strategic report a statement describing how they have had regard to the matters set out in *CA 2006, s 172(1)(a)–(f)* (see **18.24**) when performing their duties as directors. The related guidance prepared by BEIS notes that this statement should be clearly identifiable within the strategic report and suggests that directors should include information on the issues, factors and stakeholders that they need to consider, how they have engaged with stakeholders to gain an understanding of their main concerns, and the impact of this engagement on company decisions and strategies during the year. A new *CA 2006, s 426B* also requires the statement to be made available on a website maintained by or on behalf of the company. Quoted companies are already required to publish their annual report and accounts in this way (see **2.8**), but unquoted companies will need to make appropriate website arrangements, and if their statement cross-refers to other parts of the annual report will need to ensure that these are included with the website version of the statement.

There is no exemption for subsidiaries that come within the scope of the reporting requirement, so the directors of each subsidiary within a group must explain how they have met their responsibilities to their respective companies, although they may refer to group disclosures made by the parent company where appropriate.

Detailed guidance on the preparation of this statement can be found in the July 2018 version of the FRC's 'Guidance on the Strategic Report'.

## 20.6    REQUIREMENT TO PREPARE A DIRECTORS' REPORT

The directors of a company must prepare a directors' report for each financial year of the company containing specified information. However, for periods beginning on or after 1 January 2016, a company that qualifies as a micro-entity (see **5.2–5.3**: Accounts Small Companies and Micro-entities) is no longer required to prepare a directors' report. Where a company chooses in accordance with *CA 2006, s 414C(11)* (see **20.2**) to set out in the strategic report information which is required by *Schedule 7* to the *Large and Medium-sized Companies and Groups (Accounts and Reports) Regulations 2008 (SI 2008 No 410)* (see **20.9–20.21**) to be disclosed in the directors' report, it must state in the directors' report that it has done so and the information in respect of which it has done so.

**Parent companies preparing group accounts.** For a financial year in which the company is a parent company, and the directors of the company prepare group accounts, the directors' report must be a consolidated report (a *'group directors' report'*) relating to the undertakings included in the consolidation. Such a group directors' report may, where appropriate, give greater emphasis to the matters that are significant to the undertakings included in the consolidation, taken as a whole.

**Penalties.** In the case of failure to comply with the requirement to prepare a directors' report, an offence is committed by every person who

• was a director of the company immediately before the end of the period for filing accounts and reports for the financial year in question; and

• failed to take all reasonable steps for securing compliance with that requirement.

A person guilty of such an offence is liable (i) on conviction on indictment, to a fine; and (ii) on summary conviction, to a fine not exceeding the statutory maximum. See **29.1** Offences and Legal Proceedings for the statutory maximum.

[*CA 2006, s 415; SI 2013 No 1970, Reg 7(3)(a), (e); SI 2015 No 980, Reg 7*].

**Audit requirements.** The auditor must state in his report

(a)    whether, in his opinion, based on the work undertaken in the course of the audit

(i)    the information given in the directors' report is consistent with the accounts; and

(ii) the directors' report has been prepared in accordance with applicable legal requirements; and

(b) whether, in the light of his knowledge and understanding of the company and its environment gained during the course of the audit, he has identified any material misstatement in the directors' report – and the nature of any such misstatements must also be disclosed.

[*CA 2006, s 496(1); SI 2015 No 980, Reg 11*].

## 20.7 Contents of the directors' report

The detailed content of the directors' report varies as follows depending on the size and status of the company:

•   **Large and medium-sized companies** must include the information in **20.9–20.18**.

•   **Small companies** must include the information in **20.11, 20.11** (if the accounts have been audited), **20.12, 20.13** and **20.17**.

•   **Quoted companies** must also include the information in **20.19**.

•   **Companies whose securities are admitted to trading on a regulated market** must additionally include the information in **20.20**.

•   **Listed companies** must additionally include the information in **20.21**. They must also comply with the requirements of the FCA Listing Rules as to content of annual reports and accounts. See **33.32** Public and Listed Companies. The additional disclosures required may be given in the directors' report or the notes to the accounts.

## 20.8 Additional disclosures from 1 January 2019

The *Companies (Miscellaneous Reporting) Regulations 2018, SI 2018 No 860*, amend *Schedule 7 to SI 2008 No 410* to introduce new disclosures on employee and stakeholder engagement and corporate governance. Directors of subsidiaries who meet the relevant qualifying thresholds must provide the required disclosures in respect of their company.

For periods beginning on or after 1 January 2019, the previous disclosures on employee involvement (see **20.18**) are replaced with a new requirement for directors of companies where the average number of UK employees exceeds 250 to summarise in the directors' report how they have engaged with employees and had regard to their interests, and the impact of this on decisions taken during the year. They must also explain the action taken to:

(a) provide employees with regular information on matters of concern to them;

(b) consult them or their representatives on a regular basis so that their views can be taken into account when making decisions likely to affect their interests;

(c) encourage employee involvement in company performance; and

(d) achieve awareness amongst employees of the financial and other factors affecting company performance.

[*SI 2008 No 410, Sch 7 para 11; SI 2018 No 860, Reg 13*].

For the same periods, the directors of larger companies must also summarise how they have had regard to the need to foster the company's business relationships with suppliers, customers and others, and the effect that this has had on key decisions taken during the year.

## 20.8 Strategic Reports and Directors' Reports

There is an exemption from the disclosure of information about impending developments or matters in the course of negotiation if the directors are of the opinion that disclosure would be seriously prejudicial to the company's interests. A company is exempt from this disclosure requirement if it satisfies two or more of the following:

(i)     it has a turnover of not more than £36 million (adjusted proportionately if the period is more or less than a year);

(ii)    it has a balance sheet total (ie the aggregate of amounts shown as assets) of not more than £18 million;

(iii)   its number of employees is not more than 250.

[*SI 2008 No 410, Sch 7, paras 11B, 11C; SI 2018 No 860, Reg 13*].

The largest unlisted companies (both public and private) must also state in their directors' report (and also on a website maintained by or on behalf of the company):

•       which corporate governance code (if any) has been applied and how;

•       any departures from that code and the reasons for them;

•       if it has not applied a corporate governance code, why that is the case and what corporate governance arrangements have been applied.

This reporting requirement applies to a company that (a) has more than 2,000 employees, or (b) has a turnover of more than £200 million (adjusted proportionately where relevant) and a balance sheet total of more than £2 billion. [*SI 2008 No 410, Sch 7 paras 21 to 27; SI 2018 No 860, Reg 14*.] The FRC issued a consultation document, 'The Wates Corporate Governance Principles for Large Private Companies', in June 2018. This sets out six proposed Principles and supporting guidance and the aim is to finalise the document towards the end of 2018 to coincide with the introduction of the new reporting requirements.

In each case above, the average number of employees is calculated by adding together the monthly totals of individuals under contracts of service during the reporting period (excluding any who work wholly or mainly outside the UK) and dividing this by the number of months in the period. [*SI 2008 No 410, Sch 7, paras 11A(3), 11C(3), 23; SI 2018 No 860, Regs 13, 14*].

There are also certain smoothing provisions to help companies with turnover, assets and/or employee numbers that fluctuate around the specified thresholds. [*SI 2008 No 410, Sch 7, paras 11A(1), 11C(1), 24; SI 2018 No 860, Regs 13, 14*.] In effect these provide a two-year time lag before a company falls outside, or once again comes within, the scope of the reporting requirements. For instance, a company that meets the threshold in the first year must give the relevant disclosures and must continue to give them in the following year even if it is below the threshold in that year, but if it is still below the threshold in the third year, disclosure is not required. Similarly, a company that is below the threshold in the first reporting year is not required to report in the second year even if it is above the threshold in that year, but if it remains above the threshold it must report in the third year.

## 20.9 Names of directors

The directors' report must state the names of the persons who, at any time during the financial year, were directors of the company.

[*CA 2006, s 416(1)*].

## 20.10  Dividends

Unless the company is entitled to the 'small companies exemption', the directors' report must state the amount (if any) that the directors recommend should be paid by way of dividend. [*CA 2006, s 416(3); SI 2008 No 393, Reg 6*].

A company is entitled to '*small companies exemption*' in relation to the directors' report for a financial year if

- it is entitled to prepare accounts for the year in accordance with the small companies regime; or

- it would be so entitled but for being or having been a member of an ineligible group.

See 5.7–5.8 Accounts: Small Companies and Micro-entities.

[*CA 2006, s 415A; SI 2008 No 393, Reg 6*].

## 20.11  Disclosure of information to auditors

Unless the directors have taken advantage of the exemption from audit under *CA 2006, Pt 16* (see 8.29–8.35 Audit), the directors' report must contain a statement to the effect that, in the case of each of the persons who are directors at the time when the report is approved

(a)    so far as the director is aware, there is no 'relevant audit information' of which the company's auditor is unaware; and

(b)    he has taken all the steps that he ought to have taken as a director in order to make himself aware of any relevant audit information and to establish that the company's auditor is aware of that information.

'*Relevant audit information*' means information needed by the company's auditor in connection with preparing his report.

For the purposes of (*b*) above, a director is regarded as having taken all the steps that he ought to have taken if he has

- made such enquiries of his fellow directors and of the company's auditor for that purpose, and

- taken such other steps (if any) for that purpose

as are required by his duty as a director of the company to exercise reasonable care, skill and diligence.

**Penalties**. Where a directors' report containing a statement as required above is approved but the statement is false, every director of the company who

- knew that the statement was false, or was reckless as to whether it was false, and

- failed to take reasonable steps to prevent the report from being approved,

commits an offence. A person guilty of such an offence is liable (i) on conviction on indictment, to imprisonment for a term not exceeding two years or a fine (or both); and (ii) on summary conviction, to imprisonment for a term not exceeding 12 months (6 months in Scotland or Northern Ireland or a fine not exceeding the statutory maximum (or both). See 29.1 Offences and Legal Proceedings for the statutory maximum.

[*CA 2006, s 418*].

**20.12  Qualifying indemnity provisions**

If

- when a directors' report is approved, any '*qualifying indemnity provision*' (whether made by the company or otherwise) is in force for the benefit of one or more directors of the company,

- at any time during the financial year to which the directors' report relates, any such provision was in force for the benefit of one or more persons who were then directors of the company,

- when a directors' report is approved, qualifying indemnity provision made by the company is in force for the benefit of one or more directors of an 'associated company', or

- at any time during the financial year to which the directors' report relates, any such provision was in force for the benefit of one or more persons who were then directors of an associated company,

the directors' report must state that such provision was in force.

'*Qualifying indemnity provision*' means either 'qualifying third party indemnity provision' or 'qualifying pension scheme indemnity provision' as defined in **18.43 DIRECTORS**.

For these purposes, companies are associated if one is a subsidiary of the other or both are subsidiaries of the same company.

[*CA 2006, ss 236, 256*].

**20.13  Political donations and expenditure**

If a company, other than a wholly-owned subsidiary of a company incorporated in the UK, has in the financial year

(a)    made any 'political donation' to any political party or other political organisation,

(b)    made any political donation to any independent election candidate, or

(c)    incurred any 'political expenditure',

and the amount of the donation or expenditure (or the aggregate amount of all such donations and expenditure) exceeds £2,000, the directors' report for the year must contain the following particulars.

- Where (*a*) or (*b*) above applies,

    (i)    the name of each political party, other organisation or independent election candidate to whom any such donation has been made; and

    (ii)    the total amount given to that party, organisation or candidate by way of such donations in the financial year.

- Where (*c*) above applies, the total amount incurred by way of such expenditure in the financial year.

If

- at the end of the financial year, the company has subsidiaries which have, in that year, made any donations or incurred any such expenditure, and

- the company itself is not the wholly-owned subsidiary of a company incorporated in the UK,

the directors' report for the year is not required to contain such particulars unless the total amount of any such donations or expenditure (or both) made or incurred in that year by the company and the subsidiaries between them exceeds £2,000, in which case the directors' report for the year must contain those particulars in relation to each body by whom any such donation or expenditure has been made or incurred.

See **31.2** POLITICAL DONATIONS for the definitions of *'political donation'* and *'political expenditure'* for these purposes.

**Non-EU political parties.** If a company, other than a wholly-owned subsidiary of a company incorporated in the UK, has in the financial year made any 'contribution' to a 'non-EU political party', the directors' report for the year must contain

- a statement of the amount of the contribution; or

- if it has made two or more such contributions in the year, a statement of the total amount of the contributions.

If

- at the end of the financial year the company has subsidiaries which have, in that year, made any such contributions, and

- the company itself is not the wholly-owned subsidiary of a company incorporated in the UK,

the directors' report for the year is not required to contain any such statement but it must instead contain a statement of the total amount of the contributions made in the year by the company and the subsidiaries between them.

*'Contribution'* means any gift of money to the organisation (whether made directly or indirectly); any subscription or other fee paid for affiliation to, or membership of, the organisation; or any money spent (otherwise than by the organisation or a person acting on its behalf) in paying any expenses incurred directly or indirectly by the organisation.

*'Non-EU political party'* means any political party which carries on, or proposes to carry on, its activities wholly outside the Member States.

[*SI 2008 No 409, Sch 5 paras, 2, 3; SI 2008 No 410, Sch 7 paras 3, 4*].

## 20.14   Financial instruments

Unless the company is subject to the small companies regime (see **5.7–5.8** ACCOUNTS: SMALL COMPANIES AND MICRO-ENTITIES), in relation to the use of financial instruments by a company, the directors' report must contain an indication of

- the financial risk management objectives and policies of the company, including the policy for hedging each major type of forecasted transaction for which 'hedge accounting' is used, and

- the exposure of the company to 'price risk', 'credit risk', 'liquidity risk' and 'cash flow risk'

unless such information is not material for the assessment of the assets, liabilities, financial position and profit or loss of the company.

## 20.14   Strategic Reports and Directors' Reports

The expressions '*hedge accounting*', '*price risk*', '*credit risk*', '*liquidity risk*' and '*cash flow risk*' have the same meaning as they have in *Council Directive 78/660/EEC* on the annual accounts of certain types of companies, and in *Council Directive 83/349/EEC* on consolidated accounts (as amended).

In relation to a group directors' report (see **20.6**) the above provisions have effect as if the references to the company were references to the company and its subsidiary undertakings included in the consolidation.

[*SI 2008 No 410, Sch 7 para 6*].

### 20.15   Miscellaneous

Unless the company is subject to the small companies regime (see **5.7–5.8** ACCOUNTS: SMALL COMPANIES AND MICRO-ENTITIES), the directors' report must contain

(a)   particulars of all important events affecting the company which have occurred since the end of the financial year;

(b)   an indication of likely future developments in the business of the company;

(c)   an indication of the activities (if any) of the company in the field of research and development; and

(d)   (unless the company is an unlimited company) an indication of the existence of branches of the company outside the UK.

In relation to a group directors' report (see **20.6**) the above provisions in (*a*)–(*c*) above have effect as if the references to the company were references to the company and its subsidiary undertakings included in the consolidation.

[*SI 2008 No 410, Sch 7 para 7*].

### 20.16   Acquisition or charging of own shares

Unless the company is subject to the small companies regime (see **5.7–5.8** ACCOUNTS: SMALL COMPANIES AND MICRO-ENTITIES), where shares in a company are

•   purchased by the company or acquired by it by forfeiture or surrender in lieu of forfeiture, or in pursuance of *CA 2006, s 659*, see **34.1** PURCHASE OF OWN SHARES, or

•   acquired by another person in the circumstances in *CA 2006, s 662(1)*, see **34.28**(*c*) or (*d*) PURCHASE OF OWN SHARES (acquisition by a nominee of the company, or by another with financial assistance from the company, and in either case the company has a beneficial interest in the shares), or

•   made subject to a lien or other charge taken (whether expressly or otherwise) by the company and permitted under *CA 2006, s 670(2)* or *(4)*, see **34.35**(*a*) or (*c*) PURCHASE OF OWN SHARES,

the directors' report for the financial year must state

(i)    the number and nominal value of the shares so purchased, the aggregate amount of the consideration paid by the company for the shares and the reason for the purchase;

(ii)   the number and nominal value of the shares so acquired or charged during the financial year;

(iii) the maximum number and nominal value of shares which, having been so acquired or charged (whether or not during the year) are held at any time by the company or that other person during the year;

(iv) the number and nominal value of the shares so acquired or charged (whether or not during the year) which are disposed of by the company or that other person or cancelled by the company during the year;

(v) the percentage of called-up share capital represented by the number and nominal value of the shares of any particular description stated within (i) to (iv) above;

(vi) where any of the shares have been so charged, the amount of the charge in each case; and

(vii) where any of the shares have been disposed of by the company or person who acquired them for money or money's worth, the amount or value of the consideration in each case.

[*SI 2008 No 410, Sch 7 paras 8, 9*].

## 20.17 Employment of disabled persons

Where, during the financial year, the 'average number of persons employed' in each week exceeded 250, the directors' report must contain a statement on such policy as the company has applied during the financial year for

- giving full and fair consideration to applications for 'employment' made by disabled persons, having regard to their particular aptitudes and abilities;

- continuing employment of, and arranging for appropriate training for, employees who have become disabled during the period when they were employed by the company; and

- otherwise for the training, career development and promotion of disabled persons (as defined under the *Disability Discrimination Act 1995*) employed by the company.

'*Average number of persons employed*' is calculated by the formula

$$\frac{A}{B}$$

where

A = the sum of the numbers of persons who, under contracts of service, were employed by the company in each week of the financial year (whether throughout it or not)

B = the number of weeks in the financial year

'*Employment*' means employment other than employment to work wholly or mainly outside the UK, and '*employed*' and '*employee*' are to be construed accordingly.

[*SI 2008 No 409, Sch 5 para 5; SI 2008 No 410, Sch 7 para 10*].

## 20.18 Employee involvement

For periods beginning before 1 January 2019, unless the company is subject to the small companies regime (see **5.7–5.8 Accounts: Small Companies and Micro-entities**), where the average number of persons employed by the company during the financial year exceeded 250 (calculated as in **20.17** but see also below), the directors' report must contain a statement describing what action has been taken during the financial year to introduce, maintain or develop arrangements aimed at

- providing 'employees' systematically with information on matters concerning them as employees;

- consulting employees or their representatives on a regular basis so that their views can be taken into account in making decisions likely to affect their interests;

- encouraging the involvement of employees in the company's performance through a share scheme or by some other means; and

- achieving a common awareness on the part of all employees of the financial and economic factors affecting the performance of the company.

'Employee' does not include a person employed to work wholly or mainly outside the UK and in calculating the average number of persons employed, any such person is to be ignored.

[*SI 2008 No 410, Sch 7 para 11*].

See 20.8 for new disclosure requirements on employee involvement that replace the above for periods beginning on or after 1 January 2019.

## 20.19  Greenhouse gas emissions

In the case of a quoted company the directors' report must state

(a)    the annual quantity of emissions in tonnes of carbon dioxide equivalent from activities for which that company is responsible including the combustion of fuel and the operation of any facility;

(b)    the annual quantity of emissions in tonnes of carbon dioxide equivalent resulting from the purchase of electricity, heat, steam or cooling by the company for its own use;

(c)    the methodologies used to calculate the information disclosed above;

(d)    at least one ratio which expresses the quoted company's annual emissions in relation to a quantifiable factor associated with the company's activities;

(e)    where relevant, that the period for which it is reporting the information required by (*a*) and (*b*) is different to the period in respect of which the directors' report is prepared.

Comparative information must also be given for items (a), (b) and (d).

*'Emissions' means emissions into the atmosphere of a greenhouse gas as defined in Climate Change Act 2008, s 92 which are attributable to human activity.*

*'Tonne of carbon dioxide equivalent' has the meaning given in Climate Change Act 2008, s 93(2).*

[*SI 2008 No 410, Sch 7, paras 15–20; SI 2013 No 1970, Reg 7(3)(e)*].

The disclosures in (a) and (b) are only required where it is practical for the company to obtain the information, but if it is not practical the company must state what information has not been included and why.

The latest guidance from the Department for Environment, Food and Rural Affairs (DEFRA) on reporting on environmental matters, including greenhouse gas emissions, was issued in June 2013 ('Environmental Reporting Guidelines' available at www.gov.uk/measuring-and-reporting-environmental-impacts-guidance-for-businesses).

**20.20  Capital structure and control**

If a the company has 'securities' carrying 'voting rights' admitted to trading on a regulated market at the end of a financial year, the directors' report must contain detailed information, by reference to the end of that year, on the following matters, together with any necessary explanatory material.

(a)  The structure of the company's capital, including in particular

  (i)  the rights and obligations attaching to the shares or, as the case may be, to each class of shares in the company; and

  (ii)  where there are two or more such classes, the percentage of the total share capital represented by each class.

For these purposes, a company's capital includes any securities in the company that are not admitted to trading on a regulated market.

(b)  Any restrictions on the transfer of 'securities' in the company, including in particular

  (i)  limitations on the holding of securities; and

  (ii)  requirements to obtain the approval of the company, or of other holders of securities in the company, for a transfer of securities.

(c)  In the case of each person with a significant direct or indirect holding of securities in the company, such details as are known to the company of

  (i)  the identity of the person;

  (ii)  the size of the holding; and

  (iii)  the nature of the holding.

For these purposes, a person has an indirect holding of securities if they are held on his behalf or he is able to secure that rights carried by the securities are exercised in accordance with his wishes.

(d)  In the case of each person who holds securities carrying special rights with regard to control of the company

  (i)  the identity of the person; and

  (ii)  the nature of the rights.

(e)  Where

  (i)  the company has an employees' share scheme, and

  (ii)  shares to which the scheme relates have rights with regard to control of the company that are not exercisable directly by the employees, how those rights are exercisable

(f)  Any restrictions on 'voting rights', including in particular

  (i)  limitations on voting rights of holders of a given percentage or number of votes;

  (ii)  deadlines for exercising voting rights; and

  (iii)  arrangements by which, with the company's co-operation, financial rights carried by securities are held by a person other than the holder of the securities.

(g)     Any agreements between holders of securities that are known to the company and may result in restrictions on the transfer of securities or on voting rights.

(h)     Any rules that the company has about

    (i)     appointment and replacement of directors; or

    (ii)    amendment of the company's articles of association.

(i)     The powers of the company's directors, including in particular any powers in relation to the issuing or buying back by the company of its shares.

(j)     Any significant agreements to which the company is a party that take effect, alter or terminate upon a change of control of the company following a 'takeover bid', and the effects of any such agreements.

This does not apply to an agreement if

    (i)     disclosure of the agreement would be seriously prejudicial to the company; and

    (ii)    the company is not under any other obligation to disclose it.

(k)     Any agreements between the company and its directors or employees providing for compensation for loss of office or employment (whether through resignation, purported redundancy or otherwise) that occurs because of a 'takeover bid'.

'*Securities*' means shares or debentures.

'*Takeover bid*' has the same meaning as in the *Takeovers Directive* (*Directive 2004/25/EC*).

'*Voting rights*' means rights to vote at general meetings of the company in question, including rights that arise only in certain circumstances.

[*SI 2008 No 410, Sch 7 paras 13, 14*].

**20.21  Corporate governance statement**

Under the FCA Disclosure and Transparency Rules, a listed company must include a corporate governance statement as a specific section of its directors' report, or issue a separate corporate governance report published with, and in the same manner as, the directors' report. The specified contents of the corporate governance statement include the following.

(a)     A statement on compliance with the corporate governance code that applies or has been voluntarily adopted.

(b)     A description of the main features of the company's internal control and risk management systems in relation to financial reporting and (where relevant) the preparation of consolidated accounts.

(c)     The information required by *SI 2008 No 410, Sch 7, para 13(2)(c), (d), (f), (h)* and *(i)* (see **20.20**) or, where a separate corporate governance report is prepared, a cross-reference to the directors' report where these details can be found.

(d)     A description of the composition and operation of the company's administrative, management and supervisory bodies and their committees.

(e)     For periods beginning on or after 1 January 2017, a description of the diversity policy applied to the company's administrative, management and supervisory bodies (eg age, gender, educational or professional background), together with the objectives of the policy, how it has been implemented and the results in the reporting period. If the company does not have such a policy, the reason for this must be clearly explained.

Where the corporate governance statement is included within the directors' report, it will automatically be covered by the approval, signature, audit and delivery requirements in respect of that report. The legislation defines a corporate governance statement and a separate corporate governance statement for accounts and audit purposes and sets out separate but equivalent requirements on approval, signature, delivery and audit for a company that takes up the option to prepare a separate corporate governance report.

[*CA 2006, ss 419A, 446–447, 472A, 497A, 538A*].

With effect from 28 September 2018, AIM companies are also required to make certain corporate governance disclosures (see **2.9**) and for periods beginning on or after 1 January 2019, similar disclosures must be given in the directors' report of all larger unlisted companies, both public and private (see **20.8**).

## 20.22 APPROVAL AND SIGNING OF REPORTS

The strategic report, directors' report and any separate corporate governance report must be approved by the board of directors and signed on behalf of the board by a director or the secretary of the company.

**Small companies.** If in preparing the directors' report advantage is taken of the 'small companies exemption', the report must contain a statement to that effect in a prominent position above the signature.

A company is entitled to '*small companies exemption*' in relation to the directors' report for a financial year if

• it is entitled to prepare accounts for the year in accordance with the small companies regime; or

• it would be so entitled but for being or having been a member of an ineligible group.

See **5.7–5.8** ACCOUNTS: SMALL COMPANIES AND MICRO-ENTITIES.

**Offences.** If a strategic report, directors' report or separate corporate governance report is approved that does not comply with the requirements of *CA 2006*, every director of the company who

• knew that it did not comply, or was reckless as to whether it complied, and

• failed to take reasonable steps to secure compliance with those requirements or, as the case may be, to prevent the report from being approved,

commits an offence.

A person guilty of such an offence is liable (i) on conviction on indictment, to a fine; and (ii) on summary conviction, to a fine not exceeding the statutory maximum. See **29.1** OFFENCES AND PENALTIES for the statutory maximum.

[*CA 2006, ss 414D, 419, 419A; SI 2008 No 393, Reg 6; SI 2009 No 1581, Reg 2; SI 2013 No 1970, Regs 2, 3*].

See **2.11** ACCOUNTS: GENERAL for the requirement to file a copy of each report with the Registrar of Companies.

## 20.23 DEFECTIVE REPORTS

In certain circumstances, a strategic report or directors' report may be replaced or partially revised because it was originally defective. See **2.13** ACCOUNTS: GENERAL. The provisions of *CA 2006* as to the matters to be included in a strategic report or directors' report apply to a revised report as if the revised report was prepared and approved by the directors of the company as at the date of the original report.

## 20.23 Strategic Reports and Directors' Reports

*[SI 2008 No 373, Reg 3(4); SI 2013 No 2224, Reg 5].*

### 20.24 Approval and signature of revised reports

The requirement that a strategic report and directors' report must be approved by the board of directors and signed on its behalf by a director or secretary of the company (see **20.22**) also applies to any revised report, except that in the case of revision by supplementary note, it applies as if it required the signature to be on the supplementary note.

Where copies of the original strategic report or directors' report have already been sent out to members, laid before the company in general meeting in the case of a public company, or delivered to the Registrar of Companies, the directors must, before approving the revised report cause statements as to the following matters to be made in a prominent position in the revised report (or, in the case of revision by supplementary note, in that note).

(a)     In the case of revision by replacement

- that the revised report replaces the original report for the financial year (specifying it);

- that it has been prepared as at the date of the original directors' report or strategic report and not at the date of revision and accordingly does not deal with any events between those dates;

- the respects in which the original report did not comply with the requirements of the *CA 2006*; and

- any significant amendments made as a result of remedying those defects.

(b)     In the case of a revision by supplementary note

- that the note revises in certain respects the original strategic report or directors' report of the company and is to be treated as forming part of that report; and

- that the strategic report or directors' report has been revised as at the date of the original report and not as at the date of the revision and accordingly does not deal with events between those dates.

The date of approval of the revised report must be stated on the face of the report (or supplementary note).

The penalty for failure to comply with these provisions is as in **20.22**.

*[SI 2008 No 373, Reg 5; SI 2013 No 2224, Reg 10].*

### 20.25 Effect of revision of report

Subject to the provisions of the *Companies (Revision of Defective Accounts and Reports) (Amendment ) (No 2) Regulations 2013 (SI 2013 No 2224)* when the directors approve a revised report, the provisions of *CA 2006* have effect as if, the revised report was, as from the date of its approval, the strategic report or the directors' report (as the case may be) in place of the original report. This applies in particular for the purposes of

- *CA 2006, ss 431, 432* (the right to demand copies of accounts, see **2.7** ACCOUNTS: GENERAL); and

- *CA 2006, s 423* (persons entitled to receive copies, see **2.6** ACCOUNTS: GENERAL), *CA 2006, s 437* (accounts, etc of public company to be laid before company in general meeting, see **2.10** ACCOUNTS: GENERAL) and *CA 2006, s 441* (accounts, etc to be delivered to Registrar of Companies, see **2.11** Accounts: General) if the requirements of those provisions have not been complied with prior to the date of revision.

[*SI 2008 No 373, Reg 11; SI 2013 No 2224, Reg 10*].

### 20.26  Publication of revised report

Where the directors have prepared a revised report and copies of the original report have been sent to any person under *CA 2006, s 423* (persons entitled to receive copies, see **2.6** Accounts: General) or *CA 2006, s 146* (traded companies: nomination of persons to enjoy information rights, see **26.2** Members), the directors must send to any such person

- in the case of a revision by replacement, a copy of the revised report, together with a copy of the auditor's report on that report; or

- in the case of revision by supplementary note, a copy of that note together with a copy of the auditor's report on the revised report.

This must be done not more than 28 days after the date of the revision (ie the date on which the revised report is approved by the directors).

The directors must also, not more than 28 days after the revision, send a copy of the revised report and auditor's report thereon to any person who is not entitled to receive a copy under the above provisions but who is, as at the date of revision,

(a)     a member of the company,

(b)     a holder of the company's debentures, or

(c)     a person who is entitled to receive notice of general meetings

unless the company would be entitled at that date to send to that person a strategic report and supplementary material.

The exceptions from the requirement to send copies of the annual accounts and reports in **2.6** Accounts: General equally apply to sending out copies of the revised report.

In default in complying with the above provisions, an offence is committed by each of the directors who approved the revised report. A person guilty of such an offence is liable (i) on conviction on indictment, to a fine; and (ii) on summary conviction, to a fine not exceeding the statutory maximum. See **29.1** Offences and Legal Proceedings for the statutory maximum.

[*SI 2008 No 373, Reg 12; SI 2013 No 2224, Reg 11*].

### 20.27  Laying of revised report

Where the directors of a public company have prepared a revised strategic report or directors' report and the original report has already been laid before the company in general meeting, a copy of the revised report, together with a copy of the auditor's report on that report, must be laid before the next general meeting of the company held after the date of revision at which annual accounts for a financial year are laid (unless they have already been laid before an earlier general meeting).

In default, every person who is a director of the company immediately before that annual general meeting commits an offence. A person guilty of such an offence is liable, on summary conviction, to a fine not exceeding level 5 on the standard scale and, for continued contravention, a daily default fine not exceeding one-tenth of level 5 on the standard scale. See **29.1** Offences and Legal Proceedings for the standard scale. It is a defence for a person charged with such an offence to prove that he took all reasonable steps for securing that the requirements would be complied with before that annual general meeting; it is not a defence to prove that the revised report was not in fact prepared.

[*SI 2008 No 373, Reg 13*].

## 20.28  Delivery of revised report to the Registrar of Companies

Where the directors have prepared a revised strategic report or directors' report and a copy of the original report has been delivered to the Registrar of Companies, the directors must, within 28 days of the date of revision, deliver to the Registrar

- in the case of a revision by replacement, a copy of the revised report, together with a copy of the auditor's report on that report; or

- in the case of a revision by supplementary note, a copy of that note, together with a copy of the auditor's report on the revised report.

*CA 2006, ss 451* and *452* (offences and court order for default in filing accounts and reports, see **2.11** Accounts: General) also apply to a failure to comply with the above requirements but as if the reference to 'the period for filing those accounts and reports' was a reference to the 28 day period above.

[*SI 2008 No 373, Reg 14*].

## 20.29  LIABILITY FOR FALSE OR MISLEADING STATEMENTS IN REPORTS

A director of a company is liable to compensate the company for any loss suffered by it as a result of

- any untrue or misleading statement, or

- the omission of anything required to be included

in a strategic report or directors' report.

A director is so liable only if

- he knew the statement to be untrue or misleading or was reckless as to whether it was untrue or misleading; or

- he knew the omission to be dishonest concealment of a material fact.

No person can be subject to any liability to a person other than the company resulting from reliance, by that person or another, on information in a strategic report or directors' report. The reference to a person being 'subject to a liability' includes a reference to another person being entitled as against him to be granted any civil remedy or to rescind or repudiate an agreement.

The effect of this is that no persons (including directors) are liable to individual investors or third parties but auditors remain liable to the company for negligence in preparing their own report.

The above provisions do not affect liability for a civil penalty or liability for a criminal offence.

[*CA 2006, s 463*; *SI 2013 No 1970, Schedule, para 17*].

# 21   Dissolution and Restoration

General note. The provisions in this chapter apply, unless otherwise stated, with effect from 1 October 2009. For the provisions applying before that date, see the Appendix at the end of this chapter.

## 21.1   REGISTRAR OF COMPANY'S POWER TO STRIKE OFF A DEFUNCT COMPANY

If the Registrar of Companies has reasonable cause to believe that a company is not carrying on business or in operation, he may send to the company by post a letter inquiring whether it is carrying on business or in operation. [*CA 2006, s 1000(1)*]. He may take this action, for example, because he has not received documents from the company which should have been delivered to him (eg annual returns/confirmation statements and accounts) or mail sent to the registered office is returned undelivered or the company has no directors (Companies House Guidance Booklet GP4, *Strike-off, dissolution and restoration*, currently last updated 23 November 2016).

If the Registrar of Companies does not, within 14 days of sending that letter, receive any answer to it, he must within 14 days of the end of that period send to the company by post a registered letter referring to the first letter, and stating that

- no answer has been received to the first letter; and

- if an answer is not received to the second letter within 14 days from its date, a notice will be published in the Gazette with a view to striking the company's name off the register.

If the Registrar of Companies

- receives an answer to the effect that the company is not carrying on a business or in operation, or

- does not receive an answer to the second letter within one month,

a notice will be published in the *Gazette*, and sent to the company by post, to the effect that not less than three months from the date of the notice, the company will be struck off the register and the company will be dissolved unless cause is shown to the contrary.

## 21.1 Dissolution and Restoration

At the expiration of the three months, unless cause to the contrary has been shown, the Registrar of Companies may strike the company name off the register and publish notice of this in the *Gazette*. On publication, the company is dissolved although

- the liability (if any) of every director, managing officer and member of the company continues and may be enforced as if the company had not been dissolved; and

- the power of the court to wind up a company whose name has been struck off the register is not affected.

[*CA 2006, s 1000(2)–(7); SBEE 2015, s 103; SI 2015 No 1689, Reg 4*].

**Duty to act in the case of a company being wound up**. If, in a case where a company is being wound up,

- the Registrar of Companies has reasonable cause to believe that no liquidator is acting or that the affairs of the company are fully wound up, and

- the returns required to be made by the liquidator have not been made for a period of six consecutive months,

the Registrar of Companies must publish in the *Gazette*, and send to the company or the liquidator (if any), a notice to the effect that, at the expiration of two months from the date of the notice, the name of the company mentioned in it will be struck off the register and the company will be dissolved unless cause is shown to the contrary. At the expiration of the three months, unless cause to the contrary has been previously shown, the Registrar of Companies may strike the company name off the register and publish notice of this in the *Gazette*. On publication, the company is dissolved although

- the liability (if any) of every director, managing officer and member of the company continues and may be enforced as if the company had not been dissolved; and

- the power of the court to wind up a company whose name has been struck off the register is not affected.

[*CA 2006, s 1001; SBEE 2015, s 103; SI 2015 No 1689, Reg 4*].

**Addresses for notices, etc**. A letter or notice to be sent to a company may be addressed

- to the company at its registered office; or

- if no office has been registered, to the care of some officer of the company; or

- if there is no such officer whose name and address is known to the Registrar of Companies, to each of the persons who subscribed the memorandum.

A notice to a liquidator may be addressed to him at his last known place of business.

[*CA 2006, s 1002*].

Even where the company is struck off the register and dissolved, the company to be restored to the register in certain circumstances (see **21.9** and **21.10**).

## 21.2 VOLUNTARY STRIKING OFF

Subject to the restrictions in **21.3**, a company (that is any company, unlike under *CA 1985* where only private companies could make such an application) may apply to the Registrar of Companies for the company's name to be struck off the register of companies.

Once a company's name is no longer on the register, that company ceases to be a registered company. Once the company is then dissolved, it no longer exists as a legal entity. Although 'strike off' and dissolution are inextricably linked, and indeed often happen in close succession, they are legally distinct processes. Where the voluntary strike off procedure is used, the company is only deemed to be *dissolved* once the Registrar has published a notice in the *Gazette* confirming that the company's name has been struck off the register (*CA 2006, s 1003(5)*) (see below).

The company must complete Form DS01, 'Striking off application by a company', and file it with the registrar with the fee of £10. The application must be made on the company's behalf by the directors (or by a majority of them) and must contain a declaration (by the directors making the application on behalf of the company) that neither *CA 2006, s 1004* nor *CA 2006, s 1005* prevents the application from being made (see **21.3**).

[*SI 2009 No 1803, Reg 2*].

Application might be made, for example, where

- the directors want to retire and there is no one to take over the running of the company;

- the company is a subsidiary whose name is no longer needed; or

- the company was set up to exploit an idea that turned out not to be feasible.

The implications of removing a company's name from the register, where the company is no longer active, can include the following:

- **Administration** – The costs entailed in keeping a company on the register, such as in complying with the duty to prepare and file accounts and other documentation, are thus saved.

- **Directors' duties** – Even a dormant (but still registered) company will have at least one human director who owes the statutory duties to the company, and who risks personal liability if any of those duties are breached.

- **Liabilities** – A company must notify creditors before striking off. It is an offence not to notify known creditors if the directors are aware of any liabilities. Subject to this, there may nonetheless be some practical attraction to the company in being dissolved. Dissolution potentially wipes out historic debts owed by the company which are not likely to be enforced but which still create a negative balance sheet. Dissolution also spares the company exposure to potential, future claims which cannot currently be foreseen. However, this protection may be limited. Even after the company has been dissolved, future claimants can apply to restore the company to the register at any time if they have claims against it for personal injury (*CA 2006, s 1030(1)*).

The procedure is not an alternative to formal insolvency proceedings where these are appropriate. Even if a company is struck off the register and dissolved, creditors (or others) could apply for the company to be restored to the register. (Companies House Guidance Booklet GP4, *Strike-off, dissolution and restoration.*)

On receiving the request, the Registrar of Companies must publish a notice in the *Gazette* stating that he may exercise the power under these provisions in relation to the company, and inviting any person to show cause why that should not be done. If no objection is received, after the expiration of two months from the publication of the notice, the Registrar must publish a further notice in the Gazette of the company's name having been struck off. On the publication of the notice in the *Gazette*, the company is dissolved although

**21.2 Dissolution and Restoration**

- the liability (if any) of every director, managing officer and member of the company continues and may be enforced as if the company had not been dissolved; and

- the power of the court to wind up a company whose name has been struck off the register is not affected.

[*CA 2006, s 1003(3)–(6); SBEE 2015, s 103; SI 2015 No 1689, Reg 4*].

Even where the company is struck off the register and dissolved, the company may be restored to the register in certain circumstances (see **21.9** and **21.10**).

**21.3 Circumstances in which application cannot be made**

An application cannot be made under **21.2** on behalf of a company in the following circumstances.

(a) If at any time in the previous three months, the company has

    (i) changed its name;

    (ii) traded or otherwise carried on business;

    (iii) made a disposal for value of property or rights that, immediately before ceasing to trade or otherwise carry on business, it held for disposal for gain in the normal course of trading or otherwise carrying on business. For example, a company in business to sell apples could not continue selling apples during the 3 month period but it could sell the truck it once used to deliver the apples or the warehouse where they were stored; Or

    (iv) engaged in any other activity except one necessary or expedient for the purposes of making an application to strike off the company (or deciding whether to do so), concluding the affairs of the company or complying with any statutory requirement.

(b) If at the time of the application the company is the subject, or proposed subject of:

- a *section 895* (*CA 2006*) scheme (that is a compromise or arrangement with its creditors or members)

- any insolvency proceedings such as a voluntary arrangement

- an administration order

- an interim moratorium on proceedings where application to the court for an administration order has been made or notice of intention to appoint administrator has been filed, a winding up, receivership or administration by a judicial factor.

[*CA 2006, ss 1004(1)(2), 1005(1)–(3)* and Companies House Guidance Booklet GP4].

**Penalties.** It is an offence for a person to make an application in contravention of the above provisions. A person guilty of such an offence is liable (i) on conviction on indictment, to a fine; and (ii) on summary conviction, to a fine not exceeding the statutory maximum. See **29.1** OFFENCES AND LEGAL PROCEEDINGS for the statutory maximum.

In proceedings for such an offence it is a defence for the accused to prove that he did not know, and could not reasonably have known, of the existence of the facts that led to the contravention.

[*CA 2006, ss 1004(5)–(7), 1005(4)–(6)*].

**21.4    Withdrawal of application**

A director of a company which has made an application under **21.2** must ensure that the application is withdrawn forthwith (by giving notice to the Registrar of Companies) where, at any time on or after the day on which the application is made and before it is finally dealt with or withdrawn:

(a)    The company

- changes its name;

- trades or otherwise carries on business;

- makes a disposal for value of property or rights other than those which it was necessary or expedient for it to hold for the purposes of making, or proceeding with, the application; or

- engages in any activity except one necessary or expedient for the purposes of

(i)    making, or proceeding with, the application;

(ii)    concluding affairs of the company that are outstanding because of what has been necessary or expedient for the purposes of making, or proceeding with, the application; or

(iii)    complying with any statutory requirement.

For theses purposes, a company is not treated as trading or otherwise carrying on business by virtue only of the fact that it makes a payment in respect of a liability incurred in the course of trading or otherwise carrying on business.

(b)    An application to the court under *CA 2006, Pt 26* is made on behalf of the company for the sanctioning of a compromise or arrangement.

(c)    A voluntary arrangement in relation to the company is proposed.

(d)    An application to the court for an administration order in respect of the company is made.

(e)    An administrator is appointed in respect of the company or a copy of notice of intention to appoint an administrator of the company is filed with the court.

(f)    Any of the circumstances in which the company can be voluntarily wound up arise.

(g)    A petition is presented for winding up of the company by the court.

(h)    A receiver or manager of the company's property is appointed.

(i)    A judicial factor is appointed to administer the company's estate.

These circumstances are essentially the same as those which under *CA 2006, ss 1004* and *1005* would have prohibited the making of the original application, although *s 1009* is usually interpreted more narrowly.

**Penalties.** A person who fails to perform the duty imposed on him under the above provisions commits an offence. A person guilty of such an offence is liable (i) on conviction on indictment, to a fine; and (ii) on summary conviction, to a fine not exceeding the statutory maximum. See **29.1 OFFENCES AND LEGAL PROCEEDINGS** for the statutory maximum.

In proceedings for such an offence it is a defence for the accused to prove that at the time of the failure he was not aware of the fact that the company had made an application for voluntary striking off or that he took all reasonable steps to perform the duty.

## 21.4 Dissolution and Restoration

[*CA 2006, ss 1009, 1010*].

The removal of a director by the company under *CA 2006, s 168* is likely to constitute activity taken for the purpose of 'concluding affairs of the company', and hence not trigger withdrawal of the strike off application. By contrast, action such as the bringing of legal proceedings by the company is likely to amount to activity that requires its withdrawal.

The directors may also choose to withdraw their application, even if they are not obliged to do so under *CA 2006, s 1009*.

In both cases, Form DS02 ('Withdrawal of striking off application by company'), must be completed and filed with the Registrar. Currently, there is no fee for this.

## 21.5 Notification of members, employees, etc

A director (or directors) who makes an application for a voluntary striking of on behalf of a company must secure that, within seven days from the date of application, a copy of it is given to every person who on that date is

(a)     a member of the company (usually the shareholders);

(b)     an employee of the company;

(c)     a creditor of the company (including a contingent or prospective creditor). If the company is likely to have several contingent or prospective creditors whose details are difficult to obtain or verify, this may be a potential disadvantage of the voluntary strike off route. In this event, or if the company believes that it may have significant contingent or prospective liabilities, then liquidation may be the preferable avenue to follow. Further detail on voluntary liquidation and the other insolvency procedures is beyond the scope of this book;

(d)     a director of the company (other than one who was a party to the application);

(e)     a manager or trustee of any employee pension fund; or

(f)     any director(s) who has/have not signed the application to strike off (see **21.2**).

Additionally, where at any time after the date of the application and before the application is finally dealt with or withdrawn, a new person falls within (*a*)–(*e*) above, a person who is a director of the company at that time must secure that a copy of the application is given to him within seven days.

The duty imposed under these provisions ceases to apply if the application is withdrawn within the seven-day period.

[*CA 2006, ss 1006(1)–(3), 1007(1)–(3), 1011*].

**Service of documents.** For the above purposes, a document is treated as given to a person if it is delivered to him, left at his 'proper address', or sent by post to him at that address. The '*proper address*' of a person is

•       in the case of a firm incorporated or formed in the UK, its registered or principal office;

•       in the case of a firm incorporated or formed outside the UK

(i)      if it has a place of business in the UK, its principal office in the UK; or

(ii)     if it does not have a place of business in the UK, its registered or principal office; and

- in the case of an individual, his last known address.

In the case of a creditor of the company a document is treated as given to him if it is left or sent by post to him

- at the place of business of his with which the company has had dealings by virtue of which he is a creditor of the company; or

- if there is more than one such place of business, at each of them.

[*CA 2006, s 1008*].

**Penalties.** A person who fails to perform the duty imposed on him by the above provisions commits an offence. A person guilty of such an offence is liable (i) on conviction on indictment, to a fine; and (ii) on summary conviction, to a fine not exceeding the statutory maximum. See **29.1** OFFENCES AND LEGAL PROCEEDINGS for the statutory maximum.

A person commits an aggravated offence if he fails to perform the duty imposed on him by the above provisions with the intention of concealing the making of the application from the person concerned. A person guilty of an aggravated offence is liable (i) on conviction on indictment, to imprisonment for a term not exceeding seven years or a fine (or both); and (ii) on summary conviction, to imprisonment for a term not exceeding 12 months (6 months in Scotland and Northern Ireland) or to a fine not exceeding the statutory maximum (or both).

In proceedings for an offence under these provisions (aggravated or otherwise) it is a defence for the accused to prove that

- he took all reasonable steps to perform the duty; or

- in the case of a duty arising after the making of the application, that at the time of the failure he was not aware of the fact that the company had made an application.

[*CA 2006, ss 1006(4)–(7), 1007(4)–(7)*].

**21.6   Objections to proposed striking off and dissolution**

Any interested party may object to the striking off and dissolution of a company. Any objections should be in writing and sent to the Registrar of Companies, together with supporting evidence (eg copies of invoices showing that the company is trading). Examples of grounds for objecting are that

- the company has broken any of the conditions of its application;

- the directors have not informed interested parties;

- any of the prescribed information given is false;

- some form of action is being taken, or is pending, to recover any moneys owed (eg a winding-up petition or action in the small claims court);

- other legal action is being taken against the company; or

- the directors have wrongfully traded or committed a tax fraud or some other offence.

(Companies House Guidance Booklet GP4, *Strike-off, dissolution and restoration*).

**21.7   PROPERTY OF DISSOLVED COMPANY**

The provisions in this paragraph and **21.8** apply in relation to the property of a company dissolved on or after 1 October 2009 whether or not the company is dissolved under the Registrar's powers (see **21.1**) or is dissolved voluntarily (see **21.2**). They also apply to the property of a company dissolved before 1st October 2009 if at that date

(a)      no period has begun to run in relation to the property under *section 656(3)(a)* or *(b)* of the *1985 Act* or *article 607(3)(a)* or *(b)* of the *1986 Order* (period within which notice of disclaimer must be executed), and

(b)      the right to disclaim has not ceased to be exercisable in relation to the property by virtue of *section 656(2)* of the *1985 Act* or *article 607(2)* of the *1986 Order* (waiver of right to disclaim).

[*SI 2008 No 2860, Sch 2 para 88* and *SI 2009 No 2476*].

The company's assets may include both tangible property and intangible assets, such as contractual or intellectual property rights.

The law governing the ownership of property vested in a dissolved company is harsh. Therefore, if the company holds assets, it may be prudent to consider transferring them to another party – for example, to a fellow company within a group – before making the strike off application. The company should investigate all the contracts to which it is party and consider whether they may be novated to a third party, or their benefit assigned. Moreover, where the company is a member of a group, there may be terms in contracts to which *other* members of the company's group are party, by which dissolution of the company will amount to a material change to the corporate group structure and such as to trigger a breach of covenant or other issue on those contracts. Thought must be given to this in advance.

The company may also consider the possibility of lawfully returning its share capital to shareholders before applying for voluntary strike off. The company may wish to avail itself of *CA 2006, s 641*, which sets out the circumstances in which a company may reduce its share capital.

**Property of the dissolved company to be *bona vacantia*.** All property and rights whatsoever vested in or held on trust for the company immediately before its dissolution (including leasehold property, but not property held on trust for another person) are deemed to be *bona vacantia* and accordingly

•      if the company's registered office is in Lancashire, belong to the Duchy of Lancaster;

•      if the registered office is in Cornwall, belong to the Duke of Cornwall; and

•      in all other cases, belong to the Crown.

The company's bank account will be frozen and any credit balance passed to the Crown.

Except as provided for in **21.12**, the above has effect subject to any possible restoration of the company to the register under **21.9** and **21.10**.

[*CA 2006, s 1012*].

There are mechanisms by which interested parties can apply to have *bona vacantia* property vested back in themselves. However, these methods entail expense and are not guaranteed to succeed – particularly if there has been a delay since strike off.

Any rights that the company has to recover funds from its members funds which were paid by way of illegal distribution will pass to the Crown as *bona vacantia* on the company's dissolution.

Enquiries regarding *bona vacantia* should be addressed, as appropriate, to

*In England and Wales*

If the company's registered office is in Lancashire:

The Solicitor for the Affairs of the Duchy of Lancaster Farrer & Co
66 Lincoln's Inn Fields
London WC2A 3LH

If the company's registered office is in Cornwall or the Isles of Scilly:

The Solicitor for the Affairs of the Duke of Cornwall Farrer & Co
66 Lincoln's Inn Fields
London WC2A 3LH

In all other cases:

The Government Legal Department
Bona Vacantia Division (BVD)
PO Box 70165
London WC1A 9HG

*In Scotland*

The Queen's and Lord Treasurer's Remembrancer (QLTR Unit)
Scottish Government Buildings
1B-Bridge
Victoria Quay
Edinburgh EH66QQ

*In Northern Ireland*

The Crown Solicitor
Royal Courts of Justice
Chichester Street
Belfast BT1 3JY

(Companies House Guidance Booklet GP4).

## 21.8  Disclaimer of property vesting as bona vacantia

Where property vests in the Crown as *bona vacantia*, the Crown's title to it may be disclaimed by a notice signed by the Crown representative. The right to exercise a notice of disclaimer may be waived by or on behalf of the Crown either expressly or by taking possession.

Any notice of disclaimer must be executed within three years after the date on which the fact that the property may have vested in the Crown first comes to the notice of the Crown representative. But if ownership of the property is not established at that date, the relevant period runs from the end of the period reasonably necessary for the Crown representative to establish the ownership of the property. If an application in writing is made to the Crown representative by a person interested in the property requiring him to decide whether he will or will not disclaim, any notice of disclaimer must be executed within 12 months after the making of the application or such further period as may be allowed by the court.

Any notice of disclaimer must be delivered to the Registrar of Companies and retained and registered by him. Copies of it must be published in the *Gazette* and sent to any persons who have give notice to the Crown representative that they claim to be interested in the property.

The above provisions similarly apply to property vesting in the Duchy of Lancaster or the Duke of Cornwall.

## 21.8   Dissolution and Restoration

[*CA 2006, s 1013*].

Where notice of disclaimer is executed under the above provisions, the property concerned is deemed not to have vested in the Crown, Duchy of Lancaster or Duke of Cornwall as the case may be. [*CA 2006, s 1014*].

(1)   **Effect of Crown disclaimer: England and Wales and Northern Ireland**

   (a)   *General effect of disclaimer*

   The Crown's disclaimer operates so as to terminate, as from the date of the disclaimer, the rights, interests and liabilities of the company in or in respect of the property disclaimed. It does not, except so far as is necessary for the purpose of releasing the company from any liability, affect the rights or liabilities of any other person.

   (b)   *Disclaimer of leaseholds*

   The disclaimer of any property of a leasehold character does not take effect unless a copy of the disclaimer has been served (so far as the Crown representative is aware of their addresses) on every person claiming under the company as underlessee or mortgagee, and either

   (i)   no application under (*c*) below is made with respect to that property within 14 days of the day on which the last notice under this paragraph was served; or

   (ii)   where such an application has been made, the court directs that the disclaimer shall take effect.

   Where the court gives a direction under (ii) above, it may also, instead of or in addition to any order it makes under (*d*) below, make such order as it thinks fit with respect to fixtures, tenant's improvements and other matters arising out of the lease.

   (c)   *Power of court to make vesting order*

   The court may, on application by a person who

   (i)   claims an interest in the disclaimed property, or

   (ii)   is under a liability in respect of the disclaimed property that is not discharged by the disclaimer,

   make an order for the vesting of the disclaimed property in, or its delivery, to a person entitled to it (or a trustee for such a person). It may also make such an order to a person subject to a liability as in (ii) above (or a trustee for such a person) but only where it appears to the court that it would be just to do so for the purpose of compensating that person in respect of the disclaimer.

   On a vesting order being made, the property comprised in it vests in the person named without conveyance, assignment or transfer.

   (d)   *Protection of persons holding under a lease*

   The court must not make an order under (*c*) above vesting property of a leasehold nature in a person claiming under the company as underlessee or mortgagee except on terms making that person

   (i)   subject to the same liabilities and obligations as those to which the company was subject under the lease; or

(ii)     if the court thinks fit, subject to the same liabilities and obligations as if the lease had been assigned to him.

A person claiming under the company as underlessee or mortgagee who declines to accept a vesting order on such terms is excluded from all interest in the property.

If there is no person claiming under the company who is willing to accept an order on such terms, the court has power to vest the company's estate and interest in the property in any person who is liable (whether personally or in a representative character, and whether alone or jointly with the company) to perform the lessee's covenants in the lease. The court may vest that estate and interest in such a person freed and discharged from all estates, incumbrances and interests created by the company.

(e)     *Land subject to rentcharge*

Where, in consequence of the disclaimer, land that is subject to a rentcharge vests in any person, neither he nor his successors in title are subject to any personal liability in respect of sums becoming due under the rentcharge, except sums becoming due after he, or some person claiming under or through him, has taken possession or control of the land or has entered into occupation of it.

[*CA 2006, ss 1015–1019*].

(2)     **Effect of Crown disclaimer: Scotland**

(a)     *General effect of disclaimer*

The Crown's disclaimer operates to determine, as from the date of the disclaimer, the rights, interests and liabilities of the company, and the property of the company, in or in respect of the property disclaimed. It does not (except so far as is necessary for the purpose of releasing the company and its property from liability) affect the rights or liabilities of any other person.

(b)     *Power of court to make vesting order*

The court may, on application by a person who

(i)     claims an interest in disclaimed property, or

(ii)    is under a liability not discharged by *CA 2006* in respect of disclaimed property,

make an order for the vesting of the property in or its delivery to any persons entitled to it, or to whom it may seem just that the property should be delivered by way of compensation for such liability, or a trustee for him.

On a vesting order being made, the property comprised in it vests in the person named without conveyance or assignment for that purposes.

(c)     *Protection of persons holding under a lease*

Where the property disclaimed is held under a lease in favour of a person claiming under the company (whether as sub-lessee or as creditor in a duly registered or, as the case may be, recorded heritable security over a lease), the vesting order must make that person subject

> (i)     to the same liabilities and obligations as those to which the company was subject under the lease in respect of the property; or
>
> (ii)    if the court thinks fit, only to the same liabilities and obligations as if the lease had been assigned to him.

A sub-lessee or creditor declining to accept a vesting order on such terms is excluded from all interest in and security over the property.

If there is no person claiming under the company who is willing to accept an order on such terms, the court has power to vest the company's estate and interest in the property in any person liable (either personally or in a representative character, and either alone or jointly with the company) to perform the lessee's obligations under the lease. The court may vest that estate and interest in such a person freed and discharged from all interests, rights and obligations created by the company in the lease or in relation to the lease.

[*CA 2006, ss 1020–1022*]

**Liability for rentcharge on company's land in England and Wales and Northern Ireland.** Where, on the dissolution, land in England and Wales or Northern Ireland that is subject to a rentcharge vests by operation of the law in the Crown or any other person (the '*proprietor*'), neither the proprietor nor his successors in title are subject to any personal liability in respect of sums becoming due under the rentcharge, except sums becoming due after the proprietor, or some person claiming under or through him, has taken possession or control of the land or has entered into occupation of it.

[*CA 2006, s 1020*].

## 21.9 ADMINISTRATIVE RESTORATION TO THE REGISTER

An application may be made, by a former director or former member of the company, to the Registrar of Companies to restore to the register a company that has been struck off the register under **21.1** (Power of the registrar to strike off defunct companies).

It follows that a company cannot be restored under this procedure if the company was struck off voluntarily under *CA 2006, s 652A* or *CA 2006, s 1004* and *s 1005* (see **21.2**) Such an application may be made whether or not the company has in consequence been dissolved. Any application must be made within six years from the date of the dissolution of the company (an application being made when it is received by the Registrar of Companies).

*Procedure.* On an application being made (Form RTO1), the Registrar of Companies must restore the company to the register if, and only if, the following conditions are met.

- The company was carrying on business or in operation at the time of its striking off.

- If any property or right previously vested in or held on trust for the company has vested as *bona vacantia*, the Crown representative has signified to the Registrar of Companies in writing consent to the company's restoration to the register.

It is the applicant's responsibility to obtain that consent and to pay any costs (in Scotland, expenses) of the Crown representative

(i)     in dealing with the property during the period of dissolution, or

(ii)    in connection with the proceedings on the application,

that may be demanded as a condition of giving consent. Companies House refer to this consent as a *bona vacantia* waiver letter.

- The applicant has

    (i)    delivered to the Registrar of Companies such documents relating to the company as are necessary to bring up-to-date the records kept by the Registrar of Companies, together with Form RTO1 and the fee payable (for which see APPENDIX 3 COMPANIES HOUSE FEES). The most common cause for rejected applications is lack of the necessary information, and

    (ii)   paid any civil penalty for failure to deliver accounts under *CA 2006, s 453* (see **2.11** ACCOUNTS: GENERAL) or corresponding earlier provisions that were outstanding at the date of dissolution or striking off.

*Statement of compliance.* An application must be accompanied by a statement of compliance, ie a statement that

- the person making the application has standing to apply (ie was a former director or member of the company); and

- the requirements for administrative restoration above are met.

The registrar of Companies may accept the statement of compliance as sufficient evidence of those matters.

*Decision of the Registrar of Companies.* The Registrar of Companies must give notice of the decision to the applicant. If the decision is that the company should be restored to the register, the restoration takes effect as from the date that notice is sent It can take up to ten days from the receipt by Companies House of the application to restore the company. No same day service for administrative restoration is available. The Registrar of Companies must then enter on the register a note of the date as from which the company's restoration to the register takes effect, and publish notice of the restoration in the Gazette. The notice must state

- the name of the company or, if the company is restored to the register under a different name (see **21.11**), that name and its former name;

- the company's registered number; and

- the date from which the restoration takes effect.

*Effect of administrative restoration.* The general effect of administrative restoration to the register is that the company is deemed to have continued in existence as if it had not been dissolved or struck off the register. The company is not liable to a civil penalty for failure to deliver accounts under *CA 2006, s 453* (see **2.11** ACCOUNTS: GENERAL) or corresponding earlier provisions for a financial year in relation to which the period for filing accounts and reports ended

- after the date of dissolution or striking off; and

- before the restoration of the company to the register.

The court may give such directions and make such provision as seems just for placing the company and all other persons in the same position (as nearly as may be) as if the company had not been dissolved or struck off the register. An application to the court for such directions or provision may be made any time within three years after the date of restoration of the company to the register.

[*CA 2006, ss 1024–1028*].

## 21.10  Dissolution and Restoration

### 21.10  RESTORATION TO THE REGISTER BY THE COURT

An application may be made to the court by any of the persons listed below to restore to the register a company that has been

- dissolved after winding up or following administration; or

- struck off the register under 21.1 (POWER TO STRIKE OFF A DEFUNCT COMPANY) or 21.2 (VOLUNTARY STRIKE OFF) (whether or not the company has in consequence also been dissolved).

Such an application may be made by

- the Secretary of State;

- any former director of the company;

- any person having an interest in land in which the company had a superior or derivative interest;

- any person having an interest in land or other property that was subject to rights vested in the company or that was benefited by obligations owed by the company;

- any person who, but for the company's dissolution, would have been in a contractual relationship with it;

- any person with a potential legal claim against the company;

- any manager or trustee of a pension fund established for the benefit of employees of the company;

- any former member of the company (or the personal representatives of such a person);

- any person who was a creditor of the company at the time of its striking off or dissolution;

- any former liquidator of the company; or

- any other person appearing to the court to have an interest in the matter.

*When application to the court may be made.*

(1)    An application to the court for restoration of a company to the register may be made at any time for the purpose of bringing proceedings against the company for 'damages for personal injury'. No order can be made on such an application if it appears to the court that the proceedings would fail by virtue of any enactment as to the time within which proceedings must be brought. But in making that decision, the court must have regard to its power to direct that the period between the dissolution (or striking off) of the company and the making of the order is not to count for the purposes of any such enactment.

'*Personal injury*' includes any disease and any impairment of a person's physical or mental condition and '*damages for personal injury*' include

(i)    any sum in respect of funeral expenses claimed by virtue of *Law Reform (Miscellaneous Provisions) Act 1934, s 1(2)(c)* or *Law Reform (Miscellaneous Provisions) Act (Northern Ireland) 1937, s 14(2)(c)*; and

(ii)   damages under *Fatal Accidents Act 1976, Damages (Scotland) Act 1976* or *Fatal Accidents (Northern Ireland) Order 1977*.

(2)    In any other case an application to the court for restoration of a company to the register may not be made after the end of the period of six years from the date of the dissolution of the company, except that where

(i)    the company has been struck off the register under **21.1**,

(ii)    an application for administrative restoration under **21.9** has been made within the time allowed for making such an application, and

(iii)    the Registrar of Companies has refused the application,

an application to the court may be made within 28 days of notice of the Registrar's decision being issued, even if the period of six years has expired.

*Decision of the court.* The court may order the restoration of the company to the register if

- the company was struck off the register under **21.1** and the company was, at the time of the striking off, carrying on business or in operation;

- the company was struck off the register under **21.2** and any of the requirements of **21.3** to **21.5** was not complied with; and

- in any other case, the court considers it just to do so.

If the court orders restoration of the company to the register, the restoration takes effect on a copy of the court's order being delivered to the Registrar of Companies. The Registrar of Companies must then publish notice of the restoration in the Gazette. The notice must state

- the name of the company or, if the company is restored to the register under a different name (see **21.11**), that name and its former name;

- the company's registered number; and

- the date from which the restoration takes effect.

*Effect of court order for restoration to the register.* The general effect of a court order for restoration to the register is that the company is deemed to have continued in existence as if it had not been dissolved or struck off the register. The company is not liable to a civil penalty for failure to deliver accounts under *CA 2006, s 453* (see **2.11** ACCOUNTS: GENERAL) or corresponding earlier provisions for a financial year in relation to which the period for filing accounts and reports ended

- after the date of dissolution or striking off, and

- before the restoration of the company to the register.

The court may give such directions and make such provision as seems just for placing the company and all other persons in the same position (as nearly as may be) as if the company had not been dissolved or struck off the register. The court may also give directions as to

- the delivery to the Registrar of Companies of such documents relating to the company as are necessary to bring up-to-date the records kept by the Registrar of Companies;

- the payment of the costs (in Scotland, expenses) of the Registrar of Companies in connection with the proceedings for the restoration of the company to the register; and

- where any property or right previously vested in or held on trust for the company has vested as *bona vacantia*, the payment of the costs (in Scotland, expenses) of the Crown representative

## 21.10  Dissolution and Restoration

      (i)     in dealing with the property during the period of dissolution; or

      (ii)    in connection with the proceedings on the application.

[*CA 2006, ss 1029–1032*].

For details of where to apply for a court order see Companies House Guidance Booklet GP4, *Strike-off, dissolution and restoration*.

**Transitional provisions.**

(a)     The above provisions apply whether the company was dissolved or struck off the register before, on or after 1 October 2009.

(b)     Where the company was dissolved or struck off the register before 1 October 2009

     •     no application may be made under the above provisions if an application in respect of the same dissolution or striking off has been made under the *CA 1985* provisions and has not been withdrawn;

     •     the six year time limit in (2) above does not enable an application to be made in respect of a company dissolved before 1 October 2007 except that

      (i)     if the company was struck off under *CA 1985, s 652* or *652A* (see the Appendix to this Chapter, below at (1), (2)) it does not prevent an application being made at any time before 1 October 2015 or 20 years from publication in the Gazette of notice under the relevant section, whichever occurs first; and

      (ii)    the extended time limit where (2)(i)–(iii) above applies also applies to extent the time limit in (i) above.

[*SI 2008 No 2860, Sch 2 paras 90, 91*].


## 21.11  COMPANY'S NAME ON RESTORATION

A company is restored to the register with the name it had before it was dissolved or struck off the register, but subject to the following provisions.

If at the date of restoration the company could not be registered under its former name without contravening *CA 2006, s 66* (name not to be the same as another in the registrar's index of company names, see **27.6** NAMES AND BUSINESS NAMES), it must be restored to the register

(a)     under another name specified

      (i)     in the case of administrative restoration under **21.9**, in the application to the Registrar of Companies, or

      (ii)    in the case of restoration by the court under **21.10**, in the court's order, or

(b)     as if its registered number was also its name.

Where (a)(i) above applies, the provisions relating to change of name in *CA 2006, ss 80, 81* (see **27.20** NAMES AND BUSINESS NAMES) apply as if the application to the Registrar of Companies were notice of a change of name. Similarly, where (a)(ii) applies, those provisions apply as if the copy of the court order delivered to the Registrar of Companies were notice of a change a name.

Where (*b*) above applies, the company must change its name within 14 days after the date of the restoration. The change may be made by resolution of the directors (without prejudice to any other method of changing the company's name) and the company must give notice to the Registrar of Companies of the change. If the company fails to change its name within 14 days or notify the Registrar of Companies, an offence is committed by the company and every officer of the company who is in default. A person guilty of such an offence is liable, on summary conviction, to a fine not exceeding level 5 on the standard scale and, for continued contravention, to a daily default fine not exceeding one-tenth of level 5 on the standard scale. See **29.1** OFFENCES AND LEGAL PROCEEDINGS for the standard scale.

[*CA 2006, s 1033*].

### 21.12   EFFECT OF RESTORATION WHERE PROPERTY HAS VESTED AS BONA VACANTIA

The person in whom any property or right is vested under *CA 2006, s 1012* (see **21.8**) may dispose of that property or right, or any interest in it, despite the fact that the company may be restored to the register under **21.9** or **21.10**. If the company is restored to the register

- the restoration does not affect the disposition; and

- the Crown (or Duke of Cornwall) must pay to the company an amount equal to

  (i)    the consideration received, or

  (ii)   the value of any such consideration at the time of the disposition

  or, if no consideration was received, an amount equal to the value of the property, right or interest disposed of, as at the date of the disposition.

There may be deducted from the amount payable the reasonable costs of the Crown representative in connection with the disposition (to the extent that they have not been paid as a condition of administrative restoration or pursuant to a court order for restoration).

[*CA 2006, s 1034*].

**Transitional provisions**.

(1)    The above provisions apply whenever the company was dissolved.

(2)    Where the company was dissolved before 1 October 2009,

- the reference to *CA 2006, s 1012* is to be read as a reference to *CA 1985, s 654* (see the Appendix to this Chapter, below at (8)) or earlier provisions; and

- no deduction is to be made for reasonable costs of Crown representatives from consideration realised before 1 October 2009.

[*SI 2008 No 2860, Sch 2 para 92*].

### 21.13   APPLICATION TO RESTRAIN PRESENTATION OF WINDING-UP PETITION

Further detail on insolvency proceedings is beyond the scope of this Handbook.

However, in *LDX International Group LLP v Misra Ventures Ltd* [2018] EWHC 275 (Ch), the High Court evaluated the principles to be applied in response to an application from a debtor company for an injunction to restrain the presentation, advertising or otherwise publicising of a winding-up petition.

## 21.13 Dissolution and Restoration

A winding-up petition is the first stage in the process of putting a company into compulsory liquidation.

The presentation of a petition has serious consequences for the debtor company and it is vital that its directors promptly take appropriate action. The directors' immediate priority may well be to try to prevent a creditor from presenting the petition. If the debtor company disputes a creditor's statutory demand, the debtor's directors may seek an undertaking from the creditor that it will not present a petition until the dispute has been fully investigated. This may develop into an application for an injunction against the petitioning creditor.

Here, the High Court confirmed the correct approach to take when considering an application by a debtor company for an injunction to restrain presentation of the winding-up petition. In this case, neither the petition debt nor the statutory demand was contested. Instead, the injunction was sought because the debtor company had a cross-claim against the petitioning creditor which exceeded the value of the uncontested debt. The court asked itself whether the merits of the cross-claim had to be fully assessed, or whether it (the court) could simply issue an injunction on being satisfied that the cross-claim was genuine and serious and exceeded the petition debt. In the absence of exceptional circumstances, the court held that the latter approach was the correct one (this being a test set out by the Court of Appeal in *Bayoil SA, Re, Seawind Tankers Corp v Bayoil SA* [1999] 1 All ER 374, [1999] 1 WLR 147).

This decision provides some helpful clarity on how the courts are likely to respond to an application to restrain the presentation of a winding-up petition, on which there is very little authority. Most reported cases relate to applications for injunctions which are made *after* presentation of a winding-up petition.

## 21.14 INSOLVENCY AND COMPANIES COURT JUDGES

As from 26 February 2018, Registrars in Bankruptcy of the High Court have been renamed Insolvency and Companies Court Judges, pursuant to *The Alteration of Judicial Titles (Registrar in Bankruptcy of the High Court) Order 2018 (SI 2018 No 130)*. The title of Deputy Registrars will also change following the same convention.

It is understood from the explanatory memorandum that the proposed amendments are only to the name of the office, and do not change the nature of the role. Apparently, the judiciary themselves asked for the change in order that it be made clearer to court users that their cases were being heard by a *judge*, and in order to align the terminology with the name of the court itself.

The business of the Insolvency and Companies List includes corporate and personal insolvency and pure company work (such as shareholder disputes, in the Companies Court). It all forms part of the Chancery Division of the High Court and is situated in the Business and Property Court England and Wales.

## APPENDIX: PROVISIONS APPLYING BEFORE 1 OCTOBER 2009

NB that these pre-1 October 2009 notes refer to the old Companies House Guidance booklets. Please check with Companies House whether the old or new guidance applies (in many cases it remains substantially the same)

### (1) Striking off defunct companies at instigation of the Registrar of Companies

If the Registrar of Companies has reasonable cause to believe that a company is not carrying on business or in operation, he may send to the company by post a letter inquiring whether it is carrying on business or in operation. [*CA 1985, s 652(1)*].

He may take this action, for example, because he has not received documents from the company which should have been delivered to him (eg annual returns and accounts) or mail sent to the registered office is returned undelivered (Companies House Guidance Booklet GBW2 Strike-off, Dissolution and Restoration, Chapter 2 para 1).

If the Registrar of Companies does not, within one month of sending that letter, receive a reply, he must within 14 days send by post a registered letter referring to the first letter and stating that no answer has been received. The letter must also state that if no reply is received to the second letter within one month from its date, a notice will be published in the *London/Edinburgh Gazette* with a view to striking the company's name off the register.

Where the Registrar of Companies

- receives an answer from the company to the effect that the company is not carrying on a business or in operation, or

- does not receive a reply to the second letter above within one month,

he may publish a notice in the *London/Edinburgh Gazette* that, at the expiration of three months from the date of that notice, the company will be struck off the register and dissolved unless cause is shown to the contrary. The Registrar of Companies must send a copy of any such notice to the company (and will also place a copy on the company's public file). At the expiration of the three months, unless cause to the contrary has been shown, the Registrar of Companies may strike the company name off the register and publish notice of this in the *London/Edinburgh Gazette*. On publication, the company is dissolved (although this does not affect the power of the court to wind up the company).

The Registrar of Companies may also take this course of action where *a company is being wound up* and he has reasonable cause to believe that no liquidator is acting, or that the affairs of the company are fully wound up, and the returns required to be made by the liquidator have not been made for a period of six consecutive months.

[*CA 1985, s 652(2)–(5)(6)(b)*].

**Addresses for notices etc.** A letter or notice to be sent to a company may be addressed

- to the company at its registered office, or, if no office has been registered,

- to the care of some officer of the company, or if no officer is known to the Registrar of Companies,

- to each of the subscribers to the memorandum at the addresses there mentioned.

A notice to a liquidator may be addressed to him at his last known place of business.

[*CA 1985, s 652(7)*].

In England and Wales, notices are published in the Company Law Official Notifications Supplement to the *London Gazette*, published weekly on microfiche. Copies are available from The London Gazette, PO Box 7920, London SE1 5ZH (tel: 020 7394 4517). In Scotland, notices are published in the *Edinburgh Gazette*, published twice weekly. Copies are available from The Edinburgh Gazette, 73 Lothian Road, Edinburgh EH3 9AW (tel: 0870 600 5522). (Companies House Guidance Booklet GBW2, Chapter 2 para 4).

**(2) Striking off private companies on application by the company**

Subject to the conditions in (3) below being satisfied, a private company may apply to the Registrar of Companies for the company's name to be struck off the register. The application must be made on its behalf by the directors (or a majority of them) and be in the prescribed form (Form 652a).

[*CA 1985, s 652A(1)(2); Deregulation and Contracting Out Act 1994, Sch 5*].

A filing fee is payable although this will be refunded if the application is rejected or withdrawn after its registration.

Application might be made, for example, where a company is no longer required because the active directors wish to retire; the company is a subsidiary whose name is no longer needed; or the company was set up to exploit an idea that turned out not to be feasible. The procedure is not an alternative to formal insolvency proceedings where these are appropriate as creditors are likely to prevent the striking off (see (5) and (6) below). (Companies House Guidance Booklet GBW2, Chapter 1 para 1).

Following receipt of the Form 652a, the Registrar of Companies will publish a notice in the *London/Edinburgh Gazette* stating that he may exercise his power under these provisions and inviting any person to show cause why he should not do so. If cause to the contrary is not shown and the application has not been withdrawn, the Registrar of Companies will strike the company off the register not less than three months after the date of the notice. The company will be formally dissolved when the Registrar of Companies publishes a notice to that effect in the *London/Edinburgh Gazette*.

[*CA 1985, s 652A(3)–(5); Deregulation and Contracting Out Act 1994, Sch 5*].

Even where the company is struck off the register and dissolved, creditors and others may apply for the company to be restored to the register (see (9) below).

**(3) Conditions for applying**

A person cannot make an application to be struck off under (2) above if

(a)     at any time in the previous three months, it has

- changed its name;

- traded or otherwise carried on business;

- disposed for value of any property or rights which, immediately before ceasing to trade or carry on business, it held for disposal or gain in the normal course of that business or trade; or

- engaged in any other activity except one necessary or expedient for making a striking off application, concluding the affairs of the company or complying with any statutory requirement; or

(b)     the company is the subject, or proposed subject, of any insolvency proceedings or compromise or arrangement with its creditors under *CA 1985, s 425*.

For the purposes of (*a*) above, a company is not treated as trading or carrying on business by virtue only of the fact that it makes a payment in respect of a liability incurred in the course of trading or carrying on business.

[*CA 1985, s 652B(1)–(5); Deregulation and Contracting Out Act 1994, Sch 5; EmA 2002, Sch 17 para 7*].

### (4) Withdrawal of application

A director must withdraw a company's application under (2) above (using Form 652c) where, at any time after application has been made and before it is finally dealt with or voluntarily withdrawn, the company

(a)     changes its name;

(b)     trade or otherwise carries on business;

(c)     disposes for value of any property or rights (other than those which it needed to retain to make, or proceed with, the application);

(d)     engages in any other activity except one necessary or expedient for

   •      making or proceeding with a striking off application;

   •      concluding the affairs of the company which are outstanding because of what was necessary or expedient to make or proceed with the application; or

   •      complying with any statutory requirement; or

(e)     becomes the subject of any insolvency proceedings or makes a compromise or arrangement with its creditors under *CA 1985, s 425*.

For the purposes of (*b*) above, a company is not treated as trading or carrying on business by virtue only of the fact that it makes a payment in respect of a liability incurred in the course of trading or carrying on business.

[*CA 1985, s 652C(4)–(7); Deregulation and Contracting Out Act 1994, Sch 5; EmA 2002, Sch 17 para 8*].

### (5) Notification

Where an application is made under (2) above, a copy of the Form 652a must be given, within seven days of the date of application, to every person who on that date was

(a)     a member of the company;

(b)     an employee of the company;

(c)     a creditor of the company (including a contingent or prospective creditor);

(d)     a director of the company who did not sign the Form 652a; or

(e)     a manager or trustee of any employee pension fund.

[*CA 1985, ss 652B(6)(7), 652D(8); Deregulation and Contracting Out Act 1994, Sch 5*].

A copy of Form 652a must also be given to any person who becomes a member, employee etc under (a)–(e) above on a date subsequent to the application (within seven days of so becoming).

[*CA 1985, ss 652C(1)(2), 652D(8); Deregulation and Contracting Out Act 1994, Sch 5*].

There is no requirement to give notice if the application is withdrawn within the seven day period of notice.

[*CA 1985, ss 652B(8), 652C(3); Deregulation and Contracting Out Act 1994, Sch 5*].

For the above purposes, a copy of the Form 652a is treated as given to a person if it is delivered to, left at, or posted to his 'proper address' ie

(i)    in the case of an individual, his last known address;

(ii)    in the case of a company or partnership incorporated under the law outside the UK which has a place of business in the UK, its principal office in the UK;

(iii)    in the case of a company or partnership not falling within (ii) above, its registered or principal office.

Where a creditor has more than one place of business, copies of Form 652a must be left at, or sent by post to, each place of business of the creditor which the company has had dealings with in relation to the debt.

*[CA 1985, s 652D(1)–(4); Deregulation and Contracting Out Act 1994, Sch 5].*

**(6) Objections to proposed striking off and dissolution**

Any interested party may object to the striking off and dissolution of the company. Any objections should be in writing and sent to the Registrar of Companies, together with supporting evidence (eg copies of invoices showing that the company is trading). Examples of grounds for objecting are that

•    the company has broken any of the conditions of its application under (2) above;

•    the directors have not informed interested parties;

•    any of the declarations on Form 652a are false;

•    some form of action is being taken, or is pending, to recover any moneys owed (eg a winding up petition or action in the small claims court);

•    other legal action is being taken against the company; or

•    the directors have wrongfully traded or committed a tax fraud or some other offence.

(Companies House Guidance Booklet GBW2 Strike-off, Dissolution and Restoration, Chapter 1 para 8).

**(7) Offences and penalties**

The following offences and penalties are imposed for breaches in connection with the provisions in (2)–(5) above.

•    A person who breaches or fails to perform a duty imposed under (3) to (5) above is guilty of an offence and liable to a fine up. It is a defence for the accused to prove that

   (i)    in proceedings for an offence of breach of duty under (3) above (by making an application when all the conditions were not satisfied) that he did not know, and could not reasonably have known, of the existence of the facts which led to the breach;

   (ii)    in proceedings for an offence consisting of failure to give notice under *CA 1985, s 652B(6)* (see (5) above) that he took all reasonable steps to perform the duty; and

   (iii)    in proceedings for an offence consisting of failure to give notice under *CA 1985, s 652C(2)* (see (5) above) or failure to withdraw an application under (4) above, either that, at the time of the failure, he was not aware that an application had been made or he took all reasonable steps to perform the duty.

•    A person who fails to give notification as required under (5) above with the intention of concealing the making of the application is guilty of an offence and liable to a penalty.

- Where a company makes an application under (2) above, any person who, in connection with the application, knowingly or recklessly furnishes any information to the Registrar of Companies which is false or misleading in a material particular is guilty of an offence and liable to a penalty.

- Any person who knowingly or recklessly makes an application to the Registrar of Companies, which purports to be an application under (2) above, but which is not, is guilty of an offence and liable to a penalty.

[*CA 1985, ss 652E, 652F, Sch 24; Deregulation and Contracting Out Act 1994, Sch 5*].

### (8) Effect of dissolution

**Liability of directors etc**. The liability (if any) of every director, managing officer and member of the company continues and may be enforced as if the company had not been dissolved.

[*CA 1985, ss 652(6)(a), 652A(6); Deregulation and Contracting Out Act 1994, Sch 5*].

**Assets of the company**. All property and rights whatsoever vested in or held on trust for the company immediately before its dissolution (including leasehold property, but not property held on trust for any other person) are deemed to be *bona vacantia* and accordingly

- if the company's registered office is in Lancashire, belong to the Duchy of Lancaster;

- if the registered office is in Cornwall, belong to the Duchy of Cornwall; and

- in all other cases, belong to the Crown.

For enquiries regarding *bona vacantia* see **21.7**)

If the company's registered office is in Cornwall or the Isles of Scilly:

The property vesting as *bona vacantia* may be disclaimed by the Crown or Duchy as the case may be.

[*CA 1985, ss 654, 656*]. (Companies House Guidance Booklet GBW Strike-off, Dissolution and Restoration, Chapter 2 para 5).

See *CA 1985, s 657* and *Sch 20* for the effect of Crown disclaimer.

**Liability for rentcharge on company's land in England and Wales**. Where land in England and Wales vests subject to a rentcharge in the Crown or any other person (the '*proprietor*') on the dissolution of a company, the proprietor and his successors in title are not subject to any personal liability in respect of any sums becoming due under the rentcharge except sums becoming due after the proprietor, or some person claiming under or through him, has taken possession or control of the land or has entered into occupation of it.

[*CA 1985, s 658; IA 1985, Sch 6 para 47; IA 1986, Sch 13*].

### (9) Restoration to the register

Where a company has been struck off the register, the court may, on application within 20 years of dissolution, order the company's name to be restored to the register.

**If the company has been struck off at the instigation of the Registrar of Companies under (1) above**, the application may be made by the company (even though it does not legally exist) or any member or creditor. The court may order the company's name to be restored if it was carrying on business or in operation at the time it was struck off or if it is just to do so. For a consideration of these criteria for restoring to the register, see *Priceland Ltd, Re, Waltham Forest London Borough Council v Registrar of Companies* [1997] 1 BCLC 467, [1997] BCC 207.

# Appendix   Dissolution and Restoration

**If the company was struck off following an application by the company under (2) above,** the application may be made by any person to whom a copy of the application was required to be given under (5) above. The court may order the company's name to be restored to the register if that person was not given a copy of the application, or the application by the company involved a breach of the conditions of the application under (3) above, or for some other reason if it is just to do so. The court may also order restoration, on application by the Secretary of State, if satisfied that it is in the public interest to do so.

[*CA 1985, s 653(1)–(2D); Deregulation and Contracting Out Act 1994, Sch 5*].

The repeal of the above provisions with effect from 1 October 2009 does not affect an application made under those provisions before that date.

[*SI 2008 No 2860, Sch 2 para 89*].

The application for restoration may be made by any person who was legally prejudiced by the dissolution of the company. This includes a person who wishes to enforce a liability of the company and does not depend on there having been an existing cause of action when the company was struck off. The provisions are also intended to provide a remedy for a person who has a claim, whether against the company or against a third party (such as the company's insurer or guarantor), which can only be enforced if the company is restored to the register (*City of Westminster Assurance Co Ltd v Registrar of Companies* [1997] BCC 960, CA).

**Procedure**. The Registrar of Companies will provide information to assist in an application to the court but has no power to register a company without a court order.

*In England and Wales*, the application can be made to the High Court by completing a Part 8 claim form. This is the standard form that starts proceedings and can be downloaded from:

https://www.justice.gov.uk/courts/procedure-rules/civil/forms

The Registrar of the Companies Court in London usually hears restoration cases in chambers once a week on Friday afternoons. Cases are also heard at the District Registries. Alternatively, an application can be made to a County Court that has the authority to wind up the company. The claim form should be served on the solicitor dealing with any *bona vacantia* (see (8) above) and the Registrar of Companies, Restoration Section, Companies House, Crown Way, Cardiff CF14 3UZ (tel 029 2038 0069; fax 029 2038 0006). The Registrar of Companies will accept delivery by post (recorded delivery is recommended) or by hand at Companies House, Cardiff or London.

*In Scotland*, application may be made to the Court with jurisdiction to wind up the company, ie the Court of Sessions or, for a company whose paid-up capital does not exceed £120,000, the Sheriff Court in the Sheriffdom in which the company has its registered office. The petition should be served on The Lord Advocate, Crown Office, 25 Chambers Street, Edinburgh EH1 1LA and the Registrar of Companies, Companies House, 37 Castle Terrace, Edinburgh EH1 2EB. The Registrar of Companies will accept service by post (recorded delivery is recommended) or by hand. The Registrar of Companies and/or the Lord Advocate may be represented at the hearing by an agent.

*Evidence*. The Registrar of Companies will normally ask for delivery (prior to the hearing) of any statutory documents to bring the public file of the company up to date, and the correction of any irregularities in the company's structure.

The court will require an affidavit or witness statement (in Scotland, evidence) covering

(a)    service of the originating summons/petition

(b)    the circumstances of the company, including

- when it was incorporated and the nature of its objects (a copy of the certificate of incorporation and memorandum and articles of association should be attached);

- its membership and officers;

- its trading activities and, if applicable, when it stopped trading;

- an explanation of any failure to deliver accounts, returns or notices to the Registrar of Companies;

- details of the striking-off and dissolution (based on information provided by the Registrar of Companies);

- comments on the company's solvency; and

- any further information necessary to explain the reason for the application.

The applicant will normally be expected to pay the Registrar of Companies' costs in relation to the hearing.

(Companies House Guidance Booklet GBW Strike-off, Dissolution and Restoration, Chapter 3 paras 2–5 and GBW2(S) Strike-off, Dissolution and Restoration, Chapter 3 paras 2–5).

**Effect of court order.** When an office copy of the order is delivered to the Registrar of Companies, the company is deemed to have continued in existence as if its name had not been struck off. The court may, by the order, give such directions and make such provisions as seem just for placing the company and all other persons in the same position (as nearly as possible) as if the company's name had never been struck off.

[*CA 1985, s 653(3); Deregulation and Contracting Out Act 1994, Sch 5*].

### (10) Power of court to declare dissolution of company void

Where a company has been dissolved, the court may, on an application within two years (subject to below) of the date of dissolution by the liquidator or any other interested party, make an order, on such terms as it thinks fit, declaring the dissolution to have been void. Such proceedings may then be taken as if the company had not been dissolved.

The applicant must, within seven days of the order (or such further time as the court allows), deliver an office copy of the order to the Registrar of Companies. In default, he is liable to a fine.

There is no time limit where the application is for the purposes of bringing proceedings against the company for

(a)    damages in respect of 'personal injuries' including any funeral expenses claimed by virtue of the *Law Reform (Miscellaneous Provisions) Act 1934, s 1(2)(c)*, or

(b)    damages under the *Fatal Accidents Act 1976* or the *Damages (Scotland) Act 1976*,

although no order must be made if the proceedings would fail under a time limit in any other enactment. For the interaction of this provision in relation to personal injuries actions with the *Limitation Act 1980, s 33*, see *Workvale Ltd (in dissolution), Re* [1992] 1 WLR 416, [1991] BCLC 528, CA.

'*Personal injuries*' include any disease and any impairment of a person's physical or mental condition.

*Before 1 October 2008*, no application under (*a*) or (*b*) above could be made in relation to a company dissolved before 16 November 1969 [*CA 1989, s 141(4)*] but this restriction was removed from that date by *SI 2008 No 1886, Art 2*.

# Appendix   Dissolution and Restoration

[*CA 1985, s 651; CA 1989, s 141*].

The repeal of the above provisions with effect from 1 October 2009 does not affect an application made under those provisions before that date.

[*SI 2008 No 2860, Sch 2 para 89*].

The interest of an applicant under *CA 1985, s 651* above in having the company revived does not have to be firmly established or likely to prevail. It is sufficient that it is not 'merely shadowy'. It follows, therefore, that an order may be made to enable a company to meet a liability which would otherwise remain unpaid. Normally a third party should not be entitled to intervene to argue that an order should not be made. However, in cases where the making of an order would directly affect the rights of a third party, irrespective of whether the applicant has any claim against the company or the company has any claim against the third party, the third party is entitled to be joined to argue that such an order should not be made (*Forte's (Manufacturing) Ltd, Re, Stanhope Pension Trust Ltd v Registrar of Companies* (1993) 69 P & CR 238, [1994] 1 BCLC 628, CA).

## (11) Effect of company's revival after dissolution

The person in whom any property or right is vested following dissolution (see (8) above under the heading *Assets of the company*) may dispose of that property or right, or any interest in it, despite the fact that an order may be made under (9) or (10) above. Where such an order is then made,

- it does not affect the disposition; and

- the Crown (or Duke of Cornwall) must repay to the company an amount equal to

    (i)     the consideration received; or

    (ii)    the value of any such consideration at the time of the disposition; or

    (iii)   if no consideration was received, the value of the property, right or interest disposed of, as at the date of the disposition.

[*CA 1985, s 655*].

# 22   Distributions

**Cross-references.** See **47.62** SHARES for bonus issues.

**Background.** The provisions in this chapter apply, unless otherwise stated, to distributions made on or after 6 April 2008.

[*SI 2007 No 3495, Sch 4 para 33*].

## 22.1   RESTRICTIONS ON DISTRIBUTIONS

*CA 2006, ss 829–851* provide for what profits a company may lawfully distribute by way, for example, of dividends to shareholders and

- Largely restate *CA 1985, Part VIII*

- Apply to distributions made after 6 April 2008 and

- Clarify the rule in *Aveling Barford Ltd v Perion Ltd* [1989] BCLC 626, 5 BCC 677 (see **22.8**)

The basic restriction is set out in *section 830* which provides that, subject to anything in the company's articles or in any enactment which restricts what distributions can be made:

(a)   Any company may only make a distribution out of profits available for the purpose (see **22.2**).

[*CA 2006, s 830(1)*].

(b)   A *public company* may only make a distribution

- if the amount of its 'net assets' is not less than the aggregate of its called-up share capital and 'undistributable reserves'; and

- if, and to the extent that, the distribution does not reduce the amount of those assets to less than that aggregate.

'*Net assets*' means the aggregate of the company's assets (excluding any uncalled share capital) less the aggregate of its liabilities. Liabilities here include

- where the relevant accounts are Companies Act accounts,

## 22.1 Distributions

    (i)    any provisions for liabilities (or, in the case of insurance companies, provisions for other risks) which are reasonably necessary to provide for any liability the nature of which is clearly defined and which is either likely to be incurred, or certain to be incurred but uncertain as to amount or as date on which it will arise; and

    (ii)    in the case of insurance companies, any amount included under Liabilities items B (funds for future appropriations), C (technical provisions) and D (technical provisions for linked liabilities) in the balance sheet;

- where the relevant accounts are IAS accounts, provisions of any kind.

### Distribution

Distribution means every description of distribution of a company's assets to its members, whether in cash or otherwise, except for

- an issue of shares as fully or partly paid bonus shares;

- the reduction of share capital

    (i)    by extinguishing or reducing the liability of any of the members on any of the company's shares in respect of share capital not paid up, or

    (ii)    by repaying off paid up share capital;

- the redemption or purchase of any of the company's own shares out of capital (including the proceeds of any fresh issue of shares) or out of unrealised profits in accordance with *CA 2006, Pt 18, Chapter 3, 4 or 5* (see **34.2–34.18 Purchase of Own Shares**); or

- a distribution of assets to members of the company on its winding up.

[*CA 2006, s 829; SI 2007 No 3495, Sch 1 para 14; SI 2008 No 2860, art 6*].

### Undistributable reserves

A company's undistributable reserves are

(A)    its share premium account;

(B)    the capital redemption reserve;

(C)    the amount by which its accumulated, unrealised profits (so far as not previously utilised by capitalisation) exceeds its accumulated, unrealised losses (so far as not previously written off in a reduction or reorganisation of capital duly made); and

(D)    any other reserve which the company is prohibited from distributing by any other enactment or by its articles.

In (C) above, the reference to capitalisation does not include a transfer of profits of the company to its capital redemption reserve

[*CA 2006, s 831(4)*].

### Capitalisation

Capitalisation, in relation to a company's profits, means any of the following operations (whenever carried out).

- Applying the profits in wholly or partly paying up unissued shares in the company to be allotted to members of the company as fully or partly paid bonus shares.

- Transferring the profits to capital redemption reserve.

[*CA 2006, s 853(3)*].

(c)    [*CA 2006, s 831(1)–(3)(5)(6); SI 2008 No 410, Sch 9 paras 2, 4*].

See **22.4** to **22.6** for the company's accounts to be considered in determining whether a distribution may be made without contravening the above provisions.

(d)    A company must not apply an unrealised profit in paying up debentures or unpaid amounts on its issued shares.

[*CA 2006, s 849*].

## 22.2  PROFITS AVAILABLE FOR DISTRIBUTION

Insofar as a company is able to make distributions then a company's profits available for distribution are, its accumulated, realised profits (so far as not previously utilised by distribution or capitalisation) less its accumulated, realised losses (so far as not previously written off in a reduction or reorganisation of capital duly made). [*CA 2006, s 830(2)(3)*].

### Older profits and losses

Where the directors of a company are, after making all reasonable enquiries, unable to determine whether

- a particular profit made before the 'relevant date' is realised or unrealised, they may treat the profit as realised; and

- a particular loss made before the relevant date is realised or unrealised, they may treat the loss as unrealised.

The 'relevant date' is, for companies registered in Great Britain, 22 December 1980 and, for companies registered in Northern Ireland, 1 July 1983.

[*CA 2006, s 850*].

### Profits or losses

References to profits or losses of any description

- are to profits and losses of that description made at any time; and

- except where the context otherwise requires, are to profits or losses of a revenue or capital character.

[*CA 2006, s 853(2)*].

## 22.2 Distributions

**Realised profits and losses.**

References to 'realised profits' and 'realised losses', in relation to a company's accounts, are to such profits or losses of the company as fall to be treated as realised in accordance with principles generally accepted at the time when the accounts are prepared, with respect to the determination for accounting purposes of realised profits or losses. This is without prejudice to

- the construction of any other expression (where appropriate) by reference to accepted accounting principles or practice; or

- any specific provision for the treatment of profits or losses of any description as realised.

[*CA 2006, s 853(4)(5)*].

## 22.3 TREATMENT OF DEVELOPMENT COSTS

Where development costs are shown or included as an asset in the company's accounts, any amount shown or included in respect of those costs is treated as

- a realised loss for the purposes of **22.2**; and

- a realised revenue loss in the case of an investment company.

This does not apply to any part of that amount representing an unrealised profit made on revaluation of those costs. It also does not apply if

(a) there are special circumstances in the company's case justifying the directors in deciding that the amount is not to be so treated;

(b) it is stated

   (i) in the case of Companies Act accounts, in the note required to the accounts as to the reason for showing development costs as an asset, or

   (ii) in the case of IAS individual accounts, in any note to the accounts

   that the amount is not to be so treated; and

(c) the note explains the circumstances relied upon to justify the decision of the directors to that effect.

[*CA 2006, s 844*].

## 22.4 ACCOUNTING REQUIREMENTS

Subject to **22.7(1)**, whether a distribution can be made without contravening the provisions of **22.1** is determined by reference to

(i) profits, losses, assets and liabilities,

(ii) provisions of the following kind, namely

- where the relevant accounts are Companies Act accounts,

   — provisions for depreciation or diminution in value of assets;

   — any provisions for liabilities (or, in the case of insurance companies, provisions for other risks) which are reasonably necessary to provide for any liability the nature of which is clearly defined and which is either likely to be incurred, or certain to be incurred but uncertain as to amount or as date on which it will arise; and

— in the case of insurance companies, any amount included under Liabilities items Ba (funds for future appropriations), C (technical provisions) and D (technical provisions for linked liabilities) in the balance sheet; and

- where the relevant accounts are IAS individual accounts, provisions of any kind, and

(iii) share capital and reserves (including 'undistributable reserves', see **22.1**)

as stated in the company's 'relevant accounts'.

The *'relevant accounts'* for these purposes are the company's last annual accounts (see (*a*) below), except that

- where the distribution would be found to contravene the provisions of this chapter by reference to the company's last annual accounts, it may be justified by reference to interim accounts (see (*b*) below); and

- where the distribution is proposed to be declared during the company's first accounting reference period, or before any accounts have been circulated in respect of that period, it may be justified by reference to initial accounts (see (*c*) below).

The requirements of (*a*), (*b*) or (*c*) below must be complied with, as and where applicable. If any applicable requirement not complied with, the accounts may not be relied on for the purposes of this chapter and the distribution is accordingly treated as contravening the requirements for distribution.

(a) **Requirements where last annual accounts used.** The company's last annual accounts means the company's individual accounts that were last circulated to members in accordance with *CA 2006, s 423* (see **2.6** ACCOUNTS: GENERAL) or, if in accordance with *CA 2006, s 426* the company provided a strategic report instead, that formed the basis of that statement (see **6.1** ACCOUNTS: SUMMARY FINANCIAL STATEMENTS). The requirements are:

- The accounts must have been 'properly prepared' in accordance with *CA 2006* or have been so prepared subject only to matters which are not material for determining, by reference to (i)–(iii) above, whether the distribution would contravene the relevant provisions.

- Unless the company is exempt from audit and the directors take advantage of that exemption, the auditor must have made his report on the accounts. If that report was qualified, the auditor must have stated in writing (either at the time of his report or subsequently) whether in his opinion the matters in respect of which his report is qualified are material for determining whether a distribution would contravene the provisions of this chapter. A copy of that statement must, in the case of a private company, have been circulated to members in accordance with *CA 2006, s 423* (see **2.6** ACCOUNTS: GENERAL), or, in the case of a public company, have been laid before the company in general meeting. An auditor's statement is sufficient for the purposes of a distribution if it relates to distributions of a description that includes the distribution in question, even if at the time of the statement it had not been proposed.

See also *Precision Dippings Ltd v Precision Dippings Marketing Ltd* [1986] Ch 447, [1985] BCLC 385, CA.

(b) **Requirements where interim accounts used**. Interim accounts must be accounts that enable a reasonable judgment to be made as to the amounts of the items mentioned in (i)–(iii) above. Where interim accounts are prepared for a proposed distribution by a *public company*, the requirements are:

- The accounts must have been 'properly prepared', or have been so prepared subject to matters that are not material for determining, by reference to (i)–(iii) above, whether the distribution would contravene the relevant provisions.

  *'Properly prepared'* means prepared in accordance with *CA 2006, ss 395–397* (see **3.2** Accounts: Large Companies), applying those requirements with such modifications as are necessary because the accounts are prepared otherwise than in respect of an accounting reference period.

- The balance sheet comprised in the accounts must have been signed in accordance with *CA 2006, s 414* (see **2.2** Accounts: General).

- A copy of the accounts must have been delivered to the Registrar of Companies. Any requirement of as to the delivery of a certified translation into English of any document forming part of the accounts must also have been met.

(c) **Requirements where initial accounts used**. Initial accounts must be accounts that enable a reasonable judgment to be made as to the amounts of the items mentioned in (i)–(iii) above. Where initial accounts are prepared for a proposed distribution by a *public company*, the requirements are:

- The accounts must have been 'properly prepared' (see (*b*) above), or have been so prepared subject to matters that are not material for determining, by reference to (i)–(iii) above, whether the distribution would contravene the relevant provisions.

- The company's auditor must have made a report stating whether, in his opinion, the accounts have been properly prepared. If that report was qualified, the auditor must have stated in writing (either at the time of his report or subsequently) whether in his opinion the matters in respect of which his report is qualified are material for determining whether a distribution would contravene the provisions of this chapter. A copy of that statement must have been laid before the company in general meeting (see **2.6** Accounts: General).

- A copy of the accounts, of the auditor's report and of any auditor's statement must have been delivered to the Registrar of Companies. The auditor's report and any audit statement must state the name of the auditor and (where the auditor is a firm) the name of the person who signed it as senior statutory auditor. It must also be signed by the auditor or (where the auditor is a firm) in the name of the firm by a person authorised to sign on its behalf. Alternatively, if the conditions in *CA 2006, s 506* (circumstances in which names may be omitted, see **8.41** Audit) are met, the report and any statement must state that a resolution has been passed and notified to the Secretary of State in accordance with that section.

Any requirement of as to the delivery of a certified translation into English of any document forming part of the accounts must also have been met.

[*CA 2006, ss 836–839; SI 2007 No 3495, Sch 1 paras 17, 18; SI 2008 No 409, Sch 7, paras 2, 5; SI 2008 No 410, Sch 9 paras 2, 7; SI 2008 No 2860, Art 6; SI 2009 No 1941, Sch 1 para 260*].

## 22.5   Successive distributions

In determining whether a proposed distribution may be made by a company in a case where

(a)   one or more previous distributions have been made in pursuance of a determination made by reference to the same relevant accounts, or

(b)   relevant 'financial assistance' has been given, or other relevant payments have been made, since those accounts were prepared

the provision of this chapter apply as if the amount of the proposed distribution was increased by the amount of the previous distributions, financial assistance or other payments.

Financial assistance and other payments that are relevant for these purposes are

- financial assistance lawfully given by the company out of its distributable profits;

- financial assistance for the acquisition of shares given by a company in contravention of *CA 2006, s 678* or *CA 2006, s 679* (see **34.25 PURCHASE OF OWN SHARES**) in a case where the giving of that assistance reduces the company's 'net assets' or increases its 'net liabilities';

- payments made by a company in respect of the purchase by it of shares in the company (except a payment made lawfully otherwise than out of distributable profits); and

- payments of any description specified in *CA 2006, s 705* (before 1 October 2009, *CA 1985, s 168*) (payments apart from purchase price of shares to be made out of distributable profits, see **34.9 PURCHASE OF OWN SHARES**).

For the meaning of '*financial assistance*', see **34.25 PURCHASE OF OWN SHARES**.

'*Net assets*' means the amount by which the aggregate amount of the company's assets exceeds the aggregate amount of its liabilities, taking the amount of the assets and liabilities to be as stated in the company's accounting records immediately before the financial assistance is given.

'*Net liabilities*' means the amount by which the aggregate amount of the company's liabilities exceeds the aggregate amount of its assets, taking the amount of the assets and liabilities to be as stated in the company's accounting records immediately before the financial assistance is given. For this purpose, a company's liabilities include any amount retained as reasonably necessary to provide for any liability

- the nature of which is clearly defined, and

- which is either likely to be incurred or certain to be incurred but uncertain as to amount or as to the date on which it will arise.

[*CA 2006, s 840; SI 2007 No 3495, Sch 1 para 19; SI 2008 No 2860, Art 6*].

## 22.6   Realised losses and profits and revaluation of fixed assets

**Provisions to be treated as realised losses**. For the purposes of this chapter

(a)   in the case of Companies Act accounts,

(i)    provisions for depreciation or diminution in value of assets, and

(ii)   any provision for liabilities (ie any amount retained as reasonably necessary for the purpose of providing for any liability the nature of which is clearly defined and which is either likely to be incurred or certain to be incurred but uncertain as to the amount or as to the date on which it will arise, except 'revaluation provisions', and

(b)    in the case of IAS accounts, provisions of any kind (except revaluation provisions)

are treated as realised losses.

A '*revaluation provision*' means a provision in respect of a diminution in value of a fixed asset appearing on a revaluation of all the fixed assets of the company, or of all of its fixed assets other than goodwill.

For the above purposes, any consideration by the directors of the value at a particular time of a fixed asset is treated as a revaluation provided

•    the directors are satisfied that the aggregate value at that time of the fixed assets of the company that have not actually been revalued is not less than the aggregate amount at which they are then stated in the company's accounts; and

•    it is stated in a note to the accounts that

(i)    the directors have considered the value of some or all of the fixed assets of the company without actually revaluing them;

(ii)    that they are satisfied that the aggregate value of those assets at the time of their consideration was not less than the aggregate amount at which they were then stated in the company's accounts; and

(iii)    that amounts are stated in the accounts on the basis that a revaluation of fixed assets of the company is treated as having taken place at that time.

**Depreciation following revaluation of fixed asset.** Where

•    an unrealised profit is shown to have been made on the revaluation of a fixed asset, and

•    on or after the revaluation, a sum is written off or retained for depreciation of that asset over a period,

an amount equal to the amount by which that sum exceeds the sum which would have been so written off or retained for the depreciation of that asset over that period, if that profit had not been made, is treated as a realised profit made over that period.

**Fixed assets** for these purposes means assets which are intended for use on a continuing basis in the company's activities.

*Example*

|  | Asset value | Depreciation at 10% |
|---|---|---|
|  | £ | £ |
| 2005 | 10,000 | 1,000 |
| 2006 | 10,000 | 1,000 |
| 2007 | 15,000 (revaluation) | 1,500 |
| 2008 | 15,000 | 1,500 |
| 2009 | 15,000 | 1,500 |

The increase of £500 in depreciation in 2007 and subsequent years following the revaluation may be treated as a realised profit and available for distribution.

**Cost of asset unknown.** Where there is no record of the original cost of an asset, or a record cannot be obtained without unreasonable expense or delay, then in determining whether the company has made a profit or loss on the asset, its cost is taken to be the value given to it in the earliest available record of its value made on or after its acquisition by the company.

[*CA 2006, ss 841, 842; 853(6); SI 2008 No 409, Sch 7 para 6; SI 2008 No 410, Sch 9 para 2; SI 2009 No 1581, Regs 11, 12*].

## 22.7   Distribution in kind

(1) *Determination of amount*

The following provisions apply for determining the amount of a distribution consisting of or including, or treated as arising in consequence of, the sale, transfer or other disposition by a company of a non-cash asset where

- at the time of the distribution the company has 'profits available for distribution'; and

- if the amount of the distribution were to be determined in accordance with this paragraph, the company could make the distribution without contravening the provisions of this chapter.

In such circumstances, the amount of the distribution (or the relevant part of it) is taken to be

- in a case where the amount or value of the consideration for the disposition is not less than the book value of the asset, zero; and

- in any other case, the amount by which the book value of the asset exceeds the amount or value of any consideration for the disposition.

The company's '*profits available for distribution*' are treated as increased by the amount (if any) by which the amount or value of any consideration for the disposition exceeds the book value of the asset.

'*Book value*', in relation to an asset, means the amount at which the asset is stated in the relevant accounts or, where the asset is not stated in those accounts at any amount, zero.

The provisions of **22.4** and **22.5** have effect subject to the above provisions.

[*CA 2006, s 845*].

This provision is intended to remove doubts to which the decision in *Aveling Barford Ltd v Perion Ltd* [1989] BCLC 626, 5 BCC 677 had given rise. Although not disturbing the decision in that case (such that where a company which does not have distributable profits makes a distribution by way of a transfer of assets at an undervalue, this will be an unlawful distribution), it clarifies the position where the company does have distributable profits and the above conditions apply.

(2) *Treatment of unrealised profits*

Where

- a company makes a distribution consisting of or including, or treated as arising in consequence of, the sale, transfer or other disposition by the company of a non-cash asset, and

- any part of the amount at which that asset is stated in the relevant accounts represents an unrealised profit

that profit is treated as a realised profit for the purposes of

- determining the lawfulness of the distribution in accordance with this chapter (whether before or after the distribution takes place); and

- the application, in relation to anything done with a view to or in connection with the making of the distribution, of any provision of Regulations under *CA 2006, s 396* under which only realised profits are to be included in or transferred to the profit and loss account.

[*CA 2006, s 846*].

## 22.8 CONSEQUENCES OF UNLAWFUL DISTRIBUTIONS

Where

- a distribution, or part of one, made by a company to one of its members is made in contravention of the provisions of this chapter, and

- at the time of the distribution the member knows, or has reasonable grounds for believing, that it is so made,

he is liable

- to repay it (or that part of it, as the case may be) to the company; or

- in the case of a distribution made otherwise than in cash, to pay the company a sum equal to the value of the distribution (or part) at that time.

See *Precision Dippings Ltd v Precision Dippings Marketing Ltd* [1986] Ch 447, [1985] BCLC 385, CA.

The above is without prejudice to any obligation otherwise imposed, apart from these provisions, on a member to repay a distribution unlawfully made to him but does not apply to

- financial assistance for the acquisition of shares given by a company in contravention of *CA 2006, ss 678* or *CA 2006, s 679* (before 1 October 2009, *CA 1985, s 151*) (see **34.25 Purchase of Own Shares**); or

- any payment made by a company in respect of the redemption or purchase by the company of shares in itself.

[*CA 2006, s 847; SI 2007 No 3495, Sch 1 para 20; SI 2008 No 2860, Art 6*].

Directors who are parties to the payment of an unlawful dividend are jointly and severally liable to repay the amount. This applies even if the dividend is approved by a general meeting or the company's articles. See *Exchange Banking Co, Re, Flitcroft's Case* (1882) 21 Ch D 519, CA and also *Wallersteiner v Moir* [1974] 3 All ER 217, [1974] 1 WLR 991, CA; *Selangor United Rubber Estates Ltd v Cradock (a bankrupt) (No 3)* [1968] 2 All ER 1073, [1968] 1 WLR 1555 and *Belmont Finance Corpn Ltd v Williams Furniture Ltd (No 2)* [1980] 1 All ER 393, CA.

In *Bairstow v Queens Moat Houses plc* [2000] 1 BCLC 549, [2000] BCC 1025 it was held that a director who authorised the payment of an unlawful dividend in breach of his duty as a quasi trustee would be liable to repay such a dividend if

- he knew the dividends were unlawful, whether or not that actual knowledge amounted to a fraud;

- he knew the facts that established the impropriety of the payments, even though he was unaware that such impropriety rendered the payment unlawful;

- he must be taken in all the circumstances to have known all the facts which rendered the payments unlawful; or

- he ought to have known, as a reasonably competent and diligent director, that the payments were unlawful.

The decision was upheld in the Court of Appeal ([2001] 2 BCLC 531) which also held that the liability to repay applied whether the company was solvent or insolvent and that the amount to be repaid was the full amount of the unlawful dividend, not just the excess over the dividend which could lawfully have been paid.

## 22.9   APPLICATION OF RULES OF LAW RESTRICTING DISTRIBUTIONS

The provisions of this chapter are without prejudice to any rule of law restricting the sums out of which, or the cases in which, a distribution may be made. However, for the purposes of any rule of law requiring distributions to be paid out of profits or restricting the return of capital to members

- 22.7(1) applies to determine the amount of any distribution or return of capital consisting of or including, or treated as arising in consequence of the sale, transfer or other disposition by a company of a non-cash asset; and

- 22.7(2) applies as it applies for the purposes of this chapter.

[*CA 2006, s 851*].

## 22.10   PROCEDURES, ETC FOR PAYMENT OF DIVIDENDS

Because *CA 2006* and its predecessors do not regulate the procedures for payment of dividends, provision is usually made in the company's articles.

Where a company has adopted standard articles, see the provisions in

- *Table A, Regs 102–108*

- *Model Articles, Arts 30–35* (private companies)

- *Model Articles, Arts 70–77* (public companies)

There is no principle which compels a company to divide its profit among its shareholders. Whether the whole or part should be paid as dividend is a question for the directors and shareholders to decide (*Burland v Earle* [1902] AC 83, 71 LJPC 1, PC).

Unless the company's articles (whether standard or otherwise) contain provision for a dividend to be satisfied by the distribution of assets, a dividend must be made in cash (*Wood v Odessa Waterworks Co* (1889) 42 Ch D 636).

## 22.11   Listed company requirements

For the purposes of this chapter a company is listed if either

- Its securities are admitted to the Official List by the UKLA (either a standard or premium listing) and are admitted to trading on the London Stock Exchange ("LSE") main market; or

- Its shares are admitted to LSE Alternative Investment Market ("AIM")

## 22.12 Distributions

### 22.12 Companies on LSE main market: Admission and Corporate transactions

To be eligible for admission to LSE main market the company seeking admission must comply with the LSE Admission and Disclosure Standards which cover both pre-admission and ongoing continuing obligations.

Payment of dividends by a company on the main market:

- A company must contact the LSE Stock Situation Analysis team in advance of announcing a timetable for any proposed action which affects the rights of existing holders of securities traded on the LSE markets. Except in the case of a dividend timetable notification (which is subject to rule 3.8) the reference to "in advance" means that the Stock Exchange should receive the proposed timetable by no later than 09.00 on the day before the proposed announcement.

- Where applicable, dividend payments must follow the procedures set out in the guidance in Rule 3.8 of the Standards which provides (in summary) that if a dividend timetable follows the Dividend Procedure timetable it does not need to be notified to LSE in advance provided that the announcement of the dividend includes:

  – The amount of the dividend (stating whether the dividend is net or gross);

  – The record and payment dates;

  – The availability of any scrip, DRIP or dividend currency option; and

  – The election date.

Dividends outside of the guidelines must be agreed by the Stock Situation Analysis team in advance of the announcement of the dividend.

[*LSE Admission and Disclosure Standards Rules 3.5, 3.8.*]

For the purposes of the Admission and Disclosure Standards "dividend" includes all interest payments for debt securities (excluding specialist securities).

For further information on the LSE Dividend Timetable see **22.15** below **LSE DIVIDEND PROCEDURE TIMETABLE.**

### 22.13 Continuing obligations

The FCA Listing Rules regulate both the admission to the main market and continuing obligations which apply to all companies listed on that market. The Listing Rules require every company listed on the main market to notify a RIS (ie a service which disseminates regulatory information such as company announcements) as soon as possible after the board has approved any decision:

- To pay or make any dividend or other distribution on listed equity; or

- To withhold any dividend on listed securities giving details of:

  – The exact net amount payable per share;

  – The payment date;

  – The record date (where applicable); and

  – Any foreign income dividend election, together with any income tax treated as paid at the lower rate and not repayable.

For the meaning of listed equity and listed securities see the Glossary of definitions to the FCA Full Handbook.

In certain circumstances the FCA can authorise the omission of the dividend information required by LR 9.7A.2. This is where the FCA considers that disclosure of this information would be contrary to the public interest or seriously detrimental to the relevant listed company. If the FCA authorise omission it can only do so if the omission would not be likely to mislead the public with regard to facts and circumstances, knowledge of which is essential for the assessment of the shares.

[FCA Listing Rules, paras 9.7A.2, 9.7A.3]

*Disclosure by companies on the main market*

Companies listed on the main market are also obliged to comply on an ongoing basis with the Disclosure and Transparency Rules ("DTRs").

DTR 6.1.13 provides that an issuer of shares (as defined) must publish notices or distribute circulars concerning the allocation and payment of dividends.

## 22.14 Uncertificated Securities and CREST

The conditions for eligibility for admission to LSE main market provide that the company's securities must be capable of being traded electronically ie are capable of being admitted to and traded via CREST, the electronic settlement system for holding and transferring uncertificated securities. Once shares are being traded electronically then:

• Dividend payments can be mandated through CREST

• Shareholders can make dividend elections (for example in relation to scrip issues) through CREST; and

• Companies can combine payment of dividends and interest through CREST using tax vouchers in electronic form.

To take advantage of the use of electronic payment of dividends, the company's articles of association must not be inconsistent with the payment of dividends via CREST. Specimen wording for articles of association, payment mandates and dividend elections is available (guidance only) from Euroclear.

Conditions for payment mandates:

• The shareholder must elect to receive dividends payment via CREST in respect of all (and not just some) holdings;

• The company is not obliged to make payments through CREST where a holder has elected to receive dividends in that way. Each company can decide whether this is the payment mechanism they want to adopt and, if so, notify its shareholders accordingly.

See Euroclear's website – www.euroclear.com.

## 22.15 LSE Dividend Procedure Timetable

The LSE provide a dividend procedure timetable ("DP Timetable") which sets out how and when companies listed on the main market should announce dividends (whether interim or final). Provided that a company's timetable follows the DP timetable it does not need to be notified to LSE in advance provided that:

## 22.15   Distributions

- The dividend information is disseminated by a Primary Information Provider ("PIP"); and

- The announcement includes the amount of the dividend and whether net or gross the record date, the pay date and the availability of any scrip, DRIP, currency election or other alternative and if available the last day to elect for the alternative.

Conditions which apply are set out in the notes to the DP Timetable.

## 22.16  AIM companies

Payment of dividends by AIM companies is governed by the AIM rules (Rule 17) which provides that an AIM company must notify a RIS without delay of any decision to make any payments in respect of its securities (including the payment of dividends). The company must specify:

- The net amount which is payable per security;

- The payment date;

- The record date.

Information about such notifications in the past twelve months must be included on the company's website.

# 23  Insider Dealing and Market Abuse

**Cross-references**. See 33 APPENDIX PUBLIC AND LISTED COMPANIES for the Model Code for listed companies.

## 23.1  INTRODUCTION TO INSIDER DEALING AND MARKET ABUSE

This chapter deals with two pieces of legislation which regulate the manipulation of the market and market abuse. The first is the *Criminal Justice Act 1993 (CJA)* which makes it a criminal offence for an individual to (a) deal with the benefit of inside information (b) encourage another person to deal on the basis of inside information and (c) disclose inside information (see **23.2** below). The second is the *Financial Services and Markets Act 2000 (FMSA 2000)*. This does not strictly provide criminal prosecution for breach of the market abuse provisions. Instead the FCA can impose penalties (see **23.13** below).

## 23.2  THE OFFENCE OF INSIDER DEALING

Subject to the defences in **23.5**, an individual who has 'information as an insider' is guilty of the offence of insider dealing in the following circumstances.

(a)    He 'deals in securities' that are price-affected in relation to the 'inside information' in either of the following circumstances, namely

    (i)    the acquisition or disposal in question occurs on a regulated market; or

    (ii)   the person dealing relies on, or is himself acting as, a 'professional intermediary'.

    A *'professional intermediary'* is a person who carries on a business, holds himself out as willing to engage in a business or is employed in a business which (other than on an incidental or occasional basis)

        (1)    acquires and disposes of securities (as principal or agent); or

        (2)    acts as an intermediary between other persons dealing in securities.

    The person dealing in securities relies on a professional intermediary if (and only if) the person acting as a professional intermediary carries out an activity within (1) or (2) above.

(b)     He encourages another person to 'deal in securities' that are (whether or not he knows it) price-affected securities in relation to the inside information and he knows (or has reasonable cause to believe) that dealing will take place in the securities under one of the circumstances as in (a)(i) or (ii) above.

(c)     He discloses the information (otherwise than in the proper performance of the functions of his employment, office or profession) to another person.

[*CJA 1993, ss 52, 59*].

**Territorial scope.** An individual is not guilty of an offence under (a) above unless

•      he was in the UK when he is alleged to have done any act forming part of the alleged deal;

•      the regulated market on which the dealing in alleged to have occurred is identified (by order) as being regulated in the UK; or

•      the professional intermediary was in the UK at the time when he is alleged to have done anything by means of which the offence is alleged to have been committed.

An individual is not guilty of an offence under (*b*) or (*c*) above unless

•      he was in the UK at the time when he is alleged to have encouraged the dealing or disclosed the information; or

•      the alleged recipient of the information or encouragement was in the UK at the time of the alleged receipt.

[*CJA 1993, s 62*].

## 23.3   Definitions

The following definitions apply for the purposes of the insider dealing provisions in **23.2** (above) and **23.5** below.

**Acquire,** in relation to a security, includes agreeing to acquire the security and entering into a contract which creates the security.

[*CJA 1993, s 55(2)*].

**Company** means any body (whether or not incorporated and wherever incorporated or constituted) which is not a 'public sector body'.

[*CJA 1993, s 60(3)*].

**Dealing in securities.** A person deals in securities if he

•      'acquires' or 'disposes' of the securities (as principal or agent); or

•      procures (directly or indirectly) an acquisition or disposal of the securities by any other person (including his agent, his nominee or a person acting at his direction).

[*CJA 1993, s 55(1)(4)(5)*].

**Dispose,** in relation to a security, includes agreeing to disposal of the security and bringing to an end a contract which created the security.

[*CJA 1993, s 55(3)*].

**Information as an insider.** A person has information as an insider if (and only if)

- it is, and he knows that it is, 'inside information'; and

- he has it, and knows that he has it, from an inside source, ie

    (i)    through being a director, employee or shareholder of an issuer of securities or through having access to the information by virtue of his employment, office or profession; or

    (ii)    the direct or indirect source of his information is a person within (i) above.

[*CJA 1993, s 57*].

**Inside information** means information which

(a)    relates to particular securities or issuer(s) and not to securities or issuers generally (but information is treated as relating to an issuer which is a company not only where it is about the company but also where it may affect the company's business prospects);

(b)    is specific or precise;

(c)    has not been 'made public'; and

(d)    if it were made public would be likely to have a significant effect on the price of any securities.

Information is '*made public*' if

- it is published under the rules of a regulated market to inform investors and professional advisers;

- it is contained in public records;

- it can readily be obtained by those likely to 'deal in any securities'

    (i)    to which the information relates; or

    (ii)    of an the issuer to which the information relates;

- or it is derived from information which has been made public.

Information may be treated as made public even though

- it can be acquired only by persons exercising diligence or expertise;

- it is communicated only to a section of the public and not to the public at large;

- it can be acquired only by observation;

- it is communicated only on payment of a fee; or

- it is only published outside the UK.

[*CJA 1993, ss 56(1), 58, 60(4)*].

As regards (*b*) above, information such as 'our results will be much better than the market expects or knows' is not precise (as the actual results are not disclosed) but it is specific because it gives information about the results which has obviously not been made available to the public. A statement such as 'our profit will be at a certain level and the market does not know that', without stating whether they would be better or worse than the market expected, is precise information. It would be up to the recipient to judge whether the information is likely to be price-sensitive. (Hansard, Standing Committee B, col 175, 10 June 1993).

## 23.3   Insider Dealing and Market Abuse

**Market information** is information consisting of one or more of the following facts.

(a)    That securities of a particular kind have been, or are to be, acquired or disposed of (or such acquisition or disposal is under consideration or the subject of negotiation).

(b)    That securities of a particular kind have not been, or are to be, acquired or disposed of.

(c)    The number or price (or range of prices) of securities involved in a transaction within (*a*).

(d)    The identity of the persons involved or likely to be involved in any capacity in an acquisition or disposal.

[*CJA 1993, Sch 1 para 4*].

**Price-affected securities** are securities in relation to which the 'inside information' would, if made public, be likely to have a significant effect on the price of the securities.

[*CJA 1993, s 56(2)*].

**Price-sensitive information** in relation to securities means 'inside information' which would, if made public, be likely to have a significant effect on the price of the securities.

[*CJA 1993, s 56(2)*].

**Public sector body** means the government of any country or territory; any local authority (in the UK or elsewhere); any international organisation of which any Member State is a member; and the Bank of England and the central bank of any sovereign state.

[*CJA 1993, s 60(3)*].

**Securities**. The insider dealing provisions apply to any of the following securities which satisfy the conditions set out below.

(a)    Shares and stock in the share capital of a 'company'.

(b)    Debt securities (ie any instrument creating or acknowledging indebtedness which is issued by a 'company' or 'public sector body' and including, in particular, debentures, loan stock, bonds and certificates of deposit).

(c)    Warrants (ie any right to subscribe for shares or debt securities).

(d)    Depositary receipts (ie a certificate or other record which is issued by, or on behalf of, a person who holds securities within (*a*)–(*c*) above of a particular issuer and which acknowledges that another person is entitled to rights in relation to those securities or such securities of the same kind).

(e)    Options to acquire or dispose of any security within (*a*)–(*d*) above or (*f*) or (*g*) below.

(f)    Futures (ie rights under a contract for the acquisition or disposal of any securities within (*a*)–(*e*) above or (*g*) below under which delivery is to be made at a future date and at a price agreed when the contract is made).

(g)    Contracts for differences (ie rights under a contract which does not provide for the delivery of securities but whose purpose or pretended purpose is to secure a profit (or avoid a loss) by reference to fluctuations in a share index (or other similar factor) connected with securities within (*a*)–(*f*) above or the price of such securities or the interest rate offered on money placed on deposit).

The conditions are

(i)     for any security within (*a*) or (*b*) above, that it is officially listed in a State within the European Economic Area (ie any Member State of the EC or Iceland, Norway or Liechtenstein) or is admitted to dealing on, or has its price quoted on or under the rules of, a 'regulated market';

(ii)    for a warrant within (*c*) above, that *either* it satisfies the condition in (i) above *or* the right under it is a right to subscribe for any share or debt security of the same class as the share or debt security which satisfies the conditions in (i) above;

(iii)   for a depositary receipt within (*d*) above, that *either* it satisfies the condition in (i) above *or* the rights under it are in respect of any share or debt security which satisfies the condition in (i) above;

(iv)    for an option within (*e*) above or a future within (*f*) above, that *either* it satisfied the condition in (i) above *or* the option/rights under the future are in respect of any share or debt security which satisfies the condition in (i) above or any depositary receipt which satisfies that condition or the alternative condition in (iii) above); and

(v)     for a contract for differences within (*g*) above, that *either* it satisfies the condition in (i) above *or* that the purpose (or pretended purpose) of the contract is to secure a profit or avoid a loss by reference to the fluctuations in the price (or an index of the price) of any shares or debt securities which satisfy the condition in (i) above.

A '*regulated market*' is any market established under the rules of

- The London Stock Exchange Ltd
- LIFFE Administration & Management
- OMLX, the London Securities and Derivatives Exchange Ltd
- Virt-x Exchange Ltd
- The exchange known as COREDEALMTS, together with the market known as OFEX
- The Irish Stock Exchange Ltd
- The exchange known as EASDAG
- The exchange known as NASDAQ
- The exchange known as the Nouveau Marché
- The exchange known as SWX Swiss Exchange
- The stock exchanges of Amsterdam, Antwerp, Athens, Barcelona, Bavaria, Berlin, Bilbao, Bologna, Bremen, Brussels, Copenhagen, Dusseldorf, Florence, Frankfurt, Genoa, Hamburg, Hanover, Helsinki, Iceland, Lisbon, Luxembourg, Lyon, Madrid, Milan, Naples, Oporto, Oslo, Palermo, Paris, Rome, Stockholm, Stuttgart, Trieste, Turin, Valencia, Venice or Vienna

[*CJA 1993, s 54, Sch 2; SI 1994 No 187; SI 1996 No 1561; SI 2000 No 1923, Art 2; SI 2002 No 1874, Art 2*].

## 23.4   Penalties

Penalties. A person guilty of the offence of insider dealing is liable (i) on conviction on indictment, to imprisonment for up to seven years or a fine or both, or (ii) on summary conviction, to imprisonment for up to six months or a fine not exceeding the statutory maximum or both. See **29.1** OFFENCES AND LEGAL PROCEEDINGS for the statutory maximum. The consent of the Secretary of State or the Director of Public Prosecutions (in Northern Ireland, the Director of Public Prosecutions for Northern Ireland) must be obtained for proceedings to be instituted.

[*CJA 1993, s 61*].

**Time limit for proceedings.** In England and Wales, an information relating to an offence of insider dealing that is triable by a magistrates' court may be so tried if it is laid

- at any time within three years after the commission of the offence; and

- within twelve months after the date on which evidence sufficient in the opinion of the Director of Public Prosecutions or the Secretary of State (as the case may be) to justify the proceedings comes to that person's knowledge.

*In Scotland*, summary proceedings for an offence of insider dealing

- must not be commenced after the expiration of three years from the commission of the offence;

- subject to that, may be commenced at any time

  (i)   within twelve months after the date on which evidence sufficient in the Lord Advocate's opinion to justify the proceedings came to that person's knowledge; or

  (ii)  where such evidence was reported to the Lord Advocate by the Secretary of State, within twelve months after the date on which it came to the knowledge of the latter.

*In Northern Ireland*, a magistrates' court has jurisdiction to hear and determine a complaint charging the commission of a summary offence of insider dealing provided that the complaint is made

- within three years from the time when the offence was committed; and

- within twelve months from the date on which evidence sufficient in the opinion of the Director of Public Prosecutions for Northern Ireland or the Secretary of State (as the case may be) to justify the proceedings comes to that person's knowledge.

[*CJA 1993, s 61A*]

**Effect on contracts.** The fact that a person has been found guilty of the offence of insider dealing does not, in itself, make any contract void or unenforceable.

[*CJA 1993, s 63(2)*].

## 23.5  Defences

**An individual is not guilty of dealing in securities or encouraging others to deal (see 23.2(*a*) or (*b*))** if he can show any of the following.

- He did not at the time expect the dealing to result in a profit (or avoidance or loss) attributable to the fact that the information in question was 'price-sensitive information' in relation to the securities.

- At the time he believed on reasonable grounds that the information had been (or, where the offence of encouraging others to deal applies, would be) disclosed widely enough to ensure that none of those taking part in the dealing would be prejudiced by not having the information.

- He would have done what he did even if he had not had the information.

- He acted in good faith in the course of his business as a 'market maker' or his employment in the business of a market maker. A '*market maker*' is a person who holds himself out at all normal times (in compliance with the rules of a regulated market or an approved international securities self-regulating organisation) as willing to acquire or dispose of securities and who is recognised as doing so under those rules.

- The information which he had as an insider was 'market information' and it was reasonable for an individual in his position to have acted as he did despite having the information as an insider at that time. In determining whether his actions were reasonable (despite having market information) there is, in particular, to be taken into account

  (i)    the contents of the information;

  (ii)   the circumstances in which he first had the information and in what capacity; and

  (iii)  the capacity in which he now acts.

- He acted in connection with, and with a view to facilitating, an acquisition or disposal which was under consideration or the subject of negotiation (or a series of such acquisitions or disposals). The information which he had as an insider must have been 'market information' arising directly out of his involvement in that acquisition, etc.

- He acted in conformity with *Article 5* of *EU Regulation No 596/2014* on market abuse (the market abuse regulation) and each applicable EU Regulation made under that article and rules made under *FSMA 2000, s 137Q(1)* relating to buy-backs and price stabilisation.

[*CJA 1993, s 53(1)(2)(6), Sch 1 paras 1–3, 5; SI 2001 No 3649, Art 341; SI 2005 No 381, Reg 3*].

**An individual is not guilty of disclosing inside information (see 23.2(*c*) above)** if he can show that

- he did not at the time expect any person, because of the disclosure, to 'deal in securities'; or

- although he had such an expectation at that time, he did not expect the dealing to result in a profit (or avoidance of loss) attributable to the fact that the information was 'price-sensitive information' in relation to the securities.

[*CJA 1993, s 53(3)(6)*].

## 23.6   MARKET ABUSE

The market abuse regime in the *Market Abuse Regulation EU 596/2014* was brought into force on 3 July2016, providing a framework to regulate, amongst other things, dealing or attempted dealing by an insider, unlawful disclosure of inside information and other forms of market manipulation.

The regulatory framework comprises:

- *Market Abuse Regulation (EU) 596/2014 ('MAR')* an EU regulation which is directly applicable so that it automatically comes into force in all EU member states superseding any pre-existing legislation on this subject. Its scope is very wide as it applies not only to financial instruments traded on a regulated market (such as the Main Market of the London Stock Exchange) but also those trade on multi-lateral trading facilities (which include exchange regulated markets such as the Alternative Investment Market of the London Stock Exchange), other organised trading facilities and other instruments which affect the value of such financial instruments.

• EU Regulations (also directly applicable) made by the European Commission under powers delegated to them in *MAR* dealing with technical standards. Notably *annex II of EU Commission Delegated Regulation (EU) 2016/522* which deals with the indicators of market manipulation.

• Guidelines issued by the European Securities and Markets Authority ('ESMA') to assist practitioners to interpret the above Regulations.

• Supplementary guidance afforded in the FCA Handbook in Chapter 1 of the Code of Market Conduct and some of the Disclosure Guidance and Transparency Rules ('DTR') made pursuant to the *Financial Services and Markets Act 2000*.

The market abuse regime which provides for civil penalties for market abuse runs alongside the criminal insider dealing legislation (see **23.2** above) and the misleading statements/behaviour offences in ss 89–91 of the Financial Services Act 2012.

*MAR* prohibits:

• insider dealing (see **23.7**);

• unlawful disclosure (see **23.8**); and

• various other forms of market manipulation (see **23.9–23.11**).

At the same time MAR clarifies what is legitimate behaviour and the guidance afforded by ESMA and the FCA gives further examples of what is or is not permissible. Paragraph **23.12** reviews statutory exceptions to the market abuse regime.

The Code of Market Conduct promulgated by the FCA is also commonly referred to as 'MAR'. In this publication where Chapter 1 of the Code of Market Conduct (the part dealing with market abuse) is being referred to it is designated as 'MAR(1)' in order to avoid confusion.

## 23.7    Market abuse: insider dealing

The first type of market abuse is insider dealing or a recommendation of such contrary to articles 14 and 8 of MAR. Article 14 contains the prohibition and article 8 defines insider dealing as where a person possessing inside information buys or sells, financial instruments to which the information relates where that person is an insider. Article 9 of MAR contains savings for legitimate behaviour.

These concepts are considered in more detail below:

(1)    A 'person' is defined in article 3 of MAR as a natural or legal person.

(2)    'Inside information' is defined in article 7.1(a) of MAR as information which is:

    (a)    of a precise nature;

    (b)    not yet made public;

    (c)    relating to financial instruments or the issuer thereof; and

    (d)    price sensitive.

Article 7.2 of MAR states that information is precise if it indicates a set of circumstances which exist or which may reasonably be expected to come into existence where it is specific enough to enable a conclusion to be drawn. In appropriate circumstances this could include an intermediate step (MAR 7.3).

Whether or not the information is price sensitive is to be assessed by reference to whether a reasonable investor would likely take it into account in relation to their investment decisions (MAR 7.4). Further guidance on this 'reasonable investor' test can be found in the FCA Handbook in DTR 2.2.4–2.2.6.

Special provisions apply to persons responsible for executing transactions in financial instruments on behalf of clients where the definition is expanded to include information conveyed by such clients and their pending orders (MAR 7.1(d)). Likewise slightly different provisions apply to commodity derivatives and emission allowances (MAR 7.1(b) and (c) – which are beyond the scope of this publication).

(3)    Buying or selling financial instruments to which the information relates is expressed to include cancelling or amending an existing order (MAR 8.1). Recital 24 of MAR makes clear that it is assumed that a person who has inside information and subsequently deals in financial instruments does so on the basis of that information. MAR(1) 1.2.3 indicates that it is not necessary for a person to have the intention to commit market abuse.

(4)    'Financial Instruments' are defined in article 3 of MAR by reference to Annex 1 Section C of the Markets in Financial Instruments Directive 2014/65 (MiFID II) which came into force on 3 January 2018 and which lists a wide range of financial instruments including company shares and corporate bonds.

(5)    Article 8.4 of MAR provides that the prohibition on insider dealing only applies to insiders namely persons possessing inside information through being:

(a)    a member of an administrative, management or supervisory body;

(b)    a shareholder;

(c)    an employee, professional or other contractor;

(d)    engaged in crime,

or someone else who knew that the information was inside information.

Insider dealing can also occur where a person receives a recommendation or inducement to deal in financial instruments which is based on inside information (MAR 8.2) and acts on it when they knew or ought to have known that the recommendation or inducement was based on inside information (MAR 8.3).

(6)    'Legitimate behaviour' is considered in article 9 of MAR and includes where the transaction was entered into pursuant to a pre-existing commitment or legal or regulatory requirement. There are provisions to protect market makers and situations where a 'Chinese wall' is in place (ie measures designed to ensure that persons dealing in financial instruments do not have access to inside information) as well as situations where the dealing takes place in the context of a takeover bid.

The Code of Market Conduct contained in the FCA Handbook contains guidance on the provisions of MAR prohibiting insider dealing (MAR(1) 1.3) which is particularly pertinent given that MAR 9.6 provides that behaviour which overtly falls within the examples of legitimate behaviour in MAR 9 may nonetheless constitute an infringement if the FCA (being the applicable competent authority) establishes that it was done for an illegitimate reason.

## 23.7 Insider Dealing and Market Abuse

Statutory exceptions are considered in paragraph **23.12** below.

Penalties are considered in paragraph **23.13**.

### 23.8 Market abuse: unlawful disclosure

Articles 14 and 10 of MAR prohibit the unlawful disclosure of inside information. Article 14 contains the prohibition and article 10 defines unlawful disclosure as occurring if any person possessing inside information discloses that inside information otherwise than in the normal course of their employment, profession or duties and where that person is an insider. Article 11 provides a saving for market soundings provided certain conditions are met.

These concepts are considered in more detail below:

(1)   A 'person' is defined in article 3 of MAR as a natural or legal person.

(2)   'Inside information' is defined in article 7.1(a) of MAR as information which is:

    (a)   of a precise nature;

    (b)   not yet made public;

    (c)   relating to financial instruments or the issuer thereof; and

    (d)   price sensitive.

Article 7.2 of MAR states that information is precise if it indicates a set of circumstances which exist or which may reasonably be expected to come into existence where it is specific enough to enable a conclusion to be drawn. In appropriate circumstances this could include an intermediate step (MAR 7.3).

Whether or not the information is price sensitive is to be assessed by reference whether a reasonable investor would likely take it into account in relation to their investment decisions (MAR 7.4). Further guidance on this 'reasonable investor test' can be found in the FCA Handbook in DTR 2.2.4–2.2.6.

Special provisions apply to persons responsible for executing transactions in financial instruments on behalf of clients where the definition is expanded to include information conveyed by such clients and their pending orders (MAR 7.1(d)). Likewise slightly different provisions apply to commodity derivatives and emission allowances (MAR 7.1(b) and (c)) – which are beyond the scope of this publication.

(3)   Regarding 'disclosure'; article 10.1 of MAR makes it clear that disclosure encompasses disclosure of inside information to any other person.

(4)   Article 10.1 of MAR only characterises the disclosure as unlawful where the person is not acting in the normal course of their employment, profession or duties.

(5)   Regarding 'insider'; article 10.1 of MAR makes clear that it only applies to persons who are insiders within the meaning of article 8.4 of MAR namely a person possessing inside information though being:

    (a)   a member of an administrative, management or supervisory body;

    (b)   a shareholder;

    (c)   an employee, professional or other contractor;

    (d)   engaged in crime,

or someone else who knew that the information was inside information.

Article 10.2 of MAR makes clear that where a person receives a recommendation or inducement to deal in financial instruments which is based on inside information as described in MAR 8.2, the onward disclosure of that recommendation or inducement amounts to unlawful disclosure where the person disclosing it knows or ought to know that it was based on inside information.

(6)   Regarding 'market soundings'; article 11 of MAR states that where market soundings are made prior to a transaction (which could include a takeover bid) in order to gauge the level of investor interest, disclosure of inside information in the context of such soundings will be taken to be in the normal course of the employment, profession or duties of the person disclosing it (MAR 11.4). Written records should be kept for five years and made available to the FCA upon request (MAR 11.3 and 11.8). Moreover the recipient must have previously consented to receive the information on a confidential basis and not to use it to deal in affected financial instruments (MAR 11.5). The person making the market sounding should tell the recipient once the information ceases to be inside information but this does not absolve the recipient from making its own assessment (MAR 11.6–11.7). Full details of the relevant arrangements procedures and record-keeping requirements can be found in the regulation promulgated by the Commission under powers delegated to it under MAR 11.9 and 11.10 (Commission Delegated Regulations (EU) 2016/959 and 960).

(7)   The Code of Market Conduct in the FCA Handbook indicates that where a person is acting in accordance with a legal or regulatory requirement that will not normally constitute unlawful disclosure (MAR(1) 1.4).

Further statutory exceptions are considered in paragraph 23.12 below.

Penalties are considered in paragraph 23.13 below.

## 23.9   Market abuse: market manipulation under the Market Abuse Regulation

Articles 12 and 15 of MAR prohibit market manipulation. Article 15 contains the prohibition whereas article 12 defines market manipulation and article 13 of MAR contains savings for accepted market practices.

MAR 12.1 defines market manipulation as including:

(a)   behaviour which (i) may give a false or misleading signal about the supply or demand or price of a financial instrument or a related product or (ii) which is likely to secure the price of financial instruments or a related product at an abnormal or artificial level;

(b)   behaviour which employs a fictitious device to affect the price of financial instruments or related products;

(c)   knowingly disseminating false or misleading information about the supply or demand or price of financial instruments or related products; or

(d)   knowingly transmitting false or misleading information about a benchmark or other behaviour which manipulates the calculation of a benchmark.

'Knowingly' for the above purposes includes where the person ought to have known the information was false or misleading.

MAR 12.2 gives examples of manipulative behaviour which include:

(a)   securing a dominant position which is likely to affect prices or otherwise create unfair trading conditions;

(b)      buying at the opening or closing of the market in a way that is likely to mislead investors;

(c)      placing orders by electronic means (including by algorithmic or high frequency trading strategies) in such a way as to mislead or confuse or otherwise disrupt the market;

(d)      expressing an opinion on the price of a financial instrument or related product when holding an existing position in relation to it without adequately disclosing that conflict of interest.

As provided in MAR 12.3, Annex 1 of MAR (considered in paragraph **23.10** below) contains a list of indicators of manipulative behaviour relating to false and misleading signals or price securing and further indicators of manipulative behaviour involving a fictitious device or other contrivance.

Moreover, Commission Delegated Regulation (EU) 2016/522 (promulgated pursuant to powers granted under 12.5 of MAR) contains further such indicators which are considered in paragraph **23.11** below.

Article 13 of MAR provides that the prohibition on market manipulation shall not apply to accepted market practices entered into for legitimate reasons (MAR 13.1). The FCA (being the applicable competent authority) is empowered by MAR 13.2 to establish accepted market practices taking into account a range of criteria designed to ensure the transparency, liquidity and efficiency of the market and the effect of the practice on other markets within the European Union ('EU'). Such market practices must be pre-advised to ESMA and the competent authorities in other parts of the EU (MAR 13.3). ESMA is required to publish on its website a list of accepted market practices in the various member states (MAR 13.9) and the relevant competent authorities are required to keep them under review (MAR 13.8). Full details of the relevant criteria and requirements can be found in the regulation promulgated by the Commission under powers delegated to it under MAR 13.7 (Commission Delegated Regulation (EU) 2016/908).

The Code of Market Conduct contained in the FCA Handbook has a heading for 'Accepted Market Practices' but at present that section is empty. The Code of Market Conduct continues to be organised around the headings applicable to the previous market abuse regime namely: manipulating transactions (MAR(1) 1.6), manipulating devices (MAR(1) 1.7), dissemination (MAR(1) 1.8), misleading behaviour and distortion (MAR(1)1.9) and statutory exceptions (MAR(1)1.10). Large swathes of the provisions have been deleted but some useful guidance has been retained including guidance as to what would amount to legitimate reasons (MAR(1) 1.6.5–1.6.8).

### 23.10 Market abuse: indicators of manipulative behaviour under Annex 1 of the Market Abuse Regulation

MAR 12.3 provides for a non-exhaustive list of indicators of manipulative behaviour to be included in Annex 1 of MAR. Part A of Annex 1 deals with indicators of manipulative behaviour relating to false or misleading signals and to price securing. Part B deals with indicators of manipulative behaviour relating to the employment of a fictitious device or any other form of deception or contrivance.

**A: Indicators of manipulative behaviour relating to false or misleading signals and to price securing**

The following factors are to be taken into account when examining transactions for signs of manipulation of the market for a financial instrument or related product within the meaning of MAR 12.1(a):

(a)    the extent to which the transactions represent a significant proportion of the daily volume of trades;

(b)    the extent to which the transactions lead to a significant change in the price;

(c)    whether the transactions result in no change of beneficial ownership;

(d)    whether the transactions are cancelled or reversed after a short period;

(e)    the extent to which the trades result in a price change which is soon reversed;

(f)    the extent to which the trades move bid or offer prices and are removed before execution; and

(g)    the extent to which orders are placed around the specific time when reference prices, settlement prices or valuations are calculated.

**B: Indicators of manipulative behaviour relating to the employment of a fictitious device or any other form of deception or contrivance**

The following factors are to be taken into account when examining transactions for signs of manipulation of the market for a financial instrument or related product within the meaning of MAR 12.1(b):

(a)    whether trades are preceded or followed by the dissemination of false and misleading information; and

(b)    whether trades made around the time of dissemination of investment recommendations which are wrong, biased or influenced by a material interest.

The Code of Market Conduct in the FCA Handbook characterises the behaviour described in Annex 1 Part A(a) and (b) above as an 'abusive squeeze'. MAR(1) 1.6.11–1.6.13 provide further guidance on how to identify an 'abusive squeeze'.

### 23.11    Market Abuse: Further Indicators of Manipulative Behaviour under Commission Delegated Regulation (EU) 2016/522

Article 4 and Annex 2 of Commission Delegated Regulation (EU) 2016/522 (promulgated pursuant to powers granted under 12.5 of MAR) prescribe further indicators of manipulative behaviour. Section 1 of Annex 2 deals with indicators of manipulative behaviour relating to false or misleading signals and to price securing. Section 2 deals with indicators of manipulative behaviour relating to the employment of a fictitious device or any other form of deception or contrivance.

Annex 2 tracks the indicators of manipulative behaviour identified in Annex 1 of MAR and provides some well-known examples of malpractice.

**Section 1: Indicators of manipulative behaviour relating to false or misleading signals and to price securing**

(1)    Examples of bad practice indicated by unusual volumes (Annex 1 Part A(a)) are colluding in the after-market of an Initial Public Offering ('IPO'), 'creating a floor or a ceiling in the price pattern' (ie a minimum or maximum), placing 'ping orders' (ie small orders to test the level of hidden orders), 'phishing' (ie eliciting the order of other participants and trading so as to take advantage of them).

(2)    Examples of practices indicated by price movements (Annex 1 Part A(b)) are colluding in the after-market of an IPO, an 'abusive squeeze', 'inter-trading venues manipulation' and 'cross-product manipulation'.

(3)   Examples of practices indicated by transactions without change of beneficial ownership (Annex 1 Part A(c)) are 'wash trades', 'painting the tape' (ie entering into orders on public display to give an impression of activity), 'improper matched orders' and 'concealing ownership'.

(4)   Examples of practices indicated by short-term positions (Annex 1 Part A(d)) are 'painting the tape' and 'improper matched orders', but also the practice of 'pump and dump' (ie taking a long position on a financial instrument, buying or talking up the price and then selling) and its reverse 'trash and cash', 'quote stuffing' (ie placing large amounts of orders to confuse other participants) and momentum ignition – where a series of orders are placed with a view to starting or accelerating a trend.

(5)   Examples of practices indicated by a short-lived peak in the price (Annex 1 Part A(e)) are 'creating a floor or a ceiling', 'inter-trading venues manipulation', 'cross-product manipulation', 'marking the close' (ie deliberately trading as the market closes in order to try to change the reference price) and 'layering' or 'spoofing' – similar to quote stuffing and momentum ignition.

(6)   Examples of practices indicated by efforts to change the bid or offered price through cancelled trades (Annex 1 Part A(f)) are 'placing orders with no intention of executing them', 'creation of a floor or a ceiling', 'advancing the bid' (ie placing orders which are not executed with a view to increasing the bid price of a financial instrument), 'inter-trading venues manipulation', 'cross-product manipulation', 'layering' and 'spoofing', 'quote stuffing', 'momentum ignition', and 'smoking' – which in this context is placing orders to trade with a view to attracting other participants.

(7)   Examples of practices indicated by the concentration of trades around the time when reference rates are calculated (Annex 1 Part A(g)) are 'marking the close', colluding in the after-market of an IPO, 'creating a floor or a ceiling', 'inter-trading venue manipulation' and 'cross-product manipulation'.

Other provisions relate specifically to commodity contracts.

**Section 2: Indicators of manipulative behaviour relating to the employment of a fictitious device or any other form of deception or contrivance**

(1)   Examples of practices indicated by the dissemination of false or misleading information (Annex 1 Part B(a)) are trading while also spreading false information in the media, 'opening a position and closing it immediately after its public disclosure', 'pump and dump', 'trash and cash', 'concealing ownership' and other practices specifically concerning the trade in commodities.

(2)   Examples of practices indicated by trading while disseminating information which is wrong, biased or influenced by a material interest (Annex 1 Part B(b)) are trading whilst also spreading false information in the media, 'pump and dump' and 'trash and cash'.

The Code of Market Conduct in the FCA Handbook contains further guidance as to what is meant by 'dissemination' (MAR(1) 1.8.3–1.8.6).

## 23.12 Statutory Exceptions

Article 5 of MAR exempts buy-back programmes and stabilisation from the prohibitions in articles 14 and 15 on insider dealing, unlawful disclosure and market manipulation.

MAR 5.1 exempts trading in own shares in buy-back programmes where certain conditions (designed to ensure transparency and an orderly market) are met provided it is carried out in accordance with delegated regulations promulgated by the Commission under MAR 5.6

(Commission Delegated Regulation (EU) 2016/1052) and provided it accords with the objectives set out in MAR 5.2. The objectives prescribed by MAR 5.2 are that the sole purpose is a reduction of capital or to honour obligations arising from exchangeable debt financial instruments or to honour obligations arising from an employee share scheme.

MAR 5.4 exempts trading in securities for stabilisation purposes where the stabilisation is carried out for a limited period, the relevant information is notified to the FCA (the relevant competent authority) on a timely basis (including that all trades are notified within seven daily market sessions: MAR 5.5) with due limits as to price and compliance with delegated regulations promulgated by the Commission under MAR 5.6 (Commission Delegated Regulation (EU) 2016/1052).

The Code of Market Conduct contained in the FCA Handbook contains a section dealing with statutory exceptions to the market abuse regime (MAR(1) 1.10). This confirms that behaviour which conforms to MAR 5 will not amount to market abuse (MAR(1) 1.10.1). It also states that there is nothing in the FCA Rules which permits or requires market abuse (MAR(1) 1.10.2). It further states that the there is nothing in the Takeover Code which permits or requires market abuse and makes express provision for reconciling the provisions of the Takeover Code requiring the disclosure of information with the market abuse regime (MAR(1) 1.10.3–1.10.6).

[*FSMA 2000, s 131A; SI 2005 No 381*]. (MAR 1.10.1–1.10.6)

## 23.13  Penalties

The *Financial Services and Markets Act 2000 (Market Abuse) Regulations 2016* designate the FCA the competent authority for the purposes of MAR and any supplementary EU regulations and amend *Parts 6* and *8* of the *Financial Services and Markets Act 2000* ('FSMA') to confer on the FCA powers to investigate potential breaches of MAR and impose penalties if satisfied that a breach has occurred.

In summary, if market abuse is proved the FCA can:

(a)    impose an unlimited fine (*FSMA 2000, s 123*);

(b)    make a public statement that the person concerned has engaged in market abuse (*FSMA 2000, s 123*);

(c)    apply to court for an injunction (*FSMA 2000, s 381*);

(d)    require the person concerned to pay back profits made or losses avoided (*FSMA 2000, s 383*); or

(e)    require the person concerned to compensate any victims (*FSMA 2000, s 384*).

See the FCA's Decision Procedure and Penalties Manual and Enforcement Guide for full details of the enforcement procedure.

See the *Enforcement (Market Abuse Regulation) Instrument 2016 (FCA 2016/47)* for full details of the FCA's extensive powers to investigate potential breaches of MAR (see the appendix to **33 Public and Listed Companies**).

APPENDIX: FCA CODE OF MARKET CONDUCT (RELEASE 29 JULY 2018) – CHAPTER 1 – MARKET ABUSE

## 1.1 APPLICATION AND INTERPRETATION

*Application and purpose*

**1.1.1 G**   This chapter is relevant to all persons seeking guidance on the market abuse regime.

**1.1.1A G**   [deleted]

**1.1.2 G**   This chapter provides *guidance* on the *Market Abuse Regulation*. It is therefore likely to be helpful to *persons* who:

(1)   want to avoid engaging in *market abuse*; or

(2)   want to determine whether they are required by article 16 of the *Market Abuse Regulation* to report a transaction or order to the *FCA* as a suspicious one.

**1.1.3 G**   The *FCA's* statement of policy about the imposition, duration and amount of penalties in cases of *market abuse* (required by section 124 of the Act) is in DEPP 6.

*Using MAR 1*

**1.1.4 G**

(1)   Assistance in the interpretation of MAR 1 (and the remainder of the *Handbook* ) is given in the Readers' Guide to the *Handbook* and in GEN 2 (Interpreting the Handbook). This includes an explanation of the status of the types of provision used (see in particular chapter six of the Readers' Guide to the *Handbook*).

(2)   [deleted]

**1.1.5 G**   [deleted]

**1.1.6 G**   This chapter does not exhaustively describe all types of behaviour that may indicate *market abuse*. In particular, the descriptions of behaviour should be read in the light of:

(1)   the elements specified by the *Market Abuse Regulation* as making up the relevant type of *market abuse*; and

(2)   any relevant descriptions of behaviour specified by the *Market Abuse Regulation* which do not amount to *market abuse*; and

(3)   any provisions specified in any Commission legislative text made pursuant to the *Market Abuse Regulation*, and any applicable guidelines made by *ESMA*.

**1.1.7 G**   This chapter does not exhaustively describe all the factors to be taken into account in determining whether behaviour amounts to *market abuse*. The absence of a factor mentioned does not, of itself, amount to a contrary indication.

**1.1.8 G**   For the avoidance of doubt, it should be noted that any reference in this chapter to "profit" refers also to potential profits, avoidance of loss or potential avoidance of loss.

**1.1.9 G**   References are made in this chapter to provisions in the *Market Abuse Regulation* and other *EU* legislation made pursuant to the *Market Abuse Regulation* to assist readers. The fact that other provisions of the *Market Abuse Regulation* and other *EU* legislation made pursuant to the *Market Abuse Regulation* have not been referred to does not mean that they would not also assist readers or that they have a different status.

## 1.2 MARKET ABUSE: GENERAL

**1.2.1 G**   Provisions in this section are relevant to more than one of the types of behaviour which may amount to *market abuse*.

**1.2.2 UK**   [deleted]

**1.2.2-A EU**   [article 2, article 14 and article 15 of the *Market Abuse Regulation*]

**1.2.2A UK**   [deleted]

**1.2.3 G**   The *Market Abuse Regulation* does not require the person engaging in the behaviour in question to have intended to commit *market abuse*.

**1.2.4 G**   [deleted]

*Factors that may be taken into account in relation to behaviour prior to either a request for admission to trading, the admission to or the commencement of trading, or the offer for sale on a prescribed auction platform*

**1.2.5 G**   The following factors may be taken into account in determining whether or not behaviour prior to a request for admission to trading, the admission to or the commencement of trading, or the offer for sale on a *prescribed auction platform*-contravenes prohibitions and obligations in the *Market Abuse Regulation* and are indications that it does:

> if it is in relation to *financial instruments*:
>> in respect of which a request for admission to trading on a *regulated market* or *MTF* is subsequently made; and
>> if it continues to have an effect once an application has been made for the *financial instrument* to be admitted for trading, or it has been admitted to trading on a *regulated market* or *MTF*, respectively; or
> if it is in relation to *financial instruments*:
>> which are subsequently offered for sale on a *prescribed auction platform*; and
>> if it continues to have an effect once the *financial instruments* are offered for sale on a *prescribed auction platform*.

**1.2.6 G**   The following factors may be taken into account in determining whether or not refraining from action indicates behaviour which falls under the scope of the *Market Abuse Regulation*, and are indications that it does:

> if the *person* concerned has failed to discharge a legal or regulatory obligation (for example to make a particular disclosure) by refraining from acting; or
> if the *person* concerned has created a reasonable expectation of him acting in a particular manner, as a result of his representations (by word or conduct), in circumstances which give rise to a duty or obligation to inform those to whom he made the representations that they have ceased to be correct, and he has not done so.

*Insiders: factors to be taken in to account*

**1.2.7 UK**   [deleted]

**1.2.7-A EU**   [article 8(4) of the *Market Abuse Regulation*]

**1.2.7A UK**   [deleted]

**1.2.8 G**   The following factors may be taken into account in determining whether or not a *person* who possesses *inside information* ought to know that it is *inside information* for the purposes of the final indent of article 8(4) of the *Market Abuse Regulation*:

(1)    if a normal and reasonable *person* in the position of the *person* who has *inside information* would know or should have known that the *person* from whom he received it is an *insider*; and

(2)    if a normal and reasonable *person* in the position of the *person* who has *inside information* would know or should have known that it is *inside information*.

**1.2.9 G**   For the purposes of being categorised as an insider in article 8(4) of the *Market Abuse Regulation*, the *person* concerned does not need to know that the information concerned is *inside information*.

*Inside information: factors to be taken into account*

**1.2.10 UK**   [deleted]

**1.2.10A EU**   [article 7 of the *Market Abuse Regulation*]

**1.2.11 G**   [deleted]

**1.2.12 G**   The following factors may be taken into account in determining whether or not information has been made public, and are indications that it has (and therefore is not *inside information*):

(1)    whether the information has been disclosed to a *prescribed market* or a *prescribed auction platform* through a *regulatory information service or RIS* or otherwise in accordance with the rules of that market;

(2)    whether the information is contained in records which are open to inspection by the public;

(3)    whether the information is otherwise generally available, including through the Internet, or some other publication (including if it is only available on payment of a fee), or is derived from information which has been made public; and

(4)    whether the information can be obtained by observation by members of the public without infringing rights or obligations of privacy, property or confidentiality.

(5)    [deleted]

**1.2.13 G**

(1)    In relation to the factors in MAR 1.2.12G it is not relevant that the information is only generally available outside the *UK*.

(2)    In relation to the factors in MAR 1.2.12G (1) it is not relevant that the observation or analysis is only achievable by a *person* with above average financial resources, expertise or competence.

**1.2.14 G**   For example, if a passenger on a train passing a burning factory calls his broker and tells him to *sell shares* in the factory's owner, the passenger will be using information which has been made public, since it is information which has been obtained by legitimate means through observation of a public event.

**1.2.15 UK**   [deleted]

**1.2.15A UK**   [deleted]

**1.2.15B EU**   [article 7(1)(d) of the *Market Abuse Regulation*]

**1.2.16 G**   In determining whether there is a pending order for a client in relation to article 7(1)(d) of the *Market Abuse Regulation*, a factor that may be taken into account is if a person is approached by another in relation to a transaction, and:

# Insider Dealing and Market Abuse Appendix

(1)  the transaction is not immediately executed on an arm's length basis in response to a price quoted by that *person*; and

(2)  the *person* concerned has taken on a legal or regulatory obligation relating to the manner or timing of the execution of the transaction.

*Inside information: commodity derivatives*

**1.2.17 G**  [deleted]
[**Note:** article 7(1)(b) of the *Market Abuse Regulation*]

**1.2.18 UK**  [deleted]

**1.2.18A EU**  [article 7(1)(b) of the *Market Abuse Regulation*]

**1.2.19 UK**  [deleted]

**1.2.19A G**  *ESMA* has issued guidelines under article 7(5) of the *Market Abuse Regulation* which relate to the definition of *inside information* in the context of commodity derivatives.

[**Note:** the guidelines are available at www.esma.europa.eu/document/mar-guidelines-commodity-derivatives.]

**1.2.20 G**  [deleted]

**1.2.21 G**  [deleted]

*Recommending or inducing*

**1.2.22 UK**  [deleted]

**1.2.23 G**  The following are examples of behaviour that might fall within the scope of article 14(b) of the *Market Abuse Regulation*:

(1)  a director of a company, while in possession of *inside information*, instructs an employee of that company to sell a *financial instrument* in respect of which the information is *inside information*;

(2)  a *person* recommends or advises a friend to engage in behaviour which, if he himself engaged in it, would amount to *market abuse*.

## 1.3 INSIDER DEALING

**1.3.1 UK**  [deleted]

**1.3.1A EU**  [article 8 of the *Market Abuse Regulation*]

*Descriptions of behaviour that amount to insider dealing*

**1.3.2 G**  The following are examples of behaviour that may amount to insider dealing under the *Market Abuse Regulation*, but are not intended to form an exhaustive list:

(1)  [deleted]

(2)  front running/pre-positioning - that is, a transaction for a person's own benefit, on the basis of and ahead of an order (including an order relating to a bid) which he is to carry out with or for another (in respect of which information concerning the order is *inside information*), which takes advantage of the anticipated impact of the order on the market or auction clearing price;

(3)  in the context of a takeover, an *offeror* or potential *offeror* entering into a transaction in a *financial instrument*, using *inside information* concerning the

550

proposed bid, that provides merely an economic exposure to movements in the price of the target *company's* shares (for example, a spread bet on the target company's share price); and

(4)   in the context of a takeover, a person who acts for the *offeror* or potential *offeror dealing* for his own benefit in a *financial instrument* using information concerning the proposed bid.

*Factors to be taken in to account: "on the basis of"*

**1.3.3 E**   [deleted]
[**Note:** article 9 of the *Market Abuse Regulation*]

**1.3.4 E**   [deleted]

**1.3.5 E**   [deleted]
[**Note:** article 9(1)(a) of the *Market Abuse Regulation*]

*Relevant factors: legitimate business of market makers*

**1.3.6 C**   [deleted]
[**Note:** article 9(5) of the *Market Abuse Regulation*]

**1.3.7 G**   For market makers and *persons* that may lawfully *deal* in *financial instruments* on their own account, pursuing their legitimate business of such *dealing* (including entering into an agreement for the underwriting of an issue of *financial instruments*) may not in itself amount to *market abuse*.

**1.3.8 G**   [deleted]

**1.3.9 E**   [deleted]

**1.3.10 G**   The following factors may be taken into account in determining whether or not a *person's* behaviour is in pursuit of legitimate business, and are indications that it is:

(1)   the extent to which the relevant trading by the person is carried out in order to hedge a risk, and in particular the extent to which it neutralises and responds to a risk arising out of the *person's* legitimate business; or

(2)   whether, in the case of a transaction on the basis of *inside information* about a client's transaction which has been executed, the reason for it being *inside information* is that information about the transaction is not, or is not yet, required to be published under any relevant regulatory or *trading venue* obligations; or

(3)   whether, if the relevant trading by that *person* is connected with a transaction entered into or to be entered into with a client (including a potential client), the trading either has no impact on the price or there has been adequate disclosure to that client that trading will take place and he has not objected to it; or

(4)   the extent to which the *person's* behaviour was reasonable by the proper standards of conduct of the market concerned, taking into account any relevant regulatory or legal obligations and whether the transaction is executed in a way which takes into account the need for the market as a whole to operate fairly and efficiently.

**1.3.11 E**   [deleted]
[**Note:** article 9 of the *Market Abuse Regulation*]

# Insider Dealing and Market Abuse Appendix

*Relevant factors: execution of client orders*

**1.3.12 C**  [deleted]
[**Note:** article 9 of the *Market Abuse Regulation*]

**1.3.13 G**  [deleted]
[**Note:** article 9 of the *Market Abuse Regulation*]

**1.3.14 E**  [deleted]

**1.3.15 G**  The following factors may be taken into account in determining whether or not a *person's* behaviour in executing an order (including an order relating to a bid) on behalf of another is carried out legitimately in the normal course of exercise of that person's employment, profession or duties, and are indications that it is:

(1)  whether the *person* has complied with the applicable provisions of *COBS*, or their equivalents in the relevant jurisdiction; or

(2)  whether the *person* has agreed with its client it will act in a particular way when carrying out, or arranging the carrying out of, the order; or

(3)  whether the *person's* behaviour was with a view to facilitating or ensuring the effective carrying out of the order; or

(4)  the extent to which the *person's* behaviour was reasonable by the proper standards of conduct of the market or auction platform concerned and (if relevant) proportional to the risk undertaken by him; or

(5)  whether, if the relevant trading or bidding (including the withdrawal of a bid) by that *person* is connected with a transaction entered into or to be entered into with a client (including a potential client), the trading or bidding either has no impact on the price or there has been adequate disclosure to that client that trading or bidding will take place and he has not objected to it.

**1.3.16 G**  [deleted]

*Descriptions of behaviour that do not indicate insider dealing and relevant factors: take over and merger activity*

**1.3.17 G**  With reference to article 9(4) of the *Market Abuse Regulation*, examples of using *inside information* solely for the purpose of proceeding with a merger or public takeover may include:

(1)  seeking from holders of *securities*, issued by the target, irrevocable undertakings or expressions of support to accept an *offer* to acquire those securities (or not to accept such an *offer*);

(2)  making arrangements in connection with an issue of *securities* that are to be offered as consideration for the takeover or merger *offer* or to be issued in order to fund the takeover or merger *offer*, including making arrangements for the underwriting or placing of those *securities* and any associated hedging arrangements by underwriters or places which are proportionate to the risks assumed; and

(3)  making arrangements to offer cash as consideration for the takeover or merger *offer* as an alternative to *securities* consideration.

**1.3.18 G**  Categories of *inside information* relevant to MAR 1.3.17 G:

(1)  information that an offeror or potential *offeror* is going to make, or is considering making, an *offer* for the target; and

(2)  information that an *offeror* or potential *offeror* may obtain through due diligence.

**1.3.19 G**  The following factor may be taken into account in determining whether or not a *person's* behaviour is for the purpose of him proceeding with a merger with the target *company* or a public takeover of the target *company*, and is an indication that it is:

(1)  whether the transactions concerned are in the target *company's shares*.

(2)      [deleted]

*Examples of insider dealing*

**1.3.20 G**   The following descriptions are intended to assist in understanding certain behaviours which may constitute *insider dealing* under the *Market Abuse Regulation* and concern the definition of *inside information* relating to *financial instruments* other than *commodity derivatives* or *emissions allowances* or auctioned products based thereon:

(1)      X, a director at B PLC has lunch with a friend, Y. X tells Y that his company has received a takeover offer that is at a premium to the current share price at which it is trading. Y enters into a spread bet priced or valued by reference to the share price of B PLC based on his expectation that the price in B PLC will increase once the takeover offer is announced.

(2)      An employee at B PLC obtains the information that B PLC has just lost a significant contract with its main customer. Before the information is announced over the *regulatory information service* the employee, whilst being under no obligation to do so, sells his shares in B PLC based on the information about the loss of the contract.

**1.3.21 G**   The following description is intended to assist in understanding certain behaviours which may constitute *insider dealing* under the *Market Abuse Regulation* and concerns the definition of *inside information* relating to commodity derivatives.

Before the official publication of LME stock levels, a metals trader learns (from an *insider*) that there has been a significant decrease in the level of LME aluminium stocks. This information is reasonably expected to be disclosed in accordance with market practice or custom on the LME. The trader buys a substantial number of *futures* in that metal on the LME, based upon his knowledge of the significant decrease in aluminium stock levels.

**1.3.22 G**   The following description is intended to assist in understanding certain behaviours which may constitute *insider dealing* under the *Market Abuse Regulation* and concerns the definition of *inside information* relating to pending client orders.

A dealer on the trading desk of a *firm dealing* in oil derivatives accepts a very large order from a *client* to acquire a long position in oil futures deliverable in a particular *month*. Before executing the order, the dealer trades for the *firm* and on his personal account by taking a long position in those oil futures, based on the expectation that he will be able to sell them at profit due to the significant price increase that will result from the execution of his *client's* order. Both trades could constitute *insider dealing*.

**1.3.23 G**   The following connected descriptions are intended to assist in understanding certain behaviours which may constitute *insider dealing* under the *Market Abuse Regulation* and concern the differences in the definition of *inside information* for commodity derivatives and for other *financial instruments*.

(1)      A *person* deals, on a *trading venue*, in the equities of XYZ plc, a commodity producer, based on *inside information* concerning that company.

(2)      A *person* deals, in a commodity futures contract traded on a *trading venue*, based on the same information, provided that the information is reasonably expected to be disclosed or is required to be disclosed in accordance with legal or regulatory provisions at the *EU* or national level, market rules, contract, practice or custom, on the relevant commodity futures market.

**1.3.24 G**   *ESMA* has issued guidelines under article 7(5) of the *Market Abuse Regulation* which relate to the definition of *inside information* in the context of commodity derivatives.

[**Note:** the guidelines are available at www.esma.europa.eu/document/mar-guidelines -commodity-derivatives.]

# Insider Dealing and Market Abuse Appendix

## 1.4 UNLAWFUL DISCLOSURE

**1.4.1 UK** [deleted]

**1.4.1A EU** [article 10 of the *Market Abuse Regulation*]

*Descriptions of behaviour that indicate unlawful disclosure*

**1.4.2 G** The following behaviours are indications of *unlawful disclosure*:

(1) disclosure of *inside information* by the *director* of an *issuer* to another in a social context; and

(2) selective briefing of analysts by *directors* of *issuers* or others who are *persons discharging managerial responsibilities*.

*Descriptions of behaviour that does not indicate unlawful disclosure*

**1.4.3 G** The following behaviour indicates that a *person* is acting in the normal exercise of their employment, profession or duties, if a *person* makes a disclosure of *inside information*:

(1) to a government department, the Bank of England, the Competition Commission, the *Takeover Panel* or any other *regulatory body* or authority for the purposes of fulfilling a legal or regulatory obligation; or

(2) otherwise to such a body in connection with the performance of the functions of that body.

**1.4.4 G** Disclosure of *inside information* which is required or permitted by *Part 6 rules* (or any similar regulatory obligation) may not amount to *unlawful disclosure*.

**1.4.4A G** Disclosure of inside information by a broker to a potential buyer regarding the fact that the seller of financial instruments is a person discharging managerial responsibilities or the identity of the person discharging managerial responsibilities or the purpose of the sale by the person discharging managerial responsibilities where:

(1) the disclosure is made only to the extent necessary, and solely in order to dispose of the investment;

(2) the illiquidity of the stock is such that the transaction could not otherwise be completed; and

(3) the transaction could not be otherwise completed without creating a disorderly market;

may not, of itself, amount to *unlawful disclosure*.

*Factors to be taken into account in determining whether or not behaviour amounts to unlawful disclosure*

**1.4.5 G** The following factors are to be taken into account in determining whether or not the disclosure was made by a *person* in the proper course of the exercise of his employment, profession or duties, and are indications that it was:

(1) whether the disclosure is permitted by the rules of a *trading venue* a *prescribed auction platform*, of the *FCA* or the *Takeover Code*; or

(2) whether the disclosure is accompanied by the imposition of confidentiality requirements upon the *person* to whom the disclosure is made and is:

(a) reasonable and is to enable a *person* to perform the proper functions of his employment, profession or duties; or

(b) reasonable and is (for example, to a professional adviser) for the purposes of facilitating or seeking or giving advice about a transaction or *takeover bid*; or

(c) reasonable and is for the purpose of facilitating any commercial, financial or *investment* transaction (including prospective underwriters or placees of securities); or

(d)     reasonable and is for the purpose of obtaining a commitment or expression of support in relation to an *offer* which is subject to the *Takeover Code*; or

(e)     in fulfilment of a legal obligation, including to *employee* representatives or trade unions acting on their behalf.

(3)     [deleted]

**1.4.5A G**   [deleted]

*Examples of unlawful disclosure*

**1.4.6 G**   The following descriptions are intended to assist in understanding certain behaviours which may constitute *unlawful disclosure* under the *Market Abuse Regulation*:

(1)     X, a director at B PLC has lunch with a friend, Y, who has no connection with B PLC or its advisers. X tells Y that his company has received a takeover offer that is at a premium to the current share price at which it is trading.

(2)     A, a *person discharging managerial responsibilities* in B PLC, asks C, a broker, to sell some or all of As shares in B PLC. C discloses to a potential buyer that A is a *person discharging managerial responsibilities* or discloses the identity of A, in circumstances where the fact that A is a *person discharging managerial responsibilities* or the identity of A, is *inside information*.

**1.4.7 G**   [deleted]

# 1.6 MANIPULATING TRANSACTIONS

**1.6.1 UK**   [deleted]

**1.6.1-A EU**   [article 12(1)(b) of the *Market Abuse Regulation*]

**1.6.1A UK**   [deleted]

*Giving false or misleading impressions*

**1.6.2 E**   [deleted]

[**Note:** Annex 1A of the *Market Abuse Regulation*.]

**1.6.3 G**   Entering into a stock lending/borrowing or repo/reverse repo transaction, or another transaction involving the provision of collateral, does not of itself indicate behaviour described in Annex IA(c) of the *Market Abuse Regulation*.

**1.6.4 E**   [deleted]
[**Note:** Annex 1A of the *Market Abuse Regulation*.]

*Factors to be taken into account: legitimate reasons*

**1.6.5 G**   The following factors are to be taken into account when considering whether behaviour is for legitimate reasons in relation to article 12(1)(a) of the *Market Abuse Regulation*, and are indications that it is not:

(1)     if the person has an actuating purpose behind the transaction to induce others to trade in, bid for or to position or move the price of, a *financial instrument*;

(2)     if the *person* has another, illegitimate, reason behind the transactions, bid or order to trade; and

(3)     if the transaction was executed in a particular way with the purpose of creating a false or misleading impression.

**1.6.6 G**   The following factors are to be taken into account when considering whether behaviour is for legitimate reasons in relation to article 12(1)(a) of the *Market Abuse Regulation*, and are indications that it is:

(1)    if the transaction is pursuant to a prior legal or regulatory obligation owed to a third party;

(2)    if the transaction is executed in a way which takes into account the need for the market or auction platform as a whole to operate fairly and efficiently;

(3)    the extent to which the transaction generally opens a new position, so creating an exposure to market risk, rather than closes out a position and so removes market risk; and

(4)    if the transaction complied with the rules of the relevant *trading venue* about how transactions are to be executed in a proper way (for example, rules on reporting and executing cross-transactions).

**1.6.7 G**   It is unlikely that the behaviour of *trading venue* users when dealing at times and in sizes most beneficial to them (whether for the purpose of long term investment objectives, risk management or short term speculation) and seeking the maximum profit from their dealings will of itself amount to manipulation. Such behaviour, generally speaking, improves the liquidity and efficiency of *trading venues*.

**1.6.8 G**   It is unlikely that prices in the market which are trading outside their normal range will necessarily be indicative that someone has engaged in behaviour with the purpose of positioning prices at a distorted level. High or low prices relative to a trading range can be the result of the proper interplay of supply and demand.

*Factors to be taken into account: behaviour giving a false or misleading impression*

**1.6.9 E**   [deleted]

[**Note:** Annex 1A of the *Market Abuse Regulation*]

*Factors to be taken into account: behaviour securing an abnormal or artificial price level*

**1.6.10 G**   The following factors are to be taken into account in determining whether or not a *person's* behaviour amounts to manipulating transactions as described in article 12(1)(a)(ii) of the *Market Abuse Regulation*:

(1)    the extent to which the person had a direct or indirect interest in the price or value of the *financial instrument*;

(2)    the extent to which price, rate or option volatility movements, and the volatility of these factors for the *investment* in question, are outside their normal intra-day, daily, weekly or monthly range; and

(3)    whether a person has successively and consistently increased or decreased his bid, offer or the price he has paid for a *financial instrument*;

*Factors to be taken in to account: abusive squeezes*

**1.6.11 G**   The following factors are to be taken into account when determining whether a *person* has engaged in behaviour referred to in Annex IA(a) or (b) of the *Market Abuse Regulation*, commonly known as an "abusive squeeze":

(1)    the extent to which a *person* is willing to relax his control or other influence in order to help maintain an orderly market, and the price at which he is willing to do so; for example, behaviour is less likely to amount to an abusive squeeze if a *person* is willing to lend the *investment* in question;

(2)    the extent to which the *person's* activity causes, or risks causing, settlement default by other market users on a multilateral basis and not just a bilateral basis. The more widespread the risk of multilateral settlement default, the more likely that an abusive squeeze has been effected;

(3)    the extent to which prices under the delivery mechanisms of the market diverge from the prices for delivery of the *investment* or its equivalent outside those mechanisms. The greater the divergence beyond that to be reasonably expected, the more likely that an abusive squeeze has been effected; and

(4)     the extent to which the spot or immediate market compared to the forward market is unusually expensive or inexpensive or the extent to which borrowing rates are unusually expensive or inexpensive.

**1.6.12 G**  Squeezes occur relatively frequently when the proper interaction of supply and demand leads to market tightness, but this is not of itself likely to be abusive. In addition, having a significant influence over the supply of, or demand for, or delivery mechanisms for an investment, for example, through ownership, borrowing or reserving the investment in question, is not of itself likely to be abusive.

**1.6.13 G**  The effects of an abusive squeeze are likely to be influenced by the extent to which other market users have failed to protect their own interests or fulfil their obligations in a manner consistent with the standards of behaviour to be expected of them in that market. Market users can be expected to settle their obligations and not to put themselves in a position where, to do so, they have to rely on holders of long positions lending when they may not be inclined to do so and may be under no obligation to do so.

**1.6.14 E**  [deleted]

*Examples of manipulating transactions*

**1.6.15 G**  The following are examples of behaviour that may amount to manipulating transactions as described in article 12(1)(a)(ii) of the *Market Abuse Regulation*:

(1)     [deleted]
(2)     [deleted]
(3)     a trader holds a short position that will show a profit if a particular *financial instrument*, which is currently a component of an index, falls out of that index. The question of whether the *financial instrument* will fall out of the index depends on the closing price of the *financial instrument*. He places a large *sell* order in this *financial instrument* just before the close of trading. His purpose is to position the price of the *financial instrument* at a false, misleading, abnormal or artificial level so that the *financial instrument* will drop out of the index so as to make a profit; and
(4)     a fund manager's quarterly performance will improve if the valuation of his portfolio at the end of the quarter in question is higher rather than lower. He places a large order to *buy* relatively illiquid *shares*, which are also components of his portfolio, to be executed at or just before the close. His purpose is to position the price of the shares at a false, misleading, abnormal or artificial level.

**1.6.16 G**  The following is an example of an abusive squeeze:

A trader with a long position in bond *futures buys* or borrows a large amount of the cheapest to deliver bonds and either refuses to re-lend these bonds or will only lend them to parties he believes will not re-lend to the market. His purpose is to position the price at which those with short positions have to deliver to satisfy their obligations at a materially higher level, making him a profit from his original position.

## 1.7 MANIPULATING DEVICES

**1.7.1 UK**  [deleted]

**1.7.1-A EU**  [article 12(1)(b) of the *Market Abuse Regulation*]

**1.7.1A UK**  [deleted]

*Descriptions of behaviour that amount to manipulating devices*

**1.7.2 E** [deleted]

[**Note:** Article 12(2)(d) *Market Abuse Regulation*]

*Factors to be taken into account in determining whether or not behaviour amounts to manipulating devices*

**1.7.3 E** [deleted]

[**Note:** Annex 1B of the *Market Abuse Regulation*]

## 1.8 DISSEMINATION

**1.8.1 UK** [deleted]

**1.8.1A EU** [article 12(1)(c) of the *Market Abuse Regulation*]

**1.8.2 UK** [deleted]

*Descriptions of behaviour that amount to dissemination*

**1.8.3 E** [deleted]

[**Note:** article 12(1)(c) of the *Market Abuse Regulation*]

*Factors to be taken into account in determining whether or not behaviour amounts to dissemination*

**1.8.4 G** If a normal and reasonable *person* would know or ought to have known in all the circumstances that the information was false or misleading, that indicates that the *person* disseminating the information knew or ought to have known that it was false or misleading.

**1.8.5 G** If the individuals responsible for dissemination of information within an organisation could only know that the information was false or misleading if they had access to other information that was being held behind a *Chinese wall* or similarly effective arrangements, that indicates that the *person* disseminating did not know and could not reasonably be expected to have known that the information was false or misleading.

*Example of dissemination*

**1.8.6 E** The following is an example of behaviour which may amount to a contravention of article 12(1)(c) of the *Market Abuse Regulation*:

(1)    a person posts information on an Internet bulletin board or chat room which contains false or misleading statements about the takeover of a *company* whose *shares* are *financial instruments* and the *person* knows that the information is false or misleading.

[**Note:** article 12(1)(c) of the *Market Abuse Regulation*.]

## 1.9 MISLEADING BEHAVIOUR & DISTORTION

**1.9.1 UK** [deleted]

**1.9.1-A EU** [article 12(1)(c) of the *Market Abuse Regulation*]

**1.9.1A UK** [deleted]

**1.9.2 E** [deleted]

**1.9.2A E**

    (1)    [deleted]
    (2)    [deleted]

[deleted]

**1.9.2B R** [deleted]

*Short selling in relation to financial sector companies*

**1.9.2C E**

    (1)    [deleted]
    (2)    [deleted]
    (3)    [deleted]
    (4)    [deleted]

**1.9.2D E**

    (1)    [deleted]
    (2)    [deleted]
        (a)    [deleted]
        (b)    [deleted]
    (2A)    [deleted]
    (3)    [deleted]
    (4)    [deleted]
    (5)    [deleted]

**1.9.2E G** [deleted]

**1.9.3 C** [deleted]

**1.9.4 E** [deleted]

**1.9.5 E** [deleted]

## 1.10 STATUTORY EXCEPTIONS

*Behaviour that does not amount to market abuse*

**1.10.1 G**

(1)    *Behaviour* which conforms with article 5 of the *Market Abuse Regulation* or with a directly applicable *EU* regulation made under article 5 of the *Market Abuse Regulation* will not amount to *market abuse*.
(2)    [deleted]
(3)    [deleted]

*FCA rules*

**1.10.2 G**    There are no *rules* which permit or require a *person* to behave in a way which amounts to *market abuse*.

(1)    [deleted]
(2)    [deleted]

# Insider Dealing and Market Abuse Appendix

**1.10.3 G** There are no rules in the *Takeover Code*, which permit or require a *person* to behave in a way which amounts to *market abuse*.

**1.10.4 G** Behaviour conforming with any of the rules of the *Takeover Code* about the timing, dissemination or availability, content and standard of care applicable to a disclosure, announcement, communication or release of information, is unlikely to, of itself, amount to *market abuse*, if:

(1)  the rule is one of those specified in the table in MAR 1.10.5G;
(2)  the behaviour is expressly required or expressly permitted by the rule in question (the notes for the time being associated with the rules identified in the *Takeover Code* are treated as part of the relevant rule for these purposes); and
(3)  it conforms to any General Principle set out at Section B of the *Takeover Code* relevant to that rule.

**1.10.5 G** Table: Provisions of the Takeover Code conformity with which will be unlikely to, of itself, amount to market abuse (This table belongs to MAR 1.10.4G):

*Takeover Code* provisions:

| | |
|---|---|
| Disclosure of information which is not generally available | 1(a) |
| | 2.1 plus notes, 2.5, 2.6, 2.9 plus notes |
| | 8 |
| | 19.7 |
| | 20.1, 20.2, 20.3 |
| | 28.4 |
| | 37.3(b) and 37.4(a) |
| Standards of care | 2.8 first sentence and note 4 |
| | 19.1, 19.5 second sentence and note 2, 19.8 |
| | 23 plus notes |
| | 28.1 |
| Timing of announce-ments, documentation and deal-ings | 2.2, 2.4(b) |
| | 5.4 |
| | 6.2(b) |
| | 7.1 |
| | 11.1 note 6 only |
| | 17.1 |
| | 21.2 |
| | 30 |
| | 31.6(c), 31.9 |
| | 33 (in so far as it refers 31.6(c) and 31.9 only) |
| | 38.5 |
| Content of announce-ments | 2.4 (a) and (b) |
| | 19.3 |

**1.10.6 G**   Behaviour conforming with Rule 4.2 of the *Takeover Code* (in relation to restrictions on *dealings* by *offerors* and concert parties) will be unlikely to, of itself, amount to *market abuse*, if:

(1)     the *behaviour* is expressly required or expressly permitted by that rule (the notes for the time being associated with the rules identified in the *Takeover Code* are treated as part of the rule for these purposes); and

(2)     it conforms to any General Principle set out at Section B of the *Takeover Code* relevant to the rule.

*Provisions of the Buy-back and Stabilisation Regulation relating to buy- 1 back programmes*

**1.1.1 G**   [deleted]

**1.1.2 G**   [deleted]

**1.1.3 EU**   [deleted]

**1.1.4 EU**   [deleted]

**1.1.5 EU**   [deleted]

**1.1.6 G**   [deleted]

**1.1.7 G**   [deleted]

**1.1.8 G**   The FCA accepts as *"adequate public disclosure"*:

(1)     disclosure through a *regulatory information service* or otherwise in accordance with *Part 6 rules*; or

(2)     the equivalent disclosure mechanism required to be used in relation to the relevant *trading venue*.

**1.1.9 EU**   [deleted]

**1.1.10 EU**   [deleted]

**1.1.11 G**   [deleted]

**1.1.12 EU**   [deleted]

**1.1.13 G**   [deleted]

**1.1.14 G**   [deleted]

*Accepted Market Practices*

[article 13 of the *Market Abuse Regulation*.]

# 24   Interests in Public Company Shares

## 24.1   INFORMATION ABOUT INTERESTS IN A PUBLIC COMPANY'S SHARES

There are two requirements which affect the obligation to disclose interests in the shares of a company. The first is *CA 2006, ss 793–828* which re-enact (with certain modifications) the disclosure obligations previously found in *CA 1985, ss 212–220*. These provisions give public companies the right to investigate who has an 'interest' in its shares. The second requirements are the disclosure obligations in the Disclosure Guidance and Transparency Rules ('DTR') made by the FCA (see 33 PUBLIC AND LISTED COMPANIES).

The DTR 5:

- implements the provisions of the *EU Transparency Obligations Directive (Directive 2004/109/EC)*;

- applies only to companies with securities traded on a regulated or prescribed market;

- replaced *CA 1985, ss 198–220* which required the holder of shares in a public company to notify the company when that person's shareholding reached certain thresholds and also gave public companies the right to require shareholders or persons suspected of being interested in shares to disclose those interests. Those provisions were repealed in January 2007; and

- can be found in the FCA handbook (www.fca.org.uk).

The distinction between the above requirements is that the *CA 2006* provisions apply to all public companies whereas DTR 5 applies only to companies with securities traded on a regulated or prescribed market.

This chapter deals only with the *CA 2006* requirements.

**Companies and shares to which the *CA 2006* provisions apply.** The *CA 2006* provisions apply to a public company's issued shares carrying rights to vote at general meetings of the company (including any shares held as treasury shares). If voting rights are temporarily suspended (in respect of any shares) that does not affect the application of the disclosure obligations.

[*CA 2006, ss 791, 792*].

## 24.2   Power to investigate ownership of shares

Subject to the exemptions below, a public company may give notice to any person (including a person who is not a shareholder) whom it knows or has reasonable cause to believe is or, within the three years immediately preceding the date of the notice has been, 'interested' in the company's shares to confirm

(a)    whether the person does or did in fact have such an interest [s 792(2)(a)]; and

(b)    if that person does or did hold such an interest, to provide further information of that interest 'as may be required' [s 793(2)(b)].

Note the permissive words of s 793(2)(b) ie 'as may be required' so it is open to the company to decide how much information they ask for. If further information is asked for it must be 'in accordance' with ss 793(3)–(7) and so can

- Require the person to give particulars of his own past or present interests [s 793(3)]

- (Whether other interests in the shares subsist or subsisted during the three year period referred to above) require the person to give particulars about the other interests 'so far as lies within his knowledge' [s 793(4)].

- (Where the interest is a past interest) require the person to give details of the identity of the person who held the interest immediately after him 'so far as lies within his knowledge' [s 793(6)].

The particulars referred to above include

- the identity of persons interested in the shares and

- whether persons interested in the same shares were parties to a CA 2006, s 824 agreement (share acquisition agreements) or any agreement or arrangement relating to the exercise of rights conferred by the holding of the shares [s 793(5)].

**Meaning of 'interest' in shares.** The following rules apply to determine for these purposes whether a person has an interest in shares.

(1)    A reference to an interest in shares includes an interest of any kind whatsoever in the shares.

[CA 2006, s 820(2)].

(2)    Any restraints or restrictions to which the exercise of any right attached to the interest is or may be subject must be disregarded.

[CA 2006, s 820(2)].

(3)    Where an interest in shares is comprised in property held on trust, every beneficiary of the trust is treated as having an interest in the shares.

[CA 2006, s 820(3)].

(4)    A person is treated as having an interest in shares if

(i)    he enters into a contract to acquire them;

(ii)    not being the registered holder, he is entitled to exercise any right conferred by the holding of the shares or to control the exercise of any such right. For these purposes, a person is entitled to exercise or control the exercise of a right conferred by the holding of shares if he either has a right (whether subject to conditions or not) the exercise of which would make him so entitled or is under an obligation (whether subject to conditions or not) the fulfilment of which would make him so entitled;

(iii)    he has a right to call for delivery of the shares to himself or to his order (whether the right is conditional or absolute); or

(iv)    he has a right to acquire an interest in shares or is under an obligation to take an interest in shares (whether the right or obligation is conditional or absolute).

*[CA 2006, s 820(4)–(6)]*.

(5)    Persons having a joint interest are treated as each having that interest.

*[CA 2006, s 820(7)]*.

(6)    It is immaterial that shares in which a person has an interest are unidentifiable.

*[CA 2006, s 820(8)]*.

(7)    The requirement to provide information applies in relation to a person who has, or previously had, or is or was entitled to acquire, a right to subscribe for shares in the company as it applies in relation to a person who is or was interested in shares in that company.

*[CA 2006, s 821]*.

(8)    A person is taken to be interested in shares in which

(i)    his spouse or civil partner, or

(ii)    any infant child or step-child of his,

is interested.

In relation to Scotland 'infant' means a person under the age of 18 years.

*[CA 2006, s 822]*.

(9)    A person is taken to be interested in shares if a body corporate is interested in them and

(i)    the body or its directors are accustomed to act in accordance with his directions or instructions; or

(ii)    he is entitled to exercise or control the exercise of one-third or more of the voting power at general meetings of the body. A person is treated as entitled to exercise or control the exercise of voting power if

•    another body corporate is entitled to exercise or control the exercise of that voting power and he is entitled to exercise or control the exercise of one-third or more of the voting power at general meetings of that body corporate;

•    he has a right (whether or not subject to conditions) the exercise of which would make him so entitled; or

•    he is under an obligation (whether or not subject to conditions) the fulfilment of which would make him so entitled.

*[CA 2006, s 823]*.

(10)    Subject to the exceptions below, special provisions apply in relation to an agreement between two or more persons that

(a)    includes provision for the acquisition by any one or more of them of interests in shares of a particular public company (the '*target company*' for that agreement); and

(b)    imposes obligations or restrictions on any one or more of the parties to it with respect to their 'use', retention or disposal of their interests in the shares of the target company acquired in pursuance of the agreement (whether or not together with any other interests of theirs in the company's shares to which the agreement relates).

Where an interest in the target company's shares is acquired by any of the parties in pursuance of the agreement, each party to the agreement is treated as interested in all shares in the target company in which any other party to the agreement is interested 'apart from the agreement' (whether or not the interest of the other party was acquired, or includes any interest that was acquired, in pursuance of the agreement).

An interest of a party to such an agreement in shares in the target company is an interest *'apart from the agreement'* if he is interested in those shares otherwise than by virtue of the application of these provisions in relation to the agreement. Accordingly, any such interest of the person (apart from the agreement) includes any interest treated as his under (8) or (9) above or by the application of these provisions in relation to any other agreement with respect to shares in the target company to which he is a party.

Once an interest in shares in the target company has been acquired in pursuance of the agreement, the agreement (and any substituted agreement) continue to be within these provisions so long as it continues to include provisions of any description mentioned (*b*) above. This applies irrespective of

- whether or not any further acquisitions of interests in the company's shares take place in pursuance of the agreement;

- any change in the persons who are for the time being parties to it; and

- any variation of the agreement.

*'Agreement'* for these purposes includes any arrangement, and the provisions of an agreement include undertakings, expectations or understandings operative under an arrangement, and may be express or implied and absolute or not.

*Exceptions.* These provisions do not apply

(i)    to an agreement that is not legally binding unless it involves mutuality in the undertakings, expectations or understandings of the parties to it; or

(ii)   to an agreement to underwrite or sub-underwrite an offer of shares in a company, provided the agreement is confined to that purpose and any matters incidental to it.

[*CA 2006, ss 824, 825*].

For the register entries required to be made by the company following receipt of information under these provisions, see **38.12** REGISTERS. For the removal of entries, see **38.14** REGISTERS.

**Exemptions.** A person is not obliged to comply with a notice if he is for the time being exempted by the Secretary of State. But the Secretary of State must not grant any such exemption unless

- he has consulted the Governor of the Bank of England; and

- he (the Secretary of State) is satisfied that, having regard to any undertaking given by the person in question with respect to any interest held or to be held by him in any shares, there are special reasons why that person should not be subject to those obligations.

[*CA 2006, s 796*].

**24.3** *Consequences of failure to comply with notice*

(1) *Court order imposing restrictions on shares*

Where, within the time specified, a person fails to give a company the information required by a notice to under **24.2**, the company may apply to the court for an order directing that the shares in question be subject to restrictions. For the consequences of such an order, see **24.7** to **24.10**.

If the court is satisfied that such an order could unfairly affect the rights of third parties in respect of shares, the court may direct that such acts by specified persons as are set out in the order do not constitute a breach of the restrictions.

On application, the court may also make an interim order (either unconditionally or on such terms as it thinks fit).

[*CA 2006, s 794*].

(2) *Offences*

A person who

(a)   fails to comply with a notice requiring disclosure of interests under **24.2**, or

(b)   in purported compliance with such a notice

   (i)   makes a statement that he knows to be false in a material particular, or

   (ii)   recklessly makes a statement that is false in a material particular,

commits an offence except that a person does not commit an offence under (*a*) above if he proves that the requirement to give information was frivolous or vexatious.

A person guilty of such an offence is liable (i) on conviction on indictment, to imprisonment for a term not exceeding two years or a fine (or both); and (ii) on summary conviction, to imprisonment for a term not exceeding twelve months (six months in Scotland or Northern Ireland) or to a fine not exceeding the statutory maximum (or both). See **29.1** OFFENCES AND LEGAL PROCEEDINGS for the statutory maximum.

[*CA 2006, s 795*].

**24.4   Power of members to require company to act**

The members of a company may require it to exercise its powers to investigate the ownership of shares . The company is required to do so once it has received requests from members holding at least 10% of such of the paid-up capital of the company as carries a right to vote at general meetings of the company (excluding any voting rights attached to any shares in the company held as treasury shares).

A request from members may be in hard copy form or in electronic form. It must

•   state that the company is requested to exercise its powers to investigate the ownership of shares;

•   specify the manner in which the company is requested to act;

•   give reasonable grounds for requiring the company to exercise those powers in the manner specified; and

•   be authenticated by the person or persons making it.

## 24.4 Interests in Public Company Shares

[*CA 2006, s 803*].

A company that is required under the above provisions to exercise its powers must exercise those powers in the manner specified in the requests. If it defaults, an offence is committed by every officer of the company who is in default. A person guilty of such an offence is liable (i) on conviction on indictment, to a fine; and (ii) on summary conviction, to a fine not exceeding the statutory maximum. See **29.1** OFFENCES AND LEGAL PROCEEDINGS for the statutory maximum.

[*CA 2006, s 804*].

## 24.5 Power to investigate persons with significant control over a company

The *Small Business Enterprise and Employment Act 2015, Sch 3* ('*SBEE 2015*') introduces new requirements for a company to

- keep a register of people with 'significant control'; and

- to gather information to enable the company to keep such a register.

Since the definition of people with 'significant control' includes individuals who hold, directly or indirectly, either more than 25% of the shares in the company or more than 25% of the voting rights in the company a note has been added to this chapter. For full details of the new provisions including the duty to investigate obtain information and notify Companies House (see **38.18**).

[*SBEE 2015, Sch 3, Part 1; CA 2006, Part 21A; SI 2015 No 2029, Reg 4*].

## 24.6 *Report to members on outcome of investigation*

On the conclusion of an investigation carried out by a company following a members' request, the company must prepare a report of the information received. The report must be made available for inspection within a reasonable period (not more than 15 working days) after the conclusion of the investigation.

Where a company undertakes such an investigation and it is not concluded within three months from the date on which the requirement to do so arose, it must prepare an interim report of the information received in that three-month period. It must similarly prepare a report for any succeeding three-month period until the conclusion of the investigation. Each such report must be made available for inspection within a reasonable period (not more than 15 working days) after the end of the period to which it relates. The report must not contain any information which does not have to be disclosed under regulations made under *CA 2006, s 409(3)*. These *Regulations* (the *Large and Medium-sized Companies and Groups (Accounts and Reports) Regulations 2008 (SI 2008 No 410)*) provide that information about related undertakings which must be disclosed in the accounts does not apply to companies that either are established under a law outside the UK or carry on business outside the UK provided that in the opinion of the directors disclosure would be seriously prejudicial to the business of the overseas undertaking or the company or any of its subsidiaries or any other undertaking included in the consolidated accounts or if the Secretary of State agrees that the information need not be disclosed. If the information is omitted from the members' report that fact must be stated in the report.

All the reports required above must be retained by the company for at least six years from the date on which they are first made available for inspection. They must be kept available for inspection during that time at the company's registered office or at a place specified in Regulations (see **36.2** RECORDS).

See also **36.2** RECORDS for provisions as to time available for inspection and copying.

The company must, within three working days of making any report (ie interim or final) prepared under these provisions available for inspection, notify the members who made the requests under **24.4** where the report is so available.

An investigation carried out by a company is concluded when

• the company has made all such inquiries as are necessary or expedient for the purposes of the requirement; and

• in the case of each such inquiry, either a response has been received by the company or the time allowed for a response has elapsed.

*Offences.* If default is made in complying with any of the above provisions, an offence is committed by every officer of the company who is in default. A person guilty of such an offence is liable (i) on conviction on indictment, to a fine; and (ii) on summary conviction, to a fine not exceeding the statutory maximum. See **29.1** OFFENCES AND LEGAL PROCEEDINGS for the statutory maximum.

*Notice to the Registrar of Companies.* The company must give notice to the Registrar of Companies of the place at which the reports are kept available for inspection and of any change in that place (unless they have at all times been kept at the company's registered office. If default is made for 14 days in complying with this requirement, an offence is committed by the company and every officer of the company who is in default. A person guilty of such an offence is liable, on summary conviction, to a fine not exceeding level 3 on the standard scale and, for continued contravention, a daily default fine not exceeding one-tenth of level 3 on the standard scale. See **29.1** OFFENCES AND LEGAL PROCEEDINGS for the statutory maximum.

[*CA 2006, ss 805, 806, 827*].

**Right to inspect and request copy of reports.** Any report prepared must be open to inspection by any person without charge. In addition, any person is entitled, on request and on payment of such fee as may be prescribed, to be provided with a copy of any such report or any part of it. The copy must be provided within ten working days after the request is received by the company.

If an inspection is refused, or a copy not provided, an offence is committed by the company and every officer of the company who is in default. A person guilty of such an offence is liable, on summary conviction, to a fine not exceeding level 3 on the standard scale and, for continued contravention, a daily default fine not exceeding one-tenth of level 3 on the standard scale. See **29.1** OFFENCES AND LEGAL PROCEEDINGS for the standard scale.

In the case of any such refusal or default, the court may compel an immediate inspection or, as the case may be, direct that the copy required be sent to the person requiring it.

[*CA 2006, ss 807, 827*].

**24.7 ORDERS IMPOSING RESTRICTIONS ON SHARES**

The provisions below and **24.8** to **24.10** restate, without substantive change, the provisions in *CA 1985, ss 454–457*. They set out the effect of a court order imposing restrictions on shares and the penalties for attempted evasion of the restrictions. They also make provision for the relaxation or removal of restrictions or for an order for the sale of shares.

Subject to any directions by the court for protection of third parties or the terms of any interim order (see **24.3**) and subject to any relaxation of restrictions under **24.9**, the effect of a court order under *CA 2006, s 794* (see **24.3**) that shares are subject to restrictions is as follows.

## 24.7 Interests in Public Company Shares

(a)    Any transfer of the shares is void.

(b)    No voting rights are exercisable in respect of the shares.

(c)    No further shares may be issued in right of the shares or in pursuance of an offer made to their holder.

(d)    Except in a liquidation, no payment may be made of sums due from the company on the shares, whether in respect of capital or otherwise.

**Agreements to transfer**. Where shares are subject to the restriction

- in (*a*) above, an agreement to transfer the shares is also void (except for such an agreement on the making of an order for the removal of restrictions under **24.9**); and

- in (*c*) or (*d*) above, an agreement to transfer any right to be issued with other shares in right of those shares, or to receive any payment on them (otherwise than in a liquidation), is also void (except for an agreement to transfer any such right on the making of an order for the removal of restrictions under **24.9**).

[*CA 2006, s 797*].

## 24.8 Penalty for attempted evasion of restrictions

Subject to any directions by the court for protection of third parties or the terms of any interim order (see **24.3**) and subject to any relaxation or removal of restrictions under **24.9**, where shares are subject to restrictions, a person commits an offence if he

- exercises or purports to exercise any right

  (i)    to dispose of shares that to his knowledge, are for the time being subject to restrictions; or

  (ii)    to dispose of any right to be issued with any such shares;

- votes in respect of any such shares (whether as holder or proxy) or appoints a proxy to vote in respect of them;

- being the holder of any such shares, fails to notify the existence of the restrictions to any person whom he does not know to be aware of that fact but does know to be entitled (apart from the restrictions) to vote in respect of those shares (whether as holder or as proxy); or

- being the holder of any such shares, or being entitled to a right to be issued with other shares in right of them, or to receive any payment on them (otherwise than in a liquidation), enters into an agreement to transfer which is void under **24.7**.

If shares in a company are issued in contravention of the restrictions, an offence is committed by the company and every officer of the company who is in default.

A person guilty of such an offence is liable (i) on conviction on indictment, to a fine; and (ii) on summary conviction, to a fine not exceeding the statutory maximum. See **29.1** Offences and Legal Proceedings for the statutory maximum.

[*CA 2006, s 798*].

**24.9   Relaxation and removal of restrictions**

**Relaxation of restrictions.** An application may be made to the court, by the company or by any person aggrieved, on the ground that an order directing that shares are to be subject to restrictions unfairly affects the rights of third parties in respect of the shares. If the court is satisfied that the application is well-founded, it may, subject to such terms as it thinks fit, direct that specified acts by persons as set out in the order do not constitute a breach of the restrictions. [*CA 2006, s 799*].

**Removal of restrictions.** An application may be made to the court, by the company or by any person aggrieved, for an order directing that the shares cease to be subject to restrictions. The court must not make such an order unless

(a)     it is satisfied that the relevant facts about the shares have been disclosed to the company and no unfair advantage has accrued to any person as a result of the earlier failure to make that disclosure; or

(b)     the shares are to be transferred for valuable consideration and the court approves the transfer.

An order made under (*b*) above may continue, in whole or in part, the restrictions in **24.7**(*c*) or (*d*) so far as they relate to a right acquired or offer made before the transfer. Where any restrictions continue in force, an application may be made under these provisions for an order directing that the shares cease to be subject to those restrictions.

[*CA 2006, s 800*].

**24.10   Order for sale of shares**

The court may

(a)     on an application by the company, order that the shares subject to restrictions be sold, subject to the court's approval as to the sale; and

(b)     where it has made an order under (*a*) above, make such further order relating to the sale or transfer of the shares as it thinks fit on application by

(i)      the company;

(ii)     the person appointed to carry out the sale; or

(iii)    any person interested in the shares.

On making any such order, the court may also order that the applicant's costs (in Scotland, expenses) be paid out of the proceeds of sale.

**Application of proceeds of sale.** Where shares are sold in pursuance of an order as above, the proceeds of the sale, less the costs of the sale, must be paid into court for the benefit of the person or persons who are beneficially interested in the shares. On application by any person so interested, the court must order the payment to the applicant of the whole of the proceeds of sale together with any interest on them (or a proportionate part where more than one person has a beneficial interest). But where the court has ordered that the costs (in Scotland, expenses) of an applicant are to be paid out of the proceeds of sale (see above), the applicant is entitled to payment of his costs (or expenses) out of those proceeds before any person interested in the shares receives any part of those proceeds.

[*CA 2006, ss 801, 802*].

# 25   Investigations

## 25.1   INTRODUCTION TO INVESTIGATIONS

One of the few parts of the *CA 1985* which has not been subject to repeal and revision by *CA 2006* is the part relating to investigations into companies and the powers to obtain information. The references therefore in this chapter to *CA 1985, Part XIV* and *CA 1989, Part III* are still relevant. *CA 2006* also confers powers on the Secretary of State to remove inspectors, to issue directions about the scope, direction and duration of an inspection and to terminate an inspection when it is no longer in the public interest for it to continue (see **25.8** and **25.9**).

These are powers, bestowed on the Insolvency Service Civil investigators and inspectors, to investigate the suspected misconduct of companies and individuals. The powers which the investigators have include the power:

•   to require the production of documents;

•   to gain entry to premises, in order to search for and seize material; and

•   to require the disclosure of documents, or the provision of specific information.

The powers do not include a power of arrest.

Certain safeguards have been put in place with a view to keeping the exercise of these powers in check.

## 25.2   POWER OF THE SECRETARY OF STATE TO INVESTIGATE COMPANIES

The Secretary of State *may* appoint one or more inspectors to investigate and report the results of their investigation to him either

## 25.2 Investigations

(a)     on the application of

    (i)     in the case of a company having a share capital, *either* at least 200 members *or* members holding at least 10% of the shares issued (excluding any shares held as treasury shares);

    (ii)     in the case of a company not having a share capital, at least 20% in number of the persons on the company's register of members; or

    (iii)     the company itself; or

(b)     (whether or not the company is in the course of being voluntarily wound up) if it appears to the Secretary of State that

    (i)     the company's affairs are being or have been conducted

- with intent to defraud its creditors or the creditors of any other person;

- for a fraudulent or unlawful purpose; or

- in a manner unfairly prejudicial to some members (or to persons who are not members but to whom shares have been transferred or transmitted by operation of law);

    (ii)     any actual or proposed act or omission of the company or on its behalf is or would be so prejudicial;

    (iii)     the company was formed for any fraudulent or unlawful purpose;

    (iv)     persons concerned with the company's formation or management have in that connection been guilty of fraud, misfeasance or other misconduct towards the company or its members; or

    (v)     the company's members have not been given all the information with respect to its affairs which they might reasonably expect.

The Secretary of State is *required* to appoint one or more inspectors if a court having jurisdiction to wind up the company by order declares that the company's affairs ought to be so investigated.

[*CA 1985, ss 431(1), (2), 432(1), (2), (2A), (3), (4)*].

Any application either by members of the company or by the company itself under (*a*) above must be supported by such evidence as the Secretary of State requires in order to show good reason for requiring the investigation and the Secretary of State may require security (not exceeding £5,000) from the applicant(s) for payment of the costs of the investigation.

[*CA 1985, s 424(3)(4)*].

As regards (*b*) above, the appointment may be on terms that any report is not for publication, notwithstanding *CA 1985, s 437(3)* (see **25.4**).

[*CA 1985, s 432(2A)*].

**Extension of powers to subsidiaries.** Inspectors appointed as above have power, if they consider it necessary, to extend their investigation to the affairs of certain companies with a holding or subsidiary relationship to the company under investigation. Their report will then include a report on the affairs of such companies, so far as relevant to their main investigation.

[*CA 1985, s 433*].

**25.3   Production of documents and evidence**

Officers and 'agents' (past and present) of any company under investigation are under a duty to

- produce to the inspectors all 'documents' in their custody or power of or relating to the company;

- attend before the inspectors as required; and

- otherwise give them all reasonable assistance in connection with the investigation; and

- are also under the same duty if the inspectors consider they possess such information.

They are under the same duty if the inspectors consider that they possess such information.

An inspector may examine any person on oath, and an answer given by a person to a question put under any of the above powers may be used in evidence against him. However, in criminal proceedings in which that person is charged with an offence (other than an offence of making false statements under *Perjury Act 1911, ss 2* or *5, Criminal Law (Consolidation) (Scotland) Act 1995, s 44(1)* or *(2)* or *Perjury (Northern Ireland) Order 1979, Art 7* or *10*) no evidence relating to the answer may be adduced and no question relating to it may be asked by or on behalf of the prosecution unless evidence relating to it is adduced, or a question relating to it is asked, in the proceedings by or on behalf of that person. See *Saunders v United Kingdom* (Application 19187/91) (1996) 23 EHRR 313, [1998] 1 BCLC 362 where the European Court of Human Rights accepted that the use made of certain statements to inspectors was unfair and in violation of the European Convention on Human Rights and stated that the existing provisions of the *Companies Acts* could not properly override an individual's right not to be required to incriminate himself.

*'Agents'* in relation to a company includes its bankers, solicitors and auditor, whether or not they are officers but see **25.21** for privileged information.

*'Documents'* includes information recorded in any form.

The power to require production of a document includes power, in the case of a document not in hard copy form, to require the production of a copy of the document in hard copy form or in a form from which a hard copy form can readily be obtained.

Inspectors may take copies of, or extracts from, a document produced under these provisions.

[*CA 1985, s 434*].

Failure or refusal by any person to comply with any of the above requirements, or to answer any of the inspectors' questions, may be certified in writing by the inspector to the court, and may be treated as contempt of court.

[*CA 1985, s 436*].

**25.4   Inspectors' reports**

Final (and, if required, interim) reports are made by the inspectors to the Secretary of State, who is kept informed of any matters coming to the inspectors' knowledge as a result of their investigations.

[*CA 1985, s 437(1), (1A)*].

## 25.4  Investigations

Where the inspectors were appointed following a declaration by order of the court (see **25.2**), a copy of any report must be furnished to the court. If the company is registered under *CA 2006* in Northern Ireland, the Secretary of State must send a copy of any interim or final report by the inspectors to the Department of Enterprise, Trade and Investment in Northern Ireland. In any case, if he thinks fit, the Secretary of State may forward a copy of any report to the company's registered office and, on request and on payment of a fee prescribed by him by statutory instrument, he may furnish a copy to

- any member of the company or other body corporate which is the subject of the report;

- the auditor of that company or body corporate;

- any person whose conduct is referred to in the report;

- the applicants for the investigation (see **25.2**); and

- any other person whose financial interests appear to the Secretary of State to be affected by the matters dealt with in the report.

He may also cause any report to be printed and published (but see **25.2** for certain reports excluded from publication under the terms of appointment of the inspectors).

[*CA 1985, ss 437(2), (2A), (3)*].

See, however, **25.7** as regards omission of certain parts of inspectors' reports from disclosure under these provisions.

A copy of the report is admissible in any legal proceedings as evidence of the inspectors' opinion in relation to any matter in the report, and in proceedings on an application under the *CDDA 1986, s 8* (see **18.15** DIRECTORS) as evidence of any fact stated therein. The copy must be certified a true copy by the Secretary of State, and a document purporting to be such a certificate will be received in evidence as such unless the contrary is proved.

[*CA 1985, s 441*].

## 25.5  Investigation expenses

The expenses of an investigation under **25.2** (including reasonable general staff costs and overheads as determined by the Secretary of State) are defrayed, in the first place, by the Secretary of State. But he may, however, recover them as follows.

(a)  A person convicted on a prosecution instituted as a result of the investigation may in those proceedings be ordered to pay investigation expenses to a specified extent.

(b)  A company dealt with by an inspectors' report, where the inspectors were appointed otherwise than of the Secretary of State's own motion, is liable for investigation expenses, unless it was the applicant for the investigation, and except so far as the Secretary of State otherwise directs.

(c)  Where inspectors were appointed by members of the company or by the company itself (see **25.2** (*a*)) or where the investigation relates to the ownership of the company (see **25.7**), the applicant or applicants for the investigation is or are liable for investigation expenses to such extent as the Secretary of State may direct.

Except where the inspectors were appointed of the Secretary of State's own motion, their report may (and must if so required by the Secretary of State) include a recommendation as to any appropriate direction(s) under (*b*) and (*c*) above in the light of their investigations.

A liability to repay the Secretary of State under (*a*) above is, subject to satisfaction of his right to repayment, also a liability to indemnify all persons against liability under (*b*) and (*c*) above. A person liable under any of (*a*) to (*c*) above is entitled to contribution from any other person liable under the same provision, according to the amount of their respective liabilities under that provision.

[*CA 1985, s 439*].

## 25.6    OTHER POWERS OF INVESTIGATION

Various powers of investigation are available to the Secretary of State, in addition to those described at **25.2** to **25.5**, under *CA 1985, ss 442–446E*.

### 25.7    Power to investigate company ownership

If there appears to be good reason to do so, the Secretary of State may appoint inspector(s) to investigate and report on the membership of any company, and otherwise with respect to the company, to determine the true persons financially interested in the success or failure (real or apparent) of the company, or able to control or materially to influence its policy. Subject to the terms of their appointment, the inspectors' powers extend to the investigation of any circumstances suggesting the existence of a relevant arrangement or understanding which, though not legally binding, is or was observed or likely to be observed in practice.

If an application is made to the Secretary of State by members of a company for such a limited investigation, and the applicants would meet the requirements in **25.2**(*a*)(i) or (ii) as regards numbers or shares, the Secretary of State must (except as below) appoint inspectors to conduct the investigation, unless he is satisfied that the application is vexatious. The terms of appointment will, however, exclude any matter in so far as he is satisfied that it is unreasonable for it to be investigated. He may, before appointing inspectors, require security (not exceeding £5,000) from the applicant(s) for payment of the costs of the investigation.

Where it appears to the Secretary of State that his powers under *CA 1985, s 444* (see **25.8**) are sufficient for the investigation of matters which inspectors would otherwise be appointed to investigate on an application as above, he may instead conduct the investigation under *section 444*.

[*CA 1985, s 442; CA 1989, s 62; CA 2006, s 1035(5)*].

The provisions of *CA 1985, ss 433* (power to investigate subsidiaries), *434* (officers and agents duty to produce documents and evidence), *436* (obstruction of inspectors treated as contempt of court) and *437* (production of reports) apply to an investigation under *section 442* above with appropriate modifications of references to the affairs of the company to those of any other body corporate. But, in addition, they apply to

- all persons who are or have been (or whom the inspector has reasonable cause to believe to be or have been)

  (i)    financially interested in the success or failure (real or apparent) of the company or any other body corporate whose membership is investigated with that of the company, or

  (ii)   able to control or materially influence its policy (including persons concerned only on behalf of others), and

- any other person whom the inspector has reasonable cause to believe possesses relevant information,

as they apply in relation to officers or agents of the company or other body corporate.

## 25.7 Investigations

The Secretary of State may by order impose restrictions on shares and debentures under *CA 1985, ss 454–457* (see **25.23**) where there is difficulty in finding out the relevant facts about them in connection with an investigation under these provisions. But where he is satisfied that such on order may unfairly affect the rights of third parties in respect of shares, he may direct that specified acts by such persons do not constitute a breach of the restrictions.

If the Secretary of State considers there is good reason for not divulging any part of a report under these provisions, he may omit that part from the disclosure of the report under *CA 1985, s 437* (see **25.4**). He may cause a copy of any report to be kept by the Registrar of Companies, again with the omission of any part not disclosed under *CA 1985, s 437*. [*CA 1985, ss 443, 445*].

## 25.8   Power to obtain information as to those interested in shares, etc

The Secretary of State may act without the appointment of inspectors if there appears to be good reason to investigate the ownership of any shares or debentures of a company, and he considers their appointment unnecessary. He may require any person whom he has reasonable cause to believe to have, or to be able to obtain,

- any information as to the present and past interests in those shares, etc, and
- the names and addresses of the persons interested and of any persons who act or have acted on their behalf in relation to those shares etc,

to deliver such information to him.

A person has an interest for this purpose if

- he has any right to acquire or dispose of the shares, etc (or of an interest in them);
- he has any right to vote in respect of them;
- his consent is necessary for the exercise of any rights of other persons interested in them; or
- other persons interested in them can be required to, or are accustomed to, exercise their rights in accordance with his instructions.

Any person who

- fails to give information required as above,
- in giving such information makes any statement which he knows to be false in a material particular, or
- recklessly makes any statement which is false in a material particular,

commits an offence. A person guilty of such an offence is liable (i) on conviction on indictment, to imprisonment for a term not exceeding two years or a fine (or both); and (ii) on summary conviction to imprisonment for a term not exceeding twelve months (six months in Scotland or, with effect from 1 October 2009, Northern Ireland) or to a fine not exceeding the statutory maximum (or both) and, for continued contravention, a daily default fine not exceeding one-fiftieth of the greater of £5,000 or the amount corresponding to level 4 on the standard scale for summary offences. See **29.1** Offences and Legal Proceedings for the statutory maximum.

See, however, **25.21** for privileged information.

[*CA 1985, s 444; SI 2015 No 664, Sch 3*].

The Secretary of State may by order impose restrictions on shares and debentures under *CA 1985, ss 454–457* (see **25.23**) where there is difficulty in ascertaining the relevant facts about them in connection with an investigation under these provisions. But where he is satisfied that such on order may unfairly affect the rights of third parties in respect of shares, he may direct that specified acts by such persons do not constitute a breach of the restrictions.

[*CA 1985, s 445*].

## 25.9   Powers of the Secretary of State relating to inspectors

The following provisions apply where an inspector is appointed after 30 September 2007.

**General powers to give directions.** In exercising his functions an inspector must comply with any direction given to him by the Secretary of State as follows.

- The Secretary of State may give an inspector appointed under **25.2**(*a*) or (*b*) or **25.7** a direction

  (i)   as to the subject matter of his investigation (whether by reference to a specified area of a company's operation, a specified transaction, a period of time or otherwise), or

  (ii)   which requires the inspector to take (or not to take) a specified step in his investigation.

- The Secretary of State may give an inspector appointed under any provision of this chapter a direction requiring him to secure that a specified report under **25.4**

  (i)   includes the inspector's views on a specified matter;

  (ii)   does not include any reference to a specified matter;

  (iii)   is made in a specified form or manner; or

  (iv)   is made by a specified date.

Any direction under the above provisions may be given on an inspector's appointment, may vary or revoke a direction previously given, and may be given at the request of an inspector.

For the above purposes, reference to an inspector's investigation includes any investigation he undertakes, or could undertake, under *CA 1985, s 433* into the affairs of a holding company or subsidiary (see **25.2**).

[*CA 1985, s 446A*].

**Direction to terminate investigation.** Subject to below, the Secretary of State may direct an inspector to take no further steps in his investigation and, if he does so, any direction already given to the inspector in connection with the preparation of an interim report ceases to have effect and the inspector must not make a final report to the Secretary of State.

But where the inspector was appointed at the instigation of the court under *CA 1985, s 432(1)* (see **25.2**) or following an application by the members of the company under *CA 1985, s 442(3)* (see **25.7**), the Secretary of State can give a direction under these provisions only on the grounds that

- matters have come to light in the course of the inspector's investigation which suggest that a criminal offence has been committed; and

- those matters have been referred to the appropriate prosecuting authority.

Where the Secretary of State gives a direction under those circumstances, the inspector must not make a final report to the Secretary of State unless either the inspector was appointed under *CA 1985, s 432(1)* or the Secretary of State directs the inspector to make a final report to him.

## 25.9    Investigations

For the above purposes, reference to an inspector's investigation includes any investigation he undertakes, or could undertake, under *CA 1985, s 433* into the affairs of a holding company or subsidiary (see **25.2**).

[*CA 1985, s 446B*].

**Obtaining information from former inspectors, etc.** Where

• a person has been appointed as an inspector under the provisions in this chapter but has resigned or had his appointment revoked, or

• an inspector has been given a direction by the Secretary of State under *CA 1985, s 446B* (see above)

the Secretary of State may direct that person or inspector to produce documents (including information recorded in any form) obtained or generated by him during the course of his investigation to either the Secretary of State himself or a subsequent inspector appointed. Where any document is not in hard copy form, a copy of the document must be produced either in hard copy form or in a form from which a hard copy can be readily obtained.

The Secretary of State may take copies of, or extracts from, a document produced to him under these provisions. He may also direct a person to whom these provisions apply to inform him of any matters that came to that person's knowledge as a result of his investigation.

For the above purposes, reference to the investigation of a former inspector or inspector include any investigation he conducted under *CA 1985, s 433* into the affairs of a holding company or subsidiary (see **25.2**).

[*CA 1985, s 446E*].

## 25.10    Resignation, removal and replacement of inspectors

The following provisions apply where an inspector is appointed after 30 September 2007.

**Resignation and revocation of appointment.** An inspector may resign by notice in writing to the Secretary of State and the Secretary of State may revoke the appointment of an inspector by notice in writing to the inspector.

[*CA 1985, s 446C*].

**Appointment of replacement inspectors.** Where an inspector resigns or dies, or an inspector's appointment is revoked, the Secretary of State

• may appoint one or more inspectors to continue the investigation; and

• must secure that at least one inspector continues the investigation unless

    (i)    he could give any replacement inspector a direction to terminate the inspection under *CA 1985, s 446B* (see **25.9**); and

    (ii)    such a direction would under those provisions result in a final report not being made.

Any such appointment is treated as an appointment under the same provision of this chapter under which the former inspector was appointed.

For the above purposes, reference to an investigation include any investigation the former inspector conducted under *CA 1985, s 433* into the affairs of a holding company or subsidiary (see **25.2**). [*CA 1985, s 446D; CA 2006, s 1036*].

## 25.11  REQUISITION AND SEIZURE OF BOOKS AND PAPERS

Various powers set out below are available to the Secretary of State under *CA 1985, ss 447–451A* to require the production of documents, etc and to enter premises and seize books and papers.

## 25.12  Power to require production of documents

The Secretary of State may

(a)  give directions to a company requiring it to

- produce such 'documents' (or documents of such description) as may be specified in the directions; and

- provide such information (or information of such description) as may be so specified; and

(b)  authorise a person (an investigator) to require the company or any other person to

- produce such documents (or documents of such description) as the investigator may specify;

- provide such information (or information of such description) as the investigator may specify.

Any such requirement must be complied with at such time and place as may be specified in the directions or by the investigator (as the case may be). The Secretary of State or the investigator (as the case may be) may take copies of, or extracts from, a document so produced.

The production of a document under the above provisions does not affect any lien which a person has on the document.

'*Documents*' include information recorded in any form. The power to require production of a document includes power, in the case of a document not in hard copy form, to require production of a copy of it in hard copy form or in a form from which a hard copy can be readily obtained.

[*CA 1985, s 447*].

The *s 447* requirement has been extended to include a requirement to provide, not only an explanation of the contents of a document, but also to confirm its date of creation, authorship, provenance, accuracy, completeness, intended purpose, significance, and the use to which it was put (*Attorney General's Reference (No 2 of 1998)* [2000] QB 412).

A company or person can be required to provide an explanation of any discrepancy between documents produced under *s 447*, and between documents and explanations given under that section.

**Penalties**. If a person fails to comply with a requirement imposed under the above provisions, the inspector, the Secretary of State or an investigator (as the case may be) may certify the fact in writing to the court. If, after hearing any witnesses who may be produced against or on behalf of the alleged offender and any statement which may be offered in defence, the court is satisfied that the offender failed without reasonable excuse to comply with the requirement, it may deal with him as if he had been guilty of contempt of the court.

[*CA 1985, s 453C*].

**Use of information provided in evidence**. A statement made by a person in compliance with a requirement under *CA 1985, s 447* above may be used in evidence against him. But in criminal proceedings in which the person is charged with an offence (other than an offence under *CA 1985, s 451* (see **25.17**) or *Perjury Act 1911, s 5, Criminal Law (Consolidation) (Scotland) Act 1995, s 44(2)* or *Perjury (Northern Ireland) Order 1979, Art 10* (false statements made otherwise than on oath)

•      no evidence relating to the statement may be adduced by or on behalf of the prosecution, and

•      no question relating to it may be asked by or on behalf of the prosecution

unless evidence relating to it is adduced or a question relating to it is asked in the proceedings by or on behalf of that person.

[*CA 1985, s 447A*].

### 25.13  Entry and search of premises

A justice of the peace (in Scotland, a justice of the peace or a sheriff) may issue a warrant if satisfied, on information on oath (in Scotland, on evidence on oath) given by the Secretary of State or an inspector or investigator that there are reasonable grounds for believing that

(a)      there are, on any premises, 'documents' whose production has been required under any of the provisions dealt with in this chapter but which have not been produced in compliance therewith; or

(b)      an offence has been committed for which the penalty on conviction on indictment is imprisonment for a term of not less than two years, and that there are on any premises documents relating to whether the offence has been committed, provided

•      the Secretary of State, inspector or investigator has power under the provisions in this chapter to require their production; and

•      there are reasonable grounds for believing that if production was so required the documents would not be produced but would be removed from the premises, hidden, tampered with or destroyed.

'*Document*' for these purposes includes information recorded in any form.

The warrant continues in force for one month beginning with the day on which it is issued. It authorises a constable, together with any other person named on it and any other constables, to

•      enter the specified premises (using reasonable force if necessary);

•      search the premises and take possession of any documents appearing to be those referred to in (*a*) or (*b*) above (or take steps necessary to protect or prevent interference with those documents);

•      take copies; and

•      require any person named in the warrant to provide an explanation of them or state where they may be found.

See, however, **25.21** for privileged information.

A warrant issued under (*b*) above may also authorise such action in respect of other documents relevant to the investigation.

Documents taken possession of under these provisions may be retained for three months or, if within that period any proceedings to which the documents are relevant are commenced against any person for a criminal offence, until the conclusion of those proceedings.

Any person intentionally obstructing the exercise of rights under these provisions, or failing (without reasonable excuse) to provide an explanation of a document or state where it may be found when required to do so, is guilty of an offence. A person guilty of such an offence is liable (i) on conviction on indictment, to a fine; and (ii) on summary conviction, to a fine not exceeding the statutory maximum. See **29.1** Offences and Legal Proceedings for the statutory maximum.

[*CA 1985, s 448*].

Where an offence under the above provisions is committed by a body corporate, every officer of the body who is in default also commits the offence. For this purpose, any person who purports to act as a director, manager or secretary of the body is treated as an officer of the company and, if the body is a company, any shadow director is treated as an officer of the company (see **18.2(2)** Directors).

[*CA 1985, s 453D*].

## 25.14 Protection in relation to information provided to Secretary of State

A person who makes a 'relevant' disclosure is not liable, by reason only of that disclosure, in any proceedings relating to a breach of an obligation of confidence – for example, of any obligation under the *Data Protection Act 1998*. A 'relevant disclosure' is a disclosure which satisfies each of the following conditions.

(1)     It is made to the Secretary of State otherwise than in compliance with a requirement under the provisions of this chapter relating to investigations (ie it relates to information which is volunteered rather than provided in response to the exercise of an investigation power).

(2)     It is of a kind that the person making the disclosure *could* be required to make under the provisions of this chapter (ie it is relevant to a matter which could be investigated and is not covered by the provisions in **25.21** relating to privileged information).

(3)     The person who makes the disclosure does so in good faith and in the reasonable belief that the disclosure is capable of assisting the Secretary of State for the purposes of carrying out an investigation. The 'good faith' requirement means, for example, that disclosure motivated by a desire to cause harm to a business competitor is not protected.

(4)     The information disclosed is not more than is reasonably necessary for the purpose of assisting the Secretary of State in carrying out an investigation.

(5)     The disclosure is not

•       prohibited by virtue of any enactment (as defined in *CA 2006, s 1293*) whenever passed or made; or

•       made by a person carrying on the business of banking or by a lawyer and involves the disclosure of information in respect of which he owes an obligation of confidence in that capacity.

[*CA 1985, s 448A*].

## 25.15 Security of information obtained

Where information (in whatever form) is obtained

•       in pursuance of a requirement imposed under **25.12**,

•       by means of a relevant disclosure within **25.14**, or

# 25.15 Investigations

- by an investigator in consequence of the exercise of his powers under *CA 1985, s 453A* (see **25.19**),

it must not be disclosed unless the disclosure is

- made to a '*specified person*' (ie the Secretary of State, the Department of Enterprise, Trade and Investment for Northern Ireland, the Treasury, the Lord Advocate, the Director of Public Prosecutions, the Director of Public Prosecutions for Northern Ireland, the Financial Services Authority, a constable, a procurator fiscal, or the Scottish Ministers) or any officer or employee of that person; or

- of a 'specified description'. See *CA 1985, Sch 15D* for a large number of disclosures allowed, most of which are for the purpose of enabling or assisting a specified person to exercise a specific function.

Nothing in the above provisions

- prohibits the disclosure of information if it is, or has been, available to the public from any other source; or

- authorises the making of a disclosure in contravention of the *Data Protection Act 1998*.

A person who discloses any information in contravention of the above provisions is guilty of an offence. A person guilty of such an offence is liable (i) on conviction on indictment, to imprisonment for a term not exceeding two years or a fine (or both); and (ii) on summary conviction, to imprisonment for a term not exceeding twelve months (six months in Scotland or, with effect from 1 October 2009, Northern Ireland) or to a fine not exceeding the statutory maximum (or both). See **9.1** OFFENCES AND LEGAL PROCEEDINGS for the statutory maximum.

[*CA 1985, s 449, Schs 15C, 15D*].

Where an offence under the above provisions is committed by a body corporate, every officer of the body who is in default also commits the offence. For this purpose, any person who purports to act as a director, manager or secretary of the body is treated as an officer of the company and, if the body is a company, any shadow director is treated as an officer of the company (see **18.1(2)** DIRECTORS).

[*CA 1985, s 453D*].

## 25.16 Punishment for destroying, mutilating etc company documents

An officer of a company (or an officer of an authorised insurance company which is not a body corporate) who

(a) destroys, mutilates or falsifies a 'document' affecting or relating to the company's property or affairs (or is privy to such destruction, etc),

(b) makes a false entry in such a document (or is privy to any such act), or

(c) fraudulently either parts with, alters or makes an omission in any such document (or is privy to any such fraudulent act or omission)

is guilty of an offence unless, in the case of acts within (*a*) or (*b*) above, he proves that he had no intention to conceal the state of affairs of the company or to defeat the law. A person guilty of such an offence is liable (i) on conviction on indictment, to imprisonment for a term not exceeding seven years or a fine (or both); and (ii) on summary conviction, to imprisonment for a term not exceeding twelve months (six months in Scotland or, with effect from 1 October 2009, Northern Ireland) or to a fine not exceeding the statutory maximum (or both). See **29.1** Offences and Legal Proceedings for the statutory maximum.

'*Document*' includes information recorded in any form.

[*CA 1985, s 450*].

Where an offence under the above provisions is committed by a body corporate, every officer of the body who is in default also commits the offence. For this purpose, any person who purports to act as a director, manager or secretary of the body is treated as an officer of the company and is, if the body is a company, any shadow director.

[*CA 1985, s 453D*].

### 25.17  Punishment for furnishing false information

A person commits an offence if, in purporting to comply with a requirement under *CA 1985, s 447* (see **25.12**) to provide information, he

- provides information which he knows to be false in a material particular, or

- recklessly provides information which is false in a material particular.

A person guilty of such an offence is liable (i) on conviction on indictment, to imprisonment for a term not exceeding two years or a fine (or both); and (ii) on summary conviction, to imprisonment for a term not exceeding twelve months (six months in Scotland and, with effect from 1 October 2009, Northern Ireland) or to a fine not exceeding the statutory maximum (or both). See **29.1** Offences and Legal Proceedings for the statutory maximum.

[*CA 1985, s 451*].

Where an offence under the above provisions is committed by a body corporate, every officer of the body who is in default also commits the offence. For this purpose, any person who purports to act as a director, manager or secretary of the body is treated as an officer of the company and is, if the body is a company, any shadow director.

[*CA 1985, s 453D*].

### 25.18  Disclosure of information by Secretary of State or inspector

Information obtained under *CA 1985, ss 434–446E* (see **25.3** to **25.10**) or by an inspector using his powers under *CA 1985, s 453A* (see **25.19**) may be disclosed as follows.

(a)    The Secretary of State may

- disclose any such information to any person to whom, or for any purpose for which, disclosure is permitted under *CA 1985, s 449* (see **25.15**); or

- authorise or require an inspector to disclose such information to any such person or for any such purpose.

(b)    Any such information may be disclosed by an inspector to

- another inspector;

- a person appointed under

(i)    *FSMA 2000, s 167* (general investigations),

(ii)   *FSMA 2000, s 168* (investigations in particular cases),

# 25.18 Investigations

        (iii)    *FSMA 2000, s 169(1)(b)* (investigation in support of overseas regulator);

        (iv)    *FSMA 2000, s 284* (investigations into affairs of certain collective investment schemes), or

        (v)    regulations made under *FSMA 2000, s 262(2)(k)* (investigations into open-ended investment companies),

to conduct an investigation; or

- a person authorised to exercise powers under

        (i)    *CA 1985, s 447* (see **25.12**); or

        (ii)    *CA 1989, s 84* (exercise of powers to assist overseas regulatory authority).

Any information which may be so disclosed may also be disclosed to any officer or servant of that person.

The Secretary of State may also disclose any information obtained under *CA 1985, s 444* (see **25.8**) to

- the company whose ownership was the subject of the investigation,
- any member of the company,
- any person whose conduct was investigated in the course of the investigation,
- the auditor of the company, or
- any person whose financial interests appear to the Secretary of State to be affected by matters covered by the investigation.

[*CA 1985, s 451A*].

## 25.19 POWER TO ENTER AND REMAIN ON PREMISES

If an inspector appointed under **25.2** or **25.7** or an investigator authorised under **25.12** is

(a)    authorised by the Secretary of State, and

(b)    thinks that to do so will materially assist him in the exercise of his functions,

he may at all reasonable times

(i)    require entry to any of a company's premises which he believes are used (wholly or partly) for the purposes of the company's business; and

(ii)    remain there for such period as he thinks necessary for the purposes of (*b*) above.

In exercising these powers, an inspector or investigator may be accompanied by such other persons as he thinks appropriate.

Anyone who intentionally obstructs a person lawfully acting under these provisions is guilty of an offence and liable (i) on conviction on indictment, to a fine; and (ii) on summary conviction, to a fine not exceeding the statutory maximum. See **29.1** OFFENCES AND LEGAL PROCEEDINGS for the statutory maximum.

[*CA 1985, s 453A*].

Where an offence under the above provisions is committed by a body corporate, every officer of the body who is in default also commits the offence. For this purpose, any person who purports to act as a director, manager or secretary of the body is treated as an officer of the company and is, if the body is a company, any shadow director.

[*CA 1985, s 453D*].

## 25.20 Procedural matters

At the time an inspector or investigator seeks to enter the premises, he must produce evidence of his identity and evidence of his appointment or authorisation (as the case may be). Any person accompanying the inspector or investigator must also produce evidence of his identity.

**Written statement.** As soon as is practicable after obtaining entry, the inspector or investigator must give a written statement with details of his powers and the rights and obligations of the company, occupier and the persons present on the premises. The written statement must contain the list of matters contained in the *Companies Act 1985 (Power to Enter and Remain on Premises: Procedural) Regulations 2005 (SI 2005 No 684)* as follows:

- A statement that the inspector/investigator has been appointed/authorised by the Secretary of State to carry out an investigation and a reference to the enactment under which that appointment/authorisation was made.

- A statement that the inspector/investigator has been authorised by the Secretary of State under *CA 1985, s 453A* to exercise the powers in that section.

- A description of the conditions which are required by *CA 1985, s 453A(1)* to be satisfied (see **25.19**(*a*) and (*b*)) before an inspector/investigator can act.

- A description of the powers in *CA 1985, s 453A(2)* (see **25.19**(i) and (ii)).

- A statement that the inspector/investigator must, at the time he seeks to enter premises, produce evidence of his identity and evidence of his appointment/authorisation.

- A statement that any person accompanying the inspector/investigator when that person seeks to enter the premises must, at that time, produce evidence of his identity.

- A statement that entry to premises may be refused to an inspector, investigator or other person fails to produce the required evidence.

- A statement that the company, occupier and the persons present on the premises may be required by the inspector/investigator, while he is on the premises, to comply with any powers the inspector/investigator may have by virtue of his appointment/authorisation to require documents or information.

- A statement that the inspector/investigator is not permitted to use any force in exercising his powers under *CA 1985, s 453A* and is not permitted during the course of his visit to search the premises or to seize any document or other thing on the premises.

- A description of the effect of the penalty provisions in *CA 1985, s 453C* (see below) as it relates to a requirement imposed by an inspector/investigator under *CA 1985, s 453A*.

- A statement that it is an offence intentionally to obstruct an inspector, investigator or other person lawfully acting under these provisions.

- A description of the inspector's/investigator's obligations to prepare a written record of the visit and to give a copy of the record, when requested, to the company and any other occupier of the premises.

- Information about how any person entitled to receive a copy of that record can request it.

The written statement must be given to an *'appropriate recipient'*, that is

(a) where the inspector/investigator thinks that the company is the sole occupier of the premises, a person who is present on the premises and who appears to the inspector/investigator to be

    (i) an officer of the company; or

    (ii) a person otherwise engaged in the business of the company if the inspector/investigator thinks that no officer of the company is present on the premises; and

(b) if the inspector/investigator thinks that the company is not the occupier or sole occupier of the premises, a person within (a) above or (if different) a person who is present on the premises and who appears to the inspector/investigator to be an occupier of the premises or otherwise in charge of them.

If, during the time the inspector/investigator is on the premises, there is no person present who appears to him to be an appropriate recipient, he must as soon as reasonably practicable send to the company a notice of the fact and time that the visit took place, together with the written statement.

**Written record.** As soon as reasonably practicable after exercising his powers under these provisions, the inspector/investigator must prepare a written record of the visit. He must give a copy of the record, if requested, to the company or, in a case where the company is not the sole occupier of the premises, an occupier.

The written record must contain the following information.

- The name by which the company in relation to which the powers were exercised was registered at the time of the authorisation.

- The company's registered number at that time.

- The postal address of the premises visited.

- The name of the inspector/investigator who visited the premises and the name of any person accompanying him.

- The date and time when the inspector/investigator entered the premises and the duration of his visit.

- The name (if known) of the person to whom the inspector/investigator and any person accompanying him produced evidence of their identity. (If the name is not known, an account of how he produced that evidence.)

- The name (if known) of the person to whom the inspector/investigator produced evidence of his appointment/authorisation (as the case may be). (If the name is not known, an account of how he produced that evidence.)

- The name (if known) of the person who admitted the inspector/investigator to the premises. (If the name is not known, an account of how he was admitted to the premises.)

- The name (if known) of every appropriate recipient to whom the inspector/investigator, while on the premises, gave a written statement. (If any name is not known, an account of how the written statement was given to that person.)

- The name (if known) of any person physically present on the premises (to the inspector's/investigator's knowledge) at any time during his visit (other than another inspector/investigator, a person accompanying the inspector/investigator or a person to whom a copy of the written statement was given) and with whom the inspector/investigator communicated in relation to that person's presence on the premises.

- A record of any apparent failure by any person during the course of the visit to the premises to comply with any requirement imposed by the inspector/investigator.

- A record of any conduct by any person during the course of the visit to the premises which the inspector/investigator believes amounted to the intentional obstruction of him, or anyone accompanying him, in the lawful exercise of the power to enter and remain on the premises.

[*CA 1985, s 453B*].

**Penalties.** If a person fails to comply with a requirement imposed under the above provisions, the inspector, the Secretary of State or an investigator (as the case may be) may certify the fact in writing to the court. If, after hearing any witnesses who may be produced against or on behalf of the alleged offender and any statement which may be offered in defence, the court is satisfied that the offender failed without reasonable excuse to comply with the requirement, it may deal with him as if he had been guilty of contempt of the court.

[*CA 1985, s 453C*].

## 25.21 PRIVILEGED INFORMATION

There are two categories of privileged information under the provisions described at **25.2** to **25.17**.

**Legal professional privilege.** Nothing in *CA 1985, ss 431–446E* (see **25.2** to **25.10**) compels the disclosure by any person to the Secretary of State or to an inspector appointed by him of information in respect of which

(a) in an action in the High Court, a claim to legal professional privilege, or

(b) in an action in the Court of Session a claim to confidentiality of communications

could be maintained.

Similarly, nothing in *CA 1985, ss 447–451* (**25.12** to **25.17**)

- compels the production by any person of a document or the disclosure by any person of information in respect of which a claim under (*a*) or (*b*) above could be maintained; or

- authorises the taking of possession of any such document which is in the person's possession.

Despite the above, a lawyer may be compelled to disclose the name and address of his client.

**Obligation of confidence.** Unless the making of the requirement is authorised by the Secretary of State, nothing in *CA 1985, ss 434* or *443* (see **25.3** and **25.7**) requires a person to disclose information or produce documents in respect of which he owes an obligation of confidence by virtue of carrying on a banking business, unless either

- that person, or the person to whom the obligation is owed, is the company or other body corporate under investigation, or

- the person to whom the obligation is owed consents to the disclosure or production.

Similarly, under *CA 1985, s 447* (see **25.12**), the Secretary of State must not require (or authorise a person to require)

- the production by a person carrying on a banking business of a document relating to a customer's affairs, or

- the disclosure by him of information relating to those affairs,

unless

- it is necessary to do so for the purpose of investigating the affairs of the person carrying on the banking business;

- the customer is a person on whom a requirement has been imposed under *CA 1985, s 447*; or

- the customer is a person on whom a requirement to produce information or documents has been imposed by an investigator appointed by the Secretary of State under *FSMA 2000, s 171* or *s 173*. [*CA 1985, s 452*].

## 25.22 INVESTIGATION OF OVERSEAS COMPANIES

The provisions of this chapter (apart from **25.2(a)**, **25.7** and **25.8**) apply to bodies corporate incorporated outside the UK which carry on, or have carried on, business in the UK subject to such modifications and adaptations as the Secretary of State may specify by Regulations made by statutory instrument.

[*CA 1985, s 453*].

## 25.23 ORDERS IMPOSING RESTRICTIONS ON SHARES

The Secretary of State may, by order, impose restrictions on shares under *CA 1985, s 445* (see **25.7** and **25.8**). So long as shares are directed to be subject to such restrictions

(a)     any transfer or issue of those shares, or of the right to be issued with them, is void;

(b)     no voting rights are exercisable in respect of the shares;

(c)     no further shares may be issued in right of them or in pursuance of any offer made to their holder; and

(d)     (except in a liquidation) no payment may be made of any sums due from the company on them (whether in respect of capital or otherwise).

[*CA 1985, s 454(1)*].

As regards (*a*) above, any agreement to transfer the shares (or, in the case of unissued shares, any agreement to transfer the right to be issued with them) is also void (except as under **25.25**).

[*CA 1985, s 454(2)*].

As regards (*c*) and (*d*) above, an agreement to transfer any right to be issued with other shares in right of those shares (except as under **25.25**), or to receive any payment on them (other than in a liquidation), is void.

[*CA 1985, s 454(3)*].

### 25.24  Punishment for attempted evasion of restrictions

Subject to the terms of any direction by the Secretary of State and the provisions in **25.24**, a person commits an offence if he

- exercises (or purports to exercise) any right to dispose of any shares which, to his knowledge, are for the time being subject to restrictions under **25.23**, or of any right to be issued with such shares;

- votes in respect of any such shares (whether as holder or proxy), or appoints a proxy to vote in respect of them;

- being the holder of any such shares, fails to notify the existence of the restrictions to any person whom he knows is entitled (apart from the restrictions) to vote in respect of the shares (whether as holder or proxy) but whom he does not know to be aware of the restrictions; or

- being the holder of any such shares, or entitled to any right to be issued with other shares in right of them, or to receive any payment on them (other than in a liquidation), enters into any agreement which is void under *CA 1985, s 454(2) or (3)* (see **25.23**).

If shares in a company are issued in contravention of the restrictions, an offence is committed by the company and every officer of the company who is in default.

A person guilty of an offence under the above provisions is liable (i) on conviction on indictment, to a fine; and (ii) on summary conviction, to a fine not exceeding the statutory maximum. See **29.1** OFFENCES AND LEGAL PROCEEDINGS for the statutory maximum.

[*CA 1985, s 455*].

### 25.25  Relaxation and removal of restrictions

Where shares in a company are subject to restrictions because of an order under **25.23**, any aggrieved person may apply to the court for an order directing that the shares should be no longer subject to the restrictions.

[*CA 1985, s 456(1)(2)*].

Subject to below, an order lifting the restrictions may be made only if

- the relevant facts about the shares have been disclosed to the company and no unfair advantage has accrued to any person as a result of the earlier failure to make that disclosure; or

- the shares are to be transferred for valuable consideration and the court or the Secretary of State approves the transfer. [*CA 1985, s 456(3)*].

Where the court is satisfied that an order unfairly affects the rights of third parties, it may direct that specified acts by such persons do not constitute a breach of the restrictions and such an order is not subject to *CA 1985, s 456(3)* above.

[*CA 1985, s 456(1A)*].

Where shares in a company are subject to restrictions, the company or the Secretary of State may make an application to the court for the shares to be sold. The court may then order the shares to be sold, subject to its approval as to the sale, and may also direct that the restrictions be lifted. [*CA 1985, s 456(4)*]. Following such an order, the court may (on application by the Secretary of State, the company, the person appointed to effect the sale or by any person interested in the shares) make such further order relating to the sale or transfer of the shares as it thinks fit.

[*CA 1985, s 456(5)*].

The proceeds of sale (less costs) of shares sold in pursuance of a court order under *CA 1985, s 456(4)* above must be paid into court for the benefit of those beneficially interested in the shares. Any of these persons may apply to the court for payment of the whole or part of the proceeds which the court must pay together with any interest (but subject to retaining an appropriate proportion of the proceeds for other persons with a beneficial interest in the shares). Costs of a successful application under *CA 1985, s 456(4)* or *(5)* above may, if the court so orders, be a prior charge on the sale proceeds before any person interested in the shares receives any part of the proceeds. [*CA 1985, s 457*].

An order lifting any restrictions under **25.23**, if it is made under *CA 1985, s 456(4)* or expressed to be made with a view to permitting the transfer of the shares, may continue the restrictions not to issue further shares or pay any sums due on those shares (see **25.23**(*c*) and (*d*)), in whole or part, so far as they relate to any right acquired or offer made before the transfer. *CA 1985, s 456(3)* above does not apply to an order directing that such restrictions cease to apply.

[*CA 1985, s 456(6)(7)*].

# 26 Members

**Cross-references.** See 9 CLASS RIGHTS; 44 SECURITIES: CERTIFICATION AND TRANSFER; 45 SHARES.

## 26.1 THE MEMBERS OF A COMPANY

There is no definition of 'shareholder' in *CA 2006* instead the more general term 'members' is used. The 'members' of a company are defined in *CA 2006* as

- the subscribers of a company's memorandum who are deemed to have agreed to become members of the company and, on its registration, become members and must be entered as such in its register of members (see **38.6** REGISTERS); and

- every other person who agrees to become a member of a company, and whose name is entered in its register of members (see **38.6** REGISTERS).

Where an election is in force under *CA 2006, s 128B* (see **38.9** option to keep members' information on the central register) the requirement to enter particulars of members in the company register of members does not apply and the reference to "every other person . . . whose name is entered in its register of members" has effect as if that reference were a reference to a person to whom the following steps have been taken

- the person's name has been delivered to the Registrar of Companies under *CA 2006, s 128E*; and

- the document containing that information has been registered by the Registrar of Companies.

[*CA 2006, s 112; SBEE 2015, s 94, Sch 5, para 13; SI 2016 No 321, Reg 6*].

The bearer of a share warrant may, if the articles so provide, be deemed a member of the company, either to the full extent or for any purposes defined in the articles.

[*CA 2006, s 122(3)*].

# 26.1 Members

**Who may be members.**

- A *company* may normally hold shares in *another* company. But see **34 PURCHASE OF OWN SHARES** for restrictions on a company subscribing for or purchasing its own shares and **26.7** for prohibition on a subsidiary being a member of its own holding company.

- In England and Wales, *minors* (ie persons under the age of 18) may become shareholders unless the articles forbid this. On reaching majority, the minor may repudiate the contract and avoid liability for future calls but cannot recover money paid for the allotment of the shares as there has not been a total failure of consideration (*Steinberg v Scala (Leeds) Ltd* [1923] 2 Ch 452, 92 LJKB 944, CA). In Scotland, under *Age of Legal Capacity (Scotland) Act 1991*, a person has full legal capacity from the age of 16 subject to the right, while under the age of 21, to apply to the court for the setting aside of a 'prejudicial transaction' which was entered into between the ages of 16 and 18. Prior to the age of 16, contracts made will be void subject to an exception where the terms of the contract are not unreasonable and the subject matter is of a kind commonly entered into by someone of his or her age and circumstances.

- A *bankrupt* may continue to be a shareholder even after his beneficial interest has vested in the trustee in bankruptcy, unless the articles provide otherwise. He must, however vote as directed by the trustee.

- *Personal representatives and trustees in bankruptcy.* See **44.9 SECURITIES: CERTIFICATION AND TRANSFERS.**

- *Partnerships*, even though not legal persons in England and Wales, may be registered as members under the partnership name (*Land Credit Co of Ireland, Re, Weikersheim's Case* (1873) 8 Ch App 831).

**Trustees and nominees as members.** Members are defined as legal owners, that is they are the person whose names appear on the register of members. Legal and beneficial ownerships may however be separate and if that is the case the basic provision in *CA 2006* is that company only need to be concerned with the rights of the legal owner. *Section 126* of *CA 2006* provides that no notice of any trust, express or implied or constructive, must be entered on the register of members in the case of companies incorporated in England and Wales or Northern Ireland.

The company's articles also usually regulate legal and beneficial ownership of shares and the rights of beneficial owners

Where standard articles have been adopted, see

- *Table A, Reg 5*

- *Model Articles, Art 23* (private companies)

- *Model Articles, Art 45* (public companies)

Set out in **APPENDIX 4 STANDARD ARTICLES OF ASSOCIATION.**

The company is not therefore required to enquire as to whether any transfer is within the powers of the trustees and is not liable for registering a transfer which is in breach of trust (*Simpson v Molson's Bank* [1895] AC 270, PC). Equally, as the company cannot recognise any interest of a beneficiary in the shares, it has no lien on shares held by trustees for a debt due to it by a beneficiary (*Perkins, Re, ex p Mexican Santa Barbara Mining Co* (1890) 24 QBD 613, CA).

The law has however developed in response to the Final Report of the Company Law Review Steering Group who said (Vol 1 at para 7.1) that it is important that the law should provide "convenient mechanisms by which the beneficial owners or their representatives can participate in governance, and that any unnecessary obstacle to their participation should be removed" but that 'it is equally essential that any changes in the law should call into question the legal title of the registered holder'.

To that end *CA 2006, Pt 9* provides the following

- the right for members to nominate others to enjoy or exercise the rights of members (*CA 2006, s 145* see **26.2**)

- the right for the members of traded companies to nominate others to enjoy information rights (*CA 2006, s 146* see **26.4**)

- the right of the legal owner of shares to exercise rights in different ways (*CA 2006, s 152* see **26.5**) and

- the right for beneficial owners to make certain requests (*CA 2006, s 153* see **26.6**).

## 26.2    EXERCISE OF MEMBERS' RIGHTS

A member can nominate another person or persons to enjoy rights of the member in relation to the company. These fall into two categories.

(a)    Where the articles permit such nomination, anything which can be done by or in relation to the member can be done instead by, or in relation to, the nominated person. See **26.3 (this applies to all companies)**.

(b)    In the case of a company whose shares are admitted to trading on a regulated market, a member who holds shares on behalf of another person can nominate that person to enjoy information rights (whether or not the articles specifically permit nomination). See **26.4 (this applies to traded companies only)**.

## 26.3    Effect of provision of articles as to enjoyment or exercise of members' rights

*CA 2006, s 145* enables a member to nominate another person or persons to enjoy or exercise the rights of the member but only if provision is made in the company's articles. If the articles do, include such a provision then so far as is necessary to give effect to that provision, anything required/authorised by the *Companies Acts* to be done by or in relation to the member must/may instead be done by or in relation to the nominated person (or each of them) as if he were a member of the company.

This applies, in particular, to the rights conferred by

- *CA 2006, ss 291 and 293* (right to be sent proposed written resolution, see **42.7** and **42.8** RESOLUTIONS AND MEETINGS);

- *CA 2006, s 292* (right to require circulation of written resolution, see **42.8** RESOLUTIONS AND MEETINGS);

- *CA 2006, s 303* (right to require directors to call general meeting, see **42.14** RESOLUTIONS AND MEETINGS);

- *CA 2006, s 310* (right to notice of general meetings, see **42.17** RESOLUTIONS AND MEETINGS);

- *CA 2006, s 314* (right to require circulation of a statement, see **42.21** RESOLUTIONS AND MEETINGS);

## 26.3 Members

- In relation to meetings notice of which is given on or after 3 August 2009, *CA 2006, s 319A* (right to ask question at a meeting of a traded company, see **42.25** RESOLUTIONS AND MEETINGS);

- *CA 2006, s 324* (right to appoint a proxy to act at a meeting, see **42.28** RESOLUTIONS AND MEETINGS);

- *CA 2006, s 338* (right to require circulation of resolution for AGM of a public company, see **42.33** RESOLUTIONS AND MEETINGS);

- In relation to meetings notice of which is given on or after 3 August 2009, *CA 2006, s 338A* (traded companies: members power to include matters in business dealt with at AGM, see **42.33** RESOLUTIONS AND MEETINGS); and

- *CA 2006, s 423* (right to be sent a copy of annual accounts and reports, see **2.6** ACCOUNTS: GENERAL).

The above provisions do not

- confer rights enforceable against the company by anyone other than the member; and

- affect the requirements for an effective transfer or other disposition of the whole or part of a member's interest in the company.

[*CA 2006, s 145*].

## 26.4  Traded companies: nomination of persons to enjoy information rights

*Where* the shares of a company are admitted to trading on a regulated market, a member of the company who holds shares on behalf of another person may nominate that person to enjoy 'information rights'.

*'Information rights'* means

- the right to receive a copy of all communications that the company sends to its members generally (including annual accounts and reports and summary financial statements (after 1 October 2013 a strategic report will replace the summary financial statement see CHAPTER 6)), or to any class of its members that includes the person making the nomination; and

- the rights conferred by

  (i)   *CA 2006, ss 431 or 432* (right to require copies of accounts and reports, see **2.7** ACCOUNTS: GENERAL) or, before 6 April 2008, *CA 1985, s 239*; and

  (ii)  *CA 2006, s 1145* (right to require hard copy version of document or information provided in another form, see **16.34** DEALINGS WITH THIRD PARTIES).

A company need not act on a nomination purporting to relate to certain information rights only.

[*CA 2006, s 146*].

Form in which copies to be provided. If the person to be nominated wishes to receive hard copy communications, he must, before the nomination is made, request the person making the nomination to notify the company of that fact and provide an address to which such copies may be sent. If, having received such a request, the person making the nomination so notifies the company and provides the company with that address, the right of the nominated person is to receive hard copy communications. (This is subject to *CA 2006, Sch 5, paras 5–14* under which the company may take steps to enable it to communicate in electronic form or by means of a website. See **16.30** and **16.31** DEALINGS WITH THIRD PARTIES.)

If no such notification is given (or no address is provided), the nominated person is taken to have agreed that documents or information may be sent or supplied to him by the company by means of a website. That agreement may be revoked by the nominated person and does not affect his right under *CA 2006, s 1145* to require a hard copy version of a document or information provided in any other form.

[*CA 2006, s 147*].

**Termination or suspension of nomination.** The nomination is terminated in the following circumstances.

- At any time at the request of the member or of the nominated person.

- If the member or the nominated person

  (i)    in the case of an individual, dies or becomes bankrupt; and

  (ii)   in the case of a body corporate, is dissolved or is the subject of a winding-up order otherwise than for the purposes of reconstruction.

- Where the company

  (i)    enquires of a nominated person whether he wishes to retain information rights; and

  (ii)   does not receive a response within the period of 28 days beginning with the date on which the company's enquiry was sent.

  In such a case, the nomination ceases to have effect at the end of that period. Such an enquiry is not to be made of a person more than once in any 12-month period.

The effect of any nominations made by a member is suspended

- at any time when there are more nominated persons than the member has shares in the company; and

- where

  (i)    the member holds different classes of shares with different information rights, and

  (ii)   there are more nominated persons than he has shares conferring a particular right,

  to the extent that they confer that right.

The termination or suspension of a nomination means that the company is not required to act on it. But it does not prevent the company from continuing to do so, to such extent or for such period as it thinks fit.

[*CA 2006, s 148*].

**Information as to possible rights in relation to voting.** Where a company sends a copy of a notice of a meeting to a nominated person, the copy of the notice must be accompanied by a statement that

- he may have a right under an agreement between him and the member by whom he was nominated to be appointed, or to have someone else appointed, as a proxy for the meeting; and

- if he has no such right or does not wish to exercise it, he may have a right under such an agreement to give instructions to the member as to the exercise of voting rights.

CA 2006, s 325 (notice of meeting to contain statement of member's rights in relation to appointment of proxy, see **42.28 RESOLUTIONS AND MEETINGS**) does not apply to the copy, and the company must either omit the notice required by that section or include it but state that it does not apply to the nominated person. [CA 2006, s 149].

**Status of rights**.

Enjoyment by the nominated person of

- information rights (as defined above), and

- where applicable, the right to hard copy communications and the information as to possible voting rights

is enforceable against the company by the member as if they were rights conferred by the company's articles.

Any enactment, and any provision of the company's articles, having effect in relation to communications with members has a corresponding effect (subject to any necessary adaptations) in relation to communications with the nominated person. In particular

- where the members of a company entitled to receive a document or information are determined as at a date or time before it is sent or supplied, the company need not send or supply it to a nominated person

    (i)    whose nomination was received by the company after that date or time; or

    (ii)   if that date or time falls in a period of suspension of his nomination; and

- where the right of a member to receive a document or information depends on the company having a current address for him, the same applies to any person nominated by him.

The rights conferred by the nomination are in addition to the rights of the member himself and do not affect any rights exercisable by virtue of any of the provisions mentioned in 26.3.

A failure to give effect to the rights conferred by the nomination does not affect the validity of anything done by or on behalf of the company.

[CA 2006, s 150].

## 26.5 Exercise of rights where shares held on behalf of others: exercise in different ways

Where a member holds shares in a company on behalf of more than one person

- rights attached to the shares, and

- rights under any enactment exercisable by virtue of holding the shares,

    need not all be exercised, and if exercised, need not all be exercised in the same way.

Where a member

- does not exercise all his rights, he must inform the company to what extent he is exercising the rights; and

- exercises his rights in different ways, he must inform the company of the ways in which he is exercising them and to what extent they are exercised in each way.

If a member exercises his rights but fails to give such information, the company is entitled to assume that he is exercising all his rights and is exercising them in the same way.

[*CA 2006, s 152*].

**26.6    Exercise of rights where shares held on behalf of others: members' requests**

Where a company receives a request for the purposes of

- *CA 2006, s 314* (power to require circulation of statement, see **42.21** Resolutions and Meetings),

- *CA 2006, s 338* (public companies: power to require circulation of resolution for AGM, see **42.33** Resolutions and Meetings),

- in relation to meetings notice of which is given on or after 3 August 2009, *CA 2006, s 338A* (traded companies: members power to include matters in business dealt with at AGM, see **42.33** Resolutions and Meetings),

- *CA 2006, s 342* (power to require independent report on poll, see **42.36** Resolutions and Meetings), or

- *CA 2006, s 527* (power to require website publication of audit concerns, see **8.52** Audit)

it must act under any of those provisions if it receives a request in relation to which the following conditions are met.

(a)    It is made by at least 100 persons.

(b)    It is authenticated by all the persons making it.

(c)    In the case of any of those persons who is not a member of the company, it is accompanied by a statement

    (i)    of the full name and address of a person ('the member') who is a member of the company and holds shares on behalf of that person;

    (ii)    that the member is holding those shares on behalf of that person in the course of a business;

    (iii)    of the number of shares in the company that the member holds on behalf of that person;

    (iv)    of the total amount paid up on those shares;

    (v)    that those shares are not held on behalf of anyone else or, if they are, that the other person or persons are not among the other persons making the request;

    (vi)    that some or all of those shares confer voting rights that are relevant for the purposes of making a request under the provision in question; and

    (vii)    that the person has the right to instruct the member how to exercise those rights.

(d)    In the case of any of those persons who is a member of the company, it is accompanied by a statement

(i)     that he holds shares otherwise than on behalf of another person; or

(ii)    that he holds shares on behalf of one or more other persons but those persons are not among the other persons making the request.

(e)     It is accompanied by such evidence as the company may reasonably require of the matters mentioned in (c) and (d) above.

(f)     The total amount of the sums paid up on

(i)     shares held under (c) above, and

(ii)    shares held (d) above,

divided by the number of persons making the request, is not less than £100.

(g)     The request complies with any other requirements of the provision in question as to contents, timing and otherwise.

[*CA 2006, s 153*].

## 26.7   Prohibition on subsidiary being member of its holding company

**Prohibition.** Subject to the exceptions below, a body corporate cannot be a member of a company that is its holding company and any allotment or transfer of shares in a company to its subsidiary is void. [*CA 2006, s 136*]. The provisions apply

•       in relation to a company other than a company limited by shares, but substituting references to the interest of its members as such (in whatever form) for the references to shares [*CA 2006, s 143*]; and

•       to a nominee acting on behalf of a subsidiary as to the subsidiary itself. [*CA 2006, s 144*].

**Shares acquired before prohibition became applicable.** Where a body corporate became a holder of shares in a company

(a)     before 1 July 1948 (1 April 1961 in the case of a company registered in Northern Ireland), or

(b)     on or after the relevant date in (a) and before 1 October 2009 in circumstances in which the similar prohibition in *CA 1985, s 23(1)* or *Companies (Northern Ireland) Order 1986, Art 33(1)* (or any corresponding earlier enactment), as it then had effect, did not apply, or

(c)     on or after 1 October 2009 in circumstances in which the prohibition above does not apply,

it may continue to be a member of its holding company. So long as it is permitted to continue as a member, an allotment to it of fully paid shares in the company may be validly made by way of capitalisation of reserves of the company. But, so long as the prohibition would otherwise apply, it has no right to vote in respect of the shares falling within (a)–(c) above (or any shares allotted to it in respect of those shares by way of capitalisation) on a written resolution or at meetings of the company or of any class of its members.

[*CA 2006, s 137*].

**Exceptions.**

(1)     **Subsidiary acting as personal representative or trustee**

The prohibition on a subsidiary being a member of its holding company does not apply where the subsidiary is concerned only as a personal representative or trustee unless, in the latter case, the holding company, or a subsidiary of it, is beneficially interested under the trust. In determining whether the holding company or a subsidiary is so interested, there must be disregarded:

(a)     Any interest held only by way of security for the purposes of a transaction entered into by the holding company or subsidiary in the ordinary course of a business that includes the lending or money.

(b)     Where shares in a company are held on trust for the purposes of a pension scheme or employees' share scheme, any 'residual interest' that has not vested in possession.

A *residual interest* means a 'right' of the company or subsidiary ('the residual beneficiary') to receive any of the trust property in the event of

•     all the 'liabilities arising under the scheme' having been satisfied or provided for;

•     the residual beneficiary ceasing to participate in the scheme; or

•     the trust property at any time exceeding what is necessary for satisfying the liabilities arising, or expected to arise, under the scheme.

'*Right*' includes a right dependent on the exercise of a discretion vested by the scheme in the trustee or another person, and '*liabilities arising under a scheme*' include liabilities that have resulted, or may result, from the exercise of any such discretion.

(c)     Where shares in a company are held on trust for the purposes of a pension scheme or employees' share scheme, any charge or lien on, or set-off against, any benefit or other right or interest under the scheme for the purpose of enabling the employer or former employer of a member of the scheme to obtain the discharge or a monetary obligation due to him from the member.

(d)     Where shares in a company are held on trust for the purposes of a pension scheme, any right to receive from the trustee of the scheme, or as trustee of the scheme to retain, an amount that can be recovered or retained under *Pension Schemes Act 1993, s 61* or *Pension Schemes (Northern Ireland) Act 1993, s 57* (deduction of contributions equivalent premium from refund of scheme contributions) or otherwise, as reimbursement or partial reimbursement for any contributions equivalent premium paid in connection with the scheme under *Part 3* of that *Act*.

(e)     Any rights that the company or subsidiary has in its capacity as trustee, including in particular

•     any right to recover its expenses or be remunerated out of the trust property; and

•     any right to be indemnified out of the trust property for any liability incurred by reason of any act or omission in the performance of its duties as trustee.

[*CA 2006, ss 138–140*].

(2)     **Subsidiary acting as dealer in securities**

## 26.7 Members

The prohibition on a subsidiary being a member of its holding company does not apply where the shares are held by the subsidiary in the ordinary course of its business as an 'intermediary'.

An '*intermediary*' is a person who

- carries on a *bona fide* business of dealing in securities;

- is a member of or has access to a regulated market; and

- does not carry on an '*excluded business*', ie a business that consists

  (i) wholly or mainly of making or managing investments;

  (ii) wholly or mainly in providing services to connected persons (as determined in accordance with *Corporation Taxes Act 2010, s 1122*);

  (iii) in insurance business;

  (iv) in managing or acting as trustee in relation to a pension scheme or that is carried on by the manager or trustee of such a scheme in connection with or for the purposes of such a scheme; or

  (v) in operating, or acting as trustee in relation to, a collective investment scheme or that is carried on by the operator or trustee of such a scheme in connection with or for the purposes of such a scheme.

Where

(a) a subsidiary that is a dealer in securities has purportedly acquired shares in its holding company in contravention of the prohibition above, and

(b) a person acting in good faith has agreed, for value and without notice of the contravention, to acquire shares in the holding company from

  (i) the subsidiary, or

  (ii) someone who has purportedly acquired the shares after their disposal by the subsidiary,

a transfer to that person of the shares in (*a*) above has the same effect as it would have had if their original acquisition by the subsidiary had not been in contravention of the prohibition.

[*CA 2006, ss 141, 142*].

## 26.8 MINIMUM AND MAXIMUM MEMBERSHIP

**Minimum membership**. *In relation to applications for registration received by the Registrar of Companies on or after 1 October 2009*, any company can be formed with one member.

[*CA 2006, s 7*].

*For applications received before that date* (and where the requirements for registration were met), a private company limited by shares or by guarantee could have one member but any other company had to be formed with at least two members. [*CA 1985, s 1(1)(3A)* (as amended)]. If the company carries on business without having at least two members for more than six months, a person who is a member of the company and knows that it is carrying on a business with only one member is liable (jointly and severally with the company) for the payment of the company's debts contracted after that period and whilst a member of the company. For these purposes, reference to a member does not include the company itself where it is a member by virtue of its holding shares as treasury shares. [*CA 1985, s 24* (as amended; *SI 2008 No 2860, Sch 1*]. The repeal of *CA 1985, s 24* does not affect any liability under that section for debts of the company contracted before 1 October 2009.

[*SI 2008 No 2860, Sch 2 para 24*].

**Maximum membership.** There is no maximum number of members unless the company was incorporated between 1 July 1948 and 21 December 1980 and adopted *Table A, 1948* and has not since changed its articles. In such a case, there is an upper limit of 50 members (excluding employees and past employees who held when employed, and have continued to hold, shares in the company). For these purposes, joint holders are treated as a single member. There is no equivalent article in subsequent standard articles.

## 26.9    MEMBERS' POWERS, RIGHTS AND LIABILITIES

**Reserve power.** Power to manage the company is vested in the directors under the articles of association which (in the case of the Model Articles) provide that the directors are responsible for the management of the company's business. The members are however given reserve power. They may, in a case where a company has adopted the Model Articles, decide by special resolution to direct the directors to take, or refrain from taking, specified action (see *Art 4* of the *Model Articles* – APPENDIX 4).

**Rights in general.** No member has any right to any item of property owned by the company for he has no legal or equitable interest in it. The company's assets are its own property not the property of its members. See *Re George Newman & Co*, CA [1895] 1 Ch 674 and *Short v Treasury Comrs* [1948] 1 KB 116, [1947] 2 All ER 298, HL, where it was held that shareholders are not, in the eyes of the law, part owners of the undertaking which is something different from the totality of the shareholding. Neither does a member have an insurable interest in any particular assets which the company holds (*Macaura v Northern Assurance Co Ltd* [1925] AC 619, 94 LJPC 154, HL). A member is merely entitled to a *share* in the company and shares are merely a right of participation in the company on the terms of the articles of association (*Prudential Assurance Co Ltd v Newman Industries Ltd (No 2)* [1982] Ch 204, [1982] 1 All ER 354, CA). In that case it was held that a shareholder had no personal claim against a person whose actions had reduced the company's profits because the shares themselves were not directly affected and the right of participation remained intact. The correct action is one in the name of the company in respect of the loss or damage caused to it.

See also **14.12** CONSTITUTION – MEMORANDUM AND ARTICLES for the contractual effect of the articles between members and between the company and its members.

**Rights under *CA 2006*.** Members are given many rights under *CA 2006* including the right to

- receive and demand copies of the annual accounts (see **2.6** and **2.7** ACCOUNTS: GENERAL);

- receive notice of, attend, vote at, and in certain circumstances requisition, meetings of the company (see **42** RESOLUTIONS AND MEETINGS);

- inspect the statutory registers (see **38** REGISTERS), minute books (see **42.46** RESOLUTIONS AND MEETINGS), and directors' service contracts (see **18.57** DIRECTORS);

- require the company to circulate statements and resolutions (see **42.21** and **42.33** RESOLUTIONS AND MEETINGS);

- receive dividends if declared (see **22.10** DISTRIBUTIONS);

- object to the payment for the redemption or purchase of the company's shares out of capital (see **34.18** PURCHASE OF OWN SHARES);

- apply to the court for a meeting following a proposed compromise with members and/or creditors (see **35.2** RECONSTRUCTIONS AND MERGERS);

- apply to the court following the re-registration of a public company as a private company (see **41.9** RE-REGISTRATION);

- be bought out following a takeover offer where the offeror holds at least 90% of the shares (see **48.15** TAKEOVERS);

- petition the court for the winding up of the company under the *IA 1986, s 124*; and

- apply to the Secretary of State to appoint an inspector to investigate the company's affairs (see **25** INVESTIGATIONS).

**Rights of members to damages, etc.** A person is not debarred from obtaining damages or other compensation from a company by reason only that he holds, or has held,

- shares in the company; or

- any right to apply or subscribe for shares or to be included in the company's register in respect of shares.

[*CA 2006, s 655*].

**Liabilities**. The principal liabilities of a member are:

- To pay any outstanding amounts or calls on his shares as required by the company (see **47.23** SHARES). If the articles of the company provide, a member's shares may be forfeited for non-payment of calls (see **47.25** SHARES).

- In the event of a winding up, to contribute to the assets of the company in respect of any amounts unpaid on his shares.

[*IA 1986, s 74*].

If the company adopts the Model Articles, Article 2 (of both private and public company articles) provides that the liability of members is limited to the amount, if any, unpaid on the shares held by them. For companies incorporated before 1 October 2009 the limitation of liability clause was contained in the company's memorandum. See **14** CONSTITUTION – MEMORANDUM AND ARTICLES for the effect of *CA 2006, s 28* as from 1 October 2009.

## 26.10 Protection of members against unfair prejudice

**Petitions to the court**. An application may be made to the court by petition by

(a)   a member of a company (including a statutory water company),

(b)   the Secretary of State where he has

    (i)   received a report under *CA 1985, s 437* (inspector's report, see **25.3** INVESTIGATIONS),

    (ii)   exercised his powers under *CA 1985, s 447* or *448* (powers to require documents and information or to enter and search premises, see **25.12** and **25.13** INVESTIGATIONS),

    (iii)   exercised his powers under *FSMA 2000, Pt 11* (information gathering and investigations), or

    (iv)   received a report from an investigator appointed by him or the FCA under that *Part*,

(c)      the FCA where it has exercised its powers under *FSMA 2000, Pt 11*

on either of the following grounds.

•      The company's affairs are being, or have been, conducted in a manner that is unfairly prejudicial to the interests of members generally or of some part of its members (including, where (*a*) above applies, at least the member bringing the petition).

  This includes, the removal from office of the company's auditor appointed for a financial year beginning on or after 5 April 2008 on the grounds of divergence of opinion on accounting treatment or audit procedures or any other improper grounds.

•      Any actual or proposed act or omission of the company (including an act or omission on its behalf) is, or would be, so prejudicial.

Included under (*a*) above is a person who is not a member of a company but to whom shares in the company have been transferred or transmitted by operation of the law.

The powers of the Secretary of State to make an application under (*b*) above may be used in addition to, or instead of, the presenting of a winding-up petition against the company.

[*CA 2006, ss 994, 995; SI 2007 No 2194, Sch 1 para 19; SI 2007 No 3494, Reg 42*].

The unfairly prejudicial conduct must relate to members' interests *as members*. This requirement will not be narrowly interpreted, especially where quasi-partnerships features are present. Accordingly, prejudice to a member's interests as a member has been held to have occurred where:

•      A person became a member of a company on the basis that he would be involved in its management and was subsequently excluded from management (*O'Neill v Phillips* [1999] 1 WLR 1092, Lord Hoffman at *paras 1102C–1102D* and *paras 1105C–1105G*).

•      A member lent money to the company in his capacity as a creditor, and the loan was part of the basis on which he became a member of the company (*Gamlestaden Fastigheter AB v Baltic Partners Ltd* [2007] UKPC 26, [2007] 4 All ER 164, [2007] Bus LR 1521 at *paras 33–37* (A case on *article 141* of the Companies (Jersey) Law 1991 that is substantively identical to *CA 2006, s 994*)).

Both prejudice and unfairness must be shown for a petition to be successful, although there is no requirement to show discrimination as well as unfair prejudice. A member may succeed in establishing prejudice if the economic value of his or her shares has significantly decreased or is imperilled by the conduct at issue (*Re Brenfield Squash Racquets Club Ltd* [1996] 2 BCLC 184). However, not every case of established unfair prejudice involves economic detriment, especially where one or more features of a quasi-partnership exist.

Examples of the forms of conduct which courts have in certain circumstances held to amount to unfairly prejudicial conduct for this purpose include:

•      breach of fiduciary duty which results in real prejudice, such as damage to the parties' relationship of trust and confidence, the misuse or misappropriation of company assets or the procurement of an allotment of shares to dilute a minority's interests;

•      mismanagement;

•      failure to pay dividends;

- payment of excessive remuneration;

- diluting the minority's shareholding;

- failure to abide by the company's articles, any shareholders' agreements, or *CA 2006*; and

- exclusion from management where participation was part of the bargain, or failure to consult with, or provide information to, a petitioner where it was agreed that the petitioner would be consulted or provided with such information.

In the High Court case of *Wootliff v Rushton-Turner* [2016] EWHC 2802, the court decided that a claim for wrongful dismissal could be pursued in tandem with an unfair prejudice petition under *CA 2006, s 994*. The applicant was a member and chief executive officer of a company. The company dismissed him from his employment and removed him from office as director. The member brought a claim in the Employment Tribunal for, among other things, wrongful dismissal. He later withdrew those claims, but reserved his right to pursue the wrongful dismissal claim in an alternative jurisdiction (the Chancery Division). The court held – on this novel point – that it was not appropriate to strike out the unfair prejudice claim. The applicant would have to show that the affairs of the company had been conducted in a way that was both unfair and prejudicial to the interests of members. Significantly, said the court, evidence concerning his service contract could conceptually serve as evidence of the company's relationship with its members.

*Before 1 October 2007*, similar provisions applied under *CA 1985, ss 459, 460*.

See also *Meyer v Scottish Textile and Manufacturing Co Ltd (or Scottish Co-operative Wholesale Society)* 1954 SC 381, 1954 SLT 273 and *Scottish Co-operative Wholesale Society Ltd v Meyer* [1959] AC 324, [1958] 3 All ER 66, HL; *HR Harmer Ltd, Re* [1958] 3 All ER 689, [1959] 1 WLR 62, CA; *Company, a (No 004475 of 1982), Re* [1983] Ch 178, [1983] BCLC 126; *Company, a (No 002567 of 1982), Re* [1983] 2 All ER 854, [1983] BCLC 151; and *Re Bird Precision Bellows Ltd* [1986] Ch 658, [1985] BCLC 493, CA.

The above procedures are not available to a company's majority shareholders, having the power to procure the passing of any resolution of the company, such as to enable them to force the minority shareholder to give up his investment (*Morris v Hateley* [1999] 13 LS Gaz R 31, (1999) Times, 10 March, CA).

**Provisions relating to petitions.** The petition must be in the form set out in the Schedule to the *Companies (Unfair Prejudice Applications) Proceedings Rules 2009* (*SI 2009 No 2469*) with such variations, if any, as circumstances require. It must specify the grounds on which it is presented and the nature of the relief sought and be delivered to the court for filing with sufficient copies for service. The court must fix a hearing for a day (the 'return day') on which the petitioner and any respondent (including the company) must attend before the registrar or District Judge for directions to be given in relation to the procedure on the petition. On fixing the return day, the court must return to the petitioner sealed copies of the petition, each endorsed with the return day and the time of the hearing. At least 14 days before the return day the petitioner must serve a sealed copy of the petition on the company . If the petition is based on *CA 2006, s 994*, a sealed copy of the petition must be served on every respondent named in the petition at least 14 days before the return date.

On the return date or at any time after it, the court must give such directions as it thinks appropriate with respect to (i) service and advertisement of the petition; (ii) whether points of claim and defence are to be delivered; the manner in which evidence is to be given at the hearing; (iii) generally as to the procedure on the petition and the hearing and disposal of the petition and (iv) any orders, including a stay, with a view to mediation or other alternative dispute resolutions.

[*SI 2009 No 2469 Rules 1–6*].

**Powers of the court.** If the court is satisfied that a petition is well founded, it may make such order as it thinks fit for giving relief in respect of matters complained of, including

- regulating the conduct of the company's future affairs;

- requiring a company to

  (i)     refrain from doing or continuing an act complained of; or

  (ii)    do an act that the petitioner has complained it has omitted to do;

- authorising civil proceedings to be brought in the name and on behalf of the company by such persons and on such terms as it directs;

- requiring the company not to make any, or any specified, alterations in its articles without the leave of the court; and

- providing for the purchase of the shares of any members of the company by other members or by the company itself and, in the latter case, the reduction of the company's share capital accordingly.

[*CA 2006, s 996*].

**Action following a court order.**

(1)     If the court considers that the order should be advertised, it may give directions as to the manner and time the order should be advertised [*SI 2009 No 2469, Rule 6*]

(2)     Where an order of the court

- alters the company's constitution, or

- gives leave for the company to make any, or any specified, alterations to its constitution,

the company must deliver a copy of the order to the Registrar of Companies within 14 days from the making of the order or such longer period as the court may allow.

If a company makes default in complying with this provision, an offence is committed by the company and every officer of the company who is in default. A person guilty of such an offence is liable, on summary conviction, to a fine not exceeding level 3 on the standard scale and, for continued contravention, a daily default fine not exceeding one-tenth of level 3 on the standard scale. See **29.1** Offences and Legal Proceedings for the standard scale.

[*CA 2006, s 998*].

(3)     If the court order alters a company's constitution ie if the order amends

- a company's articles, or

- any resolution or agreement to which *CA 2006, ss 29, 30* apply (see **14** Constitution – Memorandum and Articles),

the copy of the order delivered to the Registrar of Companies must be accompanied by a copy of the company's articles, or the resolution or agreement in question, as amended.

Every copy of a company's articles issued by the company after the order is made must be accompanied by a copy of the order, unless the effect of the order has been incorporated into the articles by amendment.

If a company makes default in complying with these requirements, an offence is committed by the company and every officer of the company who is in default. A person guilty of such an offence is liable, on summary conviction, to a fine not exceeding level 3 on the standard scale. See **29.1** OFFENCES AND LEGAL PROCEEDINGS for the standard scale.

[*CA 2006, s 999; SI 2007 No 2194, Sch 3 para 47*].

## 26.11  DERIVATIVE CLAIMS AND PROCEEDINGS BY MEMBERS

*CA 2006, s 170(1)* provides that a directors' general duties are owed to the company rather than to individual members. It follows that only the company can enforce them. There are three main ways in which a company can take legal action against a director (or former director) for breach of duty:

- If the board of directors decides to commence proceedings.

- If a liquidator or administrator decides to commence proceedings following the commencement of a formal insolvency procedure.

- Through a derivative claim or action brought by one or more members to enforce a right which is vested not in himself/ their selves but in the company.

The third of these procedures is considered below and in **26.12** and **26.13**.

**Overview of old and new positions.**

(1)    *England and Wales and Northern Ireland*

*Before 1 October 2007*, the law relating to the ability of a member to bring proceedings on behalf of the company (a 'derivative claim') was not written down in statute but applied by common law. *Foss v Harbottle* (1843) 2 Hare 461 established the fundamental rule that to redress a wrong done to a company or to recover moneys or damages due to it, action must *prima facie* be brought by the company itself. But subsequent case law established exceptions to the rule. These were summarised in *Burland v Earle* [1902] AC 83, 71 LJPC 1, PC as applying where the persons against whom the relief was sought themselves control the majority of shares in the company and would not permit an action to be brought in the company's name. In such a case, the courts would permit the complaining shareholder to bring an action in the company's name. However, if a wrong had been effectively ratified by the company, there was a complete bar to a derivative claim and if a wrong was capable of being ratified, it might not have been possible for a minority shareholder to bring a derivative action (even if there had been no formal ratification). The cases in which the minority could maintain such an action were, therefore, largely confined to the following.

- Where the acts complained of were of a fraudulent character or *ultra vires*. See *Simpson v Westminster Palace Hotel Co* (1860) 8 HL Cas 712 and *Russell v Wakefield Waterworks Co* (1875) LR 20 Eq 474.

- Where the matter was one which could only validly be done or sanctioned, not by a simple majority, but only by a special majority. See *Cotter v National Union of Seamen* [1929] 2 Ch 58, 98 LJ Ch 323, CA and *Edwards v Halliwell* [1950] 2 All ER 1064, 94 Sol Jo 803, CA.

- Where the rights of an individual member had been infringed. See *Pender v Lushington* (1877) 6 Ch D 70.

- Where the majority were endeavouring to appropriate to themselves money, property or advantage which belonged to the company or in which the other shareholders were entitled to participate, ie a fraud on the minority. See *Atwool v Merryweather* (1867) LR 5 Eq 464n and *Burland v Earle* above.

*With effect from 1 October 2007*, the provisions in **26.12** do not form a substantive rule to replace the rule in *Foss v Harbottle* but reflect the recommendation of the Law Commission that there should be a derivative procedure with a more modern, flexible and accessible criteria for determining whether a shareholder can pursue an action. Derivative claims are expressly available for breach of the duty to exercise reasonable care, skill and diligence, even if the director has not benefited personally, and it is not necessary for the applicant to show that the directors in the wrong control the majority of the company's shares.

(2)   *Scotland*

*Before 1 October 2007*, a member's right to raise on action was conferred by substantive law. Therefore, a member had title to raise proceedings in respect of a director's breach of duty to obtain a remedy for the company. The action was raised in the name of the member but the remedy was obtained for the company and the rights which the member could enforce against a director were those of the company. The member's right arose where the action complained of was fraudulent or *ultra vires* and so could not be validated by a majority of members of the company. The remedy was not available if the majority of members acting in good faith had validated or could validate the act complained of. Two rules of substantive law applied to actions bought by members to protect the company's interests. First, the directors of the company owed a duty to the company and not to the members. Secondly, the court would not interfere in matters of internal management which could be sanctioned by a majority of the members.

*With effect from 1 October 2007*, the provisions in **26.13** seek to ensure maximum consistency between the position in England and Wales and Northern Ireland and the position in Scotland (although reflecting the different procedural requirements). In view of this they also put the rights of a member to raise actions on behalf of the company on a statutory footing.

## 26.12   Derivative claims in England and Wales or Northern Ireland

The following provisions apply to a *'derivative claim'*, ie proceedings by a member of a company

- in respect of a cause of action vested in the company; and

- seeking relief on behalf of the company.

A derivative claim may only be brought under these provisions or in pursuance of an order of the court in unfair prejudice proceedings (see **26.10** above). A derivative claim under these provisions may be brought only in respect of a cause of action arising from an actual or proposed act or omission involving negligence, default, breach of duty or breach of trust by a director of the company. The cause of action may be against the director or another person (or both). It is immaterial whether the cause of action arose before or after the person seeking to bring or continue the derivative claim became a member of the company. For these purposes

- 'director' includes a former director;

- a 'shadow director' is treated as a director; and

- references to a member of a company include a person who is not a member but to whom shares in the company have been transferred or transmitted by operation of law.

**Applications to the court.** Application to the court for permission (in Northern Ireland, leave) to continue a derivative claim is required in the following instances.

(a)  Where a member of a company brings a derivative claim.

(b)  Where

    (i)  a member of the company wishes to continue a claim brought by a company as a derivative claim on the ground that

- the manner in which the company commenced or continued the claim amounts to an abuse of the process of the court;

- the company has failed to prosecute the claim diligently; and

- it is appropriate for the member to continue the claim as a derivative claim; and

    (ii)  the cause of action on which the claim is based could be pursued as a derivative claim under these provisions.

(c)  Where a member of the company ('the applicant') wishes to continue a derivative claim which another member ('the claimant') has

- brought under (*a*) above,

- continued under (*b*) above, or

- continued under this provision

on the ground that

- the manner in which the proceedings have been commenced or continued by the claimant amounts to an abuse of the process of the court;

- the claimant has failed to prosecute the claim diligently; and

- it is appropriate for the applicant to continue the claim as a derivative claim.

If it appears to the court that the application and the evidence filed by the applicant in support of it do not disclose a *prima facie* case for giving permission (or leave), the court must dismiss the application and may make any consequential order it considers appropriate. If the application is not dismissed, the court may give directions as to the evidence to be provided by the company and may adjourn the proceedings to enable the evidence to be obtained.

On hearing the application, the court may (i) give permission (or leave) to continue the claim on such terms as it thinks fit; (ii) refuse permission (or leave) and dismiss the claim; or (iii) adjourn the proceedings on the application and give such directions as it thinks fit.

**Matters to be taken into account by the court.** In deciding whether to give permission (or leave) for an application under (*a*) or (*b*) above to be heard or, as the case may be, continued, as a derivative claim, the court must:

- Refuse permission (or leave) if it is satisfied

    (i)  that a person acting in accordance with *CA 2006, s 172* (duty to promote the success of the company, see **18.24 D**IRECTORS) would not seek to continue the claim;

(ii)      where the cause of action arises from an act or omission that is yet to occur, that the act or omission has been authorised by the company; or

(iii)      where the cause of action arises from an act or omission that has already occurred, that the act or omission was authorised by the company before it occurred or has been ratified by the company since it occurred.

•      Take into account (in particular)

(i)      whether the member is acting in good faith in seeking to continue the claim;

(ii)      the importance that a person acting in accordance with *CA 2006, s 172* (duty to promote the success of the company) would attach to continuing it;

(iii)      where the cause of action results from an act or omission that is yet to occur, whether the act or omission could be, and in the circumstances would be likely to be, authorised by the company before it occurs or ratified by the company after it occurs;

(iv)      where the cause of action arises from an act or omission that has already occurred, whether the act or omission could be, and in the circumstances would be likely to be, ratified by the company;

(v)      whether the company has decided not to pursue the claim; and

(vi)      whether the act or omission in respect of which the claim is brought gives rise to a cause of action that the member could pursue in his own right rather than on behalf of the company.

The court must have particular regard to any evidence before it as to the views of members of the company who have no personal interest, direct or indirect, in the matter.

[*CA 2006, ss 260–264*].

**The rule against reflective loss.** It is a fundamental principle of company law, established as part of the rule in *Foss v Harbottle* (1843) 2 Hare 461, that where a wrong has been done to a company, it is *the company* itself which is the proper claimant. The so-called 'rule against reflective loss' was established by the Court of Appeal in *Prudential Insurance Co Ltd v Newman Industries Ltd (No 2)* [1982] 1 Ch 204 in which the court held:

'What [a shareholder] cannot do is to recover damages merely because the company in which he is interested has suffered damage. He cannot recover a sum equal to the diminution in the market value of his shares, or equal to the likely diminution in dividend, because such a "loss" is merely a reflection of the loss suffered by the company. The shareholder does not suffer any personal loss. His only "loss" is through the company, in the diminution in the value of the net assets of the company, in which he has (say) a 3 per cent shareholding.'

In short, a *shareholder* may not recover loss which is simply reflective of the *company's* loss.

In *Breeze v The Chief Constable of Norfolk Constabulary* [2018] EWHC 485, the High Court had to decide whether the rule against reflective loss was limited to cases where there was specifically a *breach of duty* owed by a tortfeasor to the company, or whether the rule should be extended to *any* claim in which a company might have an action against a tortfeasor, to compensate it for a loss of its assets.

The claimants, being the main shareholders in a company, had been arrested and charged with fraud arising out of the way the company charged for its services. Later, they were acquitted at trial. The company then went into receivership and was ultimately dissolved. The claimants brought an action against the defendant chief constable for malicious prosecution and misfeasance in public office. As part of their claim, they tried to recover the combined value of their interest in the company, amounting to around £30 million. Essentially, they argued that the investigation and alleged malicious prosecution/misfeasance had caused the demise of the company's business, and hence the 100% diminution in the company's share value, which in turn had caused them (the two shareholders) to lose the whole value of their shares. The *company* had not brought proceedings against the police, and it had assigned no rights of action to the claimants. The defendant Chief Constable applied to strike out this aspect of the claim on the basis that it offended the reflective loss principle.

The court held that the principle of reflective loss included any situation where a company (whether or not it actually sued) had a cause of action in respect of an actionable wrong which, if pursued to its fullest extent, would enable it (the company) to seek to recoup the loss. It was *not* confined to cases of *breach of duty*, though it included such cases. Here, *the company* could have sued for misfeasance in public office in order to recover the loss of its value as reflected in the diminished share value. Therefore, in effect, the claimant shareholders were debarred from suing for that loss, which was in truth a *company* loss.

In short, the position seems to be that the rule against recovery of reflective loss will in future be taken to apply also to company causes of action *other than* pure breach of duty by the tortfeasor.

### 26.13  Derivative proceedings in Scotland

A member of a company may, in order to protect the interests of the company and obtain a remedy on its behalf, raise proceedings ('*derivative proceedings*') in respect of any actual or proposed act or omission involving negligence, default, breach of duty or breach of trust by a director of the company (the '*cause of action*'). Proceedings may be raised against the director or another person (or both). It is immaterial whether the act or omission in question arose before or after the person seeking to raise them (or continue them as below) became a member of the company.

These provisions do not affect

- any right of a member of a company to raise proceedings in respect of such an act or omission as specified above in order to protect his own interests and obtain a remedy on his own behalf; or

- the court's power to authorise civil proceedings to be brought in the name and on behalf of the company by such persons and on such terms as it directs or anything done under such an order.

For the above purposes

- 'director' includes a former director;

- a 'shadow director' (see 18.1 DIRECTORS) is treated as a director; and

- references to a member of a company include a person who is not a member but to whom shares in the company have been transferred or transmitted by operation of law.

**Requirement for leave and notice.** Derivative proceedings may be raised by a member of a company only with the leave of the court. An application for leave must specify the cause of action and summarise the facts on which the derivative proceedings are to be based.

If it appears to the court that the application and the evidence produced by the applicant in support of it do not disclose a *prima facie* case for granting it, the court must refuse the application. It may then make any consequential order it considers appropriate.

If the application is not refused, the applicant must serve the application on the company. The court may make an order requiring evidence to be produced by the company and may adjourn the proceedings on the application to enable the evidence to be obtained. The company is entitled to take part in the further proceedings on the application.

On hearing the application, the court may (i) grant the application on such terms as it thinks fit; (ii) refuse the application; or (iii) adjourn the proceedings on the application and make such order as to further procedure as it thinks fit.

**Application to continue proceedings as derivative proceedings.** Where a company has raised proceedings in respect of an act or omission which could be the basis for derivative proceedings, a member of the company may apply to the court to be substituted for the company in the proceedings, and for the proceedings to continue in consequence as derivative proceedings, on the ground that

• the manner in which the company commenced or continued the proceedings amounts to an abuse of the process of the court;

• the company has failed to prosecute the proceedings diligently; and

• it is appropriate for the member to be substituted for the company in the proceedings.

Matters then proceed as above depending upon whether or not the court accept that there is a *prima facie* case for granting the application.

**Granting of leave.** The court must refuse leave to raise derivative proceedings, or an application to continue proceedings as derivative proceedings, if it is satisfied

• that a person acting in accordance with *CA 2006, s 172* (duty to promote the success of the company, see **18.24 Directors**) would not seek to continue the proceedings;

• where the cause of action is an act or omission that is yet to occur, that the act or omission has been authorised by the company; or

• where the cause of action is an act or omission that has already occurred, that the act or omission was authorised by the company before it occurred or has been ratified by the company since it occurred.

It must also, in particular, take into account

• whether the member is acting in good faith in seeking to raise or continue the proceedings;

• the importance that a person acting in accordance with *CA 2006, s 172* (duty to promote the success of the company) would attach to raising or continuing them;

• where the cause of action is an act or omission that is yet to occur, whether the act or omission could be, and in the circumstances would be likely to be, authorised by the company before it occurs or ratified by the company after it occurs;

• where the cause of action is an act or omission that has already occurred, whether the act or omission could be, and in the circumstances would be likely to be, ratified by the company;

• whether the company has decided not to raise proceedings in respect of the same cause of action or to persist with the proceedings; and

• whether the cause of action is one which the member could pursue in his own right rather than on behalf of the company.

The court must have particular regard to any evidence before it as to the views of members of the company who have no personal interest, direct or indirect, in the matter.

**Application by member to be substituted for member pursuing derivative proceedings**. Where a member of a company ('*the claimant*') has

• raised derivative proceedings,

• continued as derivative proceedings raised by the company, or

• continued derivative proceedings under this provision,

another member of the company ('*the applicant*') may apply to the court to be substituted for the claimant in the action on the ground that

• the manner in which the proceedings have been commenced or continued by the claimant amounts to an abuse of the process of the court;

• the claimant has failed to prosecute the proceedings diligently; and

• it is appropriate for the applicant to be substituted for the claimant in the proceedings.

Matters then proceed as above depending upon whether or not the court accept that there is a *prima facie* case for granting the application.

[*CA 2006, ss 265–269*].

**Transitional provisions**. Where an application is made under the above provisions, if the cause of action arises (wholly or to any extent) from an act or omission that occurred before 1 October 2007, the court must exercise its powers under those provisions so as to secure that the proceedings in respect of that act or omission are allowed to proceed as derivative proceedings only to the extent that they could have been pursued by the applicant under the law in force immediately before that date.

[*SI 2007 No 2194, Sch 3 para 21*].

# 27 Names and Business Names

**Cross-references.** See **16.13** Dealings With Third Parties for display of name at business premises; **16.15** Dealings With Third Parties for inclusion of name in documents and communications; **18.40** Directors for re-use of company name following insolvent liquidation.

**Background.** The provisions in *CA 2006*, *Pts 6* and *41* which are considered in this chapter apply, unless otherwise stated, with effect from 1 October 2009. They replace the provisions in *CA 1985*, *Pt 1*, *Ch 2* relating to names and *BNA 1985* relating to business names.

## 27.1 NAMES

The provisions in **27.2** to **27.17** relate to the name which a company may, or may not, use and changes made in its name (whether compulsory or voluntary).

## 27.2 Indication of type of company in name

The name of a company must end

(a)     in the case of a limited company that is a public company, with 'public limited company' or 'plc'; and

(b)     subject to the exemptions below, in the case of a company that is a private company, with 'limited' or 'ltd'.

In the case of a Welsh company, its name may instead end with 'cwmni cyfyngedig cyhoeddus' or 'ccc' under (*a*) or 'cyfyngedig' or 'cyf' under (*b*).

The above provisions do not apply to community interest companies (for which see **10** Community Interest Companies).

[*CA 2006, ss 58, 59*].

**Exemptions.** A private company is exempt from the requirements to have 'limited' or 'ltd' at the end of its name in the following circumstances.

(1)     It is a charity.

[*CA 2006, s 60(1)(a)*].

(2)     It is exempted from the requirement by Regulations made by the Secretary of State. [*CA 2006, s 60(1)(b)*]. These are the *Company, Limited Liability and Business (Names and Trading Disclosures) Regulations 2015 (the 2015 Regulations)* which are referred to where relevant throughout this chapter

(3)     It is a private company limited by shares which has an existing exemption and can continue with that exemption if it meets the conditions set out in *section 61* of *CA 2006*.

[*CA 2006, ss 60(1)(c), 61*].

(4)     It is a private company limited by guarantee which has an existing exemption and can continue with that exemption if it meets the conditions set out in *CA 2006, s 62*.

[*CA 2006, ss 60(1)(c), 62*].

The Registrar of Companies may refuse to register a private limited company by a name that does not include the word 'limited' (or a permitted alternative) unless a statement has been delivered to him that the company meets the conditions for exemption. The Registrar may accept the statement as sufficient evidence of the matters stated in it.

[*CA 2006, s 60(2), (3)*].

**Restriction on amendment of articles.** A private company that is exempt by virtue of continuing an existing exemption (see (3) and (4) above), and whose name does not include 'limited' or any of the permitted alternatives, must not amend its articles so that it ceases to comply with the conditions for exemption. In contravention, an offence is committed by the company and every officer of the company who is in default. For this purpose a shadow director is treated as an officer of the company. A person guilty of such an offence is liable, on summary conviction, to a fine not exceeding level 5 on the standard scale and, for continued contravention, to a daily default fine not exceeding one-tenth of the greater of £5,000 or level 4 on the standard scale. See **29.1 OFFENCES AND LEGAL PROCEEDINGS** for the standard scale.

If, immediately before 1 October 2009, a company was exempt (by virtue of *CA 1985, s 30* (or *Companies (Northern Ireland) Order 1986, Art 40*)) from the requirement to have a name including the word limited (or a permitted alternative), and the company's memorandum or articles could not be altered without the approval of

•       the Board of Trade or a Northern Ireland department (or any other department or Minister), or

•       the Charity Commission,

that provision, in the memorandum or articles and any condition of any such licence referred to in *sections 61(1)(a)(ii)* or *(b)(ii)* which required that provision in the memorandum or articles, ceased to have effect on 1 October 2009 (unless the provision is required by or under any other enactment). [*CA 2006, s 63; SI 2015 No 664, Sch 3*].

## 27.3  Prohibited names

A company cannot be registered with a proposed name in any of the circumstances set out in **27.4** to **27.6**.

## 27.4  *Offensive name*

A company cannot be registered by a name if, in the opinion of the Secretary of State,

•       its use by the company would constitute an offence; or

•       it is offensive.

[*CA 2006, s 53*].

**27.5**  *Inappropriate indication of company type or legal form. Name same as an existing name*

The Secretary of State can, by Regulations, prohibit the use in a company name of specified words, expressions or other indications that are

- associated with, or

- similar to words, expressions or other indications associated with,

a particular type of company or form of organisation. The making of regulations does not affect the continued registration of a company by a name by which it was duly registered immediately before 1 October 2009; and in the case of a 'transitional company', on its registration or re-registration.

A *'transitional company'* is one that applied for registration (or re-registration) before 1 October 2009 (and met all the necessary requirements before that date) but which was not registered (or re-registered) until on or after that date.

[*CA 2006, s 65; SI 2008 No 2860, Sch 2 para 17*].

The Regulations referred to above made under *s 65* are the *2015 Regulations referred to above*.

Under these Regulations, the following restrictions apply.

(1)    *Generally applicable provisions*

Subject to (2)(*b*) and (3)(*b*) below, a company must not be registered under *CA 2006* by a name that includes

(a)    otherwise than at the end of the name

any of the expressions or abbreviations 'PUBLIC LIMITED COMPANY', (or with or without full stops the abbreviation) 'PLC', 'CWMNI CYFYNGEDIG CYHOEDDUS', (or with or without full stops the abbreviation) 'CCC', 'COMMUNITY INTEREST COMPANY', (or with or without full stops the abbreviation) 'CIC', 'CWMNI BUDDI-ANT CYMUNEDOL', (or with or without full stops the abbreviation) 'CBC', 'COMMUNITY INTEREST PUBLIC LIMITED COMPANY', (or with or without full stops the abbreviation) 'COMMUNITY INTEREST PLC', 'CWMNI BUDDIANT CYMUNEDOL CY-HOEDDUS CYFYNGEDIG', (or with or without full stops the abbreviation) 'CWMNI BUDDIANT CYMUNEDOL CCC';

(b)    in any part of the name

'RIGHT TO ENFRANCHISEMENT', (or with or without full stops the abbreviation) 'RTE', 'HAWL I RYDDFREINIAD'; unless that company is a RTE company within the meaning of *Leasehold Reform, Housing and Urban Development Act 1993, s 4A*;

unless that company is a RTE company within the meaning of *Leasehold Reform, Housing and Urban Development Act 1993, s 4A*;

(c)    in any part of the name

'RIGHT TO MANAGE', (or with or without full stops the abbreviation) 'RTM', 'CWMNI RTM CYFYNGEDIG'; unless that company is a RTM company within the meaning of *Commonhold and Leasehold Reform Act 2002, s 73*;

unless that company is a RTM company within the meaning of *Commonhold and Leasehold Reform Act 2002, s 73*;

(d)     in any part of the name

'EUROPEAN ECONOMIC INTEREST GROUPING' (or with or without full stops the abbreviation) 'EEIG', 'INVESTMENT COMPANY WITH VARIABLE CAPITAL', 'CWMNI BUDDSODDI A CHYFALAF NEWIDIOL', 'LIMITED PARTNERSHIP' (or with or without full stops the abbreviation) LP, 'PARTNERIAETH CYFYNGEDIG' (or with or without full stops the abbreviation) PC, 'LIMITED LIABILITY PARTNERSHIP' (or with or without full stops the abbreviation) LLP, 'PARTNERIAETH ATEBOLRWYDD CYFYNGEDIG', (or with or without full stops the abbreviation) PAC, 'OPEN-ENDED INVESTMENT COMPANY', 'CWMNI BUDDSODDIANT PENAGORED', 'CHARITABLE INCORPORATED ORGANISATION', (or with or without full stops the abbreviation) CIC, or 'SEFDYDLIAD ELUSENNOL CORFFOREDIG', (or with or without full stops the abbreviation) SEC;

An '*expressions or abbreviations specified as similar*' to the above are any in which

•      one or more permitted characters has been omitted;

•      one or more permitted characters has been added; or

•      each of one or more permitted characters has been substituted by one or more other permitted characters

in such a way as to be likely to mislead the public as to the legal form of a company or business if included in the registered name of the company or in a business name.

[*SI 2015 No 17, Reg 4, Sch 2*].

(2)     *Companies exempt from requirement to have name ending in 'limited'*

A company which is exempt under *CA 2006, s 60* from the requirement to have a name ending with 'limited' or a permitted alternative (see **27.2** above) must not be registered by a name that ends with

(a)     'UNLIMITED' or 'ANGHYFYNGEDIG' (or any 'word specified as similar'); or

(b)     'PUBLIC LIMITED COMPANY', (or with or without full stops the abbreviation), 'PLC', 'CWMNI CYFYNGEDIG CYHOEDDUS' (or with or without full stops the abbreviation) 'CCC', 'COMMUNITY INTEREST COMPANY' (or with or without full stops the abbreviation) 'CIC', 'CWMNI BUDDIANT CYMUNEDOL' (or with or without full stops the abbreviation) 'CBC', 'COMMUNITY INTEREST PUBLIC LIMITED COMPANY' (or with or without full stops the abbreviation) 'COMMUNITY INTEREST PLC', 'CWMNI BUDDIANT CYMUNEDOL CYHOEDDUS CYFYNGEDIG' (or with or without full stops the abbreviation) 'CWMNI BUDDIANT CYMUNEDOL CCC', 'LP', 'PC', 'LLP', 'PAC', 'CIO' or 'SEC' (or any 'expression or abbreviation specified as similar').

See (1) above for '*expression or abbreviation specified as similar*' which also applies to '*word specified as similar*'.

[*SI 2015 No 17, Reg 4, 5,Sch 2*].

(3)     *Unlimited companies*

An unlimited company must not be registered under *CA 2006, s 60* by a name that ends with

(a)     'LIMITED', (with or without full stops the abbreviation) 'LTD', 'CYFYNGEDIG', (with or without full stops the abbreviation) 'CYF' (or any 'word or abbreviation specified as similar'); or

(b)     'PUBLIC LIMITED COMPANY', (or with or without full stops the abbreviation), 'PLC', 'CWMNI CYFYNGEDIG CYHOEDDUS', (or with or without full stops the abbreviation) 'CCC', 'COMMUNITY INTEREST COMPANY', (or with or without full stops the abbreviation), 'CIC', 'CWMNI BUDDIANT CYMUNEDOL', (or with or without full stops the abbreviation) 'CBC', 'COMMUNITY INTEREST PUBLIC LIMITED COMPANY', (or with or without full stops the abbreviation) 'COMMUNITY INTEREST PLC', 'CWMNI BUDDIANT CYMUNEDOL CYHOEDDUS CYFYNGEDIG', (or with or without full stops the abbreviation) 'CWMNI BUDDIANT CYMUNEDOL CCC', 'LP', 'PC', 'LLP', 'PAC', 'CIO' or 'SEC' (or any 'expression or abbreviation specified as similar').

See (1) above for *'expression or abbreviation specified as similar'* which also applies to *'word specified as similar'*.

[*SI 2015 No 17, Reg 12, 13, Sch 2*].

(4)     *Overseas companies*

An overseas company must not be registered under *CA 2006* by a name that

(a)     ends with 'LIMITED', 'LTD', 'CYFYNGEDIG' or 'CYF' (or any 'word or abbreviation specified as similar') unless the liability of the members of the company is limited by its constitution;

(b)     ends with 'UNLIMITED' or 'ANGHYFYNGEDIG' (or any word specified as similar) unless the liability of the members of the company is not limited by its constitution; or

(c)     includes in any part of the name 'PUBLIC LIMITED COMPANY', (or with or without full stops the abbreviation) 'PLC, 'CWMNI CYFYNGEDIG CYHOEDDUS', (or with or without full stops the abbreviation) 'CCC, 'COMMUNITY INTEREST COMPANY', (or with or without full stops the abbreviation) 'CIC', 'CWMNI BUDDIANT CYMUNEDOL', (or with or without full stops the abbreviation) 'CBC, 'COMMUNITY INTEREST PUBLIC LIMITED COMPANY', (or with or without full stops the abbreviation) 'COMMUNITY INTEREST PLC' 'CWMNI BUDDIANT CYMUNEDOL CYHOEDDUS CYFYNGEDIG', (or with or without full stops the abbreviation) 'CWMNI BUDDIANT CYMUNEDOL CCC', 'RIGHT TO ENFRANCHISEMENT', (or with or without full stops the abbreviation) 'RTE', 'HAWL I RYDDFREINIAD', 'RIGHT TO MANAGE', (or with or without full stops the abbreviation) 'RTM', 'CWMNI RTM CYFYNGEDIG', 'EUROPEAN ECONOMIC INTEREST GROUPING', (or with or without full stops the abbreviation) 'EEIG', 'INVESTMENT COMPANY WITH VARIABLE CAPITAL', 'CWMNI BUDDSODDI A CHYFALAF NEWIDIOL', 'LIMITED PARTNERSHIP', 'PARTNERIAETH CYFYNGEDIG', 'LIMITED LIABILITY PARTNERSHIP', 'PARTNERIAETH ATEBOLRWYDD CYFYNGEDIG', 'OPEN-ENDED INVESTMENT COMPANY', 'CWMNI BUDDSODDIANT PENAGORED', 'CHARITABLE

INCORPORATED ORGANISATION', 'SEFDYDLIAD ELUSENNOL CORFFOREDIG', 'Industrial and Provident Society', Co-operative Society, Community Benefit Society 'LP', 'PC', 'LLP', 'PAC', 'CIO' or 'SEC' (or an expression or abbreviation specified as similar)

See (1) above for '*expression or abbreviation specified as similar*' which also applies to '*word specified as similar*'.

[*SI 2009 No 1085, Reg 10, Sch 2*].

**27.6**   *Name same as an existing name*

*CA 2006, s 66* provides that a company must not be registered by a name that is 'the same as' another name appearing in the Registrar of Companies' index of company names. Regulations made under *s 66* (see above **27.5** for the relevant regulations) do not affect the continued registration of a company by a name by which it was duly registered immediately before 1 October 2009 and in the case of a 'transitional company', on its registration or re-registration.

See **27.5** for '*transitional company*'.

[*CA 2006, s 66; SI 2008 No 2860, Sch 2 para 17*].

In determining whether a name is the same as another appearing in the index of company names the provisions set out in *Sch 3* to the *2015 regulations* must be followed. First there are sets of permitted characters set out in columns 1 and 2 of *para 2* of the *schedule*. Take the name remaining after the application of *para 2* then disregard any word, expression or abbreviation set out below where it appears at the end of a name.

(1)    The following words, expressions and abbreviations are to be disregarded where appearing at the end of the name.

- 'LIMITED' or (with or without full stops) the abbreviation 'LTD'

- 'CYFYNGEDIG' or (with or without full stops) the abbreviation 'CYF'

- 'UNLIMITED'

- 'ANGHYFYNGEDIG'

- 'PUBLIC LIMITED COMPANY' or (with or without full stops) the abbreviation 'PLC'

- 'CWMNI CYFYNGEDIG CYHOEDDUS' or (with or without full stops) the abbreviation 'CCC'

- 'COMMUNITY INTEREST COMPANY' or (with or without full stops) the abbreviation 'CIC'

- 'CWMNI BUDDIANT CYMUNEDOL' or (with or without full stops) the abbreviation 'CBC'

- 'COMMUNITY INTEREST PUBLIC LIMITED COMPANY' or (with or without full stops) the abbreviation 'COMMUNITY INTEREST PLC'

- 'CWMNI BUDDIANT CYMUNEDOL CYHOEDDUS CYFYNGE-DIG' or (with or without full stops) the abbreviation 'CWMNI BUDDI-ANT CYMUNEDOL CCC'

- 'RIGHT TO ENFRANCHISEMENT' or (with or without full stops) the abbreviation 'RTE'

- 'HAWL I RYDDFREINIAD'

- 'RIGHT TO MANAGE' or (with or without full stops) the abbreviation 'RTM'

- 'CWMNI RTM CYFYNGEDIG'

- 'EUROPEAN ECONOMIC INTEREST GROUPING' or (with or without full stops) the abbreviation 'EEIG'

- 'INVESTMENT COMPANY WITH VARIABLE CAPITAL'

- 'CWMNI BUDDSODDI A CHYFALAF NEWIDIOL'

- 'LIMITED PARTNERSHIP' or (with or without full stops) the abbreviation 'LP'

- 'PARTNERIAETH CYFYNGEDIG' or (with or without full stops) the abbreviation 'PC'

- 'LIMITED LIABILITY PARTNERSHIP' or (with or without full stops) the abbreviation 'LLP'

- 'PARTNERIAETH ATEBOLRWYDD CYFYNGEDIG' or (with or without full stops) the abbreviation 'PAC'

- 'OPEN-ENDED INVESTMENT COMPANY'

- 'CWMNI BUDDSODDIANT PENAGORED'

- CHARITABLE INCORPORATED ORGANISATION' or (with or without full stops) the abbreviation 'CIO'

- 'SEFDYDLIAD ELUSENNOL CORFFOREDIG' or (with or without full stops) the abbreviation 'SEC'

- Industrial and Provident Society

- Co-operative Society

- Community Benefit Society

(2)    Taking the name remaining after the application of (1) above, the following words, expressions, signs and symbols are regarded as the same as the other relevant matters set out below where each relevant matter:

(i)    is preceded by and followed by a blank space; or

(ii)    is at the beginning of the name where it is followed by a blank space.

The words, expressions, signs and symbols are

- 'AND' and '&'

- 'PLUS' and '+'

- '0', 'ZERO' and 'O'

- '1' and 'ONE'

- '2', 'TWO', 'TO' and 'TOO'

- '3' and 'THREE'

- '4', 'FOUR' and 'FOR'

- '5' and 'FIVE'

- '6' and 'SIX'

- '7' and 'SEVEN'

- '8' and 'EIGHT'

- '9' and 'NINE'

- '£' and 'POUND'

- '€' and 'EURO'

- '$' and 'DOLLAR'

- '¥' and 'YEN'

- '%', 'PER CENT', 'PERCENT', 'PER CENTUM' and 'PERCENTUM'

- '@' and 'AT'.

(3)   Taking the name remaining after the application of (1) and (2) above, disregard at the end of the name the matters set out below (or any combination of such matters) where the matter (or combination) is preceded by

(i)   a blank space;

(ii)   a full stop; or

(iii)   '@'.

The matters are

- '& Co'

- '& Company'

- 'AND CO'

- 'AND COMPANY'

- 'BIZ'

- 'CO'

- 'CO UK'

- 'CO.UK'

- 'COM'

- 'COMPANY'

- 'EU'

- 'GB'

- 'GREAT BRITAIN'

- 'NET'

- 'NI'

- 'NORTHERN IRELAND'

- 'ORG'

- 'ORG UK'

- 'ORG.UK'

- 'UK'

- 'UNITED KINGDOM'

- 'WALES'

- 'ALLFORION'

- '& CWMNI'

- 'A'R CWMNI'

- 'CWMNI'

- 'CYM'

- 'CYMRU'

- 'DU'

- 'MEWNFORION'

- 'PF'

- 'PRYDAIN FAWR'

- 'Y DEYRNAS UNEDIG'.

(4)   Taking the name remaining after the application of (1)–(3) above, disregard the following matters in any part of the name.

- Any full stop, comma, colon, semi-colon or hyphen.

- Any of the following types of punctuation but only in the forms indicated:

    (i)     Apostrophe: ' '

    (ii)    Bracket: ( ) [ ] { } < >

    (iii)   Exclamation mark: !

    (iv)    Guillemet: « »

    (v)     Inverted comma: " " "

    (vi)    Question mark: ?

    (vii)   Solidus: \ /

- *, = and #.

(5)   Taking the name remaining after the application of (1)–(4) above, disregard the letter 'S' at the end of the name.

(6)   Taking the name remaining after the application of (1)–(5) above, disregard any *'permitted character'* (see **27.8**) after the first 60 permitted characters of the name (and for this purpose, any blank space between one permitted character and another is to be counted as a permitted character).

(7)   Taking the name remaining after the application of (1)–(6) above, disregard the following matters or any combination of the following matters where they appear at the beginning of the name.

- '@'

- 'THE' (but only where followed by a blank space)

- 'WWW

(8) Taking the name remaining after the application of (1)–(7) above, disregard blank spaces.

[*SI 2015 No 17, Reg, 7, Sch 3*].

*Example of names 'the same as'*

Real Coffee Café Ltd is the same as

- Real Coffee Cafe Ltd

Plum Technology Ltd is the same as Plum Technology and Company Ltd.

(Companies House Guidance Booklet GP1 Incorporation and Names, Chr 6, para 6).

**Exceptions**. There is an exception to the rule that a company cannot be registered with the same name.

This is where the following conditions are met

- the company (company X) whose name already appears on the index of company names consents to the proposed name being the name of another company (company Y)

- company Y forms, or is to form, part of the same group as company X and

- company Y provides a statement to the Registrar of Companies made by company X indicating X's consent to the use of the name.

If the proposed same name is to be taken by a company which has not been incorporated, the copy consent must be delivered to the Registrar of Companies by the person who delivers the application for registration.

[*SI 2015 No 17, Reg 8*]

## 27.7 Sensitive words and expression

Certain names and expressions may suggest that a company has a particular status or function. If such words and expressions are included in a company's name then approval of the Secretary of State is required before a company can either be incorporated or change its name. Companies House administers this process.

The following provisions do not affect the continued registration of a company by a name by which it was duly registered immediately before 1 October 2009 and in the case of a 'transitional company', on its registration or re-registration.

See **27.5** for '*transitional company*'.

The approval of the Secretary of State is required for a company to be registered under *CA 2006* by a name that

- would be likely to give the impression that the company is connected with

  (i) Her Majesty's Government, any part of the Scottish administration, the Welsh Assembly Government or Her Majesty's Government in Northern Ireland;

(ii)     a local authority; or

(iii)    any public authority specified for these purposes by Regulations; or

• includes a word or expression 'other sensitive words or expressions' specified in the *Company, Limited liability, Partnership and Business Names (Sensitive Words and Expressions) Regulations 2014 (SI 2014 No 3140)*.

[*CA 2006, ss 54, 55, 56(1)*].

A list of all the sensitive words and expressions together with details of any necessary consents (other than the Secretary of State) is set out in the Companies House Guidance Booklet GP1 'Incorporation and Names' at Annexes A, B and C.

Annex A contains a list of sensitive words and expressions specified in regulations (referred to above) that cannot be used in a company name or business name without the prior approval of the Secretary of State.

Annex B contains a list of sensitive words and expressions that could imply a connection with a government department, a devolved administration, a local or specified public authority or a relevant body.

Annex C contains a list of words and expressions controlled by other legislation. The use of any of these words and expressions in a chosen name could be a criminal offence. This list is not exhaustive and applicants should make their own checks.

## 27.8   Permitted characters

The Regulations referred to in **27.5** above contain a list of the letters or other characters, signs or symbols (including accents and other diacritical marks) and punctuation that may be used in the name of a company registered under *CA 2006*. The Regulations do not affect the continued registration of a company by a name by which it was duly registered immediately before 1 October 2009 and in the case of a 'transitional company', on its registration or re-registration.

See **27.5** for '*transitional company*'.

[*CA 2006, s 57*].

Under these Regulations, the following permitted characters may be used in any part of the name.

• A, B, C, D, etc to X, Y, Z

• &, @, £, $, €, and ¥

• 0, 1, 2, 3, 4, 5, 6, 7, 8 or 9

• Full stop, comma, colon, semi-colon or hyphen

• Any of the following types of punctuation but only in the forms indicated:

(i)      Apostrophe: ' '

(ii)     Bracket: ( ) [ ] { } < >

(iii)    Exclamation mark: !

(iv)     Guillemet: « »

(v)      Inverted comma: " " "

(vi)     Question mark: ?

## 27.8 Names and Business Names

      (vii)    Solidus: \ /

In addition, the following signs and symbols are permitted characters that may be used but *not* as one of the first three characters of the name.

*, =, #, %, and +

[*SI 2015 No 17, Reg 2, Sch 1*].

## 27.9 Length of name

The name of a company registered under *CA 2006* must not consist of more than 160 permitted characters (see **27.8**). For the purposes of computing the number of permitted characters in the name, any blank space between one permitted character and another in the name is to be counted as though it was a permitted character. [*SI 2009 No 1085, Regs 1(3), 2(4)*].

This does affect the continued registration of a company by a name by which it was duly registered immediately before 1 October 2009; and in the case of a 'transitional company', on its registration or re-registration.

See **27.5** for '*transitional company*'.

[*CA 2006, s 57*].

## 27.10 How to register a company name

Before applying to set up a company, or do anything to change its name, it is advisable to search the index at Companies House to see if there are already any companies with names similar to the one proposed. You can do this by using Companies House free 'WebCheck' service. If in doubt, contact Companies House (tel: 0303 123 4500) or search the company names index at:

www.companieshouse.gov.uk

An applicant should also consider whether it is 'too like' another name so that, although it may be accepted by the Registrar of Companies, another company complains and a direction to change the name is made (see **27.6**).

The Registrar of Companies does not consult the Trade Marks Register when considering applications for new company names. Applicants are advised to make appropriate enquiries of the Trade Mark Register and to consider consulting a solicitor. For further advice, including how to search the Trade Mark Register, contact the Trade Marks Registry of the UK Intellectual Property Office at:

e-mail: enquiries@ipo.gov.uk

website: www.ipo.gov.uk

Registration of a company name should not be assumed to imply any subsequent acceptance of the same name for the purpose of the *Consumer Credit Act 1974*. From 1 April 2014, responsibility for consumer credit regulation has passed from the Office of Fair Trading to the Financial Conduct Authority.

If the name is not the same as one in the Index, and does not require prior approval of the Secretary of State, the incorporation documents (or, in the case of a change of name, the special resolution) should be submitted to the appropriate Registrar of Companies. If the name is acceptable and the documents correctly completed, the company name will be registered and a certificate of incorporation issued.

For all names requiring the approval of the Secretary of State applicants should seek the advice of New Companies Section at Companies House in Cardiff (companies intending to have their registered office in England or Wales) or Edinburgh (companies intending to have their registered office in Scotland). Details about the requirements on the use of the name will then be sent to the applicant.

*If the name includes any other words or expressions refer to Companies House Guidance Booklet GP1 (see 27.7).*

## 27.11 Compulsory change of name

A company may be directed to change its name in any of the circumstances in **27.12** to **27.16**.

**27.12** *Company ceasing to be entitled to exemption*

If it appears to the Secretary of State that a company whose name does not include 'limited' (or any of the permitted alternatives) has ceased to be entitled to exemption under **27.2**(1)–(4), he may direct the company to change its name within a specified period so that it ends with 'limited' (or one of the permitted alternatives).

A change of name in order to comply with such a direction can be made by resolution of the directors (without prejudice to any other method of changing the company's name). On the resolution being passed, the company must give notice to the Registrar of Companies of the change. *CA 2006, ss 80, 81* apply as regards the registration and effect of the change. See **27.17**.

If the company fails to comply with a direction an offence is committed by the company and every officer of the company who is in default. A person guilty of such an offence is liable, on summary conviction, to a fine not exceeding level 5 on the standard scale and, for continued contravention, to a daily default fine not exceeding one-tenth of the greater of £5,000 or level 4 on the standard scale. See **29.1** Offences and Legal Proceedings for the standard scale.

A company that has been directed to change its name may not, without the approval of the Secretary of State, subsequently change its name so that it does not include 'limited' (or one of the permitted alternatives). This does not apply to a change of name on re-registration or on conversion to a community interest company.

[*CA 2006, s 64; SI 2015 No 664, Sch 3*].

*Before 1 October 2009*, similar provisions applied under *CA 1985, s 31*. Where a direction was given under those provisions, it continues to apply on or after 1 October 2009 so that the company remains unable to be registered with a name that does not include 'limited' without the agreement of the Secretary of State. [*SI 2008 No 2860, Sch 2 para 20*].

**27.13** *Similarity to existing name*

The Secretary of State may direct a company to change its name following a complaint if:

- it has been registered in a name that is 'the same as' or, in the opinion of the Secretary of State, 'too like' a name appearing at the time of the registration in the Registrar of Companies' index of company names (or a name that should have appeared in that index at that time);

- misleading information to support the use of a sensitive word or expression was provided at the time of the registration;

- the name gives so misleading an indication of the company's activities it is likely to cause harm to the public;

- the company can no longer justify omitting "limited" from the end of its name; or

- the name is the same as a name associated with the applicant (complainant) in which he has goodwill or it is sufficiently similar and is likely to mislead by suggesting a connection between the company and the applicant (opportunistic registration) (see **27.14**).

[*CA 2006, s 67*].

Any such direction must be in writing and be given within 12 months of the registration of the name in question and must specify the period within which the company is to change its name. This period may be extended by a further direction in writing (but only before the end of the period for the time being specified). If a company fails to comply with the direction, an offence is committed by the company and every officer of the company who is in default. For this purpose a shadow director is treated as an officer of the company. A person guilty of such an offence is liable, on summary conviction, to a fine not exceeding level 3 on the standard scale and, for continued contravention, a daily default fine not exceeding one-tenth of level 3 on the standard scale. See **29.1** OFFENCES AND LEGAL PROCEEDINGS for the standard scale.

[*CA 2006, s 68*].

See **27.6** for '*the same as*'.

A direction may be issued, for example, as a result of an objection being lodged by an interested party because one name is 'too like' another. A company wishing to object to another company name because of similarity to its own name should write to:

*For companies incorporated in England and Wales:*

The Secretary of State
New Companies Section
Companies House
Crown Way
Cardiff
CF14 3UZ

*For companies incorporated in Scotland:*

The Secretary of State
New Companies Section
Companies House
4th Floor Edinburgh Quay 2
139 Fountainbridge
Edinburgh
EH3 9FF

Companies House takes the view that a name is 'too like' an existing name if

- it differs from another name on the index by only a few characters, signs, symbols or punctuation; or

- the names look and sound the same.

When deciding whether names are 'too like' Companies House will not consider factors such as:

- alleged trademark/patents infringement

- geographic locations

- similarity of activities

- possible passing off

- implied associations

(Companies House Guidance Booklet GP1 Incorporation and Names)

In considering whether names are similar, it is material to ascertain (i) what business has been or is intended to be carried on by the existing company and what is intended to be carried on by the new company; and (ii) what sort of name has been adopted by the existing company. See *Aerators Ltd v Tollitt* [1902] 2 Ch 319, 71 LJ Ch 727. The use of a name will not be allowed if it is intended to deceive or induce belief that the business is an extension of, or otherwise connected with, another company (*Ewing v Buttercup Margarine Co Ltd* [1917] 2 Ch 1, 86 LJ Ch 441, CA).

**27.14** *Similarity to other name in which a person has goodwill ("Opportunistic registration")*

Any person ('the applicant') may object to a company's registered name on the ground that it is

(a)    the same as a name associated with the applicant in which he has goodwill; or

(b)    sufficiently similar to such a name that its use in the UK would be likely to mislead by suggesting a connection between the company and the applicant.

The objection must be made by application to the Company Names Tribunal. The company concerned is the primary respondent to the application but any of its members or directors may be joined as respondents. Companies House does not deal with this kind of application.

If the ground in (*a*) or (*b*) above is established, it is for the respondents to show that

(i)    the name was registered before the commencement of the activities on which the applicant relies to show it has goodwill;

(ii)    the company

- is operating under the name;

- is proposing to do so and has incurred substantial start-up costs in preparation; or

- was formerly operating under the name and is now dormant;

(iii)    the name was registered in the ordinary course of a company formation business and the company is available for sale to the applicant on the standard terms of that business;

(iv)    the name was adopted in good faith; or

(v)    the interests of the applicant are not adversely affected to any significant extent.

If none of those is shown, the objection must be upheld. If the facts mentioned in (i), (ii) or (iii) above are established, the objection must nevertheless be upheld if the applicant shows that the main purpose of the respondents (or any of them) in registering the name was to obtain money (or other consideration) from the applicant or prevent him from registering the name.

'*Goodwill*' includes reputation of any description.

[*CA 2006, s 69*].

## 27.14 Names and Business Names

Full details of the application process and procedure can be found on the Company Names Tribunal website – www.ipo.gov.uk.

**27.15** *Provision of misleading information*

Where it appears to the Secretary of State that

- misleading information has been given for the purposes of the company's registration by a particular name, or

- an undertaking or assurance has been given for that purpose and has not been fulfilled

he may direct the company in writing to change its name.

Such a direction must be given within five years of the company's registration by that name. It must be complied with in the period specified in the direction (or such longer period as is allowed by further direction in writing).

If a company fails to comply with the direction, an offence is committed by the company and every officer of the company who is in default. For this purpose a shadow director is treated as an officer of the company. A person guilty of such an offence is liable, on summary conviction, to a fine not exceeding level 3 on the standard scale and, for continued contravention, a daily default fine not exceeding one-tenth of level 3 on the standard scale. See **29.1** OFFENCES AND LEGAL PROCEEDINGS for the standard scale.

[*CA 2006, s 75*].

**27.16** *Misleading indication of activities*

If, in the opinion of the Secretary of State, the name by which a company is registered is so misleading an indication of the nature of its activities as to be likely to cause harm to the public, he may direct the company to change its name. The direction must be in writing and be complied with within six weeks of the direction or such longer period as is allowed. The company may, however, within three weeks of the direction, apply to the court for the direction to be set aside. If the direction is confirmed by the court, it must specify the period within which the direction must be complied with.

If a company fails to comply with the direction, an offence is committed by the company and every officer of the company who is in default. For this purpose a shadow director is treated as an officer of the company. A person guilty of such an offence is liable, on summary conviction, to a fine not exceeding level 3 on the standard scale and, for continued contravention, a daily default fine not exceeding one-tenth of level 3 on the standard scale. See **29.1** OFFENCES AND LEGAL PROCEEDINGS for the standard scale.

[*CA 2006, s 76*].

*Before 1 October 2009*, similar provisions applied under *CA 1985, s 32*. Where such a direction was given, *CA 1985, s 32* continues to apply on or after 1 October 2009 in relation to the direction.

[*SI 2008 No 2860, Sch 2 para 21*].

## 27.17 Voluntary change of name

*Transitional provisions.* The provisions in this paragraph, to the extent that they relate to a change of name by special resolution, apply where

- the resolution was passed on or after 1 October 2009; or

- the resolution was passed before that date but no copy of the resolution was received by the Registrar of Companies under *CA 2006, s 30* (copies of resolutions affecting a company's constitution to be forwarded to the Registrar of Companies) before that date.

*CA 1985, s 28(1)(6)(7)* continues to apply to resolutions of which a copy is received by the Registrar of Companies before 1 October 2009.

[*SI 2008 No 2860, Sch 2 para 19*].

A company may change its name in the following ways.

(a) **By special resolution.** Where a change of name has been agreed to by a company by special resolution, the company must give notice to the Registrar of Companies. This is in addition to the obligation to forward a copy of the resolution to the Registrar.

Where a change of name by special resolution is conditional on the occurrence of an event, the notice given to the Registrar of Companies of the change must specify that the change is conditional and state whether the event has occurred. If the notice states that the event has not occurred,

- the Registrar of Companies is not required to act under *CA 2006, s 80* (see below) until further notice;

- when the event occurs, the company must give notice to the Registrar of Companies stating that it has occurred; and

- the Registrar of Companies may rely on the statement as sufficient evidence of the matters stated in it.

(b) **By other means provided for by the company's articles.** In such a case,

- the company must give notice to the Registrar of Companies; and

- the notice must be accompanied by a statement that the change of name has been made by means provided for by the company's articles.

The Registrar of Companies may rely on the statement as sufficient evidence of the matters stated in it.

(c) **By resolution of the directors to comply with a direction where the company ceases to be entitled to an exemption to use the word 'limited' in its name** (see **27.12**).

(d) **On the determination of a new name by the Company Names Adjudicator under** (see **27.14**).

(e) **On the determination of a new name by the court** following an appeal against a decision of the Company Names Adjudicator (see **27.14**).

(f) **On restoration of a company to the register** under *CA 2006, s 1033* (see **21.11** Dissolution and Restoration).

[*CA 2006, ss 77–79*].

### Application to change a name

Application must be made to Companies House. If the name is not the same as an existing name on the index (see **27.6**), does not include any sensitive words (see **27.7**) and is a change of name by special resolution (without conditions) the application can be sent either by Companies House software filing or by using their webfiling system. Paper applications can also be made but only if the change is made by special resolution (which may be conditional) or by other means set out in the company's articles. Each requires specific notices and/or additional documents. If the change is by means provided for in the company's articles, the application can be sent using Companies House software filing service.

**Registration and issue of new certificate of incorporation.** If the Registrar of Companies is satisfied that

- the new name complies with the provisions of this chapter,

- the requirements of the *Companies Acts* and any relevant requirements of the company's articles have been complied with,

he must enter the new name on the register in place of the former name. On the registration of the new name, the Registrar of Companies must issue a certificate of incorporation altered to meet the circumstances of the case. [*CA 2006, s 80*].

**Timing.** Electronic applications for change of name are usually processed within 24 hours. Same day service is also available. Paper applications are normally processed within five working days. Same day service is also available provided the documents are received before 3pm Monday-Friday. Fees for the cost of all these services can be found on Companies House website.

**Effect of change.** The change of a company's name has effect from the date on which the new certificate of incorporation is issued. The change does not affect any rights or obligations of the company or render defective any legal proceedings by or against it. Any legal proceedings that might have been continued or commenced against it by its former name may be continued or commenced against it by its new name. [*CA 2006, s 81*].

**Listed companies.** Any change in name must be notified to a RIS and the FCA. See **33.30(4)** PUBLIC AND LISTED COMPANIES.

In the selection of a new company's registered name, it is prudent from a general legal/commercial perspective to have regard to the risk if any of an action in trademark infringement or passing off. Further detail on these causes of action is beyond the scope of this text and the reader is invited to consult an intellectual property law volume.

Please see **16.12–16.17** on the requirements to disclose certain particulars of a company at business premises and at certain locations and in certain communications.

The Company Names Tribunal deals with complaints about cases where a company name is registered for the primary purpose of preventing someone else with legitimate interest from registering it, or demanding payment from them to release it. This Tribunal works in conjunction with the Intellectual Property Office. Further information about its procedures, fees, forms, decisions and orders, and the practice direction which governs the management of proceedings brought before the Tribunal, may be found at www.gov.uk/government/organisations/company-names-tribunal.

## 27.18  BUSINESS NAMES

The provisions in **27.19–27.26** relate to business names and are all contained in *CA 2006*. They replace the provisions formerly found in the *Business Names Act 1985*.

### 27.19  Restricted and prohibited names

The provisions in **27.20–27.22** apply to any person carrying on business (including a profession) in the UK. But they do not prevent

- an individual carrying on business under a name consisting of his 'surname' without any addition other than a 'permitted addition'; or

- individuals carrying on business in 'partnership' under a name consisting of the surnames of all the partners without any addition other than a permitted addition.

'*Surname*', in relation to a peer or person usually known by a British title different from his surname, means the title by which he is known.

'*Partnership*' means

- a partnership within the *Partnership Act 1890*; or

- a limited partnership registered under the *Limited Partnerships Act 1907*; or

- a firm or entity of a similar character formed under the law of a country or territory outside the UK.

The '*permitted additions*' are

- in the case of an individual, his forename or 'initial';

- in the case of a partnership

  (i)   the forenames of individual partners or the initials of those forenames; or

  (ii)  where two or more individual partners have the same surname, the addition of 's' at the end of that surname; and

- in either case, an addition merely indicating that the business is carried on in succession to a former owner of the business.

'*Initial*' includes any recognised abbreviation of a name.

[*CA 2006, ss 1192, 1208*].

**27.20** *Sensitive words and expressions*

Subject to the exceptions for existing names set out in **27.21**, the approval of the Secretary of State is required for a person to carry on a business in the UK by a name that

- would be likely to give the impression that the business is connected with

  (i)   Her Majesty's Government, any part of the Scottish administration, the Welsh Assembly Government or Her Majesty's Government in Northern Ireland;

  (ii)  a local authority; or

  (iii) any public authority specified for these purposes by Regulations; or

- includes a word or expression 'other sensitive words or expressions' specified in the *Company, Limited Liability Partnership and Business Names (Sensitive Words and Expressions) Regulations 2014* (see **27.7** for details).

The Regulations may require that, in connection with an application for approval, the applicant must seek the view of a specified Government department or other body.

**Offences.** A person who contravenes these provisions commits an offence. Where such an offence is committed by a body corporate, an offence is also committed by every officer of the body who is in default. A person guilty of such an offence is liable, on summary conviction, to a fine not exceeding level 3 on the standard scale and, for continued contravention, a daily default fine not exceeding one-tenth of level 3 on the standard scale. See **29.1** Offences and Legal Proceedings for the statutory maximum. The provisions of *CA 2006, ss 1121–1123* and *1125–1131* (see **29.1–29.7** Offences and Legal Proceedings) apply in relation to this offence.

[*CA 2006, ss 1193, 1194, 1195(1), 1207*].

**Withdrawal of approval.** If it appears to the Secretary of State that there are overriding considerations of public policy that require any approval given to be withdrawn, the approval may be withdrawn by notice in writing to the person concerned. The notice must state the date as from which approval is withdrawn. [*CA 2006, s 1196*].

**27.21** *Exception for existing lawful business names*

The provisions for approval of sensitive words and expressions (see **27.20**) do not apply in the following circumstances.

- To the carrying on of a business by a person who

    (i)     carried on the business immediately before 1 October 2009; and

    (ii)    continues to carry it on under the name that immediately before that date was its 'lawful business name'.

- Where

    (i)     a business is transferred to a person on or after 1 October 2009, and

    (ii)    that person carries on the business under the name that was its lawful business name immediately before the transfer,

    in relation to the carrying on of the business under that name during the period of twelve months beginning with the date of the transfer.

'*Lawful business name*', in relation to a business, means a name under which the business was carried on without contravening

- *Business Names Act 1985, s 2(1)* or *Business Names (Northern Ireland) Order 1986 (SI 1986 No 1033), Art 4(1)*, or

- after 1 October 2009, the provisions set out in **27.19–27.20**

[*CA 2006, s 1199*].

**27.22** *Misleading indication of activities*

A person must not carry on business in the UK under a name that gives so misleading an indication of the nature of the activities of the business as to be likely to cause harm to the public. A person who uses a name in contravention of this requirement commits an offence. Where such an offence is committed by a body corporate, an offence is also committed by every officer of the body who is in default. A person guilty of such an offence is liable, on summary conviction, to a fine not exceeding level 3 on the standard scale and, for continued contravention, a daily default fine not exceeding one-tenth of level 3 on the standard scale. See **29.1** Offences and Legal Proceedings for the standard scale. The provisions of *CA 2006, ss 1121–1123* and *1125–1131* (see **29.1–29.7** Offences and Legal Proceedings) apply in relation to this offence.

[*CA 2006, ss 1198, 1207*].

**27.23 Application for a business name**

For all names requiring the approval of the Secretary of State, applicants should seek the advice of Companies Registration Office in Cardiff (businesses in England or Wales) or Edinburgh (businesses in Scotland). Details about the requirements on the use of the name will then be sent to the applicant.

The application, together with any supporting information, should be submitted to the Secretary of State at the appropriate Companies Registration Office. If the name includes any word or expression which requires the consent of a relevant body (see **27.7**), the applicant must request (in writing) the relevant body to indicate whether (and if so why) it has any objection to the proposed name. A statement that such a request has been made, and a copy of any response received, must be submitted with the application to the Secretary of State, otherwise the he may refuse to consider it. [*CA 2006, s 1195(2)–(5)*].

Note that although the words in Appendix C of Companies House Guidance GP1 (see **27.7**) do not require the permission of the Secretary of State, their use may constitute a criminal offence. Owners of businesses wishing to use any of these words in a name should seek legal advice and confirmation from the body concerned that the use of the word does not contravene the legislation (although such confirmation should not be regarded as conclusive).

**27.24 DISCLOSURE REQUIRED BY INDIVIDUALS AND PARTNERSHIPS**

The provisions in **27.25–27.27** apply to an individual or 'partnership' carrying on business (including a profession) in the UK under a 'business name'. References to '*a person to whom these provisions apply*' are to such individuals or partnerships. For the provisions relating to companies trading under a business name, see **16.12 DEALINGS WITH THIRD PARTIES**.

'*Partnership*' means

- a partnership within the *Partnership Act 1890*; or

- a limited partnership registered under the *Limited Partnerships Act 1907*; or

- a firm or entity of a similar character formed under the law of a country or territory outside the UK.

'*Business name*' means a name other than

- in the case of an individual, his surname without any addition other than a 'permitted addition'; and

- in the case of a partnership

  (i)   the 'surnames' of all partners who are individuals, and

  (ii)  the corporate names of all partners who are bodies corporate,

  without any addition other than a 'permitted addition'.

'*Permitted additions*' are

- in the case of an individual, his forename or 'initial'; and

- in the case of a partnership

  (i)   the forenames of individual partners or the initials of those forenames; or

  (ii)  where two or more individual partners have the same surname, the addition of 's' at the end of that surname; and

- in either case, an addition merely indicating that the business is carried on in succession to a former owner of the business.

'*Surname*', in relation to a peer or person usually known by a British title different from his surname, means the title by which he is known.

'*Initial*' includes any recognised abbreviation of a name.

[*CA 2006, ss 1200, 1208, 1287*].

**27.25  Disclosure required in business documents, etc**

A person to whom these provisions apply (see **27.24**) must

(a)    subject to the exemption for large partnerships below, state the 'information required' in legible characters, on all

  (i)    business letters;

  (ii)   written orders for goods or services to be supplied to the business;

  (iii)  invoices and receipts issued in the course of the business; and

  (iv)   written demands for payment of debts arising in the course of the business; and

(b)    secure that the information required is immediately given, by written notice, to any person with whom anything is done or discussed in the course of the business and who asks for that information.

The Secretary of State may by Regulations require that such notices be given in a specified form.

[*CA 2006, s 1202*].

'*Information required*' is

- in the case of an individual, his name; and

- in the case of a partnership, the name of each member of the partnership

and in relation to each person so named, an address in the UK at which service of any document relating in any way to the business will be effective. If the individual or partnership has a place of business in the United Kingdom, the address must be in the United Kingdom and if the individual or partnership does not have a place of business in the United Kingdom, the address must be an address at which service of documents can be effected by physical delivery and the delivery of documents is capable of being recorded by the obtaining of an acknowledgement of delivery.

[*CA 2006, s 1201*].

**Exemption for large partnerships.** The requirements in (*a*) above do not apply in relation to a document issued by a partnership of more than 20 persons if the following conditions are met.

- The partnership must maintain at its principal place of business a list of the names of all the partners.

- No partner's name must appear in the document, except in the text or as a signatory.

- The document must state in legible characters the address of the partnership's principal place of business and that the list of the partners' names is open to inspection there.

Where a partnership maintains a list of the partners' names for these purposes, any person may inspect the list during office hours. If an inspection is refused, an offence is committed by any member of the partnership concerned who, without reasonable excuse, refused the inspection or permitted it to be refused. A person guilty of such an offence is liable, on summary conviction, to a fine not exceeding level 3 on the standard scale and, for continued contravention, a daily default fine not exceeding one-tenth of level 3 on the standard scale. See **29.1** OFFENCES AND LEGAL PROCEEDINGS for the standard scale. The provisions of *CA 2006, ss 1121–1123* and *1125–1131* (see **29.1–29.7** OFFENCES AND LEGAL PROCEEDINGS apply in relation to this offence.

[*CA 2006, s 1203, 1207*].

## 27.26 Disclosure required at business premises

A person to whom these provisions apply (see **27.24**) must, in any premises

- where the business is carried on, and

- to which customers of the business or suppliers of goods or services to the business have access,

display in a prominent position, so that it may easily be read by such customers or suppliers, a notice containing the 'information required'.

The Secretary of State may by Regulations require that such notices be displayed in a specified form. [*CA 2006, s 1204*].

'*Information required*' is the same as in **27.25**.

## 27.27 Consequence of failure to disclose

**Criminal consequences**. A person who, without reasonable excuse, fails to comply with the requirements of **27.25** or **27.26** commits an offence. Where any such offence is committed by a body corporate, an offence is also committed by every officer of the body who is in default.

A person guilty of an offence under these provisions is liable, on summary conviction, to a fine not exceeding level 3 on the standard scale and, for continued contravention, a daily default fine not exceeding one-tenth of level 3 on the standard scale. See **29.1** OFFENCES AND LEGAL PROCEEDINGS for the standard scale.

[*CA 2006, s 1205*].

**Civil consequences**. The following provisions apply to any legal proceedings, brought by an individual or partnership carrying on business in the UK under a business name, to enforce a right arising out of a contract made in the course of a business in respect of which that person was, at the time the contract was made, in breach of **27.25**(*a*) or (*b*) or **27.26**.

Such proceedings must be dismissed if the defendant (in Scotland, the defender) to the proceedings shows that

- he has a claim against the claimant (pursuer) arising out of the contract that he has been unable to pursue by reason of the latter's breach of those requirements, or

- he has suffered some financial loss in connection with the contract by reason of the claimant's (pursuer's) breach of those requirements,

unless the court before which the proceedings are brought is satisfied that it is just and equitable to permit the proceedings to continue.

# 27.27  Names and Business Names

This does not affect the right of any person to enforce such rights as he may have against another person in any proceedings brought by that person.

[*CA 2006, s 1206*].

**General provisions about offences.** The provisions of *CA 2006, ss 1121–1123* and *1125–1131* (see **29.1–29.7 OFFENCES AND LEGAL PROCEEDINGS**) apply in relation to the above offences. [*CA 2006, s 1207*].

# 28   Northern Ireland

## 28.1   EXTENSION OF LEGISLATION TO NORTHERN IRELAND

*CA 2006* creates a single company law regime which applies to the whole of the UK. Previously, provisions of GB company law were broadly replicated in separate Northern Ireland legislation. In particular the following legislation applies to Northern Ireland.

- The provisions of the *Companies Acts* (unless the context requires otherwise), ie

  (i)   the company law provisions of *CA 2006*, namely *CA 2006, Pts 1–39* together with *CA 2006, Pts 45–47* in so far as they apply for the purposes of those *Parts*;

  (ii)   *C(AICE)A 2004, Pt 2* (community interest companies); and

  (iii)   the provisions of *CA 1985* and *CC(CP)A 1985* that remain in force.

  As a result, *Companies (Northern Ireland) Order 1986 (SI 1986 No 1032)*, *Companies Consolidation (Consequential Provisions) (Northern Ireland) Order 1986 (SI 1986 No 1035)* and *Companies (Audit, Investigations and Community Enterprise) Order 2005 (SI 2005 No 1967), Part 3* cease to have effect.

- The enactments in force in GB relating to SEs extend to Northern Ireland.

  As a result, *European Public Limited-Liability Company Regulations (Northern Ireland) 2004 (SR 2004 No 417)* and *European Public Limited-Liability Company (Fees) Regulations (Northern Ireland) 2004 (SR 2004 No 418)* cease to have effect.

- The enactments in force in GB relating to

  (i)   limited liability partnerships;

  (ii)   limited partnerships;

  (iii)   open-ended investment companies; and

  (iv)   European Economic Interest Groupings

  As a result, *Limited Liability Partnerships Act (Northern Ireland) 2002, Limited Partnerships Act 1907* as it formerly had effect in Northern Ireland, *Open-Ended Investment Companies Act (Northern Ireland) 2002* and *European Economic Interest Groupings Regulations (Northern Ireland) 1989 (SR 1989 No 216)* cease to have effect.

- The provisions of *CA 2006, Pt 41* (business names).

  As a result, *Business Names (Northern Ireland) Order 1986 (SI 1986 No 1033)* ceases to have effect.

[*CA 2006, ss 2, 1284–1287*].

# 29   Offences and Legal Proceedings

**General note.** The provisions of *CA 2006* relating to offences and legal proceedings as detailed in this chapter were, unless otherwise stated, fully implemented with effect from 1 October 2009. But the provisions in this chapter do not apply to offences committed before the commencement of the relevant provision.

[*CA 2006, s 1133*].

For the provisions in *CA 1985* applying to offences committed before 1 October, see the Appendix at the end of the chapter.

## 29.1   OFFENCES UNDER THE COMPANIES ACTS

There are a large number of offences for failure to comply with the requirements of the *Companies Acts*. These are dealt with in the appropriate part of the text. For example it is an offence for a company to fail to deliver a fully completed annual return to the Registrar of Companies (see **7.4**) Punishment, depending on the offence, may be by way of imprisonment or a fine (or both). Notably, the recently amended PSC regime itself entails various offences that may be committed by investigating entities and potential or actual PSCs or 'registrable relevant legal entities' under the PSC regime. See **38** REGISTERS.

Companies are regulated by the department of Business Innovation and Skills ('BIS'). BIS also has a wide purview in promoting the interests of UK business, employers and consumers.

As part of its jurisdiction, BIS also has an investigation and prosecutorial function in relation to suspected misconduct in the course of a range of corporate activities; these include fraudulent trading, breach of bankruptcy/disqualification orders and other company offences.

In relation to financial crime, the Companies Investigation Branch of BIS carries out investigations into abuse by companies or by those involved in the running of a company who may have been engaged in fraud, serious misconduct, or material irregularities in a company's affairs.

The Secretary of State may appoint investigators under *CA 1985, ss 431 and 432*. The investigation will conclude with a report which may or may not be made public.

Moreover, under *CA 1985, s 447*, investigators may be authorised to require a company to provide documentation to assist an investigation and to require individuals to answer questions relating to the content of documents. Failure to comply with a request for assistance without reasonable excuse may constitute a contempt of court.

## 29.1   Offences and Legal Proceedings

**On conviction on indictment,** any fine imposed is unlimited.

**On summary conviction** fines in magistrates' courts are fixed up to a maximum level (the statutory maximum see below).Certain offences provide that a person guilty of the offence is liable to a fine not exceeding a specified amount (for example level 4 on the standard scale) and 'for continued contravention, a daily default fine' not exceeding a specified amount.

[*CA 2006, s 1125*].

**Statutory maximum** means, in England and Wales, the sum prescribed under the *Magistrates' Courts Act 1980, s 32* and, in Scotland, the sum prescribed under the *Criminal Procedure (Scotland) Act 1975, s 289B*. The statutory maximum is currently £5,000.

**Standard scale.** Certain penalties are determined by reference to the 'standard scale' (level 5 on which is equivalent to the statutory maximum).

'*Standard scale*' means the scale laid down by the *Criminal Justice Act 1991, s 17* (in Scotland the *Criminal Procedure (Scotland) Act 1975, s 289G*) and is as follows.

| Level on the scale | Amount of fine |
|---|---|
| 1 | £200 |
| 2 | £500 |
| 3 | £1,000 |
| 4 | £2,500 |
| 5 | £5,000 |

## 29.2   Removal of upper limit for fines imposed on summary conviction in magistrates' courts

The *Legal Aid, Sentencing and Punishment of Offenders Act 2012* was given Royal Assent on 1 May 2012. *Sections 85–87* of this *Act* provide (in summary) that offences currently punishable on summary conviction with the statutory maximum (see above) will be punishable by an unlimited fine. This means that the same sentencing principles will apply whether the offence is tried summarily or on indictment and may potentially lead to greater fines being imposed on companies and their officers.

Various provisions of this Act came into force in May 2014. They are *s 85(3), (5)–(13)* and *(15)–(17)*. They provide in summary that where an offence is relevant for the purposes of *s 85*, the Secretary of State can disapply *s 85(1)* and *(2)* (removal of upper limits) and instead substitute new maximum fines or proportionate fines.

*Section 85(1), (2)* and *(4)* came into force in March 2015. At the same time regulations made under the Act (*The Legal Aid, Sentencing and Punishment of Offenders Act 2012 (Fines on Summary Conviction) Regulations 2015 (SI 2015 No 664)*) came into force and provide at *Sch 3* for certain offences currently punishable by a fine of a proportion of level 5 on the standard scale to be punishable by a fine of a proportion of the greater of £5,000 or level 4 on the standard scale. These mainly affect daily default fines imposed under *CA 2006* and are referred to where relevant throughout the text.

## 29.3   Liability of officer in default

Where an offence is committed by a company under any provision of the *Companies Acts*, an offence is committed by every 'officer' of the company who is 'in default'. For this purpose '*officer*' includes

- any director, manager or secretary; and

- any person who is to be treated as an officer of the company for the purposes of the provision in question.

Many offences provide that a shadow director is to be treated, for the purposes of the relevant offence as a director of the company. In other words, liability can extend to those who are not, or may not necessarily be, involved in the day to day decision making of the company.

An officer is '*in default*' for the purposes of the provision if he authorises or permits, participates in, or fails to take all reasonable steps to prevent, the contravention.

[*CA 2006, s 1121*].

**Liability of company as officer in default.** Where a company is an officer of another company, it does not commit an offence as an officer in default unless one of its officers is in default. But where an offence is committed by such a company, the officer in question also commits the offence and is liable to be proceeded against and punished accordingly.

The purpose of this provision is to ensure that where a company (company B) is an officer of another company (company A) (for example a company may be the company secretary of another company in the same group of companies) liability for an offence can only be fixed on company B as an "officer in default" if one of its own officers is in default. So for example if company A fails to submit an annual return within the time limit, company B can only be liable if one of its officers is also in default in failing to submit the annual return.

[*CA 2006, s 1122*].

**Application to bodies other than companies.** *CA 2006, s 1121* above applies to a body other than a company as it applies to a company and for these purposes

(a)    in relation to a body corporate other than a company

- the reference to a director of the company must be read as referring

    (i)    where the body's affairs are managed by its members, to a member of the body; and

    (ii)   in any other case, to any corresponding officer of the body; and

- the reference to a manager or secretary of the company must be read as referring to any manager, secretary or similar officer of the body;

(b)    in relation to a partnership

- the reference to a director of the company must be read as referring to a member of the partnership; and

- the reference to a manager or secretary of the company must be read as referring to any manager, secretary or similar officer of the partnership; and

(c)    in relation to an unincorporated body other than a partnership

- the reference to a director of the company must be read as referring

    (i)    where the body's affairs are managed by its members, to a member of the body; and

    (ii)   in any other case, to a member of the governing body; and

- the reference to a manager or secretary of the company must be read as referring to any manager, secretary or similar officer of the body.

## 29.3 Offences and Legal Proceedings

[*CA 2006, s 1123*].

### 29.4 Legal professional privilege

In proceedings against a person for an offence under the *Companies Acts*, nothing in those *Acts* is to be taken to require any person to disclose any information that he is entitled to refuse to disclose on grounds of legal professional privilege (in Scotland, confidentiality of communications).

Legal professional privilege protects all communications between a professional legal advisor and his client from being disclosed without the permission of the client. *CA 2006, s 1123* therefore protects the company and/ or its officers from having to disclose something in the course of proceedings which would otherwise be protected by client confidentiality (privilege). "Communications" between a client and advisor could for example be letters written from / to a company and its solicitors provided they are confidential and are written for the purposes of giving or seeking legal advice. It would not apply if the advice was purely commercial in nature and had no legal content. If legal advice is given to a subsidiary company which then reports it to its parent company, the advice may still be protected by privilege.

[*CA 2006, s 1129*].

### 29.5 SUMMARY PROCEEDINGS

**Venue**. Summary proceedings for an offence under the *Companies Acts* may be taken

- against a body company at any place at which the body has a place of business; and

- against any other person at any place at which he is for the time being.

This is without prejudice to any jurisdiction exercisable apart from the above.

[*CA 2006, s 1127*].

**Time limit for proceedings**.

(a)    *In England and Wales*, an information relating to an offence under the *Companies Acts* that is triable by a magistrates' court may be so tried if it is laid

- at any time within three years after the commission of the offence; and

- within 12 months after the date on which evidence sufficient in the opinion of the Director of Public Prosecutions or the Secretary of State (as the case may be) to justify the proceedings comes to his knowledge.

(b)    *In Scotland*, summary proceedings for an offence under the *Companies Acts*

- must not be commenced after the expiration of three years from the commission of the offence; and

- subject to that, may be commenced at any time

    (i)    within 12 months after the date on which evidence sufficient in the Lord Advocate's opinion to justify the proceedings came to his knowledge; or

    (ii)   where such evidence was reported to him by the Secretary of State, within 12 months after the date on which it came to the knowledge of the latter.

*Criminal Procedure (Scotland) Act 1995, s 136(3)* (date when proceedings deemed to be commenced) applies for these purposes.

(c)     *In Northern Ireland*, a magistrates' court has jurisdiction to hear and determine a complaint charging the commission of a summary offence under the *Companies Acts* provided that the complaint is made

- within three years from the time when the offence was committed; and

- within 12 months from the date on which evidence sufficient in the opinion of the Director of Public Prosecutions for Northern Ireland or the Secretary of State (as the case may be) to justify the proceedings comes to his knowledge.

For the above purposes, a certificate of the Director of Public Prosecutions, the Lord Advocate, the Director of Public Prosecutions for Northern Ireland or the Secretary of State (as the case may be) as to the date on which such evidence as is referred to above came to his notice is conclusive evidence.

[*CA 2006, s 1128*].

## 29.6   CONSENT REQUIRED IN CERTAIN PROSECUTIONS

With effect from 6 April 2008, proceedings for offences under the following provisions can only be instituted in England and Wales and Northern Ireland by, or with the consent of, the appropriate authority indicated.

(a)     *CA 2006, ss 458, 460* (unauthorised disclosure of information, see **2.15** ACCOUNTS: GENERAL) and *CA 2006, s 949* (unauthorised disclosure of information, see **48.2** TAKEOVERS) — the Secretary of State or the Director of Public Prosecutions (in Northern Ireland, the Secretary of State or the Director of Public Prosecutions for Northern Ireland).

(b)     *CA 2006, s 953* (failure to comply with rules about takeover bid documents, see **48.3** TAKEOVERS) — the Secretary of State or the Director of Public Prosecutions (in Northern Ireland, the Secretary of State or the Director of Public Prosecutions for Northern Ireland).

(c)     *CA 2006, s 798* (offence of attempting to evade restrictions on shares, see **24.8** INTERESTS IN PUBLIC COMPANY SHARES) — the Secretary of State.

(d)     *CA 1985, ss 448, 449–451, 453A* (offences in connection with company investigations, see **25.12**, **25.14–25.16** and **25.18** INVESTIGATIONS) — the Secretary of State or the Director of Public Prosecutions (in Northern Ireland, the Secretary of State or the Director of Public Prosecutions for Northern Ireland).

(e)     *CA 1985, s 455* (offence of attempting to evade restrictions on shares, see **25.24** INVESTIGATIONS) — the Secretary of State.

[*CA 2006, s 1126*].

## 29.7   PROCEEDINGS AGAINST UNINCORPORATED BODIES

*CA 2006* provides for proceedings against unincorporated bodies to be brought against them as if they were corporate bodies. Proceedings for an offence under the *Companies Acts* alleged to have been committed by an unincorporated body must be brought in the name of the body (and not in that of any of its members).

## 29.7 Offences and Legal Proceedings

For the purposes of such proceedings

- any rules of court relating to the service of documents have effect as if the body were a body corporate; and

- the provisions of

  (i) in England and Wales, *Criminal Justice Act 1925, s 33* and *Magistrates' Courts Act 1980, Sch 3,*

  (ii) in Scotland, *Criminal Procedure (Scotland) Act 1995, ss 70, 143,* and

  (iii) in Northern Ireland, *Criminal Justice Act (Northern Ireland) 1945, s 18* and *Magistrates' Courts (Northern Ireland) Order 1981 (SI 1981 No 1675), Art 166, Sch 4*

  apply as they apply in relation to a body corporate.

A fine imposed on an unincorporated body on its conviction of an offence under the *Companies Acts* must be paid out of the funds of the body.

[*CA 2006, s 1130*].

## 29.8 PRODUCTION AND INSPECTION OF DOCUMENTS WHERE OFFENCE SUSPECTED

Where there is a reasonable cause to believe

- that any person has, while an officer of a company, committed an offence in connection with the management of the company's affairs, and

- that evidence of this is to be found in any 'documents' in the possession or control of the company,

on application, a court order may be made

- authorising any person named in it to inspect the documents in question, or any of them, for the purposes of investigating and obtaining evidence of the offence; and

- (except in the case of a banking company) requiring the secretary of the company, or such other officer as is named in the order, to produce the documents (or any of them) to a person named in the order at a place so named.

'*Document*' includes information recorded in any form. This could include documents in hard copy form or in electronic form such as e-mails or faxes.

There is no appeal against such an order.

An application for such an order may be made

- in England and Wales, to a judge of the High Court by the Director of Public Prosecutions, the Secretary of State or a chief officer of police;

- in Scotland, to one of the Lords Commissioners of Justiciary by the Lord Advocate; and

- in Northern Ireland, to the High Court by the Director of Public Prosecutions for Northern Ireland, the Department of Enterprise, Trade and Investment or a chief superintendent of the Police Service of Northern Ireland.

[*CA 2006, s 1132*].

## 29.9  MEANING OF 'THE COURT'

Unless it is otherwise provided, in the *Companies Acts 'the court'* means

- in England and Wales, the High Court or a county court;
- in Scotland, the Court of Session or the sheriff court; and
- in Northern Ireland, the High Court.

The provisions of the *Companies Acts* that confer jurisdiction on 'the court' as defined above have effect subject to any enactment or rule of law relating to the allocation of jurisdiction or distribution of business between courts in any part of the UK.

This section of *CA 2006* defines the term "court" for the purposes of the Companies Acts. The effect of this definition is that except where "otherwise provided" (for example in other legislation) proceedings brought under the Companies Acts can only be heard in the courts provided for in *s 1156*.

[*CA 2006, s 1156*].

## 29.10  POWER OF COURT TO GRANT RELIEF

With effect from 1 October 2008, if in any proceedings for negligence, default, breach of duty or breach of trust against

- an officer of a company, or
- a person employed by a company as auditor (whether or not an officer of the company)

it appears to the court hearing the case that the officer or person is or may be liable but that he has acted honestly and reasonably, and that having regard to all the circumstances of the case (including those connected with his employment) he ought fairly to be excused, the court may relieve him, wholly or partly, from his liability on such terms as it thinks fit. If the case is being tried by a judge with a jury, the judge, after hearing the evidence, may, if satisfied that the defendant (in Scotland, the defender) ought to be relieved in whole or part from liability, withdraw the case from the jury and direct judgment to be entered for the defendant (in Scotland, grant decree of absolvitor) on such terms and costs (in Scotland, expenses) as he thinks proper.

Where such an officer or person has reason to apprehend that a claim will or might be made against him for negligence etc, he may apply to the court for relief. The court then has the same power to relieve him as it would have had in actual proceedings for negligence, etc as above.

[*CA 2006, s 1157*].

## 29.11  SECURITY FOR COSTS (SCOTLAND)

*CA 1985, s 726(1)* and *726(2)* provided that all companies, whether in England, Wales or Scotland, could be ordered. to provide (for example) assets of the company as security for costs in specific circumstances when making a claim. *Section 726(1)* was repealed on 1 October 2009 but section *726(2)* was specifically preserved. This section provides as follows:

where, in Scotland, a limited company is pursuer in legal proceedings, the court having jurisdiction may, if it appears by credible testimony that there is reason to believe that the company will be unable to pay the defender's expenses if successful in his defence, order the company to find caution and sist the proceedings until caution is found.

In *section 726(2)* the following words have the following (equivalent) meaning in English law:

"pursuer" means plaintiff or claimant

"defender" means defendant

"caution" means security and

"sist" means to stay proceedings

[*CA 1985, s 726(2); SI 2008 No 2860, Sch 1; SI 2009 No 1941, Art 13*].

Note that the effect of *SI 2009 No 1941* is to preserve *CA 1985, s 726(2)*.

## APPENDIX: OFFENCES UNDER THE COMPANIES ACTS (*CA 1985* PROVISIONS)

The provisions of *CA 2006* relating to offences and legal proceedings as detailed in the above chapter are fully implemented with effect from 1 October 2009. But

- those provisions do not apply to offences committed before the commencement of the relevant provision.

[*CA 2006, s 1133*]; and

- the repeal of any provision in *CA 1985* creating an offence does not affect the continued operation of that provision in relation to an offence committed before 1 October 2009.

[*SI 2008 No 2860, Sch 2 para 116*].

(1) **Punishment of offences**

The penalties for conviction of offences under the *CA 1985* (other than those relating to investigations and orders imposing restrictions on shares, see INVESTIGATIONS) are listed in *CA 1985, Sch 24*. The levels of penalties in order of seriousness are as follows.

|     |                | *Punishment*                              | *Daily default fine*                    |
| --- | -------------- | ----------------------------------------- | --------------------------------------- |
| (a) | On indictment  | 7 years or a fine; or both                |                                         |
|     | Summary        | 6 months or statutory maximum; or both    |                                         |
| (b) | On indictment  | 2 years or a fine; or both                |                                         |
|     | Summary        | 6 months or statutory maximum; or both    |                                         |
| (c) | On indictment  | A fine                                     |                                         |
|     | Summary        | Statutory maximum                          | One-tenth of statutory maximum          |
| (d) | On indictment  | A fine                                     |                                         |
|     | Summary        | Statutory maximum                          |                                         |
| (e) | Summary        | Statutory maximum                          | One-tenth of statutory maximum          |
| (f) | Summary        | One-fifth of statutory maximum            | One-fiftieth of statutory maximum       |
| (g) | Summary        | One-fifth of statutory maximum            |                                         |

# Appendix   Offences and Legal Proceedings

|  |  | Punishment | Daily default fine |
|---|---|---|---|
| (h) | On indictment | A fine | |
| | Summary | Statutory maximum | £100 |

**Punishment** is the maximum fine or imprisonment which can be imposed on a person convicted of the offence in the way specified, a reference to a period of years or months being to a term of imprisonment of that duration. The fine on conviction on indictment is unlimited.

**Daily default fine.** Where a person is convicted of an offence (and incurs a penalty as under the *Punishment* column) but continues in contravention of the relevant provision, then, on a second or subsequent summary conviction of the offence, he is liable to a default fine for each day on which the contravention is continued (instead of the penalty under the *Punishment* column).

**Statutory maximum** means, in England and Wales, the sum prescribed under the *Magistrates' Courts Act 1980, s 32* and, in Scotland, the sum prescribed under the *Criminal Procedure (Scotland) Act 1975, s 289B*. The statutory maximum is currently £5,000.

[*CA 1985, s 730, Sch 24; CA 1989, Sch 19 para 17; SI 2007 No 2194, Sch 4 para 12*].

**Standard scale.** Certain new penalties under *CA 1985* are determined by reference to the 'standard scale' (level 5 on which is equivalent to the statutory maximum).

'*Standard scale*' means the scale laid down by the *Criminal Justice Act 1982, s 37* (in Scotland the *Criminal Procedure (Scotland) Act 1975, s 289G*) and is as follows.

| Level on the scale | Amount of fine |
|---|---|
| 1 | £200 |
| 2 | £500 |
| 3 | £1,000 |
| 4 | £2,500 |
| 5 | £5,000 |

## (2)   Summary proceedings

Summary proceedings for an offence under the *CA 1985* (other than *Pt 14* or *Pt 15*), the insider dealing legislation, *Companies Consolidation (Consequential Provisions) Act 1985* or *BNA 1985* may be taken

• against a company at any place at which it has a place of business; and

• against any other person at any place at which he is for the time being.

*In England and Wales*, proceedings which are triable by a magistrates' court must be brought within three years of the commission of the offence and within twelve months of the date on which evidence sufficient, in the opinion of the Director of Public Prosecutions or the Secretary of State (as the case may be), to justify the proceedings comes to his knowledge.

*In Scotland*, summary proceedings must be commenced within three years of the commission of the offence. Subject to this, proceedings may be commenced within twelve months of the date on which evidence sufficient, in the Lord Advocate's opinion, to justify the proceedings came to his knowledge or, where the evidence was reported to him by the Secretary of State, within twelve months of the date on which it came to the notice of the latter.

[*CA 1985, s 731; BNA 1985, s 7(6); Criminal Procedure (Consequential Provisions) (Scotland) Act 1995, Sch 4 para 56; SI 2007 No 2194, Sch 4 para 14*].

(3)    **Prosecution by public authorities**

*Before 6 April 2008*, proceedings in England and Wales for an offence under *CA 1985, ss 245E* or *245G* (restriction on further use/disclosure of information disclosed to HMRC or certain authorised persons) could only be brought with the consent of the Secretary of State or the Director of Public Prosecutions.

In any proceedings instituted under the *Companies Acts* (including *BNA 1985*) by the Director of Public Prosecutions, the Secretary of State or the Lord Advocate, nothing in those Acts was to be taken as requiring any person to disclose any information which he was entitled to refuse to disclose on the grounds of legal professional privilege or, in Scotland, confidentiality of communications.

[*CA 1985, s 732; BNA 1985, s 7(6); C(AICE)A 2004, Sch 2 paras 5, 7, 16, 22; SI 1995/710, Reg 5; SI 2007 No 2194, Sch 4 para 15*].

*Transitional provisions.* The repeal of the above provisions does not affect their operation in relation to offence committed before 6 April 2008.

[*SI 2007 No 3495, Sch 4 para 44*].

(4)    **Offences by bodies corporate**

*Before 6 April 2008*, where a body corporate was guilty of an offence under the provisions listed below and it was proved that the offence occurred with the consent or connivance of, or was attributable to any neglect on the part of, any director, manager, secretary or other similar officer (or any person purporting to act in such a capacity) he, as well as the body corporate, was guilty of that offence and was liable to be proceeded against and punished accordingly. If the affairs of the company were managed by the members, this also applied in relation to any act or default of a member in connection with his functions of management as if he were a director.

The relevant provisions were as follows.

(a)    *CA 1985, ss 245E(3)* and *245G(7)* (disclosure of information by HM Revenue and Customs or an authorised person).

(b)    *CA 1985, s 394A(1)* (statement by person ceasing to hold office as auditor, see **8.23 AUDIT**).

[*CA 1985, s 733; CA 1989, s 123, Sch 24; IA 1985, Sch 6 para 7; IA 1986, Sch 13 Pt I; C(AICE)A 2004, Sch 2 paras 5, 8, 16, 23; SI 2007 No 2194, Sch 4 para 16*].

Transitional provisions. The repeal of the above provisions does not affect their operation in relation to offence committed before 6 April 2008.

[*SI 2007 No 3495, Sch 4 para 44*].

(5)   **Criminal proceedings against unincorporated bodies**

*Before 6 April 2008*, proceedings for an offence alleged to have been committed by an unincorporated body under

(a)   *CA 1985, ss 245E(3)* and *245G(7)* (disclosure of information by HM Revenue and Customs or an authorised person), or

(b)   *CA 1985, s 394A(1)* (statement by person ceasing to hold office as auditor, see **8.23** AUDIT)

had to be brought in the name of that body (and not any of its members). For the purposes of such proceedings, any rules of court relating to the service of documents applied as if that body were a corporation.

Any fine imposed on an unincorporated body on conviction of such an offence had to be paid out of the funds of the body.

Where an offence within (*a*) or (*b*) above was proved to have been committed with the consent or connivance of, or to be attributable to any neglect on the part of,

•      in the case of a partnership, a partner, or

•      in the case of any other unincorporated body, an officer of the body or a member of its governing body,

that person, as well as the body, was guilty of the offence and liable to be proceeded against and punished accordingly.

[*CA 1985, s 734; CA 1989, ss 120, 123, Sch 19 para 18; Criminal Procedures (Scotland) Act 1995, Sch 4 para 56; C(AICE)A 2004, Sch 2 paras 5, 9, 16, 24; SI 2007 No 2194, Sch 2, Sch 4 para 16; SI 2007 No 3495, Sch 5 para 2*].

*Transitional provisions.* The repeal of the above provisions does not affect their operation in relation to offence committed before 6 April 2008.

[*SI 2007 No 3495, Sch 4 para 44*].

(6)   **Service of documents**

A document may be served on a company by leaving it at, or sending it by post to, the company's registered office. [*CA 1985, s 725(1)*]. See also *JC Houghton & Co v Nothard, Lowe and Wills Ltd* [1928] AC 1, 97 LJKB 76, HL.

Where a company registered in Scotland carries on business in England and Wales, the process of any court in England and Wales may be served on the company by leaving it at, or sending it by post to, the company's principal place of business in England and Wales. It should be addressed to the manager or other head officer of the company in England and Wales. The person issuing out the process must send a copy by post to the company's registered office.

[*CA 1985, s 725(2)(3)*].

(7)   **Power of court to grant relief**

*Before 1 October 2008*, if in any proceedings for negligence, default, breach of duty or breach of trust against an officer of a company or auditor it appears to the court that that person, although liable, acted honestly and reasonably and ought fairly to be excused, the court may relieve him, wholly or partly, from liability on such terms as it thinks fit. If the case is being tried by a judge with a jury, the judge may, after hearing the evidence, withdraw the case in whole or part from the jury and direct judgment to be entered for the defendant.

[*CA 1985, s 727(1)(3)*].

Where an officer of a company or auditor has reason to believe that a claim will or might be made against him for negligence etc, he may apply to the court for relief. The court has the same powers of relief on such an application as it does above in actual proceedings for negligence etc.

[*CA 1985, s 727(2)*].

(8)    **Security for costs and expenses in certain actions**

Where a limited company is plaintiff (in Scotland, pursuer) in legal proceedings and there is reason to believe that the company will be unable to pay the defendant's costs (in Scotland, the defender's expenses) if defence is successful, the court may require security to be given for those costs (in Scotland, order the company to find caution) and may determine not to proceed until such condition is satisfied. [*CA 1985, s 726*].

(9)    **Production and inspection of books where offence suspected**

Where there is a reasonable cause to believe that any person has, while an officer of a company, committed an offence in connection with the management of the company's affairs and that evidence of this is to be found in any 'books or papers' of, or under the control of, the company, the Director of Public Prosecutions, the Secretary of State or a chief officer of police (in Scotland, the Lord Advocate) may obtain a court order

- authorising any person to inspect the books and papers in question in order to investigate the offence; and

- (except in the case of a banking company) requiring an officer to produce the books etc named in the order at a place so named.

There is no appeal against such an order.

'*Books or papers*' include accounts, deeds, writings and documents.

[*CA 1985, ss 721, 744*].

# 30  Overseas Companies – Establishing a Place of Business in the UK

**Background.** The provisions in this chapter apply, unless otherwise stated, with effect from 1 October 2009. For the provisions applying before that date, see the Appendix at the end of the chapter. This chapter does not deal with the any of Listing Rules which apply to overseas companies. The *Companies Act 2006 (Strategic Report and Directors' Report) Regulations 2013* ('the *2013 Regulations*') which are referred to in various parts of this chapter, brought into force the requirement for a company to produce a strategic report for financial years ending on or after 30 September 2013.

# 30.1 Overseas Companies

## 30.1 DEFINITION OF 'OVERSEAS COMPANY'

An *'overseas company'* means a company incorporated outside the UK.

[*CA 2006, s 1044*].

## 30.2 REGISTRATION OF PARTICULARS

If an overseas company wants to establish a business in the UK it can do so either by creating a subsidiary company or by opening a branch or place of business. This chapter deals only with the latter. When opening a business in the UK an overseas company is required by regulations made under *CA 2006* to register certain particulars and documents with the Registrar of Companies.

[*CA 2006, ss 1046, 1047, 1055, 1056, 1058*].

Those regulations are the *Overseas Companies Regulations 2009 (SI 2009 No 1801)*.

## 30.3 Initial registration

The provisions in this paragraph and in **30.4** to **30.6** apply to an overseas company that opens a UK establishment. *'Establishment'* means a branch within the meaning of the *EC Eleventh Company Law Directive (89/666/EEC)* or a place of business that is not such a branch, ie is a place where the company regularly conducts its business in the UK.

The company must, within one month of having opened a UK establishment,

- deliver to the Registrar of Companies a return containing the particulars in (1) and (2) below and, where appropriate, the statement of compliance with accounting requirements (see **30.5** below); and

- deliver with the return the documents required under **30.4**.

These requirements apply each time a company opens an establishment in the UK. It should be noted that the relocation of a UK establishment from one part of the UK to another counts as the closing of one UK establishment and the opening of another (although the relocation of a UK establishment within the same part of the UK does not).

[*CA 2006, s 1059*].

The particulars required are as follows. If the company has another UK establishment for which it has already delivered a return and has no obligation to alter the particulars in that return (see **30.7–30.9** re Alterations to Particulars) then the company may instead state in the return that the particulars are included in the return delivered for the other UK establishment and give the registered number of that other establishment. Also see Companies House Guidance Booklet GP01 'Overseas Companies registered in the UK' for details of which forms must be completed and relevant fees,

(1) **Particulars of the company**

- The company's name.

- The company's legal form.

- If it is registered in the country of its incorporation, the identity of the register in which it is registered and the number with which it is so registered.

- A list of its directors giving particulars of:

(a)   *In the case of an individual,* (i) his name; (ii) any former name; (iii) a service address; (iv) usual residential address; (v) the country or state in which the individual is usually resident; (vi) nationality; (vii) business occupation (if any); and (viii) his date of birth.

(b)   *In the case of a body corporate, or a firm that is a legal person under the law by which it is governed* (i) corporate or firm name; (ii) registered or principal office; (iii) in the case of an EEA company to which the *EC First Company Law Directive* applies, particulars of the register in which the company file mentioned in *Article 3* of that Directive is kept (including details of the relevant state) and the registration number in that register; and (iv) in any other case, particulars of the legal form of the company or firm and the law by which it is governed and, if applicable, the register in which it is entered (including details of the state) and its registration number in that register.

For the purposes of (*a*)(ii) above, where a person is (or was) formerly known by more than one former name, each of them must be stated. But it is not necessary to include particulars of a former name (i) in the case of a peer or an individual normally known by a title, where the name is one by which the person was known previous to the adoption of or succession to the title; or (ii) in the case of any person, where the former name was changed or disused before the person attained the age of sixteen years or has been changed or disused for twenty years or more.

For the purposes of (*a*)(iv) above, if the person's usual residential address is the same as his service address the return need only contain a statement to that effect.

•   The secretary giving particulars of (where there are joint secretaries, with respect to each of them)

(a)   *in the case of an individual,* (i) name; (ii) any former name; and (iii) a service address; and

(b)   *in the case of a body corporate, or a firm that is a legal person under the law by which it is governed,* (i) corporate or firm name; (ii) registered or principal office; (iii) in the case of an EEA company to which the *EC First Company Law Directive* applies, particulars of the register in which the company file mentioned in *Article 3* of that Directive is kept (including details of the relevant state) and the registration number in that register; and (iv) in any other case, particulars of the legal form of the company or firm and the law by which it is governed and, if applicable, the register in which it is entered (including details of the state) and its registration number in that register.

But if all the partners in a firm are joint secretaries of the company it is sufficient to state the particulars that would be required if the firm were a legal person and the firm had been appointed secretary.

For the purposes of (*a*)(ii) above, where a person is (or was) formerly known by more than one former name, each of them must be stated. But it is not necessary to include particulars of a former name (i) in the case of a peer or an individual normally known by a title, where the name is one by which the person was known previous to the adoption of or succession to the title; or (ii) in the case of any person, where the former name was changed or disused before the person attained the age of 16 years or has been changed or disused for 20 years or more.

- The extent of the powers of the directors or secretary to represent the company in dealings with third parties and in legal proceedings, together with a statement as to whether they may act alone or must act jointly and, if jointly, the name of any other person concerned.

- Whether the company is a credit or financial institution.

- In the case of a company which is not incorporated in an EEA State,

  (a)  the law under which the company is incorporated;

  (b)  in the case of a company to which either **30.19** to **30.23** or **30.36** to **30.39** applies (companies required to prepare or disclose accounts under parent law), the period for which the company is required by its parent law to prepare accounts, together with the period allowed for the preparation and public disclosure (if any) of accounts for such a period,

  (c)  unless disclosed by company's constitution (see **30.4**(1)), the address of its principal place of business in its country of incorporation (or, if applicable, its registered office), its objects, and the amount of its issued share capital.

(2)  **Particulars of the establishment**

(a)  Address of the establishment.

(b)  Date on which it was opened.

(c)  Business carried on at it.

(d)  Name of the establishment if different from the name of the company.

(e)  Name and service address of every person resident in the UK authorised to accept service of documents on behalf of the company in respect of the establishment, or a statement that there is no such person.

(f)  A list of every person authorised to represent the company as a permanent representative of the company in respect of the establishment, containing with respect to such person

  (i)  name;

  (ii)  any former name;

  (iii)  service address; and

  (iv)  usual residential address.

(g)  Extent of the authority of any person falling within (f) above, including whether that person is authorised to act alone or jointly.

(h)  if a person falling within (f) is not authorised to act alone, the name of any person with whom they are authorised to act.

For the purpose of paragraph (f)(iv) if the person's usual residential address is the same as the person's service address the return need only contain a statement to that effect. [*SI 2009 No 1801, Regs 3–7*].

**Transitional provisions**.

(a)  An overseas company that immediately before 1 October 2009

(i)     has a branch in the UK; and

(ii)    has complied in respect of that branch with the registration requirements as set out in the Appendix to this Chapter at (6)–(10),

is treated as having complied in respect of that branch with the above requirements relating to particulars of the company and establishment.

Certain particulars, as specified in *SI 2009 No 1801, Sch 8 paras 4, 5* are treated as if delivered and registered under (1) and (2) above. For those requirements which are not treated as registered, the company must deliver a transitional return in respect of the establishment to the Registrar of Companies by no later than 31 March 2010.

(b)    An overseas company that immediately before 1 October 2009

(i)     has a place of business (other than a branch) in the UK, and

(ii)    has delivered to the Registrar of Companies in respect of that place of business the documents required as set out in the Appendix to this Chapter at (3)(a) and (b),

is treated as having complied in respect of that place of business with the requirements relating to particulars of the company and establishment.

Certain particulars, as specified in *SI 2009 No 1801, Sch 8 paras 10, 11* are treated as if delivered and registered under (1) and (2) above. For those requirements which are not treated as registered, the company must deliver a transitional return in respect of the establishment to the Registrar of Companies by no later than 31 March 2010.

A company which falls within (*a*)(i) or (*b*)(i) above but which has not complied with the requirements in (*a*)(ii) or, as the case may be, (*b*)(ii) above, is treated as if it had opened that establishment on 1 October 2009.

[*SI 2009 No 1801, Sch 8 paras 3–5, 9–11, 13(1)–(3), 14*].

**30.4**   *Documents to be delivered with the return*

The following documents must be delivered to the Registrar of Companies with the return required under **30.3**.

(1)    *Copy of company's constitution*

A certified copy of the company's 'constitution' must be delivered to the Registrar of Companies with the return. But if, at the time the return is delivered, the company

•      has another UK establishment,

•      has delivered a certified copy of the company's constitution with a return relating to that establishment, and

•      has no outstanding obligation under **30.7** to **30.9** in respect of an alteration to its constitution,

the company may instead state in the return that a certified copy of the company's constitution has been delivered in respect of another UK establishment (giving the registered number of that establishment).

Companies House requires that a certified translation of the constitution in English must also be sent if the original is in another language (see Companies House Guidance Booklet GP01 Chapter 1 para 1).

'*Constitution*', in relation to an overseas company, means the charter, statutes, memorandum and articles of association or other instrument constituting or defining the company's constitution.

[*SI 2009 No 1801, Regs 2, 8*].

(2)    *Copies of accounting documents*

If the company is one to which **30.19** to **30.23** applies (companies required to prepare and disclose accounts under parent law), copies of the company's 'latest accounting documents' must be delivered to the Registrar of Companies with the return.

'*Latest accounting documents*' means the accounting documents, prepared for a financial period of the company, last disclosed in accordance with its parent law before the end of the period allowed for delivery of the return or, if earlier, the date on which the company delivers the return.

But if, at the time the return is delivered, the company

•    has another UK establishment, and

•    has delivered the latest accounting documents in connection with a return relating to that establishment,

the company may instead state in the return that the documents are included in the material delivered in respect of another UK establishment (giving the registered number of that establishment).

[*SI 2009 No 1801, Reg 9*].

The certified translations provisions (above) apply to the accounts as they do to the constitution delivered to Companies House.

*Transitional provisions.*

(a)    An overseas company that immediately before 1 October 2009

(i)    has a branch in the UK, and

(ii)    has complied in respect of that branch with the registration requirements as set out in the Appendix to this Chapter at (6)–(10),

is treated as having complied in respect of that branch with the above requirements relating to delivering a certified copy of the company's constitution and accounting documents.

(b)    An overseas company that immediately before 1 October 2009

(i)    has a place of business (other than a branch) in the UK, and

(ii)    has delivered to the Registrar of Companies in respect of that place of business the documents required as set out in the Appendix to this Chapter at (3)(a) and (b),,

(c)    is treated as having complied in respect of that place of business with the requirements relating to delivering a certified copy of the company's constitution.

A company which falls within (*a*)(i) or (*b*)(i) above but which has not complied with the requirements in (*a*)(ii) or, as the case may be, (*b*)(ii) above, is treated as if it had opened that establishment on 1 October 2009.

[*SI 2009 No 1801, Sch 8 paras 3, 6, 7, 9, 12, 14*].

**30.5**  *Statement of future manner of compliance with accounting requirements*

If the company is one to which the provisions in **30.18** to **30.34** apply (delivery of accounting documents: general), the return required under **30.3** must state

- in the case of a company to which **30.19** to **30.23** applies (companies required to file copies of accounting documents disclosed under parent law), whether it is intended to file copies of accounting documents in accordance with those provisions in respect of the establishment to which the return relates or in respect of another UK establishment; and

- in the case of a company to which **30.24** to **30.34** applies (companies required to file accounts under UK law), whether it is intended to file accounts in accordance with the provisions in respect of the establishment to which the return relates or in respect of another UK establishment.

If the return states that it is intended to file copies of accounting documents, or accounts, in respect of another UK establishment, it must give the registered number of that establishment.

[*SI 2009 No 1801, Reg 10*].

*Transitional provisions.* An overseas company that immediately before 1 October 2009

(i)    has a branch in the UK, and

(ii)   has complied in respect of that branch with the registration requirements as set out in the Appendix to this Chapter at (6)–(10),

is treated as having complied in respect of that branch with the above requirements.

If the company is one to which **30.19** to **30.23** applies (companies required to prepare and disclose accounts under parent law), then the following, as they appear on the register immediately before 1 October 2009, are treated as if delivered and registered under *Reg 10*, namely

- the statement in the return in respect of a branch whether it is intended to file copies of accounting documents in respect of that branch or in respect of another branch; and

- if the return states that it is intended to file copies of accounting documents in respect of another branch, the registered number of that branch.

But the company must have delivered any other information required under *Reg 10* to the Registrar of Companies in a transitional return in respect of the establishment by no later than 31 March 2010.

A company which falls within (i) above but which has not complied with the requirements in (ii) above is treated as if it had opened that establishment on 1 October 2009.

[*SI 2009 No 1801, Sch 8 paras 3, 8, 13, 14*].

**30.6**  *Penalty for non-compliance*

If a company fails to comply with any of the requirements in **30.3** to **30.5**, an offence is committed by the company and every officer or agent of the company who knowingly and wilfully authorises or permits the default. A person guilty of such an offence is liable, on summary conviction, to a fine not exceeding level 3 on the standard scale, and, for continued contravention, a daily default fine not exceeding one-tenth of level 3 on the standard scale. See **29.1** OFFENCES AND LEGAL PROCEEDINGS for the standard scale.

## 30.6 Overseas Companies

[*SI 2009 No 1801, Reg 11*].

### 30.7 Alterations in registered particulars

The provisions in this paragraph and in 30.8 to 30.10 apply to an overseas company that

- has complied with the initial registration requirements in 30.3 to 30.6 in respect of one or more UK establishments; and

- has not subsequently given notice under 30.57 (notice of closure of UK establishment) in respect of all those establishments.

[*SI 2009 No 1801, Reg 12*].

(1) **Return of alteration in registered particulars**

If an alteration is made in any of the particulars delivered under 30.3(1) or (2), the company must deliver to the Registrar of Companies a return containing details of the alteration.

Where a company has more than one UK establishment, a return is required in respect of each UK establishment to which the alteration relates; but a return giving the registered numbers of more than one UK establishment is treated as a return in respect of each of them.

An alteration in any of the particulars specified in 30.3(1) (particulars of the company) is treated as relating to every UK establishment of the company.

The details required of the alteration are

- the particular that has been altered;

- details of the particular as altered; and

- the date on which the alteration was made.

The return must also state the company's name and registered number and the name (if different from the company's name) and registered number of each UK establishment to which the return relates.

The period allowed for delivery of the return is

- in the case of an alteration of any of the particulars specified in 30.3(1) (particulars of the company), 21 days after the date on which notice of the alteration in question could have been received in the UK in due course of post (if despatched with due diligence);

- in the case of an alteration of any of the particulars specified in 30.3(2) (particulars of the establishment), 21 days after the alteration is made.

[*SI 2009 No 1801, Reg 13*].

Transitional provisions. The provisions as set out in the Appendix to this Chapter at (4) and (11) continue to apply in relation to an alteration made before 1 October 2009. The above provisions apply to alterations made on or after 1 October 2009.

[*SI 2009 No 1801, Sch 8 para 15*].

(2)    **Return of alteration in company's constitution**

If any alteration is made in the company's 'constitution', the company must deliver to the Registrar of Companies a return stating

- that an alteration has been made to the company's constitution;
- the date on which the alteration was made;
- the company's name;
- the company's registered number; and
- the name (if different from the company's name) and registered number of each UK establishment to which the return relates.

The return must be accompanied by a certified copy of the constitution as altered.

'*Constitution*', in relation to an overseas company, means the charter, statutes, memorandum and articles of association or other instrument constituting or defining the company's constitution.

Where a company has more than one UK establishment, a return is required in respect of each UK establishment to which the alteration relates but a return giving the registered numbers of more than one UK establishment is treated as a return in respect of each of them.

An alteration in the company's constitution is treated as relating to a UK establishment only if a copy of the constitution is included in the material registered in respect of that establishment.

The period allowed for delivery of the return is 21 days after the date on which notice of the alteration in question could have been received in the UK in due course of post (if despatched with due diligence).

[*SI 2009 No 1801, Regs 2, 14*].

*Transitional provisions.* The provisions as set out in the Appendix to this Chapter at (4) and (11) continue to apply in relation to an alteration made before 1 October 2009. The above provisions apply to alterations made on or after 1 October 2009.

[*SI 2009 No 1801, Sch 8 para 16*].

**30.8**   *Return of alteration regarding filing of certified copy of constitution*

Where

- the company's initial return in respect of an establishment states that a certified copy of the company's 'constitution' has been delivered in respect of another UK establishment, and
- that statement ceases to be true

the company must deliver to the Registrar of Companies a further return in respect of the first-mentioned establishment

(a)    stating that the previous statement has ceased to be true

(b)    either

    (i)    accompanied by a certified copy of the company's constitution; or

   (ii)    stating that a copy of the company's constitution is included in the material delivered in respect of another UK establishment (giving the registered number of that establishment); and

(c)   stating

   (i)    the company's name;

   (ii)    the company's registered number; and

   (iii)    the name (if different from the company's name) and registered number of each UK establishment to which the return relates.

'*Constitution*', in relation to an overseas company, means the charter, statutes, memorandum and articles of association or other instrument constituting or defining the company's constitution.

Where the company has more than one UK establishment a return giving the registered numbers of more than one UK establishment is treated as a return in respect of each of them.

The period allowed for delivery of the return is 21 days after the date on which notice of the fact that the statement in the earlier return has ceased to be true could have been received in the UK in due course of post (if despatched with due diligence).

Where, after a company has made a return under this provision, the statement mentioned in (*b*)(ii) ceases to be true, the above requirements apply again.

[*SI 2009 No 1801, Regs 2, 15*].

*Transitional provisions.* The provisions of *CA 1985, Sch 21A para 8* (see the Appendix to this Chapter at (11)) continue to apply where the statement ceases to be true before 1 October 2009. The above provisions apply where that statement ceases to be true on or after 1 October 2009. [*SI 2009 No 1801, Sch 8 para 17*].

**30.9**   *Return of alteration of manner of compliance with accounting requirements*

Where

• a company's initial return in respect of a UK establishment states an intention as to whether accounting documents, or accounts, are to be filed in accordance in respect of that establishment or in respect of another UK establishment (see **30.5**), and

• that intention changes

the company must deliver to the Registrar of Companies a further return in respect of the first-mentioned establishment stating

(a)   that the intention has changed;

(b)   either

   (i)    that it is intended to file accounting documents, or accounts, in respect of the establishment to which the return relates; or

   (ii)    that it is intended to file accounting documents, or accounts, in respect of another UK establishment (giving the registered number of that establishment);

(c)   the company's name;

(d)   the company's registered number; and

(e)     the name (if different from the company's name) and registered number of each UK establishment to which the return relates.

Where the company has more than one UK establishment, a return giving the registered numbers of more than one UK establishment is treated as a return in respect of each of them.

The period allowed for delivery of the return is 21 days after the date on which notice of the fact that the intention stated in the earlier return has changed could have been received in the UK in due course of post (if despatched with due diligence).

Where, after a company has made a return under the above provisions, the intention stated in accordance with (b)(i) or (b)(ii) changes again, the above requirements apply again.

[*SI 2009 No 1801, Reg 16*].

**30.10** *Penalty for non-compliance*

If a company fails to comply with any of the requirements of **30.7** to **30.9**, an offence is committed by the company and every officer or agent of the company who knowingly and wilfully authorises or permits the default. A person guilty of such an offence is liable, on summary conviction, to a fine not exceeding level 3 on the standard scale and, for continued contravention, a daily default fine not exceeding one-tenth of level 3 on the standard scale. See **29.1** OFFENCES AND LEGAL PROCEEDINGS for the standard scale.

[*SI 2009 No 1801, Reg 17*].

## 30.11  REGISTERED NAME OF OVERSEAS COMPANY

An overseas company that is required to register particulars must register its name (see **30.3**). This may be

•       the company's corporate name (ie its name under the law of the country or territory in which it is incorporated); or

•       an alternative name (see below).

Where the overseas company is incorporated in an EEA state, it may always register its corporate name (even if it does not comply with the requirement imposed on the names of companies formed under *CA 2006*) provided that it complies with the requirements in *CA 2006, s 57* (permitted characters, etc, see **27.8** NAMES AND BUSINESS NAMES).

In any other case, the corporate name of an overseas company can only be registered if it complies with the requirements imposed on the names of companies formed and registered under *CA 2006* (apart from the requirements for the names of certain types of company to end with certain words which are not appropriate for overseas companies). See **27.3–27.10** NAMES AND BUSINESS NAMES. [*CA 2006, s 1047; SI 2015 No 17, Regs 12–15*].

**Registration under an alternative name.** An overseas company that is required to register particulars with the Registrar of Companies may at any time deliver to the Registrar for registration a statement specifying a name, other than its corporate name, under which it proposes to carry on business in the UK. An overseas company that has registered an alternative name may then subsequently deliver to the Registrar of Companies for registration a statement specifying a different name under which it proposes to carry on business in the UK (which may be its corporate name or a further alternative) in substitution for the name previously registered.

But (wherever the overseas company is incorporated) any name other than its corporate name can be registered only if it complies with the requirements imposed on the names of companies formed and registered under *CA 2006* (apart from the requirements for the names of certain types of company to end with certain words which are not appropriate for overseas companies). See **27.3–27.10** NAMES AND BUSINESS NAMES.

## 30.11 Overseas Companies

The alternative name for the time being registered under this provision is treated for all purposes of the law applying in the UK as the company's corporate name. But this does not

- affect the references in this provision or *CA 2006, s 1047* above to the company's corporate name;

- affect any rights or obligation of the company; or

- render defective any legal proceedings by or against the company.

Any legal proceedings that might have been continued or commenced against the company by its corporate name, or any name previously registered under this provision, may be continued or commenced against it by its name for the time being so registered.

[*CA 2006, s 1048*].

An overseas company, as defined by *CA 2006, s 1044*, is exempt from the obligation to keep a PSC register. See **38.18**.

An overseas company with a registered UK establishment must comply with *Part 4* of the *Company, Limited Liability Partnership and Business (Names and Trading Disclosures) Regulations 2015 (SI 2015/17)*. Details of that regime are set out at **16.12–16.16** TRADING DISCLOSURES.

## 30.12 USUAL RESIDENTIAL ADDRESSES: PROTECTION FROM DISCLOSURE

The provisions in **30.13** to **30.17** apply to an overseas company that has one or more UK establishments in respect of which it has registered particulars under **30.3**. They protect, in respect of

- a company director who is an individual and whose particulars have been delivered to the Registrar of Companies under **30.3(1)**, and

- a permanent representative of the company whose particulars have been delivered under **30.3(2)(*f*)**

information as to his usual residential address and the information that his service address is his usual residential address.

That information is referred to as *'protected information'*.

Information does not cease to be protected information on the person ceasing to be a director or permanent representative and, to that extent, references to a director or permanent representative include a former director or permanent representative.

[*SI 2009 No 1801, Regs 18, 19*].

## 30.13 Restriction on use or disclosure of protected information

(1) *By the company*

A company must not use or disclose 'protected information' (see **30.12**) about a director or permanent representative, except

- for communicating with the individual concerned;

- in order to comply with any requirement of the *Overseas Companies Regulations 2009 (SI 2009 No 1801)* as to particulars to be sent to the Registrar of Companies; or

- in accordance with **30.16** (disclosure under a court order).

But this does not prohibit any use or disclosure of protected information with the consent of the director or permanent representative concerned.

[*SI 2009 No 1801, Reg 20*].

(2) *By the Registrar of Companies*

The Registrar of Companies

(a)     must omit 'protected information' (see **30.12**) from the material on the register that is available for inspection where

   (i)     it is contained in a document delivered to him in which such information is required to be stated, and

   (ii)    in the case of a document having more than one part, it is contained in a part of the document in which such information is required to be stated;

(b)     is not obliged

   (i)     to check other documents or (as the case may be) other parts of the document to ensure the absence of protected information; or

   (ii)    to omit from the material that is available for public inspection anything registered before 1 October 2009; and

(c)     must not use or disclose protected information except as permitted under **30.14** or in accordance with **30.16**.

[*SI 2009 No 1801, Reg 21*].

*Transitional provisions* – where the protected information provisions do not apply.

•     The provisions above do not apply to

   (i)     material delivered to the Registrar of Companies before 1 October 2009; or

   (ii)    material delivered to him on or after 1 October 2009 being a return of an alteration in particulars which occurred before that date.

•     In (*b*)(ii) above, the reference to things being registered before 1 October 2009 is treated as including anything registered as a result of a return made on or after 1 October 2009 of an alteration occurring before that date.

But these transitional provisions have effect subject to the continued protection of information formerly protected by a confidentiality order.

[*SI 2009 No 1801, Sch 8 para 19*].

### 30.14  Permitted use or disclosure by the Registrar of Companies

The Registrar of Companies may use 'protected information' (see **30.12**) in the following ways.

(1)     **Communication**

For communicating with the director or permanent representative.

[*SI 2009 No 1801, Reg 22*].

(2)     **Disclosure to specified public authorities**

To disclose the protected information to a specified public authority where the following conditions are satisfied.

(a)    The specified public authority has delivered to the Registrar of Companies a statement that it intends to use the protected information only for the purpose of facilitating the carrying out by it of a 'public function' ('*the permitted purpose*').

(b)    Subject to below, the specified public authority has delivered to the Registrar of Companies a statement that it will, where it supplies a copy of the protected information to a 'processor' for the purpose of processing the information for use in respect of the permitted purpose

(i)    ensure that the processor is one who carries on business in the EEA;

(ii)    require that the information is not transmitted outside the EEA by the processor; and

(iii)    require that the processor does not disclose the information except to the authority or an employee of the authority.

But this condition does not apply where the specified public authority is the Secret Intelligence Service, Security Service or Government Communications Headquarters.

'*Processor*' means any person who provides a service which consists of putting information into data form or processing information in data form, and reference to a processor includes a reference to the processor's employees.

An employee of a person who has access to protected information is deemed to include any person working or providing services for the purposes of that person or employed by or on behalf of, or working for, any person who is so working or who is supplying such a service.

'*Public function*' includes

•    any function conferred by or in accordance with any provision contained in any enactment;

•    any function conferred by or in accordance with any provision contained in the Community Treaties or any Community instrument;

•    any similar function conferred on persons by or under provisions having effect as part of the law of a country or territory outside the UK; and

•    any function exercisable in relation to the investigation of any criminal offence or for the purpose of any criminal proceedings.

The disclosure for the purpose of facilitating the carrying out of a public function includes disclosure in relation to, and for the purpose of, any proceedings whether civil, criminal or disciplinary in which the specified public authority engages while carrying out its public functions.

The specified public authorities for these purposes are

•    the Secretary of State;

•    any Northern Ireland Department;

•    the Scottish Ministers;

•    the Welsh Ministers;

•    the Treasury;

- the Commissioners for Her Majesty's Revenue and Customs;
- the Bank of England;
- the Director of Public Prosecutions;
- the Director of Public Prosecutions for Northern Ireland;
- the Serious Fraud Office;
- the Secret Intelligence Service;
- the Security Service;
- the Government Communications Headquarters;
- the Financial Services Authority;
- the Competition Commission;
- the Pensions Regulator;
- the Panel on Takeovers and Mergers;
- the Regulator of Community Interest Companies;
- the Registrar of Credit Unions for Northern Ireland;
- the Office of the Information Commissioner;
- the Charity Commission;
- the Charity Commission for Northern Ireland;
- the Office of the Scottish Charity Regulator;
- the Postal Services Commission;
- the Gas and Electricity Markets Authority;
- the Northern Ireland Authority for Utility Regulation;
- the Gambling Commission;
- the Serious Organised Crime Agency;
- the Health and Safety Executive;
- the Health and Safety Executive for Northern Ireland;
- the Food Standards Agency;
- the Gangmasters Licensing Authority;
- the Security Industry Authority;
- a local authority (within the meaning of *CA 2006, s 54(2)*);
- an official receiver appointed under *IA 1986, s 399*;
- the Official Receiver for Northern Ireland;
- the Crown Office and Procurator Fiscal Services;
- a person acting as an insolvency practitioner within the meaning of *IA 1986, s 388* or *Insolvency (Northern Ireland) Order 1989, Art 3*;

- an inspector appointed under *CA 1985, Pt 14* or *Companies (Northern Ireland) Order 1986, Pt 15* (investigation of companies and their affairs: requisition of documents) or a person appointed under *Open-Ended Investment Companies Regulations 2001, Reg 30* or *Open-Ended Investment Companies Regulations (Northern Ireland) 2004, Reg 22* (power to investigate);

- any person authorised to exercise powers under *CA 1985, s 447* (power to require documents and information), or *CA 1989, s 84* (exercise of powers by officers, etc) or *Companies (Northern Ireland) Order 1986, Art 440*;

- any person exercising functions conferred by *FSMA 2000, Pt 6* (official listing) or the competent authority under that Part;

- a person appointed to make a report under *FSMA 2000, s 166* (reports by skilled persons);

- a person appointed to conduct an investigation under *FSMA 2000, s 167* (appointment of persons to carry out general investigations) or *FSMA 2000, s 168(3)* or *(5)* (appointment of persons to carry out investigations in particular cases);

- an inspector appointed under *FSMA 2000, s 284* (power to investigate);

- an overseas regulatory authority within the meaning of *CA 1989, s 82* (request for assistance by overseas regulatory authority); and

- a police force.

A specified public authority must deliver to the Registrar of Companies such information or evidence as he may direct to enable him to determine whether to disclose protected information. The Registrar may require such information or evidence to be verified in such manner as he may direct.

The specified public authority must inform the Registrar of Companies immediately of any change in respect of any statement delivered to him under (*a*) or (*b*) above or information or evidence provided to enabling him to determine whether to disclose protected information.

[*SI 2009 No 1801, Reg 23, Sch 1, Sch 2 paras 1–4, 11*].

(3)    **Disclosure to credit agencies**

Subject to **30.15**, to disclose the protected information to a '*credit reference agency*' (ie a person carrying on a business comprising the furnishing of information relevant to the financial standing of individuals, being information collected by the agency for that purpose) where the following conditions are satisfied.

(a)    The credit reference agency is carrying on in the UK or in another EEA State a business comprising the furnishing of information relevant to the financial standing of individuals, being information collected by the agency for that purpose.

(b)    The credit reference agency maintains appropriate procedures

(i)    to ensure that an independent person can investigate and audit the measures maintained by the agency for the purposes of ensuring the security of any protected information disclosed to that agency; and

(ii)    for the purposes of ensuring that it complies with its obligations under the *Data Protection Act 1998* or, where the agency carries on business in a EEA State other than the UK, with its obligations under legislation implementing *EC Directive 95/46/EC* on the protection of individuals with regard to the processing of personal data and on the free movement of such data.

(c)     The credit reference agency has not been found guilty of an offence under

(i)     *CA 2006, s 1112* (general false statement offence) or *Fraud Act 2006, s 2* (fraud by false representation); or

(ii)    *Data Protection Act 1998, s 47* (failure to comply with enforcement notice) in circumstances where it has used the protected information for purposes other than those in (*d*)(i)–(vi) below.

(d)     The credit reference agency has delivered to the Registrar of Companies a statement that it intends to use the protected information only for the purposes of

(i)     providing an assessment of the financial standing of a person;

(ii)    meeting any obligations contained in the *Money Laundering Regulations 2007* or any rules made pursuant to *FSMA 2000, s 146* (money laundering rules), or in any legislation of another EEA State implementing *EC Directive 2005/60/EC* on the prevention of the use of the financial system for the purpose of money laundering and terrorist financing;

(iii)   conducting conflict of interest checks required or made necessary by any enactment;

(iv)    the provision of protected information to a public authority within (2) above which has satisfied the requirements of (2)(*a*) and (*b*) above;

(v)     the provision of protected information to another credit reference agency which has itself satisfied necessary requirements for permitted disclosure to a credit reference agency; or

(vi)    conducting checks for the prevention and detection of crime and fraud.

(e)     The credit reference agency has delivered to the Registrar of Companies a statement that it intends to take delivery of and to use the protected information only in the UK or in another EEA State.

(f)     The credit reference agency has delivered to the Registrar of Companies a statement that it will, where it supplies a copy of the protected information to a 'processor' for the purpose of processing the information for use in respect of the purposes referred to in (*d*) above

(i)     ensure that the processor is one who carries on business in the EEA;

(ii)    require that the information is not transmitted outside the EEA by the processor; and

(iii)   require that the processor does not disclose the information except to the credit reference agency or an employee of the credit reference agency.

'*Processor*' means any person who provides a service which consists of putting information into data form or processing information in data form, and reference to a processor includes a reference to the processor's employees.

An employee of a person who has access to protected information is deemed to include any person working or providing services for the purposes of that person or employed by or on behalf of, or working for, any person who is so working or who is supplying such a service.

(g)    The credit reference agency has delivered to the Registrar of Companies a statement that it meets the conditions in (a)–(c) above.

The Registrar of Companies may rely on the statement under (g) above as sufficient evidence of the matters stated in it. Notwithstanding this, a credit reference agency must deliver to the Registrar such information or evidence in addition to that statement as he may direct to enable him to determine whether to disclose protected information. The Registrar may require such information or evidence to be verified in such manner as he may direct.

The credit reference agency must inform the Registrar of Companies immediately of any change in respect of any statement delivered to him under (a)–(g) above or information or evidence provided to enable him to determine whether to disclose protected information.

[*SI 2009 No 1801, Reg 24, Sch 2 paras 5–11*].

**30.15** *Application to prevent disclosure to a credit reference agency*

An application can be made to the Registrar of Companies to prevent the disclosure to a credit reference agency of protected information relating to a director or permanent representative (an '*application for higher protection*').

The Registrar of Companies must not disclose to a credit reference agency protected information relating to

- an individual in respect of whom a successful application for higher protection has been made;

- an individual in respect of whom an application for higher protection has been made where

    (i)    the Registrar of Companies has not made a determination; or

    (ii)   he has made a determination rejecting the application and an appeal against that determination has been brought but has not been determined; or

- an individual in relation to whom a confidentiality order was in force under *CA 1985, s 735B* immediately before 1 October 2009 and who, by virtue of the transitional provisions below is to be treated as having made a successful application for higher protection.

[*SI 2009 No 1801, Reg 25*].

The application must be made and determined in accordance with the following provisions.

(1)    *Application by the individual concerned*

An application for higher protection may be made to the Registrar of Companies by an individual who is, or proposes to become, a director or permanent representative of a company on the grounds that the applicant considers that there is a serious risk that the applicant, or a person who lives with the applicant, will be subjected to violence or intimidation as a result of the activities of at least one of

    (i)    the overseas companies of which the applicant is, or proposes to become, a director or permanent representative;

(ii)     the overseas companies of which the applicant was a director or permanent representative;

(iii)    the companies of which the applicant is or has been a director; or

(iv)    the limited liability partnerships of which the applicant is or has been a member.

The application must contain

- a statement of the grounds on which the application is made;

- the name and any former name of the applicant;

- the date of birth of the applicant;

- the usual residential address of the applicant;

- where the Registrar of Companies has allocated a unique identifier to the applicant, that unique identifier;

- the name and registered number of each overseas company of which the applicant is, or proposes to become, a director or permanent representative; and

- where the grounds of the application are those described in (ii), (iii) or (iv) above, the name and registered number of the overseas company, company or limited liability partnership.

The application must be accompanied by evidence which supports the applicant's statement of the grounds of the application. The Registrar of Companies may request additional information or evidence and may also refer to a 'relevant body' any question relating to an assessment of the nature and extent of any risk of violence or intimidation.

The Registrar of Companies may accept any answer from a relevant body as sufficient evidence of the matter referred to it.

A 'relevant body' means any police force and any other person whom the Registrar of Companies considers may be able to assist in answering a question referred to that person by him.

The Registrar of Companies must determine the application and send the applicant notice of his determination to his usual residential address, as stated in his application, within five working days of the determination being made.

(2)    *Application by a company*

An application for higher protection may be made to the Registrar of Companies by a company on behalf of its directors or permanent representatives on the grounds that the company considers that there is a serious risk that the director or permanent representative on behalf of whom the application is made, or a person who lives with that director or permanent representative, will be subjected to violence or intimidation as a result of the company's activities.

The application must contain

- a statement of the grounds on which the application is made;

- the name and registered number of the applicant;

- the name and any former name of each director or permanent representative on behalf of whom the application is made;

- the date of birth of each such director or permanent representative;

- the usual residential address of each such director or permanent representative;

- where the Registrar of Companies has allocated a unique identifier to any such director or permanent representative, that unique identifier; and

- the name and registered number of each UK-registered company or overseas company of which each such director or permanent representative is a director.

The application must be accompanied by evidence which supports the applicant's statement of the grounds of the application.

The Registrar of Companies may request additional information or evidence. He may also refer to a 'relevant body' (see (1) above) any question relating to an assessment of the nature and extent of any risk of violence or intimidation and may accept any answer as sufficient evidence of that risk.

The Registrar of Companies must then determine the application and send the applicant (to its registered office or, if it not registered, to the address of its principal place of business in its country of incorporation) and each director or permanent representative concerned (to their usual residential address as stated in the application) notice of his determination within five working days of the determination being made.

The Registrar of Companies must not make available for public inspection any application for higher protection, any documents provided in support of that application, or any representations received in connection with the revocation of a decision (see below).

*Appeals.* Unsuccessful applicants may, with leave of the court, appeal to the High Court (in Scotland, the Court of Session) on the grounds that the decision is unlawful, irrational or unreasonable, or has been made on the basis of a procedural impropriety or otherwise contravenes the rules of natural justice. Any appeal must be brought within 35 days of the date of the Registrar's notice (or later with the court's permission). The court may dismiss the appeal or quash the decision. In the later case, it may refer the matter to the Registrar of Companies with a direction to reconsider it and make a determination in accordance with the findings of the court.

*Duration of favourable decision.* Any decision of the Registrar of Companies in favour of the applicant on an application for higher protection continues to have effect until either

- the Registrar is notified by the individual in respect of whom the application was made (or their personal representative) of the wish that the decision should cease to apply; or

- the Registrar of Companies revokes the decision (see below).

*Revocation.* The Registrar of Companies may revoke a decision in favour of the applicant on an application for higher protection if the individual in respect of whom the application was made, or any other person, is found guilty of an offence under *CA 2006, s 1112* (general false statement offence) committed in purporting to comply with any of the above provisions.

If the Registrar of Companies proposes to make a revocation decision, he must send the individual notice of his intention

- informing the individual that he may, within 28 days of the notice, deliver representations in writing to the Registrar; and

- stating that if representations are not received by the Registrar within that period, the revocation decision will be made at the expiry of that period.

If the beneficiary delivers representations in the time allowed, the Registrar of Companies must consider them and, within five working days of making his decision, send notice of it to the beneficiary.

[*SI 2009 No 1801, Sch 3*].

*Transitional provisions* – protection of confidentiality orders

(1) A director or permanent representative of an overseas company in relation to whom a confidentiality order under *CA 1985, s 723B* was in force immediately before 1 October 2009 is treated on and after that date as if they had made an application under the above provisions and that application had been determined by the Registrar of Companies in their favour. The provisions of *SI 2009 No 1801, Sch 3* above relating to decisions of the Registrar in favour of an applicant (in particular, as to the duration and revocation of such a decision) apply accordingly. The reference to an offence under *CA 2006, s 1112* (general false statement offence) is to be read for this purpose as a reference to an offence in relation to the application for the confidentiality order.

(2) *CA 1985, s 723B(3)–(8)* (application for confidentiality order) continues to apply in relation to an application for a confidentiality order made before 1 October 2009 and (1) above applies to an individual in respect of whom such an application has been made, and has not been determined or withdrawn, as to an individual in relation to whom a confidentiality order was in force immediately before that date.

If the application is dismissed or withdrawn, (1) above ceases to apply but if the application is successful it continues to apply as in the case of an individual in relation to whom a confidentiality order was in force immediately before 1 October 2009.

[*SI 2009 No 1801, Sch 8 paras 21, 22*].

## 30.16 Disclosure under a court order

The court may make an order for the disclosure of protected information by the company or by the Registrar of Companies if

- there is evidence that service of documents at a service address other than the director or permanent representative's usual residential address is not effective to bring them to the notice of that individual; or

- it is necessary or expedient for the information to be provided in connection with the enforcement of an order or decree of the court,

and the court is otherwise satisfied that it is appropriate to make the order. The order must specify the persons to whom, and the purposes for which, disclosure is authorised.

An order for disclosure by the Registrar of Companies can only be made if the company

- does not have the director or permanent representative's usual residential address;

- no longer has a UK establishment and has given notice of that fact under **30.57**; or

- has been dissolved.

A court order can be made on the application of a liquidator, creditor or member of the company, or any other person appearing to the court to have a sufficient interest.

## 30.16    Overseas Companies

[*SI 2009 No 1801, Reg 26*].

**30.17   Circumstances in which the Registrar of Companies can put a usual residential address on the public record**

The Registrar of Companies can put a director or permanent representative's usual residential address on the public record if

- communications sent by the Registrar on or after 1 October 2009 to that individual and requiring a response within a specified period remain unanswered; or

- evidence comes to the Registrar's attention on or after 1 October 2009 that service of documents at a service address provided in place of their usual residential address is not effective to bring them to the notice of the director or permanent representative.

Before doing so, the Registrar must give notice of the proposed course of action to the director or permanent representative and to the company. The notice must state the grounds for doing so and specify a period within which representations may be made. It must be sent to the director or permanent representative at his usual residential address, unless it appears to the Registrar that service at that address may be ineffective to bring it to their notice, in which case it may be sent to any service address provided in place of that address.

On deciding that a director or permanent representative's usual residential address is to be put on the public record, the Register of Companies must proceed as if a return containing altered particulars had been made stating

- the usual residential address as the director or permanent representative's service address; and

- that their usual residential address is the same as their service address.

The Registrar must give notice of having done so to the director or permanent representative and to the company.

If the company has been notified by the director or permanent representative of a more recent address as their usual residential address, it must notify the Registrar of Companies in accordance with **30.7(1)** above. If a company fails to comply with this requirement, an offence is committed by the company and every officer of the company who is in default. A person guilty of such an offence is liable, on summary conviction, to a fine not exceeding level 5 on the standard scale and, for continued contravention, a daily default fine not exceeding one-tenth of level 5 on the standard scale. See **29.1** OFFENCES AND LEGAL PROCEEDINGS for the standard scale.

A director or permanent representative whose usual residential address has been put on the public record by the Registrar of Companies under the above provisions cannot register a service address other than his usual residential address for a period of five years from the date of the Registrar's decision.

[*SI 2009 No 1801, Regs 27–29, Sch 8 para 20*].

## 30.18   DELIVERY OF ACCOUNTING DOCUMENTS: GENERAL REQUIREMENTS

The Secretary of State has power to make provision by Regulations requiring an overseas company that is required to register particulars with the Registrar of Companies

- to prepare the like accounts and strategic report and directors' report, and

- cause to be prepared such an auditor's report,

as would be required if the company were formed and registered under *CA 2006*. The overseas company may also be required to deliver to the Registrar of Companies copies of those accounts or the accounts and reports that it is required to prepare and have audited under the law of the country in which it is incorporated.

[*CA 2006, s 1049; SI 2013 No 1970, Schedule, para 24*].

### 30.19 Companies required to prepare and disclose accounts under parent law

The provisions in **30.20** to **30.23** apply to every overseas company that has an establishment in the UK and is not

- a credit or financial institution (as to which, see **30.35** to **30.50**); or

- a company whose constitution does not limit the liability of its members;

and is either

- required by its parent law to prepare, have audited and disclose accounts; or

- incorporated in an EEA State, is required by its parent law to prepare and disclose accounts, but is not required by its parent law to have its accounts audited or deliver its accounts.

**Definitions**. For these purposes, the following definitions apply.

'*Accounting documents*' in relation to a financial period of a company, mean

(a)    the accounts of the company for the period, including if it has one or more subsidiaries, any consolidated accounts of the group;

(b)    any annual report of the directors for the period;

(c)    any report of the auditors on the accounts within (*a*) above; and

(d)    any report of the auditors on the report in (*b*) above

and for this purpose 'subsidiaries' and 'consolidated group accounts' have the meaning given to them by the company's parent law.

'*Disclosure*' means public disclosure.

'*Financial period*' means a period for which the company is required or permitted by its parent law to prepare accounts.

'*Parent law*', in relation to a company, means the law of the country in which the company is incorporated. [*SI 2009 No 1801, Regs 30, 31*].

**Transitional provisions**.

(i)    The provisions in **30.20** to **30.23** apply in relation to accounting documents first disclosed in accordance with the company's parent law on or after 1 October 2009.

(ii)    In the case of a company to which *CA 1985, s 699AA* applied before 1 October 2009, (company to which *EC 11th Company Law Directive* applies), the provisions as set out in the Appendix to this Chapter at (41) continue to apply in relation to accounting documents first disclosed in accordance with the company's parent law before 1 October 2009.

**30.19    Overseas Companies**

(iii)    In the case of a company to which *CA 1985, s 700* applied before 1 October 2009 (company with place of business but not branch in UK), the provisions as set out in the Appendix to this Chapter at (23)–(38) continue to apply in relation to the period between

- the end of the last financial year of the company beginning before 1 October 2009, and

- the beginning of the first financial period of the company in respect of which accounting documents are first disclosed in accordance with the company's parent law on or after that date,

and that period is treated as a financial year of the company (if it would otherwise not be) for the purposes of those provisions.

[*SI 2009 No 1801, Sch 8 para 23*].

**30.20** *Duty to file copies of accounting documents disclosed under parent law*

The directors of a company to which these provisions apply must deliver to the Registrar of Companies a copy of all the accounting documents prepared in relation to a financial period of the company that are disclosed in accordance with its parent law. But

(a)    where the company's parent law permits it to discharge its obligation in this respect by disclosing documents in a modified form, the directors can similarly discharge their obligation to the Registrar of Companies by delivering a copy of documents modified as permitted by that parent law;

(b)    where the company is incorporated in an EEA State

(1)    the directors are not required to deliver copies of accounting documents to the Registrar of Companies if the company's parent law does not require it to deliver accounting documents; and

(2)    the directors may discharge their obligation under this provision by delivering the accounting documents without an auditor's report if the company's parent law does not require it to have its accounts audited; and

(c)    this provision does not apply in relation to copies of accounting documents disclosed under the company's parent law before

(i)    the date on which the company first complied with the requirements of initial registration under **30.3** in respect of a UK establishment; or

(ii)    if earlier, the last day of the period allowed for delivery of a return under **30.3** in respect of its first UK establishment.

*Companies with more than one UK establishment.* A company required by the above provisions to deliver copies of accounting documents must deliver them in respect of each UK establishment that it has at the end of the financial period to which the documents relate, except that this does not apply to an establishment if

- a return in respect of that establishment has stated the intention to file copies of accounting documents in respect of another UK establishment (giving the registered number of that establishment); and

- copies of the accounting documents are delivered in respect of that establishment before the end of the period allowed for doing so.

[*SI 2009 No 1801, Reg 32*].

**30.21** *Statement of details of parent law and other information*

The accounting documents delivered to the Registrar of Companies under **30.20** must be accompanied by a statement containing the following information.

- The legislation under which the accounts have been prepared and, if applicable, audited.

- Whether those accounts have been prepared in accordance with a set of generally accepted accounting principles and, if so, the name of the organisation or other body which issued those principles.

- Whether the accounts have been audited.

- If they have been audited

  (i)  whether they have been audited in accordance with a set of generally accepted auditing standards; and

  (ii)  if so, the name of the organisation or other body which issued those standards.

- If they have not been audited, whether the company is not required to have its accounts audited.

[*SI 2009 No 1801, Reg 33*].

**30.22** *Period allowed for filing copies of accounting documents*

The period allowed for delivering copies of documents required to be delivered under **30.20** is three months from the date on which the document is required to be disclosed in accordance with the company's parent law. [*SI 2009 No 1801, Reg 34*].

**30.23** *Penalty for non-compliance*

If any of the requirements of **30.20** or **30.22** are not complied with in relation to a company's accounting documents before the end of the period allowed for delivering copies of those documents, every person who immediately before the end of that period was a director of the company commits an offence. A person guilty of such an offence is liable, on summary conviction, to a fine not exceeding level 5 on the standard scale and, for continued contravention, a daily default fine not exceeding one-tenth of level 5 on the standard scale. See **29.1** OFFENCES AND LEGAL PROCEEDINGS for the standard scales.

It is a defence for a person charged with such an offence to prove that they took all reasonable steps for securing that those requirements would be complied with before the end of that period.

[*SI 2009 No 1801, Reg 35*].

**30.24 Companies not required to prepare and disclose accounts under parent law**

The provisions in **30.25** to **30.34** apply to an overseas company that has an establishment in the UK and is not

- a credit or financial institution (as to which, see **30.35** to **30.50**);

- a company whose constitution does not limit the liability of its members; or

- a company which is required to prepare and disclose accounts under parent law (see **30.19** to **30.23**).

[*SI 2009 No 1801, Regs 30, 36*].

**Transitional provisions.**

(a)   The provisions in **30.25** to **30.34** apply in relation to accounting documents for financial years of the company beginning on or after 1 October 2009.

(b)   The provisions of

   (i)   (44) and (45) as set out in the Appendix to this Chapter (companies to which the *EC 11th Company Law Directive* applies), or

   (ii)   (23)–(38) as set out in the Appendix to this Chapter (companies with place of business but not branch in the UK),

   continue to apply in relation to accounting documents for financial years beginning before that date.

*[SI 2009 No 1801, Sch 8 para 24].*

References to provisions of *CA 2006* "as modified" are to those provisions modified for overseas companies by the *Overseas Companies Regulations 2009 (SI 2009 No 1801).*

**30.25** *Financial year, accounting reference dates and periods*

(1) *Financial year*

A company's first financial year

- begins with the first day of its first accounting reference period; and

- ends with the last day of that period or such other date, not more than seven days before or after the end of that period, as the directors may determine.

Subsequent financial years

- begin with the day immediately following the end of the company's previous financial year; and

- end with the last day of its next accounting reference period or such other date, not more than seven days before or after the end of that period, as the directors may determine.

*[CA 2006, s 390 (as modified); SI 2009 No 1801, Reg 37].*

(2) *Accounting reference periods*

A company's accounting reference periods are determined according to its accounting reference date in each calendar year.

A company's first accounting reference period is the period of more than six months, but not more than eighteen months, beginning with the date of its becoming a relevant overseas company and ending with its accounting reference date. Its subsequent accounting reference periods are successive periods of twelve months beginning immediately after the end of the previous accounting reference period and ending with its accounting reference date.

*[CA 2006, s 391 (as modified); SI 2009 No 1801, Reg 37].*

(3) *Accounting reference date*

Subject to (4) below, the accounting reference date of a company is the last day of the month in which the anniversary of its becoming a relevant overseas company falls.

*[CA 2006, s 391 (as modified); SI 2009 No 1801, Reg 37].*

(4) *Alteration of accounting reference date*

A company may by notice given to the Registrar of Companies specify a new accounting reference date having effect in relation to either

- its current accounting reference period and subsequent periods; or

- its immediately preceding accounting reference period and subsequent periods. This option is not available if the period for filing accounts for the financial year determined by reference to the immediately preceding accounting reference period has already expired.

The notice must state whether the current or immediately preceding accounting reference period is to be shortened or extended (ie whether it is to end on the first or second occasion on which the new accounting reference date falls or fell after the beginning of the period).

An accounting reference period may not be extended so as to exceed 18 months (and any notice attempting to do this is ineffective) except where the company is in administration under *IA 1986, Pt II* or *Insolvency (Northern Ireland) Order 1989, Pt III*.

[*CA 2006, s 392* (as modified); *SI 2009 No 1801, Reg 37*].

**30.26** *Individual accounts: duty to prepare*

Subject to **30.30** (duty to prepare group accounts), the directors of a company must prepare accounts for the company for each of its financial years. Those accounts are referred to as the company's 'individual accounts'.

A company's annual accounts may be prepared in accordance with one of the following.

(a)    Its parent law (*'parent law individual accounts'*) (but only if the content of those accounts includes that required under (*c*) below). Where the directors of a company prepare parent law individual accounts they must state in the notes

- that the accounts have been prepared in accordance with the company's parent law;

- the legislation under which the accounts have been prepared;

- whether the accounts have been prepared in accordance with a set of generally accepted accounting principles, and if so the name of the organisation or other body which issued those principles;

- whether the accounts have been audited; and

- if they have been audited

     (i)    whether they have been audited in accordance with a set of generally accepted auditing standards; and

     (ii)   if so, the name of the organisation or other body which issued those standards.

(b)    International accounting standards (*'IAS individual accounts'*). Where the directors of a company prepare IAS individual accounts they must state in the notes

- that the accounts have been prepared in accordance with international accounting standards;

- whether the accounts have been audited; and

- if they have been audited

     (i)    whether they have been audited in accordance with a set of generally accepted auditing standards; and

       (ii)    if so, the name of the organisation or other body which issued those standards.

(c)    *CA 2006, s 396* (as modified) (*'overseas companies individual accounts'*). This requires the individual accounts to

- comprise a balance sheet as at the last day of the financial year and a profit and loss account; and;

- comply with the provisions in **30.27** to **30.29** as to the content of the balance sheet and the profit and loss account and as to additional information to be provided by way of notes to the accounts.

Where the directors of a company prepare overseas companies individual accounts, they must state in the notes

- that the accounts have been prepared in accordance with *CA 2006, s 396*;

- whether the accounts have been prepared in accordance with a set of generally accepted accounting principles, and if so the name of the organisation or other body which issued those principles;

- whether the accounts have been audited; and

- if they have been audited

       (i)    whether they have been audited in accordance with a set of generally accepted auditing standards; and

       (ii)    if so, the name of the organisation or other body which issued those standards.

[*CA 2006, ss 394–397* (as modified); *SI 2009 No 1801, Reg 38*].

Information required to be given in notes to a company's annual accounts may be contained in the accounts or in a separate document annexed to the accounts.

[*CA 2006, s 472* (as modified); *SI 2009 No 1801, Reg 42*].

**30.27** *Individual accounts: general rules*

Every balance sheet and profit and loss account must

- show each of the line items required to be included in a balance sheet or profit and loss account in accordance with international accounting standards, and

- clearly indicate in what currency it is prepared

but subject to the following.

(1)    The company's directors must use the same line items in preparing overseas companies individual accounts for each financial year, unless in their opinion there are special reasons for a change. Particulars of any such change must be given in a note to the accounts in which the new line item is first used, and the reasons for the change must be explained.

(2)    Where the company's directors consider it appropriate, the balance sheet or the profit and loss account may show a combination of line items where they are of a similar nature.

(3)    Items that are not of a similar nature or function must be presented separately unless they are not material. For this purpose, an item is 'material' if it either supplements the information given with respect to any particular item shown in the balance sheet

and profit and loss account or is otherwise relevant to assessing the company's state of affairs. Amounts which in the particular context of any provision in this paragraph or **30.28** or **30.29** are not material may be disregarded for the purposes of that provision.

(4)     Where the nature of the company's business requires it, the company's directors must adapt the line items in the balance sheet or profit and loss account. They may combine items if

(a)     their individual amounts are not material to assessing the state of affairs or profit or loss of the company for the financial year in question, or

(b)     the combination facilitates that assessment

and where (*b*) above applies, the individual amounts of any items which have been combined must be disclosed in a note to the accounts.

(5)     The directors may exclude an item in the balance sheet or profit and loss account if there is no amount to be shown for that item for the financial year to which the balance sheet or the profit and loss account relates. But where an amount can be shown for the item in question for the immediately preceding financial year, that amount must be shown under the line item for that item.

(6)     For every item shown in the balance sheet or profit and loss account the corresponding amount for the immediately preceding financial year must also be shown. Where that corresponding amount is not comparable with the figure for the current year, the former amount may be adjusted, in which case particulars of the non-comparability and of any adjustment must be disclosed in a note to the accounts.

(7)     Amounts in respect of items representing assets or income may not be set off against amounts in respect of items representing liabilities or expenditure (as the case may be), or *vice versa.*

(8)     The company's directors must, in determining how amounts are presented within items in the profit and loss account and balance sheet, have regard to the substance of the reported transaction or arrangement, in accordance with generally accepted accounting principles or practice.

'*Line items*' for the above purposes has the same meaning as in International Accounting Standard 1 on the Presentation of Financial Statements.

[*SI 2009 No 1801, Sch 4 paras 1–9, 20*].

**30.28**  *Individual accounts: accounting principles and rules*

The amounts to be included in respect of all items shown in a company's accounts must be determined in accordance with the principles set out in (*a*)–(*e*) below. But if it appears to the company's directors that there are special reasons for departing from any of those principles in preparing the company's accounts in respect of any financial year, they may do so, in which case particulars of the departure, the reasons for it and its effect must be given in a note to the accounts.

(a)     The company is presumed to be carrying on business as a going concern.

(b)     If the accounts are not prepared on a going concern basis, that fact must be disclosed, together with the basis on which the accounts are prepared and the reason why the company is not a going concern.

(c)     Accounting policies must be applied consistently within the same accounts and from one financial year to the next.

(d)    All income and charges relating to the financial year to which the accounts relate must be taken into account, without regard to the date of receipt or payment.

(e)    In determining the aggregate amount of any item, the amount of each individual asset or liability that falls to be taken into account must be determined separately.

[*SI 2009 No 1801, Sch 4 paras 10–14*].

**30.29** *Individual accounts: notes to the accounts*

Any information required in the case of any company by the following provisions must (if not given in the company's accounts) be given by way of a note to the accounts.

(1)    *Disclosure of accounting policies*

The accounting policies adopted by the company in determining the amounts to be included in respect of items shown in the balance sheet and in determining the profit or loss of the company must be stated (including such policies with respect to the depreciation and diminution in value of assets).

The company must include in the statement of accounting policies

•    the measurement basis (or bases) used in preparing the accounts; and

•    any other accounting policies used that are relevant to an understanding of the accounts.

(2)    *Accounting standards*

It must be stated whether the accounts have been prepared in accordance with the applied accounting standards and particulars of any material departure from those standards and the reasons for it must be given.

(3)    *Assessment of the company's state of affairs*

The company must provide information which is relevant to assessing the company's state of affairs. As a minimum that information must relate, where applicable, to

•    property, plant and equipment;

•    investment property;

•    intangible assets;

•    financial assets;

•    biological assets;

•    inventories;

•    trade and other receivables (and the amount falling due after more than one year must be shown separately for each item included under receivables);

•    trade and other payables (and the amount falling due after more than one year must be shown separately for each item included under payables);

•    provisions;

•    financial liabilities;

•    issued capital and reserves;

•    finance costs;

•    finance income;

- expenses and interest paid to group undertakings (this must be shown separately from expenses and interest paid to other entities);

- income and interest derived from group undertakings (this must be shown separately from income and interest derived from other sources);

- transactions with related parties;

- dividends;

- items described as other, sundry, miscellaneous or equivalent;

- guarantees;

- contingent liabilities;

- commitments;

- other off-balance sheet arrangements; and

- financial instruments.

[*SI 2009 No 1801, Sch 1 paras 15–19*].

Information required to be given in notes to a company's annual accounts may be contained in the accounts or in a separate document annexed to the accounts.

[*CA 2006, s 472* (as modified); *SI 2009 No 1801, Reg 42*].

**30.30** *Group accounts: duty to prepare*

If at the end of a financial year a company is a parent company (see APPENDIX 1 DEFINITIONS) the directors must, instead of preparing individual accounts for the year, prepare group accounts for the year. But a parent company is exempt from the requirement to prepare group accounts where

- it has prepared parent law individual accounts under **30.26(***a***)** and that parent law does not require consolidated accounts;

- it has prepared IAS individual accounts under **30.26(***b***)** and in accordance with the international accounting standards it is not required to prepare consolidated accounts; or

- it has prepared overseas companies individual accounts under **30.26(***c***)** and all of the company's subsidiary undertakings satisfy the requirement in **30.31**.

[*CA 2006, ss 399, 402* (as modified); *SI 2009 No 1801, Reg 38*].

Where a company, being a parent company, is required under the above provisions to prepare group accounts, and that company is itself the subsidiary of another company ('the holding company'), the group accounts of the holding company are deemed to satisfy the requirements of those provisions to prepare group accounts.

[*CA 2006, s 402A* (as modified); *SI 2009 No 1801, Reg 38*.

The group accounts may be prepared in accordance with one of the following.

(a)  Its parent law ('*parent law group accounts*') but only if the content of those accounts includes that required under (*c*) below. Where the directors of a company prepare parent law group accounts they must state in the notes

- that the accounts have been prepared in accordance with the company's parent law;

- the name of the legislation under which the accounts have been prepared;

- whether the accounts have been prepared in accordance with a set of generally accepted accounting principles, and if so the name of the organisation or other body which issued those principles;

- whether the accounts have been audited; and

- if they have been audited

  (i)  whether they have been audited in accordance with a set of generally accepted auditing standards; and

  (ii)  if so, the name of the organisation or other body which issued those standards.

(b)  International accounting standards ('*IAS group accounts*'). Where the directors of a company prepare IAS group accounts they must state in the notes

- that the accounts have been prepared in accordance with international accounting standards;

- whether the accounts have been audited; and

- if they have been audited

  (i)  whether they have been audited in accordance with a set of generally accepted auditing standards; and

  (ii)  if so the name of the organisation or other body which issued those standards.

(c)  *CA 2006, s 404* as modified for overseas companies ('*overseas companies group accounts*'). This requires the individual accounts to

  (i)  comprise a consolidated balance sheet dealing with the state of affairs of the parent company and its subsidiary undertakings and a consolidated profit and loss account dealing with the profit or loss of the parent company and its subsidiary undertakings; and

  (ii)  comply with the provisions in **30.32** as to the content of the consolidated balance sheet and consolidated profit and loss account and additional information to be provided by way of notes to the accounts.

Where the directors of a company prepare overseas company group accounts, they must state in the notes

- that the accounts have been prepared in accordance with *CA 2006, s 404*;

- whether the accounts have been prepared in accordance with a set of generally accepted accounting principles, and if so the name of the organisation or other body which issued those principles;

- whether the accounts have been audited; and

- if they have been audited

  (i)  whether they have been audited in accordance with a set of generally accepted auditing standards; and

  (ii)  if so, the name of the organisation or other body which issued those standards.

[*CA 2006, ss 403, 404, 406* (as modified); *SI 2009 No 1801, Reg 38*].

Information required to be given in notes to a company's annual accounts may be contained in the accounts or in a separate document annexed to the accounts.

[*CA 2006, s 472* (as modified); *SI 2009 No 1801, Reg 42*].

**30.31**  *Group accounts: exclusion of subsidiary undertakings from consolidation*

Where a parent company prepares overseas companies group accounts, all the subsidiary undertakings of the company must normally be included in the consolidation, subject to the following exceptions.

(a)  A subsidiary undertaking may be excluded from the consolidation if its inclusion is not material. Two or more undertakings may be excluded only if they are not material taken together.

(b)  A subsidiary undertaking may be excluded from consolidation where

   (i)  severe long-term restrictions substantially hinder the exercise of the rights of the parent company over the assets or management of that undertaking;

   (ii)  the information necessary for the preparation of group accounts cannot be obtained without disproportionate expense or undue delay; or

   (iii)  the interest of the parent company is held exclusively with a view to subsequent resale.

The references in (i) and (iii) above to, respectively, the rights and the interest of the parent company are references to the right and interests held by or attributed to the company for the purposes of the definition of 'parent undertaking' (see APPENDIX 1 DEFINITIONS) in the absence of which it would not be the parent company.

[*CA 2006, s 405* (as modified); *SI 2009 No 1801, Reg 38*].

**30.32**  *Group accounts: form and content*

(1) *General rules*

•  Overseas companies group accounts must comply so far as practicable with the provisions of **30.27** to **30.29** as if the undertakings included in the consolidation ('*the group*') were a single company and, in the case of overseas companies group accounts, the minimum information listed **30.29**(3) must also relate to

   (i)  investments accounted for using the equity method; and

   (ii)  minority interest, presented within equity.

•  The consolidated balance sheet and profit and loss account must incorporate, in full, the information contained in the individual accounts of the undertakings included in the consolidation, subject to the adjustments authorised or required by the following provisions of this paragraph and to such other adjustments (if any) as may be appropriate in accordance with generally accepted accounting principles or practice.

•  Where assets and liabilities to be included in the group accounts have been valued or otherwise determined by undertakings according to accounting rules differing from those used for the group accounts, the values or amounts must be adjusted so as to accord with the rules used for the group accounts. But

   (i)  if it appears to the directors of the parent company that there are special reasons for departing from this requirement, they may do so, in which case particulars of any such departure, the reasons for it and its effect must be given in a note to the accounts; and

(ii)    adjustments need not be made if they are not material.

- Amounts that in the particular context of any provision in this paragraph are not material may be disregarded for the purposes of that provision.

## (2) *Elimination of group transactions*

- Unless the amounts concerned are not material, debts and claims between undertakings included in the consolidation, and income and expenditure relating to transactions between such undertakings, must be eliminated in preparing the group accounts.

- Unless the amounts concerned are not material, where profits and losses resulting from transactions between undertakings included in the consolidation are included in the book value of assets, they must be eliminated in preparing the group accounts. This may be effected in proportion to the group's interest in the shares of the undertakings.

- Where an undertaking becomes a subsidiary undertaking of the parent company, that acquisition must be accounted for by the acquisition method of accounting. If the generally accepted accounting principles under which the accounts have been prepared allow it to be accounted for by another method, that method may be used, but, if so, the method used must be disclosed in the notes to the accounts.

## (3) *Minority interests*

- In the balance sheet there must be shown, as a separate item and under an appropriate line item, the amount of capital and reserves attributable to shares in subsidiary undertakings included in the consolidation held by or on behalf of persons other than the parent company and its subsidiary undertakings.

- In the profit and loss account formats there must be shown, as a separate item and under an appropriate line item

    (i)    the amount of any profit or loss on ordinary activities; and

    (ii)   the amount of any profit or loss on extraordinary activities,

    attributable to shares in subsidiary undertakings included in the consolidation held by or on behalf of persons other than the parent company and its subsidiary undertakings.

## (4) *Joint ventures*

Where an undertaking included in the consolidation manages another undertaking jointly with one or more undertakings not included in the consolidation, that other undertaking ('the joint venture') may, if it is not

- a body corporate, or

- a subsidiary undertaking of the parent company,

be dealt with in the group accounts by the method of proportional consolidation. The provisions of this paragraph relating to the preparation of consolidated accounts apply, with any necessary modifications, to the proportional consolidation.

## (5) *Associated undertakings*

An '*associated undertaking*' means an undertaking in which an undertaking included in the consolidation has a participating interest and over whose operating and financial policy it exercises a significant influence, and which is not

- a subsidiary undertaking of the parent company; or

- a joint venture dealt with in accordance with (4) above.

The interest of an undertaking in an associated undertaking, and the amount of profit or loss attributable to such an interest, must be shown by the equity method of accounting. If the generally accepted accounting principles under which the accounts have been prepared allow it to be accounted for by another method, that method may be used, but, if so, the method used must be disclosed in the notes to the accounts.

Where the associated undertaking is itself a parent undertaking, the net assets and profits or losses to be taken into account are those of the parent and its subsidiary undertakings (after making any consolidation adjustments).

[*SI 2009 No 1801, Sch 5*].

Information required to be given in notes to a company's annual accounts may be contained in the accounts or in a separate document annexed to the accounts.

[*CA 2006, s 472* (as modified); *SI 2009 No 1801, Reg 42*].

**30.33** *Approval and signing of accounts*

A company's annual accounts must be approved by the board of directors and signed on behalf of the board by a director of the company. The signature must be on the company's balance sheet.

If annual accounts are approved that do not comply with the requirements of *CA 2006, Pt 15* as applied to an overseas company (with modifications) under **30.18** to **30.26**, every director of the company who

- knew that they did not comply, or was reckless as to whether they complied, and

- failed to take reasonable steps to secure compliance with those requirements or, as the case may be, to prevent the accounts from being approved,

commits an offence. A person guilty of such an offence is liable (i) on conviction on indictment, to a fine; and (ii) on summary conviction, to a fine not exceeding the statutory maximum. See **29.1** OFFENCES AND LEGAL PROCEEDINGS for the statutory maximum.

[*CA 2006, s 414* (as modified); *SI 2009 No 1801, Reg 39*].

**30.34** *Duty to file accounts and period allowed for filing*

(1) *Duty to file accounts with the Registrar of Companies*

The directors of a company must deliver to the Registrar of Companies for each financial year a copy of the company's annual accounts and such other reports as it is required to prepare. The copy of the balance sheet must state the name of the person who signed it on behalf of the board.

Accounts must be delivered in respect of each UK establishment that a company has at the end of the financial year, except that delivery of accounts is not required in respect of an establishment if

- a return under the *SI 2009 No 1801* in respect of that establishment has stated the intention to file accounts in respect of another UK establishment (giving the registered number of that establishment); and

- accounts are delivered in respect of that establishment before the end of the period allowed for doing so.

[*CA 2006, s 441* (as modified); *SI 2009 No 1801, Reg 40*].

(2) *Period allowed for filing accounts*

Subject to below, the period allowed for directors of a company to comply with their obligation under (1) above is 13 months after the end of the relevant accounting reference period.

The '*relevant accounting reference period*' is the accounting reference period by reference to which the financial year for the accounts in question was determined (see **30.25**).

*Exceptions.*

(a)     If the relevant accounting reference period is the company's first and is a period of more than 12 months, the period allowed is 13 months from the first anniversary of the company becoming a relevant overseas company.

(b)     If the relevant accounting reference period is treated as shortened by virtue of a notice given under **30.25(4)**, the period is

  (i)     that applicable in accordance with the above provisions; or

  (ii)    three months from the date of the notice;

whichever expires last.

If for any special reason the Secretary of State thinks fit, he may, on an application made before the expiry of the period otherwise allowed, give notice in writing to a company extending that period by such further period as may be specified in the notice.

[*CA 2006, s 442* (as modified); *SI 2009 No 1801, Reg 40*].

*Offences for default in filing accounts*

If the requirements of (1) above are not complied with in relation to a company's accounts for a financial year before the end of the period for filing those accounts, every person who immediately before the end of that period was a director of the company commits an offence. A person guilty of such an offence is liable, on summary conviction, to a fine not exceeding level 5 on the standard scale and, for continued contravention, a daily default fine not exceeding one-tenth of the greater of £5,000 or level 4 on the standard scale. See **29.1** Offences and Legal Proceedings for the standard scale.

It is a defence for a person charged with such an offence to prove that he took all reasonable steps for securing that those requirements would be complied with before the end of that period. It is not a defence to prove that the documents in question were not in fact prepared as required.

[*CA 2006, s 451* (as modified); *SI 2009 No 1801, Reg 41; SI 2015 No 664, Sch 3*].

## 30.35 DELIVERY OF ACCOUNTING DOCUMENTS: CREDIT OR FINANCIAL INSTITUTIONS

The Secretary of State has power to make provision by Regulations requiring a credit or financial institution

•     that is incorporated or otherwise formed outside the UK and Gibraltar;

•     whose head office is outside the UK and Gibraltar; and

•     that has a 'branch' in the UK

to prepare the like accounts and *strategic report* and directors' report, and cause to be prepared such an auditor's report, as would be required if the institution were a company formed and registered under *CA 2006*. The overseas company may also be required to deliver to the Registrar of Companies copies of those accounts or the accounts and reports that it is required to prepare and have audited under the law of the country in which it has its head office.

'*Branch*' means a place of business that forms a legally dependent part of the institution and conducts directly all or some of the operations inherent in its business.

[*CA 2006, s 1050*; the *2013 Regulations, Schedule, para 25*].

**30.36  Institutions required to prepare accounts under parent law**

The provisions in **30.37** to **30.39** apply to a credit or financial institution within **30.35** that

- is required by its parent law to prepare and have audited accounts; or

- is incorporated in an EEA State, is required by its parent law to prepare and disclose accounts, but is not required by its parent law to have its accounts audited or deliver its accounts.

**Definitions.** For these purposes, the following definitions apply.

'*Accounting documents*' in relation to a financial period of an institution are

(a)  the accounts of the institution for the period, including, if it has one or more subsidiaries, any consolidated accounts of its group,

(b)  any annual report of the directors for the period,

(c)  any report of the auditors on the accounts mentioned in (*a*) above,

(d)  any report of the auditors on the report mentioned in (*b*) above,

and for this purpose 'subsidiaries' and 'consolidated group accounts' have the meaning given to them by the institution's parent law.

'*Director*', in the case of an institution which does not have directors, means persons occupying equivalent offices.

'*Disclosure*' means public disclosure, except where an institution is not required under its parent law, any enactment having effect for the UK or its constitution to publicly disclose its accounts, in which case it means disclosure of the accounts to the persons for whose information they have been prepared.

'*Financial period*' means a period for which the institution is required or permitted by its parent law to prepare accounts.

'*Parent law*' means the law of the country in which the institution has its head office.

[*SI 2009 No 1801, Regs 43, 44*].

**30.37**  *Duty to file copies of accounting documents*

*Initial filing of copies of accounting documents.* Subject to below, a credit or financial institution must within one month of becoming an institution to which these provisions apply deliver to the Registrar of Companies copies of the latest accounting documents of the institution prepared in accordance with its parent law to have been disclosed before the end of the period allowed for compliance with this provision, or, if earlier, the date of compliance with it.

*[SI 2009 No 1801, Reg 45]*.

An institution that immediately before 1 October 2009

(i)        has a branch in the UK, and

(ii)       has complied with the requirements *CA 1985, Sch 21C para 2* (see the Appendix to this Chapter at (49)),

is treated as having complied with the requirements of *Reg 45*.

*[SI 2009 No 1801, Sch 8 para 25]*.

*Filing of copies of subsequent accounting documents.* Subject to below, a credit or financial institution must deliver to the Registrar of Companies copies of all the accounting documents of the institution prepared in accordance with its parent law that are disclosed

•        on or after 1 October 2009; and

•        on or after the end of the period allowed for compliance with *Reg 45* above, or, if earlier, the date on which it complies with that provision.

The period allowed for delivery is three months from the date on which the document is required to be disclosed in accordance with the institution's parent law.

*Transitional provisions. CA 1985, Sch 21C para 3* (see the Appendix to this Chapter at (49)) continues to apply in relation to accounting documents first disclosed in accordance with the company's parent law before 1 October 2009.

*[SI 2009 No 1801, Reg 46, Sch 8 para 25]*.

*Exceptions.*

(1)       Where an institution is incorporated or otherwise formed in an EEA State

•        it is not required to deliver copies of accounting documents if its parent law does not require it to deliver accounting documents;

•        it may discharge its obligation by delivering accounting documents without an auditor's report if its parent law does not require it to have its accounts audited; and

•        if the institution's parent law permits it to discharge an obligation with respect to the disclosure of accounting documents by disclosing documents in a modified form, it may discharge its obligation by delivering copies of documents modified as permitted by that law.

(2)       An institution is not required to deliver documents to the Registrar of Companies if, at the end of the period allowed for compliance,

(i)        it is not required by its parent law to register them;

(ii)       they are made available for inspection at each branch of the institution in the UK; and

(iii)      copies of them are available on request at a cost not exceeding the cost of supplying them.

Where by virtue of this provision an institution is not required to deliver documents under *Reg 45* or *Reg 46* above and any of the conditions specified in (i)–(iii) above ceases to be met, the institution must deliver the documents to the Registrar of Companies for registration within seven days of the condition ceasing to be met.

[*SI 2009 No 1801, Regs 48, 49*].

**30.38** *Statement of details of parent law and other information*

The copies of accounting documents delivered to the Registrar of Companies under **30.37** must be accompanied by a statement containing the following information.

- The legislation under which the accounts have been prepared and, if applicable, audited.

- Whether those accounts have been prepared in accordance with a set of generally accepted accounting principles, and if so the name of the organisation or other body which issued those principles.

- Whether the accounts have been audited.

- If they have been audited

  (i) whether they have been audited in accordance with a set of generally accepted auditing standards; and

  (ii) if so, the name of the organisation or other body which issued those standards.

- If they have not been audited, whether the institution is not required to have its accounts audited.

[*SI 2009 No 1801, Reg 47*].

**30.39** *Penalty for non-compliance*

If any of the requirements of **30.37** or **30.38** are not complied with before the end of the period allowed for delivery of copies of accounting documents, an offence is committed by every person who immediately before the end of that period was a director of the institution. A person guilty of such an offence is liable, on summary conviction, to a fine not exceeding level 5 on the standard scale and, for continued contravention, a daily default fine not exceeding one-tenth of level 5 on the standard scale. See **29.1** OFFENCES AND LEGAL PROCEEDINGS for the standard scale.

It is a defence for a person charged with such an offence to prove that he took all reasonable steps for securing that those requirements would be complied with before the end of that period.

[*SI 2009 No 1801, Reg 50*].

**30.40 Institutions not required to prepare accounts under parent law**

*In relation to accounting documents for financial years of an institution beginning on or after 1 October 2009*, the provisions in **30.41** to **30.50** apply to a credit or financial institution within **30.35** that is not an institution to which **30.36** to **30.39** applies.

*In relation to accounting documents for financial years beginning before 1 October 2009*, the provisions of *CA 1985, Sch 21C paras 9–15* (see the Appendix to this Chapter at (51)) continue to apply.

[*SI 2009 No 1801, Reg 51, Sch 8 para 26*].

**30.41** *Financial year, accounting reference dates and periods*

(1) *Financial year*

An institution's first financial year

- begins with the first day of its first accounting reference period; and

- ends with the last day of that period or such other date, not more than seven days before or after the end of that period, as the directors may determine.

Subsequent financial years

- begin with the day immediately following the end of the institution's previous financial year; and

- end with the last day of its next accounting reference period or such other date, not more than seven days before or after the end of that period, as the directors may determine.

[*CA 2006, s 390* (as modified); *SI 2009 No 1801, Reg 52*].

(2) *Accounting reference periods*

An institution's accounting reference periods are determined according to its accounting reference date in each calendar year.

An institution's first accounting reference period is the period of more than six months, but not more than eighteen months, beginning with the date of its becoming a relevant overseas institution and ending with its accounting reference date. Its subsequent accounting reference periods are successive periods of twelve months beginning immediately after the end of the previous accounting reference period and ending with its accounting reference date.

[*CA 2006, s 391* (as modified); *SI 2009 No 1801, Reg 52*].

(3) *Accounting reference date*

Subject to (4) below, the accounting reference date of an institution is the last day of the month in which the anniversary of its becoming a relevant overseas institution falls.

[*CA 2006, s 391* (as modified); *SI 2009 No 1801, Reg 52*].

(4) *Alteration of accounting reference date*

An institution may by notice given to the Registrar of Companies specify a new accounting reference date having effect in relation to either

- its current accounting reference period and subsequent periods; or

- its immediately preceding accounting reference period and subsequent periods. This option is not available if the period for filing accounts for the financial year determined by reference to the immediately preceding accounting reference period has already expired.

The notice must state whether the current or immediately preceding accounting reference period is to be shortened or extended (ie whether it is to end on the first or second occasion on which the new accounting reference date falls or fell after the beginning of the period).

An accounting reference period may not be extended so as to exceed 18 months (and any notice attempting to do this is ineffective) except where the institution is in administration under *IA 1986, Pt II* or *Insolvency (Northern Ireland) Order 1989, Pt III*.

[*CA 2006, s 392* (as modified); *SI 2009 No 1801, Reg 52*].

**30.42**  *Individual accounts: duty to prepare*

Subject to **30.46** (duty to prepare group accounts), the directors of an institution must prepare accounts for the institution for each of its financial years. Those accounts are referred to as the institution's 'individual accounts'.

An institution's annual accounts may be prepared in accordance with one of the following.

(a)    Its parent law ('*parent law individual accounts*') (but only if the content of those accounts includes that required under (*c*) below). Where the directors of an institution prepare parent law individual accounts they must state in the notes

- that the accounts have been prepared in accordance with the institution's parent law;

- the name of the legislation under which the accounts have been prepared;

- whether the accounts have been prepared in accordance with a set of generally accepted accounting principles, and if so the name of the organisation or other body which issued those principles;

- whether the accounts have been audited; and

- if they have been audited

    (i)    whether they have been audited in accordance with a set of generally accepted auditing standards; and

    (ii)   if so, the name of the organisation or other body which issued those standards.

(b)    International accounting standards ('*IAS individual accounts*'). Where the directors of an institution prepare IAS individual accounts they must state in the notes

- that the accounts have been prepared in accordance with international accounting standards;

- whether the accounts have been audited; and

- if they have been audited

    (i)    whether they have been audited in accordance with a set of generally accepted auditing standards; and

    (ii)   if so, the name of the organisation or other body which issued those standards.

(c)    *CA 2006, s 396* as modified for overseas institutions ('*overseas institutions individual accounts*'). This requires the individual accounts to

- comprise a balance sheet as at the last day of the financial year and a profit and loss account; and;

- comply with the provisions in **30.43** to **30.45** as to the content of the balance sheet and the profit and loss account and as to additional information to be provided by way of notes to the accounts.

Where the directors of an institution prepare overseas institutions individual accounts, they must state in the notes

- that the accounts have been prepared in accordance with *CA 2006, s 396*;

- whether the accounts have been prepared in accordance with a set of generally accepted accounting principles, and if so the name of the organisation or other body which issued those principles;

- whether the accounts have been audited; and

- if they have been audited

    (i)      whether they have been audited in accordance with a set of generally accepted auditing standards; and

    (ii)     if so, the name of the organisation or other body which issued those standards.

[*CA 2006, ss 394–397* (as modified); *SI 2009 No 1801, Reg 53*.

Information required to be given in notes to an institution's annual accounts may be contained in the accounts or in a separate document annexed to the accounts.

[*CA 2006, s 472* (as modified); *SI 2009 No 1801, Reg 57*].

**30.43** *Individual accounts: general rules*

Every balance sheet and profit and loss account must

- show each of the line items required to be included in a balance sheet or profit and loss account in accordance with international accounting standards, and

- clearly indicate in what currency it is prepared

but subject to the following.

(1)    The institution's directors must use the same line items in preparing overseas institutions accounts for each financial year, unless in their opinion there are special reasons for a change. Particulars of any such change must be given in a note to the accounts in which the new line item is first used, and the reasons for the change must be explained.

(2)    Where the institution's directors consider it appropriate, the balance sheet or the profit and loss account may show a combination of line items where they are of a similar nature.

(3)    Items that are not of a similar nature or function must be presented separately unless they are not material. For this purpose, an item is '*material*' if it either supplements the information given with respect to any particular item shown in the balance sheet and profit and loss account or is otherwise relevant to assessing the institution's state of affairs. Amounts which in the particular context of any provision in this paragraph or **30.44** or **30.45** are not material may be disregarded for the purposes of that provision.

(4)    Where the nature of the institution's business requires it, the directors must adapt the line items in the balance sheet or profit and loss account. They may combine items if

    (a)    their individual amounts are not material to assessing the state of affairs or profit or loss of the institution for the financial year in question, or

    (b)    the combination facilitates that assessment

and where (*b*) above applies, the individual amounts of any items which have been combined must be disclosed in a note to the accounts.

(5)    The directors may exclude an item in the balance sheet or profit and loss account if there is no amount to be shown for that item for the financial year to which the balance sheet or the profit and loss account relates. But where an amount can be shown for the item in question for the immediately preceding financial year, that amount must be shown under the line item for that item.

(6)     For every item shown in the balance sheet or profit and loss account the corresponding amount for the immediately preceding financial year must also be shown. Where that corresponding amount is not comparable with the figure for the current year, the former amount may be adjusted, in which case particulars of the non-comparability and of any adjustment must be disclosed in a note to the accounts.

(7)     Amounts in respect of items representing assets or income may not be set off against amounts in respect of items representing liabilities or expenditure (as the case may be), or *vice versa*.

(8)     The institution's directors must, in determining how amounts are presented within items in the profit and loss account and balance sheet, have regard to the substance of the reported transaction or arrangement, in accordance with generally accepted accounting principles or practice.

'*Line items*' for the above purposes has the same meaning as in International Accounting Standard 1 on the Presentation of Financial Statements.

[*SI 2009 No 1801, Sch 6 paras 1–9, 20*].

**30.44** *Individual accounts: accounting principles and rules*

The amounts to be included in respect of all items shown in a institution's accounts must be determined in accordance with the principles set out in (*a*)–(*e*) below. But if it appears to the directors that there are special reasons for departing from any of those principles in preparing the accounts in respect of any financial year, they may do so, in which case particulars of the departure, the reasons for it and its effect must be given in a note to the accounts.

(a)     The institution is presumed to be carrying on business as a going concern.

(b)     If the accounts are not prepared on a going concern basis, that fact must be disclosed, together with the basis on which the accounts are prepared and the reason why the institution is not a going concern.

(c)     Accounting policies must be applied consistently within the same accounts and from one financial year to the next.

(d)     All income and charges relating to the financial year to which the accounts relate must be taken into account, without regard to the date of receipt or payment.

(e)     In determining the aggregate amount of any item, the amount of each individual asset or liability that falls to be taken into account must be determined separately.

[*SI 2009 No 1801, Sch 6 paras 10–14*].

**30.45** *Individual accounts: notes to the accounts*

Any information required in the case of any institution by the following provisions must (if not given in the accounts) be given by way of a note to the accounts.

(1)     *Disclosure of accounting policies*

The accounting policies adopted by the institution in determining the amounts to be included in respect of items shown in the balance sheet and in determining the profit or loss of the institution must be stated (including such policies with respect to the depreciation and diminution in value of assets).

The institution must include in the statement of accounting policies

•       the measurement basis (or bases) used in preparing the accounts; and

- any other accounting policies used that are relevant to an understanding of the accounts.

(2) *Accounting standards*

It must be stated whether the accounts have been prepared in accordance with the applied accounting standards and particulars of any material departure from those standards and the reasons for it must be given.

(3) *Assessment of the institution's state of affairs*

The institution must provide information which is relevant to assessing the institution's state of affairs. As a minimum that information must relate, where applicable, to

- property, plant and equipment;
- investment property;
- intangible assets;
- financial assets;
- biological assets;
- inventories;
- trade and other receivables (and the amount falling due after more than one year must be shown separately for each item included under receivables);
- trade and other payables (and the amount falling due after more than one year must be shown separately for each item included under payables);
- provisions;
- financial liabilities;
- issued capital and reserves;
- finance costs;
- finance income;
- expenses and interest paid to group undertakings (this must be shown separately from expenses and interest paid to other entities);
- income and interest derived from group undertakings (this must be shown separately from income and interest derived from other sources);
- transactions with related parties;
- dividends;
- items described as other, sundry, miscellaneous or equivalent;
- guarantees;
- contingent liabilities;
- commitments;
- other off-balance sheet arrangements; and
- financial instruments.

[*SI 2009 No 1801, Sch 6 paras 15–19*].

Information required to be given in notes to an institution's annual accounts may be contained in the accounts or in a separate document annexed to the accounts.

[*CA 2006, s 472* (as modified); *SI 2009 No 1801, Reg 57*].

**30.46** *Group accounts: duty to prepare*

If at the end of a financial year an institution is a parent institution (see APPENDIX 1 DEFINITIONS) the directors must, instead of preparing individual accounts for the year, prepare group accounts for the year. But a parent institution is exempt from the requirement to prepare group accounts where

- it has prepared parent law individual accounts under **30.42(***a***)** and that parent law does not require consolidated accounts;

- it has prepared IAS individual accounts under **30.42(***b***)** and in accordance with the international accounting standards it is not required to prepare consolidated accounts; or

- it has prepared overseas institutions individual accounts under **30.42(***c***)** and all of the institution's subsidiary undertakings satisfy the requirement in **30.47**.

[*CA 2006, ss 399, 402* (as modified); *SI 2009 No 1801, Reg 53*].

Where an institution, being a parent institution, is required under the above provisions to prepare group accounts, and that institution is itself the subsidiary of another institution ('the holding institution'), the group accounts of the holding institution may be deemed to satisfy the requirements of those provisions to prepare group accounts.

[*CA 2006, s 402A* (as modified); *SI 2009 No 1801, Reg 53*].

The group accounts may be prepared in accordance with one of the following.

(a) Its parent law ('*parent law group accounts*') but only if the content of those accounts includes that required under (*c*) below. Where the directors of an institution prepare parent law group accounts they must state in the notes

- that the accounts have been prepared in accordance with the institution's parent law;

- the name of the legislation under which the accounts have been prepared;

- whether the accounts have been prepared in accordance with a set of generally accepted accounting principles, and if so the name of the organisation or other body which issued those principles;

- whether the accounts have been audited; and

- if they have been audited

  (i) whether they have been audited in accordance with a set of generally accepted auditing standards; and

  (ii) if so, the name of the organisation or other body which issued those standards.

(b) International accounting standards ('*IAS group accounts*'). Where the directors of an institution prepare IAS group accounts they must state in the notes

- that the accounts have been prepared in accordance with international accounting standards;

- whether the accounts have been audited; and

- if they have been audited

    (i) whether they have been audited in accordance with a set of generally accepted auditing standards; and

    (ii) if so the name of the organisation or other body which issued those standards.

(c) *CA 2006, s 404* as modified for overseas institutions (*'overseas institutions group accounts'*). This requires the individual accounts to

    (i) comprise a consolidated balance sheet dealing with the state of affairs of the parent institution and its subsidiary undertakings and a consolidated profit and loss account dealing with the profit or loss of the parent institution and its subsidiary undertakings; and

    (ii) comply with the provisions in **30.48** as to the content of the consolidated balance sheet and consolidated profit and loss account and additional information to be provided by way of notes to the accounts.

Where the directors of an institution prepare accounts in accordance with *CA 2006, s 404*, they must state in the notes

- that the accounts have been prepared in accordance with *CA 2006, s 404*;

- whether the accounts have been prepared in accordance with a set of generally accepted accounting principles, and if so the name of the organisation or other body which issued those principles;

- whether the accounts have been audited; and

- if they have been audited

    (i) whether they have been audited in accordance with a set of generally accepted auditing standards; and

    (ii) if so, the name of the organisation or other body which issued those standards.

[*CA 2006, ss 403, 404, 406* (as modified); *SI 2009 No 1801, Reg 53*].

Information required to be given in notes to an institution's annual accounts may be contained in the accounts or in a separate document annexed to the accounts.

[*CA 2006, s 472* (as modified); *SI 2009 No 1801, Reg 57*].

**30.47** *Group accounts: exclusion of subsidiary undertakings from consolidation*

Where a parent institution prepares overseas institutions group accounts, all the subsidiary undertakings of the institution must normally be included in the consolidation, subject to the following exceptions.

(a) A subsidiary undertaking may be excluded from the consolidation if its inclusion is not material. Two or more undertakings may be excluded only if they are not material taken together.

(b) A subsidiary undertaking may be excluded from consolidation where

    (i) severe long-term restrictions substantially hinder the exercise of the rights of the parent institution over the assets or management of that undertaking;

    (ii) the information necessary for the preparation of group accounts cannot be obtained without disproportionate expense or undue delay; or

(iii)    the interest of the parent institution is held exclusively with a view to subsequent resale.

The references in (i) and (iii) above to, respectively, the rights and the interest of the parent institution are references to the right and interests held by or attributed to the institution for the purposes of the definition of 'parent undertaking' (see APPENDIX 1 DEFINITIONS) in the absence of which it would not be the parent institution.

[*CA 2006, s 405* (as modified); *SI 2009 No 1801, Reg 53*].

**30.48** *Group accounts: form and content*

(1) *General rules*

•    Overseas institutions group accounts must comply so far as practicable with the provisions of **30.43** to **30.45** as if the undertakings included in the consolidation ('*the group*') were a single institution and, in the case of group accounts, the minimum information listed **30.45**(3) must also relate to

(i)    investments accounted for using the equity method; and

(ii)    minority interest, presented within equity.

•    The consolidated balance sheet and profit and loss account must incorporate, in full, the information contained in the individual accounts of the undertakings included in the consolidation, subject to the adjustments authorised or required by the following provisions of this paragraph and to such other adjustments (if any) as may be appropriate in accordance with generally accepted accounting principles or practice.

•    Where assets and liabilities to be included in the group accounts have been valued or otherwise determined by undertakings according to accounting rules differing from those used for the group accounts, the values or amounts must be adjusted so as to accord with the rules used for the group accounts. But

(i)    if it appears to the directors of the parent institution that there are special reasons for departing from this requirement, they may do so, in which case particulars of any such departure, the reasons for it and its effect must be given in a note to the accounts; and

(ii)    adjustments need not be made if they are not material.

•    Amounts that in the particular context of any provision of this paragraph are not material may be disregarded for the purposes of that provision.

(2) *Elimination of group transactions*

•    Unless the amounts concerned are not material, debts and claims between undertakings included in the consolidation, and income and expenditure relating to transactions between such undertakings, must be eliminated in preparing the group accounts.

•    Unless the amounts concerned are not material, where profits and losses resulting from transactions between undertakings included in the consolidation are included in the book value of assets, they must be eliminated in preparing the group accounts. This may be effected in proportion to the group's interest in the shares of the undertakings.

- Where an undertaking becomes a subsidiary undertaking of the parent institution, that acquisition must be accounted for by the acquisition method of accounting. If the generally accepted accounting principles under which the accounts have been prepared allow it to be accounted for by another method, that method may be used, but, if so, the method used must be disclosed in the notes to the accounts.

**(3) *Minority interests***

- In the balance sheet there must be shown, as a separate item and under an appropriate line item, the amount of capital and reserves attributable to shares in subsidiary undertakings included in the consolidation held by or on behalf of persons other than the parent institution and its subsidiary undertakings.

- In the profit and loss account formats there must be shown, as a separate item and under an appropriate line item

  (i)    the amount of any profit or loss on ordinary activities; and

  (ii)   the amount of any profit or loss on extraordinary activities,

  attributable to shares in subsidiary undertakings included in the consolidation held by or on behalf of persons other than the parent institution and its subsidiary undertakings.

**(4) *Joint ventures***

Where an undertaking included in the consolidation manages another undertaking jointly with one or more undertakings not included in the consolidation, that other undertaking ('the joint venture') may, if it is not

- a body corporate, or

- a subsidiary undertaking of the parent institution,

be dealt with in the group accounts by the method of proportional consolidation. The provisions of this paragraph relating to the preparation of consolidated accounts apply, with any necessary modifications, to the proportional consolidation.

**(5) *Associated undertakings***

An '*associated undertaking*' means an undertaking in which an undertaking included in the consolidation has a participating interest and over whose operating and financial policy it exercises a significant influence, and which is not

- a subsidiary undertaking of the parent institution; or

- a joint venture dealt with in accordance with (4) above.

The interest of an undertaking in an associated undertaking, and the amount of profit or loss attributable to such an interest, must be shown by the equity method of accounting. If the generally accepted accounting principles under which the accounts have been prepared allow it to be accounted for by another method, that method may be used, but, if so, the method used must be disclosed in the notes to the accounts.

Where the associated undertaking is itself a parent undertaking, the net assets and profits or losses to be taken into account are those of the parent and its subsidiary undertakings (after making any consolidation adjustments).

[*SI 2009 No 1801, Sch 7*].

Information required to be given in notes to an institution's annual accounts may be contained in the accounts or in a separate document annexed to the accounts.

[*CA 2006, s 472* (as modified); *SI 2009 No 1801, Reg 57*].

**30.49** *Approval and signing of accounts*

An institution's annual accounts must be approved by the board of directors and signed on behalf of the board by a director of the institution. The signature must be on the institution's balance sheet.

If annual accounts are approved that do not comply with the requirements of *CA 2006, Pt 15* as applied to an overseas institution (with modifications) under **30.40** to **30.48**, every director of the institution who

•   knew that they did not comply, or was reckless as to whether they complied, and

•   failed to take reasonable steps to secure compliance with those requirements or, as the case may be, to prevent the accounts from being approved,

commits an offence. A person guilty of such an offence is liable (i) on conviction on indictment, to a fine; and (ii) on summary conviction, to a fine not exceeding the statutory maximum. See **29.1** OFFENCES AND LEGAL PROCEEDINGS for the statutory maximum.

[*CA 2006, s 414* (as modified); *SI 2009 No 1801, Reg 54*].

**30.50** *Duty to file accounts and period allowed for filing*

(1) *Duty to file accounts with the Registrar of Companies*

The directors of an institution must deliver to the Registrar of Companies for each financial year a copy of the institution's annual accounts and such other reports as it is required to prepare. The copy of the balance sheet must state the name of the person who signed it on behalf of the board.

[*CA 2006, s 441* (as modified); *SI 2009 No 1801, Reg 55*].

(2) *Period allowed for filing accounts*

Subject to below, the period allowed for directors of an institution to comply with their obligation under (1) above is 13 months after the end of the relevant accounting reference period.

The '*relevant accounting reference period*' is the accounting reference period by reference to which the financial year for the accounts in question was determined (see **30.41**).

*Exceptions.*

(a)   If the relevant accounting reference period is the institution's first and is a period of more than 12 months, the period allowed is 13 months from the first anniversary of the institution becoming a relevant overseas institution.

(b)   If the relevant accounting reference period is treated as shortened by virtue of a notice given under **30.41(4)**, the period is

(i)    that applicable in accordance with the above provisions; or

(ii)   three months from the date of the notice;

whichever expires last.

If for any special reason the Secretary of State thinks fit, he may, on an application made before the expiry of the period otherwise allowed, give notice in writing to an institution extending that period by such further period as may be specified in the notice.

[*CA 2006, s 442* (as modified); *SI 2009 No 1801, Reg 55*].

(3) *Offences for default in filing accounts*

If the requirements of (1) above are not complied with in relation to an institution's accounts for a financial year before the end of the period for filing those accounts, every person who immediately before the end of that period was a director of the institution commits an offence. A person guilty of such an offence is liable, on summary conviction, to a fine not exceeding level 5 on the standard scale and, for continued contravention, a daily default fine not exceeding one-tenth of the greater of £5,000 or level 4 on the standard scale. See **29.1** OFFENCES AND LEGAL PROCEEDINGS for the standard scale.

It is a defence for a person charged with such an offence to prove that he took all reasonable steps for securing that those requirements would be complied with before the end of that period. It is not a defence to prove that the documents in question were not in fact prepared as required.

[*CA 2006, s 451* (as modified); *SI 2009 No 1801, Reg 56; SI 2015 No 664, Sch 3*].

## 30.51 TRADING DISCLOSURES

The Secretary of State may by Regulations make provision requiring overseas companies carrying on business in the UK to

- display specified information in specified locations;

- state specified information in specified descriptions of document or communication; and

- provide specified information on request to those they deal with in the course of their business.

[*CA 2006, s 1051*].

The provisions in **30.52** to **30.55** have been made by the *Overseas Companies Regulations 2009* and in those provisions

- a reference to any type of document is a reference to a document of that type in hard copy, electronic or any other form; and

- in relation to a company, a reference to 'its websites' includes a reference to any part of a website relating to that company which that company has caused or authorised to appear.

[*SI 2009 No 1801, Reg 58*].

## 30.52 Display of name, etc at business location

An overseas company must display the company's name and country of incorporation

(a)    at every location in the UK at which it carries on business; and

(b)    at the service address of every person resident in the UK authorised to accept service of documents on behalf of the company.

But (*a*) above does not apply to a location

- that is primarily used for living accommodation;

- at which business is carried on by a company of which every director or permanent representative who is an individual is entitled to higher protection from disclosure of their residential address (see **30.15**); or

- at which business is carried on by a company in respect of which a liquidator, administrator or administrative receiver has been appointed if the location is also a place of business of the liquidator, administrator or administrative receiver.

The company's name and country of incorporation must be displayed continuously. But if the place of business is shared by six or more companies, this requirement is treated as met if the company's name and country of incorporation are displayed for at least fifteen continuous seconds at least once in every three minutes.

The name and country of incorporation must be displayed in such a way so that they may be easily seen by any visitor to the location and must be in characters that can be read with the naked eye.

*Penalties.* Where a company fails, without reasonable excuse, to comply with any of the above requirements, an offence is committed by the company and every officer of the company who is in default. A person guilty of such an offence is liable, on summary conviction, to a fine not exceeding level 3 on the standard scale and, for continued contravention, a daily default fine not exceeding one-tenth of level 3 on the standard scale. See **29.1** OFFENCES AND LEGAL PROCEEDINGS for the standard scale. For these purposes, a shadow director is to be treated as an officer of the company. [*SI 2009 No 1801, Regs 59–61, 67*].

## 30.53 Inclusion of names and other specified information in documents and communications

(a) An overseas company must state the company's name on all

(i)     its business letters, notices and other official publications,

(ii)    its bills of exchange, promissory notes, endorsements and order forms,

(iii)   cheques purporting to be signed by or on behalf of the company,

(iv)    orders for money, goods or services purporting to be signed by or on behalf of the company,

(v)     its bills of parcels, invoices and other demands for payments, receipts, and letters of credit,

(vi)    its applications for licences to carry on a trade or activity,

(vii)   other forms of its business correspondence and documentation, and

(viii)  its websites,

that are used in carrying on the activities of its business in the UK.

(b) An overseas company that has a UK establishment in respect of which it has registered particulars under **30.3** to **30.5** must state on all its business letters, order forms and websites that are used in carrying on the activities of a UK establishment of the company

(i)     where the establishment is registered; and

(ii)    its registered number.

(c) An overseas company which is not incorporated in an EEA State must state on its business letters, order forms and its websites that are used in carrying on business in the UK

(i)      the company's country of incorporation;

(ii)     the identity of the registry, if any, in which the company is registered in its country of incorporation;

(iii)    if applicable, the number with which the company is registered in that registry;

(iv)     the location of its head office;

(v)      the legal form of the company;

(vi)     if the liability of the members of the company is limited, the fact that it is a limited company; and

(vii)    if applicable, the fact that the company is being wound up, or is subject to other insolvency proceedings or an arrangement or composition or any analogous proceedings (this does not apply where the company is required to make similar disclosures under various provisions of *IA 1986* or *Insolvency (NI) Order 1989*).

If, in the case of company having a share capital, there is reference to the amount of share capital on its business letters, order forms or websites, the reference must be to paid up share capital.

(d) Where a business letter of a company includes the name of any director of the company, other than in the text or as a signatory, the letter must disclose the name of every director of the company. In the case of a body corporate, or a firm that is a legal person under the law by which it is governed, its corporate or firm name must be given.

Any display or disclosure must be in characters that can be read with the naked eye.

*Penalties.* Where a company fails, without reasonable excuse, to comply with any of the above requirements, an offence is committed by the company and every officer of the company who is in default. A person guilty of such an offence is liable, on summary conviction, to a fine not exceeding level 3 on the standard scale and, for continued contravention, a daily default fine not exceeding one-tenth of level 3 on the standard scale. See **29.1** Offences and Legal Proceedings for the standard scale. For these purposes, a shadow director is to be treated as an officer of the company.

[*SI 2009 No 1801, Regs 59, 62–64, 67*].

## 30.54   Disclosures relating to address for service

A company must disclose the address of any person resident in the UK authorised to accept service of documents on behalf of the company to any person it deals with in the course of business who makes a written request to the company for that information. The company must send a written response to that person within five working days of the receipt of the request.

*Penalties.* Where a company fails, without reasonable excuse, to comply with any of the above requirements, an offence is committed by the company and every officer of the company who is in default. A person guilty of such an offence is liable, on summary conviction, to a fine not exceeding level 3 on the standard scale and, for continued contravention, a daily default fine not exceeding one-tenth of level 3 on the standard scale. See **29.1** Offences and Legal Proceedings for the standard scale. For these purposes, a shadow director is to be treated as an officer of the company.

[*SI 2009 No 1801, Regs 65, 67*].

**30.55 Civil consequences of failure to make a required disclosure**

Where

- any legal proceedings are brought by a company to enforce a right arising out of a contract made in the course of a business, and

- at the time the contract was made, the company was in breach of any of the requirements in **30.52** to **30.54,**

the proceedings must be dismissed if it is shown that the defendant (in Scotland, the defender)

- has a claim against the claimant (pursuer) arising out of the contract and has been unable to pursue that claim by reason of the latter's failure to comply with those requirements, or

- has suffered some financial loss in connection with the contract by reason of the claimant's (pursuer's) failure to comply with those requirements.

This does not apply if the court before which the proceedings are brought is satisfied that it is just and equitable to permit the proceedings to continue and does not affect the right of any person to enforce such rights as the person may have against another in any proceedings brought by the other. [*SI 2009 No 1801, Reg 66*].

**30.56 SERVICE OF DOCUMENTS**

(1) *Service of documents on the company*

A document may be served on an overseas company whose particulars are registered in the UK

- by leaving it at, or sending it by post to, the registered address of any person resident in the UK who is authorised to accept service of documents on the company's behalf; or

- if there is no such person, or if any such person refuses service or service cannot for any other reason be effected, by leaving it at or sending by post to any place of business of the company in the UK.

[*CA 2006, s 1139(2)*].

The place of business must exist at the time of the service and cannot merely be a former place of business (*Deverall v Grant Advertising Inc* [1955] Ch 111, [1954] 3 All ER 389, CA).

(2) *Service of documents on directors, secretaries and others*

In the case of an overseas company whose particulars are registered under the provisions in **30.3** *et seq*, a document may be served on a director, secretary or permanent representative by leaving it at, or sending it by post to, the person's registered address, ie any address for the time being shown as a current address in relation to that person in the part of the register available for public inspection.

This applies whatever the purpose of the document in question and is not restricted to service for purposes arising out of, or in connection with, the appointment or position mentioned or in connection with the company concerned.

*Change of address.* If notice of a change of that address is given to the Registrar of Companies, a person may validly serve a document at the address previously registered until the end of the period of 14 days beginning with the date on which notice of the change is registered.

Service cannot be effected under these provisions at an address

- if notice has been registered of the termination of the appointment in relation to which the address was registered and the address is not a registered address of the person concerned in relation to any other appointment; and

- if the overseas company has ceased to have any connection with the UK by virtue of which it is required to register particulars under *CA 2006, s 1046*.

[*CA 2006, s 1140; SI 2009 No 1801, Reg 75*].

### 30.57 DUTY TO GIVE NOTICE OF CLOSURE OF UK ESTABLISHMENT

If an overseas company closes a UK establishment in respect of which it has registered particulars under **30.3** *et seq*, it must forthwith give notice of that fact to the Registrar of Companies.

From the date on which such notice is given, the company is no longer obliged to deliver documents to the Registrar of Companies in respect of that establishment.

If a company fails to comply with this provision, an offence is committed by the company and every officer or agent of the company who knowingly and willingly authorises or permits the default. A person guilty of such an offence is liable, on summary conviction, to a fine not exceeding level 3 on the standard scale and, for continued contravention, a daily default fine not exceeding one-tenth of level 3 on the standard scale. See **29.1** OFFENCES AND LEGAL PROCEEDINGS for the standard scale. [*SI 2009 No 1801, Reg 77*].

### 30.58 REGISTRAR TO WHOM RETURNS, NOTICES, ETC TO BE DELIVERED

Where an overseas company is required to register or has registered particulars in more than one part of the UK, the Secretary of State may provide by Regulations that, in the case of such a company, anything authorised or required to be delivered to the Registrar is to be delivered

- to the Registrar for each part of the UK in which the company is required to register or has registered particulars; or

- to the Registrar for such part or parts of the UK as may be specified in or determined in accordance with the Regulations.

[*CA 2006, s 1057*].

### 30.59 COMPANY CONTRACTS AND EXECUTION OF DOCUMENTS

The *Overseas Companies (Execution of Documents and Registration of Charges) Regulations 2009 (SI 2009 No 1917)* provide that with effect from 1 October 2009 parts of *sections 43–51* of *CA 2006* (as modified by the regulations) apply to overseas companies (see **30.60–30.63**).

### 30.60 Company contracts

Under the law of England and Wales or Northern Ireland, a contract may be made

- by an overseas company, by writing under its common seal or in any manner permitted by the laws of the territory in which the company is incorporated for the execution of documents by such a company; and

- on behalf of an overseas company, by any person who, in accordance with the laws of the territory in which the company is incorporated, is acting under the authority (express or implied) of that company.

Unless a contrary intention appears, any formalities required by law in the case of a contract made by an individual also apply to one made by or on behalf of an overseas company.

[*CA 2006, s 43* (as modified); *SI 2009 No 1917, Reg 4*].

### 30.61   Deeds and documents: Provisions applying in England and Wales and Northern Ireland

(1) *Execution of documents*

Under the law of England and Wales or Northern Ireland a document is executed by an overseas company in either of the following ways.

(a)   By the affixing of its common seal.

(b)   if it is executed in any manner permitted by the laws of the territory in which the company is incorporated for the execution of documents by such a company.

(c)   If it is signed by a person who, in accordance with the laws of the territory in which an overseas company is incorporated, is acting under the authority (express or implied) of the company.

A document so signed and expressed, in whatever words, to be executed by the company has the same effect in relation to that company as it would have in relation to a company incorporated in England and Wales or Northern Ireland if executed under the common seal of a company so incorporated.

In favour of a 'purchaser', a document is deemed to have been duly executed by an overseas company if it purports to be signed in accordance with (*c*) above. A *'purchaser'* means a purchaser in good faith for valuable consideration and includes a lessee, mortgagee or other person who, for valuable consideration, acquires an interest in property.

Where a document is to be signed by a person on behalf of more than one overseas company, it is not duly signed by that person for the purposes of these provisions unless he signs it separately in each capacity.

References above to a document being (or purporting to be) signed by a person who, in accordance with the laws of the territory in which an overseas company is incorporated, is acting under the authority (express or implied) of the company are to be read, in a case where that person is a firm, as references to its being (or purporting to be) signed by an individual authorised by the firm to sign on its behalf.

The above provisions apply to a document that is (or purports to be) executed by an overseas company in the name of or on behalf of another person whether or not that person is also an overseas company.

[*CA 2006, s 44* (as modified); *SI 2009 No 1917, Reg 4*].

(2) *Execution of deeds*

A document is validly executed by an overseas company as a deed for the purposes of *Law of Property (Miscellaneous Provisions) Act 1989, s 1(2)(b)* and the law of Northern Ireland if, and only if, it is

- duly executed by the company; and

- delivered as a deed.

A document is presumed to be delivered for these purposes upon its being executed, unless a contrary intention is proved.

[*CA 2006, s 46* (as modified); *SI 2009 No 1917, Reg 4*].

### 30.62 Execution of documents: Provisions applying in Scotland

For the purposes of any enactment

- providing for a document to be executed by a company by affixing its common seal, or

- referring (in whatever terms) to a document so executed,

a document signed or subscribed by or on behalf of an overseas company in accordance with the provisions of the *Requirements of Writing (Scotland) Act 1995* has effect as if so executed. [[*CA 2006, s 48* (as modified); *SI 2009 No 1917, Reg 5*].].

### 30.63 Pre-incorporation contracts, deeds and obligations

A contract that purports to be made by or on behalf of an overseas company at a time when the company has not been formed has effect, subject to any agreement to the contrary, as one made with the person purporting to act for the company or as agent for it, and he is personally liable on the contract.

This also applies to

- the making of a deed under the law of England and Wales or Northern Ireland, and

- the undertaking of an obligation under the law of Scotland

as it applies to the making of a contract.

[*CA 2006, s 51* (as modified); *SI 2009 No 1917, Reg 6*].

### 30.64 REGISTRATION OF CHARGES

The regulations referred to in **30.59** (above) (as amended by the *Overseas Companies (Execution of documents and Registration of charges) Amendment Regulations* as from 1 October 2011) [*SI 2011 No 2194*] also regulate the registration of charges over property in the UK of a registered overseas company.

**In relation to charges created on or after 1 October 2009 but before 1 October 2011,** the provisions in **30.65** to **30.74** apply to an overseas company that is registered and for these purposes an overseas company

- becomes registered when it has complied with the provisions in **30.3** to **30.6** (initial registration of particulars) in respect of one or more UK establishments and those particulars have been registered; and

- ceases to be registered when it gives notice under **30.57** (notice of closure of UK establishment) in respect of *all* of its UK establishments and that notice has been registered.

For the above purposes, the particulars and notice referred to are not treated as registered unless and until they are on the register and therefore available for public inspection.

'*Establishment*' means a branch within the meaning of the *EC 11th Company Law Directive (89/666/EEC)* or a place of business that is not such a branch; and '*UK establishment*' means an establishment in the UK.

'*Charge*', in these provisions includes, in England and Wales and Northern Ireland, a mortgage and, in Scotland, any right in security.

In relation to a charge created under the law of Scotland, references to the date of creation of the charge are to

•   in the case of a floating charge, the date on which the instrument creating the floating charge was executed by the company creating the charge; and

•   in any other case, the date on which the right of the person entitled to the benefit of the charge was constituted as a real right.

[*SI 2009 No 1917, Regs 2, 8*].

*Transitional provisions.* The provisions in *CA 1985, Pt 12* relating to

•   charges created by companies incorporated outside Great Britain continue to apply in relation to charges created before 1 October 2009; and

•   charges existing on property acquired by a company incorporated outside Great Britain continue to apply to property acquired before 1 October 2009.

[*SI 2009 No 1917, Sch paras 2, 4*].

## 30.65   Charges requiring registration

A charge requires registration under these provisions if

(a)   it is created by a company to which the provisions apply (see **30.64**);

(b)   the property subject to the charge is situated in the UK; and

(c)   the charge is of a type requiring registration.

Whether the conditions in (*a*) and (*b*) above are met is determined when the charge is created.

The types of charge requiring registration are as follows.

•   A charge on land or any interest in land, other than a charge for rent or any other periodical sum issuing out of (in Scotland, payable in respect of) land. For this purpose,

   (i)    a charge on land includes a charge created by a heritable security within the meaning of *Conveyancing and Feudal Reform (Scotland) Act 1970, s 9(8)*; and

   (ii)   the holding of debentures entitling the holder to a charge on land is not an interest in the land.

•   A charge created or evidenced by an instrument that, if executed by an individual, would require registration as a bill of sale.

•   A charge for the purposes of securing any issue of debentures.

•   A charge on uncalled share capital of the company.

•   A charge on calls made but not paid.

- A charge on book debts of the company. For this purpose, the deposit by way of security of a negotiable instrument given to secure the payment of book debts is not a charge on those book debts.

- A floating charge on the company's property or undertaking.

- A charge on a ship or aircraft, or any share in a ship.

- A charge on goodwill or on any *'intellectual property'*, ie any

  (i)   patent, trade mark, registered design, copyright or design right; or

  (ii)  any licence under or in respect of any such right.

**Consequences of failure to register such a charge**. If a company creates a charge requiring registration under these provisions, the charge is void (so far as any security on the company's property or undertaking is conferred by it) against a liquidator, administrator or creditor of the company if the charge is not registered in compliance with **30.66**. This is without prejudice to any contract or obligation for repayment of the money secured by the charge; and when a charge becomes void in these circumstances, the money secured by it immediately becomes payable.

[*SI 2009 No 1917, Regs 9, 19(1)(3)*].

### 30.66  Duty to deliver particulars of charge etc for registration

A company to which these provisions apply (see **30.64**) that creates a charge requiring registration must deliver the required particulars of the charge, together with a certified copy of the instrument (if any) by which the charge is created or evidenced, to the Registrar of Companies before the end of the period allowed for registration, ie

- 21 days, beginning with the day after the day on which the charge is created; or

- if the charge is created outside the UK, 21 days beginning with the day after the day on which the instrument by which the charge is created or evidenced (or a copy of it) could, in due course of post (and if despatched with due diligence) have been received in the UK.

But there is no requirement to deliver particulars if the property subject to the charge is, at the end of the period allowed for registration, no longer situated in the UK.

The required particulars are

- the date of the creation of the charge;

- a description of the instrument (if any) creating or evidencing the charge;

- the amount secured by the charge;

- the name and address of the person entitled to the charge;

- short particulars of the property charged; and

- in the case of a floating charge created under the law of Scotland, a statement as to any provisions of the charge and of any instrument relating to it

  (i)   which prohibit or restrict or regulate the power of the company to grant further securities ranking in priority to, or *pari passu* with, the floating charge; or

  (ii)  which vary or otherwise regulate the order of ranking of the floating charge in relation to subsisting securities.

Alternatively, registration of a charge may be effected on the application of a person interested in it, in which case that person is entitled to recover from the company any fees he has properly paid to the Registrar of Companies on registration.

[*SI 2009 No 1917, Regs 10–12)*].

**30.67   Charge by way of ex facie absolute disposition (Scotland)**

For the avoidance of doubt, in the case of a charge created under the law of Scotland by way of

• an *ex facie* absolute disposition or assignation qualified by a back letter or other agreement, or

• a standard security qualified by an agreement

compliance with **30.66** does not of itself render the charge unavailable as security for indebtedness incurred after the date of compliance.

Where the amount secured by a charge so created is purported to be increased by a further back letter or agreement, a further charge is held to have been created by the *ex facie* absolute disposition or assignation or (as the case may be) by the standard security, as qualified by the further back letter or agreement. In that case, the provisions relating to the registration of charges apply to the further charge as if

• references to the charge were references to the further charge; and

• references to the date of creation of a charge were references to the date on which the further back letter or agreement was executed. [*SI 2009 No 1917, Reg 13*].

**30.68   Charges created on or after 1 October 2011**

Charges created on or after 1 October 2011 over property in the UK of a registered overseas company are regulated by *SI 2009 No 1917* (see above) as amended by *SI 2011 No 2194*. The *2011 Regulations* provide in summary that the requirement for the registration of a charge set out in the *2009 Regulations* is removed. The effect of the *2011 Regulations* is:

(i)    to remove references to the date a charge is created under the law of Scotland

   [*SI 2011 No 2194, Reg 2(1)*]

(ii)   to omit *Regulations 9–22* of the *2009 Regulations* so that a charge created on or after 1 October 2011 is no longer registrable with the Registrar of Companies

   [*SI 2011 No 2194, Reg 2(3)*]

(iii)  to require that overseas companies need to keep available for inspection copies of instruments creating charges referred to in *Regulation 24* of the 2009 regulations (as amended). *Regulation 24* now requires every overseas company to keep available for inspection a register of charges and to (as soon as practicable and in any event within 21 days of the creation of the charge) enter in the register any charge on land in the UK or any interest in such land, any charge on ships, aircraft or intellectual property registered in the UK, any floating charge on the whole or part of the company's property or undertaking situated in the UK with the exceptions set out in *Regulation 24(2A)*.

   [*SI 2011 No 2194, Reg 2(4) and 2(5)*].

(iv)    to amend the time copies of instruments and the register of charges have to be available for inspection from 14 to 21 days [*SI 2011 No 2194, Reg 2(6)*] and to provide that the right to inspect the documents and register can be carried out by electronic means

[*SI 2011 No 2194, Reg 2(8)*]

*Transitional provisions* – the provision in *Reg 2(6)* amending the time limit does not apply where the company has given notice to the Registrar of Companies of the place where documents etc are kept available for inspection in respect of a charge created before 1 October 2011.

### 30.69   Special rules about debentures: charge in series of debentures

*In circumstances where the first debenture in a series of debentures is executed on or after 1 October 2009*, where a company creates a series of debentures containing, or giving by reference to another instrument, any charge which benefits the debenture holders of that series *pari passu*, it is sufficient for the purposes **30.66** if the following are delivered to the Registrar of Companies before the end of the period of 21 days beginning with the day after the date on which that instrument is executed. If there is no such instrument, they must be delivered within 21 days beginning with the day after the day on which the first debenture of the series is executed.

(a)    Particulars of

- the total amount secured by the whole series;

- the dates of the resolutions authorising the issue of the series and the date of the covering instrument (if any) by which the series is created or defined;

- a general description of the property charged;

- the names of the trustees (if any) for the debenture holders; and

- In the case of a floating charge created under the law of Scotland, a statement as to any provisions of the charge and of any instrument relating to it

    (i)    which prohibit or restrict or regulate the power of the company to grant further securities ranking in priority to, or *pari passu* with, the floating charge; or

    (ii)   which vary or otherwise regulate the order of ranking of the floating charge in relation to subsisting securities.

(b)    A certified copy of the instrument containing the charge or, if there is no such instrument, a certified copy of one of the debentures of the series.

Particulars must also be sent for registration of

(i)    where more than one issue is made of debentures in the series, the date and amount of each issue of debentures of the series; and

(ii)   where appropriate, the amount or rate per cent of any commission, discount or allowance which has been paid or made either directly or indirectly by a company to a person in consideration of their

- subscribing or agreeing to subscribe (whether absolutely or conditionally) for debentures in the company; or

- procuring or agreeing to procure subscriptions (whether absolute or conditional) for such debentures.

The deposit of debentures as security for a debt of the company is not treated as the issue of debentures at a discount for this purpose.

But failure to comply with (i) or (ii) above does not affect the validity of the debentures issued.

[*SI 2009 No 1917, Regs 14–16, 19(2), Sch para 3*].

*Transitional provisions.* The provisions of *CA 1985, Pt 12* relating to the registration of a series of debentures of a company incorporated outside Great Britain continue to apply where the first debenture of the series was executed before 1 October 2009.

[*SI 2009 No 1917, Sch para 3*].

The *2011 Regulations* (see **30.68** above) also amend the provisions in *SI 2009 No 1917* relating to debentures for those debentures created on or after 1 October 2011. *Regulations 14–16* and *19(2)* of the *2009 Regulations* are removed and no longer apply so that particulars of any charge which benefits debenture holders no longer need to be registered. [*SI 2011 No 2194, Reg 2(3)*].

### 30.70   Endorsement of certificate on debentures

A company must cause a copy of every certificate of registration given by the Registrar of Companies under **30.71** to be endorsed on every debenture or certificate of debenture stock which is issued by the company, and the payment of which is secured by the charge so registered. But this does not require a company to cause a certificate of registration of any charge so given to be endorsed on any debenture or certificate of debenture stock issued by the company before the charge was created.

If a person knowingly and wilfully authorises or permits the delivery of a debenture or certificate of debenture stock in default of this requirement, he commits an offence. A person guilty of such an offence is liable, on summary conviction, to a fine not exceeding level 3 on the standard scale (see **29.1** OFFENCES AND LEGAL PROCEEDINGS).

[*SI 2009 No 1917, Reg 17*].

See above that these provisions do not apply to debentures created on or after 1 October 2011.

[*SI 2011, No 2194, Reg 2(3)*].

### 30.71   Register of charges to be kept by the Registrar of Companies

For each company to which these provisions apply (see **30.64**), the Registrar of Companies must keep, and make available for inspection by any person, a register of all the charges requiring registration under these provisions. The register must show

- the particulars required to be delivered to the Registrar of Companies under these provisions; and

- in the case of a charge imposed by the Enforcement of Judgments Office under *Judgments Enforcement (Northern Ireland) Order 1981, Art* 46, the date on which the charge became effective.

The Registrar must give a signed and authenticated certificate of registration of any charge so registered, stating the name of the company and the amount secured by the charge. Such a certificate is conclusive evidence that the registration requirements have been satisfied.

**Entries of satisfaction and release**. In relation to statements delivered to the Registrar of Companies on or after 1 October 2009, if a statement is delivered to the Registrar of Companies verifying with respect to a registered charge that

- the debt for which the charge was given has been paid or satisfied in whole or in part, or

- part of the property or undertaking charged has been released from the charge or has ceased to form part of the company's property or undertaking

the Registrar may enter on the register a memorandum of satisfaction of that fact.

In Scotland, if the charge is a floating charge created under the law of Scotland, the statement must be accompanied by either

- a statement by the creditor entitled to the benefit of the charge (or a person authorised by him) verifying that the statement is correct; or

- a direction obtained from the court, on the ground that such a statement could not be readily obtained, dispensing with the need for that statement,

but nothing in these provisions requires the company to submit particulars with respect to the entry in the register of a memorandum of satisfaction where the company, having created a floating charge under the law of Scotland over all or any part of its property, disposes of *part* of the property subject to the floating charge.

Where the Registrar enters a memorandum of satisfaction in whole, he must, if required, send the company a copy of it.

*Transitional provisions. CA 1985, s 403 or 419* continues to apply where the relevant statement was received by the Registrar of Companies before 1 October 2009.

[*SI 2009 No 1917, Regs 18, 21, Sch para 7*].

See above that these provisions do not apply to debentures created on or after 1 October 2011.

[*SI 2011, No 2194, Reg 2(3)*].

## 30.72 Rectification of register of charges by the court

Where there has been

- a failure to register a charge within the time required, or

- an omission or mis-statement of any particular with respect to any such charge or in a memorandum of satisfaction

the court may, on the application of the company or a person interested, order the period allowed for registration to be extended or, as the case may be, the omission or mis-statement to be rectified where it is satisfied that

- the failure or omission

    (i)    was accidental or due to inadvertence or to some other sufficient cause; or

    (ii)   is not of a nature to prejudice the position of creditors or shareholders of the company; or

- it is just and equitable to grant relief on other grounds.

*[SI 2009 No 1917, Reg 22]*.

See above that these provisions do not apply to debentures created on or after 1 October 2011

*[SI 2011, No 2194, Reg 2(3)]*

## 30.73   Appointment/cessation of receiver, etc

Subject to below, in relation to orders and appointments made on or after 1 October 2009, if a person

• obtains an order for the appointment of a receiver or manager of property of a company to which these provisions apply (see **30.64**), or

• appoints such a receiver or manager under powers contained in an instrument,

he must give notice of the fact to the Registrar of Companies within seven days of the order or of the appointment. The Registrar must then enter that fact in the register of charges.

Where a receiver or manager of a company's property appointed under powers contained in an instrument ceases to act he must give notice to that effect to the Registrar of Companies. The Registrar must then enter that fact in the register of charges.

A person who defaults in complying with the above requirements commits an offence. A person guilty of such an offence is liable, on summary conviction, to a fine not exceeding level 3 on the standard scale and, for continued contravention, a daily default fine not exceeding one-tenth of level 3 on the standard scale. See **29.1** Offences and Legal Proceedings for the standard scale.

The above provisions do not apply in relation to the appointment of a receiver under *IA 1986, s 51(1)* or *(2)* (appointment under law of Scotland by holder of floating charge or by court on application of holder) as respects which *IA 1986, s 53(1)* or *54(3)* requires the delivery to the Registrar of Companies of a copy of the instrument or interlocutor making the appointment.

*[SI 2009 No 1917, Reg 20, Sch para 6]*.

*Transitional provisions. CA 1985, s 405* continues to apply where the order or appointment was made, or the receiver or manager ceased to act before 1 October 2009.

*[SI 2009 No 1917, Sch para 6]*.

See above that these provisions do not apply to debentures created on or after 1 October 2011

*[SI 2011, No 2194, Reg 2(3)]*

## 30.74   Register of charges and copies of instruments creating charges

**Charges created on or after 1 October 2011**. The *Overseas Companies (Execution of Documents and Registration of Charges) (Amendment) Regulations 2011 (SI 2011/2194)* has abolished the obligation previously imposed on an overseas company to register at Companies House charges it creates over its UK assets. Accordingly, an overseas company now need not register any charge it creates on or after 1 October 2011 over its UK assets.

The overseas company must now enter onto its own register of charges, and make available for inspection, details of the following types of charge only:

- any charge it creates (on or after 1 October 2011) over land in the UK;

- any charge it creates (on or after 1 October 2011) over ships, aircraft and intellectual property registered in the UK; and

- any floating charge it creates (on or after 1 October 2011) over any of its property in the UK, except any charge whose terms expressly exclude all property in the UK.

Companies House has published guidance on registration of charges created by overseas companies. See *Companies House: Overseas companies in the UK: registration and filing obligations (March 2015)*.

As from 1 October 2011, a company to which these provisions apply (see **30.64**) must keep available for inspection

(a)     a copy of every instrument creating a charge requiring registration under these provisions (although in the case of a series of uniform debentures a copy of one of the debentures of the series is sufficient); and

(b)     a register of charges and enter in it as soon as practicable and in any event within 21 days of the date of creation of the charge

   (i)     any charge on land or any interest in such land of the company situated in the UK; and

   (ii)     any floating charge on the whole or part of the company's property or undertaking situated in the UK.

   (iii)     any charge on ships, aircraft or intellectual property registered in the UK.

The entry in the register under (*b*) above must in each case give

- a short description of the property and/or undertaking charged;

- the amount of the charge; and

- except in the cases of securities to bearer, the names of the persons entitled to it.

**30.74**(a)(ii) does not apply to a floating charge which expressly excludes all property or undertaking of the company situated in the UK or which purports to be a fixed charge.

If an officer of the company knowingly and wilfully authorises or permits the omission of an entry required to be made in the register, he commits an offence. A person guilty of such an offence is liable (i) on conviction on indictment, to a fine; and (ii) on summary conviction, to a fine not exceeding the statutory maximum. See **29.1** Offences and Legal Proceedings for the statutory minimum.

[*SI 2009 No 1917, Regs 23, 24; SI 2011 No 2194, Reg 2(4)* and *2(5)*].

**Inspection**. The documents under (*a*) above and the company's register of charges under (*b*) above must be kept available for inspection at a location in the UK at which it carries on business. The company must give notice to the Registrar of Companies, within 14 days, of the place at which the documents and register are kept available for inspection and of any change in that place, within 21 days of any such change.

The documents and register must be open to the inspection of any creditor or member of the company without charge and any other person on payment of £3.50 for each hour or part thereof during which the right of inspection is exercised. Where the company and the person (making the inspection) agree, the inspection may be carried out by electronic means.

[*SI 2011 No 2194, Reg 26A*]

If default is made in notifying the Registrar of Companies or an inspection is refused, an offence is committed by the company and every officer of the company who is in default. A person guilty of such an offence is liable, on summary conviction, to a fine not exceeding level 3 on the standard scale and, for continued contravention, a daily default fine not exceeding one-tenth of level 3 on the standard scale. See **29.1** Offences and Legal Proceedings for the standard scale. In the case of refusal of inspection of the register, the court may by order compel an immediate inspection of it.

**Availability for inspection.** A company to which these provisions apply (see **30.64**) must make the documents and register referred to above available for inspection by a person on a day which has been specified by that person ('the specified day') provided that

• the specified day is a working day; and

• that person gives the company the required notice of the specified day.

The required notice is at least 10 working days' notice of the specified day.

When a person gives notice of the specified day, he must also give notice of the time on that day at which he wishes to start the inspection (which must be any time between 9 am and 3 pm) and the company must make its company records available for inspection by that person for a period of at least two hours beginning with that time. If a company that fails to comply with this provision, it is treated as having refused inspection.

[*SI 2009 No 1917, Regs 25, 26; SI 2011 No 2194, Regs 2(6), 2(7) 2(8)*].

# APPENDIX: PROVISIONS APPLYING BEFORE 1 OCTOBER 2009

(1) Definition
(2) Registration and filing requirements, etc – place of business registration regime
(3) Documents to be delivered to the Registrar of Companies on establishing a place of business in Great Britain
(4) Registration of change in particulars
(5) Registration and filing requirements etc – branch registration regime
(6) Duty to register and documents to be delivered
(7) Particulars required about the company
(8) Particulars required about the branch
(9) Particulars in relation to registration of documents
(10) Documents required
(11) Registration of alteration in particulars
(12) Change in registration regime
(13) Change from place of business regime to branch regime
(14) Change from branch regime to place of business regime
(15) Miscellaneous matters
(16) Letter paper, notices etc
(17) Duty to state name etc – branches
(18) Company name
(19) Service of documents on an overseas company
(20) Penalties
(21) Channel Island and Isle of Man companies
(22) Accounts and reports
(23) Exceptions
(24) Oversea credit or financial institution with branch in Great Britain
(25) Duty to prepare annual accounts

(26) Individual accounts: form and content
(27) Group undertakings
(28) Group accounts of holding company
(29) Form and content of group accounts
(30) Small and medium-sized companies
(31) Directors' report
(32) Auditors' report
(33) Signing of the balance sheet
(34) Dormant companies
(35) Unlimited overseas companies
(36) Accounting reference dates
(37) Delivery of accounts to the Registrar of Companies
(38) Accounts and reports – companies with branches in Great Britain
(39) Companies required to make disclosure under parent law
(40) Duty to deliver accounting documents
(41) Companies not required to make disclosure under parent law
(42) Preparation of accounts and reports
(43) Duty to deliver accounts and reports
(44) Accounts and reports – credit and financial institutions with branches in Great Britain
(45) Institutions required to prepare accounts under parent law
(46) Duty to deliver accounting documents
(47) Institutions not required to prepare accounts under parent law
(48) Appropriate registrar of companies
(49) Companies within branch registration regime

# Appendix  Overseas Companies

**Background.** The provisions in this Appendix apply, unless otherwise stated, before 1 October 2009. Under transitional provisions, the provisions in *CA 1985, Chapter 1* (see (2)–(22), (48) and (49)) continue to have effect on and after 1 October 2009 so far as necessary for the purposes of the registration of returns or other documents delivered to the Registrar of Companies before that date.

[*SI 2009 No 1801, Sch 8 para 2*].

(1)  **Definition**

An '*overseas company*' is a company incorporated elsewhere than in Great Britain which

•  after 30 June 1985 'establishes a place of business' in Great Britain; or

•  before 1 July 1985 established a place of business and continues to have an established place of business in Great Britain after that date.

[*CA 1985, s 744*].

There is no precise statutory definition of the meaning of 'establishes a place of business'. In *Act Dampskib Hercules v Grand Trunk Pacific Rly Co* [1912] 1 KB 222, Buckley LJ said on this point: 'We have only to see whether the corporation is "here" . . . the best test is to ascertain whether the business is carried on here and at a defined place.' It was held that a company, whose main object was to establish and maintain a railway company in Canada and which raised capital in London to do so, had established a place of business in England.

In *South India Shipping Corpn Ltd v Export-Import Bank of Korea* [1985] 2 All ER 219, [1985] BCLC 163, CA, it was held that a bank, which had premises and staff in England and carried on there the preliminary work necessary for granting and obtaining loans and giving publicity to the bank's activities, had established a place of business there. In *Oriel Ltd, Re* [1985] 3 All ER 216, [1985] BCLC 343, CA, Oliver LJ said that the meaning of the phrase 'established place of business' connotes not only the setting up of a place of business at a specific location, but also a degree of permanence as the location of the company's business. It need not necessarily be owned, or even leased, by the company but at least must be associated with it and business must be conducted from it habitually or with some degree of regularity.

(2)  **Registration and filing requirements, etc – place of business registration regime**

As the general provisions of *CA 1985* apply only to companies formed and registered under the Act, special provisions apply regarding registration and filing require-ments of overseas companies.

The provisions in (3) and (4) below do not apply to any limited company which is incorporated outside the UK and Gibraltar and which has a *branch* in Great Britain. [*CA 1985, s 690B; SI 1992 No 3179, Sch 2 para 2*]. A special branch registration regime applies to such companies (see (5) to (14) below). Where a company so incorporated has a place of business in Great Britain that is not a branch, and has no other branch in the UK, it remains subject to the provisions in (3) and (4) below.

'*Branch*' means a branch within the meaning of the *EC 11th Company Law Directive (89/666/EEC)*, and where a branch comprises places of business in more than one part of the UK, it is treated as being situated in that part of the UK where its principal place of business is situated. [*CA 1985, s 698(2); SI 1992 No 3179, Sch 2 para 13(3)*]. In fact, the *11th Directive* does not specifically define a branch; its meaning ultimately depends on the views of the European Court of Justice when

called upon to interpret the *11th Directive*. A Department of Trade and Industry Consultative Document published in July 1992 (Implementation of EC
11th Company Law Directive and Bank Branches Directive) gives useful guidance.
It states that, in principle, a branch is a place of business which a company
establishes in another State through which the company conducts its business such
that persons resident in that State can deal with the branch instead of dealing
directly with the representatives of the company in the company's home state. Places
of business which perform operations ancillary or incidental to the company's business are, in general terms, not branches within the meaning of the *11th Directive*.
Thus, 'branch' is a narrower concept than place of business, every company with a
branch has a place of business, but not every place of business is a branch, and one
branch can cover many places of business where there is a unified management
structure.

(3)   **Documents to be delivered to the Registrar of Companies on establishing a
place of business in Great Britain**

When a company incorporated outside Great Britain establishes a place of business
in Great Britain, it must within one month deliver the following to the appropriate
Registrar of Companies for registration. See (48) below for the appropriate
Registrar.

(a)   A certified copy of the charter, statutes or memorandum and articles of the
company or other instrument constituting or defining its constitution,
together with a certified translation (if the original is not in English). The
copy of the instrument constituting or defining the company's constitution
must be certified, in the place of incorporation of the company, to be a true
copy by

(i)   an official of the government to whose custody the original is
committed;

(ii)   a notary public; or

(iii)   an officer of the company on oath taken before a person authorised
to administer oaths in that place or any of the British Officials
mentioned in the *Commissioners for Oaths Act 1889, s 6.*

(b)   A return in the prescribed form (Form 691) with details of the following.

(i)   Directors (including any person in accordance with whose instructions the directors of the company are accustomed to act) and
secretary (or any person occupying the position of secretary by
whatever name called) as in 12 COMPANY FORMATION AND TYPES
OR COMPANIES, except that it is only necessary to give details of other
directorships if the director has no business occupation in which case
details of all other current directorships must be given.

(ii)   Names and addresses of one or more persons resident in Great Britain
authorised to accept on the company's behalf service of process and
any notices required to be served on it.

(iii)   Documents delivered under (*a*) above.

(iv)   A statutory declaration by a director, secretary or person within (ii)
above stating the date on which the company's place of business in
Great Britain was established. Alternatively, in place of the statutory
declaration there may be delivered to the Registrar of Companies
using electronic communications a statement made by any person by

723

whom the declaration could have been made stating the date on which the company's place of business in Great Britain was established. Any person who makes a false statement which he knows to be false or does not believe to be true is liable to a penalty.

(c)     Where a confidentiality order is in force in respect of a director or secretary, in addition to the return under (b) above there must be also be delivered a separate return in the prescribed form containing particulars of the usual residential address of the director or secretary concerned.

[*CA 1985, ss 691, 698; CA 1989, Sch 19 para 6; SI 2000 No 3373, Art 26; SI 2002 No 912, Sch 2 para 5*].

See (20) below for penalties for non-compliance.

(4)     **Registration of change in particulars**

If any alteration is made in

(a)     any of the documents within (3)(a) above, or

(b)     the directors or secretary or the particulars contained in the list of directors under (3)(b)(i) above, or

(c)     the names and addresses of the persons authorised to accept service on behalf of the company under (3)(b)(ii) above, or

(d)     the corporate name of the overseas company,

the company must, within the specified time, deliver to the appropriate Registrar of Companies a return in the prescribed form (Forms 692(1)(a), 692(1)(b), 692(1)(c) and 692(2) respectively) containing particulars of the alteration or change. See (48) below for the appropriate Registrar.

In the case of an alteration within (3)(b)(ii) above the specified time is 21 days after the date of alteration. Otherwise it is 21 days from the date on which notice of the alteration could have been received in Great Britain by post (assuming despatched with due diligence).

*Confidentiality orders.* The following provisions apply where the rules relating to confidentiality orders are relevant.

•     If an individual in respect of whom a confidentiality order is in force becomes a director or secretary of an overseas company

    (i)     the return required to be delivered to the Registrar under the above provisions must contain the address for the time being notified by the director or secretary to the company as his service address and must not contain his usual residential address; and

    (ii)     with that return the company must deliver to the Registrar a return in the prescribed form containing the usual residential address of that director or secretary.

•     If a confidentiality order is made in respect of an existing director or secretary of an overseas company, the company must within the time specified above deliver to the Registrar for registration a return in the prescribed form containing the address for the time being notified to it by the director or secretary as his service address.

- If while a confidentiality order is in force in respect of a director or secretary of an overseas company there is an alteration in his usual residential address, the company must within the time specified above deliver to the Registrar for registration a return in the prescribed form containing the new address.

[*CA 1985, s 692; SI 2002 No 912, Sch 2 para 6*].

See (21) below for penalties for non-compliance.

(5)   **Registration and filing requirements etc – branch registration regime**

The provisions described in (6)–(14) below apply to any limited company which is incorporated outside the UK and Gibraltar and which has a 'branch' (see (2) above) in Great Britain.

[*CA 1985, s 690A; SI 1992 No 3179, Sch 2 para 2*].

(6)   **Duty to register and documents to be delivered**

A company within (5) above must, within one month of having opened a branch in a part of Great Britain (or within one month of a branch having become situated in a part of Great Britain on ceasing to be situated elsewhere), deliver to the appropriate Registrar of Companies (see (548) below), for registration, a return in the prescribed form containing the particulars set out at (7) and (8) below. Further particulars and documents are required as set out in (9) and (10) below, subject to the exceptions noted in those paragraphs.

[*CA 1985, Sch 21A para 1(1)(4); SI 1992 No 3179, Sch 2 para 3*].

*CA 1985, s 705A* governs the duties and functions of the Registrar of Companies as regards branches of overseas companies. In particular, he must keep, for each company within (5) above, a register of branches registered by it under the above provisions, and must allocate a number to each such branch (to be known as the branch's registered number).

[*CA 1985, s 705A; SI 1992 No 3179, Reg 3*].

Further returns are required, under *CA 1985, ss 703P or 703Q* (as inserted by *SI 1992 No 3179, Sch 2 para 19*) if on the date the Great Britain branch is opened, the company is subject to winding up or insolvency proceedings or if, on or before that date, a liquidator has been appointed and he continues in office at that date.

[*CA 1985, Sch 21A para 1(5); SI 1992 No 3179, Sch 2 para 3*].

See (20) below for penalties for non-compliance.

(7)   **Particulars required about the company**

The return referred to at (6) above must contain the following particulars about the company.

(a)   Its corporate name.

(b)   Its legal form.

(c)   If it is registered in the country of its incorporation, the identity of the register in which, and the number with which, it is registered.

(d)   A list of its directors and secretary, containing (subject to the provisions below relating to confidentiality orders)

       (i)     with respect to each director (if an individual): his name (meaning usually his forename and surname), any former name (but excluding certain former names, eg a married woman's maiden name), his usual residential address, his nationality, his business occupation (if any), particulars of any other directorships held by him, and his date of birth;

       (ii)    with respect to the secretary (or each of joint secretaries) (if an individual): his name (meaning usually his forename and surname), any former name (but excluding certain former names, eg a married woman's maiden name) and his usual residential address (except that where all the partners in a firm are joint secretaries, the name and principal office of the firm may be stated instead); and

       (iii)   with respect to each director and secretary (if a corporation or Scottish firm), its corporate or firm name and registered or principal office.

(e)     The extent of the powers of the directors to represent the company in dealings with third parties and in legal proceedings, together with a statement as to whether they may act alone or must act jointly and, if jointly, the name of any other person concerned.

(f)     Whether the company is a credit or financial institution within *CA 1985, s 699A* (see (44) below) (or equivalent NI provision).

The following additional particulars are required if the company is not incorporated in an EC Member State.

- The law under which the company is incorporated.

- In the case of a company within the 'delivery of accounts' requirements of either *CA 1985, Sch 21C paras 2, 3* (see (46) below) or *Sch 21D* (see (39) to (43) below), the period for which it is required, by the law under which it is incorporated, to prepare accounts, and the period allowed for the preparation and public disclosure of accounts for such an accounting period.

- Unless otherwise disclosed by the documents referred to at (10) above (where relevant)

       (i)     the address of its principal place of business in its country of incorporation;

       (ii)    its objects; and

       (iii)   the amount of its issued share capital.

Where

- at the time the return referred to in (6) above is delivered, the company has another branch in the same part of Great Britain as the branch covered by the return;

- the company has delivered the above particulars with respect to that other branch (or has done so to the extent required under the transitional provisions described in (13) below); and

- the company has no outstanding obligation to make a return in relation to any alteration of those particulars (see (11) below), then instead of providing the particulars again, the company may simply refer in the current return to the fact that the particulars have been filed in respect of the other branch, giving the number with which the other branch is registered.

*Confidentiality orders.* Where a confidentiality order is in force in respect of a director or secretary required to be specified in the list under (*d*) above

- the requirement to give particulars of his usual residential address has effect in respect of that director or secretary as if the reference to his usual residential address were a reference to his services address for the time being notified by him to the company; and

- the company must deliver to the Registrar, in addition to the return required under the above provisions, a return in the prescribed form containing particulars of the usual residential address of the director or secretary to whom the confidentiality order relates, and any such return must be delivered to the Registrar within one month of the company having opened a branch in a part of Great Britain.

[*CA 1985, Sch 21A para 2; SI 1992 No 3179, Sch 2 para 3; SI 2002 No 912, Sch 2 para 8*].

(8)    **Particulars required about the branch**

The return referred to in (6) above must also contain the following particulars about the branch.

(a)    Its address.

(b)    The date on which it was opened.

(c)    The business carried on at it.

(d)    If different from the name of the company, the name in which that business is carried on.

(e)    A list of the names and addresses of all persons resident in Great Britain authorised to accept on the company's behalf service of process in respect of the business of the branch and of any notices required to be served on the company in respect of that business.

(f)    A list of the names and, subject to the provisions below relating to confidentiality orders, usual residential addresses of all persons authorised to represent the company as its permanent representatives for the branch business.

(g)    The extent of the authority of any person within (*f*) above, including whether that person is authorised to act alone or jointly.

(h)    If a person within (*f*) above is not authorised to act alone, the name of any person with whom he is authorised to act.

*Confidentiality orders.* Where a confidentiality order is in force in respect of a permanent representative required to be specified in the list under (*f*) above

- that list has effect in respect of that permanent representative as if the reference to his usual residential address were a reference to his services address for the time being notified by him to the company; and

- the company must deliver to the Registrar, in addition to the return required under the above provisions, a return in the prescribed form containing particulars of the usual residential address of the director or secretary to whom the confidentiality order relates, and any such return must be delivered to the Registrar within one month of the company having opened a branch in a part of Great Britain.

[*CA 1985, Sch 21A para 3; SI 1992 No 3179, Sch 2 para 3; SI 2002 No 912, Sch 2 para 8*].

(9) **Particulars in relation to registration of documents**

Unless the company is a credit or financial institution to which *CA 1985, s 699A* applies (see (44) below), the return referred to at (6) above must state whether it is intended to register documents under *CA 1985, Sch 21D para 2(2)* or, as the case may be, *Sch 21D para 10(1)* (duty to deliver accounts and reports – see (38) and (42) below respectively) in respect of the branch in question or in respect of some other branch in the UK. If the latter, the place of registration of the other branch and its registered number must also be stated.

[*CA 1985, Sch 21A paras 1(1)(c), 4; SI 1992 No 3179, Sch 2 para 3*].

(10) **Documents required**

The return referred to at (6) above must be accompanied by certain documents unless

(a) at the time of delivery of the return, the company has another branch in the UK;

(b) the return contains a statement to the effect that the documents otherwise required are included in the material registered in respect of the other branch; and

(c) the return states where the other branch is registered and gives its registered number.

The documents required in respect of all companies to which the above exception does not apply are a certified copy of the company's charter, statutes or memorandum and articles (or other instrument constituting or defining the company's constitution), together with an English translation (if the document is not written in English) certified in the prescribed manner to be a correct translation.

In the case of a company which is not a credit or financial institution within *CA 1985, s 699A* (see (44) below) and which is required by its parent law (ie the law of the country in which the company is incorporated) to prepare, have audited and disclose accounts, certain accounting documents are also required (unless the above exception applies). These accounting documents (ie accounts, consolidated accounts (if any), directors' report (if any) and auditors' report) in relation to a financial period of the company (ie a period for which it is required or permitted by its parent law to prepare accounts), being the latest documents to have been publicly disclosed in accordance with the company's parent law before the earlier of the expiry of the one-month period allowed for complying with (6) above and the actual date of compliance. If any of the accounting documents is not written in English, an English translation, certified in the prescribed manner to be a correct translation, must also be provided.

[*CA 1985, Sch 21A paras 1(2)(3), 5, 6; SI 1992 No 3179, Sch 2 para 3*].

(11) **Registration of alterations in particulars**

If, after a company has delivered a return under (6) above, any alteration is made in

(a)    its charter, statutes or memorandum and articles (or other instrument constituting or defining its constitution), or

(b)    any of the particulars referred to in (7) to (9) above,

the company must deliver to the appropriate Registrar of Companies (see (48) below), for registration, a return in the prescribed form containing the prescribed particulars of the alteration. If the alteration is one within (a) above, the return must be accompanied by a certified copy of the document as altered, together with, if the document is not written in English, an English translation certified in the prescribed manner to be a correct translation.

The return must be delivered within 21 days after the making of any alteration of the particulars in (8) above (particulars about the branch) or, as regards any other alteration, within 21 days after the date on which notice of the alteration could have been received by post in Great Britain (if despatched with due diligence).

Where a company has more than one branch in Great Britain and an alteration relates to more than one such branch, a return must be delivered in respect of each branch affected. For this purpose, an alteration in any of the particulars in (7) above (particulars about the company) is to be treated as relating to every branch. However, if there is more than one branch in a part of Great Britain, one return giving the branch numbers of two or more such branches counts as a return for each branch so specified. An alteration within (a) above is only treated as relating to a branch if the document altered is included in the material registered in respect of that branch.

[*CA 1985, Sch 21A para 7; SI 1992 No 3179, Sch 2 para 3*].

Action is also needed if the return under (6) above included a statement under (10)(*b*) above and that statement ceases to be true so far as concerns the documents, other than accounting documents, mentioned in (10) above. The company must then deliver for registration either the said documents or, if applicable, a return in the prescribed form containing a further statement to the effect that those documents are included in material registered in respect of another branch of the company in the UK, and stating the place of registration and registered number of that other branch. These provisions apply in respect of any such further statement as they apply in respect of the original statement. Where there is more than one branch affected, a single return under these provisions will cover more than one branch in a part of Great Britain to the extent that the relevant branch numbers are given in the return.

The above delivery requirements must be complied with within 21 days after the date on which notice of the fact that the statement in the earlier return has ceased to be true could have been received in Great Britain by post (if despatched with due diligence).

[*CA 1985, Sch 21A para 8; SI 1992 No 3179, Sch 2 para 3*].

See (20) below for penalties for non-compliance.

*Confidentiality orders.* The following additional provisions apply where a confidentiality order is in force.

•    If an individual in respect of whom a confidentiality order is in force becomes a director, secretary or permanent representative of a company which has delivered a return under (6) above,

> (i) the return required to be delivered to the Registrar of Companies under *CA 1985, Sch 21A para 7* above must contain the address for the time being notified to the company by the director, secretary or permanent representative as his service address, but must not contain his usual residential address; and
>
> (ii) with that return the company must deliver to the Registrar a separate return in the prescribed form containing the usual residential address of that director, secretary or permanent representative.

- If, after a company has delivered a return under (6) above, a confidentiality order is made in respect of an existing director, secretary or permanent representative of the company, the company must deliver to the Registrar of Companies for registration a return in the prescribed form containing the address for the time being notified to it by the director, secretary or permanent representative as his service address. The return must be delivered within 21 days after the date on which notice of the revised address could have been received in Great Britain in due course of post (if despatched with due diligence).

- If, at any time after a company has delivered a return under (6) above, there is an alteration in the usual residential address of a director, secretary or permanent representative of the company in respect of whom a confidentiality order is in force, The company must deliver to the Registrar of Companies for registration a return in the prescribed form containing the new address. The return must be delivered within 21 days after the date on which notice of the alteration in question could have been received in Great Britain in due course of post (if despatched with due diligence).

Where a company has more than one branch in Great Britain and any provision of the above provisions requires a return to be made to the Registrar of Companies, that provision requires the company to deliver a return in respect of each of the branches; but a return which gives the branch numbers of two or more such branches is treated as a return in respect of each branch whose number is given.

[*CA 1985, Sch 21A para 9; SI 1992 No 3179, Sch 2 para 3; SI 2002 No 912, Sch 2 para 8*].

## (12)   Change in registration regime

The provisions described in (13) and (14) below cover the situation where a company makes a transition from being within the place of business registration regime to being within the branch registration regime, or vice versa. Separate transitional provisions apply in consequence of the introduction of the branch registration regime in Great Britain on 1 January 1993.

## (13)   Change from place of business regime to branch regime

The following provisions apply where a company becomes a company to which *CA 1985, s 690A* applies (branch registration regime) (see (5) above), having immediately beforehand been within *section 691* (place of business registration regime) (see (3) above).

The company need not include the particulars at (7)(*d*) above (list of directors and secretary) in its first return to be delivered under (6) above to the Registrar for a part of Great Britain (see (48) below) if, at the time of transition,

- it had an established place of business in that part;

- it had complied with (3)(*b*)(i) above (details of directors and secretary); and

- it had no outstanding obligation to make a return under *CA 1985, s 692(1)* in respect of an alteration of the kind mentioned at (4)(*b*) above (concerning directors and secretary).

To take advantage of this exemption, the company must state in the return under (6) above that the particulars have been previously filed in respect of a place of business in that part of Great Britain, giving the company's registered number.

A similar exemption applies with regard to the delivery of documents, other than accounting documents, referred to in (10) above, which broadly corresponds with the requirement at (3)(*a*) above under the place of business registration regime.

[*CA 1985, Sch 21B para 1; SI 1992 No 3179, Sch 2 para 5*].

Where a company

- becomes a company to which *CA 1985, s 690A* applies (see (5) above),

- immediately afterwards has in a part of Great Britain an established place of business but no branch, and

- immediately beforehand had an established place of business in that part of Great Britain,

then, in relation to that part of Great Britain, *CA 1985, ss 691, 692* (place of business registration regime) (see (3) and (4) above) continue to apply to the company (notwithstanding *section 690B* – see (2) above) until such time as it gives notice to the Registrar for that part of Great Britain (see (48) below) that it is a company within *section 690A* (branch registration regime).

[*CA 1985, s 692A(3); SI 1992 No 3179, Sch 2 para 4*].

(14)    **Change from branch regime to place of business regime**

The following provisions apply where a company becomes a company to which *CA 1985, s 691* applies (place of business registration regime) (see (3) above), having immediately beforehand been within *section 690A* (branch registration regime) (see (5) above).

The company need not deliver the documents referred to at (3)(*a*) above to the Registrar for a part of Great Britain (see (48) below) if, at the time of transition,

- it had a branch in that part;

- the documents, other than accounting documents, referred to in (10) above were included in the material registered in respect of the branch; and

- the company had no outstanding obligation to make a return to the Registrar for that part of Great Britain under *CA 1985, Sch 21A para 7* (return of alterations – see (11) above) as regards any alteration in the said documents.

To take advantage of this exemption, the company must state in its return under *CA 1985, s 691* (see (3)(*b*)) above that the documents have been previously filed in respect of a branch of the company, giving the branch's registered number.

A similar exemption applies with regard to the information required by *CA 1985, s 691(1)(b)(i)* (details of directors and secretary – see (3)(*b*)(i) above) which broadly corresponds with the requirement at (7)(*d*) above under the branch registration scheme.

# Appendix   Overseas Companies

[*CA 1985, Sch 21B para 2; SI 1992 No 3179, Sch 2 para 5*].

Where a company ceases to be a company to which *CA 1985, s 690A* applies (branch registration regime) (see (5) above) and, immediately afterwards,

- continues to have in Great Britain a place of business which it had immediately beforehand, and

- does not have a branch in Northern Ireland,

it is treated for *section 691* purposes (place of business registration regime) (see (3) above) as having established the place of business on the date when it ceased to be a company to which *section 690A* applies.

[*CA 1985, s 692A(1); SI 1992 No 3179, Sch 2 para 4*].

Where a limited company incorporated outside the UK and Gibraltar

- ceases to have a branch in Northern Ireland, and

- both immediately beforehand and immediately afterwards, has a place of business, but not a branch, in Great Britain,

it is treated for *CA 1985, s 691* purposes as having established the place of business on the date when it ceased to have a branch in Northern Ireland. [*CA 1985, s 692A(2); SI 1992 No 3179, Sch 2 para 4*].

(15)   **Miscellaneous matters**

**Places of business.** An overseas company must conspicuously exhibit in every place where it carries on business in Great Britain

- its name;

- its country of incorporation; and

- if applicable, the fact that its members have limited liability.

[*CA 1985, s 693(1)(b), (d); SI 1992 No 3179, Sch 2 para 6*].

See (20) below for penalties for non-compliance.

(16)   **Letter paper, notices etc**

An overseas company must state in legible characters in all bill-heads, letter paper, notices and official publications

- its name and the country of incorporation; and

- if applicable, the fact that the liability of members is limited.

[*CA 1985, s 693(1)(c), (d); SI 1992 No 3179, Sch 2 para 6*].

See (21) below for penalties for non-compliance.

(17)   **Duty to state name etc – branches**

The following provisions apply only to companies within *CA 1985, s 690A* (branch registration regime – see (5) above), and apply in addition to those relating to overseas companies generally at (13) and (14) above.

In the case of each company branch registered under *CA 1985, Sch 21A para 1* (see (6) above), the following particulars must be stated in legible characters in all letter paper and order forms used in carrying on the business of the branch.

(a)     As regards such branches of all companies within *CA 1985, s 690A* (see (5) above)

    (i)     the place of registration of the branch; and

    (ii)    the registered number of the branch.

(b)     As regards such branches of every company within *CA 1985, s 690A* which is not incorporated in an EC Member State and which is required by the law of the country in which it is incorporated to be registered

    (i)     the identity of the registry in which the company is registered in its country of incorporation; and

    (ii)    the number with which it is registered.

(c)     As regards such branches of every company within *CA 1985, s 690A* which is not incorporated in an EC Member State

    (i)     the legal form of the company;

    (ii)    the location of its head office; and

    (iii)   if applicable, the fact that it is being wound up.

[*CA 1985, s 693(2)–(4); SI 1992 No 3179, Sch 2 para 6*].

Where a company is notified by the Registrar of a change of a branch's registered number, it may continue to use the old number for three years beginning with the date of notification without contravening (a)(ii) above.

[*CA 1985, s 705A(5); SI 1992 No 3179, Reg 3*].

(18)    **Company name**

See (4) above for notification of change of name to Registrar of Companies and (16) and (17) above for disclosure of name on letter paper etc.

Notice may be served on an overseas company within twelve months of the 'relevant date' to the effect that

(a)     its name would have been prohibited under *CA 1985, s 26* if it had been formed under *CA 1985*; or

(b)     its name is too like a name already appearing in the Index of names kept by the Registrar of Companies.

The 'relevant date' is the date on which the company complied with the provisions of (3) above or those of (6) above, or the first such date, if more than one, since it became an overseas company. However, if on a later date the company's corporate name has been changed, the 'relevant date' is the date on which the company complied with the provisions of (4)(*b*) above or those of *CA 1985, Sch 21A para 7* (see (11) above) in respect of the change or, if more than one, the latest change.

The notice, which may be withdrawn within two months of service, must state the reason under (*a*) or the similar name under (*b*). The overseas company must not then, at any time after the expiration of two months from the date of notice, carry on business in Great Britain using the corporate name (although doing so does not invalidate any transaction entered into by the company). If it does, the company and every officer or agent who knowingly and wilfully authorises or permits the contravention is guilty of an offence and liable to a fine.

The company may, however, deliver to the appropriate Registrar of Companies (see (48) below) a statement in the prescribed form (Form 694(a)) specifying a name, other than its corporate name, under which it proposes to carry on business in Great Britain. This name may also be subsequently changed using Form 694(b). The new registered name is then deemed to be the company's corporate name but without affecting any rights or obligations of the company or any legal proceedings against the company under its corporate name or any previously registered name.

[*CA 1985, ss 694, 697(2), Sch 24; SI 1992 No 3179, Sch 2 para 7*].

(19)   **Service of documents on an overseas company**

Any process or notice required to be served on an overseas company within *CA 1985, s 691* (place of business regime, see (3) above) is sufficiently served if addressed to any person whose name has been delivered to the Registrar of Companies under (3) or (4) above and left at, or sent by post to, his address. Where this is not possible (because no such names have been delivered or the persons named are dead, have moved or refuse to accept service) a document may be served on the company by leaving it at, or sending it by post to, any place of business established by the company in Great Britain. [*CA 1985, s 695; SI 1992 No 3179, Sch 2 para 9*]. The place of business must exist at the time of the service and cannot merely be a former place of business (*Deverall v Grant Advertising Inc* [1955] Ch 111, [1954] 3 All ER 389, CA).

Any process or notice required to be served on a company within *CA 1985, s 690A* (branch registration regime) (see (5) above) in respect of the carrying on of the business of a registered branch is sufficiently served if addressed to any person whose name has, in respect of the branch, been delivered to the Registrar as a person falling within (8)(*e*) above and left at, or sent by post to, the address of that person which has been so delivered. Where this is not possible, the same provisions apply as under *CA 1985, s 695* (see above). Where such a company has more than one branch in Great Britain, any process or notice which does not relate to the business of any one branch is treated for these purposes as being required to be served in respect of the business of each branch.

[*CA 1985, s 694A; SI 1992 No 3179, Sch 2 para 8*].

(20)   **Penalties**

If an overseas company fails to comply with any of the provisions of (3), (4), (16), (17) above or (48) below, the company and every officer or agent of the company who knowingly and wilfully authorises or permits the default is liable to a fine.

[*CA 1985, s 697(1), Sch 24*].

If an overseas company fails to comply with any of the provisions of (6) to (11) above or (49) below, the company and every officer or agent who knowingly and wilfully authorises or permits the default is liable on summary conviction to a maximum fine of one-fifth of level 5 on the standard scale and, in the case of a continuing offence, a daily default fine £100.

[*CA 1985, s 697(3), Sch 24; SI 1992 No 3179, Sch 2 para 12*].

(21)   **Channel Islands and Isle of Man companies**

Subject to the exceptions below, the provisions of *CA 1985* and *CA 2006* requiring documents to be delivered or filed with the Registrar of Companies apply to an overseas company which is within *CA 1985, s 691* (place of business regime, see (3) above) and which is incorporated in the Channel Islands and the Isle of Man

- as if it were formed under *CA 1985*;

- if it has an established place of business in England and Wales, as if it were registered in England and Wales;

- if it has an established place of business in Scotland, as if it were registered there;

- if it has an established place of business in both England and Wales and Scotland, as if it were registered in both England and Wales and Scotland; and

- in a similar way to documents relating to things done outside Great Britain, as if they had been done in Great Britain.

The exceptions are as follows (for which the normal rules for overseas companies apply).

- *CA 1985, s 6(1)* (resolution altering the company's objects).

- *CA 1985, s 18* (alteration of memorandum and articles by statute or statutory instrument).

- *CA 1985, s 288(2)* (notice to Registrar of Companies of change of directors or secretary).

- *CA 2006, ss 29, 30* (resolutions and agreements affecting a company's constitution, so far as applicable to a resolution altering a company's memorandum or articles.

- *CA 2006, s 441* (directors' duty to file accounts).

[*CA 1985, s 699; CA 1989, Sch 10 para 12; SI 1992 No 3179, Sch 2 para 14; SI 2007 No 2194, Sch 4 para 1; SI 2008 No 948, Sch 1 para 84*].

(22)  **Accounts and reports**

Every overseas company, other than those within (23) and (24) below, must, in respect of each financial year of the company, prepare like accounts and directors' report, and cause to be prepared such an auditors' report, as would be required if the company were formed and registered under *CA 1985*. [*CA 1985, s 700(1); CA 1989, Sch 10 para 13*]. The Secretary of State may, however, modify or exempt an overseas company from these requirements [*CA 1985, s 700(2)–(4); CA 1989, Sch 10 para 13*] and this has been done by the *Overseas Companies (Accounts) (Modifications and Exemptions) Order 1990* (*SI 1990 No 440*). The effect of the order is that, for accounts purposes, overseas companies are subject to certain of the provisions of *CA 1985, Pt VII* (accounts and audit) as if that part had not been amended by *CA 1989*.

This is considered more fully in (26) to (36) below. Note that if the company is listed, it must comply with certain necessary requirements, including circulating audited financial statements to members. Such a company may not therefore be able to take advantage of the exemptions available.

(23)  **Exceptions**

*Overseas company with UK branch.* The provisions of (22) above and (26) to (38) below do not apply to any limited company which is incorporated outside the UK and Gibraltar and has a branch (as defined in (2) above) in the UK.

[*CA 1985, s 699B; SI 1992 No 3179, Sch 2 para 17*].

See also (39) to (46) below.

# Appendix   Overseas Companies

(24)   **Oversea credit or financial institution with branch in Great Britain**

The provisions of (23) and (26) to (38) below do not apply to any credit or financial institution which

- is incorporated or otherwise formed outside the UK and Gibraltar,
- whose head office is outside the UK and Gibraltar, and
- which has a branch in Great Britain.

[*CA 1985, s 699B; SI 1992 No 3179, Reg 2*].

See (44) to (47) for the provisions applying to such institutions. See (44) below for the meaning of 'credit institution', 'financial institution' and, for these purposes, 'branch'.

(25)   **Duty to prepare annual accounts**

For every oversea company, the directors must prepare a profit and loss account (or, if not trading for profit, an income and expenditure account) for each financial year and a balance sheet as at the last day of that year. In the case of a holding company, the directors must ensure that, except where there are good reasons, the financial year of its subsidiaries coincides with the company's own financial year.

[*CA 1985, s 227* as originally enacted].

(26)   **Individual accounts: form and content**

The balance sheet and profit and loss account must give a true and fair view of the state of affairs of the company as at the end of the financial year and its profit or loss for that year.

The following information must be given as appropriate on the balance sheet, profit and loss account or in the notes. The Secretary of State may, on application or with the consent of the company's directors, modify any of the requirements in relation to the company in order to adapt them to the circumstances of the company.

(i)   **Assets and liabilities generally.** Liabilities and assets must be summarised with such particulars as may be necessary to disclose their general nature. They must be classified under headings appropriate to the company's business unless a particular class is immaterial or, in the case of a class of assets, inseparable from another.

Fixed assets, current assets, and those neither fixed nor current, must be separately identified.

If the directors are of the opinion that any current assets would not realise their balance sheet value if realised in the ordinary course of business, they must state that fact in a note.

(ii)   **Fixed assets.**

(a)   The method or methods used to arrive at the amount of fixed assets under each heading must be stated.

(b)   Subject to the exceptions below, the method of arriving at the amount of any fixed asset is to be taken as the difference between its cost (or, if standing in the company's books at valuation, its valuation) and the aggregate amount provided or written off since the date of acquisition (or valuation) for depreciation or diminution in value. Such totals must be given for each heading. Where the assets are included at

736

valuation, the year of valuation (if known) must be stated in the notes. If valued during the financial year, the names and qualifications of the valuers, and basis of valuation, must also be given.

The provisions in (*b*) above does not apply to the following assets.

- Assets the replacement of which is provided either by making provision for renewals and charging the cost of replacement against that provision or by charging the cost of replacement direct to revenue. For such assets there must be stated the means by which their replacement is provided for and the aggregate amount of the provision (if any) made for renewals and not used.

- Listed or unlisted investments (see (6) and (7) below) of which the directors' valuation is shown either as a balance sheet figure or by way of note.

- Goodwill, patents or trademarks (see (4) below).

The aggregate amounts of assets acquired, and assets disposed of or destroyed, during the financial year must be stated by way of note for fixed assets under each heading.

(iii) **Preliminary expenses**. The amount of preliminary expenses (so far as not written off) must be shown in the balance sheet under a separate heading.

(iv) **Goodwill, patents etc**. The amount of goodwill, and of any patents or trademarks, so far as not written off, must be disclosed as a single item under a separate heading provided the amount is ascertainable from the company's books or from any contract or document relating to the sale or purchase.

(v) **Land**. In relation to any fixed asset shown in the balance sheet consisting of land there must be stated how much is ascribable to freehold land (or Scottish equivalent) and how much to leasehold land (or Scottish equivalent) and, of the latter, how much is ascribable to '*long leases*' (ie 'leases' with an unexpired term at the end of the financial year of at least 50 years) and how much to '*short leases*' (ie any other lease). '*Lease*' includes an agreement for a lease.

(vi) **Listed investments**.

(a) The aggregate amount of the company's 'listed investments' must be shown under a separate heading, subdivided where necessary to distinguish (i) those listed on a recognised investment exchange other than an overseas investment exchange within the meaning of the *FSMA 2000*; and (ii) those not so listed.

(b) There must be shown by way of note (i) the aggregate market value of the listed investments where it differs from the amount as stated in the balance sheet; and (ii) the stock exchange value of any investments of which the market value is shown as a higher figure.

'*Listed investments*' are those which have been granted a listing either on a recognised investment exchange (other than an overseas investment exchange within the meaning of *FSMA 2000*) or on any stock exchange of repute outside Great Britain.

(vii)   **Unlisted investments.**

(a)   The aggregate amount of the company's 'unlisted investments' must be shown under a separate heading.

(b)   In the case of such investments in equity shares of other companies, unless the directors' estimated valuation is either included as the balance sheet figure or disclosed in a note, the following information must be stated by way of note: (i) the aggregate amount of the company's income for the financial year ascribable to the investment; (ii) the amount of the company's share in the net aggregate pre-tax profits of the companies in which the investments are held, and the amount of that share after taxation; (iii) the amount of the company's share in the net aggregate undistributed profits (less losses) accumulated by those companies since the time the investments were acquired; and (iv) the manner in which any losses incurred by those companies have been dealt with in the company's accounts.

'*Unlisted investments*' are any investments other than listed investments (see (6) above).

(viii)   **Group undertakings.** Where the company is a parent company, there must be disclosed separately on the balance sheet

•   the aggregate amount of assets consisting of shares in, or amounts owing from, the company's subsidiary undertakings (distinguishing shares from indebtedness); and

•   the aggregate amount in indebtedness to the company's subsidiary undertakings.

Where the company is a subsidiary undertaking, the balance sheet must show the aggregate amount of

•   indebtedness to undertakings of which it is a subsidiary undertaking or which are fellow subsidiary undertakings;

•   indebtedness of all such undertakings to it, distinguishing in each case between indebtedness in respect of debentures and otherwise; and

•   assets consisting of shares in fellow subsidiary undertakings.

(ix)   **Current assets.**

(a)   *Stocks.* The manner in which stock and work in progress has been computed must be stated by way of note if the amount is material to the company's state of affairs or its profit or loss for the financial year.

(b)   *Foreign currencies.* The basis on which foreign currencies have been converted into sterling must be stated by way of note, if material.

(c)   *Loans to purchase own shares.* There must be stated the aggregate amount of outstanding loans: (i) to employees' share schemes under *CA 1985, s 153(4)(b)* or employees and their families under *CA 1985, s 153(4)(c)*; or (ii) by private companies under *CA 1985, s 155*, in each case for the purpose of giving financial assistance to purchase shares in the company.

(x)   **Loans.** There must be shown under separate headings

(a)   the aggregate of bank loans and overdrafts; and

(b)   the aggregate amount of other loans made to the company which are repayable (i) otherwise than by instalments and which fall due for repayment after the end of a five-year period beginning with the day after the end of the financial year; or (ii) by instalments any of which fall due after the end of that period.

For loans under (*b*) above, the terms of repayment and rate of interest for each loan must be disclosed by way of note unless, because of the number of such loans, the directors are of the opinion that compliance would result in a statement of excessive length. In such a case, a general indication of the terms and interest rates is sufficient.

A loan, or an instalment of a loan, is deemed to be due for repayment on the earliest date on which the lender could require repayment if he exercised all options and rights available to him.

(xi)   **Taxation**. There must be stated

(a)   the amount, if any, set aside to prevent undue fluctuations in charges to tax and, if during the financial year such a fund has been used for any other purpose, the amount used and the fact that it has been so used; and

(b)   particulars of any special circumstances affecting liability in respect of taxation of profits, income or capital gains for the financial year in question and/or succeeding financial years.

(xii)   **Secured liabilities**. Where any liability of the company is secured otherwise than by operation of the law on any asset of the company, that fact must be stated (although it is not necessary to specify the asset in question).

(xiii)   **Guarantees and other financial commitments**. The following information must be stated.

(a)   Particulars of any charge on the company's assets to secure the liabilities of any other person, including, where practicable, the amount secured.

(b)   The general nature of any contingent liabilities not provided for and, where practicable, the aggregate amount or estimated amount if material.

(c)   Where practicable, the aggregate amount or estimated amount, if material, of (i) contracts for capital expenditure, so far as not provided for; and (ii) capital expenditure authorised by the directors which has not been contracted for.

(xiv)   **Distributions**. The aggregate amount of recommended dividends must be disclosed under a separate heading. In addition, there must be shown by way of note

(a)   the amount of any arrears of fixed cumulative dividends on the company's shares and the period for which they are in arrears (detailing each class separately if more than one); and

(b)   any distribution by an 'investment company' which reduces the amount of its net assets to less than the aggregate of called-up share capital and 'undistributable reserves'. See 22.1 DISTRIBUTIONS for 'investment company' and 'undistributable reserves'.

739

(xv)   **Debentures.** There must be stated

    (a)    particulars of any redeemed debentures which the company has power to reissue;

    (b)    to the extent that they are not written off, and, if not, under separate headings (i) any expenses incurred in connection with any issue of debentures; (ii) any sums paid by way of commission in respect of any debentures; and (iii) any sums allowed by way of discount in respect of any debentures; and

    (c)    the nominal amount of any of the company's debentures which are held by a nominee of, or a trustee for, the company, together with the amount at which that are stated in the books of the company.

(xvi)   **Reserves and provisions.**

    (a)    'Reserves' and 'provisions' must be classified under headings appropriate to the company's business; provided that where the amount of any class is not material, it may be included under the same heading as some other class.

    (b)    There must be stated (if material) (i) the aggregate amount respectively of reserves and provisions (other than provisions for depreciation, renewals or diminution in value of assets) under separate headings; and (ii) (unless shown in the profit and loss account or by way of note) the source of any increase as compared with the amount at the end of the previous financial year and the application of any decrease.

If the reserves or provisions are divided into sub-headings, this information must be given for each sub-heading.

'*Provision*' means any amount written off or retained by way of providing for depreciation, renewals or diminution in value of assets or retained by way of providing for any known liability the amount of which cannot be determined with substantial accuracy. Where, however, such amount is in excess of that which in the opinion of the directors is reasonably necessary for the purpose, the excess is to be treated as a reserve and not as a provision.

'*Reserve*' does not include any provision (other than any excess provision as above) or any sum set aside to prevent undue fluctuations in charges for taxation.

The Secretary of State may direct that a separate statement of provisions is not required if satisfied that it would not be in the public interest and would prejudice the company.

(xvii)   **Share premium.** The amount of the share premium account must be specified on the balance sheet.

(xviii)   **Share capital.** There must be stated

    (a)    the authorised and issued share capital;

    (b)    any part of the issued share capital that consists of redeemable shares together with (i) the earliest and latest dates on which the company has power to redeem those shares; (ii) whether the shares must be redeemed in any event or are liable to be redeemed at the option of the company or the shareholder; and (iii) whether any (and, if so, what) premium is payable on redemption;

(c)   (if not stated in the profit and loss account) any share capital on which interest has been paid out of capital during the financial year; and the rate at which interest has been so paid;

(d)   to the extent that they are not written off, and if not under separate headings (i) any expenses incurred in connection with any issue of share capital; (ii) any sums paid by way of commission in respect of any shares; and (iii) the amount of the discount allowed on any issue of shares;

(e)   the number, description and amount of any shares in the company which any person has the option to subscribe for, together with details of (i) the period during which the option is exercisable; and (ii) the price to be paid for the shares subscribed for under the option; and

(f)   where shares in a public company are purchased or acquired by the company (by forfeiture or surrender in lieu) or by another person on the company's behalf, details must be given of the (i) number and nominal value of the shares involved; (ii) consideration paid, if any, and reason for the purchase; (iii) maximum number and nominal value of shares held during the year; (iv) number and nominal value of shares so acquired which are disposed of or cancelled in the year and the consideration; and (v) percentage of the called-up share capital involved for each of the above items.

(xix)   **Separate statement of certain items of income and expenditure.** The following must be stated.

(a)   The amount of interest on (i) bank loans and overdrafts and other loans made to the company which are repayable *either* otherwise than by instalments and fall due before the end of a five-year period beginning with the day after the end of the financial year *or* by instalments the last of which falls due for payment before the end of that period; and (ii) loans of any other kind made to the company. A loan or an instalment of a loan, is deemed to be due for repayment on the earliest date on which the lender could require repayment if he exercised all options and rights available to him.

(b)   The amounts respectively set aside for redemption of share capital and for redemption of loans.

(c)   The amount of income from listed investments and unlisted investments (see (6) and (7) above).

(d)   The amount of rents from land (net of ground rents, rates and other outgoings including, in Scotland, feu-duty and ground annual) but only if a substantial part of the company's revenue for the financial year consists of such rents.

(e)   The amount, if material, charged to revenue for the hire of plant and machinery.

(xx)   **Depreciation.** The amount charged to revenue by way of provision for depreciation, renewals or diminution in value of fixed assets must be shown. In the case of assets for which an amount is charged to revenue by way of provision for depreciation or diminution in value

    (a)   if an amount is also charged by way of provision for renewal, that amount must be shown separately; and

    (b)   if the amount charged to revenue has been determined otherwise than by reference to the amount of those assets as determined for balance sheet purposes, that fact must be stated. This does not apply to provisions for diminution in investments.

If depreciation or replacement of fixed assets is provided for by some method other than a depreciation charge or provision for renewals (or is not provided for), the method by which it is provided (or that fact) must be stated by way of note.

(xxi)   **Directors' emoluments.** Details must be disclosed of directors' emoluments, pensions of directors and past directors and compensation to directors for loss of office. See **3.48**, **3.50** and **3.51** ACCOUNTS: LARGE COMPANIES which apply ignoring

    (a)   amounts paid to or receivable by a connected person or a body corporate controlled by the director; and

    (b)   in relation to pensions and compensation for loss of office, the nature and estimated money value of any benefits paid otherwise than in cash.

Comparative figures for the immediately preceding financial year must also be given.

(xxii)   **Dividends and transfers to and from reserves.** There must be disclosed

    (a)   the aggregate amount of dividends paid and proposed;

    (b)   the amount, if material, set aside to, or withdrawn from, provisions other than those within (xx) above. The Secretary of State may, however, direct that the company is not obliged to show such amount if it is not in the public interest and would prejudice the company.

See (xvi) above for 'provisions' and 'reserves'.

(xxiii)   **Auditors' remuneration.** The amount of auditors' remuneration (if any) including expenses must be stated.

(xxiv)   **Miscellaneous.**

    (a)   The amount of any charge arising in consequence of the occurrence of an event in the preceding financial year and of any credit so arising must, if not included in a heading related to other matters, be stated under a separate heading.

    (b)   Where any items in the profit and loss account are materially affected by (i) transactions of a sort not usually undertaken by the company or by circumstances of an exceptional or non-recurrent nature, or (ii) any change in the basis of accounting, this fact must be stated by way of note.

(xxv)    **Comparative figures**. Comparative figures for all items in the balance sheet and profit and loss account at the end of, or for, the immediately preceding financial year must be shown.

[*CA 1985, s 258(1)(4), Sch 9, Pt I* as originally enacted; *SI 1990 No 440*].

(27)    **Group undertakings**

Where the company is a holding company (whether or not it is itself a subsidiary) the following must be disclosed separately as indicated.

(a)     The aggregate amount of assets consisting of shares in, or the amount owing from, the company's subsidiaries (distinguishing shares from indebtedness) must be shown in the balance sheet.

(b)     The aggregate amount of indebtedness to the company's subsidiaries must be shown in the balance sheet.

(c)     The number, description and amount of the shares in, and debentures of, the company held by its subsidiaries or their nominees must be shown as a note. Excluded are any shares held as personal representative or as trustee where neither the company nor any subsidiary is beneficially interested under the trust.

(d)     Where group accounts are not submitted, there must be annexed to the balance sheet a statement showing

(i)      the reasons why subsidiaries are not dealt with in group accounts;

(ii)     the net aggregate amount, so far as it concerns members of the holding company and is not dealt with in the company's accounts, of the subsidiaries' profits after deducting losses (or vice versa) for the financial years of the subsidiaries ending with, or during, the financial year of the company. Comparative figures must also be given if they were then subsidiaries;

(iii)    the net aggregate amount of the subsidiaries' profits after deducting losses (or vice versa) for the financial years of the subsidiaries ending with or during the financial year of the company so far as those profits are dealt with, or provision is made for those losses, in the company's accounts. Comparative figures must also be given if they were then subsidiaries;

(iv)     any qualifications contained in the audit reports of the subsidiaries (or notes to the accounts which would have properly been referred to in such a qualification if not so disclosed) which is not covered in the company's own accounts and is material to the members;

(v)      if any of the information required under (i) to (iv) above is not obtainable, a statement to that effect; and

(vi)     in relation to any subsidiaries whose financial years do not end with that of the company, the directors' reasons for this and the dates on which the subsidiaries' financial years ended last before the end of the company's financial year (or the earliest and latest of those dates).

The provisions of (ii) and (iii) above only apply to profits properly treated as revenue profits (with certain exceptions). They do not apply where the company is a wholly-owned subsidiary of another company incorporated in Great Britain provided a statement is attached to the balance sheet that, in the directors' opinion, the aggregate values of the shares in, and amounts owing, from the company's subsidiaries is not less than the aggregate amounts at which those assets are stated or included in the balance sheet.

*Where a company is a subsidiary* (whether or not it is itself a holding company) the balance sheet must show the aggregate amount of

- indebtedness to companies of which it is a subsidiary or a fellow subsidiary;

- indebtedness of all such companies to it, distinguishing in each case between indebtedness in respect of debentures and otherwise; and

- assets consisting of shares in fellow subsidiaries.

[*CA 1985, Sch 9 paras 19, 20* as originally enacted; *SI 1990 No 440*].

(28)   **Group accounts of holding company**

Subject to below, if an oversea company has subsidiaries at the end of its financial year, the directors must, in addition to the individual accounts, prepare a consolidated profit and loss account and balance sheet dealing with the state of affairs and profit or loss of the company and its subsidiaries. This does not apply if

(a)   the company is, at the end of the financial year, a wholly-owned subsidiary of another body corporate incorporated in Great Britain; or

(b)   the directors are of the opinion that

- it would be impracticable, disproportionately expensive or misleading;

- (provided the Secretary of State agrees) the result would be harmful or the businesses are so different that they cannot reasonably be treated as a single undertaking; or

- instead of consolidating figures for the whole group, either more than one set of consolidated accounts are prepared *or* separate accounts are prepared for each subsidiary *or* statements expanding on the information about the subsidiaries are given in the company's individual accounts *or* any combination of those forms.

[*CA 1985, s 229* as originally enacted].

(29)   **Form and content of group accounts**

The group accounts must give a true and fair view of the state of affairs and profit or loss of the company and the subsidiaries dealt with by those accounts as a whole, so far as concerns members of the company.

Where the financial year of a subsidiary does not coincide with that of the holding company, the group accounts must deal with the subsidiary's state of affairs as at the end of its 'relevant financial year' and its profit or loss for that year. The '*relevant financial year*' is the financial year ending with that of the holding company or, if the subsidiary has no financial year so ending, its financial year ending last before that date.

The consolidated balance sheet and profit and loss account must combine the information contained in the separate balance sheets and profit and loss accounts of the holding company and subsidiaries dealt with by the consolidated accounts but with such adjustments as the directors of the holding company think necessary.

Subject to that, the group accounts must comply, so far as practicable, with the provisions listed in (27) above as if the 'group' (meaning, for these purposes, all the companies included in the consolidation) were an individual company.

Where any subsidiaries of the holding company are not dealt with by the consolidated accounts

- the provisions of (28)(*a*)–(*c*) above apply as if such subsidiaries were subsidiaries of the 'group'; and

- there must be annexed to the accounts the like statement as is required by (28)(*d*)(i)–(iv) above but as if references to the holding company's accounts were references to the consolidated accounts.

In relation to any subsidiary (whether or not dealt with in the consolidated accounts) whose financial year did not end with that of the company, there must be annexed the like statement as is required under (28)(*d*)(vi) above where there are no group accounts.

[*CA 1985, s 259, Sch 9 paras 21–26, 31* as originally enacted; *SI 1990 No 440*].

(30) **Small and medium-sized companies**

The provisions for small and medium-sized companies do not apply to oversea companies. [SI *1990 No 440, Art 2(c)*].

(31) **Directors' report**

An oversea company need not prepare a directors' report or disclose any of the information required in such a report under *CA 1985, Sch 7* or *Sch 10*.

[*SI 1990 No 440, Sch 1 para 3*].

(32) **Auditors' report**

An oversea company is not required to have an auditors' report attached to its accounts.

[*SI 1990 No 440, Sch 1 para 4*].

(33) **Signing of the balance sheet**

An oversea company's accounts must be approved by the board and signed on its behalf by two directors (if there is only one director, by that one). Every copy laid before the company in general meeting or delivered to the Registrar of Companies (see (38) below) must be signed. If not, or if a copy is otherwise issued, circulated or published without being signed or bearing a copy of the signature(s), the company and every officer in default is liable to a fine.

[*CA 1985, s 238* as originally enacted; *SI 1990 No 440, Sch 1, para 4*].

(34) **Dormant companies**

The provisions of *CA 1985, ss 252, 253* as originally enacted (resolution of dormant company not to appoint auditors and laying and delivery of unaudited accounts) do not apply to oversea companies.

[*SI 1990 No 440, Reg 2(c)*].

(35) **Unlimited oversea companies**

An unlimited oversea company which at no time during the accounting reference period

- has been, to its knowledge, the subsidiary of a limited company, or

- has had, to its knowledge, shares owned or power exercised by two or more companies which if exercised by one would have made the company its subsidiary, or

- has been a promoter of a trading stamp scheme

is not required to prepare accounts or deliver them to the Registrar of Companies.

[*CA 1985, ss 241(4), 700(3)* as originally enacted; *SI 1990 No 440, Reg 2(3)*].

(36)    **Accounting reference dates**

The provisions in 2 ACCOUNTING REFERENCE DATES AND PERIODS apply to oversea companies subject to the modification in **2.5**.

(37)    **Delivery of accounts to the Registrar of Companies**

Subject to the following exceptions, the accounts and reports must be delivered to the appropriate Registrar of Companies (see (48) below), together with a certified translation if in a language other than English, within 13 months (or such longer period as the Secretary of State allows) after the end of the relevant accounting reference period. The exceptions are as follows.

- If the relevant accounting reference period is the company's first and is for a period of more than twelve months, the period allowed is 25 months from the company's establishing a place of business in Great Britain.

- If the relevant accounting period is shortened by notice under *CA 2006, s 392* (see **2.4** ACCOUNTING REFERENCE DATES AND PERIODS), the period allowed is 13 months after the end of the relevant accounting reference period or three months from the date of notice, whichever last expires.

[*CA 1985, s 702; CA 1989, Sch 10 para 13; SI 2008 No 948, Sch 1 para 86*].

**Penalties.** Where the accounts are not filed in the period allowed or do not comply with the requirements of CA 1985, the company and every person who immediately before the end of that period was a director of the company is guilty of an offence and liable to a fine. It is a defence for a person charged with such an offence to prove that he took all reasonable steps to secure that the requirements in question were complied with but it is not a defence in relation to failure to deliver copies to the Registrar to prove that the documents were not in fact prepared as required by CA 1985.

[*CA 1985, s 703, Sch 24; CA 1989, Sch 10, para 10*].

(38)    **Accounts and reports – companies with branches in Great Britain**

The provisions at (40) to (46) below apply to any company within *CA 1985, s 699AA*, ie any limited company which

- is incorporated outside the UK and Gibraltar,

- has a branch in Great Britain, and

- is not a credit or financial institution within *CA 1985, s 699A* (see (47) below).

[*CA 1985, s 699AA; SI 1992 No 3179, Sch 2 para 16*].

(39)   **Companies required to make disclosure under parent law**

The provisions at (41) and (42) below apply to any company within (39) above which is required by its parent law (ie the law of the country in which it is incorporated) to prepare, have audited and publicly disclose accounts.

(40)   **Duty to deliver accounting documents**

The following provisions apply in respect of each branch which a company within (40) above has in Great Britain.

The company must deliver to the Registrar of Companies, for registration in respect of the branch, copies of all the 'accounting documents' prepared in relation to a 'financial period' of the company which are disclosed in accordance with its parent law (ie the law of the country in which it is incorporated), where such disclosure occurs

•   after the end of the period allowed for compliance with *CA 1985, Sch 21A para 1* in respect of the branch (see (6) above), or, if earlier,

•   on or after the date on which such compliance occurs.

For these purposes, the following are *'accounting documents'* in relation to a 'financial period' of a company.

(i)   The accounts of the company for the period, including, if it has one or more subsidiaries, any consolidated accounts of the group.

(ii)   Any annual report of the directors for the period.

(iii)   The auditors' report on the accounts in (i) above.

(iv)   Any auditors' report on the report in (ii) above.

A *'financial period'* of a company means a period for which it is required or permitted by its parent law to prepare accounts.

Where the company's parent law permits it to publicly disclose accounting documents in a modified form only, the company will satisfy these provisions if it delivers copies of documents as so modified.

If any document is in a language other than English, there must be annexed to the copy delivered an English translation, certified in the prescribed manner to be a correct translation.

Documents are not required to be delivered for a particular branch if

•   they are delivered in respect of another UK branch within the time limit allowed; and

•   the particulars registered under *CA 1985, Sch 21A* in respect of the branch indicate an intention that the documents are to be registered in respect of that other branch and include the required details of that other branch. See (9) above.

*Time limit.* The period allowed for delivery, in relation to any document within these provisions, is three months from the date on which the document is first publicly disclosed in accordance with the company's parent law.

*Penalties.* On the failure of the company to comply with these provisions within the time limit, the company and every person who was a director immediately before expiry of the time limit is guilty of an offence and liable to a fine. It is a defence for a person charged with such an offence to prove that he took all reasonable steps to secure compliance.

[*CA 1985, Sch 21D paras 2–6, Sch 24; SI 1992 No 3179, Sch 2 para 18*].

(41)   **Companies not required to make disclosure under parent law**

The provisions in (44) to (46) below apply to any company within (39) above which is *not* required by its parent law (ie the law of the country in which it is incorporated) to prepare, have audited and publicly disclose accounts.

(42)   **Preparation of accounts and reports**

A company within (39) above must prepare the like accounts and directors' report, and cause to be prepared such an auditors' report, as would be required if the company were within *CA 1985, s 700* (see (23) above).

The provisions in to **2 Accounts (General) and Accounting Reference Dates and Periods** and the definition of 'financial year' in **Appendix 1 Definitions** apply with the following modifications.

(a)   For the references to the incorporation of a company, there should be substituted references to its becoming a company within (39) above; and

(b)   The restrictions in **2** on the frequency with which the current accounting reference period may be extended do not apply.

[*CA 1985, Sch 21D paras 8, 9; SI 1992 No 3179, Sch 2 para 18; SI 2008 No 948, Sch 1 para 94*].

(43)   **Duty to deliver accounts and reports**

In respect of each financial year and in respect of each branch which it has in Great Britain at the end of that financial year, a company within (39) above must deliver to the Registrar of Companies copies of the accounts and reports prepared in accordance with (40) above. If any document comprised in those accounts or reports is in a language other than English, there must be annexed to the copy delivered an English translation, certified in the prescribed manner to be a correct translation.

Documents are not required to be delivered for a particular branch if

•   they are delivered in respect of another UK branch within the time limit allowed; and

•   the particulars registered under *CA 1985, Sch 21A* in respect of the branch indicate an intention that the documents are to be registered in respect of that other branch and include the required details of that other branch. See (9) above.

*Time limits.* The period allowed for delivering accounts and reports under these provisions is 13 months after the end of the relevant accounting reference period (ie the accounting reference period by reference to which the financial year for the accounts in question was determined), subject to the following exceptions.

(i)   If the relevant accounting reference period is the company's first and it exceeds 12 months, the period allowed is 13 months from the first anniversary of the company's becoming a company within (39) above.

(ii)    If the relevant accounting reference period is treated as shortened by virtue of a notice given by the company under *CA 2006, s 392* (see **2 Accounts (General) and Accounting Reference Dates and Periods**), the period allowed is that normally applicable or three months from the date of the said notice, whichever last expires.

(iii)    The Secretary of State has the power, on an application made within the period otherwise allowed, to extend that period by such further period as he specifies in a written notice to the company.

*Penalties.* On the failure of the company to comply with these provisions within the time limit applicable, or if the accounts and reports delivered do not comply with the statutory requirements, the company and every person who was a director immediately before expiry of the time limit is guilty of an offence and liable to a fine. It is a defence for a person charged with such an offence to prove that he took all reasonable steps to secure compliance. It is not a defence, in relation to a failure to deliver copies, to prove that the documents in question were not in fact prepared as statutorily required.

[*CA 1985, Sch 21D paras 10–13, Sch 24; SI 1992 No 3179, Sch 2 para 18*].

(44)    **Accounts and reports – credit and financial institutions with branches in Great Britain**

The provisions at (45) to (46) below apply to any 'credit institution' or 'financial institution' (see below) within *CA 1985, s 699A*, ie any such institution

•    which is incorporated or otherwise formed outside the UK and Gibraltar,

•    whose head office is outside the UK and Gibraltar, and

•    which has a 'branch' (see below) in Great Britain.

'*Credit institution*' means a credit institution as defined in *EC Council Directive 2002/12/EC, Art 1(1)(a)*, ie an undertaking whose business is to receive deposits or other repayable funds from the public and to grant credits for its own account.

'*Financial institution*' means a financial institution within the meaning of *Article 1* of the EC Council Directive on the obligations of branches, established in a Member State, of credit and financial institutions having their head offices outside that Member State regarding the publication of annual accounting documents (the 'Bank Branches Directive') (*89/117/EEC*).

'*Branch*', in relation to a credit or financial institution, means a place of business which forms a legally dependent part of the institution and which conducts directly all or some of the operations inherent in its business.

[*CA 1985, s 699A; SI 1992 No 3179, Reg 2; SI 2000 No 2952; SI 2002 No 765, Reg 2*].

(45)    **Institutions required to prepare accounts under parent law**

The provisions in (49) and (50) below apply to any institution within (47) above which is required by its parent law (ie the law of the country in which it has its head office) to prepare and have audited accounts for its 'financial periods' (see (49) below) and whose only or principal 'branch' (see (47) above) within the UK is in Great Britain.

(46)    **Duty to deliver accounting documents**

*Initial requirement.* An institution within (44) above must, within one month of its becoming such an institution, deliver to the appropriate Registrar of Companies (see below), for registration, copies of the latest 'accounting documents' (see below) of the institution prepared in accordance with its parent law (ie the law of the country in which it has its head office) to have been 'disclosed' (see below) *before* the earlier of the end of the said one-month period allowed for compliance and the actual date of compliance. If any of the said documents is not written in English, there must also be delivered an English translation certified in the prescribed manner to be a correct translation.

Where an institution within (44) above had, immediately prior to becoming such an institution, a branch in Northern Ireland which was its only or principal branch within the UK, it need not deliver the said documents if they have been delivered to the Registrar for Northern Ireland pursuant to the *Companies (Northern Ireland) Order 1986 (SI 1986 No 1032)*. Instead, it may deliver a notice that it has become an institution within (44) above.

[*CA 1985, Sch 21C para 2; SI 1992 No 3179, Sch 1*].

*Subsequent requirements.* An institution within (44) above must deliver to the appropriate Registrar of Companies (see below), for registration, copies of all the 'accounting documents' (see below) of the institution prepared in accordance with its parent law which are 'disclosed' (see below) *after* the earlier of the end of the one-month period allowed for compliance with the above initial requirement and the actual date of such compliance. The same provision applies as above as regards English translations where appropriate.

The period allowed for delivery, in relation to any such document, is three months from the date on which the document is first 'disclosed'.

[*CA 1985, Sch 21C para 3; SI 1992 No 3179, Sch 1*].

*Exceptions.* An institution is excepted from both the initial and subsequent requirements above if, at the end of the period allowed for compliance with the relevant requirement,

- the institution is not required by its parent law to register the documents;

- the documents are made available for inspection at each branch of the institution in Great Britain; and

- copies of the documents are available on request at a cost not exceeding the cost of supplying them.

If any of the above conditions cease to be met, the institution must deliver copies of the documents to the Registrar, for registration, within seven days of the condition ceasing to be met.

[*CA 1985, Sch 21C para 5; SI 1992 No 3179, Sch 1*].

*General.* Where the company's parent law permits it to disclose accounting documents in a modified form only, the company will satisfy the above provisions if it delivers copies of documents as so modified.

For the purposes of these provisions, a 'financial period', in relation to an institution, means a period for which it is required or permitted by its parent law to prepare accounts. 'Accounting documents' has the same meaning as in (41) above, substituting 'institution' for 'company' and, in the case of an institution which does not have directors, substituting for 'directors' the persons occupying equivalent offices.

References in these provisions to disclosure are normally to public disclosure, except for an institution which is not required either by its parent law or by statute having effect in Great Britain or by its own constitution to publicly disclose accounts, in which case references to disclosure are to the disclosure of the accounts to the persons for whose information they have been prepared.

*[CA 1985, Sch 21C paras 4, 8; SI 1992 No 3179, Sch 1].*

*Appropriate Registrar of Companies.* The documents required to be delivered under these provisions are to be delivered to

•    the Registrar for England and Wales if the institution's only branch, or its principal branch within the UK, is in England and Wales; and

•    the Registrar for Scotland if the institution's only branch, or its principal branch within the UK, is in Scotland.

*[CA 1985, Sch 21C para 6; SI 1992 No 3179, Sch 1].*

Penalties. On the failure of the institution to comply with any of the above provisions (including the delivery requirement under 'Exceptions') within the time limit applicable, the institution and every person who was a director immediately before expiry of the time limit is guilty of an offence and liable to a fine. In the case of an institution not having directors, a person occupying an equivalent office is so liable. It is a defence for a director or other person charged with such an offence to prove that he took all reasonable steps to secure compliance.

*[CA 1985, Sch 21C para 7, Sch 24].*

(47)    **Institutions not required to prepare accounts under parent law**

As regards an institution within (45) above which is incorporated and which is *not* required by its parent law (ie the law of the country in which it has its head office) to prepare, and have audited, accounts provisions almost identical to those (44) to (46) above (substituting 'institution' for 'company') apply as regards its duty both to prepare and to deliver accounts and reports. The only differences of substance are as follows.

•    The requirement to deliver accounts and reports does not apply separately in respect of each branch in Great Britain.

•    There are additional provisions as to the appropriate Registrar of Companies to whom documents are to be delivered – these are similar to those in (49) above, substituting 'Great Britain' for 'the UK'.

•    Penalties for non-compliance apply, as they would to directors, to persons occupying an equivalent office in the case of an institution which does not have directors.

Thus, under the transitional provisions, the new provisions first apply in respect of financial years ending after 31 December 1992.

*[CA 1985, Sch 21C paras 9–15; SI 1992 No 3179, Sch 1, Sch 4 para 5; SI 2008 No 948, Sch 1 para 93].*

# Appendix Overseas Companies

(48) **Appropriate registrar of companies**

**Companies within place of business registration regime.** The documents which an oversea company within *CA 1985, s 691* (see (3) above) is required to deliver to the Registrar of Companies must be delivered to

- the Registrar for England and Wales if the company has established a place of business in England and/or Wales; and

- the Registrar for Scotland if the company has established a place of business in Scotland.

If the company has an established place of business in both parts of Great Britain, documents must be delivered to both Registrars although if it subsequently ceases to have an establishment in one part, it must give notice of that fact to the Registrar for that part and is then only obliged to deliver documents to the other Registrar.

[*CA 1985, s 696; CA 1989, Sch 19 para 13; SI 1992 No 3179, Sch 2 para 11; Sch 3 para 17*].

See (20) above for penalties for non-compliance.

(49) **Companies within branch registration regime**

The documents which a company within *CA 1985, s 690A* (see (5) above) is required to deliver to the Registrar of Companies must be delivered to

- the Registrar for England and Wales, if required to be delivered in respect of a branch in England and Wales; and

- the Registrar for Scotland, if required to be delivered in respect of a branch in Scotland.

If the company closes a branch in a part of Great Britain, or a branch ceases to be situated in that part on becoming situated elsewhere, it must give notice of that fact to the Registrar for that part and is then no longer obliged to deliver documents to that Registrar in respect of that branch.

[*CA 1985, s 695A; SI 1992 No 3179, Sch 2 para 10*].

See (20) above for penalties for non-compliance.

# 31   Political Donations

## 31.1   INTRODUCTION TO POLITICAL DONATIONS

The provisions in **31.2** to **31.8** apply to control

- political donations made by companies to political parties, to other political organisations and (with effect from 1 October 2008) to independent election candidates; and

- political expenditure incurred by companies.

They apply to

- a *political party* if

  (i)    it is registered under *Political Parties, Elections and Referendums Act 2000* (*PPERA 2000*), *Pt II*; or

  (ii)   it carries on (or proposes to carry on) activities for the purposes of, or in connection with, the participation of the party in any election or elections to public office held in a Member State other than the UK;

- a *political organisation* if it carries on (or proposes to carry on) activities that are capable of being reasonably regarded as intended to

  (i)    affect public support for a political party to which, or an independent election candidate to whom, the provisions apply, or

  (ii)   influence voters in relation to any national or regional referendum held under the law of the UK or another Member State; and

- an *independent election candidate* at any election to public office held in the UK or another Member State.

Any reference in **31.2** to **31.8** to a political party, political organisation, (with effect from 1 October 2008) independent election candidate or political expenditure is to a party, organisation, independent candidate or expenditure to which these provisions apply.

[*CA 2006, ss 362, 363*].

## 31.2   DEFINITIONS CONCERNING POLITICAL DONATIONS

**Director** includes shadow director. [*CA 2006, s 379(1)*].

**Organisation** includes any body corporate or unincorporated association and any combination of persons. [*CA 2006, s 379(1)*].

## 31.2 Political Donations

**Political donation.** Subject to below, a political donation means

- *in relation to a political party or other political organisation*, anything that in accordance with *PPERA 2000, ss 50–52* (meaning of donation) and *53* (value of donation)

    (i) constitutes a donation to a registered party for the purposes of *PPERA 2000, Pt 4, Ch 1* (control of donations to registered parties); or

    (ii) would constitute such a donation reading references in those *sections* to a registered party as references to any political party or other political organisation; and

- *in relation to an independent election* candidate, anything that in accordance with *PPERA 2000, ss 50–52* (meaning of donation) and *53* (value of donation) would constitute a donation for the purposes of *PPERA 2000, Pt 4, Ch 1* (control of donations to registered parties) reading references in those *sections* to a registered party as references to the independent election candidate.

Political donations broadly include (subject to certain specified exemptions)

- any gift to the party, organisation or candidate of money or other property;

- any 'sponsorship' provided in relation to the party, organisation or candidate;

- any subscription or other fee paid for affiliation to, or membership of, the party or organisation;

- any money spent in paying any expenses incurred directly or indirectly by the party, organisation or candidate;

- any money lent to the party, organisation or candidate otherwise than on commercial terms; and

- the provision, otherwise than on commercial terms, of any property, services or facilities for use or benefit by the party, organisation or candidate (including the services of any person).

*'Sponsorship'* is provided if any money or other property is transferred to the party, organisation or candidate or to any person for their benefit, and the purpose (or one of the purposes) of the transfer is (or must, having regard to all the circumstances, reasonably be assumed to be) to help the party, etc to meet expenses incurred (or to be incurred) by or on their behalf (or to secure that to any extent any such expenses are not so incurred) in connection with

- any conference, meeting or other event organised by or on their behalf;

- the preparation, production or dissemination of any publication by or on their behalf; or

- any study or research organised by or on their behalf.

[*CA 2006, s 364; SI 2007 No 2194, art 5*].

**Political expenditure**, in relation to a company, means expenditure incurred by the company on

(a) the preparation, publication or dissemination of advertising or other promotional or publicity material

    (i) of whatever nature, and

(ii) however published or otherwise disseminated,

that, at the time of publication or dissemination, is capable of being reasonably regarded as intended to affect public support for a political party or other political organisation or an independent election candidate; or

(b) activities on the part of the company that are capable of being reasonably regarded as intended

(i) to affect public support for a political party or other political organisation or an independent election candidate; or

(ii) to influence voters in relation to any national or regional referendum held under the law of a Member State.

For the purposes of these provisions a political donation does not count as political expenditure.

[*CA 2006, s 365*].

**Time a donation is made or expenditure is incurred**. Except as otherwise provided, any reference to the time a donation is made or expenditure is incurred is, in a case where the donation is made or expenditure incurred in pursuance of a contract, any earlier time at which that contract is entered into by the company. [*CA 2006, s 379(2)*].

## 31.3 AUTHORISATION REQUIRED FOR DONATIONS OR EXPENDITURE

Subject to the exemptions in **31.8**, a company must not

- make a political donation to a political party, other political organisation, or an independent election candidate, or

- incur any political expenditure,

unless the donation or expenditure is authorised

- in the case of a company that is not a subsidiary of another company, by a resolution of the members of the company; or

- in the case of a company that is a subsidiary of another company, by

(i) a resolution of the members of the company; *and*

(ii) a resolution of the members of any 'relevant holding company'.

But no resolution is required on the part of a company that is a wholly-owned subsidiary of a UK-registered company.

A '*relevant holding company*' means a company that, at the time the donation was made or the expenditure was incurred

- was a holding company of the company by which the donation was made or the expenditure was incurred;

- was a UK-registered company; and

- was not a subsidiary of another UK-registered company.

Any required resolution must comply with the requirements as to form (see below) and must be passed before the donation is made or the expenditure incurred.

## 31.3 Political Donations

[*CA 2006, s 366*].

**Form of authorising resolution.**

*CA 2006, Part 14* does not specify the type of resolution required to approve political donations or political expenditure. Therefore, the default position is that an ordinary resolution of the members suffices. However, the company's articles may stipulate that a higher threshold, such as a special resolution, is needed *(CA 2006, s 281(3))*.

Written resolutions under *CA 2006, Part 13, Chapter 2* can be used by private companies to pass political donations resolutions (*CA 2006, s 281*).

A resolution conferring authorisation for these purposes may relate to

- the company passing the resolution;
- one or more subsidiaries of that company; or
- the company passing the resolution and one or more subsidiaries of that company.

A resolution may be expressed to relate to all companies that are subsidiaries of the company passing the resolution

- at the time the resolution is passed, or
- at any time during the period for which the resolution has effect

without identifying them individually.

The resolution may authorise donations or expenditure under one or more of the following heads, ie

(a)  donations to political parties or independent election candidates,

(b)  donations to political organisations other than political parties, and

(c)  political expenditure

and must specify a head or heads

- in the case of a resolution relating to all companies that are subsidiaries of the company passing the resolution, for all of the companies to which it relates taken together; and
- in the case of any other resolution, for each company to which it relates.

The resolution must be expressed in general terms conforming with (a)–(c) above and must not purport to authorise particular donations or expenditure.

For each of the specified heads in (*a*)–(*c*) above, the resolution must authorise donations or expenditure (as the case may be) up to a specified amount in the period for which the resolution has effect (see below). It must also specify such amounts

- in the case of a resolution relating to all companies that are subsidiaries of the company passing the resolution, for all of the companies to which it relates taken together; and
- in the case of any other resolution, for each company to which it relates.

[*CA 2006, s 367*].

**Period for which resolution has effect.** A resolution conferring authorisation for these purposes has effect for a period of four years beginning with the date on which it is passed (unless the directors determine, or the articles require, that it is to have effect for a shorter period beginning with that date). The power of the directors to make such a determination is subject to any provision of the articles preventing them from doing so. [*CA 2006, s 368*].

### 31.4  REMEDIES IN CASES OF UNAUTHORISED DONATIONS AND EXPENDITURE

**Liability of directors.** Where a company has made a political donation or incurred political expenditure without the necessary authorisation under **31.3**, the 'directors in default' are jointly and severally liable

- to make good to the company the amount of the unauthorised donation or expenditure, with interest from the date when the expenditure was incurred at the prescribed rate (currently 8%); and

- to compensate the company for any loss or damage sustained by it as a result of the unauthorised donation or expenditure having been made.

The '*directors in default*' are

- those who, at the time the unauthorised donation was made or the unauthorised expenditure was incurred, were directors of the company by which the donation was made or the expenditure was incurred; and

- where

  (i)   that company was a subsidiary of a 'relevant holding company' (see **31.3**), and

  (ii)  the directors of the relevant holding company failed to take all reasonable steps to prevent the donation being made or the expenditure being incurred,

  the directors of the relevant holding company.

Where only part of a donation or expenditure was unauthorised, the above provisions apply only to so much of it was unauthorised.

[*CA 2006, s 369; The Companies (Interest Rate for Unauthorised Political Donation or Expenditure) Regulations 2007 (SI 2007/2242)*].

### 31.5  Enforcement of directors' liabilities by shareholder action

Subject to below, any liability of a director under **31.4** is (in addition to the right of the company to which the liability is owed to bring proceedings itself to enforce the liability) enforceable

- in the case of a liability of a director of a company to that company, by proceedings brought in the name of the company by an 'authorised group' of its members; and

- in the case of a liability of a director of a holding company to a subsidiary, by proceedings brought in the name of the subsidiary by

  (i)   an authorised group of members of the subsidiary; or

  (ii)  an authorised group of members of the holding company.

An '*authorised group*' of members of a company means

- the holders of not less than 5% in nominal value of the company's issued share capital;

- if the company is not limited by shares, not less than 5% of its members; or

- not less than 50 of the company's members.

A group of members may not bring proceedings under these provisions in the name of a company unless

- the group has given written notice to the company stating

  (i)    the cause of action and a summary of the facts on which the proceedings are to be based;

  (ii)   the names and addresses of the members comprising the group; and

  (iii)  the grounds on which it is alleged that those members constitute an authorised group; and

- not less than 28 days have elapsed between the date of the giving of the notice to the company and the bringing of the proceedings.

Where such a notice is given to a company, any director of the company may apply to the court within 28 days of the giving of the notice for an order directing that the proposed proceedings are not to be brought. An application may be made on one or more of the following grounds, namely that

(a)    the unauthorised amount has been made good to the company;

(b)    proceedings to enforce the liability have been brought, and are being pursued with due diligence, by the company; or

(c)    the members proposing to bring proceedings do not constitute an authorised group.

Where such an application is made on the ground in (b) above, the court has wide powers to direct that the proposed proceedings under these provisions are not brought or are brought on such terms and conditions as it thinks fit and that the proceedings brought by the company are to be discontinued or continued on such terms and conditions as it thinks fit.

The members by whom proceedings are brought under these provisions owe the same duties to the company in whose name they are brought as would be owed by the company's directors if the proceedings were being brought by the company itself. But proceedings to enforce any such duty may be brought by the company only with the permission of the court.

Proceedings cannot be discontinued or settled by the group except with the permission of the court, which may be given on such terms as the court thinks fit.

Nothing in the above provisions affects any right of a member of a company to bring or continue proceedings under *CA 2006, Pt 11* (derivative claims and proceedings by members, see **26.6 MEMBERS**).

[*CA 2006, ss 370, 371*].

**31.6   Costs of shareholder action**

In any proceedings brought under **31.5** in the name of the company by an authorised group, the group may apply to the court for an order directing the company to indemnify the group in respect of costs incurred, or to be incurred, by the group in connection with the proceedings. The court may then make such an order on such terms as it thinks fit. The group is not entitled to be paid any such costs out of the assets of the company except by virtue of such an order.

If no such order has been made with respect to the proceedings, then if

* the company is awarded costs in connection with the proceedings, or it is agreed that costs incurred by the company in connection with the proceedings should be paid by any defendant, or

* any defendant is awarded costs in connection with the proceedings, or it is agreed that any defendant should be paid costs incurred by him in connection with the proceedings,

the costs must be paid by the group.

In relation to Scotland, references to 'costs' are to 'expenses' and references to any 'defendant' are to any 'defender'.

[*CA 2006, s 372*].

**31.7   Information for purposes of shareholder action**

Where proceedings have been brought under **31.5** in the name of the company by an authorised group, the group is entitled to require the company to provide it with all information relating to the subject matter of the proceedings that is in the company's possession or under its control or which is reasonably obtainable by it.

If the company, having been required by the group to do so, refuses to provide the group with all or any of that information, the court may, on an application made by the group, make an order directing the company, and any of its officers or employees specified in the application, to provide the group with the information in question in such form and by such means as the court may direct.

[*CA 2006, s 373*].

**31.8   EXEMPTIONS CONCERNING POLITICAL DONATIONS**

The following exemptions to the general requirement of shareholder approval (under **31.3**) apply to the following classes of donation:

(1)   **Trade unions**

A donation to a 'trade union', other than a contribution to the union's political fund, is not a political donation for the purposes of this chapter and a trade union is not a political organisation for the purposes of the definition of '*political expenditure*' (see **31.2**).

For these purposes,

* '*trade union*' has the meaning given by *Trade Union and Labour Relations (Consolidation) Act 1992, s 1* or *Industrial Relations (Northern Ireland) Order 1992 (SI 1992 No 807), Art 3*; and

## 31.8 Political Donations

- *'political fund'* means the fund from which payments by a trade union in the furtherance of political objects are required to be made by virtue of *Trade Union and Labour Relations (Consolidation) Act 1992, s 82(1)(a)* or *Industrial Relations (Northern Ireland) Order 1992 (SI 1992 No 807), Art 57(2)(a)*.

[*CA 2006, s 374*].

(2) **Subscription for membership of trade association**

A 'subscription' paid to a 'trade association' for membership of the association is not a political donation for the purposes of **31.3**.

*'Trade association'* means an organisation formed for the purpose of furthering the trade interests of its members, or of persons represented by its members.

*'Subscription'* does not include a payment to the association to the extent that it is made for the purpose of financing any particular activity of the association.

[*CA 2006, s 375*].

(3) **All-party parliamentary groups**

An *'all-party parliamentary group'* (ie an all-party group composed of members of one or both of the Houses of Parliament (or of such members and other persons) is not a political organisation for the purposes of **31.3**.

[*CA 2006, s 376*].

(4) **Donations not amounting to more than £5,000 in any twelve month period**

Authorisation under **31.3** is not needed for a donation to a political party, other political organisation or an independent election candidate except to the extent that the total amount of

- that donation, and

- 'other relevant donations' made in the period of 12 months ending with the date on which that donation is made,

exceeds £5,000.

*'Other relevant donations'* means

(i)  in relation to a donation made by a company that is not a subsidiary, any other donations made by that company or by any of its subsidiaries; and

(ii)  in relation to a donation made by a company that is a subsidiary, any other donations made by that company, by any holding company of that company or by any other subsidiary of any such holding company.

If or to the extent that a donation is so exempt from the requirement of authorisation, it is disregarded in determining what donations are authorised by any resolution passed for the purposes of this chapter.

[*CA 2006, s 378*].

(5)   **Political expenditure exempted by order**

The *Companies (Political Expenditure Exemption) Order 2007* provides that a company whose ordinary course of business includes, or is proposed to include,

- the publication or dissemination to the public (or any part of the public) of material relating to

  (i)   news,

  (ii)  public and political affairs and events, and

  (iii) views, opinion and comment on the news and on public and political affairs and events, or

- the preparation of such material for publication or dissemination to the public (or any part of the public)

is exempt in relation to expenditure incurred in the preparation, publication or dissemination of news material which is capable of being reasonably regarded as intended to affect public support for a political party or other political organisation, or an independent election candidate, or to influence voters in relation to any national or regional referendum held under the law of a member state (for the purposes of the definition set out at **31.2** above).

For these purposes, it is irrelevant

- by which means or modes the material is prepared, etc; or

- where the public (or any part of the public) to which such material is published or disseminated is located or the identity or description of the public (or any part of it).

[*SI 2007 No 2081*].

## 31.9   INSTITUTIONAL INVESTOR GUIDANCE

The Pension and Lifetime Savings Association ('PLSA') expresses the view that it opposes the payment of, or facilitation of payment of, political donations as these are generally understood. However, given the broad definition of political donation and expenditure under *CA 2006* (which could include donations to charities or educational causes), the PLSA acknowledges that it is common for authorities to be sought on a precautionary basis. The PLSA expresses the view that it is acceptable for a company to seek a four-year authority where it has no history of making political donations. However, if the authority exceeds one year, the PLSA advises the company to clarify that, in the event that the company avails itself of that authorisation, it will seek a new authorisation at the follow AGM. See the PLSA's '*Corporate Governance Policy and Voting Guidelines 2017*', dated January 2017, at Resolution 11, '*Authorising political donations*', on the PLSA website.

# 32   Prospectuses

## 32.1   INTRODUCTION TO PROSPECTUSES

The *Prospectus Directive 2003/71/EC* harmonised requirements for the drawing up, approval and distribution of the prospectus to be published when securities are offered to the public or admitted to trading on a regulated market situated or operating within a Member State.

The provisions of the *Directive* are implemented by

- *Financial Services and Markets Act 2000 (FSMA 2000), Pt VI*;

- the Prospectus Directive Regulation (*EC Commission Regulation 809/2004 of 29 April 2004*);

- the Prospectus Rules made by the FCA (the UK Listing Authority) as the competent authority to make rules ('Part VI rules') under *FSMA 2000, s 73A(1)*;

  - the ESMA Prospectus Recommendations;

  - the ESMA Prospectus Questions and Answers;

  - the ESMA Prospectus Opinions; and

  - the Prospectus RTS Regulations.

In July 2017, *Regulation (EU) 2017/1129* on the prospectus to be published when securities are offered to the public or admitted to trading on a regulated market (the 'New Prospectus Regulation') entered into force. The New Prospectus Regulation repeals and replaces the Prospectus Directive with effect from 21 July 2019 – save for a few provisions which were repealed and replaced on 21 July 2017 and 21 July 2018.

In determining whether the rules and regulations have been complied with, the FCA will take into account whether a person has complied with the ESMA Prospectus Recommendations, the ESMA Prospectus Questions and Answers and the ESMA Prospectus Opinions. (FCA Prospectus Rules, para 1.1.8).

# 32.1 Prospectuses

Note that EU Regulations are binding and have effect in all member states ie they are directly applicable and do not have to be implemented by national legislation.

**Application of the Prospectus Rules.** Unless otherwise stated, the Prospectus Rules only apply to an offer or a request for admission to trading of transferable securities

(a)     in respect of which *FSMA 2000, s 85* applies (see **32.3**) and in relation to which the UK is the 'Home State';

(b)     where a person has elected to have a prospectus in relation to the transferable securities (see **32.7**);

(c)     where (*a*) or (*b*) above does not apply and in relation to which the UK is the Home State; or

(d)     where the competent authority of an EEA State has transferred the function of approving the prospectus to the FCA (see **32.15**).

(FCA Prospectus Rules, para 1.1.1).

'Transferable securities' means anything which is a transferable security for the purposes of *Directive 2014/65/EU* on markets in financial instruments (MiFID II), which came into force on 3 January 2018.

**Meaning of 'Home State'.** In relation to an issuer of transferable securities, the Home State is the EEA State which is the 'Home Member State' for the purposes of the *Prospectus Directive*, namely:

(i)     For all EU issuers of securities which are not mentioned in (ii), the Member State where the issuer has its registered office.

(ii)    For any issues of non-equity securities

- whose denomination per unit amounts to at least 1,000 euros, and

- giving the right to acquire any transferable securities or to receive a cash amount, as a consequence of their being converted or the rights conferred by them being exercised,

provided that the issuer of the non-equity securities is not the issuer of the underlying securities or an entity belonging to the group of the latter issuer,

- the Member State where the issuer has its registered office, or

- where the securities were or are to be admitted to trading on a regulated market or where the securities are offered to the public, at the choice of the issuer, the Member State of the offeror or the person asking for admission, as the case may be.

The same regime is also applicable to non-equity securities in a currency other than euros, provided that the value of such minimum denomination is nearly equivalent to 1,000 euro.

(iii)   For all issuers of securities incorporated in a third country, which are not mentioned in (ii) above, the Member State where

- the securities are intended to be offered to the public for the first time after 1 July 2005, or

- the first application for admission to trading on a regulated market is made,

at the choice of the issuer, the offeror or the person asking for admission, as the case may be, subject to a subsequent election by issuers incorporated in a third country if the home Member State was not determined by their choice.

[*Prospectus Directive, Art 2.1(m); FSMA 2000, ss 102A(3), 102C; SI 2005 No 1433*].

For the meaning of **EEA States** see Appendix 1 Definitions.

**Persons responsible for complying with rules.** A person must comply with all rules that are specified as being applicable to them. If a rule does not specify who is responsible for complying with it, then the following persons must comply with it.

•   In relation to an offer, the issuer and the offeror (if this is a person other than the issuer) or the offeror (if this is a person other than the issuer).

•   In relation to a request for the admission to trading of transferable securities, the issuer; and the person requesting admission to trading (if this is a person other than the issuer).

But an issuer is not responsible under either of these categories if it has not authorised or made the offer or the request for the admission to trading.

(FCA Prospectus Rules, paras 1.1.3, 1.1.4).

## 32.2   PERSONS RESPONSIBLE FOR A PROSPECTUS

The following rules only apply if the UK is the Home State (see **32.1**) for the issuer in relation to the transferable securities to which the prospectus relates.

**Equity shares.** Where a prospectus relates to

•   equity shares,

•   warrants or options to subscribe for equity shares that are issued by the issuer of the equity shares, or

•   other transferable securities that have similar characteristics

each of the following persons are, subject to below, responsible for the prospectus.

(a)   The issuer of the transferable securities.

(b)   If the issuer is a body corporate

   (i)    each person who is a director of that body corporate when the prospectus is published; and

   (ii)   each person who has authorised himself to be named, and is named, in the prospectus as a director or as having agreed to become a director of that body corporate either immediately or at a future time; and

   (iii)  each person who is a senior executive of any external management company of the issuer.

(c)   Each person who accepts, and is stated in the prospectus as accepting, responsibility for the prospectus.

   "External management company" means in relation to an issuer that is a company which is not a collective investment undertaking, a person who is appointed by the issuer (whether under contract for services or any other commercial arrangement) to perform functions that would ordinarily be performed by officers of the issuer and to make recommendations in relation to strategic matters. In considering whether the functions the person performs would ordinarily be performed by officers of the issuer, the FCA will consider, amongst other things:

(i) the nature of the board of the issuer to which the person provides services, and whether the board has the capability to act itself on strategic matters in the absence of that person's services;

(ii) whether the appointment relates to a one-off transaction or is a longer term relationship; and

(iii) the proportion of the functions ordinarily performed by officers of the issuer that is covered by the arrangements.

(d) In relation to an offer

(i) the offeror, if this is not the issuer; and

(ii) if the offeror is a body corporate and is not the issuer, each person who is a director of the body corporate when the prospectus is published.

(e) In relation to a request for the admission to trading of transferable securities

(i) the person requesting admission, if this is not the issuer; and

(ii) if the person requesting admission is a body corporate and is not the issuer, each person who is a director of the body corporate when the prospectus is published.

(f) Each person not falling within (a)–(e) above who has authorised the contents of the prospectus.

**All other securities.** Where a prospectus relates to any other transferable securities, each of the following persons is, subject to below, responsible for the prospectus.

(i) The issuer of the transferable securities.

(ii) Each person who accepts, and is stated in the prospectus as accepting, responsibility for the prospectus.

(iii) In relation to an offer, the offeror of the transferable securities, if this is not the issuer.

(iv) In relation to a request for an admission to trading of transferable securities, the person requesting admission, if this is not the issuer.

(v) If there is a guarantor for the issue, the guarantor in relation to information in the prospectus that relates to the guarantor and the guarantee.

(vi) Each person not falling within (i)–(v) above who has authorised the contents of the prospectus.

**Exclusions.**

(1) A person is not responsible for a prospectus under (a), (b) or (i) above if the issuer has not made or authorised the offer or the request for admission to trading in relation to which the prospectus was published.

(2) A person is not responsible for a prospectus under (b)(i) above if it is published without his knowledge or consent and, on becoming aware of its publication, he gives reasonable public notice as soon as practicable that it was published without his knowledge or consent.

(3) A person is not responsible for a prospectus under (d) or (iii) above if

• the issuer is responsible for the prospectus under these rules;

- the prospectus was drawn up primarily by the issuer, or by one or more persons acting on behalf of the issuer; and

- the offeror is making the offer in association with the issuer.

(4)   A person who accepts responsibility for a prospectus under (*c*) or (ii) above or authorises the contents of a prospectus under (*f*) or (vi) above, may state that they do so only in relation to specified parts of the prospectus, or only in specified respects, and in that case the person is responsible

- only to the extent specified; and

- only if the material in question is included in (or substantially in) the form and context to which the person has agreed.

Nothing in the above rules is to be construed as making a person responsible for any prospectus by reason only of the person giving advice about its contents in a professional capacity.

(FCA Prospectus Rules, paras 5.5.1–5.5.9).

## 32.3   THE NEED FOR A PROSPECTUS

If *FSMA 2000* requires a prospectus to be published then subject to the exemptions listed below, it is unlawful

(a)   for 'transferable securities' to be offered to the public in the UK, or

(b)   to request the admission of transferable securities to trading on a regulated market situated or operating in the UK

unless an 'approved prospectus' has been made available to the public before the offer or request is made.

A person who contravenes either of the above is guilty of an offence and liable

- on summary conviction, to imprisonment for a term not exceeding three months or a fine not exceeding the statutory maximum (see **29.1** OFFENCES AND LEGAL PROCEEDINGS) or both; or

- on conviction on indictment, to imprisonment for a term not exceeding two years or a fine or both.

A contravention of (*a*) or (*b*) above is actionable, at the suit of a person who suffers loss as a result of the contravention, subject to the defences and other incidents applying to actions for breach of statutory duty.

*Offer of transferable securities to the public.* There is an offer of transferable securities to the public if there is a communication to any person which presents sufficient information on

- the transferable securities to be offered, and

- the terms on which they are offered,

to enable an investor to decide to buy or subscribe for the securities in question. This includes the placing of securities through a financial intermediary but does not include a communication in connection with trading on a regulated market, a multilateral trading facility, or any other market prescribed by an *Order*.

## 32.3  Prospectuses

To the extent that an offer of transferable securities is made to a *person* in the UK, it is an offer of transferable securities to the *public* in the UK.

The communication may be made in any form and by any means.

'*Approved prospectus*' for these purposes means a prospectus approved by the competent authority of the 'Home State' (see **32.1**) in relation to the issuer of the securities.

For the meaning of "transferable securities" see **32.1**.

[*FSMA 2000, ss 85, 102B; CA 2006, Sch 15 para 10; SI 2005 No 1433*].

**Exemptions**. These fall into two categories, namely exempt offers and exempt securities.

- Certain offers to the public are exempt from the requirements of (*a*) above. See **32.4**.

- Certain securities are exempt from the requirements of (*a*) and (*b*) above under *FSMA 2000* and the FCA Prospectus Rules. See **32.5** and **32.6**.

**Information to be disclosed to all investors to whom offer addressed**. Where, in relation to an offer in the UK, no prospectus is required under *FSMA 2000*, the issuer and offeror must ensure that material information they provide to qualified investors (see **32.4**) or special categories of investors, including information disclosed in the context of meetings relating to offers, is disclosed to all qualified investors or special categories of investors to whom the offer is exclusively addressed. (FCA Prospectus Rules, para 5.6.1.)

## 32.4  Exempt offers to the public

A person does not contravene *FSMA 2000, s 85(1)* in the following circumstances.

(i)    The offer is made to or directed at 'qualified investors' only.

(ii)   The offer is made to or directed at fewer than 150 persons, other than qualified investors, per EEA State. For this purpose, the making of an offer of transferable securities to

- trustees of a trust,

- members of a partnership in their capacity as such, or

- two or more persons jointly,

is to be treated as the making of an offer to a single person.

(iii)  The minimum consideration which may be paid by any person for transferable securities acquired by him pursuant to the offer is at least 100,000 euros (or an 'equivalent amount').

(iv)   The transferable securities being offered are denominated in amounts of at least 100,000 euros (or equivalent amounts).

(v)    The total consideration for the transferable securities being offered in the EEA states cannot exceed 8,000,000 euros (or an equivalent amount). In determining whether this is satisfied in relation to an offer ('offer A'), offer A is to be taken together with any other offer of transferable securities of the same class made by the same person which

- was open at any time within the period of 12 months ending with the date on which offer A is first made; and

- had previously satisfied the 8,000,000 euros requirement.

(vi)    The offer falls within *FSMA 2000, s 86(1A)* if the transferable securities are being sold or placed through a financial intermediary where

    (a)    the transferable securities have previously been the subject of one or more offers to the public;

    (b)    in respect of one or more of those previous offers any of the paragraphs (a)–(e) of *s 86(1)* applies;

    (c)    a prospectus is available for the securities which has been approved by the FCA or the competent authority of another EEA state and meets either of the conditions in FSMA, s 86(1B); and

    (d)    the issuer or other person who was responsible for drawing up the prospectus has given written consent for the purpose of the current offer.

The conditions referred to in (c) are that the prospectus was approved by the FCA or the competent authority of another EEA state earlier than 12 months before the date the current offer is made and is supplemented by every supplementary prospectus which was required to be submitted under *FSMA 2000, s 87G(2)* or, in the case of non-equity transferable securities falling within *art 5(4)(b)* of the Prospectus Directive, that the securities concerned have not ceased to be issued in a continuous or repeated manner.

Where

- a person who is not a qualified investor ('the client') has engaged a qualified investor falling within (*a*)(i) below to act as his agent, and

- the terms on which the qualified investor is engaged enable him to make decisions concerning the acceptance of offers of transferable securities on the client's behalf without reference to the client,

an offer made to or directed at the qualified investor is not to be regarded for the above purposes as also having been made to or directed at the client.

'*Qualified investor*' in relation to an offer of transferable securities means

(a)    A person described in points (1) to (4) of Annex II to the Markets in Financial Instruments Directive ('MiFID II'), other than a person who, before the making of the offer, has agreed in writing with the relevant firm (or each of the relevant firms) to be treated as a non- professional client in accordance with MiFID II.

(b)    A person who has made a request to one or more relevant firms to be treated as a professional client in accordance with Section II of Annex II to MiFID II and has not subsequently but before the making of the offer, agreed in writing with that relevant firm (or each of the relevant firms) to be treated as a non- professional client in accordance with the final paragraph of Section 1 of Annex II of MiFID II.

(c)    A person who is an eligible counter party in accordance with Article 30 of MiFID II and has not before the making of the offer agreed in writing with the relevant firm (or each of the relevant firms) to be treated as a non-professional client in accordance with the final paragraph of Section 1 of Annex II to MiFID II.

(d)    A person whom any relevant firm is authorised to continue to treat as a professional client immediately before 3 January 2018 by virtue of Article 71(6) of the MiFID I and the firm may continue to treat as a professional client from 3 January 2018 by virtue of Section II.2 of Annex II to MiFID II.

## 32.4    Prospectuses

'Relevant firm' means an investment firm or credit institution acting in connection with the offer and "credit institution" means a credit institution authorised under the Capital Requirements Directive or an institution which would satisfy the requirements for authorisation as a credit institution under that Directive if it had its registered office (or if it does not have one its head office) in an EEA state.

Any *'equivalent amount'* not in euros is to be calculated at the latest practicable date before (but in any event not more than three working days before) the date on which the offer is first made.

[*FSMA 2000, s 86; SI 2005 No 1433; SI 2011 No 1668; SI 2012 No 1538, Reg 2, 3; SI 2013 No 3115, Sch 2 para 9; SI 2013 No 1125, Reg 2; SI 2014 No 3293, Reg 2(1)* and *SI 2018 No 786, Reg 2(2) and (3)*].

### 32.5    Exempt securities: offers to the public

The following transferable securities are exempt from the requirements of *FSMA 2000, s 85(1)*.

(a)    Units in an open-ended collective investment scheme.

(b)    Non-equity transferable securities issued by

- the government of an EEA State;
- a local or regional authority of an EEA State;
- a public international body of which an EEA State is a member;
- the European Central Bank;
- the central bank of an EEA State.

(c)    Shares in the share capital of the central bank of an EEA State.

(d)    Transferable securities unconditionally and irrevocably guaranteed by the government, or a local or regional authority, of an EEA State.

(e)    Non-equity transferable securities, issued in a continuous or repeated manner by a credit institution, where the securities

- are not subordinated, convertible or exchangeable;
- do not give a right to subscribe to or acquire other types of securities and are not linked to a derivative instrument;
- materialise reception of repayable deposits; and
- are covered by a deposit guarantee under *Directive 94/19/EC* of the European Parliament and of the Council on deposit-guarantee schemes.

(f)    Non-fungible shares of capital

- the main purpose of which is to provide the holder with a right to occupy any immoveable property; and
- which cannot be sold without that right being given up.

(g)    Transferable securities issued by one of the following bodies if, and only if, the proceeds of the offer of the transferable securities to the public will be used solely for the purposes of the issuer's objectives.

(i)    A charity.

(ii)   A housing association.

(iii)  A registered industrial and provident society.

(iv)   A non-profit making association or body recognised by an EEA State with objectives similar to those of a body falling within (i)–(iii) above.

(h)   Non-equity transferable securities, issued in a continuous or repeated manner by a credit institution, which satisfy the conditions that

• the total consideration for the transferable securities being offered in the EEA states is less than 75 million euros (or an equivalent amount); and

• the securities

(i)   are not subordinated, convertible or exchangeable; and

(ii)  do not give a right to subscribe to or acquire other types of securities and are not linked to a derivative instrument.

In determining whether the total consideration requirement is satisfied in relation to an offer ('offer A'), offer A is to be taken together with any other offer of transferable securities of the same class made by the same person which

• was open at any time within the period of 12 months ending with the date on which offer A is first made; and

• had previously satisfied the total consideration requirement.

Any *equivalent amount* not in euros is to be calculated at the latest practicable date before (but in any event not more than three working days before) the date on which the offer is first made.

(i)   Transferable securities included in an offer where the total consideration for the transferable securities being offered in the EEA states is less than 1 million euros (or an equivalent amount). Similar provisions as to the total consideration requirement and 'equivalent amount' apply as in (*h*) above.

[*FSMA 2000, s 85(5), Sch 11A; SI 2005 No 1433; SI 2011 No 1668; SI 3018 No 786, Reg 2(6)*].

(j)   Shares issued in substitution for shares of the same class already issued, if the issue of the new shares does not involve any increase in the issued capital.

(k)   Transferable securities

• offered in connection with a takeover by means of an exchange offer, or

• offered, allotted or to be allotted in connection with a merger or division,

if a document is available in either case containing information which is regarded by the FCA as being equivalent to that of the prospectus, taking into account the requirements of EU legislation.

(l)   Dividends paid out to existing shareholders in the form of shares of the same class as the shares in respect of which the dividends are paid, if a document is made available containing information on the number and nature of the shares and the reasons for and details of the offer.

(m)   Transferable securities offered, allotted or to be allotted to existing or former directors or employees by their employer to an affiliated undertaking if:

771

## 32.5   Prospectuses

- the company has its head office or registered office in the EU, provided a document is made available containing information on the number and nature of the transferable securities and the reasons for and details of the offer;

- the company is established outside the EU and has transferable securities that are admitted to trading, provided a document is made available containing information on the number and nature of the transferable securities and the reasons for and details of the offer; or

- the company is established outside the EU and has transferable securities admitted to trading on a third country market provided that:

  (i)   a document is made available containing adequate information, including the number and nature of the transferable securities;

  (ii)  the reasons for and details of the offer in a language customary in the sphere of international finance; and

  (iii) the European Commission has adopted an equivalence decision for the purpose of Article 4(1) of the Prospectus Directive regarding the third country market concerned.

(*FSMA, Sch 11A* and FCA Prospectus Rules, para 1.2.2).

## 32.6   Exempt securities: admission to trading

The following transferable securities are exempt from the requirements of *FSMA 2000, s 85(2)*.

(a)   Transferable securities as in **32.5**(*a*)–(*f*).

[*FSMA 2000, s 85(6), Sch 11A Pt 1; SI 2005 No 1433*].

(b)   Transferable securities referred to in Article 1(5)(a) of the Prospectus Regulation.

(c)   Transferable securities on their admission to trading on a regulated market:

  (i)   transferable securities referred to in Article 1(5)(a) of the Prospectus Regulation;

  (ii)  shares issued in substitution for shares of the same class already admitted to trading on the same regulated market, if the issue of the shares does not involve any increase in the issued capital;

  (iii) transferable securities offered in connection with a takeover by means of an exchange offer, if a document is available containing information which is regarded by the FCA as being equivalent to that of the prospectus, taking into account the requirements of EU legislation;

  (iv)  transferable securities offered, allotted or to be allotted in connection with a merger or a division, if a document is available containing information which is regarded by the FCA as being equivalent to that of the prospectus, taking into account the requirements of EU legislation;

  (v)   shares offered, allotted or to be allotted free of charge to existing shareholders, and dividends paid out in the form of shares of the same class as the shares in respect of which the dividends are paid, if the shares are of the same class as the shares already admitted to trading on the same regulated market and if a document is made available containing information on the number and nature of the shares and the reasons for and details of the offer;

(vi)    transferable securities offered, allotted or to be allotted to existing or former directors or employees by their employer or an affiliated undertaking, if the transferable securities are of the same class as the transferable securities already admitted to trading on the same regulated market and if a document is made available containing information on the number and nature of the transferable securities and the reasons for and detail of the offer;

(vii)   transferable securities referred to in Article 1(5)(b) of the Prospectus Regulation;

(viii)  transferable securities already admitted to trading on another regulated market, on the following conditions:

- that these transferable securities, or transferable securities of the same class, have been admitted to trading on that other regulated market for more than 18 months;

- that, for transferable securities first admitted to trading after the 31 December 2003, the admission to trading on that other regulated market was associated with an approved prospectus made available to the public in accordance with Article 14 of the Prospectus Directive except where this applies, for transferable securities first admitted to listing after 30 June 1983, listing particulars were approved in accordance with the requirements of Directive 80/390/EEC or Directive 2001/34/EC;

- that the ongoing obligations for trading on that other regulated market have been fulfilled;

- that the person requesting the admission to trading under this exemption makes a summary document available to the public in a language accepted by the competent authority of the EEA State of the regulated market where admission is sought;

- that the summary document referred to in paragraph (e) is made available to the public in the EEA State of the regulated market where admission to trading is sought in the manner set out in Article 14 of the prospectus directive;

- that the contents of the summary document comply with Article 5(2) of the Prospectus Directive. Also the document must state where the most recent prospectus can be obtained and where the financial information published by the issuer pursuant to its ongoing disclosure obligations is available; and

(ix)    transferable securities referred to in Article 1(5)(c) of the Prospectus Regulation.

[Note: Article 4(2) of the Prospectus Directive, points (a), (b) and (c) of the first subparagraph of Article 1(5) of the Prospectus Regulation and the second subparagraph of Article 1(5) of the Prospectus Regulation.]

Points (a), (b) and (c) of the first subparagraph of Article 1(5) of the Prospectus Regulation and the second subparagraph of Article 1(5) of the Prospectus Regulation provide that:

Article 1

Subject matter scope and exemptions:

. . .

## 32.6 Prospectuses

(5)     the obligation to publish a prospectus . . . shall not apply to the admission to trading on a regulated market of any of the following:

(a)     securities fungible with securities already admitted to trading on the same regulated market, provided they represent, over a period of 12 months, less than 20% of the number of securities already admitted to trading on the same regulated market;

(b)     shares resulting from the conversion or exchange of other securities or from the exercise of rights conferred by other securities where the resulting shares are of the same class as the shares already admitted to trading on the same regulated market, provided that the resulting shares represent, over a period of 12 months, less than 20% of the number of shares of the same class already admitted to trading on the same regulated market, subject to the second subparagraph of this paragraph;

(c)     securities resulting from the conversion or exchange of other securities, own funds or eligible liabilities by a resolution authority due to the exercise of a power referred to in Article 53(2), 59(2) or Article 63(1) or (2) of Directive 2014/59/ EU [establishing a framework for the recovery and resolution of credit institutions and investment firms];

. . .

The requirement that the resulting shares represent, over a period of 12 months, less than 20% of the number of shares of the same class already admitted to trading on the same regulated market as referred to in point (b) of the first sub-paragraph shall not apply in the following cases:

(a)     where a prospectus was drawn up in accordance with either this Regulation or Directive 2003/71/EC upon the offer to the public or admission to trading on a regulated market of the securities giving access to the shares;

(b)     where the securities giving access to the shares were issued before 20 July 2017;

(c)     where the shares qualify as Common Equity Tier 1 items as laid down in Article 26 of Regulation (EU) No 575/2013 of the European Parliament and of the Council of an institution as defined in point (3) of Article 4(1) of that Regulation and result from the conversion of Additional Tier 1 instruments issued by that institution due to the occurrence of a trigger event as laid down in point (a) of Article 54(1) of that Regulation;

(d)     where the shares qualify as eligible own funds or eligible basic own funds as defined in Section 3 of Chapter VI of Title I of Directive 2009/138/EC of the European Parliament and of the Council, and result from the conversion of other securities which was triggered for the purposes of fulfilling the obligations to comply with the Solvency Capital Requirement or Minimum Capital Requirement as laid down in Sections 4 and 5 of Chapter VI of Title I of Directive 2009/138/EC or of the group solvency requirement as laid down in Title III of Directive 2009/138/EC.

(FCA Prospectus Rules, paras 1.2.3 and 1.2.3A).

## 32.7   ELECTION TO HAVE A PROSPECTUS

A person who proposes to

•       issue,

- offer to the public, or

- request the admission to a regulated market of

certain transferable securities which would otherwise be exempt securities may elect to have a prospectus in relation to the securities. The transferable securities in question are those falling within **32.4**(*b*), (*d*), (*h*) or (*i*) where the UK is the Home State (see **32.1**) in relation to the issuer of the securities.

On such an election, the provisions of *FSMA 2000, Pt VI* and the FCA Prospectus Rules apply as if those securities were transferable securities for which an approved prospectus would be required under **32.3**. But FCA Listing Rules do not apply to securities which are the subject of an election.

[*FSMA 2000, s 87; SI 2005 No 1433*].

## 32.8   DRAWING UP A PROSPECTUS

A prospectus must contain the information necessary to enable investors to make an informed assessment of

- the assets and liabilities, financial position, profits and losses, and prospects of the issuer of the transferable securities and of any guarantor; and

- the rights attaching to the transferable securities.

If, in the case of transferable securities to which FSMA 2000, s 87 applies, the prospectus states that the guarantor is a specified EEA state, the prospectus is not required to include other information about the guarantor.

The necessary information must be presented in a form which is comprehensible and easy to analyse and must be prepared having regard to the particular nature of the transferable securities and their issuer.

[*FSMA 2000, s 87A(2)–(4); SI 2005 No 1433; SI 2013 No 1538, Reg 2*].

**Summary.** Unless the FCA Prospectus Rules provide otherwise, a prospectus must include a summary which conveys concisely in non-technical language, and in an appropriate structure, the key information relevant to the securities which are the subject of the prospectus and, when read with the rest of the prospectus, must be an aid to investors considering whether to invest in the securities.

The "key information" means the information which is essential to enable investors to understand the transferable securities to which the prospectus relates and to decide whether to consider the offer further. The key information must include:

(a) the essential characteristics of, and risks associated with, the issuer and any guarantor, including their assets, liabilities and financial positions;

(b) the essential characteristics of, and risks associated with investment in the transferable securities including any rights attaching to those securities;

(c) the general terms of the offer, including an estimate of the expenses charged to an investor by the issuer and the person offering the securities to the public, if not the issuer;

(d) details of the admission to trading; and

(e) the reasons for the offer and proposed use of the proceeds.

## 32.8 Prospectuses

*[FSMA 2000, s 87A(5), (6); SI 2005 No 1433; SI 2012 No 1538, Reg 4].*

A summary is not required for a prospectus relating to non–equity transferable securities that have a denomination of at least 100,000 euros (or an equivalent amount) if the prospectus relates to an admission to trading. (FCA Prospectus Rules, para 2.1.3).

The issuer, the offeror or the person asking for the admission to trading on a regulated market shall determine the detailed content of the summary. There are further technical requirements set out in Prospectus Rules, para 2.1.4. The summary must be in the language in which the prospectus was originally drawn up. The summary must also contain a warning to the effect that:

- it should be read as an introduction to the prospectus;

- any decision to invest in the transferable securities should be based on consideration of the prospectus as a whole by the investor;

- where a claim relating to the information contained in a prospectus is brought before a court, the plaintiff investor might, under the national legislation of the EEA States, have to bear the costs of translating the prospectus before the legal proceedings are initiated; and

- civil liability attaches to those persons who are responsible for the summary including any translation of the summary, but only if the summary is misleading, inaccurate or inconsistent when read together with the other parts of the prospectus or it does not provide, when read together with the other parts of the prospectus, key information in order to aid investors when considering whether to consider an offer further as set out in *FSMA 2000, s 90(12).*

(FCA Prospectus Rules, paras 2.1.4, 2.1.6, 2.1.7).

## 32.9 Format

A prospectus may be drawn up as a single document or separate documents. Where it is composed of separate documents, it must divide the required information into the following.

- *A summary.* See **32.8**.

- *A registration document* containing the information relating to the issuer.

- *A securities note* containing the information concerning the transferable securities to be offered or to be admitted to trading.

An issuer, offeror or person requesting admission who already has a registration document approved by the FCA is required to draw up only the securities note and the summary when transferable securities are offered or a request is made for admission to trading. Where there has been a material change which could affect investor's assessments since the latest updated registration document was approved (or any supplementary prospectus) was approved, the securities note must provide that information. The securities note and summary shall be subject to a separate approval.

(FCA Prospectus Rules, paras 2.2.1–2.2.5).

**Base prospectuses**. Where the transferable securities are

- non–equity transferable securities (including warrants in any form) issued under an offering programme, or

- certain non–equity transferable securities issued in a continuous or repeated manner by credit institutions the prospectus can, at the choice of the issuer, offeror or person requesting admission, consist of a base prospectus containing all relevant information concerning the issuer and the transferable securities to be offered or to be admitted to trading. For further information see FCA Prospectus Rules, paras 2.2.7–2.2.9 and *EC Commission Regulation 809/2004, Art 26*.

## 32.10  Minimum information

A prospectus must be drawn up by using one, or a combination of, the schedules and building blocks as set out in *EC Commission Regulation 809/2004, Arts 3–23* and *Annexes I–XVII* and *Annexes XX–XXX*, according to the combinations for various types of securities provided for in *Art 21* and *Annex XVIII*. These depend on the type of issuer and securities involved (see below). The provisions provide for the minimum information to be included in a prospectus. More information can be included but the FCA cannot request that a prospectus contains information items which are not included in those *Annexes* (except where *Art 4a(1)* applies). [*EC Commission Regulation 809/2004, Art 3* and FCA Prospectus Rules, para 2.3.1 and Appendix 3].

**Final offer price and amount of securities not included in prospectus**. If a prospectus for which approval is sought does not include the final offer price or the amount of transferable securities to be offered, the prospectus must disclose the criteria and/or the conditions in accordance with which the above elements will be determined or, in the case of price, the maximum price and the final offer price and the amount of transferable securities must as soon as practicable be filed with the FCA and made available to the public in accordance with Prospectus Rules, paras 2.3.2 and 3.2.4–3.2.6. See **32.21** for the right of an investor to withdraw in certain circumstances.

[*FSMA 2000, s 87A(7); SI 2005 No 1433*]. (FCA Prospectus Rules, para 2.3.2).

## 32.11  Incorporation of terms by reference

Information may be incorporated in a prospectus by reference to one or more previously or simultaneously published documents that have been approved by the competent authority of the Home State (see **32.1**) or filed with or notified to it in accordance with the *Prospectus Directive* or the *Transparency Directive*.

Information under the Transparency Directive that may be incorporated by reference includes

* annual reports and annual accounts (see **32.20**);

* interim management statements;

* half yearly reports;

* reports on payments to governments; and

* equivalent information made available to markets in the UK.

Where information is incorporated by reference, a cross-reference list must be provided in the prospectus specifying where the information can be accessed by investors.

Any information incorporated by reference must be the latest available to the issuer, offeror or person requesting admission. Where a document which may be incorporated by reference contains information which has undergone material changes, the prospectus must clearly state this and give the updated information.

Information may be incorporated by making reference only to certain parts of a document, provided that it states that the non-incorporated parts are either not relevant or covered elsewhere in the prospectus.

## 32.11  Prospectuses

Examples of information that may be incorporated by reference are set out in FCA Prospectus Rules, para 2.4.6.

The summary (see **32.8**) must not incorporate information by reference.

(FCA Prospectus Rules, paras 2.4.1–2.4.6).

### 32.12  Omission of information

The FCA may authorise the omission from a prospectus of any information, the inclusion of which would otherwise be required, on the grounds that

- its disclosure would be contrary to the public interest;

- its disclosure would be seriously detrimental to the issuer and the omission would be unlikely to mislead the public on any facts or circumstances which are essential for an informed assessment; or

- the information is only of minor importance and unlikely to influence an informed assessment.

The Secretary of State or the Treasury may issue a certificate to the effect that the disclosure of any information would be contrary to the public interest. If so, the FCA is entitled to act on any such certificate in exercising its powers under these provisions.

[*FCA 2000, s 87B; SI 2005 No 1433*].

A request to the FCA to authorise the omission of specific information must be in writing from the applicant, identify the specific information concerned and the specific reasons for its omission. It must state why, in the applicant's opinion, one or more of the above grounds apply. (FCA Prospectus Rules, para 2.5.3).

**Equivalent information.** In exceptional cases, if certain information required to be included in a prospectus is inappropriate to the issuer's activity, the legal form of the issuer or to the transferable securities in question, the prospectus must contain information equivalent to the required information (unless there is no such information). (FCA Prospectus Rules, para 2.5.1).

### 32.13  APPLICATION FOR, AND APPROVAL OF, A PROSPECTUS

An applicant must submit the following information to the FCA.

- A completed Form A.

- The prospectus.

- If the order of items in the prospectus does not coincide with the order in the schedules and building blocks in the *EC Commission Regulation* (see **32.10**), a cross-reference list identifying the pages where each item can be found in the prospectus.

- A letter identifying any items from the schedules and building blocks that have not been included because they are not applicable.

- If information is incorporated in the prospectus by reference to another document (see **32.11**), a copy of the document (annotated to indicate which item of the schedules and building blocks in the *EC Commission Regulation* it relates to).

- If the applicant is requesting the FCA to authorise the omission of information from the prospectus, the information required by FCA Prospectus Rules, paras 2.5.3 (see **32.12**).

- Contact details of individuals who are

    (i)     sufficiently knowledgeable about the documentation to be able to answer queries from the FCA; and

    (ii)    available to answer queries between the hours of 7am and 6pm.

- Any other information that the FCA may require.

An applicant must take all reasonable care to ensure that any prospectus submitted for approval for which it is responsible

- contains the necessary information required by *FSMA 2000, s 87A* and the information items in the Prospectus Directive Regulation, Annexes I to XVII and XX to XXX as appropriate to the application; and

- is to the best of its knowledge in accordance with the facts and contains no omission likely to affect its import.

The applicant must submit to the FCA the completed Form A (in final form), the relevant fee, and the other information listed above (in draft form)

(i)     if the applicant does not have transferable securities admitted to trading and has not previously made an offer, at least 20 working days before the intended approval date of the prospectus; or

(ii)    in other cases, at least 10 working days before the intended approval date of the prospectus;

(iii)   as soon as practicable in the case of a supplementary prospectus.

If the order of disclosure items in the prospectus does not coincide with the order set out in the schedules and building blocks in the PD Regulation, an applicant must provide the FCA with a cross reference list identifying the pages where each disclosure item can be found in the prospectus.

An applicant must take reasonable care to ensure any prospectus submitted for approval is contains the necessary information and is in accordance with the facts.

All drafts must be submitted in a searchable electronic format. A contact point to which the FCA can submit notifications should be specified when the first draft of the prospectus is submitted together with the further information prescribed by *Article 2 of Commission Delegated Regulation (EU) 2016/301*.

Where the applicant submits further drafts of the prospectus they shall be marked to show all changes from the previous draft and be accompanied by an unmarked draft and any necessary explanations in accordance with *Article 3 of Commission Delegated Regulation (EU) 2016/301*.

The final must not be annotated in the margin and should be accompanied by information about any changes or confirmation that there have been no changes to information previously submitted in accordance with *Article 4 of Commission Delegated Regulation (EU) 2016/301*.

The draft information must be submitted in final form before midday on the day on which approval is required to be granted.

An applicant must keep a copy of the board resolution allotting or issuing the transferable securities for six years after the application for approval of the prospectus for those securities.

## 32.13   Prospectuses

**Prospectus comprising separate documents.** In such a case, an application for approval may relate to one or more of those separate documents; if so, references above to a prospectus are, unless the context otherwise requires, to be taken to be references to the document or documents to which the application relates.

**Vetting of equivalent documents.** A person who wishes the FCA to vet an equivalent document referred 32.5(*k*) or 32.6(*d*) must submit to the FCA (together with any relevant fee)

- a copy of the document;

- a cross-reference list identifying the pages in the document where each item that is equivalent to the disclosure requirements for a prospectus may be found;

- contact details of individuals who are

   (i)    sufficiently knowledgeable about the documentation to be able to answer queries from the FCA; and

   (ii)   available to answer queries between the hours of 7am and 6pm; and

- any other information that the FCA may require.

The documents must be submitted at least ten working days before the date on which the vetting is required to be completed (20 working days if the person does not have transferable securities admitted to trading and has not previously made an offer).

(FCA Prospectus Rules, paras 3.1.1–3.1.5A, 3.1.11, 3.1.14–3.1.16).

## 32.14   Approval by FCA

The FCA may not approve a prospectus unless it is satisfied that

- the UK is the Home State (see **32.1**) in relation to the issuer of the transferable securities to which it relates;

- the prospectus contains the necessary information; and

- all of the other relevant requirements under the legislation or FCA Prospectus Rules have been complied with.

*[FSMA 2000, s 87A(1); SI 2005 No 1433].*

The 'necessary information' for the above is the information necessary to enable investors to make an informed assessment of:

(a)    the assets and liabilities, financial position, profits and losses, and prospects of the issuer of the transferable securities and of any guarantor; and

(b)    the rights attaching to the transferable securities.

If, in the case of transferable securities to which *FSMA 2000, s 87* applies, the prospectus states that the guarantor is a specified EEA state, the prospectus is not required to include other information about the guarantor. Further requirements are set out in *FSMA 2000, s 87A(3)–(10)*.

*[FSMA 2000, s 87A(2); SI 2012 No 1538, Regs 2, 4]*

The FCA must notify the applicant of its decision on an application for approval of a prospectus before the end of the period for consideration. This period

- begins on the first working day after the date on which the application is received (or, where the FCA reasonably requires further documents or information and gives notice to that effect, on the first working day after the date on which the notice is complied with); and

- ends 10 working days (in the case of a new issuer, 20 working days) thereafter.

But no notice requesting further information can be given more than 10 working days (in that case of a new issuer, 20 working days) after the date on which the application is received.

**Supplementary prospectuses.** In the case of a supplementary prospectus (see **32.19**), the FCA must notify the applicant of its decision on an application for approval before the end of the period of seven working days beginning with the date on which the application is received. It may request further documents or information if these are reasonably required.

**Failure by the FCA** to notify its decision on a prospectus or supplementary prospectus within the time limit does not constitute approval of the application in question.

[*FSMA 2000, s 87C; SI 2005 No 1433*].

**Notifying the applicant.** The FCA must notify the applicant in writing whether it decides to approve or refuse to approve a prospectus. In the latter case, it must state the reasons for refusing the application; and inform the applicant of his right to refer the matter to the Tribunal.

[*FSMA 2000, s 87D; SI 2005 No 1433*].

**Requirements imposed as condition of approval.** As a condition of approving a prospectus, the FCA may by notice in writing

- require the inclusion in the prospectus of such supplementary information necessary for investor protection it specifies;

- require a person controlling, or controlled by, the applicant to provide specified information or documents;

- require an auditor or manager of the applicant to provide specified information or documents; and

- require a financial intermediary, commissioned to assist either in carrying out the offer to the public or in requesting their admission to trading, to provide specified information or documents. [*FSMA 2000, s 87J; SI 2005 No 1433*].

## 32.15 Overseas matters

(1) *Transfer of application for approval by FCA to another EEA State*

A person seeking to have the function of approving a prospectus transferred to the competent authority of another EEA State (see **32.1**) must make a written request to the FCA at least ten working days before the date the transfer is sought. The request must

- set out the reasons for the proposed transfer;

- state the name of the competent authority to whom the transfer is sought; and

- include a copy of the draft prospectus.

The FCA will consider transferring the function of approving a prospectus to the competent authority of another EEA State

# 32.15   Prospectuses

- if requested to do so by the issuer, offeror or person requesting admission or by another competent authority; or

- in other cases if the FCA considers it would be more appropriate for another competent authority to perform that function.

The FCA may then transfer the function to the competent authority of another EEA State provided that it first obtains the agreement of the transferee authority. The FCA must inform the applicant of the transfer within three working days beginning with the first working day after the date of the transfer.

[*FSMA 2000, s 87E; SI 2005 No 1433*]. (FCA Prospectus Rules, paras 3.1.12, 3.1.13).

*(2) Transfer of application for approval to FCA by another EEA State*

Where the FCA agrees to the transfer to it of an application for the approval of a prospectus made to the competent authority of another EEA State (see **32.1**)

- the UK is to be treated as the Home State (see **32.1**) in relation to the issuer of the transferable securities to which the prospectus relates; and

- *FSMA 2000, Part VI* applies to the application as if it had been made to the FCA except that for the purposes of notification in *FSMA 2000, s 87C* (see **32.14**) the date of the transfer is taken to be the date on which the application was received by the FCA.

[*FSMA 2000, s 87F; SI 2005 No 1433*].

Final terms issued in relation to a prospectus must only contain information that relates to the securities note and must not be used to supplement the prospectus.

Where the FCA in its capacity as the competent authority of the home state receives final terms issued in relation to a prospectus it must communicate those final terms as follows

- where an offer of transferable securities to the public is to be made in another EEA state, to the competent authority of that EEA state, where possible before that offer begins or as soon as practicable following the making of that offer

- where transferable securities are to be admitted to trading on a regulated market in another EEA state, to the competent authority of that EEA state, where possible before the admission occurs or as soon as practicable following the admission of those transferable securities to trading on a regulated market.

The FCA must communicate all final terms in relation to a prospectus it receives in its capacity as the competent authority of the home state to ESMA.

[*FSMA 2000, s 87FA, B; SI 2014 No 3293, Reg 3*].

*(3) Prospectus approved in another EEA State*

A prospectus approved by the competent authority of another EEA State (see **32.1**) is not an approved prospectus for the purposes of *FSMA 2000, s 85* (see **32.3**) unless that authority has provided the FCA with

- a certificate of approval;

- a copy of the prospectus as approved; and

- if requested by the FCA, a translation of the summary of the prospectus.

A document is not a certificate of approval unless it states

- that the prospectus has been drawn up in accordance with the *Prospectus Directive* and approved, in accordance with that *Directive*, by the competent authority providing the certificate; and

- whether (and, if so, why) the competent authority providing it authorised, in accordance with the *Prospectus Directive*, the omission from the prospectus of information which would otherwise have been required to be included.

[*FSMA 2000, s 87H; SI 2005 No 1433*].

(4) *Prospectus approved in a third country*

If a prospectus relating to an issuer that has its registered office in a country that is not an EEA State (see **32.1**) is drawn up in accordance with the legislation of that country, the FCA may, if the UK is the Home State (see **32.1**) in relation to the issuer, approve the prospectus if it is satisfied that

- the prospectus has been drawn up in accordance with international standards set by international securities commission organisations, including the IOSCO disclosure standards; and

- the information requirements, including information of a financial nature, are equivalent to the requirements under *FSMA 2000, Pt VI*, the *EC Commission Regulation* and the FCA Prospectus Rules.

(FCA Prospectus Rules, paras 4.2.1.)

(5) *Provision of information to host Member State*

The FCA must, if requested to do so, supply the competent authority of a specified Host State (ie an EEA State where an offer to the public is made or admission to trading is sought, when different from the Home State, see **32.1**) with

- a certificate of approval;

- a copy of the specified prospectus (as approved by the FCA); and

- a translation of the summary of the specified prospectus (if the request states that one has been requested by the other competent authority).

The only persons who can make such a request are

- the issuer of the transferable securities in question;

- a person who wishes to offer the transferable securities in question to the public in an EEA State other than (or as well as) the UK;

- a person requesting the admission of the transferable securities in question to a regulated market situated or operating in an EEA State other than (or as well as) the UK.

Similar provisions as to the requirements of a certificate of approval apply as in (3) above.

The FCA must comply with a request under these provisions

- if the prospectus has been approved before the request is made, within three working days beginning with the date the request is received; or

- if the request is submitted with an application for the approval of a prospectus, on the first working day after the date on which it approves the prospectus.

## 32.15 Prospectuses

[FSMA 2000, s 87I; SI 2005 No 1433; SI 2012 No 1538, Reg 6].

*(6) Exercise of powers at request of competent authority of another EEA State*

If

| | |
|---|---|
| (i) | the competent authority of another EEA State (see **32.1**) has approved a prospectus, |
| (ii) | the transferable securities to which the prospectus relates have been offered to the public in the UK or their admission to trading on a regulated market has been requested, and |
| (iii) | that competent authority makes a request that the FCA assist it in the performance of its functions under the law of that State in connection with the *Prospectus Directive* |

for the purpose of complying with the request in (iii) above, the powers conferred by *FSMA 2000, ss 87K, 87L* (see **32.16**) may be exercised as if the prospectus were one which had been approved by the FCA. [*FSMA 2000, s 87P; SI 2005 No 1433*].

*(7) Use of languages*

If an offer is made, or admission to trading is sought

- only in the UK and the UK is the Home State (see **32.1**), the prospectus must be drawn up in English;

- in more than one EEA State (see **32.1**) including the UK and the UK is the Home State, the prospectus must be drawn up in English and must also be made available either in a language accepted by the competent authorities of each Host State or in a language 'customary in the sphere of international finance', at the choice of the issuer, offeror or person requesting admission (as the case may be);

- in one or more EEA States excluding the UK and the UK is the Home State, the prospectus must be drawn up in a language accepted by the competent authorities of those EEA States or in a language customary in the sphere of international finance, at the choice of the issuer, offeror or person requesting admission (as the case may be).

If admission to trading of non–equity securities whose denomination per unit amounts to at least 100,000 euros (or an equivalent amount) is sought in the UK or in one or more other EEA states, the prospectus must be drawn up in either a language accepted by the competent authorities of the Home State and Host States or in a language customary in the sphere of international finance, at the choice of the issuer, offeror, or person requesting admission (as the case may be).

The FCA consider language to be '*customary in the sphere of international finance*' if documents in that language are accepted in at least three international capital markets in each of Europe, Asia and the Americas.

For the purpose of the scrutiny by the FCA where the UK is the Home State, the prospectus must be drawn up either in English or in another language customary in the sphere of international finance, at the choice of the issuer, offeror or person requesting admission (as the case may be).

**Translation of summary into English.** If

- an offer is made in the UK,

- a prospectus relating to the transferable securities has been approved by the competent authority of another EEA State and the prospectus contains a summary, and

- the prospectus is drawn up in a language other than English that is customary in the sphere of international finance (see above),

the offeror must ensure that the summary is translated into English.

(FCA Prospectus Rules, paras 4.1.1–4.1.3, 4.1.5A, 4.1.6).

**32.16  Powers of the FCA: infringement of rules**

The FCA has the following powers where it believes the rules relating to prospectuses have been infringed.

(1)    **Power to suspend or prohibit offer to the public**

Where a person has made an offer of transferable securities to the public in the UK,

- if the FCA finds that any provision of *FSMA 2000, Pt VI* or the FCA Prospectus Rules or any other provision made in accordance with the *Prospective Directive* has been infringed, it may require the offeror to withdraw the offer;

- if the FCA has reasonable grounds for suspecting that any such provision made in accordance with the *Prospective Directive* has been infringed, it may

  (i)    require the offeror to suspend the offer for a period not exceeding ten working days; and

  (ii)   require a person not to advertise the offer, or to take such steps as the FCA may specify to suspend any existing advertisement of the offer, for a period not exceeding ten working days; and

- if the FCA has reasonable grounds for suspecting that it is likely that any such provision will be infringed, it may require the offeror to withdraw the offer.

[*FSMA 2000, s 87K; SI 2005 No 1433*].

(2)    **Power to suspend or prohibit admission to trading on a regulated market**

Where a person has requested the admission of transferable securities to trading on a regulated market situated or operating in the UK,

- if the FCA finds that any provision of *FSMA 2000, Pt VI* or the FCA Prospectus Rules or any other relevant provision made in accordance with the *Prospective Directive* has been infringed, it may require the market operator to prohibit trading in the securities on the regulated market in question;

- if the FCA has reasonable grounds for suspecting that any such provision has been infringed and the securities have not yet been admitted to trading on the regulated market in question, it may

  (i)    require the person requesting admission to suspend the request for a period not exceeding ten working days; and

  (ii)   require a person not to advertise the securities to which it relates, or to take such steps as the authority may specify to suspend any existing advertisement in connection with those securities, for a period not exceeding ten working days; and

- if the FCA has reasonable grounds for suspecting that any such provision has been infringed and the securities have been admitted to trading on the regulated market in question, it may

  (i) require the market operator to suspend trading in the securities for a period not exceeding ten working days; and

  (ii) require a person not to advertise the securities, or to take such steps as the authority may specify to suspend any existing advertisement in connection with those securities, for a period not exceeding ten working days.

[*FSMA 2000, s 87L; SI 2005 No 1433*].

(3) **Public censure of issuer**

If the FCA finds that

- an issuer of transferable securities,

- a person offering transferable securities to the public, or

- a person requesting the admission of transferable securities to trading on a regulated market,

is failing or has failed to comply with his obligations under any provision of *FSMA 2000, Pt VI* or the FCA Prospectus Rules or any other provision made in accordance with the *Prospective Directive*, it may publish a statement to that effect.

If it proposes to do so, the FCA must give the person a warning notice setting out the terms of the proposed statement. If, after considering any representations made in response to the warning notice, the FCA decides to make the proposed statement, it must give the person a decision notice setting out the terms of the statement.

A person to whom a decision notice is given can appeal to the Tribunal.

[*FSMA 2000, ss 87M, 87N; SI 2005 No 1433*].

## 32.17 FILING AND PUBLICATION OF A PROSPECTUS

A prospectus must not be published until approved by the FCA. Once it is approved, it must be filed with the FCA at the same time as it is made available to the public. A prospectus must be filed with the FCA by uploading it to the system identified by the FCA on its website. The prospectus must be made available to the public as soon as practicable and at a reasonable time in advance of, or at the latest at the beginning of, the offer or the admission to trading of the transferable securities involved. The exception is in the case of an initial public offer of a class of shares not already admitted to trading that is to be admitted to trading for the first time, in which case the prospectus must be made available to the public at least six working days before the end of the offer.

A prospectus is deemed to be made available to the public for these purposes when published in either of the following ways.

- By insertion in one or more newspapers circulated throughout, or widely circulated in, the EEA States in which the offer is made or the admission to trading is sought.

- In a printed form to be made available, free of charge, to the public at the offices of the regulated market on which the transferable securities are being admitted to trading, or at the registered office of the issuer and at the offices of the financial intermediaries placing or selling the transferable securities, including paying agents.

- In an electronic form on

    (i) the issuer's website or, if applicable, on the website of the financial intermediaries placing or selling the transferable securities, including paying agents, or

    (ii) in an electronic form on the website of the regulated market where the admission to trading is sought

    but in either case a paper copy must be delivered to the investor, upon his request and free of charge, by the issuer, the offeror, the person requesting admission or the financial intermediaries placing or selling the transferable securities.

    A person publishing a prospectus either by insertion in a newspaper or in printed form must also publish the prospectus electronically.

    The prospectus must be easily accessible when entering the website and must not contain hyper-links (apart from links to the electronic addresses where information incorporated by reference is available (see **32.11**)). The investors must have the possibility of downloading and printing the prospectus.

    The websites must avoid targeting residents in Members States or third countries where the offer of securities to the public does not take place (eg by the insertion of a disclaimer as to who are the addressees of the offer).

The text and format of the prospectus made available to the public must at all times be identical to the original version approved by the FCA.

If a prospectus consists of several documents or incorporates information by reference (see **32.11**), the documents and information making up the prospectus may be published and circulated separately if the documents are made available, free of charge, to the public, as above. Each document must indicate where the other constituent documents of the full prospectus may be obtained.

[*EC Commission Regulation, Arts 29, 30*]. (FCA Prospectus Rules, paras 3.1.10, 3.2.1– 3.2.6, 3.2.8.)

*Commission Delegated Regulation (EU) 2016/301, Recital (7)* and *Articles 6–8* contain further provisions prescribing the precise manner in which a prospectus should be published whether in electronic form or in newspapers.

(FCA Prospectus Rule, para 3.2.6A.)

## 32.18 ADVERTISEMENTS

In the case of an offer, or an admission to trading of transferable securities, for which

- a prospectus is required to be made available (see **32.3**), or

- a person elects to have a prospectus (see **32.7**),

an 'advertisement' relating to the offer or to the admission to trading must not be issued unless

- it states that a prospectus has been or will be published and indicates where investors are, or will be, able to obtain it;

- it is clearly recognisable as an advertisement;

- information in the advertisement is not inaccurate, or misleading; and

- information in the advertisement is consistent with the information contained in the prospectus (if already published) or with the information required to be in the prospectus (if the prospectus is published afterwards).

Any written advertisement must also contain a bold and prominent statement to the effect that it is not a prospectus but an advertisement and investors should not subscribe for any securities referred to in the advertisement except on the basis of information in the prospectus.

'*Advertisement*' means an announcement relating to a specific offer to the public of securities or to an admission to trading on a regulated market and aiming to specifically promote the potential subscription or acquisition of securities.

Advertisements covered by these provisions include (but are not restricted to) those communicated by any of the following means: addressed or unaddressed printed matter; electronic message or advertisement received via a mobile telephone or pager; standard letter; press advertising with or without order form; catalogue; telephone with or without human intervention; seminars and presentations; radio; videophone; videotext; electronic mail; facsimile machine (fax); television; notice; bill; poster; brochure; web posting including internet banners.

[*EC Commission Regulation, Art 34*]. (FCA Prospectus Rules, paras 3.3.1–3.3.3, Appendix 1).

*Commission Delegated Regulation (EU) 2016/301, Article 11* contains further provisions about advertisements including that an advertisement needs to be amended if a supplementary prospectus has to be published and that if no prospectus is required the advertisement should contain a warning to that effect.

(FCA Prospectus Rule, para 3.3.3A.)

## 32.19  SUPPLEMENTARY PROSPECTUS

If, during the period ("the relevant period")

- beginning with the time that the prospectus is approved, and

- ending with the closure of the offer to which the prospectus relates or when trading in the securities on a regulated market begins

there is a significant new factor, material mistake or inaccuracy relating to the information included in the prospectus, then the person on whose application the prospectus was approved must, as soon as practicable after the new factor, etc arises, submit to the FCA for its approval a supplementary prospectus containing details.

Where a prospectus relates both to an offer of transferable securities to the public and the admission of those securities to trading on a regulated market, the relevant period referred to above does not apply and the relevant period begins when the prospectus is approved and ends with the later of the closure of the offer to the public to which the prospectus relates or the time when trading in those securities on a regulated market begins.

'*Significant*' means significant for the purposes of making an informed assessment of assets and liabilities, financial position, profits and losses and prospects of the issuer (and any guarantor) and the rights attaching to the securities.

Any person responsible for the prospectus (see **32.2**) who is aware of any new factor, etc which may require the submission of a supplementary prospectus must give notice of it to

- the issuer of the transferable securities to which the prospectus relates; and

- the person on whose application the prospectus was approved.

A supplementary prospectus must provide sufficient information to correct any mistake or inaccuracy which gave rise to the need for it. It must also, if necessary, include an amendment or supplement to the summary (and any translations of the summary) to take into account the new information.

Unless the context otherwise requires, provisions in this chapter relating to prospectuses also apply to supplementary prospectuses and the provisions above also apply to any required changes for further significant factors, etc following the publication of a supplementary prospectus.

See also **32.21** for the rights of investors to withdraw their acceptances after a supplementary prospectus is published.

[*FSMA 2000, s 87G; SI 2005 No 1433; SI 2012 No 1538, Reg 5*]. (FCA Prospectus Rules, paras 3.4.2, 3.4.3).

*Commission Delegated Regulation (EU) 382/2014, Article 2* stipulates minimum situations where a supplementary prospectus must be submitted for approval including where new annual audited financial statements are published, where there is an amendment to a profit forecast contained in the prospectus, where there is a change of control, where there is a new takeover bid, where there is a change in the working capital statement, where the issuer is seeking admission to trading in additional regulated markets, where a significant new financial commitment is undertaken and where the aggregate nominal amount of the offering is increased.

(FCA Prospectus Rule, para 3.4.4.)

## 32.20  ANNUAL INFORMATION UPDATE

Subject to below, an issuer whose securities are admitted to trading and in relation to whom the UK is the Home State (see **32.1**) must prepare an annual information update (AIU) that refers to or contains all information that has been published or made available to the public over the previous 12 months in one or more EEA States and in third countries in compliance with its obligations under EU and national laws and rules dealing with the regulation of securities, issuers of securities and securities markets.

This does not apply in relation to non-equity transferable securities whose denomination per unit amounts to at least 50,000 euros (or an equivalent amount) unless the issuer has elected by notice in writing to the FCA to comply with the requirements. If an issuer so elects, it must comply with the requirements on an ongoing basis until it withdraws the election (which cannot be done within three years from the date of the initial election).

The FCA expect the AIU to refer to or contain information that is published or made available under

- *FSMA 2000, Pt VI*;

- FCA Rules made under *FSMA 2000, Pt VI*;

- *EC Regulation No 1606/2002* on the application of international accounting standards;

- *CA 2006* (or, for an overseas company, the relevant companies legislation of the place where it is incorporated, relating to the regulation of securities, issuers and securities markets); and

- laws and rules of other EEA States and third countries that relate to the regulation of securities, issuers of securities and securities markets.

The AIU must include a statement indicating that some information may be out-of-date, if such is the case.

If the AIU refers to information rather than including that information, it must

- state where the information can be obtained;

- give a short description of the nature of the information; and

- specify the date and place of filing (if applicable), and the date of publication, of the information.

**Filing and publication.** The issuer must file the AIU with the FCA, and make it available to the public, at the latest 20 working days after the publication of the annual financial statements. The AIU can be made available to the public by any of the means permitted under **32.17**.

[*EC Commission Regulation 809/2004, Art 27*].

## 32.21  REMEDIES FOR INVESTORS

**Right of investor to withdraw.** Subject to below, where a person agrees to buy or subscribe for transferable securities in circumstances where

- the final offer price, or

- the amount of transferable securities to be offered to the public

is not included in the prospectus, he may withdraw his acceptance before the end of the withdrawal period. The withdrawal period

- begins with the investor's acceptance; and

- ends at the end of the second working day after the date on which the FCA is informed of the outstanding information.

The above does not apply if the prospectus contains the criteria or conditions (or both) according to which the final offer price or amount of transferable securities will be determined, or, in the case of the offer price, the maximum price.

A person "P" may withdraw his acceptance of an offer of transferable securities to the public before the end of the second working day after the day on which the supplementary prospectus was published or such later time as may be specified in the supplementary prospectus if the following conditions are satisfied:

- a prospectus which relates to an offer of transferable securities to the public has been published

- a supplementary prospectus has been published and prior to the publication of the supplementary prospectus P agreed to buy or subscribe for transferable securities to which the offer relates and

- the significant new factor, material mistake or inaccuracy referred to in *FSMA 2000, s 87G(1)* which caused the supplementary prospectus to be published arose before delivery of the securities.

*[FSMA 2000, s 87Q; SI 2005 No 1433; SI 2012 No 1538, Reg 5].*

**32.22  Compensation for statements in prospectuses**

A remedy may be available to a person who acquires transferable securities and suffers loss in respect of them. Subject to below, there are two heads of liability.

(a)    Any person responsible for a prospectus (see **32.2**) or supplementary prospectus is liable to pay compensation to a person who has acquired securities to which the prospectus applies and suffered loss in respect of them as a result of any untrue or misleading statement in the prospectus or the omission of any matter required to be included by *FSMA 2000, ss 80* or *81*. If a prospectus is required to include information about the absence of a particular matter, the omission of that information is treated as a statement that there is no such matter.

(b)    Any person who fails to comply with the requirements relating to supplementary prospectuses is liable to pay compensation to anyone who has acquired securities and suffered loss as a result of that failure.

References to acquiring securities include contracting to acquire them or any interest in them.

**Exemption from liability.**

A person does not incur liability under the above provisions in the following circumstances.

(i)    Under (*a*) above, a person does not incur liability if he satisfies the court that, having made reasonable enquiries, he reasonably believed at the time when the prospectus was submitted to the FCA, that the statement was true and not misleading or that the matter omitted was properly omitted. He must also show that one or more of the following conditions are satisfied.

•    He continued in that belief until the securities were acquired.

•    They were acquired before it was reasonably practicable to bring a correction to the attention of potential investors.

•    He had, before the securities were acquired, taken all reasonable steps to bring a correction to the attention of potential investors.

•    he continued in that belief until after the commencement of dealings in the securities following their admission to trading and that the securities were acquired after such a lapse of time that he ought to be excused.

(ii)    Under (*a*) above, a person does not incur any liability if the statement was made (or purports to be made) by another person as an 'expert' and was stated to be included with the consent of that other person, and the person satisfies the court that, at the time the prospectus was submitted to the FCA for approval, he reasonably believed that the other person

•    was competent to make or authorise the statement; and

•    had consented to its inclusion.

He must in addition satisfy the court that one or more of the following conditions are satisfied.

•    He continued in that belief until the securities were acquired.

•    They were acquired before it was reasonably practicable to bring the fact that the expert was not competent or had not consented to the attention of potential investors.

- He had, before the securities were acquired, taken all reasonable steps to bring those facts to the attention of potential investors.

- He continued in that belief until after the commencement of dealings in the securities following their admission to trading and the securities were acquired after such a lapse of time that he ought to be excused.

'*Expert*' includes any engineer, valuer, accountant or other person whose profession, qualifications or experience give authority to a statement made by him.

(iii) Under (*a*) above, a person does not incur any liability if he satisfies the court that

- before the securities were acquired

  (i) a correction, or

  (ii) the fact that the expert was not competent or had not consented

  had been published in a manner calculated to bring it to the attention of potential investors; or

- he has taken all reasonable steps to secure such publication and reasonably believed that publication had taken place before the securities were acquired.

(iv) Under (*a*) above, a person does not incur any liability if the statement was made by an official person or contained in a public official document and he satisfies the court that it is accurately and fairly reproduced.

(v) Under (*a*) and (*b*) above, a person does not incur any liability if he satisfies the court that the person suffering the loss acquired the securities with knowledge that the statement was false or misleading or, as the case may be, knowledge of the omitted matter or the change or new matter.

(vi) Under (*b*) above, a person does not incur any liability if he satisfies the court that the change or new matter in question was not such as to call for a supplementary prospectus.

A person is not to be subject to civil liability solely on the basis of a summary (or any translation of it) in a prospectus unless the summary, when read with the rest of the prospectus, is misleading, inaccurate or inconsistent or does not provide key information as defined in *FSMA 2000, s 87A(9) and (10)*.

[*FSMA 2000, s 90, Sch 10; SI 2005 No 1433; SI 2012 No 1538, Reg 7*].

There are also other common law civil remedies in contract and tort.

## 32.23 PENALTIES CONCERNING PROSPECTUSES

The FCA may impose a penalty of such amount as it considers appropriate if it considers that

(a) an issuer of transferable securities,

(b) a person offering transferable securities to the public or requesting their admission to trading on a regulated market,

(c) an applicant for the approval of a prospectus in relation to transferable securities,

(d) a person on whom a requirement has been imposed under *FSMA 2000, ss 87K* or *87L* (see **32.16**), or

(e) any other person to whom a provision of the *Prospectus Directive* applies, has contravened a provision of *FSMA 2000, Pt VI*, the FCA Prospectus Rules, or a provision otherwise made in accordance with the *Prospectus Directive* or a requirement imposed on him under such a provision.

Where the person in (*a*)–(*e*) above is a company, if the FCA considers that a person who was at the material time a director of the company was knowingly concerned in the contravention, it may impose upon him a penalty of such amount as it considers appropriate.

As an alternative to a penalty, the FCA may instead publish a statement censuring the person concerned.

Any action (whether penalty or censure) taken by the FCA under these provisions must be within two years beginning with the first day on which it knew of the contravention unless proceedings against that person, in respect of the contravention, were begun before the end of that period.

**Procedure.** If the FCA proposes to take action against a person under these provisions, it must give him a warning notice which must state the amount of the proposed penalty or, as the case may be, set out the terms of the proposed statement.

If, after considering any representations made in response to the warning notice, the FCA decides to take action, it must issue a decision notice which must state the amount of the penalty or, as the case may be, set out the terms of the statement.

Where the FCA decides to take action against a person, that person may refer the matter to the Tribunal.

[*FSMA 2000, ss 91, 92; CA 2006, Sch 15 para 6; SI 2005 No 1433*].

In appropriate cases, there could also be criminal liability including under *Financial Services Act 2012, ss 89* and *90*.

## 32.24  APPOINTMENT OF INVESTIGATORS BY THE FCA

If it appears to the FCA that there are circumstances suggesting that

- there may have been a contravention of a provision of *FSMA 2000, Pt VI*, the FCA Prospectus Rules or a provision otherwise made in accordance with the *Prospectus Directive*, or

- a person, who was at the material time a director of a company falling within **32.23**, has been knowingly concerned in a contravention of any such provision,

the FCA may appoint one or more competent persons to conduct an investigation on its behalf.

[*FSMA 2000, s 97; CA 2006, Sch 15 para 8; SI 2005 No 433*].

## 32.25  FCA: EXEMPTION FROM LIABILITY IN DAMAGES

Neither the FCA nor any person who is a member, officer or member of staff of the FCA is to be liable in damages for anything done or omitted in the discharge of the authority's functions unless the act or omission is shown to have been in bad faith. But this exemption does not prevent an award of damages made in respect of an act or omission on the ground that it was unlawful as a result of *Human Rights Act 1998, s 6(1)*. [*FSMA 2000, s 102*].

# 33   Public and Listed Companies

## 33.1   PUBLIC COMPANIES

A public company is defined as a company limited by shares or limited by guarantee and having a share capital

- whose certificate of incorporation states that it is a public company; and

- in relation to which the requirements of the *Companies Acts* or the *'former Companies Acts'* (see APPENDIX 1 DEFINITIONS) as to registration or re-registration as a public company have been complied with

    (i) in relation to registration or re-registration in Great Britain, on or after 22 December 1980; and

    (ii) in relation to registration or re-registration in Northern Ireland, on or after 1 July 1983.

[*CA 2006, s 4*].

## 33.2   Comparison with private companies

The main differences between private and public companies are:

- **Prohibition of public offers by private companies**. A private company limited by shares or limited by guarantee and having a share capital must not

(i)    offer to the public any securities of the company; or

(ii)    allot or agree to allot any securities of the company with a view to their being offered to the public.

[*CA 2006, s 755*]. See **47.21** SHARES for full details.

• **Minimum share capital requirement for a public company**. A public company (other than a company re-registered as a public company) must not do business or exercise any borrowing rights unless the Registrar of Companies has issued it with a trading certificate. A trading certificate will only be issued if the company's allotted share capital is not less than the "authorised minimum". See **33.3**. (For the requirements when a private company is re-registered as a public company, see **41.2** RE-REGISTRATION.)

• **Directors**. A private company must have at least one director and a public company must have at least two (see **18.2** DIRECTORS).

• **Company secretaries**. A private company is not required to have a company secretary (although it may choose to do so). A public company must have a company secretary. See **13.1** COMPANY SECRETARIES).

• **Name**. The name of a limited private company must normally end in 'limited' or 'Ltd' (or the Welsh equivalent). The name of a limited public company must normally end with 'public limited company' or 'plc' (or Welsh equivalent). See **27.2** NAMES AND BUSINESS NAMES.

• **Distributions**. A public company may only make a distribution if, after that distribution, the net assets of that company are not less than the aggregate of its called-up share capital and undistributed reserves (see **22.5** DISTRIBUTIONS).

• **Accounts**. A private company, or a group of companies all of which are private companies, may take advantage of the exemptions for small and medium-sized companies (see **4** ACCOUNTS: MEDIUM-SIZED COMPANIES and **5** ACCOUNTS: SMALL COMPANIES).

• The period allowed after the end of the relevant accounting reference period for delivering a copy of the accounts and reports to the Registrar of Companies is shorter for a public company than for a private company. See **2.12** ACCOUNTS: GENERAL.

• **Regulatory provisions and corporate governance**. Public companies whose securities are admitted to trading on a regulated or prescribed market or a multilateral trading facility or organised trading facility are subject to substantial regulatory control by virtue of inter alia:

–    the Listing Rules (for companies whose securities are admitted to the Official List) – see **33.4**;

–    the Prospectus Rules (see **32** PROSPECTUSES);

–    the Disclosure Guidance and Transparency Rules (see **33.44** and **33.53**);

–    the UK Corporate Governance Code issued by the Financial Reporting Council and associated best practice guidance (for companies whose securities are admitted to the premium section of the Official List);

–    the Market Abuse Regulation and associated secondary legislation and guidance; and

–    the Aim Rules for companies admitted to the Alternative Investment Market.

**33.3    Trading certificate and minimum share capital**

**Issue of trading certificate.** See above that a public company (other than a company re-registered as a public company) must not do business or exercise any borrowing powers unless the Registrar of Companies has issued it with a trading certificate. (For the requirements when a private company is re-registered as a public company, see **41.2 RE-REGISTRATION.**)

The Registrar of Companies must issue such a certificate if, on an application made in accordance with the provisions described below, he is satisfied that the nominal value of the company's allotted share capital is not less than the authorised minimum (see below). For this purpose, a share allotted in pursuance of an employees' share scheme must not be taken into account unless paid up as to

- at least one-quarter of the nominal value of the share; and

- the whole of any premium on the share.

A trading certificate has effect from the date on which it is issued and is conclusive evidence that the company is entitled to do business and exercise any borrowing powers.

[*CA 2006, s 761*].

**Procedure for obtaining a trading certificate.** An application (Form SH50) for a certificate must

(a)    state that the nominal value of the company's allotted share capital is not less than the authorised minimum;

(b)    specify the amount, or estimated amount, of the company's preliminary expenses;

(c)    specify any amount or benefit paid or given, or intended to be paid or given, to any promoter of the company, and the consideration for the payment or benefit;

(d)    be accompanied by a statement of compliance, ie a statement that the company meets the requirements for the issue of a certificate; and

(e)    be accompanied by a statement of the aggregate amount paid up on the shares of the company on account of their nominal value.

The Registrar of Companies may accept the statement of compliance (that the company meets the requirements for the issue of a certificate under s 761) as sufficient evidence of the matters stated in it.

[*CA 2006, s 762; Small Business Enterprise and Employment Act 2015, ss 98(3)* and *164(1); SI 2016 No 321, Reg 6(f)*].

**The authorised minimum.** The '*authorised minimum*', in relation to the nominal value of a public company's allotted share capital is

- £50,000; or

- the euro equivalent as prescribed by the Secretary of State. The euro equivalent is changed from time to time.

[*CA 2006, s 763; SI 2008 No 729, Reg 2; SI 2009 No 2425, Reg 2*].

The Secretary of State may, by order, alter the sterling amount of the authorised minimum, and make a corresponding alteration of the prescribed euro equivalent. Where any such order increases the authorised minimum, it may also require a public company that has an allotted share capital of which the nominal value is less than the increased amount to

- increase the nominal value of its allotted share capital to not less than that amount; or

- re-register as a private company. [*CA 2006, s 764*].

*Application of initial requirement.* The initial requirement for a public company to have allotted share capital of a nominal value not less than the authorised minimum, must be met either by reference to allotted share capital denominated in sterling or allotted share capital denominated in euros (but not partly in one and partly in the other). Whether the requirement is met is determined, in the first case, by reference to the sterling amount and, in the second case, by reference to the prescribed euro equivalent. No account is to be taken of any allotted share capital of the company denominated in a currency other than sterling or, as the case may be, euros.

If the company could meet the requirement either by reference to share capital denominated in sterling or by reference to share capital denominated in euros, it must elect in its application for a trading certificate or, as the case may be, for re-registration as a public company which is to be the currency by reference to which the matter is determined.

[*CA 2006, s 765*].

*Application where shares denominated in different currencies etc.* The Secretary of State may make provision by Regulations as to the application of the authorised minimum in relation to a public company that

- has shares denominated in more than one currency or in a currency other than sterling or euros;

- redenominates the whole or part of its allotted share capital; or

- allots new shares.

[*CA 2006, s 766; SI 2011 No 1265, Reg 28(2)*].

**Penalties.** If a company does business or exercises any borrowing powers without having a trading certificate issued to it, an offence is committed by the company and every officer of the company who is in default. A person guilty of such an offence is liable (i) on conviction on indictment, to a fine; and (ii) on summary conviction, to a fine not exceeding the statutory maximum. See **29.1 OFFENCES AND LEGAL PROCEEDINGS** for the statutory maximum.

Any breach of the above provisions does not affect the validity of a transaction entered into by the company, but if a company

- enters into a transaction in contravention of the provisions, and

- fails to comply with its obligations in connection with the transaction within 21 days from being called on to do so

the directors of the company are jointly and severally liable to indemnify any other party to the transaction in respect of any loss or damage suffered by him by reason of the company's failure to comply with its obligations. The directors who are so liable are those who were directors at the time the company entered into the transaction.

[*CA 2006, s 767*].

## 33.4 LISTED COMPANIES – THE LISTING RULES

The Financial Conduct Authority (FCA), (which from 1 April 2013 replaced the FSA as the UK Listing Authority under *FSMA 2000*) must maintain the Official List and may admit such securities as it considers appropriate but

- nothing may be admitted to the Official List except in accordance with the provisions of *FSMA 2000, Pt VI*; and

- the Treasury may, by order, provide that anything which falls within a specified description or category may not be admitted. They have so provided in respect of securities issued by

  (i)   a private company where the securities in question are securities within the meaning of *Financial Services and Markets Act 2000 (Regulated Activities) Order 2001 (SI 2001 No 544)*; and

  (ii)  an old public company (see APPENDIX 1 DEFINITIONS).

The FCA is authorised to make rules for these purposes and those that relate to the Official List are referred to as the Listing Rules. Listing rules may provide that securities cannot be admitted to the Official List unless listing particulars have been submitted to, and approved by, the FCA and published. The Listing Rules may also specify other documents that have to be published.

Admission to the Official List can be granted only if an application is made to the FCA by (or with the consent of) the issuer and the FCA is satisfied that the requirements of the Listing Rules (and any other requirements it imposes in relation to the application) have been complied with.

[*FSMA 2000, ss 73A(1), (2), 74(1)–(3), 75(1)–(4), 79(1)*].

**Review of the Listing regime and rules**. The whole of the listing regime (the Prospectus Rules, the Listing Rules and the Disclosure and Transparency Rules) was reviewed in 2009 to clarify the structure so that investors can make more informed investment decisions and issuers have more flexibility when raising capital. As a consequence of this review the revised Listing regime and rule changes came into effect on 6 April 2010. The important changes made from 6 April 2010 were to:

- restructure the listing regime for existing and potential issuers, into two segments, premium and standard. 'Premium' indicates standards which are more stringent, super equivalent standards and 'Standard' indicates EU minimum standards;

- strengthen the corporate governance standards for overseas companies (this chapter does not specifically deal with overseas companies)

- require overseas companies with a Standard listing of shares or global depository receipts to comply with the EU Company Reporting Directive; and

- make the Standard listing segment available to UK companies as well as overseas companies.

Further major consultation took place in 2013 and the Listing Rules were amended in May 2014 with the changes coming into effect on 16 May 2014.

Major changes were necessitated by the advent of the *Market Abuse Regulation (EU) 596/2014* ('MAR') which came into force on 3 July 2016 and which the FCA says aims to insert integrity and investor protection by extending the scope of the previous UK market abuse framework to new markets (such as multilateral trading facilities or 'MTFs' which include the Alternative Investment Market of the London Stock Exchange), platforms (such as organised trading facilities or 'OTFs') and new behaviours (such as those relating to the auctioning on an auction platform organised as a regulated market of emission allowances or auctioned products based thereon). MAR was developed under the Lamfalussy process (as detailed in *s 4.3* of the FCA's Guide to the EU and its legislative processes). So it comprises several levels:

## 33.4   Public and Listed Companies

(1)    the *Market Abuse Regulation (EU) 596/2014*;

(2)    implementing measures: European Securities and Markets Authority ('ESMA') technical standards and EU Commission Delegated Acts; and

(3)    ESMA Guidelines and ESMA Questions and Answers 'Q&As',

as well as the FCAs domestic guidance. Insofar as MAR and the delegated acts take the form of EU regulations (which are directly applicable and automatically become part of domestic law), the FCA has responded to it by deleting such parts of its rules as have been superceded (notably large swathes of the former Disclosure Rules) and sign-posting the reader to the appropriate parts of MAR and its subsidiary legislation.

Further major changes were introduced by the *Markets in Financial Instruments Directive 2014/1129* 'MiFID II' which came into force on 3 January 2018. The Markets in Financial Instruments Directive 'MiFID' is the framework EU legislation for investment intermediaries who provide services to clients around financial instruments such as shares, bonds, units in collective investment schemes and derivatives. The *Markets in Financial Instruments Directive 2004* ('MiFID I') has applied in the UK since 2007 but it has been significantly overhauled by MiFID II which was designed to improve the functioning of the financial markets and to strengthen investor protection. MiFID is now made up of:

(1)    MiFID II; and

(2)    the *Markets in Financial Instruments Regulation (EU) 600/2014*.

Again, as an EU Regulation MiFIR is directly applicable and automatically becomes part of domestic law. The Treasury legislation reflecting MiFID II is found in *SI 2017 No 701, SI 2017 No 699* and *SI 2017 No 488*. The FCA has responded to MiFID II/MiFIR in the same way as for MAR by deleting such parts of its rules as have been superceded and sign-posting the reader to the appropriate EU legislation.

In addition, this chapter addresses changes which have been made to the Listing Rules up to July 2018 notably to clarify the requirements for a premium listing especially in relation to issues associated with a sovereign state.

(See www.fca.org.uk/markets/market-abuse/regulation and www.fca.org.uk/markets/mifid -ii.)

The Listing Rules are divided into 21 sections and 2 appendices as follows.

LR 1     Preliminary: All securities (see 33.8)

LR 2     Requirements for listing: All securities (see 33.9)

LR 3     Listing applications: All securities (see 33.12)

LR 4     Listing particulars for professional securities market and certain other securities: All securities (see **33.16–33.16**)

LR 5     Suspending, cancelling and restoring listing and reverse takeovers: All securities (see **33.18**)

LR 6     Additional requirements for premium listing (commercial company) (see **33.10**)

LR 7     Listing principles and Premium listing principles (see **33.19**)

LR 8     Sponsors: Premium listing (see **33.20–33.24**)

LR 9     Continuing obligations (see **33.25–33.34**)

LR 10    Significant transactions: Premium listing (see **33.35–33.37**)

LR 11    Related party transactions: Premium listing (see **33.38–33.40**)

ESMA has also issued guidance which can be accessed at www.esma.europa.eu/sites/default/files/library/2015/10/2015-esma-1415en.pdf.

Compliance with the Listing Rules falls into three categories:

(1)   all securities have to comply with LR1, 2, 3, 4 and 5

(2)   Premium listing – issuers who are commercial companies seeking a Premium listing for equity shares also need to comply with Chapters 6, 7, 8, 9, 10, 11, 12 and 13 (these are the so called 'super equivalent' provisions). Closed-ended investment funds and open-ended investment companies that have Premium listed equity shares must also comply with Chapters 15 and 16 respectively.

A 'Premium listing' is only open to equity shares that are issued by commercial companies and investment entities. An 'equity share' is a share that conveys an unlimited right to the dividends of the company and/or unlimited rights to distribution if the company is liquidated.

Special provisions applicable to Sovereign Controlled Commercial Companies with a Premium Listing are found in CHAPTER 21.

(3)   Standard listing – in addition to compliance with LR1, 2, 3, 4 and 5 a standard listing is available for securities where EU requirements (that is the Prospectus Directive, Prospectus Rules, Market Abuse Regulation, DTRs, Transparency Directive) are met. An issuer with a Standard listing is not required to comply with all the 'super equivalent' provisions (see above).

The FCA may dispense with or modify the Listing Rules in such cases and by reference to such circumstances as it considers appropriate in individual cases (subject to the terms of *EU legislation* and *FSMA 2000*). An application to dispense with or modify a Listing Rule should ordinarily be made in writing (save in circumstances of exceptional urgency):

•   in the case of a continuing obligation, at least five business days before, and

•   for any other Listing Rule, at least ten business days before

the proposed dispensation or modification is to take effect. A dispensation or modification may be either unconditional or subject to specified conditions.

Where an issuer or sponsor has applied for or been granted a dispensation or modification, it must notify the FCA immediately it becomes aware of any matter which is material to the relevance or appropriateness of the dispensation or modification.

## 33.4 Public and Listed Companies

(FCA Listing Rules, paras 1.2.1–1.2.6).

### 33.5 Standard and premium listing explained

**LR 1.5.1G**

(1)    Under the listing rules each issuer must satisfy the requirements in the rules that are specified to apply to it and its relevant securities. In some cases, a listing is described as being either a standard listing or a premium listing.

(2)    A listing that is described as a standard listing sets requirements that are based on the minimum EU directive standards. A listing that is described as a premium listing will include requirements that exceed those required under relevant EU directives.

(3)    Premium listing exists for:

    (a)    equity shares of:

        (i)    commercial companies;

        (ii)    closed-ended investment funds;

        (iii)    open-ended investment companies;

        (iv)    sovereign controlled commercial companies; and

    (b)    certificates representing shares of sovereign controlled commercial companies.

    Any other listing will be a standard listing.

(4)    In the case of equity shares of a commercial company or equity shares or certificates representing shares of a sovereign controlled commercial company, an issuer will have a choice under the listing rules as to whether it has a standard listing or a premium listing. The type of listing it applies for will therefore determine the requirements it must comply with.

(5)    LR 5.4A provides a process for the transfer of the category of listing of equity shares and for the transfer of the category of listing of certificates representing shares.

(6)    In one case, for further classes of equity shares of an investment entity, the equity shares may be admitted to a standard listing provided that, and only for so long as, the issuer has a premium listing of equity shares.

### 33.6 Misleading statements about status

**LR 1.5.2R**

An issuer that is not an issuer with a premium listing must not describe itself or hold itself out (in whatever terms) as having a premium listing or make any representation which suggests, or which is reasonably likely to be understood as suggesting, that it has a premium listing or complies or is required to comply with the requirements that apply to a premium listing.

### 33.7 Listing categories

**LR 1.6.1R**

An issuer must comply with the rules that are applicable to every security in the category of listing which applies to each security the issuer has listed. The categories of listing are:

|   |   |
|---|---|
| (1) | premium listing (commercial company); |
| (2) | premium listing (closed-ended investment fund); |
| (3) | premium listing (open-ended investment companies); |
| (3A) | premium listing (sovereign controlled commercial company); |
| (4) | standard listing (shares); |
| (5) | standard listing (debt and debt-like securities); |
| (6) | standard listing (certificates representing certain securities); |
| (7) | standard listing (securitised derivatives); |
| (8) | standard listing (miscellaneous securities). |

(Not all these categories are addressed in detail in this book in particular provisions relating specifically to close-ended investment funds and open-ended investment companies are not addressed and the focus has been on equity securities.)

**LR 1.6.2R**

An issuer must inform the FCA if the characteristics of a security change so that the security no longer meets the definition of a security in the category in which it has been placed.

**33.8   Enforcement of the Listing Rules**

Issuers must provide the FCA as soon as possible with

(a)   any information and explanations that the FCA may reasonably require to decide whether to grant an application for admission;

(b)   any information the FCA considers appropriate to protect investors or ensure the smooth operation of the market; and

(c)   any other information or explanation that the FCA may reasonably require to verify whether the Listing Rules are being and have been complied with.

The FCA may, at any time, require an issuer to publish such information (in such form and within such time limits) as it considers appropriate for the purposes of (b) above and, if the issuer fails to do so, the FCA may publish the information itself (after giving the issuer an opportunity to explain why the information should not be published).

(FCA Listing Rules, paras 1.3.1, 1.3.2).

**33.9   Requirements for listing**

The provisions of this paragraph apply to all applicants for admission to listing (unless specified otherwise). See **33.10** for additional requirements for premium listings and **33.11** for additional requirements for standard listings. The FCA may not grant an application for admission unless it is satisfied that the Listing Rules and any special requirements are complied with.

•   The applicant (other than a public sector issuer) must be

(i)   duly incorporated or otherwise validly established according to the relevant laws of its place of incorporation or establishment; and

(ii)   operating in conformity with its constitution.

•   The securities must

(i)   conform with the law of the applicant's place of incorporation;

(ii)   be duly authorised according to the applicant's constitution; and

(iii)    have any necessary statutory or other consents.

- Other than securities to which LR4 applies (ie professional securities market and certain other securities), equity shares must be admitted to trading on a regulated market for listed securities operated by a recognised investment exchange' (RIE). All other securities must be admitted to trading on a RIE's market for listed securities. For the meaning of 'equity securities' see **33.4** above.

- The securities must be freely transferable.

- Shares must be fully paid and free from all liens and from any restriction on the right of transfer (except any restriction imposed for failure to comply with a notice under *Companies Act 2006 (CA 2006), s 793* (notice by company requiring information about interests in its shares)).

- Unless the FCA agrees otherwise, the expected aggregate market value of all securities (excluding treasury shares) to be listed must be at least

    (i)    £700,000 for shares, and

    (ii)    £200,000 for debt securities

    unless either relating to a tap issue where the amount of the debt securities is not fixed or securities of the same class are already listed.

- An application for listing of securities of any class must

    (i)    if no securities of that class are already listed, relate to all securities of that class, issued or proposed to be issued; or

    (ii)    if securities of that class are already listed, relate to all further securities of that class, issued or proposed to be issued.

- If, under *FSMA 2000* or the law of another EEA State, a prospectus must be approved and published for the securities or the applicant is permitted and elects to have a prospectus (see **32.3** and **32.7** PROSPECTUSES respectively), in order to be listed

    (i)    a prospectus must have been approved by the FCA and published in relation to the securities; or

    (ii)    if another EEA State is the Home State for the securities (see **32.1** PROSPECTUSES), the relevant competent authority must have supplied the FCA with a certificate of approval, a copy of the prospectus as approved, and (if applicable) a translation of the summary of the prospectus.

- If, under LR 4 (see **33.13**), listing particulars must be approved and published for the securities, those listing particulars must have been approved and published by the FCA.

- Unless the FCA dispenses with LR 2.2.12, convertible securities and miscellaneous securities giving the holder the right to buy or subscribe for other securities may be admitted to listing only if the securities into which they are convertible or over which they give a right to buy or subscribe are already, or will become at the same time, listed securities or securities listed on a regulated, regularly operating, recognised open market.

(FCA Listing Rules, paras 2.2.1–2.2.13).

**EEA States** – see APPENDIX 1 DEFINITIONS.

**33.10**  *Additional requirements for listing for equity securities with a premium listing*

*Premium listings LR Chapter 6*

*Application LR 6.1*

*LR 6.1.1R*

This chapter applies to an applicant for the admission of equity shares to premium listing (commercial company) except where:

(1)    the applicant meets the following conditions:

    (a)    it has an existing premium listing (commercial company) of equity shares;

    (b)    it is applying for the admission of equity shares of the same class as the shares that have been admitted to premium listing; and

    (c)    it is not entering into a transaction classified as a reverse takeover; or

(2)    the following conditions are met:

    (a)    a company has an existing premium listing (commercial company) of equity shares;

    (b)    the applicant is a new holding company of the company in (a); and

    (c)    the company in (a) is not entering into a transaction classified as a reverse takeover.

*Applicant must satisfy requirements in this chapter*

*LR 6.1.2G*

An applicant to whom this chapter applies must satisfy the requirements in this chapter (in addition to those in LR 2).

*Historical financial information LR 6.2*

*LR 6.2.1R*

An applicant must have published or filed historical financial information that:

(1)    covers at least three years;

(2)    represents at least 75% of the applicant's business for the period in (1);

(3)    unless LR 5.6.21R applies, has a latest balance sheet date that is not more than:

    (a)    six months before the date of the prospectus or listing particulars for the relevant shares; and

    (b)    nine months before the date the shares are admitted to listing; and

(4)    includes the consolidated accounts for the applicant and all its subsidiary undertakings.

*LR 6.2.2G*

(1)    In determining what amounts to 75% of the applicant's business for the purpose of LR 6.2.1R(2), the FCA will consider the size, in aggregate, of all of the acquisitions that the applicant has entered into during the period required by LR 6.2.1R(1) and up to the date of the prospectus or listing particulars, relative to the size of the applicant as enlarged by the acquisitions.

(2)　In ascertaining the size of the acquisitions relative to the applicant for the purposes of LR 6.2.1R(2), the FCA will take into account factors such as the assets, profitability and market capitalisation of the businesses.

(3)　The figures used should be the latest available for the acquired entity and the applicant as enlarged by the acquisition or acquisitions.

*LR 6.2.3R*

Where an applicant has made an acquisition or series of acquisitions such that its own consolidated financial information is insufficient to meet the 75% requirement in LR 6.2.1R(2), there must be historical financial information relating to the acquired entity or entities which has been published or filed and that:

(1)　covers the period from at least three years prior to the date under LR 6.2.1R(3) up to the earlier of:

(a)　the date in LR 6.2.1R(3); or

(b)　the date of acquisition by the applicant;

(2)　is prepared and presented in a form that is consistent with the accounting policies adopted in the financial information required by LR 6.2.1R; and

(3)　in aggregate with its own historical financial information represents at least 75% of the enlarged applicant's business for the period in LR 6.2.1R(1).

*Audit requirements for historical financial information*

*LR 6.2.4R*

The historical financial information in LR 6.2.1R and LR 6.2.3R must:

(1)　have been audited or reported on in accordance with the standards acceptable under item 20.1 of Annex I of the PD Regulation; and

(2)　not be subject to a modified report, unless the circumstances set out in LR 6.2.5G apply.

*LR 6.2.5G*

The FCA may accept that LR 6.2.4R(2) has been satisfied where a modified report is present only as a result of:

(1)　the presence of an emphasis-of-matter paragraph which arises in any of the earlier periods required by LR 6.2.1R and the opinion on the final period is unmodified; or

(2)　the opinion on the historical financial information for the final period under LR 6.2.1R includes an emphasis-of-matter paragraph with regard to going concern and LR 6.7.1R (Working capital) is complied with.

*LR 6.2.6R*

An applicant must:

(1)　take all reasonable steps to ensure that the person providing the opinion in LR 6.2.4R(1) is independent of it; and

(2)　obtain written confirmation from the person providing the opinion in LR 6.2.4R(1) that it complies with guidelines on independence issued or approved by its national accountancy or auditing bodies.

*Revenue earning track record requirement LR 6.3*

LR 6.3.1R

The historical financial information required under LR 6.2.1R and LR 6.2.3R must:

(1)     demonstrate that the applicant has a revenue earning track record; and

(2)     put prospective investors in a position to make an informed assessment of the business for which admission is sought.

LR 6.3.2G

(1)     The purpose of LR 6.2.1R(2), LR 6.2.3R, and LR 6.3.1R is to ensure that the applicant has representative financial information throughout the period required by LR 6.2.1R(1) and LR 6.2.3R and to assist prospective investors to make a reasonable assessment of what the future prospects of the applicant's business might be. Investors are then able to consider the applicant's historical financial information in light of its particular competitive advantages, the outlook for the sector in which it operates and the general macro-economic climate.

(2)     The FCA may consider that an applicant does not have representative historical financial information and that its equity shares are not eligible for a premium listing if a significant part or all of the applicant's business has one or more of the following characteristics:

   (a)     a business strategy that places significant emphasis on the development or marketing of products or services which have not formed a significant part of the applicant's historical financial information;

   (b)     the value of the business on admission will be determined, to a significant degree, by reference to future developments rather than past performance;

   (c)     the relationship between the value of the business and its revenue or profit-earning record is significantly different from those of similar companies in the same sector;

   (d)     there is no record of consistent revenue, cash-flow or profit growth throughout the period of the historical financial information;

   (e)     the applicant's business has undergone a significant change in its scale of operations during the period of the historical financial information or is due to do so before or after admission;

   (f)     it has significant levels of research and development expenditure or significant levels of capital expenditure.

*Independent business LR 6.4*

LR 6.4.1R

An applicant must demonstrate that it carries on an independent business as its main activity.

LR 6.4.2G

LR 6.4.1R is intended to ensure that the protections afforded to holders of equity shares by the premium listing requirements are meaningful.

*LR 6.4.3G*

Factors that may indicate that an applicant does not satisfy LR 6.4.1R include situations where:

(1)     a majority of the revenue generated by the applicant's business is attributable to business conducted directly or indirectly with one person or group;

(2)     the applicant cannot demonstrate that it has access to financing other than from one person or group; or

(3)     the applicant does not have:

     (a)     strategic control over the commercialisation of its products; or

     (b)     strategic control over its ability to earn revenue; or

     (c)     freedom to implement its business strategy.

*Controlling shareholders LR 6.5*

*LR 6.5.1R*

An applicant with a controlling shareholder must demonstrate that, despite having a controlling shareholder, the applicant is able to carry on an independent business as its main activity.

*LR 6.5.2G*

LR 6.5.1R is intended to ensure that the protections afforded to holders of equity shares by the premium listing requirements are meaningful.

*LR 6.5.3G*

Factors that may indicate that an applicant does not satisfy the requirement in LR 6.5.1R (even where the agreement in LR 6.5.4R is in place) include:

(1)     an applicant has granted or may be required to grant security over its business in connection with the funding of a controlling shareholder or a member of a controlling shareholder's group; or

(2)     a controlling shareholder (or any associate thereof) appears to be able to influence the operations of the applicant outside its normal governance structures or via material shareholdings in one or more significant subsidiary undertakings; or

(3)     a controlling shareholder appears to be able to exercise improper influence over the applicant; or

(4)     an applicant cannot demonstrate that it has access to financing other than from a controlling shareholder (or an associate thereof).

*LR 6.5.4R*

An applicant with a controlling shareholder upon admission must have in place a written and legally binding agreement with its controlling shareholder which is intended to ensure that the controlling shareholder complies with undertakings that:

(1)     transactions and arrangements with the controlling shareholder (and/or any of its associates) will be conducted at arm's length and on normal commercial terms;

(2)     neither the controlling shareholder nor any of its associates will take any action that would have the effect of preventing the applicant from complying with its obligations under the listing rules; and

(3)     neither the controlling shareholder nor any of its associates will propose or procure the proposal of a shareholder resolution which is intended or appears to be intended to circumvent the proper application of the listing rules.

*LR 6.5.5R*

An applicant with more than one controlling shareholder is not required to enter into a separate agreement with each controlling shareholder if:

(1)     the applicant reasonably considers, in light of its understanding of the relationship between the relevant controlling shareholders, that a controlling shareholder can procure the compliance of another controlling shareholder and that controlling shareholder's associates with the undertakings in LR 6.5.4R; and

(2)     the agreement, which contains the undertakings in LR 6.5.4R, entered into with the relevant controlling shareholder also contains:

    (a)     a provision in which the controlling shareholder agrees to procure the compliance of a non-signing controlling shareholder and its associates with the undertakings in LR 6.5.4R; and

    (b)     the name of such non-signing controlling shareholder.

*Control of the business LR 6.6*

*LR 6.6.1R*

An applicant must demonstrate that it exercises operational control over the business it carries on as its main activity.

*LR 6.6.2G*

LR 6.6.1R is intended to ensure that the protections afforded to holders of holders of equity shares by the premium listing requirements are meaningful.

*LR 6.6.3G*

Factors that may indicate that an applicant does not satisfy the requirement in LR 6.6.1R include where the applicant's business consists principally of holding shares in entities that it does not control, including entities where the applicant:

(1)     owns a minority holding of shares; or

(2)     is only able to exercise negative control; or

(3)     exercises control subject to contractual arrangements which could be altered without the applicant's agreement or could result in a temporary or permanent loss of control.

*Working capital LR 6.7*

*LR 6.7.1R*

An applicant must satisfy the FCA that it and its subsidiary undertakings (if any) have sufficient working capital available for the group's requirements for at least the next 12 months from the date of publication of the prospectus or listing particulars for the shares that are being admitted.

*Warrants or options to subscribe LR 6.8*

*LR 6.8.1R*

The total of all issued warrants to subscribe for equity shares or options to subscribe for equity shares must not exceed 20% of the issued equity share capital (excluding treasury shares) of the applicant as at the time of issue of the warrants or options.

*LR 6.8.2R*

For the purpose of the 20% limit in LR 6.8.1R, rights under employees' share schemes are not included.

*Constitutional arrangements LR 6.9*

*LR 6.9.1R*

An applicant must have in place a constitution that allows it to comply with the listing rules, in particular:

(1)     LR 9.2.21R to vote on matters relevant to premium listing; and

(2)     for an applicant with a controlling shareholder, LR 9.2.2ER and LR 9.2.2FR concerning the election and re-election of independent directors.

*Pre-emption rights*

*LR 6.9.2*

If the law of the country of its incorporation does not confer on shareholders rights which are at least equivalent to LR 9.3.11R, an overseas company applying for a premium listing must:

(1)     ensure its constitution provides for rights which are at least equivalent to the rights provided in LR 9.3.11R (as qualified by LR 9.3.12R); and

(2)     be satisfied that conferring such rights would not be incompatible with the law of the country of its incorporation.

*Externally managed companies LR 6.13*

*LR 6.13.1R*

An applicant must satisfy the FCA that:

(1)     the discretion of its board to make strategic decisions on behalf of the applicant has not been limited or transferred to a person outside the applicant's group; and

(2)     its board has the capability to act on key strategic matters in the absence of a recommendation from a person outside the applicant's group.

*LR 6.13.2G*

In considering whether an applicant has satisfied LR 6.13.1R, the FCA will consider, among other things, whether the board of the applicant consists solely of non-executive directors and whether significant elements of the strategic decision-making of or planning for the applicant take place outside the applicant's group, for example with an external management company.

*Shares in public hands LR 6.14*

*LR 6.14.1R*

Where an applicant is applying for the admission of a class of equity shares to premium listing, a sufficient number of shares of that class must, no later than the time of admission, be distributed to the public in one or more EEA States.

*LR 6.14.2R*

For the purposes of LR 6.14.1R:

(1)   account may also be taken of holders in one or more states that are not EEA States, if the shares are listed in the state or states;

(2)   a sufficient number of shares will be taken to have been distributed to the public when 25% of the shares for which application for admission has been made are in public hands; and

(3)   treasury shares are not to be taken into consideration when calculating the number of shares of the class.

*LR 6.14.3R*

For the purposes of LR 6.14.1R and LR 6.14.2R, shares are not held in public hands if they are:

(1)   held, directly or indirectly by:

　　(a)   a director of the applicant or of any of its subsidiary undertakings; or

　　(b)   a person connected with a director of the applicant or of any of its subsidiary undertakings; or

　　(c)   the trustees of any employees' share scheme or pension fund established for the benefit of any directors and employees of the applicant and its subsidiary undertakings; or

　　(d)   any person who under any agreement has a right to nominate a person to the board of directors of the applicant; or

　　(e)   any person or persons in the same group or persons acting in concert who have an interest in 5% or more of the shares of the relevant class;

(2)   subject to a lock-up period of more than 180 calendar days.

*LR 6.14.4G*

When calculating the number of shares for the purposes of LR 6.14.3R(1)(e), holdings of investment managers in the same group where investment decisions are made independently by the individual in control of the relevant fund and those decisions are unfettered by the group to which the investment manager belongs will be disregarded.

*LR 6.14.5G*

(1)   The FCA may modify LR 6.14.1R to accept a percentage lower than 25% if it considers that the market will operate properly with a lower percentage in view of the large number of shares of the same class and the extent of their distribution to the public.

(2)   In considering whether to grant a modification, the FCA may take into account the following specific factors:

(a)   shares of the same class that are held (even though they are not listed) in states that are not EEA States;

(b)   the number and nature of the public shareholders; and

(c)   in relation to premium listing (commercial companies), whether the expected market value of the shares public hands at admission exceeds £100 million.

*Shares of a non-EEA company LR 6.15*

*LR 6.15.1R*

The FCA will not admit shares of an applicant incorporated in a non-EEA State that are not listed either in its country of incorporation or in the country in which a majority of its shares are held, unless the FCA is satisfied that the absence of the listing is not due to the need to protect investors.

FCA Listing Rules 6.10, 6.11 and 6.12 relate to specialist companies namely mineral companies (LR 6.10), scientific research based companies (LR 6.11) and property companies (LR 6.12).

**33.11   *Standard listings***

A company applying for a standard listing of shares (other than equity shares issued by an investment entity and preference shares that are specialist securities), must comply with the following requirements of Chapter 14 Listing Rules as well as the requirements set out in 33.9 (above).

(1)   Shares in public hands

If an application is made for the admission of a class of shares, 25% of shares of that class must, no later than the time of admission, be distributed to the public in one or more EEA States (see APPENDIX 1 DEFINITIONS). Account may also be taken of holders in non-EEA States if the shares are listed in the state or states.

For these purposes, shares are not held in public hands if they are held, directly or indirectly, by a director of the applicant or any of its subsidiaries (or a person connected with that person);

•   the trustees of any employees' share scheme or pension fund established for the benefit of any directors and employees of the applicant and its subsidiaries;

•   any person who has a right to nominate a person to the board of directors of the applicant; or

•   any person or persons in the same group, or persons acting in concert, who have an interest in 5% or more of the shares of the relevant class or

•   if the shares are subject to a lock-up period of more than 180 days.

Treasury shares are not to be taken into consideration when calculating the number of shares of the class.

The FCA can modify Listing Rule 14 and accept a lower percentage than 25% if it considers that the market will operate properly with a lower percentage in view of the large numbers of shares of the same class and the extent of their distribution to the public. For that purpose the FCA can take account of shares of the same class held in non EEA sates even though they are not listed in those non EEA states.

(2)   Shares of a non EEA company

The FCA will not admit shares of a company incorporated in a non-EEA State (see 33.9) that are not listed either in its country of incorporation or in the country in which a majority of its shares are held, unless it is satisfied that the absence of the listing is not due to the need to protect investors.

(FCA Listing Rules paras 14.1 and 14.2)

## 33.12 Application for listing

All applicants for admission must apply to the FCA by submitting

(a)   certain documents in final form by midday two business days before the FCA are to consider the application;

(b)   certain documents in final form on the day the FCA is to consider application;

(c)   all additional documents, explanations and information as required by the FCA; and

(d)   verification of any information in such manner as the FCA may specify.

The applicant must also pay the appropriate fee.

The documents to be submitted under (*a*) and (*b*) above depend upon the type of security involved and, in the case of shares, whether or not a prospectus has been produced.

For full details, see FCA Listing Rules, paras 3.3 and 3.4.

If the process of applying for admission of securities is likely to be very onerous due to the frequent or irregular nature of allotments and if no prospectus or listing particulars are required for the securities, an applicant may apply for a block listing of a specific number of securities. See FCA Listing Rules, para 3.5.

## 33.13 Listing particulars where prospectus not required

Where an issuer has applied for the admission of

(a)   securities specified in **32.5(*a*)**, (*c*), (*e*)–(*h*) Prospectuses; or

(b)   any other specialist securities for which a prospectus is not required under the *Prospectus Directive*

as no prospectus is required, listing particulars must instead be prepared, approved and published.

(FCA Listing Rules, paras 4.1.1, 4.1.2).

**General duty of disclosure.** In addition to any information required by the Listing Rules or otherwise by the FCA, listing particulars submitted to the FCA must contain all such information as investors and their professional advisers would reasonably require, and reasonably expect to find there, for the purpose of making an informed assessment of

•   the assets and liabilities, financial position, profits and losses, and prospects of the issuer of the securities; and

•   the rights attaching to the securities.

The information to be included is that which is within the knowledge of the persons responsible for the listing particulars or which it would be reasonable for them to obtain by making enquiries. In determining this, regard must be had to

- the nature of the securities and the issuer;

- the nature of the potential investors;

- the fact that certain matters may reasonably be expected to be within the knowledge of professional advisers of a kind which potential investors may reasonably be expected to consult; and

- any information available to investors or their professional advisers as a result of requirements imposed on the issuer by a recognised investment exchange, by Listing Rules or by or under any other *Act*.

[*FSMA 2000, s 80*].

**Exemptions from disclosure.** The FCA may authorise the omission from listing particulars of any information which would otherwise be required on the following grounds.

(i)   Its disclosure would be contrary to the public interest. The Secretary of State or the Treasury may issue a certificate to the effect that the disclosure of any information would be contrary to the public interest. In such a case, the FCA is entitled to act on any such certificate in exercising its powers under this provision.

(ii)  Its disclosure would be seriously detrimental to the issuer. But no authorisation can be granted, and any authorisation granted does not extend to, '*essential information*', ie information which a person considering acquiring securities of the kind in question would be likely to need in order not to be misled about any facts which it is essential for him to know in order to make an informed assessment.

(iii) In the case of specified securities, its disclosure is unnecessary for persons of the kind who may be expected normally to buy or deal in securities of that kind.

[*FSMA 2000, s 82*].

**Contents and format.**

(1)   *Summary*

The listing particulars of securities within (*a*) above must contain a summary as required for a prospectus under the Prospectus Rules (see **32.8 PROSPECTUSES**).

(2)   *Format*

The listing particulars must be in a format that complies with the relevant requirements in the Prospectus Rules and *EC Commission Regulation 809/2004* (as if those requirements applied to the listing particulars).

(3)   *Minimum information to be included*

The following minimum information must be included in listing particulars (see **32.10 PROSPECTUSES**).

- For an issue of bonds (including bonds convertible into the issuer's shares or exchangeable into a third party issuer's shares or derivative securities), irrespective of the denomination of the issue, the information required by *Annex IX*.

- The additional information required by the underlying share building block where relevant.

- For an issue of asset-backed securities, irrespective of the denomination per unit of the issue, the information required by *Annexes VII* and *VIII*.

- For an issue of certificates representing shares, irrespective of the denomination per unit of the issue, the information required by *Annex X* (except for item 13.2 relating to profit forecasts).

- For an issue of securities by the government of a non-EEA State (see **33.9**) or a local or regional authority of a non-EEA State, the information required by *Annex XVI*.

- For all issues that are guaranteed, the information in *Annex VI*.

For all other issues, the FCA would expect issuers to follow the most appropriate schedules and building blocks to determine the minimum information to be included in listing particulars.

(4) *Incorporation by reference*

An issuer may incorporate information by reference in the listing particulars as in **32.11 PROSPECTUSES**.

(5) *Equivalent information*

An issuer may include equivalent information in listing particulars as in **32.12 PROSPECTUSES**.

(6) *English language*

Listing particulars must be in English.

(7) *Omission of information*

A request to the FCA to authorise the omission of specific information in a particular case must be in writing from the issuer and identify the specific information concerned and the specific reasons for the omission. It must state why, in the issuer's opinion, one or more of the grounds for exemption from disclosure in *FSMA 2000, s 82* above applies.

(FCA Listing Rules, paras 4.2.2–4.2.10).

**Final terms.** If final terms of the offer are not included in the listing particulars,

- the final terms must be provided to investors, filed with the FCA, and made available to the public (as if the relevant requirements in **32.17 PROSPECTUSES** relating to filing and making available applied to the final terms of the offer); and

- the listing particulars must disclose the criteria and/or the conditions in accordance with which the above elements will be determined or, in the case of price, the maximum price.

(FCA Listing Rules, para 4.4.3).

**33.14** *Responsibility for listing particulars*

Subject to below, the persons responsible for listing particulars (including supplementary listing particulars) are as follows.

(a) The issuer of the securities.

(b) Where the issuer is a body corporate, each person who is a director of that body at the time when the particulars are submitted to the FCA. But a person is not to be treated as responsible in these circumstances if the particulars are published without his knowledge or consent and, on becoming aware of their publication, he forthwith gives reasonable public notice that they were published without his knowledge or consent.

(c)   Where the issuer is a body corporate, each person who has authorised himself to be named, and is named, in the particulars as a director or as having agreed to become a director of that body either immediately or at a future time.

(d)   Each person who accepts, and is stated in the particulars as accepting, responsibility for the particulars.

(e)   Each person not falling within (a)–(d) above who has authorised the contents of the particulars.

When accepting responsibility for particulars under (d) above or authorising their contents under (e) above, a person may state that he does so only in relation to certain specified parts of the particulars, or only in certain specified respects. In such a case he is responsible only to the extent specified and only if the material in question is included in (or substantially in) the form and context to which he has agreed.

Nothing in the above rules is to be construed as making a person responsible for any particulars by reason of giving advice as to their contents in a professional capacity.

[*SI 2001 No 2956, Reg 6*].

*Specialist securities.* Where listing particulars relate to securities of a kind specified by the Listing Rules for the purposes of **33.13**(iii) (disclosure of information unnecessary for persons of the kind who may be expected normally to buy or deal in securities of that kind) no person is to be treated as responsible for the particulars under (a)–(c) above but without prejudice to his being responsible under (d) above. [*SI 2001 No 2956, Reg 9*].

In the case of listing particulars for specialist securities

- the issuer must state in the listing particulars that it accepts responsibility for the listing particulars;

- the directors may state that they accept responsibility for the listing particulars; and

- other persons may state that they accept responsibility for all or part of the listing particulars, in which case the statement by the issuer or directors may be appropriately modified.

An issuer that is the government of a non–EEA State (see **33.9**) or a local or regional authority of a non–EEA State is not required to state that it accepts responsibility for the listing particulars.

(FCA Listing Rules, para 4.2.13).

**33.15**   *Supplementary listing particulars*

An issuer must submit supplementary listing particulars if at any time

- after the preparation of listing particulars which have been submitted to the FCA, and

- before the commencement of dealings in the securities concerned following their admission to the official list

there is a 'significant' change affecting any matter contained in those particulars or a significant new matter arises, the inclusion of information in respect of which would have been required.

'*Significant*' means significant for the purposes of making an informed assessment of assets and liabilities, financial position, profits and losses and prospects of the issuer and any rights attaching to the securities.

If the issuer is not aware of the change or new matter in question, he is not under a duty to comply unless he is notified of the change or new matter by a person responsible for the listing particulars. But it is the duty of any person responsible for those particulars who is aware of such a change or new matter to give notice of it to the issuer.

The provisions also apply to matter contained in any supplementary listing particulars previously published under these provisions in respect of the securities in question.

[*FSMA 2000, s 81*].

**33.16** *Approval and publication of listing particulars*

An application for approval of listing particulars or supplementary listing particulars must comply with the procedures in **32.13** Prospectuses (as if those procedures applied to the application), except that the applicant does not need to submit a completed Form A.

The FCA cannot grant an application for admission unless it is satisfied that the requirements of *FSMA 2000* and the Listing Rules are complied with.

*Notifying decision.* The FCA must notify the applicant in writing of its decision within six months of the date on which the application is received (or, where the applicant is asked to provide further information, within six months of the date on which that information is provided). [*FSMA 2000, s 76(1)–(3)*]. However, in practice, the FCA will try to notify the applicant of its decision within the same time limits as are specified in *FSMA 2000, s 87C* for approval of a prospectus or supplementary prospectus (see **32.14** Prospectuses). (FCA Listing Rules, para 4.3.3).

*Refusal of application.* The FCA may refuse an application for listing

•   if it considers that, for a reason relating to the issuer, granting it would be detrimental to the interests of the investor; or

•   in the case of securities already officially listed in another EEA State (see **33.9**), if the issuer has failed to comply with any obligations to which he is subject as a result of that listing.

If it decides to do so, the FCA must give the applicant a warning notice. If, following comments from the applicant (if any), it still decides to refuse the application, it must give the applicant a decision notice. The applicant may then refer the matter to the Tribunal.

[*FSMA 2000, ss 75(5), (6), 76(3)–(6)*].

*Publication of listing particulars.* An issuer must ensure that listing particulars or supplementary listing particulars are not published until they have been approved by the FCA. Once approved, the issuer must ensure that they are filed and published as if the relevant requirements in PR 3.2 the Prospectus Directive Regulation and Commission Delegated Regulation (EU) 2016/301 (see **32.17** Prospectuses) applied to them.

(FCA Listing Rules, paras 4.3.5 and 4.4.2).

**33.17** *Compensation for statements in listing particulars*

A remedy may be available to a person who acquires securities and suffers loss in respect of them. Subject to below, there are two heads of liability.

(a)   Any person responsible for listing particulars (see **33.14**) or supplementary listing particulars is liable to pay compensation to a person who has acquired securities to which the particulars apply and suffered loss in respect of them as a result of any untrue or misleading statement in the particulars or the omission of any matter required to be included. If listing particulars are required to include information about the absence of a particular matter, the omission of that information is treated as a statement that there is no such matter.

(b)   Any person who fails to comply with the requirements relating to supplementary listing particulars is liable to pay compensation to anyone who has acquired securities and suffered loss as a result of the failure.

References to acquiring securities include contracting to acquire them or any interest in them.

*Exemption from liability.* A person does not incur liability under the above provisions in the following circumstances.

(i)   Under (*a*) above, a person does not incur liability if he satisfies the court that, having made reasonable enquiries, he reasonably believed at the time when the listing particulars were submitted to the FCA, that the statement was true and not misleading or that the matter omitted was properly omitted. He must also show that one or more of the following conditions are satisfied.

- He continued in that belief until the securities were acquired.

- They were acquired before it was reasonably practicable to bring a correction to the attention of potential investors.

- He had, before the securities were acquired, taken all reasonable steps to bring a correction to the attention of potential investors.

- He continued in that belief until after the commencement of dealings in the securities following their admission to trading and that the securities were acquired after such a lapse of time that he ought to be excused.

(ii)   Under (*a*) above, a person does not incur any liability if the statement was made (or purports to be made) by another person as an 'expert' and was stated to be included with the consent of that other person, and the person satisfies the court that, at the time the listing particulars were submitted to the FCA for approval, he reasonably believed that the other person

- was competent to make or authorise the statement; and

- had consented to its inclusion.

He must in addition satisfy the court that one or more of the following conditions are satisfied.

- He continued in that belief until the securities were acquired.

- They were acquired before it was reasonably practicable to bring the fact that the expert was not competent, or had not consented, to the attention of potential investors.

- He had, before the securities were acquired, taken all reasonable steps to bring those facts to the attention of potential investors.

- He continued in that belief until after the commencement of dealings in the securities following their admission to trading and the securities were acquired after such a lapse of time that he ought to be excused.

*'Expert'* includes any engineer, valuer, accountant or other person whose profession, qualifications or experience give authority to a statement made by him.

(iii)   Under (*a*) above, a person does not incur any liability if he satisfies the court that

- before the securities were acquired

   (i)   a correction, or

(ii)    the fact that the expert was not competent or had not consented

had been published in a manner calculated to bring it to the attention of potential investors; or

- he has taken all reasonable steps to secure such publication and reasonably believed that publication had taken place before the securities were acquired.

(iv)    Under (*a*) above, a person does not incur any liability if the statement was made by an official person or contained in a public official document and he satisfies the court that it is accurately and fairly reproduced.

(v)    Under (*a*) and (*b*) above, a person does not incur any liability if he satisfies the court that the person suffering the loss acquired the securities with knowledge that the statement was false or misleading or, as the case may be, knowledge of the omitted matter or the change or new matter.

(vi)    Under (*b*) above, a person does not incur any liability if he satisfies the court that the change or new matter in question was not such as to call for supplementary listing particulars.

A person is not to be subject to civil liability solely on the basis of a summary (or any translation of it) in listing particulars unless the summary, when read with the rest of the listing particulars is misleading, inaccurate or inconsistent or does not provide key information as defined in *FSMA 2000*.

[*FSMA 2000, s 90, Sch 10; SI 2012 No 1538 Reg 7*].

## 33.18    Suspending, cancelling and restoring listing

**Suspending of listing by FCA.** The FCA may, in accordance with the Listing Rules

- discontinue the listing of any securities if satisfied that there are special circumstances which preclude normal dealings in the securities; and

- suspend the listing of any securities.

It may do so on its own initiative or on the application of the issuer. In the former case, the issuer may refer the matter to the Tribunal.

[*FSMA 2000, s 77; SI 2007 No 1973*].

See *FSMA 2000, ss 78, 78A* for the procedures which the FCA must follow if it proposes to discontinue or suspend a listing of securities (or does so with immediate effect) on its own initiative or at the request of the issuer respectively.

The FCA may take such action if the smooth operation of the market is, or may be, temporarily jeopardised or it is necessary to protect investors. (FCA Listing Rules, para 5.1.1).

**Cancelling of listing by FCA.** The FCA may cancel the listing of securities if satisfied that there are special circumstances that preclude normal regular dealings in them. It will generally seek to cancel the listing of an issuer's equity shares or certificates representing equity securities when the issuer completes a reverse takeover. (FCA Listing Rules, paras 5.2.1, 5.2.3).

**Cancellation of listing of equity shares at issuer's request**.

An issuer must satisfy the requirements in LR 5.2.4–5.2.12 and LR 5.3 before the FCA will cancel the listing of its securities at its request.

*LR 5.2.5R*

Subject to LR 5.2.7R, LR 5.2.10R, LR 5.2.11AR and LR 5.2.12R, an issuer with a premium listing that wishes the FCA to cancel the listing of any of its securities with a premium listing must:

<ol>
<li value="1">send a circular to the holders of the relevant securities. The circular must:
<ul>
<li>(a) comply with the requirements of LR 13.3.1R and LR 13.3.2R (contents of all circulars);</li>
<li>(b) be submitted to the FCA for approval prior to publication; and</li>
<li>(c) include the anticipated date of cancellation (which must be not less than 20 business days following the passing of the resolution referred to in paragraph (2));</li>
</ul>
</li>
<li value="2">in the case of a cancellation of listing of equity shares, obtain, at a general meeting, the prior approval of a resolution for the cancellation from:
<ul>
<li>(a) a majority of not less than 75% of the votes attaching to the shares voted on the resolution; and</li>
<li>(b) where an issuer has a controlling shareholder, a majority of the votes attaching to the shares of independent shareholders voted on the resolution;</li>
</ul>
</li>
</ol>

(2A)   in the case of a cancellation of listing of certificates representing shares, obtain, at a meeting of the holders of the certificates, the prior approval of a resolution for the cancellation from:

    (a)   a majority of not less than 75% in value of the certificates representing shares in issue at the time of the meeting that are voted on the resolution; and

    (b)   where an issuer has a controlling shareholder, a majority in value of the certificates representing shares in issue at the time of the meeting that are:

        (i)   held by holders of certificates other than the controlling shareholder; and

        (ii)   that are voted on the resolution;

<ol>
<li value="3">notify a RIS, at the same time as the circular is despatched to the relevant holders of the securities, of the intended cancellation and of the notice period and meeting; and</li>
<li value="4">notify a RIS of the passing of the resolution in accordance with LR 9.6.18R or (as applicable) LR 21.8.11R</li>
</ol>

*LR 5.2.7R*

LR 5.2.5R(2) and (2A) will not apply where an issuer of securities notifies a RIS:

<ol>
<li>that the financial position of the issuer or its group is so precarious that, but for the proposal referred to in LR 5.2.7R (2), there is no reasonable prospect that the issuer will avoid going into formal insolvency proceedings;</li>
<li>that there is a proposal for a transaction, arrangement or other form of reconstruction of the issuer or its group which is necessary to ensure the survival of the issuer or its group and the continued listing would jeopardise the successful completion of the proposal;</li>
<li>explaining:
<ul>
<li>(a) why the cancellation is in the best interests of those to whom the issuer or its directors have responsibilities (including the bodies of securities holders and creditors, taken as a whole); and</li>
</ul>
</li>
</ol>

(b)    why the approval of shareholders or, in the case of certificates representing shares, holders of certificates will not be sought prior to the cancellation of listing; and

(4)    giving at least 20 business days' notice of the intended cancellation.

**Cancellation of listing of other securities (other than equity shares with a premium listing) at the issuer's request.** The issuer must notify a RIS, giving at least 20 business days' notice of the intended cancellation, but is not required to obtain the approval of the holders of those securities as under (b) above. Where the securities are debt securities, the issuer must also notify the holders or a representative of the holders, in accordance with the terms and conditions of the issue of those securities, of intended cancellation but the prior approval of holders in general meeting does not need to be obtained.

**Cancellation in relation to takeover offers: offeror interested in 50% or less of the voting rights.**

*LR 5.2.10R*

LR 5.2.5R does not apply to the cancellation of securities with a premium listing in the case of a takeover offer if:

(1)    the offeror or any controlling shareholder who is an offeror is interested in 50% or less of the voting rights of an issuer before announcing its firm intention to make its takeover offer;

(2)    the offeror has by virtue of its shareholdings and acceptances of its takeover offer, acquired or agreed to acquire issued share capital carrying 75% of the voting rights of the issuer; and

(3)    the offeror has stated in the offer document or any subsequent circular sent to the holders of the shares that a notice period of not less than 20 business days prior to cancellation will commence either on the offeror obtaining the required 75% as described in LR 5.2.10R(2) or on the first date of issue of compulsory acquisition notices under section 979 of the Companies Act 2006 (Right of offeror to buy out minority shareholder).

For these purposes the offer document or circular must make clear that the notice period begins only when the offeror has announced that it has acquired or agreed to acquire shares representing 75% of the voting rights.

The issuer must notify shareholders and, in the case of certificates representing shares, holders of certificates that the required 75% has been obtained and that the notice period has commenced and of the anticipated date of cancellation, or the explanatory letter or other material accompanying the section 979 notice must state that the notice period has commenced and the anticipated date of cancellation.

**Cancellation in relation to takeover offers: offeror interested in more than 50% of voting rights.**

*LR 5.2.11AR*

LR 5.2.5R does not apply to the cancellation of securities with a premium listing in the case of a takeover offer if:

(1)    the offeror or any controlling shareholder who is an offeror is interested in more than 50% of the voting rights of an issuer before announcing its firm intention to make its takeover offer;

(2)    the offeror has by virtue of its shareholdings and acceptances of its takeover offer, acquired or agreed to acquire issued share capital carrying 75% of the voting rights of the issuer;

(3)    the offeror has obtained acceptances of its takeover offer or acquired or agreed to acquire shares from independent shareholders that represent a majority of the voting rights held by the independent shareholders on the date its firm intention to make its takeover offer was announced; and

(4)    the offeror has stated in the offer document or any subsequent circular sent to the holders of the shares that a notice period of not less than 20 business days prior to cancellation will commence either on the offeror obtaining the relevant shareholding and acceptances as described in LR 5.2.11AR(2) to (3) or on the first date of issue of compulsory acquisition notices under section 979 of the Companies Act 2006.

For the purposes of LR 5.2.11A(4), the offer document or circular must make clear that the notice period begins only when the offeror has announced that it has acquired or agreed to acquire shares representing 75% of the voting rights and, if relevant, has obtained acceptances of its takeover offer or acquired or agreed to acquire shares from independent shareholders that represent a majority of the voting rights held by the independent shareholders.

*LR 5.2.11CR*

The issuer must notify shareholders and, in the case of certificates representing shares, holders of certificates that the relevant thresholds described in LR 5.2.11AR(2) to (3) have been obtained and that the notice period has commenced and of the anticipated date of cancellation, or the explanatory letter or other material accompanying the section 979 notice must state that the notice period has commenced and the anticipated date of cancellation.

**Cancellation as a result of schemes of arrangement, etc. .**

*LR 5.2.12R*

LR 5.2.5R and LR 5.2.8R do not apply to the cancellation of equity shares and certificates representing shares as a result of:

(1)    a takeover or restructuring of the issuer effected by a scheme of arrangement under Part 26 of the Companies Act 2006; or

(2)    an administration or liquidation of the issuer pursuant to a court order under the Insolvency Act 1986, Building Societies Act 1986, Water Industry Act 1991, Banking Act 2009, Energy Act 2011 or the Investment Bank Special Administration Regulations 2011; or

(3)    the appointment of an administrator under paragraphs 14 (appointment by holder of floating charge) or 22 (appointment by company or directors) of Schedule B1 to the Insolvency Act 1986; or

(4)    a resolution for winding up being passed under section 84 of the Insolvency Act 1986; or

(5)    the appointment of a provisional liquidator by the court under section 135 of the Insolvency Act 1986; or

(6)    a company voluntary arrangement pursuant to Part 1 of the Insolvency Act 1986, subject to the time limits for the challenge of decisions made set out in Part 1 of the Insolvency Act 1986 having expired; or

(7)    statutory winding up or reconstruction measures in relation to an overseas issuer under equivalent overseas legislation having similar effect to those set out in (1) to (6).

(FCA Listing Rules, paras 5.2.4–5.2.12).

**Information to be supplied to the FCA.** See FCA Listing Rules, paras 5.3.1 and 5.3.2 for information to be included in, and supplied with, a request to suspend or cancel a listing.

**Timing of requests.** A written request by an issuer to have the listing of its securities

- suspended should be made as soon as practicable (suspension requests received for the opening of the market should allow sufficient time for the FCA to deal with the request before trading starts); and

- cancelled must be made not less than 24 hours before the cancellation is expected to take effect.

(FCA Listing Rules, paras 5.3.4, 5.3.5).

**Withdrawing request.** An issuer may withdraw its request at any time before the suspension or cancellation takes effect. (FCA Listing Rules, para 5.3.7).

**Restoring listing.** If an issuer has the listing of its securities cancelled, it may only have them re-admitted to the official list by re-applying for their listing.

The FCA may restore the listing of any securities that have been suspended if it considers that the smooth operation of the market is no longer jeopardised or if the suspension is no longer required to protect investors. The FCA may restore the listing even though the issuer does not request it.

An issuer that has the listing of any of its securities suspended may request the FCA to have them restored. The FCA will refuse such a request if it is not satisfied that the smooth operation of the market is no longer jeopardised or if the suspension is still required to protect investors.

(FCA Listing Rules, paras 5.4.1–5.4.4).

**Transfer between listing categories: equity shares.**

An issuer may apply to the FCA to transfer between listing categories (ie from a standard listing to a premium listing or vice versa) subject in certain cases to obtaining shareholder approval or making an announcement. The FCA will not usually review eligibility requirements where the issuer has previously been assessed as meeting those requirements but if the transfer involves a reconstitution of the capital an issuer needs to consider whether a prospectus is necessary. (FCA Listing Rules, paras 5.4A1–5.4A.17).

**Suspension, cancellation or restoration by overseas exchange or authority.** An issuer must inform the FCA if its listing has been suspended, cancelled or restored by an overseas exchange or overseas authority. (FCA Listing Rules, para 5.5.2).

**Reverse takeovers.** This section applies to companies with a premium listing and companies with a standards listing relating to shares save where the issuer is acquiring shares in a target company with the same category of listing as the issuer. It is without prejudice to the obligations a premium listed company has under LR 10 (Significant Transactions).

A reverse takeover occurs when an issuer acquires a business, company or assets which result in a fundamental change to its business or where the application of the class tests prescribed in LR 10 result in a percentage higher than 100%, ie where the issuer is buying a target bigger than it is.

In such circumstances a premium listed company needs to consult its sponsor.

The FCA will normally suspend the listing and cancel it if the takeover succeeds (so that the issuer has to reapply for a listing) unless the issuer is in a position to supply the FCA with an eligibility letter or chooses to transfer to another listing category.

## 33.18 Public and Listed Companies

Special provisions apply to shell companies.

(FCA Listing Rules, paras 5.6.1–5.6.29).

Reverse takeovers are considered in more detail in paragraph 33.35 below in the context of significant transactions by premium listed companies.

### 33.19 The Listing Principles: Premium listing

The Listing Principles apply to every listed company and in addition the Premium Listing Principles apply to every company with a premium listing of equity shares.

The purpose of the Listing Principles below is to ensure that listed companies pay due regard to the fundamental role they play in maintaining market confidence and ensuring fair and orderly markets They are designed to assist listed companies in identifying their obligations and responsibilities under the listing rules, disclosure requirements transparency rules and corporate governance rules.

The Listing Principles are as follows:

(1)     A listed company must take reasonable steps to establish and maintain adequate procedures, systems and controls to enable it to comply with its obligations.

(2)     A listed company must deal with the FCA in an open and co-operative manner.

The Premium Listing Principles are as follows:

(1)     A listed company must take reasonable steps to enable its directors to understand their responsibilities and obligations as directors.

(2)     A listed company must act with integrity towards holders and potential holders of its premium listed shares.

(3)     All equity shares in a class that have been admitted to premium listing must carry an equal number of votes on any shareholder vote.

(4)     Where a listed company has more than one class of equity shares admitted to premium listing, the aggregate voting rights of the shares in each class should be broadly proportionate to the relative interests of those classes in the equity of the listed company.

(5)     A listed company must ensure that it treats all holders of the same class of its listed equity shares that are in the same position equally in respect of the rights attaching to such listed equity shares.

(6)     A listed company must communicate information to holders and potential holders of its listed equity shares in such a way as to avoid the creation or continuation of a false market in those listed equity shares.

(FCA Listing Rules, paras 7.1.1–7.2.1A).

### Guidance on the listing and premium listing principles

Listing Principle 1 is intended to ensure that listed companies have adequate procedures, systems and controls to enable them to comply with their obligations under the listing rules, disclosure requirements, transparency rules and corporate governance rules. In particular, the FCA considers that listed companies should place particular emphasis on ensuring that they have adequate procedures, systems and controls in relation to, where applicable

•      identifying whether any obligations arise under LR 10 (Significant transactions) and LR 11 (Related party transactions); and

- the timely and accurate disclosure of information to the market.

Timely and accurate disclosure of information to the market is a key obligation of listed companies. For the purposes of Listing Principle 1 a listed company should have adequate systems and controls to be able to

- ensure that it can properly identify information which requires disclosure under the listing rules, disclosure rules, transparency rules or corporate governance rules in a timely manner; and

- ensure that any information identified under the above is properly considered by the directors and that such a consideration encompasses whether the information should be disclosed.

In assessing whether the voting rights attaching to different classes of premium listed securities are proportionate for the purposes of Premium Listing Principle 4, the FCA will have regard to the following non-exhaustive list of factors:

(1)     the extent to which the rights of the classes differ other than their voting rights, for example with regard to dividend rights or entitlement to any surplus capital on winding up;

(2)     the extent of dispersion and relative liquidity of the classes; and/or

(3)     the commercial rationale for the difference in the rights.

(FCA Listing Rules, paras 7.2.2–7.2.4).

## 33.20  Sponsors: Premium listing

*When a sponsor must be appointed*

*LR 8.2.1R*

A company with, or applying for, a premium listing of its securities must appoint a sponsor on each occasion that it:

(1)     is required to submit any of the following documents to the FCA in connection with an application for admission of securities to premium listing:

    (a)     a prospectus, supplementary prospectus or equivalent document; or

    (b)     a certificate of approval from another competent authority; or

    (c)     a summary document as required by PR 1.2.3R(8); or

    (d)     listing particulars referred to in LR 15.3.3R, LR 16.3.4R, LR 21.3.3R or LR 21.7.4R or supplementary listing particulars; or

(2)     is required to submit to the FCA a class 1 circular for approval; or

(3)     is required to submit to the FCA a circular that proposes a reconstruction or a refinancing which is required by LR 9.5.12R to include a working capital statement; or

(4)     is required to submit to the FCA a circular for the proposed purchase of own shares: which is required by LR 13.7.1R(2) to include a working capital statement; or

(Note: This does not include a circular issued by a closed-ended investment company.)

(5)    is required to do so by the FCA because it appears to the FCA that there is, or there may be, a breach of the listing rules, the disclosure requirements or the transparency rules by the listed company; or

(6)    is required by LR 11.1.10R(2)(b) to provide a listed company with a confirmation that the terms of the proposed related party transaction are fair and reasonable; or

(7)    is required to submit to the FCA a related party circular which is required by LR 13.6.1R(5) to include a statement by the board that the transaction or arrangement is fair and reasonable; or

(8)    is required by LR 8.4.3R(4) to submit to the FCA a letter from a sponsor in relation to the applicant's eligibility; or

(9)    is required to make an announcement or request a suspension in connection with a reverse takeover under LR 5.6.6R; or

(10)    provides to the FCA a disclosure regime confirmation in connection with a reverse takeover under LR 5.6.12G(1); or

(11)    makes a disclosure announcement in connection with a reverse takeover under LR 5.6.15G that contains a declaration described in LR 5.6.15G(3) or LR 5.6.15G(4); or

(12)    submits to the FCA a letter in relation to the issuer's eligibility in connection with a reverse takeover under LR 5.6.23G(2); or

(13)    provides confirmation to the FCA of its severe financial difficulty for the purposes of LR 10.8.3G(2); or

(14)    is required to provide an assessment of the appropriateness of an investment exchange or multilateral trading facility under LR 13.5.27BR; or

(15)    is required to provide a written opinion to the FCA under LR 11 Annex 1(8) (joint investment arrangements).

*LR 8.2.1AR A company must appoint a sponsor where it applies to transfer its category of listing*

A listed company with a premium listing must also obtain a sponsor's guidance if it is proposing to enter into a transaction which due to its size or nature could amount to a Class 1 transaction or a reverse takeover in order to assess the application of the listing rules, disclosure requirements and the transparency rules (see **33.35**); or enter into a transaction which is, or may be, a related party transaction in order to assess the application of the listing rules, the disclosure requirements and the transparency rules (see **33.38**).

(FCA Listing Rules, paras 8.2.1–8.2.3).

For details of the specific duties of a sponsor in relation to transactions, see FCA Listing Rules, paras 8.4.1–8.4.17.

**33.21**  *Approval, appointment and dismissal*

*Approval.* Sponsors must be approved by the FCA which maintains a list of approved sponsors on its website.

The FCA will approve a person as a sponsor only if it is satisfied that the person

•    is an authorised person or a member of a designated professional body;

•    is competent to perform sponsor services in accordance with LR8; and

•    has appropriate systems and controls in place to ensure that it can carry out its role as a sponsor in accordance with LR 8.

*LR 8.6.7*

A sponsor, or a person applying for approval as a sponsor, will not satisfy LR 8.6.5R(2) unless it has:

(1) submitted a sponsor declaration to the FCA

- for a person applying for approval as a sponsor, within three years of the date of its application; and

- for a sponsor, within the previous three years; and

(2) a sufficient number of employees with the skills, knowledge and expertise necessary for it to

- provide sponsor services in accordance with LR 8.3;

- understand

(i)  the rules, guidance and ESMA publications directly relevant to sponsor services;

(ii)  the procedural requirements and processes of the FCA;

(iii)  the due diligence process required in order to provide sponsor services in accordance with LR 8.3 and LR 8.4;

(iv)  the responsibilities and obligations of a sponsor in LR 8;

(v)  specialist industry sectors, if relevant to the sponsor services it provides or intends to provide; and

(vi)  be able to comply with the key contact requirements in LR 8.6.19 R.

To determine whether a sponsor or a person applying for approval as a sponsor is able to satisfy LR 8.6.7R(1)(a), the FCA may consider whether any of the person's employees have had material involvement in the provision of sponsor services that have required the submission of a sponsor declaration within the previous three years.

In exceptional circumstances, the FCA may consider dispensing with, or modifying, the requirement in LR 8.6.7R(1) in accordance with LR 1.2.1R.

In assessing whether a sponsor or a person applying for approval as a sponsor satisfies LR 8.6.7R(2), the FCA will consider a variety of factors including

(1)  the nature, scale and complexity of its business;

(2)  the diversity of its operations;

(3)  the volume and size of transactions it undertakes;

(4)  the volume and size of transactions it anticipates undertaking in the following year; and

(5)  the degree of risk associated with the transactions it undertakes or anticipates undertaking in the following year.

Notwithstanding LR 8.6.7CG, when considering whether a sponsor satisfies LR 8.6.7R(2)(c) the FCA expects a sponsor to have no less than two employees who are able to satisfy the key contact requirements in LR 8.6.19R(2).

(FCA Listing Rules, paras 8.6.1–8.6.20).

## 33.21   Public and Listed Companies

*Appointment*. A listed company or applicant must ensure that the FCA is informed promptly of the name and contact details of any sponsor appointed (by the listed company, applicant or sponsor).

Where more than one sponsor is appointed, the company must

(a)   ensure that one sponsor takes responsibility for contact with the FCA in respect of administrative arrangements for the sponsor service; and

(b)   inform the FCA promptly, in writing, of the name and contact details of the sponsor taking responsibility under (*a*) above.

A company should co-operate with its sponsor.

(FCA Listing Rules, paras 8.5.1–8.5.3 and 8.5.6).

### 33.22   *Responsibilities of a sponsor*

*LR 8.3.1R*

A sponsor must in relation to a sponsor service:

(1)   referred to in LR 8.2.1R(1) to (4), LR 8.2.1R(11), LR 8.2.1A R and, where relevant LR 8.2.1R(5), provide assurance to the FCA when required that the responsibilities of the company with or applying for a premium listing of its securities under the listing rules have been met;

(1A)   provide to the FCA any explanation or confirmation in such form and within such time limit as the FCA reasonably requires for the purposes of ensuring that the listing rules are being complied with by a company with or applying for a premium listing of its securities; and

(2)   guide the company with or applying for a premium listing of its securities in understanding and meeting its responsibilities under the listing rules, the disclosure requirements and the transparency rules.

A sponsor must, for so long as it provides a sponsor service, take such reasonable steps as are sufficient to ensure that any communication or information it provides to the FCA in carrying out the sponsor service is, to the best of its knowledge and belief, accurate and complete in all material respects and as soon as possible provide to the FCA any information of which it becomes aware that materially affects the accuracy or completeness of information it has previously provided.

Where a sponsor provides information to the FCA which is or is based on information it has received from a third party, in assessing whether a sponsor has complied with its obligations in LR 8.3.1A(1) the FCA will have regard, amongst other things, to whether a sponsor has appropriately used its own knowledge, judgment and expertise to review and challenge the information provided by the third party.

The sponsor will be the main point of contact with the FCA for any matter referred to in LR 8.2. The FCA expects to discuss all issues relating to a transaction and any draft or final document directly with the sponsor. However, in appropriate circumstances, the FCA will communicate directly with the company with or applying for a premium listing of its securities, or its advisers.

A sponsor remains responsible for complying with LR 8.3 even where a sponsor relies on the company with or applying for a premium listing of its securities or a third party when providing an assurance or confirmation to the FCA.

(FCA Listing Rules, paras 8.3.1, 8.3.1A, 8.3.1B, 8.3.2, 8.3.2A).

### 33.23   *Principles for sponsors*

A sponsor must keep to the following principles.

(a)   A sponsor must act with due care and skill in relation to a sponsor service.

(b)    Where, in relation to a sponsor service, a sponsor gives any guidance or advice to a listed company or applicant on the application or interpretation of the listing rules or disclosure requirements and transparency rules, the sponsor must take reasonable steps to satisfy itself that the director or directors of the listed company understand their responsibilities and obligations under those rules.

(c)    A sponsor must at all times (whether in relation to a sponsor service or otherwise)

  (i)    deal with the FCA in an open and co-operative way; and

  (ii)   deal with all enquiries raised by the FCA promptly.

(d)    If in connection with the provision of a sponsor service a sponsor becomes aware that it, or the company with or applying for a premium listing of its securities is failing or has failed to comply with its obligations under the listing rules the disclosure requirements or the transparency rules the sponsor must promptly notify the FCA.

(e)    A sponsor must, in relation to a sponsor service, act with honesty and integrity.

  The purpose of LR 8.3.7 to 8.3.13 is to ensure that conflicts of interest do not adversely affect the ability of a sponsor to perform its functions properly under the Listing Rules or market confidence in sponsors.

(f)    A sponsor must take all reasonable steps to identify conflicts of interest that could adversely affect its ability to perform its functions properly

(g)    In identifying conflicts of interest sponsors should also take into account circumstances that could create a perception in the market that a sponsor may not be able to perform its functions properly or compromise the ability of a sponsor to fulfil its obligations to the FCA in relation to the provision of sponsor services.

(h)    A sponsor must take all reasonable steps to put in place and maintain effective organisational and administrative arrangements that ensure conflicts of interest do not adversely affect its ability to perform its functions. Disclosure of a conflict of interest will not usually be considered to be an effective organisational or administrative arrangement. If a sponsor is not sure of this in relation to a sponsor service, it must decline or cease to provide the sponsor services. In case of doubt, it should discuss the issue with the FCA before it decides if it can provide a sponsor service. Listing Rules 8.3.7, 8.3.9 and 8.3.11 apply for so long as the sponsor provides a sponsor service.

(i)    If a listed company or applicant appoints more than one sponsor to provide a sponsor service then

  (i)    the appointment does not relieve either of the appointed sponsors of their obligations under Listing Rules, Chapter 8; and

  (ii)   the sponsors are each responsible for complying with the obligations under LR 8.

(j)    If a listed company or applicant appoints more than one sponsor to provide a sponsor service, the FCA expects the sponsors to co-operate with each other in relation to the sponsor service, including by establishing arrangements for the sharing of information as appropriate having regard to the sponsor service.

(FCA Listing Rules, paras 8.3.3–8.3.15).

**33.24** *Supervision of sponsors*

A sponsor must:

(a)     Pay the annual fee in order to remain on the list of sponsors.

(b)     Provide to the FCA on or after the first business day in January in each year but no later than the last business day of January in each year

    (i)     written confirmation that it continues in **33.21** to satisfy the criteria for approval as a sponsor;

    (ii)     for each of those criteria, evidence of the basis upon which it considers it meets that criterion.

(c)     Notify the FCA in writing as soon as possible if

    (i)     it ceases to satisfy the criteria for approval as a sponsor set out in LR 8.6.5. or becomes aware of any matter which in its reasonable opinion would be relevant to the FCA in considering whether the sponsor continues to comply with LR 8.6.6 or the sponsor becomes aware of any fact or circumstance relating to the sponsor or any of its employees engaged in the provision of sponsor services by the sponsor which, in its reasonable opinion, would be likely to adversely affect market confidence in the sponsors; or

    (ii)     the sponsor, or any of its employees engaged in the provision of sponsor services by the sponsor, are convicted of any offence involving fraud, theft or other dishonesty or the subject of a bankruptcy proceeding, a receiving order or an administration order;

    (iii)     any of its employees engaged in the provision of sponsor services by the sponsor are disqualified by a court from acting as a director of a company or from acting in a management capacity or conducting the affairs of any company;

    (iv)     the sponsor, or any of its employees engaged in the provision of sponsor services by the sponsor, are subject to any public criticism, regulatory intervention or disciplinary action by the FCA or any designated professional body (or any comparable body inside or outside the UK) or under any comparable legislation in any jurisdiction outside the UK;

    (v)     the sponsor resigns or is dismissed by a listed company or applicant giving details of any relevant facts or circumstances;

    (vi)     the sponsor changes its name;

    (vii)     a listed company or applicant denies the sponsor access to documents or information that have been the subject of a reasonable request by the sponsor;

    (viii)     it identifies or otherwise becomes aware of any material deficiency in the sponsor's systems and controls; or

    (ix)     there is intended to be a change of control of the sponsor, any restructuring of the sponsor's group or a reorganisation of, or a substantial change to the directors, partners or employees engaged in the provision of sponsor services by the sponsor;

    (x)     there is expected to be a change in the financial position of the sponsor or any of its group companies that would be likely to adversely affect the sponsor's ability to perform the sponsor services or otherwise comply with LR8.

Where a sponsor is of the opinion that notwithstanding the circumstances giving rise to a notification obligation under (c) above it continues to satisfy the ongoing criteria for approval as a sponsor it must include in its notification to the FCA a statement to that effect and the basis for its opinion.

(d)   Not delegate any of its functions as such, or permit another person to perform those functions

(e)   Inform the FCA in writing if it wishes to have its approval as a sponsor cancelled and must give

(i)   the sponsor's name and a clear explanation of the background and reasons for the request;

(ii)   the date on which the sponsor requests the cancellation should take effect (bearing in mind that under the statutory notice procedure a request for cancellation of approval will take a minimum of eight weeks to take effect);

(iii)   a signed confirmation that the sponsor will not provide any sponsor services as of the date the request is submitted to the FCA; and

(iv)   the name and contact details of the person at the sponsor with whom the FCA should liaise with in relation to the request.

Examples of when a sponsor should submit a cancellation request include, but are not limited to, situations where the sponsor ceases to satisfy the ongoing criteria for approval as a sponsor in accordance with LR 8.6.6 and following notification made under LR 8.7.8 there are no ongoing discussions with the FCA which could lead to the conclusion that the sponsor remains eligible or where there is a change of control of the sponsor or any restructuring of the sponsor's group that will result in sponsor services being provided by a different person, in which case the person that is intended to provide the sponsor services should apply for approval as a sponsor under LR 8.6 before it provides any sponsor services. A sponsor may withdraw its cancellation request at any time before the cancellation takes effect. The withdrawal request should initially be made by telephone and then confirmed in writing as soon as possible, with an explanation of the reasons for the withdrawal.

(FCA Listing Rules, paras 8.7.6–8.7.8, 8.7.8A, 8.7.16, 8.7.21, 8.7.21A, 8.7.22, 8.7.23).

## 33.25  Continuing obligations

Once its securities have been admitted to listing, there are still continuing obligations which a listed company must observe in order to maintain an orderly market in securities and to ensure that all users of the market have simultaneous access to the same information. The provisions of Chapter 9 of the Listing Rules only apply to a company that has a Premium listing. Companies with a Standard listing are bound by the continuing obligations of Chapter 14 para 3 of the Listing Rules.

The continuing obligations are considered in **33.26** to **33.34**.

**33.26** *Requirements with continuing application*

(1) *Admission to trading*

A listed company's securities must at all times be admitted to trading on an RIE's market for listed securities. The company must inform the FCA in writing as soon as possible if it has

•   requested an RIE to admit or re-admit any of its listed equity shares to trading;

•   requested an RIE to cancel or suspend trading of any of its listed equity shares; or

- been informed by an RIE that trading of any of its listed equity shares will be cancelled or suspended.

(2) *Independent business*

A listed company must carry on an independent business as its main activity at all times.

Where a listed company has a controlling shareholder, it must have in place at all times

- (LR 9.2.2ADR(1)) a written and legally binding agreement which is intended to ensure that the controlling shareholder complies with the independence provisions set out in LR 6.1.4D; and

- (LR9.2.2ADR(2)) a constitution that allows the election and re-election of independent directors to be conducted in accordance with the election provisions set out in LR 9.2.2ER and LR 9.2.2FR.

In order to comply with LR 9.2.2ADR(1), where a listed company will have more than one controlling shareholder, the listed company will not be required to enter into a separate agreement with each controlling shareholder if

- the listed company reasonably considers, in light of its understanding of the relationship between the relevant controlling shareholders, that a controlling shareholder can procure the compliance of another controlling shareholder and that controlling shareholder's associates with the independence provisions contained in the relevant agreement; and

- the agreement, which contains the independence provisions set out in LR 6.1.4D, entered into with the relevant controlling shareholder also contains

    (a) a provision in which the controlling shareholder agrees to procure the compliance of a non-signing controlling shareholder and its associates with the independence provisions contained within the agreement; and

    (b) the names of any such non-signing controlling shareholder.

Where as a result of changes in ownership or control of a listed company, a person becomes a controlling shareholder of the listed company, the listed company will be allowed

- a period of not more than six months from the event that resulted in that person becoming a controlling shareholder to comply with LR 9.2.2ADR(1); and

- in the case of a listed company which did not previously have a controlling shareholder, until the date of the next annual general meeting of the listed company, other than an annual general meeting for which notice has already been given or is given within a period of three months from the event that resulted in that person becoming a controlling shareholder to comply with LR 9.2.2ADR(2).

In complying with LR 9.2.2ADR(2), a listed company may allow an existing independent director who is being proposed for re-election (including any such director who was appointed by the board of the listed company until the next annual general meeting) to remain in office until any resolution required by LR 9.2.2FR has been voted on.

Where LR 9.2.2ADR applies, the election or re-election of any independent director by shareholders must be approved by

- the shareholders of the listed company; and

- the independent shareholders of the listed company.

Where applicable, if the election or re-election of an independent director is not approved by both the shareholders and the independent shareholders of the listed company, but the listed company wishes to propose that person for election or re-election as an independent director, the listed company must propose a further resolution to elect or re-elect the proposed independent director which

- must not be voted on within a period of 90 days from the date of the original vote;

- must be voted on within a period of 30 days from the end of the 90 day-period set out above and

- must be approved by the shareholders of the listed company.

A listed company must comply with the independence provisions contained in any agreement entered into under LR 6.1.4B(1) or LR 9.2.2ADR(1) at all times.

In addition to the annual confirmation required to be included in a listed company's annual financial report under LR 9.8.4(14), the FCA may request information from a listed company under LR 1.3.1(3) to confirm or verify that an independence provision contained in any agreement entered into under LR 6.1.4B(1) or LR 9.2.2ADR(1) or a procurement obligation (as set out in LR 6.1.4C(2)(a) or LR 9.2.2BR(2)(a)) contained in an agreement entered into under LR 6.1.4B(1) or LR 9.2.2ADR(1) is being or has been complied with.

*Control of business*

*LR 9.2.21R*

A listed company must exercise operational control over the business it carries on as its main activity at all times.

*LR 9.2.2JG*

LR 6.6.3G provides guidance on factors that may indicate that a listed company is not exercising operational control over the business it carries on as its main activity.

*LR 9.2.2KR makes special provisions for mineral companies.*

(3) *Compliance with the Disclosure and Transparency Rules*

A listed company whose equity shares are admitted to trading on a regulated market in the UK should consider its obligations under the disclosure requirements of Article 17 of the Market Abuse Regulation and the Transparency Rules in Parts 4, 5 and 6 of the FCA's Disclosure Guidance and Transparency Rules.

A listed company that is not already required to comply with Article 17 of the Market Abuse Regulation, must comply with those provisions as if it were an issuer for the purposes of the disclosure requirements and likewise the Transparency Rules in Parts 4, 5, and 6 of the Disclosure Guidance and Transparency Rules. See **33.37–33.51** and **33.55–33.74** respectively.

(4) *Model Code*

The provisions relating to the Model Code for dealings by directors and others in their own company's shares have been abolished and replaced with the more limited requirements of Article 19 of the Market Abuse Regulation, which is considered in **33.52** below.

(5) *Contact details*

A listed company must ensure that the FCA is provided with up-to-date contact details of at least one appropriate person nominated by it to act as the first point of contact with the FCA in relation to the company's compliance with the Listing Rules and the Disclosure and Transparency Rules. The contact person will be expected to be

(i)     knowledgeable about the listed company and the Listing Rules applicable to it;

(ii)    capable of ensuring that appropriate action is taken on a timely basis; and

(iii)   contactable on business days between the hours of 7am to 7pm.

(6) *Sponsors*

A listed company should consider its notification obligations on the appointment of sponsors (see **33.21**).

In relation to the provision of a sponsor service, a company with a premium listing of its equity shares must cooperate with its sponsor by providing the sponsor with all information reasonably requested by the sponsor for the purpose of carrying out the sponsor service in accordance with LR 8.

(7) *Shares in public hands*

A listed company must comply with the requirements in 33.7(4) at all times unless the FCA has agreed a lower percentage than 25% and not revoked that agreement.

(8) *Publication of unaudited financial information*

Where a listed company has published

•       any unaudited financial information in a Class 1 circular or a prospectus, or

•       any profit forecast or profit estimate

the first time it publishes financial information as required by disclosure and transparency rule 4.1 after the publication of unaudited financial information, it must

(a)     reproduce that material in its next annual report and accounts;

(b)     produce and disclose in the annual report and accounts the actual figures for the same period covered by that material; and

(c)     provide an explanation of the difference, if there is a difference of 10% or more between the figures required by (*b*) and those reproduced under (*a*) above.

This does not apply to pro-forma financial information prepared in accordance with Annex 1 and 2 of the Prospectus Directive Regulation or to any preliminary statements of annual results or half-yearly or quarterly reports that are reproduced with the unaudited financial information.

LR9.2.21 requires certain shareholder votes to be in addition approved by the independent shareholders subject to any modification allowed by the FCA under LR 9.2.22.

(FCA Listing Rules, paras 9.2.1–9.2.16, 9.2.2A–H, 9.2.18, 9.2.19).

LR 9.2.23–9.2.26 oblige the company to inform the FCA if it can no longer comply with certain of its continuing obligations.

**33.27**  *Continuing obligations – holders*

(1) *Proxy forms*

A listed company must ensure that, in addition to its obligation under *CA 2006*, a proxy form

•       provides for at least three-way voting on all resolutions to be proposed (except procedural resolutions); and

- states that, if it is returned without an indication as to how the proxy shall vote on any particular matter, the proxy will exercise his discretion as to whether, and if so how, he votes.

If the proposed resolutions include the re-election of more than five retiring directors, the proxy form may give shareholders the opportunity to vote for or against (or abstain from voting on) the re-election of the retiring directors as a whole but must also allow votes to be cast for or against (or for shareholders to abstain from voting on) the re-election of the retiring directors individually.

(2) *Sanctions*

Where a listed company has taken a power in its constitution to impose sanctions on a shareholder who is in default in complying with a notice served under *CA 2006, s 793* (notice by company requiring information about interests in its shares, see **24.2** INTERESTS IN PUBLIC COMPANY SHARES)

(i)     sanctions may not take effect earlier than 14 days after service of the notice;

(ii)    for a shareholding of less than 0.25% of the shares of a particular class (exclusive of treasury shares), the only sanction the constitution may provide for is a prohibition against attending meetings and voting;

(iii)   for a shareholding of 0.25% or more of the shares of a particular class (exclusive of treasury shares), the constitution may additionally provide for

- the withholding of dividends (including shares issued in lieu of dividend) on the shares concerned; and

- the placing of restrictions on the transfer of shares (other than the sale to a genuine unconnected third party such as through a RIE or an overseas exchange or by the acceptance of a takeover offer); and

(iv)    any sanctions imposed under (i) or (iii) above must cease to apply after a specified period of not more than seven days after the earlier of

- receipt by the issuer of notice that the shareholding has been sold to an unconnected third party through a RIE or an overseas exchange or by the acceptance of a takeover offer; and

- due compliance, to the satisfaction of the issuer, with the notice under *CA 2006, s 793.*

(3) *Pre-emption rights*

Subject to below, a listed company proposing to issue equity shares for cash or sell treasury shares that are equity shares for cash, must first offer them *pro rata* to

- existing holders of that class of equity shares (other than the listed company itself by virtue of its holding treasury shares); and

- holders of other equity shares of the listed company who are entitled to be offered them.

The above does not apply

- to a listed company incorporated in the UK if a general disapplication of statutory pre-emption rights has been authorised by shareholders in accordance with *CA 2006, s 570* or *571* and the issue of equity securities or sale of treasury shares that are equity shares is within the terms of the authority; or

- to a listed company undertaking a rights issue or open offer provided the disapplication of pre-emption rights is with respect to

    (i)    equity securities representing fractional entitlements; or

    (ii)   equity securities which the company considers necessary or expedient to exclude from the offer on account of the laws or regulatory requirements of a territory other than its country of incorporation unless that territory is the UK;

- to a listed company selling treasury shares for cash to an employee share scheme;

- to an overseas company with a premium listing which has obtained the consent of its shareholders to issue equity shares either within the terms of an authority equivalent to that required by *s 570* or *571* of *CA 2006* or in accordance with the law of its country of incorporation provided that the country had implemented *Article 29* of *EU Directive 77/91* or *Article 33* of *EU Directive 2012/30* and the issue of equity securities or sale of treasury shares that are equity securities by the listed company is within the terms of the authority; or

- to an open-ended investment company.

(FCA Listing Rules, paras 9.3.6, 9.3.7, 9.3.9, 9.3.11, 9.3.12).

*Use of electronic communications.* If the Listing Rules require an issuer to send documents to its security holders, the issuer may use electronic means to do so in accordance with the FCA Disclosure Guidance and Transparency Rules. See **33.71**(6). (FCA Listing Rules, para 1.4.9).

**33.28** *Share schemes, options, etc requiring prior approval*

(1) *Employees' share schemes and long-term incentive plans*

Subject to below, a listed company incorporated in the UK must ensure that any

- employees' share scheme (if the scheme involves or may involve the issue of new shares or the transfer of treasury shares), or

- long-term incentive scheme in which one or more directors of the listed company is eligible to participate

of the company or any of its 'major subsidiary undertakings' (even if incorporated or operates overseas) is approved by an ordinary resolution of the shareholders of the listed company in general meeting before it is adopted.

'*Major subsidiary undertaking*' is a subsidiary undertaking that represents 25% or more of the aggregate of the gross assets or profits (after deducting all charges except taxation) of the group.

The above does not apply to any long-term incentive scheme which is an arrangement where

(a)    participation is offered on similar terms to all (or substantially all) employees of the listed company or any of its subsidiaries whose employees are eligible to participate in the arrangement (provided that all, or substantially all, employees are not directors of the listed company); or

(b)    where the only participant is a director of the listed company (or an individual whose appointment as a director of the listed company is being contemplated) and the arrangement is established specifically to facilitate, in unusual circumstances, the recruitment or retention of the relevant individual. Instead, the information in FCA Listing Rules, paras 9.4.3 and 13.8.11 must be disclosed in the first annual report published after the date on which the relevant individual becomes eligible to participate in the arrangement.

(2) *Discounted option arrangements*

Subject to below, a listed company must not, without the prior approval by an ordinary resolution of its members in a general meeting, grant to a director or employee of the company (or any of its subsidiary companies)

- an option to subscribe,

- warrant to subscribe, or

- other similar right to subscribe

for shares in the capital of the company (or any of its subsidiary companies) if the price per share payable on the exercise of the option, etc is less than whichever of the following is used to calculate the exercise price:

- The market value of the share on the date when the exercise price is determined.

- The market value of the share on the business day before that date.

- The average of the market values for a number of dealing days within a period not exceeding 30 days immediately before that date.

The above does not apply to the grant of an option, etc

- under an employees' share scheme if participation is offered on similar terms to all (or substantially all) employees of the company or any of its subsidiary undertakings whose employees are entitled to participate in the scheme; or

- following a take-over or reconstruction, in replacement for and on comparable terms with options, etc held immediately before the take-over or reconstruction for shares in either a company of which the listed company thereby obtains control or in any of that company's subsidiary undertakings.

(FCA Listing Rules, paras 9.4.1–9.4.5).

**33.29** *Transactions*

(1) *Rights issues*

See **47.65 SHARES**.

(2) *Open offers*

A listed company must ensure that the timetable for an open offer is approved by the RIE on which its equity securities are traded and that the open offer remains open for acceptance for at least 10 business days (for the purposes of calculating the 10 business days, the first business day is the date on which the offer is first open for acceptance).

When communicating information on an open offer, a listed company must ensure that

- if the offer is subject to approval in general meeting, the announcement must state that this is the case; and

- the circular dealing with the offer must not contain any statement that might be taken to imply that the offer gives the same entitlements as a rights issue unless it is an offer with a compensatory element. If existing shareholders do not take up their rights to subscribe in an open offer with a compensatory element, the listed company must ensure that the equity securities to which the offer relates are offered for subscription or purchase on terms that any premium obtained over the subscription or purchase price (net of expenses) is to be for the account of the holders, except that if the proceeds for an existing holder do not exceed £5, the proceeds may be retained for the company's benefit and the equity securities may be allotted or sold to underwriters, if on the expiry of the subscription period no premium (net of expenses) has been obtained.

A listed company must ensure that for a subscription in an open offer with a compensatory element the following are notified to a RIS as soon as possible

(i)    the offer price and principal terms of the offer, and

(ii)   the results of the offer and, if any securities not taken up are sold, details of the sale, including the date and price per share.

(3) *Vendor consideration placing*

A listed company must ensure that in a vendor consideration placing all vendors have an equal opportunity to participate in the placing.

A *'vendor consideration placing'* is a marketing, by or on behalf of vendors, of securities that have been allotted as consideration for an acquisition.

(4) *Discounts not to exceed 10%*

Subject to below, if a listed company makes an open offer, placing, vendor consideration placing, offer for subscription of equity shares or an issue out of treasury (other than in respect of an employees' share scheme) of a class already listed, the price must not be at a discount of more than 10% to the middle market price of those shares at the time of announcing the terms of the offer for an open offer or offer for subscription of equity shares or, at the time of agreeing the placing for a placing or vendor consideration placing.

The above provisions do not apply if

•    the terms of the offer or placing at a higher discount have been specifically approved by the issuer's shareholders; or

•    it is an issue of shares for cash or the sale of treasury shares for cash under a pre-existing general authority to disapply *CA 2006, s 561* (before 1 October 2009, *CA 1985, s 89*) (existing shareholders' right of pre-emption).

If a listed company makes an open offer, placing, vendor consideration placing or offer for subscription of equity shares during the trading day it may use an appropriate on-screen intra-day price derived from another market.

On each occasion that the listed company plans to use an on-screen intra-day price it should discuss the source of the price in advance with the FCA. The FCA may be satisfied that there is sufficient justification for its use if the alternative market has an appropriate level of liquidity and the source is one that is widely accepted by the market.

The listed company must notify a RIS as soon as possible after it has agreed the terms of the offer or placing.

(5) *Offer for sale or subscription*

A listed company must ensure that for an offer for sale or an offer for subscription of equity securities

•    letters of allotment or acceptance are all issued simultaneously and numbered serially (and where appropriate split and certified by the company's registrars);

- if the equity securities may be held in uncertificated form, there is equal treatment with those who elect to hold the equity securities in certificated form and those who elect to hold them in uncertificated form;

- letters of regret are posted not later than three business days after the letters of allotment or acceptance. If not posted at the same time as those letters, a notice to that effect must be inserted in a national newspaper, to appear on the morning after the letters of allotment or acceptance are posted.

### (6) *Reconstruction or refinancing*

If a listed company produces a circular containing proposals to be put to shareholders in a general meeting relating to a reconstruction or a re-financing, the circular must be produced in accordance with **33.43** and must include a working capital statement (except for a closed-end investment fund).

### (7) *Fractional entitlements*

If, for an issue of equity securities (other than an issue in lieu of dividend), a shareholder's entitlement includes a fraction of a security, a listed company must ensure that the fraction is sold for the benefit of the holder except that if its value (net of expenses) does not exceed £5 it may be sold for the company's benefit. Sales of fractions may be made before listing is granted.

### (8) *Further issues*

When shares of the same class as shares that are listed are allotted, an application for admission to listing of such shares must be made as soon as possible and in any event within one month of the allotment.

### (9) *Temporary documents of title (including renounceable documents)*

A listed company must ensure that any temporary document of title (other than one issued in global form) for an equity security is serially numbered and states where applicable

- the name and address of the first holder and names of joint holders (if any);

- for a fixed income security, the amount of the next payment of interest or dividend;

- the pro rata entitlement;

- the last date on which transfers were or will be accepted for registration for participation in the issue;

- how the securities rank for dividend or interest;

- the nature of the document of title and proposed date of issue;

- how fractions (if any) are to be treated; and

- for a rights issue, the time (not less than 10 business days) in which the offer may be accepted, and how equity securities not taken up will be dealt with.

If renounceable, the temporary document of title must also

- state in a heading that the document is of value and negotiable;

- advise holders of equity securities who are in any doubt as to what action to take to consult appropriate independent advisers immediately;

- state that where all of the securities have been sold by the addressee (other than 'ex rights' or 'ex capitalisation'), the document should be passed to the person through whom the sale was effected for transmission to the purchaser;

- have the form of renunciation and the registration instructions printed on the back of, or attached to, the document;

- include provision for splitting (without fee) and for split documents to be certified by an official of the company or authorised agent;

- provide for the last day for renunciation to be the second business day after the last day for splitting; and

- if, at the same time as an allotment is made of shares issued for cash, shares of the same class are also allotted credited as fully paid to vendors or others, provide for the period for renunciation to be the same as but no longer than that provided for in the case of shares issued for cash.

(10) *Definitive documents of title*

A listed company must ensure that any definitive document of title for an equity share (other than a bearer security) includes the following matters on its face (or on the reverse in the case of (v) and (vi)).

(i)     The authority under which the company is constituted and the country of incorporation and registered number (if any).

(ii)    The number or amount of securities the certificate represents and, if applicable, the number and denomination of units (in the top right-hand corner).

(iii)   A footnote stating that no transfer of the security or any portion of it represented by the certificate can be registered without production of the certificate.

(iv)    If applicable, the minimum amount and multiples thereof in which the security is transferable.

(v)     The date of the certificate.

(vi)    For equity shares with preferential rights, on the face (or, if not practicable, on the reverse), a statement of the conditions thereof as to capital, dividends and (where applicable) conversion.

(FCA Listing Rules, paras 9.5.7–9.5.16).

**33.30** *Notifications*

(1) *Copies of documents*

A company must send to the FCA

- two copies of all circulars, notices, reports and other documents to which the Listing Rules apply at the same time as they are issued; and

- two copies of all resolutions passed by the company (other than ordinary business at an AGM) as soon as possible after the relevant general meeting.

The company must notify a RIS as soon as possible when a document has been forwarded to the FCA as above (unless the full text of the document is provided to the RIS). The notification must set out where copies of the relevant document can be obtained.

(2) *Notifications relating to capital*

A listed company must notify a RIS as soon as possible (unless otherwise indicated) of the following information relating to its capital.

- Any proposed change in the capital structure including listed debt securities (except that an announcement of a new issue may be delayed while marketing or underwriting is in progress).

- Any redemption of listed shares including details of the number of shares redeemed and the number of shares of that class outstanding following the redemption.

- Any extension of time granted for the currency of temporary documents of title.

- (Except in relation to a block listing of securities) the results of any new issue of equity securities or a public offering of existing equity securities.

(3) *Notification of board changes and directors' details*

A listed company must notify a RIS of any change to the board as soon as possible and in any event by the end of the business day following the decision or receipt of notice about the change by the company. This includes

- the appointment of a new director stating the appointee's name and whether the position is executive, non-executive or chairman and the nature of any specific function or responsibility of the position;

- the resignation, removal or retirement of a director (unless the director retires by rotation and is re-appointed at a general meeting of the company's shareholders);

- important changes to the role, functions or responsibilities of a director; and

- the effective date of the change if it is not with immediate effect.

Where the effective date of the board change is not yet known, the notification should state this fact and the company should notify a RIS as soon as the effective date has been decided.

In respect of any new director, a listed company must notify a RIS as soon as possible following the decision to appoint the director (and in any event within five business days of the decision) of the following (including a nil notification where appropriate).

(a)   All directorships held in any other publicly quoted company at any time in the previous five years, indicating whether or not he is still a director.

(b)   Any unspent convictions in relation to indictable offences.

(c)   Any insolvency arrangements of any

   (i)   company where the director was an executive director, or

   (ii)   partnership where he was a partner

   at the time of, or within the 12 months preceding, such arrangements.

(d)   Receiverships of any asset of such person or of a partnership of which the director was a partner at the time of, or within the 12 months preceding, such event.

(e)   Details of any public criticisms of the director by statutory or regulatory authorities (including designated professional bodies) and whether the director has ever been disqualified by a court from acting as a director of a company or from acting in the management or conduct of the affairs of any company.

A listed company must, in respect of any current director, notify a RIS as soon as possible of

- any change in the information in (*b*) to (*e*) above; and

•    any new directorships held by the director in any other publicly quoted company

(4) *Change of name*

A listed company which changes its name must, as soon as possible

•    notify a RIS of the change, stating the date on which it has taken effect;

•    inform the FCA in writing of the change; and

•    where the company is incorporated in the UK, send the FCA a copy of the revised certificate of incorporation issued by the Registrar of Companies.

(5) *Change of accounting date*

A listed company must notify a RIS as soon as possible of any change in its accounting reference date (see **2.18 ACCOUNTING REFERENCE DATES AND PERIODS**) and the new date. It must prepare and publish a second interim report in accordance with **33.57** if the effect of the change is to extend the accounting period to more than 14 months. The second interim report must be prepared and published in respect of either

•    the period up to the old accounting reference date; or

•    the period up to a date not more than six months prior to the new accounting reference date.

(FCA Listing Rules, paras 9.6.1–9.6.4, 9.6.11–9.6.15, 9.6.19–9.6.22).

**33.31**  *Preliminary statement of annual results, statement of dividends and half-yearly reports*

*Preliminary statement of annual results.* If a listed company prepares a preliminary statement of annual results, the statement must

•    be published as soon as possible after it has been approved by the board;

•    be agreed with the company's auditors prior to publication (the FRC Bulletin 'The Auditor's Association with Preliminary Announcements made in accordance with the UK Listing Rules' sets out detailed guidance on this);

•    show the figures in the form of a table, including the items required for a half-yearly report, consistent with the presentation to be adopted in the annual accounts for that financial year;

•    give details of the nature of any likely modification or emphasis –of-matter paragraphs that may be contained in the auditors' report required to be included with the annual financial report; and

•    include any significant additional information necessary for the purpose of assessing the results being announced.

*Statement of dividends.* A listed company must notify a RIS as soon as possible after the board has approved any decision to pay or make any dividend or other distribution on listed equity or to withhold any dividend or interest payment on listed securities giving details of

•    the exact net amount payable per share;

•    the payment date;

•    the record date (where applicable); and

•    any foreign income dividend election, together with any income tax treated as paid at the lower rate and not repayable.

*Omission of information.* The FCA may authorise the omission of information required by either of the above requirements if it considers that disclosure of such information would be contrary to the public interest or seriously detrimental to the listed company, provided that such omission would not be likely to mislead the public with regard to facts and circumstances, knowledge of which is essential for the assessment of the shares.

(FCA Listing Rules, paras 9.7A.1–9.7A.3).

33.32  *Annual financial report*

In addition to the requirements set out in **33.56**, a listed company must include, where applicable, the following information in its annual financial report, and the disclosures in (a)–(j) below must be given in a single identifiable section of the report, unless the report includes a cross-reference table showing where the details are set out. (See also **15.5 Corporate Governance** and **20.21 Strategic Reports and Directors' Reports** for further disclosures in respect of corporate governance issues.)

(a)    *Interest capitalised.* The amount of interest capitalised by the group during the period under review, with an indication of the amount and treatment of any related tax relief.

(b)    *Unaudited financial information.* Any information required under **33.26(8)**.

(c)    *Long-term incentive schemes.* Details of any long-term incentive scheme as required by LR 9.4.3.

(d)    *Waiver of emoluments.* Particulars of any arrangement under which a director has waived, or agreed to waive, emoluments from the company or any subsidiary. Where a director has agreed to waive future emoluments, details of such waiver together with those relating to emoluments which were waived during the period under review.

(e)    *Allotments for cash.* Where there has been an allotment of equity securities for cash in the period under review (otherwise than to the holders of the company's equity shares in proportion to their holdings of such shares) and this has not been specifically authorised by the shareholders

•    the classes of shares allotted and for each class of shares, the number allotted, their aggregate nominal value, and the consideration received by the company for the allotment;

•    the names of the allottees (if less than six) or otherwise a brief generic description of each new class of equity holder (eg holder of loan stock);

•    the market price of the securities on the date the terms of the issue were fixed; and

•    the date on which the terms of the issue were fixed.

The above information must be given for any unlisted '*major subsidiary undertaking*' of the company, ie any subsidiary undertaking that represents 25% or more of the aggregate of the gross assets or profits (after deducting all charges except taxation) of the group.

(f)    *Parent undertaking participation in a placing.* Where a company has listed shares in issue and is a subsidiary of another company, details of the participation by the parent company in any placing made during the period under review.

(g)    *Contracts of significance.* Details of any 'contract of significance' existing during the period under review

•    to which the listed company (or one of its subsidiaries) is a party and in which a director of the listed company is or was materially interested; and

- between the listed company (or one of its subsidiaries) and a controlling shareholder.

A *'contract of significance'* is one which represents, in the case of a capital transaction, 1% or more of the group's share capital and reserves and, in the case of other transactions, 1% of the group's annual purchases, sales, payments or receipts.

(h) *Contracts for services.* Details of any contract for the provision of services to the listed company (or any subsidiary) by a controlling shareholder subsisting during the period under review (unless it is a contract for the provision of services which it is the principal business of the shareholder to provide and it is not a contract of significance).

(i) *Waiver of dividends.* Details of any arrangement under which a shareholder has waived, or agreed to waive, dividends. Where a shareholder has agreed to waive future dividends, details of such waiver together with those relating to dividends which are payable during the period under review. (Details of waivers of less than 1% of the total value of any dividend need not be given, provided that some payment has been made on each share of the relevant class during the relevant calendar year.)

(j) *Statement made by the board.* A statement by the board

    (i) that the listed company has entered into any agreement required under LR 9.2.2ADR(1) (controlling shareholder – see **33.26**(2)); or

    (ii) where the listed company has not entered into an agreement required under LR 9.2.2ADR(1)

- a statement that the FCA has been notified of that non-compliance in accordance with LR 9.2.23; and

- a brief description of the background to, and reasons for, failing to enter into the agreement that enables shareholders to evaluate the impact of non-compliance on the listed company; and

    (iii) that

- the listed company has complied with the independence provisions included in any agreement entered into under LR 6.5.4R or LR 9.2.2ADR(1) during the period under review;

- so far as the listed company is aware, the independence provisions included in any agreement entered into under LR 6.5.4R or LR 9.2.2ADR(1) have been complied with during the period under review by the controlling shareholder or any of its associates; and

- so far as the listed company is aware, the procurement obligation (as set out in LR 6.5.5R(2)(a) or LR 9.2.2BR(2)(a)) included in any agreement entered into under LR 6.5.4R or LR 9.2.2ADR(1) has been complied with during the period under review by a controlling shareholder; or

    (iv) where an independence provision included in any agreement entered into under LR 6.5.4R or LR 9.2.2ADR(1) or a procurement obligation (as set out in LR 6.5.5R(2)(a) or LR 9.2.2BR(2)(a)) included in any agreement entered into under LR 6.5.4R or LR 9.2.2ADR(1) has not been complied with during the period under review

- a statement that the FCA has been notified of that non-compliance in accordance with LR 9.2.24; and

- a brief description of the background to, and reasons for, failing to comply with the relevant independence provision or procurement obligation that enables shareholders to evaluate the impact of non-compliance on the listed company.

Where an independent director declines to support a statement made under (i) or (iii) above, the board's statement must record this fact.

In the case of listed companies incorporated in the UK, the following additional items must be included:

(k) *Directors' interests in shares.* A statement setting out all the interests (in respect of which transactions are notifiable to the company under Article 19 of the Market Abuse Regulation, see **33.52**) of each person who is a director of the listed company as at the end of the period under review. All changes in the interests of each director that have occurred between the end of the period under review and a date not more than one month prior to the date of the notice of the AGM must be included (or if there have been no such changes, a statement that there have been no changes). Interests of each director include the interests of connected persons of which the listed company is, or ought upon reasonable enquiry to become, aware. The effect of this requirement is that the company is required to set out a snapshot of the total interests of a director and his or her connected persons, as at the end of the period under review (including certain information to update it as at a date not more than a month before the date of the notice of AGM). Persons who are directors during, but not at the end of the period under review, need not be included.

(l) *Major interests in shares.* A statement showing the interests disclosed to the listed company in accordance with DTR 5 as at the end of the period under review and all interests disclosed in accordance with that rule that have occurred between the end of the period under review and a date not more than one month prior to the date of the notice of the AGM. If no interests have been disclosed, a statement that no interests have been disclosed.

(m) *Going concern.* Statements by the directors on the appropriateness of adopting the going concern basis of accounting (containing the information set out in provision C.1.3 of the UK Corporate Governance Code) and their assessment of the prospects of the company (containing the information set out in provision C.2.2 of the UK Corporate Governance Code) prepared in accordance with 'Guidance on Risk Management, Internal Control and Related Financial and Business Reporting' published September 2014 by the FRC. The company must ensure that the auditors review this statement before the annual report is published.

(n) *Purchase by company of its own shares and sales for cash of treasury shares.*

- Details of any shareholders' authority for the purchase by the company of its own shares still valid at the end of the period under review;

- in the case of purchases made otherwise than through the market or by tender to all shareholders, the names of sellers of such shares purchased (or proposed to be purchased) by the listed company in the period under review;

- in the case of any purchases made otherwise than through the market or by tender or partial offer to all shareholders, or options or contracts to make such purchases entered into since the beginning of the period covered by the report, information equivalent to that required under *SI 2008 No 410, Part 2, Schedule 7* (Disclosure required by company acquiring its own shares – see **20.16**): and

- in the case of sales of treasury shares for cash made otherwise than through the market, or in connection with an employees' share scheme, or otherwise than pursuant to an opportunity which (so far as was practicable) was made to all holders of the listed company's securities (or to all holders of a relevant class of its securities) on the same terms, particulars of the names of the purchasers of such shares sold (or proposed to be sold) by the company during the period under review.

(o)   *Application of the UK Corporate Governance Code.* A statement of how the listed company has applied the Main Principles set out in the UK Corporate Governance Code, in a manner that would enable shareholders to evaluate how the principles have been applied.

(p)   *Statement on compliance with the UK Corporate Governance Code.* A statement as to whether the company has complied throughout the accounting period with all relevant provisions set out in the UK Corporate Governance Code or has not so complied. A company which has not complied must specify

- those provisions, if any, that it has not complied with;

- in the case of provisions whose requirements are of a continuing nature, the period within which, if any, it did not comply with some or all of those provisions; and

- the company's reasons for non-compliance.

The company must ensure that the auditors review each of the following before the annual report is published

- LR 9.8.6(3) (statements by the directors regarding going concern and longer term viability); and

- the parts of the statement required by LR 9.8.6(6) (corporate governance that relate to provisions C.1.1, C.2.1, C.2.3, C.3.1–C.3.8 of the UK Corporate Governance Code).

(q)   *Report to shareholders.* A report to the shareholders containing details of the unexpired term of any directors' service contract of a director proposed for election or re-election at the forthcoming annual general meeting and, if any director proposed for election or re-election does not have a directors' service contract, a statement to that effect.

An overseas company with a premium listing must include in its annual report and accounts the information required by (o), (p) and (q) above and, if it is not required to comply with equivalent requirements imposed by another EEA State, must also comply with the disclosure requirements in DTR 7.2 (corporate governance statements – see **15.5 CORPORATE GOVERNANCE**).

(FCA Listing Rules, paras 9.8.4–9.8.6, 9.8.6A, 9.8.8, 9.8.10).

Note that the UK Corporate Governance Code provisions referred to in (m) and (p) above are those in the April 2016 version of the Code, which is still referred to in the FCA Listing Rules at present. Equivalent recommendations are set out in Provisions 27 to 31 of the July 2018 version of the Code, which applies for periods beginning on or after 1 January 2019.

## 33.33   *Strategic report with supplementary information*

Any strategic report with supplementary information provided to shareholders (see **6 ACCOUNTS: STAND-ALONE STRATEGIC REPORTS**) must disclose earnings per share and the information for a strategic report set out in or under *CA 2006* and the supplementary material required under *CA 2006, s 426A*.

(FCA Listing Rules, para 9.8.13)

### 33.34 *Half-yearly report*

The requirements relating to half-yearly reports are included in the FCA Disclosure Guidance and Transparency Rules. See **33.57**.

### 33.35 Significant transactions: Premium listing

The following provisions apply to a company that has a premium listing. The purpose of the provisions is to ensure that shareholders of such a company are notified of certain transactions entered into by the company and have the opportunity to vote on larger proposed transactions.

**Transactions.** For these purposes, a '*transaction*' includes

- all agreements (including amendments to agreements) entered into by the company or its subsidiaries; and

- the grant or acquisition of an option as if the option had been exercised except that, if exercise is solely at the discretion of the company or a subsidiary, the transaction will be classified on exercise and only the consideration (if any) for the option will be classified on the grant or acquisition;

but excludes

- a transaction of a revenue nature in the ordinary course of business;

- an issue of securities, or a transaction to raise finance, which does not involve the acquisition or disposal of any fixed asset of the company or its subsidiaries; and

- any transaction between the company and a wholly-owned subsidiary or between its wholly-owned subsidiaries.

**Classification of transactions.** A transaction is classified (by assessing its size relative to that of the company proposing to make it) as follows.

- *Class 2 transaction* (where any percentage ratio is 5% or more but each is less than 25%).

- *Class 1 transaction* (where any percentage ratio is 25% or more).

If an issuer is proposing to enter into a transaction classed as a reverse takeover it should consider LR 5.6.

**The percentage ratios are:**

- The *gross assets ratio* calculated by dividing the gross assets the subject of the transaction by the gross assets of the listed company.

- The *profits ratio* calculated by dividing the profits attributable to the assets the subject of the transaction by the profits of the listed company.

- *consideration ratio* calculated by dividing the consideration for the transaction by the aggregate market value of all the ordinary shares (except treasury shares) of the listed company.

- The *gross capital ratio* calculated by dividing the gross capital of the company or business being acquired by the gross capital of the listed company.

**Transaction treated as Class 1 transaction.** The following transactions are to be treated as Class 1 transaction even if not satisfying the percentage ratio test.

(1) *Indemnities and similar arrangements*

Any exceptional agreement or arrangement with a party (other than a wholly-owned subsidiary) under which

(i) a listed company agrees to discharge any liabilities for costs, expenses, commissions or losses incurred by or on behalf of that party, whether or not on a contingent basis; and

(ii) the maximum liability is either unlimited, or is equal to or exceeds an amount equal to 25% of the average of the listed company's profits for the last three financial years (losses should be taken as 'nil' profit and included in this average).

(2) *Break fees*

An arrangement is a break fee arrangement if the purpose of the arrangement is that a compensatory sum will become payable by a listed company to another party (or parties) to a proposed transaction if the proposed transaction fails or is materially impeded and there is no independent substantive commercial rationale for the arrangement. Sums payable pursuant to break fee arrangements in respect of a transaction are to be treated as a Class 1 transaction if the total value of those sums exceeds

(i) if the listed company is being acquired, 1% of the value of the listed company calculated by reference to the offer price; and

(ii) in any other case, 1% of the market capitalisation of the listed company.

The total value of sums payable pursuant to break fee arrangements for the above purposes is the sum of

(i) any amounts paid or payable pursuant to break fee arrangements in relation to the same transaction or in relation to the same target assets or business in the 12 months prior to the date the most recent arrangements were agreed unless those arrangements were approved by shareholders; and

(ii) the aggregate of the maximum amounts payable pursuant to break fee arrangements in relation to the transaction

save that if the arrangements are such that a particular sum will only become payable in circumstances in which another sum does not, the lower sum may be left out of the calculation of the total value.

(3) *Issues by major subsidiary undertakings*

If

(i) a major subsidiary undertaking of a listed company issues equity shares for cash or in exchange for other securities or to reduce indebtedness;

(ii) the issue would dilute the listed company's percentage interest in the major subsidiary undertaking; and

(iii) the economic effect of the dilution is equivalent to a disposal of 25% or more of the aggregate of the gross assets or profits (after the deduction of all charges except taxation) of the group.

then the issue is to be treated as a Class 1 transaction.

This does not apply if the major subsidiary undertaking is itself a listed company.

'*Major subsidiary undertaking*' is a subsidiary undertaking that represents 25% or more of the aggregate of the gross assets or profits (after deducting all charges except taxation) of the group.

**Aggregating transactions**. Except in relation to a break fee arrangement (see above), transactions completed during the 12 months before the date of the latest transaction must be aggregated with that transaction for the purposes of classification if

• they are entered into by the company with the same person or with persons connected with one another;

• they involve the acquisition or disposal of securities or an interest in one particular company; or

• together they lead to substantial involvement in a business activity which did not previously form a significant part of the company's principal activities.

If, under this rule, aggregation of transactions results in a requirement for shareholder approval, then that approval is required only for the latest transaction.

(FCA Listing Rules, paras 10.1.1–10.1.3, 10.2.1–10.2.4, 10.2.6A, 10.2.7–10.2.10).

**33.36** *Reverse takeovers*

LR 5.6 applies to an issuer with:

(1)    a premium listing;

(2)    a standard listing (shares); or

(3)    a standard listing of certificates representing equity securities.

*Categories of reverse takeover to which LR 5.6 does not apply*

LR 5.6 does not apply where an issuer acquires the shares or certificates representing equity securities of a target with the same category of listing as the issuer.

*Class 1 requirements*

Notwithstanding the effect of LR 5.6.2 R, an issuer with a premium listing must in relation to a reverse takeover comply with the requirements of LR 10.5 (Class 1 requirements) for that transaction.

*Definition*

A reverse takeover is a transaction, whether effected by way of a direct acquisition by the issuer or a subsidiary, an acquisition by a new holding company of the issuer or otherwise, of a business, a company or assets:

(1)    where any percentage ratio is 100% or more; or

(2)    here any percentage ratio is 100% or more; or (2) which in substance results in a fundamental change in the business or in a change in board or voting control of the issuer.

When calculating the percentage ratio, the issuer should apply the class tests.

For the purpose of LR 5.6.4R (2), the FCA considers that the following factors are indicators of a fundamental change:

(1)     the extent to which the transaction will change the strategic direction or nature of its business; or

(2)     whether its business will be part of a different industry sector following the completion of the transaction; or

(3)     whether its business will deal with fundamentally different suppliers and end users.

*Requirement for a suspension*

An issuer, or in the case of an issuer with a premium listing, its sponsor, must contact the FCA as early as possible:

(1)     before announcing a reverse takeover which has been agreed or is in contemplation, to discuss whether a suspension of listing is appropriate; or

(2)     where details of the reverse takeover have leaked, to request a suspension.

Examples of where the FCA will consider that a reverse takeover is in contemplation include situations where:

(1)     the issuer has approached the target's board;

(2)     the issuer has entered into an exclusivity period with a target; or

(3)     the issuer has been given access to begin due diligence work (whether or not on a limited basis).

Generally, when a reverse takeover is announced or leaked, there will be insufficient publicly available information about the proposed transaction and the issuer will be unable to assess accurately its financial position and inform the market accordingly. In this case, the FCA will often consider that suspension will be appropriate, as set out in LR 5.1.2G (3) and (4). However, if the FCA is satisfied that there is sufficient publicly available information about the proposed transaction it may agree with the issuer that a suspension is not required.

LR 5.6.10 G to LR 5.6.18 R set out circumstances in which the FCA will generally be satisfied that a suspension is not required.

*Target admitted to a regulated market*

The FCA will generally be satisfied that there is sufficient information in the market about the proposed transaction if:

(1)     the target has shares or certificates representing equity securities admitted to a regulated market; and

(2)     the issuer makes an announcement stating that the target has complied with the disclosure requirements applicable on that regulated market and providing details of where information disclosed pursuant to those requirements can be obtained.

An announcement made for the purpose of LR 5.6.10G (2) must be published by means of an RIS.

*Target subject to the disclosure regime of another market*

The FCA will generally be satisfied that there is sufficient publicly available information in the market about the proposed transaction if the target has securities admitted to an investment exchange or trading platform that is not a regulated market and the issuer:

(1)     confirms, in a form acceptable to the FCA, that the disclosure requirements in relation to financial information and inside information of the investment exchange or trading platform on which the target's securities are admitted are not materially different from the disclosure requirements under DTR; and

(2)     makes an announcement to the effect that:

  (a)     the target has complied with the disclosure requirements applicable on the investment exchange or trading platform to which its securities are admitted and provides details of where information disclosed pursuant to those requirements can be obtained; and

  (b)     there are no material differences between those disclosure requirements and the disclosure requirements.

Where an issuer has a premium listing, a written confirmation provided for the purpose of LR 5.6.12G(1) must be given by the issuer's sponsor.

An announcement made for the purpose of LR 5.6.12G(2) must be published by means of an RIS.

*Target not subject to a public disclosure regime*

Where the target in a reverse takeover is not subject to a public disclosure regime, or if the target has securities admitted on an investment exchange or trading platform that is not a regulated market but the issuer is not able to give the confirmation and make the announcement contemplated by LR 5.6.12G, the FCA will generally be satisfied that there is sufficient publicly available information in the market about the proposed transaction such that a suspension is not required where the issuer makes an announcement containing:

(1)     financial information on the target covering the last three years. Generally, the FCA would consider the following information to be sufficient:

  (a)     profit and loss information to at least operating profit level;

  (b)     balance sheet information, highlighting at least net assets and liabilities;

  (c)     relevant cash flow information; and

  (d)     a description of the key differences between the issuer's accounting policies and the policies used to present the financial information on the target;

(2)     a description of the target to include key non-financial operating or performance measures appropriate to the target's business operations and the information as required under PR Appendix 3 Annex 1 item 12 (Trend information) for the target;

(3)     a declaration that the directors of the issuer consider that the announcement contains sufficient information about the business to be acquired to provide a properly informed basis for assessing its financial position; and

(4)     a declaration confirming that the issuer has made the necessary arrangements with the target vendors to enable it to keep the market informed without delay of any developments concerning the target that would be required to be released were the target part of the issuer.

An announcement made for the purpose of LR 5.6.15 must be published by means of an RIS.

Where an issuer has a premium listing, a sponsor must provide written confirmation to the FCA that in its opinion, it is reasonable for the issuer to provide the declarations described in LR 5.6.15G(3) and (4).

Where the FCA has agreed that a suspension is not necessary as a result of an announcement made for the purpose of LR 5.6.15G the issuer must comply with DTR 2.2.1R on the basis that the target already forms part of the enlarged group.

*Cancellation of listing*

The FCA will generally seek to cancel the listing of an issuer's equity shares or certificates representing equity securities when the issuer completes a reverse takeover.

LR 5.6.23G to LR 5.6.29G set out circumstances in which the FCA will generally be satisfied that a cancellation is not required.

Where the issuer's listing is cancelled following completion of a reverse takeover, the issuer must re-apply for the listing of the shares or certificates representing equity securities and satisfy the relevant requirements for listing, except that for an issuer with a premium listing, LR 6.1.3R(1)(b) and LR 6.1.3 R(1)(e) will not apply in relation to the issuer's accounts.

Notwithstanding LR 5.6.21R, financial information provided in relation to the target will need to satisfy LR 6.1.3R(1)(b) and LR 6.1.3R(1)(e).

*Acquisitions of targets from different listing categories: issuer maintaining its listing category*

Where the issuer's listing is cancelled following completion of a reverse takeover, the issuer must re-apply for the listing of the shares or certificates representing equity securities and satisfy the relevant requirements for listing, except that for an issuer with a premium listing, LR 6.2.1R(3) and LR 6.2.4R(2) will not apply in relation to the issuer's accounts.

(1)     the issuer will continue to be eligible for its existing listing category following completion of the transaction;

(2)     the issuer provides an eligibility letter setting out how the issuer as enlarged by the acquisition satisfies each listing rule requirement that is relevant to it being eligible for its existing listing category; and

(3)     the issuer makes an announcement or publishes a circular explaining:

    (a)     the background and reasons for the acquisition;

    (b)     any changes to the acquiring issuer's business that have been made or are proposed to be made in connection with the acquisition;

    (c)     the effect of the transaction on the acquiring issuer's obligations under the listing rules;

    (d)     (where appropriate) how the acquiring issuer will continue to meet the eligibility requirements referred to in LR 5.6.21R; and

    (e)     any other matter that the FCA may reasonably require.

An announcement or circular published for the purpose of LR 5.6.23G must be published by means of an RIS.

An eligibility letter prepared for the purposes of LR 5.6.23G must be provided to the FCA not less than 20 business days prior to the announcement of the transaction referred to in LR 5.6.24R.

Where an issuer has a premium listing, the eligibility letter provided for the purposes of LR 5.6.23G must be provided by a sponsor.

*Acquisitions of targets from different listing categories: issuer changing listing category*

The FCA will generally be satisfied that a cancellation is not required on completion of a reverse takeover if the target is listed with a different listing category from that of the issuer and the issuer wishes to transfer its listing to a different listing category in conjunction with the acquisition and the issuer as enlarged by the relevant acquisition complies with the relevant requirements of LR 5.4A to transfer to a different listing category.

An issuer wishing to transfer a listing of its equity shares from a premium listing (investment company) to a standard listing (shares) should note LR 5.4A.2 G which sets out limitations resulting from the application of LR 14.1.1 R (application of the listing rules to a company with or applying for a standard listing of shares).

Where an issuer is applying LR 5.4A in order to avoid a cancellation as contemplated by LR 5.6.27G, the FCA will normally waive the requirement for shareholder approval under LR 5.4A.4R(2)(c) where the issuer is obtaining separate shareholder approval for the acquisition.

(FCA Listing Rules, paras 5.6.1–5.6.29).

Special provisions apply to reverse takeovers involving shell companies, see LR 5.6.5AR, 5.6.6R, 5.6.7G, 5.6.8G, 5.6.10G, 5.6.12G, 5.6.13R, 5.6.15G, 5.6.17R and 5.6.18R.

**33.37** *Notifying significant transactions*

The notification requirements of the various classifications of transaction are as follows.

(1)   *Class 2 requirements*

A listed company must notify a RIS as soon as possible after the terms of a Class 2 transaction are agreed. Notification must include

- details of the transaction, including the name of the other party to the transaction;

- a description of the business carried on by, or using, the net assets the subject of the transaction;

- the consideration and how it is being satisfied (including the terms of any arrangement for deferred consideration);

- the value of the gross assets the subject of the transaction;

- the profit attributable to those assets;

- the effect of the transaction on the listed company including any benefits which are expected to accrue;

- details of any service contracts of proposed directors of the listed company;

- for a disposal, the application of the sales proceeds;

- for a disposal, if securities are to form part of the consideration received, a statement whether such securities are to be sold or retained; and

- details of any key individuals important to the business or company the subject of the transaction.

*Supplementary notification.* A RIS must also be notified as soon as possible if, at any time after the notification as above has been made, the company becomes aware that there has been a 'significant' change in any matter contained in the earlier notification or there is any significant new matter which requires notification. The supplementary notification must give details of the change or new matter and also contain a statement that, except as disclosed, there has been no other significant change or new matter which would have been required to be mentioned in that earlier notification if known at the time. '*Significant*' means significant for the purpose of making an informed assessment of the assets and liabilities, financial position, profits and losses and prospects of the listed company and the rights attaching to any securities forming part of the consideration. It includes a change in the terms of the transaction that affects the percentage ratios and requires the transaction to be reclassified into a higher category.

(2)   *Class 1 requirements*

In the case of a Class 1 transaction, a listed company must

- comply with the Class 2 requirements under (2) above;

- send an explanatory circular to the shareholders and obtain their prior approval in a general meeting for the transaction; and

- ensure that any agreement effecting the transaction is conditional on such approval being obtained.

If, after the production of a circular and before the completion of a Class 1 transaction or a reverse takeover, there is a material change to the terms of the transaction, the listed company must comply again separately with the above requirements in relation to the transaction. The FCA would (amongst other things) consider an increase of 10% or more in the consideration payable to be a material change.

A listed company in severe financial difficulty may find itself with no alternative but to dispose of a substantial part of its business within a short time frame to meet its ongoing working capital requirements or to reduce its liabilities. Due to time constraints, it may not be able to prepare a circular and convene an extraordinary general meeting to obtain prior shareholder approval. In such circumstances, the FCA may modify the above requirements if the company can demonstrate that it is in severe financial difficulty and satisfies the requirements set out in FCA Listing Rules, paras 10.8.2–10.8.6.

An application to modify LR 10.5 should be brought to the FCA's attention at the earliest available opportunity and at least five clear business days before the terms of the disposal are agreed.

(FCA Listing Rules, paras, 10.4.1, 10.4.2, 10.5.1, 10.5.2, 10.8.1).

## 33.38   Related party transactions: Premium listing

The following provisions of LR 11 apply to a company that has a premium listing. The purpose of the provisions generally is to set out safeguards that apply to transactions arrangements between a listed company and a related party or any other person that may benefit a related party.

*LR11.1.1AR (Controlling Shareholder – Special Provisions)*

Where a company has a premium listing and:

(1)   it is not in compliance with:

    (a)   the provisions in LR 9.2.2AR(2)(a); or

    (b)   LR 9.2.2GR; or

(2)   it becomes aware that a controlling shareholder or any of its associates is not in compliance with an independence provision contained in an agreement entered into under LR 6.1.4BR(1) or LR 9.2.2AR(2)(a);

(3)   it becomes aware that a procurement obligation (as set out in LR 6.5.5R(2)(a) or LR 9.2.2BR(2)(a) contained in an agreement entered into under LR 6.5.4R(1) or LR 9.2.2AR(2)(a) has not been complied with by a controlling shareholder; or

(4)   an independent director declines to support a statement made under LR 9.8.4R(14)(a) or LR 9.8.4R(14)(c),

the special provisions of LR 11.1.1CR apply.

In exceptional circumstances, the FCA may consider dispensing with or modifying the application of LR 11.1.1A R, in accordance with LR 1.2.1 R.

The effect of LR11.1.1C is that the company cannot rely on any of the following provisions in relation to a transaction or arrangement with or for the benefit of the relevant controlling shareholder or any associate of that controlling shareholder:

(1)    the concessions specified in LR 11.1.5R(1), LR 11.1.5R(2) and LR 11.1.5R(3) in relation to transactions or arrangements in the ordinary course of business;

(2)    LR 11.1.6R; and

(3)    LR 11.1.10R.

LR 11.1.11R provides for the aggregation of transactions conducted over a 12-month period.

If the FCA considers that it would be appropriate to do so, the FCA may dispense with or modify the application of LR 11.1.1CR(1), in accordance with LR 1.2.1R.

Where a company that has a premium listing has been subject to the provisions of LR 11.1.1AR, LR 11.1.1CR will continue to apply to the company until the publication of an annual financial report which:

(1)    contains the statements required under LR 9.8.4R(14)(a) and LR 9.8.4R(14)(c); and

(2)    does not contain a statement made under LR 9.8.4AR.

(FCA Listing Rules, paras 11.1.1A–E).

**Transactions.** For the purposes of LR 11, a reference to a transaction or arrangement by a listed company includes a transaction or arrangement by one of its subsidiaries and, unless the contrary intention appears, a transaction or arrangement includes the entering into of the agreement for the transaction or the entering into of the arrangement.

**Related party.** Related party is broadly defined to cover

•      any person who is (or was in the 12 months before the date of the transaction)

        (i)      a substantial shareholder (ie a person who controls 10% or more of the voting rights at general meeting of the company (or any subsidiary, fellow subsidiary or parent company); or

        (ii)     a director or shadow director of the company (or any subsidiary, fellow subsidiary or parent company);

•      a person exercising significant influence; or

•      an associate of any of the above.

**Related party transaction.** A related party transaction is

•      a transaction (other than a transaction in the ordinary course of business) between a listed company and a related party;

•      an arrangement(other than an arrangement in the ordinary course of business) pursuant to which a listed company and a related party each invests in, or provides finance to, another undertaking or asset; or

- any other similar transaction or arrangement (other than a transaction in the ordinary course of business) between a listed company and any other person the purpose and effect of which is to benefit a related party.

In assessing whether a transaction is in the ordinary course of business, the FCA will have regard to the size and incidence of the transaction and also whether the terms and conditions are unusual. See LRs 11.1.3, 11.1.4 and 11.1.4A for the definitions of 'transaction', 'related party' and 'substantial shareholder'.

(FCA Listing Rules, paras 11.1.1–11.1.5).

33.39   *Requirements for related party transactions*

Subject to the exemptions in **33.40**, if a listed company enters into a related party transaction, it must

(a)    make a notification in accordance with **33.37(2)** (notification of a Class 2 transaction) and in addition give details of the name of the related party and the nature and extent of the related party's interest in the transaction;

(b)    send a circular to its shareholders containing both the information required by all circulars (see **33.43**) and the specific information required of circulars for related party transactions in FCA Listing Rules, paras 13.6.1–13.6.3;

(c)    obtain approval of its shareholders for the transaction either before it is entered into or, if the transaction is expressed to be conditional on such approval, before it is completed; and

(d)    ensure that the related party does not vote on the relevant resolution and takes all reasonable steps to ensure that the related party's associates do not vote on the relevant resolution.

If after obtaining shareholder approval but before the completion of a related party transaction, there is a material change to the terms of the transaction, the listed company must comply again separately with LR11.1.7 ((*a*)–(*d*) above) in relation to the transaction. The FCA would (amongst other things) generally consider an increase of 10% or more in the consideration payable to be a material change to the terms of the transaction.

A listed company must comply with LR10.5.4 in relation to a related party transaction.

This applies to the variation or novation of an existing agreement between the listed company and a related party whether or not, at the time the original agreement was entered into, that party was a related party.

*Modified requirements for smaller related party transactions.* Where each of the percentage ratios in **33.35** is less than 5%, but one or more exceeds 0.25%, instead of having to comply with (*a*)–(*d*) above, the listed company must

(i)    [deleted]

(ii)   before entering into the transaction or arrangement obtain written confirmation from a sponsor that the terms of the proposed transaction or arrangement with the related party are fair and reasonable as far as the shareholders of the listed company are concerned; and

(iii)  as soon as possible upon entering into the transaction or arrangement make a RIS announcement which sets out the identity of the related party, the value of the consideration for the transaction or arrangement, a brief description of the transaction or arrangement, the fact that the transaction or arrangement fell within LR 11.1.10 and any other relevant circumstances.

*Aggregation of transactions.* If a listed company enters into transactions with the same related party (and any of its associates) in any 12-month period and the transactions have not been approved by shareholders, the transactions or arrangements, including transactions or arrangements falling under LR 11.1.10 or small related party transactions under LR 11 Annex 1.1 R(1) must be aggregated. If any percentage ratio in 33.35 is 5% or more for the aggregated transactions, the company must comply with (*a*)–(*d*) above in respect of the latest transaction.

If transactions that are small transactions under 33.40(1) are aggregated as above and for the aggregated small transactions each of the percentage ratios is less than 5% but one or more exceeds 0.25%, the listed company must comply with (ii) above in respect of the latest small transaction and (ii) and (iii) above in respect of the aggregated small transactions.

(FCA Listing Rules, paras 11.1.7, 11.1.9–11.1.11).

**33.40** *Exempt transactions*

The requirements in 33.39 do not apply to a transaction within (1) below or a transaction within (2)–(9) below provided it does not have any unusual features.

(1)   *Small transactions.* A small transaction, ie a transaction where each of the applicable percentage ratios in 33.35 is equal to or less than 0.25%.

(2)   *Transactions agreed before person became a related party.* A transaction the terms of which

   (i)   were agreed at a time when no party to the transaction (or person who was to receive the benefit of the transaction) was a related party; and

   (ii)   have not been amended, or required the exercise of discretion by the listed company under those terms, since the party or person became a related party.

(3)   *Issue of new securities and sale of treasury shares.* A transaction that consists of

   (i)   the take up by a related party of new securities or treasury shares under its entitlement in a pre-emptive offering; or

   (ii)   an issue of new securities made under the exercise of conversion or subscription rights attaching to a listed class of securities.

(4)   *Employees' share schemes or long-term incentive schemes.* In accordance with the terms of an employees' share scheme or a long-term incentive scheme, the transaction

   (i)   involves the receipt of any asset (including cash or securities of the company or any of its subsidiaries) by a director of the company, its parent or any of its subsidiaries;

   (ii)   is the grant of an option or other right to such a director to acquire (whether or not for consideration) any asset (including cash or new or existing securities of the company or any of its subsidiaries); or

   (iii)   is a gift or loan to the trustees of an employee benefit trust to finance the provisions of assets under (i) or (ii) above.

(5)   *Credit.* The transaction is a grant of credit (including the lending of money or the guaranteeing of a loan)

   (i)   to the related party on normal commercial terms;

   (ii)   to a director for an amount and on terms no more favourable than those offered to employees of the group generally; or

   (iii)   by the related party on normal commercial terms and on an unsecured basis.

(6)   *Directors' indemnities and loans.* The transaction is

(i)   the grant of an indemnity to, or the maintenance of a contract of insurance for, a director of the listed company (or any of its subsidiaries) which is specifically permitted under *CA 2006*; or

(ii)   a loan or assistance to a director by a listed company (or any of its subsidiaries) if the terms of the loan or assistance are in accordance with those specifically permitted under *CA 2006, s 204, 205 or 206.*

(7)   *Underwriting.* The transaction is the underwriting by a related party of all or part of an issue of securities by the listed company (or any of its subsidiaries) provided the consideration is no more than commercial consideration and is the same as that paid to other underwriters (if any).

(8)   *Joint investment arrangements.* An arrangement where a listed company (or any of its subsidiaries) and a related party each invests in, or provides finance to, another undertaking or asset if the following conditions are satisfied.

(i)   The amount invested by the related party is not more than 25% of the amount invested by the listed company (or any of its subsidiaries) and the listed company has advised the FCA in writing that this condition has been met.

(ii)   An independent adviser acceptable to the FCA has provided a written opinion to the FCA that the terms of the investment by the listed company (or any of its subsidiaries) are no less favourable than those applying to the investment by the related party.

(iii)   The advice in (i) and the opinion in (ii) are provided before the investment is made.

(9)   *Insignificant subsidiary undertakings.* A transaction where the following conditions are satisfied.

(i)   The party to the transaction is only a related party because

•   it is (or was within the 12 months before the date of the transaction) a substantial shareholder or its associate, or

•   it is a person who is (or was within the 12 months before the date of the transaction) a director or shadow director or his associate

of a subsidiary or subsidiaries of the listed company that has contributed less than 10% (10% in aggregate if more than one subsidiary) of the profits of, and represented less than 10% of the assets of, the listed company for the 'relevant period'.

'*Relevant period*' means each of the three financial years before the date of the transaction for which accounts have been published (where the subsidiary or subsidiaries have only been part of the listed company's group for more than one but less than three years, each of the financial years before the date of the transaction for which accounts have been published).

(ii)   The subsidiary has (or each of the subsidiaries as the case may be have) been in the listed company's group for one year or more.

(iii)   If the subsidiary is (or subsidiaries are) themselves party to the transaction or if securities in them or their assets are the subject of the transaction, the consideration ratio must be less than 10%.

(FCA Listing Rules, para 11.1.6, LR 11 Annex).

**33.41  Dealing in own securities and treasury shares: Premium listing**

The provisions in this paragraph apply to a company that has a premium listing and contains rules which apply to a listed company that:

(1)     purchases its own equity shares;

(2)     purchases its own securities other than equity shares;

(3)     sells or transfers treasury shares;

(4)     purchases its own securities from a related party.

The provisions in (1)–(4) below do not apply to a transaction entered into

•       in the ordinary course of business by a securities dealing business, or

•       on behalf of third parties either by the company or any member of its group

if the listed company has established and maintains effective Chinese walls between those responsible for any decision relating to the transaction and those in possession of inside information relating to the listed company.

(1)     *Prohibition on purchase of own securities*

These provisions were deleted on 3 July 2016 when the Market Abuse Regulation came into force.

(2)     *Purchases from a related party*

Where a purchase by a listed company of its own equity securities or preference shares is to be made from a related party (whether directly or through intermediaries), the related party transactions (see **33.38–33.40**) must be complied with unless

•       a tender is made to all holders of the class of securities; or

•       in the case of a market purchase authorised under a general authority granted by shareholders, it is made without prior understanding, arrangement or agreement between the company and any related party.

Where a purchase by a listed company of its own equity securities or preference shares is to be made from a related party which is a sovereign controlling shareholder or an associate of a sovereign controlling shareholder, the modifications to LR 11 (Related party transactions) in LR 21.5 (Transactions with related parties: Equity shares) and LR 21.10 (Transactions with related parties: Certificates representing shares) do not apply for the purposes of LR 12.3.1R.

(3)     *Purchases of own equity shares*

Purchases by a listed company of less than 15% of any class of its equity shares (excluding treasury shares) under a general authority granted by shareholders can only be made if

•       a tender offer is made to all holders of the class; or

•       the price to be paid is not more than the higher of 5% above the average market values of those shares for the five business days before the purchase is made and the price stipulated by Article 5.6 of the Market Abuse Regulation.

Purchases by a listed company of 15% or more of any class of equity shares (excluding treasury shares) pursuant to a general authority by the shareholders must be by way of a tender offer to all shareholders of that class. Purchases of 15% or more of any class of its own equity shares may be made by a listed company, other than by way of a tender offer, provided that the full terms of the share buyback have been specifically approved by shareholders. Where a series of purchases in aggregate amount to 15% or more, a tender offer need only be made in respect of any purchase that takes the aggregate to or above that level. Purchases that have been specifically approved by shareholders are not to be taken into account in determining whether the 15% level has been reached.

*Notification prior to purchase.* Any decision by the board to submit to shareholders a proposal for the listed company to be authorised to purchase its own equity shares (other than a renewal of an existing authority) must be notified to a RIS as soon as possible. Notification must indicate whether the proposal relates to specific purchases (in which case the names of the persons from whom the purchases are made must be given) or a general authorisation to make purchases. The outcome of the shareholders' meeting must also be notified.

*Notification of purchases.* Purchases must be notified to a RIS as soon as possible and in any event no later than 7.30am on the next business day. The notification must include

- the date of purchase;

- the number of equity shares purchased;

- the purchase price for each of the highest and lowest prices paid (where relevant);

- the number of the equity shares purchased for cancellation and purchased to be held as treasury shares; and

- where equity shares were purchased to be held as treasury shares, a statement of

    (i)    the total number of treasury shares of each class held by the company following the purchase and non-cancellation as such equity shares; and

    (ii)   the number of equity shares of each class that the company has in issue less the total number of treasury shares of each class held by the company following the purchase and non-cancellation of such equity shares.

*Consent of other classes.* Where there are in issue listed convertible securities which are convertible into the equity shares in question,

- a separate meeting of the holders of those convertible securities must be held, and

- their approval for the proposed purchase of equity shares obtained by a special resolution,

before the company enters into any agreement to purchase the shares. This does not apply if the trust deed or terms of issue of the relevant securities authorise the listed company to purchase its own equity shares.

(4)    *Purchase of own securities other than equity shares*

Except where the purchase will consist of individual transactions made in accordance with the terms of issue of the relevant securities, where a listed company intends to purchase any of its securities convertible into its equity shares with a premium listing, it must

- ensure that no dealings in the relevant securities are carried out by or on behalf of the company (or another group member) until the proposal has either been notified to a RIS or abandoned; and

- notify a RIS of its decision to purchase.

*Notification of purchases, early redemptions and cancellations.* Any purchases, early redemptions or cancellations of a company's own securities by or on behalf of the company or any other group member must be notified to a RIS when an aggregate of 10% of the initial amount of the relevant class of securities has been purchased, redeemed or cancelled and for each 5% in aggregate of the initial amount of that class acquired thereafter. This must be done as soon as possible and in any event no later than 7.30am on the next business day. Notification must include

- the amount of securities acquired, redeemed or cancelled since the last notification; and

- whether or not the securities acquired are to be cancelled and the number of that class of securities that remain outstanding.

*Warrants and options.* Where, within a period of 12 months, a listed company purchases warrants or options over its own equity shares which, on exercise, give the entitlement to equity shares representing 15% or more of the company's existing issued shares (excluding treasury shares), the company must send to its shareholders a circular containing the following information.

- A statement of the directors' intentions regarding future purchases of the company's warrants and options.

- The number and terms of the warrants or options acquired and to be acquired and the method of acquisition.

- Where warrants or options have been, or are to be, acquired from specific parties, a statement of the names of those parties and all material terms of the acquisition.

- Details of the prices to be paid.

(5)   *Treasury shares*

*Capitalisation issues and sales, transfers and cancellations of treasury shares.* Where, by virtue of it holding treasury shares (see **34.19** for the meaning of treasury shares), a company is allotted shares as part of a capitalisation issue, it must notify a RIS as soon as possible and in any event no later than 7.30 am on the next business day. The notification must state

- the date of the allotment;

- the number of shares allotted;

- a statement as to what number of the shares allotted have been cancelled and what number is being held as treasury shares; and

- where shares allotted are being held as treasury shares, a statement of

    (i)    the total number of treasury shares of each class held by the company following the allotment; and

    (ii)   the number of shares of each class that the company has in issue less the total number of treasury shares of each class held by the company following the allotment.

Any sale for cash, transfer for the purposes of or pursuant to an employees' share scheme or cancellation of treasury shares that represents over 0.5% of the listed company's share capital must be notified to a RIS as soon as possible and in any event by no later than 7.30am on the next business day. The notification must include

•   the date of the sale, transfer or cancellation;

•   the number of the shares sold, transferred or cancelled;

•   the sale or transfer price for each of the highest and lowest prices paid, where relevant; and

•   a statement of

    (i)    the total number of treasury shares of each class held by the company following the sale, transfer or cancellation; and

    (ii)   the number of shares of each class that the company has in issue less the total number of treasury shares of each class held by the company following the sale, transfer or cancellation.

(FCA Listing Rules, paras 12.1.1, 12.1.3, 12.2.1, 12.3.1, 12.3.2, 12.4.1, 12.4.2, 12.4.2A, 12.4.3, 12.4.4–12.4.8, 12.5.1–12.5.3, 12.5.7, 12.6.3–12.6.4).

### 33.42  Circulars: Premium listing

Chapter 13 of the Listing Rules applies only to a company that has a premium listing. A listed company that has a premium listing must ensure that circulars it issues to holders of listed equity shares comply with the provisions of Chapter 13.

**Incorporation by reference.** With the exception of the information in **33.43**, information may be incorporated in a circular issued by a listed company by reference to relevant information contained in an approved prospectus or listing particulars of that listed company or any other published document of that listed company that has been filed with the FCA. Such information must be the latest available to the company. When information is incorporated by reference, a cross-reference list must be provided in the circular so that security holders can easily identify specific items of information.

**Approval of circulars.** A listed company must not circulate or publish any of the following types of circular unless it has been approved by the FCA:

(1)   a class 1 circular;

(2)   a related party circular;

(3)   a circular that proposes the purchase by a listed company of its own shares which is required by LR 13.7.1R(2) to include a working capital statement; [Note LR 12.4.10G];

(4)   a circular that proposes a reconstruction or a refinancing of a listed company which is required by LR 9.5.12R to include a working capital statement;

(5)   a circular that proposes a cancellation of listing which is required to be sent to shareholders under LR 5.2.5R(1); or

(6)   a circular that proposes a transfer of listing which is required to be sent to the shareholders under LR 5.4A.4R(2).

The following documents (to the extent applicable) must be lodged with the FCA in final form before it will approve a circular.

(a)    A Sponsors Declaration for the Production of a Circular completed by the sponsor.

(b)    For a Class 1 circular or related party circular, a letter setting out any items of information required by the Listing Rules that are not applicable in that particular case.

(c)    Any other document that the FCA has asked for in advance from the listed company or its sponsor.

At least 10 clear business days before the date on which it is intended to publish the circular, two copies of the draft circular, draft copies of the letters and documents in (*a*) and (*b*) above must be submitted to the FCA.

Where a circular submitted for approval is amended, two copies of amended drafts must be resubmitted, marked to show changes made to conform with FCA comments and to indicate other changes.

A listed company must send a circular to holders of its listed equity shares as soon as practicable after it has been approved.

(FCA Listing Rules, paras 13.1.1–13.1.6, 13.2.1, 13.2.4–13.2.5, 13.2.7 and 13.2.10).

**33.43**   *Contents of circulars*

*Contents of all circulars.* Every circular sent by a listed company to holders of its listed securities must

- provide a clear and adequate explanation of its subject matter giving due prominence to its essential characteristics, benefits and risks;

- state why the security holder is being asked to vote or, if no vote is required, why the circular is being sent;

- if voting or other action is required

   (i)    contain all information necessary to allow the security holders to make a properly informed decision;

   (ii)   contain a heading drawing attention to the document's importance and advising security holders who are in any doubt as to what action to take to consult appropriate independent advisers; and

   (iii)  contain a recommendation from the Board as to the voting action security holders should take for all resolutions proposed, indicating whether or not the proposal described in the circular is, in the Board's opinion, in the best interests of security holders as a whole;

- state that if all the securities have been sold or transferred by the addressee the circular and any other relevant documents should be passed to the person through whom the sale or transfer was effected for transmission to the purchaser or transferee;

- if new securities are being issued in substitution for existing securities, explain what will happen to existing documents of title;

- not include any reference to a specific date on which listed securities will be marked 'ex' any benefit or entitlement which has not been agreed in advance with the RIE on which the company's securities are or are to be traded;

- if it relates to a transaction in connection with which securities are proposed to be listed, include a statement that application has been or will be made for the securities to be admitted and, if known, a statement of

(i)     the dates on which the securities are expected to be admitted and on which dealings are expected to commence;

(ii)    how the new securities rank for dividend or interest;

(iii)   whether the new securities rank equally with any existing listed securities;

(iv)    the nature of the document of title;

(v)     the proposed date of issue;

(vi)    the treatment of any fractions;

(vii)   whether or not the security may be held in uncertificated form; and

(viii)  the names of the RIEs on which securities are to be traded;

• if a person is named in the circular as having advised the listed company or its directors, a statement that the adviser has given and has not withdrawn its written consent to the inclusion of the reference to the adviser's name in the form and context in which it is included; and

• if the circular relates to cancelling listing, state whether it is the company's intention to apply to cancel the securities' listing.

If another part of the Listing Rules provides that a circular of a particular type must include specified information, then that information is (unless the contrary intention appears) in addition to the information required above.

(FCA Listing Rules, paras 13.3.1, 13.3.2).

*Specified information.* The Listing Rules also contain specified information to be included in certain types of circulars as follows.

| *Circular* | *FCA Listing Rules* |
|---|---|
| Class 1 circulars | Paras 13.4.1–13.4.8 and 13.5.1–13.5.34 |
| Related party circulars | Paras 13.6.1–13.6.4 |
| Circulars about purchase of own equity securities | Paras 13.7.1–13.7.2 |
| Other circulars about the allotment of shares of various types, company meetings, amendments to the constitution and the election of independent directors | Paras 13.8.1–13.8.18 |

*Sovereign Controlled Commercial Companies*

LR 21 applies to a sovereign controlled commercial company applying for, or with, a premium listing (sovereign controlled commercial company).

LR 21.2 to LR 21.5 apply in respect of a premium listing (sovereign controlled commercial company) of equity shares.

LR 21.6 to LR 21.10 apply in respect of a premium listing (sovereign controlled commercial company) of certificates representing shares and apply to: (1) a depositary; and (2) an issuer of the equity shares which are represented by certificates.

*LR 21.2 Requirements for listing: Equity shares*

*LR 21.2.1R*

To be listed, an applicant must comply with:

(1)   LR 2 (Requirements for listing: All securities);

(2)   LR 6 (Additional requirements for premium listing (commercial company)) except LR 6.1.1R and subject to the modifications and additional requirements set out in LR 21.2.2G to LR 21.2.5R; and

(3)   LR 21.2.6R and LR 21.2.7R.

*LR 21.2.2G*

For the purposes of LR 21.2.1R(2), in LR 6.4.3G, factors that may indicate that an applicant does not satisfy LR 6.4.1R (Independent Business) also include situations where an applicant has granted or may be required to grant security over its business in connection with the funding of a sovereign controlling shareholder.

*LR 21.2.3R*

For the purposes of LR 21.2.1R(2), in LR 6.5, references to a controlling shareholder must be read as excluding a sovereign controlling shareholder.

*LR 21.2.4R*

For the purposes of LR 21.2.1R(2), in LR 6.14.5G(2)(c), the reference to premium listing (commercial companies) must be read as a reference to premium listing (sovereign controlled commercial company).

*LR 21.2.5 R*

LR 21.2.1R(2) does not apply where:

(1)   the applicant meets the following conditions:

(a)   it has an existing premium listing (sovereign controlled commercial company) of equity shares;

(b)   it is applying for the admission of equity shares of the same class as the shares that have been admitted to premium listing; and

(c)   it is not entering into a transaction classified as a reverse takeover; or

(2)   the following conditions are met:

(a)   a company has an existing premium listing (sovereign controlled commercial company) of equity shares;

(b)   the applicant is a new holding company of the company in (a); and

(c)   the company in (a) is not entering into a transaction classified as a reverse takeover.

*LR 21.2.6R*

An applicant must have a sovereign controlling shareholder.

*LR 21.2.7R*

To comply with LR 21.2.6R, a State which is a sovereign controlling shareholder must be either:

(1)    recognised by the government of the UK as a State at the time the application is made; or

(2)    the UK.

*LR 21.3 Listing applications and procedures: Equity shares*

*LR 21.3.1G*

An applicant is required to comply with LR 3 (Listing applications: All securities).

*Sponsors*

*LR 21.3.2G*

An applicant that is seeking admission of its equity shares is required to retain a sponsor in accordance with LR 8 (Sponsors: Premium listing).

*LR 21.3.3R*

An applicant must appoint a sponsor on each occasion that it makes an application for admission of equity shares which requires the production of listing particulars.

*LR 21.4 Continuing obligations: Equity shares*

*LR 21.4.1R*

A listed company must comply with:

(1)    LR 9 (Continuing obligations) subject to the modifications and additional require-ments set out in LR 21.4.2G to LR 21.4.4R;

(2)    LR 10 (Significant transactions: Premium listing);

(3)    LR 12 (Dealing in own securities and treasury shares: Premium listing); and

(4)    LR 13 (Contents of circulars: Premium listing) subject to the modifications set out in LR 21.4.3R.

*LR 21.4.2G*

For the purposes of LR 21.4.1R(1), in LR 9.2.2AAG, factors that may indicate that a listed company does not satisfy LR 9.2.2AR (Independent Business) also include situations where a listed company has granted or may be required to grant security over its business in connection with the funding of a sovereign controlling shareholder.

*LR 21.4.3R*

For the purposes of LR 21.4.1R(1) and LR 21.4.1R(4), references to controlling shareholder must be read as excluding a sovereign controlling shareholder in, or for the purposes of, the following: (1) LR 9.2.2ABR and LR 9.2.2ACG; (2) LR 9.2.2ADR(1); (3) LR 9.2.2BR; (4) LR 9.2.2CR; (5) LR 9.2.2GR and LR 9.2.2HG; (6) LR 9.8.4 R(11); (7) LR 9.8.4R(14); and (8) LR 13.8.18R.

*LR 21.4.4R*

For the purposes of LR 21.4.1R(1):

(1)     in the second sentence of LR 9.2.21R the reference to the provisions of LR 5.4A.4R(3)(b)(ii) and LR 5.4A.4R(3)(c)(ii) (Approval of Independent Shareholders) must be read as a reference to the provisions of LR 5.4A.4R(3)(d)(ii);

(2)     in LR 9.2.26G (Inability to Comply) the reference to LR 9.2 must be read as a reference to LR 9.2 as modified by LR 21.4; and

(3)     in LR 9.8.4CR (Information in Annual Financial Report) the reference to LR 9.8.4R must be read as a reference to LR 9.8.4R as modified by LR 21.4.3R.

*LR 21.4.5G*

*Where a purchase by a listed company of its own equity securities or preference shares is to be made from a* related party which is a sovereign controlling shareholder or an associate of a sovereign controlling shareholder, the listed company should note LR 12.3.2R (Inapplicability of Modifications to LR11 dealing with Transactions with Related Parties).

*Additional requirements: sovereign controlling shareholder*

*LR 21.4.6R*

A listed company must at all times have a sovereign controlling shareholder.

*LR 21.4.7R*

To comply with LR 21.4.6R, a State which is a sovereign controlling shareholder must be either:

(1)     recognised by the government of the UK as a State; or

(2)     the UK.

*LR 21.4.8R*

A listed company must notify the FCA without delay if it no longer complies with the continuing obligation set out in LR 21.4.6R.

*LR 21.4.9G*

Where a listed company is unable to comply with the continuing obligation set out in LR 21.4.6R, it should consider seeking a cancellation of listing or applying for a transfer of its listing category. In particular, the listed company should note LR 5.2.2G(2) and LR 5.4A.17G (Examples of Situations where the FCA may Suspend/Cancel a Listing).

*Sponsors*

*LR 21.4.10G*

A listed company should consider the requirements in LR 8.2 (When a sponsor must be appointed or its guidance obtained) and LR 8.5 (Responsibilities of listed companies), subject to the modification to LR 8.2.3R in LR 21.5.3R.

*LR 21.5 Transactions with related parties: Equity shares*

*LR 21.5.1R*

A listed company must comply with LR 11 (Related party transactions: Premium listing) subject to the modifications in LR 21.5.2R.

*LR 21.5.2R*

For the purposes of LR 21.5.1R, in the case of a related party which is a sovereign controlling shareholder or an associate of a sovereign controlling shareholder:

(1) the following provisions do not apply: (a) LR 11.1.1AR to LR 11.1.1ER (Independent Business/Controlling Shareholder); (b) LR 11.1.7R(2) to LR 11.1.7R(4) (Requirements for Related Party transaction); (c) LR 11.1.7CR and LR 11.1.8G (Supplements); (d) LR 11.1.10R(2)(b) (Sponsor's Confirmation); and (e) LR 11.1.11R(3)(a) (Small Transactions);

(2) the following provisions are modified as follows: (a) LR 11.1.7AR must be read as if the words 'after obtaining shareholder approval but' are omitted; (b) LR 11.1.9G must be read as follows: (i) the reference to LR 11.1.7R must be read as a reference to LR 11.1.7R as modified by LR 21.5.2R(1); and (ii) as if the words 'and LR 11.1.8G' are omitted; (c) LR 11.1.11R(1) must be read as if the words 'and the transactions or arrangements have not been approved by shareholders' are replaced by 'and LR 11.1.11R(2) as modified by LR 21.5.2R(2)(d) has not been complied with in relation to these transactions or arrangements'; and (d) LR 11.1.11R(2) must be read as follows: (i) as if the first sentence is omitted and replaced by the following sentence 'If any percentage ratio is 5% or more for the aggregated transactions or arrangements, the listed company must comply with LR 11.1.7R as modified by LR 21.5.2R(1) in respect of the latest transaction or arrangement, and details of each of the transactions or arrangements being aggregated must be included in the notification required by LR 11.1.7R(1).'; and (ii) as if the 'Note' is omitted.

*LR 21.5.3R*

The requirement in LR 8.2.3R to obtain the guidance of a sponsor does not apply where a listed company is proposing to enter into a transaction which is, or may be, a related party transaction and the related party concerned is a sovereign controlling shareholder or an associate of a sovereign controlling shareholder, unless the related party transaction is, or may be, a purchase by the listed company of its own equity securities or preference shares.

*LR 21.5.4G*

Where a purchase by a listed company of its own equity securities or preference shares is to be made from a related party which is a sovereign controlling shareholder or an associate of a sovereign controlling shareholder, the listed company should note LR 12.3.2R.

*LR 21.6 Requirements for listing: Certificates representing shares*

Issuer of equity shares is taken to be the issuer.

*LR 21.6.1R*

If an application is made for the admission of certificates representing shares:

(1) the issuer of the equity shares which the certificates represent is the issuer for the purpose of the listing rules; and

(2) the application will be dealt with as if it were an application for the admission of the equity shares.

*Certificates representing shares*

*LR 21.6.2R*

For certificates representing shares to be admitted to listing, an issuer of the equity shares which the certificates represent must comply with LR 21.6.3R to LR 21.6.8R.

*LR 21.6.3R*

An issuer must be:

(1)     duly incorporated or otherwise validly established according to the relevant laws of its place of incorporation or establishment; and

(2)     operating in conformity with its constitution.

*LR 21.6.4R*

For the certificates to be listed, the equity shares which the certificates represent must:

(1)     conform with the law of the issuer's place of incorporation;

(2)     be duly authorised according to the requirements of the issuer's constitution; and

(3)     have any necessary statutory or other consents.

*LR 21.6.5R*

(1)     For the certificates to be listed, the equity shares which the certificates represent must be freely transferable.

(2)     For the certificates to be listed, the equity shares which the certificates represent must be fully paid and free from all liens and from any restriction on the right of transfer (except any restriction imposed for failure to comply with a notice under section 793 of the Companies Act 2006 (Notice by company requiring information about interests in its shares)).

*LR 21.6.6G*

The FCA may modify LR 21.6.5R to allow partly paid equity shares if it is satisfied that their transferability is not restricted and investors have been provided with appropriate information to enable dealings in the equity shares to take place on an open and proper basis.

*LR 21.6.7G*

The FCA may, in exceptional circumstances, modify or dispense with LR 21.6.5R where the issuer has the power to disapprove the transfer of equity shares if the FCA is satisfied that this power would not disturb the market in those equity shares.

*LR 21.6.8R*

(1)     For the certificates to be listed, the applicant must demonstrate that the rights attaching to the equity shares which the certificates represent are capable of being exercised by the holders of the certificates as if they were the holders of the relevant equity shares.

(2)     For the certificates to be listed, the applicant must demonstrate that it has arrangements in place which enable the holders of the certificates to exercise the rights attaching to the equity shares which the certificates represent as if they were the holders of the relevant equity shares.

*Additional requirements for the issuer*

*LR 21.6.9R*

For certificates representing shares to be admitted to listing, an issuer must comply with:

(1)     LR 6 (Additional requirements for premium listing (commercial company)) except LR 6.1.1R (Application) and LR 6.14.1R to LR 6.15.1R (Shareholdings) and subject to the modifications and additional requirements set out in LR 21.6.10G to LR 21.6.13R; and

(2)     LR 21.6.14R to LR 21.6.21R.

*LR 21.6.10G*

For the purposes of LR 21.6.9R(1), in LR 6.4.3G, factors that may indicate that an applicant does not satisfy LR 6.4.1R (Independent Business) also include situations where an applicant has granted or may be required to grant security over its business in connection with the funding of a sovereign controlling shareholder.

*LR 21.6.11R*

For the purposes of LR 21.6.9R(1), in LR 6.5 references to a controlling shareholder must be read as excluding a sovereign controlling shareholder.

*LR 21.6.12R*

For the purposes of LR 21.6.9R(1), references to shares or equity shares must be read as references to certificates representing shares in the following: (1) LR 6.3.2G(2); (2) LR 6.4.2G; (3) LR 6.5.2G; (4) LR 6.6.2G; (5) LR 6.7.1R; (6) LR 6.10.1R; (7) LR 6.10.2R; (8) LR 6.10.3R(1); (9) LR 6.11.1R; and (10) LR 6.12.1R.

*LR 21.6.13R*

LR 21.6.9R(1) does not apply where:

(1)     the applicant meets the following conditions:

    (a)     it has an existing premium listing (sovereign controlled commercial company) of certificates representing shares;

    (b)     it is applying for the admission of certificates representing shares of the same class as the certificates that have been admitted to premium listing; and

    (c)     it is not entering into a transaction classified as a reverse takeover; or

(2)     the following conditions are met:

    (a)     a company has an existing premium listing (sovereign controlled commercial company) of certificates representing shares;

    (b)     the applicant is a new holding company of the company in (a); and

    (c)     the company in (a) is not entering into a transaction classified as a reverse takeover.

*LR 21.6.14R*

If the prospectus or listing particulars for the certificates representing shares that are being admitted does not include a working capital statement which demonstrates that LR 6.7.1R is satisfied, then:

(1)     an applicant must prepare and publish a working capital statement which demonstrates that LR 6.7.1R is satisfied;

(2)     the working capital statement required by paragraph (1) must be prepared in accordance with item 3.1 of Annex 3 of the PD Regulation; and

(3)     the working capital statement required by paragraph (1) must be published at the same time as the prospectus or listing particulars, as applicable.

*LR 21.6.15R*

A working capital statement published for the purposes of LR 21.6.14R must be published by means of a RIS.

*LR 21.6.16R*

An applicant must have a sovereign controlling shareholder.

*LR 21.6.17R*

To comply with LR 21.6.16R, a State which is a sovereign controlling shareholder must be either:

(1)     recognised by the government of the UK as a State at the time the application is made; or

(2)     the UK.

*Certificates in public hands*

*LR 21.6.18R*

(1)     If an application is made for the admission of a class of certificates representing shares, a sufficient number of certificates must, no later than the time of admission, be distributed to the public in one or more EEA States.

(2)     For the purposes of paragraph (1), account may also be taken of holders in one or more states that are not EEA States, if the certificates are listed in the state or states.

(3)     For the purposes of paragraph (1), a sufficient number of certificates will be taken to have been distributed to the public when 25% of the certificates for which application for admission has been made are in public hands.

(4)     For the purposes of paragraphs (1), (2) and (3), certificates are not held in public hands if they are:

    (a)     held directly or indirectly by:

        (i)     a director of the applicant or of any of its subsidiary undertakings; or

        (ii)    a person connected with a director of the applicant or of any of its subsidiary undertakings; or

        (iii)   the trustees of any employees' share scheme or pension fund established for the benefit of any directors and employees of the applicant and its subsidiary undertakings; or

        (iv)    any person who under any agreement has a right to nominate a person to the board of directors of the applicant; or

        (v)     any person or persons in the same group or persons acting in concert who have an interest in 5% or more of the certificates of the relevant class; or

    (b)     subject to a lock-up period of more than 180 calendar days.

*LR 21.6.19G*

(1)     The FCA may modify LR 21.6.18R to accept a percentage lower than 25% if it considers that the market will operate properly with a lower percentage in view of the large number of certificates of the same class and the extent of their distribution to the public.

(2)     In considering whether to grant a modification, the FCA may take into account the following specific factors:

    (a)     certificates of the same class that are held (even though they are not listed) in states that are not EEA States;

    (b)     the number and nature of the public holders of certificates; and

    (c)     in relation to premium listing (sovereign controlled commercial company) whether the expected market value of the certificates in public hands at admission exceeds £100 million.

*LR 21.6.20G*

When calculating the number of certificates for the purposes of LR 21.6.18R(4)(a)(v), holdings of investment managers in the same group where investment decisions are made independently by the individual in control of the relevant fund and those decisions are unfettered by the group to which the investment manager belongs will be disregarded.

*Certificates of a non-EEA company*

*LR 21.6.21R*

The FCA will not admit certificates representing shares of an applicant incorporated in a non-EEA State where the class of equity shares which the certificates represent is not listed either in its country of incorporation or in the country in which a majority of its equity shares are held, unless the FCA is satisfied that the absence of listing is not due to the need to protect investors.

*Additional requirements for the certificates*

*LR 21.6.22R*

(1)     To be listed, the certificates representing shares must satisfy the requirements set out in LR 2.2.2R and LR 2.2.4R to LR 2.2.11R.

(2)     For this purpose, in those rules references to securities must be read as references to the certificates representing shares for which application for listing is made.

*LR 21.6.23R*

To be listed, the certificates representing shares must be admitted to trading on a regulated market for listed securities operated by a RIE.

*LR 21.6.24R*

To be listed, the certificates representing shares must not impose obligations on the depositary that issues the certificates except to the extent necessary to protect the certificate holders' rights to, and the transmission of entitlements of, the equity shares.

*Additional requirements for a depositary*

*LR 21.6.25R*

A depositary that issues certificates representing shares must maintain adequate arrangements to safeguard certificate holders' rights to the equity shares to which the certificates relate, and to all rights relating to the equity shares and all money and benefits that it may receive in respect of them, subject only to payment of the remuneration and proper expenses of the issuer of the certificates.

*LR 21.6.26G*

The requirement to maintain adequate arrangements to safeguard all rights relating to the equity shares includes enabling the holders of the certificates representing shares to exercise the votes attaching to the equity shares to which the certificates relate. A depositary must not vote or attempt to exercise the votes attaching to the equity shares to which the certificates relate except pursuant to and in accordance with instructions from the holders of the certificates representing shares.

*LR 21.7 Listing applications and procedures: Certificates representing shares*

*LR 21.7.1R*

An applicant for admission of certificates representing shares must comply with LR 3.2 and LR 3.4.4R to LR 3.4.6R subject to the modification and additional requirement set out in LR 21.7.2R.

*LR 21.7.2R*

In addition to the documents referred to in LR 3.4.6R, an applicant for admission of certificates representing shares must keep a copy of the executed deposit agreement for six years after the admission of the relevant certificates.

*Sponsors*

*LR 21.7.3G*

An applicant that is seeking admission of certificates representing shares is required to retain a sponsor in accordance with LR 8 (Sponsors: Premium listing).

*LR 21.7.4R*

An applicant must appoint a sponsor on each occasion that it makes an application for admission of certificates representing shares which requires the production of listing particulars.

*LR 21.8 Continuing obligations: Certificates representing shares*

*Compliance with LR 9 (Continuing obligations)*

*LR 21.8.1R*

A listed company must comply with LR 9 (Continuing obligations) except: (1) LR 9.2.1R to LR 9.2.2R (Admission to Trading); (2) LR 9.2.5G to LR 9.2.6BR (Disclosure Requirements and Transparency Rules); (3) LR 9.2.15R to LR 9.2.15AG (Shares in Public Hands); (4) LR 9.2.21R to LR 9.2.22G (Voting); and (5) LR 9.2.26G; and subject to the modifications and additional requirements set out in LR 21.8.2R to LR 21.8.12R (Inability to Comply).

*LR 21.8.2R*

For the purposes of LR 21.8.1R, references to the listed company or the issuer must be read as references to the issuer of the equity shares which the certificates represent in LR 9.

*LR 21.8.2AR*

For the purposes of LR 21.8.1R, in LR 9.2.23R, the reference to LR 9.2.21R should be read as a reference to LR 21.8.22R.

*LR 21.8.3G*

For the purposes of LR 21.8.1R, in LR 9.2.2AAG, factors that may indicate that a listed company does not satisfy LR 9.2.2AR (Independent Business) also include situations where a listed company has granted or may be required to grant security over its business in connection with the funding of a sovereign controlling shareholder.

*LR 21.8.4R*

For the purposes of LR 21.8.1R, references to controlling shareholder must be read as excluding a sovereign controlling shareholder in, or for the purposes of, the following: (1) LR 9.2.2ABR and LR 9.2.2ACG; (2) LR 9.2.2ADR(1); (3) LR 9.2.2BR; (4) LR 9.2.2CR; (5) LR 9.2.2GR and LR 9.2.2HG; (6) LR 9.8.4 R(11); and (7) LR 9.8.4R(14).

*LR 21.8.5G*

For the purposes of obtaining the shareholder approvals required by: (1) LR 9.2.2ER; (2) LR 9.2.2FR; (3) LR 9.4.1R(2); (4) LR 9.4.4R(2); and (5) LR 9.5.10R(3)(a), a listed company is required under LR 21.8.13R to ensure that the holders of its certificates representing shares are able to exercise the votes attaching to the equity shares which the certificates represent on any shareholder vote.

*LR 21.8.6G*

For the purposes of LR 9.3.11R, the listed company is required under LR 21.8.13R to ensure that, where the offer is made to holders of the class of equity shares which the certificates represent, the holders of its certificates representing shares have an equal opportunity to participate in the offer.

*LR 21.8.7R*

For the purposes of LR 21.8.1R, LR 9.5 is modified as follows: (1) in LR 9.5.1R(4), the equity securities which are the subject of the rights issue must be of the same class as the equity shares which are represented by the listed certificates representing shares; (2) LR 9.5.3G does not apply; (3) in LR 9.5.10R(1): (a) the reference to a class already listed must be read as a reference to a class of equity shares which the listed certificates represent; and (b) for the purposes of LR 9.5.10R, if the equity shares are not listed, then the middle market price of those equity shares shall be determined by reference to the middle market price of the listed certificates representing shares; and (4) a listed company must comply with the requirements in LR 9.5.15R and LR 9.5.16R so far as relevant to certificates representing shares.

*LR 21.8.8G*

For the purposes of LR 21.8.1R, in LR 9.5, the listed company is required under LR 21.8.13R to ensure that in relation to: (1) any rights issue; or (2) any open offer where the offer relates to the class of equity shares which the certificates represent, the holders of its certificates representing shares have an equal opportunity to participate in the rights issue or open offer.

*LR 21.8.9R*

In addition to complying with LR 9.6.2R, a listed company must also forward to the FCA, for publication through the document viewing facility, two copies of all resolutions passed by the holders of the listed certificates representing shares. It must also comply with the notification requirements set out in LR 9.6.3R in relation to such resolutions.

*LR 21.8.10R*

For the purposes of LR 21.8.1R: (1) in LR 9.6.4R(3) (Notifications Relating to Capital – Redemption of Shares), the reference to listed shares must be read as a reference to equity shares of the class which the certificates represent; and (2) in LR 9.8.4CR, the reference to LR 9.8.4R must be read as a reference to LR 9.8.4R (Information in Annual Financial Report) as modified by LR 21.8.4R.

*LR 21.8.11R*

In addition to complying with LR 9.6.18R, a listed company must also notify a RIS as soon as possible after a meeting of the holders of the listed certificates representing shares of all resolutions passed by the holders.

*LR 21.8.12R*

In addition to complying with LR 9.7A.2R, a listed company must comply with the notification requirements in LR 9.7A.2R in respect of the equity shares which the certificates represent.

*Additional requirements: exercise of rights attaching to the equity shares which the certificates represent*

*LR 21.8.13R*

(1)    The rights attaching to the equity shares which the certificates represent must at all times be capable of being exercised by the holders of the certificates as if they were the holders of the relevant equity shares.

(2)    A listed company must at all times have in place arrangements which enable the holders of the certificates to exercise the rights attaching to the equity shares which the certificates represent as if they were the holders of the relevant equity shares.

(3)    Every circular which is sent by a listed company to the holders of the equity shares which the certificates represent must be sent to the holders of its certificates representing shares at the same time as the circular is despatched to the holders of those equity shares.

*Additional requirements: compliance with the disclosure requirements and transparency rules*

*LR 21.8.14G*

A listed company, whose certificates representing shares are admitted to trading on a regulated market in the United Kingdom, should consider its obligations under the disclosure requirements.

*LR 21.8.15R*

A listed company that is not already required to comply with the obligations referred to under article 17 of the Market Abuse Regulation (Competent Authorities) must comply with those obligations as if it were an issuer for the purposes of the disclosure requirements and transparency rules subject to article 22 of the Market Abuse Regulation.

*LR 21.8.16G*

A listed company, whose certificates representing shares are admitted to trading on a regulated market, should consider its obligations under DTR 4 (Periodic Financial Reporting), DTR 5 (Vote Holder and Issuer Notification Rules), DTR 6 (Continuing obligations and access to information) and DTR 7 (Corporate governance).

*LR 21.8.17R*

A listed company that is not already required to comply with DTR 4, DTR 5 and DTR 6 (or with corresponding requirements imposed by another EEA Member State) must comply with DTR 4, DTR 5 and DTR 6 as if it were an issuer of shares for the purposes of the transparency rules.

*Additional requirements: certificates in public hands and admission to trading*

*LR 21.8.18R*

A listed company must comply with LR 21.6.18R at all times.

*LR 21.8.19G*

Where the FCA has modified LR 21.6.18R to accept a percentage lower than 25% on the basis that the market will operate properly with a lower percentage, but the FCA considers that in practice the market for the certificates representing shares is not operating properly, the FCA may revoke the modification in accordance with LR 1.2.1R(4).

*LR 21.8.20R*

A listed company must comply with LR 21.6.23R at all times.

*LR 21.8.21R*

A listed company must inform the FCA in writing as soon as possible if it has:

(1)     requested a RIE to admit or re-admit any of its listed certificates representing shares to trading;

(2)     requested a RIE to cancel or suspend trading of any of its listed certificates representing shares; or

(3)     been informed by a RIE that trading of any of its listed certificates representing shares will be cancelled or suspended.

*Additional requirements: voting on matters relevant to premium listing*

*LR 21.8.22R*

(1)     Where pursuant to LR 21.8, LR 21.9 or LR 21.10, the provisions of LR 9.4, LR 9.5, LR 10, LR 11 or LR 12 require a shareholder vote to be taken, that vote must be decided by a resolution of the holders of the class of equity shares which the certificates that have been admitted to premium listing represent.

(2)     Where pursuant to LR 21.8, the provisions of LR 9.2.2ER require that the resolution must in addition be approved by the independent shareholders, only:

(a)     independent shareholders who hold equity shares of the class which the certificates that have been admitted to premium listing represent; and

(b)     holders of certificates admitted to premium listing who would be independent shareholders within (a) if they held the equity shares which the certificates represent;

can vote.

(3)     Where the provisions of LR 5.2 or LR 5.4A require a vote of the holders of the certificates to be taken, that vote must be decided by a resolution of the holders of the listed company's certificates representing shares that have been admitted to premium listing.

(4)     Where the provisions of LR 5.2.5R(2A) or LR 5.4A.4R(3)(e)(ii) require that the resolution must in addition be approved by holders of certificates other than the controlling shareholder, only holders of the listed company's certificates representing shares that have been admitted to premium listing can vote.

*LR 21.8.23G*

(1)     In the case of a shareholder vote referred to in LR 21.8.22R(1), the listed company is required under LR 21.8.13R to ensure that the holders of the listed certificates representing shares are able to exercise the votes attaching to the equity shares which the certificates represent on any shareholder vote.

(2)     The purpose of LR 21.8.22R(2) is to ensure that the election or re-election of independent directors must be approved by the independent shareholders as a class. That class includes those persons whose entitlement to vote on the election of the independent directors arises as a result of their holding of certificates representing shares that have been admitted to premium listing. Accordingly, in the case of approval by the independent shareholders referred to in LR 21.8.22R(2), the listed company is required under LR 21.8.13R to ensure that the holders of the listed certificates representing shares are able to exercise the votes attaching to the equity shares which the certificates represent in relation to any such approval.

*LR 21.8.24G*

Where the provisions of LR 5.2.5R(2A) (Cancellation of Listing) or LR 5.4A.4R(3)(e)(ii) (Transfer of Categories of Lisiting) require that the resolution must in addition be approved by holders of certificates other than the controlling shareholder, the controlling shareholder will include a sovereign controlling shareholder.

*LR 21.8.25G*

The FCA may modify the operation of LR 21.8.22R in exceptional circumstances, for example to accommodate the operation of:

(1)     special share arrangements designed to protect the national interest;

(2)     dual-listed company voting arrangements; and

(3)     voting rights attaching to preference shares or similar securities that are in arrears.

*LR 21.8.26G*

Where a listed company is unable to comply with a continuing obligation set out in:

(1)     LR 9.2 as modified by LR 21.8; or

(2)     LR 21.8.13R to LR 21.8.25G,

it should consider seeking a cancellation of listing or applying for a transfer of its listing category. In particular, the listed company should note LR 5.2.2G(2) and LR 5.4A.16G.

*Additional requirements: working capital statement*

*LR 21.8.27R*

In relation to an application for admission of certificates representing shares of an applicant that has certificates representing shares already listed:

(1)     an applicant must satisfy the FCA that it and its subsidiary undertakings (if any) have sufficient working capital available for the group's requirements for at least the next 12 months from the date of publication of the prospectus or listing particulars for the certificates representing shares that are being admitted; and

(2)   if the prospectus or listing particulars for the certificates representing shares that are being admitted does not include a working capital statement which demonstrates that the requirement under paragraph (1) is satisfied, then:

  (a)   an applicant must prepare and publish a working capital statement which demonstrates that the requirement under paragraph (1) is satisfied;

  (b)   the working capital statement required by paragraph (a) must be prepared in accordance with item 3.1 of Annex 3 of the PD Regulation; and

  (c)   the working capital statement required by paragraph (a) must be published at the same time as the prospectus or listing particulars, as applicable.

*LR 21.8.28R*

A working capital statement published for the purposes of LR 21.8.27R must be published by means of a RIS.

*Additional requirements: sovereign controlling shareholder*

*LR 21.8.29R*

A listed company must at all times have a sovereign controlling shareholder.

*LR 21.8.30 R*

To comply with LR 21.8.29R, a State which is a sovereign controlling shareholder must be either:

(1)   recognised by the government of the UK as a State; or

(2)   the UK.

*LR 21.8.31R*

A listed company must notify the FCA without delay if it no longer complies with the continuing obligation set out in LR 21.8.29R.

*LR 21.8.32G*

Where a listed company is unable to comply with the continuing obligation set out in LR 21.8.29R, it should consider seeking a cancellation of listing or applying for a transfer of its listing category. In particular, the listed company should note LR 5.2.2G(2) and LR 5.4A.17G.

*Change of depositary*

*LR 21.8.33R*

Prior to any change of the depositary of certificates representing shares, the new depositary must satisfy the FCA that it meets the requirements of LR 21.6.22R to LR 21.6.26G.

*Notification of change of depositary*

*LR 21.8.34R*

(1)   An issuer of equity shares represented by listed certificates representing shares must notify a RIS of any change of depositary.

(2)   The notification required by paragraph (1) must be made as soon as possible and in any event by 7:30 am on the business day following the change of depositary, and must contain the following information:

(a)     the name, registered office and principal administrative establishment if different from the registered office of the depositary;

(b)     the date of incorporation and length of life of the depositary, except where indefinite;

(c)     the legislation under which the depositary operates and the legal form which it has adopted under the legislation; and

(d)     any changes to the information regarding the certificates representing shares.

*Sponsors*

*LR 21.8.35G*

A listed company should consider the requirements in LR 8.2 (When a sponsor must be appointed or its guidance obtained) and LR 8.5 (Responsibilities of listed companies), subject to the modification to LR 8.2.3R in LR 21.10.5R.

*LR 21.9 Transactions and circulars: certificates representing shares*

*Compliance with LR 10 (Significant transactions: Premium listing)*

*LR 21.9.1R*

A listed company must comply with LR 10 (Significant transactions: Premium listing) subject to the modifications and additional requirements set out in LR 21.9.2G to LR 21.9.9R.

*LR 21.9.2G*

Where a company has certificates representing shares listed, the purpose of LR 10 is also to ensure that holders of certificates representing shares:

(1)     are notified of certain transactions entered into by the listed company; and

(2)     have the opportunity to vote on larger proposed transactions.

*LR 21.9.3R*

For the purposes of LR 21.9.1R, references to the listed company or the issuer must be read as references to the issuer of the equity shares which the certificates represent in LR 10.

*LR 21.9.4R*

For the purposes of LR 21.9.1R, in LR 10.2.7R(1)(b), the figure used to determine the market capitalisation of the listed company is calculated as follows:

(1)     where the class of equity shares which the certificates represent is listed, the aggregate market value of all the equity shares which are listed (excluding treasury shares); and

(2)     where the class of equity shares which the certificates represent is not listed:

(a)     by dividing the aggregate market value of all the equity shares which are represented by the certificates in issue by the number of equity shares represented by the certificates; and

(b)     then multiplying the result by the total number of equity shares in the class of the equity shares which the certificates represent (excluding treasury shares).

*LR 21.9.5G*

A listed company is required under LR 21.8.13R(3) to ensure that any circular which is sent to shareholders pursuant to LR 10.5.1R(2) or LR 10.5.4R(1)(b) is sent to holders of its certificates representing shares at the same time as the circular is despatched to shareholders.

*LR 21.9.6G*

For the purposes of obtaining the prior shareholder approval required by LR 10.5.1R, a listed company is required under LR 21.8.13R to ensure that the holders of its certificates representing shares are able to exercise the votes attaching to the equity shares which the certificates represent on any shareholder vote.

*LR 21.9.7G*

For the purposes of LR 21.9.1R, in LR 10.5.5G, it may also be necessary to adjourn a convened shareholder meeting if a supplementary circular cannot be sent to holders of listed certificates representing shares at least seven days prior to the convened shareholder meeting as required by LR 13.1.9R.

*LR 21.9.8R*

For the purposes of LR 21.9.1R, paragraph 5R(5) of Annex 1 to LR 10 (Significant transactions: Premium listing) does not apply and, for the purposes of paragraph 5R(1) of Annex 1, the figure used to determine market capitalisation is calculated as at the close of business on the last business day before the announcement as follows:

(1)      where the class of equity shares which the certificates represent is listed, the aggregate market value of all the equity shares which are listed (excluding treasury shares); and

(2)      where the class of equity shares which the certificates represent is not listed:

    (a)      by dividing the aggregate market value of all the equity shares which are represented by the certificates in issue by the number of equity shares represented by the certificates; and

    (b)      then multiplying the result by the total number of equity shares in the class of the equity shares which the certificates represent (excluding treasury shares).

*LR 21.9.9R*

For the purposes of LR 21.9.1R, in paragraphs 7R(4)(a) and 7R(5)(a) of Annex 1 to LR 10, the market value of the listed company's shares is to be calculated as follows:

(1)      where the class of equity shares which the certificates represent is listed, the aggregate market value of all the equity shares which are listed (excluding treasury shares); and

(2)      where the class of equity shares which the certificates represent is not listed:

    (a)      by dividing the aggregate market value of all the equity shares which are represented by the certificates in issue by the number of equity shares represented by the certificates; and

    (b)      then multiplying the result by the total number of equity shares in the class of the equity shares which the certificates represent (excluding treasury shares).

*Compliance with LR 12 (Dealing in own securities and treasury shares: Premium listing)*

*LR 21.9.10R*

A listed company must comply with all the requirements of LR 12 (Dealing in own securities and treasury shares: Premium listing) subject to the modifications and additional requirements set out in LR 21.9.11R to LR 21.9.17G.

*LR 21.9.11R*

For the purposes of LR 21.9.10R, in LR 12:

(1)     references to the listed company must be read as references to the issuer of the equity shares which the certificates represent; and

(2)     the reference in the definition of tender offer to a class of its listed equity securities must be read as a reference to a class of equity shares which the certificates represent.

*LR 21.9.12G*

In relation to the requirement set out in LR 12.3.1R(1), the listed company is required under LR 21.8.13R to ensure that, where the tender offer is made to holders of the class of equity shares which the certificates represent, the holders of its certificates representing shares have an equal opportunity to participate in the tender offer.

*LR 21.9.13G*

Where a purchase by a listed company of its own equity securities or preference shares is to be made from a related party which is a sovereign controlling shareholder or an associate of a sovereign controlling shareholder, the listed company should note LR 12.3.2R (Inapplicability of Modifications to LR 11 dealing with Transactions with Related Parties).

*LR 21.9.14G*

For the purposes of LR 21.9.10R, in relation to the requirement set out in LR 12.4.2R (for purchases by the listed company of 15% or more of any class of its equity shares to be by way of a tender offer to all shareholders of that class), the listed company is required under LR 21.8.13R to ensure that, where the tender offer is made to holders of the class of equity shares which the certificates represent, the holders of its certificates representing shares have an equal opportunity to participate in the tender offer.

*LR 21.9.15G*

For the purposes of obtaining the shareholder approval required by LR 12.4.2AR (Purchases Other Than by Tender Offer), a listed company is required under LR 21.8.13R to ensure that the holders of its certificates representing shares are able to exercise the votes attaching to the equity shares which the certificates represent on any shareholder vote.

*LR 21.9.16R*

For the purposes of LR 21.9.10R, references to securities convertible into equity shares with a premium listing must be read as references to securities convertible into the equity shares which the certificates with a premium listing represent in the following:

(1)     LR 12.5.1R (Purchases of Own Securities Other Than Equity Shares); and

(2)     LR 12.5.2R (Notification Requirements).

*LR 21.9.17G*

A listed company is required under LR 21.8.13R(3) to ensure that any circular which is sent to shareholders pursuant to LR 12.5.7R is sent to holders of its certificates representing shares at the same time as the circular is despatched to shareholders.

*Compliance with LR 13 (Contents of circulars: Premium listing)*

*LR 21.9.18R*

A listed company must comply with all the requirements of LR 13 (Contents of circulars: Premium listing) subject to the modifications and additional requirements set out in LR 21.9.19R to LR 21.9.22R.

*LR 21.9.19R*

For the purposes of LR 21.9.18R, in LR 13, references to the listed company or to the issuer must be read as references to the issuer of the equity shares which the certificates represent.

*LR 21.9.20R*

A listed company must ensure that circulars it issues to:

(1)     holders of its listed certificates representing shares; and

(2)     holders of the class of equity shares which the certificates represent,

comply with the requirements of LR 13 as amended by this section.

*LR 21.9.21R*

For the purposes of LR 21.9.18R, references to holders of listed equity shares must be read as references to holders of listed certificates representing share and holders of the class of equity shares which the certificates represent in the following: (1) LR 13.1.9R; (2) LR 13.2.10R; and (3) LR 13.8.8R.

*LR 21.9.22R*

For the purposes of LR 21.9.18R, in LR 13.8.18R, references to controlling shareholder must be read as excluding a sovereign controlling shareholder.

*LR 21.10 Transactions with related parties: certificates representing shares*

*Transactions with related parties*

*LR 21.10.1 R*

A listed company must comply with LR 11 (Related party transactions: Premium listing) subject to the modifications and additional requirements in LR 21.10.2R to LR 21.10.8G.

*LR 21.10.2R*

For the purposes of LR 21.10.1R:

(1)     in LR 11 references to a listed company must be read as references to the issuer of the equity shares which the certificates represent; and

(2)     in LR 11.1.4AR, the reference to the company must be read as a reference to the issuer of the equity shares which the certificates represent.

*LR 21.10.3G*

For the purposes of LR 21.10.1R, a listed company that is required under LR 11.1.7CR to send a supplementary circular should have regard to the guidance in LR 21.9.5G.

*LR 21.10.4R*

In the case of a related party which is a sovereign controlling shareholder or an associate of a sovereign controlling shareholder:

(1)    the following provisions do not apply:

    (a)    LR 11.1.1AR to LR 11.1.1ER (Controlling Shareholder);

    (b)    LR 11.1.7R(2) to LR 11.1.7R(4) (Requirements for Related Party Transactions);

    (c)    LR 11.1.7CR and LR 11.1.8G (Supplementary Circular);

    (d)    LR 11.1.10R(2)(b) (Sponsor's Confirmation); and

    (e)    LR 11.1.11R(3)(a) (Small Transactions),

(2)    the following provisions are modified as follows:

    (a)    LR 11.1.7AR must be read as if the words 'after obtaining shareholder approval but' are omitted;

    (b)    LR 11.1.9G must be read as follows:

        (i)    the reference to LR 11.1.7R must be read as a reference to LR 11.1.7R as modified by LR 21.10.4R(1); and

        (ii)    as if the words 'and LR 11.1.8G' are omitted;

    (c)    LR 11.1.11R(1) must be read as if the words 'and the transactions or arrangements have not been approved by shareholders' are replaced by 'and LR 11.1.11R(2) as modified by LR 21.10.4R(2)(d) has not been complied with in relation to these transactions or arrangements'; and

    (d)    LR 11.1.11R(2) must be read as follows:

        (i)    as if the first sentence is omitted and replaced by the following sentence 'If any percentage ratio is 5% or more for the aggregated transactions or arrangements, the listed company must comply with LR 11.1.7R as modified by LR 21.10.4R(1) in respect of the latest transaction or arrangement, and details of each of the transactions or arrangements being aggregated must be included in the notification required by LR 11.1.7R(1).'; and

        (ii)    as if the 'Note' is omitted.

*LR 21.10.5R*

The requirement in LR 8.2.3R to obtain the guidance of a sponsor does not apply where a listed company is proposing to enter into a transaction which is, or may be, a related party transaction and the related party concerned is a sovereign controlling shareholder or an associate of a sovereign controlling shareholder, unless the related party transaction is, or may be, a purchase by the listed company of its own equity securities or preference shares.

*LR 21.10.6G*

Where a purchase by a listed company of its own equity securities or preference shares is to be made from a related party which is a sovereign controlling shareholder or an associate of a sovereign controlling shareholder, the listed company should note LR 12.3.2R (Inapplicability of Modifications to LR 11 dealing with Transactions with Related Parties).

*Additional requirements*

*LR 21.10.7G*

A listed company is required under LR 21.8.13R(3) to ensure that any circular which is sent to shareholders pursuant to LR 11.1.7R(2) or LR 11.1.8G(2) is sent to holders of its certificates representing shares at the same time as the circular is despatched to shareholders.

*LR 21.10.8G*

For the purposes of obtaining the shareholder approval required by LR 11.1.7R(3) (and any shareholder approval required under LR 11.1.7AR), a listed company is required under LR 21.8.13R to ensure that the holders of its certificates representing shares are able to exercise the votes attaching to the equity shares which the certificates represent on any shareholder vote.

## 33.44 LISTED COMPANIES – DISCLOSURE REGULATIONS AND DISCLOSURE GUIDANCE AND TRANSPARENCY RULES

The FCA is authorised to make rules under *FSMA 2000, Pt VI* and those rules relating to disclosure of information in respect of financial instruments which have been admitted to trading on a regulated market (or for which a request for admission to trading on such a market has been made) were known as Disclosure Rules. [*FSMA 2000, s 73A(3)*]. The Rules implemented *EC Market Abuse Directive, Art 6, EC Commission Directive 2003/124/EC, Arts 2, 3* and *EC Commission Directive 2004/72/EC, Arts 5, 6*. When the *Market Abuse Regulation (EU) 696/2014* (MAR) came into force on 3 July 2016 it superseded the EC Market Abuse Directive and large parts of the Disclosure Rules insofar as they dealt with the disclosure of inside information and dealings by directors and other persons exercising managerial responsibilities in their own company shares. The FCA has taken the approach of deleting rules which have been superseded and directing the reader to the appropriate provisions of MAR but retaining such parts of the rules as continue to provide useful guidance. Accordingly, the former Disclosure Rules are now referred to as Disclosure Guidance and Transparency Rules ('DTR') and the aggregate of the UK guidance and EU rules about disclosure are referred to elsewhere in the Pt VI rules as disclosure regulations.

**Early consultation with the FCA.** An issuer, person discharging managerial responsibilities or connected person should consult with the FCA at an early stage if they are in doubt as to how the Disclosure Regulations apply in a particular situation. Submissions should be in writing unless there is exceptional urgency.

(FCA Disclosure Guidance and Transparency Rules ('DTR'), paras 1.2.4–1.2.5).

## 33.45 Disclosure Guidance – general provisions

(1) *Supply of information to the FCA*

Deleted.

(2) *Requirements of FCA for publication of information*

Deleted.

(3) *Misleading information not to be published*

Deleted.

(4) *Notification when a RIS is not open for business*

If an issuer is required to notify information to a RIS at a time when a RIS is not open for business, it must distribute the information as soon as possible to

- not less than two national newspapers in the UK;

- two newswire services operating in the UK; and

- a RIS for release as soon as it opens.

The fact that a RIS is not open for business is not, in itself, sufficient grounds for delaying the disclosure or distribution of inside information.

(5) *English language*

(DTR 1.3.1, 1.3.3–1.3.8).

**Suspension of trading.**

Deleted – but note Article 23(2)(j) of MAR, which gives the FCA (as the relevant competent authority) power to suspend trading in affected financial instruments.

If trading in an issuer's financial instruments is suspended, the issuer, any persons discharging managerial responsibilities and any connected person must continue to comply with all applicable disclosure requirements.

Examples of when it may require the suspension of trading include

- if an issuer fails to make a required RIS announcement within the time allowed and the FCA considers this could affect the interests of investors or affect the smooth operation of the market; or

- if there is or may be a leak of inside information and the issuer is unwilling or unable to issue an appropriate RIS announcement within a reasonable period of time.

The procedure to be followed is detailed in the FCA's Decision Procedure and Penalties Manual.

(DTR 1.4.1, 1.4.2, 1.4.4).

**33.46  Disclosure and control of inside information by issuers**

The purpose of these provisions is to

- promote prompt and fair disclosure of relevant information to the market; and

- give guidance on aspects relating to disclosure of such information including the circumstance allowing delayed disclosure.

If an issuer is involved in a matter which also falls within the scope of the Takeover Code, it should be mindful of its obligations under MAR.

## 33.46 Public and Listed Companies

**Requirement to disclose inside information.**

Deleted.

However, Article 17(1) of MAR requires an issuer to inform the public as soon as possible of inside information which directly concerns the issuer.

The issuer must ensure that the inside information is made public in a manner which enables fast access and complete, correct and timely assessment of the information by the public and shall post and maintain all such information on its website for at least five years.

Commission Implementing Regulation (EU) 2016/1055, Article 2 requires issuers to disclose inside information using technical means which ensure that the inside information is disseminated widely and on a non-discriminatory basis, free of charge and simultaneously throughout the EU and which clearly identify the content of the inside information, the issuer and the date and time of its communication. Where inside information is posted on a website, Article 3 of this regulation requires this to be done on a non-discriminatory basis, free of charge, in such a way that it can easily be identified and organised in chronological order.

DTR 6.3.2 R requires an issuer or other person to disclose regulated information in the manner prescribed in DTR 6.3.3–6.3.8.

(DTR 1.5.2, 2.1.2, 2.1.3, 2.2.1, 2.2.1A and 2.2.3).

'Inside information' is defined in Article 7.1(a) of MAR as information which is:

—    of a precise nature;

—    not yet made public;

—    relating to financial instruments or the issuer thereof; and

—    price sensitive.

Article 7.2 of MAR states that information is precise if it indicates a set of circumstances which exist or which may reasonably be expected to come into existence where it is specific enough to enable a conclusion to be drawn. In appropriate circumstances this could include an intermediate step (MAR 7.3).

Whether or not the information is price sensitive is to be assessed by reference whether a reasonable investor would likely take it into account in relation to their investment decisions (MAR 7.4).

Further guidance on this 'reasonable investor' test can be found in the FCA Handbook in DTR 2.2.4–2.2.6.

**33.47** *Publication of information on the internet*

Deleted.

However, reference is made to Article 17(1) of MAR (detailed above) as well as to Article 17(9) of MAR which provides that inside information pertaining to issuers whose financial instruments are admitted to trading on an SME growth market may be posted on the trading venue's website instead of the issuer's website if the trading venue provides this facility.

(DTR 2.3.1–2.3.5).

**33.48** *Synchronised release of information*

Deleted.

However, note the provisions of MAR detailed in **33.46** above.

(DTR 2.4.1, 2.4.2).

**33.49** *Delaying disclosure of inside information*

DTR 2.5.1 is deleted but DTR 2.5.1A makes reference to Article 17(4), (5) and (8) MAR.

MAR 17(4) provides that an issuer may on its own responsibility delay disclosure of inside information provided:

(a)    immediate disclosure would prejudice its legitimate interests;

(b)    a delay is not likely to mislead the public;

(c)    the issuer is able to ensure the information is kept confidential.

Where an issuer has delayed disclosure of inside information it shall inform the FCA (being the relevant competent authority) that the information was delayed and provide a written explanation if requested to do so.

Article 17(5) provides that in order to preserve the stability of the financial system, an issuer that is a credit institution or a financial institution may delay public disclosure of inside information including information which is related to a temporary liquidity problem and in particular the need to receive temporary liquidity assistance from a central bank provided:

(a)    disclosure would risk undermining the financial stability of the issuer and the financial system;

(b)    delay is in the public interest;

(c)    confidentiality can be ensured; and

(d)    the FCA (being the relevant competent authority) has consented.

Article 17(8) of MAR provides that where an issuer discloses inside information to a third party in the normal course of their employment, profession or duties they must make public disclosure of such information simultaneously in the case of intentional disclosure and promptly in the case of non-intentional disclosure unless the person receiving the information owes them a duty of confidentiality.

Commission Implementing Regulation (EU) 2016/1055, Article 4 specifies the details which need to be retained and communicated to the FCA about the delayed disclosure of inside information including the arrangements in place for disclosing of the information in the event of a breach of confidentiality. Article 5 of the same regulation addresses the arrangements for a credit institution to delay disclosure of inside information under MAR 17(5).

As ESMA has published guidelines (ESMA/2016/1478) clarifying what would amount to legitimate interests for the purposes of MAR 17(4) and the circumstances where delaying disclosure would be likely to mislead the public.

Examples of legitimate interests which would be prejudiced by premature disclosure of inside information are:

(a)    where the issuer is in the course of negotiations;

(b)    where the issuer's financial viability is at stake;

(c)    where the issuer has a two-tier board and needs the sanction of the supervisory board;

(d)    where the issuer has a new product or invention and its intellectual property rights might be jeopardised;

(e)     where the issuer is proposing to buy or sell a major holding in another entity;

(f)     where the conditions for receiving regulatory approval for a transaction might be jeopardised.

Examples of situations where delay in disclosing inside information would be likely to mislead the public are:

(a)     where it contradicts previous public announcements;

(b)     where it indicates that objectives previously publicly announced are unlikely to be met;

(c)     where it contrasts with market expectations.

An issuer may have a legitimate interest to delay disclosing inside information concerning the provision of liquidity support by the Bank of England or by another central bank to it or to a member of the same group as the issuer.

DTR 2.5.1B averts to the ESMA guidelines and DTR 2.5.2 and 2.5.4 provide further guidance about legitimate interests. DTR 2.5.7–2.5.9 provide guidance on the persons to whom selective disclosure may be made concluding with a warning that the wider the circle of recipients the greater the likelihood that there will be a breach of confidentiality which will trigger an obligation to make full disclosure under MAR 17(8).

(DTR 1.5.2, 2.5.1, 2.5.1A, 2.5.1B, 2.5.2, 2.5.3, 2.5.4, 2.5.5A, 2.5.6 and 2.5.7–2.5.9).

**33.50**  *Control of inside information*

An issuer must establish effective arrangements to deny access to inside information to persons other than those who require it for the exercise of their functions within the issuer (DTR 2.6.1). Article 17(7) of MAR provides that where disclosure of inside information has been delayed and the confidentiality of that information is no longer ensured the issuer shall disclose that information to the public as soon as possible.

DTR 2.6.3 advises an issuer relying on Article 17(4) or (5) of MAR to prepare a holding announcement containing the details prescribed in DTR 2.2.9 ie giving as much detail as possible, explaining why a fuller announcement cannot be made and undertaking to provide further details as soon as possible.

(DTR 2.6.1–2.6.4).

**33.51**  *Insider lists*

The provisions of DTR 2.8 are deleted, but its provisions are substantially reproduced in Article 18 of MAR.

An issuer must ensure that it, and persons acting on its behalf or on its account, draw up a list of those persons working for them, under a contract of employment or otherwise, who have access to inside information relating directly or indirectly to the issuer, whether on a regular or occasional basis. On request, this list must be supplied to the FCA as soon as possible.

The insider list must include the

•      identity of each person having access to inside information;

•      reason why such person is on the insider list; and

•      date on which the insider list was created and updated

and must be promptly updated

- when there is a change in the reason why a person is already on the list;

- when any new person is provided with access to inside information; and

- to indicate the date on which a person on the list ceases to have access to inside information.

Every insider list prepared by the issuer (or by persons acting on its account or on its behalf) must be kept for at least five years from the date on which it was drawn up or updated, whichever is the latest.

*Acknowledgement of legal and regulatory duties.* An issuer must ensure that

- its employees with access to inside information acknowledge the legal and regulatory duties entailed (including dealing restrictions in relation to the issuer's financial instruments) and are aware of the sanctions attaching to the misuse or improper circulation of such information; and

- any person that is acting on its behalf or on its account and has drawn up an insider list has taken the necessary measures to ensure that every person whose name is on that list acknowledges the legal and regulatory duties entailed and is aware of the sanctions attaching to the misuse or improper circulation of such information.

Commission Implementing Regulation (EU) 2016/347 prescribes the format of insider lists and contains suitable templates.

(DTR 2.8.1–2.8.10).

## 33.52 Transactions by persons discharging managerial responsibilities and their connected persons

The substantive provisions of DTR 3 have been deleted.

DTR 3.1.1 now says the purpose of DTR 3 is to provide guidance on the provisions of Article 19 of MAR.

MAR 19.1 provides that 'persons discharging managerial responsibilities', as well as 'persons closely associated' with them, shall notify the issuer and the applicable competent authority (the FCA in the case of UK registered companies: see MAR 19.2) of every transaction conducted on their own account relating to shares or debt instruments of that issuer or to derivatives or other financial instruments relating thereto. Such notification is to be made promptly and no later than three business days after the date of the transaction. This obligation arises once the total amount of transactions has reached the threshold of 5,000 euros (MAR 19.8) in any calendar year.

MAR 3(25) defines a 'person discharging managerial responsibilities' as a person within an issuer which is:

(a)    a member of it administrative, management or supervisory body; or

(b)    a senior executive who is not a member of the bodies referred to in (a) who has regular access to inside information and power to take managerial decisions affecting the future developments and business prospects of the issuer.

DTR 3.1.2A confirms that part (b) of the above definition will apply irrespective of the contractual arrangements between the issuer and the individual concerned.

MAR 3(26) defines a 'person closely associated' as:

(a) a spouse or partner considered equivalent thereto;

(b) a dependent child;

(c) a relative who has shared the same household for at least a year;

(d) a legal person trust or partnership run or directly or indirectly controlled by any of the above or which is set up to benefit them or which has substantially the same economic interests.

DTR 3.1.2B confirms that the annual threshold of 5,000 euros will apply – despite the FCA having power to increase the threshold in MAR 19.9.

MAR 19.3 requires the issuer to ensure that information notified to it in accordance with MAR 19.1 is made public promptly and no later than three business days after the date of the transaction.

MAR 19.6 prescribes the required content of notifications required by MAR 19.1 and Commission Implementing Regulation (EU) 2016/523 prescribes the format and a template.

(DTR 3.1.1–3.1.8).

MAR 19.11 further provides that a 'person discharging managerial responsibilities' within an issuer shall not conduct any transaction on its own account or for the account of a third party, directly or indirectly, relating to shares or debt instruments of the issuer or other financial instruments relating thereto during a closed period of 30 days prior to the announcement of an interim financial report or a year-end report which the issuer is required to publish under the rules of the trading venue on which its shares are admitted to trading or national law.

MAR 19.12 provides that an issuer may nonetheless allow a 'person discharging managerial responsibilities' to trade during a closed period either in exceptional circumstances such as severe financial difficulty or in the context of a employee share scheme or other saving scheme.

Commission Delegated Regulation (EU) 2016/522, Articles 7–9 elaborate the circumstances where a 'person discharging managerial responsibilities' is allowed to trade during a closed period. Where there are exceptional circumstances Article 7 requires a prior written request to be made to the issuer explaining the need to trade during the closed period. Article 8 requires the issuer to be satisfied that circumstances are unforeseen and compelling having regard to legally enforceable commitments which cannot reasonably be satisfied other than by an immediate sale of shares. Article 9 addresses the circumstances where trading during a closed period may be permitted in the context of an employee share scheme or other saving scheme.

### 33.53 LISTED COMPANIES – THE TRANSPARENCY RULES

*CA 2006, ss 1265–1268, 1270–1272* implement the provisions of the *Transparency Obligations Directive* (*Directive 2004/109/EC*) which imposes minimum harmonisation requirements on the information to be provided to the public about 'issuers' and the control of votes attached to shares in those issuers. Under *FSMA 2000, ss 89A–89L* (as inserted by *CA 2006, ss 1266–1268*), the Financial Conduct Authority (FCA) as the competent authority are given powers to make Transparency Rules and call for information from specified persons. The FCA is also given powers in case of infringement of the rules, including public censure of the issuer and power to suspend or prohibit trading of securities.

In relation to the Transparency Rules, '*issuer*' means a legal person whose securities are admitted to trading on a regulated market or whose voting shares are admitted to trading on a UK market other than a regulated market, and in the case of depository receipts representing securities, the issuer is the issuer of the securities represented. [*FSMA 2000, s 102A(6); CA 2006, Sch 15, para 10*].

There are three main categories of obligation that are imposed and that the Transparency Rules implement in respect of UK markets and issuers.

- Requirements for issuers to make public, at regular intervals, information about their financial position and the progress and management of the business of the issuer. See **33.55–33.59**.

- Requirements for holders of votes attached to shares of issuers to notify the issuers when the number of votes they control reach a proportion of the total votes available that is specified. See **33.60–33.70**.

- Requirements for issuers to treat holders of the same securities equally. See **33.74–33.74**.

Transparency Rules are not Listing Rules, Disclosure Rules or Prospectus Rules but are Part 6 Rules. [*FSMA 2000, s 73A(6); CA 2006, Sch 15 para 3*].

**Units trusts, etc**. The provisions do not apply to an undertaking if it is a unit trust or investment company

- the object of which is the collective investment of capital provided by the public and which operates on the principle of risk spreading; and

- the units of which are, at the request of the holder of such units, repurchased or redeemed, directly or indirectly, out of the assets of that undertaking.

(DTR 1A.1).

**Modifying or dispensing with rules**. The FCA can dispense with, or modify, the Transparency Rules as it thinks fit (subject to the terms of *CA 2006* and the *Directive*). Any dispensation or modification may be either unconditional or subject to specified conditions. The FCA can subsequently revoke or modify a dispensation or modification.

An application to the FCA to dispense with or modify, a Transparency Rule must be in writing and

- contain a clear explanation of why the dispensation or modification is requested;

- include details of any special requirements;

- contain all relevant information that should reasonably be brought to the FCA's attention;

- contain any statement or information that is required by the Transparency Rules to be included for a specific type of dispensation or modification; and

- include copies of all documents relevant to the application.

An application should ordinarily be made at least five business days before the proposed dispensation or modification is to take effect.

Where a dispensation or modification has been applied for or granted, the FCA must be notified immediately of any matter which is material to the relevance or appropriateness of the dispensation or modification.

(DTR 1A.2).

### 33.54 Transparency Rules – general provisions

The purpose of the Transparency Rules is to implement parts of the Accounting Directive which requires companies to publish a corporate governance statement. For details of the DTR requirements for corporate governance statements see **15.5**.

(1)   *Early consultation with FCA*

An issuer or other person should consult with the FCA at the earliest possible stage if they are in doubt about how the Transparency Rules apply in a particular situation or consider that it may be necessary for the FCA to dispense with or modify a rule. The address for any such correspondence is:

Primary Market Monitoring

Markets Division

The Financial Conduct Authority

12 Endeavour Square

London

E20 1JN

Fax: 0207 066 8349

(2)   *Requirements of FCA for publication of information*

The FCA may, at any time, require an issuer to publish such information in such form and within such time limits as it considers appropriate to protect investors or to ensure the smooth operation of the market. If an issuer fails to comply, the FCA may itself publish the information (after giving the issuer an opportunity to make representations as to why it should not be published).

(3)   *Misleading information not to be published*

An issuer must take all reasonable care to ensure that any information it notifies to a RIS is not misleading, false or deceptive and does not omit anything likely to affect the import of the information.

(4)   *Notification when a RIS is not open for business*

If an issuer is required to notify information to a RIS at a time when a RIS is not open for business, it must distribute the information as soon as possible to

•      not less than two national newspapers in the UK;

•      two newswire services operating in the UK; and

•      a RIS for release as soon as it opens.

(5)   *Meaning of 'Home State'*

The *'Home State'* of an issuer is

(a)    in the case of an issuer of debt securities the denomination per unit of which is less than 1,000 euros or an issuer of shares

(i)    if the issuer is incorporated in the EEA, the Member State in which it has its registered office; and

(ii)   if the issuer is incorporated in a third country, the Member State in which it is required to file annual information with the competent authority; and

(b)    for an issuer not covered by (i) above, the Member State chosen by the issuer from among the Member States in which the issuer has its registered office and those Member States which have admitted its securities to trading on a regulated market on their territory. The issuer may choose only one Member State as its home Member State. Its choice remains valid for at least three years unless its securities are no longer admitted to trading on any regulated market in the EEA.

The same rules apply to debt securities in a currency other than euros, provided that the value of such minimum denomination is nearly equivalent to 1,000 euros.

(DTR 1A.2, 1A.3, FCA Glossary of definitions).

## 33.55   Periodic financial reporting

The requirements for periodic financial reporting cover the requirements for

- annual financial reports (see **33.56**);

- half-yearly financial reports (see **33.57**). In addition to the general exemption from the Transparency Rules for unit trusts, etc (see **33.53**), there are specific exemptions from the requirements for periodic financial reporting in **33.59** below.

### 33.56   *Annual financial reports*

Subject to the exemptions under **33.59** below, these provisions apply to an issuer whose transferable securities are admitted to trading and whose Home State (see **33.54(5)**) is the UK. (An issuer that is also admitted to the official list should also consider its obligations under the Listing Rules in addition to these requirements.)

An issuer must make public its annual financial report at the latest four months after the end of each financial year. It must also ensure that its annual financial report remains publicly available for at least ten years.

The annual financial report must include the following.

(a)   *Audited financial statements*

If an issuer is required to prepare consolidated accounts, the audited financial statements must comprise

- consolidated accounts prepared in accordance with International Financial Reporting Standards; and

- accounts of the parent company prepared in accordance with the national law of the EEA State in which the parent company is incorporated.

If an issuer is not required to prepare consolidated accounts, the audited financial statements must comprise accounts prepared in accordance with the national law of the EEA State in which the issuer is incorporated.

The audit report, signed by the person or persons responsible for auditing the financial statements, must be disclosed in full to the public together with the annual financial report.

An issuer which is a UK-traded non-EEA company must ensure that the person who provides the audit report is

- on the register of third country auditors (see **8.16** AUDIT);

- eligible for appointment as statutory auditor (see **8.10** AUDIT); or

- an EEA auditor (see **8.10** AUDIT).

(b)   *Management report*

The management report must

- contain a fair review of the issuer's business and a description of the principal risks and uncertainties facing the issuer;

- be a balanced and comprehensive analysis of the development and performance of the issuer's business during the financial year and the position of the issuer's business at the end of that year, consistent with the size and complexity of the business;

- include (to the extent necessary for an understanding of the development, performance or position of the issuer's business) analysis using financial key performance indicators and, where appropriate, analysis using other key performance indicators including information relating to environmental matters and employee matters; and

- include references to, and additional explanations of, amounts included in the issuer's annual financial statements, where appropriate.

The management report must also give an indication of

- any important events that have occurred since the end of the financial year unless those events are reflected in the issuer's profit and loss account or balance sheet or disclosed in the notes to the issuer's audited financial statements;

- the issuer's likely future development;

- activities in the field of research and development;

- information concerning acquisitions of own shares prescribed by Article 24(2) of EU Directive 2012/30;

- the existence of branches of the issuer; and

- in relation to the issuer's use of financial instruments and where material for the assessment of its assets, liabilities, financial position and profit or loss, the issuer's financial risk management objectives and policies (including its policy for hedging each major type of forecasted transaction for which hedge accounting is used) and the issuer's exposure to price risk, credit risk, liquidity risk and cash flow risk.

(c)   *Responsibility statements*

Responsibility statements must be made by the persons responsible within the issuer. The name and function of any person who makes a responsibility statement must be clearly indicated in that statement.

For each person making a responsibility statement, the statement must set out that to the best of his or her knowledge

- the financial statements, prepared in accordance with the applicable set of accounting standards, give a true and fair view of the assets, liabilities, financial position and profit or loss of the issuer and the undertakings included in the consolidation taken as a whole; and

- the management report includes a fair review of the development and performance of the business and the position of the issuer and the undertakings included in the consolidation taken as a whole, together with a description of the principal risks and uncertainties that they face.

ESMA has also issued guidelines under Article 16(3) of the ESMA Regulation on enforcement of financial information.

(DTR 4.1).

**33.57** *Half-yearly financial reports*

Subject to the exemptions in **33.59** below, these provisions apply to an issuer whose

- shares or debt securities are admitted to trading; and

- Home State (see **33.54(5)**) is the UK

An issuer must make public a half-yearly financial report covering the first six months of the financial year. It must be made public as soon as possible, but no later than three months, after the end of the period to which the report relates. An issuer must also ensure that the half-yearly financial report remains available to the public for at least ten years.

A half-yearly financial report must include the following information.

(a) *A condensed set of financial statements*

If an issuer is required to prepare consolidated accounts, the condensed set of financial statements must be prepared in accordance with IAS 34.

If an issuer is not required to prepare consolidated accounts, the condensed set of financial statements must contain, as a minimum, a condensed balance sheet and profit and loss account and explanatory notes on these accounts. In preparing the condensed balance sheet and profit and loss account, an issuer must follow the same principles for recognising and measuring as when preparing annual financial reports. Each must show the same headings and subtotals as were included in the most recent annual financial statements of the issuer. Additional line items must be included if, as a result of their omission, the half-yearly financial statements would give a misleading view. A comparative balance sheet as at the end of the immediate preceding financial year and a comparative profit and loss account for the first six months of the preceding financial year must be included. The explanatory notes must include sufficient information to ensure the comparability of the condensed half-yearly financial statements with the annual financial statements; and to ensure a user's proper understanding of any material changes in amounts and of any developments in the half-year period concerned.

The accounting policies and presentation applied to half-yearly figures must be consistent with those applied in the latest published annual accounts except where

- the accounting policies and presentation are to be changed in the subsequent annual financial statements (in which case the new accounting policies and presentation should be followed and the changes and the reasons for the changes should be disclosed in the half-yearly report); or

- the FCA otherwise agrees.

In practice, an entity that prepares its annual accounts under UK accounting practice will need to comply with FRS 104 'Interim Financial Reporting' (see **2.15**) when preparing a half-yearly financial report.

(b)    *An interim management report*

The interim management report must include *as a minimum*

- an indication of important events that have occurred during the first six months of the financial year, and their impact on the condensed set of financial statements, together with a description of the principal risks and uncertainties for the remaining six months of the financial year;

- in addition, an issuer of shares must disclose as a minimum,

    (i)    related parties transactions that have taken place in the first six months of the current financial year and that have materially affected the financial position or the performance of the enterprise during that period;

    (ii)    any changes in the related parties transactions described in the last annual report that could have a material effect on the financial position or performance of the enterprise in the first six months of the current financial year; and

    (iii)    if it is not required to prepare consolidated accounts, any transactions which have been entered into with related parties by the issuer, including the amount of such transactions, the nature of the related party relationship and other information about the transactions necessary for an understanding of the financial position of the issuer (but only where such transactions are material and have not been concluded under normal market conditions). Any such information may be aggregated according to their nature except where separate information is necessary for an understanding of the effects of related party transactions on the financial position of the issuer.

If the half-yearly financial report has been audited or reviewed by auditors pursuant to the Financial Reporting Council guidance on Review of Interim Financial Information, the audit report or review report must be reproduced in full. If the half-yearly financial report has not been audited or so reviewed, an issuer must make a statement to this effect in its report.

(c)    *Responsibility statements*

Responsibility statements must be made by the persons responsible within the issuer. The name and function of any person who makes a responsibility statement must be clearly indicated in that statement.

For each person making a responsibility statement, the statement must confirm that to the best of his or her knowledge

(i)    the condensed set of financial statements, prepared in accordance with the applicable set of accounting standards, gives a true and fair view of the assets, liabilities, financial position and profit or loss of the issuer, or the undertakings included in the consolidation as a whole; and

(ii)    the interim management report includes a fair review of the information required under (*b*) above.

A person making a responsibility statement satisfies the requirement in (i) above by including a statement that the condensed set of financial statements have been prepared in accordance with

- IAS 34;

- for UK issuers not using International Financial Reporting Standards, Financial Reporting Standard 104, Interim Financial Reporting issued by the FRC (see **2.15**); or

- for all other issuers not using International Financial Reporting Standards, a national accounting standard relating to interim reporting,

provided always that a person making such a statement has reasonable grounds to be satisfied that the condensed set of financial statements prepared in accordance with such a standard is not misleading.

(DTR 4.2).

**33.58**   *Reports on Payments to Governments*

Companies engaged in extractive or logging of primary forest industries whose transferable securities are admitted to trading and whose Home State is the UK must report annually on payments made to governments in each financial year. The report must be published in the prescribed manner within six months of the end of the financial year and remain publicly available for ten years.

(DTR 4.3A).

**33.59**   *Exemptions*

The following exemptions apply to the requirements in **33.56–33.57**.

(a)   *Public sector issuers*

The rules on annual financial reporting and half yearly financial reporting in **33.56–33.57** above do not apply to a state, a regional or local authority of a state, a public international body of which are least one EEA State is a member, the European Central Bank (ECB), the European Stability Facility (EFSF) established by the EFSF Framework Agreement and any other mechanism established with the objective of preserving the financial stability of European Monetary Union by providing temporary financial assistance to the EEA States whose currency is the euro and EEA States national central banks.

(b)   *Debt issuers*

The rules in **33.56–33.57** above do not apply to an issuer that issues exclusively debt securities admitted to trading, the denomination per unit of which is at least 100,000 euros (or an equivalent amount).

The rules in **33.57** above do not apply to a credit institution whose shares are not admitted to trading and which has, in a continuous or repeated manner, only issued debt securities provided that

- the total nominal amount of all such debt securities remains below 100 million euros; and

- the credit institution has not published a prospectus in accordance with the *Prospectus Directive*.

The rules in **33.57** above do not apply to an issuer already existing on 31 December 2003 which exclusively issue debt securities unconditionally and irrevocably guaranteed by the issuer's Home Member State or by a regional or local authority of that state, on a regulated market.

(c)   *Issuers of convertible securities*

The rules in **33.57** above do not apply to an issuer of transferable securities convertible into shares.

(d)     *Issuers of depository receipts*

The rules in **33.57** above do not apply to an issuer of depository receipts.

(e)     *Non-EEA States with equivalent laws*

An issuer whose registered office is in a non-EEA State is exempted from the rules in **33.56–33.57** if the law of the non-EEA State in question lays down equivalent requirements or the issuer complies with requirements of the law of a non-EEA State that the FCA considers as equivalent.

(DTR 4.4).

**33.60  Vote holder and issuer notification rules**

The Transparency Rules require holders of votes attached to shares of issuers to notify the issuers when the number of votes they control reach a specified proportion of the total votes. These provisions are considered in **33.62–33.70**.

For these purposes:

•       '*Issuer*', in relation to shares admitted to trading on a regulated market, is an issuer whose Home State (see **33.54(5)**) is the UK;

•       '*Non-UK issuer*' is an issuer whose shares are admitted to trading on a regulated market and whose Home State is the UK other than

    (i)     a public company within the meaning of s 4(2) of CA 2006; and

    (ii)    a company which is otherwise incorporated in, and whose principal place of business is in, the UK;

•       '*Shares*' means shares which are

    (i)     already issued and carry rights to vote which are exercisable in all circumstances at general meetings of the issuer including shares (eg preference shares) which, following the exercise of an option for their conversion, event of default or otherwise, have become fully enfranchised for voting purposes; and

    (ii)    admitted to trading on a regulated or prescribed market;

•       *An acquisition or disposal of shares* is to be regarded as effective when the relevant transaction is executed (unless the transaction provides for settlement to be subject to conditions which are beyond the control of the parties, in which case the acquisition or disposal is to be regarded as effective on the settlement of the transaction).

•       **Calculating percentages.** For the purposes of calculating whether any percentage threshold is reached, exceeded or fallen below and in any resulting notification, the proportion of voting rights held must, if necessary, be rounded down to the next whole number.

(DTR 5.1.1).

**33.61**  *Notification of the acquisition or disposal of major shareholdings*

A person must notify the issuer of the percentage of its voting rights he holds as shareholder or is deemed to hold through his direct or indirect holding of financial instruments (see **33.63**) falling within Rules 5.3.1(R)1 (or a combination of such holdings) if the percentage of those voting rights.

(a)     reaches, exceeds or falls below 3%, 4%, 5%, 6%, 7%, 8%, 9%, 10% and each 1% threshold thereafter up to 100% (or in the case of a non-UK issuer on the basis of thresholds at 5%, 10%, 15%, 20%, 25%, 30%, 50% and 75%) as a result of an acquisition or disposal of shares or financial instruments falls within DTR 5.3R; or

(b)     reaches, exceeds or falls below an applicable threshold in (*a*) above as a result of events changing the breakdown of voting rights and on the basis of information disclosed by the issuer in accordance with **33.66**;

and in the case of an issuer which is not incorporated in an EEA state a notification under (*b*) above must be made on the basis of equivalent events and disclosed information.

See **33.70** for an exemption for certain third country issuers.

*Voting rights that can be disregarded.* Voting rights attaching to the following shares are to be disregarded for the purposes of determining whether a person has a notification obligation under the above provisions.

•     Shares acquired or shares underlying financial instruments within DTR 5.3.1 to the extent that such financial instruments are acquired for the sole purpose of clearing and settlement within a settlement cycle not exceeding the period beginning with the transaction and ending at the close of the third trading day following the day of the execution of the transaction (irrespective of whether the transaction is conducted on-exchange).

•     Shares held or shares underlying financial instruments within DTR 5.3.1 to the extent that such financial instruments are held by a custodian (or nominee) in its custodian (or nominee) capacity (whether operating from an establishment in the UK or elsewhere) provided such a person can only exercise the voting rights attached to such shares under instructions given in writing or by electronic means.

•     Shares held or shares underlying financial instruments within DTR 5.3.1 to the extent that such financial instruments are held by a market maker acting in that capacity subject to the percentage of such shares not being equal to or in excess of 10% and subject to the market maker satisfying the criteria and complying with the conditions and operating requirements set out in the Transparency Rules.

•     Shares or shares underlying financial instruments within DTR 5.3.1(1) held by a credit institution or investment firm provided that

(i)     the shares or financial instruments are held within its trading book;

(ii)     the voting rights attached to such shares do not exceed 5%; and

(iii)     the voting rights attached to shares in or related to financial instruments the trading book are not exercised or otherwise used to intervene in the management of the issuer.

•     Shares acquired for stabilisation purposes in accordance with the *Buy-back and Stabilisation Regulation*, if the voting rights attached to those shares are not exercised or otherwise used to intervene in the management of the issuer.

*Aggregation of holdings.* The thresholds for the market making and trading book exemptions should be calculated by aggregating voting rights relating to shares with voting rights related to financial instruments (that is entitlements to acquire shares and financial instruments considered to be economically equivalent to shares) in order to ensure consistent application of the principle of aggregation of all holdings of financial instruments subject to notification requirements and to prevent a misleading representation of how many financial instruments related to an issuer are held by an entity benefiting from those exemptions.

*Aggregation of holdings in group companies.* In order to provide an adequate level of transparency in the case of a group of companies, and to take into account the fact that, where a parent undertaking has control over its subsidiaries, it may influence their management, the thresholds should be calculated at group level. Therefore all holdings owned by a parent undertaking of a credit institution or investment firm and subsidiary companies should be disclosed when the total sum of the holdings reaches the notification threshold.

- Shares acquired by a borrower under a stock lending agreement provided

    (i)    such shares (or equivalent stock) are on-lent or otherwise disposed of by the borrower by not later than close of business on the next trading day; and

    (ii)   the borrower does not declare any intention of exercising (and does not exercise) the voting rights attaching to the shares.

*Voting rights that can be disregarded except at 5%, 10% and higher thresholds.* The following can be disregarded in determining whether a person has a notification obligation under the above provisions except at the thresholds of 5% and 10% and above.

- Voting rights attaching to shares forming part of property belonging to another which that person lawfully manages under an agreement in, or evidenced in, writing. For these purposes, a person ('A') may lawfully manage investments belonging to another if

    (i)    A can manage those investments in accordance with a permission under *FSMA 2000, Part IV*;

    (ii)   A is an EEA firm other than one mentioned in *FSMA 2000, Sch 3 para 5(c) or (e)* and can manage those investments in accordance with its EEA authorisation;

    (iii)  A can, in accordance with *FSMA 2000, s 327*, manage those investments without contravening the prohibition contained in *FSMA 2000, s 19*;

    (iv)   A can lawfully manage those investments in another EEA State and would, if he were to manage those investments in the UK, require a permission under *FSMA 200, Part IV*; or

    (v)    A is a category of investment manager prescribed for this purpose by the FCA.

- Voting rights attaching to shares which may be exercisable by a person in his capacity as the operator of an authorised unit trust scheme, an authorised contractual scheme, a recognised scheme, or a UCITS scheme.

- Voting rights attaching to shares which may be exercisable by an Investment Company with Variable Capital.

(DTR 5.1.2–5.1.5).

**33.62** *Direct and indirect holders of shares (acquisition or disposal of major proportions of voting rights)*

A person is an indirect holder of shares for the purpose of the applicable definition of shareholder to the extent that he is entitled to acquire, to dispose of, or to exercise voting rights in any of the following cases or a combination of them.

(a)    Voting rights held by a third party with whom that person has concluded an agreement, which obliges them to adopt, by concerted exercise of the voting rights they hold, a lasting common policy towards the management of the issuer in question.

(b)     Voting rights held by a third party under an agreement concluded with that person providing for the temporary transfer for consideration of the voting rights in question.

(c)     Voting rights attaching to shares which are lodged as collateral with that person provided that person controls the voting rights and declares its intention of exercising them.

(d)     Voting rights attaching to shares in which that person has the life interest.

(e)     Voting rights which are held, or may be exercised within the meaning of points (a) to (d) above or, in cases (f) and (h) below, by a person undertaking investment management, or by a management company, by an undertaking controlled by that person.

In the FCA's view, this produces the result that it is always necessary for the parent undertaking of a controlled undertaking to aggregate its holding with any holding of the controlled undertaking (subject to the exemptions implicit in the wording and in **33.64**).

(f)     Voting rights attaching to shares deposited with that person which the person can exercise at its discretion in the absence of specific instructions from the shareholders.

In the FCA's view, this includes a person carrying on investment management and which is also the custodian of shares to which voting rights are attached.

(g)     Voting rights held by a third party in his own name on behalf of that person.

In the FCA's view this does not result in a unit holder in a collective investment scheme or other investment entity being treated as the holder of voting rights in the scheme property (provided always such persons do not have any entitlement to exercise, or control the exercise of, such voting rights). Neither are such persons to be regarded as holding shares 'indirectly'.

(h)     Voting rights which that person may exercise as a proxy where that person can exercise the voting rights at his discretion in the absence of specific instructions from the shareholders.

In the FCA's view, although this refers to proxies, it also describes and applies to a person undertaking investment management, and to a management company, and which is able effectively to determine the manner in which voting rights attached to shares under its control are exercised (eg through instructions given directly or indirectly to a nominee or independent custodian). Case (e) above provides for the voting rights which are under the control of such a person to be aggregated with those of its parent undertaking.

The indirect holdings within Cases (a) to (h) have to be aggregated, but also separately identified, in a notification to the issuer. Apart from those identified in the Cases (a) to (h) above, the FCA does not expect any other significant category 'indirect shareholder' to be identified.

Cases (a) to (h) above are also relevant in determining whether a person is an indirect holder of qualifying financial instruments which result in an entitlement to acquire shares (see **33.63**).

(DTR 5.2).

**33.63** *Notification of voting rights arising from the holding of certain financial instruments*

A person must make a notification in accordance with the applicable thresholds in **33.61** in respect of any financial instruments which they hold (directly or indirectly) which

(a)     on maturity give the holder under a formal agreement either the unconditional right to acquire or the discretion as the holder's right to acquire, shares to which voting rights are attached, already issued, of an issuer; or

(b)     are not included in (a) but which are referenced to shares referred to in (a) and with economic effect similar to that of the financial instruments referred to in (a) whether or not they confer a right to a physical settlement.

(DTR 5.3.1).

**33.64** *Aggregation of managed holdings*

Aggregation is not required in the following cases.

(a)     *The parent undertaking of a management company* is not required to aggregate its holdings with the holdings managed by the management company under the conditions laid down in the *Undertakings for Collective Investment in Transferable Securities (UCITS) Directive (No 85/611/EEC)*, provided such management company exercises its voting rights independently from the parent undertaking. But the requirements for the aggregation of holdings applies if the parent undertaking, or another controlled undertaking of the parent undertaking, has invested in holdings managed by such management company and the management company has no discretion to exercise the voting rights attached to such holdings and may only exercise such voting rights under direct or indirect instructions from the parent or another controlled undertaking of the parent undertaking.

(b)

(1)     The parent undertaking of an investment firm authorised under MiFID II shall not be required to aggregate its holdings with the holdings which such investment firm manages on a client-by-client basis within the meaning of Article 4(1), point 8, of MiFID, provided that:

(a)     the investment firm is authorised to provide such portfolio management;

(b)     it may only exercise the voting rights attached to such shares under instructions given in writing or by electronic means or it ensures that individual portfolio management services are conducted independently of any other services under conditions equivalent to those provided for under the UCITS Directive by putting into place appropriate mechanisms; and

(c)     the investment firm exercises its voting rights independently from the parent undertaking.

(2)     But the requirements for the aggregation of holdings applies if the parent undertaking, or another controlled undertaking of the parent undertaking, has invested in holdings managed by such investment firm and the investment firm has no discretion to exercise the voting rights attached to such holdings and may only exercise such voting rights under direct or indirect instructions from the parent or another controlled undertaking of the parent undertaking.

*Conditions for exemption.* For the purposes of the exemption to the aggregation of holdings provided in (*a*) and (*b*) above, a parent undertaking of a management company or of an investment firm must comply with the following conditions.

- It must not interfere by giving direct or indirect instructions (as defined) or in any other way in the exercise of the voting rights held by the management company or investment firm.

- The management company or investment firm must be free to exercise, independently of the parent undertaking, the voting rights attached to the assets it manages.

*FCA requirements*. A parent undertaking which wishes to make use of the exemption in relation to issuers subject to these provisions must, without delay, notify the following to the FCA.

(i)    A list of the names of the management companies, investment firms or other entities, indicating the competent authorities that supervise them, but with no reference to the issuers concerned; and

(ii)    a statement that, in the case of each such management company or investment firm, the parent undertaking complies with the conditions for exemption set out above.

The list must be updated on an ongoing basis.

Where the parent undertaking intends to benefit from the exemptions only in relation to the financial instruments referred to in the *Transparency Directive, Art 13*, it must notify to the FCA only the list referred to in (i) above.

A parent undertaking of a management company or of an investment firm must be able to demonstrate to the FCA on request that

- the organisational structures of the parent undertaking and the management company or investment firm are such that the voting rights are exercised independently of the parent undertaking (which requirement implies, as a minimum, that the parent undertaking and the management company or investment firm have established written policies and procedures reasonably designed to prevent the distribution of information between the parent undertaking and the management company or investment firm in relation to the exercise of voting rights);

- the persons who decide how the voting rights are exercised act independently; and

- if the parent undertaking is a client of its management company or investment firm or has a holding in the assets managed by the management company or investment firm, there is a clear written mandate for an arm's-length customer relationship between the parent undertaking and the management company or investment firm.

(DTR 5.4.1 to 5.4.8). See paras 5.4.9 to 5.4.11 for the position where an undertaking is involved whose registered office is in a third country.

**33.65**  *Acquisition or disposal by issuer of own shares*

An issuer of shares must, if it acquires or disposes of its own shares (either itself or through a person acting in his own name but on the issuer's behalf), make public the percentage of voting rights attributable to those shares it holds as a result of the transaction as a whole, as soon as possible, but not later than four trading days following the acquisition or disposal, where that percentage reaches, exceeds or falls below the thresholds of 5% or 10% of the voting rights. This does not apply to a third country issuer that falls within DTR 5.11.4.

The percentage must be calculated on the basis of the total number of shares to which voting rights are attached.

For additional requirements in relation to a listed company which purchases its own equity shares, see **33.41**.

(DTR 5.5).

**33.66** *Disclosures by issuers*

An issuer must, at the end of each calendar month during which an increase or decrease has occurred, disclose to the public

* the total number of voting rights and capital in respect of each class of share which it issues; and

* the total number of voting rights attaching to shares of the issuer which are held by it in treasury.

This does not apply to a third country issuer that falls within DTR 5.11.4.

Notwithstanding the above, if a relevant increase or decrease in the total number of voting rights occurs, an issuer must disclose the information (above) to the public as soon as possible and in any event no later than the end of the business day following the day on which the increase or decrease occurs. "Relevant increase or decrease" is any increase or decrease in the total number of voting rights produced when an issuer completes a transaction unless its effect on the total number of voting rights is immaterial when compared with the position before completion. It is for the issuer to assess whether the effect is immaterial. In the view of the FCA an increase or decrease of 1% or more is likely to be material both to the issuer and to the public.

The disclosure of the total number of voting rights should be in respect of each class of shares which is admitted to trading on a regulated or prescribed market.

Responsibility for all information drawn up and made public lies with the issuer.

(DTR 5.6).

**33.67** *Notification of combined holdings*

A person making a notification in accordance with **33.61** must do so by reference to each of the following.

* The aggregate of all voting rights which the person holds as shareholder and as the direct or indirect holder of financial instruments.

* The aggregate of all voting rights held as direct or indirect shareholder (disregarding for this purpose holdings of financial instruments).

* The aggregate of all voting rights held as a result of direct and indirect holdings of financial instruments falling within DTR 5.3.1.

Voting rights relating to financial instruments within DTR 5.3.1(1) that have already been notified in accordance with DTR 5.1.2 must be notified again when the person has acquired the underlying shares and such acquisition results in the total number of voting rights attached to shares issued by the same issuer reaching or exceeding the thresholds laid down by DTR 5.1.2.

The effect of this is that a person may have to make a notification if the overall percentage level of his voting rights remains the same but there is notifiable change in the percentage level of one or more of the categories of voting rights held.

(DTR 5.7).

**33.68** *Procedures for the notification and disclosure of major holdings*

(1) *Information to be included*

(a) A notification in accordance with **33.61** must include the following information.

- The resulting situation in terms of voting rights.

- The chain of controlled undertakings through which voting rights are effectively held, if applicable.

- The date on which the threshold was reached or crossed.

- The identity of the shareholder, even if that shareholder is not entitled to exercise voting rights under the conditions laid down in **33.61**, and of the person entitled to exercise voting rights on behalf of that shareholder.

(b)   A notification required of voting rights arising from the holding of financial instruments must include the following information.

- The resulting situation in terms of voting rights.

- If applicable, the chain of controlled undertakings through which financial instruments are effectively held.

- The date on which the threshold was reached or crossed.

- For instruments with an exercise period, an indication of the date or time period where shares will or can be acquired, if applicable.

- The date of maturity or expiration of the instrument.

- The identity of the holder.

- The name of the underlying issuer.

The notification must be made to the issuer of each of the underlying shares to which the financial instrument relates and, in the case of shares admitted to trading on a regulated market, to each competent authority of the Home States of such issuers.

If a financial instrument relates to more than one underlying share, a separate notification must be made to each issuer of the underlying shares.

## (2) *Time of notification*

The notification to the issuer must be effected as soon as possible, but not later than four trading days in the case of a non-UK issuer and two trading days in all other cases, the first of which is the day after the date on which the relevant person

(a)   learns of the acquisition or disposal or of the possibility of exercising voting rights, or on which, having regard to the circumstances, should have learned of it, regardless of the date on which the acquisition, disposal or possibility of exercising voting rights takes effect; or

(b)   is informed about the event mentioned in **33.61**(*b*).

For the purposes of (*a*) above a person must, in relation to a transaction to which he is a party or which he has instructed, be deemed to have knowledge of the acquisition, disposal or possibility to exercise voting rights no later than two trading days following the transaction in question and where a transaction is conditional upon the approval by public authorities of the transaction or on a future uncertain event the occurrence of which is outside the control of the parties to the agreement, the parties are deemed to have knowledge of the acquisition, disposal or possibility of exercising voting rights only when the relevant approvals are obtained or when the event happens.

### (3) *Obligation to notify*

The notification obligation following transactions of a kind mentioned in **33.62** are individual obligations of each direct shareholder or indirect shareholder there mentioned or both if the proportion of voting rights held by each party reaches, exceeds or falls below an applicable threshold.

In the circumstances in **33.62**(*h*),

- if a shareholder gives the proxy in relation to one shareholder meeting, notification may be made by means of a single notification when the proxy is given, provided it is made clear in the notification what the resulting situation in terms of voting rights will be when the proxy may no longer exercise the voting rights discretion; and

- If the proxy holder receives one or more proxies in relation to one shareholder meeting, notification may be made by means of a single notification on or after the deadline for receiving proxies, provided that it is made clear in the notification what the resulting situation in terms of voting rights will be when the proxy may no longer exercise the voting rights at its discretion.

When the duty to make notification lies with more than one person, notification may be made by means of a single common notification but this does not release any of those persons from their responsibilities in relation to the notification.

### (4) *Notification by parent undertaking, etc*

An undertaking is not required to make a notification if instead it is made by its parent undertaking or, where the parent undertaking is itself a controlled undertaking, by its own parent undertaking.

### (5) *Calculation of voting rights*

Voting rights must be calculated on the basis of all the shares to which voting rights are attached even if the exercise of such rights is suspended and must be given in respect of all shares to which voting rights are attached.

The number of voting rights to be considered when calculating whether a threshold is reached, exceeded or fallen below is the number of voting rights in existence according to the issuer's most recent disclosure made in accordance with **33.66** but disregarding voting rights attached to any treasury shares held by the issuer (in accordance with the issuer's most recent disclosure of such holdings).

### (6) *Notification to public by issuer*

An issuer must, on receipt of a notification, make public all of the information contained in it

(i)   where the issuer does not fall within (ii) below and the shares in question are admitted to trading on a regulated market, as soon as possible and in any event by not later than the end of the trading day following receipt of the notification; and

(ii)   where the issuer is a non-UK issuer or any other issuer whose shares are admitted to trading on a prescribed (but not a regulated) market, as soon as possible and in any event by not later than the end of the third trading day following receipt of the notification.

(DTR 5.8).

33.69   *Filing of information with the FCA*

A person making a notification to an issuer to which these provisions apply must, if the notification relates to shares admitted to trading on a regulated market, at the same time file a copy of such notification with the FCA.

The information to be filed with the FCA must include a contact address of the person making the notification (but such details must be in a separate annex and not included on the form which is sent to the issuer).

Information filed with the FCA for these purposes must be filed using electronic means.

(DTR 5.9, 5.10).

**33.70** *Non-EEA state issuers*

An issuer whose registered office is in a non-EEA State will be treated as meeting equivalent requirements to those set out in:

- 33.68(6)(ii) (public notifications) provided that the period of time within which the notification of the major holdings is to be effected to the issuer and is to be made public by the issuer is in total equal to or shorter than seven trading days.

- 33.65 (treasury shares) provided that

  (i)    if the issuer is only allowed to hold up to a maximum of 5% of its own shares to which voting rights are attached, a notification requirement is triggered under the law of the third country whenever this maximum threshold of 5% of the voting rights is reached or crossed;

  (ii)   if the issuer is allowed to hold up to a maximum of between 5% and 10% of its own shares to which voting rights are attached, a notification requirement is triggered under the law of the non-EEA state whenever this maximum threshold and/or the 5% threshold of the voting rights are reached or crossed; and

  (iii)  if the issuer is allowed to hold more than 10% of its own shares to which voting rights are attached, a notification requirement is triggered under the law of the non-EEA state whenever the 5% or 10% thresholds of the voting rights are reached or crossed.

  Notification above the 10% threshold is not required for this purpose.

- 33.66 (disclosure by issuers of total voting rights) provided that the issuer is required under the law of the non-EEA State to disclose to the public the total number of voting rights and capital within 30 calendar days after an increase or decrease of such total number has occurred.

An issuer whose registered office is in a non-EEA State is exempted from DTR 5.5.1, 5.6.1 and 5.8.12 if the law of the non-EEA State in question lays down equivalent requirements or the issuer complies with requirements of the law of a non-EEA State that the FCA considers an equivalent.

The FCA maintains a published list of non-EEA States, for the purposes of *Transparency Directive, Art 23.1* whose laws lay down requirements equivalent to those imposed upon issuers under these provisions or where the requirements of the law of that non-EEA State are considered to be equivalent by the FCA.

(DTR 5.11).

**33.71  Information requirements for issuers of shares and debt securities**

Unless otherwise stated, and subject to the exemptions listed at the end of the paragraph, the following provisions apply in relation to an issuer whose Home State (see 33.54(5)) is the UK and references to transferable securities, shares and debt securities are to such instruments as are admitted to trading.

# 33.71  Public and Listed Companies

**(1)  Equality of treatment**

An issuer of shares must ensure equal treatment for all holders of shares who are in the same position.

An issuer of debt securities must ensure that all holders of debt securities ranking pari passu are given equal treatment in respect of all the rights attaching to those debt securities.

**(2)  Exercise of rights by holders**

An issuer of shares or debt securities must ensure that all the facilities and information necessary to enable holders of shares or debt securities to exercise their rights are available in the Home State and that the integrity of data is preserved.

**(3)  Exercise of rights by proxy**

Shareholders and debt securities holders must not be prevented from exercising their rights by proxy, subject to the law of the country in which the issuer is incorporated.

An issuer of shares or debt securities must make available a proxy form, on paper or, where applicable, by electronic means to each person entitled to vote at a meeting of shareholders or a meeting of debt securities holders. The proxy form must be made available either together with the notice concerning the meeting or after the announcement of the meeting.

**(4)  Appointment of a financial agent**

An issuer of shares or debt securities must designate, as its agent, a financial institution through which shareholders or debt securities holders may exercise their financial rights.

**(5)  Electronic communications**

An issuer of shares or debt securities may use electronic means to convey information to shareholders or debt securities holders. To do so, it must comply with the following.

- A decision to use electronic means must be taken in a general meeting. But where the issuer is a company within the meaning of *CA 2006*, this does not prevent it from using other means to make the decision if it could have used such means before 20 January 2007.

- The use of electronic means must not depend upon the location of the seat or residence of

    (i)   the shareholder;

    (ii)  the persons referred to **33.62**(*a*)–(*h*); or

    (iii) a proxy representing a debt security holder.

- Identification arrangements must be put in place so that the shareholders, debt security holders or other persons entitled to exercise or to direct the exercise of voting rights are effectively informed.

- Shareholders, debt security holders or persons referred to **33.62**(*a*)–(*e*) who are entitled to acquire, dispose of or exercise voting rights must be

    (i)   contacted in writing to request their consent for the use of electronic means for conveying information and if they do not object within a reasonable period of time, their consent can be considered to have been given; and

(ii)   able to request at any time in the future that information be conveyed in writing.

But this does not apply in any case where *CA 2006, Sch 5* applies. See **16.29** DEALINGS WITH THIRD PARTIES.

• Any apportionment of the costs entailed in the conveyance of information by electronic means must be determined by the issuer in compliance with the principle of equal treatment in (2) above.

(6)   **Information about changes in rights attaching to securities**

An issuer of shares must without delay disclose to the public any change in the rights attaching to its various classes of shares, including changes in the rights attaching to derivative securities issued by the issuer giving access to the shares of that issuer.

An issuer of securities other than shares admitted to trading on a regulated market must disclose to the public without delay any changes in the rights of holders of securities other than shares, including changes in the terms and conditions of such securities which could indirectly affect those rights, resulting in particular from a change in loan terms or in interest rates.

An issuer of securities admitted to trading on a regulated market (other than an issuer which is a public international body of which at least one EEA State is a member) must disclose to the public without delay any new loan issues and in particular any guarantee or security in respect of such issues.

(7)   **Information about meetings, issue of new shares and payment of dividends – share issuers**

An issuer of shares must

• provide information to holders on

(i)   the place, time and agenda of meetings;

(ii)   the total number of shares and voting rights; and

(iii)   the rights of holders to participate in meetings; and

• publish notices or distribute circulars concerning the allocation and payment of dividends and the issue of new shares, including information on any arrangements for allotment, subscription, cancellation or conversion.

(8)   **Information about meetings, and payment of interest – debt security issuers**

An issuer of debt securities must publish notices or distribute circulars concerning

• the place, time and agenda of meetings of debt securities holders;

• the payment of interest;

• the exercise of any conversion, exchange, subscription or cancellation rights and repayment; and

• the rights of holders to exercise their rights in relation to the above.

If only holders of debt securities whose denomination per unit amounts to at least 50,000 euros (or an equivalent amount) are to be invited to a meeting, the issuer may choose as a venue any EEA State, provided that all the facilities and information necessary to enable such holders to exercise their rights are made available in that EEA State.

**33.71    Public and Listed Companies**

**Exemptions.**

(a)    *Non-EEA State exemption*

An issuer whose registered office is in a non-EEA State if the law of the non-EEA State in question lays down equivalent requirements or the issuer complies with requirements of the law of a non-EEA State that the FCA considers as equivalent is exempted from (2)–(9) above. The FCA maintains a published list of non-EEA States for the purposes of *Transparency Directive, Art 23.1* whose laws lay down requirements equivalent to those imposed upon issuers under these provisions or where the requirements of the law of that non-EEA State are considered to be equivalent by the FCA.

(b)    *Regional or local authorities*

A regional or local authority with securities admitted to trading is not required to comply with (3)–(6) and (9) above.

(c)    *Issuers of convertible securities, preference shares and depository receipts*

The provisions in (2)–(6), (8) and (9) above do not apply to

•       an issuer of transferable securities convertible into shares;

•       an issuer of preference shares; or

•       an issuer of depository receipts.

(DTR 6.1).

**33.72    Filing information and use of language**

The provisions in this paragraph apply to

•       an issuer whose transferable securities are admitted to trading and whose Home State (see **33.54(5)**) is the UK; and

•       a person who has requested, without the issuer's consent, the admission of its transferable securities to trading on a regulated market.

(1)    **Filing of information with the FCA**

An issuer or person that discloses regulated information must, at the same time, file that information with the FCA. Where an issuer or person is required to file regulated information under DTR 6.2.2R, the issuer or person must, at the same time, notify the following to the FCA: (1) the legal entity identifier (LEI) of the issuer concerned; and (2) the classifications relevant to the regulated information using the classes and sub-classes in DTR 6, Annex 1R. If more than one classification is relevant to the regulated information, the issuer or person must notify all relevant classes and sub-classes to the FCA. The requirement can be complied with by using a primary information provider to disseminate the information in accordance with **33.73**.

(2)    **Language**

If transferable securities are admitted to trading

(a)      only in the UK and the UK is the Home State, regulated information must be disclosed in English;

(b)      in more than one EEA State including the UK and the UK is the Home State, regulated information must be disclosed

(i)      in English; and

        (ii)      either in a language accepted by the competent authorities of each Host State or in a language customary in the sphere of international finance, at the choice of the issuer;

   (c)     in one or more EEA States excluding the UK and the UK is the Home State, regulated information must be disclosed either

        (i)       in a language accepted by the competent authorities of those Host States; or

        (ii)      in a language customary in the sphere of international finance, at the choice of the issuer; and

   (d)     without the issuer's consent, (*a*)–(*c*) above apply to the person who has requested such admission (and do not apply to the issuer).

If transferable securities whose denomination per unit amounts to at least 100,000 euros (or an equivalent amount) are admitted to trading in the UK or in one or more EEA States, regulated information must be disclosed to the public in either a language accepted by the competent authorities of the Home State and Host States or in a language customary in the sphere of international finance, at the choice of the issuer or of the person who, without the issuer's consent, has requested such admission.

(DTR 6.2).

## 33.73 Dissemination of information

This paragraph applies to

- an issuer whose transferable securities are admitted to trading and whose Home State (see 33.54(5)) is the UK;

- a person who has applied, without the issuer's consent, for the admission of its transferable securities to trading on a regulated market; and

- transferable securities that are admitted to trading only in the UK which is the Host State and not in the Home State.

An issuer or person must disclose 'regulated information' in the manner set out in (1)–(8) below. When disseminating such information, an issuer or other person must ensure that the minimum standards described below are met and must entrust a RIS with the disclosure of the information to the public, ensuring that the RIS complies with those minimum standards.

Where an issuer uses a RIS (other than a RIS which is a primary information provider or an EEA approved incoming society service or a person to whom DTR TP 1.22 applies):

(1)    the issuer or person must provide an annual written confirmation to the FCA that all regulated information disseminated by an RIS not specified in DTR 6.3.3A R(1) to DTR 6.3.3A R(3) in the previous financial year was disseminated in accordance with the minimum standards contained in DTR 6.3.4 R to DTR 6.3.8 R.

(2)    The confirmation required by DTR 6.3.3B R (1) must:

   (a)     be provided by:

        (i)       in the case of an issuer, the audit committee or the body referred to in DTR 7.1.1 R;

        (ii)      in the case of a person which is not an issuer but is a body corporate, the audit committee or the board of directors; or

(iii)    in the case of a person which is not an issuer or a body corporate, a person with corresponding powers to a director;

(b)    set out the basis for making the confirmation, including the steps taken to determine its accuracy; and

(c)    be supported by records which are:

(i)    sufficient to reasonably demonstrate the basis for making the confirmation; and

(ii)    capable of timely retrieval.

The FCA may also request information from an issuer or person under *FSMA 2000, s 89H* on an *ad hoc* basis to verify that the regulated information disseminated by a RIS (as above) has been disseminated in accordance with DTR 6.3.4 to DTR6.3.8.

'*Regulated information*' means all information which that person must disclose under the *Transparency Directive*, the *Market Abuse Regulation*, the Listing Rules or the Disclosure Guidance and Transparency Rules.

(1)    Regulated information must be disseminated in a manner ensuring that it is capable of being disseminated to as wide a public as possible, and as close to simultaneously as possible in the Home Member State and in other EEA States.

(2)    Regulated information, other than regulated information within (3) below must be communicated to the media in unedited full text.

(3)    An annual financial report that is required by **33.56** to be made public is not required to be communicated to the media in unedited full text unless the information is of a type that would be required to be disseminated in a half-yearly financial report.

(4)    The announcement relating to the publication of the following regulated information must include an indication of the website on which the relevant documents are available.

•    An annual financial report that is required by **33.56** to be made public.

•    A half-yearly financial report that is required by **33.57** to be made public.

(5)    Regulated information must be communicated to the media in a manner which ensures the security of the communication, minimises the risk of data corruption and unauthorised access, and provides certainty as to the source of the regulated information. Security of receipt must be ensured by remedying as soon as possible any failure or disruption in the communication of regulated information. An issuer or person is not responsible for systemic errors or shortcomings at the media to which the regulated information has been communicated.

(6)    Regulated information must be communicated to a RIS in a way which

•    makes clear that the information is regulated information;

•    identifies clearly

(i)    the issuer concerned;

(ii)    the subject matter of the regulated information; and

(iii)    the time and date of the communication of the regulated information by the issuer or the person.

(7)    Upon request, an issuer or other person must be able to communicate to the FCA, in relation to any disclosure of regulated information

- the name of the person who communicated the regulated information to the RIS;

- the security validation details;

- the time and date on which the regulated information was communicated to the RIS;

- the medium in which the regulated information was communicated; and

- details of any embargo placed by the issuer on the regulated information, if applicable.

(8)  An issuer or person must not charge investors any specific cost for providing regulated information.

(DTR 6.3).

### 33.74  Disclosure of information in a non-EEA State

Information that is disclosed in a non-EEA State which may be of importance to the public in the EEA must be disclosed in accordance with the provisions in **33.72** and **33.73**. This also applies to information that is not regulated information.

(DTR 6.3.10).

DTR 6 concludes with an Annex detailing the classes and sub-classes of regulated information.

### 33.75  Compensation for statements in certain publications

*FSMA 2000, s 90A* provides that *Schedule 10A* (*FSMA*) makes provision for the liability of issuers of securities to pay compensation to persons who have suffered loss as a result of

(i)  a misleading statement or dishonest omission in certain published information relating to the securities or

(ii)  a dishonest delay in publishing such information.

Schedule 10A applies to securities that are with the consent of the issuer

- admitted to trading on a securities market situated or operating in the UK; or

- traded on a regulated market situated or operating outside the UK but issued by an issuer where the UK is the issuer's home state

The issuer of securities to which these provisions apply is liable to pay compensation to a person who

(a)  acquires, continues to hold or disposes of such securities issued by it in reliance on published information to which *FSMA 2000, Schedule 10A* applies and

(b)  suffers loss in respect of the securities as a result of

(i)  any untrue or misleading statement in that published information; or

(ii)  the omission from that published information of any matter required to be included in it or

(iii)  the delay by the issuer in publishing information to which FSMA 2000 Schedule 10A relates

*FSMA 2000, Schedule 10A* only applies to information published by the issuer of securities by recognised means or by other means where the availability of the information has been announced by the issuer by recognised means. It is immaterial whether the information is required to be published (by recognised means or otherwise).

'Recognised means' are either a recognised information service as defined in *FSMA 2000, Schedule 10A, para 2(4)* or other means required or authorised to be used to communicate information to the market in question, or to the public, when a recognised information service is available.

The issuer is liable

- only if a 'person discharging managerial responsibilities' within the issuer

  (i)    knew the statement to be untrue or misleading or was reckless as to whether it was untrue or misleading; or

  (ii)   knew the omission to be a dishonest concealment of a material fact; or

  (iii)  acted dishonestly in delaying the publication of the information.

- a loss is not regarded as suffered as a result of the statement or omission unless the person suffering it acquired, continued to hold or disposed of the relevant securities

  (i)    in reliance on the information in question; and

  (ii)   at a time when, and in circumstances in which, it was reasonable for him to rely on it

An issuer is also not liable to pay compensation if the published information is contained in listing particulars or a prospectus (or supplementary listing particulars or a supplementary prospectus) and the issuer is liable under *FSMA 2000, s 90* to pay compensation.

The issuer is not subject to any liability other than provided for in respect of such loss suffered and a person other than the issuer is not subject to any liability other than to the issuer in respect of any such loss. This does not affect

- civil liability under *FSMA 2000, s 90* or *CA 2006, s 954* or for breach of contract or under the *Misrepresentation Act 1967* or arising from a person's having assumed responsibility to a particular person, for a particular purpose, for the accuracy or completeness of the information concerned

- liability to a civil penalty

- criminal liability

- the powers conferred by *FSMA 2000, ss 382* and *384*.

*'Relevant publications'* are

- any reports and statements published in response to a requirement imposed by a provision of the Transparency Rules; and

- any preliminary statement made in advance of such a report or statement to the extent that it contains information that is intended will appear in the report or statement and will be presented there is substantially the same form.

A *'person discharging managerial responsibilities'* within an issuer is

(i)    any director of the issuer (or person occupying the position of director, by whatever name called);

(ii)    in the case of an issuer whose affairs are managed by its members, any member of the issuer; and

(iii)   in the case of an issuer that has no persons within (i) or (ii) above, any senior executive of the issuer having responsibilities in relation to the information in question or its publication.

'Securities' means transferable securities within the meaning of Article 4.1.44 of the MiFID II other than money-market instruments as defined in Article 4.1.17 of MiFID II that have a maturity of less than 12 months.

'Securities market' means a regulated market as defined in Article 4.1.21 of the Directive, a multilateral trading facility as defined in Article 4.1.22 of MiFID II or a market or facility of a corresponding description outside the EEA.

[*FSMA 2000, s 90A; CA 2006, s 1270*].

## 33.76  PENALTIES CONCERNING PUBLIC AND LISTED COMPANIES

The FCA may impose a penalty of such amount as it considers appropriate in the following circumstances.

(a)    If it considers that an issuer of listed securities or an applicant for listing has contravened any provision of the Listing Rules.

(b)    If it considers that

(i)     a person has contravened a provision of the Transparency Rules or a provision otherwise made in accordance with the *Transparency Obligations Directive*,

(ii)    a person on whom a requirement has been imposed under *FSMA 2000, s 89L* (power to suspend or prohibit trading of securities in a case of infringement of an applicable transparency obligation) has contravened that requirement.

(c)    If it considers that any person has contravened a provision of the Corporate Governance Rules corresponding to Chapter 7 of the Disclosure Guidance and Transparency Rules, see Chapter 15 on Corporate Governance.

Where the person in (*a*), (*b*)(i) or (*c*) above is a company, if the FCA considers that a person who was at the material time a director of the company was knowingly concerned in the contravention, it may impose upon him a penalty of such amount as it considers appropriate.

As an alternative to a penalty, the FCA may instead publish a statement censuring the person concerned.

Any action (whether penalty or censure) taken by the FCA under these provisions must be within two years beginning with the first day on which it knew of the contravention unless proceedings against that person, in respect of the contravention, were begun before the end of that period.

**Procedure.** If the FCA proposes to take action against a person under these provisions, it must give him a warning notice which must state the amount of the proposed penalty or, as the case may be, set out the terms of the proposed statement.

If, after considering any representations made in response to the warning notice, the FCA decides to take action, it must issue a decision notice which must state the amount of the penalty or, as the case may be, set out the terms of the statement.

Where the FCA decides to take action against a person, he may refer the matter to the Tribunal.

*[FSMA 2000, ss 91, 92; CA 2006, Sch 15 para 6].*

The *Financial Services and Markets Act 2000 (Market Abuse) Regulations 2016* designate the FCA the competent authority for the purposes of MAR and any supplementary EU regulations and amend *Parts 6* and *8* of the *FSMA 2000* to confer on the FCA powers to impose penalties if satisfied that a breach has occurred.

In summary, if the FCA considers there has been a breach of the disclosure requirements of MAR, it can:

(a)   censure or fine the person who has contravened MAR (*FSMA 2000, s 123*);

(b)   censure or fine a 'person discharging managerial responsibilities' or 'person closely associated' with them (DTR 1.5.3G(1));

(c)   fine a former director if he was knowingly concerned in the breach by the issuer (DTR 1.5.3G(2));

(d)   suspend trading in the company's shares (*FSMA 2000, s 1221*); and

(e)   temporarily ban a particular individual from buying or selling financial instruments (*FSMA 2000, s 123A*).

See the FCA's Decision Procedure and Penalties Manual and Enforcement Guide for full details of the enforcement procedure.

## 33.77   APPOINTMENT OF INVESTIGATORS BY THE FCA

The *Financial Services and Markets Act 2000 (Market Abuse) Regulations 2016* amend *Parts 6* and *8* of the *FSMA 2000* to confer on the FCA powers to investigate potential breaches of MAR if satisfied that a breach has occurred.

In summary, if it appears to the FCA that there are circumstances suggesting that

•   there may have been a contravention of a

(i)   a provision of *FSMA 2000, Pt VI*,

(ii)   a provision of the Listing Rules, Transparency Rules or Corporate Governance Rules, or

(iii)   a provision otherwise made in accordance with the *Prospective Directive* or the *Transparency Obligations Directive*, or

•   a person, who was at the material time a director of a company falling within **33.76**(*a*), (*b*)(i) or (*c*) and has been knowingly concerned in a contravention of any such provision,

the FCA may appoint one or more competent persons to conduct an investigation on its behalf.

*[FSMA 2000, s 97; CA 2006, Sch 15 para 8].*

See the *Enforcement (Market Abuse Regulation) Instrument 2016 (FCA 2016/47)* for full details of the FCA's extensive powers to investigate potential breaches of MAR.

## 33.78 FCA: EXEMPTION FROM LIABILITY IN DAMAGES

Neither the FCA nor any person who is a member, officer or member of staff of the FCA is to be liable in damages for anything done or omitted in the discharge of the authority's functions unless the act or omission is shown to have been in bad faith. But this exemption does not prevent an award of damages made in respect of an act or omission on the ground that it was unlawful as a result of *Human Rights Act 1998, s 6(1)*.

[*FSMA 2000, s 102*].

APPENDIX: ENFORCEMENT (MARKET ABUSE REGULATION) INSTRUMENT 2016

## ENFORCEMENT (MARKET ABUSE REGULATION) INSTRUMENT 2016

**Powers exercised by the Financial Conduct Authority**

A. The Financial Conduct Authority makes this instrument in the exercise of the following powers and related provisions of the Financial Services and Markets Act 2000 ("the Act")
(1) section 69 (Statement of Policy);
(2) section 124 (Statement of Policy);
(3) section 139A (Power of the FCA to give guidance);
(4) section 210 (Statement of Policy); and
(5) section 395 (The FCA's and PRA's procedures).

**Commencement**

B. This instrument comes into force on 3 July 2016 immediately after the Market Abuse Regulation Instrument 2016 comes into effect.

**Amendments to the Handbook**

C. The Glossary of definitions is amended in accordance with Annex A to this instrument.
D. The Decision Procedure and Penalties Manual (DEPP) is amended in accordance with Annex B to this instrument.

**Material outside the Handbook**

E. The Enforcement Guide (EG) is amended in accordance with Annex C to this instrument.

**Citation**

F. This instrument may be cited as the Enforcement (Market Abuse Regulation) Instrument 2016.

By order of the Board
29 June 2016

**Annex A Amendments to the Glossary of definitions**

In this Annex, underlining indicates new text and striking through indicates deleted text, unless otherwise stated.

Amend the following definition as shown.

*breach*      *in DEPP*:

. . .

(4) ~~behaviour amounting to *market abuse*, in respect of which the FCA takes action pursuant to section 123 (Power to impose penalties in cases of market abuse)~~ a contravention in respect of which the *FCA* takes action pursuant to sections 123, 123A or 123B of the *Act*,

. . .

*market abuse*   (1) behaviour prohibited by:

        (a) articles 14 and 15 of the *Market Abuse Regulation*; or

        (b) articles 38 to ~~42~~ 41 of ~~Regulation (EU) No 1031/2010~~ the *auction regulation*.

**Annex B Amendments to the Decision Procedure and Penalties Manual (DEPP)**

In this Annex, underlining indicates new text and striking through indicates deleted text, unless indicated otherwise.

*1.1 Application and Purpose*

Application

1.1.1 G This manual (*DEPP*) is relevant to *firms, approved persons* and other *persons*, whether or not they are regulated by the *FCA*. It sets out:

    . . .

(2A)    the *FCA's* policy with respect to the imposition of suspensions ~~or~~ , restrictions and disciplinary prohibitions, and the period for which those ~~suspensions or restrictions~~ sanctions are to have effect, under the *Act* (see *DEPP* 6A);

. . .

**2 Annex 1 Warning notices and decision notices under the Act and certain other enactments**

    . . .

| Section of the Act | Description | Handbook reference | Decision maker |
|---|---|---|---|
| . . . | . . . | . . . | . . . |
| 126(1)/ 127(1) | when the *FCA* is proposing or deciding to impose a ~~sanction for market abuse~~ penalty or *public censure* under section 123 of the *Act*, a disciplinary prohibition under section 123A of the *Act*, or a suspension or restriction under section 123B of the *Act\** | | *RDC* |
| . . . | | | |

    . . .

2 Annex 2 Supervisory notices

| Section of the Act | Description | Handbook reference | Decision maker |
|---|---|---|---|
| . . . | | | |
| ~~96C~~ 122I | when the *FCA* is proposing to suspend or suspends trading in a *financial instrument* | *DTR* | *Executive procedures* |
| . . . | | | |

**6 Penalties**

. . .

**6.2 Deciding whether to take action**

. . .

6.2.2 G When deciding whether to take action for *market abuse* ~~or requiring or encouraging~~, the *FCA* may consider the following additional factors:

. . .

6.2.12 G ~~Persons discharging managerial responsibilities within an issuer and their connected persons, who have requested or approved the admission of a financial instrument to trading on a regulated market, and connected persons have their own responsibilities under the disclosure rules, as set out in DTR 3, for which they are primarily responsible. Accordingly, disciplinary action for a breach of the disclosure rules will not necessarily involve the issuer.~~

~~[Note: In paragraph 6.2.12, 'connected person' has the meaning in relation to a person discharging managerial responsibilities within an issuer attributed to it in subsection (5) of the definition of 'connected person' in the Handbook Glossary.]~~ [deleted]

. . .

6.2.22 G In relation to ~~behaviour~~ behaviour which may have happened or be happening in the context of a *takeover bid*, the *FCA* will refer to the *Takeover Panel* and give due weight to its views. Where the *Takeover Code* has procedures for complaint about any behaviour, the *FCA* expects parties to exhaust those procedures. The *FCA* will not, save in exceptional circumstances, take action under any of section 123 (FCA's power to impose penalties), <u>section 123A (Power to prohibit individuals from managing or dealing), section 123B (Suspending permission to carry on regulated activities etc.)</u>, section 129 (Power of court to impose penalties), section 381 (Injunctions), sections 383 or 384 (Restitution) in respect of <u>behaviour</u> behaviour to which the *Takeover Code* is relevant before the conclusion of the procedures available under the *Takeover Code*.

6.2.23 G The *FCA* will not take action against a *person* over ~~behaviour~~ behaviour which <u>does not amount to *market abuse*. Behaviour is less likely to amount to *market abuse*</u> where it (a) conforms with the *Takeover Code* or rules of an *RIE* and (b) falls within the terms of ~~any provision of the Code of Market Conduct~~ <u>MAR 1.10.4G to 1.10.6G</u> which ~~states~~ <u>state</u> that ~~behaviour~~ <u>behaviour</u> so conforming ~~does not~~ <u>is unlikely to, of itself,</u> amount to *market abuse*. The *FCA* will seek the *Takeover*

Panel's or relevant *RIE's* views on whether ~~behaviour~~ behaviour complies with the *Takeover Code* or *RIE* rules and will attach considerable weight to its views.

. . .

6.2.25 G In any case where the *FCA* considers that the use of its powers under any of sections 123, 123A, 123B, 129, 381, 383 or 384 of the *Act* may be appropriate, if that use may affect the timetable or outcome of a *takeover bid* or where it is appropriate in the context of any exercise by the *Takeover Panel* of its powers and authority, the *FCA* will consult the *Takeover Panel* before using any of those powers.

6.2.26 G Where the ~~behaviour~~ behaviour of a *person* which amounts to *market abuse* is ~~behaviour~~ behaviour to which the *Takeover Code* is relevant, the use of the *Takeover Panel's* powers will often be sufficient to address the relevant concerns. In cases where this is not so, the *FCA* will need to consider whether it is appropriate to use any of its own powers under the *market abuse regime*. The principal circumstances in which the *FCA* is likely to consider such exercise are:

(1) where the ~~behaviour~~ behaviour falls within ~~sections 118(2), 118(3) or 118(4) of the Act~~ the prohibition in article 14 of the *Market Abuse Regulation*;

(2) where the *FCA's* approach in previous similar cases (which may have happened otherwise than in the context of a *takeover bid*) suggests that a ~~financial penalty~~ sanction should be imposed;

. . .

## 6.3 Penalties for market abuse

6.3.1 G ~~Section 123(2) of the Act states that the FCA may not impose a penalty on a person if there are reasonable grounds to be satisfied that:~~

~~(1) the person concerned believed, on reasonable grounds, that his behaviour did not amount to market abuse or requiring or encouraging; or~~

~~(2) the person concerned took all reasonable precautions and exercised all due diligence to avoid engaging in market abuse or requiring or encouraging.~~ [deleted]

6.3.2 G ~~The factors which the FCA may take into account when deciding whether either of the two conditions in DEPP 6.3.1G are met include, but are not limited to:~~

~~(1) whether, and if so to what extent, the behaviour in question was or was not analogous to behaviour described in the Code of Market Conduct (see MAR 1) as amounting or not amounting to market abuse or requiring or encouraging;~~

~~(2) whether the FCA has published any guidance or other materials on the behaviour in question and if so, the extent to which the person sought to follow that guidance or take account of those materials (see the Reader's Guide to the Handbook regarding the status of guidance.) The FCA will consider the nature and accessibility of any guidance or other published materials when deciding whether it is relevant in this context and, if so, what weight it should be given;~~

~~(3) whether, and if so to what extent, the behaviour complied with the rules of any relevant prescribed market or any other relevant market or other regulatory requirements (including the Takeover Code) or any relevant codes of conduct or best practice;~~

~~(4) the level of knowledge, skill and experience of the person concerned;~~

~~(5) whether, and if so to what extent, the person can demonstrate that the behaviour was engaged in for a legitimate purpose and in a proper way;~~

~~(6) whether, and if so to what extent, the person followed internal consultation and escalation procedures in relation to the behaviour (for example, did the person discuss the behaviour with internal line management and/or internal legal or compliance departments);~~

(7)     ~~whether, and if so the extent to which, the *person* sought any appropriate expert legal or other expert professional advice and followed that advice; and~~

(8)     ~~whether, and if so to what extent, the *person* sought advice from the market authorities of any relevant *prescribed market* or, where relevant, consulted the *Takeover Panel*, and followed the advice received.~~ [deleted]

. . .

**6.5C The five steps for penalties imposed on individuals in market abuse cases**

. . .

Step 2 – the seriousness of the market abuse

**6.5C.2 G** . . .

> (13)    Factors tending to show the *market abuse* was deliberate include:
>
> . . .
>
> > (h)    for *market abuse* falling within ~~section 118(2) of the *Act*~~ the prohibition in article 14(a) of the *Market Abuse Regulation*, the individual knew or recognised that the information on which the *dealing* was based was *inside information*.

. . .

**6.7 Discount for early settlement**

**6.7.1 G** *Persons* subject to enforcement action may be prepared to agree the amount of any financial penalty, or the length of any period of suspension, restriction, condition ~~or~~ , limitation <u>or disciplinary prohibition</u> (see *DEPP* 6A), and other conditions which the *FCA* seeks to impose by way of such action. These conditions might include, for example, the amount or mechanism for the payment of compensation to consumers. The *FCA* recognises the benefits of such agreements, as they offer the potential for securing earlier redress or protection for consumers and a cost saving to the *person* concerned and to the *FCA* in contesting the financial penalty or other disciplinary action. The penalty that might otherwise be payable, or the length of the period of suspension, restriction ~~or~~ , condition <u>or disciplinary prohibition</u> that might be imposed, for a *breach* by the *person* concerned will therefore be reduced to reflect the timing of any settlement agreement.

. . .

The settlement discount scheme applied to suspensions, restrictions ~~and~~ , conditions <u>and disciplinary prohibitions</u>

**6.7.6 G** The *settlement discount scheme* which applies to the amount of a financial penalty, described in *DEPP* 6.7.2G to *DEPP* 6.7.5G, also applies to the length of the period of a suspension, restriction ~~or~~ , condition <u>or disciplinary prohibition (other than a permanent disciplinary prohibition)</u>, having regard to the *FCA's* statement of policy as set out in *DEPP* 6A.3. <u>No settlement discount is available with respect to a permanent disciplinary prohibition.</u> The *settlement discount scheme* does not apply to the length of the period for which approvals under section 59 of the Act have effect as a result of a limitation, as different considerations apply to determining the appropriate length of this period: see *DEPP* 6A.1.5G and *DEPP* 6A.3AG. However, the *FCA* will take into account that the *approved person* is willing to enter into a settlement agreement when determining the appropriate period.

. . .

# Public and Listed Companies Appendix

**6A The power to impose a suspension, restriction, condition ~~or~~ , limitation or disciplinary prohibition**

*6A.1 Introduction*

6A.1.1 G *DEPP* 6A sets out the *FCA's* statement of policy with respect to:

(1)    the imposition of suspensions or restrictions under sections 88A, 89Q and 206A of the *Act*, and the period for which those suspensions or restrictions are to have effect, as required by sections 88C(1), 89S(1) and 210(1) of the *Act* ~~.~~;

(2)    ~~It also sets out the FCA's statement of policy on~~ the imposition of suspensions, conditions or limitations under section 66 of the *Act*, the period for which suspensions or conditions are to have effect, and the period for which approvals under section 59 have effect as a result of a limitation, as required by section 69(1) ~~.~~; and

(3)    the imposition of disciplinary prohibitions, suspensions or restrictions under sections 123A and 123B of the *Act*, as required by section 124(1).

*DEPP* 6A does not concern limitations or conditions imposed under section 61(2B), 63ZA or 63ZB of the *Act*.

6A.1.2 G (1) For the purposes of *DEPP* 6A, "suspension" refers to the suspension of:

(a)    any *permission* which an *authorised person* has to carry on a *regulated activity* (under ~~section~~ sections 123B or 206A of the *Act*),

. . .

(2) "restriction" refers to limitations or other restrictions in relation to:

(a)    the carrying on of a *regulated activity* by an *authorised person* (under ~~section~~ sections 123B or 206A of the *Act*),

. . .

(3) "condition" refers to a condition imposed in relation to any approval of the performance by an *approved person* of any function to which the approval relates (under section 66 of the *Act*); ~~and~~

(4) "limitation" refers, apart from in *DEPP* 6A.1.2G(2), to a limitation of the period for which any approval of the performance by an *approved person* of any function to which the approval relates is to have effect (under section 66 of the *Act*) ~~.~~; and

(5) "disciplinary prohibition" refers to a temporary or permanent prohibition on an individual holding an office or position involving responsibility for taking decisions about the management of a *MiFID investment firm* (under section 123A(2)(a) and (3) of the *Act*) or a temporary prohibition on an individual directly or indirectly acquiring or disposing of *financial instruments* (or *emission auction products*) on his or her own account or the account of a third party, (under section 123A(2)(b) of the *Act*) or a temporary prohibition on an individual directly or indirectly making a bid at an auction conducted by a *recognised auction platform*, on his or her own account or the account of a third party (under section 123A(2)(c) of the *Act*).

[Note: see Regulation 6 and Schedule 1 to the *RAP Regulations* for application of the powers to contraventions of the *auction regulation*]

6A.1.3 G The power to impose a suspension, restriction, condition ~~or~~ , limitation or disciplinary prohibition is a disciplinary measure which the *FCA* may use in addition to, or instead of, imposing a financial penalty or issuing a *public censure*. The principal purpose of imposing such a measure is to promote high standards of regulatory and/or market conduct by deterring *persons* who have committed *breaches* from committing further *breaches*, helping to deter other *persons* from committing similar *breaches*, and demonstrating generally the benefits of compliant behaviour. These measures are tools that the *FCA* may employ to help it to achieve its *statutory objectives*. Examples of measures that we may impose include:

. . .

6A.1.4 G The powers to impose a suspension, restriction, condition or limitation in relation to *authorised persons* and *approved persons, and to impose a disciplinary prohibition in relation to individuals,* are disciplinary measures; where the *FCA* considers it necessary to take action, for example, to protect *consumers* from an *authorised person*, the *FCA* will seek to cancel or vary the *authorised person's permissions*. If the *FCA* has concerns with a *person's* fitness to be approved, and considers it necessary to take action, the *FCA* will seek to prohibit the *approved person* or withdraw their approval. For an *SMF manager*, the *FCA* may instead vary their approval by imposing one or more conditions, if the *FCA* is satisfied that they would be a fit and proper person to perform functions in relation to *regulated activities* if the conditions are imposed, and that it is appropriate to do so. While the powers to impose a suspension or a restriction in relation to *sponsors* and *primary information providers* under sections 88A(2)(b)/(c) and 89Q(2)(b)/(c) of the Act are disciplinary measures, the *FCA* can impose suspensions, limitations or other restrictions in relation to *sponsors* and *primary information providers* in other circumstances.

. . .

*6A.2 Deciding whether to take action*

6A.2.1 G The *FCA* will consider the full circumstances of each case and determine whether it is appropriate to impose a suspension, restriction, condition or , limitation, or disciplinary prohibition. The *FCA* will usually make this decision at the same time as it determines whether or not to impose a financial penalty or a *public censure*.

6A.2.2 G The *FCA* will take into account relevant factors in deciding whether it is appropriate to impose a suspension, restriction, condition or , limitation or disciplinary prohibition. These may include factors listed in *DEPP* 6.2. There may also be other factors, not listed in *DEPP* 6.2, that are relevant.

6A.2.3 G The *FCA* will consider it appropriate to impose a suspension, restriction, condition or , limitation, or disciplinary prohibition where it believes that such action will be a more effective and persuasive deterrent than the imposition of a financial penalty alone. This is likely to be the case where the *FCA* considers that direct and visible action in relation to a particular *breach* is necessary. Examples of circumstances where the *FCA* may consider it appropriate to take such action include:

. . .

(7)     where, in view of the nature and seriousness of an *approved person's* misconduct, the *FCA* considers it appropriate to impose a limitation on part or all of their approval ; and

(8)     where, in view of the nature and seriousness of an individual's misconduct, the *FCA* considers it appropriate to impose a disciplinary prohibition.

. . .

# Public and Listed Companies Appendix

*6A.3 Determining the appropriate length of the period of suspension, restriction ~~or~~ , condition or disciplinary prohibition*

6A.3.1 G The *FCA* will consider all the relevant circumstances of a case when it determines the length of the period of suspension, restriction ~~or~~ , condition <u>or disciplinary prohibition</u> (if any) that is appropriate for the *breach* concerned, and <u>is</u> also a sufficient deterrent. Set out below is a list of factors that may be relevant for this purpose. The list is not exhaustive: not all of these factors may be applicable in a particular case, and there may be other factors, not listed, that are relevant.

6A.3.2 G The following factors may be relevant to determining the appropriate length of the period of suspension, restriction ~~or~~ , condition <u>or disciplinary prohibition</u> to be imposed on a *person* under the Act:

(1)    Deterrence
When determining the appropriate length of the period of suspension, restriction ~~or~~ , condition <u>or disciplinary prohibition</u> the *FCA* will have regard to the principal purpose for which it imposes sanctions, namely to promote high standards of regulatory and/or market conduct by deterring *persons* who have committed *breaches* from committing further *breaches* and helping to deter other *persons* from committing similar *breaches*, as well as demonstrating generally the benefits of compliant business.

(2)    The seriousness of the breach
The *FCA* will have regard to the seriousness of the *breach*. In assessing this, it will consider the impact and nature of the *breach*, and whether it was committed deliberately or recklessly. Where the *breach* was committed by an *authorised person*, relevant factors may include those listed in *DEPP* 6.5A.2G(6) to (9). Where the *breach* was committed by an ~~approved person~~ individual in a non-*market abuse* case, relevant factors may include those listed in *DEPP* 6.5B.2 G(8) to (11). <u>Where the breach was committed by an individual in a *market abuse* case, relevant factors may include those listed in *DEPP* 6.5C.2G(11) to (14).</u> There may also be other factors, not listed in these sections, that are relevant.

(3)    Aggravating and mitigating factors
The *FCA* will have regard to factors that may aggravate or mitigate a breach. Where the ~~breach~~ <u>breach</u> was committed by an *authorised person*, *sponsor* or *primary information provider*, relevant factors may include those listed in *DEPP* 6.5A.3G(2). Where the *breach* was committed by an ~~approved person~~ individual in a non-*market abuse* case, relevant factors may include those listed in *DEPP* 6.5B.3G(2). <u>Where the *breach* was committed by an individual in a *market abuse* case, relevant factors may include those listed in *DEPP* 6.5C.3G(2).</u> There may also be other factors, not listed in these sections, that are relevant.

(4)    The impact of suspension, restriction ~~or~~ , condition <u>or disciplinary prohibition</u> on the person in breach

. . .

The following considerations may be relevant to the assessment of the impact of suspension or condition on an *approved person* <u>or the impact of a disciplinary prohibition on an individual</u>:

. . .

    (f)    the ~~approved~~ *person's* expected lost earnings from not being able to carry out the suspended ~~or~~ , restricted <u>or prohibited</u> activity; and

    (g)    whether the suspension ~~or~~ , restriction <u>or disciplinary prohibition</u> would cause the ~~approved~~ *person* serious financial hardship.

(5)    The impact of suspension ~~or~~ , restriction <u>or disciplinary prohibition</u> on persons other than the person in breach
The following considerations may be relevant to the assessment of the impact of suspension ~~or~~ , restriction <u>or disciplinary prohibition</u> on persons other than the *person* in *breach*:

. . .

> (b)    the impact of the suspension ~~or~~ , restriction <u>or disciplinary prohibition</u> on markets.

6A.3.3 G The *FCA* may delay the commencement of the period of suspension ~~or~~ , restriction <u>or disciplinary prohibition</u>. In deciding whether this is appropriate, the *FCA* will take into account all the circumstances of a case. Considerations that may be relevant in respect of an *authorised person, sponsor* or *primary information provider* include:

. . .

6A.3.4 G The *FCA* and the *person* on whom a suspension ~~or~~ , restriction <u>or disciplinary prohibition</u> is to be imposed may seek to agree the length of the period of suspension ~~or~~ , restriction <u>or disciplinary prohibition</u> and other terms. In recognition of the benefits of such agreements, *DEPP* 6.7 provides that the length of a period of suspension ~~or~~ , restriction <u>or disciplinary prohibition (other than a permanent disciplinary prohibition)</u> which might otherwise have been imposed will be reduced to reflect the stage at which the *FCA* and the *person* concerned reached an agreement.

. . .

*6A.4 The interaction between the power to impose suspensions, restrictions, conditions ~~and~~ , limitations <u>or disciplinary prohibitions</u> and the power to impose penalties or public censures*

6A.4.1 G The deterrent effect and impact on a *person* of a ~~suspension, restriction, condition or limitation, by itself or in combination with a financial penalty,~~ <u>combination of sanctions</u> may be greater than where only a ~~financial penalty~~ <u>single sanction</u> is imposed. The *FCA* will consider the overall impact and deterrent effect of the sanctions it imposes when determining the level of <u>any</u> penalty and the length of suspension, restriction, condition ~~or~~ , limitation <u>or disciplinary prohibition</u>.

6A.4.2 G The *FCA* expects usually to take the following approach in respect of the interaction between ~~a suspension, restriction, condition or limitation and a financial penalty or *public censure*~~ <u>sanctions</u>:

. . .

> (3)    If the *FCA*, following the approach set out in *DEPP* 6A.2, considers it appropriate to impose a suspension, restriction, condition ~~or~~ , limitation <u>or disciplinary prohibition (or some combination of these)</u>, it will calculate the appropriate length of the period <u>(or periods)</u> of ~~this measure~~ <u>sanction</u>, following the approach set out in *DEPP* 6A.3 or *DEPP* 6A.3A, as appropriate.
>
> (4)    Where the *FCA* considers it appropriate to impose ~~both a financial penalty and a suspension, restriction, condition or limitation~~ <u>a combination of sanctions</u>, it will decide whether the combined impact on the *person* is likely to be disproportionate in respect to the *breach* and the deterrent effect of the sanctions.
>
> (5)    If the *FCA* considers the combined impact on the *person* is likely to be disproportionate, it will decide whether to reduce the period of suspension, restriction, ~~or~~ condition<u>, or disciplinary prohibition, and</u> the amount of ~~the~~ <u>any</u> financial penalty or both, so that the combined impact of the sanctions is proportionate in relation to the *breach* and the deterrent effect of the sanctions. The *FCA* will decide which sanction <u>or sanctions</u> to reduce after considering all the circumstances of the case.
>
> (6)    In deciding the final level of ~~the~~ <u>any</u> financial penalty and the length of ~~the~~ <u>any</u> period of suspension, restriction, condition ~~or~~ , limitation <u>or disciplinary prohibition</u>, the *FCA* will also take into account any representations by the *person* that the

combined impact will cause them serious financial hardship. The *FCA* will take the approach set out in *DEPP* 6.5D in assessing this.

6A.4.3 G The *FCA* may depart from the approach set out in *DEPP* 6A.4.2G. For example, the *FCA* may at the outset consider that a financial penalty is the only appropriate sanction for a *breach* but, having determined the appropriate level of financial penalty, may consider it appropriate to reduce the amount of the financial penalty for serious financial hardship reasons. In such a situation, the *FCA* may consider it appropriate to impose a suspension, restriction, condition ~~or~~ , limitation or disciplinary prohibition even if the *FCA* at the outset did not consider such a sanction to be appropriate. The *FCA* will take into account whether the *person* would suffer serious financial hardship in deciding the length of the period of suspension, restriction, condition ~~or~~ , limitation or disciplinary prohibition and may decide not to impose such a measure if it considers such action would result in serious financial hardship.

**Annex C Amendments to the Enforcement Guide (EG)**
In this Annex, underlining indicates new text and striking through indicates deleted text, unless indicated otherwise.

*1 Introduction*

*1.1 Overview*
. . .

1.1.2 In the areas set out below, the *Act* expressly requires the *FCA* to prepare and publish statements of policy or procedure on the exercise of its enforcement and investigation powers and in relation to the giving of *statutory notices*.

. . .

(3)     section 124 requires the *FCA* to publish a statement of its policy on the ~~imposition and amount, of financial penalties for market abuse~~ type and level or period of administrative sanctions it may impose under Part VIII of the *Act*;

. . .

*2 The FCA's approach to enforcement*
. . .

*2.2 Case selection: Firms and individuals, market abuse cases and listing matters*
. . .

2.2.1 Other than in the area of a *firm's* failure to satisfy the *FCA's Threshold Conditions* for authorisation (see ~~paragraph~~ *EG* 2.3.1), the selection method for cases involving *firms* and individuals, *market abuse* and listing matters (for example, breaches of the listing~~,~~ or prospectus ~~or disclosure~~ *rules*) occurs at two main levels:
(1)     strategic planning~~;~~ and
(2)     decisions on individual cases.

. . .

*2.6 Assisting overseas regulators*
2.6.1 The *FCA* views co-operation with its overseas counterparts as an essential part of its regulatory functions. Section 354A of the *Act* imposes a duty on the *FCA* to

take such steps as it considers appropriate to co-operate with others who exercise functions similar to its own. This duty extends to authorities in the UK and overseas. In fulfilling this duty the *FCA* may share information which it is not prevented from disclosing, including information obtained in the course of the *FCA*'s own investigations, or exercise certain of its powers under Part XI of the *Act*. Further details of the *FCA*'s powers to assist overseas regulators are provided at *EG* 3.7.1 – 3.7.4 (Investigations to assist overseas authorities), *EG* 3.8.1 – 3.8.4 (Information requests and investigations to assist EEA regulators in relation to short selling), <u>*EG* 3.8A (Information requests and entry of premises under warrant to assist EEA regulators in relation to the Market Abuse Regulation)</u>, *EG* 4.7.1 (Use of statutory powers to require the production of documents, the provision of information or the answering of questions), *EG* 4.11.9 – 4.11.11 (Interviews in response to a request from an overseas regulator or EEA regulator), and *EG* 8.6.1 – 8.6.8 (Exercising the power under section 55Q to vary or cancel a firm's Part 4A permission or to impose requirements on a firm in support of an overseas regulator: the FCA's policy). The *FCA*'s statement of policy in relation to interviews which representatives of overseas regulators or *EEA regulators* attend and participate in is set out in *DEPP 7*.

. . .

*3 Use of information gathering and investigation powers*

*3.1 Introduction*

3.1.1 The *FCA* has various powers under sections 97, <u>122A, 122B, 122C,</u> 131E, 131FA, 165 to 169 and 284 of the *Act* and Schedule 5 to the *CRA* to gather information and appoint investigators, and to require the production of a report by a *skilled person*. In any particular case, the *FCA* will decide which powers, or combination of powers, are most appropriate to use having regard to all the circumstances. Further comments on the use of these powers are set out below.

. . .

After EG 3.2 insert the following new chapters EG 3.2A and EG 3.2B. All the text is new and is not underlined.

*3.2A Information requests (section 122A)*

3.2A.1 The *FCA* may use its section 122A power to require information and documents from an *issuer*, a *person discharging managerial responsibilities* or a *person* closely associated with a *person discharging managerial responsibilities* to support its supervisory and its enforcement functions, including those under the *Market Abuse Regulation* or any directly applicable *EU* regulation made under the *Market Abuse Regulation*.

3.2A.2 An officer with authorisation from the *FCA* may exercise the section 122A power to require information and documents. This includes an *FCA* employee or an agent of the *FCA*.

*3.2B Information requests (section 122B)*

3.2B.1 The *FCA* may use its section 122B power to require information and documents from a person to support both its supervisory and its enforcement functions under the *Market Abuse Regulation* or any directly applicable *EU* regulation made under the *Market Abuse Regulation*, or under the *auction regulation*.

[**Note:** see Regulation 6 and Schedule 1 to the *RAP Regulations* for application of the power in relation to functions under the *auction regulation*]

3.2B.2 An *officer* with authorisation from the *FCA* may exercise the section 122B power to require information and documents. This includes an *FCA* employee or an agent of the *FCA*.

After EG 3.8 insert the following new chapter EG 3.8A. All the text is new and is not underlined.

*3.8A Information requests and entry of premises under warrant to assist EEA regulators in relation to the Market Abuse Regulation or the auction regulation*

3.8A.1 The *FCA* may use its section 122B power to require information and documents from natural or legal persons to support both its supervisory and its enforcement functions.

3.8A.2 The *FCA*'s power to require information to assist *EEA regulators* in respect of the *Market Abuse Regulation* or any directly applicable *EU* regulation made under the *Market Abuse Regulation* or the *auction regulation* is contained in section 122B(6) of the *Act*. The section provides that at the request of an *EEA regulator*, the *FCA* may use its power under section 122B to require the production of information.

[**Note:** see Regulation 6 and Schedule 1 to the *RAP Regulations* in relation to the *auction regulation*]

3.8A.3 Section 122B(7) of the *Act* states that the *FCA* must, in deciding whether or not to exercise its power to require information, consider whether the exercise of that power is necessary to comply with the *Market Abuse Regulation* or any directly applicable *EU* regulation made under the *Market Abuse Regulation* or the *auction regulation*.

3.8A.4 The *FCA* may give information under 122D(1) or 176(1) (Entry of premises under warrant) at the request of an *EEA regulator* where the regulator makes the request in the exercise of its functions under the *Market Abuse Regulation*. Section 122D(11) of the *Act* states that the *FCA* must, in deciding whether or not to exercise it powers of entry of premises under warrant, consider whether the exercise of that power is necessary for the purpose of the exercise by it of its obligations under the *Market Abuse Regulation* or any directly applicable *EU* regulation made under the *Market Abuse Regulation* or the *auction regulation*.

. . .

Amend the following text as indicated

*4 Conduct of investigations*

. . .

*4.12 Search and seizure powers*

4.12.1 Under ~~section~~ sections 176 <u>and 122D</u> of the *Act*, the *FCA* has the power to apply to a justice of the peace for a warrant to enter premises where documents or information ~~is~~ are held. The circumstances under which the *FCA* may apply for a search warrant include:

. . .

4.12.2 A warrant obtained pursuant to ~~section~~ sections 176 and 122D of the *Act* authorises a police constable or an *FCA* investigator in the company, and under the supervision, of, a police constable, to do the following, amongst other things: to enter and search the premises specified in the warrant and take possession of any documents or information appearing to be documents or information of a kind in respect of which the warrant was issued or to take, in relation to any such documents or information, any other steps which may appear to be necessary for preserving them or preventing interference with them.

. . .

*7 Financial penalties and other disciplinary sanctions*

*7.1 The FCA's use of sanctions*

7.1.1 Financial penalties, suspensions, restrictions, conditions, limitations, disciplinary prohibitions, and *public censures* are important regulatory tools. However, they are not the only tools available to the *FCA*, and there will be many instances of non-compliance which the *FCA* considers it appropriate to address without the use of formal disciplinary sanctions. Still, the effective and proportionate use of the *FCA*'s powers to enforce the requirements of the *Act*, the *rules*, *COCON* and the Statements of Principle for Approved Persons (APER) will play an important role in the *FCA*'s pursuit of its *statutory objectives*. Imposing disciplinary sanctions shows that the *FCA* is upholding regulatory standards and helps to maintain market confidence and deter *financial crime*. An increased public awareness of regulatory standards also contributes to the protection of *consumers*.

7.1.2 The *FCA* has the following powers to impose ~~a financial penalty and to publish a public censure~~ sanctions.

(1)     It may publish a statement:

        . . .

        (e)     ~~where there has been *market abuse*,~~ against a *person* under section 123 of the *Act*;

        . . .

(2)     It may impose a financial penalty:

        . . .

        (c)     ~~where there has been *market abuse*,~~ on ~~any~~ a *person*, under section 123 of the *Act*;

        . . .

(3)     It may impose a suspension, *limitation* or other restriction:

        . . .

        (d)     on ~~a *firm*~~ an *authorised person* under ~~section~~ sections 123B or 206A of the *Act*.

        . . .

(5)     It may impose a disciplinary prohibition on an individual under section 123A of the *Act*.

. . .

*7.2 Alternatives to ~~financial penalties and public censures~~ sanctions*

7.2.1 The *FCA* also has measures available to it where it considers it is appropriate to take protective or remedial action. These include:

(4)     . . .

~~where there are reasonable grounds to suspect non compliance with the~~ *disclosure* ~~rules, the FCA may require the suspension of trading of a financial instrument with effect from such time as it may determine; and~~ where the *FCA* considers it necessary for the purpose of the exercise by it of functions under the *Market Abuse Regulation* or any directly applicable *EU* regulation made under the *Market Abuse Regulation*, the *FCA* may suspend trading in a *financial instrument* under section 122I of the *Act*;

(4a)     where the *FCA* considers it necessary for the purpose of the exercise by it of functions under the *auction regulation* the *FCA* may suspend trading in *emission auction products* under section 122I of the *Act*;

[Note: see Regulation 6 and Schedule 1 to the *RAP Regulations* for power in relation to *emission auction products*]

(5)     . . .

    (b)     suspend or prohibit admission of transferable securities to trading on a regulated market as set out in section 87L of the *Act* ~~:~~ ;

(6)     where the *FCA* considers it necessary for the purposes set out in section 122G of the *Act* the *FCA* may, by notice in writing, require an issuer to publish specified information or a specified statement as set out under section 122G of the *Act*; and

(7)     where the *FCA* considers it necessary for the purposes set out in section 122H of the *Act* the *FCA* may, by notice in writing, require a person to publish corrective information or a corrective statement as set out under section 122H of the *Act*.

. . .

*7.3 FCA's statements of policy*

7.3.1 The *FCA's* statement of policy in relation to the imposition of financial penalties is set out in *DEPP* 6.2 (Deciding whether to take action), ~~DEPP 6.3 (Penalties for market abuse)~~ and *DEPP* 6.4 (Financial penalty or public censure). The *FCA's* statement of policy on the amount of a financial penalty is set out in *DEPP* 6.5 to *DEPP* 6.5D. The *FCA's* statement of policy in relation to financial penalties for late submission of reports is set out in *DEPP* 6.6. The *FCA's* statement of policy in relation to the imposition of suspensions, ~~or~~ restrictions, conditions ~~and~~ , limitations and disciplinary prohibitions is set out in *DEPP* 6A (The power to impose a suspension, restriction, condition ~~or~~ , limitation or disciplinary prohibition). The *FCA's* statement of policy on the variation of an *SMF manager's* approval on its own initiative is set out in *DEPP* 8.

. . .

*8 Variation and cancellation of permission and imposition of requirements on the FCA's own initiative and intervention against incoming firms*

. . .

*8.6 Exercising the power under section 55Q to vary or cancel a firm's Part 4A permission or to impose requirements on a firm in support of an overseas regulator: the FCA's policy*

. . .

8.6.2 Relevant Community obligations which the *FCA* may need to consider include those under the Capital Requirements Directive, the *Solvency II Directive*, the Investment Services Directive/Markets in Financial Instruments Directive~~; and~~ , the Insurance Mediation Directive and the *Market Abuse Regulation*. Each of these

~~Directives~~ legislative acts imposes general obligations on the relevant *EEA competent authority* to cooperate and collaborate closely in discharging their functions under the ~~Directives~~ legislative acts.

. . .

*11 Restitution and redress*

. . .

*11.2 Criteria for determining whether to exercise powers to obtain restitution*

11.2.1 In deciding whether to exercise its powers to seek or require restitution under sections 382, 383 or 384 of the *Act*, the *FCA* will consider all the circumstances of the case. The factors which the *FCA* will consider may include, but are not limited to, those set out below.

. . .

(6)     Is redress available through another regulator?
        The *FCA* will consider the availability of redress through another regulatory authority. Where another regulatory authority, such as the *Takeover Panel*, is in a position to require appropriate redress, the *FCA* will not generally exercise its own powers to do so. If the *FCA* does consider that action is appropriate and the matters in question have happened in the context of a *takeover bid*, the *FCA* will only take action during the bid in the circumstances set out in *DEPP* ~~6.2.25G~~ 6.2.26G if the person concerned has responsibilities under the *Takeover Code*. If another *regulatory body* has required redress and a *person* has not met that requirement, the *FCA* will take this into account and (subject to all other relevant factors and circumstances) may consider it appropriate to take action to ensure that such redress is provided.

. . .

(11)    Other factors which may be relevant
        The *FCA* will consider the context of the conduct in question. In any case where the *FCA* believes that the exercise of its powers under section 383 or 384 of the *Act* may affect the timetable or outcome of a *takeover bid*, it will consult the *Takeover Panel* before taking any steps to exercise such powers, and will give due weight to its views.
        ~~Where the FCA is considering applying to court for a restitution order in relation to market abuse under section 383 of the Act, it will also consider whether the court would be prevented from making that order by section 383(3) of the Act. A similar provision to section 383(3) applies where the FCA proposes to exercise its powers to require restitution in relation to market abuse under section 384(2). The conditions set out in section 383(3)(a) and section 384(a) and (b) are the same as those that apply to penalties for market abuse and the FCA will take the same factors into account when considering whether the conditions have been met. DEPP 6.3 lists those factors.~~

. . .

*11.5 Other relevant powers*

. . .

11.5.2 The *FCA* may consider taking disciplinary action ~~for a financial penalty, or public censure,~~ using a range of powers as well as seeking restitution, if a *person* has breached a relevant requirement [13] of the *Act* or any directly applicable Community regulation or decision under *MiFID* or the *UCITS Directive* or the *auction regulation*, or has engaged in, or required or encouraged others to engage in, *market abuse*.

. . .

### 12 Prosecution of Criminal Offences

. . .

#### 12.3 Criminal prosecutions in cases of market abuse

12.3.1 In some cases there will be instances of market misconduct that may arguably involve a breach of the criminal law as well as *market abuse* as defined in section 118 of the Act. When the *FCA* decides whether to commence criminal proceedings rather than impose a sanction for *market abuse* in relation to that misconduct, it will apply the basic principles set out in the Code for Crown Prosecutors. When deciding whether to prosecute market misconduct which also falls within the definition of *market abuse*, application of these basic principles may involve consideration of some of the factors set out in paragraph *EG* 12.3.2.

. . .

### 19 Non-FSMA powers

. . .

#### 19.25 Recognised Auction Platforms Regulations 2011

19.25.1 The *FCA's* policy for using the powers given to it by the *RAP Regulations* is set out in *REC*. This includes, for example, its policy in relation to the power to impose a financial penalty on or censure an *RAP* (*REC* 2A.4) and its policy in relation to the power to give directions to an *RAP* (*REC* 4.6). The *FCA's* policy in relation to regulation 6 and Schedule 1 of the *RAP Regulations* is set out in *DEPP* and *EG*.

. . .

**Appendix 3 Appendix to the guidelines on investigation of cases of interest or concern to the Financial Conduct Authority and other prosecuting and investigating agencies**

#### 3.1 The FCA

. . .

3.1.3 Under the 2000 Act the *FCA* has powers to investigate concerns including:

. . .

- suspected *market abuse* under s.118 of the 2000 Act contraventions of the *Market Abuse Regulation* or any directly applicable *EU* regulation made under the *Market Abuse Regulation* or for contraventions of the *auction regulation*;
  [**Note:** see Regulation 6 and Schedule 1 to the *RAP Regulations* for powers in relation to contraventions of the *auction regulation*]

. . .

3.1.4 The *FCA* has the power to take the following enforcement action:

. . .

- impose civil penalties ~~in cases of market abuse~~ under s.123 of the 2000 Act; [**Note:** see Regulation 6 and Schedule 1 to the *RAP Regulations* for the application of this power and those below to contraventions of the *auction regulation*]
- temporarily prohibit an individual from exercising management functions in *MiFID investment firms* or from dealing in *financial instruments* or *emissions auction products* on their own account or on the account of a third party, under s.123A(2) of the 2000 Act;
- temporarily prohibit an individual from making a bid, on his or her own account or the account of a third party, directly or indirectly, at an auction conducted by a *recognised auction platform* under s.123A(2) of the 2000 Act;
- permanently prohibit an individual from exercising management functions in *MiFID investment firms* under s.123A(3) of the 2000 Act;
- suspend the permission of an *authorised person* or impose limitations or other restrictions in relation to the carrying on of a *regulated activity* by an *authorised person* under s.123B of the 2000 Act;
- prohibit an individual from being employed in connection with a *regulated activity*, under s.56 of the 2000 Act;

. . .

# 34   Purchase of Own Shares

**Cross-references.** See **33.32** and **33.41** PUBLIC AND LISTED COMPANIES for additional requirements of listed companies in connection with own share purchase under the Listing Rules.

## 34.1   GENERAL RULE AGAINST COMPANY ACQUIRING ITS OWN SHARES

Subject to the exceptions below, a limited company must not acquire its own shares, whether by purchase, subscription or otherwise, except in accordance with the provisions in this chapter. [*CA 2006, s 658(1)*]. See *Trevor v Whitworth* (1887) 12 App Cas 409, HL.

If a company purports to act in contravention of this,

- the purported acquisition is void; and

- an offence is committed by the company and every officer of the company who is default. A person guilty of such an offence is liable (i) on conviction on indictment, to imprisonment for a term not exceeding two years or a fine (or both); and (ii) on summary conviction, to imprisonment for a term not exceeding twelve months (six months in Scotland and Northern Ireland) or to a fine not exceeding the statutory maximum (or both). See **29.1** OFFENCES AND LEGAL PROCEEDINGS for the statutory maximum.

[*CA 2006, s 658(2)(3)*].

## 34.1 Purchase of Own Shares

**Exceptions.**

(a)   A limited company may acquire any of its own fully paid shares otherwise than for valuable consideration. See *Kirby v Wilkins* [1929] 2 Ch 444, [1929] All ER Rep 356 and *Castiglione's Will Trusts, Re, Hunter v Mackenzie* [1958] Ch 549, [1958] 1 All ER 480 for shares acquired by way of gift and bequeathed by will respectively.

(b)   The general provisions in *CA 2006, s 658* above do not prohibit

- the acquisition of shares in a reduction of share capital duly made (see **47.51** SHARES);

- the purchase of shares in pursuance of a court order under

   (i)   *CA 2006, s 98* (application to court to cancel resolution for re-registration as a private company, see **41.9** RE-REGISTRATION);

   (ii)   *CA 2006, s 721(6)* (powers of court on objection to redemption or purchase of shares out of capital, see **34.18(*d*)**);

   (iii)   *CA 2006, s 759* (remedial order in case of breach of prohibition of public offers by private company, see **47.22** SHARES); or

   (iv)   *CA 2006, ss 994–999* (protection of members against unfair prejudice, see **26.10** MEMBERS); and

- the forfeiture of shares, or the acceptance of shares surrendered in lieu, in pursuance of the articles, for failure to pay any sum payable in respect of the shares (see **47.25** SHARES).

[*CA 2006, s 659*].

The above provisions do not preclude a company from acquiring the shares of another company even in circumstances where the sole asset of the acquired company is shares in the acquiring company (*Acatos & Hutcheson plc v Watson* [1995] 1 BCLC 218, [1995] BCC 446).

## 34.2   REDEEMABLE SHARES

A limited company having a share capital may issue shares that are to be redeemed or are liable to be redeemed at the option of the company or the shareholder ('*redeemable shares*'), subject to the following provisions.

- The articles of a private limited company may exclude or restrict the issue of redeemable shares.

- A public limited company may only issue redeemable shares if it is authorised to do so by its articles.

- No redeemable shares must be issued at a time when there are no issued shares of the company that are not redeemable.

[*CA 2006, s 684*].

See **34.11–34.18** for provisions applying where a private company makes a payment for the redemption out of capital and **34.23** for the requirement to create a capital redemption reserve.

## 34.3   Provisions relating to the redemption

**Terms and manner of the redemption.** The directors of a limited company may determine the terms, conditions and manner of the redemption of shares if authorised to do so by

- the articles; or

- a resolution of the company (which may be an ordinary resolution even though it amends the articles).

Where the directors are so authorised, they must determine the terms, etc before the shares are allotted. Any obligation of the company to state in a statement of capital (see below) the rights attached to shares extends to the terms, conditions and manner of redemption.

Where the directors are not so authorised, the terms, conditions and manner of redemption of any redeemable shares must be stated in the company's articles.

[*CA 2006, s 685*].

**Payment for redeemable shares**. Redeemable shares in a limited company

(a)   may not be redeemed unless they are fully paid; and

(b)   must be paid for on the redemption date unless the terms of redemption provide that, by agreement between the company and the shareholders, the amount payable may be paid on a later date.

[*CA 2006, s 686*].

*Transitional provisions.* The provisions in (*b*) above apply to

(i)   shares issued on or after 1 October 2009; and

(ii)   shares issued before that date where the terms of redemption have been amended on or after that date to allow for payment on a date later than the redemption date.

[*SI 2008 No 2860, Sch 2 para 73*].

**Financing of the redemption**. Subject to the power of *private* companies to redeem shares out of capital (see **34.11**) and the enforcement of redemption against a company when shares have not been redeemed at the commencement of winding up (see **34.24**)

- redeemable shares in a limited company may only be redeemed out of

(i)   'distributable profits' of the company; or

(ii)   the proceeds of a fresh issue of shares made for the purpose of the redemption; and

- any premium payable on redemption of shares in a limited company must be paid out of distributable profits of the company except that if the redeemable shares were issued at a premium, any premium payable on redemption may be paid out of the proceeds of a fresh issue of shares made for the purpose of the redemption, up to an amount equal to

(i)   the aggregate of the premiums received by the company on the issue of the shares redeemed, or

(ii)   the current amount of the company's share premium account (including any amount transferred to that account in respect of premiums on the new shares),

whichever is the less. The amount of the company's share premium account is reduced by a sum corresponding (or by sums in aggregate corresponding) to the amount of any premium payable on redemption.

'*Distributable profits*' are those profits out of which the company could lawfully make a distribution (see **22.1** Distributions) equal in value to the payment. [*CA 2006, ss 687, 736*].

## 34.3 Purchase of Own Shares

**Cancellation of shares.** When shares in a limited company are redeemed, the shares are treated as cancelled and the company's issued share capital is diminished by the nominal value of those shares. [*CA 2006, s 688*].

**Notice to Registrar of Companies of redemption.** If a limited company redeems any redeemable shares, it must within one month give notice to the Registrar of Companies, specifying the shares redeemed. The notice must be accompanied by a statement of capital. This must state, with respect to the company's share capital immediately following the redemption, the following particulars.

- The total number of shares of the company.

- The aggregate nominal value of those shares and the aggregate amount (if any) unpaid on those shares (whether on account of their nominal value or by way of premium).

- For each class of shares

    (i) particulars of any voting rights attached to the shares, including rights that arise only in certain circumstances;

    (ii) particulars of any rights attached to the shares, as respects dividends, to participate in a distribution;

    (iii) particulars of any rights attached to the shares, as respects capital, to participate in a distribution (including on a winding up);

    (iv) whether the shares are to be redeemed or are liable to be redeemed at the option of the company or the shareholder;

    (v) the total number of shares of that class; and

    (vi) the aggregate nominal value of shares of that class.

- The amount paid up and the amount (if any) unpaid on each share (whether on account of the nominal value of the share or by way of premium).

If default is made in complying with this provision, an offence is committed by the company and every officer of the company who is in default. A person guilty of such an offence is liable, on summary conviction, to a fine not exceeding level 3 on the standard scale and, for continued contravention, a daily default fine not exceeding one-tenth of level 3 on the standard scale. See **29.1 OFFENCES AND LEGAL PROCEEDINGS** for the standard scale.

[*CA 2006, s 689, SBEE 2015, Sch 6, para 13; SI 2016 No 321, Art 6*].

**Listed companies.** See **33.41 PUBLIC AND LISTED COMPANIES** for provisions in the FCA Listing Rules.

## 34.4 PURCHASE OF OWN SHARES

A limited company having a share capital may purchase its own shares (including any redeemable shares) subject to the provisions in **34.5–34.10** and any restriction or prohibition in the company's articles.

A limited company may not, however, purchase its own shares

- if, as a result of the purchase, there would no longer be any issued shares of the company other than redeemable shares or shares held as treasury shares; and

- unless they are fully paid.

[*CA 2006, ss 690, 691(1)*].

### 34.5   Provisions relating to purchase

**Payment for purchase.** Where a limited company purchases its own shares, the shares must be paid for on purchase. This does not apply where a private limited company is purchasing shares for the purposes of or pursuant to an employees' share scheme. [*CA 2006, s 691(2); SI 2013 No 999, Reg 3*].

**Financing of purchase.** Subject to the power of *private* companies to redeem shares out of capital or with cash (see **34.11**) and the enforcement of redemption against a company when shares have not been redeemed at the commencement of winding up (see **34.24**)

- a limited company may only purchase its own shares out of

  (i)     'distributable profits' of the company; or

  (ii)    the proceeds of a fresh issue of shares made for the purpose of financing the purchase; and

- any premium payable on the purchase by a limited company of its own shares must be paid out of distributable profits of the company except that if the shares to be purchased were issued at a premium, any premium payable on their purchase by the company may be paid out of the proceeds of a fresh issue of shares made for the purpose of financing the purchase, up to an amount equal to

  (i)     the aggregate of the premiums received by the company on the issue of the shares purchased, or

  (ii)    the current amount of the company's share premium account (including any amount transferred to that account in respect of premiums on the new shares),

  whichever is the less. The amount of the company's share premium account is reduced by a sum corresponding (or by sums in aggregate corresponding) to the amount of any premium payable on their purchase.

'*Distributable profits*' are those profits out of which the company could lawfully make a distribution (see **22.1** DISTRIBUTIONS) equal in value to the payment.

[*CA 2006, ss 692, 736; SI 2013 No 999 Reg 4*].

**Treatment of shares purchased.** Where a limited company makes a purchase of its own shares

- if *Companies Act 2006 (CA 2006), s 724* (treasury shares) applies, the shares may be held and dealt with in accordance with **34.19–34.22**; and

- in any other case, the shares are treated as cancelled and the amount of the company's issued share capital is diminished by the nominal value of the shares cancelled.

[*CA 2006, s 706*].

### 34.6   Authority for off-market purchase

**Authority.** A company may only make an 'off-market purchase' of its own shares provided that the purchase is either authorised in accordance with CA 2006, s 693A (for an employees' share scheme), or made in pursuance of a contract which itself is approved prior to the purchase in accordance with *CA 2006, s 694*, and where:

- the terms of the contract have been authorised by resolution of the members before the contract is entered into; or

- the contract provides that no shares may be purchased in pursuance of the contract until its terms have been authorised by a resolution of the members.

An '*off-market purchase*' is one where the shares are either

- purchased otherwise than on a 'recognised investment exchange'; or

- purchased on a recognised investment exchange but

  (i)    the shares are not listed under *FSMA 2000, Pt 6;* and

  (ii)   the company has not been afforded facilities for dealings in those shares to take place on the exchange without prior permission for individual transactions from the governing authority and without limit as to the time during which those facilities are to be available.

For these purposes '*recognised investment exchange*' means a recognised investment exchange within the meaning of *FSMA 2000, Pt 18* other than an overseas exchange (within the meaning of that *Part*).

The contract may be a contract, entered into by the company and relating to shares in the company, that does not amount to a contract to purchase the shares but under which the company may (subject to any conditions) become entitled or obliged to purchase the shares.

[*CA 2006, ss 693(1)(a), (2), (3), (5), 694(1)–(3); SI 2013 No 999, Reg 5*].

**Members' resolutions.** As the type of resolution is not specified by *CA 2006, s 694(2)*, an ordinary resolution will suffice unless the articles require a higher majority.

There is no requirement to file the ordinary resolution at Companies House, though see below for the requirement to do this for an ordinary resolution giving general authority for buy-back in the context of an employees' share scheme, by *CA 2006, s 693A(8)*.

The authority conferred by a resolution made under the above provisions may be varied, revoked or (from time to time) renewed by a resolution of the members. In the case of a public company, a resolution conferring, varying or renewing authority must specify a date on which the authority is to expire, which must not be later than five years after the date on which the resolution is passed.

[*CA 2006, ss 694(4), (5), 281(3); SI 2013 No 999, Reg 5*].

A resolution conferring, varying, revoking or renewing authority as above is subject to following.

(a)    *Exercise of voting rights.*

- Where the resolution is proposed as a written resolution, a member who holds shares to which the resolution relates is not an eligible member (and therefore not entitled to receive or vote on the resolution).

- Where the resolution is proposed at a meeting of the company, it is not effective if

  (i)    any member of the company holding shares to which the resolution relates exercises the voting rights carried by any of those shares in voting on the resolution; and

  (ii)   the resolution would not have been passed if he had not done so.

For these purposes

(1)     a member who holds shares to which the resolution relates is regarded as exercising the voting rights carried by those shares not only if he votes in respect of them on a poll on the question whether the resolution should be passed, but also if he votes on the resolution otherwise than on a poll;

(2)     any member of the company may demand a poll on that question; and

(3)     a vote and a demand for a poll by a person as proxy for a member are the same respectively as a vote and a demand by the member.

(b)     A copy of the contract (if it is in writing) or of a memorandum setting out its terms (if it is not) must be made available to members

•       in the case of a written resolution, by being sent or submitted to every eligible member at or before the time at which the proposed resolution is sent or submitted to him; and

•       in the case of a resolution at a meeting, by being made available for inspection by members of the company both at the company's registered office for not less than 15 days ending with the date of the meeting and at the meeting itself.

A memorandum of contract terms so made available must include the names of the members holding shares to which the contract relates. A copy of the contract so made available must have annexed to it a written memorandum specifying such of those names as do not appear in the contract itself.

[CA 2006, ss 694(6), 695, 696].

**Variation of contract.** A company may only agree to a variation of a contract authorised under the above provisions if the terms of the variation are authorised by a resolution of the members before it is agreed to [CA 2006, s 697(1)(2); SI 2013 No 999, Reg 5]. The conditions set out in (a) and (b) (above) under the heading *Resolutions* apply to the authority for a proposed variation (with the terminology amended for variations) as they apply to the authority for a proposed contract. In addition, there must also be made available to members under (b) above a copy of the original contract or, as the case may be, a memorandum of its terms, together with any variations previously made.

[CA 2006, ss 697(3)–(5), 698, 699].

**Release of company's rights.** An agreement by a company to release its rights under a contract approved as above is void unless the terms of the release agreement are authorised by a resolution of the company before the agreement is entered into. That authority may be varied, revoked or from time to time renewed by a resolution of the company. In the case of a public company such a resolution must specify a date on which the authority is to expire which must be no later than five years after the date on which the resolution is passed.

[CA 2006, s 700(1)(2)(3)(4) SI 2009 No 1917, Reg 4; SI 2013 No 999, Reg 5].

The conditions set out in (a) and (b) (above) under the heading *Resolutions* apply to a resolution authorising a proposed release agreement as they apply to the authority for a proposed contract. In addition, there must also be made available to members under (b) above a copy of the original contract or, as the case may be, a memorandum of its terms, together with any variations previously made.

[CA 2006, ss 698, 699, 700(5)].

# 34.6   Purchase of Own Shares

**Assignment of rights.** The rights of a company under a contract authorised under *CA 2006, s 693A* (authority for an off-market purchase for the purposes of or pursuant to an employees' share scheme) or *CA 2006, s 694* (authority for an off-market purchase) are not capable of being assigned.

[*CA 2006, s 704; SI 2013 No 999, Reg 9*].

**Transitional provisions.**

(1)     The above provisions for off-market purchase apply to

- contracts entered into on or after 1 October 2009; and

- contracts entered into before that date that

    (i)     provide that no shares may be purchased in pursuance of a contract until its terms have been authorised by a special resolution of the company; and

    (ii)    are authorised by special resolution passed on or after that date.

[*SI 2008 No 2860, Sch 2 para 76*].

(2)     Where, immediately before 1 October 2009, a resolution is in force having been passed under the corresponding provisions of *CA 1985*, the resolution has effect on or after that date as if passed under the *CA 2006* provisions above.

[*SI 2008 No 2860, Sch 2 para 75*].

## 34.7   *Authority for off-market purchase for an employees' share scheme*

A company may make an off-market purchase of its own shares for the purposes of or pursuant to an employees' share scheme if the purchase has first been authorised by an ordinary resolution of the members. That authority:

- may be general or limited to the purchase of shares of a particular class or description;

- may be unconditional or subject to conditions;

- must specify the maximum number of shares authorised to be acquired and determine both the maximum and minimum prices that may be paid for the shares;

- may be varied, revoked or from time to time renewed by a resolution of the company.

So, a private company may pass an ordinary resolution granting a general authority under which the company may carry out multiple off-market buy-backs in the future in relation to an employees' share scheme.

A resolution to confer, vary or renew authority must specify a date on which it is to expire, which must be not later than five years after the date on which the resolution is passed. However, a company may make a purchase of its own shares after the expiry of the time limit specified if the contract of purchase was concluded before the authority expired and the terms of the authority permitted the company to make a contract of purchase that would or might be executed wholly or partly after its execution.

A resolution to confer or vary authority may determine the maximum or minimum price for the purchase by specifying a particular sum or by providing a basis or formula for calculating the amount of the price (but without reference to a person's discretion or opinion). *CA 2006 Chapter 3, Part 3* (Resolutions affecting a company's constitution) applies to a resolution under these provisions.

The ordinary resolution must be filed at Companies House within 15 days of it being passed.

Further guidance upon share buy-back in the context of employees' share schemes is currently still awaited from the Department for Business, Energy and Industrial Strategy, further to the Nuttall Review recommendations which were issued under the 2010 to 2015 Conservative and Liberal Democrat coalition government.

[*CA 2006 s 693A; SI 2013 No 999 Reg 7*]

## 34.8   Authority for market purchase

A limited company may only make a 'market purchase' of its own shares if the purchase has first been authorised by a resolution of the company.

A '*market purchase*' is a purchase made on a 'recognised investment exchange' other than one where

- the shares are not listed under *FSMA 2000, Pt 6;* and

- the company has not been afforded facilities for dealings in those shares to take place on the exchange without prior permission for individual transactions from the governing authority and without limit as to the time during which those facilities are to be available.

For these purposes, '*recognised investment exchange*' means a recognised investment exchange (within the meaning of *FSMA 2000, Pt 18*) other than an overseas exchange (within the meaning of that *Part*). [*CA 2006, ss 693(1)(b), (4), (5), 701(1)*].

The authority for the purchase may be

- general or limited to the purchase of shares of a particular class or description;

- unconditional or subject to conditions; and

- varied, revoked or from time to time renewed by a resolution of the company.

In addition, the authority must

- specify the maximum number of shares authorised to be acquired; and

- determine the maximum and minimum prices that may be paid for the shares. This may be done by specifying a particular sum, or by providing a formula or basis for calculating the price (but without reference to any person's discretion or opinion).

A resolution conferring, varying or renewing authority must specify a date on which it is to expire, which must not be later than five years after the date on which the resolution is passed. A company may make a purchase of its own shares after the expiry of the time limit specified if

- the contract of purchase was concluded before the authority expired; and

- the terms of the authority permitted the company to make a contract of purchase that would or might be executed wholly or partly after its expiration.

*CA 2006, ss 29, 30* (resolutions affecting a company's constitution) apply to a resolution under these provisions. See **14.10 CONSTITUTION – MEMORANDUM AND ARTICLES**. [*CA 2006, s 701(2)–(8)*].

**Assignment of rights**. The rights of a company under a contract for a market purchase are not capable of being assigned.

## 34.8 Purchase of Own Shares

[*CA 2006, s 704*].

## 34.9 Payments apart from purchase price to be made out of distributable profits

Apart from the purchase price itself (for which see **34.5**) a payment made by a company in consideration of

(a)     acquiring any right with respect to the purchase of its own shares in pursuance of a contingent purchase contract approved under **34.6**,

(b)     the variation of any contract approved under **34.6**, or

(c)     the release of any of the company's obligations with respect to the purchase of any of its own shares under a contract approved under **34.6** or authorised under **34.8**

must be made out of the company's '*distributable profits*', ie those profits out of which it could lawfully make a distribution (see **22.1** Distributions) equal in value to the payment.

If this requirement is not met in relation to a contract,

•     in a case within (*a*) above, no purchase by the company of its own shares in pursuance of that contract may be made;

•     in a case within (*b*) above, no such purchase following the variation may be made; and

•     in a case within (*c*) above, the purported release is void.

[*CA 2006, ss 705, 736*].

## 34.10 Disclosure requirements

**Copy of contract or memorandum of terms to be available for inspection.** Where a company has entered into a contract approved under **34.6** or authorised under **34.8**, it must keep available for inspection at the company's registered office or a place specified in Regulations (see **36.2** Records)

•     a copy of the contract; or

•     if the contract is not in writing, a written memorandum setting out its terms.

The contract or memorandum must be kept available for inspection from the conclusion of the contract until ten years from the date on which the purchase of all shares under the contract is completed or (as the case may be) the date on which the contract otherwise determines. This applies to any variation of the contract as it applies to the original contract.

The company must give notice to the Registrar of Companies within 14 days of the place at which the copy or memorandum is kept available for inspection and of any change in that place (unless it has at all times been kept at the company's registered office).

Every copy or memorandum required to be kept must be open to inspection without charge by any member of the company and, in the case of a public company, any other person.

In default of complying with any of the above requirements, or if an inspection is refused, an offence is committed by the company and every officer of the company who is in default. A person guilty of such an offence is liable, on summary conviction, to a fine not exceeding level 3 on the standard scale and, for continued contravention, a daily default fine not exceeding one-tenth of level 3 on the standard scale. See **29.1** Offences and Legal Proceedings for the standard scale. In the case of a refusal of an inspection, the court may compel an immediate inspection.

[*CA 2006, ss 702, 703*].

*Availability for inspection and copying.* See **36.2** RECORDS.

**Return to Registrar of Companies of purchase of own shares**. Where a company purchases shares under **34.4** above, it must deliver a return to the Registrar of Companies within 28 days from the date on which the shares are delivered to it.

The return must

(a)     distinguish treasury shares (see **34.19**) and shares which are not treasury shares;

(b)     in the case of treasury shares, distinguish those that are cancelled forthwith (see **34.21**) and those are not so cancelled;

(c)     state, with respect to shares of each class purchased

   (i)     the number and nominal value of the shares; and

   (ii)     the date on which they were delivered to the company; and

(d)     in the case of a public company, state

   (i)     the aggregate amount paid by the company for the shares; and

   (ii)     the maximum and minimum prices paid in respect of shares of each class purchased.

Particulars of shares delivered to the company on different dates and under different contracts may be included in a single return. In such a case, the amount required to be stated under (*d*)(i) above is the aggregate amount paid by the company for all the shares to which the return relates.

*Penalties.* If default is made in delivering to the Registrar of Companies any return or statement required above, an offence is committed by every officer of the company who is in default. A person guilty of such an offence is liable (i) on conviction on indictment, to a fine; and (ii) on summary conviction, to a fine not exceeding the statutory maximum and, for continued contravention, a daily default fine not exceeding one-tenth of the greater of £5,000 or the amount corresponding to level 4 on the standard scale for summary offences. See **29.1** OFFENCES AND LEGAL PROCEEDINGS for the statutory maximum.

[*CA 2006, s 707; SI 2015 No 664, Sch 3*].

**Notice to Registrar of Companies of cancellation of shares**. If, on the purchase by a company of any of its own shares,

•     *CA 2006, s 724* (treasury shares, see **34.19**) does not apply (so that the shares are treated as cancelled), or

•     *CA 2006, s 724* applies but the shares are cancelled forthwith under *CA 2006, s 729* (see **34.21**),

the company must give notice of cancellation to the Registrar of Companies within 28 days from the date on which the shares are delivered to it, specifying the shares cancelled.

The notice must be accompanied by a statement of capital (except where the statement of capital would be the same as a statement of capital that is required to be delivered to the Registrar of Companies under *CA 2006, s 720B(1)* (see **34.13(4)**) which must state the following information with respect to the company's share capital immediately following the cancellation.

## 34.10 Purchase of Own Shares

(a)     The total number of shares of the company.

(b)     The aggregate nominal value of those shares and the aggregate amount (if any) unpaid on those shares (whether on account of their nominal value or by way of premium).

(c)     For each class of shares

    (i)     particulars of any voting rights attached to the shares, including rights that arise only in certain circumstances;

    (ii)    particulars of any rights attached to the shares, as respects dividends, to participate in a distribution;

    (iii)   particulars of any rights attached to the shares, as respects capital, to participate in a distribution (including on a winding up);

    (iv)    whether the shares are to be redeemed or are liable to be redeemed at the option of the company or the shareholder;

    (v)     the total number of shares of that class; and

    (vi)    the aggregate nominal value of shares of that class.

(d)     The amount paid up and the amount (if any) unpaid on each share (whether on account of the nominal value of the share or by way of premium).

*Penalties.* If default is made in complying with the above provisions, an offence is committed by the company and every officer of the company who is in default. A person guilty of such an offence is liable, on summary conviction, to a fine not exceeding level 3 on the standard scale and, for continued contravention, a daily default fine not exceeding one-tenth of level three on the standard scale. See **29.1 OFFENCES AND LEGAL PROCEEDINGS** for the standard scale.

[*CA 2006, s 708; SBEE 2015, Sch 6, para 14; SI 2016 No 321, Art 6; SI 2009 No 388, Art 2; SI 2015 No 532, Art 4*].

## 34.11 REDEMPTION OR PURCHASE BY PRIVATE COMPANY OUT OF CAPITAL OR WITH CASH

A private limited company may purchase of its own shares (a) out of capital in accordance with *CA 2006, Ch 5* (and *Ch 5* is subject to *CA 2006, s 692(1ZA)* (purchase of own shares up toannual limit) or (b) if authorised to do so by its articles, out of capital otherwise than in accordance with *CA 2006*, Ch 5, up to an aggregate purchase price in a financial year of the lower of £15,000 or the nominal value of 5% of its fully paid share capital as at the beginning of the financial year.

If the share capital of the company is not denominated in sterling, the value of sterling shall be calculated for the purposes of (b) at an appropriate spot rate of exchange.

Provided it is made in accordance with the provisions in **34.12–34.18**, the payment that may be made out of capital (the *'permissible capital payment'*) is such an amount as, after applying for that purposes

•     any available profits of the company (see **34.12**), and

•     the proceeds of any fresh issue of shares made for the purpose of the redemption or purchase

is required to meet the price of redemption or purchase.

[*CA 2006, ss 692 (1)(1A), (1ZA), 709, 710, 736; SI 2013 No 999 Reg 4; SI 2015 No 532, Reg 3, 5*].

**Accounting consequences.** Subject to below, if the permissible capital payment for shares redeemed or purchased

(a)   is less than the nominal amount of those shares, the amount of the difference must be transferred to the company's capital redemption reserve (see **34.23**); and

(b)   is greater than the nominal amount of those shares, then

  •   the amount of any capital redemption reserve, share premium account (see **46 SHARE PREMIUM**) or fully paid share capital of the company, and

  •   any amount representing unrealised profits of the company standing to the credit of any revaluation reserve maintained by the company

may be reduced by a sum not exceeding (or by sums not in total exceeding) the amount by which the permissible capital payment exceeds the nominal amount of the shares.

Where the proceeds of a fresh issue are applied by the company in making a redemption or purchase of its own shares in addition to a payment out of capital under these provisions, the permissible capital payment for the purposes of (*a*) and (*b*) above is to be read as referring to the aggregate of that payment and those proceeds.

In relation to a payment made under *CA 2006, s 692 (1ZA)*, references to the permissible capital payment are to the purchase price of the shares or (if less) the part of it met out of the payment under *CA 2006, s 692 (1ZA)* and any proceeds of a fresh issue used to make the payment.

[*CA 2006, s 734; SI 2015 No 532, Reg 9*].

## 34.12   Available profits

The reference in **34.13** to available profits of a company is to the company's profits which are available for distribution (see generally **22 DISTRIBUTIONS**) but the question whether a company has any profits so available, and the amount of any such profits, is not determined as in **22.2–22.4 DISTRIBUTIONS** but as follows.

(1)   Determine the profits of the company by reference to the following items as stated in the 'relevant accounts'.

  (a)   Profits, losses, assets and liabilities.

  (b)   Provisions of the following kinds:

    •   Where the relevant accounts are Companies Act accounts, (i) provisions for depreciation or diminution in value of assets; and (ii) any provision for liabilities (or, in the case of insurance companies, provisions for other risks), ie any amount retained as reasonably necessary for the purpose of providing for any liability the nature of which is clearly defined and which is either likely to be incurred, or certain to be incurred but uncertain as to the amount or as to the date on which it will arise; and

    •   Where the relevant accounts are IAS accounts, provisions of any kind.

  (c)   Share capital and reserves (including undistributable reserves, see **22.1 DISTRIBUTIONS**).

(2)   Determine the amount of

  (a)   any distribution lawfully made by the company; and

(b)      any 'other relevant payment lawfully made' by the company out of distributable profits,

after the date of the relevant accounts and before the end of the 'relevant period'.

*'Other relevant payment lawfully made'* include

• financial assistance lawfully given out of distributable profits in accordance with *CA 2006, ss 677–683* (see **34.24** and **34.25**);

• payments lawfully made out of distributable profits in respect of the purchase by the company of any shares in the company; and

• payments of any description specified in **34.9**(*a*)–(*c*) lawfully made by the company.

(3)      Available profits are (1) minus (2).

The *'relevant accounts'* are any accounts that are

• prepared as at a date within the relevant period; and

• such as to enable a reasonable judgment to be made as to the amounts of the items mentioned in (1) above.

The *'relevant period'* means the period of three months ending with the date on which the solvency statement is made in accordance with *CA 2006, s 720A* or the directors' statement is made (see **34.13**).

[*CA 2006, ss 711, 712; SI 2008 No 409, Sch 7 paras 2, 4; SI 2008 No 410, Sch 9 paras 1, 2, 4; SI 2013 No 999, Reg 10*].

## 34.13   Requirements for payments out of capital

Subject to *CA 2006, s 720A* and any court order made under **34.18**, a payment out of capital by a private company for the redemption or purchase of its own shares is not lawful unless the following conditions are satisfied.

[*CA 2006, s 713; SI 2013 No 999, Reg 11*].

(1)      **Directors' statement and auditor's report**

The directors must make a statement specifying the amount of the permissible capital payment for the shares and stating that, having made full inquiry into the affairs and prospects of the company, they have formed the opinion that

(a)      as regards its initial situation immediately after the date on which the payment out of capital is proposed to be made, there will be no grounds on which the company could then be found to be unable to pay its debts (taking into account all of the company's liabilities, including any contingent or prospective liabilities); and

(b)      as regards its prospects for the year following that date (having regard to their intentions with regard to the management of the company's business, and the amount and character of the financial resources that will in their view be available, during that year), the company will be able to carry on business as a going concern (and will accordingly be able to pay its debts as they fall due) throughout that year.

It must have annexed to it a report addressed to the directors by the company's auditor stating that

- he has inquired into the company's state of affairs;

- the amount specified in the statement as the permissible capital payment for the shares in question is, in his view, properly determined in accordance with **34.11** and **34.12**; and

- he is not aware of anything to indicate that the opinion expressed by the directors in the statement under (*a*) and (*b*) above is unreasonable in all the circumstances. [*CA 2006, s 714*].

The statement must be in writing, indicate that it is a directors' statement under *CA 2006, s 714* and be signed by each of the company's directors. It must also state whether the company's business includes that of a banking company or of an insurance company.

[*SI 2009 No 388, Art 5*].

Penalties. If the directors make a statement as above without having reasonable grounds for the opinion expressed in it, an offence is committed by every director who is in default. A person guilty of such an offence is liable (i) on conviction on indictment, to imprisonment for a term not exceeding two years or a fine (or both); and (ii) on summary conviction, to imprisonment for a term not exceeding twelve months (six months in Scotland or Northern Ireland) or to a fine not exceeding the statutory maximum (or both). See **29.1** OFFENCES AND LEGAL PROCEEDINGS for the statutory maximum.

[*CA 2006, s 715*].

(2)     **Special resolution**

The payment out of capital must be approved by a special resolution passed on, or within the week immediately following, the date on which the directors make the statement under (1) above. [*CA 2006, s 716*]. The special resolution is subject to following.

*Exercise of voting rights*

Where the resolution is proposed as a written resolution, a member who holds shares to which the resolution relates is not an eligible member (and therefore not entitled to receive or vote on the resolution).

Where the resolution is proposed at a meeting of the company, it is not effective if

(i)     any member of the company holding shares to which the resolution relates exercises the voting rights carried by any of those shares in voting on the resolution; and

(ii)    the resolution would not have been passed if he had not done so.

For these purposes

- a member who holds shares to which the resolution relates is regarded as exercising the voting rights carried by those shares not only if he votes in respect of them on a poll on the question whether the resolution should be passed, but also if he votes on the resolution otherwise than on a poll;

- any member of the company may demand a poll on that question; and

- a vote and a demand for a poll by a person as proxy for a member are the same respectively as a vote and a demand by the member.

[*CA 2006, s 717*].

Disclosure of directors' statement and auditor's report

A copy of the directors' statement and auditor's report under (1) above must be made available to members

- in the case of a written resolution, by being sent or submitted to every eligible member at or before the time at which the proposed resolution is sent or submitted to him; and

- in the case of a resolution at a meeting, by being made available for inspection by members of the company at the meeting.

The resolution is ineffective if this requirement is not complied with.

[*CA 2006, s 718*].

(3)     **Public notice of proposed payment**

Within the week immediately following the date of the special resolution, the company must

(a)     cause to be published in the Gazette, and

(b)     *either* send to each of its creditors *or* cause to be published in a newspaper circulating throughout the part of the UK in which the company is registered

a notice

- stating that the company has approved a payment out of capital for the purpose of acquiring its own shares by redemption or purchase or both (as the case may be);

- specifying the amount of the permissible capital payment for the shares (see **34.11**) and the date of the resolution;

- stating where the directors' statement and auditor's report required under (1) above are available for inspection; and

- stating that any creditor of the company may, at any time within the five weeks immediately following the date of the special resolution, apply to the court under *CA 2006, s 721* (see **34.18**) for an order prohibiting the payment.

Not later than the day on which the company first publishes or gives notice under (*a*) or (*b*) above, it must deliver to the Registrar of Companies a copy of the directors' statement and auditor's report required under (1) above.

[*CA 2006, s 719*].

(4)     **Inspection of directors' statement and auditor's report**

The directors' statement and auditor's report under (1) above must be kept available for inspection at the company's registered office or a place specified in Regulations (see **36.2** RECORDS) throughout the period beginning with the day on which the company first publishes or gives notice under (3)(*a*) or (*b*) above and ending five weeks after the date of the resolution for payment out of capital.

The statement and report must be open to the inspection of any member or creditor of the company without charge.

The company must give notice to the Registrar of Companies within 14 days of the place at which the statement and report are kept available for inspection and of any change in that place (unless they have at all times been kept at the company's registered office).

If the company fails to notify the Registrar of Companies or if an inspection is refused, an offence is committed by the company and every officer of the company who is in default. A person guilty of such an offence is liable, on summary conviction, to a fine not exceeding level 3 on the standard scale and, for continued contravention, a daily default fine not exceeding one-tenth of level 3 on the standard scale. See **29.1** OFFENCES AND LEGAL PROCEEDINGS for the standard scale. In the case of a refusal of an inspection, the court may by order compel an immediate inspection.

[*CA 2006, s 720*].

*Time available for inspection and copying.* See **36.2** RECORDS.

(5)    **Timing when payment out of capital to be made or shares to be surrendered**

Subject to the exercise of the courts powers under **34.18**, the payment out of capital if made in accordance with a resolution under *CA 2006, s 716* must be surrendered no earlier than five weeks, but no more than seven weeks, after the date on which the special resolution under (2) above is passed. Shares to be purchased in accordance with a resolution under *CA 2006, s 720A* must be surrendered no earlier than five weeks after the date on which the resolution under *s 720A* is passed and no later than seven weeks after that date.

[*CA 2006, s 723; SI 2013 No 999, Reg 13*].

For cases on whether the directors and auditor owe a duty of responsibility to individual shareholders who suffer loss, see *Prudential Assurance Co Ltd v Newman Industries Ltd (No 2)* [1982] Ch 204, [1982] 1 All ER 354, CA; *Hedley Byrne & Co Ltd v Heller & Partners Ltd* [1964] AC 465, [1963] 2 All ER 575, HL; *Caparo Industries plc v Dickman* [1990] 2 AC 605, [1990] BCLC 273, HL; and *JEB Fasteners Ltd v Marks, Bloom & Co (a firm)* [1983] 1 All ER 583, [1982] Com LR 226, CA.

**34.14  Reduced requirements for payments out of capital for purchase of own shares: employees' share schemes**

*CA 2006, s 713* (see **34.13**) does not apply to the purchase out of capital by a private company of its own shares for the purposes of or pursuant to an employees' share scheme when approved by special resolution supported by a solvency statement. A resolution is supported by a solvency statement if

•    the directors of the company make a solvency statement not more than 15 days before the date on which the resolution is passed, and

•    the resolution and solvency statement are registered in accordance with *CA 2006, s 720B*.

Where the resolution is proposed as a written resolution, a copy of the solvency statement must be sent or submitted to every eligible member at or before the time at which the proposed resolution is sent or submitted to the member. Where the resolution is proposed at a general meeting, a copy of the solvency statement must be made available for members of the company throughout that meeting. The validity of a resolution is not affected by a failure to comply with either of these requirements.

[*CA 2006, s 720A; SI 2013 No 999, Reg 12*]

**34.15**  *Registration of resolution and supporting documents*

Within 15 days after the passing of the resolution for a payment out of capital by a private company for the purchase of its own shares for the purposes of or pursuant to an employees' share scheme, the company must deliver to the Registrar of Companies

## 34.15 Purchase of Own Shares

(a)    a copy of the solvency statement (see above)

(b)    a copy of the resolution

(c)    a statement of capital. The statement of capital must state with respect to the company's share capital as reduced by the resolution the total number of shares of the company; the aggregate nominal value of those shares; for each class of shares prescribed particulars of the rights attached to the shares, the total number of shares of that class and the aggregate nominal value of shares of that class and the amount (if any) unpaid on each share (whether on account of the nominal value of the share or by way of premium).

(d)    a statement by the directors of the company confirming that the solvency statement was made not more than 15 days before the date on which the resolution was passed and was provided to the members in accordance with *CA 2006, s 720A(3)* or *(4)*.

[*CA 2006, s 720B (1), (2), (5); SBEE 2015, Sch 6, para 15; SI 2013 No 999, Reg 12; SI 2016 No 321, Art 6*].

### 34.16 *Effect of delivering documents*

The Registrar of Companies must register the documents delivered to him as above. The resolution does not take effect until those documents are registered and the validity of a resolution is not affected by a failure to deliver the documents required to be delivered to the Registrar of Companies within the 15 day time specified or by a failure to comply with (d) above.

[*CA 2006 s 720B (3), (4), (6); SI 2013 No 999, Reg 12*]

### 34.17 *Default*

If the company delivers to the Registrar of Companies a solvency statement that was not provided to members in accordance with *CA 2006, s 720A(3)* or *(4)*, an offence is committed by every officer of the company who is in default. If default is made in complying with *CA 2006, s 720B*, an offence is committed by the company and every officer of the company who is in default. A person guilty of an offence under these provisions is liable on conviction on indictment to a fine or on summary conviction to a fine not exceeding the statutory maximum (see **29 Offences and Legal Proceedings**).

[*CA 2006 s 720B (7)(8)(9); SI 2013 No 999, Reg 12*]

### 34.18 Objections by members or creditors

Where a private company passes a special resolution approving a payment out of capital for the redemption or purchase of any of its shares, any creditor and any member (other than one who consented to or voted in favour of the resolution) may, within five weeks of it being passed, apply to the court for the resolution to be cancelled. The application may be made on behalf of the persons entitled to make it by one or more of their number as they may appoint in writing.

The court must make an order on such terms and conditions as it thinks fit either confirming or cancelling the special resolution. It may

(a)    adjourn the proceedings in order that an arrangement may be made to purchase the interests of dissentient members or for the protection of dissentient creditors;

(b)    give such directions as it thinks expedient for putting the arrangements into effect;

(c)    if it confirms the resolution, alter or extend any date or period of time applying to the redemption or purchase of the shares;

(d)   provide for the purchase by the company of the shares of any of its members and for the reduction accordingly of the company's capital;

(e)   make any alterations in the company's articles that may be required in consequence of any such purchase or reduction; and

(f)   require the company not to make any, or any specified, alteration in its articles without leave of the court.

[*CA 2006, s 721*].

**Notice to Registrar of Companies.** On making an application as above, the applicants, or the person making the application on their behalf, must immediately give notice to the Registrar of Companies.

On being served with notice of any such application, the company must also immediately give notice to the Registrar of Companies. Subsequently, within 15 days of the making of the court's order on the application (or such longer period as the court may at any time direct), the company must deliver to the Registrar a copy of the order. If a company fails to comply with either of these requirements, an offence is committed by the company and every officer of the company who is in default. A person guilty of such an offence is liable, on summary conviction, to a fine not exceeding level 3 on the standard scale and, for continued contravention, a daily default fine not exceeding one-tenth of level 3 on the standard scale. See **29.1** OFFENCES AND LEGAL PROCEEDINGS for the standard scale.

[*CA 2006, s 722*].

## 34.19 TREASURY SHARES

Where a limited company makes a purchase of its own shares in accordance with the provisions in *CA 2006, Ch 4* and the purchase is made out of 'distributable profits' the company may

•   hold the shares (or any of them),

•   dispose of them under the provision in **34.20**, or

•   cancel them under the provisions in **34.21**.

and in *Companies Acts* references to a company holding shares as '*treasury shares*' are to the company holding shares that

•   were (or are treated as having been) purchased by it in circumstances in which the above provisions apply; and

•   have been held by the company continuously since they were so purchased (or treated as purchased).

'*Distributable profits*' are those profits out of which the company could lawfully make a distribution (see **22.1** DISTRIBUTIONS) equal in value to the payment.

**Register of members.** Where shares are held by the company, the company must be entered in its register of members (or as the case may be the company's name must be delivered to the Registrar of Companies under *CA 2006, Part 8, Chapter 2A* (option to keep details on register kept by the Registrar)) as the member holding the shares.

[*CA 2006, ss 724, 736, SI 2013 No 999, Reg 14; SBEE 2015, Sch 5, para 25; SI 2015 No 532, Reg 7*].

## 34.19  Purchase of Own Shares

Any outstanding obligation to dispose of or cancel excess shares arising under *CA 2006, s725(3)* ceased to exist on 1 October 2009 whether or not the 12 month period in that *section 725(3)* has expired. But this does not affect the liability for offences under *CA 2006, s 732* where the 12 month period expired before 1 October 2009.

[*CA 2006, s 725* (repealed on 1 October 2009); *SI 2009 No 2022, Reg 5*].

**Exercise of rights.** The company must not exercise any right in respect of the treasury shares, and any purported exercise of such a right is void. This includes rights to attend or vote at meetings.

No dividend may be paid, and no other distribution (whether in cash or otherwise) of the company's assets (including any distribution of assets to members on a winding up) may be made, to the company in respect of the treasury shares.

The company is, however, entitled to

- any allotment of shares as fully paid bonus shares in respect of the treasury shares (in which case the shares allotted are treated as if purchased by the company at the time they were allotted); and

- the payment of any amount payable on the redemption of the treasury shares (if they are redeemable shares).

[*CA 2006, s 726*].

## 34.20  Disposal of treasury shares

Where shares are held as treasury shares, a company may at any time

(a)     sell the shares (or any of them) for a 'cash consideration'; or

(b)     transfer the shares (or any of them) for the purposes of, or pursuant to, an employees' share scheme.

*'Cash consideration'* means

- cash (including foreign currency) received by the company;

- a cheque received by the company in good faith that the directors have no reason for suspecting will not be paid;

- a release of a liability of the company for a liquidated sum;

- an undertaking to pay cash (including foreign currency) to the company on or before a date not more than 90 days after the date on which the company agrees to sell the shares; or

- payment by any other means giving rise to a present or future entitlement (of the company or a person acting on the company's behalf) to a payment, or credit equivalent to a payment, in cash. Included is a settlement bank's obligation to make a payment in respect of treasury shares under the CREST system.

But if the company receives a notice under *CA 2006, s 979* (right of offeror to buy out minority shareholders, see **48.12** TAKEOVERS) that a person desires to acquire shares held by the company as treasury shares, the company must not sell or transfer the shares to which the notice relates except to that person.

[*CA 2006, s 727; SI 2009 No 388, Art 4*].

**Notice of disposal.** Where shares held by a company as treasury shares are sold or transferred for the purposes of an employees' share scheme, the company must deliver a return to the Registrar of Companies not later than 28 days after the shares are disposed of. The return must state with respect to shares of each class disposed of

- the number and nominal value of the shares; and

- the date on which they were disposed of.

Particulars of shares disposed of on different dates may be included in a single return.

If default is made in complying with this requirement, an offence is committed by every officer of the company who is in default. A person guilty of such an offence is liable (i) on conviction on indictment, to a fine; and (ii) on summary conviction, to a fine not exceeding the statutory maximum and, for continued contravention, a daily default fine not exceeding one-tenth of the greater of £5000 or level 4 on the standard scale for summary offences. See **29.1 Offences and Legal Proceedings** for the statutory maximum.

[*CA 2006, s 728; SI 2015 No 664, Sch 3*].

**Proceeds of sale.** Where shares held as treasury shares are sold, the proceeds of sale must be dealt with as follows.

- If the proceeds of sale are equal to or less than the purchase price paid by the company for the shares, the proceeds must be treated for the purposes of distributions as a realised profit of the company.

- If the proceeds of sale exceed the purchase price paid by the company

  (i) an amount equal to the purchase price paid is treated as a realised profit of the company for the purposes of distributions; and

  (ii) the excess must be transferred to the company's share premium account.

For these purposes

- the purchase price paid by the company must be determined by the application of a weighted average price method; and

- if the shares were allotted to the company as fully paid bonus shares, the purchase price paid for them is to be treated as being nil.

[*CA 2006, s 731*].

## 34.21 Cancellation of treasury shares

Where shares are held as treasury shares, the company may at any time cancel the shares (or any of them).

If the company cancels shares held as treasury shares, the amount of the company's share capital is reduced accordingly by the nominal value of the shares cancelled.

The directors may take any steps required to enable the company to cancel its shares without complying with *CA 2006, ss 641–653* (reduction of share capital, see **47.51–47.58 Shares**).

[*CA 2006, s 729, SI 2013 No 999, Reg 15*].

**Notice of cancellation.** In relation to shares cancelled on or after 1 October 2009, where shares held by a company as treasury shares are cancelled, the company must deliver a return to the Registrar of Companies within 28 days from the date the shares are cancelled. (This does not apply to shares that are cancelled forthwith on their acquisition by the company, see **34.10**.) The return must state with respect to shares of each class cancelled

## 34.21   Purchase of Own Shares

- the number and nominal value of the shares; and

- the date on which they were cancelled.

Particulars of shares cancelled on different dates may be included in a single return.

The notice must be accompanied by a statement of capital which must state the following with respect to the company's share capital immediately following the cancellation.

(a)   The total number of shares of the company.

(b)   The aggregate nominal value of those shares and the aggregate amount (if any) unpaid on those shares (whether on account of their nominal value or by way of premium).

(c)   For each class of shares

   (i)   particulars of any voting rights attached to the shares, including rights that arise only in certain circumstances;

   (ii)   particulars of any rights attached to the shares, as respects dividends, to participate in a distribution;

   (iii)   particulars of any rights attached to the shares, as respects capital, to participate in a distribution (including on a winding up);

   (iv)   whether the shares are to be redeemed or are liable to be redeemed at the option of the company or the shareholder;

   (v)   the total number of shares of that class; and

   (vi)   the aggregate nominal value of shares of that class.

(d)   The amount paid up and the amount (if any) unpaid on each share (whether on account of the nominal value of the share or by way of premium).

*Penalties.* If default is made in complying with the above requirements, an offence is committed by the company and every officer of the company who is in default. A person guilty of such an offence is liable, on summary conviction, to a fine not exceeding level 3 on the standard scale and, for continued contravention, a daily default fine not exceeding one-tenth of level 3 on the standard scale. See **29.1** OFFENCES AND LEGAL PROCEEDINGS for the standard scale.

[*CA 2006, s 730; SBEE 2015, Sch 6 para 16; SI 2009 No 388, Art 2; SI 2016 No 32, Art 6*].

## 34.22   Offences relating to treasury shares

If a company contravenes any of the provisions of **34.19–34.21** (except notice of cancellation under **34.21**), an offence is committed by the company and every officer of the company who is in default. A person guilty of such an offence is liable (i) on conviction on indictment, to a fine; and (ii) on summary conviction, to a fine not exceeding the statutory maximum. See **29.1** OFFENCES AND LEGAL PROCEEDINGS for the statutory maximum.

[*CA 2006, s 730; SBEE 2015; Sch 6, para 16; SI 2009 No 388, Art 2; SI 2016 No 321, Art 6*].

## 34.23   THE CAPITAL REDEMPTION RESERVE

**Where shares of a limited company are redeemed or purchased wholly out of the company's profits, the amount by which the company's issued share capital is diminished in accordance with**

- *CA 2006, s 688(b)* (ie the nominal value of the redeemed shares treated as cancelled, see **34.3**); or

- *CA 2006, s 706(b)(ii)* (ie the nominal value of the shares purchased treated as cancelled, see **34.5**),

must be transferred to the capital redemption reserve.

[*CA 2006, s 733(2)*].

**Where the shares are redeemed or purchased wholly or partly out of the proceeds of a fresh issue,** and the aggregate amount of the proceeds is less than the aggregate nominal value of the shares redeemed or purchased, the amount of the difference must be transferred to the capital redemption reserve. But this does not apply in the case of a private company if, in addition to the proceeds of the fresh issue, the company applies a payment out of capital under **34.11–34.18** in making the redemption or purchase.

[*CA 2006, s 733(3)*].

**Where shares are held as treasury shares,** the amount by which a company's share capital is diminished in accordance with *CA 2006, s 729(4)* on the cancellation of any such shares (see **34.21**) must be transferred to the capital redemption reserve.

[*CA 2006, s 733(4)*].

**Use of the capital redemption reserve.** The company may use the capital redemption reserve to pay up new shares to be allotted to members as fully paid bonus shares. Subject to that, the provisions of the *Companies Acts* relating to the reduction of a company's share capital apply as if the capital redemption reserve were part of its paid up share capital.

[*CA 2006, s 733(5)(6)*].

## 34.24  EFFECT OF COMPANY'S FAILURE TO PURCHASE OR REDEEM SHARES

The following consequences apply where a company has issued shares on terms that they are (or are liable to be) redeemed or agreed to purchase any of its own shares.

(a)   The company is not liable in damages in respect of any failure on its part to redeem or purchase any of the shares. This is, however, without prejudice to any right of the holder of the shares (eg to present a petition for the company to be wound up, see *Re Holders Investment Trust Ltd* [1971] 2 All ER 289, [1971] 1 WLR 583) other than his right to sue the company for damages in respect of its failure. The court will not grant an order for specific performance of the terms of redemption or purchase if the company shows that it is unable to meet the costs of redeeming or purchasing the shares out of distributable profits.

(b)   If the company is wound up and at the commencement of the winding up any of the shares have not been redeemed or purchased, subject to below, the terms of redemption or purchase may be enforced against the company with the shares being treated as cancelled.

This does not apply if

- the terms provide for the redemption or purchase to take place at a date later than the commencement of the winding up; or

- during the period from the date on which the redemption or purchase was to have taken place to the commencement of the winding up, the company could not at any time have lawfully made a distribution equal in value to the price at which the shares were to have been redeemed or purchased.

## 34.24  Purchase of Own Shares

There must be paid, in priority to any amount that the company is liable to pay in respect of any shares at the commencement of winding up

- all other debts and liabilities of the company (other than any due to members in their character as such); and

- if other shares carry rights (whether as to capital or as to income) that are preferred to the rights as to capital attaching to the first-mentioned shares, any amount due in satisfaction of those preferred rights.

Subject to that, any such amount must be paid in priority to any amounts due to members in satisfaction of their rights (whether as to capital or income) as members.

[*CA 2006, s 735*].

## 34.25  FINANCIAL ASSISTANCE FOR PURCHASE OF OWN SHARES

The prohibitions in *CA 1985* on a private company giving financial assistance for the purchase of own shares were abolished on 1 October 2008. The following paragraphs therefore only apply to

- Public companies

- Private companies which are subsidiaries of public companies

- Private companies with public company subsidiaries (where financial assistance is being given by the public company (see (b)).

Subject to **34.26**, 'financial assistance' is prohibited in the following circumstances.

(a)  *Assistance for acquisition of shares in a public company*

    (i)  Where a person is acquiring or proposing to acquire shares in a public company, it is not lawful for that company, or a company that is a subsidiary of that company, to give financial assistance directly or indirectly for the purpose of the acquisition before or at the same time as the acquisition takes place.

    (ii)  Where a person has acquired shares in a company ('the company') and a liability has been incurred (by that or another person) for the purpose of the acquisition, it is not lawful for that company, or a company that is a subsidiary of that company, to give financial assistance directly or indirectly for the purpose of reducing or discharging the liability if, at the time the assistance is given, the company in which the shares were acquired is a public company.

(b)  *Assistance by public company for acquisition shares in its private holding company*

    (i)  Where a person is acquiring or proposing to acquire shares in a private company, it is not lawful for a public company that is a subsidiary of that company to give financial assistance directly or indirectly for the purpose of the acquisition before or at the same time as the acquisition takes place.

    (ii)  Where a person has acquired shares in a private company and a liability has been incurred (by that or another person) for the purpose of the acquisition, it is not lawful for a public company that is a subsidiary of that company to give financial assistance directly or indirectly for the purpose of reducing or discharging the liability.

For the above purposes:

- A reference to a person incurring a liability includes his changing his financial position by making an agreement or arrangement (whether enforceable or unenforceable, and whether made on his own account or with any other person) or by any other means.

- A reference to a company giving financial assistance for the purposes of reducing or discharging a liability incurred by a person for the purpose of the acquisition of shares includes its giving such assistance for the purpose of wholly or partly restoring his financial position to what it was before the acquisition took place.

**Offences.** If a company contravenes the above provisions, an offence is committed by the company and every officer of the company who is in default. A person guilty of such an offence is liable (i) on conviction on indictment, to imprisonment for a term not exceeding two years or a fine (or both); and (ii) on summary conviction, to imprisonment for a term not exceeding twelve months (six months in Scotland or Northern Ireland) or to a fine not exceeding the statutory maximum (or both).

[*CA 2006, ss 678(1)(3)(5), 679(1)(3)(5), 680*].

**Financial assistance.** '*Financial assistance*' means any of the following.

- Financial assistance by way of gift. This may include a sale or transfer at an undervalue (see *Letts v IRC* [1956] 3 All ER 588, [1957] 1 WLR 201; *A-G v Kitchin* [1941] 2 All ER 374) but possibly only to the extent of the undervalue (*Plant v Steiner* (1989) 5 BCC 352).

- Financial assistance by way of guarantee, security or indemnity (other than an indemnity in respect of the indemnifier's own neglect or default).

- Financial assistance given by way of release or waiver.

- Financial assistance given

  (i)   by way of a loan or any other agreement under which any of the obligations of the person giving the assistance are to be fulfilled at a time when, in accordance with the agreement, any obligation of another party to the agreement remains unfulfilled; or

  (ii)  by way of the novation of, or the assignment (in Scotland, assignation) of rights arising under, a loan or such other agreement.

- Any other financial assistance given by a company where

  (i)   the 'net assets' of the company are thereby reduced to a material extent by the giving of the assistance; or

  (ii)  the company has no net assets.

  '*Net assets*' means the aggregate of the company's assets less the aggregate of its liabilities. For this purpose, liabilities include

  (a)   where the company draws up Companies Act accounts, any provisions for liabilities (or, in the case of insurance companies, provisions for other risks), ie any amount retained as reasonably necessary for the purpose of providing for any liability the nature of which is clearly defined and which is either likely to be incurred, or certain to be incurred but uncertain as to amount or as to the date on which it will arise; and

  (b)   where the company draws up IAS individual accounts, any provision that is made in those accounts.

[*CA 2006, s 677; SI 2008 No 409, Sch 7 paras 2, 3; SI 2008 No 410, Sch 9 paras 2, 3*].

## 34.25 Purchase of Own Shares

For a consideration of the meaning of financial assistance, see *Charterhouse Investment Trust Ltd v Tempest Diesels Ltd* [1986] BCLC 1, 1 BCC 544 and *Wallersteiner v Moir* [1974] 3 All ER 217, [1974] 1 WLR 991, CA. Once assistance has been established, the fact that money is involved in some form will make the assistance financial assistance (*Armour Hick Northern Ltd v Whitehouse* [1980] 1 WLR 1520, 124 Sol Jo 864). It is not necessary that the assistance costs the provider anything. For example, in *Belmont Finance Corpn Ltd v Williams Furniture Ltd (No 2)* [1980] 1 All ER 393, CA the purchase of an asset for cash at full value from a potential purchaser was held to be financial assistance as it provided the purchaser with cash to buy the shares.

### 34.26 Exceptions from prohibition

The following transactions are not prohibited under **34.25**.

(a)     A distribution of the company's assets by way of dividend lawfully made.

(b)     A distribution of the company's assets made by way of distribution in the course of the company's winding up.

(c)     An allotment of bonus shares (see **47.62** SHARES).

(d)     A reduction of capital under *CA 2006, ss 641–653* (see **47.51–47.58** SHARES).

(e)     A redemption of shares under **34.2** and **34.3** or a purchase of shares under **34.4–34.10**.

(f)     Anything done in pursuance of a court order under *CA 2006, Pt 26* (order sanctioning compromise or arrangement with members or creditors, see **35.1–35.5** RECONSTRUCTIONS AND MERGERS).

(g)     Anything done under an arrangement made

- in pursuance of *IA 1986, s 110* or *Insolvency (NI) Order 1989 (SI 1989 No 2405), Art 96* (acceptance of shares by a liquidator as consideration for sale of property); or

- between a company and its creditors which is binding on the creditors under *IA 1986, Pt I* or *Insolvency (NI) Order 1989 (SI 1989 No 2405), Pt 2*.

(h)     Where the lending of money is part of the ordinary business of the company, the lending of money in the ordinary course of the company's business. This exception does not apply to a company merely because it has the power to lend money (*Steen v Law* [1964] AC 287, [1963] 3 All ER 770, PC).

(i)     The provision by the company, in good faith in the interests of the company or its holding company, of financial assistance for the purposes of an employees' share scheme.

(j)     The provision of financial assistance by the company for the purposes of, or in connection with, anything done by the company (or another company in the same group) to enable or facilitate transactions in shares in the first-mentioned company or its holding company between, and involving the acquisition of beneficial ownership of those shares by

(i)     *bona fide* employees or former employees of that company (or another company in the same group); or

(ii)     spouses or civil partners, widows, widowers or surviving civil partners, or minor children or step-children of any such employees or former employees.

For these purposes, a company is in the same '*group*' as another company if it is a holding company or a subsidiary of that company, or a subsidiary of a holding company of that company.

(k)     The making by a company of loans to persons (other than directors) employed in good faith by the company with a view to enabling those persons to acquire fully paid shares in the company or its holding company to be held by them by way of beneficial ownership.

(l)     Under **34.25**(*a*)(i), the giving of financial assistance by a company for the acquisition of shares in it or its holding company if

•     the company's principal purpose in giving the assistance is not to give it for the purpose of any such acquisition,

•     or the giving of the assistance for that purpose is only an incidental part of some larger purpose of the company,

and the assistance is given in good faith in the interests of the company.

(m)    Under **34.25**(*a*)(ii), the giving of financial assistance by a company if

•     the company's principal purpose in giving the assistance is not to reduce or discharge any liability incurred by a person for the purpose of the acquisition of shares in the company or its holding company, or

•     the reduction or discharge of any such liability is only an incidental part of some larger purpose of the company

and the assistance is given in good faith in the company's interests (see *Brady v Brady* [1989] AC 755, [1988] BCLC 579, HL).

(n)     Under **34.25**(*b*)(i) the giving of financial assistance by a company for the acquisition of shares in its holding company if

•     the company's principal purpose in giving the assistance is not to give it for the purpose of any such acquisition, or

•     the giving of the assistance for that purpose is only an incidental part of some larger purpose of the company

and the assistance is given in good faith in the interests of the company.

(o)     Under **34.25**(*b*)(ii), the giving of financial assistance by a company if

(a)     the company's principal purpose in giving the assistance is not to reduce or discharge any liability incurred by a person for the purpose of the acquisition of the shares in its holding company, or

(b)     the reduction or discharge of any such liability is only an incidental part of some larger purpose of the company

and the assistance is given in good faith in the interests of the company.

*Public companies.* If the company giving the assistance is a public company, the exceptions in (*h*)–(*k*) above only apply if

•     the company has 'net assets' that are nor reduced by the giving or assistance; or

•     to the extent that those assets are so reduced, the assistance is provided out of 'distributable profits'.

'*Net* assets' are the amount by which the aggregate of the company's assets exceeds the aggregate of its liabilities, in each case as stated in the company's accounting records immediately before the financial assistance is given. Liabilities include any amount retained as reasonably necessary for the purpose of providing for any liability the nature of which is clearly defined and that is either likely to be incurred, or certain to be incurred but uncertain as to amount or as to the date on which it will arise.

'*Distributable profits*' means those profits out of which the company could lawfully make a distribution equal in value to that assistance. It includes, in a case where the financial assistance consists of or includes, or is treated as arising in consequence of, the sale, transfer or other disposition of a non-cash asset, any profit that, if the company were to make a distribution of that character, would be available for that purpose. See **22 DISTRIBUTIONS** generally and particularly **22.1** for the meaning of '*distribution*'.

[*CA 2006, ss 678(2)(4), 679(2)(4), 681–683*].

It remains a potentially moot point whether a company is permitted to borrow in order to fund a share buy-back. Obiter remarks of Arden LJ in *Chaston v SWP Group Ltd* [2002] EWCA Civ 1999, [2003] 1 BCLC 675, [2003] BCC 140, suggest that, though borrowing to fund a buy-back would not constitute unlawful financial assistance, any security given for such borrowing would be unlawful. However, these comments were made before 1 October 2008, so the position now would seem to be that a private company may give security for any borrowing to fund a buy-back of its own shares (but not to fund the purchase of shares in its public holding company, if any).

## 34.27 SHARES HELD BY COMPANY'S NOMINEE

The provisions in (1) and (2) below apply where shares in a limited company are

(a)     taken by a subscriber to the memorandum as nominee of the company;

(b)     issued to a nominee of the company; or

(c)     acquired by a nominee of the company, partly paid up, from a third person.

(1)     **Treatment of shares**

For all purposes

- the shares are to be treated as held by the nominee on his own account; and

- the company is to be regarded as having no 'beneficial interest' in them.

This does not apply to shares acquired

- otherwise than by subscription by a nominee of a public company, where

  (i)     a person acquires shares in the company with financial assistance given to him, directly or indirectly, by the company for the purpose of or in connection with the acquisition; and

  (ii)    the company has a beneficial interest in the shares; and

- by a nominee of the company when the company has no beneficial interest in the shares.

[*CA 2006, s 660*].

(2)   **Liability of others where nominee fails to make payment in respect of shares**

If the nominee, having been called on to pay any amount for the purposes of paying up, or paying any premium on, the shares, fails to pay that amount within 21 days from being called on to do so, then

- in the case of shares that he agreed to take as subscriber to the memorandum, the other subscribers to the memorandum, and

- in any other case, the directors of the company when the shares were issued to or acquired by him,

are jointly and severally liable with him to pay that amount.

If, in proceedings for the recovery of an amount due as above, it appears to the court that the subscriber or director has acted honestly and reasonably and, having regard to all the circumstances of the case, ought fairly to be relieved from liability, the court may relieve him, either wholly or in part, from his liability on such terms as the court thinks fit.

If a subscriber to a company's memorandum or a director of a company has reason to apprehend that a claim will or might be made for the recovery of any such amount from him, he may apply to the court for relief. The court then has the same power to relieve him as it would have had in proceedings for recovery of that amount.

The above provisions do not apply to shares acquired by a nominee of the company when the company has no beneficial interest in the shares.

[*CA 2006, s 661*].

See **34.34** for '*beneficial interests*' in this context.

## 34.28 DUTY TO CANCEL SHARES IN PUBLIC COMPANY HELD BY OR FOR THE COMPANY

The following provisions apply in the case of a public company where

(a)   shares in the company are forfeited, or surrendered to the company in lieu of forfeiture, in pursuance of the articles, for failure to pay any sum payable in respect of the shares;

(b)   shares in the company are surrendered to the company in pursuance of *Building Societies Act 1986, s 102C(1)(b)*;

(c)   shares in the company are acquired by it (otherwise than in accordance with this chapter or the provisions in *CA 2006, ss 994–999*, see **26.10** MEMBERS) and the company has a 'beneficial interest' in the shares;

(d)   a nominee of the company acquires shares in the company from a third party without financial assistance being given directly or indirectly by the company and the company has a beneficial interest in the shares; or

(e)   a person acquires shares in the company, with financial assistance given to him, directly or indirectly, by the company for the purpose of or in connection with the acquisition, and the company has a beneficial interest in the shares.

Where any of the situations in (*a*)–(*e*) above apply, then, unless the shares or any interest of the company in them are previously disposed of, the company must

- cancel the shares and diminish the amount of the company's share capital by the nominal value of the shares cancelled; and

- where the effect is that the nominal value of the company's allotted share capital is brought below the authorised minimum (see **33.3** PUBLIC AND LISTED COMPANIES), apply for re-registration as a private company (see **34.30**), stating the effect of the cancellation.

It must do so no later than

(i)    in a case within (*a*) or (*b*) above, three years from the date of the forfeiture or surrender;

(ii)   in a case within (*c*) or (*d*) above, three years from the date of the acquisition; and

(iii)  in a case within (*e*) above, one year from the date of the acquisition.

The directors of the company may take any steps necessary to enable the company to comply with these requirements, and may do so without complying with the provisions of *CA 2006, ss 641–653* (reduction of capital, see **47.51–47.58** SHARES).

Neither the company nor, in a case within (*d*) or (*e*) above, the nominee or other shareholder may exercise any voting rights in respect of the shares. Any purported exercise of those rights is void.

[*CA 2006, s 662*].

See **34.34** for '*beneficial interests*' in this context.

The above provisions apply where

- the event in (*a*)–(*e*) above, or

- the event in **34.32**(*a*)–(*d*)

occurs on or after 1 October 2009. They also apply where a similar event in *CA 1985, s 146(1)* occurred before 1 October 2009 unless, before that date, the company complied with *CA 1985, s 146(2)* or the period for compliance specified in *CA 1985, s 146(3)* has expired.

**Old public companies.** In the provisions above and in **34.29–34.33** references to a public company do not include an 'old public company' (see APPENDIX 1 DEFINITIONS). [*SI 2009 No 1917, Schedule para 7*].

## 34.29   Notice of cancellation of shares

Where a company cancels shares in order to comply with **34.28**, it must within one month after the shares are cancelled give notice to the Registrar of Companies, specifying the shares cancelled. The notice must be accompanied by a statement of capital, stating the following particulars with respect to the company's share capital immediately following the cancellation.

(a)    The total number of shares of the company.

(b)    The aggregate nominal value of those shares and the aggregate amount (if any) unpaid on those shares (whether on account of their nominal value or by way of premium).

(c)    For each class of shares

(i)    particulars of any voting rights attached to the shares, including rights that arise only in certain circumstances;

(ii)    particulars of any rights attached to the shares, as respects dividends, to participate in a distribution;

(iii)   particulars of any rights attached to the shares, as respects capital, to participate in a distribution (including on a winding up);

(iv)   whether the shares are to be redeemed or are liable to be redeemed at the option of the company or the shareholder;

(v)    the total number of shares of that class; and

(vi)   the aggregate nominal value of shares of that class.

(d)    The amount paid up and the amount (if any) unpaid on each share (whether on account of the nominal value of the share or by way of premium).

If default is made in complying with this provision, an offence is committed by the company and every officer of the company who is in default. A person guilty of such an offence is liable, on summary conviction, to a fine not exceeding level 3 on the standard scale and, for continued contravention, a daily default fine not exceeding one-tenth of level 3 on the standard scale. See **29.1** OFFENCES AND LEGAL PROCEEDINGS for the standard scale.

[*CA 2006, s 663; SBEE 2015, Sch 6, para 12; SI 2009 No 388, Art 2; SI 2016 No 321, Art 6*].

### 34.30  Re-registration as a private company in consequence of cancellation

Where a company is obliged to re-register as a private company to comply with *CA 2006, s 662* (see **34.28**), the directors may resolve that the company should be so re-registered.

*CA 2006, ss 29, 30* (resolutions affecting company's constitution, see **14.10** CONSTITUTION – MEMORANDUM AND ARTICLES) apply to any such resolution. The resolution may make such changes in the company's name and in the company's articles as are necessary in connection with its becoming a private company.

The application for re-registration must contain a statement of the company's proposed name on re-registration and must be accompanied by

•    a copy of the resolution (unless a copy has already been forwarded);

•    a copy of the company's articles as amended by the resolution; and

•    a statement of compliance confirming that the requirements of these provisions as to re-registration as a private company have been complied with. The Registrar of Companies may accept the statement of compliance as sufficient evidence that the company is entitled to be re-registered as a private company.

[*CA 2006, s 664*].

**Issue of certificate of incorporation on re-registration**. If, on an application under the above provisions, the Registrar of Companies is satisfied that the company is entitled to be re-registered as a private company, the company must be re-registered accordingly. The Registrar must issue a certificate of incorporation altered to meet the circumstances of the case. It must state that it is issued on re-registration and the date on which it is issued.

On the issue of the certificate, the company becomes a private company and the changes in the company's name and articles take effect. The certificate is conclusive evidence that the requirements of *CA 2006* as to re-registration have been complied with.

[*CA 2006, s 665*].

## 34.30  Purchase of Own Shares

**Effect of failure to re-register.** If a public company that is required by **34.28** to apply to be re-registered as a private company fails to do so within the specified time, *CA 2006, ss 755–760* (prohibition of public offers by private company, see **47.21** and **47.22** SHARES) apply to it as if it were a private company. Subject to that, the company continues to be treated as a public company until it is so re-registered.

[*CA 2006, s 666*].

**Transitional provisions.** The above provisions apply in any case where *CA 2006, s 662* applies (see **34.28**).

### 34.31  Offences for failure to cancel or re-register

Where a company, when required to do by under **34.28**, fails within the specified time to

- cancel any shares,

- make an application for re-registration as a private company,

an offence is committed by the company and every officer of the company who is in default. A person guilty of such an offence is liable, on summary conviction, to a fine not exceeding level 3 on the standard scale and, for continued contravention, a daily default fine not exceeding one-tenth of level 3 on the standard scale. See **29.1** OFFENCES AND LEGAL PROCEEDINGS for the standard scale.

[*CA 2006, s 667*].

### 34.32  Application of the provisions to company re-registering as a public company

Where, after shares in a private company have been

(a)     forfeited in pursuance of the company's articles or are surrendered to the company in lieu of forfeiture,

(b)     acquired by the company (otherwise than by any of the methods permitted in this chapter or under the provisions in *CA 2006, ss 994–999*, see **26.10** MEMBERS), the company having a 'beneficial interest' in the shares,

(c)     acquired by a nominee of the company from a third party without financial assistance being given directly or indirectly by the company, the company having a beneficial interest in the shares, or

(d)     acquired by a person with financial assistance given to him, directly or indirectly, by the company for the purpose of or in connection with the acquisition, the company having a beneficial interest in the shares,

the company is re-registered as a public company, the provisions of **34.28–34.31** apply to the company as if it had been a public company at the time of the forfeiture, surrender or acquisition, subject to the following modification. The modification is that the period specified in **34.28(i)–(iii)** runs from the date of the re-registration of the company as a public company.

[*CA 2006, s 668*].

See **34.34** for '*beneficial interests*' in this context.

*Transitional provisions.* See **34.28** for transitional provisions affecting the above.

*Old public companies.* The above provisions apply to an 'old public company' (see APPENDIX 1 DEFINITIONS) as to a private company.

*[SI 2009 No 1917, Schedule para 7].*

## 34.33 Accounting treatment of shares held by public company or nominee

Where

- a public company, or a nominee of a public company, acquires shares in the company, and

- those shares are shown in a balance sheet of the company as an asset,

an amount equal to the value of the shares must be transferred out of profits available for dividend to a reserve fund and is not then available for distribution.

This applies to an interest in shares as it applies to shares, in which case the reference to the value of the shares must be read as a reference to the value to the company of its interest in the shares. [*CA 2006, s 669*].

## 34.34 BENEFICIAL INTEREST

In determining for the purposes of **34.27, 34.28** and **34.32** whether a company has a beneficial interest in shares, the following interests are to be disregarded. [*CA 2006, s 671*].

(1)   **Residual interests under pension and share schemes**

Where the shares are held on trust for the purposes of a 'pension scheme' or employees' share scheme, any 'residual interest' of the company that has not vested in possession. A *'residual interest'* means a right of the company to receive any of the trust property in the event of

(i)    all the liabilities arising under the scheme having been satisfied or provided for;

(ii)   the company ceasing to participate in the scheme; or

(iii)  the trust property at any time exceeding what is necessary for satisfying the liabilities arising or expected to arise under the scheme.

A residual interest vests in possession under (i) above on the occurrence of the event mentioned there and under (ii) and (iii) above when the company becomes entitled to require the trustee to transfer to it any of the property receivable pursuant to that right.

Where by virtue of these provisions shares are

- exempt from **34.27**(1) or (2) at the time they are taken, issued or acquired but the residual interest in question vests in possession before they are disposed of or fully paid up, **34.27**(1) and (2) apply to the shares as if they had been taken, issued or acquired on the date on which that interest vests in possession; and

- exempt from **34.28–34.32** at the time they are acquired but the residual interest in question vests in possession before they are disposed of, those provisions apply to the shares as if they had been acquired on the date on which the interest vests in possession.

[*CA 2006, s 672*].

(2)   **Employer's charges and other rights of recovery**

Where the shares are held on trust for the purposes of a 'pension scheme' there must be disregarded

- any charge or lien on, or set-off against, any benefit or other right or interest under the scheme for the purpose of enabling the employer or former employer of a member of the scheme to obtain the discharge of a monetary obligation due to him from the member; and

- any right to receive from the trustee of the scheme, or as trustee of the scheme to retain, an amount that can be recovered or retained under

    (i)   *Pension Schemes Act 1993, s 61* or otherwise, as reimbursement or partial reimbursement for any contributions equivalent premium paid in connection with the scheme under *Part 3* of that *Act*; or

    (ii)  *Pension Schemes (Northern Ireland) Act 1993, s 57* or otherwise, as reimbursement or partial reimbursement for any contributions equivalent premium paid in connection with the scheme under *Part 3* of that *Act*.

Where the shares are held on trust for the purposes of an employees' share scheme, there must be disregarded any charge or lien on, or set-off against, any benefit or other right or interest under the scheme for the purpose of enabling the employer or former employer of a member of the scheme to obtain the discharge of a monetary obligation due to him from the member. [*CA 2006, s 673*].

(3)   **Rights as personal representative or trustee**

Where the company is a personal representative or trustee, there must be disregarded any rights that the company has in that capacity including, in particular

- any right to recover its expenses or be remunerated out of the estate or trust property; and

- any right to be indemnified out of that property for any liability incurred by reason of any act or omission of the company in the performance of its duties as personal representative or trustee.

[*CA 2006, s 674*].

'*Pension scheme*' means a scheme for the provision of benefits consisting of, or including, 'relevant benefits' for, or in respect of, employees or former employees and for this purposes, employee is read as if a director of a company were employed by it. '*Relevant benefits*' means any pension, lump sum, gratuity or other like benefit given or to be given on retirement or on death or in anticipation of retirement or, in connection with past service, after retirement or death. [*CA 2006, ss 675, 676*].

## 34.35 CHARGES OF PUBLIC COMPANY ON OWN SHARES

A lien or other charge of a public company on its own shares (whether taken expressly or otherwise) is void with the following exceptions.

(a)   In the case of any description of company, a charge is permitted if the shares are not fully paid up and the charge is for an amount payable in respect of the shares.

(b)   In the case of a company whose ordinary business

    (i)   includes the lending of money, or

    (ii)  consists of the provision of credit or the bailment (in Scotland, hiring) of goods under a hire purchase agreement, or both, a charge is permitted (whether the shares are fully paid or not) if it arises in connection with a transaction entered into by the company in the ordinary course of that business.

(c)    In the case of a company that has been re-registered as a public company, a charge is permitted if it was in existence immediately before the application for re-registration.

(d)    In the case of a company that

(i)    after 22 March 1982 (if registered in Great Britain) or after 30 September 1984 (if registered in Northern Ireland) remained an 'old public company' (see APPENDIX 1 DEFINITIONS), and

(ii)    did not apply before that date to be re-registered as a public company

any charge on its own shares which was in existence on or immediately before that date. [*CA 2006, s 670; SI 2009 No 1917, Schedule para 7*].

# 35   Reconstructions and Mergers

Cross-references. See **47.51** SHARES for reduction of share capital.

## 35.1   ARRANGEMENTS AND RECONSTRUCTIONS

The provisions in **35.2** to **35.5** enable companies to apply to the court for an order sanctioning an arrangement or reconstruction. They have effect where a compromise or 'arrangement' is proposed between a 'company' and

- its creditors (or any class of them); or

- its members (or any class of them).

'*Arrangement*' for these purposes includes a reorganisation of the company's share capital by the consolidation of shares of different classes or by the division of shares into shares of different classes or both.

'*Company*' means any company liable to be wound up under *IA 1986* or *Insolvency (Northern Ireland) Order 1989* except in **35.4** where it means any company within the meaning of *CA 2006* (see **12.1** COMPANY FORMATION AND TYPES OF COMPANIES).

The provisions have effect subject to **35.6** to **35.37** (mergers and divisions of public companies) where those provisions apply (see **35.6**).

[*CA 2006, s 895*].

A '*class*' must be confined to those persons whose rights are not so dissimilar as to make it impossible for them to consult together with a view to their common interest (*Sovereign Life Assurance Co v Dodd* [1892] 2 QB 573, CA). See, for example, *Re Hellenic & General*

## 35.1　Reconstructions and Mergers

*Trust Ltd* [1975] 3 All ER 382, [1976] 1 WLR 123 where 53% of the ordinary shares were held by a company interested in the proposed arrangement. It was held that the remaining 47% of shareholders formed a separate class of whom the necessary three-quarters majority approval was required.

## 35.2　Meeting of creditors or members

Where an application is made to the court by

- a company liable to be wound up,

- any creditor or member of the company,

- if the company is being wound up, the liquidator, or

- if the company is in administration, the administrator

the court may order a meeting of the creditors (or any class of them) or the members (or any class of them) of the company, as the case may be, to be summoned in such manner as the court directs. At any such meeting, *CA 2006, s 323* (representation of corporations at meetings (see **42.27** Resolutions and Meetings) applies to a meeting of the creditors summoned under these provisions as to a meeting of the company (the references to a member of the company being read as references to the creditor).

[*CA 2006, s 896*].

**Statement to be circulated.** Where such a meeting is summoned, every notice summoning the meeting that is sent to a creditor or member must be accompanied by a statement

- explaining the effect of the compromise or arrangement;

- in particular, stating

  (i)　any material interests of the company's directors (whether as directors or as members or as creditors of the company or otherwise); and

  (ii)　the effect on those interests of the proposed compromise or arrangement, insofar as it is different from the effect on like interests of other persons; and

- where the compromise or arrangement affects the rights of debenture-holders, giving the like explanation as respects the trustees of any deed for securing the issue of the debentures as it is required to give as respects the company's directors.

Where any notice summoning the meeting is given by advertisement, it must either include such a statement as required above or state where and how creditors or members entitled to attend the meeting may obtain copies of such a statement (which must be supplied free of charge on application in the manner indicated by the notice).

[*CA 2006, s 897(1)–(4)*].

It is essential that the explanatory circulars sent out by the company are perfectly fair and, as far as possible, give all the information reasonably necessary to enable the recipients to determine how to vote (*Re Dorman, Long & Co Ltd, Re South Durham Steel and Iron Co Ltd* [1934] Ch 635, 103 LJ Ch 316).

If a company defaults in complying with any requirements set out above, an offence is committed by the company and every officer of the company who is in default. (For this purpose, a liquidator or administrator of the company and a trustee of a deed for securing the issue of debentures of the company is treated as an officer of the company.) A person guilty of such an offence is liable (i) on conviction on indictment, to a fine; and (ii) on summary conviction, to a fine not exceeding the statutory maximum. See **29.1** OFFENCES AND LEGAL PROCEEDINGS for the statutory maximum. A person is not guilty of an offence if he shows that the default was due to the refusal of a director or trustee for debenture holders to supply the necessary particulars of his interests. [*CA 2006, s 897(5)–(8)*].

**Duty of directors and trustees to provide information**. A director or trustee for debenture holders must give notice to the company of such matters relating to himself as may be necessary for the statement to be circulated. Any person in default of this requirement commits an offence and is liable, on summary conviction, to a fine not exceeding level 3 on the standard scale (see **29.1** OFFENCES AND LEGAL PROCEEDINGS).

[*CA 2006, s 898*].

### 35.3    Court sanction for compromise or arrangement

If a majority in number representing 75% in value of the creditors (or class of creditors) or members (or class of members), as the case may be, present and voting either in person or by proxy at the meeting summoned under **35.2** agree a compromise or arrangement, the court may sanction the compromise or arrangement on an application by

- the company;

- any creditor or member of the company;

- if the company is being wound up, the liquidator; or

- if the company is in administration, the administrator.

A compromise or arrangement sanctioned by the court is binding on

- all creditors/members (or class thereof) concerned; and

- the company or, where the company is being wound up, the liquidator and contributories of the company.

The court's order has no effect until a copy of it has been delivered to the Registrar of Companies.

[*CA 2006, s 899*].

In deciding whether to sanction the compromise or arrangement, the court must ensure not only that the statutory provisions are complied with but also that the majority has acted *bona fide*. It must see that the minority is not being overridden by a majority with adverse interests and that the scheme overall is reasonable. A scheme cannot be reasonable where a party gets nothing and gives up everything (*Re Alabama, New Orleans, Texas and Pacific Junction Rly Co* [1891] 1 Ch 213, CA). See also *NFU (or National Farmers' Union) Development Trust Ltd, Re* [1973] 1 All ER 135, [1972] 1 WLR 1548.

### 35.4    Powers of court to facilitate reconstruction or amalgamation

Where

- a compromise or arrangement is proposed between a company and its creditors (or any class of them) or its members (or any class of them),

- an application is made to the court to sanction that compromise or arrangement under **35.3**, and

- it is shown that the compromise or arrangement is proposed for the purposes of, or connected with,

  (i)    a scheme for the reconstruction of any two or more companies, or

  (ii)    the amalgamation of any two or more companies

under which the whole or a part of the undertaking or the 'property' of any company concerned in the scheme (a 'transferor company') is to be transferred to another (the 'transferee company'),

the court may provide, either by order sanctioning the compromise or arrangement or by any subsequent order, for all or any of the following.

- The transfer to the transferee company of the whole or any part of the undertaking, and of the property or 'liabilities', of any transferor company.

- The allotting or appropriation by the transferee company of any shares, debentures, policies, etc under the compromise or arrangement to or for any person.

- The continuation by or against the transferee company of any legal proceedings pending by or against any transferor company.

- The dissolution, without winding up, of any transferor company.

- Provision to be made for dissenters.

- Any such incidental, consequential and supplemental matters as are necessary to ensure that the reconstruction or amalgamation is fully and effectively carried out.

If the order provides for the transfer of property or liabilities, that property is thereby transferred to, and vests in, the transferee company and those liabilities are transferred to, and become liabilities of, that company.

The property (if the order so directs) vests freed from any charge that is by virtue of the compromise or arrangement to cease to have effect.

'*Property*' for these purposes includes property, rights and powers of every description.

'*Liabilities*' includes duties.

Where an order as above is made, every company in relation to which the order is made must cause a copy of the order to be delivered to the Registrar of Companies for registration within seven days after its making. In default in complying with this requirement, an offence is committed by the company and every officer of the company who is in default. A person guilty of such an offence is liable, on summary conviction, to a fine not exceeding level 3 on the standard scale and, for continued contravention, a daily default fine not exceeding one-tenth of level 3 on the standard scale. See **29.1** OFFENCES AND LEGAL PROCEEDINGS for the standard scale.

[*CA 2006, s 900*].

**35.5    Obligations with respect to articles, etc**

Where an order under the provisions in 35.3, or an order under the provisions in 35.4 altering a company's constitution, amends

- the company's articles, or

- any resolution or agreement to which *CA 2006, ss 29, 30* apply (resolution or agreement affecting a company's constitution, see **14.10** CONSTITUTION – MEMORANDUM AND ARTICLES), the copy of the order required to delivered to the Registrar of Companies by the company under those provisions must be accompanied by a copy of the company's articles' or the resolution or agreement in question, as amended.

Every copy of the company's articles issued by the company after the order is made must be accompanied by a copy of the order (unless the effect of the order has been incorporated into the articles by amendment).

In the case of a company not having articles, references above to its articles must be read as references to the instrument constituting the company or defining its constitution.

If a company makes default in complying with these requirements, an offence is committed by the company, and every officer of the company who is in default. A person guilty of such an offence is liable, on summary conviction, to a fine not exceeding level 3 on the standard scale. See **29.1** OFFENCES AND LEGAL PROCEEDINGS for the standard scale.

[*CA 2006, s 901*].

## 35.6  MERGERS AND DIVISIONS OF PUBLIC COMPANIES

The provisions in **35.7** to **35.37** apply where

- a compromise or arrangement is proposed between a public company and

    (i)    its creditors (or any class of them), or

    (ii)   its members (or any class of them)

        for the purposes of, or in connection with, a scheme for the reconstruction of any company or companies or the amalgamation of any two or more companies;

- the scheme involves

    (i)    a merger (see **35.7**); or

    (ii)   a division (see **35.20**); and

- the consideration for the transfer (or each of the transfers) envisaged is to be shares in the transferee company (or one or more of the transferee companies) receivable by members of the transferor company (or transferor companies), with or without any cash payment to members.

For these purposes

- a '*new company*' means a company formed for the purposes of, or in connection with, the scheme; and

- an '*existing company*' means a company other than one formed for the purposes of, or in connection with, the scheme.

The provisions do not apply where the company in respect of which the compromise or arrangement is proposed is being wound up. [*CA 2006, s 902*].

**Relationship to the provisions in 35.1 to 35.5 above.** The court must not sanction a compromise or arrangement unless the relevant requirements of the provisions in **35.7** to **35.37** have been complied with. For this purpose,

(1)    the requirements applicable to a merger of public companies are detailed in **35.7** to **35.18**, although certain of those requirements, and certain general requirements of **35.1** to **35.5**, are modified or excluded by the provisions in **35.19**; and

## 35.6    Reconstructions and Mergers

(2)    the requirements applicable to a division of public companies are detailed in **35.20** to **35.32**, although certain of those requirements, and certain general requirements of **35.1** to **35.5**, are modified or excluded by the provisions of **35.33**.

[*CA 2006, s 903*].

### 35.7    Mergers

A scheme involves a merger where under the scheme the undertaking, 'property' and 'liabilities' of

- one or more public companies, including the company in respect of which the compromise or arrangement is proposed, are to be transferred to another existing public company (a '*merger by absorption*'); or

- two or more public companies, including the company in respect of which the compromise or arrangement is proposed, are to be transferred to a new company, whether or not a public company, (a '*merger by formation of a new company*').

The '*merging companies*' are

- in relation to a merger by absorption, to the transferor and transferee companies; and

- in relation to a merger by formation of a new company, to the transferor companies.

'*Property*' includes property, rights and powers of every description.

'*Liabilities*' include duties.

[*CA 2006, ss 904, 941*].

### 35.8    *Draft terms of scheme*

The directors of the merging companies must draw up, and adopt, a draft of the proposed terms of the scheme. These draft terms must give particulars of *at least* the following matters.

(a)    In respect of each transferor company and the transferee company

(i)    its name;

(ii)    the address of its registered office; and

(iii)    whether it is a company limited by shares or a company limited by guarantee and having a share capital.

(b)    The number of shares in the transferee company to be allotted to members of a transferor company for a given number of their shares (the '*share exchange ratio*') and the amount of any cash payment.

(c)    The terms relating to the allotment of shares in the transferee company.

(d)    The date from which the holding of shares in the transferee company will entitle the holders to participate in profits, and any special conditions affecting that entitlement.

(e)    The date from which the transactions of a transferor company are to be treated for accounting purposes as being those of the transferee company.

(f)    Any rights or restrictions attaching to shares or other securities in the transferee company to be allotted under the scheme to the holders of shares or other securities in a transferor company to which any special rights or restrictions attach, or the measures proposed concerning them.

(g)    Any amount of benefit paid or given or intended to be paid or given

   (i)        to any of the experts referred to in **35.11** (expert's report); or

   (ii)       to any director of a merging company,

and the consideration for the payment of benefit.

But see **35.19**(1) for circumstances in which the information in (*b*), (*c*) and (*d*) is not required.

[*CA 2006, s 905*].

*Publication of draft terms.* The directors of each of the merging companies must deliver a copy of the draft terms to the Registrar of Companies. The Registrar must then publish in the Gazette notice of receipt from that company of a copy of the draft terms. That notice must be published at least one month before the date of any meeting of that company summoned for the purpose of approving the scheme. [*CA 2006, s 906*].

The requirements of *s 906* (above) do not apply if:

•    the draft terms of the merger are made available on a website which is maintained by or on behalf of the company and identifies the company;

•    and neither access to the draft terms on the website nor the supply of a hard copy of them is conditional on payment of a fee or otherwise restricted;

•    and the directors of the company deliver a notice giving details of the website to the Registrar of Companies;

•    and the Registrar publishes the notice in the Gazette at least one month before the date of any meeting summoned for the purpose of approving the scheme;

•    and the draft terms remain available on the website throughout the period beginning one month before and ending on the date of any such meeting.

   See **35.35** for disregard of website failures

[*CA 2006, s 906A*]

### 35.9    *Approval of members of merging companies*

The scheme must be approved by a majority in number, representing 75% in value, of each class of members of each of the merging companies, present and voting either in person or by proxy at a meeting. But see **35.19**(2)–(4) for circumstances in which meetings of members are not required. [*CA 2006, s 907*].

### 35.10   *Directors' explanatory report*

The directors of each of the merging companies must draw up and adopt a report consisting of

•    the statement required to be circulated under **35.2** (statement explaining effect of compromise or arrangement); and

•    insofar as that statement does not deal with the following matters, a further statement

   (i)        setting out the legal and economic grounds for the draft terms, and in particular for the share exchange ratio; and

   (ii)       specifying any special valuation difficulties.

But see **35.19**(1); **35.19**(1A) and **35.19**(5) for circumstances in which this report is not required.

## 35.10    Reconstructions and Mergers

[*CA 2006, s 908*].

### 35.11    *Expert's report*

An expert's written report to the members on the draft terms must be drawn up on behalf of each of the merging companies. On the joint application of all the merging companies, the court may approve the appointment of a joint expert to draw up a single report on behalf of all those companies but, if no such appointment is made, there must be a separate expert's report to the members of each merging company drawn up by a separate expert appointed on behalf of that company.

The expert must be a person who is eligible for appointment as a statutory auditor (see **8.10 AUDIT**) and who meets the independence requirement in **35.36(2)**.

The expert's report must

- indicate the method or methods used to arrive at the share exchange ratio;

- give an opinion as to whether the method or methods used are reasonable in all the circumstances of the case, indicate the values arrived at using each such method and (if there is more than one method) give an opinion on the relative importance attributed to such methods in arriving at the value decided on;

- describe any special valuation difficulties that have arisen;

- state whether, in the expert's opinion, the share exchange ratio is reasonable; and

- in the case of a valuation made by a person other than himself (see **35.36(1)**), state that it appeared to him reasonable to arrange for and accept the valuation.

For the purposes of making his report, the expert (or each of them) has

- the right of access to all such documents of all the merging companies, and

- the right to require from the companies' officers all such information,

as he thinks necessary.

But see **35.19(1)** and **35.19(1A)** for circumstances in which this report is not required and **35.19(5)** for agreement to dispense with an expert's report.

[*CA 2006, s 909*].

### 35.12    *Supplementary accounting statement*

If the last annual accounts of any of the merging companies relate to a financial year ending before the date seven months before the first meeting of the company summoned for the purposes of approving the scheme (or, if no meeting is required (by virtue of any of *CA 2006 ss 916–918*), the date six months before the directors of the company adopt the draft terms of the scheme, and if the company has not made public a half-yearly financial report relating to a period ending on or after the relevant date, the directors of that company must prepare a supplementary accounting statement. This must consist of

- a balance sheet dealing with the state of affairs of the company as at a date not more than three months before the draft terms were adopted by the directors; and

- where the company would be required to prepare group accounts if that date were the last day of a financial year, a consolidated balance sheet dealing with the state of affairs of the company and the undertakings that would be included in such a consolidation.

The requirements of *CA 2006* (and where relevant *IAS Regulation, Art 4*) as to matters to be included in a balance sheet and the notes to it apply to a balance sheet required under these provisions but with such modifications as are necessary by reason of its being prepared otherwise than as at the last day of a financial year. Similarly, the normal provisions as to the approval and signing of accounts (see **2.2** ACCOUNTS: GENERAL) apply to the balance sheet required for an accounting statement under these provisions.

See **35.19**(1A) for circumstances in which reports and inspection are not required and **35.19**(5) for agreement to dispense with reports etc.

[*CA 2006, s 910; SI 2011 No 1606, Reg 9(2) and (3)*].

**35.13** *Inspection of documents*

The members of each of the merging companies must be able (i) to inspect, at the registered office of that company, copies of the following documents relating to that company and every other merging company (this is however subject to the provisions in **35.14** (below)); and (ii) to obtain copies of those documents, or any part of them, on request and free of charge. The right to a hard copy of the document under *CA 2006, s 1145* does not apply here to a member who has consented to information being sent or supplied by the company by electronic means and who has not revoked that consent.

(a)    The draft terms.

(b)    The directors' explanatory report (subject to the exceptions in **35.19**(1) and **35.19**(5)).

(c)    The expert's report (subject to the exceptions in **35.19**(1) and **35.19**(5)).

(d)    The company's annual accounts and reports for the last three financial years ending on or before the first meeting of the members (or any class of members) of the company summoned for the purposes of approving the scheme.

(e)    Any supplementary accounting statement required under **35.12**; and

(f)    If no supplementary accounting statement is required under **35.12** because the company has made public a recent half-yearly financial report that report.

The period for inspection or obtaining copies begins one month before, and ends on the date of, the first meeting of the members (or any class of members) of the company for the purposes of approving the scheme.

*CA 2006, s 1145* (right to hard copy) does not apply to a document sent or supplied in accordance with (b) (above) to a member who has consented to information being sent or supplied by the company by electronic means and has not revoked that consent and *CA 2006, Schedule 5, Part 4* (communications by means of a website) also does not apply for the purposes of (b).

All of the requirements of *s 911* are subject to **35.19**(1A).

[*CA 2006, s 911; SI 2011 No 1606, Reg 10*].

**35.14** *Publication of documents on company website*

The right in **35.13** for members to inspect documents does not apply if

•    the document is made available on a website which is maintained on or behalf of the company and identifies the company; and

•    access to the document on the website is not conditional on payment of a fee or otherwise restricted; and

•    the document remains available on the website throughout the period beginning one month before, and ending on the date of any meeting of the company summoned for the purpose of approving the scheme.

## 35.14 Reconstructions and Mergers

A person is able to obtain a copy of a document free of charge (see **35.13** (above)) if the document is made available on the website and the person is able throughout the period beginning one month before and ending on the date set out above to retain a copy of the document made available on the website and to produce a hard copy of it. Where members are only able to obtain copies of a document in this way, the requirement to make the documents available for inspection set out in **35.13** still applies even if the conditions set out in this paragraph are met.

See **35.35** for disregard of website failures.

[*CA 2006, s 911A; SI 2011 No 1606, Reg 11*]

**35.15** *Report on material changes of assets of merging companies*

The directors of each of the merging companies must report to every meeting of members, or any class of members, of that company summoned for the purpose of agreeing to the scheme and to the directors of every other merging company, any material changes in the property and liabilities of that company between the date when the draft terms were adopted and the date of the meeting in question. The directors of each of the merging companies must in turn report those matters to every meeting of the members or any class of members of the company summoned for the purpose of agreeing to the scheme or must send a report of those matters to every member entitled to receive notice of the meeting. This requirement is subject to the exceptions in **35.19(1)A** and **35.19(5)**.

[*CA 2006, s 911B; SI 2011 No 1606, Reg 12*]

**35.16** *Approval of articles of new transferee company*

In the case of a merger by formation of a new company, the articles of the transferee company, or a draft of them, must be approved by ordinary resolution each of the transferor companies. [*CA 2006, s 912*].

**35.17** *Protection of holders of securities with special rights*

The scheme must provide that where any securities of a transferor company (other than shares) to which special rights are attached are held by a person otherwise than as a member or creditor of the company, that person is to receive rights in the transferee company of equivalent value unless

•     the holder has agreed otherwise; or

•     the holder is, or under the scheme is to be, entitled to have the securities purchased by the transferee company on terms that the court considers reasonable.

[*CA 2006, s 913*].

**35.18** *No allotment of shares to transferor company or transferee company*

The scheme must not provide for any shares in the transferee company to be allotted to

•     a transferor company (or its nominee) in respect of shares in the transferor company held by the transferor company itself (or its nominee); or

•     the transferee company (or its nominee) in respect of shares in a transferor company held by the transferee company (or its nominee).

[*CA 2006, s 914; SI 2008 No 690, Reg 3*].

**35.19** *Exceptions*

(1) *Circumstances in which certain particulars and reports not required*

In the case of a merger by absorption (see **35.7**), if all of the 'relevant securities' of the transferor company (or, if there is more than one transferor company, of each of them) are held by or on behalf of the transferee company

(a)     the draft terms of the scheme need not give the particulars mentioned in **35.8**(*b*), (*c*) or (*d*) (particulars relating to allotment of shares to members of transferor company);

(b)     the requirement for an explanatory statement to be circulated or made available (see **35.2**) does not apply;

(c)     the provisions in **35.10** (directors' explanatory report) and **35.11** (expert's report) do not apply;

(d)     the requirements for inspection of documents under **35.13** do not apply so far as relating to any document required to be drawn up under the provisions mentioned in (*c*) above.

[*CA 2006, s 915*].

(1A) *Other circumstances in which reports and inspection not required*

In the case of a merger by absorption (see **35.7**), where 90% or more (but not all) of the relevant securities of the transferor company (or, if there is more than one transferor company, each of them) are held by or on behalf of the transferee company then if the scheme provides that every other holder of relevant securities has the right to require the transferee company to acquire those securities, if a holder of securities exercises that right and the consideration to be given for those securities is fair and reasonable then the following do not apply

(a)     *CA 2006, s 908* (directors' explanatory report)

(b)     *CA 2006, s 909* (expert's report)

(c)     *CA 2006, s 910* (supplementary accounting statement)

(d)     *CA 2006, s 911* (inspection of documents) and

(e)     *CA 2006, s 911B* (report on material· changes of assets of merging company).

[*CA 2006, s 915A; SI 2011 No 1606, Reg 14*].

(2) *Circumstances in which meeting of members of transferee company not required*

In the case of a merger by absorption (see **35.7**), if 90% or more (but not all) of the relevant securities of the transferor company (or, if there is more than one transferor company, of each of them) are held by or on behalf of the transferee company, it is not necessary for the scheme to be approved at a meeting of the members (or any class of members) of the transferee company if the court is satisfied that the following conditions have been complied with.

(a)     Publication of notice of receipt of the draft terms by the Registrar of Companies took place in respect of the transferee company at least one month before the date of the first meeting of members (or any class of members) of the transferor company summoned for the purpose of agreeing to the scheme or the draft terms are made available on a website which is maintained by the company and identifies the company and access to the draft terms on the website is not conditional on the payment of a fee or otherwise restricted and the directors of the company deliver a notice to the Registrar giving details of the website and the Registrar published that notice in the *Gazette* at least one month before the date of the first meeting of members (or any class of members) of the transferor company summoned for the purpose of agreeing to the scheme and the draft terms remained available on the website throughout the period beginning one month before, and ending on, that date.

(b)     The members of the transferee company were able during the period beginning one month before, and ending on, the date mentioned in **35.2**(a) to

(i) inspect copies of the documents listed in the applicable paragraphs of 35.13(a)–(f) relating to the transferee company and the transferor company (or, if there is more than one transferor company, each of them) at the registered office of that company or the document is made available on a website which is maintained by the company and identifies the company and access to the. document on the website is not conditional on the payment of a fee or otherwise restricted and the document remains available on the website throughout the period beginning one month before and ending on the date mentioned in 35.17(2)(a); and

(ii) obtain copies of those documents, or any part of them, on request and free of charge throughout the period beginning one month before, and ending on, the date mentioned in 35.17(2)(a)

(c) One or more members of the transferee company, who together held not less than 5% of the paid-up capital of the company which carried the right to vote at general meetings of the company (excluding any shares in the company held as treasury shares) would have been able, during that period, to require a meeting of each class of members to be called for the purpose of deciding whether or not to agree to the scheme and no such requirement was made.

For these purposes, 'relevant securities', in relation to a company, means shares or other securities carrying the right to vote at general meetings of the company.

See 35.35 for disregard of website failures. [CA 2006, s 916, SI 2011 No 1606, Reg 15(2)–(4)].

(3) Circumstances in which no meetings required

In the case of a merger by absorption (see 35.7) if all of the relevant securities of the transferor company (or, if there is more than one transferor company, of each of them) are held by or on behalf of the transferee company, it is not necessary for the scheme to be approved at a meeting of the members (or any class of members) of any of the merging companies (see 35.7) if the court is satisfied that the following conditions have been complied with.

(a) Publication of notice of receipt of the draft terms by the Registrar of Companies took place in respect of all the merging companies at least one month before the date of the court's order or the draft terms are made available on a website which is maintained by or on behalf of the company and identifies the company and access to those draft terms or the supply of a hard copy of them is not conditional on the payment of a fee or otherwise restricted and the directors deliver a notice giving details of the website to the Registrar and in each case the Registrar published the notice in the Gazette at least one month before the date of the court's order and the draft terms remain available on the website throughout the period beginning one month before and ending on that date.

(b) The members of the transferee company were able during the period beginning one month before, and ending on, that date to

(i) inspect at the registered office of that company copies of the applicable documents listed in 35.13(a)–(f) relating to the transferee company and the transferor company (or, if there is more than one transferor company, each of them) or the document is made available on a website which is maintained by or on behalf of the transferee company and identifies the company and access to the document is not conditional on the payment of a fee or otherwise restricted and the document remains available on the website throughout the period beginning one month before and ending on the date mentioned in (a) above; and

(ii)    obtain copies of those documents, or any part of them, on request and free of charge throughout the period beginning one month before, and ending on, the date mentioned in (a) above.

(c)    One or more members of the transferee company, who together held not less than 5% of the paid-up capital of the company which carried the right to vote at general meetings of the company (excluding any shares in the company held as treasury shares) would have been able, during that period, to require a meeting of each class of members to be called for the purpose of deciding whether or not to agree to the scheme and no such requirement was made.

For these purposes, '*relevant securities*', in relation to a company, means shares or other securities carrying the right to vote at general meetings of the company.

[*CA 2006, s 917; SI 2011 No 1606, Reg 16(2)–(4)*].

(4) *Other circumstances in which meeting of members of transferee company are not required*

In the case of any merger by absorption (see 35.7), it is not necessary for the scheme to be approved by the members of the transferee company if the court is satisfied that the following conditions have been complied with.

(a)    Publication of notice of receipt of the draft terms by the Registrar of Companies took place in respect of the transferee company at least one month before the date of the first meeting of members (or any class of members) of the transferor company (or, if there is more than one transferor company, any of them) summoned for the purposes of agreeing to the scheme or the draft terms are made available on a website which is maintained by the company and identifies the company and access to the draft terms on the website is not conditional on the payment of a fee or otherwise restricted and the directors of the company deliver a notice to the Registrar giving details of the website and the Registrar published that notice in the Gazette at least one month before the date of the first meeting of members (or any class of members) of the transferor company (or, if there is more than one transferor company, any of them) summoned for the purpose of agreeing to the scheme and the draft terms remained available on the website throughout the period beginning one month before, and ending on, that date.

(b)    The members of that company were able during the period beginning one month before, and ending on, the date of any such meeting to

(i)    inspect at the registered office of that company copies of the documents specified in the applicable paragraphs of 35.13(a)–(f) relating to the transferee company and the transferor company (or, if there is more than one transferor company, each of them) or the document is made available on a website which is maintained by or on behalf of the transferee company and identifies the company and access to the document is not conditional on the payment of a fee or otherwise restricted and the document remains available on the website throughout the period beginning one month before and ending on the date mentioned in (a) above; and

(ii)    obtain copies of those documents or any part of them on request and free of charge throughout the period beginning one month before and ending on the date of any such meeting mentioned in (a) above.

(c)    One or more members of that company, who together held not less than 5% of the paid-up capital of the company which carried the right to vote at general meetings of the company (excluding any shares in the company held as treasury shares) would have been able, during that period, to require a meeting of each class of members to be called for the purpose of deciding whether or not to agree to the scheme and no such requirement was made.

[*CA 2006, s 918; SI 2011 No 1606, Reg 17(2)–(4)*].

(5) *Agreement to dispense with reports etc*

If all members holding shares in, and all persons holding other securities of, the merging companies, being shares or securities that carry a right to vote in general meetings of the company in question, so agree, the following requirements do not apply

- *CA 2006, s 908* (directors' explanatory report)

- *CA 2006, s 909* (expert's reports)

- *CA 2006, s 910* (supplementary accounting statement)

- *CA 2006, s 911B* (report on material changes of company assets of merging company) and

- *CA 2006, s 911* (inspection of documents) so far as relating to any documents required to be drawn up under *CA 2006, ss 908, 909* or *910*.

For these purposes

- the members, or holders of other securities, of a company, and

- whether shares or other securities carry a right to vote in general meetings of the company,

are determined as at the date of the application to the court under *CA 2006, s 896* (see **35.2**).

[*CA 2006, s 918A; SI 2011 No 1606, Reg 18(2)–(4)*].

## 35.20 Divisions

A scheme involves a division where under the scheme the undertaking, 'property' and 'liabilities' of the company in respect of which the compromise or arrangement is proposed are to be divided among and transferred to two or more companies each of which is either

- an existing public company; or

- a new company (whether or not a public company).

References to the companies involved in the division are to the transferor company and any existing transferee companies.

'*Property*' includes property, rights and powers of every description.

'*Liabilities*' include duties.

[*CA 2006, ss 919, 941*].

### 35.21 *Draft terms of scheme*

A draft of the proposed terms of the scheme must be drawn up and adopted by the directors of each of the companies involved in the division. The draft terms must cover at least the following.

(a)    In respect of the transferor company and each transferee company,

(i)    its name;

(ii)   the address of its registered office; and

(iii)  whether it is a company limited by shares or a company limited by guarantee and having a share capital.

(b)    The number of shares in a transferee company to be allotted to members of the transferor company for a given number of their shares (the '*share exchange ratio*') and the amount of any cash payment.

(c)    The terms relating to the allotment of shares in a transferee company.

(d)    The date from which the holding of shares in a transferee company will entitle the holders to participate in profits, and any special conditions affecting that entitlement.

(e)    The date from which the transactions of the transferor company are to be treated for accounting purposes as being those of a transferee company.

(f)    Any rights or restrictions attaching to shares or other securities in a transferee company to be allotted under the scheme to the holders of shares or other securities in the transferor company to which any special rights or restrictions attach, or the measures proposed concerning them.

(g)    Any amount of benefit paid or given or intended to be paid or given

(i)    to any of the experts referred to in 35.25, or

(ii)   to any director of a company involved in the division,

and the consideration for the payment of benefit.

(h)    Particulars of the 'property' and 'liabilities' to be transferred (to the extent that these are known to the transferor company) and their allocation among the transferee companies.

(i)    Provision for the allocation among, and transfer to, the transferee companies of any other property and liabilities that the transferor company has acquired or may subsequently acquire.

(j)    Specify the allocation to members of the transferor company of shares in the transferee companies and the criteria upon which that allocation is based.

[CA 2006, s 920].

'*Property*' includes property, rights and powers of every description.

'*Liabilities*' include duties. [*CA 2006, s 941*].

*Publication of draft terms by Registrar.* The directors of each company involved in a division must deliver a copy of the draft terms to the Registrar of Companies. The Registrar must then publish in the Gazette notice of receipt from that company of a copy of the draft terms. That notice must be published at least one month before the date of any meeting of that company summoned for the purpose of approving the scheme. But these requirements are subject to 35.22 (publication of draft terms on company website) and 35.33(4) (power of court to exclude certain requirements).

[*CA 2006, s 921; SI 2011 No 1606, Reg 19(1) and (2)*].

**35.22** *Publication of draft terms on company website*

The provisions set out in 35.21 do not apply if

- the draft terms are available on a website which is maintained by or on behalf of the company and identifies the company

- access to the draft terms on the website or the supply of a hard copy of them is not conditional on payment of a fee or otherwise restricted

- directors of the company deliver a notice to the Registrar giving details of the website

- the Registrar publishes the notice in the Gazette at least one month before the date of any meeting of the company summoned for the purpose of approving the scheme and

- the draft terms remain available on the website throughout the period beginning one month before, and ending on, the date of any such meeting.

[*CA 2006, s 921A; SI 2011, No 1606 Reg 20*]

**35.23** *Approval of members of companies involved in the division*

The compromise or arrangement must be approved by a majority in number, representing 75% in value, of each class of members of each of the companies involved in the division, present and voting either in person or by proxy at a meeting. But see **35.33**(1) and (2) for circumstances in which meetings of members are not required. [*CA 2006, s 922*].

**35.24** *Directors' explanatory report*

The directors of the transferor and each existing transferee company must draw up and adopt a report consisting of

- the statement required to be circulated under **35.2** (statement explaining effect of compromise or arrangement); and

- insofar as that statement does not deal with the following matters, a further statement

  (i)   setting out the legal and economic grounds for the draft terms, and in particular for the share exchange ratio and for the criteria on which the allocation to the members of the transferor company of shares in the transferee companies was based; and

  (ii)  specifying any special valuation difficulties.

The report must also state

- whether a report has been made to any transferee company under *CA 2006, s 593* (valuation of non–cash consideration for shares, see **47.31** SHARES); and

- if so, whether that report has been delivered to the Registrar of Companies.

But see **35.33**(3) and **35.33**(3A) for circumstances in which this report is not required.

[*CA 2006, s 923*].

**35.25** *Expert's report*

An expert's written report to the members on the draft terms must be drawn up on behalf of each company involved in the division. On the joint application of the companies involved in the division, the court may approve the appointment of a joint expert to draw up a single report on behalf of all those companies but, if no such appointment is made, there must be a separate expert's report to the members of each company involved in the division drawn up by a separate expert appointed on behalf of that company.

The expert must be a person who is eligible for appointment as a statutory auditor (see **8.10** AUDIT) and who meets the independence requirement in **35.36**(2).

The expert's report must

- indicate the method or methods used to arrive at the share exchange ratio;

- give an opinion as to whether the method or methods used are reasonable in all the circumstances of the case, indicate the values arrived at using each such method and (if there is more than one method) give an opinion on the relative importance attributed to such methods in arriving at the value decided on;

- describe any special valuation difficulties that have arisen;

- state whether, in the expert's opinion, the share exchange ratio is reasonable; and

- in the case of a valuation made by a person other than himself (see **35.36**(1)), state that it appeared to him reasonable to arrange for and accept the valuation.

For the purposes of making his report, the expert (or each of them) has

- the right of access to all such documents of the companies involved in the division, and

- the right to require from the companies' officers all such information,

as he thinks necessary.

But see **35.33**(3) and **35.33**(3A) for circumstances in which this report is not required.

[*CA 2006, s 924*].

**35.26** *Supplementary accounting statement*

If the last annual accounts of a company involved in the division relate to a financial year ending before the date seven months before the first meeting of the company summoned for the purposes of approving the scheme (or if no meeting of the company is required (by virtue of *CA 2006, ss 931 or 932*) the date six months before the directors of the company adopt the draft terms of the scheme) and if the company has not made public a half-yearly financial report relating to a period ending on or after the relevant date, the directors of that company must prepare a supplementary accounting statement. This must consist of

- a balance sheet dealing with the state of affairs of the company as at a date not more than three months before the draft terms were adopted by the directors; and

- where the company would be required to prepare group accounts if that date were the last day of a financial year, a consolidated balance sheet dealing with the state of affairs of the company and the undertakings that would be included in such a consolidation.

The requirements of *CA 2006* (and where relevant *IAS Regulation, Art 4*) as to matters to be included in a balance sheet and the notes to it apply to a balance sheet required under these provisions but with such modifications as are necessary by reason of its being prepared otherwise than as at the last day of a financial year. Similarly, the normal provisions as to the approval and signing of accounts (see **2.2** ACCOUNTS: GENERAL) apply to the balance sheet required for an accounting statement under these provisions.

But see **35.33**(3) and **35.33**(3A) for circumstances in which a supplementary accounting statement is not required.

[*CA 2006, s 925; SI 2011 No 1606, Reg 23(2)–(4)*].

# 35.27 Reconstructions and Mergers

**35.27** *Inspection of documents*

The members of each company involved in the division must be able (i) to inspect, at the registered office of that company, copies of the following documents relating to that company and every other company involved in the division; and (ii) to obtain copies of those documents, or any part of them, on request free of charge.

(a)     The draft terms.

(b)     The directors' explanatory report.

(c)     The expert's report.

(d)     The company's annual accounts and reports for the last three financial years ending on or before the first meeting of the members (or any class of members) of the company summoned for the purposes of approving the scheme.

(e)     Any supplementary accounting statement required under **35.26**.

(f)     If no statement is required under **35.26** because the company has not made public a recent half-yearly financial report, that report.

The period of for inspection or obtaining copies begins one month before, and ends on the date of, the first meeting of the members (or any class of members) of the company for the purposes of approving the scheme.

The right to inspect documents is subject to the provisions set out in **35.28** and the requirements in (b), (c) and (e) above are subject to **35.33(3)** (Agreement to dispense with reports), **35.33(3A)** (Certain requirements excluded where shareholders given proportional rights) and **35.33(4)** (Power of court to exclude certain requirements).

*CA 2006, s 1145* (right to hard copy) does not apply to a document sent or supplied in accordance with (b) (above) to a member who has consented to information being sent or supplied by the company by electronic means and has not revoked that consent and *CA 2006, Sch 5, Pt 4* (communications by means of a website) also does not apply for the purposes of (b).

[*CA 2006, s 926; SI 2011 No 1606, Reg 24(4)*].

**35.28** *Publication of documents on company website*

The rights in **35.27** for members to inspect documents do not apply if

•     the document is made available on a website which is maintained on or behalf of the company and identifies the company; and

•     access to the document on the website is not conditional on payment of a fee or otherwise restricted; and

•     the document remains available on the website throughout the period beginning one month before, and ending on the date of any meeting of the company summoned for the purpose of approving the scheme.

A person is able to obtain a copy of a document free of charge if the document is made available on the website and the person is able throughout the period beginning one month before and ending on the date set out above to retain a copy of the document made available on the website and to produce a hard copy of it. Where members are only able to obtain copies of a document in this way, the requirement to make the documents available for inspection set out in **35.27** still applies even if the conditions set out in this paragraph are met. [*CA 2006, s 926A; SI 2011 No 1606, Reg 25*].

**35.29** *Report on material changes of assets of transferor company*

The directors of the transferor company must report to

- every meeting of the members (or any class of members) of that company summoned for the purpose of agreeing to the scheme, and

- the directors of each existing transferee company,

any material changes in the 'property' and 'liabilities' of the transferor company between the date when the draft terms were adopted and the date of the meeting in question.

The directors of each existing transferee company must in turn

- report those matters to every meeting of the members (or any class of members) of that company summoned for the purpose of agreeing to the scheme, or

- send a report of those matters to every member entitled to receive notice of such a meeting.

'*Property*' includes property, rights and powers of every description.

'*Liabilities*' include duties.

But see **35.33(3)** and **35.33(3A)** for circumstances in which such a report is not required.

[*CA 2006, ss 927, 941, SI 2011 No 1606, Reg 26*].

**35.30** *Approval of articles of new transferee company*

The articles of every new transferee company, or a draft of them, must be approved by ordinary resolution of the transferor company. [*CA 2006, s 928*].

**35.31** *Protection of holders of securities with special rights*

The scheme must provide that where any securities of a transferor company (other than shares) to which special rights are attached are held by a person otherwise than as a member or creditor of the company, that person is to receive rights in the transferee company of equivalent value unless

- the holder has agreed otherwise; or

- the holder is, or under the scheme is to be, entitled to have the securities purchased by a transferee company on terms that the court considers reasonable.

[*CA 2006, s 929*].

**35.32** *No allotment of shares to transferor company or to transferee company*

The scheme must not provide for any shares in a transferee company to be allotted to

- the transferor company (or its nominee) in respect of shares in the transferor company held by the transferor company itself (or its nominee); or

- a transferee company (or its nominee) in respect of shares in the transferor company held by the transferee company (or its nominee).

[*CA 2006, s 930; SI 2008 No 690, Reg 4*].

**35.33** *Exceptions*

(1) *Circumstances in which meeting of members of transferor company not required (division)*

In the case of a division where all of the shares or other securities of the transferor company carrying the right to vote at general meetings of the company are held by or on behalf of one or more existing transferee companies, it is not necessary for the scheme to be approved by a meeting of the members (or any class of members) of the transferor company if the court is satisfied that the following conditions have been complied with.

## 35.33 Reconstructions and Mergers

(a) Publication of notice of receipt of the draft terms by the Registrar of Companies took place in respect of all the companies involved in the division at least one month before the date of the court's order or the draft terms are made available on a website which is maintained by or on behalf of the company and identifies the company and access to the draft terms on the website or the supply of a hard copy of them from the website is not conditional on payment of a fee or otherwise restricted and the directors of the company deliver a notice giving details of the website to the Registrar of Companies.

This must be satisfied in respect of each of the companies involved in the division. In each case the Registrar must have published the notice in the *Gazette* at least one month before the date of the court's order and the draft terms must have remained available on the website throughout the period beginning one month before, and ending on, that date.

(b) The members of every company involved in the division were able, during the period beginning one month before, and ending on, the date of the court's order, to

(i) inspect at the registered office of their company copies of the documents listed in the applicable paragraphs of **35.27**(*a*)–(*f*) relating to every company involved in the division or the document is made available on a website which is maintained by or on behalf of the company to which it relates and identifies the company, access to the document on the website is not conditional on payment of a fee or otherwise restricted and the document remains available on the website throughout the period beginning one month before, and ending on, the date of the court's order.

(ii) obtain copies of those documents, or any part of them, on request and free of charge throughout the period beginning one month before, and ending on, the date of the court's order.

(c) No such requirement as under (*c*) above was made.

(d) The directors of the transferor company have sent to

(i) every member who would have been entitled to receive notice of a meeting to agree to the scheme (had any such meeting been called), and

(ii) the directors of every existing transferee company,

a report of any material change in the 'property' and 'liabilities' of the transferor company between the date when the terms were adopted by the directors and the date one month before the date of the court's order.

'*Property*' includes property, rights and powers of every description.

'*Liabilities*' include duties. [*CA 2006, ss 931, 941, SI 2011 No 1606, Reg 27(2)–(4)*].

(2) *Circumstances in which meeting of members of transferee company not required (division)*

In the case of a division, it is not necessary for the scheme to be approved by the members of a transferee company if the court is satisfied that the following conditions have been complied with in relation to that company.

(a) Publication of notice of receipt of the draft terms by the Registrar of Companies took place in respect of the transferee company at least one month before the date of the first meeting of members of the transferor company summoned for the purposes of agreeing to the scheme or the draft terms are made available on a website which is maintained by or on behalf of the company and identifies the company and access to the draft terms on the website or the supply of a hard copy of them from the website is not conditional on payment of a fee or otherwise restricted and the directors of the company deliver a notice giving details of the website to the Registrar of Companies.

In each case the Registrar must have published the notice in the Gazette at least one month before the date of first meeting of the transferor company summoned for the purpose of agreeing to the scheme and the draft terms must have remained available on the website throughout the period beginning one month before, and ending on, that date.

(b)    The members of the transferee company were able, during the period beginning one month before and ending on that date, to

    (i)    inspect at the registered office of that company copies of the documents listed in the applicable paragraphs of **35.27**(*a*)–(*f*) relating to that company and every other company involved in the division or the document is made available on a website which is maintained by or on behalf of the transferee company and identifies the company, access to the document on the website is not conditional on payment of a fee or otherwise restricted and the document remains available on the website throughout the period beginning one month before, and ending on, the date in **35.33**(2)(a); and

    (ii)    obtain copies of those documents or any part of them on request and free of charge throughout the period beginning one month before and ending on the date in **35.33**(2)(a).

(c)    One or more members of that company, who together held not less than 5% of the paid-up capital of the company which carried the right to vote at general meetings of the company (excluding any shares in the company held as treasury shares) would have been able, during that period, to require a meeting of each class of members to be called for the purpose of deciding whether or not to agree to the scheme and no such requirement was made.

But the conditions in (*a*) and (*b*) above are subject to (4) below.

[*CA 2006, s 932, SI 2011 No 1606, Reg 28(2)–(5)*].

(3) *Agreement to dispense with reports, etc*

If all members holding shares in, and all persons holding other securities of, the companies involved in the division (being shares or securities that carry a right to vote in general meetings of the company in question) so agree, the following requirements may be dispensed with.

•    The requirement for a

    (i)    directors' explanatory report (see **35.24**);

    (ii)    expert's report (see **35.25**);

    (iii)    supplementary accounting statement (see **35.26**); and

    (iv)    report on material changes in the assets of the transferor company (see **35.29**).

•    The requirements for inspection of documents under **35.27** do not apply so far as relating to any document required to be drawn up under the provisions mentioned in (i)–(iii) above.

For these purposes, the members, or holders of other securities, of a company, and whether shares or other securities carry a right to vote in general meetings of the company, are determined as at the date of the application to the court under **35.2**.

## 35.33   Reconstructions and Mergers

*[CA 2006, s 933].*

*(3A) Certain requirements excluded where shareholders given proportional rights*

In the case of a division where each of the transferee companies is a new company, if all the shares in each of the transferee companies are to be allotted to the members of the transferor company in proportion to their rights in the allotted share capital of the transferor company, the following requirements do not apply

- *CA 2006, s 923* (directors' explanatory report)
- *CA 2006, s 924* (expert's report)
- *CA 2006, s 925* (supplementary accounting statement)
- *CA 2006, s 927* (report on material changes in assets of the transferor company) and
- *CA 2006, s 926* (inspection of documents) so far as they relate to any documents required to be drawn up under *CA 2006, ss 923, 924* and *925.*

*[CA 2006, s 933A, SI 2011 No 1606, Reg 29].*

*(4) Power of court to exclude certain requirements*

In the case of a division, the court may by order direct that

- in relation to any company involved in the division, the requirements for publication of the draft terms under **35.21** and inspection of documents under **35.27** do not apply, and
- in relation to an existing transferee company, (2) above has effect with the omission of conditions (2)(*a*) and (*b*)

if it is satisfied that the following conditions will be fulfilled in relation to that company.

(a)   The members of that company will have received, or will have been able to obtain free of charge, copies of the documents listed in **35.27**

    (i)   in time to examine them before the date of the first meeting of the members (or any class of members) of that company summoned for the purposes of agreeing to the scheme; or

    (ii)   in the case of an existing transferee company where in the circumstances described in (2) above no meeting is held, in time to require a meeting as mentioned in (2)(*d*) above.

(b)   The creditors of that company will have received, or will have been able to obtain free of charge, copies of the draft terms in time to examine them

    (i)   before the date of the first meeting of the members (or any class of members) of the company summoned for the purposes of agreeing to the scheme; or

    (ii)   in the circumstances mentioned in (*a*)(ii) above, at the same time as the members of the company.

(c)   No prejudice would be caused to the members or creditors of the transferor company or any transferee company by making the order in question. *[CA 2006, s 934; SI 2011 No 1606, Reg 30].*

### 35.34   *Liability of transferee companies for each other's defaults*

Subject to below, in the case of a division, each transferee company is jointly and severally liable for any liability transferred to any other transferee company under the scheme to the extent that the other company defaults in satisfying that liability.

But

- this does not apply to liabilities owed to the creditors (or a class of creditors) of the transferor company if a majority in number representing 75% in value of the creditors (or class of creditors), present and voting either in person or by proxy at a meeting summoned for the purposes of agreeing to the scheme, so agree in relation to the liabilities owed to them; and

- a transferee company is not liable under this provision for an amount greater than the 'net value transferred' to it under the scheme. '*Net value transferred*' is the value (at the time of the transfer) of the property transferred to it under the scheme less the amount at that date of the liabilities so transferred.

'*Liabilities*' include duties. [*CA 2006, s 940, 941*].

## 35.35   Disregard of website failures beyond control of company

A failure to make information or a document available on the website throughout the period specified in the following provisions is to be disregarded if it is made available on the website for any part of that period and the failure to make it available is wholly attributable to circumstances that it would not be reasonable to have expected the company to prevent or avoid. The provisions are

- *CA 2006, s 906A(6);*

- *CA 2006, s 911A(4);*

- *CA 2006, s 916(3B)* and *(4B)*;

- *CA 2006, s 917(3B)* and *(4B)*;

- *CA 2006, s 918(2B)* and *(3B)*;

- *CA 2006, s 921A(6)*;

- *CA 2006, s 926A(4)*;

- *CA 2006, s 931(3B)* and *(4B)*;

- *CA 2006, s 932(2B)* and *(3B)*; and

- *CA 2006, s 940A.*

## 35.36  Expert's report: supplementary provisions

(1) *Valuation by another person*

Where an expert thinks that it is reasonably necessary for a valuation to be made to enable him to draw up his report, he can arrange for another person, who appears to him to have the requisite knowledge and experience, to make the valuation. The person must meet the independence requirement in (2) below.

In such a case, the expert's report must state that fact and must also

- state the valuer's name and what knowledge and experience he has to carry out the valuation; and

- describe so much of the undertaking, 'property' and 'liabilities' as was valued by the other person, and the method used to value them, and specify the date of the valuation.

'*Property*' includes property, rights and powers of every description.

'*Liabilities*' include duties.

[*CA 2006, ss 935, 941*].

(2) *Experts and valuers: independence requirement*

A person meets the independence requirement for the purposes of **35.11, 35.25** and (1) above only if

- he is not

    (i) an officer or employee of any of the 'companies concerned in the scheme'; or

    (ii) a partner or employee of such a person, or a partnership of which such a person is a partner;

- he is not

    (i) an officer or employee of an 'associated undertaking' of any of the companies concerned in the scheme; or

    (ii) a partner or employee of such a person, or a partnership of which such a person is a partner; and

- there does not exist between

    (i) the person or an associate of his, and

    (ii) any of the companies concerned in the scheme or an associated undertaking of such a company,

    a connection of any such description as may be specified by Regulations.

For these purposes, an auditor of a company is not regarded as an officer or employee of the company.

The '*companies concerned in the scheme*' are every transferor and existing transferee company.

An '*associated undertaking*', in relation to a company, means *either* a parent undertaking or subsidiary undertaking of the company *or* a subsidiary undertaking of a parent undertaking of the company.

'*Associate*' means

(a) in relation to an individual,

    (i) that individual's spouse or civil partner or minor child or step-child;

    (ii) any body corporate of which that individual is a director (or, in the case of a LLP, member); and

    (iii) any employee or partner of that individual.

(b) in relation to a body corporate,

    (i) any body corporate of which that body is a director (or, in the case of a LLP, member);

    (ii) any body corporate in the same group as that body; and

    (iii) any employee or partner of that body or of any body corporate in the same group;

(c)     in relation to a partnership that is a legal person under the law by which it is governed,

    (i)     any body corporate of which that partnership is a director (or, in the case of a LLP, member);

    (ii)    any employee of or partner in that partnership; and

    (iii)   any person who is an associate of a partner in that partnership; and

(d)     in relation to a partnership that is not a legal person under the law by which it is governed, any person who is an associate of any of the partners.

[*CA 2006, ss 936, 937*].

## 35.37 Powers of the court

**Power of court to summon meeting of members or creditors of existing transferee company.** The court may order a meeting of the members or creditors of an existing transferee company (or any class of them), to be summoned on an application by

• the company concerned;

• a member or creditor of the company;

• if the company is being wound up, the liquidator; or

• if the company is in administration, the administrator.

*CA 2006, s 323* (representation of corporations at meetings, see **42.27** RESOLUTIONS AND MEETINGS) applies to a meeting of creditors summoned under these provisions as to a meeting of the company (the references to a member of the company being read as references to a creditor).

**Court to fix date for transfer of undertaking, etc of transferor company.** Where the court sanctions a compromise or arrangement, it must fix a date on which the transfer (or transfers) to the transferee company (or transferee companies) of the undertaking, 'property' and 'liabilities' of the transferor company is (or are) to take place. This may be done in the order sanctioning the compromise or arrangement or in a subsequent order under **35.4**. Any such order that provides for the dissolution of the transferor company must fix the same date for the dissolution.

If it is necessary for the transferor company to take steps to ensure that the undertaking, property and liabilities are fully transferred, the court must fix a subsequent date, not later than six months after the date fixed above, by which such steps must be taken. In such a case, the court may postpone the dissolution of the transferor company until that subsequent date. The court may postpone (or further postpone) that subsequent date if it is satisfied that the necessary steps cannot be completed by the date (or latest date) fixed.

'*Property*' includes property, rights and powers of every description.

'*Liabilities*' include duties.

[*CA 2006, ss 938, 939, 941*].

## 35.38 MERGER REFERENCES

A merger control regime applies under *Enterprise Act 2002, Part 3 and the Enterprise and Regulatory Reform Act 2013*. Merger notification in the UK is voluntary and is regulated by the Competition and Markets Authority (CMA). Full details of how to notify a merger and receive approval for a merger are available on the CMA website at www.gov.uk.

## 35.39 Reconstructions and Mergers

### 35.39 EC MERGER CONTROL REGULATIONS

The *EC Council Regulation of 20 January 2004 [139/2004]* is designed to deal specifically with cross-border mergers. The provisions have direct effect in the UK in relation to concentrations with a *'community dimension'*, ie where

- the combined aggregate worldwide turnover of all the undertakings concerned is more than €5,000 million; and

- the aggregate Community-wide turnover of each of at least two of the undertakings concerned is more than €250 million,

unless each of the undertakings concerned achieves more than two-thirds of its aggregate Community-wide turnover within the same Member State.

A concentration that does not meet the above thresholds still has a community dimension where

- the combined aggregate worldwide turnover of all the undertakings concerned is more than €2,500 million;

- in each of at least three Member States, the combined aggregate turnover of all the undertakings concerned is more than €100 million and the aggregate turnover of each of at least two of those undertakings is more than €25 million; and

- the aggregate Community-wide turnover of each of at least two of the undertakings concerned is more than €100 million,

unless each of the undertakings concerned achieves more than two-thirds of its aggregate Community-wide turnover within the same Member State.

Any concentration having a community dimension is dealt with by the European Commission unless remitted to a Member State. Conversely, a concentration falling short of having a community dimension is dealt with by the Member State applying its own national law (see **35.38** for the UK provisions) although the Member State can chose to refer the matter to the Commission.

### 35.40 CROSS-BORDER MERGERS

The provisions of *The Companies (Cross-border Mergers) Regulations 2007 (SI 2007 No 2974)* in **35.41** to **35.66** implement *EC Directive 2005/56/EC* (the Cross-border Mergers Directive), which was repealed and codified with effect from 20 July 2017 by *Directive (EU) 2017/1132* of the European Parliament and of the Council of 14 June 2017 relating to certain aspects of company law. *The Companies (Cross-border Mergers) Regulations 2007* provide a framework for limited liability companies to engage in cross-border mergers.

### 35.41 Meaning of 'cross-border merger'

Cross-border merger means a merger by one of the following three methods.

(1)    **Merger by absorption**, ie an operation in which

- there are one or more transferor companies;

- there is an existing transferee company. The meaning of 'existing transferee' was at issue in the case *Re Itau BBA International Ltd* [2012] ALL ER (D) 206. The merger was between a company registered in Portugal and a UK company, purchased as a shelf company for the purposes of the merger. The issue for the court was whether the shelf company could be an 'existing' company as this is defined in the *Companies (Cross-border) Regulations* (see above) as a 'transferee company other than one formed for the purposes of or in connection with a cross-border merger'. The court concluded that a literal interpretation of the definition would put an entirely pointless and unexplained restriction in the *Regulations* and it was therefore open to the court to correct the drafting error in the *Regulations*;

• at least one of those companies is a UK company;

• at least one of those companies is an '*EEA company*' (ie a body corporate governed by the law of an EEA State other than the UK). *In the matter of Easynet Global Services Ltd* [2016] EWHC 2681 (Ch), the court ruled that there must be a genuine cross-border element to the merger and that the inclusion of an EEA company in the transaction must not simply be a device so as to fall within *The Companies (Cross-Border Mergers) Regulations 2007*;

• every transferor company is dissolved without going into liquidation, and on its dissolution transfers all its assets and liabilities to the transferee company; and

• the consideration for the transfer is

　(i)　shares or other securities representing the capital of the transferee company, and

　(ii)　if so agreed, a cash payment,

receivable by members of the transferor company.

(2)　**Merger by absorption of a wholly-owned subsidiary**, ie an operation in which

• there is one transferor company, of which all the shares or other securities representing its capital are held by an existing transferee company. In *Formenta and the Companies (Cross-Border Merger Regulations 2007*, the court concluded that it had no problem with the concept of a reverse cross-border merger, being where the transferor is the parent company that is merged into its subsidiary;

• either the transferor company or the transferee company is a UK company;

• either the transferor company or the transferee company is an EEA company (see above); and

• the transferor company is dissolved without going into liquidation, and on its dissolution transfers all its assets and liabilities to the transferee company.

(3)　**Merger by formation of a new company**, ie an operation in which

• there are two or more transferor companies, at least two of which are each governed by the law of a different EEA State;

• every transferor company is dissolved without going into liquidation, and on its dissolution transfers all its assets and liabilities to a transferee company formed for the purposes of, or in connection with, the operation;

• the consideration for the transfer is

　(i)　shares or other securities representing the capital of the transferee company, and

    (ii)    if so agreed, a cash payment,

receivable by members of the transferor company; and

- at least one of the transferor companies or the transferee company is a UK company.

[*SI 2007 No 2974, Reg 2*].

## 35.42 Pre-merger requirements

A UK merging company may apply to the court for an order certifying for the purposes of *EC Directive 2005/56/EC, Art 10.2* (issue of pre-merger certificate) that the company has completed properly the pre-merger acts and formalities for the cross-border merger. The court must not make such an order unless the requirements of **35.43** to **35.50** (pre-merger requirements) have been complied with.

[*SI 2007 No 2974, Reg 6*].

## 35.43 *Draft terms of merger*

The directors of the UK merging company must draw up and adopt a draft of the proposed terms of the cross-border merger. Subject to below, the draft must give particulars of at least the following matters.

(a)    In relation to each transferor company and transferee company

    (i)    its name,

    (ii)    its registered office, and

    (iii)    its legal form and the law by which it is governed.

(b)    The share exchange ratio and the amount of any cash payment.

(c)    The terms relating to the allotment of shares or other securities in the transferee company.

(d)    The likely effects of the cross-border merger for employees of each merging company.

(e)    The date from which the holding of shares or other securities in the transferee company will entitle the holders to participate in profits, and any special conditions affecting that entitlement. In *Re iTouch Ltd* [2016] EWHC 3448 (Ch), the court held that, as the date may be omitted for a merger by absorption of a wholly-owned subsidiary under *Reg 7(3)*, it could not be said that there had been a failure to comply with the regulation due to the specified effective date being a date that had passed by the time the draft terms were put before the authorities. *iTouch* was distinguished from the merger of two sister companies in *Get Business Services Ltd and ICT Business Services GmbH Re Companies (Cross-Border Mergers) Regulations 2007 [2017] EWHC 2677 (Ch)*, where it was held that the date is a matter for agreement between the merging parties. *Regulation 7(2)(e)* does not contain any implied restriction on the date that can be specified and a date preceding the effective date of the transaction is not excluded.

(f)    The date from which the transactions of the transferor companies are to be treated for accounting purposes as being those of the transferee company.

(g)    Any rights or restrictions attaching to shares or other securities in the transferee company to be allotted under the cross-border merger to the holders of shares or other securities in a transferor company to which any special rights or restrictions attach, or the measures proposed concerning them.

(h)     Any amount or benefit paid or given (or intended to be paid or given) to the independent expert (see **35.45**) or to any director of a merging company, and the consideration for the payment of benefit.

(i)     The transferee company's articles of association, or if it does not have articles, the instrument constituting the company or defining its constitution. (Before 1 October 2008, 'articles' include the company's memorandum of association.)

(j)     Information on the procedures by which any employee participation rights are to be determined in accordance with **35.57** *et seq.*

(k)     Information on the evaluation of the assets and liabilities to be transferred to the transferee company.

(l)     The dates of the accounts of every merging company which were used for the purpose of preparing the draft terms of merger.

But particulars of the matters referred to in (*b*), (*c*) and (*e*) may be omitted in the case of a merger by absorption of a wholly-owned subsidiary.

The draft must

•       *not* provide for any shares in the transferee company to be allotted to

   (i)     a transferor company (or its nominee) in respect of shares in the transferor company held by the transferor company itself (or its nominee); or

   (ii)    the transferee company (or its nominee) in respect of shares in the transferor company held by the transferee company (or its nominee); and

•       provide that where any securities of a UK transferor company (other than shares) to which special rights are attached are held by a person other than as a member or creditor of the company, that person is to receive rights in the transferee company of equivalent value, unless

   (i)     the holder has agreed otherwise; or

   (ii)    the holder is (or under the draft will be) entitled to have the securities purchased by the transferee company on terms which the court considers reasonable.

[*SI 2007 No 2974, Reg 7, Sch 1 para 3*].

**35.44**  *Directors' report*

The directors of the UK merging company must draw up and adopt a report which must

•       explain the effect of the cross-border merger for members, creditors and employees of the company;

•       state

   (i)     the legal and economic grounds for the draft terms;

   (ii)    any material interests of the directors (whether as directors or as members or as creditors or otherwise); and

   (iii)   the effect on those interests of the cross-border merger, in so far as it is different from the effect on the like interests of other persons; where information to be provided explains the effect of the cross-border merger for employees (see above), it must include suitable information relating to the use of agency workers (this provision came into force on 1 October 2011 – see *Reg 8 para (2A)* inserted by the *Agency Workers Regulations 2010 (SI 2010 No 93)*; and

- (where the cross-border merger affects the rights of debenture holders of the company), state

  (i)   any material interests of the trustees of any deed for securing the issue of the debentures (whether as trustees or as members or as creditors or otherwise); and

  (ii)  the effect on those interests of the cross-border merger, in so far as it is different from the effect on the like interests of other persons.

  Any trustee for the company's debenture holders must give notice to the company's directors of such matters relating to himself as may be necessary for these purposes. Any person in default commits an offence. A person guilty of such an offence is liable, on summary conviction, to a fine not exceeding level 3 on the standard scale. See **29.1** OFFENCES AND LEGAL PROCEEDINGS.

The directors must deliver copies of the report to its employee representatives (or if there are no such representatives, the employees) not less than two months before the date of the first meeting of the members (or any class of members) of the company (see **35.48**). If the employee representatives deliver an opinion on the report to the company's registered office not less than one month before the date of the first meeting of the members (or any class of members) of the company, every copy of the report issued after the date on which the opinion was delivered must be accompanied by the opinion.

[*SI 2007 No 2974, Reg 8*].

**35.45** *Independent expert's report*

Apart from the exceptions below, a report must be drawn up by

- an 'independent expert' who has been appointed for the UK merging company by its directors;

- an independent expert who has been appointed for all the merging companies by the court on the joint application of all the merging companies; or

- a person who has been appointed for all the merging companies by a competent authority of another EEA State.

An '*independent expert*' is a person who is eligible for appointment as a statutory auditor (see **8.10** AUDIT) and is independent. A person is not independent unless he satisfies the independence test for a statutory auditor in respect of all the merging companies (on the assumption that all these companies were required to appoint an auditor). See **8.11** AUDIT.

Where he thinks it is necessary to enable him to draw up the report, an independent expert may arrange for a valuation (or accept one which has already been made) by another person, together with a report which will enable him to prepare his own report. That other person must be someone who appears to him to have the requisite knowledge and experience to make the valuation and who is independent (applying the same test as above).

In the report the independent expert must

- indicate

  (i)   the methods used to arrive at the share exchange ratio; and

  (ii)  the values arrived at using each such method;

- describe any special valuation difficulties which have arisen;

- give an opinion

(i)     as to whether the methods used are reasonable in all the circumstances of the case;

(ii)    if there is more than one method, on the relative importance attributed to each method in arriving at the value decided on; and

(iii)   as to whether the share exchange ratio is reasonable;

- in the case of a valuation made by another person

(i)     state that fact and the date of the valuation;

(ii)    state the person's name and what knowledge and experience he has to carry out the valuation;

(iii)   describe so much of the assets and liabilities as was valued by the other person, and the method used to value them; and

(iv)    state that it appeared to him reasonable to arrange for the valuation to be so made or to accept a valuation so made.

In making his report, the independent expert has the right of access to all such documents, and information from officers, of every merging company as he thinks necessary for the purpose of making his report.

*Exceptions.* A report need not be drawn up where

- the cross-border merger is a merger by absorption of a wholly-owned subsidiary;

- the cross-border merger is a merger by absorption where 90% or more (but not all) of the 'relevant securities' of the transferor company (or, if there is more than one transferor company, of each of them) are held by or on behalf of the transferee company; or

- every member of every merging company agrees that such a report is not required.

'*Relevant securities*', in relation to a transferor company, means shares or other securities carrying the right to vote at general meetings of the company. [*SI 2007 No 2974, Reg 9*].

**35.46** *Inspection of documents*

The members of the UK merging company and its employee representatives (or if there are no such representatives, the employees) must be able

- to inspect at the registered office of the company copies of

(i)     the draft terms of merger;

(ii)    the directors' report;

(iii)   the independent expert's report, if such a report is required; and

- to obtain copies of those documents or any part of them on request free of charge

during the period beginning one month before, and ending on the date of, the first meeting of the members (or any class of members) of the company. [*SI 2007 No 2974, Reg 10*].

**35.47** *Public notice of receipt of registered documents*

The directors of the UK merging company must deliver to the Registrar of Companies particulars of the date, time and place of every meeting summoned by the court under **35.51**, together with

(a)    a copy of the court order;

(b)    a copy of the draft terms of merger; and

(c)    documents giving particulars in relation to each merging company of

(i)    its name;

(ii)    its registered office;

(iii)    its legal form and the law by which it is governed;

(iv)    in the case of a UK company, its registered number;

(v)    in the case of an EEA company (ie a body corporate governed by the law of an EEA State other than the UK) to which the *First Company Law Directive* applies, particulars of the register in which the company file mentioned in *Article 3* of that *Directive* (file for each registered company to be kept in national register) is kept (including details of the relevant State) and its registration number in that register; and

(vi)    in the case of any other EEA company, particulars, if any, of the register in which it is entered (including details of the relevant State) and its registration number in that register.

The documents must be delivered to the Registrar of Companies not less than two months before the date of the first meeting of the members (or any class of members) of the company (see **35.48**).

The Registrar of Companies must publish notice of his receipt of the documents at least one month before the date of the first meeting of the members (or any class of members) of the company. His notice must state

•    the date of receipt of the documents;

•    the particulars referred to in (*c*) above;

•    in relation to each UK merging company, a statement that information related to the company is kept in the UK register;

•    a statement that the *Regulations* require copies of the draft terms of merger, the directors' report and (if there is one) the independent expert's report to be kept available for inspection; and

•    the date, time and place of every meeting summoned under **35.51**.

[*SI 2007 No 2974, Reg 12*].

**35.48**  *Approval of members in meeting*

Subject to below, the draft terms of merger must be approved by a majority in number, representing 75% in value, of each class of members of the UK merging company, present and voting either in person or by proxy at a meeting summoned under **35.51**. The approval of the members may be made subject to

•    ratification of any arrangements adopted for employee participation in the transferee company; or

•    an order of a competent authority of another EEA State which amends the share exchange ratio in accordance with *EC Directive 2005/56/EC, Art 10.3* (national procedure allowing for amendment of share exchange ratio).

The approval of the members is not required

- in the case of a transferor company concerned in a merger by absorption of a wholly-owned subsidiary; and

- in the case of an existing transferee company if

  (i)    the publication of the notice required under **35.47** took place in respect of the company at least one month before the date of the first meeting of members of the transferor companies;

  (ii)   the members of the transferee company were able during a period beginning one month before, and ending on, the date of the first such meeting to inspect at the registered office of the transferee company copies of the documents listed in **35.46** in relation to all the merging companies, and to obtain copies of those documents or any part of them on request; and

  (iii)  one or more members of the transferee company, who together held not less than 5% of the paid-up capital of the company which carried the right to vote at general meetings of the company (excluding any shares held as treasury shares), would have been able, during that period, to require a meeting of each class of members to be called for the purpose of deciding whether or not to agree to the scheme, and no such requirement was made.

[*SI 2007 No 2974, Reg 13; SI 2011 No 1606, Reg 38(3)*].

**35.49** *Approval of creditors in meeting*

If a meeting of creditors or a class of creditors is summoned under **35.51**, the draft terms of merger must be approved by a majority in number, representing 75% in value, of the creditors or class of creditors (as the case may be), present and voting either in person or by proxy at the meeting. [*SI 2007 No 2974, Reg 14*].

**35.50** *Documents to be circulated or made available*

Where a meeting is summoned under **35.51**,

- every notice summoning the meeting that is sent to a member or creditor must include copies of the documents referred to **35.46**; and

- every notice summoning the meeting that is given by advertisement must

  (i)    include copies of those documents, or

  (ii)   state where and how members or creditors may obtain copies of those documents free of charge.

[*SI 2007 No 2974, Reg 15*].


**35.51  Power of court to summon meeting of members or creditors**

The court may, on an application by

- the UK merging company,

- any member of the UK merging company in the case of a meeting of members or a class of members,

- any creditor of the UK merging company in the case of a meeting of creditors or a class of creditors, or

- in the case of a UK merging company in administration, the administrator order a meeting of members (or a class of members) for the purposes of **35.48** or creditors (or a class of creditors) for the purposes of **35.49** to be summoned in such manner as the court directs.

*CA 2006, s 323* (representation of corporations at meetings, see **42.27** RESOLUTIONS AND MEETINGS) applies to a meeting of the creditors summoned under these provisions as to a meeting of the company (the references to a member of the company being read as references to a creditor). In *Easynet Global Services Limited [2018] EWHC Civ 10* it was noted that the usual application process made to a Registrar of the Companies Court has developed and the application made under *Regulation 11* is now made to a judge in the Companies Court. This process allows for any serious problems with a cross-border merger proposal to be flushed out at an early stage of the merger. An application under *Regulation 11* will raise novel or substantial issues arising either at that stage or on a later application under *Regulation 16* for an order approving the completion of the merger.

[*SI 2007 No 2974, Reg 11*].

### 35.52 Court approval of cross-border merger

The court may, on the joint application of all the merging companies, make an order approving the completion of the cross-border merger for the purposes of *EC Directive 2005/56/EC, Art 11* (scrutiny of completion of merger) if

(a)     the transferee company is a UK company;

(b)     a court order has been made under **35.42** in relation to each UK merging company;

(c)     an order has been made by a competent authority of another EEA State for the purposes of *EC Directive 2005/56/EC, Art 10.2* (issue of pre-merger certificate) in relation to each merging company which is an EEA company (ie a body corporate governed by the law of an EEA State other than the UK);

(d)     the application is made to the court on a date not more than six months after the making of any order under (*b*) or (*c*) above;

(e)     the draft terms of merger approved by every order referred under (*b*) or (*c*) above are the same; and

(f)     where appropriate, any arrangements for employee participation in the transferee company have been determined in accordance with **35.57** *et seq*.

Where the court makes such an order, it must in the order fix a date on which the consequences of the cross-border merger (see **35.53**) are to have effect That date must be not less than 21 days after the date on which the order is made. After the consequences of the cross-border merger have taken effect (see **35.53**), an order made under these provisions is conclusive evidence that the conditions set out above have been satisfied and the requirements in **35.43–35.50** have been complied with and the cross-border merger may not be declared null and void.

In *Easynet Global Services Ltd* [2018] EWHC Civ 10, it was held that *Regulation 16* of the *Regulations* gives the domestic court discretion as to whether to give final approval for the implementation of a cross-border merger. However, *Regulation 16* is intended to reflect *Article 11* of the *2005 Directive* and does not introduce any distinct restriction on the EU rights under *Article 49* of the *Treaty on the Functioning of the EU and the Cross-Border Mergers Directive 2005* to engage in a cross-border merger. The discretion conferred by *Regulation 16* should be exercised in a manner compatible with rights under EU law. Accordingly, the court was obliged to exercise its power under *Regulation 16* and give effect to the cross-border merger in this case. This judgment was approved and applied in *Re M2 Property Invest Ltd* [2017] EWHC 3218 (Ch).

[*SI 2007 No 2974, Reg 16; SI 2015 No 180, Reg 2*].

### 35.53  Consequences of a cross-border merger

The consequences of a cross-border merger are that

- the assets and liabilities of the transferor companies are transferred to the transferee company;

- the rights and obligations arising from the contracts of employment of the transferor companies are transferred to the transferee company;

- the transferor companies are dissolved; and

- in the case of a merger by absorption or a merger by formation of a new company, the members of the transferor companies except the transferee company (if it is a member of a transferor company) become members of the transferee company.

The consequences take effect

- where a court order has been made **35.52**, on the date fixed in that order; or

- where an order has been made by a competent authority of another EEA State for the purposes of *EC Directive 2005/56/EC, Art 11* (scrutiny of completion of merger), on the date fixed in accordance with the law of that State.

The transferee company must take such steps as are required by law (including by the law of another EEA State) for the transfer of the assets and liabilities of the transferor companies to be effective in relation to other persons.

[*SI 2007 No 2974, Reg 17*].

### 35.54  Copies of order to be provided to members and delivered to the Registrar of Companies

Where an order is made under **35.52** approving the completion of a cross-border merger,

(a)  the UK transferee company must, on request by any member, send him a copy of the order; and

(b)  the UK transferee company and every UK transferor company must deliver the following documents and particulars to the Registrar of Companies for registration not more than seven days after the date on which it was made.

  - A copy of the court order made under **35.52**. See also **35.55**.

  - In the case of a transferor company which is an EEA company (ie a body corporate governed by the law of an EEA State other than the UK) to which the *First Company Law Directive* applies, particulars of the register in which the company file mentioned in *Article 3* of that *Directive* (file for each registered company to be kept in national register) is kept (including details of the relevant State) and its registration number in that register.

  - In the case of any other transferor company which is a EEA company, particulars, if any, of the register in which it is entered (including details of the relevant State) and its registration number in that register.

(c)     Where an order is made by a competent authority of another EEA State approving the completion of a cross-border merger for the purposes of *EC Directive 2005/56/EC, Art 11* (scrutiny of completion of merger), every transferor company which is a UK company must deliver a copy of the order to the Registrar of Companies for registration not more than 14 days after the date on which it was made.

If a company defaults in complying with (*a*) above, an offence is committed by every officer of the company who is in default. If a UK merging company defaults in complying with (*b*) or (*c*) above, an offence is committed by the company and every officer of the company who is in default. A person guilty of either offence is liable, on summary conviction, to a fine not exceeding level 3 on the standard scale and for continued contravention, in the case of (*b*) above to a daily default fine not exceeding one-tenth of level 3 on the standard scale. See **29.1** OFFENCES AND LEGAL PROCEEDINGS for the standard scale.

[*SI 2007 No 2974, Regs 18, 19; SI 2008 No 583, Reg 2*].

### 35.55   Amendment of transferee company's articles, etc

If an order made under **35.52** amends

•       the articles of association of the UK transferee company, or

•       any resolution or agreement in relation to the UK transferee company to which *CA 2006, ss 29, 30* apply (resolutions and agreements affecting a company's constitution, see **14.10** COMPANY CONSTITUTION),

the copy of the court order delivered to the Registrar of Companies by the UK transferee company under **35.54** must be accompanied by a copy of the company's articles, or the resolution or agreement in question, as amended.

Every copy of the company's articles issued by the company after the order is made must be accompanied by a copy of the order, unless the effect of the order has been incorporated into the articles by amendment.

In the case of a company not having articles, references above to its articles are to be read as references to the instrument constituting the company or defining its constitution.

If a UK transferee company defaults in complying with the above provisions, an offence is committed by the company and every officer of the company who is in default. A person guilty of such an offence is liable, on summary conviction, to a fine not exceeding level 3 on the standard scale. See **29.1** OFFENCES AND LEGAL PROCEEDINGS for the standard scale.

[*SI 2007 No 2974, Reg 20*].

### 35.56   Notification of registration by Registrar of Companies

Where the Registrar of Companies receives a copy of a court order made under **35.52** approving the completion of a cross-border merger, he must without undue delay

(a)     in relation to each transferor company which is an EEA company (ie a body corporate governed by the law of an EEA State other than the UK) to which the *First Company Law Directive* applies, give notice of that order to the register in which the company file mentioned in *Article 3* of that *Directive* (file for each registered company to be kept in national register) is kept;

(b)     in relation to any other transferor company which is a EEA company, give notice of the order to the register, if any, in which it is entered; and

(c)    on or after the date fixed in the order as the date on which the consequences of the cross-border merger are to have effect,

    (i)    strike the name of the UK transferor company from the UK register; and

    (ii)    place a note in the register stating that, as from that date, the assets and liabilities of the UK transferor company were transferred to the transferee company.

Where the Registrar of Companies receives from the registry of another EEA State notice for the purposes of *EC Directive 2005/56/EC, Art 13* (notification of registries in other Member States) of an order approving the completion of a cross-border merger, he must on, or without undue delay after, the date fixed for the purposes of *EC Directive 2005/56/EC, Art 12* (entry into effect of the cross-border merger) take the steps specified in (*c*)(i) and (ii) above in relation to every UK transferor company.

[*SI 2007 No 2974, Reg 21*].

## 35.57   Employee participation

The provisions in **35.58** to **35.64** apply where the transferee company is a UK company and where

- a merging company has, in the six months before the publication of the draft terms of merger, an average number of employees that exceeds 500 and has a system of 'employee participation',

- For the purposes of calculating the average number of employees, agency workers whose contract was not a contract of employment with one or more temporary work agencies which were merging companies at the relevant time, are treated as having been employed by such a temporary work agency or agencies for the duration of their assignment with a hirer (see *Reg, para 22(1A)* inserted by the *Agency Worker Regulations 2010 (SI 2010 No 93)* and *reg 3(1)(b)* of those regulations for the meaning of 'contract). *Reg 22(1A)* came into force on 1 October 2011.

- a UK merging company has a proportion of employee representatives amongst the directors, or

- a merging company has 'employee representatives' amongst members of the administrative or supervisory organ or their committees or of the management group which covers the profit units of the company

except that the provisions for ballot arrangements (see **35.60**) and the provisions for confidential information and protection for employees (see **35.62** to **35.64**) apply to a UK merging company, its employees or their representatives, regardless of whether the transferee company is a UK company.

'*Employee participation*' means the influence of the employees and/or the employee representatives in the transferee company or a merging company by way of the right to

- elect or appoint some of the members of the transferee company's or the merging company's supervisory or administrative organ; or

- recommend and/or oppose the appointment of some or all of the members of the transferee's or the merging company's supervisory or administrative organ.

'*Employee representatives*' mean

- if the employees are of a description in respect of which an independent trade union is recognised by their employer for the purpose of collective bargaining, representatives of the trade union who normally take part as negotiators in the collective bargaining process; and

- any other employees of their employer who are elected or appointed as employee representatives to positions in which they are expected to receive, on behalf of the employees, information

  (i)   which is relevant to the terms and conditions of employment of the employees; or

  (ii)  about the activities of the undertaking which may significantly affect the interests of the employees,

  but excluding representatives who are expected to receive information relevant only to a specific aspect of the terms and conditions or interests of the employees (eg health and safety, collective redundancies or pension schemes).

[*SI 2007 No 2974, Regs 3, 22*].

**35.58** *Merging companies and the special negotiating body*

(1) *Duty on merging company to provide information*

As soon as possible after adopting the draft terms of merger, each merging company must provide information to the employee representatives of that company or, if no such representatives exist, the employees themselves. This information must include, as a minimum, information

- identifying the merging companies;

- of any decision of the merging companies to select standard rules of employee participation, see **35.61(1)**); and

- giving the number of employees employed by each merging company.

When a special negotiating body has been formed in accordance with (2) below, each merging company must provide that body with such information as is necessary to keep it informed of the plan and progress of establishing the UK transferee company until the date upon which the consequences of the cross-border merger take effect.

[*SI 2007 No 2974, Reg 23*].

The information to be provided under *reg 23* must include suitable information relating to the use of agency workers (if any) in that company (see *reg 23(4)* inserted by the *Agency Workers Regulations 2010* which came into force on 1 October 2011).

See *SI 2007 No 2974, Reg 24, Sch 2 para 1* for the complaints procedure where an employee representative or, where no such representative exists, any employee believes that a merging company has failed to provide the required information or that the information provided is false or incomplete in a material particular.

(2) *The special negotiating body*

Subject to the merging companies selecting standard rules of employee participation (see **35.61(1)**), each merging company must make arrangements for the establishment of a special negotiating body. The task of this body is to reach an employee participation agreement with the merging companies (see **35.59**).

[*SI 2007 No 2974, Reg 25*].

Employees of merging companies registered in each EEA State (including the UK) must be given an entitlement to elect one member of the special negotiating body for each 10% (or fraction thereof) which employees of merging companies registered in that State represent of the total workforce of the merging companies (the '*constituent members*'). [*SI 2007 No 2974, Reg 26(1)*]. But if, following that election, the members elected to the special negotiating body do not include at least one constituent member in respect of each merging company, the employees of any merging company in respect of which there is no constituent member are given the entitlement (subject to limitations) to elect an additional member to the special negotiating body.

[*SI 2007 No 2974, Reg 26(2)(3)*].

Each merging company must, as soon as reasonably practicable and in any event no later than one month after the establishment of the special negotiating body, inform their employees of the outcome of any elections held under these provisions.

[*SI 2007 No 2974, Reg 26(4)*].

There are also special rules for re-elections if changes to the merging bodies result in the number of members which employees would be entitled to elect either increasing or decreasing, and for the election of a substitute member if a member is no longer willing or able to continue serving.

[*SI 2007 No 2974, Reg 26(5)*].

See *SI 2007 No 2974, Reg 27, Sch 2 para 2* for the complaints procedure about the establishment of a special negotiating body (that is a complaint that a special negotiating body has not been established).

**35.59** *Negotiation of the employee participation agreement*

(1) *Negotiations*

Subject to below the merging companies selecting standard rules of employee participation (see **35.61(1)**), the parties are under a duty to negotiate in a spirit of cooperation with a view to reaching an employee participation agreement. The duty commences one month after the election of the members of the special negotiating body (or the last member if there is more than one election) and lasts for a period of six months (or until the completion of the negotiations, if earlier). The period can be extended by a further six months.

[*SI 2007 No 2974, Reg 28*].

(2) *The employee participation agreement*

The agreement must be in writing and must specify

- the scope of the agreement;

- if, during negotiations, the parties decide to establish arrangements for employee participation, the substance of those arrangements including (if applicable) the number of directors of the UK transferee company which the employees will be entitled to elect, appoint, recommend or oppose, the procedures as to how these directors may be elected, appointed, recommended or opposed by the employees, and their rights; and

- the date of entry into force of the agreement, its duration, the circumstances, if any, in which the agreement is required to be re-negotiated and the procedure for its re-negotiation.

If the transferee company is to provide information on the employment situation in the transferee company under the employee participation agreement, the information must include suitable information relating to the use of agency workers (if any) in that company (see *reg 29(2A)*) inserted by the *Agency Workers Regulations 2010 (SI 2010 No 93)* which came into force on 1 October 2011.

The employee participation agreement must not be subject to the standard rules of employee participation (see **35.61**), unless it contains a provision to the contrary.

[*SI 2007 No 2974, Reg 29*].

(3) *Decisions of the special negotiating body*

Each member of the special negotiating body has one vote. Subject to (4) below, the special negotiating body must take decisions by an absolute majority vote, although where at least 25% of the employees of the merging companies have participation rights, any decision which would result in a 'reduction of participation rights' must be taken by a two-thirds majority vote.

A '*reduction of participation rights*' means that the proportion of directors of the UK transferee company who may be elected or appointed (or whose appointment may be recommended or opposed) by virtue of employee participation is lower than the proportion of such directors or members in the merging company which had the highest proportion of such directors or members.

The special negotiating body must publish the details of any decision taken (including under (4) below) in such a manner as to bring the decision, so far as reasonably practicable, to the attention of the employees whom they represent. Publication must take place as soon as reasonably practicable and, in any event, no later than 14 days after the decision has been taken.

For the purpose of negotiations, the special negotiating body may be assisted by experts of its choice.

The merging companies must pay for any reasonable expenses of the functioning of the special negotiating body and any reasonable expenses relating to the negotiations that are necessary to enable the special negotiating body to carry out its functions in an appropriate manner. But where the special negotiating body is assisted by more than one expert, the merging companies are not required to pay such expenses in respect of more than one of them. [*SI 2007 No 2974, Reg 30*].

(4) *Decision not to open or to terminate negotiations*

The special negotiating body may decide, by a majority vote of two-thirds of its members, representing at least two-thirds of the employees of the merging companies, including the votes of members representing employees in at least two different EEA States, not to open negotiations under (1) above or to terminate negotiations already opened.

Following any such decision, the duty of the parties under (1) above to negotiate with a view to establishing an employee participation agreement cease as from the date of the decision. [*SI 2007 No 2974, Reg 31*].

(5) *Complaints about decisions of special negotiating body.*

A member of the special negotiating body, an employee representative, or where there is no such representative in respect of an employee, that employee may present a complaint to the Central Arbitration Committee (CAC) if he believes that the special negotiating body has taken a decision referred to in *SI 2007 No 2974, Reg 30* or *31* and—

(a)    that the decision was not taken by the majority required by *SI 2007 No 2974, Reg 30 or 31*; or

(b)    that the special negotiating body failed to publish the decision in accordance with *SI 2007 No 2974, Reg 30(5)*.

The complaint must be presented to the CAC—

(a)     in the case of a complaint under (a) within 21 days of publication of the decision of the special negotiating body;

(b)     in the case of a complaint under (b) within 21 days of the date by which the decision should have been published.

(3) Where the CAC finds the complaint well-founded it shall make a declaration that the decision was not taken properly and that it shall have no effect.

[*SI 2007 No 2974, Reg 32*].

**35.60** *Election of UK members of the special negotiating body*

(1) *Ballot arrangements*

*SI 2007 No 2974, Reg 33, Sch 2, para 1* contains detailed provisions for the holding of ballots for the UK members of the special negotiating body. This includes the appointment of one or more independent ballot supervisors and a complaints procedure if the requirements are not followed.

(2) *Conduct of the ballot*

There are detailed provisions relating to the conduct of ballots. As soon as reasonably practicable after the holding of the ballot, the ballot supervisor must publish the results of the ballot in such manner as to make them available to the directors and, so far as reasonably practicable, the UK employees entitled to vote in the ballot and the persons who stood as candidates. He must also publish a report where he considers that

•       any of the requirements as to the conduct of the ballot was not satisfied with the result that the outcome of the ballot would have been different; or

•       there was interference with the carrying out of his functions or a failure by the directors to comply with all reasonable requests made by him with the result that he was unable to form a proper judgement as to whether each of the requirements as to the conduct of the ballot was satisfied.

A fresh ballot or ballots must then be held.

All costs relating to the holding of a ballot of UK employees, including payments made to a ballot supervisor for supervising the conduct of the ballot, must be borne by the UK merging company (whether or not an ineffective ballot report has been published).

[*SI 2007 No 2974, Reg 34*].

(3) *Representation of employees*

A constituent member elected to the special negotiating body in accordance with *Regulation 26(1)* (see **35.58(2)**) is to be treated as representing the employees for the time being of the merging company whose employees were entitled to vote in the ballot in which he was elected. But if an additional member is elected in accordance with *Regulation 26(2)(3)* (see **35.58(2)**) he, and not any member elected in accordance with *Regulation 26(1)*, is to be treated as representing those employees.

[*SI 2007 No 2974, Reg 35*].

**35.61** *Standard rules of employee participation in a UK transferee company*

(1) *Selection of standard rules of employee participation*

The merging companies may choose, without negotiating with the special negotiating body, the employee representatives or the employees, that a UK transferee company is to be subject to the standard rules of employee participation (see (3) below) from the date upon which the consequences of the cross-border merger take effect.

# 35.61   Reconstructions and Mergers

[*SI 2007 No 2974, Reg 36*].

(2) *Application of the standard rules*

The standard rules of employee participation also apply to a UK transferee company where the circumstances in (*a*) and (*b*) apply.

(a)     Before registration of the UK transferee company, one or more forms of employee participation existed in at least one of the merging companies and either

    (i)     that participation applied to at least one-third of the total number of employees of the merging companies; or

    (ii)    that participation applied to less than one third of the total number of employees of the merging companies but the special negotiating body has decided that the standard rules of employee participation should apply.

    (iii)   For the purposes of calculating the number of employees in (a) agency workers are treated as having been employed by a temporary work agency or agencies (see **35.57**) and *reg 37(2A)* inserted by the *Agency Workers Regulations 2010 (SI 2010 No 93)* which came into force on 1 October 2011.

(b)     Either

    (i)     the merging companies and the special negotiating body agree that the standard rules should apply; or

    (ii)    the period specified in **35.59**(1) for them to negotiate an employee participation agreement has expired without the parties reaching an agreement, the merging companies agree that the standard rules should apply, and the special negotiating body has *not* taken any decision under **35.59**(4) either not to open or to terminate the negotiations.

Where the standard rules of employee participation apply and more than one form of employee participation existed in the merging companies, the special negotiating body must decide which of the existing forms of participation apply in the UK transferee company. If it fails to do so (or where one or more form of employee participation existed in the merging companies and the merging companies have chosen, without any prior negotiation, to be directly subject to the standard rules of employee participation), the merging companies are responsible for determining the form of employee participation in the UK transferee company.

[*SI 2007 No 2974, Reg 37*].

(3) *The standard rules*

Under the standard rules, the employee representatives of the UK transferee company (or if there are no such representatives, the employees)

•     subject to (4) below, have the right to elect, appoint, recommend or oppose the appointment of a number of directors of the transferee company, such number being equal to the number in the merging company which had the highest proportion of directors (or their EEA equivalent) so elected or appointed; and

•     taking into account the proportion of employees of the transferee company formerly employed in each merging company, must decide on the allocation of directorships, or on the means by which the transferee's employees may recommend or oppose the appointment of directors. In making this decision, if the employees of one or more merging company are not covered by the proportional criterion, they must appoint a member from one of those merging companies including one from the UK, if appropriate.

Every director of the transferee company so elected, appointed or recommended must be a full director with the same rights and obligations as the directors representing shareholders, including the right to vote.

If under the standard rules of employee participation the transferee company has to provide information on the employment situation in that company, that must include suitable information relating to the use of agency workers (if any) in that company (see *reg 38(5)*) inserted by the *Agency Workers Regulations 2010 (SI 2010 No 93)* which came into force on 1 October 2011.

[*SI 2007 No 2974, Reg 38*].

(4) *Limit on level of employee participation*

Where, following prior negotiation, the standard rules of employee participation apply, the UK transferee company may limit the proportion of directors elected, appointed, recommended or opposed through employee participation to a level which is the lesser of

•     the highest proportion in force in the merging companies prior to registration; and

•     one third of the directors.

[*SI 2007 No 2974, Reg 39*].

(5) *Subsequent domestic mergers*

A transferee company resulting from a cross-border merger that operates under an employee participation system must ensure that employees' rights to employee participation are not affected, before the end of the period of three years beginning with the date on which the consequences of the cross-border merger have effect (see **35.53**) by any court order under *CA 2006, s 899* for the purposes of

•     a reconstruction of the company or the amalgamation of the company with another company; or

•     a merger involving a public company.

[*SI 2007 No 2974, Reg 40*].

**35.62** *Confidential information*

*Duty of confidentiality.* Where a transferee company or merging company entrusts a person, pursuant to any provision relating to employee participation in **35.57** to **35.64**, with any information or document on terms requiring it to be held in confidence, the person must not disclose it except in accordance with the terms on which it was disclosed to him. Procedures are laid down for the recipient to apply to the Central Arbitration Committee (in Northern Ireland, the Industrial Court) for a declaration as to whether it was reasonable for the company to require him to hold the information or document in confidence.

[*SI 2007 No 2974, Reg 41, Sch 2 para 4*].

*Withholding of information by the transferee or merging company.* Neither a transferee company nor a merging company is required to disclose any information or document to a person for the purposes of **35.57** to **35.64** where the nature of the information or document is such that, according to objective criteria, the disclosure would seriously harm or be prejudicial to the transferee company or merging company. Where there is any dispute, application may be made to the Central Arbitration Committee (in Northern Ireland, the Industrial Court) for a declaration as to whether the information or document is of such a nature.

[*SI 2007 No 2974, Reg 42, Sch 2 para 5*].

## 35.63   Reconstructions and Mergers

**35.63** *Protection for employees and members of special negotiating body, etc*

(1) *Right to time off for members of special negotiating body, etc*

An employee who is

- a member of a special negotiating body,

- a director of a transferee company, or

- a candidate in an election in which any person elected will, on being elected, be such a director or member,

is entitled to be permitted by his employer to take reasonable time off during the employee's working hours in order to perform his functions as such a member, director or candidate.

[*SI 2007 No 2974, Reg 43*].

(2) *Right to remuneration for time off under (1) above*

An employee who is permitted to take time off under (1) above is entitled to be paid remuneration by his employer for the time taken off at the '*appropriate hourly rate*', ie the amount of one week's pay divided by the number of normal working hours in a week for that employee when employed under the contract of employment in force on the day when the time is taken. There are special provisions where the number of normal working hours differs from week to week or over a longer period.

[*SI 2007 No 2974, Reg 44*].

(3) *Complaints to employment tribunals*

An employee may present a complaint to an employment tribunal (in Northern Ireland, an industrial tribunal) that his employer has

- unreasonably refused to permit him to take time off as required under (1) above; or

- failed to pay the whole or any part of any amount to which the employee is entitled under (2) above.

The complaint must be made within three months of the date on which the time off was taken or on which it is alleged the time off should have been permitted (or such longer period as the tribunal allows).

[*SI 2007 No 2974, Reg 45; Sch 2 para 6*].

(4) *Unfair dismissal of employee*

An employee who is dismissed is regarded as unfairly dismissed for the purposes of *Employment Rights Act 1996, Pt 10* if the reason (or, if more than one, the principal reason) for the dismissal is that he

(i)     took, or proposed to take, any proceedings before an employment tribunal (in Northern Ireland, an industrial tribunal) to enforce any right conferred on him by *SI 2007 No 2974* (and for these purposes it is immaterial whether or not the employee has the right or entitlement and whether or not the right has been infringed provided the employee has acted in good faith);

(ii)    exercised, or proposed to exercise, any entitlement to apply or complain to the Central Arbitration Committee or the Employment Appeal Tribunal (in Northern Ireland, the Industrial Court and the High Court in Northern Ireland) conferred by *SI 2007 No 2974* or exercised or proposed to exercise the right to appeal in connection with any rights conferred by those Regulations;

(iii)    acted with a view to securing that a special negotiating body did or did not come into existence;

(iv)    indicated that he did or did not support the coming into existence of a special negotiating body;

(v)    stood as a candidate in an election in which any person elected would, on being elected, be a member of a special negotiating body or a director of a UK transferee company;

(vi)    influenced or sought to influence by lawful means the way in which votes were to be cast by other employees in a ballot arranged under *SI 2007 No 2974*;

(vii)    voted in such a ballot;

(viii)    expressed doubts, whether to a ballot supervisor or otherwise, as to whether such a ballot had been properly conducted; or

(ix)    proposed to do, failed to do, or proposed to decline to do, any of the things mentioned in (v) to (viii) above.

[*SI 2007 No 2974, Reg 46, Sch 2 para 7*].

(5) *Unfair dismissal of member of special negotiating body, etc*

An employee who is

•    a member of a special negotiating body,

•    a director of a transferee company, or

•    a candidate in an election in which any person elected will, on being elected, be such a director or member,

who is dismissed is regarded as unfairly dismissed for the purposes of *Employment Rights Act 1996, Pt 10* if the reason (or, if more than one, the principal reason) for the dismissal is that

(i)    the employee performed or proposed to perform any functions or activities as such a member, director or candidate; or

(ii)    the employee or a person acting on his behalf made or proposed to make a request to exercise an entitlement conferred on the employee under (1) or (2) above.

[*SI 2007 No 2974, Reg 47*].

(6) *Detriment*

An employee has the right not to be subjected to any detriment by any act, or deliberate failure to act, by his employer, done on a ground specified in (4)(i)–(ix) above, unless the detriment in question amounts to dismissal.

[*SI 2007 No 2974, Reg 49, Sch 2 para 9*].

(7) *Detriment for member of special negotiating body, etc*

An employee who is

•    a member of a special negotiating body,

•    a director of a transferee company, or

•    a candidate in an election in which any person elected will, on being elected, be such a director or member, has the right not to be subjected to any detriment by any act, or deliberate failure to act, by his employer, done on a ground specified in (5)(i) or (ii) above, unless the detriment in question amounts to dismissal. [*SI 2007 No 2974, Reg 50*].

(8) *Detriment: enforcement*

An employee may present a complaint to an employment tribunal (in Northern Ireland, an industrial tribunal) that he has been subjected to a detriment in contravention of (6) or (7) above.

[*SI 2007 No 2974, Reg 51, Sch 2 para 10*].

**35.64** *Compliance and enforcement*

(1) *Disputes about the operation of an employee participation agreement or the standard rules of employee participation*

Where

- an employee participation agreement has been agreed, or
- the standard rules of employee participation apply,

a complaint may be presented to the CAC (in Northern Ireland, the Industrial Court) by

- a special negotiating body, or
- in a case where no special negotiating body has been elected or appointed, or has been dissolved, an employee representative or employee of the transferee company

who considers that the transferee company has failed to comply with the terms of the employee participation agreement or, where applicable, the standard rules of employee participation.

Such a complaint must be brought within the three months beginning with the date of the alleged failure (or where the failure takes place over a period, the last day of that period).

Where the CAC (in Northern Ireland, the Industrial Court) finds the complaint well founded, it must make a declaration to that effect and may make an order requiring the transferee company, by a specified date, to take such steps as are necessary to comply with the terms of the employee participation agreement or, where applicable, the standard rules of employee participation. The applicant may then, within three months of the decision, make an application to the Employment Appeal Tribunal (in Northern Ireland, the High Court in Northern Ireland) for a penalty notice to be issued. On such an application, that body must issue a written penalty notice to the transferee company requiring it to pay a penalty to the Secretary of State in respect of the failure (up to a maximum of £75,000) unless satisfied, on hearing representations from the transferee company, that the failure resulted from a reason beyond its control or that it has some other reasonable excuse for its failure.

No order of the CAC (in Northern Ireland, the Industrial Court) has the effect of suspending or altering the effect of any act done or of any agreement made by the transferee company or merging company.

[*SI 2007 No 2974, Regs 53, 55, Sch 2 para 12*].

(2) *Misuse of procedures*

If an employee representative (or where there is no such representative in relation to an employee, an employee) believes that a transferee company or merging company is misusing or intending to misuse the transferee company or the powers in *SI 2007 No 2974* for the purpose of

- depriving the employees of that merging company or the transferee company of their rights to employee participation, or

- withholding such rights from any of those people,

he may make a complaint to the CAC (in Northern Ireland, the Industrial Court).

Such a complaint must be made before the date upon which the consequences of the cross-border merger take effect (see 35.53) or within a period of 12 months after that date.

The CAC (in Northern Ireland, the Industrial Court) must uphold the complaint unless the respondent proves the contrary. Where it finds the complaint to be well-founded, it must make a declaration to that effect and may make an order requiring the transferee company or merging company to take action to ensure that the employees involved are not deprived of their rights to employee participation or that such rights are not withheld from them. The complainant may then, within three months of the decision, make an application to the Employment Appeal Tribunal (in Northern Ireland, the High Court in Northern Ireland) for a penalty notice to be issued. On such an application, that body must issue a written penalty notice to the transferee company or merging company requiring it to pay a penalty to the Secretary of State in respect of the failure (up to a maximum of £75,000) unless satisfied, on hearing representations from the transferee company or merging company, that the failure resulted from a reason beyond its control or that it has some other reasonable excuse for its failure.

No order of the CAC (in Northern Ireland, the Industrial Court) has the effect of suspending or altering the effect of any act done or of any agreement made by the transferee company or merging company.

[*SI 2007 No 2974, Regs 54, 55, Sch 2 para 13*].

## 35.65  Unregistered companies

The provisions in **35.40** to **35.64** apply to an unregistered company as they apply to a company formed and registered under *CA 2006* (or earlier provisions). In the application of the provisions to an unregistered company

- any reference to a UK company's registered office is to be read as a reference to the unregistered company's principal office in the UK;

- any reference to a part of the UK in which a UK company is registered is to be read as a reference to the part of the UK in which the unregistered company's principal office is situated; and

- **35.47**(*c*) applies with the omission of (iv) (duty to state company's registered number).

[*SI 2007 No 2974, Reg 5*].

## 35.66  Application of certain provisions of CA 2006

The following provisions apply for the purposes of **35.40** to **35.64** as they apply for the purposes of the Companies Acts.

- *CA 2006, s 1081* (annotation of the register, see **39.10** REGISTRAR OF COMPANIES).

- *CA 2006, ss 1102–1104, 1107* (language requirements for documents delivered to Registrar, see **39.13** REGISTRAR OF COMPANIES).

- *CA 2006, s 1105* (documents that may be drawn up and delivered in other languages, see **39.13** REGISTRAR OF COMPANIES) applies to the documents required to be delivered to the Registrar of Companies under **35.47**(*b*) (draft terms of merger) and **35.54**(*c*) (order of competent authority of another EEA State).

## 35.66   Reconstructions and Mergers

- *CA 2006, s 1106* (voluntary filing of translations, see **39.13 R**EGISTRAR OF **C**OMPANIES) applies in relation to

  (i)    all official languages of EEA States; and

  (ii)   all documents required to be delivered to the Registrar of Companies under *SI 2007 No 2974*.

- *CA 2006, s 1112* (offence of false statement to Registrar, see **39.18 R**EGISTRAR OF **C**OMPANIES) with effect from 1 October 2008.

- *CA 2006, s 1113* (enforcement of company's filing obligations, see **39.16 R**EGISTRAR OF **C**OMPANIES).

- *CA 2006, ss 1121–1123* (liability of officer in default, see **29.3 O**FFENCES AND **L**EGAL **P**ROCEEDINGS).

- *CA 2006, s 1125* (meaning of 'daily default fine', see **29.1 O**FFENCES AND **L**EGAL **P**ROCEEDINGS).

- *CA 2006, ss 1127, 1128* (summary proceedings, see **29.5 O**FFENCES AND **L**EGAL **P**ROCEEDINGS).

- *CA 2006, s 1129* (legal professional privilege, see **29.4 O**FFENCES AND **L**EGAL **P**ROCEEDINGS).

- *CA 2006, s 1130* (proceedings against unincorporated bodies, see **29.7 O**FFENCES AND **L**EGAL **P**ROCEEDINGS).

[*SI 2007 No 2974, Reg 4, Sch 1 para 2*].

# 36   Records

**Cross-references.** See **38** REGISTERS; **42.43, 42.44** RESOLUTIONS AND MEETINGS for minutes of directors' meetings and general meetings respectively.

## 36.1   FORM OF RECORDS GENERALLY

'Company records' may be

- kept in 'hard copy' or 'electronic form', and

- arranged in such manner as the directors of the company think fit,

provided the information in question is adequately recorded for future reference.

Any provision of an instrument made by a company before 12 February 1979 that requires a register of holders of the company's debentures to be kept in hard copy form is to be read as requiring it to be kept in hard copy or electronic form.

Where the records are kept in electronic form, they must be capable of being reproduced in hard copy form.

'*Company records*' means

(a)    any register, index, accounting records, agreement, memorandum, minutes or other document required by the *Companies Acts* to be kept by a company; and

(b)    any register kept by the company of its debenture holders.

See APPENDIX 1 DEFINITIONS for the meaning of '*hard copy*' and '*electronic form*'.

*Offences.* If a company fails to comply with these requirements, an offence is committed by every officer of the company who is in default. A person guilty of such an offence is liable, on summary conviction, to a fine not exceeding level 3 on the standard scale and, for continued contravention, a daily default fine not exceeding one-tenth of level 3 on the standard scale. See **29.1** OFFENCES AND LEGAL PROCEEDINGS for the standard scale.

[*CA 2006, ss 1134, 1135*].

## 36.2   Inspection of records and provision of copies

(1)    **Inspection location**

Certain specified records (see below) may be kept available for inspection at

- the company's registered office; or

- at one location other than the registered office provided that

  (i)    it is situated in the same part of the UK in which the company is registered;

  (ii)   all the specified records are kept at that same place; and

  (iii)  the place has been notified to the Registrar of Companies as being the company's alternative inspection location, on Form AD03, within 14 days.

See **7.2** and **7.3** for details to be included in a company's annual return of the company's registered office address and alternative inspection location (SAIL) and how changes must be notified to Companies House.

[*CA 2006, s 1136(1); SI 2008 No 3006, Reg 3*].

The specified records are

- the register of members (see **38.8** REGISTERS);

- the historic register of members (see **38.9** REGISTERS);

- the register of directors (see **38.3** REGISTERS);

- directors' service contracts (see **18.53** DIRECTORS);

- directors' indemnities (see **18.44** DIRECTORS);

- the register of secretaries (see **38.6** REGISTERS);

- records of resolution (see **42.44** RESOLUTIONS);

- contracts relating to purchase of own shares (see **34.10** PURCHASE OF OWN SHARES);

- documents relating to redemption or purchase of own shares out of capital by private company (see **34.13** PURCHASE OF OWN SHARES);

- the register of debenture holders (see **38.16** REGISTERS);

- the register of people with significant control over a company (PSC register);

- the historic PSC register (where the company has chosen to keep its PSC register centrally with the Registrar (instead of in its own register), the company must retain a copy of the PSC register containing all the information that was required to be included as at the time immediately before the election took effect; this historic register must remain open for inspection, and for requests for copies, in the same way as a normal PSC register);

- report to members of outcome of investigation by public company into interests in its shares (see **24.6** INTERESTS IN PUBLIC COMPANY SHARES);

- the register of interests in shares disclosed to public company (see **38.12** REGISTERS); and

- the register of charges and copies of instruments creating charges (see **38.15** REGISTERS).

[*CA 2006, s 1136(2)*].

(2)    **Availability for inspection – private companies**

A private company must make its company records available for inspection by a person on a day which has been specified by that person ('the specified day') provided that

•    the specified day is a working day; and

•    the person gives the company the required notice of the specified day.

The required notice is:

•    At least two working days' notice if

(i)    the notice is given during the period of notice for a general meeting or a class meeting; or

(ii)    where the company circulates a written resolution, the notice is given during the period provided for in *CA 2006, s 297(1)*, ie the period specified for the purpose in the company's articles or, if none is specified, the period of 28 days beginning with the circulation date

provided that the notice given both begins and ends during the period referred to in (i) or (ii) above (as the case may be).

•    In all other cases, at least 10 working days' notice of the specified day.

When the person gives notice of the specified day, he must also give notice of the time on that day at which he wishes to start the inspection (which must be any time between 9am and 3pm) and the company must make its company records available for inspection by that person for a period of at least two hours beginning with that time.

*[SI 2008 No 3006, Reg 4]*.

By the *Company, Limited Liability Partnership and Business (Names and Trading Disclosures) Regulations 2015*, where a company has specified an alternative inspection location for its records, it must disclose the address of that place, and the type of records kept at that place, to any person it deals with in the course of business who makes a written request for such information. The company must send a written response to that person within five working days of receiving the request.

*[SI 2015 No 17, Reg 27]*

(3)    **Option to hold a central register: private companies**

*Schedule 5* to the *Small Business Enterprise and Employment Act 2015* (*SBEE 2015*) amended the *CA 2006*, with effect from 30 June 2016, to give private companies the option of keeping certain information – that is, information which must be recorded in certain statutory registers – on the central, public register maintained by the Registrar of Companies only. In this way the company can dispense with the need to keep and maintain these registers separately.

The registers to which this applies include:

•    registers of members;

•    the PSC register; an election to exercise this option may be made on incorporation by the subscribers, or at any time following incorporation by the company itself;

•    registers of directors;

•    registers of directors' residential addresses; and

## 36.2    Records

- registers of secretaries.

(*CA 2006, ss 790W–790ZE, 167A–167F, 279A–279F*).

**(4)    Option to keep information relating to directors and secretaries on central register**

As explained above, new sections of the *CA 2006* came into force on 30 June 2016 which set out a procedure by which private companies may keep information on the *central* register, instead of in 'internal' statutory books at the registered office. Notably:

- A private company may choose to hold the register of directors and/or the register of directors' residential addresses on the central register. The election may be made by the company's subscribers on incorporation, or by the company itself at any time after incorporation by giving notice to the registrar.

- An election takes effect when it is registered by the registrar. It remains valid until the company either (i) ceases to be a private company, or (ii) withdraws the election.

- So long as an election remains in force, a company does not have to keep a register of directors and/or a register of directors' residential addresses.

- While an election is in force, the company must deliver information to the Registrar that would otherwise have to be notified under *CA 2006, s 167* if an election was not in force. It is an offence for a company and every officer in default not to comply with this duty.

- An election made under *CA 2006, s 167A* can be withdrawn by giving notice of withdrawal to the Registrar.

[*CA 2006, ss 167A–167F*].

There are similar provisions concerning the register of secretaries.

[*CA 2006, ss 279A–279F*].

**(5)    Availability for inspection – public companies**

A public company must make its company records available for inspection for at least two hours between 9am and 5pm on each working day.

[*SI 2008 No 3006, Reg 5*].

**(6)    Inspection: general**

A company is not required for the purposes of inspection of any its records to present information in that record in a different order, structure or form from that set out in that record.

[*SI 2008 No 3006, Reg 6(1)*].

See APPENDIX 3 (FEES PAYABLE TO COMPANIES) for details of fees payable for inspection of certain documents.

**(7)    Copying of information**

A company must permit a person to make a copy of the whole or any part of a company record in the course of inspection at the location at which the record is made available for inspection and at any time during which the record is made available for inspection, but a company is not required to assist that person in making his copy of that record.

Where a person requests a company to provide a copy of a company record

- in hard copy form, the company must provide that copy in hard copy form; and

- in electronic form, the company must provide that copy in such electronic form as the company decides except that where the company keeps a company record in hard copy form only, it is not required to provide a copy of that record in electronic form.

Where a company provides a copy of a company record in electronic form to a member of the company or to a holder of the company's debentures, the company is not also required to provide a hard copy of that record in accordance with *CA 2006, s 1145*.

A company is not required to present information in a copy of a company record that it provides in a different order, structure or form from that set out in the record.

[*SI 2008 No 3006, Regs 6(2), 7–9*].

See APPENDIX 3 (FEES PAYABLE TO COMPANIES) for details of fees payable for inspection of certain documents.

(8)   **Inspection of accounting records**

Subject to (1)–(7) above no right is given to inspect the accounting records or other books and documents of the company unless that right is given by the articles. Where a company has adopted standard articles, see

- *Table A 1985, Reg 109* (which provides in summary that no member has the right to inspect accounting records or "other book or document of the company" unless the right is conferred by law or authorised by the directors or by an ordinary resolution of members)"

- *Model Articles, Art 50* (private companies)

- *Model Articles, Art 83* (public companies)

  (which both provide in summary that no person is entitled to inspect any of the company's accounting records or "other records or documents" except as provided by law or authorised by the directors or by an ordinary resolution of members.)

set out in APPENDIX 4 STANDARD ARTICLES OF ASSOCIATION.

See also *McCusker v McRae* 1966 SC 253 and *Conway v Petronius Clothing Co Ltd* [1978] 1 All ER 185, [1978] 1 WLR 72.

**36.3   Duty to take precautions against falsification**

Where company records are kept otherwise than in bound books, adequate precautions must be taken to guard against falsification and to facilitate the discovery of falsification. This does not apply to documents required to be kept under

(a)   *CA 2006, s 228* (copies of director's service contract or memoranda of their terms); or

(b)   *CA 2006, s 237* (qualifying indemnity provisions made for directors).

If a company fails to comply with this requirement, an offence is committed by every officer of the company who is in default. A person guilty of such an offence is liable, on summary conviction, to a fine not exceeding level 3 on the standard scale and, for continued contravention, a daily default fine not exceeding one-tenth of level 3 on the standard scale. See **29.1** OFFENCES AND LEGAL PROCEEDINGS for the standard scale.

## 36.3  Records

*[CA 2006, s 1138]*.

## 36.4  Preservation of records

Where there are specific provisions in the legislation relating to the preservation of records (eg accounting records as under **36.7**), these are covered in the relevant part of this book. Otherwise, companies' legislation does not set out any general provisions as to the period for preservation of a company's records. It is recommended practice to keep

- memorandum of association, articles of association, certificate of incorporation, statutory registers and copies of published accounts for the life of the company;

- invoices, receipts, returned cheques, paying-in books, bank statements, etc for six years;

- title deeds and related correspondence for twelve years after disposal; and

- contracts and agreements for six years after expiry (twelve years if under seal).

Where standard articles have been adopted, see

- *Model Articles, Art 82* (public companies) which provides which documents may be destroyed and when. The Model Articles for private companies do not contain the same or similar provisions.

The Model Articles are set out in APPENDIX 4 STANDARD ARTICLES OF ASSOCIATION.

## 36.5  DUTY TO KEEP ACCOUNTING RECORDS

Every company must keep adequate accounting records sufficient to show and explain the company's transactions and to

- disclose with reasonable accuracy, at any time, the financial position of the company at that time; and

- enable the directors to ensure that any accounts required to be prepared comply with the requirements of *CA 2006* and, where applicable, *International Accounting Standards Regulation, Art 4*.

The accounting records must, in particular, contain

- entries from day-to-day of all sums of money received and expended by the company and the matters in respect of which the receipt and expenditure takes place; and

- a record of the assets and liabilities of the company.

If the company's business involves dealing in goods, the accounting records must also contain

(i)     statements of stock held by the company at the end of each financial year;

(ii)    all statements of stock-taking from which any statement of stock in (i) above has been or is to be prepared; and

(iii)   (except in the case of goods sold by way of ordinary retail trade) statements of all goods sold and purchased, showing sufficient detail of the goods, buyers and sellers to enable all these to be identified.

A parent company with a subsidiary undertaking in relation to which the above requirements do not apply must take reasonable steps to ensure that the undertaking keeps such accounting records as to enable the directors of the parent company to ensure that any accounts required to be prepared comply with the requirements of *CA 2006* and, where applicable, *IAS Regulation, Art 4*.

[*CA 2006, s 386*].

*Offences*. If a company fails to comply with the above provisions, an offence is committed by every officer of the company who is in default. A person guilty of such an offence is liable (i) on conviction on indictment, to imprisonment for a term not exceeding two years or a fine (or both); and (ii) on summary conviction, to imprisonment for a term not exceeding twelve months (six months in Scotland or Northern Ireland) or to a fine not exceeding the statutory maximum (or both). See 29.1 OFFENCES AND LEGAL PROCEEDINGS for the statutory maximum. It is a defence for a person charged with such an offence to show that he acted honestly and that in the circumstances in which the company's business was carried on the default was excusable.

[*CA 2006, s 387*].

**Interpretation of the above provisions.** See the ICAEW technical release (TECH 01/11) "Guidance for directors on accounting records under the Companies Act 2006"

**Lien over accounting records.** As *CA 2006, s 386* above imposes mandatory duties on a company in connection with the keeping of accounting records and criminal penalties for breach of those duties. An accountant (or solicitor) cannot claim a lien over books and documents for unpaid fees. See *DTC (CNC) Ltd v Gary Sargeant & Co (a firm)* [1996] 2 All ER 369, [1996] 1 BCLC 529 where an accountant asserted a lien over sales and purchase invoices, cheque books, paying-in books and bank statements.

See also ICAEW guidance "Documents and records : ownership, lien and rights of access".

## 36.6 Location and inspection of accounting records

The accounting records must be kept at the company's registered office or such other place as the directors think fit and must at all times be open to inspection by the company's officers.

If the accounting records are kept outside the UK, accounts and returns which

- disclose with reasonable accuracy the financial position of the business at intervals of not more than six months, and

- enable the directors to ensure that the accounts required to be prepared comply with the requirements of *CA 2006* (and, where applicable, the requirements of *IAS Regulation, Art 4*)

must be sent to, and kept in, a place in the UK, and must at all times be open to inspection by the company's officers.

[*CA 2006, s 388(1)–(3)*].

*Offences*. If a company fails to comply with the above provisions, an offence is committed by every officer of the company who is in default. A person guilty of such an offence is liable (i) on conviction on indictment, to imprisonment for a term not exceeding two years or a fine (or both); and (ii) on summary conviction, to imprisonment for a term not exceeding twelve months (six months in Scotland and Northern Ireland) or to a fine not exceeding the statutory maximum (or both). See 29.1 OFFENCES AND LEGAL PROCEEDINGS for the statutory maximum. It is a defence for a person charged with such an offence to show that he acted honestly and that in the circumstances in which the company's business was carried on the default was excusable.

## 36.6 Records

[*CA 2006, s 389(1)(2)(4)*].

### 36.7 Preservation of accounting records

The accounting records that a company is required to keep under **36.5** must be preserved

- in the case of a private company, for three years from the date on which they are made; and

- in the case of a public company, for six years from the date on which they are made.

This is subject to any provision contained in rules made under *IA 1986, s 411* or *Insolvency (Northern Ireland) Order 1989 (SI 1989 No 2405), Art 359.*

[*CA 2006, s 388(4)(5)*].

It should also be noted that records may be required to be preserved longer for other purposes. HM Revenue and Customs require VAT records to be preserved for six years (or such lesser period as they allow) and direct tax assessments may be raised for up to six years after the chargeable accounting period (20 years in the case of fraud or negligent conduct).

*Offences.* An officer of a company commits an offence if he

- fails to take all reasonable steps for securing compliance by the company with *CA 2006, s 388(4)*; or

- intentionally causes any default by the company under that provision.

A person guilty of such an offence is liable (i) on conviction on indictment, to imprisonment for a term not exceeding two years or a fine (or both); and (ii) on summary conviction, to imprisonment for a term not exceeding twelve months (six months in Scotland and Northern Ireland) or to a fine not exceeding the statutory maximum (or both). See **29.1** OFFENCES AND LEGAL PROCEEDINGS for the statutory maximum. It is a defence for a person charged with such an offence to show that he acted honestly and that in the circumstances in which the company's business was carried on the default was excusable.

[*CA 2006, s 389(3)(4)*].

### 36.8 Criminal destruction etc of accounting records

Where a person dishonestly, with a view to gain for himself or another or intent to cause loss to another,

- destroys, defaces, conceals or falsifies any account or any other record or document made or required for any accounting purpose, or

- makes use of any such account, etc which he knows to be materially misleading, false or deceptive

he is, on conviction, liable to imprisonment for a term not exceeding seven years.

[*Theft Act 1968, s 17*].

# 37   Registered Office

**Cross-references.** See **16.13–16.17** DEALINGS WITH THIRD PARTIES for various disclosure requirements concerning the registered office.

**Background.** The provisions in this chapter apply, unless otherwise stated, with effect from 1 October 2009.

## 37.1   REQUIREMENT TO HAVE A REGISTERED OFFICE

A company must at all times have a registered office to which all communications and notices may be addressed. [*CA 2006, s 86*]. On formation, the address is that specified in the registration documents sent to the Registrar of Companies under *CA 2006, s 9* (see **12.3** COMPANY FORMATION AND TYPES OF COMPANIES).

## 37.2   CHANGE OF ADDRESS

A company may change the address of its registered office by giving notice to the Registrar of Companies. The change takes effect upon the notice being registered by the Registrar of Companies but for the next 14 days any document can still be validly served at the address previously registered.

Where a company has given notice, for the purposes of any duty

(a)     to keep available for inspection at its registered office any register, index or other document, or

(b)     to mention the address of its registered office in any document,

the company may act on the change as from such date, not more than 14 days after the notice is given, as it may determine.

Where a company unavoidably ceases to perform at its registered office any duty within (*a*) above in circumstances in which it was not practicable to give prior notice to the Registrar of Companies of a change in the address of its registered office (eg in the case of fire), it is not to be treated as having failed to comply with that duty provided it

•       resumes performance of that duty at other premises as soon as practicable; and

•       gives notice accordingly to the Registrar of Companies of a change in the situation of its registered office within 14 days of doing so.

[*CA 2006, s 87*].

## 37.3   WELSH COMPANIES

A '*Welsh company*' means a company as to which it is stated in the register that its registered office is to be situated in Wales (as opposed to England and Wales). A company can be set up as a Welsh company by delivering to the Registrar of Companies a statement to this effect on formation (see **12.3** COMPANY FORMATION AND TYPES OF COMPANIES).

## 37.3   Registered Office

(a)   **Becoming a Welsh company**. A company

- whose registered office is in Wales, and

- as to which it is stated in the register that its registered office is to be situated in England and Wales,

may by special resolution require the register to be amended so that it states that the company's registered office is to be situated in Wales.

(b)   **Ceasing to be a Welsh company**. A company

- whose registered office is in Wales, and

- as to which it is stated in the register that its registered office is to be situated in Wales,

may by special resolution require the register to be amended so that it states that the company's registered office is to be situated in England and Wales.

Where a company passes a resolution under (*a*) or (*b*) above it must give notice to the Registrar of Companies who must amend the register accordingly and issue a new certificate of incorporation altered to meet the circumstances of the case.

[*CA 2006, s 88*]


## 37.4   REGISTERED OFFICE DISPUTES

On 6 April 2016 the *Companies (Address of Registered Office) Regulations 2016* came into force. The regulations, with new *CA 2006, s 1097A* (Rectification of register relating to company registered office), introduce a new procedure to allow the Registrar to change the registered office of a company or limited liability partnership where, following an application by any person, the registrar considers that the entity is not authorised to use that address.

Under the regulations, briefly:

- An application to change a company's or LLP's registered office may be made by any person.

- Unless the registrar dismisses the application immediately because there is no reasonable prospect of success, the registrar must give notice to the entity of the application and invite it to provide evidence that the entity is authorised to use the address as its registered office.

- Unless the entity itself decides to change its registered office, it must respond with evidence that it is authorised to use the address.

- If the entity fails to provide adequate evidence, the Registrar must change the address of the registered office to a default address (which will be a PO Box at Companies House).

- The Registrar may refer applications or questions relating to the application to the court.

- The Registrar may also rely on certain evidence to be satisfied that the entity is authorised to use the address, including evidence suggesting the entity or a related group undertaking has a proprietary interest at the address.

- On determining an application, the Registrar must give notice to both parties.

- The applicant or the entity may appeal the decision to the court within 28 days.

- Where the address of a registered office is changed by the Registrar (after a successful application or following direction from the court), certain duties of the entity (which relate to inspection of records, or disclosure or display of information) will be suspended for 28 days or, where an appeal is brought by the entity, throughout the appeal process.

- The default address may not be used for the purpose of keeping, or making available for inspection, the entity's registers, indexes or other documents; the Registrar will not be required to open any documents delivered to the entity at the default address; and the Registrar must provide for the collection by the entity of any documents delivered to the entity at the default address, and may destroy any documents uncollected after 12 months.

- If an entity gives notice to change of its registered office from a default address, the Registrar may require evidence that the entity is authorised to use the new address.

The application is made using Form RP07. The relevant documents a private individual might submit to show an address is being used without their authority, include documents showing the applicant's proprietary rights in the address, a written agreement entitling the applicant to use the address and a utility bill sent to the applicant at the address provided it is dated within the last six months.

[*SI 2016 No 423*].

# 38  Registers

## 38.1  FORM IN WHICH REGISTER KEPT

Subject to **38.2** (option to keep information on the central Register) any register or index which a company is required to keep under the *Companies Acts* may be kept in hard copy or electronic form and may be arranged in such manner as the directors of the company think fit, provided the information in question is adequately recorded for future reference. This is subject to the requirements that where the records are kept

- in electronic form, they must be capable of being reproduced in hard copy form; and

- otherwise than in bound books, adequate precautions must be taken to guard against falsification and to facilitate its discovery.

If a company fails to comply with the above provisions, an offence is committed by every officer of the company who is in default. A person guilty of such an offence is liable, on summary conviction, to a fine not exceeding level 3 on the standard scale and, for continued contravention, a daily default fine not exceeding one-tenth of level 3 on the standard scale. See **29.1** OFFENCES AND LEGAL PROCEEDINGS for the standard scale.

[*CA 2006, ss 1135(1)–(4), 1138(1)–(3)*].

## 38.2  OPTION TO KEEP INFORMATION ON THE CENTRAL (PUBLIC) REGISTER

*SBEE 2015, s 94* and *Sch 5* introduce a new *CA 2006, Chapter 2A* which provides for private companies to elect to keep information on the register kept by the Registrar of Companies instead of entering that information in their own registers. The provisions come into force on 30 June 2016. The provisions cover the register of directors and directors' residential addresses (see **38.4**), register of secretaries (see **38.7**), register of members (see **38.9**) and register of people with significant control (see **38.18**).

## 38.3 Registers

Subject to **38.4** (option to keep directors information on the central register) every company must

- keep a register of its directors containing the required particulars of each person who is a director;

- keep the register available for inspection at the company's registered office or at a place specified in Regulations. The regulations are the *Companies (Company Records) Regulations 2008 (SI 2008 No 3006)* (see **36.2** Records). It must be open to the inspection of any member of the company without charge and any other person on payment of such fee as may be prescribed. The fee is £3.50 for each hour or part of an hour during which the right of inspection of exercised (see Appendix **3** Fees);

- give notice to the Registrar of Companies of the place at which the register is kept available for inspection and any change in that place (unless it has at all times been kept at the company's registered office); and

- give notice to the Registrar of Companies, within 14 days, of any change in the particulars contained on the register and the date on which the change occurred. Where

  - (i)    a company gives notice of a change of a director's service address as stated in the company's register of directors, and

  - (ii)    the notice is not accompanied by notice of any resulting change in the particulars contained in the company's register of directors' residential addresses (see **38.5**),

  the notice must be accompanied by a statement that no such change is required.

**Offences**. If

- default is made in complying with the requirements to

  - (i)    keep a register with the required particulars,

  - (ii)    keep the register available for inspection at the correct location,

  - (iii)    notify the Registrar of Companies of the place, or any change in the place, where the register is available for inspection, or

  - (iv)    notify the Registrar of Companies of any changes in the particulars contained on the register, or

- an inspection is refused,

an offence is committed by the company and every officer of the company who is in default. For these purposes, a shadow director is treated as an officer of the company. A person guilty of such an offence is liable, on summary conviction, to a fine not exceeding level 5 on the standard scale and, for continued contravention, a daily default fine not exceeding one-tenth of the greater of £5,000 or level 4 on the standard scale. See **29.1** Offences and Legal Proceedings for the standard scale. In the case of a refusal of inspection of the register, the court may by order compel an immediate inspection of it.

**Particulars of directors to be disclosed**. A company's register of directors must contain the following particulars.

- (a)    In the case of an individual

  - (i)    'name' and any 'former name';

(ii)     a service address (which may be stated to be 'the company's registered office');

(iii)     the country or state (or part of the UK) in which he is usually resident;

(iv)     nationality;

(v)     business occupation (if any); and

(vi)     date of birth.

*'Name'* means a Christian name (or other forename) and surname. But in the case of a peer or an individual usually known by a title, the title may be stated instead of his Christian name (or other forename) and surname or in addition to either or both of them.

*'Former name'* means a name by which the individual was formerly known for business purposes. Where a person is (or was) formerly known by more than one such name, each of them must be stated. It is not necessary for the register to contain particulars of a former name

• in the case of a peer or an individual normally known by a British title, where the name is one by which the person was known previous to the adoption of or succession to the title; and

• in the case of any person, where the former name *either* was changed or disused before the person attained the age of 16 *or* has been changed or disused for 20 years or more.

(b)     In the case of a body corporate, or a firm that is a legal person under the law by which it is governed

(i)     corporate or firm name;

(ii)     registered or principal office;

(iii)     in the case of an EEA company to which the *First Company Law Directive* applies, particulars of

• the register in which the company file mentioned in *Article 3* of that *Directive* is kept (including details of the relevant state); and

• the registration number in that register; and

(iv)     in any other case, particulars of

• the legal form of the company or firm and the law by which it is governed; and

• if applicable, the register in which it is entered (including details of the state) and its registration number in that register.

The Secretary of State may, by Regulations, add to or remove items from the above requirements.

[*CA 2006, ss 162–164, 166, 167*].

**Directors' residential addresses**. See **38.5** for obligations to keep a register and **18.73** Directors for entries required to be made in the company's register following action by the Registrar of Companies under *Companies Act 2006 (CA 2006), ss 245, 246* (putting usual residential address on public record). The requirement for entries in the company's register is subject to any election in force (see **38.4**).

## 38.3   Registers

**Time available for inspection and copying.** See **36.2** Records.

Obligation to keep separate registers

(1)     On or after 1 October 2009, the register of directors and secretaries kept by a company under *CA 1985, s 288(1)* is treated as two separate registers, ie a register of directors under *CA 2006, s 162* (see above) and a register of secretaries under *CA 2006, s 275* (see **38.6**).

[*SI 2008 No 2860, Sch 2 para 25*].

(2)     A company incorporated before 1 October 2009 does not need to comply with the any provision of *CA 2006* requiring the company's register of directors or secretaries to contain particulars additional to those required by *CA 1985* until the earlier of

  •     the date to which the company makes up its first annual return made up to a date on or after 1 October 2009; and

  •     the last date to which the company should have made up that return

except that this provision

  (i)     does not apply in relation to a director of whom particulars are first registered on or after 1 October 2009 (whether the director was appointed before or on or after that date); and

  (ii)    ceases to apply in relation to a director whose registered particulars fall to be altered on or after 1 October 2009 because they have changed (whether the change occurred before, on or after that date).

None of the above provisions affect the particulars required to be included in the company's annual return.

[*SI 2008 No 2860, Sch 2 para 26*].

(3)     In the case of a company incorporated before 1 October 2009,

  •     the 'relevant existing address' of a director is deemed, on or after 1 October 2009, to be a service address; and

  •     any entry in the company's register of directors stating that address is treated, on or after that date, as complying with the obligation under (*a*)(ii) (particulars of director above) to state a service address.

The 'relevant service address' is

  (i)     the address that immediately before 1 October 2009 appears in the company's register of directors and secretaries as having been notified to the company as the service address notified by an individual applying for a confidentiality order in respect of a usual residential address; or

  (ii)    if no such address appeared, the address that immediately before 1 October 2009 appears in the company's register of directors and secretaries as the director's usual residential address.

Any notification of a change of a relevant existing address before 1 October 2009 that is received by the company on or after that date is treated as being or, as the case may be, including notification of a change of service address.

The operation of this provision does not give rise to any duty to notify the Registrar of Companies under *CA 2006, s 167* (duty to notify the Registrar of Companies of change of particulars in the register).

[*SI 2008 No 2860, Sch 2 para 27*].

(4) A company incorporated before 1 October 2009, must have removed from its register of directors on 1 October 2009 any entry relating to a 'shadow director'. *CA 2006, s 167* (duty to notify the Registrar of Companies of changes in particulars in the register) applies as if the shadow director had ceased to be a director on that date.

[*SI 2008 No 2860, Sch 2 para 28*].

(5) The removal by a company incorporated before 1 October 2009, from its register of directors on or after 1 October 2009 of particulars required by *CA 1985* but not required by *CA 2006* does not give rise to any duty to notify the Registrar of Companies under *CA 2006, s 167* (duty to notify Registrar of Companies of changes of particulars in the register).

[*SI 2008 No 2860, Sch 2 para 29*].

(6) *CA 2006, s 167* (duty to notify Registrar of Companies of changes of particulars in the register) applies in relation to

- a change among a company's directors, or

- a change in the particulars contained in the register

occurring on or after 1 October 2009.

## 38.4 OPTION TO KEEP DIRECTORS' INFORMATION ON THE CENTRAL REGISTER

**Right to make an election**

An election may be made in respect of a register of directors or a register of directors' residential addresses (or both).

An election may be made by giving notice to the Registrar of Companies

- by the subscribers wishing to form a private company under CA 2006; or

- by the private company itself once it is formed and registered.

If the notice is given by subscribers wishing to form a private company, it must be given when the documents required to be delivered under *s 9* are delivered to the registrar.

**Effective date of election**

The same provisions apply as in **38.2**.

**Effect of election on obligations under *CA 2006, ss 162–167***

If an election is in force with respect to a company, the company's obligations under *CA 2006, ss 162–167* to keep and maintain a register of the relevant kind, and to notify the Registrar of changes to it, do not apply with respect to the period when the election is in force.

The reference to a register "of the relevant kind" is to a register (whether a register of directors or a register of directors' residential addresses) of the kind in respect of which the election is made.

## 38.4    Registers

### Duty to notify Registrar of changes

When an election under the above is in force the company must deliver to the Registrar any information of which the company would during that period have been obliged to give notice under *CA 2006, s 167*, had the election not been in force, and any statement that would have had to accompany such a notice.

The information (and any accompanying statement) must be delivered as soon as reasonably practicable after the company becomes aware of the information and, in any event, no later than the time by which the company would have been required under *CA 2006, s 167* to give notice of the information.

### Offences

If default is made in complying with this section, an offence is committed by the company, and every officer of the company who is in default. For this purpose a shadow director is treated as an officer of the company. A person guilty of an offence under this section is liable on summary conviction in England and Wales, to a fine and, for continued contravention, a daily default fine not exceeding the greater of £500 and one-tenth of level 4 on the standard scale and in Scotland or Northern Ireland, to a fine not exceeding level 5 on the standard scale and, for continued contravention, a daily default fine not exceeding one-tenth of level 5 on the standard scale. See **29.1** Offences and Legal Proceedings for the standard scale.

### Withdrawing the election

A company may withdraw an election made by or in respect of the register of directors or directors' residential addresses. Withdrawal is achieved by giving notice of withdrawal to the Registrar and the withdrawal takes effect when the notice is registered by the Registrar.

The effect of withdrawal is that the company's obligation to keep and maintain a register of the relevant kind, and its obligation to notify the Registrar of changes to that register, applies from then on with respect to the period going forward.

This means that, when the withdrawal takes effect

(i)     the company must enter in that register all the information that is required to be contained in that register in respect of matters that are current as at that time; but

(ii)    the company is not required to enter in its register information relating to the period when the election was in force that is no longer current.

[*CA 2006, ss 167A–167F; SBEE 2015, s 94, Sch 5, paras 5, 6, 7; SI 2016 No 321, Reg 6*].


## 38.5    REGISTER OF DIRECTORS' RESIDENTIAL ADDRESSES

Subject to **38.4** (option to keep information on the central register) every company must comply with the requirement to

• keep a register of directors' residential addresses stating the usual residential address of each of the company's directors; and

• give notice to the Registrar of Companies, within 14 days, of any change in the particulars contained on the register and the date on which the change occurred. If a director's usual residential address is the same as his service address (as stated in the company's register of directors under **38.3**), the register of directors' residential addresses need only contain an entry to that effect. But this does not apply if his service address is stated to be 'The company's registered office'.

If default is made in complying with the above provisions, an offence is committed by the company and every officer of the company who is in default. For this purpose, a 'shadow director' is treated as an officer of the company. A person guilty of such an offence is liable, on summary conviction, to a fine not exceeding the greater of £5000 or level 4 on the standard scale and, for continued contravention, a daily default fine not exceeding one-tenth of the greater of £5,000 or level 4 on the standard scale. See 29.1 OFFENCES AND LEGAL PROCEEDINGS for the standard scale.

The above provisions apply only to directors who are individuals, not where the director is a body corporate or a firm that is a legal person under the law by which it is governed.

[*CA 2006, ss 165, 167; SI 2015 No 664, Sch 3; CA 2006, ss 167A–167F; SBEE 2015, s 94, Sch 5, paras 5, 6, 7; SI 2016 No 321, Reg 6*].

## 38.6   REGISTER OF SECRETARIES

Subject to **38.7** – (option to keep company secretary information on the central register) every company must

- keep a register of its secretaries containing the required particulars of the person who is, or persons who are, the secretary or joint secretaries of the company;

- keep the register available for inspection at the company's registered office or at a place specified in Regulations (see **36.2** RECORDS). It must be open to the inspection of any member of the company without charge and any other person on payment of such fee as may be prescribed (see APPENDIX 3 FEES);

- give notice to the Registrar of Companies, within 14 days, of the place at which the register is kept available for inspection and any change in that place (unless it has at all times been kept at the company's registered office); and

- give notice to the Registrar of Companies, within 14 days, of any change in the particulars contained on the register.

**Offences.** If

- default is made in complying with the requirements to

    (i)     keep a register with the required particulars,

    (ii)    keep the register available for inspection at the correct location,

    (iii)   notify the Registrar of Companies of the place, or any change in the place, where the register is available for inspection, or

    (iv)    notify the Registrar of Companies of any changes in the particulars contained on the register, or

- an inspection is refused,

an offence is committed by the company and every officer of the company who is in default. For these purposes, a 'shadow director' is treated as an officer of the company. A person guilty of such an offence is liable, on summary conviction, to a fine not exceeding the greater of £5000 or level 4 on the standard scale and, for continued contravention, a daily default fine not exceeding one-tenth of the greater of £5,000 or level 4 on the standard scale. See **29.1** OFFENCES AND LEGAL PROCEEDINGS for the standard scale. In the case of a refusal of inspection of the register, the court may by order compel an immediate inspection of it.

**Particulars of secretaries to be disclosed.** A company's register of secretaries must contain the following particulars.

## 38.6 Registers

(a)    In the case of an individual:

    (i)    Name, ie Christian name (or other forename) and surname. In the case of a peer or an individual usually known by a title, the title may be stated instead of his Christian name (or other forename) and surname or in addition to either or both of them.

    (ii)    Any former name, ie any name by which the individual was formerly known for business purposes. Where a person is (or was) formerly known by more than one such name, each of them must be stated. It is not necessary for the register to contain particulars of a former name

- in the case of a peer or an individual normally known by a British title, where the name is one by which the person was known previous to the adoption of or succession to the title; and

- in the case of any person, where the former name *either* was changed or disused before the person attained the age of 16 *or* has been changed or disused for 20 years or more.

    (iii)    A service address. This may be stated to be 'The company's registered office'.

(b)    In the case of a body corporate, or a firm that is a legal person under the law by which it is governed

    (i)    corporate or firm name;

    (ii)    registered or principal office;

    (iii)    in the case of an EEA company to which the *First Company Law Directive* applies, particulars of

- the register in which the company file mentioned in *Article 3* of that *Directive* is kept (including details of the relevant state); and

- the registration number in that register; and

    (iv)    in any other case, particulars of

- the legal form of the company or firm and the law by which it is governed; and

- if applicable, the register in which it is entered (including details of the state) and its registration number in that register.

If all the partners in a firm are joint secretaries it is sufficient to state the particulars that would be required if the firm were a legal person and the firm had been appointed secretary. [*CA 2006, ss 275, 276(1), 277–279*].

**Time available for inspection and copying.** See **36.2** RECORDS.

For companies incorporated before 1 October 2009 see **38.3** (above) *Obligation to keep separate registers* which also apply to the keeping of the register of secretaries.

## 38.7    OPTION TO KEEP INFORMATION ABOUT THE COMPANY SECRETARY ON THE CENTRAL REGISTER

The provisions relating to options for the directors register are provided in exactly the same way for the register of secretaries which a company must keep, excepting those provisions where it refers to "register of the relevant kind" read "register of company secretaries". See **38.4** for full details.

[*CA 2006, ss 279A–279E; SBEE 2015, s 94, Sch 5, para 10; SI 2016 No 321, Reg 6*].

## 38.8 REGISTER OF MEMBERS

**Particulars to be disclosed**. Subject to **38.9** (option to keep information about members on the central register) every company must keep a register of its members containing the following information.

(a)    The names and addresses of the members.

(b)    The date on which each person was registered as a member.

(c)    The date at which any person ceased to be a member.

(d)    In the case of a company having a share capital, with the names and addresses of the members, a statement of

- the shares held by each member, distinguishing each share by its number (where applicable) and, where the company has more than one class of issued shares, by its class; and

- the amount paid (or agreed to be considered as paid) on the shares of each member.

If the company has converted any of its shares into stock, and given notice of the conversion to the Registrar of Companies, the amount and class of stock held by each member must be shown instead of the amount of shares and the particulars relating to shares specified above.

In the case of joint holders of shares or stock in a company, the names of each joint holder must be stated but, in other respects, joint holders are regarded as a single member (so that the register must show a single address).

(e)    In the case of a company that does not have a share capital but has more than one class of members, the class to which each member belongs.

[*CA 2006, s 113(1)–(6)*].

*Treasury shares*. Where a company purchases its own shares as treasury shares (see **34.19** Purchase of Own Shares),

- the requirements of (*a*)–(*d*) above need not be complied with if the company cancels all of the shares forthwith after the purchase; and

- if the company does not cancel all of the shares forthwith after the purchase, any share that is so cancelled can be disregarded for those purposes.

Subject to this, where a company holds shares as treasury shares, it must be entered in the register as the member holding those shares.

[*CA 2006, s 124*].

**Index of members**. Every company with more than 50 members must keep an index of the names of the members of the company, unless the register of members is in such a form as to constitute an index. The index must enable the account of each member in the register to be readily found. Any necessary alteration in the index must be made within 14 days of any alteration to the register of members.

[*CA 2006, s 115(1)–(3)*].

**Single member companies**. If a limited company is formed under *CA 2006* with only one member, a statement that the company has only one member must be entered in the company's register of members, together with the name and address of that sole member.

If

- the number of members of a limited company falls to one (or, as the case may be, increases from one to two or more), or

- an unlimited company with only one member becomes a limited company or re-registration

a statement that the company has (or, as the case may be, has ceased to have) one member, and the date on which the event occurred, must at that time be entered in the register of members, together with the name and address of the sole member (or, as the case may be, the former sole member).

[*CA 2006, s 123(1)–(3)*].

**Offences by the company**. If a company makes default in complying with the above provisions relating to particulars to be disclosed, index of members or single member companies, an offence is committed by the company and every officer of the company who is in default. A person guilty of such an offence is liable, on summary conviction, to a fine not exceeding level 3 on the standard scale and, for continued contravention, to a daily default fine not exceeding one-tenth of level 3 on the standard scale. See **29.1** Offences and Legal Proceedings for the standard scale.

[*CA 2006, ss 113(7), (8), 115(5), (6), 123(4), (5)*].

**Share warrants**. Until a share warrant issued by a company is surrendered, the following are deemed to be the particulars required to be entered in the register of members:

- the fact of the issue of the warrant;

- a statement of the shares included in the warrant, distinguishing each share by its number (if it has one); and

- the date of the issue of the warrant.

The bearer of a share warrant may, if the articles of the company so provide, be deemed a member of the company within the meaning of *CA 2006*, either to the full extent or for any purposes defined in the articles.

The company is responsible for any loss incurred by any person by reason of the name of a bearer of a share warrant being entered in the register in respect of the shares specified in it without the warrant being surrendered and cancelled.

See **44.12** that as from May 2015 share warrants to bearer have been abolished.

[*CA 2006, s 122; SBEE 2015, Sch 4 para 23*].

**Removal of entries relating to former members**. An entry relating to a former member of the company may be removed from the register 10 years after the date on which he ceased to be a member (whenever the period of 10 years expired). A copy of any details that were included in the register immediately 6 April 2008 and that are removed from the register must be retained by the company until 6 April 2018 or, if earlier, 20 years after the member concerned ceased to be a member.

[*CA 2006, s 121; SI 2007 No 3495, Art 3, Sch 4 para 2*].

**Shares held in trust.** No notice of any trust (expressed, implied or constructive) must be entered on the register of members of a company registered in England and Wales or Northern Ireland, or be receivable by the Registrar of Companies. [*CA 2006, s 126*]. A company is not, therefore, required to enquire as to whether a transfer is within the powers of the trustees.

**Power of court to rectify register.** If

• any person's name is, without sufficient cause, entered in or omitted from the register of members, or

• there is default or unnecessary delay in entering on the register the fact of any person having ceased to be a member,

that person, the company or any member of the company can apply to the court for rectification of the register. The court may decide any question relating to the title of a person who is a party to the application to have his name entered in or omitted from the register. It may either refuse the application or may order rectification of the register. It may also order payment by the company of any damages sustained by any party aggrieved. Where the company is required to send a list of its members to the Registrar of Companies, the court must, when making an order for rectification of the register, direct such notice to be given to the Registrar of Companies. [*CA 2006, s 125*]. See also *Re Sussex Brick Co* [1904] 1 Ch 598.

**Register to be evidence.** The register of members is *prima facie* evidence of any matters which are directed or authorised by *CA 2006* to be inserted in it except for any matters of which the central register is prima facie evidence by virtue of *CA 2006, s 128H* (see **38.9**).

[*CA 2006, s 127*].

**Time limit for claims arising from entry in register.** *In relation to causes of action arising on or after 6 April 2008*, liability incurred by a company from the making or deletion of an entry in the register of members (or a failure to do so) is not enforceable more than 10 years after the date of the error or failure. This is without prejudice to any lesser period of limitation and, in Scotland, to any rule that the obligation giving rise to the liability prescribes before the expiry of that period. [*CA 2006, s 128*].

*In relation to causes of action arising before 6 April 2008*, the time limit is either 6 April 2018 or 20 years from when the cause of action arose (as provided by *CA 1985 s 52(7)*) whichever expires first. This is similarly without prejudice to any lesser period of limitation and, in Scotland, to any rule that the obligation giving rise to the liability prescribes before the expiry of that period.

[*SI 2007 No 3495, Art 3, Sch 4 para 3*].

**Changes in particulars.** It is the responsibility of members to keep the company informed of any changes in address or name. Any change of address should be signed by the member. In practice, companies frequently send out a standard form for the member to sign and return. On a change of name, more formal documentary proof is required to avoid fraud (eg production of the marriage certificate). On the change of name of a corporate member, a copy of the new certificate of incorporation should be produced. All such amendments have to be approved by the directors.

## 38.9    OPTION TO KEEP MEMBERS' DETAILS ON THE CENTRAL REGISTER

### Right to make an election

An election may be made by giving notice to the Registrar of Companies

- by the subscribers wishing to form a private company under *CA 2006*; or

- by the private company itself once it is formed and registered. In this case, the election is of no effect unless, before it is made all the members of the company have assented to the making of the election, and any overseas branch registers that the company was keeping under *CA 2006, Chapter 3* have been discontinued and all the entries in those registers transferred to the company's register of members in accordance with *CA 2006, s 135.*

If the notice is given by subscribers wishing to form a private company

(i)    it must be given when the documents required to be delivered under *CA 2006, s 9* are delivered to the Registrar of Companies, and

(ii)   it must be accompanied by a statement containing all the information that;

- would be required (in the absence of the notice) to be entered in the company's register of members on incorporation of the company; and

- is not otherwise included in the documents delivered under *CA 2006, s 9.*

If the notice is given by the company, it must be accompanied by

(i)    a statement by the company

- that all the members of the company have assented to the making of the election; and

- if the company was keeping any overseas branch registers, that all such registers have been discontinued and all the entries in them transferred to the company's register of members in accordance with *CA 2006, s 135*; and

(ii)   a statement containing all the information that is required to be contained in the company's register of members as at the date of the notice in respect of matters that are current as at that date.

The company must where necessary update the statement sent under (ii) to ensure that the final version delivered to the Registrar contains all the information that is required to be contained in the company's register of members as at the time immediately before the election takes effect in respect of matters that are current as at that time. This obligation to update the statement includes an obligation to rectify it (where necessary) in consequence of the company's register of members being rectified (whether before or after the election takes effect).

**Offences**

If default is made in complying with the obligation to update the statement an offence is committed by the company, and every officer of the company who is in default. For this purpose a shadow director is treated as an officer of the company. A person guilty of an offence is liable on summary conviction to a fine not exceeding level 3 on the standard scale and, for continued contravention, a daily default fine not exceeding one-tenth of level 3 on the standard scale. See **29.1** Offences and Legal Proceedings for the standard scale.

A reference to matters that are current as at a given date or time is a reference to persons who are members of the company as at that date or time, and any other matters that are current as at that date or time.

**Effective date of election**

An election made under the above takes effect when the notice of election is registered by the Registrar.

The election remains in force until either the company ceases to be a private company, or a notice of withdrawal sent by the company (see below) is registered by the Registrar whichever occurs first.

**Effect of an election on obligations under *CA 2006, Chapter 2* (obligation to keep a register of members)**

The company's obligation to maintain a register of members does not apply with respect to the period when the election is in force. This means that, during that period

- the company must continue to keep a register of members in accordance with *CA 2006, Chapter 2* (a 'historic' register) containing all the information that was required to be stated in that register as at the time immediately before the election took effect; but

- the company does not have to update that register to reflect any changes that occur after that time.

This also applies to the index of members (if the company is obliged to keep an index of members) as it applies to the register of members.

The provisions of *CA 2006, Chapter 2* (including the rights to inspect or require copies of the register and to inspect the index) continue to apply to the historic register and, if applicable, the historic index during the period when the election is in force.

The company must place a note in its historic register

- stating that an election under *CA 2006, s 128B* is in force;

- recording when that election took effect; and

- indicating that up-to-date information about its members is available for public inspection on the central register.

The obligations with respect to a historic register and historic index do not apply in a case where the election was made by subscribers wishing to form a private company.

**Offences by the company**

If a company makes default in complying with the above provisions an offence is committed by the company and every officer of the company who is in default. A person guilty of such an offence is liable, on summary conviction, to a fine not exceeding level 3 on the standard scale and, for continued contravention, to a daily default fine not exceeding one-tenth of level 3 on the standard scale. See **29.1** Offences and Legal Proceedings for the standard scale.

**Duty to notify Registrar of Companies of changes**

When an election is in force under the above provisions, the company must deliver to the Registrar any 'relevant information' that the company would during that period have been obliged under *CA 2006* to enter in its register of members, had the election not been in force.

'Relevant information' means information other than

(i)     the date mentioned in *CA 2006, s 113(2)(b)* (date when person registered as member);

(ii)    the date mentioned in *CA 2006, s 123(3)(b)* (date when membership of limited company increases from one to two or more members); and

(iii)     the dates mentioned in the following provisions, but only in cases where the date to be recorded in the central register is to be the date on which the document containing information of the relevant change is registered by the Registrar

- *CA 2006, s 113(2)(c)* (date when person ceases to be member); and

- *CA 2006, s 123(2)(b)* (date when company becomes single member company).

and in either of these cases the company must, when it delivers information of the relevant change, indicate to the Registrar that, in accordance with *CA 2006, s 1081(1A)*, the date to be recorded in the central register is to be the date on which the document containing that information is registered by the Registrar.

The relevant information must be delivered as soon as reasonably practicable after the company becomes aware of it and, in any event, no later than the time by which the company would have been required to enter the information in its register of members.

**Offences**

If default is made in complying with this obligation an offence is committed by the company, and every officer of the company who is in default. For this purpose a shadow director is treated as an officer of the company. A person guilty of an offence is liable on summary conviction to a fine not exceeding level 3 on the standard scale and, for continued contravention, a daily default fine not exceeding one-tenth of level 3 on the standard scale. See **29.1** Offences and Legal Proceedings for the standard scale.

**Information as to the state of the central register**

When a person inspects or requests a copy of material on the central register relating to a company in respect of which an election is in force, the person may ask the company to confirm that all information that the company is required to deliver to the Registrar has been delivered.

If a company fails to respond to such a request an offence is committed by the company, and every officer of the company who is in default. A person guilty of an offence under this section is liable on summary conviction to a fine not exceeding level 3 on the standard scale.

**Power of court to order company to remedy default or delay**

If

- the name of a person is without sufficient cause included in, or omitted from, information that a company delivers to the Registrar under these provisions concerning its members; or

- default is made or unnecessary delay takes place in informing the Registrar of either the name of a person who is to be a member of the company, or the fact that a person has ceased or is to cease to be a member of the company,

then the following provisions apply.

The person aggrieved, or any member of the company, or the company, may apply to the court for an order requiring the company to deliver to the Registrar the information (or statements) necessary to rectify the position, and where applicable, requiring the Registrar to record under *CA 2006, s 1081(1A)* the date determined by the court.

The court may

- either refuses the application or may make the order and order the company to pay any damages sustained by any party aggrieved.

- on such an application decide either any question relating to the title of a person who is a party to the application to have the person's name included in or omitted from information delivered to the Registrar about the company's members, (whether the question arises between members or alleged members, or between members or alleged members on the one hand and the company on the other hand) or any question necessary or expedient to be decided for rectifying the position.

Nothing in the above affects a person's rights under *CA 2006, s 1095* or *1096* (rectification of register on application to registrar or under court order).

### Central register to be evidence

The central register is prima facie evidence of any matters about which a company is required to deliver information to the Registrar under *CA 2006, Chapter 2A*. This does not apply to information to be included in a statement under *CA 2006, s 128B(5)(b)* (statement accompanying the notice of election) or in any updated statement under *CA 2006, s 128B(6)*.

### Time limits for claims arising from delivery to Registrar

Liability incurred by a company from the delivery to the Registrar of information under *CA 2006, Chapter 2A* or from a failure to deliver any such information is not enforceable more than ten years after the date on which the information was delivered or, as the case may be, the failure first occurred.

This is without prejudice to any lesser period of limitation (and, in Scotland, to any rule that the obligation giving rise to the liability prescribes before the expiry of that period).

### Withdrawing the election

A company may withdraw an election made by or in respect of it. Withdrawal is achieved by giving notice of withdrawal to the Registrar and the withdrawal takes effect when the notice is registered by the Registrar.

The effect of withdrawal is that the company's obligation under *CA 2006, Chapter 2* to maintain a register of members applies from then on with respect to the period going forward. This means that, when the withdrawal takes effect

(i)   the company must enter in its register of members all the information that is required to be contained in that register in respect of matters that are current as at that time;

(ii)  the company must also retain in its register all the information that it was required to keep in a historic register while the election was in force; but

(iii) the company is not required to enter in its register information relating to the period when the election was in force that is no longer current.

The company must place a note in its register of members stating that the election under *CA 2006, s 128B* has been withdrawn, recording when that withdrawal took effect, and indicating that information about its members relating to the period when the election was in force that is no longer current is available for public inspection on the central register.

### Offences

If default is made in complying with this obligation an offence is committed by the company, and every officer of the company who is in default. For this purpose a shadow director is treated as an officer of the company. A person guilty of an offence is liable on summary conviction to a fine not exceeding level 3 on the standard scale and, for continued contravention, a daily default fine not exceeding one-tenth of level 3 on the standard scale. See 29.1 OFFENCES AND LEGAL PROCEEDINGS for the standard scale.

[*CA 2006, ss 128B–J; SBEE 2015, s 94, Sch 5, para 3; SI 2016 No 321, Reg 6*].

### 38.10   Location and inspection of register

**Location of register.** A company's register of members must be kept available for inspection at its registered office or a place specified in the *Companies (Company Records) Regulations 2008 (SI 2008 No 3006)* which provide that the specified place is a place that is situated in a part of the UK in which the company is registered. It must be the same specified place for all relevant provisions of *CA 2006* dealing with inspection and must be notified to the Registrar of Companies as the alternative inspection location.

[*CA 2006, s 114(1)*].

**Notice to Registrar of Companies.** A company must give notice to the Registrar of Companies of the place where its register of members is kept available for inspection and of any change in that place. No such notice is required if the register has, at all times since it came into existence (or, in the case of a register in existence on 1 July 1948 (1 April 1961 in Northern Ireland), at all times since then) been kept available for inspection at the company's registered office.

[*CA 2006, s 114(2)–(4)*].

**Location of index.** The index must be at all times kept available for inspection at the same place as the register of members.

[*CA 2006, s 115(4)*].

**Right to inspect and request copies.** The register and index of members' names must be open to inspection by any member without charge and any other person on payment of a fee The fee is £3.50 per hour or part of an hour during which the right of inspection is exercised. See APPENDIX 3 FEES PAYABLE TO COMPANIES.

Any person may require a copy of a company's register of members, or of any part of it, on payment of such fee as may be prescribed. These are prescribed at a set rate per number of copies and the 'reasonable costs' incurred by the company (see APPENDIX 3 FEES PAYABLE TO COMPANIES)

A person seeking to exercise either of the above rights (ie inspection or copy) must make a request to the company to that effect. The request must contain the following information.

- In the case of an individual, his name and address.

- In the case of an organisation, the name and address of an individual responsible for making the request on behalf of the organisation.

- The purpose for which the information is to be used.

- Whether the information will be disclosed to any other person, and if so

  (i)    where that person is an individual, his name and address;

  (ii)   where that person is an organisation, the name and address of an individual responsible for receiving the information on its behalf; and

  (iii)  the purpose for which the information is to be used by that person.

On receipt of such a request, the company must, within five working days, either comply with the request or apply to the court (and notify the person making the request that it has done so). If, on an application, the court is satisfied that the inspection or copy is not sought for a proper purpose, it must direct the company not to comply with the request. It may also further order that the company's costs (in Scotland, expenses) on the application be paid in whole or in part by the person who made the request (even if he is not a party to the application). Where the court makes such a direction and it appears to the court that the company is (or may be) subject to other requests made for a similar purpose (whether made by the same person or different persons), it may direct that the company is not to comply with any such request. If, on an application, the court does not direct the company not to comply with the request, the company must comply with the request immediately upon the court giving its decision or, as the case may be, the proceedings being discontinued.

[*CA 2006, ss 116, 117*].

In *Fox-Davies v Burberry plc* [2017] EWCA Civ 1129, [2017] All ER (D) 201 (Jul), the Court of Appeal (in a decision handed down in July 2017) upheld a High Court decision that a request made by a tracing agent under *CA 2006, s 116* to inspect or copy a company's register of members was invalid, since it did not contain all information required by the statute and it was made for an improper purpose.

In dismissing the appeal, the Court of Appeal held that a company did not have to comply with a request to inspect or copy the company's register of members which was made (under *CA 2006, s 116*) by a person who was not a member of the company and who ran an agency to trace lost members of public quoted companies. The Court of Appeal held that, in the particular case, the request was invalid, since it did not contain the names and addresses of any individuals with whom the tracing agent was going to share the information, as required by *CA 2006, s 116(4)(d)*.

The court also found that the request had been made for an improper purpose. Two of the judges found that the tracing agent had not provided sufficient information about the terms on which the lost shareholders would be reconnected with the company to enable a proper assessment of the stated purpose to be made. One judge found that the agent's purpose was to extract a commission or fee from traced lost members, whilst not disclosing the asset to which they might be entitled before they agree to pay commission, and that such purpose was not proper.

The court agreed however that, for the purposes of *CA 2006, s 117*, the onus was on the company to show that the purpose was improper. The test of whether a purpose was improper was objective, in that the decision was made by the court on the basis of its evaluation of the purpose. The court also held that:

•   to decide whether a purpose was proper, it might be necessary to look at both the objective and the *means* of achieving that objective;

•   the test was the same for requests by members or non-members; and

•   the test did not depend on whether the request was in the interests of the shareholders.

*Offences in connection with request for or disclosure of information.* It is an offence for a person, when requesting an inspection or copy of a register of members, knowingly or recklessly to make a statement that is misleading, false or deceptive in a material particular. It is also an offence for a person in possession of information obtained in such a way to

•   do anything that results in the information being disclosed to another person, or

•   fail to do anything with the result that the information is disclosed to another person,

knowing or having reason to suspect that person may use the information for a purpose that is not a proper purpose.

## 38.10 Registers

A person guilty of such an offence is liable (i) on conviction on indictment, to imprisonment for a term not exceeding two years or a fine (or both); and (ii) on summary conviction, to imprisonment for a term not exceeding twelve months (six months in Scotland or Northern Ireland) or to a fine not exceeding the statutory maximum (or both). See **29.1 OFFENCES AND LEGAL PROCEEDINGS** for the statutory maximum. [*CA 2006, s 119*].

*Time available for inspection and copying.* See **36.2 RECORDS**.

**Information as to the state of the register and index**. When a person

- inspects the register, or the company provides him with a copy of the register or any part of it, the company must inform him of the most recent date (if any) on which alterations were made to the register and there were no further alterations to be made; and

- inspects the index of members' names, the company must inform him whether there is any alteration to the register that is not reflected in the index.

[*CA 2006, s 120(1), (2)*].

**Offences by company**. If a company

(a)   fails to give notice to the Registrar of Companies of where the register of members is kept available for inspection within 14 days of any change,

(b)   refuses to allow an inspection of the register, or fails to provide a copy, as required above (otherwise than in accordance with a court order), or

(c)   fails to provide the necessary information as to the state of the register or index

an offence is committed by the company and every officer of the company who is in default. A person guilty of such an offence is liable, on summary conviction, to a fine not exceeding level 3 on the standard scale and, for continued contravention under (*a*) or (*b*) above, a daily default fine not exceeding one-tenth of level 3 on the standard scale. See **29.1 OFFENCES AND LEGAL PROCEEDINGS** for the standard scale.

In the case of any refusal or failure under (*b*) above, the court may by order compel an immediate inspection or, as the case may be, direct that the copy required be sent to the person requesting it.

[*CA 2006, ss 114(5), (6), 118, 120(3), (4)*].

## 38.11 Overseas branch registers

A company having a share capital which transacts business in any of the countries or territories listed below may cause to be kept a branch register of members resident there. Such a branch register is known as an '*overseas branch register*' and a reference in any Act or the articles of a company to a 'dominion register' or 'colonial register' are to be read as referring to such an overseas branch register (unless the context requires otherwise).

The countries and territories referred to above are any part of the dominions outside the UK, Channel Islands or Isle of Man, together with

| | | |
|---|---|---|
| Bangladesh | Cyprus | Dominica |
| The Gambia | Ghana | Guyana |
| The Hong Kong Special Administrative Region of the People's Republic of China | India | Ireland |

| | | |
|---|---|---|
| Kenya | Kiribati | Lesotho |
| Malawi | Malaysia | Malta |
| Nigeria | Pakistan | Seychelles |
| Sierra Leone | Singapore | South Africa |
| Sri Lanka | Swaziland | Trinidad and Tobago |
| Uganda | Zimbabwe | |

[*CA 2006, s 129*].

**Notice of opening of overseas branch register**. A company that begins to keep an overseas branch register must give notice to the Registrar of Companies within 14 days of doing so, stating the country or territory in which the register is kept.

[*CA 2006, s 130(1)*].

**Keeping of overseas branch register**. An overseas branch register is regarded as part of the company's register of members ('the main register') and must therefore be kept in the same manner (see **38.8**) unless the Secretary of State provides otherwise by Regulations. Subject to this, a company may by its articles make such provision as it thinks fit as to the keeping of overseas branch registers. [*CA 2006, s 131*].

**Register or duplicate to be kept available for inspection in UK**. A company that keeps an overseas branch register must keep the register, or a duplicate of the register duly entered up from time to time, available for inspection at the place in the UK where the company's main register is kept available for inspection. Any such duplicate is treated for all purposes of *CA 2006* as part of the main register.

[*CA 2006, s 132(1), (2)*].

**Transactions in shares registered in overseas branch register**. Shares registered in an overseas branch register must be distinguished from those registered in the main register and no transaction with respect to such shares may be registered in any other register. An instrument of transfer of a share registered in an overseas branch register

• is regarded as a transfer of property situated outside the UK; and

• unless executed in a part of the UK, is exempt from stamp duty.

[*CA 2006, s 133*].

**Discontinuance of overseas branch register**. A company may discontinue an overseas branch register. If it does so, all the entries in that register must be transferred to some other overseas branch register kept in the same country or territory or to the main register. The company must give notice to the Registrar of Companies of the discontinuance within 14 days.

[*CA 2006, s 135(1)–(3)*].

**Offences**. If default is made in complying with the provisions above relating to

• notice of opening,

• keeping the register or a duplicate available for inspection in the UK, or

• discontinuance

an offence is committed by the company and every officer of the company who is in default. A person guilty of such an offence is liable, on summary conviction, to a fine not exceeding level 3 on the standard scale and, for continued contravention, a daily default fine not exceeding one-tenth of level 3 on the standard scale. See **29.1** OFFENCES AND LEGAL PROCEEDINGS for the standard scale.

## 38.11  Registers

[*CA 2006, ss 130(2), (3), 132(3, (4), 135(4), (5)*].

**Jurisdiction of local courts**. A competent court in a country or territory where an overseas branch register is kept may exercise the same jurisdiction as is exercisable by a court in the UK to rectify the register (see **38.8**) or in relation to a request for inspection or a copy of the register (see **38.10**). The offences of refusing inspection, failing to provide a copy of the register and making a false, misleading or deceptive statement in a request for inspection or a copy (see **38.10**) may be prosecuted summarily before any tribunal having summary criminal jurisdiction in the country or territory where the register is kept.

These provisions on jurisdiction extend only to those countries and territories to which *CA 1985, Sch 14 para 3* (which made similar provision) extended immediately before 1 October 2009. [*CA 2006, s 134*].

## 38.12  REGISTER OF DISCLOSED INTERESTS IN PUBLIC COMPANY SHARES

Automatic disclosure rules are set out in the Transparency Rules made by the FCA (under power given to them by *FSMA 2000*) and notification is to the FCA rather than the company. A company is only therefore required to maintain a register covering disclosures following its own investigations into shareholdings. Any separate part of the register kept by the company before 20 January 2007 relating to investigations must continue to be kept and is treated as part of the register kept for these purposes.

[*SI 2006 No 3428, Sch 5 para 2*].

**Updating the register**. A company which receives information in pursuance of a requirement imposed by it under *CA 2006, s 793* (see **24.2** INTERESTS IN PUBLIC COMPANY SHARES) must, within three days (see below) of receipt of the information, enter in the register

•      the fact that the requirement was imposed and the date on which it was imposed; and

•      the information received in pursuance of the requirement.

The information must be entered against the name of the present holder of the shares in question or, if there is no present holder or the present holder is not known, against the name of the person holding the interest. Entries against each name entered must appear in chronological order.

The company is not, by virtue of anything done for these purposes, affected with notice of, or put upon inquiry as to, the rights of any person in relation to any shares (eg it is not concerned with the existence of any trust over the shares).

[*CA 2006, s 808(1)–(4), (7)*].

**Associated index**. Unless the register kept as above is kept in such a form as itself to constitute an index, the company must keep an index of the names entered in it. It must make any necessary entry or alteration in the index within 10 days (see below) after the date on which any entry or alteration is made in the register. The index must contain, in respect of each name, a sufficient indication to enable the information entered against it to be readily found.

[*CA 2006, s 810(1)–(3)*].

**Reckoning of number of days**. Where the period allowed above for fulfilling an obligation is expressed as a number of days, any day that is a Saturday, Sunday or a bank holiday in the part of the UK in which the company is registered is to be disregarded.

[*CA 2006, s 827*].

**Duty of company ceasing to be public company.** If a company ceases to be a public company, it must continue to keep any register and any associated index until the end of the period of six years after it ceased to be such a company.

[*CA 2006, s 819(1)*].

**Penalties.** If a company fails to

(a)    keep and update the register as required,

(b)    keep and properly update any associated index required, or

(c)    continue to keep any register and any associated index for the required period after ceasing to be a public company

an offence is committed by the company and every officer of the company who is in default. A person guilty of such an offence is liable, on summary conviction, to a fine not exceeding level 3 on the standard scale and, for continued contravention, a daily default fine not exceeding one-tenth of level 3 on the standard scale. See **29.1** OFFENCES AND LEGAL PROCEEDINGS for the standard scale. [*CA 2006, ss 808(5), (6), 810(5), (6), 819(2), (3)*].

**Adjustment of entry relating to share acquisition agreement.** If a person who is identified in the register as being a party to an agreement to which *CA 2006, s 824* applies (certain share acquisition agreements, see **24.1** INTERESTS IN PUBLIC COMPANY SHARES) ceases to be a party to the agreement, he may apply to the company for the inclusion of that information in the register. If the company is satisfied that he has ceased to be a party to the agreement, it must record that information (if not already recorded) in every place where his name appears in the register as a party to the agreement. If an application to the company is refused (otherwise than on the ground that the information has already been recorded), the applicant may apply to the court for an order directing the company to include the information in question in the register. The court may then make such an order if it thinks fit.

[*CA 2006, s 818*].

### 38.13   Location and inspection of register

**Location of register.** The register must be kept available for inspection at the company's registered office or a place specified in Regulations (see **36.2** RECORDS).

[*CA 2006, s 809(1)*].

**Notice to Registrar of Companies.** A company must give notice to the Registrar of Companies within 14 days of the place where the register is kept available for inspection and of any change in that place. No such notice is required if the register has at all times been kept available for inspection at the company's registered office. [*CA 2006, s 809(2), (3)*]. In calculating the 14 days allowed, any day that is not a working day is to be disregarded.

[*CA 2006, s 827*].

**Location of index.** The index must be at all times kept available for inspection at the same place as the register.

[*CA 2006, s 810(4)*].

**Right to inspect and request copies of entries.** The register (and any associated index) must be open to inspection by any person without charge. Any person is also entitled, on request and on payment of such fee as may be prescribed (see **38.3** above for details of prescribed fees and APPENDIX 3 FEES), to be provided with a copy of any entry in the register.

## 38.13 Registers

A person seeking to exercise either of the rights conferred by these provisions (ie inspection or copy) must make a request to the company to that effect. The request must contain the following information.

• In the case of an individual, his name and address.

• In the case of an organisation, the name and address of an individual responsible for making the request on behalf of the organisation.

• The purpose for which the information is to be used.

• Whether the information will be disclosed to any other person, and if so

    (i) where that person is an individual, his name and address;

    (ii) where that person is an organisation, the name and address of an individual responsible for receiving the information on its behalf; and

    (iii) the purpose for which the information is to be used by that person.

Where a company receives such a request, it must

• comply with the request if satisfied that it is made for a proper purpose; or

• refuse the request if not so satisfied and inform the person making the request, stating the reason why it is not satisfied.

A person whose request is refused may then apply to the court. If he does so, he must notify the company which in turn must use its best endeavours to notify any persons whose details would be disclosed if the company were required to comply with the request. If the court is not satisfied that the inspection or copy is sought for a proper purpose, it must direct the company not to comply with the request. Where the court makes such a direction and it appears to the court that the company is (or may be) subject to other requests made for a similar purpose (whether made by the same person or different persons), it may direct that the company is not to comply with any such request. If the court does not direct the company not to comply with the request, the company must comply with the request immediately upon the court giving its decision or, as the case may be, the proceedings being discontinued.

[*CA 2006, ss 811, 812*].

*Offences in connection with request for or disclosure of information*. It is an offence for a person, when requesting an inspection or copy of the register, knowingly or recklessly to make a statement that is misleading, false or deceptive in a material particular. It is also an offence for a person in possession of information obtained in such a way to

• do anything that results in the information being disclosed to another person, or

• fail to do anything with the result that the information is disclosed to another person,

knowing, or having reason to suspect, that person may use the information for a purpose that is not a proper purpose.

A person guilty of such an offence is liable (i) on conviction on indictment, to imprisonment for a term not exceeding two years or a fine (or both); and (ii) on summary conviction, to imprisonment for a term not exceeding twelve months (six months in Scotland or Northern Ireland) or to a fine not exceeding the statutory maximum (or both). See **29.1 OFFENCES AND LEGAL PROCEEDINGS** for the statutory maximum.

[*CA 2006, s 814*].

*Information protected from wider disclosure.* Information about related undertakings must not be made available for inspection if the company is for the time being entitled to any exemption from disclosing the information in the notes to its accounts because to do so would be harmful to the company's business.

[*CA 2006, s 826*].

*Time available for inspection and copying.* See **36.2** RECORDS.

**Penalties.** If a company fails to

(a)     keep a register or any index available for inspection as required,

(b)     notify the Registrar of Companies of the place where the register is kept within the time allowed, or

(c)     allow inspection of the register or provide copies of entries when required to do so (otherwise than in accordance *CA 2006, s 812*)

an offence is committed by the company and every officer of the company who is in default. A person guilty of such an offence is liable, on summary conviction, to a fine not exceeding level 3 on the standard scale and, for continued contravention, a daily default fine not exceeding one-tenth of level 3 on the standard scale. See **29.1** OFFENCES AND LEGAL PROCEEDINGS for the standard scale.

Where (*c*) above applies, the court may by order compel an immediate inspection or, as the case may be, direct that the copy required be sent to the person requiring it.

[*CA 2006, ss 809(4), (5), 810(5), (6), 813; SBEE 2015, s 83*].

## 38.14 Removal of entries from the register

Entries in the register of interests disclosed in shares must not be deleted except in the following circumstances.

•     A company may remove an entry from the register if more than six years have elapsed since the date the entry was made.

•     Where, in pursuance of an obligation imposed by a notice under *CA 2006, s 793* (see **24.2** INTERESTS IN PUBLIC COMPANY SHARES) a person gives to a company the name and address of another person as being interested in shares in the company, that other person may apply to the company for the removal of the entry from the register. If the company is satisfied that the information is incorrect, it must remove the entry. If such an application is refused, the applicant may apply to the court for an order directing the company to remove the entry in question from the register.

If an entry is deleted for any other reason, the company must restore it as soon as reasonably practicable.

**Penalties.** If the company defaults in complying with any of the above requirements, an offence is committed by the company and every officer of the company who is in default. A person guilty of such an offence is liable, on summary conviction, to a fine not exceeding level 3 on the standard scale and, for continued contravention of failure to restore an entry, a daily default fine not exceeding one-tenth of level 3 on the standard scale. See **29.1** OFFENCES AND LEGAL PROCEEDINGS for the standard scale.

[*CA 2006, ss 815–817*].

## 38.15   REGISTER OF CHARGES AND COPIES OF INSTRUMENTS CREATING CHARGES

As from 6 April 2013, *CA 2006, Pt 25, Chs 1* and *2* were repealed and replaced by provisions in the *Companies Act 2006 (Amendment of Part 25) Regulations 2013 (SI 2013 No 600)* which apply to charges created on or after 6 April 2013. The provisions of *CA 2006, Part 25* as they stood immediately before 6 April 2013 continue to apply to charges created before that date. This chapter covers both pre and post 6 April 2013 regulatory provisions

**Charges created before 6 April 2013** — documents available for inspection

Every company must keep available for inspection

(a)   a copy of every instrument creating a charge requiring registration (see **40** REGISTRATION OF CHARGES) (although in the case of a series of uniform debentures a copy of one debenture in the series is sufficient); and

(b)   a register of charges and enter in it

   (i)   all charges specifically affecting property of the company; and

   (ii)   all floating charges on the whole or part of the company's property or undertaking.

The entry in the register under (*b*) above must give

• a short description of the property charged;

• the amount of the charge; and

• except in the case of securities to bearer, the names of the persons entitled to it.

If an officer of the company knowingly and wilfully authorises or permits the omission of an entry required to be made in the register, he commits an offence. A person guilty of such an offence is liable (i) on conviction on indictment, to a fine; and (ii) on summary conviction, to a fine not exceeding the statutory maximum. See **29.1** OFFENCES AND LEGAL PROCEEDINGS for the statutory maximum.

[*CA 2006, ss 875, 876, 890, 891*].

The documents under (*a*) above and the register under (*b*) above must be kept available for inspection at the company's registered office or a place specified in *Regulations* (see **36.2** RECORDS). They must be open to the inspection of any creditor or member of the company without charge and any other person on payment of such fee as may be prescribed (see APPENDIX 3 FEES).

The company must give notice to the Registrar of Companies, within 14 days, of the place at which the documents and register are kept available for inspection and of any change in that place (unless they have at all times been kept at the company's registered office).

If default is made in notifying the Registrar of Companies or an inspection required is refused, an offence is committed by the company and every officer of the company who is in default. A person guilty of such an offence is liable, on summary conviction, to a fine not exceeding level 3 on the standard scale and, for continued contravention, to a daily default fine not exceeding one-tenth of level 3 on the standard scale. See **29.1** OFFENCES AND LEGAL PROCEEDINGS for the standard scale. In the case of refusal of inspection of the register, the court may by order compel an immediate inspection of it.

[*CA 2006, ss 877, 892*].

*Time available for inspection and copying.* See **36.2 Records**.

**Charges created on or after 6 April 2013**

Every company must keep available for inspection

(a)     a copy of every instrument creating a charge capable of registration (see **40 Registration of Charges**) (although in the case of a charge contained in a series of uniform debentures a copy of one of the debentures of the series is sufficient);

(b)     a copy of every instrument effecting any variation or amendment of such a charge; and

(c)     a copy of any other documents which contain the particulars referred to in *CA 2006, s 859D(1)* or the particulars of the property or undertaking charged which are not contained in the instrument creating the charge but are instead contained in those other documents which are referred to or otherwise incorporated into the instrument.

It is sufficient for the purposes of the inspection requirements above if the company keeps a copy of the instrument in the form delivered to the Registrar of Companies under *CA 2006, s 859A(3), 859B(3), 859B(4)* or *859C(3)*.

Where a translation has been delivered to the Registrar of Companies in accordance with *CA 2006, s 1105*, the company must keep a copy of the translation available for inspection.

[*CA 2006, s 859P; SI 2013 No 600, Schedule 1*]

The documents under the above provisions must be kept available for inspection at the company's registered office or a place specified in *Regulations* (see **36.2 Records**). They must be open to the inspection of any creditor or member of the company without charge and any other person on payment of such fee as may be prescribed (see **Appendix 3 Fees**).

The company must give notice to the Registrar of Companies, within 14 days, of the place at which the documents are kept available for inspection and of any change in that place (unless they have at all times been kept at the company's registered office).

If default is made in notifying the Registrar of Companies or an inspection required is refused, an offence is committed by the company and every officer of the company who is in default. A person guilty of such an offence is liable, on summary conviction, to a fine not exceeding level 3 on the standard scale and, for continued contravention, to a daily default fine not exceeding one-tenth of level 3 on the standard scale. See **29.1 Offences and Legal Proceedings** for the standard scale. In the case of refusal of inspection of the register, the court may by order compel an immediate inspection of it.

Where the company and a person wishing to carry out an inspection agree, the inspection may be carried out by electronic means.

[*CA 2006, s 859Q; SI 2013 No 600, Schedule 1*]

### 38.16 REGISTER OF DEBENTURE HOLDERS

A company is not obliged to keep a register of debenture holders but, where it does, the following provisions apply with effect from 6 April 2008 (unless otherwise stated).

**Location of register.** Any register of debenture holders of a company must be kept available for inspection at the company's registered office or a place specified in *Regulations*. The regulations are the *Companies (Company Records) Regulations 2008 (SI 2008 No 3006)*. See **38.10** above and **36.2 Records**).

## 38.16 Registers

*[CA 2006, s 743(1); SI 2007 No 3495, Art 3].*

**Notice to Registrar of Companies.** A company must give notice to the Registrar of Companies within 14 days of the place where the register is kept available for inspection and of any change in that place. No such notice is required if the register has, at all times since it came into existence, been kept available for inspection at the company's registered office. If a company defaults in complying with these requirements, an offence is committed by the company and every officer of the company who is in default. A person guilty of such an offence is liable, on summary conviction, to a fine not exceeding level 3 on the standard scale and, for continued contravention, to a daily default fine not exceeding one-tenth of level 3 on the standard scale. See **29.1 OFFENCES AND LEGAL PROCEEDINGS** for the standard scale.

*[CA 2006, s 743(2)–(5); SI 2007 No 3495, Art 3].*

**Rights to inspect and request copies.** The register, except when 'duly closed', must be open to the inspection of

- a registered debenture holder or any shareholder in the company, without charge; and

- any other person on payment of such fee as may be prescribed (see **APPENDIX 3 FEES**).

A register is '*duly closed*' if it is closed in accordance with provision contained in the articles, debentures, stock certificates (in the case of debenture stock), trust deed or other document securing the debentures or debenture stock. The total period for which a register is closed in any year must not exceed 30 days.

Any person may require a copy of the register, or of any part of it, on payment of such fee as may be prescribed (see **APPENDIX 3 FEES**).

A person seeking to exercise either of the above rights (ie inspection or copy) must make a request to the company to that effect. The request must contain the following information.

- In the case of an individual, his name and address.

- In the case of an organisation, the name and address of an individual responsible for making the request on behalf of the organisation.

- The purpose for which the information is to be used.

- Whether the information will be disclosed to any other person, and if so

  (i)     where that person is an individual, his name and address;

  (ii)    where that person is an organisation, the name and address of an individual responsible for receiving the information on its behalf; and

  (iii)   the purpose for which the information is to be used by that person.

On receipt of such a request, the company must, within five working days, either comply with the request or apply to the court (and notify the person making the request that it has done so). If, on an application the court is satisfied that the inspection or copy is not sought for a proper purpose, it must direct the company not to comply with the request. It may also further order that the company's costs (in Scotland, expenses) on the application be paid in whole or in part by the person who made the request (even if he is not a party to the application). Where the court makes such a direction and it appears to the court that the company is (or may be) subject to other requests made for a similar purpose (whether made by the same person or different persons), it may direct that the company is not to comply with any such request. If, on an application, the court does not direct the company not to comply with the request, the company must comply with the request immediately upon the court giving its decision or, as the case may be, the proceedings being discontinued.

[*CA 2006, s 744, 745*].

*Offences in connection with request for or disclosure of information.* It is an offence for a person, when requesting an inspection or copy of a register of members, knowingly or recklessly to make a statement that is misleading, false or deceptive in a material particular. It is also an offence for a person in possession of information obtained in such a way to

•   do anything that results in the information being disclosed to another person, or

•   fail to do anything with the result that the information is disclosed to another person,

knowing or having reason to suspect that person may use the information for a purpose that is not a proper purpose.

A person guilty of such an offence is liable (i) on conviction on indictment, to imprisonment for a term not exceeding two years or a fine (or both); and (ii) on summary conviction, to imprisonment for a term not exceeding twelve months (six months in Scotland or Northern Ireland) or to a fine not exceeding the statutory maximum (or both). See **29.1** OFFENCES AND LEGAL PROCEEDINGS for the statutory maximum.

[*CA 2006, s 747*].

*Time available for inspection and copying.* See **36.2** RECORDS.

**Offences by company.** If a company refuses to allow an inspection of the register, or fails to provide a copy as required above (otherwise than in accordance with a court order), an offence is committed by every officer of the company who is in default and, in addition in the case of (*a*) above, by the company. A person guilty of such an offence is liable, on summary conviction, to a fine not exceeding level 3 on the standard scale and, for continued contravention, a daily default fine not exceeding one-tenth of level 3 on the standard scale. See **29.1** OFFENCES AND LEGAL PROCEEDINGS for the standard scale. The court may also compel an immediate inspection or, as the case may be, direct that the copy required be sent to the person requiring it.

[*CA 2006, s 746*].

**Duplicate register.** References above to a register of debenture holders include a duplicate of a register of debenture holders that is kept outside the UK or any part of such a register.

[*CA 2006, ss 743(6), 744(6)*].

**Time limit for claims arising from entry in register.** In respect of causes of action arising on or after 6 April 2008, liability incurred by a company from the making or deletion of an entry in the register (or from a failure to do so) is not enforceable more than 10 years after the date on which the entry was made or deleted or, as the case may be, the failure first occurred. This is without prejudice to any lesser period of limitation (and, in Scotland, to any rule that the obligation giving rise to the liability prescribes before the expiry of that period). [*CA 2006, s 748; SI 2007 No 3495, Art 3*]. The time limit for causes of action arising before 6 April 2008 is

•   10 years after 6 April 2008, or

•   20 years from the date when the cause of action arose,

whichever expires first. This is without prejudice to any lesser period of limitation (and, in Scotland, to any rule that the obligation giving rise to the liability prescribes before the expiry of that period).

## 38.16    Registers

[*SI 2007 No 3495, Sch 4 para 23*].

**Form in which register to be kept.** The register can be kept in hard copy or electronic form. With effect from 1 October 2009, any provision of an instrument made by a company before 12 February 1979 that requires a register of holders of the company's debentures to be kept in hard copy form is to be read as requiring it to be kept in hard copy or electronic form.

[*CA 2006, s 1135(5)*].

## 38.17  REGISTER OF DIRECTORS' INTERESTS

**With effect from 6 April 2007**, a company is no longer required to keep a register of directors' interests. [*CA 2006, s 1177*].

## 38.18  REGISTER OF PEOPLE WITH SIGNIFICANT INTERESTS

Provisions which came into force on 6 April 2016 in the *Small Business, Enterprise and Employment Act 2015 (SBEE 2015) (s 81 and Sch 3)* introduced *CA 2006, Part 21A* and require certain companies (see below) to keep a register of people who have significant control over the company ('a PSC register') and also to elect to keep such information on the central register kept by the Registrar of Companies (see **38.2**). The primary legislation has been supported by the *Register of People with Significant Control Regulations 2016, SI 2016/339* (the '*PSC Regulations*').

These provisions have been further amended by the *Information about People with Significant Control (Amendment) Regulations 2017, SI 2017/693*, which came into force on 26 June 2017 (the '*2017 PSC Regulations*'). Companies House has also issued various items of guidance available on Gov.uk, including '*Guidance for Companies, LLPs and ESPs*', referred to below.

In short, the *2017 PSC Regulations*:

*   widen the scope of companies required to comply with this regime;

*   insert 14-day time limits for companies to comply with the duties to keep information up to date (*CA 2006, s 790E(5)*), and enter required particulars and additional matters in the company's PSC register (*CA 2006, s 790M*); and

*   add a new obligation that a company must give notice to the registrar of changes to the company's PSC register.

Companies House/Department for Business, Energy and Industrial Strategy have issued a series of guidance documents which are available on Gov.uk; these include the document entitled '*Register of People with Significant Control – Guidance for Registered and Unregistered Companies, Societates Europeae, Limited Liability Partnerships and Eligible Scottish Partnerships*', referred to below. The reader is encouraged to consult these documents for further detailed guidance on the procedures to be followed.

**Companies to which the provisions apply**

These provisions apply to UK incorporated companies limited by shares or guarantee (including community interest companies – see **10 COMMUNITY INTEREST COMPANIES**), limited liability partnerships, unlimited companies, unregistered companies, and dormant companies.

They do *not* currently apply to other 'non-corporate' entities, such as English limited partnerships, co-operative or community benefit societies, charitable trusts, or charitable incorporated organisations.

The provisions apply to all UK companies, other than those admitted to trading on a regulated market in the UK or an EEA state (other than the UK), or on specified markets listed in *Schedule 1* to the *PSC Regulations*. This is a departure from the previous position whereby companies that are subject to the FCA's Disclosure Guidance and Transparency Rule 5 (DTR 5) did not need to keep a register.

Hence the regime now applies to companies listed on prescribed markets such as AIM or the NEX Exchange Growth Market. Overseas entities operating in the UK might be subject to requirements in their home country; however they are not subject to the requirements of *CA 2006, Pt 21A* to hold a register.

These companies must collect information about their PSCs from 26 June 2017, and must keep a PSC register from 24 July 2017.

Thereafter they must update PSC information on their own registers within 14 days, and must provide the information to Companies House within a further 14 days.

**Where should the PSC register be kept?**

A company must record its PSC information in two different forms of register:

• the *central* register, maintained by Companies House; and

• the company's *own* register, usually maintained at the company's registered office.

[*CA 2006, s 790N*].

Since 30 June 2016, private limited companies may choose to keep PSC information on the central register rather than maintaining their own PSC register. Notably, if the information is only kept centrally, it will reveal the full date of birth of the PSCs (which will not appear if the company maintains its own PSC register). Individuals may however apply to have such information shielded from disclosure save in exceptional circumstances.

**Persons with "significant control" to which the provisions apply**

A person with significant control is an individual who meets one or more of the following conditions in relation to the company. The person:

• holds, directly or indirectly, more than 25% of the shares in the company;

• holds, directly or indirectly, more than 25% of the voting rights in the company;

• holds the right, directly or indirectly, to appoint or remove a majority of the board of directors of the company;

• has the right to exercise, or actually exercises, significant influence or control over the company; or

• has the right to exercise, or actually exercises, significant influence or control over the activities of a trust or firm. and the trustees of a trust or the members of a firm that, under the law by which it is governed, is not a legal person meet any of the other specified conditions (in their capacity as such) in relation to the company or would do so if they were individuals.

Individuals with significant control are either "registrable" or "non-registrable". They are non-registrable if they do not "hold any interest in the company" except through one or more legal entities over each of which they have significant control and

(i) as respects any shares or right in the company which they hold indirectly by virtue of having a majority stake in a legal entity which holds the shares or right directly, the legal entity through which the shares or right are held is a relevant legal entity in relation to the company; and

(ii)  as respects any shares or right in the company which they hold indirectly by virtue of a majority stake in a legal entity (L) that is part of a chain of legal entities that includes L, at least one of the legal entities in the chain is a relevant legal entity in relation to the company.

A relevant legal entity is either "registrable" or "non-registrable". It is "non-registrable" if it does not "hold any interest in the company" except through one or more other legal entities over each of which it has significant control and

(i)  as respects any shares or right in the company which it holds indirectly by virtue of having a majority stake in a legal entity which holds the shares or right directly, the legal entity through which the shares or right are held is also a relevant legal entity in relation to the company; and

(ii)  as respects any shares or right in the company which it holds indirectly by virtue of a majority stake in a legal entity (L) that is part of a chain of legal entities that includes L, at least one of the legal entities in the chain is also a relevant legal entity in relation to the company.

Whether an individual or a relevant legal entity "holds an interest in a company" or holds that interest through another legal entity is determined in accordance with *CA 2006, Sch 1A, Part 2* which specifies the circumstances in which both apply and whether someone has significant control over that other legal entity is determined in accordance with *CA 2006, Sch 1A, Part 1(2) and (3)* ie that the person or legal entity holds, directly or indirectly, more than 25% of the shares in the company or more than 25% of the voting rights in the company.

A "legal entity" is a body corporate or a firm that is a legal person under the law by which it is governed and in relation to a company, a legal entity is a "relevant legal entity" ("RLE") if

•  it would have come within the definition of a person with significant control over the company if it had been an individual; and

•  it is subject to its own disclosure requirements.

A legal entity is "subject to its own disclosure requirements" if

•  *CA 2006, Part 21A* applies to it (whether by virtue of *CA 2006, s 790B* or another enactment that extends the application of this Part);

•  it is a DTR5 issuer;

•  it is of a description specified in regulations under *CA 2006, s 790B* (or that section as extended); or

•  it is of a description specified by the Secretary of State by regulations made under *CA 2006, s 790C, para 7.*

[*CA 2006, s 790C(2), (3), (4), (5), (6), (7), (8), (9); SBEE 2015, s 81, Sch 3; SI 2015 No 2029, Reg 4; SI 2016 No 136, Reg 2*].

## 38.19  Obligation to keep a PSC register and required particulars

A company to which *CA 2006, Part 21A* applies must keep a register of people with significant control over the company but only those who are "registrable" as defined above.

The "required particulars" of any individual with significant control over the company who is "registrable" in relation to the company must be entered in the register once all the required particulars of that individual have been confirmed.

The company must not enter any of the individual's particulars in the register until they have all been confirmed (see below for definition), but the required particulars of any entity that is a registrable relevant legal entity in relation to the company must be noted in the register once the company becomes aware of the entity's status as such. If the company becomes aware of a relevant change (within the meaning of *CA 2006, s 790E*) with respect to a registrable person or registrable relevant legal entity whose particulars are stated in the register

- details of the change and the date on which it occurred must be entered in the register; but

- in the case of a registrable person, the details and date must not be entered there until they have all been confirmed.

Particulars of any individual with significant control over the company who is "non-registrable" in relation to the company must not be entered in the register.

A person's required particulars, and the details and date of any relevant change with respect to a person, are considered for the purposes of this section to have been "confirmed" if

- the person supplied or confirmed them to the company (whether voluntarily, pursuant to a duty imposed by *CA 2006, Part 21A* or otherwise);

- another person did so but with that person's knowledge; or

- they were included in a statement of initial significant control delivered to the Registrar of Companies under *CA 2006, s 9* by subscribers wishing to form the company.

In the case of someone who was a registrable person or a registrable relevant legal entity in relation to the company on its incorporation

- the date to be entered in the register as the date on which the individual became a registrable person, or the entity became a registrable relevant legal entity, is to be the date of incorporation; and

- in the case of a registrable person, that particular is deemed to have been "confirmed".

For the purposes of *CA 2006, Part 21A* provisions if a person's usual residential address is the same as his or her service address, the entry for him or her in the register may state that fact instead of repeating the address (but this does not apply in a case where the service address is stated to be "The company's registered office").

Nothing in *CA 2006, s 126* (trusts not to be entered on register) affects what may be entered in a company's PSC register or is receivable by the Registrar of Companies in relation to people with significant control over a company (even if they are members of the company).

## Offences

If a company makes default in complying with these provisions an offence is committed by the company, and every officer of the company who is in default. A person guilty of an offence is liable on summary conviction to a fine not exceeding level 3 on the standard scale and, for continued contravention, a daily default fine not exceeding one-tenth of level 3 on the standard scale. (See **29.1** Offences and Legal Proceedings for the standard scale.)

[*CA 2006, s 790M; SBEE 2015, Sch 3; SI 2016 No 2029, Reg 4*].

## 38.19　Registers

### Required particulars of "registrable" individuals etc

(a)　The "required particulars" of an individual who is a registrable person are

- name;

- a service address;

- the country or state (or part of the United Kingdom) in which the individual is usually resident;

- nationality;

- date of birth;

- usual residential address;

- the date on which the individual became a registrable person in relation to the company in question;

- the nature of his or her control over that company; and

- if, in relation to that company, restrictions on using or disclosing any of the individual's PSC particulars are in force under regulations made under *CA 2006, s 790ZG* (Regulations requiring the Registrar of Companies or a company from using or disclosing PSC particulars), that fact.

(b)　In the case of a corporation sole, a government or government department of a country or territory or part of a country or territory, an international organisation whose members include two or more countries or territories (or their governments) or a local authority or local government body in the UK or elsewhere the "required particulars" are

- name;

- principal office;

- the legal form of the person and the law by which it is governed;

- the date on which it became a registrable person in relation to the company in question; and

- the nature of its control over the company.

(c)　The "required particulars" of a registrable relevant legal entity are

- corporate or firm name;

- registered or principal office;

- the legal form of the entity and the law by which it is governed;

- if applicable, the register of companies in which it is entered (including details of the state) and its registration number in that register;

- the date on which it became a registrable relevant legal entity in relation to the company in question; and

- the nature of its control over that company.

[*CA 2006, s 790K; SBEE 2015, Sch 3; SI 2016 No 2029, Reg 4*].

## Duty to supply and update information

*Duty to investigate—'reasonable steps'*

The company must:

- take 'reasonable steps' to find out if there is anyone who is a registrable PSC or RLE in relation to itself; and

- if there is such an entity, identify it/them. This entails serving a notice on anyone whom the company knows or has reasonable cause to believe to be a PSC, and requiring the addressee to confirm or correct the particulars of the notice.

[*CA 2006, s 790D*].

*What are reasonable steps?*

As above, a company must take reasonable steps to identify its PSCs or registrable RLEs:

- The company should first consider all the documents and information already available to it to identify if it might have a PSC.

- It should consider interests held by individuals, legal entities and trusts or firms (partnerships without legal personality).

- The company must consider if it knows about any joint arrangements or rights held through a variety of means which might ultimately be controlled by the same person.

- The company should then pursue certain lines of enquiry depending on which of the five Conditions indicating a potential PSC (as set out at **38.18** above) is relevant in the particular case.

The Companies House/Department for Business, Energy and Industrial Strategy document, 'Register of People with Significant Control - Guidance for Registered and Unregistered Companies, Societates Europeae, Limited Liability Partnerships and Eligible Scottish Partnerships' sets out at page 15 a detailed table which summarises what constitutes the key (reasonable) steps which a company should take when investigating its PSCs and RLEs, based on these five conditions. The reader is encouraged to consult this table for further guidance.

| Condition | Steps to be taken |
|---|---|
| 1 Directly or indirectly owning more than 25% of the shares | Review the register of members, articles of association and statement of capital to identify whether anyone holds more than 25% of the shares (note that under paragraph 7.1 of the Guidance for Companies, LLPs and ESPs a company without shares should consider the position relating to profit or capital). |
| 2 Directly or indirectly holding more than 25% of the voting rights | Review the register of members and articles of association to identify whether anyone holds more than 25% of the voting rights. Identify any shareholder agreements which might result in shareholdings of more than 25% and consider whether voting patterns suggest some parties (for example members of the same family) might be acting together. |
| 3 Directly or indirectly holding the right to appoint or remove the majority of directors | Review any provisions in the articles of association or other covenants or agreements which concern the appointment or removal of directors holding the majority of votes at board level. |

| 4 | Otherwise having the right to exercise, or actually exercising, *significant influence or control* | Consider whether anyone else who does not meet one or more of Conditions 1–3 has significant influence or control over the way the company is run, irrespective of any formal role. Statutory guidance provides guidance on the meaning of significant influence or control. Regard must be had to this guidance when considering whether a person meets this Condition. |
| 5 | Where a trust or firm would satisfy one or more of the first four Conditions if it were an individual. Any individual holding the right to exercise, or actually exercising, significant influence or control over the activities of that trust or firm. | Consider whether anyone who meets the first four Conditions is a trust or firm. Where this is the case, the trustees would be entered on the PSC register and shown as meeting whichever of Conditions 1–4 apply. Then consider whether anyone has significant influence or control over the activities of that trust or firm. The Statutory PSC Guidance for Companies provides guidance on the meaning of significant influence or control over the activities of a trust or firm. Regard must be had to this guidance when considering whether a person meets this Condition. |

### *Duty to confirm information*

Once the company has determined that it has a PSC, it must ensure it has the relevant information to enter on the PSC register. See under *Information notices* below.

Information about *individuals* must be confirmed before it is put on the PSC register.

[*CA 2006, s 790D*].

If the company has determined that it has a registrable RLE, it must also make sure that it has the information about that legal entity to enter it on the PSC register. However information about a registrable *RLE*, unlike a PSC, does *not* need to be *confirmed* before it can go on the PSC register.

### *Confirming information*

Information may be treated as being confirmed if:

• the PSC supplied the information;

• the information was provided with the knowledge of the PSC;

• the company asked the PSC to confirm the information was correct, and they replied that it was so; or

• the company holds previously confirmed information and has no reason to believe it has changed.

### *Service of information notices*

If the company:

• lacks the information it needs; or

• in the case of a PSC, lacks confirmed information,

it must serve notice on the individual or legal entity.

It may serve such notice by post or email, and must keep a record of its communications.

[*CA 2006, s 790D*].

In general, investigating entities must serve a notice seeking details of any suspected change to PSC information *'as soon as reasonably practicable'*. Since 26 June 2017, the company must send such notice within 14 days of becoming aware of the change.

- If addressed to *an individual*, the notice ('S790D Notice') must require the addressee to state whether or not he or she is a registrable person in relation to the company, and, if so, to confirm or correct any particulars of his or hers that are included in the notice, and supply any that are missing.

- If addressed to *a legal entity*, the notice ('S790D Notice') must require the addressee to state whether or not it is a registrable relevant legal entity in relation to the company, and, if so, to confirm or correct any of its particulars that are included in the notice, and supply any that are missing.

The company may also give notice to a person where the company knows, or has reasonable cause to believe, that that person knows the identity of a potential PSC or RLE, or knows the identity of someone likely to have that knowledge. Such notice should ask the addressee to state whether or not any particulars being supplied are being supplied with the knowledge of the persons concerned.

A person to whom such a notice is given is not required by that notice to disclose any information in respect of which a claim to legal professional privilege could be maintained in legal proceedings.

The notice must state that the addressee is to comply with the notice within one month.

A company is not required to take steps or give notice under *s 790D* if:

- the company has already been informed of the person's status as a registrable person or registrable relevant legal entity in relation to it;

- the company has been supplied with all the particulars; and

- in the case of a registrable person, the information and particulars were provided either by the person concerned or with his or her knowledge.

[*CA 2006, s 790D*].

*Duty of company to update information*

A company must enter newly confirmed information on its PSC register within 14 days and must file such information with Companies House within a further 14 days.

The company must keep its PSC information up to date, including by serving further investigation notices on any relevant person or entity if it knows or has reasonable cause to believe that a 'relevant change' has occurred.

*Updating the company's own maintained PSC register*

A company must enter updated information on its own PSC register within 14 days if it:

- has been informed of the change;

- has all of the updated information needed; and

- has confirmed that updated information if it relates to a PSC and has not been provided by the PSC or with his or her knowledge.

The above applies even if the company does not have all the information it needs about any of its other PSCs or registrable RLEs. It should continue to take reasonable steps to identify those PSCs or registrable RLEs and may be required to record additional matters during that time.

## 38.19    Registers

[*CA 2006, s 790E*].

If the company knows or has reason to believe a relevant change (see below) has occurred but needs more information, then it must serve notice as soon as practicable, and in any case within 14 days.

In such notice, the company must:

•    ask the individual or legal entity to confirm that the change has occurred;

•    give the date that the change occurred; and

•    give the correct and up to date information.

The individual or legal entity must respond to the notice within one month. If they do not, the company must not enter incomplete or suspected information in the register.

[*CA 2006, s 790E*].

A 'relevant change' for this purpose means that:

•    the person or entity ceases to be a registrable person or entity in relation to the company; or

•    any other change occurs as a result of which the particulars stated for the person in the PSC register are incorrect or incomplete.

The notice must require the addressee to:

•    confirm whether or not the change has occurred;

•    if so, state the date of the change; and

•    confirm or correct the particulars included in the notice, and supply any that are missing from the notice.

*Filing the information on the central register*

Since 26 June 2017:

•    a company must enter any changes to PSC information on its own PSC register within 14 days; and

•    within a further 14 days, the company must then file the information at Companies House, where it will be entered on the central register.

As from 24 July 2017, the above also applies to those unregistered companies and companies on prescribed markets which fall within the scope of the PSC regime for the first time.

Failure to comply with these requirements is a criminal offence.

Companies which have elected to keep their PSC register at Companies House need only file confirmed information with Companies House within 14 days.

*Confirming the content of the central public register (the confirmation statement)*

As from 26 June 2017 (24 July 2017 for new scope entities), companies must confirm their information with Companies House at least once a year via a confirmation statement.

Where individuals or entities have ceased to be a PSC or RLE, the information about them must nonetheless be kept on the company's register for ten years.

*Recording information in the register*

*CA 2006, s 790K* sets out the particulars required as to the nature of control to be recorded on the PSC register (see above).

[*CA 2006, s 790K*].

**38.20    Inspection and copying of PSC register**

**Register to be kept available for inspection.** A company's PSC register must be kept available for inspection at its registered office, or at a place specified in regulations under *CA 2006, s 1136*.

A company must give notice to the Registrar of Companies of the place where its PSC register is kept available for inspection and of any change in that place. No such notice is required if the register has, at all times since it came into existence, been kept available for inspection at the company's registered office.

**Offences**

If a company makes default for 14 days in complying with the above an offence is committed by the company, and every officer of the company who is in default. A person guilty of such an offence is liable on summary conviction to a fine not exceeding level 3 on the standard scale and, for continued contravention, a daily default fine not exceeding one-tenth of level 3 on the standard scale. See **29.11** Offences and Legal Proceedings for the standard scale.

**Rights to inspect and require copies.** Subject to the provisions of *CA 2006, s 790ZF* (protection of usual residential addresses) and *s 790ZG* (protection of certain other materials to be made by Regulations), a company's PSC register must be open to the inspection of any person without charge. Any person may require a copy of a company's PSC register, or any part of it, on payment of such fee as may be prescribed. A person seeking to exercise either of the above rights must make a request to the company to that effect and the request must contain the following information

(a)    in the case of an individual, his or her name and address;

(b)    in the case of an organisation, the name and address of an individual responsible for making the request on behalf of the organisation; and

(c)    the purpose for which the information is to be used.

Where a company receives a request to inspect or copy the register, it must within five working days either comply with the request, or apply to the court. If it applies to the court, it must notify the person making the request.

If on such an application

•    the court is satisfied that the inspection or copy is not sought for a proper purpose it must direct the company not to comply with the request, and it may further order that the company's costs (in Scotland, expenses) on the application be paid in whole or in part by the person who made the request, even if that person is not a party to the application; and

•    the court does not direct the company not to comply with the request, the company must comply with the request immediately upon the court giving its decision or, as the case may be, the proceedings being discontinued.

If the court makes such a direction and it appears to the court that the company is or may be subject to other requests made for a similar purpose (whether made by the same person or different persons), it may direct that the company is not to comply with any such request. The order must contain such provision as appears to the court appropriate to identify the requests to which it applies.

## 38.20    Registers

### Offences

If an inspection required is refused or default is made in providing a copy required under the above, otherwise than in accordance with an order of the court, an offence is committed by the company, and every officer of the company who is in default. A person guilty of such an offence is liable on summary conviction to a fine not exceeding level 3 on the standard scale and, for continued contravention, a daily default fine not exceeding one-tenth of level 3 on the standard scale. In the case of any such refusal or default the court may by order compel an immediate inspection or, as the case may be, direct that the copy required be sent to the person requesting it.

It is an offence for a person knowingly or recklessly to make, in a request for inspection or copies, a statement that is misleading, false or deceptive in a material particular.

It is an offence for a person in possession of information obtained by exercise of either of the rights conferred by the above to do anything that results in the information being disclosed to another person, or to fail to do anything with the result that the information is disclosed to another person, knowing, or having reason to suspect, that person may use the information for a purpose that is not a proper purpose.

A person guilty of an offence under this section is liable on conviction on indictment, to imprisonment for a term not exceeding two years or a fine (or both) or on summary conviction in England and Wales, to imprisonment for a term not exceeding 12 months or to a fine (or both) ,and in Scotland, to imprisonment for a term not exceeding 12 months or to a fine not exceeding the statutory maximum (or both) and in Northern Ireland, to imprisonment for a term not exceeding six months or to a fine not exceeding the statutory maximum (or both).

### Information as to state of register

Where a person inspects the PSC register, or the company provides a person with a copy of the register or any part of it, the company must inform the person of the most recent date (if any) on which alterations were made to the register and whether there are further alterations to be made.

If a company fails to provide that information an offence is committed by the company, and every officer of the company who is in default. A person guilty of an offence under this section is liable on summary conviction to a fine not exceeding level 3 on the standard scale.

[*CA 2006, ss 790N–790T; SBEE 2015, Sch 3; SI 2016 No 2029, Reg 4*].

## 38.21   Duty to investigate and obtain information

A company which is obliged to keep a PSC register (the "company") must

- take reasonable steps to find out if there is anyone who is a registrable person or a registrable relevant legal entity in relation to the company, and if so, to identify them; and

- must give notice to anyone whom it knows or has reasonable cause to believe to be a registrable person or a registrable relevant legal entity in relation to it.

But the company is not required to take steps or give notice with respect to a registrable person or registrable relevant legal entity if the company has already been informed of the person's status as a registrable person or registrable relevant legal entity in relation to it, and been supplied with all the particulars, and in the case of a registrable person, the information and particulars were provided either by the person concerned or with his or her knowledge.

The notice, if addressed to an individual or legal entity, must require the addressee to state whether or not he or she is a registrable person or registrable legal entity (as the case may be) in relation to the company and, if so, to confirm or correct any particulars of his or hers or its that are included in the notice, and supply any that are missing.

The company may also give notice to a person if it knows or has reasonable cause to believe that the person knows the identity of (including knowing information from which that person can be identified) any of the following

• any registrable person in relation to the company;

• any relevant legal entity in relation to the company;

• any entity which would be a relevant legal entity in relation to the company but for the fact that *CA 2006, s 790C(6)(b)* (company subject to its own disclosure requirements) does not apply in respect of it; or

• knows the identity of someone likely to have that knowledge.

Such a notice

(a)   may require the addressee to state whether or not the addressee knows the identity of

• any person who falls within subsection (6); or

• any person likely to have that knowledge; and

if so, to supply any particulars of theirs that are within the addressee's knowledge, and state whether or not the particulars are being supplied with the knowledge of each of the persons concerned; and

(b)   must state that the addressee is to comply with the notice by no later than the end of the period of one month beginning with the date of the notice.

"Particulars" means

(i)   in the case of a registrable person or a registrable relevant legal entity, the required particulars (see **38.19**); and

(ii)   in any other case, any particulars that will allow the person to be contacted by the company.

A person to whom such notice is given is not required by that notice to disclose any information in respect of which a claim to legal professional privilege (in Scotland, to confidentiality of communications) could be maintained in legal proceedings.

[*CA 2006, s 790D; SBEE 2015, Sch 3; SI 2016 No 2029, Reg 4*].

**Company's duty to keep information up to date**

If particulars of a registrable person or registrable relevant legal entity are stated in a company's PSC register, the company must give notice to the person or entity if the company knows or has reasonable cause to believe that a relevant change has occurred.

In the case of a registrable person or registrable legal entity, a "relevant change" occurs if

• the person or the entity ceases to be a registrable person or registrable legal entity in relation to the company; or

• any other change occurs as a result of which the particulars stated for the person or the entity in the PSC register are incorrect or incomplete.

The company must give the notice as soon as reasonably practicable after it learns of the change or first has reasonable cause to believe that the change has occurred and the notice must require the addressee to confirm whether or not the change has occurred, and if so

- to state the date of the change; and

- to confirm or correct the particulars included in the notice, and supply any that are missing from the notice.

The notice must state that the addressee is to comply with the notice by no later than the end of the period of one month beginning with the date of the notice.

A company is not required to give such notice if the company has already been informed of the relevant change, and in the case of a registrable person, that information was provided either by the person concerned or with his or her knowledge.

**Offences**

If a company fails to comply with a duty to take steps or give notice, an offence is committed by the company, and every officer of the company who is in default. A person guilty of an offence under this section is liable on conviction on indictment, to imprisonment for a term not exceeding two years or a fine (or both) ,on summary conviction in England and Wales, to imprisonment for a term not exceeding 12 months or a fine (or both),in Scotland, to imprisonment for a term not exceeding 12 months or to a fine not exceeding the statutory maximum (or both) and in Northern Ireland, to imprisonment for a term not exceeding six months or to a fine not exceeding the statutory maximum (or both). See **29.11** Offences and Legal proceedings for the statutory maximum.

[*CA 2006, ss 790E, 790F; SBEE 2015, Sch 3; SI 2016 No 2029, Reg 4*].

**Enforcement of disclosure**

If a notice under either of the above provisions is served by a company on a person who has a relevant interest in the company, and the person fails to comply with that notice within the time specified in it, the company may give the person a notice (a "warning notice") informing the person that it is proposing to issue the person with a notice (a "restrictions notice") with respect to the relevant interest. A restrictions notice is issued on a person by sending the notice to the person.

The company may issue the restrictions notice if, by the end of the period of one month beginning with the date on which the warning notice was given the person has not complied with the notice and the company has not been provided with a valid reason sufficient to justify the person's failure to comply with the notice.

In deciding whether to issue a restrictions notice, the company must have regard to the effect of the notice on the rights of third parties in respect of the "relevant interest" and for these purposes a person has a relevant interest in a company if the person holds any shares in the company or holds any voting rights in the company, or holds the right to appoint or remove any member of the board of directors of the company.

**Effect of restrictions notice**

The effect of a restrictions notice is as follows

- any transfer of the interest or agreement to transfer the interest (unless it is a court approved transfer) or to transfer any associated right (otherwise than in a liquidation) (unless it is a court approved transfer) is void;

- no rights are exercisable in respect of the interest;

- no shares may be issued in right of the interest or in pursuance of an offer made to the interest-holder; and

- except in a liquidation, no payment may be made of sums due from the company in respect of the interest, whether in respect of capital or otherwise.

An "associated" right is a right to be issued with any shares issued in right of the relevant interest, or a right to receive payment of any sums due from the company in respect of the relevant interest.

## Protection of third-party rights

The court may give a direction if, on application by any person aggrieved, the court is satisfied that a restrictions notice issued by the company unfairly affects the rights of third parties in respect of the relevant interest. The direction

- is given for the purpose of protecting those third-party rights;

- is a direction that certain acts will not constitute a breach of the restrictions placed on the relevant interest by the restrictions notice; and

- may be given subject to such terms as the court thinks fit.

An order containing a direction must specify the acts that will not constitute a breach of the restrictions, and may confine the direction to cases where those acts are done by persons, or for purposes, described in the order.

## Offences

A person commits an offence if the person does of the following knowing that the interest is subject to restrictions.

The things are

- exercising or purporting to exercise any right to dispose of a relevant interest;

- exercising or purporting to exercise any right to dispose of any right to be issued with a relevant interest; or

- voting in respect of a relevant interest (whether as holder of the interest or as proxy) or appointing a proxy to vote in respect of a relevant interest.

A person who has a relevant interest that the person knows to be subject to restrictions commits an offence if the person

- knows a person to be entitled (apart from the restrictions) to vote in respect of the interest, whether as holder or as proxy;

- does not know the person to be aware of the fact that the interest is subject to restrictions; and

- fails to notify the person of that fact.

A person commits an offence if the person

- either has a relevant interest that the person knows to be subject to restrictions or is entitled to an associated right; and

- enters in that capacity into an agreement that is void by virtue of the above provisions.

If shares in a company are issued in contravention of a restriction imposed by virtue of a restrictions notice an offence is committed by the company, and every officer of the company who is in default. A person guilty of such an offence is liable on conviction on indictment, to a fine, on summary conviction in England and Wales, to a fine or in Scotland or Northern Ireland, to a fine not exceeding the statutory maximum.

### Relaxation of restrictions

An application may be made to the court by the company in question or by any person aggrieved for an order directing that the relevant interest cease to be subject to restrictions.

The court must not make an order under this paragraph unless it is satisfied that the information required by the notice has been disclosed to the company and no unfair advantage has accrued to any person as a result of the earlier failure to make that disclosure, or the relevant interest is to be transferred for valuable consideration and the court approves the transfer.

An order made by the court may continue, in whole or in part, the restrictions so far as they relate to a right acquired or offer made before the transfer and where any restrictions continue in force, an application may be made for an order directing that the relevant interest cease to be subject to those restrictions, and the provision restricting the court from making an order (above) does not apply in relation to the making of such an order.

### Orders for sale

The court may order that the relevant interest subject to restrictions be sold subject to the court's approval as to the sale. An application for such an order may only be made by the company in question. If the court makes an order, it may make such further order relating to the sale or transfer of the interest as it thinks fit.

An application for such further order may be made by the company in question, by the person appointed by or in pursuance of the order to affect the sale, or by any person with an interest in the relevant interest.

On making either of the above orders the court may order that the applicant's costs (in Scotland, expenses) be paid out of the proceeds of sale and where such costs order is made, the applicant is entitled to payment of those costs (or expenses) out of the proceeds before any person receives any part of the proceeds of sale.

If a relevant interest is sold in pursuance of such a court order, the proceeds of the sale, less the costs of the sale, must be paid into court for the benefit of those who are beneficially interested in the relevant interest and a person who is beneficially interested in the relevant interest may apply to the court for the whole or part of those proceeds to be paid to that person.

On such an application, the court must order the payment to the applicant of the whole of the proceeds of sale together with any interest on the proceeds, or if another person was also beneficially interested in the relevant interest at the time of the sale, such proportion of the proceeds (and any interest) as the value of the applicant's interest bears to the total value of the relevant interest.

### Company's power to withdraw restrictions notice

A company that issues a person with a restrictions notice must by notice withdraw the restrictions notice if

- it is satisfied that there is a valid reason sufficient to justify the person's failure to comply with the notice;

- the notice served is complied with; or

- it discovers that the rights of a third party in respect of the relevant interest are being unfairly affected by the restrictions notice.

### Offences for failing to comply with notices

A person to whom a notice under *CA 2006, s 790D or 790E* (above) is addressed commits an offence if the person fails to comply with the notice, or in purported compliance with the notice makes a statement that the person knows to be false in a material particular, or recklessly makes a statement that is false in a material particular.

Where the person is a legal entity, an offence is also committed by every officer of the entity who is in default.

A person does not commit an offence if the person proves that the requirement to give information was frivolous or vexatious.

A person guilty of an offence under this paragraph is liable on conviction on indictment, to imprisonment for a term not exceeding two years or a fine (or both), on summary conviction in England and Wales, to imprisonment for a term not exceeding 12 months or to a fine (or both), in Scotland, to imprisonment for a term not exceeding 12 months or to a fine not exceeding the statutory maximum (or both) and in Northern Ireland, to imprisonment for a term not exceeding six months or to a fine not exceeding the statutory maximum (or both).

### Offences for failing to provide information

A person commits an offence if the person fails to comply with a duty to give information under *CA 2006, s 790G or 790H*, or in purported compliance with such a duty makes a statement that the person knows to be false in a material particular, or recklessly makes a statement that is false in a material particular.

Where the person is a legal entity, an offence is also committed by every officer of the entity who is in default.

A person guilty of an offence under this paragraph is liable on conviction on indictment, to imprisonment for a term not exceeding two years or a fine (or both),on summary conviction in England and Wales, to imprisonment for a term not exceeding 12 months or to a fine (or both), in Scotland, to imprisonment for a term not exceeding 12 months or to a fine not exceeding the statutory maximum (or both) and in Northern Ireland, to imprisonment for a term not exceeding six months or to a fine not exceeding the statutory maximum (or both).

[*CA 2006, s 790I, Sch 1B; SBEE 2015, Sch 3; SI 2016 No 2029, Reg 4*].

## 38.22   Removal of entries and rectifying the PSC register

An entry relating to an individual who used to be a registrable person or an entity that used to be a registrable relevant legal entity may be removed from the company's PSC register after the expiration of ten years from the date on which the individual ceased to be a registrable person or the entity ceased to be a registrable relevant legal entity in either case in relation to the company.

If the name of any person is, without sufficient cause, entered in or omitted from a company's PSC register as a registrable person or registrable relevant legal entity, or default is made or unnecessary delay takes place in entering on the PSC register the fact that a person has ceased to be a registrable person or registrable relevant legal entity, the person aggrieved or any other interested party may apply to the court for rectification of the register.

The court may either refuse the application or may order rectification of the register and payment by the company of any damages sustained by any party aggrieved. On such an application, the court may decide any question as to whether the name of any person who is a party to the application should or should not be entered in or omitted from the register, and more generally, decide any question necessary or expedient to be decided for rectification of the register.

## 38.22   Registers

In the case of a company required by *CA 2006* to send information stated in its PSC register to the Registrar of Companies, the court, when making an order for rectification of the register, must by its order direct notice of the rectification to be given to the Registrar.

The reference to "any other interested party" is to any member of the company, and any other person who is a registrable person or a registrable relevant legal entity in relation to the company.

[*CA 2006, ss 790U, 790V, Sch 1B; SBEE 2015, Sch 3; SI 2016 No 2029, Reg 4*].

### 38.23   ENFORCEMENT OF THE PSC REGIME

On 5 April 2018, Companies House published its 2018 to 2019 business plan. The plan recorded that, as at the time of publication, 98% of companies had provided PSC information to Companies House. However, Companies House indicated its recognition that improvements could be made. According to the business plan, Companies House intends to:

- contact companies where it believes they have misunderstood the requirements, in order to ensure that records are correct;

- pursue companies that have not provided PSC information in their confirmation statement or that have not provided a statement of additional matters;

- investigate with companies which have issued notices to their PSC (asking PSCs to provide information) or restrictions (where a PSC has failed to provide information), but have not since updated that information;

- enforce compliance by companies where there has been a complaint about missing or incorrect PSC information.

- develop data and intelligence sharing facilities with law enforcement and government departments in order to facilitate the sharing of information and the tackling of economic crime; and

- follow-up complaints about PSC information; Companies House aspires to respond within ten working days.

The business plan also announces Companies House's intention to work in partnership with BEIS to gather evidence. That evidence will be used to support the review of the effectiveness of the PSC regime which the Government plans to undertake in 2019.

### 38.24   OPTION TO KEEP PSC DETAILS ON THE CENTRAL REGISTER

**Right to make an election**

An election may be made by giving notice to the Registrar of Companies

- by the subscribers wishing to form a private company under *CA 2006*; or

- by the private company itself once it is formed and registered. In this case, the election is of no effect unless notice of the intention to make the election was given to each eligible person at least 14 days before the date on which the election was made and no objection was received by the subscribers or, as the case may be, the company from any eligible person within that notice period.

A person is an "eligible person" if

- in a case of an election by the subscribers wishing to form a private company, the person's particulars would, but for the election, be required to be entered in the company's PSC register on its incorporation; and

- in the case of an election by the company itself the person is a registrable person or a registrable relevant legal entity in relation to the company, and the person's particulars are stated in the company's PSC register.

If the notice is given by subscribers wishing to form a private company

(i)    it must be given when the documents required to be delivered under *CA 2006*, *s 9* are delivered to the Registrar of Companies; and

(ii)   it must be accompanied by a statement confirming that no objection was received by the subscribers or, as the case may be from any eligible person. If the notice is given by the company, it must be accompanied by a statement by the company that no objection was received as above, and a statement containing all the information that is required to be contained in the company's PSC register as at the date of the notice in respect of matters that are current as at that date.

The company must where necessary update the statement sent under (ii) to ensure that the final version delivered to the Registrar contains all the information that is required to be contained in the company's PSC register as at the time immediately before the election takes effect in respect of matters that are current as at that time. This obligation to update the statement includes an obligation to rectify it (where necessary) in consequence of the company's register of members being rectified (whether before or after the election takes effect).

**Offences**

If default is made in complying with the obligation to update the statement an offence is committed by the company, and every officer of the company who is in default. For this purpose a shadow director is treated as an officer of the company. A person guilty of an offence is liable on summary conviction to a fine not exceeding level 3 on the standard scale and, for continued contravention, a daily default fine not exceeding one-tenth of level 3 on the standard scale. See **29.1** Offences and Legal Proceedings for the standard scale.

A reference to matters that are current as at a given date or time is a reference to persons who are a registrable person or registrable relevant legal entity in relation to the company as at that date or time, and whose particulars are required to be contained in the company's PSC register as at that date or time any other matters that are current as at that date or time.

[*CA 2006*, *s 790X; SBEE 2015*, *s 81, Sch 3; SI 2015 No 2019, Reg 4*].

**Effective date of election**

An election made under the above takes effect when the notice of election is registered by the Registrar.

The election remains in force until either the company ceases to be a private company, or a notice of withdrawal sent by the company (see below) is registered by the Registrar whichever occurs first.

[*CA 2006*, *s 790Y; SBEE 2015*, *s 81, Sch 3; SI 2015 No 2019, Reg 4*].

**Effect of an election on obligations under *CA 2006*, *Chapter 3* (obligation to keep a PSC register)** The company's obligation to maintain a PSC register does not apply with respect to the period when the election is in force. This means that, during that period

- the company must continue to keep a PSC register in accordance with *CA 2006*, *Chapter 3* (a "historic" register) containing all the information that was required to be stated in that register as at the time immediately before the election took effect; but

# 38.24  Registers

- the company does not have to update that register to reflect any changes that occur after that time.

The provisions of *CA 2006, Chapter 3* (including the rights to inspect or require copies of the register) continue to apply to the historic register during the period when the election is in force.

The company must place a note in its historic register

- stating that an election under *CA 2006, s 790X* is in force;

- recording when that election took effect; and

- indicating that up-to-date information about people with significant control over the company is available for public inspection on the central register.

The obligations with respect to a historic register do not apply in a case where the election was made by subscribers wishing to form a private company.

[*CA 2006, s 790Z; SBEE 2015, s 81, Sch 3; SI 2015 No 2019, Reg 4*].

### Duty to notify Registrar of Companies of changes

When an election is in force under the above provisions, the company must deliver to the Registrar any information that the company would during that period have been obliged under *CA 2006* to enter in its PSC register, had the election not been in force.

The information must be delivered as soon as reasonably practicable after the company becomes aware of it and, in any event, no later than the time by which the company would have been required to enter the information in its PSC register.

### Offences

If default is made in complying with this obligation an offence is committed by the company, and every officer of the company who is in default. For this purpose a shadow director is treated as an officer of the company. A person guilty of an offence is liable on summary conviction to a fine not exceeding level 3 on the standard scale and, for continued contravention, a daily default fine not exceeding one-tenth of level 3 on the standard scale. See **29.1** Offences and Legal Proceedings for the standard scale

[*CA 2006, s 790ZA; SBEE 2015, s 81, Sch 3; SI 2015 No 2019, Reg 4*].

### Information as to the state of the central register

When a person inspects or requests a copy of material on the central register relating to a company in respect of which an election is in force, the person may ask the company to confirm that all information that the company is required to deliver to the Registrar has been delivered.

If a company fails to respond to such a request an offence is committed by the company, and every officer of the company who is in default. A person guilty of an offence under this section is liable on summary conviction to a fine not exceeding level 3 on the standard scale.

[*CA 2006, s 790ZB; SBEE 2015, s 81, Sch 3; SI 2015 No 2019, Reg 4*].

### Power of court to order company to remedy default or delay

If

- the name of a person is without sufficient cause included in, or omitted from, information that a company delivers to the Registrar under these provisions concerning persons who are a registrable person or a registrable relevant legal entity; or

1078

- default is made or unnecessary delay takes place in informing the Registrar that a person has become a registrable person or registrable relevant legal entity or has ceased to be a registrable person or a registrable relevant legal entity in relation to it then the following provisions apply.

- The person aggrieved, or any other interested party may apply to the court for an order requiring the company to deliver to the Registrar the information (or statements) necessary to rectify the position.

The court may

- refuse the application or may make the order and order the company to pay any damages sustained by any party aggrieved.

- on such an application decide either any question relating to the title of a person who is a party to the application to have the person's name included in or omitted from information delivered to the Registrar about persons who are a registrable person or a registrable relevant legal entity in relation to the company and any question necessary or expedient to be decided for rectifying the position.

Nothing in the above affects a person's rights under *CA 2006, s 1095* or *1096* (rectification of register on application to Registrar or under court order).

[*CA 2006, s 790ZC; SBEE 2015, s 81, Sch 3; SI 2015 No 2019, Reg 4*].

**Withdrawing the election**

A company may withdraw an election made by or in respect of it. Withdrawal is achieved by giving notice of withdrawal to the Registrar and the withdrawal takes effect when the notice is registered by the Registrar.

The effect of withdrawal is that the company's obligation under *CA 2006, Chapter 3* to maintain a PSC register applies from then on with respect to the period going forward. This means that, when the withdrawal takes effect

(i)     the company must enter in its PSC register all the information that is required to be contained in that register in respect of matters that are current as at that time;

(ii)    the company must also retain in its register all the information that it was required to keep in a historic register while the election was in force; but

(iii)   the company is not required to enter in its register information relating to the period when the election was in force that is no longer current.

The company must place a note in its PSC register stating that the election under *CA 2006, s 790X* has been withdrawn, recording when that withdrawal took effect, and indicating that information about people with significant control over the company relating to the period when the election was in force that is no longer current is available for public inspection on the central register.

[*CA 2006, s 790ZD; SBEE 2015, s 94, Sch 5, para 3; SI 2016 No 321, Reg 6*].

**Definitions and interpretation for the purposes of *CA 2006, Sch 1A***

*Joint interests*

If two or more persons each hold a share or right jointly, each of them is treated for the purposes of *CA 2006, Sch 1A* as holding that share or right.

*Joint arrangements*

If shares or rights held by a person and shares or rights held by another person are the subject of a joint arrangement between those persons, each of them is treated as holding the combined shares or rights of both of them.

A "joint arrangement" is an arrangement between the holders of shares (or rights) that they will exercise all or substantially all the rights conferred by their respective shares (or rights) jointly in a way that is pre-determined by the arrangement.

"Arrangement" includes-

(a)     any scheme, agreement or understanding, whether or not it is legally enforceable; and

(b)     any convention, custom or practice of any kind.

*Calculating shareholdings*

In relation to a legal entity that has a share capital, a reference to holding "more than 25% of the shares" in that entity is to holding shares comprised in the issued share capital of that entity of a nominal value exceeding (in aggregate) 25% of that share capital.

In relation to a legal entity that does not have a share capital a reference to holding shares in that entity is to holding a right to share in the capital or, as the case may be, profits of that entity and a reference to holding "more than 25% of the shares" in that entity is to holding a right or rights to share in more than 25% of the capital or, as the case may be, profits of that entity.

*Voting rights*

A reference to the voting rights in a legal entity is to the rights conferred on shareholders in respect of their shares (or, in the case of an entity not having a share capital, on members) to vote at general meetings of the entity on all or substantially all matters.

In relation to a legal entity that does not have general meetings at which matters are decided by the exercise of voting rights a reference to exercising voting rights in the entity is to be read as a reference to exercising rights in relation to the entity that are equivalent to those of a person entitled to exercise voting rights in a company and a reference to exercising more than 25% of the voting rights in the entity is to be read as a reference to exercising the right under the constitution of the entity to block changes to the overall policy of the entity or to the terms of its constitution.

In applying these provisions, the voting rights in a legal entity are to be reduced by any rights held by the entity itself.

*Rights to appoint or remove members of the board*

A reference to the right to appoint or remove a majority of the board of directors of a legal entity is to the right to appoint or remove directors holding a majority of the voting rights at meetings of the board on all or substantially all matters.

References to a board of directors, in the case of an entity that does not have such a board, are to be read as references to the equivalent management body of that entity.

*Shares or rights held 'indirectly'*

A person holds a share "indirectly" if the person has a majority stake in a legal entity and that entity holds the share in question, or is part of a chain of legal entities

(i)     each of which (other than the last) has a majority stake in the entity immediately below it in the chain; and

(ii)    the last of which holds the share.

A person holds a right 'indirectly' if the person has a majority stake in a legal entity and that entity holds that right, or is part of a chain of legal entities

(i)     each of which (other than the last) has a majority stake in the entity immediately below it in the chain; and

(ii)    the last of which holds that right.

For these purposes, A has a 'majority stake' in B if

(a)     A holds a majority of the voting rights in B; and

(b)     A is a member of B and has the right to appoint or remove a majority of the board of directors of B;

(c)     A is a member of B and controls alone, pursuant to an agreement with other shareholders or members, a majority of the voting rights in B; or

(d)     A has the right to exercise, or actually exercises, dominant influence or control over B. In the application of this to the right to appoint or remove a majority of the board of directors, a legal entity is to be treated as having the right to appoint a director if

      (a)     a person's appointment as director follows necessarily from that person's appointment as director of the legal entity; or

      (b)     the directorship is held by the legal entity itself.

*Shares held by nominees*

A share held by a person as nominee for another is to be treated as held by the other (and not by the nominee).

*Rights treated as held by person who controls their exercise*

Where a person controls a right, the right is to be treated as held by that person (and not by the person who in fact holds the right, unless that person also controls it).

A person 'controls' a right if, by virtue of any arrangement between that person and others, the right is exercisable only

(a)     by that person;

(b)     in accordance with that person's directions or instructions; or

(c)     with that person's consent or concurrence.

"Arrangement" includes

(a)     any scheme, agreement or understanding, whether or not it is legally enforceable; and

(b)     any convention, custom or practice of any kind.

But something does not count as an arrangement unless there is at least some degree of stability about it (whether by its nature or terms, the time it has been in existence or otherwise).

## 38.24  Registers

*Rights exercisable only in certain circumstances etc*

Rights that are exercisable only in certain circumstances are to be taken into account only

(a)    when the circumstances have arisen, and for so long as they continue to obtain; or

(b)    when the circumstances are within the control of the person having the rights.

But rights that are exercisable by an administrator or by creditors while a legal entity is in relevant insolvency proceedings are not to be taken into account even while the entity is in those proceedings.

"Relevant insolvency proceedings" means

(a)    administration within the meaning of the *IA 1986*;

(b)    administration within the meaning of the *Insolvency (Northern Ireland) Order 1989 (SI 1989/2405 (NI 19))*; or

(c)    proceedings under the insolvency law of another country or territory during which an entity's assets and affairs are subject to the control or supervision of a third party or creditor.

Rights that are normally exercisable but are temporarily incapable of exercise are to continue to be taken into account.

*Rights attached to shares held by way of security*

Rights attached to shares held by way of security provided by a person are to be treated as held by that person

(a)    where apart from the right to exercise them for the purpose of preserving the value of the security, or of realising it, the rights are exercisable only in accordance with that person's instructions, and

(b)    where the shares are held in connection with the granting of loans as part of normal business activities and apart from the right to exercise them for the purpose of preserving the value of the security, or of realising it, the rights are exercisable only in that person's interests.

[*CA 2006, Sch 1A; SBEE 2015, s 81, Sch 3; SI 2015 No 2019, Reg 4*].


## 38.25  THE GENERAL DATA PROTECTION REGULATION

The *General Data Protection Regulation, Regulation (EU) 2016/679 (GDPR)* introduces substantial amendments to data protection law in the UK, replacing the *Data Protection Act 1998 (DPA 1998)* and *Directive 95/46/EC* (the Data Protection Directive). Its provisions are directly applicable and fully enforceable in all EU Member States from 25 May 2018. While the GDPR allows Member States to introduce further domestic provisions in a number of areas, specific implementing legislation is not required. The GDPR represents the biggest overhaul in data protection law in over two decades and introduces a raft of changes covering key conceptual changes, rights for data subjects, additional obligations and liabilities for data controllers and data processors and changes in regulatory oversight.

The GDPR is a complex and principles-based regulation. Personal data and technology are becoming increasingly important aspects of most businesses as the majority of businesses process information about employees, customers/clients, suppliers etc. Data is becoming an increasingly valuable and strategic corporate asset and can therefore be critical to the valuation of a company or, in the context of a mergers and acquisitions (M&A) transaction, of the target group or a target business. There will be some M&A transactions where personal data will be particularly crucial, for example where the target group or target business relies heavily on data for the success of its business model or for its operations or which relies on special categories of personal data (ie sensitive personal data). Therefore, data protection compliance under the GDPR is likely to be relevant to most companies and to most M&A transactions, to a greater or lesser degree depending upon the amount of, and type of, data processing undertaken by the target group or target business.

The fast pace of technological developments is reflected in the wider definition of 'personal data' under the GDPR. This now includes location data, online identifiers and genetic data. Special categories of personal data under the GDPR now include the processing of genetic and/or biometric data where the purpose is to uniquely identify the data subject (biometric data includes facial recognition and 'dactyloscopic' data, more commonly known as fingerprinting). These additions to what is considered personal data will mean that a company will need to closely examine the personal data that it holds in order to determine whether and, if so, subject to what safeguards, it must provide data, to its shareholders, directors and third parties.

More broadly this issue is likely to acquire ever greater significance as there are growing numbers of very high value companies worldwide that possess relatively few tangible assets but have their value in intangible information, data and creativity.

The GDPR is distinct from a company's statutory obligations under the *Companies Act* which are the main focus of this Handbook. The GDPR is ably dealt with in other volumes, and more detailed coverage of it is beyond the scope of this text. Nonetheless, there are key ramifications here for all companies and their operations.

# 39   Registrar of Companies

## 39.1   REGISTRARS AND THEIR CONTACT DETAILS

There must be a Registrar of Companies for England and Wales, Scotland and Northern Ireland, each appointed by the Secretary of State. [*CA 2006, s 1060*]

Company information can be obtained by post, fax, courier or through a personal visit to any one of the Information Centres at the offices in Cardiff, London and Edinburgh.

| | |
|---|---|
| **Contact centre**—this is the main route for all general enquiries | |
| Telephone (open 8.30am – 6pm Monday to Friday) | +44 (0)303 1234 500 |
| Email | enquiries@companies-house.gov.uk |
| Please see Companies House website (companieshouse.gov.uk) for the latest contact details including opening hours. | |
| **Companies House Information Centres** | |
| For England and Wales: *Cardiff*: Crown Way, Maindy, Cardiff CF14 3UZ (open 24 hours a day for the receipt of documents) | |
| *London*: 4 Abbey Orchard Street, Westminster, London SW1P 2HT | |
| Office hours | Monday to Friday 9.00am – 5.00pm |
| For Scotland: *Edinburgh*: 4th Floor, Edinburgh Quay 2, 139 Fountainbridge, Edinburgh, EH3 9FF | |
| For Northern Ireland: 2nd Floor, The Linenhall, 32–38 Linenhall Street, Belfast BT28BG | Monday to Friday 9.00am – 5.00pm |

## 39.2 Registrar of Companies

### 39.2 GUIDANCE BOOKLETS

There is a wealth of useful guidance booklets which are available from Companies House and on its website (freely downloadable from the internet on: www.companieshouse.gov.uk) about registering, filing and disclosing information with Companies House. These guides cover UK companies, overseas companies and LLPs. They also cover recent developments, such as the confirmation statement and the people with significant control (PSC) requirements (see **38.19** OPTION TO KEEP A **PCS** REGISTER AND REQUIRED PARTICULARS).

### 39.3 DUTIES AND POWERS OF THE REGISTRAR OF COMPANIES

The Registrar of Companies must perform a wide range of duties conferred on him by and under the *Companies Acts* and other legislation, together with other functions in relation to the registration of companies and other matters which the Secretary of State may from time to time direct him to perform. [*CA 2006, s 1061*]. Some of these duties and related powers are considered in **39.4** to **39.19** below. Unless the context requires otherwise, the provisions apply to an overseas company. [*CA 2006, s 1059A(5)*].

### 39.4 Certificates of incorporation

**Public notice of issue.** The Registrar of Companies must cause to be published, in the Gazette or in accordance with **39.17**, notice of the issue of any certificate of incorporation of a company on formation, change of name or re-registration. He must also publish notice on a company becoming, or ceasing to become, a Welsh company under **37.3** REGISTERED OFFICE. The notice must state the name and registered number of the company and the date of issue of the certificate.

[*CA 2006, s 1064*].

Any person may require the Registrar of Companies to provide him with a copy of any certificate of incorporation of a company (whenever issued), signed by the Registrar or authenticated by the registrar's seal.

[*CA 2006, s 1065*].

### 39.5 Registered numbers

The Registrar of Companies must allocate a number (the company's 'registered number') to every company. This includes an overseas company whose particulars have been registered under *CA 2006, s 1046* unless the Registrar is of the opinion that the company is not required to register particulars under that section.

The Registrar may determine what form registered numbers take (eg one or more sequences of figures or letters) and may adopt a new form of registered number, making such changes to existing registered numbers as appear necessary. Any such change has effect from the date on which the company is notified by the Registrar of the change. For a period of three years beginning with that date, any requirement to disclose the company's registered number imposed by the provisions relating to trading disclosures (see **16.12** DEALINGS WITH THIRD PARTIES) is satisfied by the use of either the old number or the new.

[*CA 2006, s 1066*].

Similar provisions apply to the allocation to every UK establishment of an overseas company whose particulars are registered under *CA 2006, s 1046* of a number to be known as the UK establishment's registered number.

[*CA 2006, s 1067*].

**39.6    Delivery of documents to the Registrar of Companies**

Under the *Companies Acts* and other legislation, a wide variety of documents must be delivered to the Registrar of Companies for filing. The Registrar of Companies may impose requirements as to the form, authentication and manner of delivery of these documents. [*CA 2006, s 1068(1)*].

The requirements in (1)–(3) below apply to documents delivered to the Registrar of Companies on or after 1 October 2013.

[*SI 2009 No 1802, Schedule; SI 2013 No 1947, Reg 2*].

(1)    **Form**

The Registrar of Companies may

- require the contents of a document to be in a standard form; and

- impose requirements for the purpose of enabling the document to be scanned or copied.

[*CA 2006, s 1068(2)*].

Documents delivered to the Registrar of Companies are scanned to produce an electronic image. The original documents are stored away and the electronic image is used as the working document. If documents are filed electronically, the Registrar automatically creates an electronic image from the data provided. Documents delivered to the Registrar must, therefore, comply with requirements set out below as specified by the Registrar. If they do not, the Registrar can reject them.

Documents filed electronically must comply with the Registrar's specifications in the rules on electronic filing (the formats are in the rules published on Companies House website).

Paper documents. Every document sent to the Registrar of Companies must state in a prominent position the registered name and number of the company and must comply with any requirements specified by the Registrar relating to the legibility of that document.

Briefly, documents should be on A4 size, plain white paper with a matt finish. Text should be black, clear, legible, and of uniform density. Letters and numbers must be clear and legible so that Companies House can make an acceptable copy.

There are guidelines for completing forms and documents and a warning that failure to follow the guidelines is likely to result in the document being rejected.

GP2 Life of a Company – Part 1 Chapter 14.

(2)    **Authentication**

The Registrar of Companies may

- require the document to be authenticated by a particular person or a person of a particular description;

- specify the means of authentication; and

- require the document to contain, or be accompanied by, the name or registered number (or both) of the company (or other body) to which it relates.

[*CA 2006, s 1068(3)*].

## 39.6 Registrar of Companies

    (3)    **Manner of delivery**

The Registrar of Companies may specify requirements as to

- the physical form of the document (eg hard copy or electronic form);

- the means to be used for delivering the document (eg by post or electronic means);

- the address to which the document is to be sent; and

- in the case of a document to be delivered by electronic means, the hardware and software to be used, and technical specifications (eg matters relating to protocol, security, anti-virus protection or encryption).

All documents subject to the Directive disclosure requirements (see **39.8**) *may* be delivered to the Registrar by 'electronic means' (see APPENDIX 1 DEFINITIONS). But nothing in these provisions authorises the Registrar to require documents to be delivered by electronic means unless the Secretary of State has made the appropriate Regulations and the Registrar's rules covering the detailed requirements for electronic delivery have been published.

    [*CA 2006, ss 1068(4)–(6), 1069*].

    (4)    **Option to keep members' (see 38.9)** or PSC information (see **38.18**) on the central register

Where there is an option in force *CA 2006, s 1068* authorises the Registrar to require any document permitted or required to be delivered to the Registrar under *CA 2006, Part 8, Chapter 2A* to be delivered by electronic means.

[*CA 2006, ss 1068(4)–(6A), 1069; SBEE 2015, s 94, Sch 5, para 29; SI 2016 No 321, Reg 6, Sch 3 Part 2, para 6*].

Any requirements imposed by the Registrar under (1)–(3) above must not be inconsistent with requirements imposed by any enactment.

[*CA 2006, s 1068(7)*].

**Agreement for delivery by electronic means**. In relation to all documents delivered to the Registrar of Companies, the Registrar may agree with a company (or other body) that documents relating to the company (or other body) that are required or authorised to be delivered to the Registrar will be delivered by electronic means, except as provided for in the agreement. Documents in relation to which an agreement is in force must then be delivered in accordance with the agreement.

[*CA 2006, s 1070*].

**Documents not delivered until received**. In relation to documents delivered on or after 1 October 2009 (other than those delivered in pursuance of an obligation arising before that date, in which case the provisions which would have applied if the document had been delivered before that date continue to apply), a document is not delivered to the Registrar of Companies until it is received by him.

[*CA 2006, s 1071; SI 2008 No 2860, Sch 2 para 99; SI 2009 No 1802, Sch*].

**39.7**    *Requirements for proper delivery*

The provisions in this paragraph apply to documents delivered to the Registrar of Companies (other than those delivered in pursuance of an obligation arising before 1 October 2009, in which case the provisions which would have applied if the document had been delivered before that date and the Registrar of Companies former practice continue to apply).

[*SI 2008 No 2860, Sch 2 paras 100–102; SI 2009 No 1802, Sch*].

A document delivered to the Registrar of Companies is not properly delivered unless all the following requirements are met.

- The requirements of the appropriate provision as regards the contents of the document and form, authentication and manner of delivery.

- Any applicable requirements under **39.6**.

- Any requirements as to the language in which the document is drawn up and delivered or as to its being accompanied on delivery by a certified translation into English.

- In so far as it consists of or includes names and addresses, any requirements as to permitted characters, letters or symbols or as to its being accompanied on delivery by a certificate as to the transliteration of any element.

- Any applicable requirement as to certification or verification (see **39.15**).

- Any requirement as to the use of unique identifiers (see **39.9**).

- Any requirements as regards payment of a fee in respect of its receipt by the Registrar.

A document that is not properly delivered is treated for the purposes of the provision requiring it or authorising it to be delivered as not having been delivered (subject to below).

[*CA 2006, s 1072*].

*Power to accept documents not meeting requirements for proper delivery*. The Registrar of Companies can accept (and register) a document that does not comply with the above requirements. If he does so, the document is treated as received for the purposes **39.8**. No objection may be taken to the legal consequences of a document being so accepted (or registered) by the Registrar of Companies on the ground that the requirements for proper delivery were not met.

The acceptance of a document by the Registrar of Companies under this provision does not affect

- the continuing obligation to comply with the requirements for proper delivery; or

- subject to what follows, any liability for failure to comply with those requirements.

For the purposes of *CA 2006, s 453* (civil penalty for failure to file accounts and reports, see **2.11** ACCOUNTS: GENERAL) and any enactment imposing a daily default fine for failure to deliver the document, the period after the document is accepted does not count as a period during which there is default in complying with the requirements for proper delivery. But if, subsequently,

- the Registrar of Companies issues a notice under **39.11(1)** in respect of the document (notice of administrative removal from the register), and

- the requirements for proper delivery are not complied with before the end of the period of 14 days after the issue of that notice,

any subsequent period of default does count for the purposes of those provisions.

[*CA 2006, s 1073*].

*Documents containing unnecessary material*. Where a document delivered to the Registrar of Companies contains 'unnecessary material',

- if the unnecessary material cannot readily be separated from the rest of the document, the document is treated as not meeting the requirements for proper delivery; and

- if the unnecessary material can readily be separated from the rest of the document, the Registrar of Companies may register the document either

    (i)    with the omission of the unnecessary material; or

    (ii)   as delivered.

'*Unnecessary material*' means material that is not necessary in order to comply with an obligation under any Act and is not specifically authorised to be delivered to the Registrar of Companies. [*CA 2006, s 1074*].

*Informal correction of document.* Where a document has not been registered under *CA 2006, s 1073* above, the Registrar of Companies may corrected a document delivered to him if it appears to him to be incomplete or internally inconsistent but only on instructions and with the consent of the company (or other body) concerned. Any document that is so corrected is treated as having been delivered when the correction is made. This provision applies in relation to documents delivered in connection with registration of charges by a person other than the company (or other body) as if the references to the company (or other body) were to the company (or other body) or the person by whom the document was delivered.

[*CA 2006, s 1075*].

*Replacement of a document not meeting requirements for delivery.* The Registrar of Companies may accept a replacement for a document previously delivered that did not comply with the requirements for proper delivery or contained unnecessary material. The replacement document must be delivered by the same person who delivered the original document or the company (or other body) to which the original document relates. This provision for voluntary replacement does not apply where the original document related to company charges (for which see *CA 2006, s 859M* at **39.9** and **39.17** REGISTRATION OF CHARGES.

[*CA 2006, s 1076; SI 2013 No 600, Schedule 2, para 3*].

### 39.8   Public notice of receipt of certain documents

The Registrar of Companies must cause to be published, in the *Gazette* or in accordance with **39.17**, notice of the receipt of any document that, on receipt, is subject to the requirements of *First Company Law Directive (68/151/EEC), Art 3* (the '*Directive disclosure requirements*'). The notice must state the name and registered number of the company, the description of document and the date of receipt. The Registrar is not required to cause notice of the receipt of a document to be published before the date of incorporation of the company to which the document relates.

[*CA 2006, s 1077*].

The documents subject to the *Directive* disclosure requirements are as follows.

**All companies**

(A) *Constitutional documents*

    (1)    The company's memorandum and articles.

    (2)    Any amendment of the company's articles (including every resolution or agreement required to be embodied in or annexed to copies of the company's articles issued by the company) and, before 1 October 2009, any amendment of the company's memorandum.

    (3)    After any amendment of the company's articles (or, before 1 October 2009, memorandum), the text of the document as amended.

    (4)    With effect from 1 October 2009, any notice of a change of the company's name.

(B) *Directors*

    (1)    The statement of proposed officers required on formation of the company.

    (2)    Notification of any change among the company's directors.

    (3)    Notification of any change in the particulars of directors required to be delivered to the Registrar.

(C) *Accounts, reports and returns*

    (1)    All documents required to be delivered to the Registrar under *CA 2006, s 441* (annual accounts and reports).

    (2)    All documents delivered to the Registrar under *CA 2006, ss 394A(2)(e), 448A(2)(e)* and *479A(2)(e)* (qualifying subsidiary companies: conditions for exemption from the audit, preparation and filing of individual accounts)

    (3)    The company's annual return.

(D) *Registered office*

Notification of any change of the company's registered office.

(E) *Winding up*

    (1)    Copy of any winding-up order in respect of the company.

    (2)    Notice of the appointment of liquidators.

    (3)    Order for the dissolution of a company on a winding up.

    (4)    Return by a liquidator of the final meeting of a company on a winding up.

**Public companies**

(A) *Share capital*

    (1)    Any statement of capital and initial shareholdings.

    (2)    Any return of allotment and, with effect from 1 October 2009, the statement of capital accompanying it.

    (3)    Copy of any resolution under *CA 2006, ss 570, 571* (disapplication of pre-emption rights).

    (4)    Copy of any report under *CA 2006, ss 593* as to the value of a non-cash asset.

(5)    A statement of capital accompanying notice given under *CA 2006, s 625* (notice by company of redenomination of shares).

(6)    A statement of capital accompanying notice given under *CA 2006, s 627* (notice by company of reduction of capital in connection with redenomination of shares).

(7)    Notice delivered under *CA 2006, s 636* (notice of new name of class of shares) or *CA 2006, s 637* (notice of variation of rights attached to shares) (registration of particulars of specified rights)).

(8)    A statement of capital accompanying order delivered under *CA 2006, s 649* (order of court confirming reduction of capital).

(9)    Notification (under *CA 2006, s 689*) of the redemption of shares and the statement of capital accompanying it.

(10)    A statement of capital accompanying return delivered under *CA 2006, s 708* (notice of cancellation of shares on purchase of own shares or *CA 2006, s 730* (notice of cancellation of shares held as treasury shares).

(11)    Any statement of compliance delivered under *CA 2006, s 762* (statement that company meets conditions for issue of trading certificate) (public company share capital requirements)).

(12)    Any statement delivered under *CA 2006, s 762(1)(e)* (statement of the aggregate amount (if any) unpaid up on shares (whether on account of their nominal value or by way of premium)).

(B)    *Mergers and divisions*

(1)    Copy of any draft of the terms of a scheme required to be delivered to the Registrar under *CA 2006, s 906* or *CA 2006, s 921*.

(2)    Copy of any order under *CA 2006, s 899* or *CA 2006, s 900* in respect of a compromise or arrangement to which *CA 2006, Pt 27* (mergers and divisions of public companies) applies.

**Private company re-registering as a public company**

(1)    The last statement of capital relating to the company received by the Registrar of Companies under any provision of the *Companies Acts* becomes subject to the Directive disclosure requirements. *CA 2006, s 1077* above applies as if the statement had been received by the Registrar of Companies when the re-registration takes effect. In this case the company must provide a statement of the aggregate amount paid upon shares on account of their nominal value.

**Overseas companies**

(1)    Any return or document delivered under *Overseas Companies Regulations 2009, Part 2* (initial registration of particulars, see **30.3–30.5** Overseas Companies).

(2)    Any return or document delivered under *Overseas Companies Regulations 2009, Part 3* (alterations in registered particulars, see **30.8** and **30.9** Overseas Companies).

(3)    Any document delivered under *Overseas Companies Regulations 2009, Part 5* (delivery of accounting documents: general, see **30.18** *et seq* Overseas Companies).

(4)    Any document delivered under *Overseas Companies Regulations 2009, Part 6* (delivery of accounting documents: credit or financial institutions, see **30.35** *et seq* Overseas Companies).

(5)     Any notice under *Overseas Companies Regulations 2009, Reg 77* (duty to give notice of closure of UK establishment, see **30.57** OVERSEAS COMPANIES).

[*CA 2006, s 1078; SBEE 2015, s 98(4); SI 2009 No 1801, Reg 76; SI 2009 No 1801 Overseas Companies Regulations 2009, Reg 76; SI 2012 No 2301, Reg 19; SI 2016 No 321, Reg 6*].

**39.9   Maintaining company records on the register**

The Registrar of Companies must keep records of

•       the information contained in documents delivered to the Registrar under any enactment; and

•       certificates issued by the Registrar under any enactment.

The records relating to companies are referred to collectively as '*the register*'.

Information deriving from documents subject to the *Directive* disclosure requirements (see **39.8**) must be kept by the Registrar in electronic form. Otherwise, information contained in documents delivered to the Registrar may be recorded and kept in any form the Registrar thinks fit, provided it is possible to inspect it and produce a copy of it and provided the records enable all the information relating to a particular company or other registered body to be retrieved.

[*CA 2006, s 1080*].

**Annotation of the register**. *In relation to documents delivered to the Registrar of Companies on or after 1 October 2009* the Registrar of Companies

(a)     *must* place a note in the register recording

•       the date on which a document is delivered to the Registrar;

•       if a document is corrected (see **39.7**), the nature and date of the correction;

•       if a document is replaced (whether or not material derived from it is removed), the fact that it has been replaced and the date of delivery of the replacement; and

•       if material is removed

        (i)     what was removed (giving a general description of its contents);

        (ii)    under what power; and

        (iii)   the date on which that was done;

                •       if a document is rectified under *CA 2006, s 859M*, the nature and date of rectification; and

                •       if a document is replaced under *CA 2006, s 859N*, the fact that it has been replaced and the date of delivery of the replacement.

(b)     *may* place a note in the register containing such information as appears to the Registrar to be necessary to remedy, as far as possible, any material on the register that is misleading or confusing.

A note may be removed if it no longer serves any useful purpose. Any duty or power of the Registrar with respect to annotation of the register is subject to the court's power under *CA 2006, s 1097* (see **39.11(4)**) to direct that a note be removed from the register or that no note should made of the removal of material that is the subject of the court's order.

## 39.9 Registrar of Companies

[CA 2006, s 1081; SI 2009 No 1802, Sch; SI 2009 No 1803, Reg 3; SI 2013 No 600, Schedule 2, para 3].

**Allocation of unique identifiers.** The Secretary of State may make provision for the use, in connection with the register, of reference numbers ('unique identifiers') to identify each person who

- is a director of a company;

- is secretary (or a joint secretary) of a company; or

- in the case of an overseas company whose particulars are registered under *CA 2006, s 1046*, holds any such position as may be specified for the purposes of these provisions.

[*CA 2006, s 1082*].

**Preservation of original documents.** The originals of documents delivered to the Registrar of Companies in hard copy form must be kept for three years after they are received by the Registrar, after which they may be destroyed provided the information contained in them has been recorded. But material not available for public inspection (see **39.10**) need only be kept as long as appears necessary to the Registrar for the purposes for which the material was delivered to him.

The Registrar is under no obligation to keep the originals of documents delivered in electronic form, provided the information contained in them has been recorded.

[*CA 2006, s 1083*].

**Records relating to companies that have been dissolved, etc**. Where a company is dissolved, at any time after two years from the date of dissolution the Registrar of Companies may direct that records relating to the company may be removed to the Public Record Office or, as the case may be, the Public Records Office for Northern Ireland. The records must then be disposed of under the rules relating to that Office.

Similar rules apply to records where an overseas company ceases to have any connection with the UK by virtue of which it is required to register particulars.

The above provisions do not extend to Scotland.

[*CA 2006, s 1084*].

## 39.10 Inspection and copying of the register

Any person may inspect the register or require a copy of any material on the register (subject to a fee). The right of inspection extends to the originals of documents delivered to the Registrar of Companies in hard copy form if, and only if, the record kept by the Registrar of the contents of the document is illegible or unavailable (but note that the period for which hard copy originals are kept is limited under **39.9**). Certain material as specified in *CA 2006, s 1087* is not, however, available for public inspection or copying. This includes (see *s 1087* for a full list of materials not available for inspection)

- protected information under *CA 2006, s 242(1)* (directors' residential addresses, see **18.71** DIRECTORS) or corresponding provisions relating to overseas companies;

- any address in respect of which a successful application under **39.19** is made to make as address on the public register unavailable for public inspection;

- the contents of any instrument creating or evidencing a charge, or the certified or verified copy of such an instrument, and delivered to the Registrar in Companies for filing;

- information about a person's date of birth; and

- information relating to residential addresses of people with significant control over the company (see **38.18**).

*Disclosure of date of birth information*

*CA 2006, ss 1087A* and *1087B* provide that the Registrar of Companies must not disclose "restricted DOB information" unless

- the same information about the "relevant person"(see definition below) (whether in the same or a different capacity) is made available for public inspection as a result of being contained in another description of document in relation to which no restriction under *CA 2006, s 1087(2)* applies; or

- disclosure by the Registrar is permitted to a public authority or to a credit reference agency.

Information about a person does not cease to fall within this provision when he or she ceases to be a relevant person and, to that extent, references to a "relevant person" include someone who used to be a relevant person.

These provisions do not apply to restricted DOB information about a relevant person in his or her capacity as someone whose particulars are stated in the company's PSC register if an application under regulations made under *CA 2006, s 790ZG* (regulations for protecting PSC particulars) has been granted with respect to that information and not been revoked.

"Restricted DOB information" means information which at any time (the "relevant time")

- is DOB information (information as to the day of the month (but not the month or year)) on which a relevant person was born;

- is contained in a document delivered to the Registrar that is "protected" at "the relevant time" as regards that information and the document is one in which such information is required to be stated; and

- if the document has more than one part, the part in which the information is contained is a part in which such information is required to be stated.

A document delivered to the registrar is "protected" at any time unless it is an "election period document," or *CA 2006, s 1087(7)* applies to it at the time, or it was registered before these provisions come into force.

A "relevant person" is an individual who is a director of a company, or whose particulars are stated in a company's PSC register as a registrable person in relation to that company (see **38.18**).

An "election period document" is

- in relation to a director a statement of the company's proposed officers delivered under *CA 2006, s 9* in circumstances where the subscribers gave notice of election under *CA 2006, s 167A* (election to keep information on central register) in respect of the company's register of directors when the statement was delivered or a document delivered by the company under *CA 2006, s 167D* (duty to notify Registrar of changes while election in force).

- in relation to a person whose particulars are stated in the PSC register (see **38.18**), a statement of initial significant control delivered under CA 2006 s 9( in circumstances where the subscribers gave notice of election under section 790X in respect of the company when the statement was delivered) or a document containing a statement or updated statement delivered by the company under *CA 2006, s 790X(6)(b)* or *(7)* (statement accompanying notice of election made after incorporation) or a document delivered by the company under *CA 2006, s 790ZA* (duty to notify Registrar of changes while election in force).

*Permitted disclosure to specified public authorities and credit reference agencies*

Disclosure is permitted to specified public authorities if the specified public authority

- has delivered to the Registrar a statement that it intends to use the restricted DOB information only for the purpose of facilitating the carrying out by that specified public authority of a public function; and

- has also delivered to the Registrar a statement that it will comply with the processing requirements set out in *SI 2015 No 1694, Sch 2.*

This does not apply where the specified public authority is the Secret Intelligence Service, Security Service or Government Communications Headquarters.

A list of specified public authorities is set out in *SI 2015 No 1694, Sch 1.*

Disclosure is also permitted to credit reference agencies if the credit reference agency

- is carrying on in the UK or in another EEA State a business comprising the furnishing of information relevant to the financial standing of individuals, being information collected by the agency for that purpose;

- maintains appropriate procedures to ensure that an independent person can investigate and audit the measures maintained by the agency for the purposes of ensuring the security of any restricted DOB information disclosed to that agency and for the purposes of ensuring that it complies with its obligations under the Data Protection Act 1998 or, where the agency carries on business in a EEA State other than the UK, with its obligations under legislation implementing Directive 95/46/EC of the European Parliament and of the Council of 24 October 1995 on the protection of individuals with regard to the processing of personal data and on the free movement of such data;

- has not been found guilty of an offence under *CA 2006, s 1112* (general false statement offence) or of the *Fraud Act 2006, s 2* (fraud by false representation) or *Data Protection Act 1998, s 47* (failure to comply with enforcement notice) in circumstances where it has used the restricted DOB information for purposes other than those described in (a)–(e) of below; and

- has delivered to the Registrar a statement that it intends to use the restricted DOB information only for the purposes of

  (a)   providing an assessment of the financial standing of a person;

  (b)   meeting any obligations contained in the Money Laundering Regulations 2007 or any rules made pursuant to *FSMA 2000, s 137A* which relate to the prevention and detection of money laundering in connection with the carrying on of regulated activities by authorised persons, or in any legislation of another EEA State implementing Directive 2005/60/EC of the European Parliament and of the Council of 26 October 2005 on the prevention of the use of the financial system for the purpose of money laundering and terrorist financing;

  (c)   conducting conflict of interest checks required or made necessary by any enactment;

(d)    the provision of restricted DOB information to a specified public authority which has satisfied the requirements above or a credit reference agency which has satisfied the requirements above; or

(e)    conducting checks for the prevention and detection of crime and fraud

- has delivered to the Registrar a statement that it intends to take delivery of and to use the restricted DOB information only in the UK or in another EEA State;

- has delivered to the Registrar a statement that it will, where it supplies a copy of the restricted DOB information to a processor for the purpose of processing the information for use in respect of the purposes referred to in *SI 2015 No 1694 Sch 2, para 7*; and

- has delivered to the Registrar a statement that it meets the conditions in *Sch 2, para 6*.

See also **18.70** and **18.71** for circumstances in the Registrar may disclose "protected information" which apply to DOB disclosures.

[*CA 2006, ss 1087A, 1087B: SBEE 2015, s 96; SI 2015 No 1694, Reg 2, Sch 1 and Sch 2*].

*Application for inspection or copy.* The Registrar of Companies can specify the form and manner in which an application for inspection or copies should be made except that applications in respect of documents subject to the Directive disclosure requirements (see **39.8**) may be submitted to the Registrar in hard copy or electronic form, as the applicant chooses.

*Form and manner in which copies to be provided.* Copies of documents subject to the Directive disclosure requirements (see **39.8**) must be provided in hard copy or electronic form, as the applicant chooses except that the Registrar is not obliged to provide copies in electronic form of a document that was delivered to the Registrar in hard copy form if

- the document was delivered on or before 31 December 1996; or

- the document was delivered on or before 31 December 2006 and ten years or more elapsed between the date of delivery and the date of receipt of the first application for a copy on or after 1 January 2007.

Subject to this, the Registrar may determine the form and manner in which copies are to be provided.

*Certification of copies as accurate.* Copies provided in hard copy form must be certified as true copies (unless the applicant dispenses with such certification).

Copies provided in electronic form must not be certified as true copies unless the applicant expressly requests such certification. Where he does so request, the Registrar's certificate must be authenticated by means of an electronic signature that

- is uniquely linked to the Registrar;

- indicates that the Registrar has caused it to be applied;

- is created using means that the Registrar can maintain under his sole control; and

- is linked to the certificate and to the copy provided in such a manner that any subsequent change of the data comprised in either is detectable.

Any copy certified by the Registrar of Companies to be an accurate record of the contents of the original document is in all legal proceedings admissible in evidence as

- of equal validity with the original document; and

- evidence (in Scotland, sufficient evidence) of any fact stated in the original document of which direct oral evidence would be admissible.

*[CA 2006, ss 1085–1087B, 1089–1091; SBEE 2015, s 96, Sch 3 para 8; SI 2006 No 3429, Reg 2; SI 2015 No 1689, Reg 4; SI 2015 No 842, Reg 2; SI 2015 No 2029, Reg 4].*

**Application to Registrar to make address unavailable for public inspection. See 39.19.**

See Appendix 1 Definitions for the meaning of 'hard copy' and 'electronic form'.

### 39.11   Correction or removal of material on the register

In relation to documents delivered to, and certificates issued by, the Registrar of Companies the Registrar has various powers and duties to rectify the register.

(1)    **Inconsistencies**

Where it appears that the information contained in a document delivered to the Registrar of Companies is inconsistent with other information on the register, the Registrar may give notice to the company requiring it to take steps to resolve the inconsistency within 14 days. If the necessary documents are not delivered within that period, an offence is committed by the company and every officer of the company who is in default. A person guilty of such an offence is liable, on summary conviction, to a fine not exceeding level 5 on the standard scale; for continued contravention, a daily default fine not exceeding one-tenth of the greater of £5000 or level 4 on the standard scale. See 29.1 Offences and Legal Proceedings for the standard scale.

See Companies House guidance "Inconsistencies on the public register" for more information.

*[CA 2006, s 1093; SI 2015 No 664, Sch 3].*

(2)    **Administrative removal of material**

The Registrar of Companies may remove from the register anything that there was power, but no duty, to include. This covers, in particular, unnecessary material (see **39.7**) and material derived from a document that has been replaced by voluntary replacement under 39.7 or because of inconsistencies under (*a*) above.

On or before removing any material under this provision (otherwise than at the request of the company) the Registrar must give notice

(i)     to the person by whom the material was delivered (if the identity, and name and address of that person are known); or

(ii)    to the company to which the material relates (if notice cannot be given under (i) above and the identity of that company is known).

*[CA 2006, s 1094].*

(3)    **Rectification of register on application to Registrar of Companies**

On application (but not if there is a valid objection to the application, see below) the Registrar of Companies must remove from the register any 'relevant material' that

- derives from anything invalid or ineffective or that was done without the authority of the company or overseas company to which the material relates; or

- is factually inaccurate, or is derived from something that is factually inaccurate or forged.

'*Relevant material*', in the case of a company, is material concerning its officers or registered office and that was included in, or is derived from material that was included in, a company form delivered to the Registrar of Companies by any person. In the case of an overseas company, it is material concerning its officers, permanent representatives, persons authorised to accept service of documents and addresses of UK establishments.

An application relating to the address of a registered office or UK establishment can only be made by the company or overseas company concerned. Any other application can only be made by the person who delivered the form in question, the company or overseas company to which it relates, or any other person to whom the material relates.

The application must

- specify what is to be removed from the register and indicate where on the register it is;

- be accompanied by a statement that the material specified in the application complies with these provisions;

- state the applicant's name and address;

- where the application relates to the address of a registered office or UK establishment, confirm that the applicant is the company or overseas company to which the relevant material relates;

- in any other case, state whether the applicant is

    (i)     the person who delivered the form in question;

    (ii)    the company or overseas company to which it relates; or

    (iii)   another person to whom the material relates; and

- state whether the relevant material which is the subject of the application

    (i)     derives from anything invalid or ineffective;

    (ii)    derives from anything that was done without the authority of the company or overseas company to which the material relates;

    (iii)   is factually inaccurate or is derived from something that is factually inaccurate; or

    (iv)    is derived from something that is forged.

The Registrar is obliged to give notice of the application to specified person including the company, every person who (to the Registrar's knowledge) was a director or secretary of the company and, in the case of an overseas company, every person who, at the time the application was delivered to the Registrar, was authorised to accept documents on behalf of the overseas company or was the permanent representative of one of its UK establishments. The notice must, amongst other things,

- specify what is to be removed from the register and indicate where on the register it is;

- give particulars of the recipient's right to object to the application and the requirements applying to that right; and

- explain the effect of a valid objection.

An objection to an application may be made to the Registrar of Companies in writing by any person, stating the name and address of the person making the objection and identify the application to which the objection relates, within 28 days of the Registrar's notice.

If no valid objection is made to an application, the Registrar of Companies may accept the statement as sufficient evidence that the material specified in the application should be removed from the register and must notify the applicant of that fact. This does not apply if the material specified in the application is material naming a person in a statement of a company's proposed officers as a person who is to be a director of the company, or in a notice given by a company under *CA 2006, s 167 or 167D* as a person who has become a director of the company, and the application is made by or on behalf of the person named and is accompanied by a statement that the person did not consent to act as director of the company. If the company provides the Registrar with the necessary evidence within the time required, the Registrar must not remove the material from the register.

If the company does not provide the Registrar with the necessary evidence within that time the material is conclusively presumed to be derived from something that is factually inaccurate, and the Registrar must accept the applicant's statement as sufficient evidence that the material should be removed from the register.

"The necessary evidence" is

(a)     evidence sufficient to satisfy the Registrar that the person did consent to act as director of the company; plus

(b)     a statement by the company that the evidence provided by it is true and is not misleading or deceptive in any material particular.

These provisions do apply to material contained in a statement of proposed officers or notice given under *CA 2006, s or 167D* if the statement or notice was received by the Registrar before *SBEE 2015, s 102* came into force (6 April 2016).

But if a valid objection is made to the application, the Registrar of Companies must reject the application and

- send an acknowledgment of receipt to the person who made the objection;

- notify the applicant of the fact that an objection has been made; and

- notify every other person to whom he gave notice of the application.

[*CA 2006, s 1095; SBEE 2015, s 102; SI 2009 No 1802, Schedule; SI 2009 No 1803, Regs 4, 5; SI 2016 No 321, Reg 3*].

*The Registrar of Companies and Applications for Striking Off (Amendment) Regulations 2016 (SI 2016/441)* came into force on 6 April 2016. These regulations introduced a new administrative procedure for removing material naming a person as a company director from the public register. They implemented *SBEEA 2015, s 102*. This latter section in turn amended *CA 2006, s 1095*, by ensuring that an application to take a director's details off the register could only be blocked if the company provided sufficient evidence to show that the person did in fact consent to be a director. Further guidance is awaited from Companies House upon the new procedure.

(4)     **Rectification of the register under court order**

The Registrar of Companies must remove from the register any material that

- derives from anything that the court has declared to be invalid or ineffective, or to have been done without the authority of the company, or

- a court declares to be factually inaccurate, or to be derived from something that is factually inaccurate, or forged,

and that the court directs should be removed from the register.

A copy of the court's order must be sent to the Registrar of Companies for registration.

[*CA 2006, ss 1096, 1097*].

(5)   **Rectification of the register relating to a company's registered office**

*Section 99* of the *SBEE 2015* inserts *CA 2006, s 1097A*. This enables the Registrar of Companies, on application, to change the address of a company's registered office. Enabling regulations will need to be made to allow the new powers to be used. As at May 2016 the new provisions are not in force and regulations have not been published.

**Public notice of removal of certain material from the register.** *With effect from 1 October 2009*, the Registrar of Companies must cause to be published, in the *Gazette* or in accordance with **39.17**, notice of the removal from the register of any document subject to the Directive disclosure requirements (see **39.8**) or of any material derived from such a document. The notice must state the name and registered number of the company, the description of document and the date of receipt.

[*CA 2006, s 1098*].

## 39.12   Index of company names

The Registrar of Companies must keep an index of the names of the following companies and other bodies (the '*Registrar's index of company names*').

- UK-registered companies.

- Any body to which any provision of the *Companies Acts* applies by virtue of regulations under *CA 2006, s 1043* (unregistered companies).

- Overseas companies that have registered particulars with the Registrar under *CA 2006, s 1046*, other than companies that appear to the Registrar not to be required to do so.

- Limited partnerships registered in the UK.

- Limited liability partnerships incorporated in the UK.

- European Economic Interest Groupings registered in the UK.

- Open-ended investment companies authorised in the UK.

- Societies registered under the *Industrial and Provident Societies Act 1965* or the *Industrial and Provident Societies Act (Northern Ireland) 1969*.

[*CA 2006, s 1099*].

Any person may inspect the registrar's index of company names.

[*CA 2006, s 1100*].

## 39.13 Registrar of Companies

**39.13 Language requirements: translation**

The provisions in (1) to (4) below apply to all documents required to be delivered to the Registrar of Companies under any provision of the *Companies Acts* or the *Insolvency Act 1986* or the *Insolvency (Northern Ireland) Order 1989 (SI 1989 No 2405)*.

[*CA 2006, s 1102*].

(1) **Documents to be drawn up and delivered in English**

Subject to (2) and (3) below, the general rule is that all documents required to be delivered to the Registrar of Companies must be drawn up and delivered in English.

[*CA 2006, s 1103*].

(2) **Documents relating to Welsh companies**

Documents relating to a Welsh company may be drawn up and delivered to the Registrar of Companies in Welsh. Any such document must be accompanied by a certified translation into English with the following exceptions.

- A non-traded company's memorandum of association.

- A non-traded company's articles.

- A community interest company report prepared for a non-traded company under *C(AICE)A 2004, s 34* (see **10.18 COMMUNITY INTEREST COMPANIES**).

- A resolution or agreement which was agreed to by members of a non-traded company and to which *CA 2006, ss 29, 39* apply (see **14.10 COMPANY CONSTITUTION**) apart from

  (a) a special resolution that (i) a private company should be re-registered as a public company; (ii) a public company should be re-registered as a private limited company; (iii) a private limited company should be re-registered as an unlimited company; or (iv) an unlimited company should be re-registered as a limited company;

  (b) a special resolution agreeing to the change of a company's name;

  (c) a special resolution required by *C(AICE)A 2004, s 37* (requirements for an existing company to become a community interest company, see **10.5 COMMUNITY INTEREST COMPANIES**);

  (d) a resolution or agreement as altered by an enactment other than an enactment amending the general law, required to be delivered to the Registrar of Companies under *CA 2006, s 34* (see **14.13 CONSTITUTION – MEMORANDUM AND ARTICLES**);

  (e) a resolution or agreement as altered by an order of a court or other authority, required to be delivered to the Registrar of Companies under *CA 2006, s 35* (see **14.13 CONSTITUTION – MEMORANDUM AND ARTICLES**) or *CA 2006, s 999* (see **26.5 MEMBERS**);

  (f) a special resolution under *CA 2008, s 88(2)* requiring the register to be amended so that it states that a company's registered office is to be situated in Wales;

  (g) a special resolution under *CA 2006, s 626* (reduction of capital in connection with redenomination);

(h)    a special resolution under *CA 2006, s 641(1)(a)* (resolution for reducing the share capital of a private limited company supported by a solvency statement); or

(i)    a resolution under *CA 2006, s 664(1)* that a public company should be re-registered as a private company to comply with *CA 2006, s 662*.

• Annual accounts and reports of a non-traded company required to be delivered to the Registrar of Companies.

• A declaration referred to in *C(AICE)A 2004, s 11(1)(b)* (see **10.4(*b*)** COMMUNITY INTEREST COMPANIES) or *C(AICE)A 2004, s 12(1)(b)* or *(c) (see 10.5(b)(c)* COMMUNITY INTEREST COMPANIES) which relates to a non-traded company.

• Revised accounts and any revised report of a non-traded company, and any auditor's report on such revised accounts and reports, required to be delivered to the Registrar of Companies.

• A document required to be appended to the group accounts of a non-traded company by *SI 2008 No 410, Sch 6 para 30(2)* (banking groups: information as to undertaking in which shares held as a result of financial assistance operation).

• All documents to be delivered to the Registrar by a non-traded company under *CA 2006, ss 394A(2)(e), 448A(2)(e)* and *479(2)(e)* (qualifying subsidiaries: conditions for exemption from the audit, preparation and filing of individual accounts).

• A document in a form prescribed in Welsh (or partly in Welsh and partly in English) by virtue of *Welsh Language Act 1993, s 26*.

Where a document is properly delivered to the Registrar of Companies in Welsh without a certified translation into English, the Registrar must obtain such a translation if the document is to be available for public inspection. The translation is treated as if delivered to the Registrar in accordance with the same provision as the original.

A Welsh company may deliver to the Registrar of Companies a certified translation into Welsh of any document in English that relates to the company and is, or has been, delivered to the Registrar.

The provisions of *CA 2006, s 1105* in (3) below do not apply to a document relating to a Welsh company that is drawn up and delivered in Welsh.

[*CA 2006, s 1104; SI 2009 No 1803, Reg 6; SI 2012 No 2301, Reg 21*].

(3)    **Documents that may be drawn up and delivered in other languages**

The documents listed below may be drawn up and delivered to the Registrar of Companies in a language other than English, but when delivered they must be accompanied by a certified translation into English. The documents in question are

• agreements required to be forwarded to the Registrar of Companies under *CA 2006, ss 29, 30* (agreements affecting the company's constitution, see **14.10** CONSTITUTION – MEMORANDUM AND ARTICLES)

• documents required to be delivered under *CA 2006, s 400(2)(e)* or *s 401(2)(f)* (company included in accounts of larger group);

• certified copies required to be delivered relating to registration of charges; and

- a memorandum of association;

- a company's articles;

- a valuation report required to be delivered to the Registrar of Companies under *CA 2006, s 94(2)(d)* (application for a private company to be re-registered as a public company, see **41.6 Re-Registration**);

- any order made by a competent court in the UK or elsewhere;

- copies of the consolidated accounts, the auditor's report and the consolidated annual report to be delivered to the Registrar under *CA 2006, ss 394A(2)(e), 448A(2)(e)* or *479A(2)(e)* (qualifying subsidiaries: conditions for exemption from the audit, preparation and filing of individual accounts).

- in the case of an overseas company,

  (i)   a certified copy of the constitution required to be delivered to the Registrar of Companies under *Overseas Companies Regulations 2009, Reg 8, 14* or *15* (see **30.4, 30.7** and **30.8 Overseas Companies** respectively);

  (ii)  copies of accounting documents required to be delivered under *Overseas Companies Regulations 2009, Reg 9, 32, 45* or *46* (see **30.4, 39.20,** and **30.37 Overseas Companies** respectively);

  (iii) copies of accounts required to be delivered under *CA 2006, s 441* as modified by *Overseas Companies Regulations 2009, Regs 40* and *55* (see **30.44** and **30.50 Overseas Companies** respectively); and

  (iv)  a certified copy of a debenture or other instrument creating or evidencing a charge over the property of the company to which *Overseas Companies (Execution of Documents and Registration of Charges) Regulations 2009, Pt 3* applies.

[*CA 2006, s 1105; SI 2006 No 3429, Reg 4; SI 2007 No 2974; SI 2009 No 1801, Reg 78; SI 2009 No 1803, Reg 7; SI 2009 No 1917, Reg 27; SI 2012 No 2301, Reg 21; SI 2013 No.600, Schedule 2, para 3*].

(4)   **Certified translations**

In the case of any discrepancy between the original language version of a document and a 'certified translation'

- the company may not rely on the translation as against a 'third party'; but

- a third party may rely on the translation unless the company shows that the third party had knowledge of the original.

A '*certified translation*' means a translation certified to be a correct translation.

A '*third party*' means a person other than the company or the Registrar of Companies.

[*CA 2006, s 1107*]

**Voluntary filing of translations.** A company may deliver to the Registrar of Companies one or more certified translations of any document relating to the company that is, or has been, delivered to the Registrar.

The Secretary of State may by *Regulations* specify the languages and descriptions of document in relation to which this facility is available. The facility must be available in relation to all the official languages of the EU and all documents subject to the *Directive* disclosure requirements (see **39.8**).

These provisions do not apply where the original document was delivered to the Registrar of Companies before 8 November 2006.

[*CA 2006, s 1106; SI 2006 No 3429, Reg 5; SI 2007 No 2974*].

**39.14    Language requirements: transliteration**

The following provisions apply in relation to all documents delivered to the Registrar of Companies.

**Permitted characters.** Subject to the exceptions below, names and addresses in a document delivered to the Registrar of Companies must contain only letters, characters and symbols (including accents and other diacritical marks) that are permitted. Those permitted are:

•    Letters A to Z (in upper and lower case)

•    Numerals 0, 1, 2, 3, 4, 5, 6, 7, 8 and 9

•    &, @, £, $, €, ¥, *, =, #, %, and +

•    Any of the following types of punctuation but only in the forms indicated:

   (i)    Apostrophe: ' ' '

   (ii)    Bracket: ( ) [ ] { } < >

   (iii)    Exclamation mark: !

   (iv)    Guillemet: « »

   (v)    Inverted comma: " " ″

   (vi)    Question mark: ?

   (vii)    Solidus: \ /

•    Full stop, comma, colon, semi-colon or hyphen

The above requirement does not apply to the following documents.

(a)    A memorandum of association.

(b)    A company's articles.

(c)    An order made by a competent court in the UK or elsewhere.

(d)    An agreement required to be forwarded to the Registrar of Companies under *CA 2006, ss 29, 30* (agreements affecting a company's constitution see **14.10** CONSTITUTION – MEMORANDUM AND ARTICLES).

(e)    A valuation report required to be delivered to the Registrar of Companies under *CA 2006, s 94(2)(d)* (application for a private company to be re-registered as a public company).

(f)    A document required to be delivered to the Registrar of Companies under *CA 2006, s 400(2)(e)* or *s 401(2)(f)* (company included in accounts of larger group: requirement to deliver copy of group accounts).

(g)    An instrument or copy instrument required to be delivered to the Registrar of Companies under *CA 2006, Pt 25* (company charges).

(h)    A certified copy of the constitution of an overseas company required to be delivered to the Registrar of Companies under *Overseas Companies Regulations 2009, Reg 8, 14* or *15*.

## 39.14 Registrar of Companies

(i)    A copy of accounting documents of an overseas company required to be delivered to the Registrar of Companies under *Overseas Companies Regulations 2009, Reg 9, 32, 45 or 46.*

(j)    A copy of the annual accounts of an overseas company, or of a credit or financial institution to which *Overseas Companies Regulations 2009, Pt 6 Chapter 2* applies, required to be delivered to the Registrar of Companies under *CA 2006, s 441.*

(k)    copies of the consolidated accounts, the auditor's report and the consolidated annual report to be delivered to the Registrar under *CA 2006, ss 394A(2)(e), 448A(2)(e)* or *479A(2)(e)* (qualifying subsidiaries: conditions for exemption from the audit, preparation and filing of individual accounts).

[*CA 2006, s 1108; SI 2009 No 1803, Reg 8, Sch; SI 2012 No 2301, Reg 21*].

**Voluntary transliteration into Roman characters.** Where a name or address is, or has been, delivered to the Registrar of Companies in a permitted form using other than Roman characters, the company (or other body) to which the document relates may deliver to the Registrar a transliteration into Roman characters.

[*CA 2006, s 1109*].

**Certification.** The Secretary of State may make provision by Regulations requiring the certification of transliterations and prescribing the form of certification.

[*CA 2006, s 1110*].

## 39.15 Requirements as to certification or verification

Where a document required or authorised to be delivered to the Registrar of Companies under any enactment is required

•    to be certified as an accurate translation or transliteration, or

•    to be certified as a correct copy or verified,

the Registrar may impose requirements as to the person, or description of person, by whom the certificate or verification is to be given provided such requirements are not inconsistent with requirements imposed by any enactment with respect to the certification or verification of the document concerned.

The power conferred on the Registrar of Companies under *CA 2006, s 1068* (see **39.6**) is exercisable in relation to the certificate or verification as if it were a separate document.

[*CA 2006, s 1111*].

## 39.16 Enforcement of company's filing obligations

Where a company has made default in complying with any obligation under the *Companies Acts* to

•    deliver a document to the Registrar of Companies, or

•    give notice to the Registrar of Companies of any matter

the Registrar, or any member or creditor of the company, may give notice to the company requiring it to comply with the obligation.

If the company fails to make good the default within 14 days after service of the notice, the Registrar, or any member or creditor of the company, may apply to the court for an order directing the company, and any specified officer of it, to make good the default within a specified time. The court's order may provide that all costs (in Scotland, expenses) of, or incidental to, the application are to be borne by the company or by any officers of it responsible for the default.

These provisions do not affect the operation of any enactment making it an offence, or imposing a civil penalty, for the default.

[*CA 2006, s 1113*].

### 39.17 ALTERNATIVE TO PUBLICATION IN THE GAZETTE

Notices that would otherwise need to be published by the Registrar in the Gazette may instead be published by such means as may from time to time be approved by the Registrar in accordance with Regulations made by the Secretary of State.

Nothing in these provisions prevents the Registrar from giving public notice both in the Gazette and by means approved under these provisions. In such a case, the requirement of public notice is met when notice is first given by either means.

[*CA 2006, s 1116*].

### 39.18 OFFENCE OF GENERAL FALSE STATEMENT

It is an offence for a person knowingly or recklessly to

• deliver or cause to be delivered to the Registrar of Companies, for any purpose of the *Companies Acts*, a document, or

• to make to the Registrar, for any such purpose, a statement

that is misleading, false or deceptive in a material particular.

A person guilty of such an offence is liable (i) on conviction on indictment, to imprisonment for a term not exceeding two years or a fine (or both); and (ii) on summary conviction, to imprisonment for a term not exceeding twelve months (six months in Scotland and Northern Ireland) or to a fine not exceeding the statutory maximum (or both). See **29.1** OFFENCES AND LEGAL PROCEEDINGS for the statutory maximum.

[*CA 2006, s 1112*].

### 39.19 APPLICATION TO MAKE AN ADDRESS UNAVAILABLE FOR PUBLIC INSPECTION

An application may be made to the Registrar of Companies requiring him to make an address on the register unavailable for public inspection. The application can be made as follows.

(1)    **By an individual**

An application may be made by an individual whose usual residential address was placed on the register after 31 December 2002

• under *CA 1985, s 10* (documents to be sent to Registrar of Companies), *CA 1985, s 288* (register of directors and secretaries), *CA 2006, s 363* (duty to deliver annual returns), *CA 1985, s 691* (documents to be delivered to Registrar of Companies), *CA 1985, s 692* (registration of altered particulars), or *CA 1985, Sch 21A, para 2* (registration of UK branch by overseas company);

- under the equivalent NI legislation; or

- as a service address under *CA 2006, s 12* (statement of proposed officers), *CA 2006, s 167* (duty to notify Registrar of Companies of changes of director's particulars) or *CA 2006, s 855* (contents of annual return) or under regulations made under *CA 2006, s 1046*.

The grounds on which an application may be made are that the individual concerned

- considers that there is a serious risk that he, or a person who lives with him, will be subjected to violence or intimidation as a result of the activities of at least one of the companies of which

    (i)   he is, or proposes to become, a director; or

    (ii)  he is not a director but of which he has been at any time a director, secretary or permanent representative;

- he is or has been employed by a 'relevant organisation';

- he has made, or has had made on his behalf, a successful application requiring the Registrar of Companies not to disclose protected information about him to credit reference agencies under *CA 2006, s 243* (see **18.73** DIRECTORS); or

- had a confidentiality order in force in relation to him immediately before 1 October 2009.

A *'relevant organisation'* means the Government Communications Headquarters, the Secret Intelligence Service, the Security Service or a police force.

The application must contain

- a statement of the grounds on which the application is made;

- the name and any former name of the applicant;

- the usual residential address of the applicant that is to be made unavailable for public inspection;

- an address for correspondence in respect of the application;

- the name and registered number of each company of which the applicant is or has been at any time since 1 January 2003 a director, secretary or permanent representative;

- the service address which is to replace that usual residential address on the register;

- Subject to below

    (i)   the date of birth of the applicant;

    (ii)  the name of each company of which the applicant proposes to become a director; and

    (iii) where the Registrar of Companies has allotted a unique identifier to the applicant, that unique identifier.

except that the application need not contain this information where the application is delivered to the Registrar of Companies on the same day as the applicant delivers an application under *CA 2006, s 243* (application not to disclose protected information to credit reference agencies, see **18.73** DIRECTORS).

The application must be accompanied by evidence that the relevant grounds apply.

The Registrar of Companies may request additional information and evidence and may refer to a 'relevant body' any question relating to an assessment of the nature and extent of any risk of violence or intimidation or, as the case may be, as to whether the applicant is or has been employed by a relevant organisation. He may accept any answer from the relevant body as sufficient evidence of the matter referred to it.

A *'relevant body'* means any police force and any other person whom the Registrar of Companies considers may be able to assist in answering a question referred to that person by him.

The Registrar of Companies must determine the application and send the applicant, to the address for correspondence stated in his application, notice of his determination within five working days of that determination being made.

(2) **Application by a company**

An application may be made by a company in respect of the addresses of

- all of its members and former members whose addresses were contained in an annual return or a return of allotment of shares, or

- the subscribers to its memorandum of association.

where the relevant document was delivered to the Registrar of Companies after 31 December 2002.

The grounds on which an application may be made are that the company making the application considers that, as a result of its activities, the availability to members of the public of those addresses creates a serious risk that its members or former members or subscribers, or persons who live at those addresses, will be subjected to violence or intimidation.

The application must contain

- the name of the applicant and its registered number; and

- a statement of the grounds on which the application is made.

It must be accompanied by evidence which supports the applicant's assertion that its application falls within the grounds stated. Alternatively, where the court has made an order under *CA 2006, s 117(3)* (register of members: response to request for inspection or copy) directing the applicant not to comply with a request under *CA 2006, s 116* (rights to inspect and require copies), a copy of that order can be submitted.

The Registrar of Companies may direct that additional information or evidence be delivered to him and he may also refer to a 'relevant body' (see (1) above) any question relating to the assessment of the nature and extent of any risk of violence or intimidation. He may accept any answer from the relevant body as sufficient evidence of the matter referred to it.

The Registrar of Companies must determine the application and send the applicant, to its registered office, notice of his determination within five working days of that determination being made.

(3)  **Application by a person who registers a charge**

An application may be made to the Registrar of Companies by a person who

- registered a charge under *CA 1985, Pt 12* (or NI equivalent) after 31 December 2002 or has registered a charge under *CA 2006, Pt 25* or regulations made under *CA 2006, s 1052*, and

- is not the company which created the charge or acquired the property subject to a charge,

in respect of his address delivered to the Registrar of Companies for the purposes of that registration.

The grounds on which an application may be made are that the person making the application considers that there is a serious risk that he, or if applicable his employees, or persons who live with him or his employees, will be subjected to violence or intimidation as a result of the activities of the company which is, or was, subject to the charge.

The application must contain

- a statement of the grounds on which the application is made;

- the name of the applicant, and where the applicant is a company, its registered number;

- the address of the applicant that is to be made unavailable for public inspection;

- the name and registered number of the company which is or was subject to the charge;

- an address for correspondence with the Registrar of Companies in respect of the application;

- where the applicant is the chargee, the service address which is to replace the address of the applicant on the register.

It must be accompanied by evidence which supports the applicant's assertion that there is a serious risk that he or, if applicable, his employees, or persons who live with him or his employees, will be subjected to violence or intimidation as a result of the activities of the company which is or was subject to the charge.

The Registrar of Companies may direct that additional information or evidence should be delivered to him and he may also refer to a 'relevant body' (see (1) above) any question relating to the assessment of the nature and extent of any risk of violence or intimidation. He may accept any answer from the relevant body as sufficient evidence of the matter referred to it.

The Registrar of Companies must determine the application and send the applicant, to the address stated in the application, notice of his determination within five working days of that determination being made.

**Effect of a successful application.** Where an application has been determined in favour of the applicant, the Registrar of Companies must

- in the case of an application made under (1) or (3) above, make the specified address unavailable for public inspection; and

- in the case of an application under (2) above, make all of the members', former members' or subscribers' addresses unavailable for public inspection.

A person in relation to whom a confidentiality order was in force immediately before 1 October 2009 is treated, on or after that date, as if they had made a successful application to make their usual residential address unavailable for inspection under these provisions. [*SI 2008 No 2860, Sch 2 para 36*]. The Registrar of Companies must therefore continue to make that address unavailable for public inspection.

**Appeals.** Unsuccessful applicants may, with leave of the court, appeal to the High Court (in Scotland, the Court of Session) on the grounds that the decision is unlawful, irrational or unreasonable, or has been made on the basis of a procedural impropriety or otherwise contravenes the rules of natural justice. Any appeal must be brought within 21 days of the date of the Registrar's notice (or later with the court's permission). The court may dismiss the appeal or quash the decision. In the later case, it may refer the matter to the Registrar of Companies with a direction to reconsider it and make a determination in accordance with the findings of the court.

**Duration of decision.** A decision continues to have effect until the Registrar of Companies revokes the decision.

**Revocation.** The Registrar of Companies may revoke a decision at any time if he is satisfied that the 'beneficiary' of that decision or any other person, in purported compliance with any of the above provisions, is found guilty of an offence under *CA 2006, s 1112* (general false statement offence).

If the Registrar of Companies proposes to make a revocation decision, he must send the beneficiary notice of his intention

- informing the beneficiary that he may, within 28 days of the notice, deliver representations in writing to the Registrar; and

- stating that if representations are not received by the Registrar within that period, the revocation decision will be made at the expiry of that period.

If the beneficiary delivers representations in the time allowed, the Registrar of Companies must consider them and, within five working days of making his decision, send notice of it to the beneficiary.

[*CA 2006, s 1088; SI 2009 No 214, Regs 9–16; SI 2009 No 1917, Reg 27*].

As to recent developments in this area, on 22 February 2018, a set of draft *Companies (Disclosure of Address) (Amendment) Regulations 2018* and an accompanying explanatory memorandum were published.

These draft regulations make certain amendments to the *Companies (Disclosure of Address) Regulations 2009*.

Notably, a new *regulation 9* is substituted; this provides that an individual whose usual residential address is on the central register may apply to the registrar under *CA 2006, s 1088* for that residential address to be made unavailable for public inspection, *without* having to rely on any specified grounds. The *2009 Regulations* had curtailed the scope of such application by laying down certain limited grounds – such as, that the individual considered himself or herself, or a person living with them, to be at serious risk of violence or intimidation as a result of the activities of a company with which they were involved. The new *2018 Regulations* should in principle make it easier for a director to succeed in, effectively, protecting the privacy of their home address.

## 39.19  Registrar of Companies

The Government has previously announced that the draft *2018 Regulations* would come into force by the end of summer 2018. We will update the position in a future edition of the Handbook as matters unfold.

## 39.20  COMPANIES HOUSE WEBFILING

Instead of filling and updating certain company details in paper form, it is possible to use the Companies House WebFiling service on its website. Nearly 90% of companies are already filing some or all of their information electronically.

Newcomers to WebFiling must first register (free of charge) for the following two codes.

- *Security code* — this identifies the company as a user. It is sent by email when a company registers and is linked to its email address.

- *Company authentication code* — this is posted to the company's registered office address and is the electronic equivalent of a company director's signature. Companies must keep it safe and only share it with someone they trust to file information for the company.

For most companies, WebFiling covers all the information they will need to file in a typical year. It covers all of the most commonly filed document types, including

- the annual return;
- change of accounting reference date;
- change of name;
- appointment of a director or secretary;
- terminating appointment as director or secretary;
- change of particulars for director or secretary;
- change in situation or address of registered office;
- return of allotments of shares – excluding non-cash;
- audit-exempt abbreviated accounts;
- location of register of members;
- location of register of debenture holders;
- dormant company accounts; and
- particulars of a charge.

Documents can be submitted between 7.00am and midnight Monday to Saturday, but will only be examined during working hours (7.30am to 6.30pm, Monday to Friday). More information on this service is available on the Companies House website.

Companies House aims to expand WebFiling further to provide a 100% electronic filing capability by 2018/2019. It is available 24 hours seven days a week.

Currently, all information filing options on the service are free, except for the annual return and change of name (see APPENDIX 3: COMPANIES HOUSE FEES). Annual return fees can be paid online by credit or debit card. Alternatively, companies filing ten or more annual returns each year can apply for a Companies House e-filing credit account. The main advantages of Webfiling are:

- time-saving information can be filed directly from a PC;

- security of information;

- cost-annual returns are filed at half the cost of a paper filing;

- benefit from PROOF (a Protected Online Filing scheme, of which more information may be found on the Companies House website)

- less chance of forms and returns being rejected;

- web filing users get access to additional services including email reminders for accounts and annual returns (confirmation statements) and PROOF.

# 40   Registration of Charges

**Cross-references.** See **38.15** REGISTERS for the requirement for a company to keep a register of charges and copies of instruments creating charges; **45** for security taken when a charge is given; **30.64** for registration of charges over UK property of an overseas company

## 40.1   INTRODUCTION TO REGISTRATION OF CHARGES

Companies are able to use all or any of their assets as security for loans. This usually involves the creation of a charge over its assets. Certain charges on a company's property must be registered with the Registrar of Companies. The provisions for companies registered in England and Wales and Northern Ireland are covered in **40.2** and those for companies registered in Scotland are covered in **40.13–40.19**. As from 6 April 2013, *Companies Act 2006 (CA 2006), Pt 25, Chs 1* and *2* were repealed and *SI 2008 No 2296* referred to in this chapter is revoked. Both are replaced by provisions in the *Companies Act 2006 (Amendment of Part 25) Regulations 2013 (SI 2013 No 600)* which came into force on 6 April 2013 and which apply to charges created on or after that date. The provisions of *CA 2006, Pt 25* as they stood immediately before 6 April 2013 continue to apply to charges created before that date together with new provisions (*CA 2006, s 859K, 859L* and *859O*) which also apply to charges created before 6 April 2013. This chapter includes covers both pre and post 6 April 2013 regulatory provisions.

### ENGLAND AND WALES AND NORTHERN IRELAND

## 40.2   Charges created before 6 April 2013

**Charges created by a company.** A company registered in England and Wales or in Northern Ireland that creates a charge (which includes a mortgage see definition below) must deliver the prescribed particulars of the charge, together with the instrument (if any) by which the charge is created or evidenced, to the Registrar of Companies for registration before the end of the period allowed for registration, ie

- 21 days beginning with the day after the day on which the charge is created; or

- if the charge is created outside the UK (see **40.7**), 21 days beginning with the day after the day on which the instrument by which the charge is created or evidenced (or a copy of it) could, in due course of post (and if despatched with due diligence) have been received in the UK.

The prescribed particulars for these purposes are

- the date of the creation of the charge;

- a description of the instrument (if any) creating or evidencing the charge;

- the amount secured by the charge;

- the name and address of the person entitled to the charge; and

- short particulars of the property charged.

Alternatively, registration of a charge may be effected on the application of a person interested in it, in which case that person is entitled to recover from the company any fees he has properly paid to the Registrar of Companies on the registration.

If the company fails to comply with these provisions then, unless the registration of charge has been effected by another person, an offence is committed by the company and every officer of the company who is in default. A person guilty of such an offence is liable (i) on conviction on indictment, to a fine; or (ii) on summary conviction, to a fine not exceeding the statutory maximum. See **29.1** OFFENCES AND LEGAL PROCEEDINGS for the statutory maximum.

The charges to which these provisions apply are as follows.

- A charge on land (wherever situated) or any interest in land, other than a charge for any rent or other periodical sum issuing out of land. The holding of debentures entitling the holder to a charge on land is not, for this purpose, an interest in the land.

- A charge created or evidenced by an instrument which, if executed by an individual, would require registration as a bill of sale.

- A charge for the purposes of securing any issue of debentures.

- A charge on uncalled share capital of the company.

- A charge on calls made but not paid.

- A charge on book debts of the company. The deposit by way of security of a negotiable instrument given to secure the payment of book debts is not, for this purpose, a charge on those book debts.

- A floating charge on the company's property or undertaking.

- A charge on a ship or aircraft, or any share in a ship.

- A charge on goodwill or on any 'intellectual property'. For this purpose, '*intellectual property*' means

    (i)     any patent, trade mark, registered design, copyright or design right; and

    (ii)    any licence under or in respect of any such right.

[*CA 2006, ss 860, 861, 870(1); SI 2008 No 2996, Reg 2*].

**40.3    UK registered companies: Charges created on or after 6 April 2013**

A UK registered company (irrespective of the place of incorporation of the company within the UK) that creates a charge (see below for definition) must (or a person interested in such a charge must) deliver a *'section 859D* statement of particulars' and, where the charge is created or evidenced by an instrument, a certified copy of the instrument, to the Registrar of Companies for registration before the 'period allowed for delivery'.

For the purposes of delivering the *section 859D* statement of particulars, persons interested in a charge would include the charge holder. Companies House have clarified that this would also include legal advisers to the company and the charge holder. Companies House have also confirmed that legal advisers to the company and the charge holder may sign Form MR01 in relation to the charge. Given the consequences of non-registration (see below), in practice, the charge holder (or its legal advisers) will often take responsibility for arranging registration. The filing of the *section 859D* statement of particulars and Form MR01 (or MR08 if there is no instrument) can be done through the Companies House WebFiling service (see **39.20 COMPANIES HOUSE WEBFILING**). For this purpose, a lender (or anyone other than the company who created the charge) would need to apply to Companies House for a lender authentication code.

The period allowed for delivery is a period of 21 days beginning with the day after the date of creation of the charge unless a court order allowing an extended period is made under *CA 2006, s 859F(3)* (see below). If such an order is made, a copy of the order must be delivered to the Registrar of Companies with the *section 859D* statement of particulars. If these provisions are complied with the Registrar of Companies must register the charge.

Extension of the period allowed for delivery may be granted under *CA 2006, s 859F* where the court is satisfied that neither the company nor any other person interested in the charge has delivered to the Registrar of Companies the documents required under *s 859A* or *859B* before the end of the period allowed for delivery and that the failure to deliver those documents was accidental or due to inadvertence or to some other sufficient cause or is not of a nature to prejudice the position of creditors or shareholders of the company or that on other grounds it is just and equitable to grant relief. The court may, on the application of the company or a person interested, and on such terms and conditions as seem to the court just and expedient, order that the period allowed for delivery be extended.

For the purposes of the provisions in *CA 2006, Part 25* a charge includes a mortgage, a standard security, assignation in security and any other right in security constituted under the law of Scotland including any heritable security, but not including a pledge. A charge does not include a charge in favour of a landlord on a cash deposit given as security in connection with the lease of land or a charge created by a member of Lloyd's (within the meaning of the *Lloyd's Act 1982*) to secure its obligations in connection with its underwriting business at Lloyd's and "cash" includes foreign currency.

Where a certified copy of an instrument is delivered to the Registrar of Companies the following information is not required to be included:

• personal information relating to an individual (other than the name of the individual);

• the number or other identifier of a bank or securities account of a company or individual;

• a signature.

But the Registrar of Companies is entitled, without further enquiry, to accept the certified copy of an instrument whether or not any of the above information is contained within the instrument.

## 40.3  Registration of Charges

The "date of creation of a charge" is defined in the Table set out in *CA 2006, s 859E.*

For the purposes of (*CA 2006, Pt 25*) a charge of a type described in column 1 of the Table is taken to be created on the date given in relation to it in column 2.

| 1. Type of charge | 2. When charge created |
|---|---|
| Standard security | The date of its recording in the Register of Sasines or its registration in the Land Register of Scotland |
| Charge other than a standard security, where created or evidenced by an instrument | Where the instrument is a deed that has been executed and has immediate effect on execution and delivery, the date of delivery |
| | Where the instrument is a deed that has been executed and held in escrow, the date of delivery into escrow |
| | Where the instrument is a deed that has been executed and held as undelivered, the date of delivery |
| | Where the instrument is not a deed and has immediate effect on execution, the date of execution |
| | Where the instrument is not a deed and does not have immediate effect on execution, the date on which the instrument takes effect |
| Charge other than a standard security, where not created or evidenced by instrument | The date on which the charge comes into effect |

Where a charge is created or evidenced by an instrument made between two or more parties, references in the above Table to "execution" are to execution by all the parties to the instrument whose execution is essential for the instrument to take effect as a charge.

*CA 2006, s 859E* applies for the purposes of *CA 2006, Part 25, Chapter 1* even if further forms, notices, registrations or other actions or proceedings are necessary to make the charge valid or effectual for any other purposes.

For the purposes of *CA 2006, Part 25, Chapter 1*, the Registrar of Companies is entitled without further enquiry to accept a charge as created on the date given as the date of creation of the charge in a *section 859D* statement of particulars (see below).

In *CA 2006, s 859E*, "deed" means a deed governed by the law of England and Wales and Northern Ireland or an instrument governed by a law other than the law of England or Wales or Northern Ireland which requires delivery under that law in order to take effect and references to "delivery", in relation to a deed includes delivery as a deed where required.

[*CA 2006, s 859A, s 859E, s 859F, s 859G; SI 2013 No 600, Schedule 1.*]

A statement of particulars relating to a charge created by a company is a *section 859D* statement of particulars if it contains the following particulars:

- the registered name and number of the company;

- the date of the creation of the charge and (if the charge is one to which *CA 2006, s 859C* applies) the date of acquisition of the property or undertaking concerned;

- where the charge is created or evidenced by an instrument the following particulars;

    (a)    any of the following: the name of each of the persons in whose favour the charge has been created or of the security agents or trustees holding the charge for the benefit of one or more persons or where there are more than four such persons; security agents or trustees; the names of any four such persons; security agents or trustees listed in the charge instrument and a statement that there are other such persons, security agents or trustees;

(b)   whether the instrument is expressed to contain a floating charge and, if so, whether it is expressed to cover all the property and undertaking of the company;

(c)   whether any of the terms of the charge prohibit or restrict the company from creating further security that will rank equally with or ahead of the charge;

(d)   whether (and if so a short description of) any land, ship, aircraft or intellectual property that is registered or required to be registered in the United Kingdom, is subject to a charge (which is not a floating charge) or fixed security included in the instrument;

(e)   whether the instrument includes a charge (which is not a floating charge) or fixed security over any tangible or corporeal property or any intangible or incorporeal property not described in (d);

•   where the charge is not created or evidenced by an instrument the following particulars:

(a)   a statement that there is no instrument creating or evidencing the charge;

(b)   the names of each of the persons in whose favour the charge has been created or the names of any security agents or trustees holding the charge for the benefit of one or more persons;

(c)   the nature of the charge;

(d)   a short description of the property or undertaking charged;

(e)   the obligations secured by the charge.

"Fixed security" has the meaning given in *CA 1985, s 486(1)* and "intellectual property" includes any patent, trade mark, registered design, copyright or design right and any licence under or in respect of any such right.

[*CA 2006, s 859D; SI 2013 No 600, Schedule 1*]

**Consequence of failure to register such a charge. Charges created before 6 April 2013**. If a company creates a charge within the above provisions, the charge is void (so far as any security on the company's property or undertaking is conferred by it) against a liquidator, administrator or creditor of the company unless it is registered as required above. This is without prejudice to any contract or obligation for repayment of the money secured by the charge; and when a charge becomes void in these circumstances, the money secured by it immediately becomes payable.

[*CA 2006, s 874*].

The charge is void even if the liquidator or creditor has notice of the unregistered charge (*Monolithic Building Co, Re, Tacon v Monolithic Building Co* [1915] 1 Ch 643, 84 LJ Ch 441, CA).

**Consequence of failure to register such a charge. Charges created on or after 6 April 2013**. If a company creates a charge to which *CA 2006, s 859A* (charges created by a company) or *s 859B* (charge in a series of debentures) applies and the documents required by the relevant section are not delivered to the Registrar of Companies by the company or by another person interested in the charge before the end of the relevant period allowed for delivery (see above for definition), the charge is void (so far as any security on the company's property or undertaking is conferred by it) against a liquidator, administrator or creditor of the company. This is without prejudice to any contract or obligation for repayment of the money secured by the charge; and when a charge becomes void in these circumstances, the money secured by it immediately becomes payable.

[*CA 2006, s 859H; SI 2013 No 600, Schedule 1*]

### 40.4    Charges existing on property acquired

#### Charges created before 6 April 2013

Where a company registered in England and Wales or in Northern Ireland acquires property which is subject to a charge which would, if it had been created by the company after the acquisition of the property, require registration under the provisions in **40.2** to **40.12**, the company must deliver

- particulars of the charge, and

- a certified copy of the instrument (if any) by which the charge was created or evidenced

to the Registrar of Companies for registration before the end of the period allowed for registration, ie

- 21 days beginning with the day after the day on which the acquisition is completed; or

- if the property is situated and the charge was created outside the UK (see **40.7**), 21 days beginning with the day after the day on which the instrument by which the charge is created or evidenced (or a copy of it) could, in due course of post (and if despatched with due diligence) have been received in the UK.

The prescribed particulars for these purposes are

- the date of the creation of the charge;

- a description of the instrument (if any) creating or evidencing the charge;

- the amount secured by the charge;

- the name and address of the person entitled to the charge;

- short particulars of the property charged; and

- the date of the acquisition of the property which is subject to the charge.

If default is made in complying with these provisions, an offence is committed by the company and every officer of the company in default. A person guilty of such an offence is liable (i) on conviction on indictment, to a fine; or (ii) on summary conviction, to a fine not exceeding the statutory maximum. See **29.1** OFFENCES AND LEGAL PROCEEDINGS for the statutory maximum.

[*CA 2006, ss 862, 870(2); SI 2008 No 2996, Reg 4*].

#### Charges created on or after 6 April 2013

Where a company acquires property which is subject to a charge which would have been capable of being registered under **40.3** if it had been created by the company after the acquisition of the property or undertaking, the company or any person interested in the charge must deliver a *section 859D* statement of particulars (see **40.3**) to the Registrar of Companies for registration together with, where the charge is created or evidenced by an instrument, a certified copy of the instrument.

[*CA 2006, s 859C; SI 2013 No 600, Schedule 1*]

**40.5    Special rules about debentures**

**Debentures created before 6 April 2013**

Where a company registered in England and Wales or in Northern Ireland creates a series of debentures containing, or giving by reference to another instrument, a charge which benefits the debenture holders of the series *passu*, it is sufficient for the purposes of **40.2** if the following are delivered to the Registrar of Companies within 21 days after the day on which the deed containing the charge is executed. If there is no such deed, they must be delivered within 21 days after the day on which the first debenture of the series is executed.

(a)    Particulars of

- the total amount secured by the whole series;

- the dates of the resolutions authorising the issue of the series and the date of the covering deed (if any) by which the security is created or defined;

- a general description of the property charged; and

- the names of the trustees for the debenture-holders (if any).

(b)    The deed containing the charge or, if there is no deed, one of the debentures of the series.

Particulars must also be sent for registration of

(i)    the date and amount of each issue of debentures of a series; and

(ii)    where appropriate, the amount or rate per cent of any commission, discount or allowance which has been paid or made directly or indirectly by a company to a person in consideration of his

- subscribing or agreeing to subscribe (whether absolutely or conditionally) for debentures of the company; or

- procuring or agreeing to procure subscriptions (whether absolute or conditional) for such debentures.

The deposit of debentures as security for a debt of the company is not to be treated as the issue of debentures at a discount for these purposes.

But failure to register particulars under (i) or (ii) above does not affect the validity of the debentures issued.

Registration of a series of debentures may be effected by the company or on the application of a person interested in them, in which case that person is entitled to recover from the company any fees he has properly paid to the Registrar of Companies on the registration.

If the company fails to comply with these provisions then, unless the registration of the series of debentures has been effected by another person, an offence is committed by the company and every officer of the company who is in default. A person guilty of such an offence is liable (i) on conviction on indictment, to a fine; or (ii) on summary conviction, to a fine not exceeding the statutory maximum. See **29.1** OFFENCES AND LEGAL PROCEEDINGS for the statutory maximum.

# 40.5   Registration of Charges

[*CA 2006, ss 863, 864, 870(3)*].

### Debentures created on or after 6 April 2013

Where a company creates a series of debentures containing, or giving by reference to another instrument, a charge which benefits the debenture holders of the series *pari passu*, the company must (or a person interested in such a charge must) deliver a "*section 859D* statement of particulars" and, where the charge is created or evidenced by an instrument, a certified copy of the instrument, to the Registrar of Companies for registration before the "period allowed for delivery". The period allowed for delivery is, if there is a deed containing the charge, 21 days beginning with the day after the date on which the deed is executed or, if there is no deed containing the charge, 21 days beginning with the day after the date on which the first debenture of the series is executed unless a court order allowing an extended period is made under *CA 2006, s 859F(3)* (see **40.3** for details of when the court may make such an order). If such an order is made, a copy of the order must be delivered to the Registrar of Companies with the *section 859D* statement of particulars. If these provisions are complied with the Registrar of Companies must register the charge. Where the charge is not created or evidenced by an instrument, the Registrar of Companies is required to register it only if a certified copy of one of the debentures in the series is delivered to the Registrar of Companies with the *section 859D* statement of particulars.

Where the charge is contained in a series of debentures the *section 859D* statement of particulars must, in addition to the matters set out in **40.3**, also contain the following:

- either the name of each of the trustees for the debenture holders or where there are more than four such persons, the names of any four persons listed in the charge instrument as trustees for the debenture holders ,and a statement that there are other such persons;

- the dates of the resolutions authorising the issue of the series;

- the date of the covering instrument (if any) by which the series is created or defined.

For the purposes of *CA 2006, s 859B*, a statement of particulars is taken to be a *section 859D* statement of particulars even if it does not contain the names of the debenture holders.

In *CA 2006, s 859B*, "deed" means a deed governed by the law of England and Wales and Northern Ireland or an instrument governed by a law other than the law of England or Wales or Northern Ireland which requires delivery under that law in order to take effect.

[*CA 2006, s 859B; SI 2013 No 600, Schedule 1*]

## 40.6   Endorsement of certificate on debentures

### Charges created before 6 April 2013

A company must cause a copy of every certificate of registration given by the Registrar of Companies under **40.9** to be endorsed on every debenture or certificate of debenture stock which is issued by the company, and the payment of which is secured by the charge so registered. But this does not require a company to cause a certificate of registration of any charge so given to be endorsed on any debenture or certificate of debenture stock issued by the company before the charge was created.

If a person knowingly and wilfully authorises or permits the delivery of a debenture or certificate of debenture stock in default of this requirement, he commits of an offence. A person guilty of such an offence is liable, on summary conviction, to a fine not exceeding level 3 on the standard scale (see **29.1** OFFENCES AND LEGAL PROCEEDINGS).

[*CA 2006, s 865*].

There are no corresponding provisions for charges created on or after 6 April 2013.

### 40.7    Charges in other jurisdictions

**Charges created before 6 April 2013**

**Charges created outside the UK comprising property situated outside the UK.** The delivery to the Registrar of Companies of a verified copy of the instrument by which the charge is created or evidenced has the same effect for the purposes of **40.2** to **40.12** as the delivery of the instrument itself. [*CA 2006, s 866(1)*].

**Charges created in the UK comprising property situated outside the UK.** The instrument creating or purporting to create the charge may be sent for registration under **40.2** even though further proceedings may be necessary to make the charge valid or effectual according to the law of the country where the property is situated.

[*CA 2006, s 866(2)*].

**Charges created in, or over property in, another UK jurisdiction.** Where

• a charge comprises property situated in a part of the UK other than the part in which the company is registered, and

• registration in that other part is necessary to make the charge valid or effectual under the law of that part of the UK,

the delivery to the Registrar of Companies of a verified copy of the instrument by which the charge is created or evidenced, together with a certificate stating that the charge was presented for registration in that other part of the UK on the date on which it was so presented, has the same effect for the purposes of **40.2** to **40.12** as the delivery of the instrument itself.

[*CA 2006, s 867*].

There are no corresponding provisions for charges created on or after 6 April 2013.

### 40.8    Northern Ireland: registration of certain charges affecting land

**Charges created before 6 April 2013**

Where a charge imposed by an order under *Judgments Enforcement (Northern Ireland) Order 1981, Art 46* or notice of such a charge is registered in the Land Registry against registered land or any estate in registered land of a company, the Registrar of Titles must, as soon as may be, cause two copies of that order or notice to be delivered to the Registrar of Companies.

Where a charge imposed by an order under *Judgments Enforcement (Northern Ireland) Order 1981, Art 46* is registered in the Registry of Deeds against any unregistered land or estate in land of a company, the Registrar of Deeds must, as soon as may be, cause two copies of the order to be delivered to the Registrar of Companies.

On delivery of copies under either of the above provisions, the Registrar of Companies must

• register one of them in accordance with **40.9**; and

• not later than seven days from that date of delivery, cause the other copy, together with a certificate of registration, to be sent to the company against which judgment was given.

## 40.8    Registration of Charges

Where a charge to which the above provisions applies is vacated, the Registrar of Titles or, as the case may be, the Registrar of Deeds must cause a certified copy of the certificate of satisfaction lodged under *Judgments Enforcement (Northern Ireland) Order 1981, Art 132(1)* to be delivered to the Registrar of Companies for entry of a memorandum of satisfaction in accordance with **40.9**.

[*CA 2006, s 868*].

There are no corresponding provisions for charges created on or after 6 April 2013.

### 40.9    Register of charges to be kept by the Registrar of Companies

#### Charges created before 6 April 2013

For every company, the Registrar of Companies must keep, and make available for inspection by any person, a register of all the charges requiring registration under the provisions in **40.2** to **40.12**. The register must show

- in the case of a charge to the benefit of which the holders of a series of debentures are entitled, the particulars specified in **40.5(*a*)**;

- in the case of a charge imposed by the Enforcement of Judgments Office under *Judgments Enforcement (Northern Ireland) 1981, Art 46*, the date on which the charge became effective; and

- in the case of any other charge

    (i)     the date of creation (in the case of a charge created by the company) or the date of acquisition of the property (in the case of a charge which was existing on property acquired by the company);

    (ii)    the amount secured by the charge;

    (iii)   short particulars of the property charged; and

    (iv)    the persons entitled to the charge.

The Registrar of Companies must give a signed or authenticated certificate of registration of any charge so registered, stating the amount secured by the charge. Such a certificate is conclusive evidence that the registration requirements have been complied with. See *Exeter Trust Ltd v Screenways Ltd* [1991] BCLC 888, [1991] BCC 477, CA.

[*CA 2006, s 869*].

#### Charges created on or after 6 April 2013

For every company, the Registrar of Companies must allocate to the charge a unique reference code and place a note in the register recording that reference code and include in the register any documents delivered under *CA 2006, s 859A(3)* (certified copy of an instrument where the charge is created or evidenced by an instrument), *s 859A(5)* (a court order made under *s 859F(3)* extending the period for delivering a charge), *s 859B(3)* (certified copy of an instrument where the charge is created or evidenced by an instrument), *s 859B(4)* (certified copy of one of the debentures in the series), *s 859B(7)* (a court order made under *s 859F(3)* extending the period for delivering a charge) or *s 859C(3)* (certified copy of an instrument where the charge is created or evidenced by an instrument).

The Registrar of Companies must give a signed or authenticated certificate of registration of the charge to the person who delivered the *section 859* statement of particulars to that Registrar. The certificate must state the registered name and number of the company in respect of which the charge was registered and the unique reference code allocated to the charge. In the case of registration under *s 859A* or *859B* the certificate is conclusive evidence that the documents required by the section concerned were delivered to the Registrar of Companies before the end of the relevant period allowed for delivery.

The relevant period allowed for delivery is the period allowed for delivery under the section in question or if a court order under *CA 2006, s 859F(3)* has been made, the period allowed by the order.

Where a company is acting as trustee of property or undertaking which is the subject of a charge delivered for registration, the company or any person interested in the charge may deliver to the Registrar of Companies a statement to that effect. A statement which is delivered after the delivery for registration of the charge must include the registered name and number of the company and the unique reference code allocated to the charge.

[*CA 2006, s 859L, s 859J; SI 2013 No 600, Schedule 1*]

*Entries of satisfaction and release.* **Charges created before, on or after 6 April 2013**

If a statement is delivered to the Registrar of Companies with respect to a registered charge to the effect that:

- the debt for which the charge was given has been paid or satisfied in whole or in part, or

- all or part of the property or undertaking charged has been released from the charge or has ceased to form part of the company's property or undertaking (and where the statement relates to part only of the property or undertaking charged, the statement must include a short description of that part).

and also the following particulars with respect to the registered charge are delivered to the Registrar of Companies

- the name and address of the person delivering the statement and an indication of their interest in the charge;

- the registered name and number of the company that created the charge or acquired the property or undertaking subject to the charge;

- in respect of a charge created before 6 April 2013 the date of creation of the charge, a description of the instrument (if any) by which the charge is created or evidenced, short particulars of the property or undertaking charged; and

- in respect of a charge created on or after 6 April 2013, the unique reference code allocated to the charge.

the Registrar of Companies must include in the register a statement of satisfaction in whole or in part or a statement of the fact that all or part of the property or undertaking has been released from the charge or has ceased to form part of the company's property or undertaking (as the case may be).

[*CA 2006, s 859L; SI 2013 No 600, reg 3* and *Schedule 1*]

**40.10 Rectification of register of charges by court**

**Charges created before 6 April 2013**

Where there has been

- a failure to register a charge within the time required, or

- an omission or mis-statement of any particulars with respect to any such charge or in a memorandum of satisfaction.

the court may, on the application of the company or a person interested, order the period allowed for registration to be extended or, as the case may be, the omission or mis-statement to be rectified where it is satisfied that

- the failure or omission

  (i) was accidental or due to inadvertence or to some other sufficient cause; or

  (ii) is not of a nature to prejudice the position of creditors or shareholders of the company; or

- it is just and equitable to grant relief on other grounds.

[*CA 2006, s 873*].

**Charges created on or after 6 April 2013**

Where there has been an omission or mis-statement in any statement or notice delivered to the Registrar in accordance with *CA 2006, Chapter 1, Part 25* and the court is satisfied that:

- the omission or mis-statement

  (i) was accidental or due to inadvertence or to some other sufficient cause; or

  (ii) is not of a nature to prejudice the position of creditors or shareholders of the company; or

- that on other grounds it is just and equitable to grant relief,

the court may, on the application of the company or a person interested, and on such terms and conditions as seem to the court just and expedient, order that the omission or mis-statement be rectified.

A copy of the court order must be sent by the applicant to the Registrar of Companies for registration.

[*CA 2006, s 859M; SI 2013 No 600, Schedule 1*]

If the court is satisfied that a copy of an instrument or debenture delivered to the Registrar of Companies contains material which could have been omitted (see **40.3**) or the wrong instrument or debenture was delivered to the Registrar of Companies or the copy was defective, the court may, on the application of the company or a person interested, and on such terms as seem to the court just and expedient, order that the copy of the instrument or debenture be removed from the register and replaced. A copy of the court order must be sent by the applicant to the Registrar of Companies for registration.

[*CA 2006, s 859N; SI 2013 No 600, Schedule 1*]

An application to rectify such an error must be made to the Central London County Court. Further guidance on the procedure to be followed in such an application, and on the claim form to be used (Form LOC009), may be found on the HM Courts and Tribunals Service website. The guidance currently appearing there was prepared in relation to the pre-6 April 2013 regime. However, the Central London County Court have advised that the application and forms there can now be used for an application under *CA 2006, s 859M*, with appropriate amendments being made to the forms. Even though Form LOC009 refers to the Companies Court, the Central London County Court is the appropriate forum for this application.

There is also an informal correction procedure under *CA 2006, s 1075*, by which the Registrar may in certain circumstances, before registering a charge, informally correct a document delivered to it if that document appears to be incomplete or internally inconsistent. Companies House has produced guidance on this informal process.

**40.11   Notification of addition to or amendment of charge: charges created before, on or after 6 April 2013**

Where after the creation of a charge, the charge is amended by adding or amending a term:

(a)     that prohibits or restricts the creation of any fixed security or any other charge having priority over or ranking *pari passu* with the charge; or

(b)     varies or otherwise regulates the order of the ranking of the charge in relation to any fixed security or any other charge,

either the company that created the charge or the person taking the benefit of the charge (or another charge referred to in (b)) may deliver the following to the Registrar of Companies for registration.

•       a certified copy of the instrument effecting the amendment, variation or regulation and

•       a statement of the following particulars

    (i)      the registered name and number of the company

    (ii)     in the case of a charge created before 6 April 2013 the date of creation of the charge, a description of the instrument (if any) by which the charge was created or evidenced and short particulars of the property or undertaking charged as set out when the charge was registered and in the case of a charge created on or s 6 April 2013, (where allocated) the unique reference code allocated to the charge.

"Fixed security" has the meaning given in *CA 1985, s 486(1)* and the provisions above do not affect the continued application of *CA 1985, s 466*.

[*CA 2006, s 859O; SI 2013 No 600, Schedule 1*]

**40.12   Registration of enforcement of security**

**Charges created before, on or after 6 April 2013**

If a person

•       obtains an order for the appointment of a receiver or manager of a company's property or undertaking, or

•       appoints such a person under powers contained in an instrument.

he must, within seven days of the order or appointment, give notice of the fact to the Registrar of Companies and also if the order was obtained, or the appointment made, by virtue of a registered charge held by the person give the Registrar of Companies a notice containing the following:

•       in the case of a charge created before 6 April 2013, the date of the creation of the charge, a description of the instrument (if any) creating or evidencing the charge and short particulars of the property or undertaking charged;

- in the case of a charge created on or after 6 April 2013, the unique reference code allocated to the charge.

The Registrar of Companies must then enter that fact on the register of charges.

Where a receiver or manager of a company's property appointed under powers contained in an instrument ceases so to act the person must on so ceasing, give notice of that fact to the Registrar of Companies and give the Registrar of Companies a notice containing:

- in the case of a charge created before 6 April 2013, the date of the creation of the charge, a description of the instrument (if any) creating or evidencing the charge and short particulars of thee property or undertaking charged;

- in the case of a charge created on or after 6 April 2013, the unique reference code allocated to the charge.

The Registrar of Companies must then enter that fact on the register of charges.

A person who defaults in complying with the above provisions commits an offence. A person guilty of such an offence is liable, on summary conviction, to a fine not exceeding level 3 on the standard scale and, for continued contravention, a daily default fine not exceeding one-tenth of level 3 on the standard scale. See **29.1** OFFENCES AND LEGAL PROCEEDINGS for the standard scale.

*CA 2006, s 859K* applies only to a receiver or manager appointed by a court in England and Wales or Northern Ireland or under an instrument governed by the law of England and Wales or Northern Ireland but does not apply to a receiver appointed under *Chapter 2* of *Part 3* of the *Insolvency Act 1986* (Receivers (Scotland)).

[*CA 2006, s 859K; SI 2013 No 600, reg 3* and *Schedule 1*].

## 40.13  SCOTLAND

The provisions set out in **40.13–40.19** apply only to charges created before 6 April 2013. See above for provisions which apply to charges created on or after that date.

**Charges created by a company.** An incorporated company registered in Scotland that creates a charge listed below must deliver the prescribed particulars of the charge, together with a copy certified as a correct copy of the instrument (if any) by which the charge is created or evidenced, to the Registrar of Companies for registration before the end of the period allowed for registration, ie

- 21 days beginning with the day after the 'date of creation of the charge'; or

- if the charge is created outside the UK (see **40.17**), 21 days beginning with the day after the day on which a copy of the instrument by which the charge is created or evidenced could, in due course of post (and if despatched with due diligence) have been received in the UK.

The prescribed particulars for these purposes are

- the date of the creation of the charge;
- a description of the instrument (if any) creating or evidencing the charge;
- the amount secured by the charge;
- the name and address of the person entitled to the charge;

- short particulars of the property charged; and

- in the case of a floating charge, a statement as to any provisions of the charge and of any instrument relating to it which prohibit or restrict or regulate the power of the company to grant further securities ranking in priority to, or *pari passu* with, the floating charge, or which vary or otherwise regulate the order of ranking of the floating charge in relation to subsisting securities.

Alternatively, registration of a charge may be effected on the application of a person interested in it, in which case that person is entitled to recover from the company any fees he has properly paid to the Registrar of Companies on the registration.

If the company fails to comply with these provisions then, unless the registration of charge has been effected by another person, an offence is committed by the company and every officer of the company who is in default. A person guilty of such an offence is liable (i) on conviction on indictment, to a fine; or (ii) on summary conviction, to a fine not exceeding the statutory maximum. See **29.1** OFFENCES AND LEGAL PROCEEDINGS for the statutory maximum.

The charges to which these provisions apply are as follows.

(a)   A charge on land (wherever situated) or any interest in such land This does not include a charge for any rent or other periodical sum payable in respect of the land but does include a charge created by a heritable security within the meaning of *Conveyancing and Feudal Reform (Scotland) Act 1970, s 9(8)*. The holding of debentures entitling the holder to a charge on land is not for these purposes deemed to be an interest in land.

(b)   A security over incorporeal moveable property comprising

   (i)      goodwill;

   (ii)     a patent or a licence under a patent;

   (iii)    a trade mark;

   (iv)    a copyright or a licence under a copyright;

   (v)     a registered design or a licence in respect of such a design;

   (vi)    a design right or a licence under a design right;

   (vii)   book debts (whether book debts of the company or assigned to it);

   (viii)  uncalled share capital of the company or calls made but not paid.

(c)   A security over a ship or aircraft or any share in a ship.

(d)   A floating charge.

For the purposes of (*b*)(vii) above, the deposit by way of security of a negotiable instrument given to secure the payment of book debts is not to be treated as a charge on those book debts.

The '*date of creation of the charge*' is

- in the case of a floating charge, the date when the instrument creating it was executed by the company; and

- in any other case, the date when the right of the person entitled to the benefit of the charge was constituted as a real right.

## 40.13 Registration of Charges

[*CA 2006, ss 878, 879, 886(1); SI 2008 No 2996, Reg 3*].

**Consequence of failure to register such a charge**. If a company creates a charge within the above provisions, the charge is void (so far as any security on the company's property or any part of it is conferred by the charge) against a liquidator, administrator or creditor of the company unless it is registered as required above. This is without prejudice to any contract or obligation for repayment of the money secured by the charge; and when a charge becomes void in these circumstances, the money secured by it immediately becomes payable. [*CA 2006, s 889*].

The charge is void even if the liquidator or creditor has notice of the unregistered charge (*Monolithic Building Co, Re, Tacon v Monolithic Building Co* [1915] 1 Ch 643, 84 LJ Ch 441, CA).

## 40.14 Charges existing on property acquired

Where a company registered in Scotland acquires property which is subject to a charge which would, if it had been created by the company after the acquisition of the property, have been required to be registered under the provisions in **40.13** to **40.19**, the company must deliver

- the prescribed particulars of the charge, and

- a copy (certified to be a correct copy) of the instrument (if any) by which the charge was created or is evidenced

to the Registrar of Companies for registration before the end of the period allowed for registration, ie

- 21 days beginning with the day after the day on which the transaction is settled; or

- if the property is situated and the charge was created outside the UK (see **40.17**), 21 days beginning with the day after the day on which a copy of the instrument by which the charge is created or evidenced could, in due course of post (and if despatched with due diligence) have been received in the UK.

The prescribed particulars for these purposes are

- the date of the creation of the charge;

- a description of the instrument (if any) creating or evidencing the charge;

- the amount secured by the charge;

- the name and address of the person entitled to the charge;

- short particulars of the property charged; and

- the date of the acquisition of the property which is subject to the charge.

If default is made in complying with these provisions, an offence is committed by the company and every officer of the company in default. A person guilty of such an offence is liable (i) on conviction on indictment, to a fine; or (ii) on summary conviction, to a fine not exceeding the statutory maximum. See **29.1** Offences and Legal Proceedings for the statutory maximum.

[*CA 2006, s 880, 888(2); SI 2008 No 2996, Reg 4*].

## 40.15 Charges by way of *ex facie* absolute disposition, etc

For the avoidance of doubt, in the case of a charge created by way of

- an *ex facie* absolute disposition or assignation qualified by a back letter or other agreement, or

- a standard security qualified by an agreement

compliance with **40.13** does not of itself render the charge unavailable as security for indebtedness incurred after the date of compliance.

Where the amount secured by a charge so created is purported to be increased by a further back letter or agreement, a further charge is held to have been created by the *ex facie* absolute disposition or assignation or (as the case may be) by the standard security, as qualified by the further back letter or agreement. In that case, the provisions in **40.13** to **40.19** apply to the further charge as if

- references to the charge were references to the further charge; and

- references to the date of creation of the charge were references to the date on which the further back letter or agreement was executed.

[*CA 2006, s 881*].

### 40.16 Special rules about debentures

Where a company registered in Scotland creates a series of debentures containing, or giving by reference to any other instrument, any charge to the benefit of which the debenture holders of that series are entitled *pari passu*, it is sufficient for the purposes of **40.13** if the following are delivered to the Registrar of Companies within 21 days after the day on which the deed containing the charge is executed. If there is no such deed, they must be delivered within 21 days after the day on which the first debenture of the series is executed.

(a)    Particulars of

- the total amount secured by the whole series;

- the dates of the resolutions authorising the issue of the series and the date of the covering deed (if any) by which the security is created or defined;

- a general description of the property charged;

- the names of the trustees for the debenture-holders (if any); and

- in the case of a floating charge, a statement of any provision of the charge and of any instrument relating to it which *either* prohibit, restrict or regulate the company's power to grant further securities ranking in priority to, or *pari passu* with, the floating charge *or* otherwise regulate the order of ranking of the floating charge in relation to subsisting securities.

(b)    A copy of the deed containing the charge or, if there is no deed, one of the debentures of the series.

Particulars must also be sent for registration of

(i)    where more than one issue is made of debentures in a series, the date and amount of each issue of debentures of the series; and

(ii)    where appropriate, the amount or rate per cent of any commission, discount or allowance which has been paid or made directly or indirectly by a company to a person in consideration of his

- subscribing or agreeing to subscribe (whether absolutely or conditionally) for debentures of the company; or

- procuring or agreeing to procure subscriptions (whether absolute or conditional) for such debentures.

(iii)    The deposit of debentures as security for a debt of the company is not to be treated as the issue of debentures at a discount for these purposes.

But failure to register particulars under (i) or (ii) above does not affect the validity of the debentures issued.

Registration of a series of debentures may be effected by the company or on the application of a person interested in them, in which case that person is entitled to recover from the company any fees he has properly paid to the Registrar of Companies on the registration.

If the company fails to comply with these provisions then, unless the registration of series of debentures has been effected by another person, an offence is committed by the company and every officer of the company who is in default. A person guilty of such an offence is liable (i) on conviction on indictment, to a fine; or (ii) on summary conviction, to a fine not exceeding the statutory maximum. See **29.1** OFFENCES AND LEGAL PROCEEDINGS for the statutory maximum.

[*CA 2006, ss 882, 883, 886(3)*].

## 40.17  Charges on property outside the UK

**Charges created in the UK but comprising property outside the UK**. The copy of the instrument creating or purporting to create the charge may be sent for registration under **40.12** even if further proceedings may be necessary to make the charge valid or effectual according to the law of the country where the property is situated.

[*CA 2006, s 884*].

## 40.18  Register of charges to be kept by the Registrar of Companies

For every company, the Registrar of Companies must keep, and make available for inspection by any person, a register of all charges requiring registration. The register must show

- in the case of a charge to the benefit of which the holders of a series of debentures are entitled; the particulars specified in **40.16**(*a*); and

- in the case of any other charge

  (i)    the date of creation (if created by the company) or the date of acquisition of the property (if the charge was existing on property acquired by the company);

  (ii)    the amount secured by the charge;

  (iii)    short particulars of the property charged;

  (iv)    the persons entitled to the charge; and

  (v)    in the case of a floating charge, a statement of any of the provisions of the charge and of any instrument relating to it which *either* prohibit, restrict or regulate the company's power to grant further securities ranking in priority to, or *pari passu* with, the floating charge *or* regulate the order of ranking of the floating charge in relation to subsisting securities.

The Registrar of Companies must give a signed or authenticated certificate of registration of any charge so registered, stating the name of the company, the person first-named in the charge among those entitled to the benefit of the charge (or, in the case of a series of debentures, the name of the holder of the first such debenture issued) and the amount secured by the charge. Such a certificate is conclusive evidence that the registration requirements have been complied with.

[*CA 2006, s 885*].

**Entries of satisfaction and relief.** If a statement is delivered to the Registrar of Companies verifying with respect to a registered charge that

- the debt for which the charge was given has been paid or satisfied in whole or in part, or

- part of the property charged has been released from the charge or has ceased to form part of the company's property

the Registrar of Companies may enter on the register a memorandum of satisfaction (in whole or in part) regarding that fact. If the charge is a floating charge, the statement must be accompanied by either

- a statement by the creditor entitled to the benefit of the charge (or a person authorised by him) verifying that the statement is correct; or

- a direction obtained from the court, on the ground that such a statement could not be readily obtained, dispensing with the need for that statement.

Where the Registrar of Companies enters a memorandum of satisfaction in whole, he must, if required, supply a copy of it to the company.

Nothing in any of the above provisions requires the company to submit particulars with respect to an entry in the register of a memorandum of satisfaction where, having created a floating charge over all or any part of its property, it disposes of part of the property subject to the floating charge.

[*CA 2006, s 887*].

## 40.19  Rectification of register of charges by court

Where there has been

- a failure to register a charge within the time required, or

- an omission or mis-statement of any particulars with respect to any such charge or in a memorandum of satisfaction,

the court may, on the application of the company or a person interested, order the period allowed for registration to be extended or, as the case may be, the omission or mis-statement to be rectified where it is satisfied that

- the failure or omission

    (i)    was accidental or due to inadvertence or to some other sufficient cause, or

    (ii)   is not of a nature to prejudice the position of creditors or shareholders of the company; or

- it is just and equitable to grant relief on other grounds.

[*CA 2006, s 888*].

## 40.20  REGISTRATION IN SPECIAL REGISTER, AND ELSEWHERE

### Charges created before 6 April 2013

## 40.20   Registration of Charges

Charges over certain assets, such as land, intellectual property, ships and aircraft, must be registered at other asset-specific institutions as well as at Companies House.

The Secretary of State has been empowered to make provision for facilitating information-sharing between registries. He/she is also empowered to provide, by order, that the Registrar of Companies need not register a charge of a specified description under the provisions in **40.2–40.19**, but that the charge is instead registered in a special register. Any charge that is properly registered in the special register is to be treated as if it had been registered (and certified by the Registrar of Companies as registered) in accordance with those provisions. The person responsible for maintaining the special register and the Registrar of Companies must have information-sharing arrangements in place which must ensure that persons inspecting the register are made aware of the existence of charges in the special register and are able to obtain information from the special register about any such charge. [*CA 2006, s 893; SI 2013 No 600, Schedule 2, para 3*].

There are no corresponding provisions for charges created on or after 6 April 2013.

These powers have yet to be used. It may be that, if they are in the future deployed, the need for charges to be registered both at Companies House and at an asset-specific registry may change.


## 40.21   COMPANIES' RECORDS AND REGISTERS

See **36** (RECORDS) and **38.15** (REGISTER OF CHARGES) for details of copies which must be kept for inspection.

# 41 Re-Registration

**Cross-references.** See **30.2** OVERSEAS COMPANIES for registration of overseas companies.

## 41.1 INTRODUCTION TO RE-REGISTRATION

A company may alter its status by re-registration. The following possibilities are allowed for under *CA 2006*.

- A private company becoming a public company (see **41.2** to **41.7**).
- A public company becoming a private company (see **41.8** to **41.11**).
- A private limited company becoming unlimited (see **41.13** to **41.15**).
- An unlimited private company becoming a limited (see **41.16** to **41.19**).
- A public company becoming a private and unlimited (see **41.20** to **41.22**).

[*CA 2006, s 89*].

## 41.2 A PRIVATE COMPANY BECOMING A PUBLIC COMPANY

A private company (whether limited or unlimited) may be re-registered as a public company limited by shares if the following conditions are met.

- A special/written resolution that it should be so re-registered is passed.
- The company has a share capital and the requirements in **41.3** are met as regards its share capital.

- The requirements of **41.4** are met as regards its net assets.

- If **41.5** applies (recent allotment of shares for non-cash consideration), the requirements of that paragraph are met.

- The company has not previously been re-registered as unlimited.

- An application for re-registration is delivered to the Registrar of Companies, together with the other documents required and a statement of compliance (see **41.6**).

- The company makes such changes in its name and in its articles as are necessary in connection with its becoming a public company.

- If the company is unlimited, it makes such changes in its articles as are necessary in connection with its becoming a company limited by shares.

[*CA 2006, s 90*].

## 41.3 Share capital requirements

The following requirements must be met at the time the special resolution is passed that the company should be re-registered as a public company.

(a)     The nominal value of the company's allotted share capital must be not less than the authorised minimum. See 33.3 PUBLIC AND LISTED COMPANIES.

(b)     Each of the company's allotted shares must be paid up at least as to one-quarter of the nominal value of that share and the whole of any premium on it.

(c)     If any shares in the company or any premium on them have been fully or partly paid up by an undertaking given by any person that he or another should do work or perform services (whether for the company or any other person), the undertaking must have been performed or otherwise discharged.

(d)     If shares have been allotted as fully or partly paid up as to their nominal value or any premium on them otherwise than in cash, and the consideration for the allotment consists of or includes an undertaking to the company (other than one to which (*c*) above applies), then either

(i)     the undertaking must have been performed or otherwise discharged; or

(ii)     there must be a contract between the company and some person pursuant to which the undertaking is to be performed within five years from the time the special resolution is passed.

**Disregarded shares.** For the purpose of determining whether the requirements in (*b*), (*c*) and (*d*) are met, the following may be disregarded.

(i)     Shares allotted before

- 22 June 1982 in the case of a company then registered in Great Britain; or

- 31 December 1984 in the case of a company then registered in Northern Ireland.

But no more than one-tenth of the nominal value of the company's allotted share capital (excluding shares disregarded under (ii) below) is to be disregarded under this provision.

(ii)     Shares allotted in pursuance of an employees' share scheme by reason of which the company would, but for this provision, be precluded under (*b*) above (but not otherwise) from being re-registered as a public company.

Any shares so disregarded are treated as not forming part of the allotted share capital for the purposes of (*a*) above.

**Proposed reduction in share capital**. A company must not be re-registered as a public company if it appears to the Registrar of Companies that

• the company has resolved to reduce its share capital;

• the reduction

(i)     is made under *CA 2006, s 626* (reduction of capital in connection with redenomination of share capital, see **47.50** SHARES);

(ii)    is supported by a solvency statement in accordance with *CA 2006, s 643* (see **47.53** SHARES); or

(iii)   has been confirmed by an order of the court under *CA 2006, s 648* (see **47.55** SHARES); and

• the effect of the reduction is, or will be, that the nominal value of the company's allotted share capital is below the authorised minimum.

[*CA 2006, s 91*].

**41.4   Net assets requirements**

A company applying to re-register as a public company must obtain the following.

(a)     A balance sheet prepared as at a date not more than seven months before the date on which the application is delivered to the Registrar of Companies.

(b)     An 'unqualified report' by the company's auditor on that balance sheet.

An '*unqualified report*' means

(i)     if the balance sheet was prepared for a financial year of the company, a report stating without material qualification the auditor's opinion that the balance sheet has been properly prepared in accordance with the requirements of *CA 2006*; or

(ii)    if the balance sheet was not prepared for a financial year of the company, a report stating without material qualification the auditor's opinion that the balance sheet has been properly prepared in accordance with the provisions of *CA 2006* which would have applied if it had been prepared for a financial year of the company.

A qualification is 'material' unless the auditor states in his report that the matter giving rise to the qualification is not material for these purposes.

(c)     A written statement by the company's auditor that, in his opinion, at the balance sheet date the amount of the company's 'net assets' was not less than the aggregate of its called-up share capital and 'undistributable reserves'. See **22.5** DISTRIBUTIONS for the meaning of '*net assets*' and **22.1** DISTRIBUTIONS for the meaning of '*undistributable reserves*'.

Between the balance sheet date and the date on which the application for re-registration is delivered to the Registrar of Companies, there must be no change in the company's financial position that results in the amount of its net assets becoming less than the aggregate of its called-up share capital and undistributable reserves.

[*CA 2006, s 92*].

## 41.5   Re-Registration

**41.5   Recent allotment of shares for non-cash consideration**

Where the company has, between the date as at which the balance sheet required under **41.4** is prepared and the passing of the special resolution, allotted shares as fully or partly paid up (as to their nominal value or any premium on them) otherwise than in cash, the Registrar of Companies cannot entertain an application by the company for re-registration as a public company unless *one* of the following conditions is satisfied.

(1)     The requirements of *CA 2006, s 593(1)(a)* and *(b)* have been have been complied with (independent valuation of non-cash consideration; valuer's report to company not more than six months before allotment, see **47.32**(*a*)(*b*) SHARES).

(2)     The allotment is in connection with a share exchange, ie

  •     the shares are allotted in connection with an 'arrangement' under which the whole or part of the consideration for the shares allotted is provided by

   (i)     the transfer to the company allotting the shares of shares (or shares of a particular class) in another company; or

   (ii)    the cancellation of shares (or shares of a particular class) in another company; and

  •     the allotment is open to all the holders of the shares of the other company in question (or, where the arrangement applies only to shares of a particular class, to all the holders of the company's shares of that class) to take part in the arrangement in connection with which the shares are allotted.

In determining whether a person is a holder of shares for these purposes, there must be disregarded

  •     shares held by, or by a nominee of, the company allotting the shares; and

  •     shares held by, or by a nominee of

   (i)     the holding company of the company allotting the shares;

   (ii)    a subsidiary of the company allotting the shares; or

   (iii)   a subsidiary of the holding company of the company allotting the shares.

In deciding whether an allotment is in connection with a share exchange, it is immaterial whether or not the arrangement in connection with which the shares are allotted involves the issue to the company allotting the shares of shares (or shares of a particular class) in the other company.

'*Arrangement*' means any agreement, scheme or arrangement, including an arrangement sanctioned in accordance with *CA 2006, Pt 26* (company compromise with creditors and members, see **35** RECONSTRUCTIONS AND MERGERS) or *IA 1986, s 110* or *Insolvency (Northern Ireland) Order 1989 (SI 1989 No 2405), Art 96* (liquidator in winding up accepting shares as consideration for sale of company's property).

(3)     The allotment is in connection with a proposed merger with another company, ie where one of the companies concerned proposes to acquire all the assets and liabilities of the other in exchange for the issue of its shares or other securities to shareholders of the other (whether or not accompanied by a cash payment).

[*CA 2006, s 93*].

**41.6   Application and accompanying documents**

An application for re-registration as a public company on Form RRO1 must contain/be accompanied by the following.

- A statement of the company's proposed name on re-registration.

- In the case of a company without a secretary, a statement of the company's proposed secretary. This must contain particulars that will be required to be stated in the company's register of secretaries (see **38.6** REGISTERS) of the person who is (or the persons who are) to be the secretary or joint secretaries of the company. The statement must also contain a consent by the person named as secretary (or each of the persons named as joint secretaries) to act in the relevant capacity. If all the partners in a firm are to be joint secretaries, consent may be given by one partner on behalf of all of them.

- A copy of the special/written resolution that the company should re-register as a public company (unless a copy has already been forwarded to the Registrar of Companies under *CA 2006, ss 29, 30*, see **14.10** CONSTITUTION – MEMORANDUM AND ARTICLES).

- A copy of the company's articles as proposed to be amended.

- A copy of the balance sheet and other documents referred to in **41.4**(*a*)–(*c*).

- If **41.5** applies, a copy of the valuation report (if any) under those provisions.

- A statement of compliance that the requirements as to re-registration as a public company have been complied with. The Registrar of Companies may accept this statement as sufficient evidence that the company is entitled to be re-registered as a public company.

*Companies Act 2006, s 94* is amended by the *Small Business, Enterprise and Employment Act 2015 (SBEE 2015), s 98* which provides that a company's application will also have to be accompanied by a statement of the aggregate amount paid up on the shares of the company on account of their nominal value.

[*CA 2006, ss 94, 95; SBEE 2015, s 98; SI 2016 No 321, Reg 6*].

**41.7   Issue of certificate of incorporation on re-registration**

If, on an application for re-registration as a public company, the Registrar of Companies is satisfied that the company is entitled to be so re-registered, the company must be re-registered accordingly. The Registrar must then issue a certificate of incorporation, altered to meet the circumstances of the case, stating that it is issued on re-registration and the date on which it is issued.

On the issue of the certificate

- the company by virtue of the issue of the certificate becomes a public company;

- the changes in the company's name and articles take effect; and

- where the application contained a statement of the company's proposed secretary, that person is (or the persons named as joint secretaries are) deemed to have been appointed to that office.

The certificate is conclusive evidence that the requirements of *CA 2006* as to re-registration have been complied with.

## 41.7 Re-Registration

[*CA 2006, s 96*].

## 41.8 A PUBLIC COMPANY BECOMING A PRIVATE COMPANY

A public company may be re-registered as a private limited company if the following conditions are met.

- A special resolution that it should be so re-registered is passed.
- Where no application under **41.9** for cancellation of the resolution has been made

    (i)    having regard to the number of members who consented to or voted in favour of the resolution, no such application may be made; or

    (ii)   the period within which such an application could be made has expired.

- Where an application under **41.9** for cancellation of the resolution has been made

    (i)    the application has been withdrawn; or

    (ii)   an order has been made confirming the resolution and a copy of that order has been delivered to the Registrar of Companies.

- An application for re-registration is delivered to the Registrar of Companies, together with the other documents required and a statement of compliance (see **41.10**).
- The company makes such changes in its name and in its articles as are necessary in connection with its becoming a private company limited by shares or, as the case may be, by guarantee.

[*CA 2006, s 97*].

## 41.9 Application to court to cancel resolution

Where a special resolution under **41.8** has been passed, an application may be made to the court for the cancellation of the resolution by

- the holders of not less in aggregate than 5% in nominal value of the company's issued share capital or any class of the company's issued share capital (disregarding any shares held by the company as treasury shares, see **34.19** PURCHASE OF OWN SHARES),
- if the company is not limited by shares, not less than 5% of its members, or
- not less than 50 of the company's members

but not by a person who has consented to or voted in favour of the resolution.

The application must be made within 28 days after the passing of the resolution and may be made on behalf of the persons entitled to make it by one or more of their number as they appoint for the purpose.

On making the application, the applicants, or the person making the application on their behalf, must immediately give notice to the Registrar of Companies. On being served with notice of any such application, the company must immediately give notice to the Registrar of Companies.

The court, on hearing the application, must make an order either cancelling or confirming the resolution. It may

- make that order on such terms and conditions as it thinks fit;

- adjourn the proceedings in order that an arrangement may be made to the satisfaction of the court for the purchase of the interests of dissentient members;

- provide for the purchase by the company of the shares of any of its members and for the reduction accordingly of the company's capital;

- make such alteration in the company's articles as may be required in consequence; and

- require the company *not* to make any, or any specified, amendments to its articles without the leave of the court.

Within 15 days of the making of the court's order on the application (or such longer period as the court may direct), the company must deliver to the Registrar a copy of the order.

**Offences.** If the company fails to

- notify the Registrar of Companies that it has been served with notice of an application, or

- send the Registrar a copy of the court order in the time allowed

an offence is committed by the company and every officer of the company who is in default. A person guilty of such an offence is liable, on summary conviction, to a fine not exceeding level 3 on the standard scale and, for continued contravention, a daily default fine not exceeding one-tenth of level 3 on the standard scale. See **29.1** OFFENCES AND LEGAL PROCEEDINGS for the standard scale.

[*CA 2006, ss 98, 99*].

## 41.10  Application and accompanying documents

An application for re-registration as a private limited company on Form RRO2 must contain/be accompanied by the following.

- A statement of the company's proposed name on re-registration.

- A copy of the resolution that the company should re-register as a private limited company (unless a copy has already been forwarded to the Registrar of Companies under *CA 2006, ss 29, 30*, see **14.10** CONSTITUTION – MEMORANDUM AND ARTICLES).

- A copy of the company's articles as proposed to be amended.

- A statement of compliance that the requirements as to re-registration as a private limited company have been complied with. The Registrar of Companies may accept this statement as sufficient evidence that the company is entitled to be re-registered as a private limited company.

[*CA 2006, s 100*].

## 41.11  Issue of certificate of incorporation on re-registration

If, on an application for re-registration as a private limited company, the Registrar of Companies is satisfied that the company is entitled to be so re-registered, the company must be re-registered accordingly. The Registrar must then issue a certificate of incorporation, altered to meet the circumstances of the case, stating that it is issued on re-registration and the date on which it is issued.

On the issue of the certificate

- the company by virtue of the issue of the certificate becomes a private limited company; and

- the changes in the company's name and articles take effect.

The certificate is conclusive evidence that the requirements of *CA 2006* as to re-registration have been complied with. [*CA 2006, s 101*].

## 41.12    Re-registration as a private company in consequence of cancellation of shares

A public company may be required by *CA 2006, s 662* to re-register as a private company where shares are cancelled and as a consequence the value of the company's nominal share capital is brought below the authorised minimum. Form RRO9 is used for these purposes (see 34.25 Purchase of own shares).

## 41.13    A PRIVATE COMPANY BECOMING UNLIMITED

A private limited company may be re-registered as an unlimited company if the following conditions are met.

- All the members of the company have assented to its being so re-registered.

- The company has not previously been re-registered as limited.

- An application for re-registration is delivered to the Registrar of Companies, together with the other documents required and a statement of compliance (see **41.14**).

- The company makes such changes in its name and its articles

    (i)     as are necessary in connection with its becoming an unlimited company; and

    (ii)    if the company is to have a share capital, as are necessary in connection with its becoming an unlimited company having a share capital.

For the above purposes,

- a trustee in bankruptcy of a member of the company (including, in Scotland, a permanent trustee or an interim trustee on the sequestrated estate of a member of the company and a trustee under a protected trustee deed granted by a member of the company) is entitled, to the exclusion of the member, to assent to the company's becoming unlimited; and

- the personal representative of a deceased member of the company may assent on behalf of the deceased.

[*CA 2006, s 102*].

## 41.14    Application and accompanying documents

An application for re-registration as an unlimited company on Form RRO5 must contain/be accompanied by the following.

- A statement of the company's proposed name on re-registration.

- The form of assent to the company's being registered as an unlimited company (see *SI 2008 No 3014, Sch 3*), authenticated by or on behalf of all the members of the company.

- A copy of the company's articles as proposed to be amended.

- A statement of compliance that the requirements as to re-registration as an unlimited company have been complied with. The statement must contain a statement by the directors of the company that

  (i)     the persons by whom or on whose behalf the form of assent is authenticated constitute the whole membership of the company; and

  (ii)    if any of the members have not authenticated that form themselves, the directors have taken all reasonable steps to satisfy themselves that each person who authenticated it on behalf of a member was lawfully empowered to do so.

The Registrar of Companies may accept the statement of compliance as sufficient evidence that the company is entitled to be re-registered as an unlimited company.

[*CA 2006, s 103; SI 2008 No 3014, Reg 5*].

## 41.15  Issue of certificate of incorporation on re-registration

If, on an application for re-registration of a private company as an unlimited company, the Registrar of Companies is satisfied that the company is entitled to be so re-registered, the company must be re-registered accordingly. The Registrar must then issue a certificate of incorporation, altered to meet the circumstances of the case, stating that it is issued on re-registration and the date on which it is issued.

On the issue of the certificate

- the company by virtue of the issue of the certificate becomes an unlimited company; and

- the changes in the company's name and articles take effect.

The certificate is conclusive evidence that the requirements of *CA 2006* as to re-registration have been complied with.

[*CA 2006, s 104*].

## 41.16  AN UNLIMITED PRIVATE COMPANY BECOMING A PRIVATE LIMITED COMPANY

An unlimited company may be re-registered as a private limited company if the following conditions are met.

- A special resolution that it should be so re-registered is passed. The resolution must state whether the company is to be limited by shares or by guarantee.

- The company has not previously been re-registered as unlimited.

- An application for re-registration is delivered to the Registrar of Companies, together with the other documents required and a statement of compliance (see **41.17**).

- The company makes such changes in its name and in its articles as are necessary in connection with its becoming a company limited by shares or, as the case may be, by guarantee.

[*CA 2006, s 105*].

## 41.17 Re-Registration

### 41.17 Application and accompanying documents

An application for re-registration as a limited company on Form RRO6 must contain/be accompanied by the following.

- A statement of the company's proposed name on re-registration.

- A copy of the resolution that the company should re-register as a private limited company (unless a copy has already been forwarded to the Registrar of Companies under *CA 2006, ss 29, 30*, see **14.10** CONSTITUTION – MEMORANDUM AND ARTICLES).

- If the company is to be limited by guarantee, a statement of guarantee which must state that each member undertakes that, if the company is wound up while he is a member or within one year after he ceases to be a member, he will contribute to the assets of the company such amount as may be required for

    (i)   payment of the debts and liabilities of the company contracted before he ceases to be a member,

    (ii)  payment of the costs, charges and expenses of winding up, and

    (iii) adjustment of the rights of the contributories among themselves

    (iv)  not exceeding a specified amount.

- A copy of the company's articles as proposed to be amended.

- A statement of compliance that the requirements as to re-registration as a limited company have been complied with. The Registrar of Companies may accept the statement of compliance as sufficient evidence that the company is entitled to be re-registered as a limited company.

[*CA 2006, s 106*].

### 41.18 Issue of certificate of incorporation on re-registration

If, on an application for re-registration of an unlimited company as a limited company, the Registrar of Companies is satisfied that the company is entitled to be so re-registered, the company must be re-registered accordingly. The Registrar must then issue a certificate of incorporation, altered to meet the circumstances of the case, stating that it is issued on re-registration and the date on which it is issued.

On the issue of the certificate

- the company by virtue of the issue of the certificate becomes a limited company; and

- the changes in the company's name and articles take effect.

The certificate is conclusive evidence that the requirements of *CA 2006* as to re-registration have been complied with.

[*CA 2006, s 107*].

### 41.19 Statement of capital required where company already has share capital

A company which on re-registration under **41.18** already has allotted share capital must, within 15 days after the re-registration, deliver a statement of capital to the Registrar of Companies. This does not apply if the information which would be included in the statement has already been sent to the Registrar in a statement of capital and initial shareholdings under *CA 2006, s 10* (see **12.3** COMPANY FORMATION AND TYPES OF COMPANIES) or (if different) the last statement of capital sent by the company (see **7.2** ANNUAL RETURNS).

The statement of capital must state with respect to the company's share capital on re-registration:

(a)     The total number of shares of the company.

(b)     The aggregate nominal value of those shares. and the amount (if any) unpaid on each share (whether on account of the nominal value of the share or by way of premium).

(c)     For each class of shares

  (i)     particulars of any voting rights attached to the shares, including rights that arise only in certain circumstances;

  (ii)    particulars of any rights attached to the shares, as respects dividends, to participate in a distribution;

  (iii)   particulars of any rights attached to the shares, as respects capital, to participate in a distribution (including on a winding up);

  (iv)    whether the shares are to be redeemed or are liable to be redeemed at the option of the company or the shareholder;

  (v)     the total number of shares of that class; and

  (vi)    the aggregate nominal value of shares of that class.

(d)     The amount paid up and the amount (if any) unpaid on each share (whether on account of the nominal value of the share or by way of premium).

If default is made in complying with these provisions, an offence is committed by the company and every officer of the company who is in default. A person guilty of such an offence is liable, on summary conviction, to a fine not exceeding level 3 on the standard scale and, for continued contravention, a daily default fine not exceeding one-tenth of level 3 on the standard scale. See 29.1 OFFENCES AND LEGAL PROCEEDINGS for the standard scale.

[*CA 2006, s 108; SBEE 2015, s 93(4); SI 2009 No 388, Art 2; SI 2016 No 321, Reg 6*].

## 41.20  A PUBLIC COMPANY BECOMING PRIVATE AND UNLIMITED

A public company limited by shares may be re-registered as an unlimited private company if the following conditions are met.

•     All the members of the company have assented to its being so re-registered.

•     The company has not previously been re-registered as limited or as unlimited.

•     An application for re-registration is delivered to the Registrar of Companies, together with the other documents required and a statement of compliance (see **41.21**).

•     The company makes such changes in its name and its articles as are necessary in connection with its becoming an unlimited private company.

For the above purposes,

•     a trustee in bankruptcy of a member of the company (including, in Scotland, a permanent trustee or an interim trustee on the sequestrated estate of a member of the company and a trustee under a protected trustee deed granted by a member of the company) is entitled, to the exclusion of the member, to assent to the company's re-registration; and

- the personal representative of a deceased member of the company may assent on behalf of the deceased.

[*CA 2006, s 109*].

## 41.21  Application and accompanying documents

An application for re-registration of a public company as an unlimited private company on Form RRO7 must contain/be accompanied by the following.

- A statement of the company's proposed name on re-registration.

- The form of assent to the company's being registered as a private and unlimited company (see *SI 2008 No 3014, Sch 4*), authenticated by or on behalf of all the members of the company.

- A copy of the company's articles as proposed to be amended.

- A statement of compliance that the requirements as to re-registration as an unlimited private company have been complied with. The statement must contain a statement by the directors of the company that

    (i)    the persons by whom or on whose behalf the form of assent is authenticated constitute the whole membership of the company; and

    (ii)   if any of the members have not authenticated that form themselves, the directors have taken all reasonable steps to satisfy themselves that each person who authenticated it on behalf of a member was lawfully empowered to do so.

The Registrar of Companies may accept the statement of compliance as sufficient evidence that the company is entitled to be re-registered as an unlimited private company.

[*CA 2006, s 110; SI 2008 No 3014, Reg 6*].

## 41.22  Issue of certificate of incorporation on re-registration

If, on an application for re-registration of a public company as an unlimited private company, the Registrar of Companies is satisfied that the company is entitled to be so re-registered, the company must be re-registered accordingly. The Registrar must then issue a certificate of incorporation, altered to meet the circumstances of the case, stating that it is issued on re-registration and the date on which it is issued.

On the issue of the certificate

- the company by virtue of the issue of the certificate becomes an unlimited private company; and

- the changes in the company's name and articles take effect.

The certificate is conclusive evidence that the requirements of *CA 2006* as to re-registration have been complied with.

[*CA 2006, s 111*].

## 41.23  OLD PUBLIC COMPANY RE-REGISTERING AS A PUBLIC COMPANY

The provisions in **41.2** to **41.7** also apply to an old public company (see APPENDIX 1 DEFINITIONS) but with

- references to a private company being read as references to an old public company; and

- references to a special resolution of the company being read as references to a resolution of the directors.

*CA 2006, ss 29, 30* (resolutions affecting a company's constitution, see **14.10** Constitution – Memorandum and Articles) apply to any such resolution.

[*SI 2009 No 1941, Sch 3 para 3*].

### 41.24  OLD PUBLIC COMPANY BECOMING A PRIVATE COMPANY

An old public company (see Appendix 1 Definitions) may pass a special resolution *not* to be re-registered as a public company. The provisions in **41.9** (application to the court to cancel the resolution) apply to such a resolution as they would apply to a special resolution by a public company to be re-registered as private.

The Registrar of Companies must issue the company with a certificate stating that it is a private company if

(a)  a special resolution not to be re-registered as a public company has been passed and either

  (i)  28 days from the passing of the resolution elapse without an application being made under **41.9** (as applied); or

  (ii)  such an application is made and proceedings are concluded on the application without the court making an order for the cancellation of the resolution; or

(b)  an old public company delivers a statutory declaration by a director or secretary of the company that the company does not at the time of the declaration satisfy the conditions for the company to be re-registered as public.

For the purposes of (a)(ii) above, proceedings on the application are concluded

- at the expiration of the period of 15 days from the making of the court's order on the application (or such longer period as the court may direct); or

- when the company has been notified that the application has been withdrawn.

The company then becomes a private company by virtue of the issue of the certificate.

[*SI 2009 No 1941, Sch 3 paras 4, 5*].

**Failure by old public company to obtain new classification.** If, at any time, an old public company has not delivered to the Registrar of Companies a statutory declaration under (*b*) above, then unless at the time the company has

- applied to be re-registered as a public company (and the application has not been refused or withdrawn), or

- passed a special resolution under (*a*) above not to be re-registered as a public company (and the resolution has not been revoked and has not been cancelled by the court as above)

the company and any officer of it who is in default is guilty of an offence. A person guilty of such an offence is liable, on summary conviction, to a fine not exceeding level 3 on the standard scale and, for continued contravention, a daily default fine not exceeding one-tenth of level 3 on the standard scale. See **29.1** Offences and Legal Proceedings for the standard scale.

# 41.24   Re-Registration

*[SI 2009 No 1941, Sch 3 para 6]*.

# 42 Resolutions and Meetings

**Cross-references.** See **2.10** ACCOUNTS: GENERAL for laying of accounts and reports before company in general meeting; **8.45** AUDIT for rights of an auditor to attend company general meetings.

## 42.1 RESOLUTIONS: GENERAL PROVISIONS

*Extraordinary resolutions*: The term "extraordinary resolution" does not appear in the *2006 Act*. Articles of association based on *Table A, 1985* may continue to refer to such resolutions (unless amended). If this is the case any reference to an extraordinary resolution in a provision of a contract or a company's memorandum or articles continues to have effect and continues to be construed in accordance with *CA 1985, s 378* as if that section had not been repealed.

[*SI 2007 No 2194, Sch 3 para 23*].

*Resolutions.* A resolution of the members (or of a class of members)

- of a private company must be passed

    (i)     as a written resolution in accordance with **42.5** to **42.11**; or

    (ii)    at a meeting of the members to which the provisions in **42.12** to **42.31** apply; and

- of a public company must be passed at a meeting of the members to which the provisions in **42.12** to **42.31** and, where relevant, **42.32** and **42.33** apply. If the company is also quoted, there are additional requirements in **42.34** to **42.40**.

Where a provision of *CA 2006* requires a resolution of a company (or of the members or a class of members of a company) and does not specify what kind of resolution is required, then an ordinary resolution is required unless the company's articles require a higher majority (or unanimity). [*CA 2006, s 281(1)–(3)*].

But none of the provisions in this chapter affect any enactment or rule of law as to

- things done otherwise than by passing a resolution;

- circumstances in which a resolution is or is not treated as having been passed; or

- cases in which a person is precluded from alleging that a resolution has not been duly passed.

[*CA 2006, s 281(4)*].

This preserves the common law unanimous consent rule. Unless *CA 2006* provides otherwise, a number of decided cases have held that a company is bound in a matter *intra vires* by the unanimous but informal agreement of its members. See, for example, *Re Express Engineering Works Ltd* [1920] 1 Ch 466, 89 LJ Ch 379, CA. This applies even if there is no actual meeting but only informal discussions (*Parker & Cooper Ltd v Reading* [1926] Ch 975, 96 LJ Ch 23). The agreement must, however, be unanimous; it is not enough that a majority sufficient to pass the appropriate resolution agrees to the proposal (*EBM Co Ltd v Dominion Bank* [1937] 3 All ER 555, 81 Sol Jo 814, PC). See also *Re Duomatic Ltd* [1969] 2 Ch 365, [1969] 1 All ER 161 where it was held that, where all shareholders who have a right to attend and *vote* at a general meeting of the company assent to some matter which a general meeting could carry into effect, that assent is as binding as a resolution in general meeting would be.

The case of *Randhawa v Turpin* [2016] EWHC 2156 (Ch) sheds light on the *Duomatic* principle. The court considered whether the quorum provisions for a directors' meeting set out in a company's articles of association had been informally amended by the unanimous consent of the company's shareholders under *Duomatic*.

The issue was whether a purported directors' appointment of administrators was invalid, where the board meeting which resolved to make the appointment was inquorate. The company's articles required a quorum of two for a board meeting, and limited the powers of a sole director to convening a general meeting or appointing an additional director. However, at the time of the purported administrators' appointment (and for the four preceding years), the company had a sole director (D). The administrators' appointment was made at a meeting at which D was the only director present.

D was the registered holder of 75% of the company's share capital, which he held on bare trust for his father (R). The remaining 25% of the share capital was registered in the name of an Isle of Man company ('IMCo') which had been dissolved in 1996. The beneficial ownership of that part of the company's share capital was unclear, but R was probably also the beneficial owner of the shares registered in the dissolved company's name.

The court at first instance held that the administrators' appointment was valid. It found that there had been a consistent course of conduct under which D and R had informally sanctioned the exercise of all the directors' powers by *one* director alone. This had served as informal amendment to, or variation of, the articles, which was binding on the company under *Duomatic*. Hence, the acquiescence of the 75% shareholder alone ought to be sufficient to trigger the *Duomatic* principle; no one could have voted for the remaining 25% of the company's share capital because the registered holder of those shares no longer existed, and no one else was on the register of members in its place.

The case went to appeal. As at August 2017, the Court of Appeal has just handed down its decision. The Court of Appeal unanimously allowed the appeal, holding that the administrators' appointment was invalidly made and that the *Duomatic* principle was incapable of applying in the circumstances. The court found that *Duomatic* required the assent of all the shareholders who had the right to attend and vote at a general meeting of the company, not just those shareholders who were available at the time. The principle simply could not apply in a situation where one of the registered shareholders was a dissolved corporation which no longer existed. This is because *Duomatic* requires the consent of all the registered shareholders and one of them was incapable of consenting. IMCo's assent could not be inferred for the purposes of triggering *Duomatic* by looking to the intentions of those who may previously have had an interest in IMCo.

## 42.2  Ordinary resolutions

An ordinary resolution of the members (or of a class of members) of a company means a resolution that is passed by a simple majority.

- *A written resolution* is passed by a simple majority if it is passed by members representing a simple majority of the total voting rights of eligible members (see **42.6**).

- *A resolution passed at a meeting on a show of hands* is passed by a simple majority if it is passed by a simple majority of the votes cast by those entitled to vote.

- *A resolution passed at a meeting on a poll taken* is passed by a simple majority if it is passed by members representing a simple majority of the total voting rights of members who (being entitled to do so) vote

    (i)    in person or by proxy, or

    (ii)   (in relation to meetings notice of which is given on or after 3 August 2009) in advance (see **42.26**)

    on the resolution.

Anything that may be done by ordinary resolution may also be done by special resolution (see **42.3**). [*CA 2006, s 282*].

## 42.3  Special resolutions

A special resolution of the members (or of a class of members) of a company means a resolution passed by a majority of not less than 75%.

- *A written resolution* is passed by a majority of not less than 75% if it is passed by members representing not less than 75% of the total voting rights of eligible members (see **42.6**).

    Where a resolution of a private company is passed as a written resolution,

    (i)    the resolution is not a special resolution unless it stated that it was proposed as a special resolution; and

    (ii)   if the resolution so stated, it may only be passed as a special resolution.

- *A resolution passed at a meeting on a show of hands* is passed by a majority of not less than 75% if it is passed by not less than 75% of the votes cast by those entitled to vote.

## 42.3 Resolutions and Meetings

- *A resolution passed at a meeting on a poll taken* is passed by a majority of not less than 75% if it is passed by members representing not less than 75% of the total voting rights of the members who (being entitled to do so) vote

  (i)      in person or by proxy, or

  (ii)      in advance (see **42.26**)

  on the resolution.

Where a resolution is passed at a meeting

(a)      the resolution is not a special resolution unless the notice of the meeting included the text of the resolution and specified the intention to propose the resolution as a special resolution; and

(b)      if the notice of the meeting so specified, the resolution may only be passed as a special resolution.

[*CA 2006, s 283*].

## 42.4   Members' votes

(1) *General rules*

The following provisions have effect subject to any provision of the company's articles.

- *On a vote on a written resolution*

  (i)      in the case of a company having a share capital, every member has one vote in respect of each share or each £10 of stock held by him; and

  (ii)      in any other case, every member has one vote.

- *On a vote on a resolution on a show of hands at a meeting*, every member present in person has one vote. See (2) below for proxies.

- *On a vote on a resolution on a poll taken at a meeting*

  (i)      in the case of a company having a share capital, every member has one vote in respect of each share or each £10 of stock held by him; and

  (ii)      in any other case, every member has one vote.

Nothing in the above provisions is to be read as restricting the effect of *CA 2006, s 152* (exercise of rights by nominees, see **26.5 MEMBERS**), voting by proxies (see (2) below), voting on a poll (see **42.26(3)**), votes cast in advance (see **42.26(4)**), or representation of corporations at meetings (see **42.27**).

[*CA 2006, s 284*].

(2) *Voting by proxies*

*On a vote on a resolution on a show of hands at a meeting:*

(a)      Subject to (*b*) below, every proxy present who has been duly appointed by one or more members entitled to vote on the resolution has one vote.

(b)      A proxy has one vote for and one vote against the resolution if

  (i)      the proxy has been duly appointed by more than one member entitled to vote on the resolution; and

(ii)    the proxy has been instructed by one or more of those members to vote for the resolution and by one or more other of those members to vote against it.

But this has effect subject to any provision of the company's articles.

*On a poll taken at a meeting of a company*, all or any of the voting rights of a member may be exercised by one or more duly appointed proxies. But where a member appoints more than one proxy, this does not authorise the exercise by the proxies taken together of more extensive voting rights than could be exercised by the member in person.

[*CA 2006, s 285*].

(3) *Voting rights on a poll or written resolution*

In relation to a resolution required or authorised by an enactment, if a private company's articles provide that a member has a different number of votes in relation to a resolution when it is passed as a written resolution and when it is passed on a poll taken at a meeting

•    the provision about how many votes a member has in relation to the resolution passed on a poll is void; and

•    a member has the same number of votes in relation to the resolution when it is passed on a poll as the member has when it is passed as a written resolution.

[*CA 2006, s 285A*].

(4) *Votes of joint holders of shares*

Subject to any provision of the company's articles, in the case of joint holders of shares of a company, only the vote of the 'senior holder' who votes (and any proxies duly authorised by him) may be counted by the company. The *'senior holder'* for these purposes is determined by the order in which the names of the joint holders appear in the register of members or, if an election is in force under *CA 2006, s 128B*, in the register kept by the Registrar of Companies (see **38.9** (Option to keep members' details on the central register)).

[*CA 2006, s 286; SBEE 2015, s 94, Sch 5, para 16; SI 2016 No 321, Reg 6*]

(5) *Provisions of articles as to determination of entitlement to vote*

Nothing in **42.1** to **42.3** or the provisions above affects

•    any provision of a company's articles

(i)    requiring an objection to a person's entitlement to vote on a resolution to be made in accordance with the articles; and

(ii)   for the determination of any such objection to be final and conclusive; or

•    the grounds on which such a determination may be questioned in legal proceedings.

[*CA 2006, s 287*].

See also *Wall v London and Northern Assets Corpn* [1899] 1 Ch 550, 68 LJ Ch 248 and *Wall v Exchange Investment Corpn* [1926] Ch 143, 95 LJ Ch 132, CA.

(6) *Exercise of members' rights*

A member may nominate another person or persons to enjoy rights of the member in relation to the company. See **26.3** MEMBERS.

## 42.4    Resolutions and Meetings

(7) *Standard articles*

Where the company has adopted standard articles, see:

*   *Table A, 1985, Regs 54–59*,

*   *Model Articles, Art 43* (private companies),

*   *Model Articles, Art 35* (public companies),

set out in APPENDIX 4 STANDARD ARTICLES OF ASSOCIATION.

(8) *Bankruptcy*

Unless there is any contrary provision in the articles, a bankrupt still remains a member of the company as long as his name appears on the register and his trustee in bankruptcy has not secured registration in his own name (*Morgan v Gray* [1953] Ch 83, [1953] 1 All ER 213).

## 42.5    WRITTEN RESOLUTIONS OF PRIVATE COMPANIES

**General provisions**. In the *Companies Acts* a *'written resolution'* means a resolution of a private company proposed and passed in accordance with the provisions in this paragraph and **42.6** to **42.11**. It does not mean that there is a requirement for 'writing' in the sense of a hard copy.

With certain exceptions, a private company may pass any resolution using the written resolution procedure. Any provision of the articles of a private company is void in so far as it would have the effect that a resolution that is required by or otherwise provided for in an enactment could not be proposed and passed as a written resolution. The exceptions are a resolution under

*   *CA 2006, s 168* (removing a director before the expiration of his period of office, see **18.9** DIRECTORS); and

*   *CA 2006, s 510* (removing an auditor before the expiration of his term of office, see **8.18** AUDIT).

A resolution may be proposed as a written resolution by the directors (see **42.7**) or by the members (see **42.8**).

From 1 October 2007 there has been no requirement to pass written resolutions unanimously. As a result

(a)    references in enactments passed or made before 1 October 2007 to

(i)    a resolution of a company in general meeting, or

(ii)    a resolution of a meeting of a class of members of the company,

have effect as if they included references to a written resolution of the members, or of a class of members, of a private company (as appropriate); and

(b)    a written resolution of a private company has effect as if passed (as the case may be)

(i)    by the company in general meeting, or

(ii)    by a meeting of a class of members of the company,

and references in enactments passed or made before 1 October 2007 to a meeting at which a resolution is passed or to members voting in favour of a resolution are construed accordingly.

[*CA 2006, ss 288, 300; SI 2007 No 2194, Art 1, Sch 1 para 13; SI 2007 No 3495, Art 10*].

**42.6  Eligible members and circulation date**

The '*eligible members*' in relation to a resolution proposed as a written resolution of a private company are the members who would have been entitled to vote on the resolution on the 'circulation date' of the resolution.

If the persons entitled to vote on a written resolution change during the course of the day that is the circulation date, the eligible members are the persons entitled to vote on the resolution at the time that the first copy of the resolution is sent or submitted to a member for his agreement.

[*CA 2006, s 289*].

The '*circulation date*' of a written resolution is the date on which copies of it are sent or submitted to members (or if copies are sent or submitted to members on different days, to the first of those days).

[*CA 2006, s 290*].

**42.7  Written resolutions proposed by directors**

Where a resolution is proposed as a written resolution by the directors of the company, the company must send or submit a copy of the resolution to every eligible member by

(a)    sending copies at the same time (so far as reasonably practicable) to all eligible members in hard copy form, in electronic form or by means of a website;

(b)    if it is possible to do so without undue delay, submitting the same copy to each eligible member in turn (or different copies to each of a number of eligible members in turn); or

(c)    a combination of (*a*) and (*b*).

The copy of the resolution must be accompanied by a statement informing the member how to signify agreement to the resolution and as to the date by which the resolution must be passed if it is not to lapse. See **42.9**.

In the event of default in complying with these provisions, an offence is committed by every officer of the company who is in default. A person guilty of such an offence is liable (i) on conviction on indictment, to a fine; and (ii) on summary conviction, to a fine not exceeding the statutory maximum. See **29.1** Offences and Legal Proceedings for the statutory maximum. The validity of the resolution, if passed, is not affected by a failure to comply with these provisions. [*CA 2006, s 291*].

**42.8  Written resolutions proposed by members**

The members of a private company may require the company to circulate a resolution that may properly be moved, and is proposed to be moved, as a written resolution. Any resolution may properly be moved as a written resolution unless

•    it would, if passed, be ineffective (whether by reason of inconsistency with any enactment or the company's constitution or otherwise);

•    it is defamatory of any person; or

•    it is frivolous or vexatious.

Where the members require the company to circulate a resolution, they may also require the company to circulate with it a statement (of not more than 1,000 words) on the subject matter of the resolution.

The company is required to circulate the resolution, and any accompanying statement, once it has received requests from members representing not less than 5% (or such lower percentage as is specified for this purpose in the company's articles) of the total voting rights of all members entitled to vote on the resolution.

A request may be in hard copy form or in electronic form. It must identify the resolution and any accompanying statement and must be authenticated by the person or persons making it.

[*CA 2006, s 292*].

**Circulation of resolution.** Where a company is required under the above provisions to circulate a written resolution, it must send or submit to every eligible member a copy of the resolution and a copy of any accompanying statement (but see below for expenses of circulation and application to the court). The company must do so by

(a)    sending copies at the same time (so far as reasonably practicable) to all eligible members in hard copy form, in electronic form or by means of a website;

(b)    if it is possible to do so without undue delay, submitting the same copy to each eligible member in turn (or different copies to each of a number of eligible members in turn); or

(c)    a combination of (*a*) and (*b*).

The company must send or submit the copies (or, if copies are sent or submitted to members on different days, the first of those copies) not more than 21 days after it becomes subject to the requirement to circulate the resolution. The copy of the resolution must be accompanied by guidance as to how to signify agreement to the resolution and the date by which the resolution must be passed if it is not to lapse. See **42.9**.

In the event of default in complying with these provisions, an offence is committed by every officer of the company who is in default. A person guilty of such an offence is liable (i) on conviction on indictment, to a fine; and (ii) on summary conviction, to a fine not exceeding the statutory maximum. See **29.1** OFFENCES AND LEGAL PROCEEDINGS for the statutory maximum. The validity of the resolution, if passed, is not affected by a failure to comply with these provisions.

[*CA 2006, s 293*].

**Expenses of circulation.** The expenses of the company in circulating a written resolution of members must be paid by the members who requested it, unless the company resolves otherwise. Unless the company has previously resolved to pay the expenses, it is not bound to circulate the resolution unless a sum reasonably sufficient to meet its expenses is deposited with, or tendered to, it.

[*CA 2006, s 294*].

**Application to court not to circulate members' statement.** A company is not required to circulate a members' statement if, on an application by the company or another person who claims to be aggrieved, the court is satisfied that the rights conferred by the above provisions are being abused. The court may order the members who requested the circulation of the statement to pay the whole or part of the company's costs (in Scotland, expenses) on such an application, even if they are not parties to the application.

[*CA 2006, s 295*].

**42.9    Agreeing to written resolutions**

A written resolution is passed when the required majority of eligible members have signified their agreement to it. A member signifies his agreement to a proposed written resolution when the company receives from him (or from someone acting on his behalf) an authenticated document

•       identifying the resolution to which it relates; and

•       indicating his agreement to the resolution.

The document must be sent to the company in hard copy form or in electronic form.

A member's agreement to a written resolution, once signified, may not be revoked.

[*CA 2006, s 296*].

**Period for agreeing to written resolution.** A proposed written resolution lapses if it is not passed before the end of

•       the period specified for this purpose in the company's articles; or

•       if none is specified, the period of 28 days beginning with the circulation date.

The agreement of a member to a written resolution is ineffective if signified after the expiry of that period.

[*CA 2006, s 297*].

**42.10    Sending relevant documents by electronic means**

Where a company has given an 'electronic address' in any document containing or accompanying a proposed written resolution, it is deemed to have agreed that any document or information relating to that resolution may be sent by electronic means to that address (subject to any conditions or limitations specified in the document).

'*Electronic address*' means any address or number used for the purposes of sending or receiving documents or information by electronic means.

[*CA 2006, s 298*].

**42.11    Publication on website**

Where a company sends a written resolution, or a statement relating to a written resolution, to a person by means of a website, the resolution or statement is not validly sent for these purposes unless the resolution is available on the website throughout the period beginning with the circulation date and ending on the date on which the resolution lapses under **42.10**. [*CA 2006, s 299*].

**42.12    MEETINGS AND RESOLUTIONS AT MEETINGS**

A resolution of the members of a company is validly passed at a general meeting if

•       notice of the meeting and of the resolution is given, and

•       the meeting is held and conducted,

in accordance with the provisions in **42.14** to **42.31** (and, where relevant, **42.32** and **42.33**) and the company's articles.

## 42.12   Resolutions and Meetings

[*CA 2006, s 301*].

**Amendments to resolutions**. Where standard articles have been adopted, see

- *Model Articles, Art 47* (private companies),

- *Model Articles, Art 40* (public companies),

set out in APPENDIX 4 STANDARD ARTICLES OF ASSOCIATION. Both these provisions allow for the amendment of both ordinary and special resolutions but only if certain conditions are met.

## 42.13 Electronic meetings and voting

Nothing in *CA 2006, Part 13* (Resolutions and Meetings) precludes the holding and conducting of a meeting in such a way that persons who are not present together at the same place may, by electronic means, attend and speak and vote at it.

In the case of a traded company (see APPENDIX 1 DEFINITIONS) the use of electronic means for the purpose of enabling members to participate in a general meeting may be made subject only to such requirements and restrictions as are

- necessary to ensure the identification of those taking part and the security of the electronic communication; and

- proportionate to the achievement of those objectives,

but this does not affect any power of a company to require reasonable evidence of the entitlement of any person who is not a member to participate in the meeting.

[*CA 2006, s 360A; SI 2009 No 1632, Reg 8*].

## 42.14 Calling meetings

(1) *Directors' power to call general meetings*

The directors of a company may call a general meeting of the company. [*CA 2006, s 302*].

Where standard articles have been adopted, if there are not sufficient directors in the UK to call a meeting, see

- *Table A, 1985, Reg 37*

set out in APPENDIX 4 STANDARD ARTICLES OF ASSOCIATION.

(2) *Meetings called by members*

*Directors' duty to call meetings required by members*. The members of a company may require the directors to call a general meeting of the company. The directors must do so once the company has received requests to do so from

- members representing at least 5% of such of the paid-up capital of the company as carries the right of voting at general meetings of the company (excluding any paid-up capital held as treasury shares); or

- in the case of a company not having a share capital, members who represent at least 5% of the total voting rights of all the members having a right to vote at general meetings.

A request must state the general nature of the business to be dealt with at the meeting and may include the text of a resolution that may properly be moved, and is intended to be moved, at the meeting. A resolution may properly be moved at a meeting unless

- it would, if passed, be ineffective (whether by reason of inconsistency with any enactment or the company's constitution or otherwise);

- it is defamatory of any person; or

- it is frivolous or vexatious.

A request may be in hard copy form or in electronic form and must be authenticated by the person or persons making it.

[*CA 2006, s 303*].

*Directors' duty to call meetings required by members.* Where the directors are required to call a general meeting of the company, they must call it within 21 days from the date on which they become subject to the requirement. It must be held on a date not more than 28 days after the date of the notice convening the meeting.

If the members' requests for the meeting identify a resolution to be moved at the meeting, the notice of the meeting must include notice of the resolution. If the resolution is to be proposed as a special resolution, the directors are treated as not having duly called the meeting if they do not give the required notice of the resolution in accordance with **42.3**.

[*CA 2006, s 304*].

*Power of members to call meeting at company's expense.* If the directors are required as above to call a meeting and do not do so, the members who requested the meeting, or any of them representing more than one half of the total voting rights of all of them, may themselves call a general meeting. Where the requests received by the company included the text of a resolution intended to be moved at the meeting, the notice of the meeting must include notice of the resolution.

The meeting must be called for a date not more than three months after the date on which the directors become subject to the requirement to call a meeting. It must be called in the same manner, as nearly as possible, as that in which meetings are required to be called by directors of the company.

Any reasonable expenses incurred by the members requesting the meeting because of the failure of the directors must be reimbursed by the company. Any sum so reimbursed must then be retained by the company out of any sums due or becoming due from the company by way of fees or other remuneration in respect of the services of such of the directors as were in default.

[*CA 2006, s 305*].

(3) *Resigning auditor*

In certain circumstances, a resigning auditor may request the directors to call a general meeting. See **8.22 AUDIT**.

(4) *Power of court to order meeting*

If, for any reason, it is impracticable to

- call a meeting of a company in any manner in which meetings of that company may be called, or

- to conduct the meeting in the manner prescribed by the company's articles or *CA 2006*,

the court may (either of its own motion, on the application of a director or on the application of a member of the company who would be entitled to vote at the meeting) order a meeting to be called, held and conducted in any manner the court thinks fit.

Where such an order is made, the court may give such ancillary or consequential directions as it thinks expedient (including that one member of the company present at the meeting be deemed to constitute a quorum).

A meeting called, held and conducted in accordance with an order under this provision is deemed, for all purposes, to be a meeting of the company duly called, held and conducted.

[*CA 2006, s 306; SI 2008 No 2860, Art 6*].

The power of the court, on application, to call a meeting cannot be used by one group of shareholders to defeat the class rights of another group. See *BML Group Ltd v Harman* (1994) Times, 8 April, CA.

For a case where the court exercised its discretion under these provisions, see *Re Sticky Fingers Restaurant Ltd* [1992] BCLC 84, [1991] BCC 754 where the only two directors and members of the company were in dispute and one was refusing to attend meetings so that the company was effectively deadlocked. The court stipulated that any director appointed at the meeting would not be allowed to act unless he gave specified undertakings designed to protect the existing directors (eg not to vote for their dismissal).

### 42.15 Notice of meetings

**(1) Companies other than traded companies and opted in companies** (see (*b*) below)

The following provisions apply to all general meetings where the company is

(a)     not a traded company (see APPENDIX 1 DEFINITIONS); or

(b)     a traded company that is an opted-in company (see **48.9** TAKEOVERS) where

> (i)     the meeting is held to decide whether to take any action that might result in the frustration of a takeover bid for the company; or
>
> (ii)    the meeting is held by virtue of *CA 2006, s 969* (power of offeror to require general meeting to be held).

Subject to below,

* a general meeting of a private company (other than an adjourned meeting) must be called by notice of at least 14 days; and

* a general meeting of a public company (other than an adjourned meeting) must be called by notice of

> (i)     in the case of an annual general meeting (see **42.32**), at least 21 days, and
>
> (ii)    in any other case, at least 14 days.

In calculating the periods of notice referred to above, the day on which notice is given and the day of the meeting are excluded.

The above requirements for notice are subject to the following.

* A company's articles may require a longer period of notice.

* A general meeting may be called by shorter notice if agreed to by the members. Apart from the AGM of a public company (for which see **42.32**) the shorter notice must be agreed to by a majority in number of the members having a right to attend and vote at the meeting, being a majority who

> (i)     together hold not less than the 'requisite percentage' in nominal value of the shares giving a right to attend and vote at the meeting (excluding any shares in the company held as treasury shares); or

(ii)     in the case of a company not having a share capital, together represent not less than the requisite percentage of the total voting rights at that meeting of all the members.

The '*requisite percentage*' is, in the case of a private company, 90% (or such higher percentage not exceeding 95% as may be specified in the company's articles) and, in the case of a public company, 95%.

Elective resolutions of private companies

Before 1 October 2007, private companies (only) could pass an elective resolution authorising shorter notice of meeting than required by *CA 1985 s 369(4)*. If, immediately before 1 October 2007, there was such an elective resolution in force under *CA 1985, s 369(4)* which

•     specified 90% as the requisite percentage (or under which resolution the company in general meeting had determined that the percentage should be 90%), or

•     specified a percentage greater than 90% but less than 95% as the requisite percentage (or under which resolution the company in general meeting had determined a percentage greater than 90% but less than 95%),

any provision in the company's articles adopted before 1 October 2007 specifying a different percentage is to be disregarded.

[*CA 2006, ss 307, 360; SI 2007 No 2194, Sch 3 paras 26, 26A; SI 2008 No 674, Sch 3 para 2*].

(2) *Traded companies (other than an opted in company see (1)(b) above)*

Unless the company's articles require a longer period of notice, a general meeting of a traded company (see **Appendix 1 Definitions**) must be called by notice of

•     in the case where conditions A to C below are met, at least 14 days; and

•     in any other case, at least 21 days.

In calculating the periods of notice referred to above, the day on which notice is given and the day of the meeting are excluded.

Condition A is that the general meeting is not an AGM.

Condition B is that the company offers the facility for members to vote by electronic means accessible to all members who hold shares that carry rights to vote at general meetings. This condition is met if there is a facility, offered by the company and accessible to all such members, to appoint a proxy by means of a website.

Condition C is that a special resolution reducing the period of notice to not less than 14 days has been passed at the immediately preceding AGM or at a general meeting held since that AGM. In the case of a company which has not yet held an AGM, the condition is that a special resolution reducing the period of notice to not less than 14 days has been passed at a general meeting.

Where a general meeting is adjourned, the adjourned meeting may be called by shorter notice than required above except that, in the case of an adjournment for lack of a quorum, this applies only if

•     no business is to be dealt with at the adjourned meeting the general nature of which was not stated in the notice of the original meeting; and

•     the adjourned meeting is to be held at least 10 days after the original meeting.

## 42.15   Resolutions and Meetings

[*CA 2006, ss 307A, 360*].

**42.16** *Ways of giving notice*

Notice of a general meeting of a company must be given

- in hard copy form;

- in electronic form;

- by means of a website (see below); or

- by a combination of the above.

[*CA 2006, s 308*].

*Publication of notice of meeting on website.* Notice of a meeting is not validly given by a company by means of a website unless

- when the company notifies a member of the presence of the notice on the website, the notification

  (i) states that it concerns a notice of a company meeting;

  (ii) specifies the place, date and time of the meeting; and

  (iii) in the case of a public company, states whether the meeting will be an annual general meeting; and

- the notice is available on the website throughout the period beginning with the date of that notification and ending with the conclusion of the meeting.

[*CA 2006, s 309*].

Where standard articles have been adopted, for general provisions relating to the giving of notice, see *Table A, 1985, Regs 111–116*, set out in Appendix 4 Standard Articles of Association.

**42.17** *Persons entitled to receive notice*

Subject to any enactment and the provisions of the company's articles, notice of a general meeting of a company must be sent to

(a) every member (including any person who is entitled to a share in consequence of the death or bankruptcy of a member, if the company has been notified of their entitlement); and

(b) every director.

The reference in (*a*) above to the bankruptcy of a member includes the sequestration of the estate of a member and a member's estate being the subject of a protected trust deed (within the meaning of the *Bankruptcy (Scotland) Act 1985*).

[*CA 2006, s 310*].

**42.18** *Contents of notice*

(1) *General requirements*

Notice of a general meeting of a company is given must state:

- The time and date of the meeting.

- The place of the meeting.

• The general nature of the business to be dealt with at the meeting. In relation to a company other than a traded company (in relation to meetings of which notice is given before 3 August 2009, in relation to any company) this has effect subject to any provision of the company's articles.

[*CA 2006, s 311(1)(2)*].

Where standard articles have been adopted, for general provisions relating to the giving of notice, see *Table A, 1985, Reg 38*, set out in APPENDIX 4 STANDARD ARTICLES OF ASSOCIATION.

See *Tiessen v Henderson* [1899] 1 Ch 861. The time and place of the meeting are at the discretion of the directors but this must be exercised in good faith. See *Cannon v Trask* (1875) LR 20 Eq 669 where the company was restrained from bringing forward the date of a meeting before share transfers were registered to persons opposed to the board.

(2) *Traded companies: additional disclosures in notice*

Notice of a general meeting of a 'traded company' (see APPENDIX 1 DEFINITIONS) must also include:

• A statement giving the address of the website on which the information required under (3) below is published.

• A statement

    (i) that the right to vote at the meeting is determined by reference to the register of members or, if an election is in force under *CA 2006, s 128B*, in the register kept by the Registrar of Companies (see 38.9 (Option to keep members' details on the central register)); and

    (ii) of the time when that right is determined in accordance with *CA 2006, s 360B(2)* (traded companies: share dealings before general meetings, see **42.41**).

• A statement of the procedures with which members must comply in order to be able to attend and vote at the meeting (including the date by which they must comply).

• A statement giving details of any forms to be used for the appointment of a proxy.

• Where the company offers the facility for members to vote in advance (see **42.26**) or by electronic means (see **42.13**), a statement of the procedure for doing so (including the date by which it must be done and details of any forms to be used).

• A statement of the right of members to ask questions in accordance with *CA 2006, s 319A* (traded companies: questions at meetings, see **42.25**).

[*CA 2006, s 311(3); SBEE 2015, s 98, Sch 5, para 17; SI 2016 No 321, Reg 6*].

(3) *Traded companies: publication of information in advance of general meeting*

A traded company (see APPENDIX 1 DEFINITIONS) must publish ensure that the information in (a)–(d) below relating to a general meeting is available on a website that identifies the company and is maintained by or on behalf of the company.

(a) The matters set out in the notice of the meeting (see (1) and (2) above).

(b) The total numbers of

    (i) shares in the company, and

    (ii) shares of each class,

in respect of which members are entitled to exercise voting rights at the meeting.

(c)    The totals of the voting rights that members are entitled to exercise at the meeting in respect of the shares of each class.

(d)    Members' statements, members' resolutions and members' matters of business received by the company after the first date on which notice of the meeting is given.

Access to the information on the website, and the ability to obtain a hard copy of the information from the website, must not be conditional on payment of a fee or otherwise restricted.

The information

*    must be made available

(i)    in the case of (*a*)–(*c*) above, on or before the first date on which notice of the meeting is given; and

(ii)    in the case of (*d*) above, as soon as reasonably practicable; and

*    must be kept available throughout the period of two years beginning with the date on which it is first made available on a website under these provisions, although a failure to do so is disregarded if

(i)    the information is made available on the website for part of that period; and

(ii)    the failure is wholly attributable to circumstances that it would not be reasonable to have expected the company to prevent or avoid.

The amounts in (*b*) and (*c*) above must be ascertained at the latest practicable time before the first date on which notice of the meeting is given.

If these provisions are not complied with in respect of any meeting, an offence is committed by every officer of the company who is in default. A person guilty of such an offence is liable, on summary conviction, to a fine not exceeding level 3 on the standard scale. See **29.1** Offences and Legal Proceedings for the standard scale. Failure to comply does not, however, affect the validity of the meeting or of anything done at the meeting.

[*CA 2006, s 311A*].

**42.19**  *Resolutions requiring special notice*

Where by any provision of the *Companies Acts* special notice is required of a resolution, the resolution is not effective unless notice of the intention to move it has been given to the company at least 28 days before the meeting at which it is moved.

The company must, where practicable, give its members notice of any such resolution in the same manner and at the same time as it gives notice of the meeting. But where that is not practicable, the company must give its members notice at least 14 days before the meeting

*    by advertisement in a newspaper having an appropriate circulation; or

*    in any other manner allowed by the company's articles.

If, after notice of the intention to move such a resolution has been given to the company, a meeting is called for a date 28 days or less after the notice has been given, the notice is deemed to have been properly given, though not given within the time required.

[*CA 2006, s 312*].

In calculating the periods of notice referred to above, the day on which notice is given and the day of the meeting are excluded.

[*CA 2006, s 360*].

**42.20** *Accidental failure to give notice of resolution or meeting*

Where a company gives notice of a general meeting or a resolution intended to be moved at a general meeting, any accidental failure to give notice to one or more persons is disregarded for the purpose of determining whether notice of the meeting or resolution (as the case may be) is duly given.

The above has effect subject to any provision of the companies articles, except in relation to notice given under

- *CA 2006, s 304* (directors' duty to call meetings required by members, see **42.14**);

- *CA 2006, s 305* (notice of meetings called by members following failure of directors, see **42.14**); and

- *CA 2006, s 339* (notice of resolutions at AGMs proposed by members, see **42.33**).

[*CA 2006, s 313; SI 2007 No 2194, Sch 3 para 28*].

Where standard articles have been adopted, for general provisions relating to the giving of notice, see *Table A, 1985, Reg 39*, set out in APPENDIX 4 STANDARD ARTICLES OF ASSOCIATION.

See also *Re West Canadian Collieries Ltd* [1962] Ch 370, [1962] 1 All ER 26. Failure to give notice under the mistaken belief that a person is not a shareholder for the purpose of a particular meeting is not an accidental omission (*Musselwhite v C H Musselwhite & Son Ltd* [1962] Ch 964, [1962] 1 All ER 201).

## 42.21  Members' statements

**Members' power to require circulation of statement**. The members of a company may require the company to circulate, to members of the company entitled to receive notice of a general meeting, a statement of not more than 1,000 words with respect to a matter referred to in a proposed resolution to be dealt with at that meeting or other business to be dealt with at that meeting.

A company is required to circulate a statement once it has received requests to do so from

- members representing at least 5% of the total voting rights of all the members who have a right to vote on the matter in question (excluding any voting rights attached to any shares in the company held as treasury shares); or

- at least 100 members who have a right to vote on the matter in question and hold shares in the company on which there has been paid up an average sum, per member, of at least £100.

A request may be in hard copy form or in electronic form. It must identify the statement to be circulated, be authenticated by the person or persons making it, and be received by the company at least one week (excluding the day the request is received and the day of the meeting) before the meeting to which it relates.

[*CA 2006, ss 314, 360*].

**Company's duty to circulate members' statement**. A company that is required under the above provisions to circulate a statement must send a copy of it to each member of the company entitled to receive notice of the meeting in the same manner as the notice of the meeting and at the same time as, or as soon as reasonably practicable after, it gives notice of the meeting (but see below for expenses of circulation and application to the court).

# 42.21 Resolutions and Meetings

In the event of default in complying with this requirement, an offence is committed by every officer of the company who is in default. A person guilty of such an offence is liable (i) on conviction on indictment, to a fine; and (ii) on summary conviction, to a fine not exceeding the statutory maximum. See 29.1 OFFENCES AND LEGAL PROCEEDINGS for the statutory maximum.

*[CA 2006, s 315]*.

**Expenses of circulating members' statement**. The expenses of the company in circulating a members' statement need not be paid by the members who requested the circulation of the statement if

- the meeting to which the requests relate is an annual general meeting of a public company; and

- requests sufficient to require the company to circulate the statement are received before the end of the financial year preceding the meeting.

Apart from this exception, the expenses of the company must be paid by the members who requested the circulation of the statement unless the company resolves otherwise. Unless the company has previously resolved to pay the expenses, it is not bound to circulate the resolution unless a sum reasonably sufficient to meet its expenses is deposited with it, or tendered to it, not later than one week before the meeting. In calculating the period of one week, the day the sum is deposited or tendered and the day of the meeting are excluded.

*[CA 2006, ss 316, 360]*.

**Application to court not to circulate members' statement**. A company is not required to circulate a members' statement if, on an application by the company or another person who claims to be aggrieved, the court is satisfied that the rights conferred by the above provisions are being abused. The court may order the members who requested the circulation of the statement to pay the whole or part of the company's costs (in Scotland, expenses) on such an application, even if they are not parties to the application.

*[CA 2006, s 317]*.

## 42.22 Procedure at meetings

Where standard articles have been adopted, see

(a)    for attendance and speaking at general meetings

- *Model Articles, Art 37* (private companies)

- *Model Articles, Art 29* (public companies)

(b)    for no voting of shares on which money is owed to the company

- *Model Articles, Art 41* (public companies)

set out in APPENDIX 4 STANDARD ARTICLES OF ASSOCIATION.

## 42.23 *Quorum*

In the case of a company limited by shares or guarantee and having only one member, one 'qualifying person' present at a meeting is a quorum. In any other case, subject to the provisions of the company's articles, two qualifying persons present at a meeting are a quorum, unless each is a qualifying person only because he is

- authorised under 42.27 to act as the representative of a corporation in relation to the meeting, and they are representatives of the same corporation; or

1166

- he is appointed as proxy of a member in relation to the meeting, and they are proxies of the same member.

A '*qualifying person*' means

- an individual who is a member of the company;

- a person authorised under **42.27** to act as the representative of a corporation in relation to the meeting; or

- a person appointed as proxy of a member in relation to the meeting.

[*CA 2006, s 318*].

Where standard articles have been adopted, see

- *Table A, 1985, Regs 40, 41*

- *Model Articles, Art 38* (private companies)

- *Model Articles, Art 38* (public companies)

set out in APPENDIX 4 STANDARD ARTICLES OF ASSOCIATION.

**42.24** *Chairman and directors*

Subject to any provision of the company's articles that states who may or may not be chairman, a member may be elected to be the chairman of a general meeting by a resolution of the company passed at the meeting.

[*CA 2006, s 319*].

Where standard articles have been adopted, see

- *Table A 1985, Regs 42, 43*

- *Model Articles, Art 39* (private companies),

- *Model Articles, Art 31* (public companies),

set out in APPENDIX 4 STANDARD ARTICLES OF ASSOCIATION.

*Directors.* A director, even if not a member, will normally be entitled to attend and speak at any general meeting and any separate meeting of the holders of any class of shares. Where standard articles have been adopted, see

- *Table A 1985, Reg 44*

- *Model Articles, Art 40* (private companies),

- *Model Articles, Art 32* (public companies),

set out in APPENDIX 4 STANDARD ARTICLES OF ASSOCIATION.

**42.25** *Traded companies: questions at meetings*

At a general meeting of a traded company (see APPENDIX 1 DEFINITIONS), the company must answer any question relating to the business being dealt with at the meeting put by a member attending the meeting unless

- to do so would

  (i)   interfere unduly with the preparation for the meeting; or

## 42.25 Resolutions and Meetings

    (ii)    involve the disclosure of confidential information;

- the answer has already been given on a website in the form of an answer to a question; or

- it is undesirable in the interests of the company or the good order of the meeting that the question be answered.

[*CA 2006, s 319A*].

**42.26** *Voting procedure*

(1) *Declaration by chairman on a show of hands*

On a vote on a resolution at a meeting on a show of hands, a declaration by the chairman that the resolution has or has not been passed, or passed with a particular majority, is conclusive evidence of that fact without proof of the number or proportion of the votes recorded in favour of or against the resolution. An entry in respect of such a declaration in minutes of the meeting recorded in accordance with **42.44** is also conclusive evidence of that fact without such proof.

These provisions do not have effect if a poll is demanded in respect of the resolution (and the demand is not subsequently withdrawn).

[*CA 2006, s 320*].

Where standard articles have been adopted, see

- *Table A 1985, Regs 46, 47,*
- *Model Articles, Art 42* (private companies),
- *Model Articles, Art 34* (public companies),

set out in Appendix 4 Standard Articles of Association.

Where no poll is demanded, a resolution is passed on a show of hands even if, on a poll, a different result would have been obtained (*Re Horbury Bridge Coal, Iron and Waggon Co* (1879) 11 Ch D 109, CA).

(2) *Demanding a poll*

Where standard articles have been adopted, see

- *Table A 1985, Regs 46, 48, 51,*
- *Model Articles, Art 44* (private companies),
- *Model Articles, Arts 36, 37* (public companies),

set out in Appendix 4 Standard Articles of Association.

A provision of a company's articles is void in so far as it would have the effect of

- excluding the right to demand a poll at a general meeting on any question other than
  - (i)    the election of the chairman of the meeting; or
  - (ii)   the adjournment of the meeting; or
- making ineffective a demand for a poll on any such question which is made by
  - (i)    not less than five members having the right to vote on the resolution;

(ii)   a member or members representing not less than 10% of the total voting rights of all the members having the right to vote on the resolution (excluding any voting rights attached to any shares in the company held as treasury shares); or

(iii)   a member or members holding shares in the company conferring a right to vote on the resolution, being shares on which an aggregate sum has been paid up equal to not less than 10% of the total sum paid up on all the shares conferring that right (excluding shares in the company conferring a right to vote on the resolution which are held as treasury shares).

[*CA 2006, s 321*].

For these purposes, where a member has appointed a proxy to vote on his behalf, the proxy is treated as the member.

[*CA 2006, s 329(2)*].

(3) *Voting on a poll*

Where standard articles have been adopted, for general provisions relating to the giving of notice, see *Table A, 1985, Regs 49–52*, set out in APPENDIX 4 STANDARD ARTICLES OF ASSOCIATION.

On a poll taken at a general meeting of a company, a member entitled to more than one vote need not, if he votes, use all his votes or cast all the votes he uses in the same way.

[*CA 2006, s 322*].

(4) *Votes cast in advance*

A company's articles may contain provision to the effect that on a vote on a resolution on a poll taken at a meeting, the votes may include votes cast in advance.

(a)   Any provision of a company's articles is void in so far as it would have the effect of requiring any document casting a vote in advance to be received by the company or another person earlier than

•   in the case of a poll taken more than 48 hours after it was demanded, 24 hours before the time appointed for the taking of the poll; and

•   in the case of any other poll, 48 hours before the time for holding the meeting or adjourned meeting.

In calculating these periods, no account is to be taken of any part of a day that is not a working day.

(b)   In the case of a traded company (see APPENDIX 1 DEFINITIONS), any provision in the articles in relation to advance voting at a general meeting may be made subject only to such requirements and restrictions as are

•   necessary to ensure the identification of the person voting; and

•   proportionate to the achievement of that objective.

But nothing in this provision affects any power of a company to require reasonable evidence of the entitlement of any person who is not a member to vote.

[*CA 2006, s 322A*].

(5) *Casting vote of chairman*

Where, immediately before 1 October 2007, the articles of a company provided that, in the event of equality of votes on an ordinary resolution (whether on a show of hands or on a poll), the chairman should have a casting vote in addition to any other vote that he might have

- if that provision has not been removed by a subsequent alteration of the articles, it continues to have effect notwithstanding *CA 2006, s 282* (see **42.2**); and

- if that provision has been removed by a subsequent alteration of the articles, the company may at any time restore the provision which has effect notwithstanding *CA 2006, s 282*.

In relation to meetings of which notice is given on or after 3 August 2009, nothing in the above applies in relation to a traded company (see APPENDIX 1 DEFINITIONS) (in other words traded companies cannot in any circumstances use the casting vote of a chairman on an ordinary resolution).

[*SI 2007 No 2194, Sch 3 para 23A; SI 2007 No 3495, Sch 5 para 2(5); SI 2009 No 1632, Reg 22*].

**42.27** *Representation of corporations at meetings*

If a corporation (whether or not a company within the meaning of *CA 2006*) is a member of a company, it may, by resolution of its directors or other governing body, authorise a person or persons to act as its representative or representatives at any meeting of the company. Where it does so, the position is as follows.

(a)   Subject to (*b*) below, a person authorised by a corporation is entitled to exercise (on behalf of the corporation) the same powers as the corporation could exercise if it were an individual member of the company.

(b)   Where a company authorises more than one person,

    (i)   on a vote on a resolution on a show of hands at a meeting of the company, each authorised person has the same voting rights as the corporation would be entitled to; and

    (ii)   where (i) above does not apply and more than one authorised person purport to exercise a power under (*a*) above in respect of the same shares

- if they purport to exercise the power in the same way as each other, the power is treated as exercised in that way; and

- if they do not purport to exercise the power in the same way as each other, the power is treated as not exercised.

*In relation to meeting of which notice is given before 3 August 2009*, where the corporation authorises more than one person and more than one of them purport to exercise such power

- if they purport to exercise the power in the same way, the power is treated as exercised in that way; and

- if they do not purport to exercise the power in the same way, the power is treated as not exercised.

[*CA 2006, s 323*].

**42.28 Proxies**

Nothing in *CA 2006, ss 324–330* (below) prevents a company's articles from conferring more extensive rights on members or proxies.

[*CA 2006, s 331*].

(1)    **Rights to appoint proxies**

A member of a company is entitled to appoint another person as his proxy to exercise all or any of his rights to attend and to speak and vote at a meeting of the company.

In the case of a company having a share capital, a member may appoint more than one proxy in relation to a meeting, provided that each proxy is appointed to exercise the rights attached to a different share or shares held by him, or (as the case may be) to a different £10, or multiple of £10, of stock held by him.

[*CA 2006, s 324*].

(2)    **Obligation of proxy to vote in accordance with instructions**

A proxy must vote in accordance with any instructions given by the member by whom the proxy is appointed.

[*CA 2006, s 324A*].

(3)    **Notice of meeting to contain statement of rights**

In every notice calling a meeting of a company there must appear, with reasonable prominence, a statement informing the member of his rights under (1) above and any more extensive rights conferred by the company's articles to appoint more than one proxy.

Failure to comply with this requirement does not affect the validity of the meeting or of anything done at the meeting but an offence is committed by every officer of the company who is in default. A person guilty of such an offence is liable, on summary conviction, to a fine not exceeding level 3 on the standard scale. See **29.1** Offences and Legal Proceedings for the standard scale.

[*CA 2006, s 325*].

(4)    **Company-sponsored invitations to appoint proxies**

If, for the purposes of a meeting, a company issues at its own expense invitations to members to appoint as proxy a specified person or a number of specified persons, the invitations must be issued to all members entitled to vote at the meeting. This is not contravened if

•       there is issued to a member at his request a form of appointment naming the proxy or a list of persons willing to act as proxy; and

•       the form or list is available on request to all members entitled to vote at the meeting.

If this provision is contravened as respects a meeting, an offence is committed by every officer of the company who is in default. A person guilty of such an offence is liable, on summary conviction, to a fine not exceeding level 3 on the standard scale. See **29.1** Offences and Legal Proceedings for the standard scale.

[*CA 2006, s 326*].

(5) **Notice required of appointment of proxy, etc**

    (a) *All companies*

Any provision of a company's articles is void if would have the effect of requiring

- the appointment of a proxy, or

- any document necessary to show the validity of, or otherwise relating to, the appointment of a proxy

to be received by the company or another person earlier than the following time.

- In the case of a meeting or adjourned meeting, 48 hours before the time for holding the meeting or adjourned meeting.

- In the case of a poll taken more than 48 hours after it was demanded, 24 hours before the time appointed for the taking of the poll.

- In the case of a poll taken not more than 48 hours after it was demanded, the time at which it was demanded.

In calculating these periods, no account must be taken of any part of a day that is not a working day.

[*CA 2006, s 327(1)–(3)*].

    (b) *Traded companies*

In the case of a traded company (see Appendix 1 Definitions)

- the appointment of a person as proxy for a member must be notified to the company in writing; and

- where such an appointment is made, the company may require reasonable evidence of (i) the identity of the member and of the proxy; (ii) the member's instructions (if any) as to how the proxy is to vote; and (iii) where the proxy is appointed by a person acting on behalf of the member, authority of that person to make the appointment. The company may not require to be provided with anything else related to the appointment.

[*CA 2006, s 327(A1)*].

(6) **Chairing meetings**

Subject to any provision of the company's articles that states who may or who may not be chairman, a proxy may be elected to be the chairman of a general meeting by a resolution of the company passed at the meeting.

[*CA 2006, 328*].

(7) **Right of proxy to demand a poll**

The appointment of a proxy to vote on a matter at a meeting of a company authorises the proxy to demand, or join in demanding, a poll on that matter.

[*CA 2006, s 329(1)*].

(8)     **Notice required of termination of proxy's authority**

*In relation to meetings of a traded company* (see APPENDIX 1 DEFINITIONS) the termination of the authority of a person to act as proxy must be notified to the company in writing.

[*CA 2006, s 330(A1)*].

*In relation to meetings generally*, the following provisions apply in the case of *any* company as regards notice that the authority of a person to act as proxy is terminated.

Any provision of the company's articles is void if it would have the effect of requiring notice of termination to be received by the company or another person earlier than the following time.

•       In the case of a meeting or adjourned meeting, 48 hours before the time for holding the meeting or adjourned meeting.

•       In the case of a poll taken more than 48 hours after it was demanded, 24 hours before the time appointed for the taking of the poll.

•       In the case of a poll taken not more than 48 hours after it was demanded, the time at which it was demanded.

In calculating these periods, no account must be taken of any part of a day that is not a working day.

Subject to the above, and subject to any provision of the company's articles which has the effect of requiring notice of termination to be received by the company or another person at a time earlier than that specified below, the termination of the authority of a person to act as proxy

(a)     does not affect

(i)      whether he counts in deciding whether there is a quorum at a meeting;

(ii)     the validity of anything he does as chairman of a meeting;

(iii)    the validity of a poll demanded by him at a meeting;

unless the company receives notice of the termination before the commencement of the meeting; and

(b)     does not affect the validity of a vote given by that person unless the company receives notice of the termination

(i)      before the commencement of the meeting or adjourned meeting at which the vote is given; or

(ii)     in the case of a poll taken more than 48 hours after it is demanded, before the time appointed for taking the poll. In calculating this period, no account must be taken of any part of a day that is not a working day.

If the company's articles require or permit members to give notice of termination to a person other than the company, the references above to the company receiving notice have effect as if they were or (as the case may be) included a reference to that person.

[*CA 2006, s 330(1)–(7)*].

Where a shareholder has given a proxy, in the absence of any special circumstances or any special contract expressly excluding the right to vote in person, his right to vote at a meeting is paramount to the right of the proxy to vote (*Cousins v International Brick Co Ltd* [1931] 2 Ch 90, 100 LJ Ch 404, CA).

(9)   **Listed companies – special provisions**

A proxy form must be sent, to each person entitled to vote at the meeting, with the notice convening a meeting of holders of listed securities. The proxy form must provide for at least three way voting on all resolutions (except procedural resolutions) and must state that if it is returned without an indication as to how the proxy shall vote on any particular matter, the proxy will exercise his discretion as to whether, and if so how, he votes. Where the resolutions to be proposed include the re-election of retiring directors and the number of retiring directors standing for re-election exceeds five, the proxy must give each shareholder the opportunity to vote for or against (or abstain from voting on) the re-election of the retiring directors as a whole but must also allow votes to be cast for or against(or for shareholders to abstain from voting on) the re-election of them individually. (FCA Listing Rules, paras 9.3.6, 9.3.7).

(10)   **Standard articles**

Where standard articles have been adopted, see

- *Table A, 1985, Regs 59–63,*
- *Model Articles, Arts 45, 46* (private companies),
- *Model Articles, Arts 38, 39* (public companies),

set out in Appendix 4 Standard Articles of Association.

## 42.29  Adjourned meetings

**Adjournment of meeting.** Where standard articles have been adopted, see

- *Table A, 1985, Reg 45*
- *Model Articles, Art 41* (private companies)
- *Model Articles, Art 33* (public companies)

set out in Appendix 4 Standard Articles of Association.

A chairman cannot adjourn a meeting at his own will and pleasure. If he no longer wishes to take part, the meeting itself can resolve to go on and appoint a new chairman (*National Dwellings Society v Sykes* [1894] 3 Ch 159).

**Resolution passed at adjourned meeting.** Where a resolution is passed at an adjourned meeting of a company, the resolution is for all purposes to be treated as having been passed on the date on which it was in fact passed, and is not to be deemed passed on any earlier date.

[*CA 2006, s 332*].

## 42.30  Sending documents relating to meetings, etc in electronic form

Where a company has given an 'electronic address' in

(a)   a notice calling a meeting,

(b)   an instrument of proxy sent out by the company in relation to the meeting, or

(c)     an invitation to appoint a proxy issued by the company in relation to the meeting,

it is deemed to have agreed that any document or information relating to proceedings at the meeting or, as the case may be, proxies for that meeting may be sent by electronic means to that address (subject to any conditions or limitations specified in the notice).

'*Electronic address*' means any address or number used for the purposes of sending or receiving documents or information by electronic means.

For these purposes, documents relating to proxies include

- the appointment of a proxy in relation to a meeting;

- any document necessary to show the validity of, or otherwise relating to, the appointment of a proxy; and

- notice of the termination of the authority of a proxy.

[*CA 2006, s 333*].

**Traded companies: duty to provide electronic address for receipt of proxies, etc.** A traded company (see APPENDIX 1 DEFINITIONS) must provide an electronic address for the receipt of any document or information relating to proxies for a general meeting.

The company must provide the address either

- by giving it when sending out an instrument of proxy for the purposes of the meeting or issuing an invitation to appoint a proxy for those purposes; or

- by ensuring that it is made available, throughout the period beginning with the first date on which notice of the meeting is given and ending with the conclusion of the meeting, on the website on which the information required by **42.18**(3) above is made available.

The company is deemed to have agreed that any document or information relating to proxies for the meeting may be sent by electronic means to the address provided (subject to any limitations specified by the company when providing the address).

Documents relating to proxies include

- the appointment of a proxy for a meeting;

- any document necessary to show the validity of, or otherwise relating to, the appointment of a proxy; and

- notice of the termination of the authority of a proxy.

'*Electronic address*' has the same meaning as in *CA 2006, s 333* above.

[*CA 2006, s 333A*].

## 42.31  Class meetings

The provisions in **42.12** to **42.30** apply (with necessary modifications) in relation to a meeting of holders of a class of shares (or meeting of a class of members of a company without a share capital) as they apply in relation to a general meeting but with the following variations.

(a)     The provisions in **42.14**(2) and (4).

(b)     The additional requirements relating to traded companies (see APPENDIX 1 DEFINITIONS) in *CA 2006, ss 311(3), 311A, 319A, 327(A1), 330(A1)* and *333A* (see **42.18**(2), **42.18**(3), **42.25**, **42.28**(5)(*b*), **42.28**(8) and **42.30** respectively) do not apply.

(c) The provisions in **42.15(1)** apply in relation to a meeting of holders of a class of shares in a traded company as they apply in relation to a meeting of holders of a class of shares in a company other than a traded company (and, accordingly the provisions in **42.15(2)** do not apply in relation to such a meeting).

(d) The provisions in *CA 2006, s 318* (quorum, see **42.23**) and *CA 2006, s 321* (right to demand a poll, see **42.26(2)**) do not apply in relation to a meeting in connection with the variation of rights attached to a class of shares (or class of members of a company without a share capital). Instead the following provisions apply.

*Quorum.* The quorum for such a meeting is:

- In the case of a meeting of holders of a class of shares

  (i) for a meeting other than an adjourned meeting, two persons present holding at least one-third in nominal value of the issued shares of the class in question (excluding any shares of that class held as treasury shares); and

  (ii) for an adjourned meeting, one person present holding shares of the class in question.

  Where a person is present by proxy or proxies, he is treated as holding only the shares in respect of which those proxies are authorised to exercise voting rights.

- In the case of a meeting of a class of members of a company without a share capital

  (i) for a meeting other than an adjourned meeting, two members of the class present (in person or by proxy) who together represent at least one-third of the voting rights of the class; and

  (ii) for an adjourned meeting, one member of the class present (in person or by proxy).

*Right to demand a poll.* At a variation of class rights meeting

- in the case of a meeting of holders of a class of shares, any holder of shares of the class in question present may demand a poll; and

- in the case of a meeting of a class of members of a company without a share capital, any member present (in person or by proxy) may demand a poll.

For the purposes of the above provisions,

- any amendment of a provision contained in a company's articles for the variation of the rights attached to a class of shares (class of members in the case of a company without a share capital), or the insertion of any such provision into the articles, is itself to be treated as a variation of those rights; and

- references to the variation of rights attached to a class of shares (class of members in the case of a company without a share capital) include references to their abrogation.

[*CA 2006, ss 334, 335*].

## 42.32  PUBLIC COMPANIES AND TRADED COMPANIES: ANNUAL GENERAL MEETINGS

(1) *Public companies: holding meetings*

Every public company must hold a general meeting as its annual general meeting (AGM)

(a)     where it has given notice of the alteration of its accounting reference date under *CA 2006, s 392* (see **2.20** Accounting Reference Dates and Periods), specifying a new accounting reference date and stating that the current accounting reference period or the previous accounting reference period is to be shortened, within three months of giving that notice; and

(b)     in all other circumstances, in each period of six months beginning with the day following its accounting reference date (see **2.19** Accounting Reference Dates and Periods).

Before 6 April 2008, the period was seven months. The reduction from seven to six months also does not have effect in relation to a company until

(i)     the directors of the company have complied with *CA 1985, s 241* (laying of accounts and reports before the company in general meeting) in respect of its last financial year beginning before 6 April 2008; or

(ii)    the first financial year of the company beginning on or after that date comes to an end.

This is in addition to any other meetings held during that period.

If a company fails to comply with this requirement, an offence is committed by every officer of the company who is in default. A person guilty of such an offence is liable (i) on conviction on indictment, to a fine; and (ii) on summary conviction, to a fine not exceeding the statutory maximum. See **29.1** Offences and Legal Proceedings for the statutory maximum.

[*CA 2006, s 336(1)(2)–(4)*].

In the case of a company formed and registered before 1 October 2007 that is a public company immediately before that date,

•     *CA 1985, s 366* (duty to hold AGM) continues to apply to determine the date by which the company must hold its first AGM after 30 September 2007; and

•     *CA 2006, s 336* (see above) applies in relation to subsequent AGMs.

Private companies are not required to hold an AGM after 1 October 2007 but the repeal of *CA 1985, s 366* (duty to hold AGM) does not affect any provision of a private company's memorandum or articles that expressly requires the company to hold an AGM. Any such provision continues to have such effect as it had immediately before 1 October 2007. But for this purpose, a provision specifying that one or more directors are to retire at an AGM is not provision expressly requiring the company to hold an AGM.

With effect from 31 December 2007, a company is not to be treated as one whose articles expressly require it to hold an AGM if, immediately before 1 October 2007, there was in force in relation to the company a resolution under *CA 1985, s 366A* (election to dispense with AGM).

(2) *Traded companies that are private companies: holding meetings*

Every private company that is a traded company (see Appendix 1 Definitions) must hold a general meeting as its annual general meeting (AGM)

- where it has given notice of the alteration of its accounting reference date under *CA 2006, s 392* (see **2.19** ACCOUNTING REFERENCE DATES AND PERIODS), specifying a new accounting reference date and stating that the current accounting reference period or the previous accounting reference period is to be shortened, within 3 months of giving that notice; and

- in all other circumstances, in each period of nine months beginning with the day following its accounting reference date (in addition to any other meetings held during that period).

This is in addition to any other meetings held during that period.

If a company fails to comply with this requirement, an offence is committed by every officer of the company who is in default. A person guilty of such an offence is liable (i) on conviction on indictment, to a fine; and (ii) on summary conviction, to a fine not exceeding the statutory maximum. See **29.1** OFFENCES AND LEGAL PROCEEDINGS for the statutory maximum.

[*CA 2006, s 336(1A)(2)–(4)*].

(3) *Public companies and traded companies: Notice of AGM*

A notice calling an AGM must state that the meeting is an AGM.

See **42.15** for notice of general meetings which also applies to AGMs. An AGM of a public company may be called by shorter notice than that required under **42.15** or by the company's articles (as the case may be), if *all* the members entitled to attend and vote at the meeting agree to the shorter notice.

Where a notice calling an AGM of a traded company is given more than six weeks before the meeting, the notice must include

- if the company is a public company, a statement of the right under *CA 2006, s 338* (see **42.33**) to require the company to give notice of a resolution to be moved at the meeting; and

- whether or not the company is a public company, a statement of the right under *CA 2006, s 338A* (see **42.33**) to require the company to include a matter in the business to be dealt with at the meeting.

In calculating the six-week period referred to above, the day on which the notice is given and the day of the meeting are excluded.

[*CA 2006, ss 337, 360*].

(4) *Business of the meeting*

There is no set business which must be held at the AGM but it is usual to consider the annual accounts, declare the final dividend (if any), deal with the election of directors, approve directors' remuneration and re-appoint the auditor, fixing the level of his remuneration.

### 42.33 Circulation of members' resolutions

### (1) Public companies: power to require circulation of resolutions for AGM

The members of a public company may require the company to give, to members of the company entitled to receive notice of the next AGM, notice of a resolution which may properly be moved and is intended to be moved at that meeting. A resolution may properly be moved at an AGM unless

- it would, if passed, be ineffective (whether by reason of inconsistency with any enactment or the company's constitution or otherwise);

- it is defamatory of any person; or

- it is frivolous or vexatious.

A company must give notice of a resolution once it has received requests that it do so from

- members representing at least 5% of the total voting rights of all the members who have a right to vote on the resolution at the AGM to which the requests relate (excluding any voting rights attached to any shares in the company held as treasury shares); or

- at least 100 members who have a right to vote on the resolution at the AGM to which the requests relate and hold shares in the company on which there has been paid up an average sum, per member, of at least £100.

Under *CA 2006, s 153*, a company must also act under these provisions where it receives the necessary number of requests from persons nominated by members to enjoy their rights in relation to the company. See **26.6 MEMBERS** for full details.

The request may be in hard copy form or in electronic form. It must identify the resolution of which notice is to be given and must be authenticated by the person or persons making it. It must be received by the company not later than six weeks (excluding the day the request is received and the day of the meeting) before the AGM to which the requests relate or, if later, the time at which notice is given of that meeting.

[*CA 2006, ss 338, 360*].

### (2) Traded companies: members' power to include other matters in business dealt with at AGM

The members of a traded company (see **APPENDIX 1 DEFINITIONS**) may request the company to include in the business to be dealt with at an AGM any matter (other than a proposed resolution) unless it is defamatory of any person, frivolous or vexatious.

A company is required to include such a matter once it has received requests that it do so from

- members representing at least 5% of the total voting rights of all the members who have a right to vote at the meeting; or

- at least 100 members who have a right to vote at the meeting and hold shares in the company on which there has been paid up an average sum, per member, of at least £100.

See also *CA 2006, s 153* (exercise of rights where shares held on behalf of others, see **26.6 MEMBERS**).

A request

- may be in hard copy form or in electronic form;

- must identify the matter to be included in the business;

- must be accompanied by a statement setting out the grounds for the request;

- must be authenticated by the person or persons making it; and

- must be received by the company not later than

> (i)　　six weeks (excluding the day the request is received and the day of the meeting) before the meeting; or
>
> (ii)　　if later, the time at which notice is given of that meeting.

[*CA 2006, ss 338A, 360*].

**(3) Public companies: company's duty to circulate members' resolutions for AGMs**

A public company required under (1) above to give notice of a resolution must send a copy of it to each member of the company entitled to receive notice of the AGM in the same manner as notice of the meeting and at the same time as, or as soon as reasonably practicable after, it gives notice of the meeting. But see below for the requirement to deposit or tender a sum in respect of expenses of circulation.

In the event of default in complying with this requirement, an offence is committed by every officer of the company who is in default. A person guilty of such an offence is liable (i) on conviction on indictment, to a fine; and (ii) on summary conviction, to a fine not exceeding the statutory maximum. See **29.1 Offences and Legal Proceedings** for the statutory maximum.

[*CA 2006, s 339*].

*Expenses of circulating members' resolutions for AGM.* The expenses of the company in complying with the above requirements need not be paid by the members who requested the circulation of the resolution if

- 　　requests sufficient to require the company to circulate it are received before the end of the financial year preceding the meeting; or

- 　　company resolves otherwise.

Otherwise, the expenses of the company must be paid by the members who requested the circulation of the resolution and the company is not bound to circulate the resolution unless there is deposited with it, or tendered to it, a sum reasonably sufficient to meet its expenses not later than

- 　　six weeks before the AGM to which the requests relate; or

- 　　if later, the time at which notice is given of that meeting.

In calculating the periods of six weeks, the day the sum is deposited or tendered and the day of the meeting are excluded.

[*CA 2006, ss 340, 360*].

**(4) Traded companies: company's duty to circulate members' matters for AGM**

A traded company that is required under (2) above to include any matter in the business to be dealt with at an AGM must give notice of it to each member of the company entitled to receive notice of the AGM in the same manner as notice of the meeting and at the same time as, or as soon as reasonably practicable after, it gives notice of the meeting. It must also publish it on the same website as that on which the company published the information required by *CA 2006, s 311A* (publication of information in advance of the AGM, see **42.18**). But see below where the members concerned need to deposit or tender a sum to cover the expenses of circulation.

In the event of default in complying with this requirement, an offence is committed by every officer of the company who is in default. A person guilty of such an offence is liable (i) on conviction on indictment, to a fine; and (ii) on summary conviction, to a fine not exceeding the statutory maximum. See **29.1 Offences and Legal Proceedings** for the statutory maximum. [*CA 2006, s 340A*].

*Expenses of circulating members' matters to be dealt with at AGM.* The expenses of the company in complying with the above requirements need not be paid by the members who requested the inclusion of the matter in the business to be dealt with at the AGM if

- requests sufficient to require the company to include the matter are received before the end of the financial year preceding the meeting; or

- company resolves otherwise.

Otherwise, the expenses of the company must be paid by the members who requested the inclusion of the matter and the company is not bound to comply with those provisions unless there is deposited with it, or tendered to it, a sum reasonably sufficient to meet its expenses not later than

- six weeks before the AGM to which the requests relate; or

- if later, the time at which notice is given of that meeting.

In calculating the six-week period, the day on which the sum is deposited or tendered and the day of the AGM are excluded.

[*CA 2006, s 340B*].

## 42.34   QUOTED COMPANIES AND TRADED COMPANIES: ADDITIONAL REQUIREMENTS

**Quoted companies** (APPENDIX 1 DEFINITIONS) must comply with the relevant requirements in **42.35–42.40** in relation to meetings.

**Traded companies** (see APPENDIX 1 DEFINITIONS) must comply with the relevant requirements in **42.35–42.40** in relation to meetings.

## 42.35   Website publication of poll results

(1) *Quoted companies other than traded companies*

Where a poll is taken at a general meeting of a quoted company that is not a traded company, the company must ensure that the following information is made available on a website.

- The date of the meeting.

- The text of the resolution or, as the case may be, a description of the subject matter of the poll.

- The number of votes cast in favour and the number of votes cast against.

The information must be made available on a website that is maintained by or on behalf of the company and identifies the company in question. Access to the information on the website, and the ability to obtain a hard copy of the information from the website, must not be conditional on the payment of a fee or otherwise restricted. The information must be made available as soon as reasonably practicable and must be kept available throughout the period of two years beginning with the date on which it is first made available on a website in accordance with this requirement. A failure to make information available on a website throughout this period can, however, be disregarded if

- the information is made available on the website for part of that period; and

- the failure is wholly attributable to circumstances that it would not be reasonable to have expected the company to prevent or avoid.

In the event of default in complying with the above requirements, an offence is committed by every officer of the company who is in default. A person guilty of such an offence is liable, on summary conviction, to a fine not exceeding level 3 on the standard scale. See **29.1** OFFENCES AND LEGAL PROCEEDINGS for the standard scale. But failure to comply does not affect the validity of the poll or the resolution or other business (if passed or agreed to) to which the poll relates.

[*CA 2006, ss 341(1)(2)–(6), 353*].

(2) *Traded companies*

Where a poll is taken at a general meeting of a traded company, the company must ensure that the following information is available on a website.

- The date of the meeting.

- The text of the resolution or, as the case may be, a description of the subject matter of the poll.

- The number of votes validly cast.

- The proportion of the company's issued share capital determined at the time at which the right to vote is determined under *CA 2006, s 360B(2)* (see **42.41**) represented by those votes.

- The number of votes cast in favour.

- The number of votes cast against.

- The number of abstentions (if counted).

A traded company must comply with these requirements by

- the end of 16 days beginning with the date of the meeting; or

- if later, the end of the first working day after the day on which the result of the poll is declared.

The information must be made available on a website that is maintained by or on behalf of the company and identifies the company in question. Access to the information on the website, and the ability to obtain a hard copy of the information from the website, must not be conditional on the payment of a fee or otherwise restricted. The information must be made available as soon as reasonably practicable and must be kept available throughout the period of two years beginning with the date on which it is first made available on a website in accordance with this requirement. A failure to make information available on a website throughout this period can, however, be disregarded if

- the information is made available on the website for part of that period; and

- the failure is wholly attributable to circumstances that it would not be reasonable to have expected the company to prevent or avoid.

In the event of default in complying with the above requirements, an offence is committed by every officer of the company who is in default. A person guilty of such an offence is liable, on summary conviction, to a fine not exceeding level 3 on the standard scale. See **29.1** OFFENCES AND LEGAL PROCEEDINGS for the standard scale. But failure to comply does not affect the validity of the poll or the resolution or other business (if passed or agreed to) to which the poll relates. [*CA 2006, ss 341(1A)(1B)(2)–(6), 353*].

**42.36  Quoted companies: Independent report on poll**

The members of a quoted company may require the directors to obtain an independent report on any poll taken, or to be taken, at a general meeting of the company. The directors must obtain an independent report if they receive requests to do so from

(a)     members representing not less than 5% of the total voting rights of all the members who have a right to vote on the matter to which the poll relates (excluding any voting rights attached to any shares in the company held as treasury shares); or

(b)     not less than 100 members who have a right to vote on the matter to which the poll relates and hold shares in the company on which there has been paid up an average sum, per member, of not less than £100.

Where the requests relate to more than one poll, the requirements of (*a*) or (*b*) above must be satisfied in relation to each of them.

Under *CA 2006, s 153*, a company must also act under these provisions where it receives the necessary number of requests from persons nominated by members to enjoy their rights in relation to the company. See **26.6 MEMBERS** for full details.

A request may be in hard copy form or in electronic form. It must identify the poll or polls to which it relates and be authenticated by the person or persons making it. It must be received by the company not later than one week after the date on which the poll is taken.

[*CA 2006, s 342*].

**The report**. The independent assessor's report must state his name and his opinion whether

•     the procedures adopted in connection with the poll or polls were adequate;

•     the votes cast (including proxy votes) were fairly and accurately recorded and counted;

•     the validity of members' appointments of proxies was fairly assessed;

•     the notice of the meeting contained the necessary statement of rights to appoint a proxy (see **42.28**(3); and

•     the provisions relating to company-sponsored invitations to appoint proxies (see **42.28**(4)) were complied with in relation to the meeting.

The report must give the assessor's reasons for the opinions stated. If he is unable to form an opinion on any of those matters, the report must record that fact and state the reasons for it.

[*CA 2006, s 347*].

**42.37**  *Appointment of independent assessor*

Where the directors are required to obtain an independent report on a poll or polls, they must within one week appoint a person they consider to be appropriate to prepare the report. They must not appoint a person who does not meet the independence requirement (see below) or who has another role in relation to any poll on which he is to report (including, in particular, a role in connection with collecting or counting votes or with the appointment of proxies).

In the event of default in complying with this requirement, an offence is committed by every officer of the company who is in default. A person guilty of such an offence is liable, on summary conviction, to a fine not exceeding level 5 on the standard scale. See **29.1 OFFENCES AND LEGAL PROCEEDINGS** for the standard scale.

If, at the meeting, no poll on which a report is required is taken, the directors are not required to obtain a report from the independent assessor and his appointment ceases (but without prejudice to any right to be paid for work done before the appointment ceased).

[*CA 2006, s 343*].

*Independence requirement.* A person may not be appointed as an independent assessor if

- he is

    (i)     an officer or employee of the company; or

    (ii)    a partner or employee of such a person, or a partnership of which such a person is a partner;

- he is

    (i)     an officer or employee of an 'associated undertaking' of the company; or

    (ii)    a partner or employee of such a person, or a partnership of which such a person is a partner; or

- there exists between

    (i)     the person or an 'associate' of his, and

    (ii)    the company or an associated undertaking of the company,

    a connection of any such description as may be specified by Regulations made by the Secretary of State.

An auditor of the company is not regarded as an officer or employee of the company for this purpose.

'*Associated undertaking*' means a

- parent undertaking or subsidiary undertaking of the company; or

- subsidiary undertaking of a parent undertaking of the company.

'*Associate*' means

- in relation to an individual,

    (i)     that individual's spouse or civil partner or minor child or step-child;

    (ii)    any body corporate of which that individual is a director; and

    (iii)   any employee or partner of that individual;

- in relation to a body corporate,

    (i)     any body corporate of which that body is a director;

    (ii)    any body corporate in the same group as that body; and

    (iii)   any employee or partner of that body or of any body corporate in the same group; and

- in relation to a partnership that is a legal person under the law by which it is governed,

    (i)     any body corporate of which that partnership is a director;

    (ii)    any employee of or partner in that partnership; and

(iii)    any person who is an associate of a partner in that partnership.

In relation to a partnership that is not a legal person under the law by which it is governed, 'associate' means any person who is an associate of any of the partners.

[*CA 2006, ss 344, 345*].

*Effect of appointment of a partnership.* Where a partnership that is not a legal person under the law by which it is governed is appointed as an independent assessor, unless a contrary intention appears, the appointment is of the partnership as such and not of the partners. Where the partnership ceases, the appointment is to be treated as extending to the following.

- Any partnership that succeeds to the practice of that partnership.

- Any other person who succeeds to that practice having previously carried it on in partnership.

For these purposes

- a partnership is regarded as succeeding to the practice of another partnership only if the members of the successor partnership are substantially the same as those of the former partnership; and

- a partnership or other person is regarded as succeeding to the practice of a partnership only if it or he succeeds to the whole or substantially the whole of the business of the former partnership.

Where the partnership ceases and the appointment is not so treated as extending to any partnership or other person, the appointment may, with the consent of the company, be treated as extending to a partnership, or other person, who succeeds to the business of the former partnership (or such part of it as is agreed by the company is to be treated as comprising the appointment).

[*CA 2006, s 346*].

**42.38** *Rights of independent assessor*

*Right to attend meeting, etc.* Where an independent assessor has been appointed to report on a poll, he is entitled to attend the meeting at which the poll may be taken and any subsequent proceedings in connection with the poll. If the independent assessor is a firm, such rights are exercisable by an individual authorised by the firm in writing to act as its representative for that purpose.

The independent assessor is also entitled to be provided by the company with a copy of the notice of the meeting and any other communication provided by the company in connection with the meeting to persons who have a right to vote on the matter to which the poll relates.

These rights are only to be exercised to the extent that the independent assessor considers necessary for the preparation of his report.

[*CA 2006, s 348*].

*Right to information.* The independent assessor is entitled to access to the company's records relating to any poll on which he is to report and the meeting at which the poll or polls may be, or were, taken. He may require anyone who at any material time was a director, secretary, employee, member or agent (including banker, solicitor and auditor) of the company, or a person holding or accountable for any of the company's records, to provide him with information or explanations for the purpose of preparing his report.

Any statement made by a person in response to a requirement under this provision may not be used in evidence against him in criminal proceedings except proceedings for an offence under *CA 2006, s 350* (see below).

A person is not required to disclose information in respect of which a claim to legal professional privilege (in Scotland, to confidentiality of communications) could be maintained in legal proceedings.

[*CA 2006, s 349*].

*Offences relating to provision of information.* A person who fails to comply with a requirement under *CA 2006, s 349* above without delay commits an offence unless it was not reasonably practicable for him to provide the required information or explanation. A person guilty of such an offence is liable, on summary conviction, to a fine not exceeding level 3 on the standard scale. See **29.1** OFFENCES AND LEGAL PROCEEDINGS for the standard scale.

A person also commits an offence who knowingly or recklessly makes to an independent assessor a statement (oral or written) that

- conveys, or purports to convey, any information or explanations which the independent assessor requires, or is entitled to require; and

- is misleading, false or deceptive in a material particular.

A person guilty of such an offence is liable (i) on conviction on indictment, to imprisonment for a term not exceeding two years or a fine (or both); and (ii) on summary conviction, to imprisonment for a term not exceeding twelve months (six months in Scotland and Northern Ireland) or to a fine not exceeding the statutory maximum (or both). See **29.1** OFFENCES AND LEGAL PROCEEDINGS for the statutory maximum.

Nothing in these provisions relating to offences affects any right of an independent assessor to apply for an injunction (in Scotland, an interdict or an order for specific performance) to enforce his rights.

[*CA 2006, s 350*].

**42.39** *Making information available on the website*

Where an independent assessor has been appointed to report on a poll, the company must ensure that the following information is made available on a website.

- The fact of his appointment.

- His identity.

- The text of the resolution or, as the case may be, a description of the subject matter of the poll to which his appointment relates.

- A copy of a report by him which complies with the requirements in **42.36**.

The information must be made available on a website that is maintained by or on behalf of the company and identifies the company in question. Access to the information on the website, and the ability to obtain a hard copy of the information from the website, must not be conditional on the payment of a fee or otherwise restricted. The information must be made available as soon as reasonably practicable and must be kept available throughout the period of two years beginning with the date on which it is first made available on a website in accordance with this requirement. A failure to make information available on a website throughout this period can, however, be disregarded if

- the information is made available on the website for part of that period; and

- the failure is wholly attributable to circumstances that it would not be reasonable to have expected the company to prevent or avoid.

In the event of default in complying with the above requirements, an offence is committed by every officer of the company who is in default. A person guilty of such an offence is liable, on summary conviction, to a fine not exceeding level 3 on the standard scale. See **29.1** Offences and Legal Proceedings for the standard scale. But failure to comply does not affect the validity of the poll or the resolution or other business (if passed or agreed to) to which the poll relates.

[*CA 2006, ss 351, 353*].

## 42.40   Class meetings

The provisions of

- **42.35** apply (with any necessary modification) in relation to a meeting of holders of a class of shares of a quoted company or traded company in connection with the variation of the rights attached to such shares as they apply in relation to a general meeting of the company; and

- **42.36** to **42.39** apply (with any necessary modifications) in relation to a meeting of holders of a class of shares of a quoted company in connection with the variation of the rights attached to such shares as they apply in relation to a general meeting of the company.

For these purposes

- any amendment of a provision contained in a company's articles for the variation of the rights attached to a class of shares, or the insertion of any such provision into the articles, is itself to be treated as a variation of those rights; and

- references to the variation of rights attached to a class of shares include references to their abrogation.

[*CA 2006, s 352*].

## 42.41   TRADED COMPANIES: REQUIREMENTS FOR PARTICIPATING IN AND VOTING AT GENERAL MEETINGS

The requirements are—

(a)   Any provision of the articles of a traded company (see Appendix 1 Definitions) is void in so far as it would have the effect of

   (i)   imposing a restriction on a right of a member to participate in and vote at a general meeting of the company unless the member's shares have (after having been acquired by the member and before the meeting) been deposited with, or transferred to, or registered in the name of another person.

   (ii)   imposing a restriction on the right of a member to transfer shares in the company during the period of 48 hours before the time for the holding of a general meeting of the company if that right would not otherwise be subject to that restriction; and

(b)   A Traded company must determine the right to vote at a general meeting of the company by reference to the register of members as at a time (determined by the company) that is not more than 48 hours before the time for the holding of the meeting.

## 42.41 Resolutions and Meetings

In calculating the period mentioned in (*a*)(ii) and (*b*) above, no account is to be taken of any part of a day that is not a working day.

Nothing in the above provisions affects

- the operation of *CA 2006, Pt 22* or *CA 1985, Pt 15* (see **24 Interests in Public Company Shares**) or any provision in a company's articles relating to the application of those provisions; or

- the validity of articles prescribed, or to the same effect as articles prescribed, under *CA 2006, s 19* (power of Secretary of State to prescribe model articles).

[*CA 2006, s 360A; SI 2009 No 1632, Reg 20*].

## 42.42 DIRECTORS' MEETINGS

Apart from the provisions relating to minutes in **42.43**, there are no provisions in *CA 2006* with regard to the holding of directors' meetings and, subject to the terms of the articles, the directors may regulate their proceedings as they think fit. Where the company has adopted standard articles, see

- *Table A 1985, Regs 88–98*,

- *Model Articles, Arts 7–14* (private companies),

- *Model Articles, Arts 7–17* (public companies),

set out in **Appendix 4 Standard Articles of Association**.

Standard articles may stipulate that written resolutions, signed by all directors entitled to receive notice of a directors' meeting, are as valid as if passed at a duly convened meeting (see, for example *Table A 1985, Reg 93* and Model Articles, *Art 18* (public companies)). This, however, does not override a requirement of the articles that a quorum exists for board meetings. For example, where the quorum to conduct business is two directors, a written resolution signed by one director is invalid even if the only other director is outside the UK and not entitled to receive notice of the meeting (see *Hood Sailmakers Ltd v Axford* [1996] 4 All ER 830, [1997] 1 BCLC 721).

## 42.43 Minutes of directors' meetings

Every company must cause minutes of all proceedings at meetings of its directors to be recorded. Such records must be then be kept for at least ten years from the date of the meeting.

If a company fails to comply with this requirement, an offence is committed by every officer of the company who is in default. A person guilty of such an offence is liable, on summary conviction, to a fine not exceeding level 3 on the standard scale and, for continued contravention, a daily default fine not exceeding one-tenth of level 3 on the standard scale. See **29.1 Offences and Legal Proceedings** for the standard scale.

[*CA 2006, s 248*].

Where standard articles have been adopted, for general provisions relating to the giving of notice, see *Model Articles, Art 15*, set out in **Appendix 4 Standard Articles of Association**.

**Minutes as evidence**. Where minutes of a directors' meeting have been duly recorded as above, then

- if purporting to be authenticated by the chairman of the meeting or by the chairman of the next directors' meeting, they are evidence (in Scotland, sufficient evidence) of the proceedings at the meeting; and

- until the contrary is proved

   (i)    the meeting is deemed duly held and convened;

   (ii)   all proceedings at the meeting are deemed to have duly taken place; and

   (iii)  all appointments at the meeting are deemed valid.

[*CA 2006, s 249*].

## 42.44 RECORDS OF RESOLUTIONS AND MEETINGS

Every company must keep records comprising the following.

(a)    Copies of all resolutions of members passed otherwise than at general meetings.

Such a record, if purporting to be signed by a director of the company or by the company secretary, is evidence (in Scotland, sufficient evidence) of the passing of the resolution.

Where there is a record of a written resolution of a private company, the requirements of *CA 2006* with respect to the passing of the resolution are deemed to be complied with unless the contrary is proved.

(b)    Minutes of all proceedings of general meetings.

Such minutes, if purporting to be signed by the chairman of that meeting or by the chairman of the next general meeting, are evidence (in Scotland, sufficient evidence) of the proceedings at the meeting.

Where there is a record of proceedings of a general meeting of a company, then, until the contrary is proved

- the meeting is deemed duly held and convened;

- all proceedings at the meeting are deemed to have duly taken place; and

- all appointments at the meeting are deemed valid.

(c)    Details provided to the company in accordance with **42.45**.

The records must be kept for at least ten years from the date of the resolution, meeting or decision (as appropriate).

If a company fails to comply with these requirements, an offence is committed by every officer of the company who is in default. A person guilty of such an offence is liable, on summary conviction, to a fine not exceeding level 3 on the standard scale and, for continued contravention, a daily default fine not exceeding one-tenth of level 3 on the standard scale. See **29.1 OFFENCES AND LEGAL PROCEEDINGS** for the standard scale. [*CA 2006, ss 355, 356*].

Where standard articles have been adopted, see *Table A 1985, Reg 100*, set out in **APPENDIX 4 STANDARD ARTICLES OF ASSOCIATION**.

**Form of minute book.** See **36.1 RECORDS** for the provisions relating to form of records generally.

## 42.45 Resolutions and Meetings

### 42.45 Records of decisions of sole member

If a company limited by shares or by guarantee has only one member, where the member takes any decision that

- may be taken by the company in general meeting, and

- has effect as if agreed by the company in general meeting,

he must (unless that decision is taken by way of a written resolution) provide the company with details of that decision. If he fails to comply with this requirement, he commits an offence and is liable, on summary conviction, to a fine not exceeding level 2 on the standard scale. See **29.1** OFFENCES AND LEGAL PROCEEDINGS for the standard scale.

Failure to comply with these requirements does not affect the validity of any decision referred to above.

[*CA 2006, s 357*].

### 42.46 Inspection of records of resolutions and meetings

The records referred to in **42.44** relating to the previous ten years must be kept available for inspection at the company's registered office or at a place specified in Regulations (see **36.2** RECORDS).

The company must give notice to the Registrar of Companies of

- the place at which the records are kept available for inspection, and

- any change in that place,

unless they have at all times been kept at the company's registered office.

The records must be open to the inspection of any member of the company without charge and a member may require a copy of any of the records on payment of such fee as may be prescribed.

**Time available for inspection and copying**. See **36.2** RECORDS.

**Offences**. If

- default is made for 14 days in notifying the Registrar of Companies as above,

- inspection is refused, or

- a copy requested is not sent,

an offence is committed by every officer of the company who is in default. A person guilty of such an offence is liable, on summary conviction, to a fine not exceeding level 3 on the standard scale and, for continued contravention, to a daily default fine not exceeding one-tenth of level 3 on the standard scale. See **29.1** OFFENCES AND LEGAL PROCEEDINGS for the standard scale.

In a case in which an inspection is refused or a copy requested is not sent, the court may by order compel an immediate inspection of the records or direct that the copies required be sent to the persons who requested them.

[*CA 2006, s 358*].

### 42.47 Resolutions and meetings of class of members

The provisions in **42.44–42.46** apply (with necessary modifications) in relation to resolutions and meetings of

- holders of a class of shares, and

- in the case of a company without a share capital, a class of members,

as they apply in relation to resolutions of members generally and to general meetings.

[*CA 2006, s 359*].

## 42.48 INFORMATION AS TO EXERCISE OF VOTING RIGHTS BY INSTITUTIONAL INVESTORS

The Treasury or the Secretary of State may make provision by Regulations requiring certain institutions to provide information about the exercise of voting rights attached to specific shares.

The institutions to which the provisions apply are

- unit trust schemes;

- open-ended investment companies;

- investment trusts;

- pension schemes;

- undertakings authorised to carry on long-term insurance; and

- collective investment schemes.

Regulations may require the provision of specified information about, amongst other things,

- the exercise or non-exercise of voting rights by the institution or any person acting on its behalf;

- any instructions given by the institution or any person acting on its behalf as to the exercise or non-exercise of voting rights; and

- any delegation by the institution or any person acting on its behalf of any functions in relation to the exercise or non-exercise of voting rights or the giving of such instructions.

[*CA 2006, ss 1277–1280*].

Although Regulations have not been published which require voting information, the UK Stewardship Code (see **15 CORPORATE GOVERNANCE**) requires institutional investors to have a clear policy on voting and to disclose their voting activity under the principles and guidance set out in the Code.

# 43   Scotland

**Cross-references**. See **16.22** Dealing With Third Parties for service of documents on a company registered in Scotland carrying on a business in England and Wales; **17.17** Debt Finance–Debentures and Other Borrowing for debentures to bearer; **29.5** Offences and Legal Proceedings for summary proceedings in Scotland; **39.1** Registrar of Companies for Companies Registration Office in Scotland; **44.12** Securities: Certification and Transfers for offences in connection with share warrants.

## 43.1   INTRODUCTION TO THE COMPANIES ACTS IN SCOTLAND

The *Companies Acts* apply in Scotland as they do in the rest of the UK but subject to certain variations and modifications to allow for the different legal system applying there. Apart from the cross-references above, the main provisions which specifically refer to Scotland are as follows.

- Registration of charges (see **40** Registration of Charges).

- Floating charges (see **43.2** to **43.5**).

- Charitable companies (see **43.6** and **43.7**).

- Execution of documents (see **16.7** Dealing With Third Parties).

## 43.2   FLOATING CHARGES

**Note**. The provisions in this paragraph and in **43.3** to **43.5** are repealed by *Bankruptcy and Diligence etc (Scotland) Act 2007, s 46(1)* with effect from a date to be appointed. They will then be replaced by provisions in *Part 2* of that *Act*.

Under the law of Scotland, an incorporated company (whether within the meaning of *CA 1985* or not) may, for the purpose of securing any debt or other obligation incurred or binding upon the company or any other person, create in favour of the creditor a floating charge over all or any part of its property (including uncalled capital) or undertaking.

Subject to the provisions of *CA 1985*, a floating charge in relation to any heritable property in Scotland has effect in accordance with these provisions and *IA 1986, Pt III* notwithstanding that the instrument creating it is not recorded in the Register of Sasines or, as appropriate, registered in accordance with the *Land Registration (Scotland) Act 1979*.

[*CA 1985, s 462*].

Any floating charge which purported to subsist as a floating charge before 17 November 1972 and which, if created on or after that date, would have been validly created under *Companies (Floating Charges and Receivers) (Scotland) Act 1972* is deemed to have subsisted as a valid floating charge from the day of its creation. [*CA 1985, s 465(1)*].

## 43.3  Scotland

### 43.3  Effect of floating charge on winding up

Where a company goes into liquidation, a floating charge created by the company attaches to the relevant property or undertaking but subject to the rights of any person who

- has executed diligence on the property (or part); or

- holds a fixed security or another floating charge over the property (or part) ranking in priority to that floating charge.

Subject to the above, the provisions of *IA 1986, Pt IV* (except *section 185*) apply in relation to the floating charge as if it were a fixed security over the property to which it has attached in respect of

- the principal amount of the debt or obligation; and

- any interest which accrues thereon until payment of the sum due under the charge.

[*CA 1985, ss 463, 486*].

### 43.4  Priority of floating charge

The order of ranking of floating charges and fixed securities is as follows.

(a)  Where all or part of a company's property is subject to a floating charge *and* a fixed security arising by operation of the law, the fixed security has priority.

(b)  Subject to (*a*) above the instrument creating a floating charge over all or any part of the company's property may

(i)  determine the order of ranking by prohibiting or restricting the creation, after the date of the instrument, of a fixed security or other floating charge having priority over it or ranking *pari passu* with it (and such a provision is effective to confer priority); or

(ii)  determine the order in which the floating charge is to rank over the same property (or part) with any other subsisting or future floating charges or fixed securities. The consent is required of the holders of any subsisting floating charge or fixed security which would be adversely affected.

(c)  Subject to (*a*) and (*b*) above

(i)  a fixed security, the right to which has been constituted as a real right before a floating charge has attached to all or any part of the company's property, has priority over a floating charge;

(ii)  floating charges rank with one another according to the time of registration (see **40 REGISTRATION OF CHARGES**); and

(iii)  floating charges received by the Registrar of Companies for registration by the same postal delivery rank equally with one another.

Where the holder of a floating charge within (ii) or (iii) above has received notice in writing of the subsequent registration of another floating charge over the same property (or part), the preference in ranking of the first-mentioned floating charge is restricted to security for

- the holder's present advances;

- any further advances he is required to make under the instrument creating the floating charge or any ancillary document;

- interest due or becoming due on all such advances;

- expenses etc reasonably incurred; and

- in the case of a floating charge to secure a contingent liability (other than a liability arising under any further advances made from time to time), the maximum sum to which that contingent liability is capable of amounting whether or not it is contractually limited. [*CA 1985, ss 464, 486*].

For the above purposes, any provision relating to ranking of charges contained in an instrument creating a floating charge (or any ancillary document) executed prior to 17 November 1972 and which, if made on or after that date would have been a valid provision under *Companies (Floating Charges and Receivers) (Scotland) Act 1972* is deemed to have been a valid provision from the date of its making. [*CA 1985, s 465(2)*].

## 43.5   Alteration of a floating charge

The instrument creating a floating charge (or any ancillary document) may be altered by the execution of an instrument of alteration by the company, the holder of the charge and the holder of any other charge (including a fixed security) which would be adversely affected by the alteration.

Without prejudice to any enactment or rule of law regarding the execution of documents, such an instrument of alteration is validly executed if it is executed

(a)   where trustees for debenture-holders are acting in accordance with a trust deed, by those trustees; or

(b)   where, in the case of a series of debentures, no such trustees are acting, by or on behalf of

- a majority in nominal value of those present (or represented by proxy) and voting at a meeting of debenture-holders at which holders of at least one-third in nominal value of the outstanding debentures of the series are present (or so represented); or

- where no such meeting is held, the holders of at least one-half in nominal value of the outstanding debentures of the series.

The provisions of **43.4** apply to the instrument of alteration as they apply to the instrument creating a floating charge. [*CA 1985, ss 466, 486*].

*CA 1985, s 466(4A)* applies to an alteration of a floating charge where the alteration is one which

- prohibits or restricts the creation of any fixed security or any other floating charge having priority over, or ranking *pari passu* with, the floating charge, or

- varies, or otherwise regulates, the ranking of the floating charge in relation to fixed securities or to other floating charges, or

- releases property from a floating charge, or

- increases the amount secured by a floating charge

[*CA 1985, s 466(4)*].

## 43.5    Scotland

Every alteration to a floating charge created by a company is, so far as any security on the company's property or any part of it is conferred by the alteration, void against the liquidator or administrator and any creditor of the company, unless the documents referred to in the following paragraph are delivered by the company or any person interested in the charge to the Registrar of Companies for registration before the end of the relevant period allowed for delivery.

This is without prejudice to any contract or obligation for repayment of the money secured by the alteration to the charge and when an alteration becomes void the money secured by it immediately becomes payable.

The "relevant period allowed for delivery" is the period of 21 days beginning with the day after the date of execution of the instrument of alteration or, if an order under *CA 2006, s 859F(3)* has been made (see **40.3**) the period allowed by the order

The documents which must be delivered are

- a certified copy of the instrument of alteration, and

- a statement of particulars including the registered name and number of the company, the date of creation of the charge, a description of the instrument (if any) by which the charge was created or evidenced, shot particulars of the property or undertaking charged as set out when the charge was registered, date(s) of execution of the instrument of alteration and names and address(es) of the persons who have executed the instrument of alteration.

*CA 2006, s 859F* (Extension of period allowed for delivery), *s 859G*, (Personal information in certified copies), *s 859I* (Entries on the register), *s 859M* (rectification of register) and *s 859N* (Replacement of instrument or debenture) (see Chapter **40** for all details) apply to an alteration to a floating charge to which the above applies as they apply to a charge as if:

(a)    references to the documents required or delivered under *CA 2006, s 859A or 859B* were the documents referred to above;

(b)    references to the period allowed for delivery under the section concerned were to the relevant period allowed for delivery period referred to above;

(c)    references to delivery of a certified copy of an instrument to the Registrar of Companies for the purposes of *CA 2006, Chapter A1, Part 25* were to the delivery of a certified copy of an instrument of alteration to the Registrar of Companies;

(d)    references to registration in accordance with a provision of *CA 2006, Chapter A1, Part 25*, were to registration in accordance with CA 1985, s 466

(e)    references to registration under *CA 2006, s 859A or 859B* were to registration under *CA 1985, s 466*; and

(f)    references to a statement or notice delivered to the Registrar of Companies in accordance with *CA 2006, Chapter A1, Part 25* were to a statement delivered to the Registrar of Companies in accordance with this *CA 1985, s 466(4A)*.

[*CA 1985, s 466(4A), SI 2013 No 600, Schedule 2, para 1*]


## 43.6    CHARITABLE COMPANIES

In Scotland, where a charity is a company or other body corporate having power to alter the instruments establishing or regulating it, no exercise of that power which has the effect of the body ceasing to be a charity is valid so as to affect the application of

(a)    any property acquired by virtue of any transfer, contract or obligation previously effected otherwise than for full consideration in money or money's worth;

(b)    any property representing property acquired under (*a*);

(c)    any property representing income which has accrued before the alteration is made; or

(d)    the income from any property in (*a*) to (*c*) above.

[*CA 1989, s 112(2); SI 2006 No 242, Sch*].

See also **16.4** DEALINGS WITH THIRD PARTIES for the restriction on the provisions of *CA 2006, s 39* (company's capacity) and *CA 2006, s 40* (power of directors to bind the company) in relation to such a charitable company.

## 43.7    Name of company not including 'charity', etc

Where a company is a charity and its name does not include the word 'charity' or 'charitable', the fact that the company is a charity must be stated in English in legible characters in all

(a)    business letters;

(b)    notices and other official publications;

(c)    bills of exchange, promissory notes, endorsements, cheques and orders for money or goods purporting to be signed by or on behalf of the company;

(d)    documents for the creation, transfer, variation or extinction of an interest in land purporting to be executed by the company; and

(e)    bills of parcels, invoices, receipts and letters of credit.

If a company fails to comply with these requirements, it commits an offence. An officer of the company, or a person acting on its behalf, also commits an offence if he

(i)    issues, or authorises the issue of, any document within (*a*), (*b*) or (*e*) above, or

(ii)    signs, or authorises to be signed on behalf of the company, any document within (*c*) above

in which the required statement required does not appear. A person guilty of such an offence is liable, on summary conviction, to a fine not exceeding level 3 on the standard scale (see **29.1** OFFENCES AND LEGAL PROCEEDINGS).

Additionally, a person in breach of (ii) above is personally liable to the holder of the bill of exchange, promissory note, endorsement, cheque or order for money or goods for the amount of it (unless it is duly paid by the company).

[*CA 1989, s 112(6)–(11); SI 2008 No 948, Sch 3 para 6*].

## 43.8    Bankruptcy (Scotland) Act 2016

A new Act entitled the *Bankruptcy (Scotland) Act 2016* came into force on 30 November 2016. This Act consolidates various amendments to existing Scottish bankruptcy legislation and effectively brings Scottish law on insolvency together into one piece of legislation. The detail of this new legislation is beyond the scope of this book, which does not purport to cover Scottish law.

# 44   Securities: Certification and Transfers

**Cross-references.** See 17 DEBT FINANCE–DEBENTURES AND OTHER BORROWINGS; 47 SHARES.

## 44.1   SHARE CERTIFICATES

**In the case of a company registered in England and Wales or Northern Ireland**, a certificate under the common seal of the company specifying any shares held by a member is *prima facie* evidence of his title to the shares.

**In the case of a company registered in Scotland,**

- a certificate under the common seal of the company specifying any shares held by a member, or

- a certificate specifying any shares held by a member and subscribed by the company in accordance with the *Requirements of Writing (Scotland) Act 1995*,

is sufficient evidence, unless the contrary is shown, of his title to the shares.

[*CA 2006, s 768*].

Share certificates are issued for the benefit of the company in general; they are a declaration by the company to all the world that the person in whose name the certificate is made out, and to whom it is given, is a shareholder in the company. The company is therefore estopped from denying the accuracy of a vendor's certificate and the purchaser is entitled to damages (*Bahia and San Francisco Rly Co, Re* (1868) LR 3 QB 584).

Where a company issues an incorrect certificate, the company may also be estopped from denying the correctness of the certificate against the person to whom it is issued, in the absence of fraud or forgery, where he enters into a contract to sell the shares (*Dixon v Kennaway & Co* [1900] 1 Ch 833). See also *Bloomenthal v Ford* [1897] AC 156, HL.

## 44.2   ISSUE OF CERTIFICATES, ETC ON ALLOTMENT

Subject to below, a company must, within two months after the allotment of any of its shares, debentures or debenture stock, complete and have ready for delivery

- the certificates of the shares allotted;

- the debentures allotted; or

- the certificates of the debenture stock allotted.

This does not apply in the following circumstances.

- If the conditions of issue of the shares, debentures or debenture stock provide otherwise.

- Where shares, debentures or debenture stock are allotted to a 'financial institution' a company is not required, in consequence of that allotment, to comply with the above provisions. A '*financial institution*' means

  (i)    a recognised clearing house acting in relation to a recognised investment exchange; or

  (ii)   a nominee of a recognised clearing house acting in that way or a recognised investment exchange, in either case designated for these purposes in the rules of the recognised investment exchange in question.

- In the case of an allotment of shares if, following the allotment, the company has issued a share warrant in respect of the shares (see **44.12**).

If default is made in complying with these requirements, an offence is committed by every officer of the company who is in default. A person guilty of such an offence is liable, on summary conviction, to a fine not exceeding level 3 on the standard scale and, for continued contravention, a daily default fine not exceeding one-tenth of level 3 on the standard scale. See **29.1** OFFENCES AND LEGAL PROCEEDINGS for the statutory maximum.

[*CA 2006, ss 769, 778*].

See **44.13** for the court's power to order a company to make good any default under these provisions.

## 44.3    TRANSFERS OF SECURITIES

The shares or other interest of any member in a company are transferable in accordance with the company's articles, subject to

- the *Stock Transfer Act 1963* or the *Stock Transfer Act (Northern Ireland) 1963* (which enable securities of certain descriptions to be transferred by a simplified process, see **44.4**); and

- regulations which enable title to securities to be evidenced and transferred without a written instrument (see **44.13**).

[*CA 2006, s 544*].

The procedure for transferring securities is outlined in **44.4** to **44.8**. Special provisions apply in relation to Stock Exchange transactions. These are outlined in **44.14**.

## 44.4    Stock Transfer Act 1963

*STA 1963* provides a simplified procedure for the transfer of *fully paid-up* 'registered securities' of any description, being

(a)    securities issued by any company as defined in *Companies Act 2006 (CA 2006)*, *s 1(1)* (see **12.1** COMPANY FORMATION AND TYPES OF COMPANIES) except a company limited by guarantee or an unlimited company;

(b)     securities issued by any other body incorporated in Great Britain by or under any enactment or by Royal Charter, except a building society or industrial and provident society;

(c)     UK Government securities, except stock or bonds in the National Savings Stock Register and national savings certificates;

(d)     local authority securities;

(e)     units of an authorised unit trust scheme, an authorised contractual scheme or a recognised scheme within the meaning of *FSMA 2000, Pt 17*; and

(f)     shares issued by an open-ended investment company within the meaning of the *Open-Ended Investment Companies Regulations 2001 (SI 2001 No 1228)*.

[*STA 1963, s 1(4); SI 2013 No 1388, Reg 4*].

'*Registered securities*' means transferable securities the holders of which are entered in a register, whether or not maintained in Great Britain.

'*Securities*' means shares, stock, debentures, debenture stock, loan stock, bonds, units of a collective investment scheme within the meaning of *FSMA 2000*, and other securities of any description.

[*STA 1963, s 4(1)*].

Registered securities within (*a*) to (*d*) above may be transferred by means of an instrument in the form set out in *STA 1963, Sch 1* (as amended) (a stock transfer), executed by the transferor only and specifying

•     the full name and address of the transferee;

•     the consideration;

•     the description and number or amount of the securities; and

•     the transferor.

The form need not be attested. Where the transfer has been executed for the purpose of a Stock Exchange transaction, the particulars of the consideration and of the transferee may either be inserted in that transfer or supplied by means of a broker's transfers.

[*STA 1963, s 1(1)(2)*].

Nothing in the above provisions affects the validity of what would otherwise be a valid instrument of transfer. [*STA 1963, s 1(3)*]. For example, where a company has adopted standard articles, see

•     *Table A, 1985, Reg 23*

•     *Model Articles, Art 26* (private companies)

set out in Appendix 4 Standard Articles of Association.

Note that *STA 1963* does not apply to transfers of partly-paid shares. Where such shares are being transferred, the instrument of transfer will require execution by the transferee and attestation. This is because the liability to pay up the sum outstanding on the shares is being transferred from the transferor to the transferee.

Similar provisions apply in Northern Ireland under *Stock Transfer Act (Northern Ireland) 1963*.

## 44.5 Securities: Certification and Transfers

**44.5 Action by transferor/transferee of securities**

**Stock Exchange transactions.** See **44.14**.

**Other transactions.** The procedure required depends on the circumstances.

(a) *Transferor disposing of entire holding to one transferee.* The transferor executes a 'proper instrument of transfer' (normally a stock transfer form – see **44.4**) in favour of the transferee, which he hands to the transferee, together with the share certificate(s), in exchange for the agreed consideration. The transferee then pays the necessary stamp duty on the transfer and delivers the transfer, duly stamped, together with the share certificate(s), to the company for registration. If the company's directors approve the transfer (see **44.6**), the transferee's name is entered in the register of members, the previous share certificate is cancelled, and a new certificate issued to the transferee.

(b) *Transferor disposing of part only of holding to one transferee.* The transferor executes a 'proper instrument of transfer' (normally a stock transfer form – see **44.4**) and hands it, together with the share certificate(s), to the company (rather than the transferee). The form of transfer is then certificated by the company, ie it is endorsed with the words 'certificate lodged' or similar words (see **44.8**). The company returns the certificated transfer to the transferor, but retains the share certificate. The transferor then hands the certified transfer form to the transferee, in exchange for the agreed consideration. The transferee pays the necessary stamp duty on the transfer and delivers the stamped transfer to the company for registration. If the company's directors approve the transfer (see **44.6**), new share certificates are issued to the transferor (for the balance retained) and the transferee (for the shares acquired) and the transferee's name is also entered in the register of members.

(c) *Transferor disposing of shares to more than one transferee.* A similar procedure applies as in (*b*) above) but the transferor executes a separate form of transfer for each transferee.

**44.6 Registration of transfer**

A company may not register a transfer of shares in, or debentures of, the company unless

• a 'proper instrument of transfer' has been delivered to it; or

• the transfer is

    (i) an exempt transfer within the *Stock Transfer Act 1982*; or

    (ii) a Stock Exchange transaction in accordance with **44.14**.

But this does not affect any power of the company to register as shareholder or debenture holder a person to whom the right to any shares in, or debentures of, the company has been transmitted by operation of law. See **44.9**.

If an election is in force under *CA 2006, Pt 8, Chapter 2A* in respect of the company (election to keep certain details on the public register kept by the Registrar), references in the above to registering a transfer (or a person) are to be read as references to delivering particulars of that transfer to the Registrar under *Chapter 2A*.

[*CA 2006, s 770; SBEE 2015, Sch 5, para 26; SI 2016 No 321, Reg 6*].

A conventional stock transfer form is a '*proper instrument of transfer*' even if it does not state the consideration money and is not stamped. The defects in the form are mere irregularities and the registration of the transfer is not invalid (*Nisbet v Shepherd* [1994] 1 BCLC 300, [1994] BCC 91, CA).

**Procedure on transfer being lodged**. Subject to below, when a transfer of shares in, or debentures of, a company has been lodged with the company on or after 6 April 2008, the company must either

- register the transfer, or

- give the transferee notice of refusal to register the transfer, together with its reasons for the refusal

as soon as practicable and in any event within two months after the date on which the transfer is lodged with it. If the company refuses to register the transfer (see **44.7**), it must provide the transferee with such further information about the reasons for the refusal as the transferee may reasonably request (but this does *not* include copies of minutes of meetings of directors).

If a company fails to comply with this requirement, an offence is committed by the company and every officer of the company who is in default. A person guilty of such an offence is liable, on summary conviction, to a fine not exceeding level 3 on the standard scale and, for continued contravention, a daily default fine not exceeding one-tenth of level 3 on the standard scale. See **29.1** OFFENCES AND LEGAL PROCEEDINGS for the standard scale.

These provisions do not apply in relation to the transmission of shares or debentures by operation of law (see **44.9**) or a transfer of shares if the company has issued a share warrant in respect of the shares (see **44.12**). If an election is in force under *CA 2006, Pt 8, Chapter 2A* in respect of the company (election to keep certain details on the public register kept by the Registrar), references in the above to registering a transfer (or a person) are to be read as references to delivering particulars of that transfer to the Registrar under *Chapter 2A*.

[*CA 2006, s 771; SBEE 2015, Sch 5, para 27; SI 2016 No 321, Reg 6*].

Failure to notify within the time limit means that the power of refusal to register is lost and the court may grant an application for rectification of the register under *CA 2006, s 125*, see **38.8** REGISTERS (*Re Inverdeck Ltd* [1998] 2 BCLC 242, [1998] BCC 256).

**Transfer of shares on application of transferor**. On the application of the transferor of any share or interest in a company, the company must enter in its register of members the name of the transferee or, as the case may be, deliver the name to the Registrar of Companies under *CA 2006, Pt 8, Chapter 2A*, in the same manner and subject to the same conditions as if the application for the entry were made by the transferee.

[*CA 2006, s 772; SBEE 2015, Sch 5, para 28; SI 2016 No 321, Reg 6*].

**Standard articles**. A company's articles may contain provisions relating generally to the transfer of shares. Where a company has adopted standard articles, see

- *Table A, 1985, Regs 23–28*;

- *Model Articles, Art 26* (private companies); and

- *Model Articles, Arts 63, 64* (public companies),

set out in APPENDIX 4 STANDARD ARTICLES OF ASSOCIATION.

A company's articles may also contain provisions restricting the right of its members to transfer their shares (see **44.7**).

## 44.7  Restrictions on transfers

A public company which wishes to have its shares quoted on the Stock Exchange cannot impose restrictions on the transfer of its shares (other than in exceptional circumstances), since to do so would adversely affect their marketability. By contrast, the articles of a private company frequently contain such restrictions. Where restrictions are imposed, they are normally either refusal powers or pre-emption provisions.

## 44.7   Securities: Certification and Transfers

**Refusal powers**. A company's articles may empower the directors to refuse to register a transfer, either at their complete discretion or on specified grounds. Such a power, as with any other power conferred on the directors, must be exercised in good faith for the benefit of the company (*Smith & Fawcett Ltd, Re* [1942] Ch 304, [1942] 1 All ER 542, CA) and not for some personal motive of the directors (see *Tett v Phoenix Property and Investment Co Ltd* [1984] BCLC 599). Furthermore, the power must be exercised by the making of a positive decision at a board meeting (see *Moodie v W and J Shepherd (Bookbinders) Ltd* [1949] 2 All ER 1044, 94 Sol Jo 95, HL), failing which the transfer must be registered (*Re Hackney Pavilion Ltd* [1924] 1 Ch 276, 93 LJ Ch 193).

Where a company has adopted standard articles, see

- *Table A, 1985, Reg 24*

- *Model Articles, Art 26* (private companies)

- *Model Articles, Arts 63, 64* (public companies)

set out in APPENDIX 4 STANDARD ARTICLES OF ASSOCIATION.

The remedy for the refusal to register a transfer is for the person aggrieved to apply to the court for rectification of the register of members under *CA 2006, s 125*. See **38.8** REGISTERS.

**Pre-emption provisions**. A company's articles may contain pre-emption provisions, ie provisions requiring any member who wishes to sell his shares to offer them first to existing members, normally at a fair price to be determined by the articles. The effect of such a provision will depend on its precise wording, and there have been numerous decided cases on the subject. See, for example, *Lyle & Scott Ltd v Scott's Trustees; Lyle & Scott Ltd v British Investment Trust Ltd* [1959] AC 763, [1959] 2 All ER 661, HL.

## 44.8   Certification of instrument of transfer

An instrument of transfer (normally a stock transfer form – see **44.4**) is certificated if it bears the words 'certificate lodged' (or words to the like effect). The certification is made by a company if

- the person issuing the instrument is a person authorised to issue certificated instruments of transfer on the company's behalf; and

- the certification is signed by a person authorised to certificate transfers on the company's behalf or by an officer or employee either of the company or of a body corporate so authorised. A certification is treated as signed by a person if

  (i)  it purports to be authenticated by his signature or initials (whether handwritten or not); and

  (ii) it is not shown that the signature or initials was or were placed there neither by himself nor by a person authorised to use the signature or initials for the purpose of certificating transfers on the company's behalf.

  [*CA 2006, s 775(4)*].

The certification by a company of an instrument of transfer of any shares in, or debentures of, the company is to be taken as a representation by the company, to any person acting on the faith of the certification, that documents have been produced to the company that on their face show a *prima facie* title to the shares or debentures in the transferor named in the instrument. However, the certification is not to be taken as a representation that the transferor has any title to the shares or debentures.

[*CA 2006, s 775(1)(2)*].

Where a person acts on the faith of a false certification by a company made negligently, the company is under the same liability to him as if the certification had been made fraudulently. [*CA 2006, s 775(3)*].

Where a company erroneously returned a share certificate to the transferor together with the certificated transfer, and the transferor purported to execute a second 'transfer' in favour of a third party, it was held that the company's duty in relation to the share certificate was owed only to the original transferees, and not to the third party (*Longman v Bath Electric Tramways Ltd* [1905] 1 Ch 646, 74 LJ Ch 424, CA).

## 44.9   TRANSMISSION OF SHARES

Transmission occurs most commonly on the death or bankruptcy of a shareholder but it can also arise on a person becoming of unsound mind and the subject of an order of the Court of Protection. Following the death of a shareholder, the legal title to his shares vests in his personal representatives or, where the shares were held jointly, in the surviving holder(s).

**Execution of share transfer by personal representatives and trustees in bankruptcy.** An instrument of transfer of the share or other interest of a deceased member of a company may be made by his personal representative, although the personal representative is not himself a member of the company, and is as effective as if the personal representative had been such a member at the time of the execution of the instrument. [*CA 2006, s 773*].

If the personal representative does have the shares transferred into his own name and becomes registered as a member, he is personally liable for calls on outstanding shares (with a right of indemnity against the deceased's estate); otherwise he will only be liable for outstanding calls to the extent of the deceased's assets in his hands (*Cheshire Banking Co, Re, Duff's Executors' Case* (1886) 32 Ch D 301, CA).

A trustee in bankruptcy may similarly transfer the bankrupt's shares without first becoming registered as a member.

[*Insolvency Act 1986, s 314, Sch 5*].

**Evidence of grant of probate, etc.** The production to a company of any document that is, by law, sufficient evidence of the grant of

- probate of the will of a deceased person,

- letters of administration of the estate of a deceased person, or

- confirmation as executor of a deceased person,

must be accepted by the company as sufficient evidence of the grant.

[*CA 2006, s 774*].

**Standard articles.** The transmission of shares may be regulated by a company's articles. Where a company has adopted standard articles, see

- *Table A, 1985, Regs 29–31*:

- *Model Articles, Arts 27, 28* (private companies); and

- *Model Articles, Arts 65–68* (public companies),

set out in APPENDIX 4 STANDARD ARTICLES OF ASSOCIATION.

### 44.10  ISSUE OF CERTIFICATES, ETC ON TRANSFER

**Duty of company as to issue of certificates, etc on transfer**. Subject to below, a company must, within two months after the date on which a transfer of any of its shares, debentures or debenture stock is lodged with the company, complete and have ready for delivery

- the certificates of the shares transferred;

- the debentures transferred; or

- the certificates of the debenture stock transferred.

For this purpose a '*transfer*' means either a transfer duly stamped and otherwise valid or an exempt transfer within *Stock Transfer Act 1982* and does not include a transfer that the company is for any reason entitled to refuse to register and does not register.

The provisions above do not apply in the following circumstances.

(a)     If the conditions of issue of the shares, debentures or debenture stock provide otherwise.

(b)     If a transfer for transferring shares, debentures or debenture stock to a 'financial institution' is lodged with a company, the company is not required, in consequence of that transfer, to comply with the above provisions. A '*financial institution*' means

     (i)     a recognised clearing house acting in relation to a recognised investment exchange; or

     (ii)     a nominee of a recognised clearing house acting in that way or a recognised investment exchange, in either case designated for these purposes in the rules of the recognised investment exchange in question.

(c)     In the case of a transfer of shares if, following the transfer, the company has issued a share warrant in respect of the shares (see **44.12**).

(d)     In the case of a transfer to a person where, by virtue of Regulations under *Stock Transfer Act 1982, s 3* the transferee is not entitled to a certificate or other document evidencing title in respect of the securities transferred. But if, in such a case, the transferee subsequently becomes entitled to such a certificate, etc by virtue of any provision of those Regulations, and gives notice in writing of that fact to the company, the provisions then apply as if the reference to the date of the lodging of the transfer were a reference to the date of the notice.

If default is made in complying with the above requirements, an offence is committed by every officer of the company who is in default. A person guilty of such an offence is liable, on summary conviction, to a fine not exceeding level 3 on the standard scale and, for continued contravention, a daily default fine not exceeding one-tenth of level 3 on the standard scale. See **29.1** OFFENCES AND LEGAL PROCEEDINGS for the standard scale.

[*CA 2006, s 776–778*].

Where a company has adopted standard articles, see, *Model Articles, Art 46* (public companies), set out in APPENDIX 4 STANDARD ARTICLES OF ASSOCIATION.

See **44.13** for the court's power to order a company to make good any default under these provisions.

**44.11   Contents and replacement of share certificates**

A company's articles frequently include provisions with respect to the contents of, and replacement of lost or destroyed, share certificates including that the shareholder is entitled to a replacement and that the directors may decide that an indemnity must be provided. Where a company has adopted standard articles, see

•   *Table A, 1985, Regs, 6, 7*;

•   *Model Articles, Arts 24, 25* (private companies); and

•   *Model Articles, Arts 47–49* (public companies),

set out in APPENDIX **4** STANDARD ARTICLES OF ASSOCIATION.

**44.12   SHARE WARRANTS**

A company limited by shares may, if authorised by its articles, issue with respect to any fully paid shares a warrant (known as a 'share warrant') stating that the bearer of the warrant is entitled to the shares specified in it. A share warrant issued under the company's common seal (or, in the case of a company registered in Scotland, subscribed in accordance with the *Requirements of Writing (Scotland) Act 1995*) entitles the bearer to the shares specified in it and the shares may be transferred by delivery of the warrant.

A company that issues a share warrant may also, if authorised by its articles, provide (by coupons or otherwise) for the payment of the future dividends on the shares included in the warrant.

As from May 2015 share warrants to bearer have been abolished by *Small Business, Enterprise and Employment Act 2015 (SBEE 2015), ss 84, 85, 86 and Sch 4*. The effect of these provisions is as follows:

•   *CA 2006, s 779* is amended to include a new *s 779(4)* which provides that no share warrants may be issued by a company on or after the date *SBEE 2015, s 84* comes into force irrespective of whether the company's articles purport to authorise it to do so.

•   *SBEE 2015, s 84* came into force May 2015 (see *SBEE 2015, s 164*).

•   share warrants issued before May 2015 have to be either converted into registered shares or cancelled in accordance with *SBEE 2015, Sch 4*.

•   if the company's articles authorise the issue of share warrants the company must amend its articles to remove the provision and can so amend without the need for a special resolution or without complying with any provision for entrenchment relevant to that provision.

A copy of the articles as amended must be sent to the Registrar of Companies

[*CA 2006, s 779; SBEE 2015, ss 84, 85, 86, 164, Sch 4*].

See **38.6** REGISTERS regarding entries in a company's register of members in relation to share warrants.

**Duty of company to issue certificate on surrender of share warrant.** In relation to share warrants surrendered to a company unless the articles provide otherwise, the company must, within two months of the surrender of the share warrant for cancellation, complete and have ready for delivery the certificates of the shares specified in the warrant.

If default is made in complying with this requirement, an offence is committed by every officer of the company who is in default. A person guilty of such an offence is liable on summary conviction to a fine not exceeding level 3 on the standard scale and, for continued contravention, a daily default fine not exceeding one-tenth of level 3 on the standard scale. See **29.1** OFFENCES AND LEGAL PROCEEDINGS for the standard scale.

[*CA 2006, s 780*].

See **44.13** for the court's power to order a company to make good any default under this provision.

**Standard articles**. Where a company has adopted standard articles, see *Model Articles, Art 51* (public companies), set out in APPENDIX **4** STANDARD ARTICLES OF ASSOCIATION.

**Offences in connection with share warrants (Scotland)**. In Scotland, a person commits an offence if

(a)   with intent to defraud, he forges or alters, or offers, utters, disposes of, or puts off, knowing the same to be forged or altered, any share warrant or coupon, or any document purporting to be a share warrant or coupon issued under *CA 2006*;

(b)   by means of any such forged or altered share warrant, coupon or document, he demands or tries to obtain or receive

•   any share or interest in a company under *CA 2006*, or

•   any dividend or money payment in respect of any such share or interest,

knowing the warrant, coupon or document to be forged or altered;

(c)   without lawful authority or excuse (of which proof lies on him), he

•   engraves, or makes on any plate or other material, any share warrant or coupon purporting to be

(i)   a share warrant or coupon issued or made by any particular company; or

(ii)   a blank share warrant or coupon so issued or made; or

(iii)   a part of such a share warrant or coupon; or

•   uses any such plate or other material for the making or printing of any such share warrant or coupon, or of any such blank share warrant or coupon or of any part of such a share warrant or coupon; or

•   he knowingly has in his custody or possession any such plate or other material.

A person guilty of an offence under (*a*) or (*b*) above is liable, on summary conviction, to imprisonment for a term not exceeding six months or to a fine not exceeding level 5 on the standard scale (or both). A person guilty of an offence under (*c*) above is liable (i) on conviction on indictment, to imprisonment for a term not exceeding seven years or a fine (or both); and (ii) on summary conviction, to imprisonment for a term not exceeding six months or a fine not exceeding the statutory maximum (or both). See **29.1** OFFENCES AND LEGAL PROCEEDINGS for the standard scale and statutory maximum.

[*CA 2006, s 781*].

## 44.13   ISSUE OF CERTIFICATES: COURT ORDER TO MAKE GOOD DEFAULT

If a company, on which a notice has been served requiring it to make good any default in complying with its duty as to the issue of certificates, etc under **44.2**, **44.10** or **44.12** above, fails to make good the default within ten days after service of the notice, the person entitled to have the certificates or the debentures delivered to him may apply to the court. The court may make an order directing the company, and any officer of it, to make good the default within such time as is specified in the order. The order may also provide that all costs (in Scotland, expenses) of, and incidental to, the application are to be borne by the company or by an officer of it responsible for the default.

[*CA 2006, s 782*].

## 44.14 STOCK EXCHANGE TRANSFERS

A more complex system of transfers is required for dealings carried out on the Stock Exchange to provide an effective centralised method for the settlement of bargains.

The *Uncertificated Securities Regulations 2001 (SI 2001 No 3755)* (as amended by the *Companies Act 2006 (Consequential Amendments) (Uncertificated Securities) Order 2009 (SI 2009 No 1889)* and the *Uncertificated Securities (Amendment) Regulations 2013 (SI 2013 No 632)*), contain the concept of a '*relevant system*' which is defined as a computer-based system and procedures which enable title to units of security to be evidenced and transferred without a written instrument.

The Bank of England has powers (which it has delegated to the FCA) to approve a person who wishes to be the 'Operator' of a relevant system. [*SI 2001 No 3755, Regs 4–13, Sch 1*]. Euroclear UK (formerly CRESTCo) has been approved as Operator of a relevant system in respect of CREST. Euroclear is responsible for establishing and running the central computer system and for specifying the technical requirements which must be met by networks through which messages are sent to and from the central computer system.

CREST enables 'participating securities' to be held without the need for a share certificate to be issued and to be transferred without the need for an executed stock transfer form to be submitted to the company. It is a voluntary system in two ways. First, an issuer may choose whether or not a particular class of securities issued by it is to be eligible for transfer through CREST. (There is no requirement that listed securities should be eligible for CREST although in practice most securities listed on the London Stock Exchange or dealt in on the Alternative Investment Market have joined CREST.) Secondly, even if a particular security is admitted to CREST, a shareholder may choose whether to hold the security in certificated or uncertificated form.

The CREST central computer system maintains records called 'stock accounts'. A stock account is maintained for each separate 'participating security' held by each 'system-member'. The account relates to the entries on the register maintained by the 'participating issuer'. When the central computer system receives an instruction from a system-member transferor and a system-member transferee in relation to a transfer, it checks that the transferor is able to transfer the relevant number of securities and that the transferee has a payment bank which is willing to make the payment for the transfer. The computer system then itself generates an 'operator instruction' to the company instructing it to register the transfer which it is required to do within two hours. All messages are sent to and from the central computer system and the participants in the system (eg companies and their shareholders) do not communicate directly with each other. At no point does Euroclear act as a principal either in holding securities itself or as obligor under the payment arrangements.

A '*participating security*' is a security title to units of which is permitted by an Operator to be transferred by means of a relevant system. [*SI 2001 No 3755, Reg 3(1)*]. The Regulations allow most securities issued by companies incorporated in the UK under the Companies Acts to be eligible for CREST (including debenture and loan stocks, preference shares and subscription warrants). In order for a security to be admitted to CREST, an issuer must comply with the CREST procedures for admission of securities. Securities are admitted by class and so, for example, the ordinary shares of a particular company may be a participating security whilst its preference shares exist only in certificated form.

A company's articles normally contain provisions concerning the transfer of shares in the company. If the articles are in all respects consistent with

(i)      holding shares of a class in uncertificated form,

(ii)     transfer of title to shares of the class by means of a relevant system, and

(iii)    the Regulations,

that class of shares may become a participating security. To the extent that a company's articles are inconsistent with (i)–(iii) above, the directors may pass a resolution that title to shares of that class may be transferred by means of a relevant system. Notice must be given to each member of the company either of the intention to pass such a resolution or that such a resolution has been passed. In the latter case, notice must be given within 60 days of the passing of the resolution. [*SI 2001 No 3755, Regs 14–19*]. In the case of convertible and redeemable shares, other changes to the articles may be necessary to disapply the provisions relating to the *means* by which convertible shares are converted or redeemable shares are redeemed. For example, articles may require amendment so that a system message can constitute a conversion notice.

A '*participating issuer*' is a person who has issued a security which is a participating security. Except where an issuer acts as its own registrar, CREST is unlikely to have any significant impact on the issuer. The company's registrar needs to participate in CREST and be in a position to send and receive messages (or have them latter sent and received on their behalf).

A '*system-member*' is a person who has been permitted by Euroclear to transfer through CREST title to uncertificated units of a participating security held by him. [*SI 2001 No 3755, Reg 3(1)*]. The system-member is the person whose name appears on the register of securities maintained by the participating issuer. The only requirements imposed by Euroclear on a person wishing to be a system-member are that

•        a settlement bank has agreed to provide settlement bank facilities; and

•        the system-member has the ability to send and receive messages through the system (either himself or through a 'sponsor').

A '*sponsored member*' is a system-member who has appointed a sponsor to send and receive messages on his behalf. Individuals are unlikely to have the necessary computer network to enable them to send and receive messages directly. The concept of a sponsored member enables a person to hold shares in uncertificated form, and therefore to be a registered shareholder, by appointing another person (eg a broker or bank) to send and receive electronic messages relating to those shares.

A '*system-participant*' or '*user*' is a person permitted by the Operator to send and receive messages. In practical terms this is the person with the computer and network connection. A '*sponsoring system-participant*' is a person who has been permitted to send and receive instructions on behalf of other persons. Thus a system member may, but need not be, a system-participant. A company which does not maintain its own register is not a system-participant – its registrar will be a system-participant and will be a sponsoring system-participant for the issuer.

**Changes of form.** There are special provisions to enable a unit of a security to be changed from certificated to uncertificated form and vice versa (whether at the time of a transfer of title or without there being a change of holder).

**Registers of members.** A company any of whose securities can be transferred through CREST must subdivide its register of those securities to show how many securities each person holds in uncertified form and certified form respectively. [*SI 2001 No 3755, Reg 20*]. For these purposes, any overseas branch register (see **38.11** REGISTERS) maintained by a company is not regarded as forming part of the company's register of members. It is not therefore possible to hold shares in uncertificated form on an overseas branch register. A person who is recorded on such a register who wishes to hold shares in uncertificated form must first have his entry transferred to the principal register and then take the necessary steps to convert his holding from certificated to uncertificated form.

*Rectification of a register.* A participating issuer can only rectify a register of securities in relation to uncertificated units with the consent of the Operator or by order of the court. [*SI 2001 No 3755, Reg 25*].

*Registration of transfers.* A participating issuer

(a)     must register a transfer of title to uncertificated units in accordance with an operator instruction unless the transfer is prohibited by court order or the issuer has actual notice that the transfer is prohibited or avoided by or under an enactment or a transfer to a deceased person; and

(b)     must not register a transfer of title to uncertificated units unless required to do so

•       by an operator instruction;

•       by court order; or

•       by or under any enactment.

An issuer who registers a transfer other than under (*b*) above is in breach of statutory duty and may incur liability in damages to anyone who suffers loss as a result of the default.

An issuer may refuse to register a transfer if, *inter alia*, the instruction requires a transfer of units to an entity which is not a natural or legal person or to a minor.

[*SI 2001 No 3755, Regs 28, 46*].

**Standard articles.** Where a company has adopted standard articles, see, *Model Articles, Art 50* (public companies), set out in APPENDIX 4 STANDARD ARTICLES OF ASSOCIATION.

# 45   Security for Company Borrowing

*Cross-references*: See 17 DEBT FINANCE-DEBENTURES AND OTHER BORROWING, 40 REGISTRATION OF CHARGES.

## 45.1   INTRODUCTION TO SECURITY FOR COMPANY BORROWING

A company may need to borrow for a variety of reasons for example to expand the company through asset or share acquisitions. The purpose for which the money is being borrowed will usually determine the nature of the loan. Project finance for example is usually used for long term financing of building and industrial projects. The finance is usually a mixture of equity investment and syndicated bank loans, secured over the project assets. See 17.4 for types of company borrowing. This chapter is concerned only with the types of security a lender can take for company loans and the validity and priority of that secured lending in the event (usually) of company insolvency. It does not deal with details of insolvency law and procedures. For further information see *Tolley's Insolvency Law*.

## 45.2   TAKING SECURITY AND GIVING FINANCIAL ASSISTANCE

"Security" is defined in the *Insolvency Act 1986* as, in relation to England and Wales, any mortgage, charge, lien, or other security (*IA 1986, s 248 (1)(b)*) and "secured creditor" in relation to a company, means a creditor of the company who holds in respect of his/her debt a security over property of the company (*IA 1986, s 248(1)(a)*) Taking security for a loan to a company provides a degree of protection which an unsecured loan often does not. The main protection is that subject to the validity and priority of any security taken, a fixed charge secured creditor, when enforcing the security, ranks ahead of preferential and unsecured creditors. Generally also a secured charge holder is able (subject to the validity of the charge) to sell the assets secured by the charge in the event of the borrower's default in payment and is able to appoint a receiver to realise the property subject to the charge. The appointment and powers of receivers and administrators is outside the scope of this chapter. The lender may also take additional/ other security from for example members of the same group of companies as the primary borrower and/or from the company's directors (by way of personal guarantees). The personal liabilities of directors under such guarantees are outside the scope of this chapter. Future assets of the company may also be secured by a charge. Historically only floating charges were created over future assets, but given the disadvantages of floating charges (see 45.5) fixed charges also now are created over future as well as present assets of the company. There is a distinction in the priorities afforded to charges depending on whether the security is by way of fixed or floating charge. See 17.5 and 45.4 and 45.5 below for the meaning of fixed and floating charges, 45.5 below for the meaning of preferential creditors and 45.7 for priority of charges.

## 45.2  Security for Company Borrowing

*Financial assistance*

On 1 October 2008 the prohibition on a private company giving financial assistance for the purchase of its own shares was abolished. The prohibition was retained for public companies (*CA 2006, s 678*). When giving financial assistance (for example as part of an acquisition finance arrangement) pre 1 October 2008, private companies would have to go through what was called the "whitewash" procedure. Although strictly *CA 2006*, in abolishing the financial assistance provisions for private companies does not require the whitewash procedure to be followed, commercial practice still dictates that lenders need some comfort when what would have amounted to financial assistance is involved on a loan transaction. The Financial Law and Company Law committees of the City of London Law Society issued a joint memorandum in September 2008 recommending that certain general company law principles should continue to be taken into account when a private company is giving what would have amounted to financial assistance. These principles are:

- that the transaction must be in the best interests of the company ("likely to promote the success of the company for the benefit of its members");

- the transaction must not breach the rules on distributions or otherwise constitute an illegal reduction in the capital of the company;

- that the validity of the transaction may be called into question as a transaction at an undervalue for the purposes of the *Insolvency Act ("IA") 1986, s 238*. See the City of London Law Society website at www.citysolicitors.org.uk (go to Committees tab and then Company Law) for the full text of the paper "*The implications for leveraged transactions of the repeal of the statutory prohibition of financial assistance by private companies*": The paper further commented on the following practical issues involved.

*Best interests of the company*

The requirement to show that the transaction is in the best interests of the company may be considered in the same way as any other "upstream" commitment by a subsidiary for the benefit of other members of the group and the following may be considered as practical measures to give assurance that this requirement is met:

- board minutes that confirm the board has considered the matter and concluded that the transaction should be approved. It may be helpful to identify the "corporate benefit" in the minutes (whether tangible (guarantee fees) or intangible (the benefit of remaining part of the group)) and the board's assessment of the solvency of the company;

- approval by a shareholder resolution, which can reduce or eliminate the risk of a company/shareholder challenge based on breach of duty by the directors (the risk remains of a challenge if the company is insolvent, or is threatened by insolvency but as to this, see below).

*No reduction of capital*

If the transaction involves an outright transfer of assets to or for the benefit of the shareholders of the company it may amount to a distribution, in which case the statutory rules on distributions must be complied with:

- if it is gratuitous, or

- if it involves a transfer at less than the lower of fair market value and book value (if the company has distributable reserves) or less than fair market value (if the company does not have distributable reserves).

Any other transaction which involves (or may in future involve) the transfer of assets to or for the benefit of shareholders and involves:

- a gift (not amounting to a distribution),

- a loan, or

- a guarantee or indemnity, the grant of security or any other assumption of a liability by the company

may amount to an unlawful reduction of capital if, as a result of the transaction, there would be a reduction in the net assets recorded in the company's books and that reduction exceeds the amount of the distributable reserves of the company.

If a transaction is on arm's length terms, it may be lawful even if the transaction would result in accounting net assets being reduced by more than the distributable reserves of the company. However, such situations are likely to be relatively rare and will require case-by-case analysis.

The effect on net assets should be determined according to normal accounting principles, so that if the transaction does not require an immediate accounting loss to be recognised there will be no effect on net assets. Accordingly, none of the issue of an upstream guarantee, the creation of upstream security or the making of an upstream loan will offend the rules concerning the maintenance of capital unless in the books of the company concerned the loan receivable falls to be recorded at less than the amount advanced or the guarantee or security requires the immediate recognition of a liability (and then only to the extent that the amount of the loss exceeds the distributable reserves of the company).

The steps that should be taken to provide assurance that the validity of the transaction cannot be challenged effectively will depend on the circumstances, but may include:

- being able to demonstrate that the directors of the company entering into the transaction have considered whether it will lead to a reduction in net assets and, if so, the amount of profits available for distribution. This will involve an assessment of the likelihood of any guarantee being called or any loan not being repaid and, under some accounting standards, the market value of a guarantee given or of a loan made. The amount of detail considered appropriate in any such assessment may depend on the degree of uncertainty as to (a) the possibility of a payment having to be made and (b) the potential magnitude of the payment (taking into account any right of indemnity and any right of contribution);

- in some circumstances the directors may wish to arrange for an independent review of the cash flows and projections relied on for this purpose or of the processes used to develop them. However, we expect this to be an exception rather than the usual case;

- if the transaction will reduce the accounting net assets of the company and therefore requires distributable reserves in order to be lawful, it may be appropriate to arrange for a detailed review of the distributable reserves position to be carried out and for the auditors to be consulted on the conclusions of that review.

*Insolvency / potential insolvency*

If the company concerned is, or is at risk of becoming, insolvent (or if the transaction causes the company to become insolvent), the risk of challenge to the transaction is much increased. The usual assessment of the creditworthiness of the overall transaction should identify any solvency issues that may exist independent of the proposed transaction. It is likely that the steps outlined above will identify any threat to solvency created by the transaction itself.

## 45.2 Security for Company Borrowing

*Conclusion: impact on financing transactions*

Although some more cautious views have been expressed, the City of London Law Society believe there is a significant consensus supporting the approach set out above. As a result, they consider that the abolition of the prohibition on financial assistance for private companies will not, by itself, throw up any problems additional to those which have always required consideration when dealing with cross guarantees, upstream loans and upstream security.

They expect, therefore, that procedures adopted to assure interested parties that financing and refinancing of share acquisitions are not vulnerable to legal challenge should now come into line with those familiar to practitioners in other financing transactions. There remain significant implications here for company directors in terms of their need to justify any decision or transaction by reference to their statutory duties – notably, their duty under *CA 2006, s 172* to promote the success of the company.

### 45.3 CHARGES

Charges are the most common form of security granted over a company's assets and can be fixed or floating (see **45.4** and **45.5**). Mortgages over the company's real property are an additional and other usual form of security. A "charge" is not defined in either *CA 2006* or *IA 1986* – see **17.5** and does not transfer legal or equitable title to the chargee. A mortgage by contrast transfers the title subject to the mortgage to the lender by way of security and can be by way of a legal or equitable mortgage. Creation of a mortgage over property prevents the borrower dealing with the asset in any way without the consent of the chargeholder.

### 45.4 Fixed charges

A fixed charge is a direct charge over a specific asset or category of assets and has the effect that the company is not free to deal with or dispose of the charged asset(s) even in the ordinary course of business without the consent of the chargee. With a view to improving the security of creditors, an increasing proportion of assets are being made the subject of fixed charges rather than floating charges: in particular, book debts have been targeted. The court, in deciding whether a charge is fixed or floating, will look not only at the intention of the parties when creating the charge but also at the effect of that charge. If the company can use the book debts as cash flow this is not consistent with a fixed charge. The debts must be put in a blocked account or otherwise controlled by the chargee for the fixed charge to be considered as such. There have been decisions in which it has been held that there can be a valid fixed charge over book debts (*Re Siebe Gorman & Co Ltd v Barclays Bank Ltd* [1979] 2 Lloyd's Rep 142, 10 LDAB 94), (*Re Keenan Bros* [1986] BCLC 242, 2 BCC 98, 970, Ir SC) and (*New Bullas Trading Ltd* [1994] 1 BCLC 485, [1994] BCC 36, CA). Where a charge lacks the relevant control provisions, a charge on book debts may be held to be only a floating charge (*Re Armagh Shoes Ltd* [1982] NI 59, [1984] BCLC 405 and *Brumark Investments Limited reported under the name of Richard Dale Agnew and Kevin James Bearsley v The Commissioner of Inland Revenue and Official Assignee for the estate in bankruptcy of Bruce William Birtwhistle and Mark Leslie Birtwhistle* [2001] 3 WLR 454 and [2001] BCC 259) with the consequence that the charged assets must be used to pay any preferential claims. Following the decision in Brumark Investments Limited it is believed that the majority of fixed charges over book debts encountered by the official receiver will be floating charges as the elements of control over the collection and disposition of the debts will be absent.

### 45.5 Floating charges

A floating charge (by contrast to a fixed charge) constitutes a present security, on a class of assets. It leaves a company free to deal with its assets in the ordinary course of business until some further step by or on behalf of those interested in the charge causes the charge to crystallise. In addition, when the charge is enforced it can help to preserve the business as a going concern by enabling an appointed receiver to trade on and to sell the business to a purchaser without the need for court involvement. A floating charge has three elements:

- it is a charge on a class of assets of a company present and future;

- the class of assets may change from time to time; and

- the company may carry on business in the ordinary way until action is taken by the chargeholder.

Certain events cause crystallisation of a floating charge:

- the winding up of the company,

- the appointment of a receiver, and

- the cessation of the company's business.

(See In *Re Woodroffes (Musical Instruments) Ltd* [1986] Ch 366, [1985] 3 WLR 543, [1985] 2 All ER 908.) Crystallisation takes place on the occurrence of any of those events, even though nothing is stated in the debenture and even if it is contrary to what is stated in the debenture.

In addition, the parties to the charge can agree contractually that a floating charge, created by a debenture, may be crystallised into a fixed charge by intervention of the debenture holder. Most commonly this intervention will take the form of the appointment of a receiver out of court by the debenture holder but it may take other forms, eg the service of a notice converting the floating charge into a fixed charge in respect of specified assets.

Floating chargeholders are disadvantaged by the following:

- preferential creditors are paid in priority insofar as the company's assets available for payment of general creditors are insufficient to meet them. This includes a floating charge which has subsequently (ie after it is made) become a fixed charge (*IA 1986, s 175(2)(b)* and *(3)*). "Preferential creditors" are defined in *IA 1986, Schedule 6* and comprise in the main payments to occupational pension funds and payments to employees (*Schedule 6, paras 8–14*). The *Enterprise Act 2002* reduced the number of preferred creditors and abolished the right of Crown departments (such as HMRC) to be preferred creditors where the petition for winding up was presented on or after 15 September 2003;

- fixed charge holders may sell assets the subject of the charge (see above);

- payment of expenses of winding up, insofar as the company's assets available for general creditors are insufficient to meet those expenses, have priority over the claims of floating charge holders (*IA 1986, s 176ZA*). This applies to winding up orders made after 6 April 2008 (see **45.7**). Before that date ie where a winding up order is made after 6 April 2008 following a resolution for a voluntary winding up passed before that date, payment is subject to the decision in *Buchler and another v Talbot and another and others* [2004] UKHL 9 (known as the *Leyland DAF Limited* case). The judgment substantially altered the way in which liquidators of companies, which had granted floating charges over their assets, could attempt to recover the payment of the liquidation expenses and pay the (liquidation) preferential creditors .In the *Leyland DAF Limited* case their Lordships concluded that the assets of a company that has gone into liquidation are comprised in two separate funds:

  - charged assets (ie those which are subject to a floating or fixed charge), and

  - free assets (ie those which are not subject to a floating or fixed charge but which are held in trust for the unsecured creditors).

## 45.5 Security for Company Borrowing

Each fund should bear its own costs and there is no reason why either interested group (the debenture holder and the unsecured creditors) should contribute towards the costs of the other fund. A debenture holder has no liability for the general costs of the winding-up. See above that *IA 1986, s 176ZA* effectively reversed this decision for a winding up after 6 April 2008; and

- *ring fencing*: IA 1986, s 176A provides (in summary) that: where a floating charge relates to property of a company:

  (a)    which has gone into liquidation,

  (b)    which is in administration,

  (c)    of which there is a provisional liquidator, or

  (d)    of which there is a receiver.

then the liquidator, administrator or receiver must set aside a prescribed part of the company's net property which is available for the satisfaction of unsecured debts, and must not distribute that part to the floating charge holder except in so far as it exceeds the amount required for the satisfaction of unsecured debts. In other words the liquidator, administrator or receiver must ring fence a prescribed part of the assets for unsecured creditors.

The calculation of the prescribed part of the company's assets which must be set apart is set out in the *Insolvency Act 1986 (Prescribed Part) Order 2003 (SI 2003 No 2097)* which provides that where the company's net property does not exceed £10,000 in value the prescribed part is 50% of that property. Subject to *art 2* of the *Order*, where the company's net property exceeds £10,000 in value the prescribed part is the sum of—

(i)    50% of the first £10,000 in value; and

(ii)    20% of that part of the company's net property which exceeds £10,000 in value.

*Article 2* of the *Order* says that the value of the prescribed part of the company's net property to be made available for the satisfaction of unsecured debts of the company pursuant to *IA 1986, s 176A* shall not exceed £600,000.

## 45.6    REGISTRATION OF CHARGES

In order to be valid a charge must be properly registered at Companies House within the time limits imposed by *CA 2006, s 860*. If the charge is not registered within the statutory time limits, the charge is void (so far as any security on the company's property or undertaking is conferred by it) against a liquidator, administrator or creditor of the company [*CA 2006, s 874*]. The charge is void even if the liquidator or creditor has notice of the unregistered charge (*Monolithic Building Co, Re Tacon v Monolithic Building Co* [1915] 1 Ch 643, 84 LJ Ch 441, CA). See CHAPTER 40 of this book for full details of the registration of charges under *CA 2006* and APPENDIX 2 for details of forms to be used when registering a charge. As mentioned above a company may also grant security by way of a mortgage over real property. Where this is the case the charge must be registered with the Land Registry.

## 45.7    VALIDITY AND PRIORITY

In order for a charge to be effective against the borrower or against a liquidator, administrator or receiver it must be valid. To be valid:

- the company must have the power to create the charge. This type of power would historically have been set out in the company's objects (in its memorandum.) As from 1 October 2009 a company's objects are unrestricted unless the company's articles provide otherwise [*CA 2006, s 31(1)*]. A company incorporated on or after 1 October 2009 may adopt restricted objects which have to be set out in the company's articles of association. A charge may still be valid even if the company has exceeded its powers in creating the charge.

- the document must be properly executed. An agreement to dispose of an interest in land must be in writing and signed by or on behalf of each party to the agreement and must incorporate all the agreed terms in one document [*Law of Property (Miscellaneous Provisions) Act 1989, s 2*]. A mortgage or charge of an equitable interest or trust must be made in writing and signed by the chargor [*Law of Property Act 1925, s 53(1)(c)*]. The person who signed it should have had the power to do so on behalf of the company. Where the document was signed by the director(s), or someone authorised by them to do so, and provided that the chargeholder acted in good faith, the charge will be valid even if the director(s) exceeded their powers [*CA 2006, s 40*].

The director(s) may be personally liable in an action for misfeasance or breach of duty if they caused the company to act outside the scope of its constitution [*CA 2006, s 40(5)*].

- the charge must be registered (see **45.6**) If the company does not register a charge within the time prescribed by *CA 2006, s 860*, the charge is void against a liquidator, administrator or creditor of the company and cannot be enforced in priority to a subsequent charge which is properly registered (see below for priority ) but the charge remains enforceable against the company (provided the company is not in administration or liquidation ) and the debt secured by the charge remains enforceable [*CA 2006, s 874(3)*]. Additionally the company and every officer of the company commit an offence [*CA 2006, s 860(4) and (5)*]. CA 2006 contains provisions to enable a company to register a charge out of time. This involves an application to the court by the company itself or by "a person interested" [*CA 2006, s 873(2)*]. The court has the discretion on hearing the application to order that the period allowed for registration shall be extended provided it is satisfied that the failure to register the charge before the end of the time period allowed was accidental or due to inadvertence or to some other sufficient cause or is not of a nature to prejudice the position of the company's creditors or shareholders [*CA 2006, s 873(1)*]. In making the order the court can impose such terms and conditions as seem to the court to be just and expedient.

[*CA 2006, s 873(2)*].

## Priority

In addition to ensuring that a charge is valid, the chargeholder will also want to ensure that they have priority over other creditors. "Priority" means the order in which creditors are paid in the event for example of company liquidation.

The basic rules of priority are:

- *unsecured creditors*: (apart from preferential creditors (see **45.5** above) who may take priority) all other unsecured creditors rank *pari passu*, that is equally amongst themselves.

[*IA 1986, s 107*]

- *secured creditors*. As a general rule a fixed charge created first in time and duly registered (see **45.6**) takes priority over later fixed charges [*James v Boythorpe Colliery Co* [1890] 2 Meg 55]. A fixed charge takes priority over a floating charge even if created after the floating charge unless the fixed charge is made subject to the prior floating charge [*Re Robert Stephenson & Co Ltd* [1913] 2 Ch 201]. This can be done by a deed of priority which is made between the company and the chargeholders. A deed of priority is effective even if results in a floating charge taking priority over a fixed charge [*Re Portabase Clothing Ltd* [1993] BCC 96]. A floating charge created first in time takes priority over later floating charges even if the later chargeholder has notice that the earlier charge exists [*Re Benjamin Cope & Sons Ltd* [1914] 1 Ch 800].

• *debenture holders.* See **17.14** that where debentures are secured by a floating charge, if possession is taken of property subject to the charge and the company is not, at the time, being wound up, the preferential debts must be paid in priority to any claims under the debenture (either for the principal sum or interest).

[*CA 2006, s 754*].

*Expenses of liquidation – winding-up order made after 6 April 2008*

*IA 1986, s 176ZA* provides that the liquidator's general expenses shall, where the unencumbered assets are insufficient to meet those expenses, be paid in priority to the claims of preferential creditors and floating charge-holders, therefore effectively reversing the decision in *Leyland DAF Ltd*. This section may not be applied retrospectively and therefore applies only to winding-up orders made after 6 April 2008. Where the winding-up order is made following a resolution for a voluntary winding up passed by the company before 6 April 2008 the provisions of *IA 1986, s 176ZA* will not apply.

# 46   Share Premium

## 46.1   TRANSFERS TO, AND APPLICATIONS OF, SHARE PREMIUM ACCOUNT

A company issues shares at a premium if the consideration which it receives for them exceeds in value the nominal amount of the shares issued.

Subject to **46.2** and **46.3**, if a company issues shares at a premium, whether for cash or otherwise, a sum equal to the aggregate amount or value of the premiums on those shares must be transferred to an account called the 'share premium account'. See *Henry Head & Co Ltd v Ropner Holdings Ltd* [1952] Ch 124, [1951] 2 All ER 994 for a consideration of the words 'or otherwise' and also Viscount Simon's opinion in *Gold Coast Selection Trust Ltd v Humphrey (Inspector of Taxes)* [1948] AC 459, [1948] 2 All ER 379, HL where an asset is difficult to value.

The share premium account can be used as follows.

• To pay up new shares to be allotted to members as fully paid bonus shares.

• Where, on issuing shares, a company has transferred a sum to the share premium account, it may use that sum to write off

  (i)   the expenses of the issue of those shares; and

  (ii)  any commission paid on the issue of those shares.

Subject to this, the provisions of the *Companies Acts* relating to the reduction of a company's share capital apply as if the share premium account were part of its paid up share capital. See also **47.51** SHARES for the reduction of share capital.

[*CA 2006, s 610*].

The Secretary of State may make Regulations relieving companies from the above requirements in relation to premiums other than cash premiums or otherwise restricting or modifying any relief from the requirements above and in **46.2** to **46.4**.

[*CA 2006, s 614*].

## 46.2   MERGER RELIEF

Unless the issue falls within **46.3**, the provisions of **46.1** do not apply to the premiums on any 'equity shares' issued in pursuance of an 'arrangement' providing for the allotment of equity shares in the issuing company ('company A') on terms that the consideration for shares allotted is to be provided by

• the issue or transfer to company A of equity shares in the other company ('company B'), or

• the cancellation of any such shares not held by company A

on condition that Company A must have secured at least a 90% equity holding in company B.

## 46.2 Share Premium

In determining whether the 90% test is satisfied, Company A has secured at least a 90% equity holding in company B if, in consequence of an acquisition or cancellation of equity shares in company B (in pursuance of the arrangement) it holds equity shares in company B of an aggregate amount equal to 90% or more of the nominal value of that company's equity share capital. For this purposes

- it is immaterial whether any of those shares were acquired in pursuance of the arrangement; and

- shares in the company B held by the company as treasury shares (see **34.19 PURCHASE OF OWN SHARES**) are excluded in determining the nominal value of company B's share capital.

Where the equity share capital of company B is divided into different classes of shares, company A is not regarded as having secured at least a 90% equity holding in company B unless the 90% test is met in relation to each of those classes taken separately.

For these purposes, shares held by

- a company that is company A's holding company or subsidiary,

- a subsidiary of company A's holding company, or

- its or their nominee

are treated as held by company A.

*Non-equity shares.* Where the arrangement also provides for the allotment of any shares in company A on terms that the consideration for those shares is to be provided by

- the issue or transfer to company A of *non-equity* shares in company B, or

- the cancellation of any such shares in that company not held by company A

relief extends to any shares in company A allotted on those terms in pursuance of the arrangement.

'*Equity shares*' means shares comprised in a company's '*equity share capital*' (see **APPENDIX 1 DEFINITIONS**) and '*non-equity shares*' means shares (of any class) that are not so comprised.

'*Arrangement*' means any agreement, scheme or arrangement (including an arrangement sanctioned under *CA 2006, Pt 26* (arrangements and reconstructions, see **35.1 RECONSTRUCTIONS AND MERGERS**) or *IA 1986, s 110* (liquidator accepting shares as consideration for sale of company property)).

[*CA 2006, ss 612, 613, 616(1)*].

**Reflection of relief in the company's balance sheet.** The amount corresponding to the amount representing the premiums (or part of the premiums) on shares issued by a company that, by virtue of any relief under these provisions, is not included in the company's share premium account may also be disregarded in determining the amount at which any shares, or other consideration provided for the shares issued, is to be included in the company's balance sheet. [*CA 2006, s 615*].

See also **46.4**.

ccccffdffffffccfff

## 46.3 GROUP RECONSTRUCTION RELIEF

Where the issuing company

- is a wholly-owned subsidiary of another company (the 'holding company'), and
- allots shares at a premium to
  - (i) the holding company, or
  - (ii) another wholly-owned subsidiary of the holding company

  in consideration for the transfer to the issuing company of non-cash assets of a company (the 'transferor company') that is a member of the group of companies that comprises the holding company and all its wholly-owned subsidiaries

it is not required by the provisions in **46.1** to transfer any amount in excess of the 'minimum premium value' to the share premium account.

The *'minimum premium value'* is the amount (if any) by which the base value of the consideration for the shares allotted exceeds the aggregate nominal value of the shares and is calculated using the formula

$$(A - L) - N$$

where

- A = the base value of the assets transferred, which is to be taken as the lesser of
  - the cost of those assets to the transferor company; or
  - the amount at which those assets are stated in the transferor company's accounting records immediately before the transfer.
- L = the base value of the liabilities of the transferor company assumed by the issuing company as part of the consideration for the assets transferred, which is to be taken as the amount at which they are stated in the transferor company's accounting records immediately before the transfer.
- N = the aggregate nominal value of the shares issued.

[*CA 2006, s 611*].

**Reflection of relief in the company's balance sheet.** The amount corresponding to the amount representing the premiums (or part of the premiums) on shares issued by a company that, by virtue of any relief under these provisions, is not included in the company's share premium account may also be disregarded in determining the amount at which any shares, or other consideration provided for the shares issued, is to be included in the company's balance sheet. [*CA 2006, s 615*].

See also **46.4**.

## 46.4 SUPPLEMENTARY PROVISIONS FOR SHARE PREMIUM

For the purposes of **46.2** and **46.3**

- references to
  - (i) the acquisition by a company of shares in another company, and
  - (ii) the issue or allotment of shares to, or the transfer of shares to or by, a company

include (respectively) the acquisition of shares by, and the issue or allotment or transfer of shares to or by, a nominee of that company;

- references to the transfer of shares in a company include the transfer of a right to be included in the company's register of members in respect of those shares; and

- 'company', except in references to the issuing company, includes any body corporate.

[*CA 2006, s 616*].

# 47 Shares

**Cross-references.** See 9 CLASS RIGHTS; 17 DEBT FINANCE–DEBENTURES AND OTHER BORROWING; 22 DISTRIBUTIONS; 23 INSIDER DEALING AND MARKET ABUSE; 24 INTERESTS IN PUBLIC COMPANY SHARES; 32 PROSPECTUSES; 34 PURCHASE OF OWN SHARES; 35 RECONSTRUCTIONS AND MERGERS; 44 SECURITIES: CERTIFICATION AND TRANSFERS; 46 SHARE PREMIUM; 48 TAKEOVERS.

## 47.1 SHARES

In the *Companies Acts*, '*share*', in relation to a company, means a share in the company's share capital and references to:

- shares include stock (except where a distinction between share and stock is express or implied); and

- a number of shares include an amount of stock (where the context allows the reference to shares being read as including stock).

A company's shares may not be converted into stock. This does not affect any conversion of shares into stock carried out pursuant to a resolution of the company in general meeting passed, or a written resolution agreed to, before 1 October 2009. Stock created before 1 October 2009 (including stock created under a resolution of the company in general meeting ) may be reconverted into shares (see **47.48**).

[*CA 2006, s 540*].

**Nature of shares**. The shares (or other interest of a member in a company) are personal property (in Scotland, moveable property) and are not in the nature of real estate (or heritage). [*CA 2006, s 541*]. See also the judicial definitions in *Borland's Trustee v Steel Bros & Co Ltd* [1901] 1 Ch 279, 70 LJ Ch 51 and *IRC v Crossman* [1937] AC 26, 66, [1936] 1 All ER 762, HL.

The assets of a company are owned by the company itself and the ownership of shares does not entitle the holder to any property rights to the company's assets; he is merely entitled to a *share* in the company and *not* to an interest in every asset the company owns. Shares may be of different classes (see **47.5**) and the rights and obligations of the holders of each class are normally set out in the company's constitution.

## 47.2 Nominal value of shares

Shares in a limited company having a share capital must each have a fixed nominal value and an allotment of a share that does not have a fixed nominal value is void. If a company purports to allot shares in contravention of this provision, an offence is committed by every officer of the company who is in default. A person guilty of such an offence is liable (i) on conviction on indictment, to a fine; and (ii) on summary conviction, to a fine not exceeding the statutory maximum. See **29.1** OFFENCES AND LEGAL PROCEEDINGS for the statutory maximum.

[*CA 2006, s 542(1)(2)(4)(5)*].

Although shares must have a nominal value (ie no-par value shares are not permitted) this need not be paid at the time of issue. Shares may therefore be nil paid, partly paid or fully paid but where they are not fully paid the shareholder has a liability to pay up the nominal amount of his shares in the event of a call (see **47.25**) or on the winding up of the company. See, however, **47.26** for the minimum amount to be paid on shares allotted by a public company.

**Currency**. Shares in a limited company having a share capital may be denominated in any currency, and different classes of shares may be denominated in different currencies. But see **33.3** PUBLIC AND LISTED COMPANIES for the requirement that the initial authorised minimum share capital requirement for a public company must be denominated in sterling or euros. [*CA 2006, s 542*]. See **47.49** for the redenomination of shares into a different currency.

## 47.3 Numbering of shares

Each share in a company having a share capital must be distinguished by its appropriate number, unless, at any time:

- all the issued shares in a company are fully paid up and rank *pari passu* for all purposes, or

- all the issued shares of a particular class in a company are fully paid up and rank *pari passu* for all purposes, in which case none of those shares need thereafter have a distinguishing number so long as it remains fully paid up and ranks *pari passu* for all purposes with all shares of the same class for the time being issued and fully paid up. [*CA 2006, s 543*].

### 47.4   Transferability of shares

The shares (or other interest of any member in a company) are transferable in accordance with the company's articles, but subject to the *Stock Transfer Act 1963* (or, in Northern Ireland, the S*tock Transfer Act (Northern Ireland) 1963*) and Regulations which enable title to securities to be evidenced and transferred without a written instrument. See **44** Securities: Certification and Transfer generally.

[*CA 2006, s 544*].

### 47.5   Classification of shares

Where there are no different or separate rights attaching to a particular class of shares in a company then all shares rank equally (*Birch v Cropper, Re Bridgewater Navigation Co Ltd* (1889) 14 App Cas 525, HL). A company may, however, subject to the provisions of *CA 2006* and its constitution and without prejudice to any rights attaching to existing shares, issue any shares with such rights and restrictions as the company determines by ordinary resolution. Where a company has adopted standard articles, see:

- *Table A, 1985, Art 2*

- *Model Articles, Art 22* (private companies)

- *Model Articles, Art 43* (public companies)

set out in Appendix **4** Standard Articles of Association which all (in summary) enable a company to issue shares with different rights and restrictions provided the company in general meeting determine those rights etc.

Different classes of shares are most commonly distinguished by different rights and restrictions relating to dividends, voting, return of capital in a winding up and transferability. The more common classifications of shares are as follows.

(1)   **Ordinary shares**

Ordinary shares, sometimes referred to as 'equity' or 'risk' capital, are the basic shares of a company and confer residual rights on their holders, ie after all other classes of shares have been satisfied. Generally, the ordinary shares carry voting rights and rights to dividends (if any after preferred holders are paid), and give a right to participate on a winding up in any excess assets. Some companies do, however, issue ordinary shares (sometimes referred to as 'A' ordinary shares) which do not carry voting rights.

(2)   **Preference shares**

Generally, preference shares carry no voting rights but are are entitled to a dividend and to other rights, whether to income or capital, in preference to ordinary shareholders. Any rights expressed as attaching to the shares on their creation are, *prima facie*, a definition of the whole of their rights (see *Scottish Insurance Corpn Ltd v Wilsons & Clyde Coal Co Ltd* [1949] AC 462, [1949] 1 All ER 1068, HL) and negative any other rights to which, but for the specified rights, they would have been entitled (*Re National Telephone Co* [1914] 1 Ch 755, 83 LJ Ch 552). Preference shares include the following:

- *Cumulative preference shares* where the right to a dividend, if profits are insufficient in any year, accumulates until profits become sufficient. Unless otherwise stated, the right to receive a preference dividend is cumulative (*Webb v Earle* (1875) LR 20 Eq 556). Even where dividends are cumulative, there is no absolute right to the dividend unless and until the dividend is declared out of available profits (compare interest on debentures). See *Buenos Ayres Great Southern Rly Co Ltd, Re, Buenos Ayres Great Southern Rly Co Ltd v Preston* [1947] Ch 384, [1947] 1 All ER 729.

- Non–cumulative preference shares where there is no right to the accumulation of unpaid dividends because this has been rebutted by the terms of issue (see, for example, *Staples v Eastman Photographic Materials Co* [1896] 2 Ch 303, CA where dividends were to be paid 'out of the net profits each year').

- *Participating preference shares* where there is a right to a dividend and/or return of capital on winding up in preference to the ordinary shares, together with a right to participate in a further distribution of income or capital as the case may be if there remains a surplus after a dividend and/or return of capital to the ordinary shareholders. The right to participate in surplus profits must be expressly stated (*Will v United Lankat Plantations Co Ltd* [1914] AC 11, 83 LJ Ch 195, HL) as must the rights to participate in capital (*Scottish Insurance Corporation v Wilsons & Clyde Coal Co Ltd supra*; *Isle of Thanet Electric Supply Co Ltd, Re* [1950] Ch 161, [1949] 2 All ER 1060, CA).

- *Redeemable preference shares* which a company may redeem at a fixed time or at its option. See **34.2 Purchase of Own Shares** which applies to the redemption of any class of shares (not just preference shares) and **34.5** for the relaxation of rules relating to the payment by private companies for share buy backs from employees' share scheme.

(3)   **Founders', management and deferred shares**

Such shares are normally subscribed for by the promoters and are usually deferred in priority to the ordinary shares, ie. the rights of the holders to receive a dividend are deferred until a dividend at a specific rate has been paid out on other shares.

(4)   **Redeemable shares**

A company limited by shares may issue redeemable shares. See **34.2 Purchase of Own Shares**.

(5)   **Employees' or workers' shares**

In recent years, many companies have issued shares to their employees under one of the many employees' share schemes (see **Appendix 1 Definitions**). As well as encouraging employee involvement in the company, they offer considerable tax incentives. In the early years of ownership there are normally restrictions on transfers. See **47.16** for the disapplication of the pre-emption rules to shares allotted to such schemes.

## 47.6   SHARE CAPITAL

**Company having a share capital**. References in the *Companies Acts* to a 'company having a share capital' are to a company that has power under its constitution to issue shares.

**Allotted share capital** means the shares of a company that have been allotted. It includes shares taken on the formation of the company by the subscribers to the company's memorandum.

**Authorised share capital.** Companies formed on or after 1 October 2009 are not required to have an authorised share capital. Companies formed before that date may continue to have an authorised share capital but, as such a provision is treated as a provision of the company's articles, it can be amended in the same way as any other change in the articles. See **14** CONSTITUTION – MEMORANDUM AND ARTICLES.

If a company has an authorised share capital, it cannot issue shares beyond the amount of that authorised capital. If it does so, the issue is void and the allottee can recover any money paid (*Bank of Hindustan, China and Japan Ltd v Alison* (1871) LR 6 CP 222).

Companies incorporated before 1 October 2009 with an authorised share capital.

(1) Any provision of a company's memorandum as to the amount of the company's authorised share capital that was in force immediately before 1 October 2009 is treated, on or after that date, as a provision of the company's articles setting out the maximum amount of shares that may be allotted by the company. As such, it may be amended or revoked by the company by ordinary resolution in the same way as any other change in the articles. See **14** CONSTITUTION – MEMORANDUM AND ARTICLES.

(2) The provisions in (1) above do not affect the power of a company, by special resolution, to adopt new articles (with effect from 1 October 2009 or any later date) that make no provision as to the maximum number of shares that may be allotted by the company.

(3) Any amendment of a company's articles on or after 1 October 2009 authorising the directors to allot shares in excess of the amount of the authorised share capital that was in force immediately before that date has effect although not expressed as amending or revoking that amount.

[*SI 2008 No 2860, Sch 2 para 42*]

**Called-up share capital** means so much of a company's share capital as equals the aggregate amount of the calls made on its shares (whether or not those calls have been paid), together with:

• any share capital paid up without being called; and

• any share capital to be paid on a specified future date under the articles, the terms of allotment of the relevant shares or any other arrangements for payment of those shares.

**Equity share capital** means a company's issued share capital excluding any part of that capital that, neither as respects dividends nor as respects capital, carries any right to participate beyond a specified amount in a distribution.

**Issued share capital** means the shares of a company that have been issued, ie the shares which have been taken up by shareholders who agree to pay for them either in cash or in kind, together with shares issued as fully paid bonus shares (see **47.62**). It includes shares taken on the formation of the company by the subscribers to the company's memorandum.

**Uncalled share capital** is construed from the definition of called-up share capital.

[*CA 2006, ss 545–548*].

**Reserve liability.** *Before 1 October 2009*, a limited company could, by special resolution, determine that any part of its share capital not already called up could only be called up in the event, and for the purposes of, winding up. [*CA 1985, s 120*]. This reserve liability was also known as the reserve capital. Any mortgage of reserve capital is void, see *Mayfair Property Co, Re, Bartlett v Mayfair Property Co* [1898] 2 Ch 28, CA. With effect from 1 October 2009, *CA 1985, s 120* was repealed.

## 47.6 Shares

[*CA 2006, Sch 16*].

## 47.7 Minimum share capital requirements for public companies

A public company must not do business or exercise any borrowing powers unless the Registrar of Companies has issued it with a trading certificate on being satisfied that the nominal value of the company's allotted share capital is not less than the 'authorised minimum'.

See **33.3** PUBLIC AND LISTED COMPANIES for full details.

## 47.8 ALLOTMENT OF SHARES

The provisions in **47.9** to **47.22** deal with the general requirements of *CA 2006* relating to the allotment of shares. They have no application in relation to the taking of shares by the subscribers to the memorandum on the formation of the company.

For the purposes of the *Companies Acts*, shares in a company are taken to be allotted when a person acquires the unconditional right to be included in the company's register of members in respect of the shares or, as the case may be, to have the person's name and other particulars delivered to the Registrar of Companies under *CA 2006, Part 8, Chapter 2A* and registered by the Registrar (see **38.9** – Option to keep members' information on the public register). See also *Florence Land and Public Works Co, Re, Nicol's Case, Tufnell and Ponsonby's Case* (1885) 29 Ch D 421, CA.

[*CA 2006, ss 558, 559; SBEE 2015, s 94; SI 2016 No 321, Reg 6*].

## 47.9 Power of directors to allot shares

For cases involving the contractual aspects of application for, and allotment of, shares, see *Jackson v Turquand* (1869) LR 4 HL 305 (application for shares is normally the offer with acceptance being the notification of the allotment but a letter of rights from a company is an offer which may be accepted by the shareholder); *Brewery Assets Corpn, Re, Truman's Case* [1894] 3 Ch 272, *Byrne & Co v Leon Van Tienhoven & Co* (1880) 5 CPD 344, *London and Northern Bank, Re, ex p Jones* [1900] 1 Ch 220 (revocation of offer); *Household Fire and Carriage Accident Insurance Co v Grant* (1879) 4 Ex D 216, CA, *Holwell Securities Ltd v Hughes* [1974] 1 All ER 161, [1974] 1 WLR 155, CA (notification of allotment by post); and *Ramsgate Victoria Hotel Co v Montefiore* (1866) LR 1 Exch 109 (allotment must be made within a reasonable time of application).

The directors of a company must not exercise any power of the company:

(a)     to allot shares in the company, or

(b)     to grant rights to subscribe for, or to convert any security into, shares in the company,

except in accordance with the provisions in (1) or (2) below. But:

- this does not apply to the allotment of shares in pursuance of an employees' share scheme or to the grant of a right to subscribe for, or to convert any security into, shares so allotted;

- where (*b*) above applies, the requirement does not apply in relation to the allotment of shares pursuant to that right;

- nothing in these provisions affects the validity of an allotment or other transaction; and

- the directors' actions can be subsequently ratified by the company in general meeting (*Bamford v Bamford* [1970] Ch 212, [1969] 1 All ER 969, CA).

A director who knowingly contravenes, or permits or authorises a contravention of these provisions commits an offence. A person guilty of such an offence is liable (i) on conviction on indictment, to a fine; and (ii) on summary conviction, to a fine not exceeding the statutory maximum. See **29.1** OFFENCES AND LEGAL PROCEEDINGS for the statutory maximum.

[*CA 2006, s 549*].

(1) **Private company with only one class of shares**

Where a private company has only one class of shares, the directors may allot shares or grant rights to subscribe for, or convert any security into, shares in the company except to the extent that they are prohibited from doing so by the company's articles ie the directors no longer need shareholder authority unless the articles provide otherwise. [*CA 2006, s 550*].

*Transitional provisions: companies incorporated before 1 October 2009 and "transitional companies".*

(i) The power of the directors of a private company to allot shares referred to above only applies to a company existing immediately before 1 October 2009 or a 'transitional company' if the members of the company have resolved that the directors should have such power. The resolution may be by ordinary resolution (even if taking the form of an alteration of the company's articles). Once the members of the company have passed such a resolution, the application of *CA 2006, s 550* in relation to the company is not affected by any subsequent resolution (except one altering the company's articles so as to prohibit, to any extent, exercise of the powers mentioned in that section).

A '*transitional company*' means a company that was formed and registered (or re-registered) under *CA 1985* on or after 1 October 2009 where an application for registration (or re-registration) was received by the Registrar of Companies and the requirements as to registration or re-registration (as the case may be) were met before 1 October 2009.

(ii) For the purposes of *CA 2006, s 550*, provisions of the articles of a company existing on 1 October 2009 or a transitional company (see (i) above):

- authorising the directors to allot shares in accordance with *CA 1985, s 80*, or

- added following an elective resolution under *CA 1985, s 80A* and authorising the directors to allot shares,

are not to be treated as provisions prohibiting the directors from exercising the powers conferred by *CA 2006, s 550* in cases to which the authority does not extend.

[*SI 2008 No 2860, Sch 2 paras 43, 44*].

(2) **Other companies not covered by (1) above ie private companies with more than one class of shares and public companies**

The directors of these companies may allot shares or grant rights to subscribe for, or convert any security into, shares in the company if they are authorised to do so by the company's articles or by resolution of the company.

Authorisation may be given for a particular exercise of the power or for its exercise generally, and may be unconditional or subject to conditions. The authorisation must:

- state the maximum amount of shares that may be allotted under it; and

- specify the date on which it will expire, which must be not more than five years from:

    (i) in the case of authorisation contained in the company's articles at the time of its original incorporation, the date of that incorporation;

    (ii) in any other case, the date on which the resolution is passed by virtue of which the authorisation is given.

*Renewal of authorisation.* Authorisation may be renewed or further renewed by resolution of the company for a further period not exceeding five years. It may also be revoked or varied at any time by resolution of the company. Any resolution renewing authorisation must:

- state (or restate) the maximum amount of shares that may be allotted under the authorisation or, as the case may be, the amount remaining to be allotted under it; and

- specify the date on which the renewed authorisation will expire.

Where (*b*) above applies, references above to the maximum amount of shares that may be allotted under the authorisation are to the maximum amount of shares that may be allotted pursuant to the rights.

*Allotment after expiration of authority.* The directors may allot shares (or grant rights to subscribe for or to convert any security into shares) after authorisation has expired if:

- the shares are allotted (or the rights are granted) in pursuance of an offer or agreement made by the company before the authorisation expired; and

- the authorisation allowed the company to make an offer or agreement which would or might require shares to be allotted (or rights to be granted) after the authorisation had expired.

*Resolutions.* A resolution of a company to give, vary, revoke or renew authorisation under these provisions may be an ordinary resolution, even though it amends the company's articles.

*CA 2006, ss 29, 30* (resolutions affecting a company's constitution) apply to a resolution under these provisions. See **14.10** CONSTITUTION – MEMORANDUM AND ARTICLES. [*CA 2006, s 551*].

Pre 1 October 2009 authorisations. An authorisation in force immediately before 1 October 2009 under *CA 1985, ss 80* or *80A* has effect on or after that date as if given under *CA 2006, s 551*.

[*SI 2008 No 2860, Sch 2 para 45*].

See also **47.21** for prohibition of public offers by private companies.

## 47.10 Commissions, discounts and allowances

**Permitted commission.** A company may pay a commission to a person in consideration of his subscribing or agreeing to subscribe (whether absolutely or conditionally) for shares in the company, or procuring or agreeing to procure subscriptions (whether absolute or conditional) for shares in the company if the following conditions are satisfied:

- The payment of the commission is authorised by the company's articles.

- The commission paid or agreed to be paid does not exceed:

    (i)     10% of the price at which the shares are issued, or

    (ii)    the amount or rate authorised by the articles,

    whichever is the less.

[*CA 2006, s 553(1)(2)*].

Where standard articles have been adopted, see:

- *Table A, 1985, Reg 4*

- *Model Articles, Art 44* (public companies)

set out in Appendix 4 standard articles of association.

**Commission paid by other persons.** A vendor to, or promoter of, or other person who receives payment in money or shares from, a company may apply any part of the money or shares so received in payment of any commission the payment of which directly by the company would be permitted under the above provisions. [*CA 2006, s 553(3)*].

**General prohibition of commissions, discounts and allowances.** Except as permitted above, a company must not apply any of its shares or capital money, either directly or indirectly, in payment of any commission, discount or allowance to any person in consideration of his

- subscribing or agreeing to subscribe (whether absolutely or conditionally) for shares in the company; or

- procuring or agreeing to procure subscriptions (whether absolute or conditional) for shares in the company.

This applies whether the shares or money are so applied by being added to the purchase money of property acquired by the company or to the contract price of work to be executed for the company, or being paid out of the nominal purchase money or contract price, or otherwise.

But this does not affect the payment of such brokerage as has previously been lawful.

[*CA 2006, s 552*].

## 47.11 Registration of allotment

A company must register an allotment of shares as soon as practicable, and in any event within two months after the date of the allotment. This does not apply if the company has issued a share warrant in respect of the shares (see **44.12** Securities: Certification and Transfers). If an election is in force under *CA 2006, Part 8, Chapter 2A* (option to keep information on the public register – see **38** Registers), the obligation to register the allotment of shares is replaced by an obligation to deliver particulars of the allotment to the Registrar of Companies in accordance with *Chapter 2A*.

## 47.11 Shares

If a company fails to comply with these requirement, an offence is committed by the company and every officer of the company who is in default. A person guilty of such an offence is liable, on summary conviction, to a fine not exceeding level 3 on the standard scale and, for continued contravention, a daily default fine not exceeding one-tenth of level 3 on the standard scale. See 29.1 Offences and Legal Proceedings for the standard scale.

For the company's duties as to the issue of share certificates, see 44 Securities: Certification and Transfers

[CA 2006, s 554; SBEE 2015, s 98, Sch 5, para 19; SI 2016 No 321, Reg 6].

### 47.12 Return of allotments

**Limited companies**. A company:

- limited by shares, or

- limited by guarantee and having a share capital

must, within one month of making an allotment of shares, deliver to the Registrar of Companies for registration a return of the allotment on form SSSHO1. The return must contain the following information.

(i)     The class of shares and the number of shares allotted.

(ii)    The currency (if this is not completed Companies House will assume currency is in pounds sterling).

(iii)   The number of shares allotted.

(iv)    The amount paid up and the amount (if any) unpaid on each allotted share (whether on account of the nominal value of the share of by way of premium).

(v)     Where the shares are allotted as fully or partly paid (as to their nominal value or any premium on them) otherwise than in cash, the consideration for the allotment together, in the case of a public company, a valuation of the consideration.

The return must also be accompanied by a statement of capital that states the following information with respect to the company's share capital at the date to which the return is made up.

- The total number of shares of the company.

- The class of shares, the number of those shares, the aggregate nominal value of those shares and the aggregate amount (if any) unpaid on those shares (whether on account of their nominal value or by way of premium).

- For each class of shares:

    (i)     particulars of any voting rights attached to the shares, including rights that arise only in certain circumstances;

    (ii)    particulars of any rights attached to the shares, as respects dividends, to participate in a distribution;

    (iii)   particulars of any rights attached to the shares, as respects capital, to participate in a distribution (including on a winding up);

    (iv)    whether the shares are to be redeemed or are liable to be redeemed at the option of the company or the shareholder.

[CA 2006, s 555; SBEE 2015, s 97; SI 2009 No 388, Arts 2, 3; SI 2016 No 321, Reg 6].

**Unlimited companies allotting a new class of shares.** An unlimited company that allots shares of a class with rights that are not in all respects uniform with shares previously allotted must, within one month of making such an allotment, deliver to the Registrar of Companies for registration a return of the allotment. The return must contain the following information of the rights attached to the shares.

(i)     Particulars of any voting rights attached to the shares, including rights that arise only in certain circumstances.

(ii)    Particulars of any rights attached to the shares, as respects dividends, to participate in a distribution.

(iii)   Particulars of any rights attached to the shares, as respects capital, to participate in a distribution (including on a winding up).

(iv)    Whether the shares are to be redeemed or are liable to be redeemed at the option of the company or the shareholder.

For these purposes, shares are not to be treated as different from shares previously allotted by reason only that the former do not carry the same rights to dividends as the latter during the twelve months immediately following the former's allotment.

[*CA 2006, s 556; SI 2009 No 388, Art 2*].

**Failure to make return.** If a company defaults in complying with any of the above provisions, an offence is committed by every officer of the company who is in default. A person guilty of such an offence liable (i) on conviction on indictment, to a fine; and (ii) on summary conviction, to a fine not exceeding the statutory maximum and, for continued contravention, a daily default fine not exceeding one-tenth of the greater of £5000 or the amount corresponding to level 4 on the standard scale for summary offences. See **29.1** OFFENCES AND LEGAL PROCEEDINGS for the statutory maximum.

In the case of default in delivering the required return to the Registrar of Companies within one month period allowed, any person liable for the default may apply to the court for relief. If the court is satisfied that:

•     the omission to deliver the document was accidental or due to inadvertence, or

•     it is just and equitable to grant relief,

it may make an order extending the time for delivery of the document for such period as it thinks proper.

[*CA 2006, s 557; SI 2015 No 664, Sch 3*].

## 47.13  Existing shareholders' right of pre-emption

In addition to the general restrictions on the powers of directors of a company to allot shares (see **47.9**) there are also restrictions on their power to allot shares to persons other than existing members of the company. These are considered in this paragraph and in **47.14–47.19**. The provisions have no application in relation to the taking of shares by the subscribers to the memorandum on the formation of the company.

[*CA 2006, s 577*].

For these purposes:

(a)    '*equity securities*' means:

(i)     ordinary shares in the company; or

(ii)   rights to subscribe for, or to convert securities into, ordinary shares in the company;

(b)   '*ordinary shares*' means shares other than shares that as respects dividends and capital carry a right to participate only up to a specified amount in a distribution; and

(c)   the '*allotment of equity securities*' includes:

(i)   the grant of a right to subscribe for, or to convert any securities into, ordinary shares in the company but does not include the allotment of shares pursuant to such a right; and

(ii)   the sale of ordinary shares in the company that immediately before the sale are held by the company as treasury shares.

[*CA 2006, s 560*].

Subject to **47.16–47.19**, a company must not allot equity securities to a person on any terms unless:

(i)   it has made an offer to each person who holds ordinary shares in the company to allot to him on the same or more favourable terms a proportion of those securities that is as nearly as practicable equal to the proportion in nominal value held by him of the ordinary share capital of the company, and

(ii)   the period during which any such offer may be accepted has expired or the company has received notice of the acceptance or refusal of every offer so made.

Securities that a company has offered to allot to a holder of ordinary shares may be allotted to him, or anyone in whose favour he has renounced his right to their allotment, without contravening (ii) above.

*Treasury shares.* Shares held by the company as treasury shares are disregarded for the purposes of these provisions (so that the company is not treated as a person who holds ordinary shares and the shares are not treated as forming part of the ordinary share capital of the company).

[*CA 2006, s 561; SI 2008 No 2860, Sch 2 para 49*].

'*Holder of the shares*'. References above (however expressed) to the 'holder' of shares of any description is to whoever was the holder of shares of that description at the close of business on a date to be specified in the offer. That date must fall within the period of 28 days immediately before the date of the offer. [*CA 2006, s 574*].

**47.14** *Communication of pre-emption offers*

Offers that are required to be made to holders of a company's shares under **47.13** may be made in hard copy or electronic form. See APPENDIX 1 DEFINITIONS for the meaning of these terms.

If the holder:

•   has no registered address in an EEA State and has not given the company an address in an EEA State for the service of notices on him, or

•   is the holder of a share warrant,

the offer may be made by either publishing it in the *Gazette* or publishing a notice in the *Gazette* specifying where a copy of it can be obtained or inspected.

The offer must state a period during which it may be accepted and cannot be withdrawn before the end of that period. The period must be one of at least 14 days beginning in the case of an offer made:

- in hard copy form, with the date on which the offer is sent or supplied;

- in electronic form, with the date on which the offer is sent; and

- by publication in the Gazette, with the date of publication.

[*CA 2006, s 562; SI 2009 No 2022, Reg 2*].

See also **16.23–16.35** Dealings With Third Parties for the 'company communication provisions' relating to communications sent by companies, including the provisions in **16.33** relating to communications to joint holders and communications following the death or bankruptcy of the shareholder.

**47.15** *Liability in case of contravention*

Where there is a contravention of **47.13** or **47.14**, the company, and every officer of it who knowingly authorised or permitted the contravention, are jointly and severally liable to compensate any person to whom an offer should have been made for any loss, damage, costs or expenses which the person has sustained or incurred by reason of the contravention. But no proceedings to recover any such loss, etc may be commenced after the expiration of two years:

- from the delivery to the Registrar of Companies of the return of allotment; or

- where equity securities other than shares are granted, from the date of the grant.

[*CA 2006, s 563*].

**47.16** *Exceptions to right of pre-emption*

The provisions in **47.13** do not apply:

- in relation to the allotment of bonus shares;

- to a particular allotment of equity securities if these are, or are to be, wholly or partly paid up otherwise than in cash; and

- to the allotment of securities that would, apart from any renunciation or assignment of the right to their allotment, be held under an employees' share scheme (see Appendix 1 Definitions).

[*CA 2006, ss 564–566*].

**47.17** *Exclusion of pre-emption rights*

(1) *Private companies*

All or any of the requirements of **47.13** and **47.14** may be excluded by provision contained in the articles of a private company. They can be excluded:

- generally in relation to the allotment by the company of equity securities; or

- in relation to allotments of a particular description.

Any requirement or authorisation contained in the articles of a private company that is inconsistent with the requirements of paragraph **47.13** or **47.14** (as the case may be) is treated for these purposes as a provision excluding that paragraph.

A provision to which (2) below applies is not to be treated as inconsistent with the provisions set out in **47.13**.

[*CA 2006, s 567*].

Exclusion of pre-emption rights in force pre 1 October 2009. Where provision was made under *CA 1985, s 91* excluding the pre-emption requirements of *CA 1985, ss 89 or 90* and was in force immediately before 1 October 2009, the provision has effect on or after that date as if it was, or included, provision made by *CA 2006, s 567* above excluding the corresponding requirements of **47.3** and **47.14**. [*SI 2008 No 2860, Sch 2 para 50*].

(2) *Articles conferring corresponding right*

The provisions of *CA 2006, s 568* apply where in a case in which *CA 2006, s 561* (see **47.13**) would otherwise apply:

- a company's articles contain provision ('pre-emption provision') prohibiting the company from allotting ordinary shares of a particular class unless it has complied with the condition that it makes a pre-emption offer as is described in **47.13** to each person who holds ordinary shares of that class, and

- in accordance with that provision:

  (i)    the company makes an offer to allot shares to such a holder, and

  (ii)   he or anyone in whose favour he has renounced his right to their allotment accepts the offer.

In that case *CA 2006, s 561* does not apply to the allotment of those shares and the company may allot them accordingly. The provisions of **47.14** regarding the communication of pre-emption offers to shareholders also apply in relation to offers made in pursuance of the pre-emption provision of the company's articles (but subject to (1) above).

If there is a contravention of the pre-emption provision of the company's articles, the company, and every officer of it who knowingly authorised or permitted the contravention, are jointly and severally liable to compensate any person to whom an offer should have been made under the provision for any loss, damage, costs or expenses which the person has sustained or incurred by reason of the contravention. But no proceedings to recover any such loss, etc may be commenced after the expiration of two years:

- from the delivery to the Registrar of Companies of the return of allotment; or

- where equity securities other than shares are granted, from the date of the grant.

[*CA 2006, s 568*]

'*Holder of the shares*'. See **47.13** for the meaning of.

**47.18** *Disapplication of pre-emption rights*

(1) *Private company with only one class of shares*

The directors of a private company that has only one class of shares may be given power by the articles, or by a special resolution of the company, to allot equity securities of that class as if the provisions in **47.13**:

- did not apply to the allotment; or

- applied to the allotment with such modifications as the directors determine.

Where the directors make such an allotment, the provisions in **47.13–47.19** have effect accordingly.

[*CA 2006, s 569*].

(2) *Directors acting under general authorisation*

Where the directors of a company are generally authorised to allot shares under *CA 2006, s 551* (see **47.9**(2)), they may be given power by the articles, or by a special resolution of the company, to allot equity securities pursuant to that authorisation as if the provisions of **47.13**:

- did not apply to the allotment; or

- applied to the allotment with such modifications as the directors may determine.

Where the directors make such an allotment, the provisions in **47.13–47.19** have effect accordingly.

The power conferred by these provisions ceases to have effect when the authorisation to which it relates is revoked or would (if not renewed) expire. But if the authorisation is renewed, the power may also be renewed, for a period not longer than that for which the authorisation is renewed, by a special resolution of the company.

Despite the fact that the power conferred by these provisions has expired, the directors may allot equity securities in pursuance of an offer or agreement previously made by the company if the power enabled the company to make an offer or agreement that would or might require equity securities to be allotted after it expired.

[*CA 2006, s 570*].

Exclusion of pre-emption in force pre 1 October 2009. Where pre-emption provisions excluding or modifying *CA 1985, s 89(1)* were made by virtue of *CA 1985, s 95(1)* and were in force immediately before 1 October 2009, the provisions have effect on or after that date as if they had been made by virtue of *CA 2006, s 570* above and excluded or modified *CA 2006, s 561* (see **47.13**). The power conferred to allot equity securities may accordingly be renewed under *CA 2006, s 570(3)*. [*SI 2008 No 2860, Sch 2 para 52*].

(3) *Disapplication by special resolution*

Where the directors of a company are authorised to allot shares under **47.9**(2), whether generally or otherwise, the company may by special resolution resolve that the provisions in **47.13**:

- do not apply to a specified allotment of equity securities to be made pursuant to that authorisation; or

- apply to such an allotment with such modifications as may be specified in the resolution.

Where such a resolution is passed, the provisions in **47.13–47.19** have effect accordingly.

A special resolution under these provisions ceases to have effect when the authorisation to which it relates is revoked or would (if not renewed) expire. But if the authorisation is renewed, the resolution may also be renewed, for a period not longer than that for which the authorisation is renewed, by a special resolution of the company.

[*CA 2006, s 571(1)–(3)*].

Despite the fact that any such resolution has expired, the directors may allot equity securities in pursuance of an offer or agreement previously made by the company if the resolution enabled the company to make an offer or agreement that would or might require equity securities to be allotted after it expired.

A special resolution under these provisions, or a special resolution to renew such a resolution, must not be proposed unless:

- it is recommended by the directors; and
- the directors have made a written statement setting out:
  - (i) their reasons for making the recommendation;
  - (ii) the amount to be paid to the company in respect of the equity securities to be allotted; and
  - (iii) the directors' justification of that amount.

If the resolution is proposed at a general meeting, the directors' statement must be circulated to the members entitled to notice of the meeting with that notice. Alternatively, if the resolution is proposed as a written resolution, it must be sent or submitted to every eligible member at or before the time at which the proposed resolution is sent or submitted to him.

[*CA 2006, s 571(4)–(7)*].

Exclusion of pre-emption rights pre 1 October 2009.

(a) Where a special resolution excluding or modifying *CA 1985, s 89(1)* was passed by virtue of *CA 1985 s 95(2)* and was in force immediately before 1 October 2009, the resolution has effect on or after that date as if it had been passed by virtue of *CA 2006, s 571* above and excluded or modified *CA 2006, s 561*. The resolution may accordingly be renewed under *CA 2006, s 571(3)*.

(b) It is immaterial whether the directors' statement required before a resolution can be proposed under *CA 2006, s 571* above is made, or is sent, submitted or circulated as required by that section, before on or after 1 October 2009.

[*SI 2008 No 2860, Sch 2 paras 53, 54(1)*].

Liability for false statement in directors' statement. Where a directors' statement is sent, submitted or circulated to a member, a person who knowingly or recklessly authorises or permits the inclusion of any matter that is misleading, false or deceptive in a material particular in such a statement commits an offence. A person guilty of such an offence is liable (i) on conviction on indictment, to imprisonment for a term not exceeding two years or a fine (or both); and (ii) on summary conviction, to imprisonment for a term not exceeding 12 months (in Scotland or Northern Ireland, 6 months) or to a fine not exceeding the statutory maximum (or both). See **29.1** Offences and Legal Proceedings for the statutory maximum.

[*CA 2006, s 572*].

(4) *Sale of treasury shares*

Where a sale of treasury shares is an allotment of equity securities by virtue of **47.13**(*c*)(ii), the directors of a company may be given power by the articles, or by a special resolution of the company, to allot equity securities as if **47.13**:

- did not apply to the allotment; or
- applied to the allotment with such modifications as the directors may determine.

Where the directors make such an allotment, the provisions in **47.13–47.19** have effect accordingly.

The power conferred by these provisions ceases to have effect when the authorisation to which it relates is revoked or would (if not renewed) expire. But if the authorisation is renewed, the power may also be renewed, for a period not longer than that for which the authorisation is renewed, by a special resolution of the company.

Despite the fact that the power conferred by these provisions has expired, the directors may allot equity securities in pursuance of an offer or agreement previously made by the company if the power enabled the company to make an offer or agreement that would or might require equity securities to be allotted after it expired.

The company may by special resolution resolve that the provisions of **47.13**:

- do not apply to a specified allotment of securities; or

- do apply to the allotment with such modifications as may be specified in the resolution.

In such a case, the provisions in **47.13–47.19** have effect accordingly and, in particular, the provisions of *CA 2006, s 571(4)–(7)* (see (3) above) apply.

[*CA 2006, s 573*].

Exclusion of pre-emption rights pre 1 October 2009.

Where provision excluding or modifying *CA 1985, s 89(1)* was made by virtue of *CA 1985, s 95(2A)* and was in force immediately before 1 October 2009, the provision has effect on or after that date as if it had been made by virtue of *CA 2006, s 573* above and excluded or modified *CA 2006, s 561* (see **47.13**). The power conferred to allot equity securities may accordingly be renewed under *CA 2006, s 570(3)* or *CA 2006, s 571(3)*.

[*SI 2008 No 2860, Sch 2 para 55*].

**47.19** *Saving provisions*

*Other restrictions on offer or allotment.* The provisions in **47.13–47.18** are without prejudice to any other Act by virtue of which a company is prohibited (whether generally or in specified circumstances) from offering or allotting equity securities to any person. Where a company cannot by virtue of such an Act offer or allot equity securities to a holder of ordinary shares of the company, those shares are disregarded for the purposes of **47.13** so that:

- the person is not treated as a person who holds ordinary shares; and

- the shares are not treated as forming part of the ordinary share capital of the company.

[*CA 2006, s 575*].

*Older pre-emption requirements.*

(1) In the case of a public company, the provisions in **47.13–47.18** do not apply to an allotment of equity securities that are subject to a pre-emption requirement in relation to which *CA 1985, s 96(1)* or *Companies (Northern Ireland) Order 1986, Art 106(1)* applied before 1 October 2009 (ie allotments of equity securities subject to a requirement imposed before 22 June 1982, whether by the company's memorandum or articles or otherwise, that the company must, when allotting securities, offer to allot them, or some of them, in a manner which is inconsistent with these provisions).

(2) In the case of a private company, a pre-emption requirement to which *CA 1985, s 96(3)* or *Companies (Northern Ireland) Order 1986, Art 106(3)* applied before 1 October 2009 has effect, so long as the company remains a private company, as if it were contained in the company's articles. Under those provisions, a requirement which was imposed on a private company before 22 June 1982, otherwise than by the company's memorandum or articles, and which would have had the effect of excluding the pre-emption provisions if contained in the memorandum or articles, has effect as if it were so contained.

(3) A pre-emption requirement to which *CA 1985, s 96(4)* or *Companies (Northern Ireland) Order 1986, Art 106(4)* applied before 1 October 2009 is treated for the purposes of the provisions in **47.13–47.18** as if it were contained in the company's articles.

[*CA 2006, s 576*].

**47.20 Public companies: allotment where issue not fully subscribed**

No allotment must be made of shares of a public company offered for subscription unless:

- the issue is subscribed for in full; or

- the offer is made on terms that the shares subscribed for may be allotted in any event or if specified conditions are met (and those conditions are met).

If shares are prohibited from being allotted by the above provisions and 40 days have elapsed after the first making of the offer, all money received from applicants for shares must be repaid forthwith, initially without interest. But if any of the money is not repaid within 48 days after the first making of the offer, the directors of the company are jointly and severally liable to repay it, with interest at the rate for the time being specified under *Judgments Act 1838, s 17* from the expiration of the 48th day. A director is not so liable if he proves that the default in the repayment of the money was not due to any misconduct or negligence on his part.

Any condition requiring or binding an applicant for shares to waive compliance with any requirement of this section is void. [*CA 2006, s 578(1)–(3), (6)*].

**Shares offered as wholly or partly payable otherwise than in cash.** The above provisions also apply to such shares, the word 'subscribed' being construed accordingly. References to repayment of money received from applicants include:

- the return of any other consideration received (including, if the case so requires, the release of the applicant from any undertaking); or

- if it is not reasonably practicable to return the consideration, the payment of money equal to its value at the time it was so received;

[*CA 2006, s 578(4)(5)*].

**Effect of irregular allotment.** Where an allotment is made in contravention of the *CA 2006, s 578*, it is voidable at the instance of the applicant within one month after the date of the allotment, and not later. This applies even if the company is in the course of being wound up. A director of the company who knowingly contravenes, or permits or authorises the contravention of, any of the provisions of *section 578* (above) with respect to allotment is liable to compensate the company and the allottee respectively for any loss, damages, costs or expenses that the company or allottee may have sustained or incurred by the contravention provided proceedings are brought within two years of the date of the allotment.

[*CA 2006, s 579*].

**47.21 Prohibition of public offers by private companies**

A private company limited by shares, or limited by guarantee and having a share capital, must not:

- 'offer to the public' any 'securities' of the company; or

- allot or agree to allot any securities of the company with a view to their being offered to the public.

Unless the contrary is proved, an allotment or agreement to allot securities is presumed to be made with a view to their being offered to the public if an offer of the securities (or any of them) to the public is made:

- within six months after the allotment or agreement to allot; or

- before the receipt by the company of the whole of the consideration to be received by it in respect of the securities.

But a company does not contravene these provisions if:

(a) it acts in good faith in pursuance of arrangements under which it is to re-register as a public company before the securities are allotted; or

(b) as part of the terms of the offer it undertakes to re-register as a public company within a period ending not later than six months after the day on which the offer is made (or, in the case of an offer made on different days, first made), and that undertaking is complied with.

[*CA 2006, s 755(1)–(4)*].

**'Offer to the public'.** An offer to the public includes an offer to any section of the public, however selected.

An offer is not regarded as an offer to the public if it can properly be regarded, in all the circumstances, as:

- not being calculated to result, directly or indirectly, in securities of the company becoming available to persons other than those receiving the offer; or

- otherwise being a '*private concern of the person receiving it and the person making it*'. Unless the contrary is proved, this means that:

    (a) it is made to a '*person already connected with the company*' and, where it is made on terms allowing that person to renounce his rights, the rights may only be renounced in favour of another person already connected with the company; or

    (b) it is an offer to subscribe for securities to be held under an employees' share scheme (see APPENDIX 1 DEFINITIONS) and, where it is made on terms allowing that person to renounce his rights, the rights may only be renounced in favour of:

        (i) another person entitled to hold securities under the scheme; or

        (ii) a person already connected with the company.

For these purposes, a '*person already connected with the company*' means

    (i) an existing member or employee of the company;

    (ii) a member of the family of a person who is or was a member or employee of the company (ie that person's spouse or civil partner and children, including step-children, and their descendants);

    (iii) the widow or widower, or surviving civil partner, of a person who was a member or employee of the company;

    (iv) an existing debenture holder of the company; or

    (v) a trustee (acting in his capacity as such) of a trust of which the principal beneficiary is a person within any of (i)–(iv) above.

[*CA 2006, s 756*].

**'Securities'** means shares or debentures. [*CA 2006, s 755(5)*].

**Validity of allotment, etc.** Nothing in the above provisions or in **47.22** affects the validity of any allotment or sale of securities or of any agreement to allot or sell securities.

[*CA 2006, s 760*].

**47.22** *Enforcement of prohibition*

Contravention of the provisions in **47.21** can be enforced in any of the following ways.

(1)    *Court order restraining proposed contravention*

If it appears to the court:

- on an application under these provisions made by:

    (i)    a member or creditor of the company, or

    (ii)    the Secretary of State, or

- in proceedings under *CA 2006, Pt 30* (protection of members against unfair prejudice, see **26.5 MEMBERS**),

that a company is *proposing to act* in contravention of the provisions in **47.21**, the court must make an order restraining it from so doing.

[*CA 2006, s 757*].

(2)    *Orders available to the court after contravention*

If it appears to the court:

- on an application under these provisions made by:

    (i)    a member of the company who *either* was a member at the time the offer was made (or, if the offer was made over a period, at any time during that period) *or* became a member as a result of the offer,

    (ii)    a creditor of the company who was a creditor at the time the offer was made (or, if the offer was made over a period, at any time during that period), or

    (iii)    the Secretary of State, or

- in proceedings under *CA 2006, Pt 30* (protection of members against unfair prejudice, see **26.10 MEMBERS**),

that a company *has acted* in contravention of the provisions in **47.21**, the court must make an order requiring the company to re-register as a public company unless it appears to the court that:

- the company does not meet the requirements for re-registration as a public company; and

- it is impractical or undesirable to require it to take steps to do so.

If the court does not make an order for re-registration, it may make a remedial order under (3) below and/or an order for the compulsory winding up of the company.

[*CA 2006, s 758*].

(3)    *Remedial orders*

A '*remedial order*' is an order for the purpose of putting a person affected by anything done in contravention of the provisions in **47.21** in the position he would have been in if it had not been done. Without prejudice to the generality of the power of the court to make such an order:

- where a private company has:

    (i)     allotted securities pursuant to an offer to the public, or

    (ii)    allotted or agreed to allot securities with a view to their being offered to the public,

a remedial order may require any person knowingly concerned in the contravention to offer to purchase any of those securities at such price and on such other terms as the court thinks fit;

- a remedial order may be made:

    (i)     against any person knowingly concerned in the contravention, whether or not an officer of the company;

    (ii)    notwithstanding anything in the company's constitution (which includes, for this purpose, the terms on which any securities of the company are allotted or held); and

    (iii)   whether or not the holder of the securities subject to the order is the person to whom the company allotted or agreed to allot them; and

- where a remedial order is made against the company itself, the court may provide for the reduction of the company's capital accordingly.

[*CA 2006, s 759*].

## 47.23 PAYMENT FOR SHARES

Where shares are issued in a company, a shareholder is liable to pay up the nominal value of each of his shares, together with any premium, and the amount owing to the company is a debt which can be 'called up' (see **47.25**). The company may not require him to pay the full amount when he first takes up the shares (but see **47.26** for the minimum value which must be paid up on allotment of public company shares).

Subject to **47.26**, shares allotted by a company, and any premium on them, may be paid up in money or money's worth (including goodwill and know-how). This does not prevent a company from:

- allotting bonus shares to its members; or

- paying up, with sums available for the purpose, any amounts for the time being unpaid on any of its shares (whether on account of the nominal value of the shares or by way of premium).

[*CA 2006, s 582*].

## 47.24 Allotment of shares at a discount not permitted

A company's shares must not be allotted at a discount. If shares are allotted in contravention of this, the allottee is liable to pay the company an amount equal to the amount of the discount, with interest at the 'appropriate rate'. [*CA 2006, s 580*]. The '*appropriate rate*' of interest is 5% a year or such other rate as specified by statutory instrument.

## 47.24    Shares

[*CA 2006, s 592*].

See *Ooregum Gold Mining Co of India v Roper* [1892] AC 125, HL. See also *Welton v Saffrey* [1897] AC 299 where, although a company being wound up could pay all its creditors, it was held that holders of shares issued at a discount were still liable to account to the company for the discount in order to adjust the rights of the shareholders *inter se*.

## 47.25  Calls

Generally, a company will call up the amount it is owed on its shares rateably for all shareholders. But, if so authorised by its articles, it may:

- make arrangements on the issue of shares for a difference between the shareholders in the amounts and times of payment of calls on their shares; and

- accept from any member the whole or part of the amount remaining unpaid on any shares held by him, although no part of that amount has been called up.

Where it does so, and where the articles permit, the company may subsequently pay any dividends in proportion to the amount paid up on each share where a larger amount is paid up on some shares than on others. [*CA 2006, s 581*].

Where a company has adopted standard articles, see:

- *Table A, 1985, Reg 17*

- *Model Articles, Art 55* (public companies)

set out in APPENDIX 4 STANDARD ARTICLES OF ASSOCIATION.

**General provisions relating to calls in the articles**. A company's articles will usually contain provisions relating to the procedure, timing and liability for calls on shares. Where a company has adopted standard articles, see:

- *Table A, 1985, Regs 12–16*

- *Model Articles, Art 21* (private companies)

- *Model Articles, Arts 54–57* (public companies)

set out in APPENDIX 4 STANDARD ARTICLES OF ASSOCIATION.

**Lien on shares for unpaid calls**. A company's articles will usually contain provisions relating to its lien on shares for outstanding calls, etc. Where a company has adopted standard articles, see:

- *Table A, 1985, Regs 8–11*

- *Model Articles, Arts 52, 53* (public companies)

set out in APPENDIX 4 STANDARD ARTICLES OF ASSOCIATION.

Where a shareholder has lodged his share certificate with a bank as security for a loan and the bank has given notice of this to the company, the company cannot, in respect of moneys due to it from the shareholder after notice of the bank's security, claim priority over advances made by the bank after such notice (*Bradford Banking Co v Briggs, Son & Co Ltd* (1886) 12 App Cas 29, HL).

**Forfeiture for non-payment of calls**. If the articles of a company provide, the company may forfeit shares for failure to pay calls. It may also accept surrender in lieu of forfeiture. [*CA 2006, s 659(2)(c)*]. Where a company has adopted standard articles, see:

- *Table A, 1985, Regs 18–22*

- *Model Articles, Arts 58–62* (public companies)

set out in APPENDIX 4 STANDARD ARTICLES OF ASSOCIATION.

See also *Ladies' Dress Association Ltd v Pulbrook* [1900] 2 QB 376, CA and *Bolton, Re, ex p North British Artificial Silk Ltd* [1930] 2 Ch 48, 99 LJ Ch 209.

See **34.28** PURCHASE OF OWN SHARES for cancellation of the shares forfeited in the case of a public company.

### 47.26    Additional rules for public companies

(1) *Shares taken by subscribers to the memorandum*

Shares taken by a subscriber to the memorandum of a public company, in pursuance of an undertaking of his in the memorandum, and any premium on the shares, must be paid up in cash. [*CA 2006, s 584*].

*Meaning of payment in cash.* For the purposes of *CA 2006*, a share in a company is deemed '*paid up in cash*' (as to its nominal value or any premium on it) or '*allotted for cash*', if the consideration received for the allotment or payment up is a 'cash consideration', ie:

- cash received by the company;

- a cheque received by the company in good faith that the directors have no reason for suspecting will not be paid;

- a release of a liability of the company for a liquidated sum;

- an undertaking to pay cash to the company at a future date; or

- in relation to consideration received in pursuance of an obligation entered into on or after 1 October 2009, payment by any other means giving rise to a present or future entitlement (of the company or a person acting on the company's behalf) to a payment, or credit equivalent to payment, in cash. Included is a settlement bank's obligation to make a payment in respect of the allotment or payment up of shares under the CREST system.

"Cash" includes foreign currency.

Except for the purpose of existing shareholders rights of pre-emption under **47.13–47.19**, the payment of cash, or an undertaking to pay cash, to a person *other than* the company counts as consideration other than cash.

[*CA 2006, s 583; SI 2009 No 388, Art 4*].

(2) *Prohibition on accepting undertaking to do work or perform services*

A public company must not accept at any time, in payment up of its shares or any premium on them, an undertaking given by any person that he or another will do work or perform services for the company or any other person.

If a public company accepts such an undertaking, when the shares or the premium are treated as paid up (in whole or in part) by the undertaking, the 'holder of the shares':

(a)    remains liable to pay the company an amount equal to the nominal value of the shares, together with the whole of any premium (or, if the case so requires, such proportion of that amount as is treated as paid up by the undertaking); and

# 47.26 Shares

(b)   is liable to pay interest at the 'appropriate rate' on the amount payable under (*a*) above. The '*appropriate rate*' of interest is 5% a year or such other rate as specified by statutory instrument.

The '*holder of the shares*' includes a person who has an unconditional right to:

*   be included in the company's register of members in respect of those shares; or

*   have an instrument of transfer of them executed in his favour.

[*CA 2006, ss 585, 592*].

(3) *Shares must be at least one-quarter paid up*

Apart from shares allotted under an employees' share scheme (see APPENDIX 1 DEFINITIONS), a public company must not allot a share unless it is paid up at least as to one-quarter of its nominal value and the whole of any premium on it.

If a company allots a share in contravention of this:

*   the share is to be treated as if one-quarter of its nominal value, together with the whole of any premium on it, had been received; and

*   the allottee is liable to pay the company the minimum amount which should have been received in respect of the share under this provision (less the value of any consideration actually applied in payment up, to any extent, of the share and any premium on it), with interest at the 'appropriate rate'. The '*appropriate rate*' of interest is 5%pa or such other rate as specified by statutory instrument.

This does not apply to the allotment of bonus shares, unless the allottee knew (or ought to have known) the shares were allotted in contravention of this provision.

[*CA 2006, s 586*].

(4) *Payment by long-term undertaking*

A public company must not allot shares as fully or partly paid up (as to their nominal value or any premium on them) otherwise than in cash if the consideration for the allotment is, or includes, an undertaking which is to be, or *may be*, performed more than five years after the date of the allotment.

[*CA 2006, s 587(1)*].

If:

(a)   a company allots shares in contravention of this provision, or

(b)   an undertaking which is to be performed within five years of the allotment is not performed within the period allowed by the contract for the allotment of the shares,

the allottee is liable to pay the company (where (*b*) applies, at the end of the period so allowed) an amount equal to the aggregate of the nominal value of the shares and the whole of any premium (or, if the case so requires, so much of that aggregate as is treated as paid up by the undertaking), with interest at the 'appropriate rate'. The '*appropriate rate*' of interest is 5% pa or such other rate as specified by statutory instrument.

[*CA 2006, s 587(2)(4)*].

Where a contract for the allotment of shares does not contravene this provision, any variation of the contract (which includes an ancillary contract relating to payment for the shares) is void if its effect is that the contract would have contravened this provision if the terms of the contract as varied had been its original terms. This also applies to the variation by a public company of the terms of a contract entered into before the company was re-registered as a public company.

[*CA 2006, s 587(3)*].

### 47.27  Liability of subsequent holder of shares

If a person (A) becomes a 'holder' of shares in respect of which:

- there has been a contravention of any provision relating to payment for shares in **47.23–47.30** (including a failure to carry out an undertaking under **47.26(4)(*b*)**), and

- by virtue of that contravention another is liable to pay any amount under the provision contravened,

then A is also liable to pay that amount (jointly and severally with any other person so liable) unless:

- he is a purchaser for value and, at the time of the purchase, he did not have actual notice of the contravention concerned; or

- he derived title to the shares (directly or indirectly) from a person who became a holder of them after the contravention and was not liable under the above provisions.

'Holder of shares' for these purposes includes any person who has an unconditional right:

- to be included in the company's register of members in respect of the shares or as the case may be to have his name and other particulars delivered to the Registrar of Companies under *CA 2006, Part 8, Chapter 2A* and registered by the Registrar (see **38.9** – Option to keep information on the public register); or

- to have an instrument of transfer of the shares executed in his favour.

[*CA 2006, s 588; SBEE 2015, s 94, Sch 5, para 21; SI 2016 No 321, Reg 6*].

### 47.28  Power of court to grant relief

Where, under **47.26(2)** or **(4)** or **47.27**, a person is liable to a company:

(a)   in relation to payment in respect of shares in the company, or

(b)   by virtue of an undertaking given to it in, or in connection with, payment for shares in the company,

that person may apply to the court to be exempted in whole or in part from the liability.

There are two overriding principles to which the court must have regard in determining whether it should exempt the applicant in whole or in part from any liability. First, a company that has allotted shares should receive money or money's worth at least equal in value to the aggregate of the nominal value of those shares and the whole of any premium or, if the case so requires, so much of that aggregate as is treated as paid up. Subject to that, secondly, where a company would, if the court did not grant the exemption, have more than one remedy against a particular person, it should be for the company to decide which remedy it should remain entitled to pursue. Because these are 'overriding principles', a court will need very good reasons to accept that it is just and equitable to exempt an applicant from liability where the company has not received sufficient value (*Bradford Investments plc (No 2), Re* [1991] BCLC 688, [1991] BCC 379).

Otherwise, the court may exempt the applicant from the liability only if and to the extent that it appears to the court just and equitable to do so. In reaching its decision, the court must have regard to the following (except in relation to a decision whether to grant relief in respect of a liability for interest arising before 1 October 2009).

Where (*a*) above applies,

- whether the applicant has paid, or is liable to pay, any amount in respect of:

    (i)     any other liability arising in relation to those shares under any provision relating to payment for shares in **47.23–47.27** or any provision relating to independent valuation of non-cash consideration in **47.32–47.42**; or

    (ii)    any liability arising by virtue of any undertaking given in or in connection with payment for those shares;

- whether any person other than the applicant has paid or is likely to pay, whether in pursuance of any order of the court or otherwise, any such amount; and

- whether the applicant or any other person:

    (i)     has performed in whole or in part, or is likely so to perform, any such undertaking; or

    (ii)    has done, or is likely to do, any other thing in payment or part payment for the shares.

Where (*b*) above applies,

- whether the applicant has paid or is liable to pay any amount in respect of liability arising in relation to the shares under any provision relating to payment for shares in **47.23–47.30** or any provision relating to independent valuation of non-cash consideration in **47.31–47.45**; or

- whether any person other than the applicant has paid or is likely to pay, whether in pursuance of any order of the court or otherwise, any such amount.

[*CA 2006, s 589(1)–(5)*].

**Proceedings against a contributor.** Certain powers are conferred on the court where a person brings proceedings against another (the '*contributor*') for a contribution in respect of liability to a company arising under any provision relating to payment for shares in **47.23–47.30** or any provision relating to independent valuation of non-cash consideration in **47.31–47.45** and it appears to the court that the contributor is liable to make such a contribution. The court may, if and to the extent that it appears to be just and equitable to do so, having regard to the respective culpability (in respect of the liability to the company) of the contributor and the person bringing the proceedings:

- exempt the contributor in whole or in part from his liability to make such a contribution; or

- order the contributor to make a larger contribution than, but for this provision, he would be liable to make.

[*CA 2006, s 589(6)*].

### 47.29  Penalty for contravention

If a company contravenes any of the provisions in **47.23–47.27**, an offence is committed by the company and every officer of the company who is in default. A person guilty of such an offence is liable (i) on conviction on indictment, to a fine; and (ii) on summary conviction, to a fine not exceeding the statutory maximum. See **29.1 OFFENCES AND LEGAL PROCEEDINGS** for the statutory maximum.

[*CA 2006, s 590*].

**47.30 Enforceability of undertakings to do work, etc**

Without prejudice to **47.28**, where:

- an undertaking to do work or perform services or to do any other thing is given by any person, in or in connection with payment for shares in a company, and

- that undertaking is enforceable by the company apart from any of the provisions in **47.23–47.27**

the undertaking is so enforceable notwithstanding that there has been a contravention in relation to it of any provision relating to payment for shares in **47.23–47.30** or any provision relating to independent valuation of non-cash consideration in **47.31–47.45**.

[*CA 2006, s 591*].

**47.31 PUBLIC COMPANIES: INDEPENDENT VALUATION OF NON-CASH CONSIDERATION**

There are two situations in which a public company may be required to obtain an independent valuer's report of non-cash consideration.

- Where a public company seeks to allot shares as fully or partly paid otherwise than in cash, the consideration for the allotment must be independently valued. See **47.32–47.35**.

- Where a public company formed as such enters unto an agreement with a subscriber to the memorandum for the transfer by him to the company, or another, of non-cash assets within two years of commencing to trade and the consideration for the transfer to be given by the company is one-tenth or more of the company's issued share capital. See **47.36–47.40**.

See also **47.41** for the requirements of independent valuations and **47.42–47.44** for supplementary provisions.

**47.32 Non-cash consideration for shares**

Subject to **47.33**, a public company must not allot shares as fully or partly paid up (as to their nominal value or any premium on them) otherwise than in cash unless:

(a) the consideration for the allotment has been independently valued;

(b) the valuer's report has been made to the company in the six months immediately preceding the allotment of the shares; and

(c) a copy of the report has been sent to the proposed allottee.

See **47.26**(1) above for the meaning of '*allotted for cash*'.

**Effect of contravention.** If a company allots shares in contravention of the above and either:

- the allottee has not received the valuer's report required to be sent to him, or

- there has been some other contravention of the requirements of this provision or the valuation and reporting requirements (see **47.34**) that the allottee knew, or ought to have known, amounted to a contravention, the allottee is liable to pay the company an amount equal to the aggregate of the nominal value of the shares and the whole of any premium (or, if the case so requires, so much of that aggregate as is treated as paid up by the consideration), with interest at the 'appropriate rate'. The 'appropriate rate' of interest is 5% pa or such other rate as specified by statutory instrument.

[*CA 2006, ss 593(1)(3)(4), 609*].

**47.33** *Exceptions to the valuation requirement*

(1) *Application of reserves*

The application of an amount standing to the credit of any of a company's reserve accounts or its profit and loss account in paying up (to any extent) shares allotted to members of the company, or premiums on shares so allotted, does not count as consideration for the allotment. Accordingly, the requirement for a report does not apply in that case.

[*CA 2006, s 593(2)*].

(2) *Arrangements with another company*

The provisions in **47.32** do not apply to an 'arrangement' for the allotment of shares in a company (company A) on terms that the whole or part of the consideration for the shares allotted is to be provided by:

- the transfer to that company A, or

- the cancellation,

of all or some of the shares (or shares of a particular class) in another company (company B). It is immaterial whether the arrangement provides for the issue to company A of shares (or shares of any particular class) in company B. The arrangement must be open to all the holders of the shares in company B (or, where the arrangement applies only to shares of a particular class, to all the holders of shares of that class) but disregarding shares held:

- by, or by a nominee of, company A;

- by, or by a nominee of, a company which is:

    (i)     the holding company, or a subsidiary, of company A; or

    (ii)    a subsidiary of such a holding company;

- shares held as treasury shares by company B.

'*Arrangement*' means any agreement, scheme or arrangement, including an arrangement sanctioned in accordance with:

- *CA 2006, Pt 26* (see **35.1** to **35.5** RECONSTRUCTIONS AND MERGERS); or

- *IA 1986, s 110* or *Insolvency (Northern Ireland) Order 1989, Art 96* (liquidator in winding up accepting shares as consideration for sale of company property).

[*CA 2006, s 594*].

(3) *Mergers or divisions*

The provisions in **47.32** do not apply to the allotment of shares by a company as part of a scheme to which *CA 2006, Pt 27* (Mergers and Divisions of public companies) applies if, in the case of a scheme involving a merger, an expert's report is drawn up as required by *CA 2006, s 909* or, in the case of a scheme involving a division, an expert's report is drawn up as required by *CA 2006, s 924*.

[*CA 2006, s 595*].

**47.34** *Valuation and reporting requirements*

The provisions in **47.41** (general provisions as to independent valuation and report) apply to the valuation and report required under **47.32**.

The valuer's report must state:

- the nominal value of the shares to be wholly or partly paid for by the consideration in question;

- the amount of any premium payable on the shares;

- the description of the consideration and, as respects so much of the consideration as he himself has valued, a description of that part of the consideration, the method used to value it and the date of the valuation;

- the extent to which the nominal value of the shares and any premium are to be treated as paid up:

  (i)   by the consideration;

  (ii)  in cash (see **47.26**(1) above for the meaning of '*allotted for cash*'); and

- either in the report itself or an accompanying note that:

  (i)   in the case of a valuation made by another person, it appeared to the valuer reasonable to arrange for it to be so made or to accept a valuation so made;

  (ii)  whoever made the valuation, that the method of valuation was reasonable in all the circumstances;

  (iii) it appears to the valuer that there has been no material change in the value of the consideration in question since the valuation; and

  (iv)  on the basis of the valuation, the value of the consideration, together with any cash by which the nominal value of the shares or any premium payable on them is to be paid up, is not less than so much of the aggregate of the nominal value and the whole of any such premium as is treated as paid up by the consideration and any such cash.

*Position where consideration accepted is only partly for shares.* Where the consideration to be valued is accepted partly in payment up of the nominal value of the shares and any premium and partly for some other consideration given by the company, the provisions above and those in **47.32** apply as if references to the consideration accepted by the company included the proportion of that consideration that is properly attributable to the payment up of that value and any premium. In such a case:

(a)   the valuer must carry out, or arrange for, such other valuations as will enable him to determine that proportion; and

(b)   his report must state what valuations have been made under (*a*) above and also the reason for, and method and date of, any such valuation and any other matters which may be relevant to that determination.

[*CA 2006, s 596*].

**47.35** *Copy report to be delivered to the Registrar of Companies*

A company to which a report is made as to the value of any consideration for which, or partly for which, it proposes to allot shares must deliver a copy of the report to the Registrar of Companies for registration. This must be done at the same time that the company files the return of the allotment of those shares under **47.12**.

If default is made in complying with these requirements, an offence is committed by every officer of the company who is in default. A person guilty of such an offence is liable (i) on conviction on indictment, to a fine; and (ii) on summary conviction, to a fine not exceeding the statutory maximum and, for continued contravention, a daily default fine not exceeding one-tenth of the greater of £5000 or the amount corresponding to level 4 on the standard scale for summary offences. See 29.1 OFFENCES AND LEGAL PROCEEDINGS for the statutory maximum.

In the case of default in delivering to the Registrar of Companies any document as required by these provisions, any person liable for the default may apply to the court for relief. If the court is satisfied that:

•      the omission to deliver the document was accidental or due to inadvertence, or

•      it is just and equitable to grant relief,

it may extend the time for delivery of the document for such period as it thinks proper.

[*CA 2006, s 597; SI 2015 No 664, Sch 3*].

**47.36   Transfer of non-cash assets to a public company in the initial period**

Subject to the exceptions below, a public company formed as such must not enter into an agreement:

(a)      with a subscriber to the company's memorandum,

(b)      for the transfer by him to the company, or another, before the end of the company's 'initial period' of one or more 'non-cash assets',

(c)      under which the consideration for the transfer to be given by the company is, at the time of the agreement, equal in value to one-tenth or more of the company's issued share capital

unless the conditions below have been complied with. The company's '*initial period*' means the period of two years beginning with the date of the company being issued with a trading certificate under *CA 2006, s 761* (see 33.3 PUBLIC AND LISTED COMPANIES). See APPENDIX 1 DEFINITIONS for '*non-cash assets*'.

[*CA 2006, s 598(1)–(3)*].

**Conditions**. The conditions are as follows.

(1)      *Independent valuation*

The consideration to be received by the company (ie the asset to be transferred to it or, as the case may be, the advantage to the company of the asset's transfer to another person) and any non-cash consideration to be given by the company must have been independently valued.

The valuer's report must have been made to the company during the six months immediately preceding the date of the agreement.

A copy of the report must have been sent to the 'other party' to the proposed agreement not later than the date on which copies have to be circulated to members under (2) below. The '*other party*' is the person referred to in (*a*) above but if he has received a copy of the report under the provisions in (2) below in his capacity as a member of the company, it is not necessary to send another copy under this provision.

These provisions do not affect any requirement to value any consideration for purposes of **47.32** (non-cash consideration for shares).

[*CA 2006, s 599*].

(2)    *Approval by members*

- The terms of the agreement must have been approved by an ordinary resolution of the company.

- Copies of the valuer's report must have been circulated to the members entitled to notice of the meeting at which the resolution is proposed, not later than the date on which notice of the meeting is given.

- A copy of the proposed resolution must have been sent to the other party to the proposed agreement (ie the person referred to (*a*) above).

[*CA 2006, s 601; SI 2009 No 1941, Sch 1 para 260*].

**Exceptions.** The above provisions do not apply (and no valuer's report is required):

- where it is part of the company's ordinary business to acquire, or arrange for other persons to acquire, assets of a particular description, and the agreement is entered into by the company in the ordinary course of that business; or

- to an agreement entered into by the company under the supervision of the court or of an officer authorised by the court for the purpose.

[*CA 2006, s 598(4), (5)*].

**47.37**  *Valuation and reporting requirements*

The provisions in **47.41** below (general provisions as to independent valuation and report) apply to the valuation and report required under **47.36** above.

The valuer's report must state:

- the consideration to be received by the company, describing the asset in question (specifying the amount to be received in cash) and the consideration to be given by the company (specifying the amount to be given in cash);

- the method and date of valuation; and

- either in the report itself or an accompanying note that:

    (i)    in the case of a valuation made by another person, it appeared to the valuer reasonable to arrange for it to be so made or to accept a valuation so made;

    (ii)   whoever made the valuation, the method of valuation was reasonable in all the circumstances;

    (iii)  it appears to the valuer that there has been no material change in the value of the consideration in question since the valuation; and

    (iv)   on the basis of the valuation, the value of the consideration to be received by the company is not less than the value of the consideration to be given by it.

*Position where consideration given only partly for transfer of asset.* Any reference above or in **47.36** to consideration given for the transfer of an asset includes consideration given partly for its transfer. In such a case:

- the value of any consideration partly so given is to be taken as the proportion of the consideration properly attributable to its transfer;

- the valuer must carry out or arrange for such valuations of anything else as will enable him to determine that proportion; and

- his report must state what valuations have been made for that purpose and also the reason for, and method and date of, any such valuation and any other matters which may be relevant to that determination.

[*CA 2006, s 600*].

**47.38** *Copy report to be delivered to the Registrar of Companies*

A company that has passed a resolution under **47.36**(2) with respect to the transfer of an asset must, within 15 days of doing so, deliver to the Registrar of Companies a copy of the resolution together with the valuer's report.

If a company fails to comply to do so, an offence is committed by the company and every officer of the company who is in default. A person guilty of such an offence is liable, on summary conviction, to a fine not exceeding level 3 on the standard scale and, for continued contravention, to a daily default fine not exceeding one-tenth of level three on the standard scale. See **29.1** OFFENCES AND LEGAL PROCEEDINGS for the standard scale.

[*CA 2006, s 602*].

**47.39** *Company re-registering as a public company*

The provisions in **47.36–47.38** apply with the following adaptations in relation to a company re-registered as a public company.

- The reference in **47.36**(*a*) to a person who is a subscriber to the company's memorandum should be read as a reference to a person who is a member of the company on the date of re-registration.

- The 'initial period' is the period of two years beginning with the date of re-registration.

[*CA 2006, s 603*].

**47.40** *Effect of contravention*

Where a public company enters into an agreement in contravention of **47.36** above and either:

- the other party to the agreement has not received the valuer's report required to be sent to him, or

- there has been some other contravention of the requirements of these provisions that the other party to the agreement knew or ought to have known amounted to a contravention,

the company is entitled to recover from that person any consideration given by it under the agreement, or an amount equal to the value of the consideration at the time of the agreement. The agreement, so far as not carried out, is void.

But if the agreement is or includes an agreement for the allotment of shares in the company, then:

- whether or not the agreement also contravenes **47.32** (valuation of non-cash consideration for shares), this provision does not apply to it in so far as it is for the allotment of shares; and

- the allottee is liable to pay the company an amount equal to the aggregate of the nominal value of the shares and the whole of any premium (or, if the case so requires, so much of that aggregate as is treated as paid up by the consideration), with interest at the 'appropriate rate'. The '*appropriate rate*' of interest is 5% pa or such other rate as specified by statutory instrument.

[*CA 2006, ss 604, 609*].

**47.41 Requirements as to independent valuation**

The provisions in this paragraph apply to the valuation and report required under **47.32** and **47.36**. They also apply to the valuation and report required under *CA 2006, s 93* (see **41.5 Re-Registration**).

[*CA 2006, s 1149*].

**Requirements for being a valuer.** The valuation and report must be made by a person (the valuer) who is eligible for appointment as a statutory auditor under *CA 2006, s 1212* (see **8.10 Audit**) and who meets the independence requirement.

[*CA 2006, s 1150(1)*].

*The independence requirement.* A person meets the independence requirement only if:

- he is not:
    - (i)    an officer or employee of the company; or
    - (ii)   a partner or employee of such a person, or a partnership of which such a person is a partner;
- he is not:
    - (i)    an officer or employee of an 'associated undertaking' of the company; or
    - (ii)   a partner or employee of such a person, or a partnership of which such a person is a partner; and
- there does not exist between:
    - (i)    the person or an 'associate' of his, and
    - (ii)   the company or an associated undertaking of the company,

    a connection of any such description as may be specified by regulations.

For this purposes, an auditor of the company is not regarded as an officer or employee of the company.

'*Associated undertaking*' means:

- a parent undertaking or subsidiary undertaking of the company; or
- a subsidiary undertaking of a parent undertaking of the company.

'*Associate*' means:

(a)   in relation to an individual,
   - (i)    that individual's spouse or civil partner or minor child or step-child;
   - (ii)   any body corporate of which that individual is a director; and
   - (iii)  any employee or partner of that individual;

(b)   in relation to a body corporate,
   - (i)    any body corporate of which that body is a director;
   - (ii)   any body corporate in the same group as that body; and

(iii)    any employee or partner of that body or of any body corporate in the same group;

(c)    in relation to a partnership that is a legal person under the law by which it is governed,

(i)    any body corporate of which that partnership is a director;

(ii)    any employee of or partner in that partnership; and

(iii)    any person who is an associate of a partner in that partnership; and

(d)    in relation to a partnership that is not a legal person under the law by which it is governed, any person who is an associate of any of the partners.

In relation to a limited liability partnership, in (a)–(d) above for 'director' read 'member'.

[*CA 2006, ss 1151, 1152*].

**Use of other valuers.** Where the valuer thinks that it is reasonable for the valuation of the consideration (or part of it) to be made by another person who:

•    appears to him to have the requisite knowledge and experience to value the consideration or that part of it, and

•    is not an officer or employee of:

(i)    the company, or

(ii)    any other body corporate that is that company's subsidiary or holding company or a subsidiary of that company's holding company,

or a partner of or employed by any such officer or employee,

he may arrange for such a valuation, together with a report which will enable him to make his own report under this provision. For these purposes, however, an auditor is not regarded as an officer or employee.

Where the consideration (or part of it) is valued by a person other than the valuer himself, the latter's report must state that fact and must also:

•    state the former's name and what knowledge and experience he has to carry out the valuation; and

•    describe so much of the consideration as was valued by the other person, and the method used to value it, and specify the date of that valuation.

[*CA 2006, s 1150(2)-(4)*].

**Valuer entitled to full disclosure.** A person carrying out a valuation or making a report with respect to any consideration proposed to be accepted or given by a company, is entitled to require from the officers of the company such information and explanation as he thinks necessary to enable him to carry out the valuation or make the report and provide any note required where the valuation is carried out by another person.

Where a person knowingly or recklessly makes a statement (whether orally or in writing) to a person carrying out a valuation or making a report which conveys (or purports to convey) any information or explanation which that person requires and which is misleading, false or deceptive in a material particular, the person making the statement commits an offence. A person guilty of such an offence is liable (i) on conviction on indictment, to imprisonment for a term not exceeding two years or a fine (or both); and (ii) on summary conviction to imprisonment for a term not exceeding twelve months (in Scotland and Northern Ireland, six months) or to a fine not exceeding the statutory maximum (or both). See **29.1** Offences and Legal Proceedings for the statutory maximum.

[*CA 2006, s 1153*].

**47.42  Liability of subsequent holders of shares**

A person (A) who subsequently becomes a 'holder' of shares may incur liable in the following cases.

(a)    Where:

- there has been a contravention of **47.32** (valuation of non-cash consideration for shares), and

- by virtue of that contravention another person is liable to pay any amount under the provision contravened,

then, subject to below, A is also liable to pay that amount (jointly and severally with any other person so liable).

(b)    If a company enters into an agreement in contravention of **47.36** (agreement for transfer of non-cash asset in initial period) and:

- the agreement is or includes an agreement for the allotment of shares in the company,

- A becomes a holder of shares allotted under the agreement, and

- by virtue of the agreement and allotment under it another person is liable to pay an amount under **47.40**,

then, subject to below, A is also liable to pay that amount (jointly and severally with any other person so liable). This applies whether or not the agreement also contravenes **47.32**.

A is exempt from liability under (*a*) and (*b*) above if:

- he is a purchaser for value and, at the time of the purchase, he did not have actual notice of the contravention concerned; or

- he derived title to the shares (directly or indirectly) from a person who became a holder of them after the contravention and who was not liable under the above provision.

'*Holder*', in relation to shares in a company, include any person who has an unconditional right to be included in the company's register of members in respect of those shares or as the case may be to have his name and other particulars delivered to the Registrar of Companies under *CA 2006, Part 8, Chapter 2A* and registered by the Registrar (see **38.9** – Option to keep information on the public register) or to have an instrument of transfer of the shares executed in his favour.

[*CA 2006, s 605; SBEE 2015, s 94, Sch 5, para 21; SI 2016 No 321, Reg 6*].

**47.43  Power of court to grant relief**

A person who is liable to a company:

- under any provision in **47.32–47.42** in relation to payment in respect of any shares in the company, or

- by virtue of an undertaking given to it in, or in connection with, payment for any shares in the company,

may apply to the court to be exempted in whole or in part from the liability.

There are two overriding principles to which the court must have regard in determining whether it should exempt the applicant in whole or in part from any liability. First, a company that has allotted shares should receive money or money's worth at least equal in value to the aggregate of the nominal value of those shares and the whole of any premium or, if the case so requires, so much of that aggregate as is treated as paid up. Subject to that, secondly, where a company would, if the court did not grant the exemption, have more than one remedy against a particular person, it should be for the company to decide which remedy it should remain entitled to pursue. Because these are 'overriding principles', a court will need very good reasons to accept that it is just and equitable to exempt an applicant from liability where the company has not received sufficient value (*Bradford Investments plc (No 2), Re* [1991] BCLC 688, [1991] BCC 379).

Otherwise, the court may exempt the applicant from the liability only if and to the extent that it appears to the court just and equitable to do so. In reaching its decision, the court must have regard to the following (except in relation to a decision whether to grant relief in respect of a liability for interest arising before 1 October 2009).

Where (*a*) above applies,

- whether the applicant has paid, or is liable to pay, any amount in respect of:

    (i)    any other liability arising in relation to those shares under any provision in **47.32–47.42** relating to independent valuation of non-cash consideration or **47.23–47.27** relating to payment for shares; or

    (ii)   any liability arising by virtue of any undertaking given in or in connection with payment for those shares;

- whether any person other than the applicant has paid or is likely to pay, whether in pursuance of any order of the court or otherwise, any such amount; and

- whether the applicant or any other person:

    (i)    has performed in whole or in part, or is likely so to perform, any such undertaking; or

    (ii)   has done, or is likely to do, any other thing in payment or part payment for the shares.

Where (*b*) above applies,

- whether the applicant has paid or is liable to pay any amount in respect of liability arising in relation to the shares under any provision in **47.32–47.42** relating to independent valuation of non-cash consideration or **47.23–47.27** relating to payment for shares; or

- whether any person other than the applicant has paid, or is likely to pay, whether in pursuance of any order of the court or otherwise, any such amount.

[*CA 2006, s 606(1)–(4)*].

**Proceedings against a contributor.** Certain powers are conferred on the court where a person brings proceedings against another (the '*contributor*') for a contribution in respect of liability to a company arising under any provision relating to payment for shares in

47.23–47.27 or any provision relating to independent valuation of non-cash consideration in 47.32–47.42 and it appears to the court that the contributor is liable to make such a contribution. The court may, if and to the extent that it appears to be just and equitable to do so, having regard to the respective culpability (in respect of the liability to the company) of the contributor and the person bringing the proceedings:

- exempt the contributor in whole or in part from his liability to make such a contribution; or

- order the contributor to make a larger contribution than, but for this provision, he would be liable to make.

[*CA 2006, s 606(5)*].

Where a person is liable to a company under **47.40**, the court may, on application, exempt him in whole or in part from that liability if and to the extent that it appears to the court to be just and equitable to do so having regard to any benefit accruing to the company by virtue of anything done by him towards the carrying out of the agreement.

[*CA 2006, s 606(6)*].

## 47.44 Penalty for contravention

In relation to consideration received in pursuance of an obligation entered into on or after 1 October 2009, where a company contravenes the requirements of **47.32** or **47.36**, an offence is committed by the company, and every officer of the company who is in default. A person guilty of such an offence is liable (i) on conviction on indictment, to a fine; and (ii) on summary conviction, to a fine not exceeding the statutory maximum. See **29.1** OFFENCES AND LEGAL PROCEEDINGS for the statutory maximum.

[*CA 2006, s 607*].

## 47.45 Enforceability of undertakings to do work, etc

Without prejudice to **47.43**, where:

- an undertaking to do work or perform services or to do any other thing is given by any person, in or in connection with payment for shares in a company, and

- that undertaking is enforceable by the company apart from any of the provisions in **47.32–47.43**

the undertaking is so enforceable notwithstanding that there has been a contravention in relation to it of any provision relating to payment for shares in **47.23–47.30** or any provision relating to independent valuation of non-cash consideration in **47.32–47.43**.

[*CA 2006, s 608*].

## 47.46 ALTERATION OF SHARE CAPITAL

A limited company having a share capital can only alter its share capital by:

- increasing its share capital by allotting new shares (see **47.8**);

- reducing its share capital (see **47.51**);

- sub-dividing or consolidate all or any of its share capital (see **47.47**); or

- reconverting stock into shares (see **47.48**).

The company may redenominate all or any of its shares in accordance **47.49** and may reduce its share capital in connection with such a redenomination (see **47.50**).

[*CA 2006, s 617(1)–(4)*].

Nothing in the above provisions affects:

- the power of a company to purchase its own shares or to redeem shares (see **34** PURCHASE OF OWN SHARES);

- the power of a company to purchase its own shares in pursuance of an order of the court under:

  (i)   *CA 2006, s 98* (application to court to cancel resolution for re-registration as a private company, see **41.9** RE-REGISTRATION);

  (ii)  *CA 2006, s 721(6)* (powers of court on objection to redemption or purchase of shares out of capital, **34.18** PURCHASE OF OWN SHARES);

  (iii) *CA 2006, s 759* (remedial order in case of breach of prohibition of public offers by private company, see **47.22**), or

  (iv)  *CA 2006, Pt 30* (protection of members against unfair prejudice, see **26.10** MEMBERS);

- the forfeiture of shares, or the acceptance of shares surrendered in lieu, in pursuance of the company's articles, for failure to pay any sum payable in respect of the shares;

- the cancellation of shares under *CA 2006, s 662* (duty to cancel shares held by or for a public company, see **34.28** PURCHASE OF OWN SHARES); or

- the power of a company to:

  (i)   to enter into a compromise or arrangement in accordance with *CA 2006, Pt 26* (arrangements and reconstructions, see **35.1** to **35.5** RECONSTRUCTIONS AND MERGERS), or

  (ii)  to do anything required to comply with an order of the court on an application under that *Part*.

[*CA 2006, s 617(5)*].

**47.47 Sub-division or consolidation of shares**

A limited company having a share capital may:

- sub-divide its shares, or any of them, into shares of a smaller nominal amount than its existing shares; or

- consolidate and divide all or any of its share capital into shares of a larger nominal amount than its existing shares.

In any sub-division, consolidation or division of shares, the proportion between the amount paid and the amount (if any) unpaid on each resulting share must be the same as it was in the case of the share from which that share is derived.

[*CA 2006, s 618(1)(2)*].

**Authorisation**. A company may only exercise a power to sub-divide or consolidate if its members have passed a resolution authorising it to do so. The resolution may authorise the company to exercise:

- more than one of the powers;

- a power on more than one occasion; or

- a power at a specified time or in specified circumstances.

The articles may exclude or restrict the exercise of any power conferred by *CA 2006, s 618*. [*CA 2006, s 618(3)–(5)*].

Where standard articles have been adopted, see:

- *Table A, 1985, Regs 32, 33*

- *Model Articles, Art 69* (public companies)

Set out in APPENDIX 4 STANDARD ARTICLES OF ASSOCIATION.

**Notice to Registrar of Companies**. If a company exercises the power conferred above, it must, within one month after doing so, give notice to the Registrar of Companies, specifying the shares affected. The notice must be accompanied by a statement of capital giving details of the following with respect to the company's share capital immediately following the exercise of the power.

- The total number of shares of the company.

- The aggregate nominal value of those shares and the aggregate amount (if any) unpaid on those shares (whether on account of their nominal value or by way of premium).

- For each class of shares:

    (i) particulars of any voting rights attached to the shares, including rights that arise only in certain circumstances;

    (ii) particulars of any rights attached to the shares, as respects dividends, to participate in a distribution;

    (iii) particulars of any rights attached to the shares, as respects capital, to participate in a distribution (including on a winding up);

    (iv) whether the shares are to be redeemed or are liable to be redeemed at the option of the company or the shareholder;

    (v) the total number of shares of that class; and

    (vi) the aggregate nominal value of shares of that class.

If default is made in complying with this requirement, an offence is committed by the company and every officer of the company who is in default. A person guilty of such an offence is liable, on summary conviction, to a fine not exceeding level 3 on the standard scale and, for continued contravention, a daily default fine not exceeding one-tenth of the standard scale. See **29.1 OFFENCES AND LEGAL PROCEEDINGS** for the standard scale.

[*CA 2006, s 619; SBEE 2015, s 97, Sch 6, para 6; SI 2009 No 388, Art 2; SI 2016 No 321, Reg 6*].

**47.48 Reconversion of stock into shares**

A limited company that has converted paid-up shares into stock (before the repeal by *CA 2006* of the power to do so) may reconvert that stock into paid-up shares of any nominal value.

This power may only be exercised if its members have passed an ordinary resolution authorising it to do so. The resolution may authorise the company to exercise the power:

- on more than one occasion; or

- at a specified time or in specified circumstances.

[*CA 2006, s 620*].

**Notice to Registrar of Companies.** If a company exercises the power conferred above, it must, within one month after doing so, give notice to the Registrar of Companies, specifying the stock affected. The notice must be accompanied by a statement of capital giving details of the following with respect to the company's share capital immediately following the exercise of the power.

- The total number of shares of the company.

- The aggregate nominal value of those shares and the aggregate amount (if any) unpaid on those shares (whether on account of their nominal value or by way of premium).

- For each class of shares:

    (i)     particulars of any voting rights attached to the shares, including rights that arise only in certain circumstances;

    (ii)    particulars of any rights attached to the shares, as respects dividends, to participate in a distribution;

    (iii)   particulars of any rights attached to the shares, as respects capital, to participate in a distribution (including on a winding up);

    (iv)    whether the shares are to be redeemed or are liable to be redeemed at the option of the company or the shareholder;

    (v)     the total number of shares of that class; and

    (vi)    the aggregate nominal value of shares of that class.

If default is made in complying with this requirement, an offence is committed by the company and every officer of the company who is in default. A person guilty of such an offence is liable, on summary conviction, to a fine not exceeding level 3 on the standard scale and, for continued contravention, a daily default fine not exceeding one-tenth of the standard scale. See **29.1** OFFENCES AND LEGAL PROCEEDINGS for the standard scale.

[*CA 2006, s 621; SBEE 2015, s 97, Sch 6, para 7; SI 2009 No 388, Art 2; SI 2016 No 321, Reg 6*].

**47.49 Redenomination of share capital**

Subject to its articles (which may prohibit or restrict the exercise of the power), a limited company having a share capital may, by resolution, 'redenominate' its share capital or any class of its share capital, ie convert shares from having a fixed nominal value in one currency to having a fixed nominal value in another currency. The resolution may specify conditions which must be met before the redenomination takes effect.

The conversion must be made at a spot rate of exchange specified in the resolution. The rate must be either:

- a rate prevailing on a day specified in the resolution, or

- a rate determined by taking the average of rates prevailing on each consecutive day of a period specified in the resolution

and the day or period specified must be within the period of 28 days ending on the day before the resolution is passed.

Redenomination in accordance with a resolution under these provisions takes effect on the day on which the resolution is passed or on such later day as determined in accordance with the resolution.

A resolution under this provision lapses if the redenomination for which it provides has not taken effect at the end of the period of 28 days beginning on the date on which it is passed.

*CA 2006, ss 29, 30* (resolutions affecting a company's constitution, see **14.10** CONSTITUTION – MEMORANDUM AND ARTICLES) apply to a resolution under this provision.

[*CA 2006, s 622*].

**Calculation of new nominal values.** For each class of share, the new nominal value of each share is calculated as follows.

(1)   Take the aggregate of the old nominal values of all the shares of that class.

(2)   Translate that amount into the new currency at the rate of exchange specified in the resolution.

(3)   Divide that amount by the number of shares in the class.

[*CA 2006, s 623*].

**Effect of redenomination.** The redenomination of shares does not affect any rights or obligations of members under the company's constitution, or any restrictions affecting members under the company's constitution. In particular, it does not affect entitlement to dividends (including entitlement to dividends in a particular currency), voting rights or any liability in respect of amounts unpaid on shares. For this purpose, the company's constitution includes the terms on which any shares of the company are allotted or held.

Subject to this, references to the old nominal value of the shares in any agreement or statement, or in any deed, instrument or document, are (unless the context otherwise requires) be read after the resolution takes effect as references to the new nominal value of the shares.

[*CA 2006, s 624*].

**Notice to Registrar of Companies.** A company must, within one month after redenomination, give notice to the Registrar of Companies specifying the shares redenominated and stating the date on which the resolution was passed. The notice must be accompanied by a statement of capital giving details of the following with respect to the company's share capital as redenominated by the resolution.

- The total number of shares of the company

- The aggregate nominal value of those shares and the aggregate amount (if any) unpaid on those shares (whether on account of their nominal value or by way of premium).

- For each class of shares:

    (i)   particulars of any voting rights attached to the shares, including rights that arise only in certain circumstances;

(ii)    particulars of any rights attached to the shares, as respects dividends, to participate in a distribution;

(iii)   particulars of any rights attached to the shares, as respects capital, to participate in a distribution (including on a winding up);

(iv)    whether the shares are to be redeemed or are liable to be redeemed at the option of the company or the shareholder;

(v)     the total number of shares of that class; and

(vi)    the aggregate nominal value of shares of that class.

If default is made in complying with this requirement, an offence is committed by the company and every officer of the company who is in default. A person guilty of such an offence is liable, on summary conviction, to a fine not exceeding level 3 on the standard scale and, for continued contravention, a daily default fine not exceeding one-tenth of level 3 on the standard scale. See 29.1 OFFENCES AND LEGAL PROCEEDINGS for the standard scale.

[*CA 2006, s 625; SBEE 2015, s 97, Sch 6, para 8; SI 2009 No 388, Art 2; SI 2016 No 321, Reg 6*].

**47.50**  *Reduction of capital in connection with redenomination*

A limited company that passes a resolution under **47.49** may, for the purpose of adjusting the nominal values of the redenominated shares to obtain values that are, in the opinion of the company, more suitable, reduce its share capital. The reduction of capital:

•     requires a special resolution of the company (which must be passed within three months of the resolution effecting the redenomination); and

•     does not extinguish or reduce any liability in respect of share capital not paid up.

The amount by which share capital is reduced must not exceed 10% of the nominal value of the company's allotted share capital immediately after the reduction.

The provisions in **47.51–47.58** (reduction of share capital) do not apply to a reduction of capital under this provision.

[*CA 2006, s 626*].

**Notice to Registrar of Companies**. Where such a resolution is passed, the company must, within 15 days after the resolution is passed, give notice to the Registrar of Companies stating the date of the resolution and the date of the resolution to redenominate share capital under **47.49** in connection with which it was passed. This is in addition to the copies of the resolutions themselves that are required to be delivered to the Registrar of Companies under **14.10** CONSTITUTION – MEMORANDUM AND ARTICLES.

The notice must be accompanied by a statement of capital giving details of the following with respect to the company's share capital as reduced by the resolution.

•     The total number of shares of the company.

•     The aggregate nominal value of those shares and the aggregate amount (if any) unpaid on those shares (whether on account of their nominal value or by way of premium.

•     For each class of shares:

(i)     particulars of any voting rights attached to the shares, including rights that arise only in certain circumstances;

(ii)     particulars of any rights attached to the shares, as respects dividends, to participate in a distribution;

(iii)    particulars of any rights attached to the shares, as respects capital, to participate in a distribution (including on a winding up);

(iv)    whether the shares are to be redeemed or are liable to be redeemed at the option of the company or the shareholder;

(v)     the total number of shares of that class; and

(vi)    the aggregate nominal value of shares of that class.

On receipt, the Registrar of Companies must register the notice and the statement. The reduction of capital is not effective until those documents are registered.

The company must also deliver to the Registrar of Companies, within 15 days after the resolution is passed, a statement by the directors confirming that the reduction in share capital does not exceed 10% of nominal value of allotted shares immediately after reduction.

If default is made in complying with any of these requirements, an offence is committed by the company and every officer of the company who is in default. A person guilty of such an offence is liable (i) on conviction on indictment to a fine; and (ii) on summary conviction, to a fine not exceeding the statutory maximum. See **29.1** OFFENCES AND LEGAL PROCEEDINGS for the statutory maximum.

[*CA 2006, s 627; SBEE 2015, s 97, Sch 6, para 9; SI 2009 No 388, Art 2; SI 2016 No 321, Reg 6*].

**Redenomination reserve**. The amount by which a company's share capital is reduced must be transferred to a reserve, called the '*redenomination reserve*'. This reserve may be applied by the company in paying up shares to be allotted to members as fully paid bonus shares. But, subject to that, the provisions of the *Companies Acts* relating to the reduction of a company's share capital apply as if the redenomination reserve were paid-up share capital of the company.

[*CA 2006, s 628*].

## 47.51  REDUCTION OF SHARE CAPITAL

Subject to any provision of the company's articles (or, before 1 October 2009, the company's memorandum) restricting or prohibiting the reduction of the company's share capital, a limited company having a share capital may reduce its share capital:

(a)     in the case of a private company limited by shares, by special resolution supported by a solvency statement (see **47.52–47.54**);

(b)     in any case, by special resolution confirmed by the court (see **47.55–47.57**).

A company may not reduce its capital under (*a*) above if, as a result of the reduction, there would no longer be any member of the company holding shares other than redeemable shares.

A company may not reduce its share capital under (a) or (b) as part of a scheme by virtue of which a person, or a person together with its associates, is to acquire all the shares in the company or (where there is more than one class of shares in a company) all the shares of one or more classes, in each case other than shares that are already held by that person or its associates. This does not apply to a scheme under which

(a)    the company is to have a new parent undertaking;

(b)    all or substantially all of the members of the company become members of the parent undertaking; and

(c)    the members of the company are to hold proportions of the equity share capital of the parent undertaking in the same or substantially the same proportions as they hold the equity share capital of the company.

For the purposes of the above

'associate' has the meaning given by *CA 2006, s 988* (meaning of 'associate'), reading references in that section to an offeror as references to the person acquiring the shares in the company; and

'scheme' means a compromise or arrangement sanctioned by the court under *CA 2006, Part 26* (arrangements and reconstructions).

But subject to those provisions a company may reduce its share capital under *CA 2006, s 641* in any way and, in particular, it may:

• extinguish or reduce the liability on any of its shares in respect of share capital not paid up (see *Doloswella Rubber and Tea Estates Ltd and Reduced, Re* [1917] 1 Ch 213, 86 LJ Ch 223); or

• either with or without extinguishing or reducing liability on any of its shares:

    (i)    cancel any paid-up share capital that is lost or unrepresented by available assets; or

    (ii)    repay any paid-up share capital in excess of the company's wants.

    See *Westburn Sugar Refineries Ltd, ex p* [1951] AC 625, [1951] 1 All ER 881, HL; *Thomas De La Rue & Co Ltd and Reduced, Re* [1911] 2 Ch 361, 81 LJ Ch 59; and *Re Jupiter House Investments (Cambridge) Ltd* [1985] 1 WLR 975, [1985] BCLC 222.

The special resolution may not provide for a reduction of share capital to take effect later than the date on which the resolution has effect.

[*CA 2006, s 641; SI 2015 No 472, Reg 3*].

Where the company has adopted standard articles, see *Table A, 1985, Reg 34*, set out in APPENDIX 4 STANDARD ARTICLES OF ASSOCIATION.

**47.52 Private companies: reduction of capital supported by a solvency statement**

A resolution for reducing share capital of a private company under **47.51**(*a*) is supported by a solvency statement if:

• the directors of the company make a statement of the solvency of the company in accordance with **47.53** not more than 15 days before the date on which the resolution is passed; and

• the resolution and solvency statement are registered in accordance with **47.53**.

Where the resolution is proposed:

• as a written resolution, a copy of the solvency statement must be sent or submitted to every eligible member at or before the time at which the proposed resolution is sent or submitted to him; and

- at a general meeting, a copy of the solvency statement must be made available for inspection by members of the company throughout that meeting.

The validity of a resolution is not affected by a failure to comply with this requirement.

[*CA 2006, s 642*].

**47.53** *Solvency statement*

A solvency statement is a statement that each of the directors:

- has formed the opinion, as regards the company's situation at the date of the statement, that there is no ground on which the company could then be found to be unable to pay (or otherwise discharge) its debts; and

- has also formed the opinion:

    (i)    if it is intended to commence the winding up of the company within twelve months of that date, that the company will be able to pay (or otherwise discharge) its debts in full within twelve months of the commencement of the winding up; or

    (ii)   in any other case, that the company will be able to pay (or otherwise discharge) its debts as they fall due during the year immediately following that date.

In forming those opinions, the directors must take into account all of the company's liabilities (including any contingent or prospective liabilities).

The solvency statement must be in writing in the prescribed form and must:

- state the date on which it is made;

- state the name of each director of the company;

- indicate that it is a solvency statement for the purposes of *CA 2006, s 642*; and

- be signed by each of the directors of the company.

*Offence.* If the directors make a solvency statement without having reasonable grounds for the opinions expressed in it, and the statement is delivered to the Registrar of Companies, an offence is committed by every director who is in default. A person guilty of such an offence is liable (i) on conviction on indictment, to imprisonment for a term not exceeding two years or a fine (or both); and (ii) on summary conviction, to imprisonment for a term not exceeding twelve months (in Scotland and Northern Ireland, six months) or to a fine not exceeding the statutory maximum (or both). See **29.1** OFFENCES AND LEGAL PROCEEDINGS for the statutory maximum.

[*CA 2006, s 643; SI 2008 No 1915, Art 2*].

**47.54** *Registration of resolution and supporting documents*

Within 15 days after the resolution for reducing share capital is passed, the company must deliver the following documents to the Registrar of Companies.

(a)    A copy of the resolution (see **14.10** CONSTITUTION – MEMORANDUM AND ARTICLES).

(b)    A copy of the solvency statement under **47.53**.

(c)    A statement of capital which must state, with respect to the company's share capital as reduced by the resolution:

- The total number of shares of the company.

- The aggregate nominal value of those shares and the aggregate amount (if any) unpaid on those shares (whether on account of their nominal value or by way of premium).

- For each class of shares:

    (i)     particulars of any voting rights attached to the shares, including rights that arise only in certain circumstances;

    (ii)    particulars of any rights attached to the shares, as respects dividends, to participate in a distribution;

    (iii)   particulars of any rights attached to the shares, as respects capital, to participate in a distribution (including on a winding up);

    (iv)    whether the shares are to be redeemed or are liable to be redeemed at the option of the company or the shareholder;

    (v)     the total number of shares of that class; and

    (vi)    the aggregate nominal value of shares of that class.

(d)     A statement by the directors confirming that the solvency statement was:

- made not more than 15 days before the date on which the resolution was passed; and

- provided to members in accordance with **47.52**.

The Registrar of Companies must register the documents delivered to him under (*b*)–(*d*) above and the resolution does not take effect until those documents are registered.

The validity of a resolution is not affected by a failure to deliver the documents under (*b*)–(*e*) above within the time specified.

*Offences.* If the company delivers to the Registrar of Companies a solvency statement that was not provided to members in accordance with **47.52**, an offence is committed by every officer of the company who is in default. Additionally, if default is made in complying with the above requirements as to delivery of documents to the Registrar of Companies, an offence is committed by the company and every officer of the company who is in default. A person guilty of an offence under either of these provisions is liable (i) on conviction on indictment, to a fine; and (ii) on summary conviction, to a fine not exceeding the statutory maximum. See **29.1** Offences and Legal Proceedings for the statutory maximum.

[*CA 2006, s 644; SBEE 2015, s 97, Sch 6, para 10; SI 2009 No 388, Art 2; SI 2016 No 321, Reg 6*].

### 47.55 Reduction of capital confirmed by the court

Where a company has passed a resolution for reducing share capital, it may apply to the court for an order confirming the reduction.

[*CA 2006, s 645(1)*].

Where such an application is made the provisions in this paragraph and in **47.56** and **47.57** apply.

**Creditors entitled to object to reduction**. If the proposed reduction of capital involves either:

- diminution of liability in respect of unpaid share capital, or

- the payment to a shareholder of any paid-up share capital,

and in any other case where the court directs, every creditor of the company who:

- at a date fixed by the court, is entitled to any debt or claim that would be admissible in a winding up of the company commencing on that date, and

- can show that there is a real likelihood that the reduction would result in the company being unable to discharge his debt or claim when it fell due

is entitled to object to the reduction of capital.

The court must settle a list of creditors entitled to object. For that purpose, it must ascertain, as far as possible without requiring an application from any creditor, the names of those creditors and the nature and amount of their debts or claims. It may then publish notices fixing a time within which creditors not entered on the list are to claim to be so entered or are to be excluded from the right of objecting to the reduction of capital.

If a creditor entered on the list whose debt or claim is not discharged (or has not determined) does not consent to the reduction, the court may, if it thinks fit, dispense with the consent of that creditor if the company secures payment of his debt or claim. For this purpose, the debt or claim must be secured by appropriating (as the court may direct) the full amount of the debt or claim or, if the company does not admit the full amount (or the amount is contingent or not ascertained) an amount fixed by the court.

[*CA 2006, ss 645(2)(4), 646; SI 2009 No 2022, Reg 3*].

The court may, however,

- direct that this is not to apply; or

- if, having regard to any special circumstances it thinks proper to do so, direct that this is not to apply as regards any class or classes of creditors.

[*CA 2006, ss 645(2)(3), 646*].

(In most schemes for reduction of capital this power will be used because the company will either have agreed the capital reduction with creditors or secured its liabilities by means of a guarantee.)

See also *Re Lucania Temperance Billiard Halls (London) Ltd* [1966] Ch 98, [1965] 3 All ER 879 and *Re Antwerp Waterworks Co Ltd* [1931] WN 186, 172 LT Jo 75.

As well as the position of creditors the court must also consider present and future shareholders (see *Poole v National Bank of China Ltd* [1907] AC 229, 76 LJ Ch 458, HL). See also *Ratners Group plc, Re [1988] BCLC 685*, 4 BCC 293. It must carefully scrutinise any scheme which does not provide for uniform treatment of shareholders with similar rights and must be satisfied that it is not unjust or inequitable, although this does not mean that it cannot sanction such a scheme (*British and American Trustee and Finance Corpn v Couper* [1894] AC 399, HL).

*Offences in connection with list of creditors.* If an officer of the company:

- intentionally or recklessly:

  (i) conceals the name of a creditor entitled to object to the reduction of capital, or

 (ii)    misrepresents the nature or amount of the debt or claim of a creditor, or

- is knowingly concerned in any such concealment or misrepresentation,

he commits an offence. A person guilty of such an offence is liable (i) on conviction on indictment, to a fine; and (ii) on summary conviction, to a fine not exceeding the statutory maximum. See **29.1** Offences and Legal Proceedings for the statutory maximum.

[*CA 2006, s 647*].

**Court order confirming reduction**. The court may make an order confirming the reduction of capital on such terms and conditions as it thinks fit. But it must not confirm the reduction unless it is satisfied, with respect to every creditor of the company who is entitled to object to the reduction of capital that either:

- his consent to the reduction has been obtained; or

- his debt or claim has been discharged, or has determined or has been secured.

Where the court confirms the reduction, it may order the company to publish the reasons for reduction of capital or any other information in connection with the reduction where it thinks expedient to give proper information to the public. This can include the causes that led to the reduction.

The court may also, if for any special reason it thinks proper to do so, make an order directing that the company must, during a period commencing on or at any time after the date of the order, add to its name as its last words the words 'and reduced'. If such an order is made, those words are, until the end of the period specified, deemed to be part of the company's name.

[*CA 2006, s 648*].

**47.56** *Registration of order and statement of capital*

The Registrar of Companies, on production of an order of the court confirming the reduction of a company's share capital and the delivery of a copy of the order and of a statement of capital (approved by the court), must register the order and statement. This is subject to the provisions set out in **47.57**. Notice of the registration must be published in such manner as the court may direct.

The statement of capital must give details of the following with respect to the company's share capital as altered by the order.

- The total number of shares of the company.

- The aggregate nominal value of those shares and the aggregate amount (if any) unpaid on those shares (whether on account of their nominal value or by way of premium).

- For each class of shares:

 (i)    particulars of any voting rights attached to the shares, including rights that arise only in certain circumstances;

 (ii)    particulars of any rights attached to the shares, as respects dividends, to participate in a distribution;

 (iii)    particulars of any rights attached to the shares, as respects capital, to participate in a distribution (including on a winding up);

 (iv)    whether the shares are to be redeemed or are liable to be redeemed at the option of the company or the shareholder;

(v)     the total number of shares of that class; and

(vi)    the aggregate nominal value of shares of that class.

The resolution for reducing share capital, as confirmed by the court's order, takes effect:

• in the case of a reduction of share capital that forms part of a compromise or arrangement sanctioned by the court under *CA 2006, Pt 26* (arrangements and reconstructions):

  (i)    on delivery of the order and statement of capital to the Registrar of Companies; or

  (ii)   if the court so orders, on the registration of the order and statement of capital; and

• in any other case, on the registration of the order and statement of capital.

*Certification.* The Registrar of Companies must also certify the registration of the order and statement of capital. The certificate must be signed by the Registrar (or authenticated by the Registrar's official seal) and is conclusive evidence that the requirements of CA 2006 with respect to the reduction of share capital have been complied with and that the company's share capital is as stated in the statement of capital. [*CA 2006, ss 644, 649; SBEE 2015, s 97, Sch 6, paras 10, 11; SI 2009 No 388, Art 2; SI 2016 No 321, Reg 6*].

### 47.57 Public company reducing capital below the authorised minimum

Where the court makes an order confirming a reduction of a public company's capital that has the effect of bringing the nominal value of its allotted share capital below the authorised minimum (see **29.4 OFFENCES AND LEGAL PROCEEDINGS**), the Registrar of Companies must not register the order unless either:

• the court so directs; or

• the company is first re-registered as a private company.

[*CA 2006, s 650*].

In these circumstances, the court may authorise the company to be re-registered as a private company without its having passed the special resolution otherwise required by *CA 2006, s 97* (see **41.8 RE-REGISTRATION**). If it does so, the court must specify in the order the changes to the company's name and articles to be made in connection with the re-registration. The company may then be re-registered as a private company if an application to that effect is delivered to the Registrar of Companies together with:

• a copy of the court's order; and

• notice of the company's name, and a copy of the company's articles, as altered by the court's order.

The Registrar of Companies must issue a certificate of incorporation stating that it is issued on re-registration and the date on which it is issued. On the issue of the certificate:

• the company becomes a private company; and

• the changes in the company's name and articles take effect.

The certificate is conclusive evidence that the requirements of *CA 2006* as to re-registration have been complied with.

## 47.57 Shares

[*CA 2006, s 651*].

Where a public company reduces its share capital to less than the authorised minimum but immediately increases it again to more than authorised minimum by a resolution which takes effect before, or at the same time as, the reduction resolution, the company is not obliged to re-register as a private company (*Re MB Group Ltd* [1989] BCLC 672, 5 BCC 684).

## 47.58 Effect of reduction of capital

(1) *Liability of members generally*

Subject to (2) below, where a company's share capital is reduced, a member of the company (past or present) is not liable in respect of any share to any call or contribution exceeding in amount the difference (if any) between:

- the nominal amount of the share as notified to the Registrar of Companies in the statement of capital delivered under **47.54** or **47.56**; and

- the amount paid on the share or the reduced amount (if any) which is deemed to have been paid on it, as the case may be.

Nothing in the above affects the rights of the contributories among themselves. [*CA 2006, s 652*].

(2) *Liability of members to creditor in case of omission from list of creditors*

Where, in the case of a reduction of capital confirmed by the court under **47.55**,

- a creditor entitled to object to the reduction of share capital is, by reason of his ignorance of the proceedings for reduction of share capital or of their nature and effect with respect to his debt or claim, not entered on the list of creditors, and

- after the reduction of capital the company is unable (within the meaning of the *Insolvency Act 1986, s 123* or *Insolvency (Northern Ireland) Order 1989, Art 103*) to pay the amount of his debt or claim,

every member of the company at the date on which the resolution for reducing capital took effect (see **47.56**) is liable to contribute for the payment of the debt or claim an amount not exceeding that which he would have been liable to contribute if the company had commenced to be wound up on the day before that date.

If the company is wound up, the court may, on the application of the creditor in question and proof of his ignorance,

- settle a list of persons liable to contribute under this provision; and

- make and enforce calls and orders on them as if they were ordinary contributories in a winding up.

[*CA 2006, s 653*].

## 47.59 Treatment of reserve arising from reduction of capital

A reserve arising from the reduction of a company's share capital is not distributable with the following exceptions.

(a)     Where an unlimited company reduces its share capital.

(b)     If a private company limited by shares reduces its share capital and the reduction is supported by a solvency statement but has not been the subject of an application to the court for an order confirming it.

(c) If a limited company having a share capital reduces its share capital and the reduction is confirmed by order of the court.

In such cases, the reserve arising from the reduction is to be treated for the purposes of *CA 2006, Pt 23* (distributions) as a realised profit (unless, where (c) applies, the court orders otherwise). The exceptions do not, however, affect the operation of anything to the contrary in:

- an order of, or undertaking to, the court;

- the resolution for, or any other resolution relevant to, the reduction; or

- the company's memorandum or articles of association.

[*CA 2006, s 645; SI 2008 No 1915, Art 3*].

## 47.60 MAINTENANCE OF CAPITAL

There are a number of provisions in *CA 2006* which seek to ensure that a company's capital is maintained other than by being lost in the ordinary course of business. This is because the issued share capital is the ultimate fund for payment of the company's creditors. See *Exchange Banking Co, Re, Flitcroft's Case* (1882) 21 Ch D 519, CA.

(1) **Allotment of shares at a discount**

A company's shares must not be allotted at a discount. See **47.24**.

(2) **Company not to acquire own shares**

Subject to certain exceptions, a company must not acquire its own shares whether by purchase, subscription or otherwise. See **34.1** PURCHASE OF OWN SHARES for details and exceptions.

(3) **Acquisition of shares by company's nominee**

With certain exceptions, shares issued to or acquired by a nominee of the company are treated as held by the nominee on his own account. See **34.27** PURCHASE OF OWN SHARES.

## 47.61 Duty of directors to call meeting on serious loss of capital

Where the net assets of a public company are half or less of its called-up share capital, the directors must, within 28 days from the earliest date on which that fact is known to any director, call a general meeting of the company, for a date not later than 56 days from that date, to consider what (if any) steps should be taken to deal with the situation.

In default, each director who knowingly authorises or permits the failure, or after the 56-day period knowingly authorises or permits the failure to continue, commits an offence. A person guilty of such an offence is liable (i) on conviction on indictment, to a fine; and (ii) on summary conviction, to a fine not exceeding the statutory maximum. See **29.1** OFFENCES AND LEGAL PROCEEDINGS for the statutory maximum.

Nothing in *CA 2006, s 656* authorises the consideration at a convened meeting of any matter that could not have been considered at that meeting apart from (this) *section 656*.

[*CA 2006, s 656*].

**47.62    Shares**

**47.62  BONUS ISSUES**

A company may 'capitalise' its profits by applying them in wholly or partly paying up unissued shares in the company to be allotted to members as fully or partly paid bonus shares. [*CA 2006, s 853(3)*]. The procedure is known as a 'bonus issue' or alternatively a 'scrip issue' or 'capitalisation issue'. To make a bonus issue, a company must be authorised by its articles to do so. Where standard articles have been adopted, see:

- *Table A, 1985, Reg 110*

- *Model Articles, Art 36* (private companies

- *Model Articles, Art 78* (public companies)

set out in APPENDIX 4 STANDARD ARTICLES OF ASSOCIATION.

In practice, the bonus shares will generally be fully paid. If this is a requirement under the articles, any alteration of the articles to allow for partly-paid bonus shares would require written agreement by a member before he became liable for any unpaid share capital. [*CA 2006, s 25*]. See **14.7** CONSTITUTION – MEMORANDUM AND ARTICLES.

**Effect of *CA 2006* provisions.** The general rule that shares, and any premium payable on them, must be paid up in money or money's worth does not prevent a company from allotting bonus shares to its members. [*CA 2006 s 582(2)*]. However, like other shares, bonus shares must not be allotted at a discount (*Welton v Saffery* [1897] AC 299, HL). See **47.24**.

The provisions in **47.32** which require a public company allotting shares otherwise than in cash to have the consideration independently valued do not apply to bonus shares. See **47.33(1)**.

**Return of allotments.** Where a company makes any allotment of shares (including a bonus issue), it must within one month thereafter deliver to the Registrar of Companies a return in the prescribed form. See **47.12**.

**47.63  Funds available for making bonus issues**

A company's profits available for distribution are the excess of its accumulated, realised profits over its accumulated, realised losses. [*CA 2006, s 830(2)*]. However, an issue of fully or partly paid bonus shares is not a distribution for this purpose [*CA 2006, s 829(2)(a)*] and *unrealised* profits may therefore be utilised for paying up bonus shares, although they cannot be applied in paying up bonus *debentures* [*CA 2006, s 849*]. In addition, the share premium account [*CA 2006, s 610(3)*] and the capital redemption reserve [*CA 2006, s 733(5)*] may also be utilised in paying up fully paid bonus shares (but not debentures).

Where standard articles have been adopted, see:

- *Table A, 1985, Reg 110*

- *Model Articles, Art 36* (private companies)

- *Model Articles, Art 78* (public companies)

set out in APPENDIX 4 STANDARD ARTICLES OF ASSOCIATION.

Where, immediately before 22 December 1980 (1 July 1983 in Northern Ireland) a company was authorised by a provision of its articles to apply unrealised profits in paying up in full or in part unissued shares to be allotted to members as fully or partly paid bonus shares, the provision continues (subject to any alteration in the articles) as authority for those profits to be applied after that date.

[*CA 2006, s 848*].

## 47.64 RIGHTS ISSUES

In order to raise new capital, a company may make a rights issue to existing members or debenture-holders by which they are given the right to subscribe for new securities in a fixed proportion to their existing holdings. The price at which the new securities are offered is normally below the market price. It should be noted that under *CA 2006, ss 560–577* there are pre-emption provisions restricting the allotment of shares to persons other than existing members of the company (see **47.13–47.19**).

**Procedure for making rights issues**. The directors must ensure that the company has authority to issue the securities (see **47.9**).

In the case of a private company, the procedure is relatively straightforward, an issue being made to existing members in accordance with the articles of association and the securities normally being paid for in cash at that time.

## 47.65  Listed companies

A rights offer is made by a renounceable letter (or other negotiable document) which may be traded (as 'nil paid' rights) for a period before payment for the securities is due. The offer must remain open for acceptance for at least 10 business days.

For a placing of rights arising from a rights issue before the official start of dealings, a listed company must ensure that:

- the placing relates to at least 25% of the maximum number of equity securities offered;

- the placees are committed to take up whatever is placed with them;

- the price paid by the placees does not exceed the price at which the equity securities which are the subject of the rights issue are offered by more than one half of the calculated premium over that offer price (that premium being the difference between the offer price and the theoretical ex-rights price); and

- the equity securities which are the subject of the rights issue are of the same class as the equity securities already listed.

The FCA may modify LR 9.5.1(1) to allow the placing to relate to less than 25% if it is satisfied that requiring at least 25% would be detrimental to the success off the issue and may list the equity securities at the same time as they are admitted to trading in 'nil paid' form. On the equity securities being paid up and the allotment becoming unconditional, the listing will continue without any need for a further application to list fully paid securities.

If the existing shareholders do not take up their rights to subscribe in a rights issue:

- the listed company must ensure that the equity securities to which the offer relates are offered for subscription or purchase on terms that any premium obtained over the subscription or purchase price (net of expenses) is to be for the account of the holders, except that if the proceeds for an existing holder do not exceed £5, the proceeds may be retained for the company's benefit; and

- the equity securities may be allotted or sold to underwriters, if on the expiry of the subscription period no premium (net of expenses) has been obtained.

A listed company must ensure that for a rights issue a Regulatory Information Service must be notified, as soon as possible, of the issue price and principal terms of the issue; the results of the issue; and details of the sale (including date and price per share) if any rights not taken up are sold.

## 47.65    Shares

A listed company must ensure that the offer relating to a rights issue remains open for acceptance for at least 10 business days. For the purposes of calculating the period of ten business days, the first business day is the date on which the offer is first open for acceptance. (FCA Listing Rules, paras 9.5.1–9.5.6).

# 48   Takeovers

**Cross-references.** See 35 RECONSTRUCTIONS AND MERGERS.

## 48.1   BACKGROUND TO TAKEOVERS

From 1968, takeover regulation in the UK has been overseen by the Panel on Takeovers and Mergers ('the Panel') which, prior to the *European Directive on Takeover Bids* (*EC Directive 2004/25/EC*) (the '*Takeovers Directive*'), administered non statutory rules and principles contained in the City Code on Takeovers and Mergers (the 'Code').

*Companies Act 2006 (CA 2006)*, Pt 28 was brought into force on 6 April 2007. It put both the Takeover Panel and the Code on a statutory footing and also provided for full implementation of the Takeovers Directive (see **48.2**).

## 48.2   THE PANEL ON TAKEOVERS AND MERGERS

The Panel may do anything that it considers necessary for the purposes of, and in connection with, its functions. [*CA 2006, s 942(2)*].

**Rules.** The Panel must make rules giving effect to the following *Articles* of the *Takeovers Directive*.

- *Art 3.1* (general principles);
- *Art 4.2* (jurisdictional rules);
- *Art 5* (matters related to the protection of minority shareholders, mandatory bid and equitable price);
- *Art 6.1–6.3* (contents of the bid documentation);
- *Arts 7, 8* (time allowed for the acceptance of a bid and publication of a bid);
- *Art 9* (obligations of the management of the target company); and
- *Art 13* (other rules applicable to the conduct of bids).

[*CA 2006, s 943(1)*].

## 48.2 Takeovers

The rules made may also make other provision

- for or in connection with the regulation of

    (i)     takeover bids;

    (ii)    merger transactions, and

    (iii)   other transactions that have or may have, directly or indirectly, an effect on the ownership or control of companies;

- for or in connection with the regulation of things done in consequence of, or otherwise in relation to, any such bid or transaction; and

- about cases where

    (i)     any such bid or transaction is, or has been, contemplated or apprehended; or

    (ii)    an announcement is made denying that any such bid or transaction is intended.

[*CA 2006, s 943(2)*].

All rules must be made by an instrument in writing. Immediately after an instrument containing rules is made, the text must be made available to the public, with or without payment, in whatever way the Panel thinks appropriate. A person is not to be taken to have contravened a rule if he shows that, at the time of the alleged contravention, the text of the rule had not been so made available.

[*CA 2006, s 944(2)–(4)*].

**The City Code on Takeovers and Mergers.** The rules made under the above are contained in the City Code on Takeovers and Mergers. See Appendix to this chapter for a summary of the provisions of the Code.

**Rulings.** The Panel may give rulings on the interpretation, application or effect of rules. To the extent and in the circumstances specified in rules, and subject to any review or appeal, a ruling has binding effect.

[*CA 2006, s 945*].

**Directions.** Rules may contain provisions conferring power on the Panel to give any direction that appears necessary to restrain a person from acting or potentially acting in breach of the rules.

[*CA 2006, s 946*].

**Power to require documents and information.** The Panel may, by notice in writing, require a person (at a place specified and within a reasonable time) to

- produce any documents that are specified in the notice; and

- provide such information as may be reasonably required in connection with the exercise of its functions.

It may require any document to be authenticated or any information to be verified in such manner as it may reasonably require. It may take copies of or extracts from a document produced.

The production of a document does not affect any lien that a person has on the document and a person is not required to disclose documents or information in respect of which a claim to legal professional privilege (in Scotland, to confidentiality of communications) could be maintained in legal proceedings.

[*CA 2006, s 947*].

**Restrictions on disclosure of information**. Information concerning the private affairs of an individual or a business provided to the Panel in connection with its functions may not be disclosed during the individual's lifetime or while the business is carried on without the consent of the individual or business in question except for

- the purposes of carrying out the Panel's functions; or

- disclosure to a person, or for a purpose, set out in *CA 2006, Sch 2*.

The provisions do not prohibit the disclosure of information if it is or has been available to the public from any other source.

Nothing in the provisions authorises the making of a disclosure in contravention of the data protection legislation.

A person who discloses information in contravention of these provisions is guilty of an offence unless *either* he did not know, and had no reason to suspect, that the information fell within the provisions *or* he took all reasonable steps and exercised all due diligence to avoid the commission of the offence.

[*CA 2006, ss 948, 949, Sch 2; SI 2009 No 1208; Data Protection Act 2018, s 212(1), Sch 19, para 123 (with ss 117, 209 and 210); SI 2018 No 625, Reg 2(1)(g)*].

**Duty of co-operation**. The Panel must take such steps as it considers appropriate to co-operate with

- the FCA;

- an authority designated as a supervisory authority for the purposes of *Takeovers Directive, Art 4.1*; and

- any other person or body that exercises functions of a public nature, under legislation in any country or territory outside the UK, that appear to the Panel to be similar to its own functions or those of the FCA.

[*CA 2006, s 950*].

**Hearings and appeals**. Rules must provide for a decision of the Panel to be subject to review by a committee of the Panel (the 'Hearings Committee') and for there to be a right of appeal against a decision of the Hearings Committee to an independent tribunal (the 'Takeover Appeal Board').

[*CA 2006, s 951(1)(3)*].

**Sanctions**. Rules may contain provision conferring power on the Panel to impose sanctions on a person who has acted in breach of rules or failed to comply with a direction (see above). [*CA 2006, s 952*].

**Compensation**. Rules may confer power on the Panel to order a person to pay such compensation (with interest) as it thinks just and reasonable if he is in breach of a rule the effect of which is to require the payment of money.

[*CA 2006, s 954*].

**Isle of Man**. With effect from 1 March 2009, the provisions in *CA 2006, Pt 28 Chap 1* are extended to the Isle of Man, with certain modification to reflect the differences in the legal system and governmental and regulatory structures of the Isle of Man. Among other things, the modifications impose a duty on the Island's Financial Supervision Commission to co-operate with the Takeover Panel. The modifications also provide for the exchange of information about takeovers.[*SI 2008 No 3122*]. See *SI 2008 No 3122, Sch* for full details of the modifications.

**48.3  Failure to comply with rules about bid documentation**

Provisions relating to bid documentation are laid down in *Takeovers Directive, Arts 6.3, 9.5* which are implemented in the UK by rules which the Panel are obliged to make under *CA 2006, s 943* (see **48.2**). The offences detailed below apply in relation to bid documentation where a takeover bid is made for a company that has securities carrying voting rights admitted to trading on a regulated market in the UK.

(a)     Where an offer document published in respect of the bid does not comply with offer document rules, an offence is committed by

   (i)      the person making the bid; and

   (ii)     where the person making the bid is a body of persons, any director, officer or member of that body who caused the document to be published.

A person commits an offence for these purposes only if

   •        he knew that the offer document did not comply, or was reckless as to whether it complied; and

   •        he failed to take all reasonable steps to secure that it did comply.

(b)     Where a response document published in respect of the bid does not comply with response document rules, an offence is committed by any director or other officer of the company subject to the bid who

   (i)      knew that the response document did not comply, or was reckless as to whether it complied, and

   (ii)     failed to take all reasonable steps to secure that it did comply.

Where either offence is committed by a corporate body (eg a corporate director), it is also committed by the director, officers or members of that body.

A person guilty of an offence under the above provisions is liable (i) on conviction on indictment, to a fine; and (ii) on summary conviction, to a fine not exceeding the statutory maximum. See **29.1** OFFENCES AND LEGAL PROCEEDINGS for the statutory maximum.

[*CA 2006, s 953*].

**48.4  Enforcement by the court**

If, on the application of the Panel, the High Court (in Scotland the Court of Session) is satisfied that

   •        there is a reasonable likelihood that a person will contravene a rule-based requirement, or

   •        a person has contravened a rule-based requirement or a disclosure requirement,

the court may make any order it thinks fit to secure compliance with the requirement. Apart from this, no person has a right to seek an injunction (in Scotland, has title or interest to seek an interdict or an order for specific performance) to prevent a person from contravening (or continuing to contravene) a rule-based requirement or a disclosure requirement. [*CA 2006, s 955*].

**48.5** **Effect of non-compliance with rules**

Compliance with the rules made by the Panel is a matter solely for the Panel. It is therefore specifically provided that

- contravention of a rule-based requirement or a disclosure requirement does not give rise to any right of action for breach of statutory duty; and

- contravention of a rule-based requirement does not make any transaction void or unenforceable or (subject to any provision of the rules) affect the validity of any other thing (although transactions will be capable of being set aside or unravelled in cases of, for example, misrepresentation or fraud).

[*CA 2006, s 956*].

**48.6** **Exemption from liability in damages**

Neither the Panel nor any person who is a member, officer or member of staff of the Panel is to be liable in damages for anything done or omitted in the discharge of the Panel's functions unless the act or omission is shown to have been in bad faith. But this exemption does not prevent an award of damages made in respect of an act or omission on the ground that it was unlawful as a result of *Human Rights Act 1998, s 6(1)* (acts of public authorities incompatible with Convention rights). [*CA 2006, s 962*].

**48.7** **IMPEDIMENTS TO TAKEOVERS**

The *Takeovers Directive, Art 11* seeks to override, in certain circumstances, a number of defensive mechanisms that may be adopted by companies prior to a bid. These include

- differential share structures under which minority shareholders can exercise disproportionate voting rights;

- restrictions on transfers of shares in the company articles or in contractual agreements; and

- limitations on share ownership.

As permitted by *Takeovers Directive, Art 12*, the UK has decided not to apply the provisions of *Art 11* in all cases but instead to include in *CA 2006* provisions for companies with voting shares traded on regulated markets to opt in to its provisions should they choose to do so.

These provisions are outlined in **48.8** and **48.9**.

**48.8** **Opting in and opting in**

A company may by special resolution (an '*opting-in resolution*') opt in for the purposes of these provisions if the following three conditions are met in relation to the company.

(1) The company has voting shares admitted to trading on a regulated market.

(2) The company's articles of association

    (i) do not contain any such restrictions as are mentioned in *Takeovers Directive, Art 11* or, if they do contain any such restrictions, provide for the restrictions not to apply at a time when (or in circumstances in which) they would be disapplied by that *Article*; and

    (ii) do not contain any other provision which would be incompatible with that *Art 11*.

*Takeovers Directive, Art 11* relates to both the takeover bid period and the time following the bid when the bidder has acquired 75% or more of the company's capital carrying voting rights. It provides that restrictions both on the right to transfer shares and on voting rights that are contained in the articles of the company should not apply. It also provides that, in certain circumstances, shares carrying multiple voting rights will only have one vote and extraordinary rights of shareholders concerning the appointment or removal of board members should be disapplied.

(3)    No shares conferring special rights in the company are held by

(a)    a 'minister',

(b)    a nominee of, or any other person acting on behalf of, a minister, or

(c)    a company directly or indirectly controlled by a minister,

and no such rights are exercisable by or on behalf of a minister under any Act.

By order, this can be extended to include a specified person or body that exercises functions of a public nature as it applies in relation to a minister.

*'Minister'* means the holder of an office in Her Majesty's Government in the UK, the Scottish Ministers, a minister within the meaning given by *Northern Ireland Act 1998, s 7(3)* and the Welsh Ministers.

A company may revoke an opting-in resolution by a further special resolution (an *'opting-out resolution'*).

[*CA 2006, s 966*].

An opting-in or an opting-out resolution must specify the date from which it is to have effect.

• The effective date of an opting-in resolution may not be earlier than the date on which the resolution is passed. Conditions (2) and (3) above must be met at the time when an opting-in resolution is passed but condition (1) does not need to be met until the effective date. An opting-in resolution passed before the time when voting shares of the company are admitted to trading on a regulated market complies with this requirement if, instead of specifying a particular date, it provides for the resolution to have effect from that time.

• The effective date of an opting-out resolution may not be earlier than the first anniversary of the date on which a copy of the opting-in resolution was forwarded to the Registrar of Companies.

Where a company has passed an opting-in resolution, any alteration of its articles of association that would prevent condition (2) above from being met is of no effect until the effective date of an opting-out resolution passed by the company.

[*CA 2006, s 967*].

**Communication of decisions.** A company that has passed an opting-in or an opting-out resolution must notify

(a)    the Panel, and

(b)    where the company has voting shares admitted to trading on a regulated market in an EEA State other than the UK (or has requested such admission), the takeover supervisory authority of that state.

Notification must be given within 15 days after the resolution is passed and, if any admission or request under (*b*) above occurs at a later time, within 15 days after that time.

If a company fails to comply with these provisions, an offence is committed by the company and every officer of it who is in default. A person guilty of such an offence is liable, on summary conviction, to a fine not exceeding level 3 on the standard scale and, for continued contravention, a daily default fine not exceeding one-tenth of level 3 on the standard scale. See **29.1** Offences and Legal Proceedings for the standard scale. [*CA 2006, s 970*].

## 48.9   Consequences of opting out

**Effect on contractual restrictions**. Where a takeover bid is made for an '*opted-in company*' (ie one to which an opting-in resolution has effect and to which the conditions in **48.8**(1) and (3) still apply), an agreement entered into

- between a person holding shares in the company and another such person on or after 21 April 2004, or

- at any time between such a person and the company,

is invalid in so far as it places any restriction on the following.

(a)    On the transfer to the offeror, or at his direction to another person, of shares in the company during the offer period.

(b)    On the transfer to any person of shares in the company at a time during the offer period when the offeror holds shares amounting to not less than 75% in value of all the 'voting shares' in the company.

(c)    On rights to vote at a general meeting (including rights to vote on a written resolution) of the company that decides whether to take any '*action which might result in the frustration of the bid*' ie any action of that kind specified in rules under *CA 2006, s 943(1)* giving effect to *Takeovers Directive, Art 9* (see **48.2**).

(d)    On rights to vote at a general meeting of the company that

   (i)    is the first such meeting to be held after the end of the offer period; and

   (ii)   is held at a time when the offeror holds shares amounting to not less than 75% in value of all the voting shares in the company.

The above applies to such an agreement even if the law applicable to the agreement (apart from these provisions) is not the law of a part of the UK.

If a person suffers loss as a result of any act or omission that would, but for these provisions, be a breach of an agreement to which the provisions apply (ie as a result of a contractual agreement being overridden), he is entitled to compensation, of such amount as the court considers just and equitable, from any person who would (but for these provisions) be liable to him for committing or inducing the breach.

For the above purposes, '*voting shares*' in the company do not include

- debentures; or

- shares that, under the company's articles of association, do not normally carry rights to vote at its general meetings (eg shares carrying rights to vote that, under those articles, arise only where specified pecuniary advantages are not provided).

[*CA 2006, ss 968, 971*].

**Power of offeror to require general meeting to be called.** Where a takeover bid is made for an opted-in company, the offeror may by making a request to the directors of the company require them to call a general meeting of the company if, at the date at which the request is made, he holds shares amounting to not less than 75% in value of all the 'voting shares' (see above) in the company.

*CA 2006, ss 303–305* (members' power to require general meetings to be called, see **42.14(2)** RESOLUTIONS AND MEETINGS) apply as if a request by the offeror for a meeting in the circumstances above was substituted for requests from members representing the required percentage under those provisions.

[*CA 2006, s 969, 972*].

## 48.10  'SQUEEZE-OUT' AND 'SELL-OUT'

The concepts of 'squeeze-out' and 'sell-out' are designed to address problems of, and for, residual minority shareholders following a successful takeover bid. Squeeze-out rights enable a successful bidder to compulsorily purchase the shares of remaining minority shareholders who have not accepted the bid. Sell-out rights enable minority shareholders, following a bid, to require the majority shareholder to purchase their shares. As they both involve the compulsory acquisition of shares against the will of one of the parties, high thresholds apply to the exercising of such rights and there are protective rules on the price that must be paid for the shares concerned.

The provisions of *CA 2006, ss 974–991* in **48.11–48.19** restate *CA 1985, Part 13A* in a clearer form but also make changes to comply with the *Takeovers Directive, Arts 15, 16*.

### 48.11  Takeover offers and related terms

The following definitions and related terms apply for the purposes of **48.12–48.19**.

(1)     **Meaning of 'takeover offer'**

An offer to acquire 'shares' in a company is a *'takeover offer'* if the following two conditions are satisfied in relation to the offer.

(a)     It is an offer to acquire

- all the shares in a company; or

- where there is more than one class of shares in a company, all the shares of one or more classes,

other than 'shares already held by the offeror' at the date of the offer.

This condition is treated as satisfied where the offer does not extend to shares that associates of the offeror hold or have contracted to acquire (whether unconditionally or subject to conditions being met) *and* the condition would be satisfied if the offer did extend to those shares.

*'Shares already held by the offeror'* includes a reference to shares that he has contracted to acquire (whether unconditionally or subject to conditions being met) but *excludes* a reference to shares that are the subject of a contract

- intended to secure that the holder of the shares will accept the offer when it is made; and

- entered into *either* by deed and for no consideration (in Scotland, for no consideration) *or* for consideration of negligible value *or* for consideration consisting of a promise by the offeror to make the offer.

(b)     The terms of the offer are the same

- in relation to all the shares to which the offer relates; or

- where the shares to which the offer relates include shares of different classes, in relation to all the shares of each class.

This condition is treated as satisfied

- where

    (i)     shares carry an entitlement to a particular dividend which other shares of the same class, by reason of being allotted later, do not carry;

    (ii)    there is a difference in the value of consideration offered for the shares allotted earlier as against that offered for those allotted later;

    (iii)   that difference merely reflects the difference in entitlement to the dividend; and

    (iv)    the condition would be satisfied but for that difference; *or*

- where

    (i)     the law of a country or territory outside the UK precludes an offer of consideration in the form, or any of the forms, specified in the terms of the offer ('the specified form') or precludes it except after compliance by the offeror with conditions with which he is unable to comply or which he regards as unduly onerous;

    (ii)    the persons to whom an offer of consideration in the specified form is precluded are able to receive consideration in another form that is of substantially equivalent value; and

    (iii)   the condition would be satisfied but for the fact that an offer of consideration in the specified form to those persons is precluded.

For the above purposes, '*shares*' means shares, other than 'relevant treasury shares', that have been allotted on the date of the offer. But a takeover offer *may* include among the shares to which it relates

- all or any shares that are allotted after the date of the offer but before a specified date;

- all or any relevant treasury shares that cease to be held as treasury shares before a specified date; and

- all or any other relevant treasury shares.

'*Relevant treasury shares*' means shares that are held by the company as treasury shares on the date of the offer or become shares held by the company as treasury shares after that date but before a date specified in, or determined in accordance with, the terms of the offer.

*Revised offers.* Where the terms of an offer make provision for their revision and for acceptances on the previous terms to be treated as acceptances on the revised terms, then, if the terms of the offer are revised in accordance with that provision, the revision is not to be regarded for these purposes as the making of a fresh offer. References to the date of the offer are accordingly to be read as references to the date of the original offer.

*Effect of impossibility, etc of communicating or accepting offer.* Where there are holders of shares in a company to whom an offer to acquire shares in the company is not communicated, that does not prevent the offer from being a takeover offer for these purposes if

- those shareholders have no registered address in the UK;

- the offer was not communicated to those shareholders in order not to contravene the law of a country or territory outside the UK, and

- either

  (i) the offer is published in the Gazette; or

  (ii) the offer can be inspected, or a copy of it obtained, at a place in an EEA State or on a website, and a notice is published in the Gazette specifying the address of that place or website.

Where an offer is made to acquire shares in a company and there are persons for whom, by reason of the law of a country or territory outside the UK, it is impossible to accept the offer, or more difficult to do so, that does not prevent the offer from being a takeover offer for these purposes.

[*CA 2006, s 974–976, 978*].

(2) **Shares to which the offer relates**

Subject to *CA 2006, s 979(8)(9)* in **48.12** below, for these purposes

(a) where a takeover offer is made and, during the period beginning with the date of the offer and ending when the offer can no longer be accepted, the offeror

- acquires or unconditionally contracts to acquire any of the shares to which the offer relates, but

- does not do so by virtue of acceptances of the offer,

those shares are treated as excluded from those to which the offer relates; and

(b) shares that an associate of the offeror holds or has 'contracted' to acquire, whether at the date of the offer or subsequently, are not treated as shares to which the offer relates, even if the offer extends to such shares.

'*Contracted*' means contracted unconditionally or subject to conditions being met.

[*CA 2006, s 977*].

(3) **Associates**

'*Associate*', in relation to an offeror, means any of the following.

- A nominee of the offeror.

- A holding company, subsidiary or fellow subsidiary of the offeror or a nominee of such a holding company, subsidiary or fellow subsidiary.

  For these purposes, a company is a fellow subsidiary of another body corporate if both are subsidiaries of the same body corporate but neither is a subsidiary of the other.

- A body corporate in which the offeror is substantially interested.

For these purposes, an offeror has a substantial interest in a body corporate if

(i) the body or its directors are accustomed to act in accordance with his directions or instructions; or

(ii) he is entitled to exercise, or control the exercise of, one-third or more of the voting power at general meetings of the body. See **24.1** INTERESTS IN PUBLIC COMPANY SHARES for when a person is treated as entitled to exercise or control the exercise of voting power, which provisions also apply for these purposes.

- A person who is, or is a nominee of, a party to a 'share acquisition agreement' with the offeror.

For these purposes, an agreement is a *'share acquisition agreement'* if

(i) it is an agreement for the acquisition of, or of an interest in, shares to which the offer relates;

(ii) it includes provisions imposing obligations or restrictions on any one or more of the parties to it with respect to their use, retention or disposal of such shares, or their interests in such shares, acquired in pursuance of the agreement (whether or not together with any other shares to which the offer relates or any other interests of theirs in such shares); and

(iii) it is not an 'excluded agreement'. An agreement is an *'excluded agreement'* if it is not legally binding, unless it involves mutuality in the undertakings, expectations or understandings of the parties to it. It is also an excluded agreement if it is an agreement to underwrite or sub-underwrite an offer of shares in a company, provided the agreement is confined to that purpose and any matters incidental to it.

The reference in (ii) above to the use of interests in shares is to the exercise of any rights or of any control or influence arising from those interests (including the right to enter into an agreement for the exercise, or for control of the exercise, of any of those rights by another person).

- Where the offeror is an individual, his spouse or civil partner and any minor child or step-child of his.

[*CA 2006, s 988*].

(4) **Convertible securities**

For these purposes, securities of a company are treated as shares in the company if they are convertible into, or entitle the holder to subscribe for, such shares. References to the 'holder of shares' or a 'shareholder' are to be read accordingly.

This is not to be read as requiring any securities to be treated as shares of the same class as

- those into which they are convertible or for which the holder is entitled to subscribe; or

- other securities by reason only that the shares into which they are convertible or for which the holder is entitled to subscribe are of the same class.

*[CA 2006, s 989].*

(5)    **Debentures carrying voting rights**

For these purposes, debentures issued by a company that has voting shares, or debentures carrying voting rights, which are admitted to trading on a regulated market are treated as shares in the company if they carry voting rights.

In relation to debentures so treated as shares, references to

- the 'holder of shares' or a 'shareholder' are to be read accordingly; and

- shares being allotted are to be read as references to debentures being issued.

*[CA 2006, s 990].*

(6)    **Date of the offer**

'Date of the offer' means

- where the offer is published, the date of publication; and

- where the offer is not published, or where any notices of the offer are given before the date of publication, the date when notices of the offer (or the first such notices) are given.

See (1) above where an offer is revised.

*[CA 2006, s 991(1)].*

(7)    **Unconditional contracts**

For these purposes, a person contracts unconditionally to acquire shares if his entitlement under the contract to acquire them is not (or is no longer) subject to conditions or if all conditions to which it was subject have been met.

*[CA 2006, s 991(2)].*

(8)    **When shares are allotted**

Shares in a company are taken to be allotted when a person acquires the unconditional right to be included in the company's register of members in respect of the shares.

*[CA 2006, s 558].*

## 48.12 Squeeze-out: right of offeror to buy out minority shareholder

**Entitlement to give notice.** If the offeror has, by virtue of acceptances of the offer, acquired or unconditionally contracted to acquire

- not less than 90% in value of the 'shares to which the offer relates' (see **48.11(2)**), and

- in a case where the shares to which the offer relates are voting shares, not less than 90% of the voting rights carried by those shares,

he may give notice to the holder of any shares to which the offer relates which the offeror has not acquired, or unconditionally contracted to acquire, that he desires to acquire those shares.

If the offer relates to shares of different classes, similar provisions apply but to each class separately.

*[CA 2006, s 979(1)–(4)].*

**Treatment of options, etc and treasury shares.** In the case of a takeover offer which includes among the shares to which it relates

•      shares that are allotted after the date of the offer, or

•      relevant treasury shares (see **48.11(1)**) that cease to be held as treasury shares after the date of the offer,

the offeror's entitlement to give a notice as above on any particular date is determined as if the shares to which the offer relates did not include any allotted, or ceasing to be held as treasury shares, on or after that date.

[*CA 2006, s 979(5)*].

The effect of this is that the offeror need only bring into the calculation shares which are actually in issue (ie allotted) at the relevant time. If more share are subsequently allotted which takes the percentage of acceptances then received below 90%, that will not invalidate squeeze-out notices already issued. But if the offeror wishes to serve further squeeze-out notices, he must have at least 90% of shares (or shares in a class) then in issue and subject to the offer at the time he sends the notices out.

**Contracts to acquire shares which have not become unconditional.** Where

(a)     the requirements for giving notice as above are satisfied, and

(b)     there are shares in the company which the offeror (or an associate of his) has contracted to acquire subject to conditions being met, and in relation to which the contract has not become unconditional,

the offeror's entitlement to give a notice is determined as if

•      the shares to which the offer relates included shares falling within (*b*) above; and

•      in relation to those shares, the words 'by virtue of acceptances of the offer' above were omitted.

[*CA 2006, s 979(6), (7)*].

**Other shares acquired during the offer period.** Where a takeover offer is made and during the period beginning with the date of the offer and ending when the offer can no longer be accepted, the offeror

•      acquires, or unconditionally contracts to acquire, any of the shares to which the offer relates but otherwise than by acceptances of the offer, and

•      the value of the consideration for which they are acquired or contracted to be acquired ('the acquisition consideration') does not exceed the value of the consideration specified in the terms of the offer (or as subsequently increased on a revised offer),

then for these purposes those shares are not excluded under **48.11(2)(***a***)** from those to which the offer relates, and the offeror is treated as having acquired or contracted to acquire them by virtue of acceptances of the offer.

Where, in similar circumstances, an associate (see **48.11(3)**) of the offeror acquires, or unconditionally contracts to acquire, any of the shares to which the offer relates, those shares are not excluded by **48.11(2)(***b***)** above from those to which the offer relates.

[*CA 2006, s 979(8)–(10)*].

## 48.12    Takeovers

*Example*

A Ltd makes an offer for the 1 million issued shares in B Ltd at £1 per share which is subsequently increased to £1.20 per share. It receives acceptances from holders of 800,000 shares. During the offer period, A Ltd also buys 110,000 shares on the open market at £1.10 per share.

A Ltd will be treated as having acquired the 110,000 shares under the terms of the offer. Although £1.10 is higher than the offer price at the time the shares are purchased, it is less than the subsequently increased offer price of £1.20. A Ltd has therefore acquired 910,000 (800,000 + 110,000) shares under the offer and as this represents 91% it can buy out the minority. If, on the other hand, A Ltd had bought the 110,000 shares at £1.30 per share, these shares would have been excluded from the shares subject to the offer. A Ltd would be treated as having acquired 800,000 out of 890,000 (1,000,000 – 110,000) shares under the offer (ie 89.89%) and would not therefore be able to buy out the minority.

**48.13** *Provisions relating to the giving of notice*

*Method of giving notice.* The notice to shareholders by the offeror under **48.12** must be given

(a)     personally; or

(b)     by recorded delivery post to

(i)     his address in the UK registered in the company's books; or

(ii)    if no such address is registered, the address (if any) in the UK given by him to the company for the giving of notices; or

(c)     if no address is registered under (*b*)(i) above or has been notified under (*b*)(ii) above, by air mail (if available) to the address outside the UK registered in the company's books.

Where notice cannot be given under (*a*) to (*c*) above because the holder of the shares is the holder of a share warrant to bearer, it must be given by advertisement as provided in the company's articles or, if no such provision is made, by advertisement in the *Gazette*.

[*SI 1987 No 752, Reg 4*].

*Time limit.* No notice may be given after the end of

• the period of three months beginning with the day after the last day on which the offer can be accepted; or

• the period of six months beginning with the date of the offer, where that period ends earlier and the offer is one under which the time allowed for acceptance of the offer is not governed by rules under *CA 2006, s 943(1)* that give effect to *Takeovers Directive, Art 7*. (This will apply to the takeover of most private companies.)

*Notice to the company.* At the time when the offeror first gives a notice in relation to an offer, he must send to the company a copy of the notice and a statutory declaration by him in the prescribed form, stating that the conditions for the giving of the notice are satisfied. Where the offeror is a company, the statutory declaration must be signed by a director.

A person commits an offence if he

• fails to send a copy of a notice or a statutory declaration as required; or

• makes such a declaration knowing it to be false or without having reasonable grounds for believing it to be true.

It is a defence for a person charged with an offence for failing to send a copy of a notice to prove that he took reasonable steps for securing compliance.

1292

A person guilty of an offence under this section is liable (i) on conviction on indictment, to imprisonment for a term not exceeding two years or a fine (or both); and (ii) on summary conviction, to imprisonment for a term not exceeding twelve months (six months in Scotland and Northern Ireland) or to a fine not exceeding the statutory maximum (or both) and, for continued contravention, a daily default fine not exceeding one-fiftieth of the greater of £5000 or the amount corresponding to level 4 on the standard scale for summary offences. See **29.1** OFFENCES AND LEGAL PROCEEDINGS for the statutory maximum.

[*CA 2006, s 980; SI 2015 No 664, Sch 3*].

**48.14**   *Effect of notice*

Subject to **48.18**, where notice is given, the offeror is *entitled and bound* to acquire the shares to which the notice relates on the terms of the offer. Where the terms of an offer give the shareholder a choice of consideration, the notice must give particulars of the choice and state

•        that the shareholder may, within six weeks from the date of the notice, indicate his choice in writing to the offeror at an address specified in the notice; and

•        which consideration specified in the offer will apply if he does not indicate a choice.

This applies whether or not any time-limit or other conditions applicable to the choice under the terms of the offer can still be complied with.

If the consideration offered to or (as the case may be) chosen by the shareholder

•        is not cash and the offeror is no longer able to provide it, or

•        was to have been provided by a third party who is no longer bound or able to provide it,

the consideration is to be taken to consist of an amount of cash, payable by the offeror, which at the date of the notice is equivalent to the consideration offered or (as the case may be) chosen.

At the end of six weeks from the date of the notice, the offeror must immediately

(a)      send a copy of the notice to the company, together with

(i)       if the shares to which the notice relates are registered, an instrument of transfer executed on behalf of the holder of the shares by a person appointed by the offeror (on receipt of which the company must register the offeror as holder of those shares); or

(ii)      if the shares to which the notice relates are transferable by the delivery of warrants or other instruments, a statement to that effect (on receipt of which the company must issue the offeror with warrants or other instruments in respect of the shares, and those warrants, etc already in issue in respect of the shares become void).

(b)      Pay or transfer to the company the consideration for the shares to which the notice relates (or where the consideration consists of shares or securities to be allotted by the offeror, allot the shares or securities to the company).

*Consideration held on trust by the company.* The company must hold any money or other consideration received by it on trust for the person who, before the offeror acquired them, was entitled to the shares in respect of which the money or other consideration was received. Any money that it receives, together with any dividends or other sum accruing, must be paid into a separate bank account bearing interest at an appropriate rate.

If the person entitled to the consideration held on trust

- cannot be found,

- reasonable enquiries have been made at reasonable intervals to find the person, and

- either 12 years have elapsed since the consideration was received or the company is wound up

then

- for companies registered in England and Wales or Northern Ireland, the consideration (together with any interest, dividend or other benefit that has accrued from it) must be paid into court; and

- for companies registered in Scotland,

    (i)     the trust terminates;

    (ii)    the company or (if the company is wound up) the liquidator must sell any consideration other than cash and any benefit other than cash that has accrued from the consideration; and

    (iii)   a sum representing the consideration so far as it is cash, the proceeds of any sale under (ii) above, and any interest, dividend or other benefit that has accrued from the consideration,

    must be deposited in the name of the Accountant of Court in a separate bank account and the receipt for the deposit must be transmitted to the Accountant of Court.

    *Bankruptcy (Scotland) Act 2016, s 150* (so far as consistent with *CA 2006*) applies (with any necessary modifications) to sums so deposited as it applies to sums deposited under *s 148(3)* of that *Act.*

The expenses of any reasonable enquiry that is made may be paid out of the money or other property held on trust for the person to whom the enquiry relates.

[*CA 2006, ss 981, 982*].

## 48.15  Sell-out: right of minority shareholder to be bought out by offeror

### Offers relating to all the shares in a company

(a)     The holder of any *voting* shares to which the offer relates who has not accepted the offer may write to the offeror and require him to acquire those shares if, at any time before the end of the period within which the offer can be accepted

    (i)     the offeror (or an associate of his) has, by virtue of acceptances of the offer, acquired or unconditionally contracted to acquire some (but not all) of the shares to which the offer relates; and

    (ii)    those shares, with or without any other shares in the company which he has acquired or contracted to acquire (whether unconditionally or subject to conditions being met)

        - amount to not less than 90% in value of all the voting shares in the company (or would do so but for **48.11(5)**); and

        - carry not less than 90% of the voting rights in the company (or would do so but for **48.11(5)**).

(b)     The holder of any *non-voting* shares to which the offer relates who has not accepted the offer may write to the offeror and require him to acquire those shares if, at any time before the end of the period within which the offer can be accepted

    (i)     the offeror (or an associate of his) has by virtue of acceptances of the offer acquired or unconditionally contracted to acquire some (but not all) of the shares to which the offer relates; and

    (ii)    those shares, with or without any other shares in the company which he has acquired or contracted to acquire (whether unconditionally or subject to conditions being met), amount to not less than 90% in value of all the shares in the company (or would do so but for **48.11(5)**).

**Offers for shares of one or more classes only**

(c)     If a takeover offer relates to shares of one or more classes and at any time before the end of the period within which the offer can be accepted

    (i)     the offeror (or an associate of his) has by virtue of acceptances of the offer acquired or unconditionally contracted to acquire some (but not all) of the shares of any class to which the offer relates; and

    (ii)    those shares, with or without any other shares of that class which he has acquired or contracted to acquire (whether unconditionally or subject to conditions being met)

      •     amount to not less than 90% in value of all the shares of that class; and

      •     in a case where the shares of that class are voting shares, carry not less than 90% of the voting rights carried by the shares of that class,

the holder of any shares of that class to which the offer relates who has not accepted the offer may write to the offeror and require him to acquire those shares.

For the purposes of (*a*) and (*b*) above, a takeover offer relates to all the shares in a company if it is an offer to acquire all the shares in the company within the meaning of *CA 2006, s 974* (see **48.11(1)**).

[*CA 2006, ss 983(1)–(4)(8), 984(1)*].

**Treasury shares.** For the above purposes, in calculating 90% of the value of any shares, shares held by the company as treasury shares are to be treated as having been acquired by the offeror.

[*CA 2006, s 983(5)*].

**Contracts to acquire shares which have not become unconditional.** Where

•     a shareholder exercises rights conferred on him in (*a*)–(*c*) above,

•     at the time when he does so, there are shares in the company which the offeror (or an associate of his) has contracted to acquire subject to conditions being met, and in relation to which the contract has not become unconditional, and

•     the appropriate 90% test(s) in (*a*)(ii), (*b*)(ii) or (*c*)(ii) (as the case may be) would not be satisfied if those shares were not taken into account,

the shareholder is treated for the purposes of **48.17** as not having exercised his rights unless the 90% test(s) would be satisfied if

- the reference in (*a*)(ii), (*b*)(ii) or (*c*)(ii) (as the case may be) to other shares in the company which the offeror (or an associate of his) has contracted to acquire unconditionally or subject to conditions being met were a reference to such shares which he has unconditionally contracted to acquire; and

- the reference in (*a*), (*b*) or (*c*) above (as the case may be) to the period within which the offer can be accepted were a reference to the period referred to in **48.16** below.

[*CA 2006, s 983(6)(7)(8)*].

**48.16** *Provisions relating to giving notice*

*Time limit.* Rights conferred on a shareholder under **48.15** are not exercisable after the end of the period of three months from

- the end of the period within which the offer can be accepted; or

- if later, the date of the notice that must be given below.

Within one month of the time specified in **48.15**(*a*), (*b*) or (*c*) (as the case may be), the offeror must give any shareholder who has not accepted the offer notice in the prescribed manner of the rights that are exercisable by the shareholder under that provision and the period within which the rights are exercisable. If the notice is given before the end of the period within which the offer can be accepted, it must state that the offer is still open for acceptance. This requirement to give notice does not apply if the offeror has given the shareholder a notice in respect of the shares in question under **48.12** (notice of intention to buy the shares).

An offeror who fails to comply with this requirement commits an offence. If the offeror is a company, every officer of that company who is in default, or to whose neglect the failure is attributable, also commits an offence. If an offeror other than a company is charged with such an offence, it is a defence for him to prove that he took all reasonable steps for securing compliance with the requirement.

A person guilty of such an offence is liable (i) on conviction on indictment, to a fine; and (ii) on summary conviction, to a fine not exceeding the statutory maximum and, for continued contravention, a daily default fine not exceeding one-fiftieth of the greater of £5000 or level 4 on the standard scale for summary offences. See **29.1** OFFENCES AND LEGAL PROCEEDINGS for the statutory maximum.

[*CA 2006, s 984; SI 2015 No 664, Sch 3*].

*Method of giving notice by the offeror.* The notice to shareholders by the offeror must be given

(a)     personally; or

(b)     by recorded delivery post to

    (i)     his address in the UK registered in the company's books; or

    (ii)    if no such address is registered, the address (if any) in the UK given by him to the company for the giving of notices; or

(c)     if no address is registered under (*b*)(i) above or has been notified under (*b*)(ii) above, by air mail (if available) to the address outside the UK registered in the company's books.

Where notice cannot be given under (*a*) to (*c*) above because the holder of the shares is the holder of a share warrant to bearer, it must be given by advertisement as provided in the company's articles or, if no such provision is made, by advertisement in the *Gazette*.

[*SI 1987 No 752, Reg 4*].

**48.17** *Effect of notice*

Subject to **48.18**, where a shareholder exercises his rights under **48.16** in respect of any shares held by him, the offeror is entitled and bound to acquire those shares on the terms of the offer or on such other terms as may be agreed.

Where the terms of an offer are such as to give the shareholder a choice of consideration

- the shareholder may indicate his choice when requiring the offeror to acquire the shares; and

- the notice given to the shareholder under **48.16**

    (i)    must give particulars of the choice and of the shareholder's rights to chose; and

    (ii)   may state which consideration specified in the offer will apply if he does not indicate a choice.

This applies whether or not any time limit or other conditions applicable to the choice under the terms of the offer can still be complied with.

If the consideration offered to or (as the case may be) chosen by the shareholder

- is not cash and the offeror is no longer able to provide it, or

- was to have been provided by a third party who is no longer bound or able to provide it,

the consideration is to be taken to consist of an amount of cash, payable by the offeror, which at the date when the shareholder requires the offeror to acquire the shares is equivalent to the consideration offered or (as the case may be) chosen.

[*CA 2006, s 985*].


**48.18 Applications to the court**

Application may be made to the court in the following circumstances.

(a)    Where a notice is given under **48.12** to a shareholder, the shareholder may apply to the court within six weeks from the date of notice. The court may order that

    - the offeror is not entitled and bound to acquire the shares to which the notice relates; or

    - the terms on which the offeror is entitled and bound to acquire the shares are such as the court thinks fit.

If such an application is pending at the end of that six-week period, the requirements of **48.14**(*a*) and (*b*) do not have to be complied with until the application has been disposed of.

In the ordinary case of such an offer where the 90% who accepted the offer are unconnected with the offeror, the court will pay the greatest attention to the views of the majority. Where, however, as a matter of substance the persons putting forward the offer are the majority shareholders, the onus must fall on the majority shareholders to satisfy the court that the scheme is one with which the minority shareholders ought reasonably to be compelled to fall in with (*Bugle Press Ltd, Re, Re Houses and Estates Ltd* [1961] Ch 270, [1960] 1 All ER 768).

(b)     Where a shareholder exercises his rights under **48.15** (right of minority shareholder to be bought out) the court may, on an application made by him or the offeror, order that the terms on which the offeror is entitled and bound to acquire the shares are such as the court thinks fit.

(c)     Where a takeover offer has not been accepted to the extent necessary for entitling the offeror to give notices under **48.12**, the court may, on an application made by him, make an order authorising him to give notices under those provisions if it is satisfied that

  (i)     the offeror has, after reasonable enquiry, been unable to trace one or more of the persons holding shares to which the offer relates;

  (ii)    the requirements would have been met if the person, or all the persons, in (i) above had accepted the offer;

  (iii)   the consideration offered is fair and reasonable; and

  (iv)    it is just and equitable to do so having regard, in particular, to the number of shareholders who have been traced but who have not accepted the offer.

On an application

•     a shareholder who has made an application under (*a*) or (*b*) above must give notice of the application to the offeror;

•     an offeror who is given notice of such an application under (*a*) or (*b*) above must then give a copy of the notice to

  (i)     any person (other than the applicant) to whom a notice has been given under **48.12**; and

  (ii)    any person who has exercised his rights under **48.15**;

•     an offeror who makes an application under (*b*) above must give notice of the application to

  (i)     any person to whom a notice has been given under **48.12**; and

  (ii)    any person who has exercised his rights under **48.15**.

•     the court may not require consideration of a

  (i)     higher value than that specified in the terms of the offer ('the offer value') to be given for the shares to which the application relates unless the holder of the shares shows that the offer value would be unfair; and

  (ii)    lower value than the offer value to be given for the shares; and

•     no order for costs or expenses may be made against a shareholder unless the court considers that

  (i)     the application was unnecessary, improper or vexatious;

  (ii)    there has been unreasonable delay in making the application; or

  (iii)   there has been unreasonable conduct on the shareholder's part in conducting the proceedings on the application.

[*CA 2006, s 986*].

**48.19 Joint offers**

Where a takeover offer is made by two or more persons jointly, the conditions for the exercise of the rights conferred by **48.12** and **48.15** are satisfied

- in the case of acquisitions by virtue of acceptances of the offer, by the joint offerors acquiring or unconditionally contracting to acquire the necessary shares jointly; and

- in other cases, by the joint offerors

  (i)     (where **48.12** applies) acquiring or unconditionally contracting to acquire the necessary shares either jointly or separately; and

  (ii)    (where **48.15** applies) acquiring or contracting (whether unconditionally or subject to conditions being met) to acquire the necessary shares either jointly or separately.

The rights and obligations of the offeror under **48.12**–**48.17** are respectively joint rights and joint and several obligations of the joint offerors, subject to certain exceptions in *CA 2006, s 987(5)–(10)*.

[*CA 2006, s 987(1)–(4)*].

# APPENDIX: THE CITY CODE ON TAKEOVERS AND MERGERS

## THE CITY CODE ON TAKEOVERS AND MERGERS

The City Code on Takeovers and Mergers is produced in order to provide an orderly framework within which takeovers are conducted. It is produced by an independent body, the Panel on Takeovers and Mergers, whose main functions are to issue and administer the Code and to supervise and regulate takeovers and other matters to which the Code applies, its central objective being to ensure fair treatment for all shareholders in takeover bids.

The Panel maintains a website at www.thetakeoverpanel.org.uk/, where the latest version of the City Code on Takeovers and Mergers is available.

# Appendix 1 – Definitions

### GENERAL DEFINITIONS

The following definitions apply for the purposes of this book.

**Accounting reference date.** See **2.18** ACCOUNTS (GENERAL) AND ACCOUNTING REFERENCE DATES AND PERIODS.

**Accounting reference period.** See **2.17** ACCOUNTS (GENERAL) AND ACCOUNTING REFERENCE DATES AND PERIODS.

**Accounting standards.** Accounting standards mean statements of standard accounting practice issued by prescribed bodies, and references to 'accounting standards applicable to a company's annual accounts' are to such standards as are, in accordance with their terms, relevant to the company's circumstances and to the accounts. [*CA 2006, s 464*]. The FRC is a prescribed body for these purposes. [*SI 2012 No 1471, Reg 23*].

**Accounts meeting** means (in relation to a public company) a general meeting of the company at which the company's annual accounts and reports are (or are to be) laid in accordance with *CA 2006, s 437*. [*CA 2006, s 437(3)*]

**Annual accounts,** mean

- any individual accounts prepared by the company for that year (see *CA 2006, s 394*); and

- any group accounts prepared by the company for that year

and include notes to the accounts giving information which is required by any provision of *CA 2006* or international accounting standards, and required or allowed by any such provision to be given in a note to company accounts.

This is subject to *CA 2006, s 408* (option to omit individual profit and loss account from annual accounts where information given in notes to the individual balance sheet , see **3.60** ACCOUNTS: LARGE COMPANIES).

[*CA 2006, ss 471(1), 472(2); SI 2012 No 2301, Reg 18; SI 2013 No 3008, Reg 7(3)*].

**Annual accounts and reports.** *In the case of an unquoted company*, its annual accounts and reports for a financial year are

- its annual accounts;

- the strategic report (if any) (see CHAPTER 2)

- the directors' report, and

- the auditor's report on those accounts for financial years ending on or after 30 September 2013 on the strategic report (where this is covered by the auditor's report) (see CHAPTER 2)) and the directors' report (unless the company is exempt from audit).

*In the case of a quoted company*, its annual accounts and reports for a financial year are

- its annual accounts;

# Appendix 1 – Definitions

- the directors' remuneration report, (for financial years ending on or after 30 September 2013 the strategic report (if any) (see CHAPTER 2))

- the directors' report; and

- the auditor's report on those accounts (for financial years ending on or after 30 September 2013 on the strategic report (where this is covered by the auditor's report) (see CHAPTER 2)) and the directors' report (unless the company is exempt from audit).

[*CA 2006, s 471(2)(3); SI 2013 No 1970, Schedule, para 18*].

**Asset-locked body**

- a CIC, a charity or (with effect from 1 October 2009, a permitted industrial and provident society); or

- a body established outside the UK that is equivalent to either of those.

**Associated undertaking**. See **3.65** ACCOUNTS: LARGE COMPANIES.

**Balance sheet**, includes notes to the accounts giving information which is required by any provision of *CA 2006* or international accounting standards, and required or allowed by any such provision to be given in a note to company accounts.

[*CA 2006, s 472(2)*].

**BIS** the Department for Business, Innovation and Skills

**Body corporate** includes a body incorporated outside the UK, but does not include

- a corporation sole; or

- a partnership that, whether or not a legal person, is not regarded as a body corporate under the law by which it is governed.

[*CA 2006, s 1173*].

**Called-up share capital** means so much of the share capital of a company as equals

- the aggregate amount of calls made on its shares (whether or not these calls have been paid);

- any share capital paid up without being called; and

- any share capital to be paid on a specified future date under the articles, under the terms of allotment of the relevant shares or under any other arrangements for payment of those shares.

[*CA 2006, s 547*].

**Capital redemption reserve**. See **34.23** PURCHASE OF OWN SHARES.

**Class of shares**. See **9.1** CLASS RIGHTS.

**Companies Acts** means

(a)     the company law provisions of *CA 2006*;

(b)     *C(AICE)A 2004, Pt 2* (community interest companies); and

(c)     the provisions of *CA 1985* and the *CC(CP)A 1985* that remain in force.

Note that the provisions under (*b*) and (*c*) above are extended to Northern Ireland by *CA 2006, s 1284.*

[*CA 2006, s 2*].

**Company** means a company formed and registered under *CA 2006*, ie

• a company so formed and registered after the commencement of *CA 2006, Pt 1* (1 October 2009); or

• a company that immediately before that date

(i) was formed and registered under *CA 1985* or the *Companies (Northern Ireland) Order 1986 (SI 1986 No 1032)*, or

(ii) was an existing company for the purposes of that *Act* or that *Order*,

(which is to be treated on commencement as if formed and registered under *CA 2006*).

[*CA 2006, s 1(1)*].

**Constitution.** Unless the context requires otherwise, references in the *Companies Acts* to a company's constitution include the company's articles and any resolutions or agreements to which *CA 2006, ss 29, 30* apply (see **14.10 CONSTITUTION – MEMORANDUM AND ARTICLES**). [*CA 2006, s 17*]. Unless the context requires otherwise, references to a company's articles in any *CA 2006* provisions that were brought fully into force before 1 October 2009 include the company's memorandum.

[*SI 2007 No 2194, Sch 1 para 1*].

**Contributory.** In the Companies Acts, contributory means every person liable to contribute to the assets of the company in the event of it being wound up except for persons liable to contribute by virtue of a declaration by the court under *IA 1986, s 213* (fraudulent trading) or *IA 1986, s 214* (wrongful trading).

For the purposes of all proceedings for determining, and all proceedings prior to the final determination of, the persons who are to be deemed contributories, the expression includes any person alleged to be a contributory.

[*CA 2006, s 1170B; SI 2009 No 1941, Sch 1 para 260*].

**Corporate governance statement** means the statement required by the FCA Disclosure and Transparency Rules, paras 7.2.1 to 7.2.11. A 'separate' corporate governance statement means one that is not included in the directors' report. See **15.5 CORPORATE GOVERNANCE**.

[*CA 2006, ss 472A, 538A; SI 2009 No 1581, Regs 5, 8*].

**Corporation** includes a body incorporated outside the UK, but does not include

• a corporation sole; or

• a partnership that, whether or not a legal person, is not regarded as a body corporate under the law by which it is governed.

[*CA 2006, s 1173*].

**Court.** Except as otherwise provided, the court means

• in England and Wales, the High Court or a county court;

• in Scotland, the Court of Session or sheriff court; and

# Appendix 1 – Definitions

in Northern Ireland, the High Court.

[*CA 2006, s 1156(1)*].

**Debenture** includes debenture stock, bonds and any other securities of a company, whether or not constituting a charge on the assets of the company. [*CA 2006, s 738*]. See **17.6 Debt Finance–Debentures and Other Borrowing**.

**Director**. Director includes any person occupying the position of director by whatever name called.

[*CA 2006, s 250*].

**Dormant company**. A company is dormant during any period in which it has no 'significant accounting transaction'. A '*significant accounting transaction*' means a transaction which is required by *CA 2006, s 386* to be entered in the company's accounting records, but disregarding

(a) a transaction arising from the taking of shares in the company by a subscriber to the memorandum as a result of an undertaking of his in connection with the formation of the company; or

(b) a transaction consisting of the payment of

   (i) a fee to the Registrar of Companies on a change of name;

   (ii) a fee to the Registrar of Companies on the re-registration of a company;

   (iii) a penalty under *CA 2006, s 453* (penalty for failure to file accounts, see **2.11 Accounts: General**), or

   (iv) a fee to the Registrar of Companies for the registration of an annual return.

Any reference to a body corporate other than a company being dormant has a corresponding meaning.

[*CA 2006, s 1169*].

**EEA state** in relation to any time, means a state which at that time is a Member State or any other state which at that time is a party to the EEA agreement, ie the agreement on the European Economic Area signed at Oporto on 2 May 1992 (together with the Protocol adjusting that Agreement signed at Brussels on 17 March 1993, as modified or supplemented from time to time).

[*CA 2006, s 1170*].

The current Member States are Austria, Belgium, Bulgaria, Croatia, Cyprus, Czech Republic, Denmark, Estonia, Finland, France, Germany, Greece, Hungary, Iceland, Ireland, Italy, Latvia, Lichtenstein, Lithuania, Luxembourg, Malta, The Netherlands, Norway, Poland, Portugal, Romania, Slovakia , Slovenia, Spain, Sweden and the UK

**EEA company** and **EEA undertaking** mean a company or undertaking governed by the law of an EEA State.

[*CA 2006, s 1170*].

**Electronic form**. A document or information is sent or supplied in electronic form if it is sent or supplied

• by electronic means (eg by e-mail or fax); or

• by any other means while in an electronic form (eg sending a disk by post).

A document or information authorised or required to be sent or supplied in electronic form must be sent or supplied in a form, and by a means, that the sender or supplier reasonably considers will enable the recipient to read it and to retain a copy of it. A document or information can be read only if

- it can be read with the naked eye, or

- to the extent that it consists of images (eg photographs, pictures, maps, plans or drawings), it can be seen with the naked eye.

[*CA 2006, s 1168(3)(5)(6)(7)*].

**Electronic means.** A document or information is sent or supplied by electronic means if it is

- sent initially and received at its destination by means of electronic equipment for the processing (which expression includes digital compression) or storage of data; and

- entirely transmitted, conveyed and received by wire, by radio, by optical means or by other electromagnetic means.

[*CA 2006, s 1168(4)(7)*].

**Employees' share scheme** is a scheme for encouraging or facilitating the holding of shares or debentures of a company by or for the benefit of

- *bona fide* employees or former employees of the company, any subsidiary of the company, or the company's holding company or any subsidiary of the company's holding company; or

- the spouses, civil partners, surviving spouses, surviving civil partners or minor children or step-children of such employees or former employees.

[*CA 2006, s 1166*].

**Equity share capital** means a company's issued share capital excluding any part of that capital that does not carry any right (either as respects dividends or capital) to participate beyond a specified amount in a distribution.

[*CA 2006, s 548*].

**Fellow subsidiary undertakings** are undertakings which are 'subsidiary undertakings' of the same 'parent undertaking' but are not parent undertakings or subsidiary undertakings of each other.

[*CA 2006, s 1161(4)*].

**Financial year.** A company's first financial year begins with the first day of its first accounting reference period (see 2.17 ACCOUNTS (GENERAL) AND ACCOUNTING REFERENCE DATES AND PERIODS) and ends with the last day of that period or such other date, not more than seven days before or after the end of that period, as the directors may determine.

Subsequent financial years begin with the day immediately following the end of the company's previous financial year and end with the last day of its next accounting reference period or such other date, not more than seven days before or after the end of that period, as the directors may determine.

The seven-day variation allows accounts either to be prepared for a 52-week period or always to end on a specific day of the week.

# Appendix 1 – Definitions

In relation to an undertaking which is not a company, a reference to its financial year is to any period in respect of which a profit and loss account of the undertaking is required to be made up (by its constitution or by the law under which it is established), whether that period is a year or not..

The directors of a parent company must secure that, except where in their opinion there are good reasons against it, the financial year of each of its subsidiary undertakings coincides with the company's own financial year.

[*CA 2006, s 390*].

**Firm** means any entity, whether or not a legal person, that is not an individual and includes a body corporate, a corporation sole and a partnership or other unincorporated association.

[*CA 2006, s 1173*].

**Former Companies Acts** means

- the 'Joint Stock Companies Acts', *Companies Act 1862, Companies (Consolidation) Act 1908, Companies Act 1929, Companies Act (Northern Ireland) 1932, Companies Acts 1948 to 1983, Companies Act (Northern Ireland) 1960, Companies (Northern Ireland) Order 1986* and *Companies Consolidation (Consequential Provisions) (Northern Ireland) Order 1986*, and

- the provisions of the *CA 1985* and the *CC(CP)A 1985* that are no longer in force.

For these purposes the '*Joint Stock Companies Acts*' means *Joint Stock Companies Act 1856, Joint Stock Companies Acts 1856, 1857, Joint Stock Banking Companies Act 1857*, and the *Act to enable Joint Stock Banking Companies to be formed on the principle of limited liability*, but does not include *Joint Stock Companies Act 1844*.

[*CA 2006, s 1171*].

**The Gazette** means

- as respects companies registered in England and Wales, the London Gazette;

- as respects companies registered in Scotland, the Edinburgh Gazette; and

- as respects companies registered in Northern Ireland, the Belfast Gazette.

[*CA 2006, s 1173*].

**Group** means a 'parent undertaking' and its 'subsidiary undertakings' (see below).

[*CA 2006, s 474(1)*].

**Group undertaking** in relation to an 'undertaking' means an undertaking which is

- a 'parent undertaking' or 'subsidiary undertaking' of that undertaking; or

- a subsidiary undertaking of any parent undertaking of that undertaking.

[*CA 2006, s 1161(5)*].

**Hard copy.** A document or information is sent or supplied in hard copy form if it is sent or supplied in a paper copy or similar form capable of being read. A document or information can be read only if

- it can be read with the naked eye; or

- to the extent that it consists of images (eg photographs, pictures, maps, plans or drawings), it can be seen with the naked eye.

[*CA 2006, s 1168(2)(6)(7)*].

**Holding company**. See, by implication, under definition of 'subsidiary' below.

**IAS Regulation** means EC Regulation No. 1606/2002 of the European Parliament and of the Council of 19 July 2002 on the application of international accounting standards.

[*CA 2006, s 474(1)*].

**International accounting standards** means the international accounting standards, within the meaning of the IAS Regulation (see above), adopted from time to time by the European Commission in accordance with that Regulation.

[*CA 2006, s 474(1)*].

**Limited by guarantee**. See 12 COMPANY FORMATION AND TYPES OF COMPANIES.

**Limited by shares**. See 12 COMPANY FORMATION AND TYPES OF COMPANIES.

**Limited company**. See 12 COMPANY FORMATION AND TYPES OF COMPANIES.

**Members**. The members of a company are

- the subscribers to the company's memorandum (who are deemed to have agreed to become members on subscribing their names and who become members on the company's registration); and

- every other person who agrees to become a member of the company and whose name is entered in the register of members.

[*CA 2006, s 112*].

**MiFID investment firm** means an investment firm within the meaning of *EC Directive 2004/39/EC, Art 4.1.1* other than

- a company to which that Directive does not apply by virtue of *Art 2* of that Directive;

- a company which is an exempt investment firm within the meaning of *SI 2007 No 126, Reg 4A(3)*;

- any other company which fulfils all the requirements set out in *SI 2007 No 126, Reg 4C(3)*; and

- in respect of a financial year beginning before, but ending on or after 1 November 2007 (the '*transitional financial year*'), any person who satisfies the following conditions.

  (a) Condition A is satisfies if, at any time that is within the transitional financial year and before 1 November 2007, the person would have been a MiFID investment firm if the Directive had had effect at that time.

  (b) Condition B is satisfied if the person

    (i) was not, at any time that is within the transitional financial year and before 1 November 2007, an ISD investment firm within the meaning of *CA 1985, s 262* (as it had effect at that time); and

    (ii) would not, at any time that is within the transitional financial year and is on or after 1 November 2007, have been such a firm if that section had had effect at that time as it had effect immediately before 1 November 2007.

# Appendix 1 – Definitions

[CA 2006, ss 474, 539].

**Non-cash asset** means any property or interest in property, other than cash (which includes foreign currency). Any reference to the transfer or acquisition of a non-cash asset includes

- the creation or extinction of an estate or interest in, or a right over, any property; and

- the discharge of a liability of any person, other than a liability for a liquidated sum.

[CA 2006, s 1163].

**Officer** in relation to a body corporate includes a director, manager or secretary.

[CA 2006, s 1173].

**Old public company.** An old public company is a company limited by shares, or a company limited by guarantee and having a share capital, which

- existed on 22 December 1980 (in Northern Ireland, 1 July 1983) or was incorporated after that date pursuant to an application made before that date;

- was not a private company within the meaning of *CA 1948, s 28* (in Northern Ireland, *CA (Northern Ireland) 1960, s 28*) on that date or, if later, on the day of the company's incorporation; and

- has not since that date or the day of the company's incorporation (as the case may be) either been re-registered as a public company or become a private company.

Subject to below, references in the Companies Acts to

- a public company, or

- a company other than a private company,

are to be read (unless the context otherwise requires) as including an old public company and references to a private company are to be read accordingly.

But this does not apply in relation to *CA 2006, Pt 7* (re-registration as a means of altering a company's status) and *CA 2006 662–669* (treatment of shares held by or for public company) and does not restrict the power to make provision by regulations under *CA 2006, s 65* (inappropriate use of indications of company type or legal form).

[SI 2009 No 1941, Sch 3 paras 1, 2].

**Ordinary resolution.** See **42.2** RESOLUTIONS AND MEETINGS.

**Overseas company** means a company incorporated outside the UK.

[CA 2006, ss 1044, 1173].

**Parent undertakings.** See *'Meaning of 'parent' and 'subsidiary' undertaking'* below.

**Participating interests.** A participating interest means an 'interest in shares' held by an undertaking in another undertaking which it holds on a long-term basis for the purpose of securing a contribution to its activities by the exercise of control or influence arising from (or related to) that interest. Unless the contrary is shown, a holding of 20% or more of the shares of the undertaking is presumed to be a participating interest.

*'Interest in shares'* includes an interest which is convertible into an interest in shares and an option to acquire shares or any such interest (even if the relevant shares are, until the conversion or the exercise of the option, unissued).

An interest held on behalf of an undertaking is to be treated as held by it.

For the purposes of the expression 'participating interest'

- In the balance sheet and profit and loss formats set out in 3 ACCOUNTS: LARGE COMPANIES and 5 ACCOUNTS: SMALL COMPANIES, 'participating interest' does not include an interest in a group undertaking; and

- in those formats as they apply in relation to group accounts and in the definition of associated undertakings, the references above to the interest held by, and the purposes and activities of, the undertaking concerned are to be construed as references to the interest held by, and the purposes and activities of, the group.

[*SI 2008 No 409, Sch 8 para 8; SI 2008 No 410, Sch 10 para 11*].

**Prescribed** means prescribed (by Order or by Regulations) by the Secretary of State.

[*CA 2006, s 1167*].

**Private company.** See 12 COMPANY FORMATION AND TYPES OF COMPANIES.

**Profit and loss account** includes

- notes to the accounts giving information which is required by any provision of *CA 2006* or international accounting standards, and required or allowed by any such provision to be given in a note to company accounts; and

- in relation to a company that prepares IAS accounts, an income statement or other equivalent financial statement required to be prepared by international accounting standards.

In the case of an undertaking not trading for profit, any reference to a profit and loss account is to an income and expenditure account (and references to profit and loss and, in relation to group accounts, to a consolidated profit and loss account are construed accordingly).

[*CA 2006, ss 472(2), 474(1)(2)*].

**Public company.** See 12 COMPANY FORMATION AND TYPES OF COMPANIES.

**Quoted company.** A quoted company means a company whose equity share capital

- has been included in the official list in accordance with the provisions of *FSMA 2000, Part VI*;

- is officially listed in an EEA State; or

- is admitted to dealing on either the New York Stock Exchange or the exchange known as Nasdaq.

A company is a quoted company in relation to a financial year if it is a quoted company immediately before the end of the accounting reference period by reference to which that financial year was determined.

[*CA 2006, s 385(1)(2)*].

**Receiver or manager** (and certain related references). Any reference in the Companies Acts to a receiver or manager of the property of a company, or to a receiver of it, includes a receiver or manager or (as the case may be) a receiver of part only of that property and a receiver only of the income arising from the property or from part of it.

Any reference in the Companies Acts to the appointment of a receiver or manager under powers contained in an instrument includes an appointment made under powers that, by virtue of an enactment, are implied in and have effect as if contained in the instrument.

# Appendix 1 – Definitions

*[CA 2006, s 1170A]*.

**Redeemable shares**. See **34.2 Purchase of Own Shares**.

**Requirements of *CA 2006***. References in the company law provisions of *CA 2006* to the requirements of *CA 2006* include the requirements of Regulations and Orders made under it.

*[CA 2006, s 1172]*.

**Service address**. A service address in relation to a person means an address at which documents may be effectively served on that person.

*[CA 2006, s 1141]*.

**Shadow director**. See **18.1 Directors**.

**Share** means share in a company's share capital, and includes stock (except where a distinction between shares and stock is expressed or implied).

*[CA 2006, s 540(1)(4)]*.

References to shares

•	in relation to an undertaking with capital but no share capital, are to rights to share in the capital of the undertaking; and

•	in relation to an undertaking without capital, are to interests

(i)	conferring any right to share in the profits, or liability to contribute to the losses, of the undertaking; or

(ii)	giving rise to an obligation to contribute to the debts or expenses of the undertaking in the event of a winding up.

*[CA 2006, s 1161(2)]*.

**Share premium account**. See **46.1 Share Premium**.

**Special notice** (in relation to a resolution). See **42.19 Resolutions and Meetings**.

**Special resolution**. See **42.3 Resolutions and Meetings**.

**Subsidiary**

A company is a subsidiary of another company, (its holding company)

in any of the following circumstances.

•	If that other company holds a majority of the 'voting rights' in it.

•	If that other company is a member of it and has the right to appoint or remove a majority of its board of directors, ie the right to appoint or remove directors holding a majority of the voting rights at meetings of the board on all, or substantially all, matters. For these purposes, a company is treated as having the right to appoint to a directorship if

(i)	a person's appointment to it follows necessarily from his appointment as director of the company; or

(ii)	the directorship is held by the company itself.

A right to appoint or remove which is exercisable only with the consent or concurrence of another person is left out of account unless no other person has a right to appoint or, as the case may be, remove in relation to that directorship.

- If that other company is a member of it and controls alone, pursuant to an agreement with other members, a majority of the voting rights in it.

- If it is a subsidiary of a company which is itself a subsidiary of that other company.

'*Voting rights*' are rights conferred on shareholders in respect of their shares (or, in the case of a company not having a share capital, on members) to vote at general meetings of the company on all, or substantially all, matters.

For the above purposes,

(a) rights which are exercisable only in certain circumstances are taken into account only

- when the circumstances have arisen, and for so long as they continue to obtain; or

- when the circumstances are within the control of the person having the rights

and rights which are normally exercisable but are temporarily incapable of exercise continue to be taken into account;

(b) rights held by a person in a fiduciary capacity are treated as not held by him;

(c) rights held by a person as nominee for another are treated as held by the other; and rights are regarded as held as nominee if they are exercisable only on that other person's instructions or with his consent or concurrence;

(d) rights attached to shares held by way of security are treated as held by the person providing the security where

- apart from the right to exercise them to preserve the value of, or realise, the security, the rights are exercisable only in accordance with his instructions; or

- the shares are held in connection with the granting of loans as part of normal business activities and apart from the right to exercise them to preserve the value of, or realise, the security, the rights are exercisable only in his interests.

For these purposes, rights are treated as being exercisable in accordance with the instructions of, or in the interests of, a company if they are exercisable in accordance with the instructions of, or in the interests of, any subsidiary or holding company of that company or any subsidiary of a holding company of that company;

(e) rights are treated as held by a company if they are held by any of its subsidiaries and nothing in (c) or (d) above is to be construed as requiring rights held by a holding company to be treated as held by any of its subsidiaries; and

(f) voting rights in a company are reduced by any rights held by the company itself.

References in the provisions of (b) to (f) above to rights held by a person include rights falling to be treated as held by him by virtue of any other of those provisions but not rights which by virtue of any such provision are to be treated as not held by him.

[*CA 2006, ss 1159, 1160, Sch 6*].

**Subsidiary undertakings.** See '*Meaning of 'parent' and 'subsidiary' undertaking*' below.

**Traded company.** A traded company means a company any shares of which

- carry rights to vote at general meetings; and

# Appendix 1 – Definitions

- are admitted to trading on a regulated market in an EEA state by or with the consent of the company.

[*CA 2006, s 360C*].

**Treasury shares**. See **34.19 Purchase of Own Shares**.

**Turnover**, in relation to a company, means the amounts derived from the provision of goods and services falling within the company's ordinary activities, after deduction of trade discounts, value added tax and any other taxes based on the amounts so derived.

[*CA 2006, ss 474(1), 539(1)*].

**UK-registered company** means a company registered under *CA 2006* but does not include an overseas company that has registered particulars under *CA 2006, s 1046*.

[*CA 2006, ss 547, 1158*].

**Undertaking** (see also *'Meaning of 'parent' and 'subsidiary' undertaking'* below) means

- a body corporate or partnership, or

- an unincorporated association carrying on a trade or business, with or without a view to profit.

Where an undertaking is not a company, expressions appropriate to companies must be construed as references to the corresponding persons, officers, document or organs, as the case may be, appropriate to undertakings of that description.

[*CA 2006, s 1161(1)(3)*].

**Unlimited company**. See **12 Company Formation and Types of Companies**.

**Unquoted company** means a company that is not a quoted company (see above).

[*CA 2006, s 385(3)*].

**Wholly-owned subsidiary**. A company is a wholly-owned subsidiary of another company if it has no members except that other company and that other company's wholly-owned subsidiaries or persons acting on behalf of that other company or its wholly-owned subsidiaries. [*CA 2006, s 1159(2)*]. A similar definition applied under *CA 1985, s 736(2)*.

**Working day**, in relation to a company, means a day that is not a Saturday or Sunday, Christmas Day, Good Friday or any day that is a bank holiday under *Banking and Financial Dealings Act 1971* in the part of the UK where the company is registered.

[*CA 2006, s 1173*].

**Written resolution**. See **42.5 Resolutions and Meetings**.

## MEANING OF 'PARENT' AND 'SUBSIDIARY' UNDERTAKING

An 'undertaking' is a *'parent undertaking'* in relation to another undertaking (a 'subsidiary undertaking') if

(a) it holds a majority of the 'voting rights' in the undertaking;

(b) it is a member of the undertaking and has the right to appoint or remove a majority of its board of directors;

(c) it has the right to exercise a dominant influence over the undertaking by virtue of

# Appendix 1 – Definitions

(i)     provisions in the undertaking's articles; or

(ii)     a 'control contract');

(d)     it is a member of the undertaking and controls alone, pursuant to an agreement with other shareholders or members, a majority of the 'voting rights';

(e)     it has the power to exercise, or actually exercises, dominant influence or control over it; or

(f)     the two undertakings in question are managed on a unified basis.

For the above purposes, an undertaking is to be treated as a member of another undertaking if

• any of its subsidiary undertakings is a member of that undertaking; or

• any shares in that other undertaking are held by persons acting on behalf of the undertaking or any of its subsidiary undertakings.

A parent undertaking is treated as a parent undertaking of undertakings in relation to which any of its subsidiary undertakings are, or are treated as being, parent undertakings (and references to its subsidiary undertakings are construed accordingly).

References to shares are to allotted shares.

[*CA 2006, s 1162*].

## Voting rights

'*Voting rights*' means the rights conferred on shareholders in respect of their shares (or, if the undertaking does not have a share capital, on members) to vote at general meetings of the undertaking on all (or substantially all) matters. In the case of an undertaking which does not have general meetings at which matters are decided by the exercise of voting rights, references to holding 'a majority of the voting rights' in the undertaking should be construed as having the right, under the constitution of the undertaking, to direct its overall policy or to alter the terms of its constitution.

[*CA 2006, Sch 7 para 2*].

## Right to appoint or remove a majority of the directors

The reference to the right to appoint or remove a majority of the board of directors is to the right to appoint or remove directors holding a majority of the voting rights at board meetings on all (or substantially all) matters.

An undertaking is treated as having the right to appoint to a directorship if

• a person's appointment to it follows necessarily from his appointment as director of the undertaking; or

• the directorship is held by the undertaking itself.

No account is to be taken of a right to appoint (or remove) which can be exercised only with the consent or concurrence of another person, except where, in relation to that directorship, no-one else has the right to appoint (or remove).

[*CA 2006, Sch 7 para 3*].

# Appendix 1 – Definitions

## Right to exercise dominant influence

An undertaking is not to be regarded as having the right to exercise a dominant influence over another undertaking unless it has the right to give directions, with respect to the operating and financial policies of that other undertaking, which its directors are obliged to comply with whether or not they are for the benefit of that other undertaking.

A '*control contract*' means a written contract, conferring a right to exercise a dominant influence, which

- is of a kind authorised by the articles of the undertaking in relation to which the right is exercisable; and

- is permitted by the law under which that undertaking is established.

[*CA 2006, Sch 7 para 4*].

## General rules on 'rights'

The following rules apply for the purposes of 'rights' referred to above

(a)     Rights exercisable only in certain circumstances are taken into account only

    (i)     when the circumstances have arisen and for so long as they continue; or

    (ii)     when the circumstances are within the control of the persons having the rights.

(b)     Rights normally exercisable but temporarily incapable of being exercised must continue to be taken into account.

(c)     Rights held by a person in a fiduciary capacity are treated as not held by him.

(d)     Rights held by a person as nominee for another (ie rights exercisable only on the other's instructions or with his consent or concurrence) are treated as held by the other.

(e)     Rights attached to shares held by way of security are treated as held by the person providing the security

    (i)     where the rights are exercisable only in accordance with that person's instructions (apart from the right to exercise them to preserve the value of, or realise, the security); and

    (ii)     if the shares are held in connection with the granting of loans as part of normal business activities, where the rights are exercisable only in that person's interests (apart from any right to exercise them to preserve the value of, or realise, the security).

    Rights are treated as being exercisable in accordance with the instructions of, or in the interests of, an undertaking if they are exercisable in accordance with the instructions of, or in the interests of, any 'group undertaking'

(f)     Rights are treated as held by a parent undertaking if they are held by any of its subsidiary undertakings.

(g)     The voting rights in an undertaking must be reduced by any rights held by the undertaking itself.

Nothing in (*d*) or (*e*) above is to be construed as requiring rights held by a parent undertaking to be treated as held by any of its subsidiary undertakings.

References in (*c*) to (*g*) above to rights held by a person include rights falling to be treated as held by him, but exclude rights falling to be treated as not held by him, by virtue of any of these provisions.

[*CA 2006, Sch 7 paras 5–11*].

# Appendix 2 – Forms

### FORMS – GENERAL COMPANY USE

Companies are required to submit a variety of information on their business activities to the Registrar of Companies. All statutory forms are available on request and free of charge from Companies House Cardiff and from Companies House Edinburgh (see **39.1** REGISTRAR OF COMPANIES). Forms can be obtained or submitted online or by post.

See **39.6** REGISTRAR OF COMPANIES for use of forms and completion of forms generally.

The forms which are currently prescribed for *CA 2006* are divided into Webcheck (ie on line filing) and paper forms. Please see Companies House website for help in completing forms and for a complete list of forms. This Appendix does not include forms for LLPs, LPs, EEIGs, SEs, Cross Border Mergers, *Newspaper Libel and Registration Act*, UK companies not formed under *CA 2006*, pre 6 April 2013 mortgages, and those forms listed on Companies House website as *Companies Act 1985* paper forms.

**CA 2006 forms**
**Online filing**

| | |
|---|---|
| AR01 | Annual Return (£14 charge) |
| Annual Accounts | Audit Exempt Small Full Accounts (with Abbreviated Option) |
| Annual Accounts | Audit Exempt Abbreviated Accounts—Annual Accounts, Micro-entity accounts |
| AA01 | Change of accounting reference date |
| AA02 | Dormant Company Accounts |
| AD01 | Change of registered office address |
| AP01 | Appointment of Director |
| AP02 | Appointment of Corporate Director |
| AP03 | Appointment of Secretary |
| AP04 | Appointment of Corporate Secretary |
| NM01 | Change of company name (only file online if permission is not needed for the new company name) |
| TM01 | Terminating appointment as Director |
| TM02 | Terminating appointment as Secretary |
| CH01 | Change of particulars for Director |
| CH02 | Change of particulars for Corporate Director |
| CH03 | Change of particulars for Secretary |
| CH04 | Change of particulars for Corporate Secretary |
| AD02 | Notification of single alternative inspection location (SAIL) |
| AD03 | Change of location of the company records to the single alternative inspection location (SAIL) |
| AD04 | Change of location of the company records to the registered office |
| IN01 | Register a private company (only online if a private company and is limited by shares and is adopting model articles and permission is not needed for company name) |

# Appendix 2 – Forms

*CA 2006* forms

| | |
|---|---|
| TM02 | Termination of appointment of secretary |
| CH01 | Change of director's details |
| CH02 | Change of corporate director's details |
| CH03 | Change of secretary's details |
| CH04 | Change of corporate secretary's details |
| DS01 | Striking off application by a company |
| DS02 | Withdrawal of striking off application by a company |
| IN01 | Application to register a private or public company |
| Pro Forma Memorandum CA 2006 (with a share capital) | Pro Forma of CA 2006 Memorandum for a company with a share capital (notice of subscribers) |
| Pro Forma Memorandum CA 2006 (without a share capital) | Pro Forma of CA 2006 Memorandum for a company without a share capital (notice of subscribers) |
| IC01 | Notice of intention to carry on business as an investment company |
| IC02 | Notice that a company no longer wishes to be an investment company |
| RM01 | Notice of appointment of an administrative receiver, receiver or manager |
| RM02 | Notice of ceasing to act as an administrative receiver, receiver or manager |
| MR01 | Particulars of a mortgage or charge (where date or creation of charge is on or after 6/4/2013) |
| MR02 | Particulars of a charge subject to which property or undertaking has been acquired (where date or creation of charge is on or after 6/4/2013) |
| MR03 | Particulars for the registration of a charge to secure a series of debentures (where date or creation of charge is on or after 6/4/2013) |
| MR04 | Register a statement of satisfaction (where charge is created before, on or after 6/4/2013) |
| MR05 | Statement that part (or the whole) of the property charged has been released from the charge (where charge is created before, on or after 6/4/2013) |
| MR06 | Statement of company acting as trustee (where date or creation of charge is on or after 6/4/2013) |
| MR07 | Particulars of alteration of charge (negative pledge) |
| MR08 | Particulars of charge where there is no instrument (where date or creation of charge is on or after 6/4/2013) |
| MR09 | Particulars of a charge subject to which property or undertaking has been acquired where there is no instrument (where date or creation of charge is on or after 6/4/2013) |
| MR10 | Particulars for the registration of a charge to secure a series of debentures where there is no instrument (where date or creation of charge is on or after 6/4/2013) |
| AD06 | Notice of opening of overseas branch register |
| AD07 | Notice of discontinuance of overseas branch register |

# Appendix 2 – Forms

## *CA 2006* forms

| | |
|---|---|
| AP05 | Appointment of a manager under Section 47 of the Companies (Audit, Investigations and Community Enterprise) Act 2004 or receiver and manager under Section 18 of the Charities Act 1993 or judicial factor (Scotland) |
| TMO3 | Termination of appointment of manager under Section 47 of the Companies (Audit, Investigations and Community Enterprise) Act 2004 or receiver and manager under Section 18 of the Charities Act 1993 or judicial factor (Scotland) |
| CH05 | Change of service address for manager appointed under Section 47 of the Companies (Audit, Investigations and Community Enterprise) Act 2004 or receiver and manager under Section 18 of the Charities Act 1993 or judicial factor (Scotland) |
| RP01 | Replacement of document not meeting requirements for proper delivery |
| RP02A | Application for rectification by the Registrar of Companies |
| RP02B | Application for rectification of a registered office or a UK establishment address by the Registrar of Companies |
| RP03 | Notice of an objection to a request for the Registrar of Companies to rectify the Register |
| RP04 | Second filing of a document previously delivered |
| VT01 | Certified voluntary translation of an original document that is or has been delivered to the Registrar of Companies |
| RR01 | Application by a private company for re-registration as a public company |
| RR02 | Application by a public company for re-registration as a private limited company |
| RR03 | Notice by the company of application to the court for cancellation of resolution for re-registration |
| RR04 | Notice by the applicants of application to the court for cancellation of resolution for re-registration |
| RR05 | Application by a private limited company for re-registration as an unlimited company |
| Pro-Forma form of assent for re-registration of private company as unlimited | Pro-Forma form of assent for re-registration of private limited company as unlimited |
| RR06 | Application by an unlimited company for re-registration as a private limited company |
| RR07 | Application by a public company for re-registration as a private unlimited company |
| Pro-Forma form of assent for re-registration of public company as private and unlimited | Pro-Forma form of assent for re-registration of public company as private and unlimited |
| RR08 | Application by a public company for re-registration as a private limited company following a court order reducing capital |
| RR09 | Application by a public company for re-registration as a private company following a cancellation of shares |
| Res CA2006 | Special resolution on change of name |

**CA 2006 forms**

| | |
|---|---|
| Written Res CA2006 | Written special resolution on change of name |
| 980(1) | Notice of takeover offer to non-assenting shareholders |
| 980(dec) | Notice of declaration to non-assenting shareholders |
| 984 | Notice of takeover to non-assenting shareholders |
| SH01 | Return of allotment of shares |
| SH02 | Notice of consolidation, sub-division, redemption of shares or re-conversion of stock into shares |
| SH03 | Return of purchase of own shares |
| SH04 | Notice of sale or transfer of treasury shares |
| SH05 | Notice of cancellation of treasury shares |
| SH06 | Notice of cancellation of shares |
| SH07 | Notice of cancellation of shares held by or for a public company |
| SH08 | Notice of name or other designation of class of shares |
| SH09 | Return of allotment by an unlimited company allotting new class of shares |
| SH10 | Notice of particulars of variation of rights attached to shares |
| SH11 | Notice of new class of members |
| SH12 | Notice of particulars of variation of class rights |
| SH13 | Notice of name or other designation of class of members |
| SH14 | Notice of redenomination of shares |
| SH15 | Notice of reduction of capital following redenomination |
| SH16 | Notice by the applicants of application to court for cancellation of the special resolution approving a redemption or purchase of shares out of capital |
| SH17 | Notice by the company of application to court for cancellation of the special resolution approving a redemption or purchase of shares out of capital |
| SH19 | Statement of capital |
| SH50 | Application for trading certificate for a public company |
| 466 | Particulars of an instrument of alteration to a floating charge created by a company registered in Scotland |

# Appendix 3 – Companies House Fees

## 1  FEES PAYABLE

Companies House fees payable can be found at www.gov.uk/government/organisations/companies-house/about-our-services#companies -house-fees. This is the definitive source for up to date fees.

Companies House charge a statutory filing fee for:

- company incorporation and registration;
- limited liability partnership (LLP) incorporation and registration fees;
- overseas company incorporation and registration fees;
- European economic interest groupings (EEIG) incorporation and registration fees;
- European company – sociates europea (SE) incorporation and registration fees;
- community interest company (CIC) and 'other' incorporation types;
- limited partnership (LP) incorporation fees; and
- extractives filing service.

They charge a statutory search fee on:

- Companies House Direct (CHD) search fees;
- WebCHeck search fees;
- information centre search fees;
- contact centre search fees;
- XML gateway search fees;
- extranet search fees;
- bulk product fees; and
- DVD product fees.

Some of Companies House fees are set by regulations and confirmed by Parliament. Some fees are administratively set by a fees determination.

All statutory fees on this list have been confirmed by Parliament and are set by the following statutory fees regulations:

- *The Registrar of Companies (Fees) (Companies, Overseas Companies and Limited Liability Partnerships) Regulations 2012 (SI 2012/1907)* as amended by *The Registrar of Companies (Fees) (Amendment) Regulations 2016 (SI 2016/621).*
- *The Registrar of Companies (Fees) (European Economic Interest Grouping and European Public Limited-Liability Company) Regulations 2012 (SI 2012/1908)* as amended by *The Registrar of Companies (Fees) (Amendment) Regulations 2016 (SI 2016/621).*

# 1   Appendix 3 – Companies House Fees

- *The Registrar of Companies (Fees) (Limited Partnerships and Newspaper Proprietors) Regulations 2009 (SI 2009/2392)* as amended by *The Registrar of Companies (Fees) (Limited Partnerships) (Amendment) Regulations 2011 (SI 2011/319)* and *The Registrar of Companies (Fees) (Amendment) Regulations 2016 (SI 2016/621).*

Not all fees are set by the above regulations, some fees are administratively set by a fees determination (see www.gov.uk/government/uploads/system/uploads/ attachment _data/file/629335/Fees_Determination__17_July_2017-.pdf) under *CA 2006, s 1063(5).* These include fees for new products, products that are in decline and products that have a small customer base.

The registration fees above do not apply to documents delivered under the *Companies Act 1985* or the *Companies (Northern Ireland) Order 1986.*

Any document delivered to the Registrar of Companies under the *Companies Act 1985* or the *Companies (Northern Ireland) Order 1986* will be free of charge.

# Appendix 4 – Standard Articles of association

(1) Companies Act 1985 Table A (SI 1985/805)
(2) Model articles: private companies limited by shares (SI 2008/3229, Sch 1). CA 2006
(3) Model articles: public companies (SI 2008/3229, Sch 3). CA 2006

## COMPANIES ACT 1985 TABLE A (SI 1985/805) MODEL ARTICLES: COMPANIES LIMITED BY SHARES (SI 2008 NO 3229, SCH 1).

### 1 Regulations for management of a company limited by shares

In these regulations

"the Act" means the Companies Act 1985 including any statutory modification or re-enactment thereof for the time being in force [and any provisions of the Companies Act 2006 for the time being in force][2].

"the articles" means the articles of the company.

"clear days" in relation to the period of a notice means that period excluding the day when the notice is given or deemed to be given and the day for which it is given or on which it is to take effect.

["communication" means the same as in the Electronic Communications Act 2000.][1]

["electronic communication" means the same as in the Electronic Communications Act 2000.][1]

"executed" includes any mode of execution.

"office" means the registered office of the company.

"the holder" in relation to shares means the member whose name is entered in the register of members as the holder of the shares.

"the seal" means the common seal of the company.

"secretary" means the secretary of the company or any other person appointed to perform the duties of the secretary of the company, including a joint, assistant or deputy secretary.

"the United Kingdom" means Great Britain and Northern Ireland.

Unless the context otherwise requires, words or expressions contained in these regulations bear the same meaning as in the Act but excluding any statutory modification thereof not in force when these regulations become binding on the company.

**Notes**

---

1  Inserted by SI 2000 No 3373, art 32(1), Sch 1 para 1 with effect from 22 December 2000.

2  Inserted by SI 2007 No 2541, Reg 3 in relation to a company registered on or after 1 October 2007.

---

## 2 Share capital

Subject to the provisions of the Act and without prejudice to any rights attached to any existing shares, any share may be issued with such rights or restrictions as the company may by ordinary resolution determine.

## 3

Subject to the provisions of the Act, shares may be issued which are to be redeemed or are to be liable to be redeemed at the option of the company or the holder on such terms and in such manner as may be provided by the articles.

## 4

The company may exercise the powers of paying commissions conferred by the Act. Subject to the [provisions] of the Act, any such commission may be satisfied by the payment of cash or by the allotment of fully or partly paid shares or partly in one way and partly in the other.

**Note**

Word in square brackets substituted for the word 'provision' by SI 1985 No 1052 as from 1 August 1985.

## 5

Except as required by law, no person shall be recognised by the company as holding any share upon any trust and (except as otherwise provided by the articles or by law) the company shall not be bound by or recognise any interest in any share except an absolute right to the entirety thereof in the holder.

## 6 Share certificates

Every member, upon becoming the holder of any shares, shall be entitled without payment to one certificate for all the shares of each class held by him (and, upon transferring a part of his holding of shares of any class, to a certificate for the balance of such holding) or several certificates each for one or more of his shares of any class, to a certificate for the balance of such holding) or several certificates each for one or more of his shares upon payment for every certificate after the first of such reasonable sum as the directors may determine. Every certificate shall be sealed with the seal and shall specify the number, class and distinguishing numbers (if any) of the shares to which it relates and the amount or respective amounts paid up thereon. The company shall not be bound to issue more than one certificate for shares held jointly by several persons and delivery of a certificate to one joint holder shall be a sufficient delivery to all of them.

## 7

If a share certificate is defaced, worn-out, lost or destroyed, it may be renewed on such terms (if any) as to evidence and indemnity and payment of the expenses reasonably incurred by the company in investigating evidence as the directors may determine but otherwise free of charge, and (in the case of defacement or wearing-out) on delivery up of the old certificate.

## 8 Lien

The company shall have a first and paramount lien on every share (not being a fully paid share) for all moneys (whether presently payable or not) payable at a fixed time or called in respect of that share. The directors may at any time declare any share to be wholly or in part exempt from the provisions of this regulation. The company's lien on a share shall extend to any amount payable in respect of it.

## 9

The company may sell in such manner as the directors determine any shares on which the company has a lien if a sum in respect of which the lien exists is presently payable and is not paid within fourteen clear days after notice has been given to the holder of the share or to the person entitled to it in consequence of the death or bankruptcy of the holder, demanding payment and stating that if the notice is not complied with the shares may be sold.

## 10

To give effect to a sale the directors may authorise some person to execute an instrument of transfer of the shares sold to, or in accordance with the directions of, the purchaser. The title of the transferee to the shares shall not be affected by any irregularity in or invalidity of the proceedings in reference to the sale.

## 11

The net proceeds of the sale, after payment of the costs, shall be applied in payment of so much of the sum for which the lien exists as is presently payable, and any residue shall (upon surrender to the company for cancellation of the certificate for the shares sold and subject to a like lien for any moneys not presently payable as existed upon the shares before the sale) be paid to the person entitled to the shares at the date of the sale.

## 12 Calls on shares and forfeiture

Subject to the terms of allotment, the directors may make calls upon the members in respect of any moneys unpaid on their shares (whether in respect of nominal value or premium) and each member shall (subject to receiving at least fourteen clear days' notice specifying when and where payment is to be made) pay to the company as required by the notice the amount called on his shares. A call may be required to be paid by instalments. A call may, before receipt by the company of any sum due thereunder, be revoked in whole or part and payment of a call may be postponed in whole or part. A person upon whom a call is made shall remain liable for calls made upon him notwithstanding the subsequent transfer of the shares in respect whereof the call was made.

## 13

A call shall be deemed to have been made at the time when the resolution of the directors authorising the call was passed.

## 14

The joint holders of a share shall be jointly and severally liable to pay all calls in respect thereof.

## 15

If a call remains unpaid after it has become due and payable the person from whom it is due and payable shall pay interest on the amount unpaid from the day it became due and payable until it is paid at the rate fixed by the terms of allotment of the share or in the notice of the call or, if no rate is fixed, at the appropriate rate (as defined by the Act) but the directors may waive payment of the interest wholly or in part.

## 16

An amount payable in respect of a share on allotment or at any fixed date, whether in respect of nominal value or premium or as an instalment of a call, shall be deemed to be a call and if it is not paid the provisions of the articles shall apply as if that amount had become due and payable by virtue of a call.

**17**

Subject to the terms of allotment, the directors may make arrangements on the issue of shares for a difference between the holders in the amounts and times of payment of calls on their shares.

**18**

If a call remains unpaid after it has become due and payable the directors may give to the person from whom it is due not less than fourteen clear days' notice requiring payment of the amount unpaid together with any interest which may have accrued. The notice shall name the place where payment is to be made and shall state that if the notice is not complied with the shares in respect of which the call was made will be liable to be forfeited.

**19**

If the notice is not complied with any share in respect of which it was given may, before the payment required by the notice has been made, be forfeited by a resolution of the directors and the forfeiture shall include all dividends or other moneys payable in respect of the forfeited shares and not paid before the forfeiture.

**20**

Subject to the provisions of the Act, a forfeited share may be sold, re-alloted or otherwise disposed of on such terms and in such manner as the directors determine either to the person who was before the forfeiture the holder or to any other person and at any time before sale, re-allotment or other disposition, the forfeiture may be cancelled on such terms as the directors think fit. Where for the purposes of its disposal a forfeited share is to be transferred to any person the directors may authorise some person to execute an instrument of transfer of the share to that person.

**21**

A person any of whose shares have been forfeited shall cease to be a member in respect of them and shall surrender to the company for cancellation the certificate for the shares forfeited but shall remain liable to the company for all moneys which at the date of forfeiture were presently payable by him to the company in respect of those shares with interest at the rate at which interest was payable on those moneys before the forfeiture or, if no interest was so payable, at the appropriate rate (as defined in the Act) from the date of forfeiture until payment but the directors may waive payment wholly or in part or enforce payment without any allowance for the value of the shares at the time of forfeiture or for any consideration received on their disposal.

**22**

A statutory declaration by a director or the secretary that a share has been forfeited on a specified date shall be conclusive evidence of the facts stated in it as against all persons claiming to be entitled to the share and the declaration shall (subject to the execution of an instrument of transfer if necessary) constitute a good title to the share and the person to whom the share is disposed of shall not be bound to see to the application of the consideration, if any, nor shall his title to the share be affected by any irregularity in or invalidity of the proceedings in reference to the forfeiture or disposal of the share.

**23 Transfer of shares**

The instrument of transfer of a share may be in any usual form or in any other form which the directors may approve and shall be executed by or on behalf of the transferor and, unless the share is fully paid, by or on behalf of the transferee.

**24**

The directors may refuse to register the transfer of a share which is not fully paid to a person of whom they do not approve and they may refuse to register the transfer of a share on which the company has a lien. They may also refuse to register a transfer unless

(a)     it is lodged at the office or at such other place as the directors may appoint and is accompanied by the certificate for the shares to which it relates and such other evidence as the directors may reasonably require to show the right of the transferor to make the transfer;

(b)     it is in respect of only one class of shares; and

(c)     it is in favour of not more than four transferees.

**25**

If the directors refuse to register a transfer of a share, they shall within two months after the date on which the transfer was lodged with the company send to the transferee notice of the refusal.

**26**

The registration of transfers of shares or of transfers of any class of shares may be suspended at such times and for such periods (not exceeding thirty days in any year) as the directors may determine.

**27**

No fee shall be charged for the registration of any instrument of transfer or other document relating to or affecting the title to any share.

**28**

The company shall be entitled to retain any instrument of transfer which is registered, but any instrument of transfer which the directors refuse to register shall be returned to the person lodging it when notice of the refusal is given.

**29 Transmission of shares**

If a member dies the survivor or survivors where he was a joint holder, and his personal representatives where he was a sole holder or the only survivor of joint holders, shall be the only persons recognised by the company as having any title to his interest; but nothing herein contained shall release the estate of a deceased member from any liability in respect of any share which had been jointly held by him.

**30**

A person becoming entitled to a share in consequence of the death or bankruptcy of a member may, upon such evidence being produced as the directors may properly require, elect either to become the holder of the share or to have some person nominated by him registered as the transferee. If he elects to become the holder he shall give notice to the company to that effect. If he elects to have another person registered he shall execute an instrument of transfer of the share to that person. All the articles relating to the transfer of shares shall apply to the notice or instrument of transfer as if it were an instrument of transfer executed by the member and the death or bankruptcy of the member had not occurred.

**31**

A person becoming entitled to a share in consequence of the death or bankruptcy of a member shall have the rights to which he would be entitled if he were the holder of the share, except that he shall not, before being registered as the holder of the share, be entitled in respect of it to attend or vote at any meeting of the company or at any separate meeting of the holders of any class of shares in the company.

**32 Alteration of share capital**

The company may by ordinary resolution

(a)     increase its share capital by new shares of such amount as the resolution prescribes;

(b)     consolidate and divide all or any of its share capital into shares of larger amount than its existing shares;

(c)    subject to the provisions of the Act, sub-divide its shares, or any of them, into shares of smaller amount and the resolution may determine that, as between the shares resulting from the sub-division, any of them may have any preference or advantage as compared with the others; and

(d)    cancel shares which, at the date of the passing of the resolution, have not been taken or agreed to be taken by any person and diminish the amount of its share capital by the amount of the shares so cancelled.

**33**

Whenever as a result of a consolidation of shares any members would become entitled to fractions of a share, the directors may, on behalf of those members, sell the shares representing the fractions for the best price reasonably obtainable to any person (including, subject to the provisions of the Act, the company) and distribute the net proceeds of sale in due proportion among those members, and the directors may authorise some person to execute an instrument of transfer of the shares to, or in accordance with the directions of, the purchaser. The transferee shall not be bound to see to the application of the purchase money nor shall his title to the shares be affected by any irregularity in or invalidity of the proceedings in reference to the sale.

**34**

Subject to the provisions of the Act, the company may by special resolution reduce its share capital, any capital redemption reserve and any share premium account in any way.

**35 Purchase of own shares**

Subject to the provisions of the Act, the company may purchase its own shares (including any redeemable shares) and, if it is a private company, make a payment in respect of the redemption or purchase of its own shares otherwise than out of distributable profits of the company or the proceeds of a fresh issue of shares.

**36 General meetings**

All general meetings other than annual general meetings shall be called extraordinary general meetings.

**Note**

This Article ceases to apply to a company registered on or after 1 October 2007. [*SI 2007 No 2541, Reg 4*].

**37**

The directors may call general meetings and, on the requisition of members pursuant to the provisions of the Act, shall forthwith proceed to convene an extraordinary general meeting for a date not later than eight weeks after receipt of the requisition. If there are not within the United Kingdom sufficient directors to call a general meeting, any director or any member of the company may call a general meeting.

**Note**

This article is amended by *SI 2007 No 2541, Reg 5* in relation to companies registered on or after 1 October 2007 as follows.

•    For the words 'an extraordinary' substitute the word 'a'.

•    For the words 'for a date not later than eight weeks after receipt of the requisition' substitute 'in accordance with the provisions of the Act'.

**38 Notice of general meetings**

An annual general meeting and an extraordinary general meeting called for the passing of a special resolution or a resolution appointing a person as a director shall be called by at least twenty-one clear days' notice. All other extraordinary general meetings shall be called by at least fourteen clear days' notice but a general meeting may be called by shorter notice if is so agreed

    (a)    in the case of an annual general meeting, by all the members entitled to attend and vote thereat; and

    (b)    in the case of any other meeting by a majority in number of the members having a right to attend and vote being a majority together holding not less than ninety-five per cent in nominal value of the shares giving that right.

The notice shall specify the time and place of the meeting and the general nature of the business to be transacted and, in the case of an annual general meeting, shall specify the meeting as such.

Subject to the provisions of the articles and to any restrictions imposed on any shares, the notice shall be given to all the members, to all persons entitled to a share in consequence of the death or bankruptcy of a member and to the directors and auditors.

**Note**

This Article is amended by *SI 2007 No 2541, Regs 9, 20* in relation to companies registered on or after 1 October 2007 as follows.

*In relation to a private company limited by shares*

    •    Omit the words 'An annual general meeting and an extraordinary general meeting called for the passing of a special resolution or a resolution appointing a person as a director shall be called by at least twenty-one clear days' notice. All other extraordinary'.

    •    Omit paragraph (a).

    •    In paragraph (b), omit the words 'in the case of any other meeting' and '– five'.

    •    Omit the words 'and, in the case of an annual general meeting, shall specify the meeting as such'.

*In relation to public companies limited by shares*

    •    After the words 'annual general meeting' omit the words 'and an extraordinary general meeting called for the passing of a special resolution or a resolution appointing a person as a director'.

    •    After the words 'All other' omit the word 'extraordinary'.

**39**

The accidental omission to give notice of a meeting to, or the non-receipt of notice of a meeting by, any person entitled to receive notice shall not invalidate the proceedings at that meeting.

## 40 Proceedings at general meetings

No business shall be transacted at any meeting unless a quorum is present. Two persons entitled to vote upon the business to be transacted, each being a member or a proxy for a member or a duly authorised representative of a corporation, shall be a quorum.

**Note**

This Article is amended by *SI 2007 No 2541, Reg 10* in relation to private companies limited by shares registered on or after 1 October 2007 as follows.

    •    At the beginning of the second sentence insert the words 'Save in the case of a company with a single member'.

**41**

If such a quorum is not present within half an hour from the time appointed for the meeting, or if during a meeting such a quorum ceases to be present, the meeting shall stand adjourned to the same day in the next week at the same time and place or [to] such time and place as the directors may determine.

**Note**

Word in square brackets substituted by *SI 1985 No 1052* with effect from 1 August 1985

**42**

The chairman, if any, of the board of directors or in his absence some other director nominated by the directors shall preside as chairman of the meeting, but if neither the chairman nor such other director (if any) be present within fifteen minutes after the time appointed for holding the meeting and willing to act, the directors present shall elect one of their number to be chairman and, if there is only one director present and willing to act, he shall be chairman.

**43**

If no director is willing to act as chairman, or if no director is present within fifteen minutes after the time appointed for holding the meeting, the members present and entitled to vote shall choose one of their number to be chairman.

**44**

A director shall, notwithstanding that he is not a member, be entitled to attend and speak at any general meeting and at any separate meeting of the holders of any class of shares in the company.

**45**

The chairman may, with the consent of a meeting at which a quorum is present (and shall if so directed by the meeting), adjourn the meeting from time to time and from place to place, but no business shall be transacted at an adjourned meeting other than business which might properly have been transacted at the meeting had the adjournment not taken place. When a meeting is adjourned for fourteen days or more, at least seven clear days' notice shall be given specifying the time and place of the adjourned meeting and the general nature of the business to be transacted. Otherwise it shall not be necessary to give any such notice.

**46**

A resolution put to the vote of a meeting shall be decided on a show of hands unless before, or on the declaration of the result of, the show of hands a poll is duly demanded. Subject to the provisions of the Act, a poll may be demanded

(a)     by the chairman; or
(b)     by at least two members having the right to vote at the meeting; or
(c)     by a member or members representing not less than one-tenth of the total voting rights of all the members having the right to vote at the meeting; or
(d)     by a member or members holding shares conferring a right to vote at the meeting being shares on which an aggregate sum has been paid up equal to not less than one-tenth of the total sum paid up on all the shares conferring that right;

and a demand by a person as proxy for a member shall be the same as a demand by the member.

**47**

Unless a poll is duly demanded a declaration by the chairman that a resolution has been carried or carried unanimously, or by a particular majority, or lost, or not carried by a particular majority and an entry to that effect in the minutes of the meeting shall be conclusive evidence of the fact without proof of the number or proportion of the votes recorded in favour of or against the resolution.

**48**

The demand for a poll may, before the poll is taken, be withdrawn but only with the consent of the chairman and a demand so withdrawn shall not be taken to have invalidated the result of a show of hands declared before the demand was made.

**49**

A poll shall be taken as the chairman directs and he may appoint scrutineers (who need not be members) and fix a time and place for declaring the result of the poll. The result of the poll shall be deemed to be the resolution of the meeting at which the poll was demanded.

**50**

In the case of an equality of votes, whether on a show of hands or on a poll, the chairman shall be entitled to a casting vote in addition to any other vote he may have.

Note

This Article ceases to have effect in relation to a company registered on or after 1 October 2007.

[*SI 2007 No 2826, Reg 3*].

**51**

A poll demanded on the election of a chairman or on a question of adjournment shall be taken forthwith. A poll demanded on any other question shall be taken either forthwith or at such time and place as the chairman directs not being more than thirty days after the poll is demanded. The demand for a poll shall not prevent the continuance of a meeting for the transaction of any business other than the question on which the poll was demanded. If a poll is demanded before the declaration of the result of a show of hands and the demand is duly withdrawn, the meeting shall continue as if the demand had not been made.

**52**

No notice need be given of a poll not taken forthwith if the time and place at which it is to be taken are announced at the meeting at which it is demanded. In any other case at least seven clear days' notice shall be given specifying the time and place at which the poll is to be taken.

**53**

A resolution in writing executed by or on behalf of each member who would have been entitled to vote upon it if it had been proposed at a general meeting at which he was present shall be as effectual as if it had been passed at a general meeting duly convened and held and may consist of several instruments in the like form each executed by or on behalf of one or more members.

Note

This Article ceases to have effect in relation to a company registered on or after 1 October 2007.

[*SI 2007 No 2826, Reg 6*].

**54 Votes of members**

Subject to any rights or restrictions attached to any shares, on a show of hands every member who (being an individual) is present in person or (being a corporation) is present by a duly authorised representative, not being himself a member entitled to vote, shall have one vote and on a poll every member shall have one vote for every share of which he is the holder.

# Appendix 4 – Standard Articles of association, art 54

Note

This Article is amended by *SI 2007 No 2826, Reg 4* in relation to companies registered on or after 1 October 2007 as follows.

- After the words 'is present in person' insert the words 'or by proxy'.

- After the words 'is present by a duly authorised representative, insert the words 'or proxy'.

- Substitute for the words 'not being' the words 'unless the proxy (in either case) or the representative is'.

**55**

In the case of joint holders the vote of the senior who tenders a vote, whether in person or by proxy, shall be accepted to the exclusion of the votes of the other joint holders; and seniority shall be determined by the order in which the names of the holders stand in the register of members.

**56**

A member in respect of whom an order has been made by any court having jurisdiction (whether in the United Kingdom or elsewhere) in matters concerning mental disorder may vote, whether on a show of hands or on a poll, by his receiver, *curator bonis* or other person authorised in that behalf appointed by that court, and any such receiver, *curator bonis* or other person may, on a poll, vote by proxy. Evidence to the satisfaction of the directors of the authority of the person claiming to exercise the right to vote shall be deposited at the office, or at such other place as is specified in accordance with the articles for the deposit of instruments of proxy, not less than 48 hours before the time appointed for holding the meeting or adjourned meeting at which the right to vote is to be exercised and in default the right to vote shall not be exercisable.

Note

By virtue of the *Adults with Incapacity (Scotland) Act 2000, s 88(2), Sch 5, para 1* the references to a *curator bonis* shall be construed as references to a guardian with similar powers appointed under that Act.

**57**

No member shall vote at any general meeting or at any separate meeting of the holders of any class of shares in the company, either in person or by proxy, in respect of any share held by him unless all moneys presently payable by him in respect of that share have been paid.

**58**

No objection shall be raised to the qualification of any voter except at the meeting or adjourned meeting at which the vote objected to is tendered, and every vote not disallowed at the meeting shall be valid. Any objection made in due time shall be referred to the chairman whose decision shall be final and conclusive.

**59**

On a poll votes may be given either personally or by proxy. A member may appoint more than one proxy to attend on the same occasion.

**60**

[The appointment of][1] a proxy shall be [in writing][2] executed by or on behalf of the appointor and shall be in the following form (or in a form as near thereto as circumstances allow or in any other form which is usual or which the directors may approve)—

. . . . . . . . . . . PLC/Limited

I/We, . . . . . . . . . . of . . . . . . . . . . , being a member/members of the above-named company, hereby appoint . . . . . . . . . . of . . . . . . . . . . , or failing him, . . . . . . . . . . of . . . . . . . . . . , as my/our proxy to vote in my/our names[s] and on my/our behalf at the annual/extraordinary general meeting of the company, to be held on . . . . . . . . . . . 19 . . . . . . . . . . . , and at any adjournment thereof.

Signed on . . . . . . . . . 19. . . . . . . . ."[3]

**Notes**

[1] Substituted for the words 'An instrument appointing' by *SI 2000 No 3373, art 32(1), Sch 1 para 2* with effect from 22 December 2000.

[2] Words in italics revoked by *SI 2000 No 3373, art 32(1), Sch 1 para 2* with effect from 22 December 2000.

[3] This Article is amended by *SI 2007 No 2541, Regs 11, 21* in relation to companies registered on or after 1 October 2007 as follows.

*In relation to a private company limited by shares*

- After the words 'our behalf at the' omit the words 'annual/extraordinary'.

*In relation to public companies limited by shares*

- After the words 'our behalf at the annual/' omit the word 'extraordinary' and insert the words 'any other'.

## 61

Where it is desired to afford members an opportunity of instructing the proxy how he shall act the [appointment of][1] a proxy shall be in the following form (or in a form as near thereto as circumstances allow or in any other form which is usual or which the directors may approve) . . . . . . . . . . . PLC/Limited

I/We, . . . . . . . . . . . of . . . . . . . . . . . , being a member/members of the above-named company, hereby appoint . . . . . . . . . . . of . . . . . . . . . . . , or failing him, . . . . . . . . . . . of . . . . . . . . . . . , as my/our proxy to vote in my/our names[s] and on my/our behalf at the annual/extraordinary general meeting of the company, to be held on . . . . . . . . . . . 19 . . . . . . . . . . . , and at any adjournment thereof.

Signed on . . . . . . . . . 19. . . . . . . . ."

This form is to be used in respect of the resolutions mentioned below as follows:

Resolution No. 1 *for *against

Resolution No. 2 *for *against.

*Strike out whichever is not desired.

Unless otherwise instructed, the proxy may vote as he thinks fit or abstain from voting.

Signed this . . . . . . . . . day of . . . . . . . . . ."

**Notes**

[1] Substituted for the words 'instrument appointing' by *SI 2000 No 3373, art 32(1), Sch 1 para 3* with effect from 22 December 2000.

*In relation to a private company limited by shares*

- After the words 'our behalf at the' omit the words 'annual/extraordinary'.

*In relation to public companies limited by shares*

- After the words 'our behalf at the annual/' omit the word 'extraordinary' and insert the words 'any other'.

## 62

[The appointment of] a proxy and any authority under which it is executed or a copy of such authority certified notarially or in some other way approved by the directors may

(a)     [in the case of an instrument in writing] be deposited at the office or at such other place within the United kingdom as is specified in the notice convening the meeting or in any instrument of proxy sent out by the company in relation to the meeting not less than 48 hours before the time for holding the meeting or adjourned meeting at which the person named in the instrument proposes to vote; or

[(aa)    in the case of an appointment contained in an electronic communication, where an address has been specified for the purpose of receiving electronic communications

    (i)    in the notice convening the meeting, or

    (ii)    in any instrument of proxy sent out by the company in relation to the meeting, or

    (iii)    in any invitation contained in an electronic communication to appoint a proxy issued by the company in relation to the meeting,

be received at such address not less than 48 hours before the time for holding the meeting or adjourned meeting at which the person named in the appointment proposes to vote;]

(b)    in the case of a poll taken more than 48 hours after it is demanded, be deposited [or received] as aforesaid after the poll has been demanded and not less than 24 hours before the time appointed for the taking of the poll; or

(c)    where the poll is not taken forthwith but is taken not more than 48 hours after it was demanded, be delivered at the meeting at which the poll was demanded to the chairman or to the secretary or to any director;

[and an appointment of proxy which is not deposited, delivered or received] in a manner so permitted shall be invalid.

[In this regulation and the next, "address", in relation to electronic communications, includes any number or address used for the purposes of such communications.]

**Note**

Words 'The appointment of' substituted for the words 'The instrument appointing', words 'and an appointment of proxy which is not deposited, delivered or received' substituted for 'and an instrument of proxy which is not deposited or delivered', and other word in square brackets inserted by *SI 2000 No 3373, art 32(1), Sch 1 para 4* with effect from 22 December 2000.

### 63

A vote given or poll demanded by proxy or by the duly authorised representative of a corporation shall be valid notwithstanding the previous determination of the authority of the person voting or demanding a poll unless notice of the determination was received by the company at the office or at such other place at which the instrument of proxy was duly deposited [or, where the appointment of the proxy was contained in an electronic communication, at the address at which such appointment was duly received] before the commencement of the meeting or adjourned meeting at which the vote is given or the poll demanded or (in the case of a poll taken otherwise than on the same day as the meeting or adjourned meeting) the time appointed for taking the poll.

**Note**

Words in square brackets inserted by *SI 2000 No 3373, art 32(1), Sch 1 para 5* with effect from 22 December 2000.

### 64 Number of directors

Unless otherwise determined by ordinary resolution, the number of directors (other than alternate directors) shall not be subject to any maximum but shall be not less than two.

### 65 Alternate directors

Any director (other than an alternate director) may appoint any other director, or any other person approved by resolution of the directors and willing to act, to be an alternate director and may remove from office an alternate director so appointed by him.

**66**

An alternate director shall be entitled to receive notice of all meetings of directors and of all meetings of committees of directors of which his appointor is a member, to attend and vote at any such meeting at which the director appointing him is not personally present and generally to perform all the functions of his appointor as a director in his absence but shall not be entitled to receive any remuneration from the company for his services as an alternate director. But it shall not be necessary to give notice of such a meeting to an alternate director who is absent from the United Kingdom.

**67**

An alternate director shall cease to be an alternate director if his appointor ceases to be a director; but, if a director retires by rotation or otherwise but is reappointed or deemed to have been reappointed at the meeting at which he retires, any appointment of an alternate director made by him which was in force immediately prior to his retirement shall continue after his reappointment.

**68**

Any appointment or removal of an alternate director shall be by notice to the company signed by the director making or revoking the appointment or in any other manner approved by the directors.

**69**

Save as otherwise provided in the articles, an alternate director shall be deemed for all purposes to be a director and shall alone be responsible for his own acts and defaults and he shall not be deemed to be the agent of the director appointing him.

**70 Powers of directors**

Subject to the provisions of the Act, the memorandum and the articles and to any directions given by special resolution, the business of the company shall be managed by the directors who may exercise all the powers of the company. No alteration of the memorandum or articles and no such direction shall invalidate any prior act of the directors which would have been valid if that alteration had not been made or that direction had not been given. The powers given by this regulation shall not be limited by any special power given to the directors by the articles and a meeting of directors at which a quorum is present may exercise all powers exercisable by the directors.

**71**

The directors may, by power of attorney or otherwise, appoint any person to be the agent of the company for such purposes and on such conditions as they determine, including authority for the agent to delegate all or any of his powers.

**72 Delegation of directors' powers**

The directors may delegate any of their powers to any committee consisting of one or more directors. They may also delegate to any managing director or any director holding any other executive office such of their powers as they consider desirable to be exercised by him. Any such delegation may be made subject to any conditions the directors may impose, and either collaterally with or to the exclusion of their own powers and may be revoked or altered. Subject to any such conditions, the proceedings of a committee with two or more members shall be governed by the articles regulating the proceedings of directors so far as they are capable of applying.

**73 Appointment and retirement of directors**

At the first annual general meeting all the directors shall retire from office, and at every subsequent annual general meeting one-third of the directors who are subject to retirement by rotation or, if their number is not three or a multiple of three, the number nearest to one-third shall retire from office; but, if there is only one director who is subject to retirement by rotation, he shall retire.

**Note**

This Article ceases to have effect in relation to private companies limited by shares registered on or after 1 October 2007. [*SI 2007 No 2541, Reg 13*].

**74**

Subject to the provisions of the Act, the directors to retire by rotation shall be those who have been longest in office since their last appointment or reappointment, but as between persons who became or were last reappointed directors on the same day those to retire shall (unless they otherwise agree among themselves) be determined by lot.

**Note**

This Article ceases to have effect in relation to private companies limited by shares registered on or after 1 October 2007. [*SI 2007 No 2541, Reg 13*].

**75**

If the company, at the meeting at which a director retires by rotation, does not fill the vacancy the retiring director shall, if willing to act, be deemed to have been reappointed unless at the meeting it is resolved not to fill the vacancy or unless a resolution for the reappointment of the director is put to the meeting and lost.

**Note**

This Article ceases to have effect in relation to private companies limited by shares registered on or after 1 October 2007. [*SI 2007 No 2541, Reg 13*].

**76**

No person other than a director retiring by rotation shall be appointed or reappointed a director at any general meeting unless

    (a)    he is recommended by the directors; or

    (b)    not less than fourteen nor more than thirty-five clear days before the date appointed for the meeting, notice executed by a member qualified to vote at the meeting has been given to the company of the intention to propose that person for appointment or reappointment stating the particulars which would, if he were so appointed or reappointed, be required to be included in the company's register of directors together with notice executed by that person of his willingness to be appointed or reappointed.

**Note**

This Article is amended by *SI 2007 No 2541, Reg 14* in relation to private companies limited by shares registered on or after 1 October 2007 as follows.

    •    After the words 'No person' omit the words 'other than a director retiring by rotation'.

**77**

Not less than seven nor more than twenty-eight clear days before the date appointed for holding a general meeting notice shall be given to all who are entitled to receive notice of the meeting of any person (other than a director retiring by rotation at the meeting) who is recommended by the directors for appointment or reappointment as a director at the meeting or in respect of whom notice has been duly given to the company of the intention to propose him at the meeting for appointment or reappointment as a director. The notice shall give the particulars of that person which would, if he were so appointed or reappointed, be required to be included in the company's register of directors.

**Note**

This Article is amended by *SI 2007 No 2541, Reg 15* in relation to private companies limited by shares registered on or after 1 October 2007 as follows.

- After the words 'meeting of any person' omit the words '(other than a director retiring by rotation at the meeting)'.

**78**

Subject as aforesaid, the company may by ordinary resolution appoint a person who is willing to act to be a director either to fill a vacancy or as an additional director and may also determine the rotation in which any additional directors are to retire.

**Note**

This Article is amended by *SI 2007 No 2541, Reg 16* in relation to private companies limited by shares registered on or after 1 October 2007 as follows.

- Omit the words 'Subject as aforesaid,'.

**79**

The directors may appoint a person who is willing to act to be a director, either to fill a vacancy or as an additional director, provided that the appointment does not cause the number of directors to exceed any number fixed by or in accordance with the articles as the maximum number of directors. A director so appointed shall hold office only until the next following annual general meeting and shall not be taken into account in determining the directors who are to retire by rotation at the meeting. If not reappointed at such annual general meeting, he shall vacate office at the conclusion thereof.

**Note**

This Article is amended by *SI 2007 No 2541, Reg 17* in relation to private companies limited by shares registered on or after 1 October 2007 as follows.

- Omit the second and third sentences.

**80**

Subject as aforesaid, a director who retires at an annual general meeting may, if willing to act, be reappointed. If he is not reappointed, he shall retain office until the meeting appoints someone in his place, or if it does not do so, until the end of the meeting.

**Note**

This Article ceases to have effect in relation to private companies limited by shares registered on or after 1 October 2007. [*SI 2007 No 2541, Reg 18*].

**81 Disqualification and removal of directors**

The office of a director shall be vacated if

    (a)    he ceases to be a director by virtue of any provision of the Act or he becomes prohibited by law from being a director; or

    (b)    he becomes bankrupt or makes any arrangement or composition with his creditors generally; or

(c)    he is, or may be, suffering from mental disorder and either

    (i)    he is admitted to hospital in pursuance of an application for admission for treatment under the Mental Health Act 1983 or, in Scotland, an application for admission under the Mental Health (Scotland) Act 1960, or

    (ii)   an order is made by a court having jurisdiction (whether in the United Kingdom or elsewhere) in matters concerning mental disorder for his detention or for the appointment of a receiver, curator bonis or other person to exercise powers with respect to his property or affairs; or

(d)    he resigns his office by notice to the company; or

(e)    he shall for more than six consecutive months have been absent without permission of the directors from meetings of directors held during that period and the directors resolve that his office be vacated.

**Note**

By virtue of the *Adults with Incapacity (Scotland) Act 2000, s 88(2), Sch 5, para 1* the references to a curator bonis shall be construed as references to a guardian with similar powers appointed under that Act.

## 82  Remuneration of directors

The directors shall be entitled to such remuneration as the company may by ordinary resolution determine and, unless the resolution provides otherwise, the remuneration shall be deemed to accrue from day to day.

## 83  Directors' expenses

The directors may be paid all travelling, hotel, and other expenses properly incurred by them in connection with their attendance at meetings of directors or committees of directors or general meetings or separate meetings of the holders of any class of shares or of debentures of the company or otherwise in connection with the discharge of their duties.

## 84  Directors' appointments and interests

Subject to the provisions of the Act, the directors may appoint one or more of their number to the office of managing director or to any other executive office under the company and may enter into an agreement or arrangement with any director for his employment by the company or for the provision by him of any services outside the scope of the ordinary duties of a director. Any such appointment, agreement or arrangement may be made upon such terms as the directors determine and they may remunerate any such director for his services as they think fit. Any appointment of a director to an executive office shall terminate if he ceases to be a director but without prejudice to any claim to damages for breach of the contract of service between the director and the company. A managing director and a director holding any other executive office shall not be subject to retirement by rotation.

## 85

Subject to the provisions of the Act, and provided that he has disclosed to the directors the nature and extent of any material interest of his, a director notwithstanding his office

    (a)    may be a party to, or otherwise interested in, any transaction or arrangement with the company or in which the company or in which the company is otherwise interested;

    (b)    may be a director or other officer of, or employed by, or a party to any transaction or arrangement with, or otherwise interested in, any body corporate promoted by the company or in which the company is otherwise interested; and

    (c)    shall not, by reason of his office, be accountable to the company for any benefit which he derives from any such office or employment or from any such transaction or arrangement or from any interest in any such body corporate and no such transaction or arrangement shall be liable to be avoided on the ground of any such interest or benefit.

**86**

For the purposes of regulation 85

    (a)      a general notice given to the directors that a director is to be regarded as having an interest of the nature and extent specified in the notice in any transaction or arrangement in which a specified person or class of persons is interested shall be deemed to be a disclosure that the director has an interest in any such transaction of the nature and extent so specified; and

    (b)      an interest of which a director has no knowledge and of which it is unreasonable to expect him to have knowledge shall not be treated as an interest of his.

## 87 Directors' gratuities and pensions

The directors may provide benefits, whether by the payment of gratuities or pensions or by insurance or otherwise, for any director who has held but no longer holds any executive office or employment with the company or with any body corporate which is or has been a subsidiary of the company or a predecessor in business of the company or of any such subsidiary, and for any member of his family (including a spouse and a former spouse) or any person who is or was dependent on him, and may (as well before as after he ceases to hold such office or employment) contribute to any fund and pay premiums for the purchase or provision of any such benefit.

## 88 Proceedings of directors

Subject to the provisions of the articles, the directors may regulate their proceedings as they think fit. A director may, and the secretary at the request of a director shall, call a meeting of the directors. It shall not be necessary to give notice of a meeting to a director who is absent from the United Kingdom. Questions arising at a meeting shall be decided by a majority of votes. In the case of an equality of votes, the chairman shall have a second or casting vote. A director who is also an alternate director shall be entitled in the absence of his appointor to a separate vote on behalf of his appointor in addition to his own vote.

**89**

The quorum for the transaction of the business of the directors may be fixed by the directors and unless so fixed at any other number shall be two. A person who holds office only as an alternate director shall, if his appointor is not present, be counted in the quorum.

**90**

The continuing directors or a sole continuing director may act notwithstanding any vacancies in their number, but, if the number of directors is less than the number fixed as the quorum, the continuing directors or director may act only for the purpose of filling vacancies or of calling a general meeting.

**91**

The directors may appoint one of their number to be the chairman of the board of directors and may at any time remove him from that office. Unless he is unwilling to do so, the director so appointed shall preside at every meeting of directors at which he is present. But if there is no director holding that office, or if the director holding it is unwilling to preside or is not present within five minutes after the time appointed for the meeting, the directors present may appoint one of their number to be chairman of the meeting.

**92**

All acts done by a meeting of directors, or of a committee of directors, or by a person acting as a director shall, notwithstanding that it be afterwards discovered that there was a defect in the appointment of any director or that any of them were disqualified from holding office, or had vacated office, or were not entitled to vote, be as valid as if every such person had been duly appointed and was qualified and had continued to be a director and had been entitled to vote.

**93**

A resolution in writing signed by all the directors entitled to receive notice of a meeting of directors or of a committee of directors shall be as valid and effectual as it if had been passed at a meeting of directors or (as the case may be) a committee of directors duly convened and held and may consist of several documents in the like form each signed by one or more directors; but a resolution signed by an alternate director need not also be signed by his appointor and, if it is signed by a director who has appointed an alternate director, it need not be signed by the alternate director in that capacity.

**94**

Save as otherwise provided by the articles, a director shall not vote at a meeting of directors or of a committee of directors on any resolution concerning a matter in which he has, directly or indirectly, an interest or duty which is material and which conflicts or may conflict with the interests of the company unless his interest or duty arises only because the case falls within one or more of the following paragraphs

| | |
|---|---|
| (a) | the resolution relates to the giving to him of a guarantee, security, or indemnity in respect of money lent to, or an obligation incurred by him for the benefit of, the company or any of its subsidiaries; |
| (b) | the resolution relates to the giving to a third party of a guarantee, security, or indemnity in respect of an obligation of the company or any of its subsidiaries for which the director has assumed responsibility in whole or part and whether alone or jointly with others under a guarantee or indemnity or by the giving of security; |
| (c) | his interest arises by virtue of his subscribing or agreeing to subscribe for any shares, debentures, or other securities of the company or any of its subsidiaries, or by virtue of his being, or intending to become, a participant in the underwriting or sub-underwriting of an offer of any such shares, debentures, or other securities by the company or any of its subsidiaries for subscription, purchase or exchange; |
| (d) | the resolution relates in any way to a retirement benefits scheme which has been approved, or is conditional upon approval, by the Board of Inland Revenue for taxation purposes. |

For the purposes of this regulation, an interest of a person who is, for any purpose of the Act (excluding any statutory modification thereof not in force when this regulation becomes binding on the company), connected with a director shall be treated as an interest of the director and, in relation to an alternate director, an interest of his appointor shall be treated as an interest of the alternate director without prejudice to any interest which the alternate director has otherwise.

**95**

A director shall not be counted in the quorum present at a meeting in relation to a resolution on which he is not entitled to vote.

**96**

The company may by ordinary resolution suspend or relax to any extent, either generally or in respect of any particular matter, any provision of the articles prohibiting a director from voting at a meeting of directors or of a committee of directors.

**97**

Where proposals are under consideration concerning the appointment of two or more directors to offices or employments with the company or any body corporate in which the company is interested the proposals may be divided and considered in relation to each director separately and (provided he is not for another reason precluded from voting) each of the directors concerned shall be entitled to vote and be counted in the quorum in respect of each resolution except that concerning his own appointment.

**98**

If a question arises at a meeting of directors or of a committee of directors as to the right of a director to vote, the question may, before the conclusion of the meeting, be referred to the chairman of the meeting and his ruling in relation to any director other than himself shall be final and conclusive.

**99 Secretary**

Subject to the provisions of the Act, the secretary shall be appointed by the directors for such term, at such remuneration and upon such conditions as they may think fit; and any secretary so appointed may be removed by them.

**100 Minutes**

The directors shall cause minutes to be made in books kept for the purpose

(a)     of all appointments of officers made by the directors; and

(b)     of all proceedings at meetings of the company, of the holders of any class of shares in the company, and of the directors, and of committees of directors, including the names of the directors present at each such meeting.

**101 The seal**

The seal shall only be used by the authority of the directors or of a committee of directors authorised by the directors. The directors may determine who shall sign any instrument to which the seal is affixed and unless otherwise so determined it shall be signed by a director and by the secretary or by a second director.

**102 Dividends**

Subject to the provisions of the Act, the company may by ordinary resolution declare dividends in accordance with the respective rights of the members, but no dividend shall exceed the amount recommended by the directors.

**103**

Subject to the provisions of the Act, the directors may pay interim dividends if it appears to them that they are justified by the profits of the company available for distribution. If the share capital is divided into different classes, the directors may pay interim dividends on shares which confer deferred or non-preferred rights with regard to dividend as well as on shares which confer preferential rights with regard to dividend, but no interim dividend shall be paid on shares carrying deferred or non-preferred rights if, at the time of payment, any preferential dividend is in arrear. The directors may also pay at intervals settled by them any dividend payable at a fixed rate if it appears to them that the profits available for distribution justify the payment. Provided the directors act in good faith they shall not incur any liability to the holders of shares conferring preferred rights for any loss they may suffer by the lawful payment of an interim dividend on any shares having deferred or non-preferred rights.

**104**

Except as otherwise provided by the rights attached to shares, all dividends shall be declared and paid according to the amounts paid up on the shares on which the dividend is paid. All dividends shall be apportioned and paid proportionately to the amounts paid up on the shares during any portion or portions of the period in respect of which the dividend is paid; but, if any share is issued on terms providing that it shall rank for dividend as from a particular date, that share shall rank for dividend accordingly.

**105**

A general meeting declaring a dividend may, upon the recommendation of the directors, direct that it shall be satisfied wholly or partly by the distribution of assets and, where any difficulty arises in regard to the distribution, the directors may settle the same and in particular may issue fractional certificates and fix the value for distribution of any assets and may determine that cash shall be paid to any member upon the footing of the value so fixed in order to adjust the rights of members and may vest any assets in trustees.

## 106

Any dividend or other moneys payable in respect of a share may be paid by cheque sent by post to the registered address of the person entitled or, if two or more persons are the holders of the share or are jointly entitled to it by reason of the death or bankruptcy of the holder, to the registered address of that one of those persons who is first named in the register of members or to such person and to such address as the person or persons entitled may in writing direct. Every cheque shall be made payable to the order of the person or persons entitled or to such other person as the person or persons entitled may in writing direct and payment of the cheque shall be a good discharge to the company. Any joint holder or other person jointly entitled to a share as aforesaid may give receipts for any dividend or other moneys payable in respect of the share.

## 107

No dividend or other moneys payable in respect of a share shall bear interest against the company unless otherwise provided by the rights attached to the share.

## 108

Any dividend which has remained unclaimed for twelve years from the date when it became due for payment shall, if the directors so resolve, be forfeited and cease to remain owing by the company.

## 109 Accounts

No member shall (as such) have any right of inspecting any accounting records or other book or document of the company except as conferred by statute or authorised by the directors or by ordinary resolution of the company.

## 110 Capitalisation of profits

The directors may with the authority of an ordinary resolution of the company

(a) subject as hereinafter provided, resolve to capitalise any undivided profits of the company not required for paying any preferential dividend (whether or not they are available for distribution) or any sum standing to the credit of the company's share premium account or capital redemption reserve;

(b) appropriate the sum resolved to be capitalised to the members who would have been entitled to it if it were distributed by way of dividend and in the same proportions and apply such sum on their behalf either in or towards paying up the amounts, if any, for the time being unpaid on any shares held by them respectively, or in paying up in full unissued shares or debentures of the company of a nominal amount equal to that sum, and allot the shares or debentures credited as fully paid to those members, or as they may direct, in those proportions, or partly in one way and partly in the other: but the share premium account, the capital redemption reserve, and any profits which are not available for distribution may, for the purposes of this regulation, only be applied in paying up unissued shares to be allotted to members credited as fully paid;

(c) make such provision by the issue of fractional certificates or by payment in cash or otherwise as they determine in the case of shares or debentures becoming distributable under this regulation in fractions; and

(d) authorise any person to enter on behalf of all the members concerned into an agreement with the company providing for the allotment to them respectively, credited as fully paid, of any shares or debentures to which they are entitled upon such capitalisation, any agreement made under such authority being binding on all such members.

[111 Notices

Any notice to be given to or by any person pursuant to the articles (other than a notice calling a meeting of the directors) shall be in writing or shall be given using electronic communications to an address for the time being notified for that purpose to the person giving the notice.

In this regulation, "address", in relation to electronic communications, includes any number or address used for the purposes of such communications.]

Note

*Article 111* substituted by *SI 2000 No 3373, art 32(1), Sch 1 para 6* as from 22 December 2000. The text previously read 'Any notice to be given to or by any person pursuant to the articles shall be in writing except that a notice calling a meeting of the directors need not be in writing.'

### 112

The company may give any notice to a member either personally or by sending it by post in a prepaid envelope addressed to the member at his registered address or by leaving it at that address [or by giving it using electronic communications to an address for the time being notified to the company by the member]. In the case of joint holders of a share, all notices shall be given to the joint holder whose name stands first in the register of members in respect of the joint holding and notice so given shall be sufficient notice to all the joint holders. A member whose registered address is not within the United Kingdom and who gives to the company an address within the United Kingdom at which notices may be given to him[, or an address to which notices may be sent using electronic communications,] shall be entitled to have notices given to him at that address, but otherwise no such member shall be entitled to receive any notice from the company. [In this regulation and the next, "address", in relation to electronic communications, includes any number or address used for the purposes of such communications.]

Note

Words in square brackets inserted by *SI 2000 No 3373, art 32(1), Sch 1 para 7* with effect from 22 December 2000.

### 113

A member present, either in person or by proxy, at any meeting of the company or of the holders of any class of shares in the company shall be deemed to have received notice of the meeting and, where requisite, of the purposes for which it was called.

### 114

Every person who becomes entitled to a share shall be bound by any notice in respect of that share which, before his name is entered in the register of members, has been duly given to a person from whom he derives his title.

### 115

Proof that an envelope containing a notice was properly addressed, prepaid and posted shall be conclusive evidence that that the notice was given. [Proof that a notice contained in an electronic communication was sent in accordance with guidance issued by the Institute of Chartered Secretaries and Administrators shall be conclusive evidence that the notice was given.] A notice shall, . . . be deemed to be given at the expiration of 48 hours after the envelope containing it was posted [or, in the case of a notice contained in an electronic communication, at the expiration of 48 hours after the time it was sent].

Note

Words in square brackets inserted by *SI 2000 No 3373, art 32(1), Sch 1 para 8* with effect from 22 December 2000.

## 116

A notice may be given by the company to the persons entitled to a share in consequence of the death or bankruptcy of a member by sending or delivering it, in any manner authorised by the articles for the giving of notice to a member, addressed to them by name, or by the title of representatives of the deceased, or trustee of the bankrupt or by any like description at the address, if any, within the United Kingdom supplied for that purpose by the persons claiming to be so entitled. Until such an address has been supplied, a notice may be given in any manner in which it might have been given if the death or bankruptcy had not occurred.

## 117 Winding up

If the company is wound up, the liquidator may, with the sanction of an extraordinary resolution of the company and any other sanction required by the Act, divide among the members in specie the whole or any part of the assets of the company and may, for that purpose, value any assets and determine how the division shall be carried out as between the members or different classes of members. The liquidator may, with the like sanction, vest the whole or any part of the assets in trustees upon such trusts for the benefit of the members as he with the like sanction determines, but no member shall be compelled to accept any assets upon which there is a liability.

### Note

This Article is amended by *SI 2007 No 2541, Reg 7* in relation to companies registered on or after 1 October 2007 as follows.

- For the words 'an extraordinary' substitute the words 'a special'.

## 118 Indemnity

Subject to the provisions of the Act but without prejudice to any indemnity to which a director may otherwise be entitled, every director or other officer or auditor of the company shall be indemnified out of the assets of the company against any liability incurred by him in defending any proceedings, whether civil or criminal, in which judgment is given in his favour or in which he is acquitted or in connection with any application in which relief is granted to him by the court from liability for negligence, default, breach of duty or breach of trust in relation to the affairs of the company.

## MODEL ARTICLES: PRIVATE COMPANIES LIMITED BY SHARES (SI 2008 NO 3229, SCH 1). COMPANIES ACT 2006 AS AMENDED BY THE MENTAL HEALTH DISCRIMINATION ACT 2013

### INDEX

# Appendix 4 – Standard Articles of association

## PART 1: INTERPRETATION AND LIMITATION OF LIABILITY

### 1 Defined terms

In the articles, unless the context requires otherwise

"articles" means the company's articles of association;

"bankruptcy" includes individual insolvency proceedings in a jurisdiction other than England and Wales or Northern Ireland which have an effect similar to that of bankruptcy;

"chairman" has the meaning given in article 12;

"chairman of the meeting" has the meaning given in article 39;

"Companies Acts" means the Companies Acts (as defined in section 2 of the Companies Act 2006), in so far as they apply to the company;

"director" means a director of the company, and includes any person occupying the position of director, by whatever name called;

"distribution recipient" has the meaning given in article 31;

"document" includes, unless otherwise specified, any document sent or supplied in electronic form;

"electronic form" has the meaning given in section 1168 of the Companies Act 2006;

"fully paid" in relation to a share, means that the nominal value and any premium to be paid to the company in respect of that share have been paid to the company;

"hard copy form" has the meaning given in section 1168 of the Companies Act 2006;

"holder" in relation to shares means the person whose name is entered in the register of members as the holder of the shares;

"instrument" means a document in hard copy form;

"ordinary resolution" has the meaning given in section 282 of the Companies Act 2006;

"paid" means paid or credited as paid;

"participate", in relation to a directors' meeting, has the meaning given in article 10;

"proxy notice" has the meaning given in article 45;

"shareholder" means a person who is the holder of a share;

"shares" means shares in the company;

"special resolution" has the meaning given in section 283 of the Companies Act 2006;

"subsidiary" has the meaning given in section 1159 of the Companies Act 2006;

"transmittee" means a person entitled to a share by reason of the death or bankruptcy of a shareholder or otherwise by operation of law; and

"writing" means the representation or reproduction of words, symbols or other information in a visible form by any method or combination of methods, whether sent or supplied in electronic form or otherwise.

Unless the context otherwise requires, other words or expressions contained in these articles bear the same meaning as in the Companies Act 2006 as in force on the date when these articles become binding on the company.

## 2 Liability of members

The liability of the members is limited to the amount, if any, unpaid on the shares held by them.

### PART 2: DIRECTORS

*Directors' powers and responsibilities*

## 3 Directors' general authority

Subject to the articles, the directors are responsible for the management of the company's business, for which purpose they may exercise all the powers of the company.

## 4 Shareholders' reserve power

(1) The shareholders may, by special resolution, direct the directors to take, or refrain from taking, specified action.

(2) No such special resolution invalidates anything which the directors have done before the passing of the resolution.

## 5 Directors may delegate

(1) Subject to the articles, the directors may delegate any of the powers which are conferred on them under the articles

    (a)     to such person or committee;

    (b)     by such means (including by power of attorney);

    (c)     to such an extent;

    (d)     in relation to such matters or territories; and

    (e)     on such terms and conditions;

  as they think fit.

(2) If the directors so specify, any such delegation may authorise further delegation of the directors' powers by any person to whom they are delegated.

(3) The directors may revoke any delegation in whole or part, or alter its terms and conditions.

## 6 Committees

(1) Committees to which the directors delegate any of their powers must follow procedures which are based as far as they are applicable on those provisions of the articles which govern the taking of decisions by directors.

(2) The directors may make rules of procedure for all or any committees, which prevail over rules derived from the articles if they are not consistent with them.

# Appendix 4 – Standard Articles of association, art 7

*Decision-making by directors*

## 7 Directors to take decisions collectively

(1) The general rule about decision-making by directors is that any decision of the directors must be either a majority decision at a meeting or a decision taken in accordance with article 8.

(2) If

    (a)      the company only has one director, and

    (b)      no provision of the articles requires it to have more than one director,

the general rule does not apply, and the director may take decisions without regard to any of the provisions of the articles relating to directors' decision-making.

## 8 Unanimous decisions

(1) A decision of the directors is taken in accordance with this article when all eligible directors indicate to each other by any means that they share a common view on a matter.

(2) Such a decision may take the form of a resolution in writing, copies of which have been signed by each eligible director or to which each eligible director has otherwise indicated agreement in writing.

(3) References in this article to eligible directors are to directors who would have been entitled to vote on the matter had it been proposed as a resolution at a directors' meeting.

(4) A decision may not be taken in accordance with this article if the eligible directors would not have formed a quorum at such a meeting.

## 9 Calling a directors' meeting

(1) Any director may call a directors' meeting by giving notice of the meeting to the directors or by authorising the company secretary (if any) to give such notice.

(2) Notice of any directors' meeting must indicate

    (a)      its proposed date and time;

    (b)      where it is to take place; and

    (c)      if it is anticipated that directors participating in the meeting will not be in the same place,

how it is proposed that they should communicate with each other during the meeting.

(3) Notice of a directors' meeting must be given to each director, but need not be in writing.

(4) Notice of a directors' meeting need not be given to directors who waive their entitlement to notice of that meeting, by giving notice to that effect to the company not more than 7 days after the date on which the meeting is held. Where such notice is given after the meeting has been held, that does not affect the validity of the meeting, or of any business conducted at it.

## 10 Participation in directors' meetings

(1) Subject to the articles, directors participate in a directors' meeting, or part of a directors' meeting, when

    (a)      the meeting has been called and takes place in accordance with the articles, and

    (b)      they can each communicate to the others any information or opinions they have on any particular item of the business of the meeting.

(2) In determining whether directors are participating in a directors' meeting, it is irrelevant where any director is or how they communicate with each other.

(3) If all the directors participating in a meeting are not in the same place, they may decide that the meeting is to be treated as taking place wherever any of them is.

## 11 Quorum for directors' meetings

(1) At a directors' meeting, unless a quorum is participating, no proposal is to be voted on, except a proposal to call another meeting.

(2) The quorum for directors' meetings may be fixed from time to time by a decision of the directors, but it must never be less than two, and unless otherwise fixed it is two.

(3) If the total number of directors for the time being is less than the quorum required, the directors must not take any decision other than a decision

    (a)      to appoint further directors, or

    (b)      to call a general meeting so as to enable the shareholders to appoint further directors.

## 12 Chairing of directors' meetings

(1) The directors may appoint a director to chair their meetings.

(2) The person so appointed for the time being is known as the chairman.

(3) The directors may terminate the chairman's appointment at any time.

(4) If the chairman is not participating in a directors' meeting within ten minutes of the time at which it was to start, the participating directors must appoint one of themselves to chair it.

## 13 Casting vote

(1) If the numbers of votes for and against a proposal are equal, the chairman or other director chairing the meeting has a casting vote.

(2) But this does not apply if, in accordance with the articles, the chairman or other director is not to be counted as participating in the decision-making process for quorum or voting purposes.

## 14 Conflicts of interest

(1) If a proposed decision of the directors is concerned with an actual or proposed transaction or arrangement with the company in which a director is interested, that director is not to be counted as participating in the decision-making process for quorum or voting purposes.

(2) But if paragraph (3) applies, a director who is interested in an actual or proposed transaction or arrangement with the company is to be counted as participating in the decision-making process for quorum and voting purposes.

(3) This paragraph applies when

    (a)      the company by ordinary resolution disapplies the provision of the articles which would otherwise prevent a director from being counted as participating in the decision-making process;

    (b)      the director's interest cannot reasonably be regarded as likely to give rise to a conflict of interest; or

    (c)      the director's conflict of interest arises from a permitted cause.

(4) For the purposes of this article, the following are permitted causes

    (a)      a guarantee given, or to be given, by or to a director in respect of an obligation incurred by or on behalf of the company or any of its subsidiaries;

    (b)      subscription, or an agreement to subscribe, for shares or other securities of the company or any of its subsidiaries, or to underwrite, sub-underwrite, or guarantee subscription for any such shares or securities; and

    (c)      arrangements pursuant to which benefits are made available to employees and directors or former employees and directors of the company or any of its subsidiaries which do not provide special benefits for directors or former directors.

(5) For the purposes of this article, references to proposed decisions and decision-making processes include any directors' meeting or part of a directors' meeting.

(6) Subject to paragraph (7), if a question arises at a meeting of directors or of a committee of directors as to the right of a director to participate in the meeting (or part of the meeting) for voting or quorum purposes, the question may, before the conclusion of the meeting, be referred to the chairman whose ruling in relation to any director other than the chairman is to be final and conclusive.

(7) If any question as to the right to participate in the meeting (or part of the meeting) should arise in respect of the chairman, the question is to be decided by a decision of the directors at that meeting, for which purpose the chairman is not to be counted as participating in the meeting (or that part of the meeting) for voting or quorum purposes.

## 15 Records of decisions to be kept
The directors must ensure that the company keeps a record, in writing, for at least 10 years from the date of the decision recorded, of every unanimous or majority decision taken by the directors.

## 16 Directors' discretion to make further rules
Subject to the articles, the directors may make any rule which they think fit about how they take decisions, and about how such rules are to be recorded or communicated to directors.

*Appointment of directors*

## 17 Methods of appointing directors
(1) Any person who is willing to act as a director, and is permitted by law to do so, may be appointed to be a director
- (a) by ordinary resolution, or
- (b) by a decision of the directors.

(2) In any case where, as a result of death, the company has no shareholders and no directors, the personal representatives of the last shareholder to have died have the right, by notice in writing, to appoint a person to be a director.

(3) For the purposes of paragraph (2), where 2 or more shareholders die in circumstances rendering it uncertain who was the last to die, a younger shareholder is deemed to have survived an older shareholder.

## 18 Termination of director's appointment
A person ceases to be a director as soon as
- (a) that person ceases to be a director by virtue of any provision of the Companies Act 2006 or is prohibited from being a director by law;
- (b) a bankruptcy order is made against that person;
- (c) a composition is made with that person's creditors generally in satisfaction of that person's debts;
- (d) a registered medical practitioner who is treating that person gives a written opinion to the company stating that that person has become physically or mentally incapable of acting as a director and may remain so for more than three months;
- (f) notification is received by the company from the director that the director is resigning from office, and such resignation has taken effect in accordance with its terms.

## 19 Directors' remuneration
(1) Directors may undertake any services for the company that the directors decide.

(2) Directors are entitled to such remuneration as the directors determine
- (a) for their services to the company as directors, and
- (b) for any other service which they undertake for the company.

(3) Subject to the articles, a director's remuneration may
- (a) take any form, and
- (b) include any arrangements in connection with the payment of a pension, allowance or gratuity, or any death, sickness or disability benefits, to or in respect of that director.

(4) Unless the directors decide otherwise, directors' remuneration accrues from day to day.

(5) Unless the directors decide otherwise, directors are not accountable to the company for any remuneration which they receive as directors or other officers or employees of the company's subsidiaries or of any other body corporate in which the company is interested.

## 20 Directors' expenses

The company may pay any reasonable expenses which the directors properly incur in connection with their attendance at

|       |                                                                                          |
|-------|------------------------------------------------------------------------------------------|
| (a)   | meetings of directors or committees of directors,                                        |
| (b)   | general meetings, or                                                                      |
| (c)   | separate meetings of the holders of any class of shares or of debentures of the company,  |

or otherwise in connection with the exercise of their powers and the discharge of their responsibilities in relation to the company.

### PART 3: SHARES AND DISTRIBUTIONS

*Shares*

## 21 All shares to be fully paid up

(1) No share is to be issued for less than the aggregate of its nominal value and any premium to be paid to the company in consideration for its issue.

(2) This does not apply to shares taken on the formation of the company by the subscribers to the company's memorandum.

## 22 Powers to issue different classes of share

(1) Subject to the articles, but without prejudice to the rights attached to any existing share, the company may issue shares with such rights or restrictions as may be determined by ordinary resolution.

(2) The company may issue shares which are to be redeemed, or are liable to be redeemed at the option of the company or the holder, and the directors may determine the terms, conditions and manner of redemption of any such shares.

## 23 Company not bound by less than absolute interests

Except as required by law, no person is to be recognised by the company as holding any share upon any trust, and except as otherwise required by law or the articles, the company is not in any way to be bound by or recognise any interest in a share other than the holder's absolute ownership of it and all the rights attaching to it.

## 24 Share certificates

(1) The company must issue each shareholder, free of charge, with one or more certificates in respect of the shares which that shareholder holds.

(2) Every certificate must specify

|       |                                                           |
|-------|-----------------------------------------------------------|
| (a)   | in respect of how many shares, of what class, it is issued; |
| (b)   | the nominal value of those shares;                        |
| (c)   | that the shares are fully paid; and                       |
| (d)   | any distinguishing numbers assigned to them.              |

(3) No certificate may be issued in respect of shares of more than one class.

(4) If more than one person holds a share, only one certificate may be issued in respect of it.

(5) Certificates must

|       |                                                              |
|-------|--------------------------------------------------------------|
| (a)   | have affixed to them the company's common seal, or           |
| (b)   | be otherwise executed in accordance with the Companies Acts. |

## 25 Replacement share certificates

(1) If a certificate issued in respect of a shareholder's shares is

|       |                                    |
|-------|------------------------------------|
| (a)   | damaged or defaced, or             |
| (b)   | said to be lost, stolen or destroyed, |

that shareholder is entitled to be issued with a replacement certificate in respect of the same shares.

(2) A shareholder exercising the right to be issued with such a replacement certificate

    (a)      may at the same time exercise the right to be issued with a single certificate or separate certificates;

    (b)      must return the certificate which is to be replaced to the company if it is damaged or defaced; and

    (c)      must comply with such conditions as to evidence, indemnity and the payment of a reasonable fee as the directors decide.

## 26 Share transfers

(1) Shares may be transferred by means of an instrument of transfer in any usual form or any other form approved by the directors, which is executed by or on behalf of the transferor.

(2) No fee may be charged for registering any instrument of transfer or other document relating to or affecting the title to any share.

(3) The company may retain any instrument of transfer which is registered.

(4) The transferor remains the holder of a share until the transferee's name is entered in the register of members as holder of it.

(5) The directors may refuse to register the transfer of a share, and if they do so, the instrument of transfer must be returned to the transferee with the notice of refusal unless they suspect that the proposed transfer may be fraudulent.

## 27 Transmission of shares

(1) If title to a share passes to a transmittee, the company may only recognise the transmittee as having any title to that share.

(2) A transmittee who produces such evidence of entitlement to shares as the directors may properly require

    (a)      may, subject to the articles, choose either to become the holder of those shares or to have them transferred to another person, and

    (b)      subject to the articles, and pending any transfer of the shares to another person, has the same rights as the holder had.

(3) But transmittees do not have the right to attend or vote at a general meeting, or agree to a proposed written resolution, in respect of shares to which they are entitled, by reason of the holder's death or bankruptcy or otherwise, unless they become the holders of those shares.

## 28 Exercise of transmittees' rights

(1) Transmittees who wish to become the holders of shares to which they have become entitled must notify the company in writing of that wish.

(2) If the transmittee wishes to have a share transferred to another person, the transmittee must execute an instrument of transfer in respect of it.

(3) Any transfer made or executed under this article is to be treated as if it were made or executed by the person from whom the transmittee has derived rights in respect of the share, and as if the event which gave rise to the transmission had not occurred.

## 29 Transmittees bound by prior notices

If a notice is given to a shareholder in respect of shares and a transmittee is entitled to those shares, the transmittee is bound by the notice if it was given to the shareholder before the transmittee's name has been entered in the register of members.

*Dividends and other distributions*

## 30 Procedure for declaring dividends

(1) The company may by ordinary resolution declare dividends, and the directors may decide to pay interim dividends.

(2) A dividend must not be declared unless the directors have made a recommendation as to its amount. Such a dividend must not exceed the amount recommended by the directors.

(3) No dividend may be declared or paid unless it is in accordance with shareholders' respective rights.

(4) Unless the shareholders' resolution to declare or directors' decision to pay a dividend, or the terms on which shares are issued, specify otherwise, it must be paid by reference to each shareholder's holding of shares on the date of the resolution or decision to declare or pay it.

(5) If the company's share capital is divided into different classes, no interim dividend may be paid on shares carrying deferred or non-preferred rights if, at the time of payment, any preferential dividend is in arrear.

(6) The directors may pay at intervals any dividend payable at a fixed rate if it appears to them that the profits available for distribution justify the payment.

(7) If the directors act in good faith, they do not incur any liability to the holders of shares conferring preferred rights for any loss they may suffer by the lawful payment of an interim dividend on shares with deferred or non-preferred rights.

### 31 Payment of dividends and other distributions

(1) Where a dividend or other sum which is a distribution is payable in respect of a share, it must be paid by one or more of the following means

(a)     transfer to a bank or building society account specified by the distribution recipient either in writing or as the directors may otherwise decide;

(b)     sending a cheque made payable to the distribution recipient by post to the distribution recipient at the distribution recipient's registered address (if the distribution recipient is a holder of the share), or (in any other case) to an address specified by the distribution recipient either in writing or as the directors may otherwise decide;

(c)     sending a cheque made payable to such person by post to such person at such address as the distribution recipient has specified either in writing or as the directors may otherwise decide; or

(d)     any other means of payment as the directors agree with the distribution recipient either in writing or by such other means as the directors decide.

In the articles, "the distribution recipient" means, in respect of a share in respect of which a dividend or other sum is payable

(a)     the holder of the share; or

(b)     if the share has two or more joint holders, whichever of them is named first in the register of members; or

(c)     if the holder is no longer entitled to the share by reason of death or bankruptcy, or otherwise by operation of law, the transmittee.

### 32 No interest on distributions

The company may not pay interest on any dividend or other sum payable in respect of a share unless otherwise provided by

(a)     the terms on which the share was issued, or

(b)     the provisions of another agreement between the holder of that share and the company.

### 33 Unclaimed distributions

(1) All dividends or other sums which are

(a)     payable in respect of shares, and

(b)     unclaimed after having been declared or become payable,

may be invested or otherwise made use of by the directors for the benefit of the company until claimed.

(2) The payment of any such dividend or other sum into a separate account does not make the company a trustee in respect of it.

(3) If

    (a)       twelve years have passed from the date on which a dividend or other sum became due for payment, and

    (b)       the distribution recipient has not claimed it,

the distribution recipient is no longer entitled to that dividend or other sum and it ceases to remain owing by the company.

## 34 Non-cash distributions

(1) Subject to the terms of issue of the share in question, the company may, by ordinary resolution on the recommendation of the directors, decide to pay all or part of a dividend or other distribution payable in respect of a share by transferring non-cash assets of equivalent value (including, without limitation, shares or other securities in any company).

(2) For the purposes of paying a non-cash distribution, the directors may make whatever arrangements they think fit, including, where any difficulty arises regarding the distribution

    (a)       fixing the value of any assets;

    (b)       paying cash to any distribution recipient on the basis of that value in order to adjust the rights of recipients; and

    (c)       vesting any assets in trustees.

## 35 Waiver of distributions

Distribution recipients may waive their entitlement to a dividend or other distribution payable in respect of a share by giving the company notice in writing to that effect, but if

    (a)       the share has more than one holder, or

    (b)       more than one person is entitled to the share, whether by reason of the death or bankruptcy of one or more joint holders, or otherwise,

the notice is not effective unless it is expressed to be given, and signed, by all the holders or persons otherwise entitled to the share.

*Capitalisation of profits*

## 36 Authority to capitalise and appropriation of capitalised sums

(1) Subject to the articles, the directors may, if they are so authorised by an ordinary resolution

    (a)       decide to capitalise any profits of the company (whether or not they are available for distribution) which are not required for paying a preferential dividend, or any sum standing to the credit of the company's share premium account or capital redemption reserve; and

appropriate any sum which they so decide to capitalise (a "capitalised sum") to the persons who would have been entitled to it if it were distributed by way of dividend (the "persons entitled") and in the same proportions.

(2) Capitalised sums must be applied

    (a)       on behalf of the persons entitled, and

    (b)       in the same proportions as a dividend would have been distributed to them.

(3) Any capitalised sum may be applied in paying up new shares of a nominal amount equal to the capitalised sum which are then allotted credited as fully paid to the persons entitled or as they may direct.

(4) A capitalised sum which was appropriated from profits available for distribution may be applied in paying up new debentures of the company which are then allotted credited as fully paid to the persons entitled or as they may direct.

(5) Subject to the articles the directors may

    (a)       apply capitalised sums in accordance with paragraphs (3) and (4) partly in one way and partly in another;

(b)    make such arrangements as they think fit to deal with shares or debentures becoming distributable in fractions under this article (including the issuing of fractional certificates or the making of cash payments); and

(c)    authorise any person to enter into an agreement with the company on behalf of all the persons entitled which is binding on them in respect of the allotment of shares and debentures to them under this article.

## MODEL ARTICLES: PUBLIC COMPANIES (SI 2008 NO 3229, SCH 3). COMPANIES ACT 2006 AS AMENDED BY THE MENTAL HEALTH DISCRIMINATION ACT 2013

### INDEX

# Appendix 4 – Standard Articles of association

## PART 1: INTERPRETATION AND LIMITATION OF LIABILITY

### 1 Defined terms

In the articles, unless the context requires otherwise

"alternate" or "alternate director" has the meaning given in article 25;

"appointor" has the meaning given in article 25;

"articles" means the company's articles of association;

"bankruptcy" includes individual insolvency proceedings in a jurisdiction other than England and Wales or Northern Ireland which have an effect similar to that of bankruptcy;

"call" has the meaning given in article 54;

"call notice" has the meaning given in article 54;

"certificate" means a paper certificate (other than a share warrant) evidencing a person's title to specified shares or other securities;

"certificated" in relation to a share, means that it is not an uncertificated share or a share in respect of which a share warrant has been issued and is current;

"chairman" has the meaning given in article 12;

"chairman of the meeting" has the meaning given in article 31;

"Companies Acts" means the Companies Acts (as defined in section 2 of the Companies Act 2006), in so far as they apply to the company;

"company's lien" has the meaning given in article 52;

"director" means a director of the company, and includes any person occupying the position of director, by whatever name called;

"distribution recipient" has the meaning given in article 72;

"document" includes, unless otherwise specified, any document sent or supplied in electronic form;

"electronic form" has the meaning given in section 1168 of the Companies Act 2006;

"fully paid" in relation to a share, means that the nominal value and any premium to be paid to the company in respect of that share have been paid to the company;

"hard copy form" has the meaning given in section 1168 of the Companies Act 2006;

"holder" in relation to shares means the person whose name is entered in the register of members as the holder of the shares, or, in the case of a share in respect of which a share warrant has been issued (and not cancelled), the person in possession of that warrant;

"instrument" means a document in hard copy form;

"lien enforcement notice" has the meaning given in article 53;

"member" has the meaning given in section 112 of the Companies Act 2006;

"ordinary resolution" has the meaning given in section 282 of the Companies Act 2006;

"paid" means paid or credited as paid;

"participate", in relation to a directors' meeting, has the meaning given in article 9;

"partly paid" in relation to a share means that part of that share's nominal value or any premium at which it was issued has not been paid to the company;

"proxy notice" has the meaning given in article 38;

"securities seal" has the meaning given in article 47;

"shares" means shares in the company;

"special resolution" has the meaning given in section 283 of the Companies Act 2006;

"subsidiary" has the meaning given in section 1159 of the Companies Act 2006;

"transmittee" means a person entitled to a share by reason of the death or bankruptcy of a shareholder or otherwise by operation of law;

"uncertificated" in relation to a share means that, by virtue of legislation (other than section 778 of the Companies Act 2006) permitting title to shares to be evidenced and transferred without a certificate, title to that share is evidenced and may be transferred without a certificate; and

"writing" means the representation or reproduction of words, symbols or other information in a visible form by any method or combination of methods, whether sent or supplied in electronic form or otherwise.

Unless the context otherwise requires, other words or expressions contained in these articles bear the same meaning as in the Companies Act 2006 as in force on the date when these articles become binding on the company.

## 2 Liability of members

The liability of the members is limited to the amount, if any, unpaid on the shares held by them.

## PART 2: DIRECTORS

### *Directors' powers and responsibilities*

### 3 Directors' general authority

Subject to the articles, the directors are responsible for the management of the company's business, for which purpose they may exercise all the powers of the company.

### 4 Members' reserve power

(1)The members may, by special resolution, direct the directors to take, or refrain from taking, specified action.

(2) No such special resolution invalidates anything which the directors have done before the passing of the resolution.

### 5 Directors may delegate

(1) Subject to the articles, the directors may delegate any of the powers which are conferred on them under the articles

| | |
|---|---|
| (a) | to such person or committee; |
| (b) | by such means (including by power of attorney); |
| (c) | to such an extent; |
| (d) | in relation to such matters or territories; and |

(e)      on such terms and conditions;

as they think fit.

(2) If the directors so specify, any such delegation may authorise further delegation of the directors' powers by any person to whom they are delegated.

(3) The directors may revoke any delegation in whole or part, or alter its terms and conditions.

## 6 Committees

(1) Committees to which the directors delegate any of their powers must follow procedures which are based as far as they are applicable on those provisions of the articles which govern the taking of decisions by directors.

(2) The directors may make rules of procedure for all or any committees, which prevail over rules derived from the articles if they are not consistent with them.

*Decision-making by directors*

## 7 Directors to take decisions collectively

Decisions of the directors may be taken

(a)      at a directors' meeting, or

(b)      in the form of a directors' written resolution.

## 8 Calling a directors' meeting

(1) Any director may call a directors' meeting.

(2) The company secretary must call a directors' meeting if a director so requests.

(3) A directors' meeting is called by giving notice of the meeting to the directors.

(4) Notice of any directors' meeting must indicate

(a)      its proposed date and time;

(b)      where it is to take place; and

(c)      if it is anticipated that directors participating in the meeting will not be in the same place, how it is proposed that they should communicate with each other during the meeting.

(5) Notice of a directors' meeting must be given to each director, but need not be in writing.

(6) Notice of a directors' meeting need not be given to directors who waive their entitlement to notice of that meeting, by giving notice to that effect to the company not more than 7 days after the date on which the meeting is held. Where such notice is given after the meeting has been held, that does not affect the validity of the meeting, or of any business conducted at it.

## 9 Participation in directors' meetings

(1) Subject to the articles, directors participate in a directors' meeting, or part of a directors' meeting, when—

(a)      the meeting has been called and takes place in accordance with the articles, and

(b)      they can each communicate to the others any information or opinions they have on any particular item of the business of the meeting.

(2) In determining whether directors are participating in a directors' meeting, it is irrelevant where any director is or how they communicate with each other.

(3) If all the directors participating in a meeting are not in the same place, they may decide that the meeting is to be treated as taking place wherever any of them is.

## 10 Quorum for directors' meetings

(1) At a directors' meeting, unless a quorum is participating, no proposal is to be voted on, except a proposal to call another meeting.

(2) The quorum for directors' meetings may be fixed from time to time by a decision of the directors, but it must never be less than two, and unless otherwise fixed it is two.

## 11 Meetings where total number of directors less than quorum

(1) This article applies where the total number of directors for the time being is less than the quorum for directors' meetings.

(2) If there is only one director, that director may appoint sufficient directors to make up a quorum or call a general meeting to do so.

(3) If there is more than one director

    (a)     a directors' meeting may take place, if it is called in accordance with the articles and at least two directors participate in it, with a view to appointing sufficient directors to make up a quorum or calling a general meeting to do so, and

    (b)     if a directors' meeting is called but only one director attends at the appointed date and time to participate in it, that director may appoint sufficient directors to make up a quorum or call a general meeting to do so.

## 12 Chairing directors' meetings

(1) The directors may appoint a director to chair their meetings.

(2) The person so appointed for the time being is known as the chairman.

(3) The directors may appoint other directors as deputy or assistant chairmen to chair directors' meetings in the chairman's absence.

(4) The directors may terminate the appointment of the chairman, deputy or assistant chairman at any time.

(5) If neither the chairman nor any director appointed generally to chair directors' meetings in the chairman's absence is participating in a meeting within ten minutes of the time at which it was to start, the participating directors must appoint one of themselves to chair it.

## 13 Voting at directors' meetings: general rules

(1) Subject to the articles, a decision is taken at a directors' meeting by a majority of the votes of the participating directors.

(2) Subject to the articles, each director participating in a directors' meeting has one vote.

(3) Subject to the articles, if a director has an interest in an actual or proposed transaction or arrangement with the company

    (a)     that director and that director's alternate may not vote on any proposal relating to it, but

    (b)     this does not preclude the alternate from voting in relation to that transaction or arrangement on behalf of another appointor who does not have such an interest.

## 14 Chairman's casting vote at directors' meetings

(1) If the numbers of votes for and against a proposal are equal, the chairman or other director chairing the meeting has a casting vote.

(2) But this does not apply if, in accordance with the articles, the chairman or other director is not to be counted as participating in the decision-making process for quorum or voting purposes.

## 15 Alternates voting at directors' meetings

A director who is also an alternate director has an additional vote on behalf of each appointor who is

    (a)     not participating in a directors' meeting, and

    (b)     would have been entitled to vote if they were participating in it.

## 16 Conflicts of interest

(1) If a directors' meeting, or part of a directors' meeting, is concerned with an actual or proposed transaction or arrangement with the company in which a director is interested, that director is not to be counted as participating in that meeting, or part of a meeting, for quorum or voting purposes.

(2) But if paragraph (3) applies, a director who is interested in an actual or proposed transaction or arrangement with the company is to be counted as participating in a decision at a directors' meeting, or part of a directors' meeting, relating to it for quorum and voting purposes.

(3) This paragraph applies when

    (a)    the company by ordinary resolution disapplies the provision of the articles which would otherwise prevent a director from being counted as participating in, or voting at, a directors' meeting;

    (b)    the director's interest cannot reasonably be regarded as likely to give rise to a conflict of interest; or

    (c)    the director's conflict of interest arises from a permitted cause.

(4) For the purposes of this article, the following are permitted causes

    (a)    a guarantee given, or to be given, by or to a director in respect of an obligation incurred by or on behalf of the company or any of its subsidiaries;

    (b)    subscription, or an agreement to subscribe, for shares or other securities of the company or any of its subsidiaries, or to underwrite, sub-underwrite, or guarantee subscription for any such shares or securities; and

    (c)    arrangements pursuant to which benefits are made available to employees and directors or former employees and directors of the company or any of its subsidiaries which do not provide special benefits for directors or former directors.

(5) Subject to paragraph (6), if a question arises at a meeting of directors or of a committee of directors as to the right of a director to participate in the meeting (or part of the meeting) for voting or quorum purposes, the question may, before the conclusion of the meeting, be referred to the chairman whose ruling in relation to any director other than the chairman is to be final and conclusive.

(6) If any question as to the right to participate in the meeting (or part of the meeting) should arise in respect of the chairman, the question is to be decided by a decision of the directors at that meeting, for which purpose the chairman is not to be counted as participating in the meeting (or that part of the meeting) for voting or quorum purposes.

## 17 Proposing directors' written resolutions

(1) Any director may propose a directors' written resolution.

(2) The company secretary must propose a directors' written resolution if a director so requests.

(3) A directors' written resolution is proposed by giving notice of the proposed resolution to the directors.

(4) Notice of a proposed directors' written resolution must indicate

    (a)    the proposed resolution, and

    (b)    the time by which it is proposed that the directors should adopt it.

(5) Notice of a proposed directors' written resolution must be given in writing to each director.

(6) Any decision which a person giving notice of a proposed directors' written resolution takes regarding the process of adopting that resolution must be taken reasonably in good faith.

## 18 Adoption of directors' written resolutions

(1) A proposed directors' written resolution is adopted when all the directors who would have been entitled to vote on the resolution at a directors' meeting have signed one or more copies of it, provided that those directors would have formed a quorum at such a meeting.

(2) It is immaterial whether any director signs the resolution before or after the time by which the notice proposed that it should be adopted.

(3) Once a directors' written resolution has been adopted, it must be treated as if it had been a decision taken at a directors' meeting in accordance with the articles.

(4) The company secretary must ensure that the company keeps a record, in writing, of all directors' written resolutions for at least ten years from the date of their adoption.

## 19 Directors' discretion to make further rules

Subject to the articles, the directors may make any rule which they think fit about how they take decisions, and about how such rules are to be recorded or communicated to directors.

*Appointment of directors*

## 20 Methods of appointing directors

Any person who is willing to act as a director, and is permitted by law to do so, may be appointed to be a director

- (a)   by ordinary resolution, or
- (b)   by a decision of the directors.

## 21 Retirement of directors by rotation

(1) At the first annual general meeting all the directors must retire from office.

(2) At every subsequent annual general meeting any directors

- (a)   who have been appointed by the directors since the last annual general meeting, or
- (b)   who were not appointed or reappointed at one of the preceding two annual general meetings,

must retire from office and may offer themselves for reappointment by the members.

## 22 Termination of director's appointment

A person ceases to be a director as soon as

- (a)   that person ceases to be a director by virtue of any provision of the Companies Act 2006 or is prohibited from being a director by law;
- (b)   a bankruptcy order is made against that person;
- (c)   a composition is made with that person's creditors generally in satisfaction of that person's debts;
- (d)   a registered medical practitioner who is treating that person gives a written opinion to the company stating that that person has become physically or mentally incapable of acting as a director and may remain so for more than three months;
- (f)   notification is received by the company from the director that the director is resigning from office as director, and such resignation has taken effect in accordance with its terms.

## 23 Directors' remuneration

(1) Directors may undertake any services for the company that the directors decide.

(2) Directors are entitled to such remuneration as the directors determine

- (a)   for their services to the company as directors, and
- (b)   for any other service which they undertake for the company.

(3) Subject to the articles, a director's remuneration may

- (a)   take any form, and
- (b)   include any arrangements in connection with the payment of a pension, allowance or gratuity, or any death, sickness or disability benefits, to or in respect of that director.

(4) Unless the directors decide otherwise, directors' remuneration accrues from day to day.

(5) Unless the directors decide otherwise, directors are not accountable to the company for any remuneration which they receive as directors or other officers or employees of the company's subsidiaries or of any other body corporate in which the company is interested.

## 24 Directors' expenses

The company may pay any reasonable expenses which the directors properly incur in connection with their attendance at

- (a)   meetings of directors or committees of directors,

(b)      general meetings, or

(c)      separate meetings of the holders of any class of shares or of debentures of the company,

or otherwise in connection with the exercise of their powers and the discharge of their responsibilities in relation to the company.

*Alternate directors*

## 25 Appointment and removal of alternates

(1) Any director (the "appointor") may appoint as an alternate any other director, or any other person approved by resolution of the directors, to

(a)      exercise that director's powers, and

(b)      carry out that director's responsibilities,

in relation to the taking of decisions by the directors in the absence of the alternate's appointor.

(2) Any appointment or removal of an alternate must be effected by notice in writing to the company signed by the appointor, or in any other manner approved by the directors.

(3) The notice must

(a)      identify the proposed alternate, and

(b)      in the case of a notice of appointment, contain a statement signed by the proposed alternate that the proposed alternate is willing to act as the alternate of the director giving the notice.

## 26 Rights and responsibilities of alternate directors

(1) An alternate director has the same rights, in relation to any directors' meeting or directors' written resolution, as the alternate's appointor.

(2) Except as the articles specify otherwise, alternate directors

(a)      are deemed for all purposes to be directors;

(b)      are liable for their own acts and omissions;

(c)      are subject to the same restrictions as their appointors; and

(d)      are not deemed to be agents of or for their appointors.

(3) A person who is an alternate director but not a director

(a)      may be counted as participating for the purposes of determining whether a quorum is participating (but only if that person's appointor is not participating), and

(b)      may sign a written resolution (but only if it is not signed or to be signed by that person's appointor).

No alternate may be counted as more than one director for such purposes.

(4) An alternate director is not entitled to receive any remuneration from the company for serving as an alternate director except such part of the alternate's appointor's remuneration as the appointor may direct by notice in writing made to the company.

## 27 Termination of alternate directorship

An alternate director's appointment as an alternate terminates

(a)      when the alternate's appointor revokes the appointment by notice to the company in writing specifying when it is to terminate;

(b)      on the occurrence in relation to the alternate of any event which, if it occurred in relation to the alternate's appointor, would result in the termination of the appointor's appointment as a director;

(c)      on the death of the alternate's appointor; or

(d)      when the alternate's appointor's appointment as a director terminates, except that an alternate's appointment as an alternate does not terminate when the appointor retires by rotation at a general meeting and is then re-appointed as a director at the same general meeting.

PART 3: DECISION-MAKING BY MEMBERS

*Organisation of general meetings*

## 28 Members can call general meeting if not enough directors

If

(a)      the company has fewer than two directors, and

(b)      the director (if any) is unable or unwilling to appoint sufficient directors to make up a quorum or to call a general meeting to do so,

then two or more members may call a general meeting (or instruct the company secretary to do so) for the purpose of appointing one or more directors.

## 29 Attendance and speaking at general meetings

(1) A person is able to exercise the right to speak at a general meeting when that person is in a position to communicate to all those attending the meeting, during the meeting, any information or opinions which that person has on the business of the meeting.

(2) A person is able to exercise the right to vote at a general meeting when

(a)      that person is able to vote, during the meeting, on resolutions put to the vote at the meeting, and

(b)      that person's vote can be taken into account in determining whether or not such resolutions are passed at the same time as the votes of all the other persons attending the meeting.

(3) The directors may make whatever arrangements they consider appropriate to enable those attending a general meeting to exercise their rights to speak or vote at it.

(4) In determining attendance at a general meeting, it is immaterial whether any two or more members attending it are in the same place as each other.

(5) Two or more persons who are not in the same place as each other attend a general meeting if their circumstances are such that if they have (or were to have) rights to speak and vote at that meeting, they are (or would be) able to exercise them.

## 30 Quorum for general meetings

No business other than the appointment of the chairman of the meeting is to be transacted at a general meeting if the persons attending it do not constitute a quorum.

## 31 Chairing general meetings

(1) If the directors have appointed a chairman, the chairman shall chair general meetings if present and willing to do so.

(2) If the directors have not appointed a chairman, or if the chairman is unwilling to chair the meeting or is not present within ten minutes of the time at which a meeting was due to start

(a)      the directors present, or

(b)      (if no directors are present), the meeting,

must appoint a director or member to chair the meeting, and the appointment of the chairman of the meeting must be the first business of the meeting.

(3) The person chairing a meeting in accordance with this article is referred to as "the chairman of the meeting".

## 32 Attendance and speaking by directors and non-members

(1) Directors may attend and speak at general meetings, whether or not they are members.

(2) The chairman of the meeting may permit other persons who are not

(a)      members of the company, or

(b) otherwise entitled to exercise the rights of members in relation to general meetings,

to attend and speak at a general meeting.

## 33 Adjournment

(1) If the persons attending a general meeting within half an hour of the time at which the meeting was due to start do not constitute a quorum, or if during a meeting a quorum ceases to be present, the chairman of the meeting must adjourn it.

(2) The chairman of the meeting may adjourn a general meeting at which a quorum is present if

(a) the meeting consents to an adjournment, or

(b) it appears to the chairman of the meeting that an adjournment is necessary to protect the safety of any person attending the meeting or ensure that the business of the meeting is conducted in an orderly manner.

(3) The chairman of the meeting must adjourn a general meeting if directed to do so by the meeting.

(4) When adjourning a general meeting, the chairman of the meeting must

(a) either specify the time and place to which it is adjourned or state that it is to continue at a time and place to be fixed by the directors, and

(b) have regard to any directions as to the time and place of any adjournment which have been given by the meeting.

(5) If the continuation of an adjourned meeting is to take place more than 14 days after it was adjourned, the company must give at least 7 clear days' notice of it (that is, excluding the day of the adjourned meeting and the day on which the notice is given)

(a) to the same persons to whom notice of the company's general meetings is required to be given, and

(b) containing the same information which such notice is required to contain.

(6) No business may be transacted at an adjourned general meeting which could not properly have been transacted at the meeting if the adjournment had not taken place.

*Voting at general meetings*

## 34 Voting: general

A resolution put to the vote of a general meeting must be decided on a show of hands unless a poll is duly demanded in accordance with the articles.

## 35 Errors and disputes

(1) No objection may be raised to the qualification of any person voting at a general meeting except at the meeting or adjourned meeting at which the vote objected to is tendered, and every vote not disallowed at the meeting is valid.

(2) Any such objection must be referred to the chairman of the meeting whose decision is final.

## 36 Demanding a poll

(1) A poll on a resolution may be demanded

(a) in advance of the general meeting where it is to be put to the vote, or

(b) at a general meeting, either before a show of hands on that resolution or immediately after the result of a show of hands on that resolution is declared.

(2) A poll may be demanded by

(a) the chairman of the meeting;

(b) the directors;

(c) two or more persons having the right to vote on the resolution; or

(d) a person or persons representing not less than one tenth of the total voting rights of all the members having the right to vote on the resolution.

(3) A demand for a poll may be withdrawn if

(a)      the poll has not yet been taken, and

(b)      the chairman of the meeting consents to the withdrawal.

## 37 Procedure on a poll

(1) Subject to the articles, polls at general meetings must be taken when, where and in such manner as the chairman of the meeting directs.

(2) The chairman of the meeting may appoint scrutineers (who need not be members) and decide how and when the result of the poll is to be declared.

(3) The result of a poll shall be the decision of the meeting in respect of the resolution on which the poll was demanded.

(4) A poll on

(a)      the election of the chairman of the meeting, or

(b)      a question of adjournment,

must be taken immediately.

(5) Other polls must be taken within 30 days of their being demanded.

(6) A demand for a poll does not prevent a general meeting from continuing, except as regards the question on which the poll was demanded.

(7) No notice need be given of a poll not taken immediately if the time and place at which it is to be taken are announced at the meeting at which it is demanded.

(8) In any other case, at least 7 days' notice must be given specifying the time and place at which the poll is to be taken.

## 38 Content of proxy notices

(1) Proxies may only validly be appointed by a notice in writing (a "proxy notice") which

(a)      states the name and address of the member appointing the proxy;

(b)      identifies the person appointed to be that member's proxy and the general meeting in relation to which that person is appointed;

(c)      is signed by or on behalf of the member appointing the proxy, or is authenticated in such manner as the directors may determine; and

(d)      is delivered to the company in accordance with the articles and any instructions contained in the notice of the general meeting to which they relate.

(2) The company may require proxy notices to be delivered in a particular form, and may specify different forms for different purposes.

(3) Proxy notices may specify how the proxy appointed under them is to vote (or that the proxy is to abstain from voting) on one or more resolutions.

(4) Unless a proxy notice indicates otherwise, it must be treated as

(a)      allowing the person appointed under it as a proxy discretion as to how to vote on any ancillary or procedural resolutions put to the meeting, and

(b)      appointing that person as a proxy in relation to any adjournment of the general meeting to which it relates as well as the meeting itself.

## 39 Delivery of proxy notices

(1) Any notice of a general meeting must specify the address or addresses ("proxy notification address") at which the company or its agents will receive proxy notices relating to that meeting, or any adjournment of it, delivered in hard copy or electronic form.

(2) A person who is entitled to attend, speak or vote (either on a show of hands or on a poll) at a general meeting remains so entitled in respect of that meeting or any adjournment of it, even though a valid proxy notice has been delivered to the company by or on behalf of that person.

(3) Subject to paragraphs (4) and (5), a proxy notice must be delivered to a proxy notification address not less than 48 hours before the general meeting or adjourned meeting to which it relates.

(4) In the case of a poll taken more than 48 hours after it is demanded, the notice must be delivered to a proxy notification address not less than 24 hours before the time appointed for the taking of the poll.

(5) In the case of a poll not taken during the meeting but taken not more than 48 hours after it was demanded, the proxy notice must be delivered

    (a)      in accordance with paragraph (3), or

    (b)      at the meeting at which the poll was demanded to the chairman, secretary or any director.

(6) An appointment under a proxy notice may be revoked by delivering a notice in writing given by or on behalf of the person by whom or on whose behalf the proxy notice was given to a proxy notification address.

(7) A notice revoking a proxy appointment only takes effect if it is delivered before

    (a)      the start of the meeting or adjourned meeting to which it relates, or

    (b)      (in the case of a poll not taken on the same day as the meeting or adjourned meeting) the time appointed for taking the poll to which it relates.

(8) If a proxy notice is not signed by the person appointing the proxy, it must be accompanied by written evidence of the authority of the person who executed it to execute it on the appointor's behalf.

## 40 Amendments to resolutions

(1) An ordinary resolution to be proposed at a general meeting may be amended by ordinary resolution if

    (a)      notice of the proposed amendment is given to the company secretary in writing by a person entitled to vote at the general meeting at which it is to be proposed not less than 48 hours before the meeting is to take place (or such later time as the chairman of the meeting may determine), and

    (b)      the proposed amendment does not, in the reasonable opinion of the chairman of the meeting, materially alter the scope of the resolution.

(2) A special resolution to be proposed at a general meeting may be amended by ordinary resolution, if

    (a)      the chairman of the meeting proposes the amendment at the general meeting at which the resolution is to be proposed, and

    (b)      the amendment does not go beyond what is necessary to correct a grammatical or other non-substantive error in the resolution.

(3) If the chairman of the meeting, acting in good faith, wrongly decides that an amendment to a resolution is out of order, the chairman's error does not invalidate the vote on that resolution.

*Restrictions on members' rights*

## 41 No voting of shares on which money owed to company

No voting rights attached to a share may be exercised at any general meeting, at any adjournment of it, or on any poll called at or in relation to it, unless all amounts payable to the company in respect of that share have been paid.

*Application of rules to class meetings*

## 42 Class meetings

The provisions of the articles relating to general meetings apply, with any necessary modifications, to meetings of the holders of any class of shares.

## PART 4: SHARES AND DISTRIBUTIONS

*Issue of shares*

### 43 Powers to issue different classes of share

(1) Subject to the articles, but without prejudice to the rights attached to any existing share, the company may issue shares with such rights or restrictions as may be determined by ordinary resolution.

(2) The company may issue shares which are to be redeemed, or are liable to be redeemed at the option of the company or the holder, and the directors may determine the terms, conditions and manner of redemption of any such shares.

### 44 Payment of commissions on subscription for shares

(1) The company may pay any person a commission in consideration for that person

    (a)      subscribing, or agreeing to subscribe, for shares, or

    (b)      procuring, or agreeing to procure, subscriptions for shares.

(2) Any such commission may be paid

    (a)      in cash, or in fully paid or partly paid shares or other securities, or partly in one way and partly in the other, and

    (b)      in respect of a conditional or an absolute subscription.

*Interests in shares*

### 45 Company not bound by less than absolute interests

Except as required by law, no person is to be recognised by the company as holding any share upon any trust, and except as otherwise required by law or the articles, the company is not in any way to be bound by or recognise any interest in a share other than the holder's absolute ownership of it and all the rights attaching to it.

*Share certificates*

### 46 Certificates to be issued except in certain cases

(1) The company must issue each member with one or more certificates in respect of the shares which that member holds.

(2) This article does not apply to

    (a)      uncertificated shares;

    (b)      shares in respect of which a share warrant has been issued; or

    (c)      shares in respect of which the Companies Acts permit the company not to issue a certificate.

(3) Except as otherwise specified in the articles, all certificates must be issued free of charge.

(4) No certificate may be issued in respect of shares of more than one class.

(5) If more than one person holds a share, only one certificate may be issued in respect of it.

### 47 Contents and execution of share certificates

(1) Every certificate must specify

    (a)      in respect of how many shares, of what class, it is issued;

    (b)      the nominal value of those shares;

    (c)      the amount paid up on them; and

    (d)      any distinguishing numbers assigned to them.

(2) Certificates must

(a)     have affixed to them the company's common seal or an official seal which is a facsimile of the company's common seal with the addition on its face of the word "Securities" (a "securities seal"), or

(b)     be otherwise executed in accordance with the Companies Acts.

## 48 Consolidated share certificates

(1) When a member's holding of shares of a particular class increases, the company may issue that member with

(a)     a single, consolidated certificate in respect of all the shares of a particular class which that member holds, or

(b)     a separate certificate in respect of only those shares by which that member's holding has increased.

(2) When a member's holding of shares of a particular class is reduced, the company must ensure that the member is issued with one or more certificates in respect of the number of shares held by the member after that reduction. But the company need not (in the absence of a request from the member) issue any new certificate if

(a)     all the shares which the member no longer holds as a result of the reduction, and

(b)     none of the shares which the member retains following the reduction,

were, immediately before the reduction, represented by the same certificate.

(3) A member may request the company, in writing, to replace

(a)     the member's separate certificates with a consolidated certificate, or

(b)     the member's consolidated certificate with two or more separate certificates representing such proportion of the shares as the member may specify.

(4) When the company complies with such a request it may charge such reasonable fee as the directors may decide for doing so.

(5) A consolidated certificate must not be issued unless any certificates which it is to replace have first been returned to the company for cancellation.

## 49 Replacement share certificates

(1) If a certificate issued in respect of a member's shares is

(a)     damaged or defaced, or

(b)     said to be lost, stolen or destroyed,

that member is entitled to be issued with a replacement certificate in respect of the same shares.

(2) A member exercising the right to be issued with such a replacement certificate

(a)     may at the same time exercise the right to be issued with a single certificate or separate certificates;

(b)     must return the certificate which is to be replaced to the company if it is damaged or defaced; and

(c)     must comply with such conditions as to evidence, indemnity and the payment of a reasonable fee as the directors decide.

*Shares not held in certificated form*

## 50 Uncertificated shares

(1) In this article, "the relevant rules" means

(a)     any applicable provision of the Companies Acts about the holding, evidencing of title to, or transfer of shares other than in certificated form, and

(b)     any applicable legislation, rules or other arrangements made under or by virtue of such provision.

(2) The provisions of this article have effect subject to the relevant rules.

(3) Any provision of the articles which is inconsistent with the relevant rules must be disregarded, to the extent that it is inconsistent, whenever the relevant rules apply.

(4) Any share or class of shares of the company may be issued or held on such terms, or in such a way, that

(a)     title to it or them is not, or must not be, evidenced by a certificate, or

(b)     it or they may or must be transferred wholly or partly without a certificate.

(5) The directors have power to take such steps as they think fit in relation to

(a)     the evidencing of and transfer of title to uncertificated shares (including in connection with the issue of such shares);

(b)     any records relating to the holding of uncertificated shares;

(c)     the conversion of certificated shares into uncertificated shares; or

(d)     the conversion of uncertificated shares into certificated shares.

(6) The company may by notice to the holder of a share require that share

(a)     if it is uncertificated, to be converted into certificated form, and

(b)     if it is certificated, to be converted into uncertificated form,

to enable it to be dealt with in accordance with the articles.

(7) If

(a)     the articles give the directors power to take action, or require other persons to take action, in order to sell, transfer or otherwise dispose of shares, and

(b)     uncertificated shares are subject to that power, but the power is expressed in terms which assume the use of a certificate or other written instrument,

the directors may take such action as is necessary or expedient to achieve the same results when exercising that power in relation to uncertificated shares.

(8) In particular, the directors may take such action as they consider appropriate to achieve the sale, transfer, disposal, forfeiture, re-allotment or surrender of an uncertificated share or otherwise to enforce a lien in respect of it.

(9) Unless the directors otherwise determine, shares which a member holds in uncertificated form must be treated as separate holdings from any shares which that member holds in certificated form.

(10) A class of shares must not be treated as two classes simply because some shares of that class are held in certificated form and others are held in uncertificated form.

## 51 Share warrants

(1) The directors may issue a share warrant in respect of any fully paid share.

(2) Share warrants must be

(a)     issued in such form, and

(b)     executed in such manner,

as the directors decide.

(3) A share represented by a share warrant may be transferred by delivery of the warrant representing it.

(4) The directors may make provision for the payment of dividends in respect of any share represented by a share warrant.

(5) Subject to the articles, the directors may decide the conditions on which any share warrant is issued. In particular, they may

(a)     decide the conditions on which new warrants are to be issued in place of warrants which are damaged or defaced, or said to have been lost, stolen or destroyed;

(b)     decide the conditions on which bearers of warrants are entitled to attend and vote at general meetings;

(c)     decide the conditions subject to which bearers of warrants may surrender their warrant so as to hold their shares in certificated or uncertificated form instead; and

(d)     vary the conditions of issue of any warrant from time to time, and the bearer of a warrant is subject to the conditions and procedures in force in relation to it, whether or not they were decided or specified before the warrant was issued.

(6) Subject to the conditions on which the warrants are issued from time to time, bearers of share warrants have the same rights and privileges as they would if their names had been included in the register as holders of the shares represented by their warrants.

(7) The company must not in any way be bound by or recognise any interest in a share represented by a share warrant other than the absolute right of the bearer of that warrant to that warrant.

*Partly paid shares*

## 52 Company's lien over partly paid shares

(1) The company has a lien ("the company's lien") over every share which is partly paid for any part of

    (a)        that share's nominal value, and

    (b)        any premium at which it was issued,

which has not been paid to the company, and which is payable immediately or at some time in the future, whether or not a call notice has been sent in respect of it.

(2) The company's lien over a share

    (a)        takes priority over any third party's interest in that share, and

    (b)        extends to any dividend or other money payable by the company in respect of that share and (if the lien is enforced and the share is sold by the company) the proceeds of sale of that share.

(3) The directors may at any time decide that a share which is or would otherwise be subject to the company's lien shall not be subject to it, either wholly or in part.

## 53 Enforcement of the company's lien

(1) Subject to the provisions of this article, if

    (a)        a lien enforcement notice has been given in respect of a share, and

    (b)        the person to whom the notice was given has failed to comply with it,

the company may sell that share in such manner as the directors decide.

(2) A lien enforcement notice

    (a)        may only be given in respect of a share which is subject to the company's lien, in respect of which a sum is payable and the due date for payment of that sum has passed;

    (b)        must specify the share concerned;

    (c)        must require payment of the sum payable within 14 days of the notice;

    (d)        must be addressed either to the holder of the share or to a person entitled to it by reason of the holder's death, bankruptcy or otherwise; and

    (e)        must state the company's intention to sell the share if the notice is not complied with.

(3) Where shares are sold under this article

    (a)        the directors may authorise any person to execute an instrument of transfer of the shares to the purchaser or a person nominated by the purchaser, and

    (b)        the transferee is not bound to see to the application of the consideration, and the transferee's title is not affected by any irregularity in or invalidity of the process leading to the sale.

(4) The net proceeds of any such sale (after payment of the costs of sale and any other costs of enforcing the lien) must be applied

    (a)        first, in payment of so much of the sum for which the lien exists as was payable at the date of the lien enforcement notice,

    (b)        second, to the person entitled to the shares at the date of the sale, but only after the certificate for the shares sold has been surrendered to the company for cancellation or a suitable indemnity has been given for any lost certificates, and subject to a lien equivalent to the company's lien over the shares before the sale for any money payable in respect of the shares after the date of the lien enforcement notice.

(5) A statutory declaration by a director or the company secretary that the declarant is a director or the company secretary and that a share has been sold to satisfy the company's lien on a specified date

(a) is conclusive evidence of the facts stated in it as against all persons claiming to be entitled to the share, and

(b) subject to compliance with any other formalities of transfer required by the articles or by law, constitutes a good title to the share.

## 54 Call notices

(1) Subject to the articles and the terms on which shares are allotted, the directors may send a notice (a "call notice") to a member requiring the member to pay the company a specified sum of money (a "call") which is payable in respect of shares which that member holds at the date when the directors decide to send the call notice.

(2) A call notice

(a) may not require a member to pay a call which exceeds the total sum unpaid on that member's shares (whether as to the share's nominal value or any amount payable to the company by way of premium);

(b) must state when and how any call to which it relates it is to be paid; and

(c) may permit or require the call to be paid by instalments.

(3) A member must comply with the requirements of a call notice, but no member is obliged to pay any call before 14 days have passed since the notice was sent.

(4) Before the company has received any call due under a call notice the directors may

(a) revoke it wholly or in part, or

(b) specify a later time for payment than is specified in the notice,

by a further notice in writing to the member in respect of whose shares the call is made.

## 55 Liability to pay calls

(1) Liability to pay a call is not extinguished or transferred by transferring the shares in respect of which it is required to be paid.

(2) Joint holders of a share are jointly and severally liable to pay all calls in respect of that share.

(3) Subject to the terms on which shares are allotted, the directors may, when issuing shares, provide that call notices sent to the holders of those shares may require them

(a) to pay calls which are not the same, or

(b) to pay calls at different times.

## 56 When call notice need not be issued

(1) A call notice need not be issued in respect of sums which are specified, in the terms on which a share is issued, as being payable to the company in respect of that share (whether in respect of nominal value or premium)

(a) on allotment;

(b) on the occurrence of a particular event; or

(c) on a date fixed by or in accordance with the terms of issue.

(2) But if the due date for payment of such a sum has passed and it has not been paid, the holder of the share concerned is treated in all respects as having failed to comply with a call notice in respect of that sum, and is liable to the same consequences as regards the payment of interest and forfeiture.

## 57 Failure to comply with call notice: automatic consequences

(1) If a person is liable to pay a call and fails to do so by the call payment date

| | |
|---|---|
| (a) | the directors may issue a notice of intended forfeiture to that person, and |
| (b) | until the call is paid, that person must pay the company interest on the call from the call payment date at the relevant rate. |

(2) For the purposes of this article

| | |
|---|---|
| (a) | the "call payment date" is the time when the call notice states that a call is payable, unless the directors give a notice specifying a later date, in which case the "call payment date" is that later date; |
| (b) | the "relevant rate" is |

| | | |
|---|---|---|
| | (i) | the rate fixed by the terms on which the share in respect of which the call is due was allotted; |
| | (ii) | such other rate as was fixed in the call notice which required payment of the call, or has otherwise been determined by the directors; or |
| | (iii) | if no rate is fixed in either of these ways, 5 per cent per annum. |

(3) The relevant rate must not exceed by more than 5 percentage points the base lending rate most recently set by the Monetary Policy Committee of the Bank of England in connection with its responsibilities under Part 2 of the Bank of England Act 1998(a).

(4) The directors may waive any obligation to pay interest on a call wholly or in part.

## 58 Notice of intended forfeiture

A notice of intended forfeiture

| | |
|---|---|
| (a) | may be sent in respect of any share in respect of which a call has not been paid as required by a call notice; |
| (b) | must be sent to the holder of that share or to a person entitled to it by reason of the holder's death, bankruptcy or otherwise; |
| (c) | must require payment of the call and any accrued interest by a date which is not less than 14 days after the date of the notice; |
| (d) | must state how the payment is to be made; and |
| (e) | must state that if the notice is not complied with, the shares in respect of which the call is payable will be liable to be forfeited. |

## 59 Directors' power to forfeit shares

If a notice of intended forfeiture is not complied with before the date by which payment of the call is required in the notice of intended forfeiture, the directors may decide that any share in respect of which it was given is forfeited, and the forfeiture is to include all dividends or other moneys payable in respect of the forfeited shares and not paid before the forfeiture.

## 60 Effect of forfeiture

(1) Subject to the articles, the forfeiture of a share extinguishes

| | |
|---|---|
| (a) | all interests in that share, and all claims and demands against the company in respect of it, and |
| (b) | all other rights and liabilities incidental to the share as between the person whose share it was prior to the forfeiture and the company. |

(2) Any share which is forfeited in accordance with the articles

| | |
|---|---|
| (a) | is deemed to have been forfeited when the directors decide that it is forfeited; |
| (b) | is deemed to be the property of the company; and |
| (c) | may be sold, re-allotted or otherwise disposed of as the directors think fit. |

(3) If a person's shares have been forfeited

| | |
|---|---|
| (a) | the company must send that person notice that forfeiture has occurred and record it in the register of members; |
| (b) | that person ceases to be a member in respect of those shares; |
| (c) | that person must surrender the certificate for the shares forfeited to the company for cancellation; |

| (d) | that person remains liable to the company for all sums payable by that person under the articles at the date of forfeiture in respect of those shares, including any interest (whether accrued before or after the date of forfeiture); and |
| (e) | the directors may waive payment of such sums wholly or in part or enforce payment without any allowance for the value of the shares at the time of forfeiture or for any consideration received on their disposal. |

(4) At any time before the company disposes of a forfeited share, the directors may decide to cancel the forfeiture on payment of all calls and interest due in respect of it and on such other terms as they think fit.

## 61 Procedure following forfeiture

(1) If a forfeited share is to be disposed of by being transferred, the company may receive the consideration for the transfer and the directors may authorise any person to execute the instrument of transfer.

(2) A statutory declaration by a director or the company secretary that the declarant is a director or the company secretary and that a share has been forfeited on a specified date

| (a) | is conclusive evidence of the facts stated in it as against all persons claiming to be entitled to the share, and |
| (b) | subject to compliance with any other formalities of transfer required by the articles or by law, constitutes a good title to the share. |

(3) A person to whom a forfeited share is transferred is not bound to see to the application of the consideration (if any) nor is that person's title to the share affected by any irregularity in or invalidity of the process leading to the forfeiture or transfer of the share.

(4) If the company sells a forfeited share, the person who held it prior to its forfeiture is entitled to receive from the company the proceeds of such sale, net of any commission, and excluding any amount which

| (a) | was, or would have become, payable, and |
| (b) | had not, when that share was forfeited, been paid by that person in respect of that share, |

but no interest is payable to such a person in respect of such proceeds and the company is not required to account for any money earned on them.

## 62 Surrender of shares

(1) A member may surrender any share

| (a) | in respect of which the directors may issue a notice of intended forfeiture; |
| (b) | which the directors may forfeit; or |
| (c) | which has been forfeited. |

(2) The directors may accept the surrender of any such share.

(3) The effect of surrender on a share is the same as the effect of forfeiture on that share.

(4) A share which has been surrendered may be dealt with in the same way as a share which has been forfeited.

*Transfer and transmission of shares*

## 63 Transfers of certificated shares

(1) Certificated shares may be transferred by means of an instrument of transfer in any usual form or any other form approved by the directors, which is executed by or on behalf of

| (a) | the transferor, and |
| (b) | (if any of the shares is partly paid) the transferee. |

(2) No fee may be charged for registering any instrument of transfer or other document relating to or affecting the title to any share.

(3) The company may retain any instrument of transfer which is registered.

(4) The transferor remains the holder of a certificated share until the transferee's name is entered in the register of members as holder of it.

(5) The directors may refuse to register the transfer of a certificated share if

    (a)    the share is not fully paid;

    (b)    the transfer is not lodged at the company's registered office or such other place as the directors have appointed;

    (c)    the transfer is not accompanied by the certificate for the shares to which it relates, or such other evidence as the directors may reasonably require to show the transferor's right to make the transfer, or evidence of the right of someone other than the transferor to make the transfer on the transferor's behalf;

    (d)    the transfer is in respect of more than one class of share; or

    (e)    the transfer is in favour of more than four transferees.

(6) If the directors refuse to register the transfer of a share, the instrument of transfer must be returned to the transferee with the notice of refusal unless they suspect that the proposed transfer may be fraudulent.

### 64 Transfer of uncertificated shares

A transfer of an uncertificated share must not be registered if it is in favour of more than four transferees.

### 65 Transmission of shares

(1) If title to a share passes to a transmittee, the company may only recognise the transmittee as having any title to that share.

(2) Nothing in these articles releases the estate of a deceased member from any liability in respect of a share solely or jointly held by that member.

### 66 Transmittees' rights

(1) A transmittee who produces such evidence of entitlement to shares as the directors may properly require

    (a)    may, subject to the articles, choose either to become the holder of those shares or to have them transferred to another person, and

    (b)    subject to the articles, and pending any transfer of the shares to another person, has the same rights as the holder had.

(2) But transmittees do not have the right to attend or vote at a general meeting in respect of shares to which they are entitled, by reason of the holder's death or bankruptcy or otherwise, unless they become the holders of those shares

### 67 Exercise of transmittees' rights

(1) Transmittees who wish to become the holders of shares to which they have become entitled must notify the company in writing of that wish.

(2) If the share is a certificated share and a transmittee wishes to have it transferred to another person, the transmittee must execute an instrument of transfer in respect of it.

(3) If the share is an uncertificated share and the transmittee wishes to have it transferred to another person, the transmittee must

    (a)    procure that all appropriate instructions are given to effect the transfer, or

    (b)    procure that the uncertificated share is changed into certificated form and then execute an instrument of transfer in respect of it.

(4) Any transfer made or executed under this article is to be treated as if it were made or executed by the person from whom the transmittee has derived rights in respect of the share, and as if the event which gave rise to the transmission had not occurred.

## 68 Transmittees bound by prior notices

If a notice is given to a member in respect of shares and a transmittee is entitled to those shares, the transmittee is bound by the notice if it was given to the member before the transmittee's name has been entered in the register of members.

*Consolidation of shares*

## 69 Procedure for disposing of fractions of shares

(1) This article applies where

    (a)      there has been a consolidation or division of shares, and

    (b)      as a result, members are entitled to fractions of shares.

(2) The directors may

    (a)      sell the shares representing the fractions to any person including the company for the best price reasonably obtainable;

    (b)      in the case of a certificated share, authorise any person to execute an instrument of transfer of the shares to the purchaser or a person nominated by the purchaser; and

    (c)      distribute the net proceeds of sale in due proportion among the holders of the shares.

(3) Where any holder's entitlement to a portion of the proceeds of sale amounts to less than a minimum figure determined by the directors, that member's portion may be distributed to an organisation which is a charity for the purposes of the law of England and Wales, Scotland or Northern Ireland.

(4) The person to whom the shares are transferred is not obliged to ensure that any purchase money is received by the person entitled to the relevant fractions.

(5) The transferee's title to the shares is not affected by any irregularity in or invalidity of the process leading to their sale.

*Distributions*

## 70 Procedure for declaring dividends

(1) The company may by ordinary resolution declare dividends, and the directors may decide to pay interim dividends.

(2) A dividend must not be declared unless the directors have made a recommendation as to its amount. Such a dividend must not exceed the amount recommended by the directors.

(3) No dividend may be declared or paid unless it is in accordance with members' respective rights.

(4) Unless the members' resolution to declare or directors' decision to pay a dividend, or the terms on which shares are issued, specify otherwise, it must be paid by reference to each member's holding of shares on the date of the resolution or decision to declare or pay it.

(5) If the company's share capital is divided into different classes, no interim dividend may be paid on shares carrying deferred or non-preferred rights if, at the time of payment, any preferential dividend is in arrear.

(6) The directors may pay at intervals any dividend payable at a fixed rate if it appears to them that the profits available for distribution justify the payment.

(7) If the directors act in good faith, they do not incur any liability to the holders of shares conferring preferred rights for any loss they may suffer by the lawful payment of an interim dividend on shares with deferred or non-preferred rights.

## 71 Calculation of dividends

(1) Except as otherwise provided by the articles or the rights attached to shares, all dividends must be

(a)      declared and paid according to the amounts paid up on the shares on which the dividend is paid, and

(b)      apportioned and paid proportionately to the amounts paid up on the shares during any portion or portions of the period in respect of which the dividend is paid.

(2) If any share is issued on terms providing that it ranks for dividend as from a particular date, that share ranks for dividend accordingly.

(3) For the purposes of calculating dividends, no account is to be taken of any amount which has been paid up on a share in advance of the due date for payment of that amount.

## 72 Payment of dividends and other distributions

(1) Where a dividend or other sum which is a distribution is payable in respect of a share, it must be paid by one or more of the following means

(a)      transfer to a bank or building society account specified by the distribution recipient either in writing or as the directors may otherwise decide;

(b)      sending a cheque made payable to the distribution recipient by post to the distribution recipient at the distribution recipient's registered address (if the distribution recipient is a holder of the share), or (in any other case) to an address specified by the distribution recipient either in writing or as the directors may otherwise decide;

(c)      sending a cheque made payable to such person by post to such person at such address as the distribution recipient has specified either in writing or as the directors may otherwise decide; or

(d)      any other means of payment as the directors agree with the distribution recipient either in writing or by such other means as the directors decide.

(2) In the articles, "the distribution recipient" means, in respect of a share in respect of which a dividend or other sum is payable

(a)      the holder of the share; or

(b)      if the share has two or more joint holders, whichever of them is named first in the register of members; or

(c)      if the holder is no longer entitled to the share by reason of death or bankruptcy, or otherwise by operation of law, the transmittee.

## 73 Deductions from distributions in respect of sums owed to the company

(1) If

(a)      a share is subject to the company's lien, and

(b)      the directors are entitled to issue a lien enforcement notice in respect of it,

they may, instead of issuing a lien enforcement notice, deduct from any dividend or other sum payable in respect of the share any sum of money which is payable to the company in respect of that share to the extent that they are entitled to require payment under a lien enforcement notice.

(2) Money so deducted must be used to pay any of the sums payable in respect of that share.

(3) The company must notify the distribution recipient in writing of

(a)      the fact and amount of any such deduction;

(b)      any non-payment of a dividend or other sum payable in respect of a share resulting from any such deduction; and

(c)      how the money deducted has been applied.

## 74 No interest on distributions

The company may not pay interest on any dividend or other sum payable in respect of a share unless otherwise provided by

(a)      the terms on which the share was issued, or

(b)      the provisions of another agreement between the holder of that share and the company.

## 75 Unclaimed distributions

(1) All dividends or other sums which are

    (a)       payable in respect of shares, and

    (b)       unclaimed after having been declared or become payable,

may be invested or otherwise made use of by the directors for the benefit of the company until claimed.

(2) The payment of any such dividend or other sum into a separate account does not make the company a trustee in respect of it.

(3) If

    (a)       twelve years have passed from the date on which a dividend or other sum became due for payment, and

    (b)       the distribution recipient has not claimed it,

the distribution recipient is no longer entitled to that dividend or other sum and it ceases to remain owing by the company.

## 76 Non-cash distributions

(1) Subject to the terms of issue of the share in question, the company may, by ordinary resolution on the recommendation of the directors, decide to pay all or part of a dividend or other distribution payable in respect of a share by transferring non-cash assets of equivalent value (including, without limitation, shares or other securities in any company).

(2) If the shares in respect of which such a non-cash distribution is paid are uncertificated, any shares in the company which are issued as a non-cash distribution in respect of them must be uncertificated.

(3) For the purposes of paying a non-cash distribution, the directors may make whatever arrangements they think fit, including, where any difficulty arises regarding the distribution

    (a)       fixing the value of any assets;

    (b)       paying cash to any distribution recipient on the basis of that value in order to adjust the rights of recipients; and

    (c)       vesting any assets in trustees.

## 77 Waiver of distributions

Distribution recipients may waive their entitlement to a dividend or other distribution payable in respect of a share by giving the company notice in writing to that effect, but if

    (a)       the share has more than one holder, or

    (b)       more than one person is entitled to the share, whether by reason of the death or bankruptcy of one or more joint holders, or otherwise,

the notice is not effective unless it is expressed to be given, and signed, by all the holders or persons otherwise entitled to the share.

*Capitalisation of profits*

## 78 Authority to capitalise and appropriation of capitalised sums

(1) Subject to the articles, the directors may, if they are so authorised by an ordinary resolution

    (a)       decide to capitalise any profits of the company (whether or not they are available for distribution) which are not required for paying a preferential dividend, or any sum standing to the credit of the company's share premium account or capital redemption reserve; and

    (b)       appropriate any sum which they so decide to capitalise (a "capitalised sum") to the persons who would have been entitled to it if it were distributed by way of dividend (the "persons entitled") and in the same proportions.

(2) Capitalised sums must be applied

    (a)       on behalf of the persons entitled, and

(b)    in the same proportions as a dividend would have been distributed to them.

(3) Any capitalised sum may be applied in paying up new shares of a nominal amount equal to the capitalised sum which are then allotted credited as fully paid to the persons entitled or as they may direct.

(4) A capitalised sum which was appropriated from profits available for distribution may be applied

(a)    in or towards paying up any amounts unpaid on existing shares held by the persons entitled, or

(b)    in paying up new debentures of the company which are then allotted credited as fully paid to the persons entitled or as they may direct.

(5) Subject to the articles the directors may

(a)    apply capitalised sums in accordance with paragraphs (3) and (4) partly in one way and partly in another;

(b)    make such arrangements as they think fit to deal with shares or debentures becoming distributable in fractions under this article (including the issuing of fractional certificates or the making of cash payments); and

(c)    authorise any person to enter into an agreement with the company on behalf of all the persons entitled which is binding on them in respect of the allotment of shares and debentures to them under this article.

## PART 5: MISCELLANEOUS PROVISIONS

*Communications*

## 79 Means of communication to be used

(1) Subject to the articles, anything sent or supplied by or to the company under the articles may be sent or supplied in any way in which the Companies Act 2006 provides for documents or information which are authorised or required by any provision of that Act to be sent or supplied by or to the company.

(2) Subject to the articles, any notice or document to be sent or supplied to a director in connection with the taking of decisions by directors may also be sent or supplied by the means by which that director has asked to be sent or supplied with such notices or documents for the time being.

(3) A director may agree with the company that notices or documents sent to that director in a particular way are to be deemed to have been received within a specified time of their being sent, and for the specified time to be less than 48 hours.

## 80 Failure to notify contact details

(1) If

(a)    the company sends two consecutive documents to a member over a period of at least 12 months, and

(b)    each of those documents is returned undelivered, or the company receives notification that it has not been delivered,

that member ceases to be entitled to receive notices from the company.

(2) A member who has ceased to be entitled to receive notices from the company becomes entitled to receive such notices again by sending the company

(a)    a new address to be recorded in the register of members, or

(b)    if the member has agreed that the company should use a means of communication other than sending things to such an address, the information that the company needs to use that means of communication effectively.

## 81 Company seals

(1) Any common seal may only be used by the authority of the directors.

(2) The directors may decide by what means and in what form any common seal or securities seal is to be used.

(3) Unless otherwise decided by the directors, if the company has a common seal and it is affixed to a document, the document must also be signed by at least one authorised person in the presence of a witness who attests the signature.

(4) For the purposes of this article, an authorised person is

    (a)    any director of the company;

    (b)    the company secretary; or

    (c)    any person authorised by the directors for the purpose of signing documents to which the common seal is applied.

(5) If the company has an official seal for use abroad, it may only be affixed to a document if its use on that document, or documents of a class to which it belongs, has been authorised by a decision of the directors.

(6) If the company has a securities seal, it may only be affixed to securities by the company secretary or a person authorised to apply it to securities by the company secretary.

(7) For the purposes of the articles, references to the securities seal being affixed to any document include the reproduction of the image of that seal on or in a document by any mechanical or electronic means which has been approved by the directors in relation to that document or documents of a class to which it belongs.

## 82 Destruction of documents

(1) The company is entitled to destroy

    (a)    all instruments of transfer of shares which have been registered, and all other documents on the basis of which any entries are made in the register of members, from six years after the date of registration;

    (b)    all dividend mandates, variations or cancellations of dividend mandates, and notifications of change of address, from two years after they have been recorded;

    (c)    all share certificates which have been cancelled from one year after the date of the cancellation;

    (d)    all paid dividend warrants and cheques from one year after the date of actual payment; and

    (e)    all proxy notices from one year after the end of the meeting to which the proxy notice relates.

(2) If the company destroys a document in good faith, in accordance with the articles, and without notice of any claim to which that document may be relevant, it is conclusively presumed in favour of the company that

    (a)    entries in the register purporting to have been made on the basis of an instrument of transfer or other document so destroyed were duly and properly made;

    (b)    any instrument of transfer so destroyed was a valid and effective instrument duly and properly registered;

    (c)    any share certificate so destroyed was a valid and effective certificate duly and properly cancelled; and

    (d)    any other document so destroyed was a valid and effective document in accordance with its recorded particulars in the books or records of the company.

(3) This article does not impose on the company any liability which it would not otherwise have if it destroys any document before the time at which this article permits it to do so.

(4) In this article, references to the destruction of any document include a reference to its being disposed of in any manner.

### 83 No right to inspect accounts and other records

Except as provided by law or authorised by the directors or an ordinary resolution of the company, no person is entitled to inspect any of the company's accounting or other records or documents merely by virtue of being a member.

### 84 Provision for employees on cessation of business

The directors may decide to make provision for the benefit of persons employed or formerly employed by the company or any of its subsidiaries (other than a director or former director or shadow director) in connection with the cessation or transfer to any person of the whole or part of the undertaking of the company or that subsidiary.

*Directors' indemnity and insurance*

### 85 Indemnity

(1) Subject to paragraph (2), a relevant director of the company or an associated company may be indemnified out of the company's assets against

(a)  any liability incurred by that director in connection with any negligence, default, breach of duty or breach of trust in relation to the company or an associated company,

(b)  any liability incurred by that director in connection with the activities of the company or an associated company in its capacity as a trustee of an occupational pension scheme (as defined in section 235(6) of the Companies Act 2006),

(c)  any other liability incurred by that director as an officer of the company or an associated company.

(2) This article does not authorise any indemnity which would be prohibited or rendered void by any provision of the Companies Acts or by any other provision of law.

(3) In this article

(a)  companies are associated if one is a subsidiary of the other or both are subsidiaries of the same body corporate, and

(b)  a "relevant director" means any director or former director of the company or an associated company.

### 86 Insurance

(1) The directors may decide to purchase and maintain insurance, at the expense of the company, for the benefit of any relevant director in respect of any relevant loss.

(2) In this article

(a)  a "relevant director" means any director or former director of the company or an associated company,

(b)  a "relevant loss" means any loss or liability which has been or may be incurred by a relevant director in connection with that director's duties or powers in relation to the company, any associated company or any pension fund or employees' share scheme of the company or associated company, and

(c)  companies are associated if one is a subsidiary of the other or both are subsidiaries of the same body corporate.

# Table of Cases

# Table of Cases

## C

## D

# Table of Cases

# Table of Cases

# Table of Cases

## S

# Table of Cases

## Y

# Table of Statutory Instruments

# Table of Statutory Instruments

# Table of Statutory Instruments

# Table of Statutory Instruments

# Table of Statutory Instruments

# Table of Statutory Instruments

# Table of Statutory Instruments

# Table of Statutory Instruments

# Table of Statutory Instruments

# Table of EU Legislation

# Table of EU Legislation

# Table of Statutes

# Table of Statutes

# Table of Statutes

# Table of Statutes

# Table of Statutes

# Table of Statutes

# Table of Statutes

# Table of Statutes

# Table of Statutes

# Table of Statutes

# Table of Statutes

# Table of Statutes

# Index

## A

# Index

# Index

# Index

# Index

# Index

# Index

# Index

# Index

# Index

# Index

# Index

# Index

# Index

# Index

# Index

# Index

# Index

# Index

# Index

# Index

# Index

# Index

# Index

# Index

# Index

# Index

# Index

# Index

# Index

# Index

# Index

Index

**Registration of charges, – *cont.***
overseas companies, – *cont.*
Scotland 30.67
requirement 40.1
Scotland 40.13–40.19
Scotland,
creation of charge 40.13
debentures 40.16
ex facie absolute disposition 40.15
failure to register 40.13
property acquired 40.14
property outside UK 40.17
rectification by court 40.19
register 40.18
Registrar of Companies 40.18
special register 40.20
**Registration of company,**
application for 12.3
certificate 12.4
overseas company 30.2–30.10
re-registration 34.30–34.32
**Regulations,**
EU Regulations, prospectuses 32.1
large and medium sized companies and
groups 3.2
requirements of CA 2006 App 1
**Regulatory framework,**
UK Corporate Governance Code 15.2–15.6
**Related party transactions,**
Listing Rules 33.38
small companies 5.38
**Related undertakings,**
accounts disclosures 3.36–3.44, 3.68–3.77
**Relevant market, trading on,**
annual return 7.2
**Removal of directors,**
community interest companies 10.21
generally 18.9
**Remuneration,**
auditor,
disclosure 3.53, 5.39
fixing 8.17
directors,
accounts disclosure 3.45–3.52, 3.78
approval by members 18.48
charitable companies 18.48
determined by 18.46
payment 18.49
payment for loss of office 18.47
resolution, voting on 18.49
directors' remuneration reports,
See also Directors' remuneration reports
generally 19.11–9.34

**Remuneration, – *cont.***
policy,
See also Directors' remuneration policy
contents 19.6
generally 19.3
**Remuneration committee,**
UK Corporate Governance Code 15.10
**Reports, annual,**
financial, listed companies 33.32
publication of 2.3
**Requisition of documents,**
destruction of documents 25.16
disclosure of information 25.18
entry of premises 25.13
furnishing false information 25.17
introduction 25.11–25.18
mutilation of documents 25.16
power of Secretary of State 25.12
protection as to information provided 25.14
search of premises 25.13
security of information obtained 25.15
**Reserve liability,**
historical meaning 47.6
**Reserves,**
accounts disclosure 3.18, 3.27, 5.27
reduction of share capital 47.59
types,
capital redemption reserve 34.23
revaluation reserve 3.16, 5.25
undistributable 22.1
**Residential addresses of directors,**
overseas company 30.12–30.17
protection from disclosure,
application by Registrar of Companies, 39.19
application not to disclose via credit reference
agencies 18.71
application to make unavailable for inspection 18.74
court order for disclosure 18.72
overseas company 30.1230.17
permitted use or disclosure 18.70
protection from disclosure 18.68–18.74
public record, on 18.73
register 38.5
restriction on use or disclosure 18.69
register 38.5
**Resolutions,**
articles, entitlement to vote 42.4
class of members 42.47
constitutional matters 14.10
directors' meetings 42.42–42.43
extraordinary,
term not used in CA 2006 42.1
institutional investors 42.48

# Index

# Index

# Index

# Index